The Heath Anthology of American Literature

Volume D

Modern Period: 1910–1945

The Heath Anthology of American Literature

Seventh Edition

Volume D
Modern Period: 1910–1945

Paul Lauter
Trinity College
General Editor

John Alberti
Northern Kentucky University
Editor, Instructor's Guide

Mary Pat Brady
Cornell University

Kirk Curnutt
Troy University

Daniel Heath Justice
University of British Columbia

James Kyung-Jin Lee
University of California, Irvine

Richard Yarborough
University of California, Los Angeles
Associate General Editor

Wendy Martin
Claremont Graduate University

D. Quentin Miller
Suffolk University

Bethany Schneider
Bryn Mawr College

Ivy T. Schweitzer
Dartmouth College

Sandra A. Zagarell
Oberlin College

CENGAGE

Australia • Brazil • Mexico • Singapore • United Kingdom • United States

CENGAGE

The Heath Anthology of American Literature, **Seventh Edition**
Volume D, *Modern Period: 1910–1945*

Edited by Paul Lauter, Richard Yarborough, John Alberti, Mary Pat Brady, Kirk Curnutt, Daniel Heath Justice, James Kyung-Jin Lee, Wendy Martin, D. Quentin Miller, Bethany Schneider, Ivy T. Schweitzer, and Sandra A. Zagarell

Editor in Chief: Lyn Uhl
Publisher: Michael Rosenberg
Senior Development Editor: Leslie Taggart
Development Editor: Craig Leonard
Assistant Editor: Erin Bosco
Editorial Assistant: Rebecca Donahue
Media Editor: Janine Tangney
Marketing Brand Manager: Lydia LeStar
Content Project Manager: Rosemary Winfield
Art Director: Marissa Falco
Production Technology Analyst: Jeff Joubert
Manufacturing Planner: Betsy Donaghey
Rights Acquisition Specialist: Jessica Elias
Production Service: Tania Andrabi, Cenveo Publisher Services
Text Designer: Shawn Girsberger
Cover Designer: Tani Hasegawa
Cover Image: Jacob Lawrence, *Untitled (Street Scene with Policeman)*, 1938. Tempera on paper, 11 1/2 × 13 in. Photo © copyright 2011 The Jacob and Gwendolyn Lawrence Foundation, Seattle/Artists Rights Society (ARS), NY
Compositor: Cenveo Publisher Services

For product information and technology assistance, contact us at **Cengage Customer & Sales Support, 1-800-354-9706**.

For permission to use material from this text or product, submit all requests online at **www.cengage.com/permissions**.
Further permissions questions can be emailed to **permissionrequest@cengage.com**.

Library of Congress Control Number: 2012916935

ISBN 13: 978-1-133-31025-9
ISBN 10: 1-133-31025-7

Cengage
20 Channel Center Street
Boston, MA 02210
USA

Cengage is a leading provider of customized learning solutions with office locations around the globe, including Singapore, the United Kingdom, Australia, Mexico, Brazil and Japan. Locate your local office at **international.cengage.com/region**.

Cengage products are represented in Canada by Nelson Education, Ltd.

To learn more about Cenagage platforms and services, register or access you online learning solution, or purchase materials for your course, visit **www.cengage.com**.

Instructors: Please visit **login.cengage.com** and log in to access instructor-specific resources.

Printed in the United States of America
4 5 6 7 8 9 10 23 22 21 20 19

CONTENTS

ISSUES AND VISIONS IN MODERN AMERICA 2299

PREFACE

The *Heath Anthology of American Literature* represents a remarkable success story. It is not the story of a book, a small board of editors, or even a few publishing houses. It is, rather, the story of the thousands of students and faculty who have in the last quarter century transformed the study of American literature.

LITERATURE AS AN INCLUSIVE CULTURAL FORM

When in 1978 we began the Reconstructing American Literature project (from which the anthology developed), the definition of what constituted American literature was very narrow in terms of the authors covered, the forms of writing included, and the ideas of literary study then dominant. Today's students would hardly recognize the anthologies or the syllabi that characterized the work of critics and teachers back in the 1950s or 1960s. That work would appear as odd today as 1900 baseball uniforms or perhaps Victorian hoop skirts—recognizable but remote from our society or culture.

The Heath Anthology of American Literature was part of a movement for cultural change. That movement took as its goal conceiving American literature as an inclusive cultural form, a form of creativity that spoke of and to the lives of all Americans and that spoke with many voices and in many different ways. It has always been our intent and practice to represent the writers who traditionally had constituted American literature. It was and remains our goal to be as inclusive as the limits of these five volumes permit.

A DIVERSE COMMUNITY OF SCHOLARS

Because societies and cultures change, our understanding of the meaning of *inclusive* likewise changes. As readers will see, today's seventh edition of the *Heath Anthology* differs in what we think are interesting and useful ways from the first edition of 1980 or even from the more recent sixth edition. We have updated a large number of headnotes as well as introductions. And we have made certain changes in the literary texts contained in the anthology. Many of these changes are specified below.

Most of the ideas for change originated with teachers and students who have used the anthology. The particular character of the *Heath Anthology* has always depended on the participation in the project of a wide community of scholars and teachers. Unlike other anthologies, the *Heath* includes introductory notes that have been written by scholars who specialize in a particular author. In their diverse yet consistent approaches, these headnotes illustrate for students how writing about literature is not limited to any single standard.

More important, perhaps, these contributing editors, together with readers, consultants, and users of the anthology, have provided guidance to our large and diverse editorial board as we determine the changes that will make the anthology most useful. We hope that a new generation of students and teachers will share with us their ideas about what works in the anthology and what does not, what texts and configurations might be changed, and what more we might provide so that they can make the best use of these books.

BROADENING THE "LITERARY"

What is the "best use"? The answers to that question will, of course, vary enormously depending on the students and teachers involved. One could teach a fairly traditional course using *The Heath Anthology of American Literature*, emphasizing only the writers historically considered significant. There are rich selections in these volumes of writers like Edwards, Franklin, Emerson, Hawthorne, Melville, Thoreau, Whitman, Dickinson, James, Twain, and modernists like Eliot, Fitzgerald, Hemingway, Pound, Stevens, Wharton, and the like. But we have from the beginning of this project striven to include many writers who would not have been part of such a traditional course, like Frederick Douglass, Lydia Maria Child, Frances Harper, Sarah Piatt, Charles W. Chesnutt, Mary Wilkins Freeman, Kate Chopin, José Martí, and Randolph Bourne, just to name a few from earlier times. One of the accomplishments that we are most proud of is the transformative impact of the *Heath Anthology* on the American literary canon. The inclusion of a number of important new (that is, underappreciated) authors in the *Heath* has played an important role in catalyzing a wider and deeper awareness of their significance.

Likewise, these books contain abundant selections of fiction, poetry, drama, and also nonfictional prose, polemical and historical essays, songs, chants, speeches, and the like. Another major goal of the *Heath Anthology* has been to broaden our understanding of what constitutes the "literary." On the one hand, we want to provide students with a large selection of well-known texts whose literary power and cultural relevance had been established by generations of critics and teachers—William Bradford's "Of Plymouth Plantation," Benjamin Franklin's *Autobiography*, poetry by Bradstreet and Dickinson, "Young Goodman Brown," "Self-Reliance," "Civil Disobedience," "Annabel Lee," "Daisy Miller," "The Open Boat," *The Awakening,* *The Waste Land,* "Hills Like White Elephants," "Sonny's Blues," "Howl."

At the same time, we wish to provide exemplary texts that, because of their forms or subjects, have seldom been taught and often little read. Thus, we include, for example, "sorrow songs" or spirituals, nineteenth-century folk songs and stories, *corridos* and blues lyrics, and poems written on the walls of Angel Island prison by Chinese detainees.

Likewise, we include nonfictional forms such as the spiritual autobiographies of Thomas Shepard and Elizabeth Ashbridge, sketches by Fanny Fern, polemical letters by Angelina and Sarah Grimké, columns by Finley Peter Dunne, José Martí's important "Our America," Randolph Bourne's "Trans-National America," Martin Luther King's "I Have a Dream," and chapters from Gloria Anzaldúa's *Borderlands/La Frontera*. The sixth edition extended this goal by incorporating journal entries from several members of the Lewis and Clark expedition, letters protesting Cherokee removal, "proletarian" folk songs, and graphic narratives by Art Spiegelman, Lynda Barry, and others.

The seventh edition widens the lens still further by including a broader span of written texts by Native American authors from all parts of the country, the work of many more Spanish-language writers of all centuries, including those from the period of the Mexican Revolution, Chinese American immigrants such as novelist and future actor H. T. Tsiang, and essays such as Carlos Bulosan's "The Freedom from Want" that dramatize both the allure and the pitfalls of nationalism. A section of Spoken Word poetry now concludes the anthology. It is our hope that teachers and students will be able to take advantage of what remains, by far, the most inclusive and varied anthology in the field.

LONG AND SHORT WORKS

The *Heath Anthology* has also from its beginning balanced longer complete works with shorter texts by the wide variety of authors included. Thus, this edition includes the full texts of Royall Tyler's "The Contrast," Susanna Rowson's play *Slaves in Algiers; or, A Struggle for Freedom*, Melville's "Benito Cereno" and "Billy Budd," Frederick Douglass's *Narrative*, Abraham Cahan's "The Imported Bridegroom," Kate Chopin's *The Awakening*, Nella Larsen's *Passing*, George C. Wolfe's *The Colored Museum*, and Arthur Miller's *A View From the Bridge*, among many other longer works.

HISTORICAL AND SOCIAL CONTEXTS

It has always been our view that literature, like any art form, must in part be studied in relation to the historical and social contexts from which it develops and to which it speaks. We have therefore systematically included in the volumes important historical texts ranging from the Declaration of Independence to decisive court decisions like that enabled Indian "removal" or imposed and finally helped end racial segregation. These "In Focus" sections can be read for their own interest, since they are vivid documents in and of themselves. But they can also be read to provide contexts to the more traditionally literary texts that constitute the primary content of the anthology. With the *Heath Anthology*'s unusually wide selection, they provide instructors with broadened opportunities to help students perceive continuity and change in the literary and cultural history of what is now the United States.

Likewise, in this electronic age, we have the following electronic resources for both instructors and students:

- **Heath Anthology Premium Website for Volumes A, B, C, D, and E.** This robust Premium Website includes a wide variety of multimedia resources to help bring to life the works and time periods featured in the *Anthology*. The website can be navigated by volume and centers around thirty of the most commonly taught works for each volume. Each is supported by reading comprehension quizzes, interactive media such as audio or video, Web links, and author biographies. In addition, the Premium Website features materials to help provide historical, social, and political context for these works, such as maps and images. A glossary of literary terms is also provided, in both list form and as interactive flashcards. A variety of eBooks are available as an optional add-on to the Premium Website, including *The Scarlet Letter* and *Adventures of Huckleberry Finn*. Access the Premium Website at www.cengagebrain.com.

- **The Heath Blog.** Available as a link from the Instructor Companion Site and from the Premium Website, the Heath Blog is dedicated to providing tools, information, and pedagogical approaches for instructors and students of American literature and culture. It provides virtual space for conversations about what choices we make when we anthologize texts, how these texts are presented and received in the classroom, and how they resonate with contemporary concerns. All users are encouraged to respond to the blog articles with their own commentary and suggestions. Instructors may access the Instructor Companion Site at www.login.cengage.com, and the Premium Website is available for students via www.cengagebrain.com.

- ***Online Instructor's Manual.*** The *Online Instructor's Manual*, edited by John Alberti, offers suggestions for approaching texts and authors, model assignments, and useful exam and discussion questions. This helpful resource is available on the Instructor Companion Site, which can be accessed at www.login.cengage.com.

- **Instructor Companion Site.** This password-protected website provides access to both the downloadable Online Instructor's Manual and the Heath Blog.

CHANGES IN THE SEVENTH EDITION

The seventh edition includes 176 new works across the five volumes.

WHAT IS NEW IN VOLUME A, BEGINNINGS TO 1800

Changes to Volume A, Beginnings to 1800, are relatively few but draw on the latest scholarship to update translations and headnotes as well as enrich our offerings from Native and Spanish America. As in the other volumes in the seventh edition, we have added a new "In Focus: Northern New York—Mohegan/Brotherton Tribes" section that highlights the region of Northern New York. Included in this section are writers pulled from other places in the sixth edition, such as Handsome Lake, Samson Occom, and Hendrick Aupaumut, complemented by a new excerpt from Joseph Johnson, son-in-law and close associate of Occom, capped by an introductory headnote that discusses the many interrelations among these figures across tribal affiliation and the larger cultural movements they shaped. We have added Corn Tassel to "Native American Political Texts and Oratory" to continue integrating Native American writing and oratory throughout Volume A.

The selections from Gaspar Perez de Villagrá have been expanded and newly translated and form the hub of a group of hemispheric Spanish American writers recounting the exploration and conquest of North and South America, including new entries by Juan de Oñate, Fray Alonso Gregorio de Escobedo on the conquest of Florida, and Felipe Guaman Poma de Ayala on the conquest of Peru. Excerpts from Gaspar de Villagrá and Fray Alonso Gregorio de Escobedo are reprinted in the original Spanish.

Later in the volume, we have included two new selections from the revolutionary literature of Spanish America—a popular broadside by José Álvarez de Toledo and one of the founding documents of Latin American history, Simón Bolívar's "Letter from Jamaica," which now concludes Volume A.

The selections from New Netherland writer Adriaen van der Donck have been updated with a new translation, and we have added the entirety of Susanna Rowson's popular play *Slaves in Algiers* in the place of excerpts from her novel *Charlotte Temple*.

In the critical sections, we have added significant excerpts from Bartolomé de las Casas on the plight of the Indians, Aníbal Quijano and Immanuel Wallerstein on "Americanity," Trish Loughran on eighteenth-century print culture, and a blog post on "Decolonial Aesthetics" that reinforces the salience of colonial literature and coloniality to the present postmodern moment.

WHAT IS NEW IN VOLUME B, EARLY NINETEENTH CENTURY: 1800–1865

Volume B, Early Nineteenth Century: 1800–1865, has a newly restructured section on Native American literature, with new selections that include excerpts from Black Hawk and Mary Jemison, which frame the opening section as an exploration of complex and often misunderstood Native identities. Other Native writers, like William Appess and Jane Johnston Schoolcraft, are interspersed throughout the volume, working against the notion that Native voices precede other voices. A new "In Focus" section dedicated to the Cherokee nation and the literature surrounding Cherokee removal has been added. This enables instructors to focus on a particular Native nation, gaining a nation-specific focus that helps students understand both the Cherokee context in specific, and the larger imperative to encounter Native writing as nationally specific.

The "Cultures of Spanish America" section has been restructured and greatly expanded, with new works in English and in Spanish (with translations provided) by Victoria Moreno, José María Heredia, José María Tornel, and Vicente Pérez Rosales.

Finally, a new section focusing on "The Caribbean in the Antebellum Imagination," with works by Martin Delany, Lucy Holcombe Pickens, and Miguel Tolón, has been added.

WHAT IS NEW IN VOLUME C, LATE NINETEENTH CENTURY: 1865–1910

Thoroughly reconceived, Volume C, Late Nineteenth Century: 1865–1910, reflects even more vividly the extraordinary writing that flourished as the United States became a modern, diverse nation with an international presence. The overarching concept of this volume is that the literature written between 1865 and 1910 was so plentiful and so diverse that no single set of organizational categories does it justice. We have therefore devised several complementary categories to showcase this variety in a comprehensible manner.

Now book-ending the volume are sections on significant literary trends—"Varieties of Postwar Realism: Prose and Poetry" and literature "On the Cusp of a New Century." Of the other four sections in Volume C, one centers on Siouxian peoples ("Nation within a Nation: Lakotas/Dakotas/Nakotas"); two are organized geographically ("Writing and Place" and "Redefining the South"); and another ("Outside/Inside U.S.A.: Expansion and Immigration") foregrounds the era's cultural and political ferment with writing by or about immigrants and literature created in response to the shifting borders of the nation and to its geopolitical expansion.

All of these sections contain new material in addition to the literature of past editions. Most notably, we now feature four authors new to the *Heath Anthology*—the "Hoosier poet" James Whitcomb Riley, the witty Vermont regionalist Rowland E. Robinson, the Southern plantation tradition writer Thomas Nelson Page, and the proto-modernist poet Sadakichi Hartmann.

There are many new selections by familiar authors, among them Henry James's "The Figure in the Carpet," a section of Zitkala-Sa's "Impressions of an Indian Childhood," Mary E. Wilkins Freeman's "Old Woman Magoun," and Charles W. Chesnutt's "The Doll." We also restored the Frank Norris section.

Still further, we introduce two exciting, little-known Latino narratives— "Memories of California"/"Recuerdos de California" by Carlos F. Galán and "The Tale of a Glove"/"Historia de un guante" by N. Bolet Peraza. These selections are presented in Spanish and in English translations produced for the *Heath Anthology* by contributing editor John Alba Cutler.

In addition, Volume C now offers new or substantially revised headnotes on a number of authors included in earlier editions—Henry James, Sarah Orne Jewett, Mary E. Wilkins Freeman, Frances E. W. Harper, Alice Dunbar-Nelson, and Jack London. Finally, we also present new and revised "In Focus" sections, complete with new and updated introductory essays.

WHAT IS NEW IN VOLUME D, MODERN PERIOD: 1910–1945

Volume D, Modern Period: 1910–1945, continues to demonstrate the diversity of the literary period known as modernism by introducing readers to the array of modernisms that constitute it—the hermetic experiments of Ezra Pound and T. S. Eliot, the more commercial expression of loss and uncertainty in popular efforts by F. Scott Fitzgerald and Edna St. Vincent Millay, the ethnically complex fusion of African American and dominant-culture aesthetics that typify the Harlem Renaissance, and the political activism of the proletarian movement of the 1930s and its internal debates over the social functions of art.

Volume D continues to expand notions of both modernity and modernism by widening the scope of literary experience. Included here for the first time is a section on the literature of the Mexican Revolution, featuring Industrial Workers of the World (IWW) organizer Ricardo Flores Magón's *cri de guerre* "Land and Liberty" and a newly translated excerpt from the Spanish version of Leonor Villegas de Magnon's "La Rebelde," among others. There are two stories from Maria Cristina Mena, and a poem and two novel excerpts of H. T. Tsiang, who captures the despair of New York Chinatown like no other 1930s' writer. The famous "rent party" chapter from Wallace Thurman's *Infants of the Spring* (1932) features thinly veiled portraits of leading Harlem Renaissance writers. Also included are Meridel LeSueur's story "Annunciation" and an excerpt from her posthumously published novel, *The Girl*; Jose Garcia Villa's "Footnote to Youth" (the most famous Filipino short story of the 1930s); and a selection of poetry that expands our notions of modernist experimentation. Mexican American folklorist Jovita Gonzalez's essay "Shades of the Tenth Muses" provides a hallucinatory meditation on canon inclusion.

WHAT IS NEW IN VOLUME E, CONTEMPORARY PERIOD: 1945 TO THE PRESENT

Volume E, Contemporary Period: 1945 to the Present, has been radically restructured to reflect ongoing changes in what is considered contemporary and to make it easier for instructors and students to locate major trends and developments in the contemporary period. We have organized this section by decades, basing their placement on the date of publication rather than by the birth date of authors.

Some of the period's prolific, established authors such as Tennessee Williams, Arthur Miller, Toni Cade Bambara, Ishmael Reed, Sherman Alexie, and John Updike are represented by different works from the ones we included in previous editions.

Although we have had to reduce or cut some selections by authors previously represented in this section in the interest of limiting the volume to a reasonable length, more striking is the list of writers we have added to this volume. New authors to the seventh edition include John Cheever, Mitsuye Yamada, Kurt Vonnegut, Ralph Molina, Luís Valdez, Richard Ford, George C. Wolfe, Ann Beattie, Percival Everett, Martin Espada, Demetria Martinez, T. C. Boyle, Stephen Dunn, Natasha Trethewey, Junot Díaz, Dave Eggers, Jane Trenka, ZZ Packer, Francisco Goldman, and Manuel Munoz.

We have also added substantial new "In Focus" sections of Ojibway writings from the contemporary period, and the volume concludes with a section of "Spoken Word Poetry," which showcases some important new voices and the genre that they have helped to develop but which connects a current trend to the oral traditions that form the origin of American literature in its earliest years.

ACKNOWLEDGMENTS

We want to extend our thanks to all of the contributing editors who devoted their time and scholarship to introductory notes, choices of texts, and teaching materials. For the current edition, they include the following:

Katherine Bassard, Virginia Commonwealth University

Paula Bernat Bennett (Emerita), Southern Illinois University

Renée Bergland, Simmons College

Leah Blatt Glasser, Mount Holyoke College

David Budbill, poet and independent scholar

Raul Bueno, Dartmouth College

Keith Byerman, Indiana State University

Floyd Cheung, Smith College

Jonathan Chua, Ateneo de Manila

Hillary Chute, Harvard University

Michael C. Cohen, University of California, Los Angeles

Raúl Coronado, University of Chicago

Denise Cruz, Indiana University

Suzanne del Gizzo, Chestnut Hill College

Jared Demick, University of Connecticut

Joseph Dewey, University of Pittsburgh, Johnstown

Lyn Di Lorio, The City College of New York

Amy Doherty Mohr, Amerika Institut, Ludwig Maximilians Universität, Munich

Jennifer Emery-Peck, Oberlin College

Armando García, University of Pittsburgh

Caroline Gebhard, Tuskegee University

June Howard, University of Michigan

Caren Irr, Brandeis University

Gene Jarrett, Boston University

Ann Keniston, University of Nevada, Reno

Ryan James Kernan, Rutgers University

Kathy Knapp, University of Connecticut

Sara Kosiba, Troy University

Rodrigo Lazo, University of California, Irvine

Katherine E. Ledford, Appalachian State University

Marissa López, University of California, Los Angeles

Crystal J. Lucky, Villanova University

Manuel Martin-Rodriguez, University of California, Merced

Lauren R. Maxwell, The Citadel

Keith Mitchell, University of Massachusetts, Lowell

Charles Molesworth, City University of New York, Queens

Paula Moya, Stanford University

Viet Nguyen, University of Southern California

Ben V. Olguin, University of Texas, San Antonio

Yolana Padilla, University of Pennsylvania

Josephine Park, University of Pennsylvania

Robert Dale Parker, University of Illinois, Urbana-Champaign

Soojin Pate, Minneapolis Community and Technical College

Elizabeth Petrino, Fairfield University

Peter Reed, University of Mississippi

Domino Renee Perez, University of Texas, Austin

Ana Patricia Rodriguez, University of Maryland, College Park

Ramón Saldívar, Stanford University

James Schiff, University of Cincinnati

Lavina Dhingra, Bates College

E. Thomson Shields, East Carolina University

Susan Shillinglaw, San Jose State University

Amjrit Singh, Ohio University

Scott Slovic, University of Nevada, Reno

James Smethurst, University of Massachusetts, Amherst

Mayumi Takada, Bryn Mawr College

Justine Tally, Universidad de la Laguna

Kara Thompson, College of William and Mary

Lisa Thompson, State University of New York, Albany

Darlene Unrue, University of Nevada, Las Vegas

Joanne van der Woude, Columbia University

Ariana Vigil, University of North Carolina, Chapel Hill

Jennifer Wallach, University of North Texas

Hilary Wyss, Auburn University

Yvonne Yarbro-Bejarano, Stanford University

Thanks to Oberlin College for funding student researchers and to Amanda Shubert and Hillary Smith for the incomparable work they have done in that capacity. We also want to thank student researchers Carson Thomas and Kyle Lewis from Dartmouth College and Brandy Underwood from the University of California, Los Angeles for excellent editorial help.

We especially want to thank those who reviewed this edition:

David Anderson, University of North Texas

Craig Barrette, Brescia University

Robert Bennett, Montana State University

Brett Bodily, North Lake College

Kathryn Brewer-Strayer, Stillman College

Delmar Brewington, Piedmont Technical College

Brad Campbell, California Polytechnic State University

Beth Capo, Illinois College

Charles Cuthbertson, Southern Utah University

Joshua Dickinson, Jefferson Community College

Sharynn Owens Etheridge-Logan, Claflin University

April Gentry, Savannah State University

Wendy Gray, J. Sargeant Reynolds Community College

Deirdre Hall, University of North Carolina, Greensboro

Amy Hankins, Ottawa University

Tena Helton, University of Illinois, Springfield

Tai Houser, Broward College

Melanie Jenkins, Snow College

Bruce Johnson, Providence College

David Jones, University of Wisconsin, Eau Claire

Thomas Long, University of Connecticut

Marit MacArthur, California State University, Bakersfield

Bridget Marshall, University of Massachusetts, Lowell

John Miller, Longwood University

Keith Mitchell, University of Massachusetts, Lowell

Emmanuel Ngwang, Claflin University

Miles Orvell, Temple University

Priscilla Perkins, Roosevelt University

Jane Rosecrans, J. Sargeant Reynolds Community College

Christopher Schroeder, Northeastern Illinois University

Claudia Slate, Florida Southern College

Jimmy Smith, Union College

Blythe Tellefsen, Fullerton College

Ruthe Thompson, Southwest Minnesota State University

Stephanie Tingley, Youngstown State University

Terri Tucker, Southwest Texas Junior College

Tondalaya VanLear, Dabney S. Lancaster Community College

Trent Watts, Missouri University of Science and Technology

Michelle Weisman, College of the Ozarks

Eric Wertheimer, Arizona State University

Julie Wilhelm, Lamar University

We would like to continue to thank the many scholars who contributed to this as well as to earlier editions of this work. Their names are listed in the *Online Instructor's Manual* that accompanies this anthology.

The Heath Anthology of American Literature

Volume D

Modern Period: 1910–1945

The Heath Anthology
of American Literature

Volume D

Modern Period 1910–1945

AN IMAGE GALLERY
1910–1945

■ **MARCEL DUCHAMP**, *NUDE DESCENDING A STAIRCASE*
(NO. 2) (1912). Marcel Duchamp's (1887–1968) painting achieved
notoriety at the 1913 International Exhibition of Modern Art, called
the Armory Show after the building in New York City where the
show was held. The show introduced American visitors to European
artists such as Vincent Van Gogh, Paul Gauguin, Paul Cézanne, Pablo
Picasso, Georges Braque, and many others. Duchamp's *Nude* came
to symbolize the disturbing vision of the world displayed in many
modernist works. Some described the painting as an explosion in a
shingle factory or an earthquake on the subway. For more on the
Armory Show, see pages 1–2. (© *2012 Artists Rights Society (ARS),
New York/ADAGP, Paris/Succession Marcel Duchamp. Digital Image* ©
The Museum of Modern Art/Licensed by SCALA/Art Resource, NY)

■ **WORLD WAR I BOND POSTER (1917).** This poster advertising U.S. government bonds depicts a ship of immigrants entering New York Harbor. Symbols of freedom (the Statue of Liberty and an American flag) greet the aspiring citizens as they approach Ellis Island. This poster encouraged participation in the second Liberty Loan drive of 1917, one of three bond campaigns that took place in the United States during World War I. The muted red, white, and blue tones appealed to the patriotism of the newest Americans. The poster was also published with text in Yiddish and Italian. For a critique of patriotism, see John Dos Passos's "The Body of an American," pages 1036–1041.

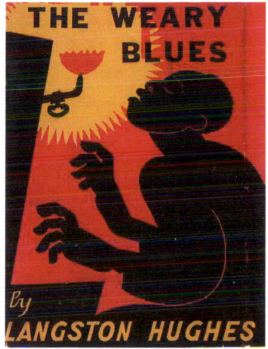

Harry Ransom Center, The University of Texas at Austin

■ **LANGSTON HUGHES,** *THE WEARY BLUES* **(1926).** The dust jacket of Langston Hughes's (1902–1967) first book, *The Weary Blues*, was illustrated by Miguel Covarrubias and published by Knopf, New York, in 1926. Covarrubias was a Mexican painter, writer, and anthropologist. He came to New York in 1923, and soon his caricatures were appearing in magazines such as *Vanity Fair* and *The New Yorker*. His illustrations also appeared in various magazines and books. "The Weary Blues" itself is featured on page 963, followed by a selection of period blues lyrics.

shutterstock.com

■ **THE STYLING OF CONSUMER DESIGN (1930s).** Although the first U.S. patent for a stove-top coffee percolator dates back to 1865, it was not until the introduction of electric versions near the turn of the century that the appliance became associated with style and home sophistication, largely by removing it from the "labor" of stove work. Percolators are just one of thousands of consumer items that began to be sold by form instead of function in the burgeoning consumer age. Composed of basic technology, such home devices relied on design to distinguish themselves in the marketplace. Their appeal was to allow consumers the illusion of a chosen "look" that would express their personality even in the most mundane of domestic utensils. For an analysis of this emphasis on style, see Earnest Elmo Calkins's "Beauty: The New Business Tool," pages 359–361.

■ **THE UTILITY OF TECHNOLOGY (c. 1900).** Thomas Edison patented phonograph technology in 1878, but more than any other of his many inventions, this one demonstrates the tension between innovation and novelty in the marketplace. For many consumers, the limitations of cylinders (originally made of tin foil and subsequently of wax) reduced the functionality of the device to a mere toy. The phonograph industry struggled against this perception for two decades until 1901, when the Victor Talking Machine Company began marketing discs whose audio capacity better approximated the experience of live music. For a critique of consumerism, see Thorstein Veblen's *The Theory of the Leisure Class: A Study of Economic Institutions*, pages 119–120.

■ **TEN DAYS IN FEBRUARY (1913).** The February 22, 1913, assassinations of President Francisco I. Madero and Vice President José María Pino Suárez were the culmination of the siege known as "La Decena Tragica" or "The Ten Tragic Days." Forced to resign from office after a coup staged by José Victoriano Huerta Márquez—remembered in Mexico today as "The Jackal" and "The Usurper"—the men were supposed to have been guaranteed safe passage into exile. Their murders were central events in the Mexican Revolution. For a discussion of assassinations, see Leonor Villegas de Magnon, "Laredo and the Constitutionalists," pages 277–283.

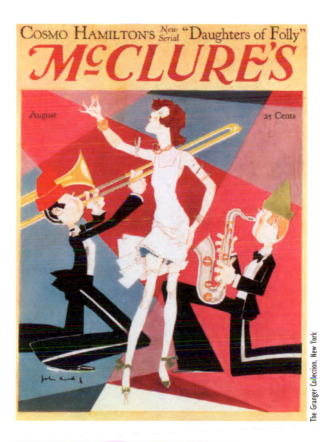

■ **JOHN HELD, *McCLURE'S* COVER (c. 1925).** John Held's (1889–1958) illustrations in popular magazines such as *Life*, *Vanity Fair*, *Harper's Bazaar*, and *Redbook* capture the great changes of the 1920s. Jazz entered the cultural scene, and young women wore more daring clothes as they danced the Charleston and other new dances. The older generation enjoyed the humor of Held's art, and the younger generation looked to his images for style and role models. Held designed two memorable F. Scott Fitzgerald jacket covers—*Tales of the Jazz Age* (1922) and *The Vegetable* (1923). Fitzgerald's "Babylon Revisited," on pages 594–609, is an eloquent testimonial to the excesses of the Jazz Age.

■ **WILLIAM VAN ALEN, CHRYSLER BUILD-
ING (1930).** Architect William Van Alen (1883–
1954) created an homage to the automobile in
the Chrysler Building. He designed a frieze of
Chrysler hubcaps at the thirtieth floor running
around the building with "gargoyles" in the form
of Chrysler radiator caps at each corner. Triangular windows reach to the sky like the spokes of
the wheel. Ironically, by the time this paean to
American industry was completed in 1930, the
stock market had crashed. Although not about
this particular skyscraper, Hart Crane's "The
Bridge," pages 704–705, dramatizes the spectato-
rial amazement structures such as this inspired.

■ **DOROTHEA LANGE,** *MIGRANT MOTHER* **(1936).** Dorothea Lange's (1895–1965) famous *Migrant Mother* series was taken in 1936 in Nipomo, California. The pictures show Florence Owens Thompson and her family. Lange describes the photo: "Nipomo, Calif. Mar. 1936. Migrant agricultural worker's family. Seven hungry children. Mother aged 32, the father is a native Californian. Destitute in a pea pickers camp, because of the failure of the early pea crop. These people had just sold their tent in order to buy food. Most of the 2,500 people in this camp were destitute." Lange's photos brought widespread attention to the destitute migrant farm laborers in California. The works of Meridel LeSueur on pages 1090–1109 capture the bonds between women forged as a survival tactic during the Great Depression.

■ **JACOB LAWRENCE,** *GREAT MIGRATION* **(1940).** Jacob Lawrence (1917–2000) received a commission in 1940 to complete a series of sixty panels on the Great Migration of African Americans during and after World War I. Lawrence's epic begins and ends with train stations. In this panel, African Americans leave the South and crowd toward three major cities. In the first half of the series, Lawrence displays a Southern landscape stricken by poverty and violence. The second half shows improved conditions in the communities of the urban North as well as race riots and overcrowding. For a discussion of the Great Migration, see Alain Locke's "The New Negro," pages 743–752. (*Jacob Lawrence, The Migration Series, Panel no. 1: During World War I there was a great migration north by southern African Americans., 1940–41, Casein tempera on hardboard, 12 × 18 in., Acquired 1942, The Phillips Collection, Washington, D.C.* © 2012 Artists Rights Society [ARS], New York.)

■ **THE POWER OF THE IMAGE (1910).** Jessie Tarbox Beals's 1910 photograph "Family in Airshaft," was originally commissioned for a newsletter called *Bagdad on the Subway*, published by the New York Association for Improving the Condition of the Poor (AICP), a benevolent society dedicated to alleviating urban poverty. The image, first published under the title "Little Prisoners of the Slums," offers gritty insight into tenement squalor. Along with Lewis Hine and Jacob Riis, Beals helped define the art of social-documentary photography. Anzia Yezierska's "America and I," pages 1006–1014, complements photographs such as this. (*"Family in Airshaft" by Jessie Tarbox Beals, ca. 1910, Community Service Society Records, Box 297, Folder 5, Rare Book & Manuscript Library, Columbia University in the City of New York*)

■ **FEDERAL ART PROJECT, A YOUNG MAN'S OPPORTUNITY FOR WORK, PLAY, STUDY & HEALTH (1941).** When President Franklin D. Roosevelt established the Works Progress Administration in 1935, Federal Project Number One was established to fund arts-related projects. The Federal Art Project employed more than five thousand arts projects, including poster divisions through the United States. The New Deal administrators believed that art should be a part of the daily lives of all Americans. This poster for the U.S. Civilian Conservation Corps, one of the earliest New Deal programs, advertises opportunities for young men to work on various conservation projects. The period folk music lyrics on pages 1015–1027, give a different, less smiling view of the difficulties of labor.

Modern Period:
1910–1945

The Centers of the Modern

In 1913 the initial shock of modernism reached the United States in the form of the Armory Show. Staged in a New City building that had once housed military operations, this art exhibit outraged much of the population. Derided by the press as either hoaxes or insults to good taste, many of the works were abstract paintings, mainly by living artists, European and American, who were not well known. Most notorious was the piece by Marcel Duchamp, a radical French artist who eventually came to live in America: an abstract painting of a nude woman descending a staircase; three years later he exhibited a urinal installed upside down and signed "R. Mutt." The show was international in terms of the artists represented, but it was thoroughly American in its optimism and its brashness.

When William Carlos Williams, then a practicing physician in New Jersey, saw the Duchamp painting, he laughed out loud. That laugh represented several emotions, and behind them a newly developing cultural frame of reference. Williams, like Duchamp, wanted art and poetry to be in contact with everyday life and everyday objects, even if it meant attacking the normal placidity of cultural conventions. Williams laughed at Duchamp's boldness, at his irreverence, and through a shock of recognition, he was also laughing at himself. For a great many people, the advent of modernism in America was definitely not a laughing matter. But for others, including many who would become identified as the country's leading writers, the irreverence and exuberance of the Armory Show were importantly echoed by the cultural energy that was taking shape in America in the first decades of the new century. Gertrude Stein once teasingly redefined old and new when she remarked that America was the oldest country in the world, because it had lived in the twentieth century longer than any other nation. Many historical and social forces helped make America modern, and in turn American writers helped make modernism what it was, and is.

Defining modernism is a difficult task. A comprehensive definition would refer to its stylistic innovations, its willingness to disrupt traditional syntax and form, to mix together modes or levels of writing that had often been kept separate, and to risk incoherence and experimentation in order to challenge the audience's preconceived notions of value and order. A historical definition would say that modernism is the artistic movement in which the artist's self-consciousness about questions of form and structure became uppermost. Some people saw modernism in terms of its obsession with so-called primitive

"If it had not been for these thing, I might have live out my life talking at street corners to scorning men. I might have die, unmarked, unknown, a failure. Now we are not a failure. This is our career and our triumph. Never in our full life could we hope to do such work for tolerance, for joostice, for man's onderstanding of man as now we do by accident. Our words—our lives—our pains— nothing! The taking of our lives—lives of a good shoemaker and a fish-peddler—all! That last moment belongs to us—that agony is our triumph."

Bartolomeo Vanzetti

material and attitudes, while yet others maintained that its essential ingredient was an international perspective on cultural matters. To the extent that both groups have support for their argument, we can also say that modernism realigns the center of culture, either by reaching out beyond its national or regional boundaries or by reincorporating material that had previously been considered "subliterary." In brief, modernism asks us to reconsider what we normally understand by the center and the margins.

One consensus argues simply that modernism is a cultural movement or period style that was dominant in the arts internationally, between the first years of the twentieth century and the end of World War II. But then the disagreement sets in: Was it profoundly anticultural in its impulses (as "R. Mutt" would seem to suggest)? Was it only a bankrupt form of romanticism? Artists who shared the beliefs of romanticism had for several generations been increasingly disheartened by the way society had marginalized artistic creativity. Was modernism's glorification of the artist a form of self-serving grandiosity that only masked a deep social despair?

All these questions are negatively phrased, but each can be converted into a positive claim. Many American writers, people otherwise as diverse as H.D. (Hilda Doolittle) and Ernest Hemingway, Theodore Dreiser and Jean Toomer, might have been willing to accept some of the following positive claims. Modernism rests on the belief that the artist is generally less appreciated but more sensitive, even more heroic, than the average person. By trusting in the power of art to save us from the deadening features of everyday life, especially the desensitizing elements in urban, industrial society, the artist both challenges tradition and reinvigorates it. New styles of writing were necessary to express new ideas and values, and modernism created what one critic called a "tradition of the new." This would mean a strong commitment to breaking away from both patterned responses and predictable forms.

The principle of experimentalism had to be rigorously defended, in the view of most modernists, since it would keep art from turning into something stale or pious. This attitude, however, was not the only one prevalent among modern writers. African American writers, for instance, sometimes drew consciously on traditional material and forms. Native American writers frequently wanted to restore ancient tales to a new, contemporary audience and so reclaim some of the cultural patrimony that was threatened by the modern age. But much modern art tried to avoid grandiosity and pompous themes, such as were often voiced by figures in organized religion or mainstream politics, working instead with the artist's individual perceptions and celebrating the ordinary textures and rhythms of life in an extraordinary way. Better to focus on a red wheelbarrow than on some worn-out public or classical monument, regardless of the disruption this might cause the expectations of the audience. Modernism shocked because it had to, and it used irony and an assortment of disruptive techniques to penetrate any and all the pious beliefs that kept us from knowing our true selves and our true values.

Modernism, in these general terms, contains several contradictory elements. For example, it was democratic in its impulses, tilting against the hierarchies that sustain historically sanctioned values—values such as the stability of the individual self, the importance of the patriarchal family as a cornerstone in society, and the need to honor long-established laws and customs. Modernism was also elitist, since it made claims for the artist that it was not always willing to extend to ordinary men and women. This is one reason why modernism was not wholly embraced by African American, Native American, or immigrant authors. Modernism, however, could redraw tradition so that some hidden or forgotten values might be reasserted. But in its more impatient forms it appeared to throw overboard traditional values altogether. And, very much to the point in our context, some modernist writers celebrated indigenous or national traditions, such as America's technological expertise, seeing in them a source of great emotional force in a world that was otherwise rootless and overstandardized—what many people seven decades ago called "deracinated." On the other hand, many modernist masterpieces deliberately assaulted the faith of simple views and simple people and even saw in the national spirit a jingoism or provinciality that is everything an international cultural movement must try to avoid or eliminate.

The struggle for freer expression, especially in sexual and political matters, was one of the main issues in modernism. Writers committed to such expression often found themselves pursuing a kind of exile. Much of American literature in this period took place in foreign lands, but those settings sometimes had a very American feel to them, especially the sidewalk cafes and bars of Hemingway's Paris, or the Riviera of F. Scott Fitzgerald's *Tender Is the Night*. Still other writers fled from the small towns of their birth, not to Europe or other foreign places, but to the large and growing urban centers of America, especially Chicago, Los Angeles, and New York City. Many also deliberately headed for Greenwich Village or Harlem, centers within centers, as it were, but desirable in part because they were places where the marginal could be celebrated. In fleeing to the big cities, these writers were part of a great social and historical movement in America that swept along not only artists but also thousands of black Americans and immigrants from many countries. This growth of what we can call "mass society"—that is, large urban concentrations of millions of people, living in great density and working in factory jobs or other forms of wage labor—was at once the setting of modern art and often its focus of attack or celebration.

When American writers in large numbers fled their native shores during the first decades of the twentieth century, many to Paris or London, they did so seeking the broadest possible base for their experience, at the same time fleeing what they felt was a constrictive society. For many years, American artists had reacted negatively to what they identified as the Puritanical and repressive elements in our culture; this reaction grew stronger in the period before and after World War I. The Committee for the Suppression of Vice, headed by a man named Comstock, was operating visibly; it had lent its name to the term "Comstockery," an attitude that censored all reference to any immoral or even sexual behavior. Laws were passed in this period, for example, that prohibited sending any information about birth control through the mail. In 1900 Dreiser had difficulty publishing his novel *Sister Carrie* and was able to do so only in a "sanitized" version. However, in 1925, his novel *An American Tragedy* was received with great praise, though it, too, told of a woman who wandered from the path of rectitude.

In some sense, the very efforts at repression suggest the strength of the movements to change American culture: at contest in the struggle over birth control, for example, was what might today be called "women's liberation"— whether the greater access to education or work, in the professions staffed by women since the late nineteenth century, would finally be translated into wider opportunities for self and sexual expression and for freedom from the cycle of pregnancy, childbirth, and family-rearing that continued to entrap many poor and working women. Family-planning advocates, led by women like Margaret Sanger, argued that access to birth control was critical if society were to fulfill its implicit promises to women. Writers like Agnes Smedley (in *Daughter of Earth*) dramatized from a female perspective the savage internal conflicts many women experienced between their own sexuality and the consequences of its expression; more broadly still, Edith Wharton created characters like Lily Bart (in *The House of Mirth*) and Charity Royall (in *Summer*) for whom the social promises of wider opportunity outside traditional marriage proved altogether illusory. The issues of free expression with which modernist writers were concerned were thus related to deeply conflicted questions of social policy and cultural norms.

That connection was also illustrated in 1925, by the Scopes trial in Tennessee, in which a man was charged with corrupting young people by teaching them the theory of evolution, thus challenging one of the central myths of our culture, namely that humans were created by a divine being at a specific time as revealed in the Old Testament. In 1920 the editors of a magazine called *The Little Review* were fined $100 for publishing a portion of James Joyce's novel *Ulysses*, whose language had been described as "obscene." But in 1936, Judge John Woolsey wrote a landmark decision in the United States District Court clearing the way for the unhampered publication of this and other important modernist works. What society often treasured as its central beliefs—in decency, in the necessity for hard work, in the desirability of order and respect—was what modern art called into question.

One way to view modern art and modern society in the same framework is to see that both phenomena pose questions about the center and the periphery. Previously societies tended to have a visible center and to produce a centrally located culture—the obvious model being that of the court and the monarch in early modern European societies. But with the coming of fully modern forms of life, many countries, the United States chief among them, evolved social forms in which the palpable sources of power and influence were harder to identify. Many forms of authority were questioned, especially in the 1920s and 1930s, because the forces that gave society its shape were changing, often with incredible speed. Ezra Pound spoke of the age as one that demanded an "accelerated grimace." The city was certainly one of the places where the tempo of modern life was noticeably faster, and with this speed went a blurring of the outlines and a need to capture the panorama through rapidly shifting perspectives.

Some earlier writers such as Whitman, William Dean Howells, and Stephen Crane had begun to open up urban vistas in the late nineteenth century. Of course, the worlds of the raft and the whaling ship in Twain and Melville or of the New England village in Mary E. Wilkins Freeman and Sarah Orne Jewett could show middle-class readers a great deal about their experience, but eventually such exotic locales would prove insufficient to their increasingly urbanized consciousness. Dreiser's fiction is unimaginable outside of an urban setting, as is that of Toomer, Hughes, Yezierska, and Fitzgerald. Hemingway and Wharton, on the other hand, write about Paris and New York, but also about trout streams and small Michigan and New England towns. Indeed, the pastoral or rural spirit remained a part of American literature in the first half of the twentieth century and its debunking a frequent theme. But it was largely within the concentration of cities that writers, especially the male modernists, found subject material and stimulation. Cities, however, do not easily sort themselves out into manageable shapes. The modern city is a challenge, even a threat, to the idea of order, and as such it can present a problem to the aesthetic impulse. But American authors rose to this challenge, often attempting to resolve this artistic dilemma through experiments in artistic form.

When writers like Sherwood Anderson, Jean Toomer, Theodore Dreiser, Zora Neale Hurston, and Marianne Moore came to New York City, they were in some ways consciously coming to the center of literary life in America. But when these writers tried to capture what lay at the heart of America, they often looked to other locales as well. When H.D., Ezra Pound, and Hemingway went off to Paris or London, they, too, had a longing for a center, though each at some point in their careers settled in a small town considerably removed from the metropolis and its concentrations of wealth and influence. As the environments of these writers changed, so too did their sense of subject matter. Not only might the center and the margins be redrawn, but the very notions of centrality and marginality would receive a modernist configuration. Hemingway could address the cosmic forces through the tale of a lone and primitive fisherman. H.D. might use the colossi of ancient myth to plumb her own psychic strength. The common men and women of New Jersey, marginalized by their economic and social status, could enter the art of Williams and find there a recognizable world, though not necessarily one that had a simple, old-fashioned celebration of stability as its centering principle.

But not all the literature in the modernist period in America focused on marginal figures. Or, to put it slightly differently, not all writers felt their material or characters to be marginalized. Robert Frost, for example, drew heavily on a tradition of nature and transcendentalism in his poetry, and Edith Wharton dissected the established power of "old New York" in her novels and stories, just as Edwin Arlington Robinson, Ellen Glasgow, and Zora Neale Hurston confidently wrote of small-town citizens who lived in an ostensibly stable world. Underneath the surface, however, all five writers were able to reveal fissures and tremors suggestive of modernist anxiety and cultural despair. The small-town and rural locales were favored by some writers, but only for the most blinkered witnesses were the old social forms still valid.

Many of the developments in the modern world tended to de-emphasize the importance of place altogether, at least in the older nostalgic sense. Strong impulses toward regionalism and local color could exist at the same time, however, and an important writer such as Frost could make use of these interests. But the workforce, for example, was increasingly made up of minorities: blacks and immigrants who had been called upon to do the backbreaking physical labor that made many of the advancements of modernity possible and who were often treated as little more than exchangeable parts in a great social mechanism.

In the 1920s the population of New York City grew immensely. But by the end of the decade, engineers had built a tunnel to New Jersey, creating an important link outside the island confines of Manhattan and a step toward the creation of what came to be called the "megalopolis." The end of the decade also saw work begin on the Empire State Building, soon to become a symbol not only of the city, but also of America itself throughout the world. This elegant structure epitomized the way skyscrapers converted space into something like a commodity, to be bought, sold, or rented as the business world saw fit. Large cities were able to expand both vertically and horizontally, and with their expansion came architecture and forms of life that were more and more bureaucratically organized—a bureaucracy that political philosopher Hannah Arendt called a system that featured "rule by nobody," a way of constantly displacing the center of responsibility and authority.

Culture is in complex ways always engaged in questions of authority, of course. The culture of modernism is structured by many themes, but one of the chief concerns it addresses is the idea that the older forms of authority are decayed or useless and that the authority of the individual must be strengthened, or people will be overwhelmed by what many in the 1930s called the "forces of collectivism." Indeed, the fear of collectivism was largely the result of the success of the 1917 Bolshevik Revolution in Russia. There was, however, a strong native strain of collectivist sentiment in the United States; Eugene Debs ran for president in 1920 on a socialist ticket and captured almost one million votes. Many American writers were seriously attracted by Marxism, despite the ostracism it sometimes entailed. In the America of the 1930s, the social crisis triggered by the Depression was often argued about, and physically fought over, in terms of individualism and collectivism.

But even before the Depression brought the decade of the 1920s to a brutal conclusion, the social struggles of the country were being bitterly contested. After World War I, the so-called Palmer raids of 1919, under the leadership of then Attorney General A. Mitchell Palmer, rounded up people with Communist affiliations, suspected subversive designs, or even activist labor backgrounds. These raids were only one of several efforts, private or government-sponsored, to "cleanse" the body politic of any radical or "foreign" influence. The Sacco and Vanzetti case, a direct outgrowth of the climate of fear produced by the Palmer raids, provided a particularly striking instance of this clash over political values. Accused of murder in connection with a payroll robbery, these two Italian anarchists were prosecuted, judged, and ultimately executed by members of the older Yankee aristocracy and were defended over the seven years of appeals by, among others, a large group of writers and intellectuals, including Hemingway, John Dos Passos, Edna St. Vincent Millay, and Maxwell Anderson, many of whom participated in activities and wrote works focused on the case; Millay, in fact, was arrested on a picket line protesting their innocence.

Important strikes in the steel, coal, and textile industries in the late 1910s and early 1920s gave ample warning that America had to do more to meet the needs of ordinary workers than had so far been accomplished by the reform-minded liberalism of Theodore Roosevelt and Woodrow Wilson.

Still, those strikes were generally lost by the relatively weak mine and steel unions, and the 1920s became a period dominated by business interests. While the postwar years brought widespread prosperity—except to significant areas of the farm belt—wealth and power continued to be concentrated throughout this period. Working conditions, wages, and the length of the work week were all issues contested between those who held power and control of America's growing industries and those who worked in its increasingly modernized shops and assembly lines. However, it was not until after the stock-market crash of 1929, the subsequent depression, and the general discrediting of business interests that these conflicts became widely visible or were much written about. Only then, too, did the pendulum of social and economic power swing in some degree back toward working people, who began to find ways to amass and control social power.

It wasn't only working people who developed new ways of amassing and controlling power in and after the Great Depression. There was also a challenging structure for generating new financial strength and, by extension, social force as well: the American corporation. Again, America was not alone here, for other advanced industrial societies had corporations, some of great extensiveness and sophistication. But America and the modern world seemed united in their fascination with big business. And in America big business had increasingly come in the twentieth century to mean corporate business. In 1924 the newly elected President Coolidge proclaimed that "the chief business of the American people is business. The man who builds a factory builds a temple.... The man who works there worships there." Needless to say, five years later such religiosity took on an especially bitter irony for many.

However, after the depression, American business rebounded with a strength that amazed the world. In part this new strength was increased by the industrial retooling of the economy made necessary by World War II. And collectivism might at times have seemed a mere phantom, for the strength of American business was finally not curtailed by such "advanced" social legislation as the Social Security Act and the Labor Relations Act, both of which became law in 1935. Even the Republican candidate for President in 1936, Alf Landon, ran on a platform that supported social security. The depression had the ineradicable effect of turning the boom period of the first two decades of the century into a period of social reorganization and planning. The forces of progressivism, with their belief in the power of masses of people to determine their own political destiny, had prospered under Teddy Roosevelt and Wilson and had been chastened by Harding, Coolidge, and Hoover; these forces were still vitally at work in American society in the 1930s.

Locating the sources of power in the people themselves had always been one of the cornerstones of American political thought. Such a broad base of power was often centered, however, in institutions that were hard to change, slow to reflect greater diversity, and quick to justify their own mistakes. In 1920 the Nineteenth Amendment giving women the right to vote was adopted. Some saw suffrage as the culmination of a long struggle that had begun almost eighty years before with the Seneca Falls convention of 1848; they took it to symbolize the emergence of women into full equality, a significant place at the center of political power. And it is certainly true that the efforts to achieve women's suffrage and related reforms continued unabated throughout much of the nineteenth and early twentieth centuries. For others, the achievement of suffrage represented a more equivocal "victory," one which did little to change women's marginal status.

The historical evidence offers an ambiguous answer. It was certainly true, for example, that more and more women had since at least the 1890s been working for wages outside the home, that significant numbers of them had become professionals, and that women were no longer so utterly compelled to marry for support. But the professions they entered were primarily new ones: social work, nursing, and librarianship, which, like the old standby teaching, offered low status and pay. The traditional, and more lucrative, male professions, like medicine, law, and the clergy, remained largely closed to women for another half century. Women were barred from the skilled trades, and, in fact, as many as forty percent of working women, especially blacks, were engaged in household labor. Even within the home, the vaunted development of "labor-saving" household appliances carried its own ambiguities: machines often simply "freed" women to shift time to other household work, like child care, and the machines also changed the very nature of the chores, imposing higher standards of cleanliness on the "modern" housewife. The ambiguities extended in still other directions: if the new ideas of Freud suggested that women had and should be able to enjoy sexual feelings, and if the twenties "flapper" emerged in her bobbed hair and short skirts as an embodiment of female sexuality, most Americans probably continued to hold contrary Victorian ideas condemnatory of such new freedoms.

To point to the ambiguities of "progress" is not to deny that profound and significant changes had taken place in the lives of large numbers of women. Nothing suggests this so much as the falling birth rate: white women in 1800 bore, on average, more than *seven* children; in 1860, 5.21; by 1920, the rate was down to 3.17. Opportunities for higher and graduate education did broaden steadily, at least into the 1920s. Women made many of the "new professions" their own: the Settlement House movement, and organizations established during this era from the Junior Leagues to the League of Women Voters to the Consumers League, offered women of all ages structured opportunities for participating effectively in public life. At the same time, perhaps precisely because more women were entering and competing in the job market and were leading ultimately successful campaigns for suffrage, the prohibition of alcoholic beverages and lynching, and other progressive reforms, tensions over women's role and status increased markedly in the decades surrounding World War I.

In 1911 the philosopher George Santayana had attacked what he described as the "feminized" American intellect as an expression of an outmoded "genteel tradition." He and other writers of the period, like Sinclair Lewis and Joseph Herge-sheimer, mocked the provinciality and presumed intellectual backwardness of small-town club ladies, as well as what some saw as the androgynous eccentricities of their bohemian sisters. While such critics assailed "genteel" male writers like William Dean Howells, the polemics of the time took on a distinctly gendered quality, which historians have only recently come to note. Perhaps this "war of words" developed because the experiences and outlooks of many male modernist writers differed from those of their female counterparts. For T. S. Eliot, the social life of the time might be represented by Prufrock's tea:

> In the room the women come and go
> Talking of Michelangelo.

But for Amy Lowell it might be an afternoon of chatty visits with her sister poets, Sappho, Elizabeth Barrett Browning, and Emily Dickinson ("The Sisters"), who seem strange to her,

> but near,
> Frightfully near, and rather terrifying,
> I understand you all, for in myself—
> Is that presumption? Yet indeed it's
> true—
> We are one family.

Recent critics have noted that the disintegration of the pre–World War order, so alarming to many male writers, seemed, perhaps, less a shock to women than a kind of liberation from, to quote Lowell again, Queen Victoria, Martin Luther, and "the long line of Church Fathers."

However that might be, it was certainly the case that the "woman question" was one of the main reasons why the 1920s felt to many who lived through it like a very modern time indeed. Where interest in modernism flourished, as in New York's Greenwich Village, the hub of social and literary experimentalism, feminism was a prominent part of the culture. Much of the bohemianism of the Village could be traced back to models in nineteenth-century France, but the mix of artists and social radicals had an American flavor all its own. There was a famous salon run by Mabel Dodge Luhan, a wealthy woman known for bringing together social and political radicals such as John Reed, who was to write *Ten Days That Shook the World*, a powerful history of the Bolshevik Revolution in Russia; Margaret Sanger, the proponent of birth control; and Big Bill Heywood, a leader of the Industrial Workers of the World (known as the IWW or "Wobblies"). Though Luhan herself was eventually to back away from the more radical positions of her guests, the salon was a focus for discussion and organization about a host of social and aesthetic issues. Another key figure in the bohemian culture of the Village was Edna St. Vincent Millay, whose poetry celebrated freedom in love and the equal rights of women and men in moral questions, and whose writing and triumphantly flippant public stance helped shape the notion of the avant-garde writer for an entire generation of readers.

For many centuries the traditional roles of Western European culture had tended to divide the work of art into things made by men and things inspired or conserved by women. Few modernist writers pictured themselves as aggressively a maker as did Gertrude Stein; she was a woman who broke the rules. Her contemporary Amy Lowell also existed, in the public mind especially, in a category reserved for the outrageous; Lowell smoked cigars and expressed her opinions very forthrightly. She stood in contrast to a poet like Millay, who redefined the possibilities for women writers in more elusive and indirect ways. But Stein worked hard and inventively at virtually remaking the rules of English syntax. What she produced was often baffling to people who still believed in the genteel tradition, that is, those who looked to literature only to reassure themselves about the world. Stein pursued a most ungenteel lifestyle, and her prose style was called upon to perform in ways that only a marginal figure could readily imagine. Stein's marginality came from being a woman and a lesbian, but in the context of modernism she earned for herself what is to many people a central place. Though she spent much of her life as an expatriate in France, she is also regarded as one of the most American of authors. Categories and definitions were not safe with her; her only constant was a desire to experiment.

At about the same time women were winning the right to vote, another Constitutional amendment was passed, making the production, sale, and consumption of alcoholic beverages illegal. Prohibition was, like suffrage, a social experiment. However, Prohibition failed and suffragism did not. What the two movements had in common, however, (besides many people who supported them both, often for reasons that were linked) is that they both suggested that the social order could be in some sense "engineered"; that is, through political edicts, people's habits and conditions of life could be fundamentally altered. The idea that society was in an important way a product of political institutions appealed to the American mind, for after all, in many ways America itself had begun as an experiment, an idea. America was not the only country to have a suffragist movement or to experiment with Prohibition, but because these were implemented in the 1920s, they seemed to be especially "modern" ideas—or vice versa.

Prohibition sponsored a culture all its own, as it produced or enhanced the visibility of speakeasies, bathtub gin, and organized crime. From the beginning, many people in America saw such an attempt to regulate alcohol as thoroughly hypocritical and doomed to failure. But the root of Prohibition in the temperance movement of the previous century was one of the remnants of religion in our national life. (There were other important elements in the temperance movement, such as a feminist revolt against family violence and the loss of income that alcoholism often entailed. The movement also included some who were disturbed by the "foreign" influence in saloon life.) Though modernism was in many ways a thoroughly secular, even antireligious movement, the nation's cultural life could not be thoroughly restructured overnight. This truth cut both ways, for neither the forces of experimentalism nor those of traditionalism were able to settle the questions raised by Prohibition. In 1933 the amendment was overturned, but what many people called "the noble experiment" had nevertheless left its mark on our collective identity.

The amendments giving women the vote and prohibiting the use of alcohol were important expressions of the spirit of the '20s. They represented both social experimentalism and political trust, something startlingly new and something reaffirmed. But if America was itself an experiment and Prohibition and

As stated before, every colored man who moves into Hyde Park knows that he is damaging his white neighbors' property. Therefore, he is making war on the white man. Consequently, he is not entitled to any consideration and forfeits his right to be employed by the white man. If employers should adopt a rule of refusing to employ Negroes who persist in residing in Hyde Park to the damage of the white man's property, it would soon show good results.

The Negro is using the Constitution and its legal rights to abuse the moral rights of the white....

There is nothing in the make-up of a Negro, physically or mentally, which should induce anyone to welcome him as a neighbor. The best of them are insanitary, insurance companies class them as poor risks, ruin alone follows in their path. They are as proud as peacocks, but have nothing of the peacock's beauty. Certain classes of the Negroes, such as the Pullman porters, political heelers and hairdressers are clamoring for equality. They are not content with remaining with the creditable members of their race, they seem to want to mingle with the whites. Their inordinate vanity, their desire to shine as social lights caused them to stray out of their paths and lose themselves. We who would direct them back where they belong, towards their people, are censured and called "unjust." Far more unjust are their actions to the members of their race who have no desire to interfere with the homes of the white citizens of this district.

Property Owner's Journal, "Protect Your Property!" (1919), 1920

women's suffrage two of its more challenging chapters, on a Friday in October 1929, the country experienced one of its most severe failures. The stock market crash of 1929 and subsequent Great Depression were a shock to all forms of political and social stability. It eventually required a great social experiment—the New Deal—to reset the shaken foundations. But in the meantime, the conflicting impulses of reformism, collectivism, individualism, and experimentalism that took on many forms in the early part of the 1920s faced each other on a stage marked by suspicion, fear, and dislocation. People waited in soup lines for food and sold apples on the street in an effort to support themselves and their families. By now such images are so familiar to us that they are almost clichés, but to the men and women who first experienced them, the sensations of rage and helplessness were overwhelming. Many people talked of a loss of American innocence, referring back to a Puritan metaphor that echoed the fall from the Garden of Eden. The Puritans had themselves discovered a world far from innocent, and their fate showed how difficult it was to build a city on the hill to replace the lost innocence of the Garden.

The depression showed Americans many things. It demonstrated, for example, the importance of the United States in the world of other nations, for the effects of our economic collapse soon spread throughout the Western industrialized world. The effects of the depression also were greatly magnified by the Dust Bowl, a prolonged period of drought that left the agricultural center of the country in severe hardship. This devastation challenged the idea of the country as a land full of natural bounty. It also entered the national mythology—that storehouse of images and stories by which a people tells itself who they are—and became a part of some of our classic literature, such as John Steinbeck's *The Grapes of Wrath*. Also important was the fact that many Americans experienced migration and mobility in new ways; in desperate search for work, people took to the road and headed west or to big cities such as Chicago and New York. Many currents of American literature maintained a regional force, and there was also a new character in our midst: the drifter, often a man with a buried past and little to recommend him except an ability to survive at the edges of society.

What we can now see slightly more clearly than those who suffered through it is that the depression represented the high point of the historical development of the powers of the state in America. The many federal agencies that were created to help re-energize the economy, the power that accrued to the office of the presidency, and the realization that America's promise was only as sound as its economic system: all these helped to enhance governmental power in a way that challenged the virtually sacred tenets of American individualism. At the same time, a fierce argument had raged for over a decade regarding how a balance might be struck between collectivism and individualism; questions about such a balance had animated the American political tradition since its beginnings. In fact, in the midst of the depression, President Roosevelt entitled one of his 1936 campaign speeches, "The Period of Social Pioneering Is Only at Its Beginning." The use of the pioneer metaphor enabled Roosevelt to invoke some of the cultural power of the myth of individualism even as he advanced the forms of activist government and social planning.

Though many might think that active resentment and resistance to the most obvious abuses of such power did not occur until the 1960s, the roots of the conflict go back at least thirty years to the time when an indigenous American radicalism set itself against what it saw as the enormous development of state power. Many of our poets mistrusted the trend towards concentration of power and official authority: E. E. Cummings, for example, praised the conscientious objector, and William Faulkner seemed to express a sneaking admiration for outcasts and renegades. Others, such as William Carlos Williams in his poem "To Elsie," depicted the victims of the system with something approaching clinical detachment. Again, modernism used irony to challenge "normal" perspectives and values.

If the 1920s were a period dominated by experimentalism, and one that altered the arts as well as traditional structures of social power, the 1930s were a period of solidarity and political experimentation. The Communist Party, for example, the largest political organization of the Left in the 1930s, sponsored a wide range of activities, from unemployment councils and tenant unions to the literary John Reed clubs and Writers' Congresses, as well as newspapers and magazines. Party intellectuals, like Mike Gold, developed aesthetic theories of "proletarian realism" based on Marxist principles. And Party organizers, though later subject to 1950s purges, played key roles in starting the new industrial

unions, which came together in 1935 in the Congress of Industrial Organizations (CIO), led by John L. Lewis and William Green. Early in the depression,
the principle that workers had a *right* to organize collectively had been written
into law; translating that theoretical right into practice, especially for the semi-
skilled or unskilled workers of mass-production industries, proved no easy matter, for major manufacturers sharply resisted the new unions. In the intense
and often violent struggles that characterized organizing campaigns in major
industries like rubber, auto, and electrical, the government played a relatively
neutral role—sometimes implicitly supporting unionization—which some interpreted as an effort to insure its own power or at least to build the political coalition headed by F.D.R.

For many writers, the 1930s offered as compelling, though strikingly different, a cultural milieu as that of 1920s bohemianism. Left-wing groups urged
artists to support working-class organizing efforts, to help move the masses, in
Edward Seaver's words, "through the maze of history toward Socialism and the
classless society." Writers argued vigorously about the virtues and possibilities
of the "proletarian novel." The American Writers' Congress of 1935 provided a
platform for debating such issues, as did a variety of magazines whose names
express their times: *Partisan Review, New Masses*, the *Anvil*. And as the decade
wore on, more and more writers, like Dorothy Parker, Lillian Hellman, and Ernest Hemingway, turned their talents toward the struggle against the rising
threat of fascism.

Some authors, like Meridel LeSueur and Langston Hughes, tried to find
ways of utilizing modernist formal techniques to pursue socialist political goals.
But LeSueur insisted that the major departure of the period's culture was vali-
dating the lives and experiences of working people. For such goals, certain modernist tactics, like ironic detachment and linguistic complexity, offered little of
value, though its interest in industrial processes, cinematic movement, and flat,
ordinary language could be turned to political ends.

By no means was all 1930s culture defined by the Left. In the South, particularly around Vanderbilt University, the group of "Southern Agrarians" offered
their alternative to liberal and left-wing movements. Relatively isolated during
the thirties, a number of these men became influential literary critics in succeeding decades, and their depoliticized formal mode of reading texts, the "New Criticism," a later academic orthodoxy. However, precisely because so much in the
thirties was given shape by organizers and intellectuals of the Left, the profound
anti-communism of the late 1940s and the 1950s obscured much of what had
gone on in that earlier time. Until very recently, books and writers of the thirties were often cited only in order to deplore or condemn them as politically
naive or formally backward. Some are. But many works, like the novels of Josephine Herbst and Fielding Burke, and the shorter pieces contained in this volume, have increased in critical estimation. While it was a contentious,
frequently sectarian time, it was also a period of considerable and varied literary
accomplishment. And it was the seedbed for some of the most significant of our
contemporary writers, like Tillie Olsen, Muriel Rukeyser, and Richard Wright, all
of whom honed their literary talents in 1930s political conflicts.

There were also other forces at work, chief among them the development of
a new form of business management. For at least two decades before the war,

that is, in the 1920s and 1930s, American business had moved away from the ideal of the mogul or buccaneering entrepreneur to a safer, more settled agent of economic stewardship. The business executive, by replacing the tycoon, reflected a new sense of how to organize all forms of power: economic, political, and social. Companies like General Motors and Standard Oil would come to dominate international commerce in the second half of the twentieth century, but they began amassing their enormous wealth in the decades immediately after the depression. Many writers deplored the new economic formations of what came to be called corporate capitalism; they saw them as unresponsive to human needs, wasteful of resources, and generally smug about their own prerogatives.

These new organizations of power often justified themselves as pursuing policies much more enlightened than those of the rapacious robber-barons of an earlier era. Such justifications were supported by the creation of massive amounts of wealth, demonstrated in very real ways, such as the production of automobiles, which changed the face of the cities and the countryside as well. Modernism in some of its aspects was quite thrilled by such manifestations. In his poem about Brooklyn Bridge, Hart Crane, for example, tried to capture the spirit of inventiveness and material progress in the mechanical age by using lyric forms. But the corporations extended their business theories, which prized inventiveness and progressively greater technical control, to society as a whole, as they argued for rational organization, the control of markets, and the desirability of new products and increased consumption. Many apologists for capitalism argued that an alliance between business and government should replace the oppositional politics of "trust-busting" and thereby offer to the people what would rightly become the dominant shaping force in American society. The benign form of this alliance was known as corporate liberalism, a belief that all the parts must support the good of the whole, and such parts would prosper best if they appreciated the special needs and benefits of that whole. Some writers were reluctant, however, to accept such arguments, and they frequently opposed what others celebrated as the genius of American "know how."

Such opposition as writers offered was not necessarily heeded, much less appreciated. But this did not lessen its vigor or frequency. A well-known historian, Henry Steele Commager, wrote in *The American Mind* (1950) that the "all but unanimous repudiation of the accepted economic order by its literary representatives is one of the curious phenomena of American culture." Commager traced this repudiating spirit back to Thoreau and Emerson, which is surely one correct lineage. But some of the opposition spirit was fed by the modern concern with alienation. This notion was not especially connected to America; in fact, it was first explored in European Romanticism and in the writings of Karl Marx. But because it is such a central idea in the structure of modernity, it also had very strong and vivid manifestations in American literature.

Modernism and the Self

When Gertrude Stein told Hemingway that he and his fellow writers were all a "lost generation," she was speaking of alienation. When T. S. Eliot spoke about a "pair of ragged claws/Scuttling across the floors of silent seas," he was expressing a strong sense of alienation. When Louise Bogan speaks as "The Alchemist" who

... burned my life, that I might find
A passion wholly of the mind,
Thought divorced from eye and bone,
Ecstasy come to breath alone

she is registering what Eliot called the "dissociation of sensibility." And when Langston Hughes talked of "a dream deferred," he, too, spoke from a feeling of alienation. Stein's remark refers to the aftermath of World War I; Eliot's deals with sexual and social insecurity; Hughes is describing particular historical conditions of racial discrimination and oppression. Indeed, Hughes's living conditions were markedly different from those of privileged émigrés such as Eliot and Hemingway. But each writer is treating one of the central themes of modern literature: how can I form any basis for meaningful values and experience when I feel separated from my truest self, cut off from any sense of belonging in the world in a secure way? Alienation can be viewed as a condition of permanent marginality.

Alienation can take on very different meanings and tonalities depending on a person's immediate circumstances. Stein's remark about a lost generation, for example, clearly refers to the aftermath of World War I. In that war, America lost more than 100,000 people through battlefield deaths and the effects of disease; the number of deaths suffered by the European countries, however, was even more staggering. More than seven million people perished on both sides. Mass society had produced a form of mass destruction. The loss of social purpose, heightened by the feeling of absurdity when confronted with the stupidity of the battle strategies and the "efficiency" of such lethal means as poison gas and motorized armaments, gave a special meaning to alienation in the postwar years. The scale of unnecessary suffering and the enormous loss of life changed the value systems of society for many people. Any notion that war contained chivalrous elements, or that it could be used to advance the causes of civilization, became harder and harder to sustain.

While America escaped the physical destruction of its cities and industrial capacities, it nevertheless remained scarred by the war in ways that were deep and pervasive. Pound spoke of the aftermath by describing civilization as "an old bitch gone in the teeth." Hemingway objected to the use of big and noble words; he felt that patriotism and duty had been corrupted by the uses to which they had been put by those who managed the war machines of the modern age. No longer could writers applaud sentiments such as President Wilson's when he explained that the purpose of the war was to "make the world safe for democracy." H.D. turned increasingly to a private order of myth that would, she hoped, show the way forward to a system of universal love. Even the technique of modernist irony was hard pressed to capture the split many felt between ideals and events. Alienation could mean that the person felt like a stranger, but it could also convey the feeling that it was the world that had become strange.

One way to think about alienation is to imagine how the very notion of the self altered as the modern world was formed. One of the most important changes was the development of a very acute sense of awareness about one's inner life. In European Romanticism, this inner life was often seen as the true source of meaning and value in one's experience. At the same time, this interiority was a source of confusion, self-doubt, and self-questioning, since its states and emotions and insights were frequently unstable, infinitely changeable, or self-contradictory. The writings of Freud did much to put this exploration on a scientific basis, but even Freudian schemes of selfhood left many questions unanswered. The Freudian self, or "ego" as it was called, was often seen as a location of deep-seated conflicts and unerasable memories that constantly distorted one's ability to understand the past or adjust to the future. One way to resolve such contradictions was to adopt an ironic stance about everything, even about one's own stance. This consequently put a strain on the uses to which outside sources of authority—such as social norms or political structures—could be put in telling us who we "truly" are. Such lack of a clear identity can readily be experienced as a feeling of homelessness or marginality.

Because so much of the modern world seems "open"—in part because of our greater control over the physical environment, our ability to travel further and more quickly, the systems of distribution, and so forth—and because it seems possible as well to open up our models of artistic form, the modern self is sometimes confused by its own freedom. This confusion can be illusory. Immigrant writers, for example, often discover that their new home has more than a fair share of problems and limitations; what started as a quest for freedom produces a disillusioning awareness of restrictions and limits. One of the great themes of immigrant writing is the paradox of a new beginning that turns into a series of new losses and failures. In this, immigrants are thoroughly American, since from the country's beginnings this paradoxical reversal of expectations has shadowed our culture. Much immigrant writing, to be sure, tells a standard version of the success story, as the newcomer eventually rises to a social and economic position of prominence, or at least security. One of the standard histories on the subject, Oscar Handlin's *The Uprooted*, captures this double sense of the experience. As Crèvecoeur put it in *Letters from an American Farmer* (1782), for all successful immigrants "those (new) lands confer on them the title of freemen, and to that title every benefit is affixed which men can possibly require." However, titles are very unstable in the modern world. Consequently, there are also many stories that focus on the dislocation instead of the security, that examine the persistence of margins rather than the pursuit of a new center.

Such dislocation or redefinition of the self is a cultural theme that makes the role of the immigrant one of special interest. And of course it is such conflict and questioning about the self (and *through* the self) that form much of the background of artistic experimentalism prevalent in the modern period. We can also hear these concerns with the self expressed and explored in material that some have called "pre-modernist," however. In Dreiser's story "Typhoon," for example, the young woman slowly comes to a realization that the man she is involved with will not marry her and acknowledge the child she is expecting. Dreiser characterizes this realization as "some wild, unbelievable misery and fatality which had seemingly descended on her and yet could not be real." The woman knows and doesn't know, or rather she recognizes her state of mind even as she questions its very existence.

Native American writers often experienced something similar to this dislocation of the self. For many of them, however, this dislocation was experienced in terms of the loss of their legacy of land and their tribal culture. The

Allotment Act of 1887 began with another social experiment, somewhat like those of Prohibition and suffrage. By giving parcels of the tribal land to individual Native Americans, the federal government hoped to break up the system of reservations, which had produced passivity, alcoholism, and a lack of economic development. Too often, however, individuals became the prey of unscrupulous speculators, who tricked the Native Americans out of their small parcels of "real estate" and left them even more ill-equipped to deal with modern "Anglo" society.

Alienation, for the Native American population, therefore meant the loss of one's tribal name, one's land, and one's identity as a member of a historically rich cultural community. One can see this very clearly in the extracts from *Sundown* (1934), the novel by John Joseph Matthews in which the spread of oil-derricks across the landscape becomes a haunting symbol of how the central social powers, in the search for raw materials to fuel a society, very remote from the concerns of the Native Americans, can seemingly at will make and remake the land in their own designs. The derricks move in gradually from east to west, and then as bust follows boom in the capitalist economy, the derricks slowly disappear as the wave of "development" flows back eastward. Alienation and marginality for the Native American are all too forcibly defined by a society that operates with unseen motives and purposes.

T. S. Eliot's strategy in *The Waste Land* is to divide the self among a heap of cultural fragments; Dreiser splits the woman's consciousness into two contradictory (but seemingly complete) states of awareness. Some immigrant writers come to America in this period wishing for a new life, yet often carrying a baggage of selfhood—in the form of ethnic traits, language, and physical characteristics—that is sometimes used against them by members of the dominant culture. Can the immigrant say that he or she has a true self that is defined by the very quest for a new home and a new identity? Can the immigrant proceed to establish this identity without taking full measure of the new environment? What if such full measure involves the surrendering of much, if not all, of the identity that the immigrant arrived with? Can a new center be drawn up out of a space and time that are shaped by so many other forces besides personal will? Anzia Yezierska asks these questions with an urgency every bit as deeply felt as Eliot's fragmented speaker. They are also asked in novels like *My Antonia* by American-born writers like Willa Cather who are deeply interested in the processes by which European immigrants became midwestern pioneers.

Some poems, such as Gwendolyn Bennett's "To Usward" (which asks that its readers "be contained/By entities of self") and Claude McKay's "Harlem Dancer" ("I knew her self was not in that strange place"), directly raise issues about how the self can offer to define its very structure. Other works, such as the fiction of Mike Gold, can generally avoid any use of introspection, relying instead on the externally focused observation of daily life to make their point. Immigrant writing treats issues such as alienation, but often without the elaborate aesthetic devices developed by more experimental writers. This is not because immigrant writers are not aware of the complexity of their fates, but rather because in many instances the needs of audiences and the demands of artistic consistency don't allow for elaboration at a level of form and structure.

In the 1920s immigration to America reached new levels, comparable to those of the earlier period of the 1880s. (However, many Asians were excluded from the quotas during this period; the history of immigration patterns is complex and often marked by a bigotry and fear engendered by national conditions.) However, the earlier immigrant groups had the advantage of being able to participate in a sense of settling the frontier. In the 1920s many of the newcomers to America ended up living in cities, especially those large urban conglomerations that were such an important part of the modern world; this continued the pattern set by immigrants at the end of the nineteenth century and further increased the concern of many that such concentrations of foreigners were dangerous and unhealthy. These urban-dwelling immigrants of the twentieth century saw their own stories differently from those of their previous counterparts. Often they experienced the pains of dislocation and alienation, but they did so against a background of a bustling and driven commercial economy. It was not easy for them to cultivate the modes of introspection and self-analysis that were a part of other modern literature.

Even in works that are occupied with external description, and in those works by and about immigrants where the themes of nineteenth-century realism, such as social placement, family life, and economic success, are predominant, alienation is present. Sometimes this alienation can be detected in the distance we sense between the author's control of the material and the emotional demands that seem to come from the material itself. Such distance is usually called irony; many readers experience it as a form of detachment, even coldness. Modernists, however, felt that to give in to the full emotional impact of the material would involve them in a sentimentalism that they believed to be inaccurate—even dishonest. Readers who mistrusted modernism and yet shared some of its dislike of the modernized structures of society might well have said that irony itself was the end result of alienation.

Modernism and the New Negro Renaissance

The relations between modernism and the New Negro (or Harlem) Renaissance were complex. The Renaissance is generally considered the period that extends from just after World War I until the Great Depression. It is true that in this period a tremendous amount of work in all forms—poetry, fiction, drama, and essays—was produced by a group of diversely talented African American writers. Some of them, like Jean Toomer, were well known outside Harlem through their appearance in leading white publications. Some, like Zora Neale Hurston, were well known for a while but mostly in Harlem, and have had to be more widely "discovered" later by groups of white readers. Others, such as Langston Hughes, went on to full careers that extended beyond the period called the Renaissance. But it was a chapter in America's literary life that had a set of questions and qualities all its own. The Harlem Renaissance is sometimes referred to as the "New Negro Movement," in part as a result of the Alain Locke essay and anthology that use this term. Although most of the writing took place in Harlem, some critics acknowledge that the movement had centers of activity located throughout the country.

In an important sense, the history of the Harlem Renaissance begins with the publication of W.E.B. Du Bois's *The Souls of Black Folk* (1903). Du Bois was

I'll Take My Stand

... Nobody now proposes for the South, or for any other community in this country, an independent political destiny. That idea is thought to have been finished in 1865. But how far shall the South surrender its moral, social, and economic autonomy to the victorious principle of Union? That question remains open. The South is a minority section that has hitherto been jealous of its minority right to live its own kind of life. The South scarcely hopes to determine the other sections, but it does propose to determine itself, within the utmost limits of legal action. Of late, however, there is the melancholy fact that the South itself has wavered a little and shown signs of wanting to join up behind the common or American industrial ideal. It is against that tendency that this book is written. The younger Southerners, who are being converted frequently to the industrial gospel, must come back to the support of the Southern tradition. They must be persuaded to look very critically at the advantages of becoming a "new South" which will be only an undistinguished replica of the usual industrial community.

But there are many other minority communities opposed to industrialism, and wanting a much simpler economy to live by. The communities and private persons sharing the agrarian tastes are to be found widely within the Union. Proper living is a matter of the intelligence and the will, does not depend on the local climate or geography, and is capable of a definition which is general and not Southern at all. Southerners have a filial duty to discharge to their own section. But their cause is precarious and they must seek alliances with sympathetic communities everywhere. The members of the present group would be happy to be counted as members of a national agrarian movement.

Industrialism is the economic organization of the collective American society. It means the decision of society to invest its economic resources in the applied sciences. But the word science has acquired a certain sanctitude. It is out of order to quarrel with science in the abstract, or even with the applied sciences when their applications are made subject to criticism and intelligence. The capitalization of the applied sciences has now become extravagant and uncritical; it has enslaved our human energies to a degree now clearly felt to be burdensome. The apologists of industrialism do not like to meet this charge directly; so they often take refuge in saying that they are devoted simply to science! They are really devoted to the applied sciences and to practical production. Therefore it is necessary to employ a certain skepticism even at the expense of the Cult of Science, and to say, It is an Americanism, which looks innocent and disinterested, but really is not either....

Religion can hardly expect to flourish in an industrial society. Religion is our submission to the general intention of a nature that is fairly inscrutable; it is the sense of our rôle as creatures within it. But nature industrialized, transformed into cities and artificial habitations, manufactured into commodities, is no longer nature but a highly simplified picture of nature. We receive the illusion of having power over nature, and lose the sense of nature as something mysterious and contingent. The God of nature under these conditions is merely an amiable expression, a superfluity, and the philosophical understanding ordinarily carried in the religious experience is not there for us to have.

Nor do the arts have a proper life under industrialism, with the general decay of sensibility which attends it. Art depends, in general, like religion, on a right attitude to nature; and in particular on a free and disinterested observation of nature that occurs only in leisure. Neither the creation nor the understanding of works of art is possible in an industrial age except by some local and unlikely suspension of the industrial drive.

The amenities of life also suffer under the curse of a strictly-business or industrial civilization. They consist in such practices as manners, conversation, hospitality, sympathy, family life, romantic love—in the social exchanges which reveal and develop sensibility in human affairs. If religion and the arts are founded on right relations of man-to-nature, these are founded on right relations of man-to-man. . . .

It is strange, of course, that a majority of men anywhere could ever as with one mind become enamored of industrialism: a system that has so little regard for individual wants. There is evidently a kind of thinking that rejoices in setting up a social objective which has no relation to the individual. Men are prepared to sacrifice their private dignity and happiness to an abstract social ideal, and without asking whether the social ideal produces the welfare of any individual man whatsoever. But this is absurd. The responsibility of men is for their own welfare and that of their neighbors; not for the hypothetical welfare of some fabulous creature called society. . . .

For, in conclusion, this much is clear: If a community, or a section, or a race, or an age, is groaning under industrialism, and well aware that it is an evil dispensation, it must find the way to throw it off. To think that this cannot be done is pusillanimous. And if the whole community, section, race, or age thinks it cannot be done, then it has simply lost its political genius and doomed itself to impotence.

1930

to become one of the founders of the National Association for the Advancement of Colored People (NAACP), and the editor of its important journal, *Crisis*, which published many of the prominent writers of the Renaissance. But it was Du Bois's book that set a course for black people different from the cultural assimilationism of Booker T. Washington. The approach of Du Bois was built on a recognition of what he called a "twoness," a divided awareness of one's identity on the part of African Americans:

> It is a peculiar sensation, this double consciousness, this sense of always looking at one's self through the eyes of others, of measuring one's soul by the tape of a world that looks on in amused contempt and pity. One ever feels his two-ness,—an American, a Negro, two souls, two thoughts, two unreconciled strivings; two warring ideals in one dark body, whose dogged strength alone keeps it from being torn asunder.

This sounds very much like a description of alienation, of course. However, it would be too easy simply to supply such a term to cover the distinct experience of black Americans. It is the fact that such terms as *alienation* both do and do not describe the experience of people who figured largely in the New Negro Renaissance that makes its relation to modernism so complex. Modernism was largely a European movement, and the New Negro Renaissance exhibited many features that owe little to European avant-garde art. In fact, it is possible to see modernism as drawing on some of the Renaissance's concerns in order to develop its energies: such questions as marginality, the use of folk or so-called "primitive" material, and the problem of writing for an elite audience, show that the channels of influence ran in both directions. One of the sources of the interest and complexity of the Renaissance is how it illustrates that the center and the margins of culture are always subject to redefinition.

Blacks experienced an outburst of oppressive and even murderous prejudice in the years immediately following World War I. In part, the bloody racial assaults of 1919—in Chicago, East St. Louis, and elsewhere—reflected intensified competition for jobs, housing, and even for recreational space between entrenched and hostile whites and blacks recently arrived from the more formally segregated South. In some measure, the continued racial strife was fueled in large part by that most benighted and despicable of American phenomena, the Ku Klux Klan. These organized bigots and vigilantes gained considerable increase in membership in part from the widespread xenophobia that was awakened by the flux of immigrants after World War I. However, the Klan also grew because the issues addressed by the Reconstruction period after the Civil War were never resolved. The liberal reformism of the first years of the century was of course potentially extendable to all, regardless of race, although it had largely been conceived of and designed for whites. But the racism in American society was such that even in prosperity blacks were not extended full civil and political rights; so, when the postwar period saw mounting concerns about "foreign" influence in American life, especially in the market place and the factory, the situation of blacks worsened.

The leading writers of the New Negro Renaissance were themselves divided to some extent about the conflicting claims of advancement through cultural and educational "progress," or political protection and power gained through activist struggles and mass organizations and movements. One attempt at mass organization was the "Back to Africa" movement led by Marcus Garvey, founder of the Universal Negro Improvement Association, whose ideas attracted many blacks at this same time. Du Bois himself, at the end of *Souls of Black Folk*, said that improvement of the black masses was possible only through the cultivation of an educated elite, what he called the "talented Tenth." Many of the ideas of Du Bois were echoed in an essay that can be read as a manifesto of the Renaissance, Alain Locke's "The New Negro" (1925).

In this compendium of themes for a modernist revolution in black art and consciousness, Locke speaks of the importance of urbanization for blacks in the new century. There is also a strong sense of a new life as part of an experiment, a willful excursion into unknown territory that recalls one of the major themes of European Romanticism. Locke also speculates on the role of Harlem as the center of this new revolutionary movement: Harlem "is—or promises at least to be—a race capital." And he goes on to raise the issue of internationalism, arguing at one point that the "possible role of the American Negro in the future development of Africa is one of the most constructive and universally helpful missions that any modern people can lay claim to." This last point was especially significant because it showed that the Renaissance had posited a forward-looking aspect to its consciousness. Such consciousness would serve as an important source of cultural as well as political strength for black people.

Though Locke mentions Garvey favorably, he himself inclined toward the argument that proposed the leavening effect of a cultural elite. Hardly any black writer would say, however, that the masses were simply to be led by more educated blacks. Nor would they deny that it was through direct experience of the widespread and inescapable injustice of racism in America that all blacks must come to expect and demand greater justice. Still, the question about black leadership, and whether that leadership should take on a cultural or a political form, remained of prime importance throughout the Renaissance, and beyond. There were strong feelings that artistic forms should be made to fit into the general advancement of the lives and political fortunes of blacks, but just how this would be done was extremely difficult to settle. One key consideration was the economic fact that earlier black writers such as Charles Chesnutt and Paul Laurence Dunbar could not have hoped to sustain themselves by writing only for black audiences; indeed, Dunbar turned to writing musicals to make a living. Eventually a market for black art and culture developed among blacks, due largely to increasing urbanization, increased racial awareness, and spreading literacy. Initially, that market was focused on the sale of "race records," the powerfully evocative work of black musicians like Bessie Smith and Louis Armstrong, who became known outside the black community. Ultimately, however, the market widened sufficiently, among whites as well as blacks, so that black writers and even visual artists, as well as musicians, could hope to make a living through their art.

The New Negro Renaissance was made possible in large measure by this new black audience. However, it was an audience very much in transition. Somehow its writers had to build a consciousness of the history of their community even as they worked toward progressive ideals. The question of the political uses of artistic forms became highly charged in this context. And the Renaissance writers could not simply assume, as did the white modernist authors, that the use of innovative forms was automatically a cultural advance. Any one-to-one relationship between political desires and artistic choices might well prove too restrictive. Claude McKay, for example, used fairly traditional forms in his poetry, but his ideas and values were radical when it came to issues of justice and freedom.

The tensions between modernist principles and the other, more pressing needs of black writers produced several important extended discussions. Chief among these were the question of whether or not the use of experimental forms limited the audience for black literature and whether or not the use of folk material was advantageous or implicitly condescending. These issues were complicated by whether the person who argued one point of view or the other was addressing a strictly black readership, or whether reference was being made, explicitly or not, to a larger white audience. These debates came up many times, and in different forms. For example, some people felt that if black authors were to be fully part of the artistic mainstream, they must be conversant with the latest artistic experiments. The counter-argument suggested that since many black readers were far from enjoying the benefits of middle-class society, with its consumerism, its suburban luxuries, and its extended educational system, they could hardly be expected to take an interest in highly complex aesthetic theories, issues, and forms.

The question of folk material arose in two contexts: the life and culture of blacks who lived in the South, and the world of folk music, especially its more modern forms, blues and jazz. Many of the black writers of this period "discovered" the culture of the black South, for they had been born in northern and urban areas and were by and large removed from the region that had long developed forms of life quite different from those of an industrialized society. Sterling Brown and Jean Toomer were two such writers. On the other hand, Nella Larsen left Alabama after studying and working there for a number of years, and her work is mainly concerned with urban experience. The traditions of narrative in the South were those of the folktale, with its use of mythic material and schematic patterning, and the slave narrative, with its emphasis on testimony and integrity. Slave narratives would serve as an important artistic context for Hurston and Richard Wright, and later for several contemporary black novelists, such as Alice Walker and Toni Morrison. The North, on the other hand, was filled with readers whose sense of a story was shaped by the traditions of European realism. Often a writer can combine both; Zora Neale Hurston, for example, was trained as an anthropologist and used characters and motifs from rural Florida, but she often crafted her stories with details and structures similar to those of famous modern short story writers such as Chekhov and Maupassant.

The use of the blues tradition was also a matter of great artistic debate. The world that was represented in blues lyrics could be understood to be one based on mere complaint about one's repressed and exploited condition. Yet there is in the blues tradition a series of images and themes that point the way toward liberation and even revolt. By using this tradition, with its roots in the world of slavery and peonage, a skillful writer could extend the richness of his or her vision back in time and acknowledge the original situation of blacks in America.

The blues also owed an important debt to the post-Reconstruction chaingangs of black prisoners, who adopted the "answer-and-call" format of black spirituals. Jazz, by extension, became a way for the black artist to create links to the past while at the same time forging one of the most complex and sophisticated of all indigenous American art forms. The poetry of Sterling Brown and Langston Hughes exemplifies some of these possibilities, possibilities that are further explored in the black literature of the 1960s and 1970s.

Black artists face questions of social justice and aesthetic form in particular ways, of course, and when the questions overlap, the tensions can be considerable. Jean Toomer managed these tensions with a special talent, as he used the poetic approach of a very lyrical prose to work with material that had not been granted a full voicing in American literature. He was an extremely self-conscious artist, who was very aware of the "twoness" of which Du Bois had spoken. (In fact, Toomer was a mulatto, and was sometimes accused of trying to "pass" in white society; this condition obviously complicated his situation in terms of "twoness.") The entirety of his book *Cane*, which is available here in excerpts, demonstrates how inventive artistic solutions are often found in changing the center of the work, or at least redefining what we normally understand as the central structure of a poem or story. In writing about *Cane*, Toomer explained that he had built a structure that went "aesthetically from simple forms to complex forms, and back to simple forms. Regionally (it went) from the South up into the North, and back into the South, and then a return North."

Toomer faced the questions of folk material, and experimental forms, and he also implicitly addressed himself to another issue that in a sense stands behind both of these other questions: individual expressiveness. Here the Renaissance writer shared some of the concerns of those artists who grappled with the problem of the modernist idea of the self. Was it possible to find the truth of one's own individual experience and still be true to the larger pressures of one's social and political identity? Modernism tried to insist that the eye of the artist could be transcendently placed above such categories as race and nation. Modernist artists also often made the very divided and fragmented nature of the self into the focus of their art. Native American writers were less directly concerned with subjective individual experience and instead vacillated between using folk materials and trying to adapt other literary traditions to express their concerns. The *Coyote Stories* (1933) of Mourning Dove can be compared and contrasted with the use of similar material by writers such as Toomer. Other available forms, such as journalism and drama, were attractive to both African American and Native American writers who were pledged to speak for groups of people and to do so in ways that grievances and oppression could be directly and widely moving to audiences. Black writers in different ways adopted both of these strategies, the subjective and introspective as well as the directly rhetorical or public speech, but they nevertheless had special problems of their own that such strategies would not address fully.

The hopes of Americans were often tested in this period by various celebrated trials, including that of Sacco and Vanzetti, noted earlier. For the black community, a somewhat similar case was that of the "Scottsboro Boys," a group of young black men unfairly charged and jailed for the assault of two white women in 1931. (Through a long process of appeals and demonstrations, the last of the Scottsboro "boys" was finally released in 1950.) In fact, we can say that if the Harlem Renaissance begins with Toomer's *Cane* (1923) and ends with the important anthology edited by Sterling Brown and others, *The Negro Caravan* (1941), then the Scottsboro trial becomes a sort of half-way marker. But if the Scottsboro incident represented a historical moment in the awakening of white consciousness (at least among liberals) about black oppression, to many black Americans it could hardly serve as a comforting chapter in their history. By extension, many incidents in our common historical self-awareness are valued very differently by blacks than by whites.

This is preeminently the time to speak the truth, the whole truth, frankly and boldly. Nor need we shrink from honestly facing conditions in our country today. This great Nation will endure as it has endured, will revive and will prosper. So, first of all, let me assert my firm belief that the only thing we have to fear is fear itself—nameless, unreasoning, unjustified terror which paralyzes needed efforts to convert retreat into advance. In every dark hour of our national life a leadership of frankness and vigor has met with that understanding and support of the people themselves which is essential to victory. I am convinced that you will again give that support to leadership in these critical days.

I see millions of families trying to live on incomes so meager that the pall of family disaster hangs over them day by day.

I see millions whose daily lives in city and on farm continue under conditions labeled indecent by a so-called polite society half a century ago.

I see millions denied education, recreation, and the opportunity to better their lot and the lot of their children.

I see millions lacking the means to buy the products of farm and factory and by their poverty denying work and productiveness to many other millions.

I see one-third of a nation ill-housed, ill-clad, ill-nourished.

It is not in despair that I paint you that picture. I paint it for you in hope—because the Nation, seeing and understanding the injustice in it, proposes to paint it out. We are determined to make every American citizen the subject of his country's interest and concern; and we will never regard any faithful, law-abiding group within our borders as superfluous. The test of our progress is not whether we add more to the abundance of those who have much; it is whether we provide enough for those who have too little.

Franklin Delano Roosevelt, *First and Second Inaugural Addresses*

Nonetheless, the Harlem Renaissance was a truly important chapter for black readers and writers; it should become the same for whites. One way to begin reading the cultural importance of the Renaissance for both whites and blacks is to see it as a chapter in a yet-unwritten history of modern literature, a history that will give modernism and the Renaissance—as well as their tangled relations—fair representation. Locke's hope that Harlem would be a capital of a new black consciousness reflects many of these tangles, for it seeks to establish a center. This, however, would have the possible effect of relegating some of the indigenous black experience—slave narratives, say, and the blues, and rural folk culture—to the periphery. The proper balance between such a center and such a periphery was often heatedly discussed among the writers of the Renaissance, and it remains a matter of significant conflict today.

Modernism and the South

Some artists devoted their work to a striving for cultural and ethnic specificity and rooted-ness that the high orders of modernism seldom permitted. The Fugitive-Agrarian movement of the 1920s and 1930s in the South actually made this sort of contradiction within modernism a sustaining engine of creativity.

T. S. Eliot, one of the figureheads of international modernism in the 1920s, was, first as poet and then as cultural critic, one of the sparks to this Southern movement. Restless under the prescription to supply an outdated "local color" regionalism, the chief poets of the Fugitive movement (John Crowe Ransom, Allen Tate, and Robert Penn Warren) deliberately sought a kind of poetry that would acknowledge their regional history and character, yet achieve at the same time a rigor and historical–cultural sweep and sophistication such as they had seen and (in varying degrees) admired in "The Waste Land."

In the late 1920s, a few years after their careers as Fugitives waned, they reorganized themselves as Agrarians to resist what they saw as the imposition of an international and uniform culture by "the New Humanists," a group of scholars led by Eliot's former professor at Harvard, Irving Babbitt. The Agrarian manifesto, *I'll Take My Stand* (1930), is a collection of essays that argues for several and separate cultures, not a single and intellectualized one, such as modernism promised (or threatened). This manifesto was deeply contradictory: it formulated a scorching and radical criticism of industrial society and all its modernization and offered as a "solution" a return to traditional social forms based on agricultural values. Such an attempt to turn back historical development, or at least to redirect it, can be seen as yet another American "experiment."

With the success of the centralization and federalization of political and social life in the United States during the Great Depression, the Agrarian experimental agenda failed to reach a powerful audience—not even the Southern farmers the Agrarians envisioned went for the program—and the writers returned, one by one, to poetry and literary criticism.

By the end of the 1930s, they had come up with the New Criticism and a literary–historical definition of themselves, the Southern Renaissance, that put them on the U.S. literary map. With the success of William Faulkner and his winning the Nobel Prize in 1950, this regional movement was well established. Nor is this happy ending to the story without irony and self-contradiction, for

Faulkner's fiction was not a complete success with the Agrarians-turned-critics, and the feeling was mutual.

At the end of the time spectrum, the literary–historical story is somewhat similar to its beginning. As Southern "regional" writing seemed to fill magazines and bookstores, and win prizes, another "regional" group, urban Jewish writers and critics (Saul Bellow, Bernard Malamud, Philip Roth, Alfred Kazin, Irving Howe, and others) began a renaissance of their own. A new tradition helped to cross-hatch and round out the modernist contours. Literary works and understandings were reworked; literary stock fluctuated; tempers flared, died down. Modernism, which had actually been a system of several energy cores, ascended to the status of a single literary movement; it became a fixture of academic understanding by the mid-1950s.

Modernism, Popular Culture, and the Media

Modernism approached all forms of traditional meaning with wariness, if not suspicion. This did not by any means entail a total rejection of all tradition, but instead modernists often looked for new ways to revivify and challenge traditional values. Because it was in many ways a very self-conscious movement, modernism also turned its attention to the ways in which values and experience are passed on to wider audiences, in both a temporal and spatial sense. This attention resulted in the artistic exploration of the media—the modern forms of information and (implicit) evaluation that came into being with such "outlets" as the mass audience newspaper, the radio, and the best seller. These media were part of the very large pattern of modernization that included developments in transportation, housing, the standardization of market activities, and so forth. In short, mass society developed new ways to communicate with itself. However, communicating with itself caused an exponential increase in complexity. Modernization in industrial society involved the widespread availability of different forms of communication. This availability was problematic, however, because there was no longer a unequivocally dominant culture subject to central control, and yet some people and classes had more power over communication than others. In the past one of the chief functions of culture, and by extension literature, was to resolve tensions between different social factions or classes and even to celebrate the unity that a nation relied on for their security, wealth, and happiness. In modernized societies, culture was often called upon to play a similar role, but at the same time there was added a new possibility, namely, contesting the official version or representing alternative versions of such unity. As we have seen, sometimes these alternative versions took the more or less coherent forms called "modernism," but sometimes they even took shape outside or in opposition to modernist tenets. In nearly every case, however, the control and understanding of the media of communication and self-representation were at issue.

Many artists were fascinated with these media, but many were also appalled by them. "We have the press for wafer": here Pound, for example, bitingly refers to the distorted use of the newspaper, the press, for something sacred, the wafer, used by Christian churches in their communion services. Dos Passos, however, tried to replicate the effect of the newspaper and newsreel headline in the very text of his fiction in order to be true to the tempo of his times. The phonograph shows up in Eliot's *The Waste Land* as a symbol of mechanization and the deadening of emotion; the cinema (and even the elevator!) appears in Crane's "To Brooklyn Bridge" as something like a magic carpet. On the other hand, in Langston Hughes's "Air Raid over Harlem," a movie script is envisioned as a way to make the unimaginable terror of racial war into a palpable image. It wasn't until later, perhaps in the heyday of Pop Art in the 1960s, that such media were unequivocally celebrated by artists. However, modern artists saw that despite whatever wariness they experienced, the new media were definitely an unignorable part of modern life and as such had to be dealt with in art.

Many writers even pursued careers in some of the media, or at least sought gainful employment there for a time. Crane and Sherwood Anderson worked in advertising, for example. Many other writers went to Hollywood, especially in the 1940s, to work as screenwriters. True, they were often drawn there by the prospect of monetary reward (it was not unusual for writers to be paid $1500 per week in the 1940s, a large salary, especially for that time), and they often left disappointed. It was not only Scott Fitzgerald, however, who sojourned a while in Babylon; so, too, did Faulkner, Yezierska, Odets, and many more. And there was also the work on newspapers, engaged in by LeSueur and others, but perhaps best typified by Hemingway, that came to form an important part of modern fiction's prose style.

In the decades after 1910, the main inventions to be widely circulated in American society were the movies, the model T, and the telephone. The first sound film was shown in 1927, but for years previously, the silent movies had developed a sophisticated set of techniques and a star system that involved millions of fans in its success. Indeed, Charlie Chaplin had become a household word and a favorite of artists as well, as Hart Crane's poem demonstrates. After 1930, the radio and the phonograph became increasingly widespread. The first commercial radio broadcast was actually made in 1920, but a number of years elapsed before the average household owned a receiver. Likewise, television made an appearance at the 1939 New York City World's Fair, but a national TV network did not exist until ten years later.

The Chicago Exposition in 1893 marked an important watershed in America's cultural history. The World's Fair can serve as a similar marker of change. It was organized around exhibits sponsored by large corporations; these companies were one of the main forces at work in presenting the new media and technologies to the American public. It was not long before some people began to suggest that all these media were in effect mainly useful as elements of social control. The fact that radio programs and newspapers were produced at centralized locations, and often used material already selected and shaped by a group of professionals who had certain attitudes and outlooks, contributed to this realization. Still, such media were most often presented as advantages of modern living, allowing a kind of important democratization of knowledge by making available to people from all walks of life what had once been restricted to a small group.

Such centered forms of control over the production and distribution of the news, not to mention our views of history, politics, and other public forms of knowledge, were not completely new. Earlier societies had also utilized symbolic forms of narrative and other explanations and controlled them by exercising royal prerogatives, for example. However, modern media seemed to have an extensiveness, and something like a transparency, that gave them special force. It was tempting for writers to be a part of this network, and at the same time it was hard to resist it if their predilections lay in that direction. This is why the story of Hollywood and the writers who went there is so fascinating and so often retold—but beyond that, what hope would writers have if their time-honored devices were to be slowly but steadily replaced by other forms of information and storytelling?

Modernism had always cultivated its fascination with what it saw in the primitive. Part of the anticultural impulse in the movement took the form of a high valuation of the life forms of people who had not been thoroughly industrialized, or even "civilized" in the modern sense. This fascination goes back to William Wordsworth and other Romantic writers of the nineteenth century. The so-called "primitive" forms of storytelling became a focus of this modernist interest in different forms of knowledge. In many ways, the media were at the opposite end of the spectrum from such forms. Where the ancient storyteller used a background of shared belief and invoked a spiritual realm that gave credibility to the tale, the modern news report was, as it were, self-contained. It referred only to the surfaces of life and to either the most immediately plausible context or to some form of sensationalism or escapism.

For all these differences in assumptions and effects, however, both the ancient tale and the media news story serve as a way for the society to represent itself to its members, and hence for its members to come to a fuller understanding of their social identities. The writer has to choose, consciously or unconsciously, to accept the validity of the media's version of people's characters and lives or to adopt some critical distance from it. This was yet another area where modernist irony would come into play. The consequence of such irony, however, would almost certainly be to limit the writer's audience, since many people would not easily be able to read against the grain of so much "popular" wisdom.

The phenomenon of the best seller in the modern period is tied up with the beginning of a mass readership fostered by the book clubs, many of which began in the 1930s. In 1931, for example, *The Good Earth* by Pearl Buck entered the best-seller lists for an extended stay of two years. In 1937, *Gone with the Wind* was published, and within ten years it had sold three and a half million copies. Some of the writers who earned critical acclaim were economically very successful and were also "bestsellers," though that term was generally avoided for novels that were considered artistically "serious." Hemingway became a wealthy man through his fiction, and Fitzgerald also prospered, at least for a time. Many others, however, such as Moore, Stein, and Crane, had to settle for the esteem of the academy or of a relatively small group of intellectuals. The relation between popular success and artistic talent has never been simple, and writers are often the first to bemoan this situation. In the modern age, however, such disjunctions were sometimes seen to be a result of the influence of the media. In a sense this issue can be put this way: what some readily refer to as "popular" art others insist on calling "mass art." Such people prefer to reserve the term "popular" art for the kinds of folk expression that thrives without any recourse to advanced forms of distribution such as those offered by the media.

Again, we can turn to notions of marginality in order to put these points in a context that relates them to parts of the foregoing discussion. What follows is a very brief explanation of a process that is undoubtedly more complicated than what can be shown here, since many forces are at work in such matters. Popular art might once, in premodern society, have had a central role to play in a society's self-representation. Tales and heroes and motifs transformed by fantasy and desire would help a social group to recognize and understand itself and its members. However, with the advent of modern mass society, the media displaced truly popular forms of representation, substituting "mass art" images and ideas that best fit into the new media forms. This displacement created two marginalized sources of cultural images: the surviving remnants of popular culture, which we can see in work from the Harlem Renaissance writers, for example, and the more complex forms of cultural experiments that we associate with the modernist spirit.

Modern literature is marked by a willingness to engage itself with a wide variety of cultural forms. In this sense, much of modernism is in dialogue with popular art, alternately drawn to it and trying to outstrip it. The Harlem Renaissance writer may have a different reason for engaging in this sort of dialogue with popular forms from that of the experimental modernist; both may in turn be quite different from a poet such as Frost or Robert Penn Warren, who questions much of what passes for popular wisdom or "common sense." But even an immigrant writer like Yezierska can sharply attack the very widely circulated notions that pass for accepted opinion, while at the same time longing to set aside her alienated condition and fit into the narrative frames that she has heard and read about in all the popular media. And so modern culture can be understood—in at least one version—as a struggle among various artistic forms and audiences for the central interpretative myths, images, and stories of the age.

What some would argue against this account is that it assumes that societies do not always get exactly the cultural representations they desire. How, one might ask, can anyone say that the modernist or the Harlem Renaissance writer or the immigrant writer possessed a version of the culture that was any more valid than that which existed in the popular media? Of course, no one can. In a very real and important sense, the culture does contain all the expressive forms that its members produce, and that culture is no more (and no less) than the sum of all such expressions. One thing we can claim for the writer, however, is that he or she does have access to a vast and complex array of devices that allow for many various forms of expressiveness. This array of forms also suggests that many different attitudes can be registered: acceptance, rejection, praise, condemnation, and many sorts of variations and combinations thereof.

The following selections, therefore, are highly varied. The writers share only two things in common; they identified themselves as American, and they were born at a time when the modern world had unmistakably come into being. Their reactions to that world were diverse in terms of attitude and artistic form. Such variety is perhaps best appreciated by multiple perspectives, cross-readings, and even eccentric explorations.

TOWARD THE MODERN AGE

Modernism has become a very broad term, and like terms such as Classicism and Romanticism, it not only includes many diverse elements, but it also attracts "forerunners." Because the temporal limits of such cultural styles are hard to fix, readers and critics often end up talking about "premodern" works. This can occasionally be distorting, for few writers actually compose their work self-consciously as an advance version of some later style or movement. However, there are writers in certain periods whose work can be interestingly and usefully placed in a context of later developments. In the case of writers who are seen as heading "towards modernism," this often means their work has some of the themes and styles of what is generally regarded as the highwater mark of modernism itself, from the first years of the twentieth century until after World War II. Other writers working in the same period can be seen as outside Modernism altogether and yet working with problems and themes that dominate the modern age.

Women writers are especially interesting in this context. For example, Edith Wharton can readily be seen as a representative writer of realist novels, much like those by nineteenth-century masters such as George Eliot or Thackeray, but because of her concern with certain mental and emotional states, and their origins in the conflict of the individual faced with oppressive social values, her work also reflects some of the concern of psychological and ironic realism. Furthermore, her sensibility and talent as a woman make her a keen observer of forces in social and personal relations that are hidden from many male novelists. Wharton's work also stands in the tradition of women novelists of America who wrote with an eye to sentiment and family values, but it also sharply challenges many of the features of this tradition. Likewise, Willa Cather is a novelist who borrows heavily from the tradition of regional literature, but her work goes far beyond the more expectable limits of such work. Simply by being writers who challenge the traditions in which they work, Cather and Wharton are seen by many as moving toward modernism.

The same sort of argument applies to poets such as Masters, Millay, and Jeffers. None of these poets are especially noted for their technical innovations, which is to say they don't break the norms of syntax and diction as readily or as often as poets such as Pound and Eliot. Nevertheless, their poetry is infused with a feeling of challenge: for Jeffers, this challenge sets itself against any sense of nature as a source of comfort; for Masters, the challenge is to redefine the sense of heroism and scale in people's lives; for Millay, there is an attack, often implicit, against the sentimental, especially as it pertains to women's roles and limitations.

Writers could also approach modern issues of great import in the medium of prose. Some especially significant social issues such as race were discussed in essays, novels, or autobiography. Three African Americans might be seen as originating a modern conversation about the "color line"—what W.E.B. Du Bois called the main political problem of the twentieth century. It was Du Bois himself, in conversation with Booker T. Washington and James Weldon Johnson, who traced the complex curves and intersections of race and modern life.

The writings of these three people not only raise questions of historical justice and memory, but they also provoke reflection about key modern issues involving personal testimony, the right to represent or speak for others, and movement between audiences in both dominant and repressed groups in society. The modernity of the traditions of African American writing is clearly anticipated by Du Bois and his compatriots.

Much of the reception of modernism was contested on such matters as propriety and stylistic innovation; readers simply refused to accept the notion that poems and novels should look and sound that way. But the writers in this section may not have generated the same sort of audience resistance. The work here doesn't fit comfortably into a set historical framework, because some of its elements are forward-looking and some are not. In each case, however, the writer may have been less consciously preoccupied with such matters as the historical fate of a certain style and instead has decided to work with words and forms that are more locally responsive or even deliberately out of the rush of contemporary developments.

Charles Molesworth
Queens College, City University of New York

BOOKER T. WASHINGTON
1856–1915

Booker Taliaferro Washington's life and most important literary work embodied the American myth of the poor boy who pulls himself up by his own bootstraps to become a success. As he wrote in his autobiography, *Up from Slavery*, he was born a slave in Franklin County, Virginia, "in the midst of the most miserable, desolate, and discouraging surroundings." He received no help from his white father, whose identity has never been ascertained. It was his mother, Jane, the cook for a small planter named James Burroughs, who taught young Booker his survival lessons. Booker (he did not take the name Washington until he began to attend school) spent his first nine years as a slave on the Burroughs farm. When the Civil War ended, his mother took him and his three siblings to Malden, West Virginia, to join her husband, Washington Ferguson, a former slave who had found employment in the salt mines. Booker soon went to work at a salt furnace; by the time he was twelve years old, he had seen considerable dangerous work in the Malden coal mines. Nevertheless the boy had his dream—he wanted to go to school.

By attending night school sporadically, Washington achieved fundamental literacy, but he was unable to get any regular schooling until he went to work as a houseboy for Mrs. Viola Ruffner, the wife of a Malden mine owner. She was the first of many well-placed white people whom Washington learned to please in exchange for their support of his ambitions. From her he learned lessons that in 1872 enabled him to gain admission into the Hampton Institute, an industrial school for blacks and American Indians near Norfolk, Virginia. He studied not only the academic curriculum at Hampton, but also the ways in which its president, Samuel C. Armstrong, won the admiration of his black students and the goodwill of the white community. After graduating from Hampton with honors in 1875, Washington soon returned as a faculty member. In 1881 the Alabama legislature asked Armstrong to recommend someone who could found a school for black teachers at Tuskegee in the heart of the state's "Black Belt." Washington was his choice.

From 1881 until his death, Washington concentrated on three goals: (1) the creation and maintenance of Tuskegee Institute as a major black-run educational institution, (2) the advancement of his own power as a national racial leader, and (3) the publicizing and defense of his philosophy of African American education and socioeconomic progress. With a modest tone, Washington provides considerable evidence of the lofty status he attained in the eyes of powerful whites. The text of his most famous address, which he gave at the opening of the Cotton States and International Exposition in Atlanta, is followed by a letter from President Grover Cleveland congratulating him on the wisdom of his ideas about how to solve America's race problem. Without expounding these ideas systematically in his autobiography, Washington makes *Up from Slavery* demonstrate their efficacy in his life and in the life of Tuskegee.

As many post-war African American leaders believed, Washington felt the key to his race's advancement was education. However, the kind of education that Tuskegee offered was what Washington called "practical knowledge"— "knowing how to make a living." This attitude toward education gave Washington his reputation as a realist. When he urged fellow blacks in his Atlanta Exposition address "to draw the line between the superficial and the substantial, the ornamental gewgaws of life and the useful," he concerned himself with the here and now, rather than romantic hopes and distant ideals.

Washington's brand of realism had profound political implications. Black leaders like Frederick Douglass had traditionally laid claim to the principles of full citizenship embodied in the U.S. Constitution and Bill of Rights. Washington's pragmatism, however, implied that African Americans had to prove they were qualified for civil rights by making a success of themselves first in the economic arena.

For a half century after its publication, *Up from Slavery* was the best-known book written by an African American. This was mainly attributable to Washington's skill in subtly revising his literary models, the autobiographies of Benjamin Franklin and Frederick Douglass. *Up from Slavery* is a slave narrative whose opening recalls Douglass's 1845 *Narrative*, but Washington's agenda is radically different from that of his predecessor's. W.E.B. Du Bois took exception to this agenda, however, as did other critics of Washington. While Douglass depicts slavery as a hell on earth, Washington blandly calls it a "school" that helped prepare blacks for the role that he argues they were ready and willing to assume in the postwar economic order. Washington attributes his successes to his adherence to many of the virtues celebrated in Franklin's archetypal American success story: selflessness, industry, honesty, and optimism. As recent scholarship has shown, however, behind the mask of the public-spirited, humble, and plainspoken schoolmaster, one can often find a devious and self-centered power broker. To read *Up from Slavery* is to explore the rhetorical means by which Washington constructed the most powerful and disingenuous myth of black selfhood in his era.

William L. Andrews
University of North Carolina at Chapel Hill

PRIMARY WORKS

The Future of the American Negro, 1899; *Up from Slavery*, 1901; *Working with the Hands*, 1904; *My Larger Education*, 1911; *The Booker T. Washington Papers*, Vols. 1–14, 1972–1989.

from Up from Slavery

Chapter I. A Slave among Slaves

I was born a slave on a plantation in Franklin County, Virginia. I am not quite sure of the exact place or exact date of my birth, but at any rate I suspect I must have been born somewhere and at some time. As nearly as I have been able to learn, I was born near a crossroads post-office called Hale's Ford, and the year was 1858 or 1859.[1] I do not know the month or the day. The earliest impressions I can now recall are of the plantation and the slave quarters—the latter being the part of the plantation where the slaves had their cabins.

My life had its beginning in the midst of the most miserable, desolate, and discouraging surroundings. This was so, however, not because my owners were especially cruel, for they were not, as compared with many others. I was born in a typical log cabin, about fourteen by sixteen feet square. In this cabin I lived with my mother and a brother and sister till after the Civil War, when we were all declared free.

Of my ancestry I know almost nothing. In the slave quarters, and even later, I heard whispered conversations among the coloured people of the tortures which the slaves, including, no doubt, my ancestors on my mother's side, suffered in the middle passage of the slave ship while being conveyed from Africa to America. I have been unsuccessful in securing any information that would throw any accurate light upon the history of my family beyond my mother. She, I remember, had a half-brother and a half-sister. In the days of slavery not very much attention was given to family history and

---

[1]1858 or 1859: Washington was probably born in the spring of 1856.

family records—that is, black family records. My mother, I suppose, attracted the attention of a purchaser who was afterward my owner and hers. Her addition to the slave family attracted about as much attention as the purchase of a new horse or cow. Of my father I know even less than of my mother. I do not even know his name. I have heard reports to the effect that he was a white man who lived on one of the near-by plantations. Whoever he was, I never heard of his taking the least interest in me or providing in any way for my rearing. But I do not find especial fault with him. He was simply another unfortunate victim of the institution which the Nation unhappily had engrafted upon it at that time.

The cabin was not only our living-place, but was also used as the kitchen for the plantation. My mother was the plantation cook. The cabin was without glass windows; it had only openings in the side which let in the light, and also the cold, chilly air of winter. There was a door to the cabin—that is, something that was called a door—but the uncertain hinges by which it was hung, and the large cracks in it, to say nothing of the fact that it was too small, made the room a very uncomfortable one. In addition to these openings there was, in the lower right-hand corner of the room, the "cat-hole"—a contrivance which almost every mansion or cabin in Virginia possessed during the ante-bellum period. The "cat-hole" was a square opening, about seven by eight inches, provided for the purpose of letting the cat pass in and out of the house at will during the night. In the case of our particular cabin I could never understand the necessity for this convenience, since there were at least a half-dozen other places in the cabin that would have accommodated the cats. There was no wooden floor in our cabin, the naked earth being used as a floor. In the centre of the earthen floor there was a large, deep opening covered with boards, which was used as a place in which to store sweet potatoes during the winter. An impression of this potato-hole is very distinctly engraved upon my memory, because I recall that during the process of putting the potatoes in or taking them out I would often come into possession of one or two, which I roasted and thoroughly enjoyed. There was no cooking-stove on our plantation, and all the cooking for the whites and slaves my mother had to do over an open fireplace, mostly in pots and "skillets." While the poorly built cabin caused us to suffer with cold in the winter, the heat from the open fireplace in summer was equally trying.

The early years of my life, which were spent in the little cabin, were not very different from those of thousands of other slaves. My mother, of course, had little time in which to give attention to the training of her children during the day. She snatched a few moments for our care in the early morning before her work began, and at night after the day's work was done. One of my earliest recollections is that of my mother cooking a chicken late at night, and awakening her children for the purpose of feeding them. How or where she got it I do not know. I presume, however, it was procured from our owner's farm. Some people may call this theft. If such a thing were to happen now, I should condemn it as theft myself. But taking place at the time it did, and for the reason that it did, no one could ever make me believe that my mother was guilty of thieving. She was simply a victim of the system of slavery. I cannot remember having slept in a bed until after our family was declared free by the Emancipation Proclamation. Three children—John, my older brother, Amanda, my sister, and myself—had a pallet on the dirt floor, or, to be more correct, we slept in and on a bundle of filthy rags laid upon the dirt floor.

I was asked not long ago to tell something about the sports and pastimes that I engaged in during my youth. Until that question was asked it had never occurred to me that there was no period of my life that was devoted to play. From the time that I can remember anything, almost every day of my life has been occupied in some kind of labour; though I think I would now be a more useful man if I had had time for sports. During the period that I spent in slavery I was not large enough to be of much service, still I was occupied most of the time in cleaning the yards, carrying water to the men in the fields, or going to the mill, to which I used to take the corn, once a week, to be ground. The mill was about three miles from the plantation. This work I always dreaded. The heavy bag of corn would be thrown across the back of the horse, and the corn divided about evenly on each side; but in some way, almost without exception, on these trips, the corn would so shift as to become unbalanced and would fall off the horse, and often I would fall with it. As I was not strong enough to reload the corn upon the horse, I would have to wait, sometimes for many hours, till a chance passerby came along who would help me out of my trouble. The hours while waiting for some one were usually spent in crying. The time consumed in this way made me late in reaching the mill, and by the time I got my corn ground and reached home it would be far into the night. The road was a lonely one, and often led through dense forests. I was always frightened. The woods were said to be full of soldiers who had deserted from the army, and I had been told that the first thing a deserter did to a Negro boy when he found him alone was to cut off his ears. Besides, when I was late in getting home I knew I would always get a severe scolding or a flogging.

I had no schooling whatever while I was a slave, though I remember on several occasions I went as far as the schoolhouse door with one of my young mistresses to carry her books. The picture of several dozen boys and girls in a schoolroom engaged in study made a deep impression upon me, and I had the feeling that to get into a schoolhouse and study in this way would be about the same as getting into paradise.

So far as I can now recall, the first knowledge that I got of the fact that we were slaves, and that freedom of the slaves was being discussed, was early one morning before day, when I was awakened by my mother kneeling over her children and fervently praying that Lincoln and his armies might be successful, and that one day she and her children might be free. In this connection I have never been able to understand how the slaves throughout the South, completely ignorant as were the masses so far as books or newspapers were concerned, were able to keep themselves so accurately and completely informed about the great National questions that were agitating the country. From the time that Garrison, Lovejoy,[2] and others began to agitate for freedom, the slaves throughout the South kept in close touch with the progress of the movement. Though I was a mere child during the preparation for the Civil War and during the war itself, I now recall the many late-at-night whispered discussions that I heard my mother and the other slaves on the plantation indulge in. These discussions showed that they understood the situation, and that they kept themselves informed of events by what was termed the "grape-vine" telegraph.

During the campaign when Lincoln was first a candidate for the Presidency, the slaves on our far-off plantation, miles from any railroad or large city or daily newspaper, knew what the issues involved were. When war was begun between the North and the South, every slave on our plantation felt and knew that, though other issues were discussed, the primal one was that of slavery. Even the most ignorant members of my race on the remote plantations felt in their hearts, with a certainty that admitted of no doubt, that the freedom of the slaves would be the one great result of the war, if the Northern armies conquered. Every success of the Federal armies and every defeat of the Confederate forces was watched with the keenest and most intense interest. Often the slaves got knowledge of the results of great battles before the white people received it. This news was usually gotten from the coloured man who was sent to the post-office for the mail. In our case the post-office was about three miles from the plantation, and the mail came once or twice a week. The man who was sent to the office would linger about the place long enough to get the drift of the conversation from the group of white people who naturally congregated there, after receiving their mail, to discuss the latest news. The mail-carrier on his way back to our master's house would as naturally retail the news that he had secured among the slaves, and in this way they often heard of important events before the white people at the "big house," as the master's house was called.

I cannot remember a single instance during my childhood or early boyhood when our entire family sat down to the table together, and God's blessing was asked, and the family ate a meal in a civilized manner. On the plantation in Virginia, and even later, meals were gotten by the children very much as dumb animals get theirs. It was a piece of bread here and a scrap of meat there. It was a cup of milk at one time and some potatoes at another. Sometimes a portion of our family would eat out of the skillet or pot, while some one else would eat from a tin plate held on the knees, and often using nothing but the hands with which to hold the food. When I had grown to sufficient size, I was required to go to the "big house" at mealtimes to fan the flies from the table by means of a large set of paper fans operated by a pulley. Naturally much of the conversation of the white people turned upon the subject of freedom and war, and I absorbed a good deal

[2]William Lloyd Garrison (1805–1879) and Elijah Parish Lovejoy (1802–1837), prominent abolitionist editors.

of it. I remember that at one time I saw two of my young mistresses and some lady visitors eating ginger-cakes, in the yard. At that time those cakes seemed to me to be absolutely the most tempting and desirable things that I had ever seen; and I then and there resolved that, if I ever got free, the height of my ambition would be reached if I could get to the point where I could secure and eat ginger-cakes in the way that I saw those ladies doing.

Of course as the war was prolonged the white people, in many cases, often found it difficult to secure food for themselves. I think the slaves felt the deprivation less than the whites, because the usual diet for the slaves was corn bread and pork, and these could be raised on the plantation; but coffee, tea, sugar, and other articles which the whites had been accustomed to use could not be raised on the plantation, and the conditions brought about by the war frequently made it impossible to secure these things. The whites were often in great straits. Parched corn was used for coffee, and a kind of black molasses was used instead of sugar. Many times nothing was used to sweeten the so-called tea and coffee.

The first pair of shoes that I recall wearing were wooden ones. They had rough leather on the top, but the bottoms, which were about an inch thick, were of wood. When I walked they made a fearful noise, and besides this they were very inconvenient, since there was no yielding to the natural pressure of the foot. In wearing them one presented an exceedingly awkward appearance. The most trying ordeal that I was forced to endure as a slave boy, however, was the wearing of a flax shirt. In the portion of Virginia where I lived it was common to use flax as part of the clothing for the slaves. That part of the flax from which our clothing was made was largely the refuse, which of course was the cheapest and roughest part. I can scarcely imagine any torture, except, perhaps, the pulling of a tooth, that is equal to that caused by putting on a new flax shirt for the first time. It is almost equal to the feeling that one would experience if he had a dozen or more chestnut burrs, or a hundred small pin-points, in contact with his flesh. Even to this day I can recall accurately the tortures that I underwent when putting on one of these garments. The fact that my flesh was soft and tender added to the pain. But I had no choice. I had to wear the flax shirt or none; and had it been left to me to choose, I should have chosen to wear no covering. In connection with the flax shirt, my brother John, who is several years older than I am, performed one of the most generous acts that I ever heard of one slave relative doing for another. On several occasions when I was being forced to wear a new flax shirt, he generously agreed to put it on in my stead and wear it for several days, till it was "broken in." Until I had grown to be quite a youth this single garment was all that I wore.

One may get the idea, from what I have said, that there was bitter feeling toward the white people on the part of my race, because of the fact that most of the white population was away fighting in a war which would result in keeping the Negro in slavery if the South was successful. In the case of the slaves on our place this was not true, and it was not true of any large portion of the slave population in the South where the Negro was treated with anything like decency. During the Civil War one of my young masters was killed, and two were severely wounded. I recall the feeling of sorrow which existed among the slaves when they heard of the death of "Mars' Billy." It was no sham sorrow, but real. Some of the slaves had nursed "Mars' Billy"; others had played with him when he was a child. "Mars' Billy" had begged for mercy in the case of others when the overseer or master was thrashing them. The sorrow in the slave quarter was only second to that in the "big house." When the two young masters were brought home wounded, the sympathy of the slaves was shown in many ways. They were just as anxious to assist in the nursing as the family relatives of the wounded. Some of the slaves would even beg for the privilege of sitting up at night to nurse their wounded masters. This tenderness and sympathy on the part of those held in bondage was a result of their kindly and generous nature. In order to defend and protect the women and children who were left on the plantations when the white males went to war, the slaves would have laid down their lives. The slave who was selected to sleep in the "big house" during the absence of the males was considered to have the place of honour. Any one attempting to harm "young Mistress" or "old Mistress" during the night would have had to cross the dead body of the slave to do so. I do not know how many have noticed it, but I think that it will be found to be true that there are few instances, either in slavery or freedom, in which a member of my race has been known to betray a specific trust.

As a rule, not only did the members of my race entertain no feelings of bitterness against the whites before and during the war, but there are many instances of Negroes tenderly caring for their former masters and mistresses who for some reason have become poor and dependent since the war. I know of instances where the former masters of slaves have for years been supplied with money by their former slaves to keep them from suffering. I have known of still other cases in which the former slaves have assisted in the education of the descendants of their former owners. I know of a case on a large plantation in the South in which a young white man, the son of the former owner of the estate, has become so reduced in purse and self-control by reason of drink that he is a pitiable creature; and yet, notwithstanding the poverty of the coloured people themselves on this plantation, they have for years supplied this young white man with the necessities of life. One sends him a little coffee or sugar, another a little meat, and so on. Nothing that the coloured people possess is too good for the son of "old Mars' Tom," who will perhaps never be permitted to suffer while any remain on the place who knew directly or indirectly of "old Mars' Tom."

I have said that there are few instances of a member of my race betraying a specific trust. One of the best illustrations of this which I know of is in the case of an ex-slave from Virginia whom I met not long ago in a little town in the state of Ohio. I found that this man had made a contract with his master, two or three years previous to the Emancipation Proclamation, to the effect that the slave was to be permitted to buy himself, by paying so much per year for his body; and while he was paying for himself, he was to be permitted to labour where and for whom he pleased. Finding that he could secure better wages in Ohio, he went there. When freedom came, he was still in debt to his master some three hundred dollars. Notwithstanding that the Emancipation Proclamation freed him from any obligation to his master, this black man walked the greater portion of the distance back to where his old master lived in Virginia, and placed the last dollar, with interest, in his hands. In talking to me about this, the man told me that he knew that he did not have to pay the debt, but that he had given his word to his master, and his word he had never broken. He felt that he could not enjoy his freedom till he had fulfilled his promise.

From some things that I have said one may get the idea that some of the slaves did not want freedom. This is not true. I have never seen one who did not want to be free, or one who would return to slavery.

I pity from the bottom of my heart any nation or body of people that is so unfortunate as to get entangled in the net of slavery. I have long since ceased to cherish any spirit of bitterness against the Southern white people on account of the enslavement of my race. No one section of our country was wholly responsible for its introduction, and, besides, it was recognized and protected for years by the General Government. Having once got its tentacles fastened on to the economic and social life of the Republic, it was no easy matter for the country to relieve itself of the institution. Then, when we rid ourselves of prejudice, or racial feeling, and look facts in the face, we must acknowledge that, notwithstanding the cruelty and moral wrong of slavery, the ten million Negroes inhabiting this country, who themselves or whose ancestors went through the school of American slavery, are in a stronger and more hopeful condition, materially, intellectually, morally, and religiously, than is true of an equal number of black people in any other portion of the globe. This is so to such an extent that Negroes in this country, who themselves or whose forefathers went through the school of slavery, are constantly returning to Africa as missionaries to enlighten those who remained in the fatherland. This I say, not to justify slavery—on the other hand, I condemn it as an institution, as we all know that in America it was established for selfish and financial reasons, and not from a missionary motive—but to call attention to a fact, and to show how Providence so often uses men and institutions to accomplish a purpose. When persons ask me in these days how, in the midst of what sometimes seem hopelessly discouraging conditions, I can have such faith in the future of my race in this country, I remind them of the wilderness through which and out of which, a good Providence has already led us.

Chapter III. The Struggle for an Education

One day, while at work in the coal-mine,[3] I happened to overhear two miners talking about a great school for coloured people somewhere in Virginia.

[3]Washington went to work in a coal mine in Malden, West Virginia, at about the age of ten to supplement his family's meager income.

This was the first time that I had ever heard anything about any kind of school or college that was more pretentious than the little coloured school in our town.

In the darkness of the mine I noiselessly crept as close as I could to the two men who were talking. I heard one tell the other that not only was the school established for the members of my race, but that opportunities were provided by which poor but worthy students could work out all or a part of the cost of board, and at the same time be taught some trade or industry.

As they went on describing the school, it seemed to me that it must be the greatest place on earth, and not even Heaven presented more attractions for me at that time than did the Hampton Normal and Agricultural Institute in Virginia,[4] about which these men were talking. I resolved at once to go to that school, although I had no idea where it was, or how many miles away, or how I was going to reach it; I remembered only that I was on fire constantly with one ambition, and that was to go to Hampton. This thought was with me day and night.

After hearing of the Hampton Institute, I continued to work for a few months longer in the coal-mine. While at work there, I heard of a vacant position in the household of General Lewis Ruffner, the owner of the salt-furnace and coal-mine. Mrs. Viola Ruffner, the wife of General Ruffner, was a "Yankee" woman from Vermont. Mrs. Ruffner had a reputation all through the vicinity for being very strict with her servants, and especially with the boys who tried to serve her. Few of them had remained with her more than two or three weeks. They all left with the same excuse: she was too strict. I decided, however, that I would rather try Mrs. Ruffner's house than remain in the coal-mine, and so my mother applied to her for the vacant position. I was hired at a salary of $5 per month.

I had heard so much about Mrs. Ruffner's severity that I was almost afraid to see her, and trembled when I went into her presence. I had not lived with her many weeks, however, before I began to understand her. I soon began to learn that, first of all, she wanted everything kept clean about her, that she wanted things done promptly and systematically, and that at the bottom of everything she wanted absolute honesty and frankness. Nothing must be sloven or slipshod; every door, every fence, must be kept in repair.

I cannot now recall how long I lived with Mrs. Ruffner before going to Hampton, but I think it must have been a year and a half. At any rate, I here repeat what I have said more than once before, that the lessons that I learned in the home of Mrs. Ruffner were as valuable to me as any education I have ever gotten anywhere since. Even to this day I never see bits of paper scattered around a house or in the street that I do not want to pick them up at once. I never see a filthy yard that I do not want to clean it, a

[4]A co-educational school founded in 1868 for the training of teachers, farmers, and the development of trades among southern blacks.

paling off of a fence that I do not want to put it on, an unpainted or unwhitewashed house that I do not want to paint or whitewash it, or a button off one's clothes, or a grease-spot on them or on a floor, that I do not want to call attention to it.

From fearing Mrs. Ruffner I soon learned to look upon her as one of my best friends. When she found that she could trust me she did so implicitly. During the one or two winters that I was with her she gave me an opportunity to go to school for an hour in the day during a portion of the winter months, but most of my studying was done at night, sometimes alone, sometimes under some one whom I could hire to teach me. Mrs. Ruffner always encouraged and sympathized with me in all my efforts to get an education. It was while living with her that I began to get together my first library. I secured a dry-goods box, knocked out one side of it, put some shelves in it, and began putting into it every kind of book that I could get my hands upon, and called it my "library."

Notwithstanding my success at Mrs. Ruffner's I did not give up the idea of going to the Hampton Institute. In the fall of 1872 I determined to make an effort to get there, although, as I have stated, I had no definite idea of the direction in which Hampton was, or of what it would cost to go there. I do not think that any one thoroughly sympathized with me in my ambition to go to Hampton unless it was my mother, and she was troubled with a grave fear that I was starting out on a "wild-goose chase." At any rate, I got only a half-hearted consent from her that I might start. The small amount of money that I had earned had been consumed by my stepfather and the remainder of the family, with the exception of a very few dollars, and so I had very little with which to buy clothes and pay my travelling expenses. My brother John helped me all that he could, but of course that was not a great deal, for his work was in the coal-mine, where he did not earn much, and most of what he did earn went in the direction of paying the household expenses.

Perhaps the thing that touched and pleased me most in connection with my starting for Hampton was the interest that many of the older coloured people took in the matter. They had spent the best days of their lives in slavery, and hardly expected to live to see the time when they would see a member of their race leave home to attend a boarding-school. Some of these older people would give me a nickel, others a quarter, or a handkerchief.

Finally the great day came, and I started for Hampton. I had only a small, cheap satchel that contained what few articles of clothing I could get. My mother at the time was rather weak and broken in health. I hardly expected to see her again, and thus our parting was all the more sad. She, however, was very brave through it all. At that time there were no through trains connecting that part of West Virginia with eastern Virginia. Trains ran only a portion of the way, and the remainder of the distance was travelled by stage-coaches.

The distance from Malden to Hampton is about five hundred miles. I had not been away from home many hours before it began to grow painfully evident that I did not have enough money to pay my fare to Hampton. One experience I shall long remember. I had been travelling over the mountains most of the afternoon in an old-fashioned stage-coach, when, late in the evening, the coach stopped for the night at a common, unpainted house called a hotel. All the other passengers except myself were whites. In my ignorance I supposed that the little hotel existed for the purpose of accommodating the passengers who travelled on the stage-coach. The difference that the colour of one's skin would make I had not thought anything about. After all the other passengers had been shown rooms and were getting ready for supper, I shyly presented myself before the man at the desk. It is true I had practically no money in my pocket with which to pay for bed or food, but I had hoped in some way to beg my way into the good graces of the landlord, for at that season in the mountains of Virginia the weather was cold, and I wanted to get indoors for the night. Without asking as to whether I had any money, the man at the desk firmly refused to even consider the matter of providing me with food or lodging. This was my first experience in finding out what the colour of my skin meant. In some way I managed to keep warm by walking about, and so got through the night. My whole soul was so bent upon reaching Hampton that I did not have time to cherish any bitterness toward the hotel-keeper.

By walking, begging rides both in wagons and in the cars, in some way, after a number of days, I reached the city of Richmond, Virginia, about eighty-two miles from Hampton. When I reached there, tired, hungry, and dirty, it was late in the night. I had never been in a large city, and this rather added to my misery. When I reached Richmond, I was completely out of money. I had not a single acquaintance in the place, and, being unused to city ways, I did not know where to go. I applied at several places for lodging, but they all wanted money, and that was what I did not have. Knowing nothing else better to do, I walked the streets. In doing this I passed by many food-stands where fried chicken and half-moon apple pies were piled high and made to present a most tempting appearance. At that time it seemed to me that I would have promised all that I expected to possess in the future to have gotten hold of one of those chicken legs or one of those pies. But I could not get either of these, nor anything else to eat.

I must have walked the streets till after midnight. At last I became so exhausted that I could walk no longer. I was tired, I was hungry, I was everything but discouraged. Just about the time when I reached extreme physical exhaustion, I came upon a portion of a street where the board sidewalk was considerably elevated. I waited for a few minutes, till I was sure that no passers-by could see me, and then crept under the sidewalk and lay for the night upon the ground, with my satchel of clothing for a pillow. Nearly all night I could hear the tramp of feet over my head. The next morning I found myself somewhat refreshed, but I was extremely hungry, because it had been a long time since I had had sufficient food. As soon as it became light enough for me to see my surroundings I noticed that I was near a large ship, and that this ship seemed to be unloading a cargo of pig iron. I went at once to the vessel and asked the captain to permit me to help unload the vessel in order to get money for food. The captain, a white man, who seemed to be kind-hearted, consented. I worked long enough to earn money for my breakfast, and it seems to me, as I remember it now, to have been about the best breakfast that I have ever eaten.

My work pleased the captain so well that he told me if I desired I could continue working for a small amount per day. This I was very glad to do. I continued working on this vessel for a number of days. After buying food with the small wages I received there was not much left to add to the amount I must get to pay my way to Hampton. In order to economize in every way possible, so as to be sure to reach Hampton in a reasonable time, I continued to sleep under the same sidewalk that first gave me shelter the first night I was in Richmond. Many years after that the coloured citizens of Richmond very kindly tendered me a reception at which there must have been two thousand people present. This reception was held not far from the spot where I slept the first night I spent in that city, and I must confess that my mind was more upon the sidewalk that first gave me shelter than upon the reception, agreeable and cordial as it was.

When I had saved what I considered enough money with which to reach Hampton, I thanked the captain of the vessel for his kindness, and started again. Without any unusual occurrence I reached Hampton, with a surplus of exactly fifty cents with which to begin my education. To me it had been a long, eventful journey; but the first sight of the large, three-story, brick school building seemed to have rewarded me for all that I had undergone in order to reach the place. If the people who gave the money to provide that building could appreciate the influence the sight of it had upon me, as well as upon thousands of other youths, they would feel all the more encouraged to make such gifts. It seemed to me to be the largest and most beautiful building I had ever seen. The sight of it seemed to give me new life. I felt that a new kind of existence had now begun—that life would now have a new meaning. I felt that I had reached the promised land, and I resolved to let no obstacle prevent me from putting forth the highest effort to fit myself to accomplish the most good in the world.

As soon as possible after reaching the grounds of the Hampton Institute, I presented myself before the head teacher for assignment to a class. Having been so long without proper food, a bath, and change of clothing, I did not, of course, make a very favourable impression upon her, and I could see at once that there were doubts in her mind about the wisdom of admitting me as a student. I felt that I could hardly blame her if she got the idea that I was a worthless loafer or tramp. For some time she did not refuse to admit me, neither did she decide in my favour, and I continued to linger about her, and to impress her in all the ways I could with my worthiness. In the meantime I saw her admitting other students, and that added greatly to my discomfort, for I felt, deep down in my heart, that I could do as well as they, if I could only get a chance to show what was in me.

After some hours had passed, the head teacher said to me: "The adjoining recitation-room needs sweeping. Take the broom and sweep it."

It occurred to me at once that here was my chance. Never did I receive an order with more delight. I knew that I could sweep, for Mrs. Ruffner had thoroughly taught me how to do that when I lived with her.

I swept the recitation-room three times. Then I got a dusting-cloth and I dusted it four times. All the woodwork around the walls, every bench, table, and desk, I went over four times with my dusting-cloth. Besides, every piece of furniture had been moved and every closet and corner in the room had been thoroughly cleaned. I had the feeling that in a large measure my future depended upon the impression I made upon the teacher in the cleaning of that room. When I was through, I reported to the head teacher. She was a "Yankee" woman who knew just where to look for dirt. She went into the room and inspected the floor and closets; then she took her handkerchief and rubbed it on the woodwork about the walls, and over the table and benches. When she was unable to find one bit of dirt on the floor, or a particle of dust on any of the furniture, she quietly remarked, "I guess you will do to enter this institution."

I was one of the happiest souls on earth. The sweeping of that room was my college examination, and never did any youth pass an examination for entrance into Harvard or Yale that gave him more genuine satisfaction. I have passed several examinations since then, but I have always felt that this was the best one I ever passed.

I have spoken of my own experience in entering the Hampton Institute. Perhaps few, if any, had anything like the same experience that I had, but about that same period there were hundreds who found their way to Hampton and other institutions after experiencing something of the same difficulties that I went through. The young men and women were determined to secure an education at any cost.

The sweeping of the recitation-room in the manner that I did it seems to have paved the way for me to get through Hampton. Miss Mary. F. Mackie, the head teacher, offered me a position as janitor. This, of course, I gladly accepted, because it was a place where I could work out nearly all the cost of my board. The work was hard and taxing, but I stuck to it. I had a large number of rooms to care for, and had to work late into the night, while at the same time I had to rise by four o'clock in the morning, in order to build the fires and have a little time in which to prepare my lessons. In all my career at Hampton, and ever since I have been out in the world, Miss Mary F. Mackie, the head teacher to whom I have referred, proved one of my strongest and most helpful friends. Her advice and encouragement were always helpful and strengthening to me in the darkest hour.

I have spoken of the impression that was made upon me by the buildings and general appearance of the Hampton Institute, but I have not spoken of that which made the greatest and most lasting impression upon me, and that was a great man—the noblest, rarest human being that it has ever been my privilege to meet. I refer to the late General Samuel C. Armstrong.

It has been my fortune to meet personally many of what are called great characters, both in Europe and America, but I do not hesitate to say that I never met any man who, in my estimation, was the equal of General Armstrong. Fresh from the degrading influences of the slave plantation and the coal-mines, it was a rare privilege for me to be permitted to come into direct contact with such a character as General Armstrong. I shall always remember that the first time I went into his presence he made the impression upon me of being a perfect man; I was made to feel that there was something about him that was superhuman. It was my privilege to know the General personally from the time I entered Hampton till he died, and the more I saw of him the greater he grew in my estimation. One might have removed from Hampton all the buildings, class-rooms, teachers, and industries, and given the men and women there the opportunity of coming into daily contact with General Armstrong, and that alone would have been a liberal education. The older I grow, the more I am convinced that there is no education which one can get from books and costly apparatus that is equal to that which can be gotten from contact with great men and women. Instead of studying books so constantly, how I wish that our schools and colleges might learn to study men and things!

General Armstrong spent two of the last six months of his life in my home at Tuskegee. At that time he was paralyzed to the extent that he had lost control of his body and voice in a very large degree. Notwithstanding his affliction, he worked almost constantly night and day for the cause to which he had given his life. I never saw a man who so completely lost sight of himself. I do not believe he ever had a selfish thought. He was just as happy in trying to assist some other institution in the South as he was when working for Hampton. Although he fought the Southern white man in the Civil War, I never heard him utter a bitter word against him afterward. On the other hand, he was constantly seeking to find ways by which he could be of service to the Southern whites.

It would be difficult to describe the hold that he had upon the students at Hampton, or the faith they had in him. In fact, he was worshipped by his students. It never occurred to me that General Armstrong could fail in anything that he undertook. There is almost no request that he could have made that would not have been complied with. When he was a guest at my home in Alabama, and was so badly paralyzed that he had to be wheeled about in an invalid's chair, I recall that one of the General's former students had occasion to push his chair up a long, steep hill that taxed his strength to the utmost. When the top of the hill was reached, the former pupil, with a glow of happiness on his face, exclaimed, "I am so glad that I have been permitted to do something that was real hard for the General before he dies!" While I was a student at Hampton, the dormitories became so crowded that it was impossible to find room for all who wanted to be admitted. In order to help remedy the difficulty, the General conceived the plan of putting up tents to be used as rooms. As soon as it became known that General Armstrong would be pleased if some of the older students would live in the tents during the winter, nearly every student in school volunteered to go.

I was one of the volunteers. The winter that we spent in those tents was an intensely cold one, and we suffered severely—how much I am sure General Armstrong never knew, because we made no complaints. It was enough for us to know that we were pleasing General Armstrong, and that we were making it possible for an additional number of students to secure an education. More than once, during a cold night, when a stiff gale would be blowing, our tent was lifted bodily, and we would find ourselves in the open air. The General would usually pay a visit to the tents early in the morning, and his earnest, cheerful, encouraging voice would dispel any feeling of despondency.

I have spoken of my admiration for General Armstrong, and yet he was but a type of that Christlike body of men and women who went into the Negro schools at the close of the war by the hundreds to assist in lifting up my race. The history of the world fails to show a higher, purer, and more unselfish class of men and women than those who found their way into those Negro schools.

Life at Hampton was a constant revelation to me; was constantly taking me into a new world. The matter of having meals at regular hours, of eating on a tablecloth, using a napkin, the use of the bath-tub and of the toothbrush, as well as the use of sheets upon the bed, were all new to me.

I sometimes feel that almost the most valuable lesson I got at the Hampton Institute was in the use and value of the bath. I learned there for the first time some of its value, not only in keeping the body healthy, but in inspiring self-respect and promoting virtue. In all my travels in the South and elsewhere since leaving Hampton I have always in some way sought my daily bath. To get it sometimes when I have been the guest of my own people in a single-roomed cabin has not always been easy to do, except by slipping away to some stream in the woods. I have always tried to teach my people that some provision for bathing should be a part of every house.

For some time, while a student at Hampton, I possessed but a single pair of socks, but when I had worn these till they became soiled, I would wash them at night and hang them by the fire to dry, so that I might wear them again the next morning.

The charge for my board at Hampton was ten dollars per month. I was expected to pay a part of this in cash and to work out the remainder. To meet this cash payment, as I have stated, I had just fifty cents when I reached the institution. Aside from a very few dollars that my brother John was able to send me once in a while, I had no money with which to pay my board. I was determined from the first to make my work as janitor so valuable that my services would be indispensable. This I succeeded in doing to such an extent that I was soon informed that I would be allowed the full cost of my board in return for my work. The cost of tuition was seventy dollars a year. This, of course, was wholly beyond my ability to provide. If I had been compelled to pay the seventy dollars for tuition, in addition to providing for my board, I would have been compelled to leave the Hampton school. General Armstrong, however, very kindly got Mr. S. Griffitts Morgan, of New Bedford, Mass., to defray the cost of my tuition during the whole time that I was at Hampton. After I finished the course at Hampton and had entered upon my lifework at Tuskegee, I had the pleasure of visiting Mr. Morgan several times.

After having been for a while at Hampton, I found myself in difficulty because I did not have books and clothing. Usually, however, I got around the trouble about books by borrowing from those who were more fortunate than myself. As to clothes, when I reached Hampton I had practically nothing. Everything that I possessed was in a small hand satchel. My anxiety about clothing was increased because of the fact that General Armstrong made a personal inspection of the young men in ranks, to see that their clothes were clean. Shoes had to be polished, there must be no buttons off the clothing, and no grease-spots. To wear one suit of clothes continually, while at work and in the schoolroom, and at the same time keep it clean, was rather a hard problem for me to solve. In some way I managed to get on till the teachers learned that I was in earnest and meant to succeed, and then some of them were kind enough to see that I was partly supplied with second-hand clothing that had been sent in barrels from the North. These barrels proved a blessing to hundreds of poor but deserving students. Without them I question whether I should ever have gotten through Hampton.

When I first went to Hampton I do not recall that I had ever slept in a bed that had two sheets on it. In those days there were not many buildings there, and room was very precious. There were seven other boys in the same room with me; most of them, however, students who had been there for some time. The sheets were quite a puzzle to me. The first night I slept under both of them, and the second night I slept on top of both of them; but by watching the other boys I learned my lesson in this, and have been trying to follow it ever since and to teach it to others.

I was among the youngest of the students who were in Hampton at that time. Most of the students were men and women—some as old as forty years of age. As I now recall the scene of my first year, I do not believe that one often has the opportunity of coming into contact with three or four hundred men and women who were so tremendously in earnest as these men and women were. Every hour was occupied in study or work. Nearly all had had enough actual contact with the world to teach them the need of education. Many of the older ones were, of course, too old to master the text-books very thoroughly, and it was often sad to watch their struggles; but they made up in earnestness much of what they lacked in books. Many of them were as poor as I was, and, besides having to wrestle with their books, they had to struggle with a poverty which prevented their having the necessities of life. Many of them had aged parents who were dependent upon them, and some of them were men who had wives whose support in some way they had to provide for.

The great and prevailing idea that seemed to take possession of every one was to prepare himself to lift up the people at his home. No one seemed to think of himself. And the officers and teachers, what a rare set of human beings they were! They worked for the students night and day, in season

and out of season. They seemed happy only when they were helping the students in some manner. Whenever it is written—and I hope it will be—the
part that the Yankee teachers played in the education of the Negroes immediately after the war will make one of the most thrilling parts of the history
of this country. The time is not far distant when the whole South will appreciate this service in a way that it has not yet been able to do.

Chapter VI. Black Race and Red Race

During the year that I spent in Washington,[5] and for some little time before
this, there had been considerable agitation in the state of West Virginia over
the question of moving the capital of the state from Wheeling to some other
central point. As a result of this, the Legislature designated three cities to
be voted upon by the citizens of the state as the permanent seat of government. Among these cities was Charleston, only five miles from Malden, my
home. At the close of my school year in Washington I was very pleasantly
surprised to receive, from a committee of white people in Charleston, an invitation to canvass the state in the interests of that city. This invitation I
accepted, and spent nearly three months in speaking in various parts of the
state. Charleston was successful in winning the prize, and is now the permanent seat of government.

The reputation that I made as a speaker during this campaign induced a
number of persons to make an earnest effort to get me to enter political life,
but I refused, still believing that I could find other service which would prove
of more permanent value to my race. Even then I had a strong feeling that
what our people most needed was to get a foundation in education, industry,
and property, and for this I felt that they could better afford to strive than
for political preferment. As for my individual self, it appeared to me to be reasonably certain that I could succeed in political life, but I had a feeling that it
would be a rather selfish kind of success—individual success at the cost of
failing to do my duty in assisting in laying a foundation for the masses.

At this period in the progress of our race a very large proportion of the
young men who went to school or to college did so with the expressed determination to prepare themselves to be great lawyers, or Congressmen, and
many of the women planned to become music teachers; but I had a reasonably fixed idea, even at that early period in my life, that there was need for
something to be done to prepare the way for successful lawyers, Congressmen, and music teachers.

I felt that the conditions were a good deal like those of an old coloured
man, during the days of slavery, who wanted to learn how to play on the
guitar. In his desire to take guitar lessons he applied to one of his young
masters to teach him; but the young man, not having much faith in the ability of the slave to master the guitar at his age, sought to discourage him by

---

[5]In the fall of 1878, Washington left a position as a schoolteacher in the Kanawha Valley, West Virginia, to pursue a year of
theological study at the Wayland Seminary
in Washington, D.C.

telling him: "Uncle Jake, I will give you guitar lessons; but, Jake, I will have to charge you three dollars for the first lesson, two dollars for the second lesson, and one dollar for the third lesson. But I will charge you only twenty-five cents for the last lesson."

Uncle Jake answered: "All right, boss, I hires you on dem terms. But, boss! I wants yer to be sure an' give me dat las' lesson first."

Soon after my work in connection with the removal of the capital was finished, I received an invitation which gave me great joy and which at the same time was a very pleasant surprise. This was a letter from General Armstrong, inviting me to return to Hampton at the next Commencement to deliver what was called the "post-graduate address." This was an honour which I had not dreamed of receiving. With much care I prepared the best address that I was capable of. I chose for my subject "The Force That Wins."

As I returned to Hampton for the purpose of delivering this address, I went over much of the same ground—now, however, covered entirely by railroad—that I had traversed nearly six years before, when I first sought entrance into Hampton Institute as a student. Now I was able to ride the whole distance in the train. I was constantly contrasting this with my first journey to Hampton. I think I may say, without seeming egotism, that it is seldom that five years have wrought such a change in the life and aspirations of an individual.

At Hampton I received a warm welcome from teachers and students. I found that during my absence from Hampton the institute each year had been getting closer to the real needs and conditions of our people; that the industrial teaching, as well as that of the academic department, had greatly improved. The plan of the school was not modelled after that of any other institution then in existence, but every improvement was made under the magnificent leadership of General Armstrong solely with the view of meeting and helping the needs of our people as they presented themselves at the time. Too often, it seems to me, in missionary and educational work among undeveloped races, people yield to the temptation of doing that which was done a hundred years before, or is being done in other communities a thousand miles away. The temptation often is to run each individual through a certain educational mould, regardless of the condition of the subject or the end to be accomplished. This was not so at Hampton Institute.

The address which I delivered on Commencement Day seems to have pleased every one, and many kind and encouraging words were spoken to me regarding it. Soon after my return to my home in West Virginia, where I had planned to continue teaching, I was again surprised to receive a letter from General Armstrong, asking me to return to Hampton partly as a teacher and partly to pursue some supplementary studies. This was in the summer of 1879. Soon after I began my first teaching in West Virginia I had picked out four of the brightest and most promising of my pupils, in addition to my two brothers, to whom I have already referred, and had given them special attention, with the view of having them go to Hampton. They had gone there, and in each case the teachers had found them so well prepared that they entered advanced classes. This fact, it seems, led to my being called back to Hampton as a teacher. One of the young men that I sent to Hampton in this way is now Dr. Samuel E. Courtney, a successful physician in Boston, and a member of the School Board of that city.

About this time the experiment was being tried for the first time, by General Armstrong, of educating Indians at Hampton. Few people then had any confidence in the ability of the Indians to receive education and to profit by it. General Armstrong was anxious to try the experiment systematically on a large scale. He secured from the reservations in the Western states over one hundred wild and for the most part perfectly ignorant Indians, the greater proportion of whom were young men. The special work which the General desired me to do was to be sort of "house father" to the Indian young men—that is, I was to live in the building with them and have the charge of their discipline, clothing, rooms, and so on. This was a very tempting offer, but I had become so much absorbed in my work in West Virginia that I dreaded to give it up. However, I tore myself away from it. I did not know how to refuse to perform any service that General Armstrong desired of me.

On going to Hampton, I took up my residence in a building with about seventy-five Indian youths. I was the only person in the building who was not a member of their race. At first I had a good deal of doubt about my ability to succeed. I knew that the average Indian felt himself above the white man, and, of course, he felt himself far above the Negro, largely on account of the fact of the Negro having submitted to slavery—a thing which the Indian would never do. The Indians, in the Indian Territory, owned a large number of slaves during the days of slavery. Aside from this, there was a general feeling that the attempt to educate and civilize the red men at Hampton would be a failure. All this made me proceed very cautiously, for I felt keenly the great responsibility. But I was determined to succeed. It was not long before I had the complete confidence of the Indians, and not only this, but I think I am safe in saying that I had their love and respect. I found that they were about like any other human beings; that they responded to kind treatment and resented ill-treatment. They were continually planning to do something that would add to my happiness and comfort. The things that they disliked most, I think, were to have their long hair cut, to give up wearing their blankets, and to cease smoking; but no white American ever thinks that any other race is wholly civilized until he wears the white man's clothes, eats the white man's food, speaks the white man's language, and professes the white man's religion.

When the difficulty of learning the English language was subtracted, I found that in the matter of learning trades and mastering academic studies there was little difference between the coloured and Indian students. It was a constant delight to me to note the interest which the coloured students took in trying to help the Indians in every way possible. There were a few of the coloured students who felt that the Indians ought not to be admitted to Hampton, but these were in the minority. Whenever they were asked to do so, the Negro students gladly took the Indians as roommates, in order that they might teach them to speak English and to acquire civilized habits.

I have often wondered if there was a white institution in this country whose students would have welcomed the incoming of more than a hundred companions of another race in the cordial way that these black students at Hampton welcomed the red ones. How often I have wanted to say to white students that they lift themselves up in proportion as they help to lift others, and the more unfortunate the race, and the lower in the scale of civilization, the more does one raise one's self by giving the assistance.

Chapter XIII. Two Thousand Miles for a Five-Minute Speech

... On the morning of September 17, together with Mrs. Washington and my three children, I started for Atlanta. I felt a good deal as I suppose a man feels when he is on his way to the gallows. In passing through the town of Tuskegee I met a white farmer who lived some distance out in the country. In a jesting manner this man said: "Washington, you have spoken before the Northern white people, the Negroes in the South, and to us country white people in the South; but in Atlanta, to-morrow, you will have before you the Northern whites, the Southern whites, and the Negroes all together. I am afraid that you have got yourself into a tight place." This farmer diagnosed the situation correctly, but his frank words did not add anything to my comfort.

In the course of the journey from Tuskegee to Atlanta both coloured and white people came to the train to point me out, and discussed with perfect freedom, in my hearing, what was going to take place the next day. We were met by a committee in Atlanta. Almost the first thing that I heard when I got off the train in that city was an expression something like this, from an old coloured man near by: "Dat's de man of my race what's gwine to make a speech at de Exposition to-morrow. I'se sho' gwine to hear him."

Atlanta was literally packed, at the time, with people from all parts of this country, and with representatives of foreign governments, as well as with military and civic organizations. The afternoon papers had forecasts of the next day's proceedings in flaring headlines. All this tended to add to my burden. I did not sleep much that night. The next morning, before day, I went carefully over what I intended to say. I also kneeled down and asked God's blessing upon my effort. Right here, perhaps, I ought to add that I make it a rule never to go before an audience, on any occasion, without asking the blessing of God upon what I want to say.

I always make it a rule to make especial preparation for each separate address. No two audiences are exactly alike. It is my aim to reach and talk to the heart of each individual audience, taking it into my confidence very much as I would a person. When I am speaking to an audience, I care little for how what I am saying is going to sound in the newspapers, or to another audience, or to an individual. At the time, the audience before me absorbs all my sympathy, thought, and energy.

Early in the morning a committee called to escort me to my place in the procession which was to march to the Exposition grounds. In this procession were prominent coloured citizens in carriages, as well as several Negro military organizations. I noted that the Exposition officials seemed to go out of their way to see that all of the coloured people in the procession were properly placed and properly treated. The procession was about three hours in reaching the Exposition grounds, and during all of this time the sun was shining down upon us disagreeably hot. When we reached the grounds, the heat, together with my nervous anxiety, made me feel as if I were about ready to collapse, and to feel that my address was not going to be a success. When I entered the audience-room, I found it packed with humanity from bottom to top, and there were thousands outside who could not get in.

The room was very large, and well suited to public speaking. When I entered the room, there were vigorous cheers from the coloured portion of the audience, and faint cheers from some of the white people. I had been told, while I had been in Atlanta, that while many white people were going to be present to hear me speak, simply out of curiosity, and that others who would be present would be in full sympathy with me, there was a still larger element of the audience which would consist of those who were going to be present for the purpose of hearing me make a fool of myself, or, at least, of hearing me say some foolish thing, so that they could say to the officials who had invited me to speak, "I told you so!"

One of the trustees of the Tuskegee Institute, as well as my personal friend, Mr. William H. Baldwin, Jr., was at the time General Manager of the Southern Railroad, and happened to be in Atlanta on that day. He was so nervous about the kind of reception that I would have, and the effect that my speech would produce, that he could not persuade himself to go into the building, but walked back and forth in the grounds outside until the opening exercises were over.

Chapter XIV. The Atlanta Exposition Address

The Atlanta Exposition,[6] at which I had been asked to make an address as a representative of the Negro race, as stated in the last chapter, was opened with a short address from Governor Bullock. After other interesting exercises, including an invocation from Bishop Nelson, of Georgia, a dedicatory ode by Albert Howell, Jr., and addresses by the President of the Exposition and Mrs. Joseph Thompson, the President of the Woman's Board, Governor Bullock introduced me with the words, "We have with us to-day a representative of Negro enterprise and Negro civilization."

When I arose to speak, there was considerable cheering, especially from the coloured people. As I remember it now, the thing that was uppermost in my mind was the desire to say something that would cement the friendship of the races and bring about hearty cooperation between them. So far as my

[6]Washington spoke at the opening ceremonies of the Atlanta (Georgia) Cotton States and International Exposition, September 18, 1895.

outward surroundings were concerned, the only thing that I recall distinctly now is that when I got up, I saw thousands of eyes looking intently into my face. The following is the address which I delivered:—

Mr. President and Gentlemen of the Board of Directors and Citizens:

One-third of the population of the South is of the Negro race. No enterprise seeking the material, civil, or moral welfare of this section can disregard this element of our population and reach the highest success. I but convey to you, Mr. President and Directors, the sentiment of the masses of my race when I say that in no way have the value and manhood of the American Negro been more fittingly and generously recognized than by the managers of this magnificent Exposition at every stage of its progress. It is a recognition that will do more to cement the friendship of the two races than any occurrence since the dawn of our freedom.

Not only this, but the opportunity here afforded will awaken among us a new era of industrial progress. Ignorant and inexperienced, it is not strange that in the first years of our new life we began at the top instead of at the bottom; that a seat in Congress or the state legislature was more sought than real estate or industrial skill; that the political convention or stump speaking had more attractions than starting a dairy farm or truck garden.

A ship lost at sea for many days suddenly sighted a friendly vessel. From the mast of the unfortunate vessel was seen a signal, "Water, water; we die of thirst!" The answer from the friendly vessel at once came back, "Cast down your bucket where you are." A second time the signal, "Water, water; send us water!" ran up from the distressed vessel, and was answered, "Cast down your bucket where you are." And a third and fourth signal for water was answered, "Cast down your bucket where you are." The captain of the distressed vessel, at last heeding the injunction, cast down his bucket, and it came up full of fresh, sparkling water from the mouth of the Amazon River. To those of my race who depend on bettering their condition in a foreign land or who underestimate the importance of cultivating friendly relations with the Southern white man, who is their next-door neighbour, I would say: "Cast down your bucket where you are"—cast it down in making friends in every manly way of the people of all races by whom we are surrounded.

Cast it down in agriculture, mechanics, in commerce, in domestic service, and in the professions. And in this connection it is well to bear in mind that whatever other sins the South may be called to bear, when it comes to business, pure and simple, it is in the South that the Negro is given a man's chance in the commercial world, and in nothing is this Exposition more eloquent than in emphasizing this chance. Our greatest danger is that in the great leap from slavery to freedom we may overlook the fact that the masses of us are to live by the productions of our hands, and fail to keep in mind that we shall prosper in proportion as we learn to dignify and glorify common labour and put brains and skill into the common occupations of life; shall prosper in proportion as we learn to draw the line between the superficial and the substantial, the ornamental gewgaws of life and the useful. No race can prosper till it learns that there is as much dignity in tilling a field as in writing a poem. It is at the bottom of life we must begin, and not at the top. Nor should we permit our grievances to overshadow our opportunities.

To those of the white race who look to the incoming of those of foreign birth and strange tongue and habits for the prosperity of the South, were I permitted I would repeat what I say to my own race, "Cast down your bucket where you are." Cast it down among the eight millions of Negroes whose habits you know, whose fidelity and love you have tested in days when to have proved treacherous meant the ruin of your firesides. Cast down your bucket among these people who have, without strikes and labour wars, tilled your fields, cleared your forests, builded your railroads and cities, and brought forth treasures from the bowels of the earth, and helped make possible this magnificent representation of the progress of the South. Casting down your bucket among my people, helping and encouraging them as you are doing on these grounds, and to education of head, hand, and heart, you will find that they will buy your surplus land, make blossom the waste places in your fields, and run your factories. While doing this, you can be sure in the future, as in the past, that you and your families will be surrounded by the most patient, faithful, law-abiding, and unresentful people that the world has seen. As we have proved our loyalty to you in the past, in nursing your children, watching by the sick-bed of your mothers and fathers, and often following them with tear-dimmed eyes to their graves, so in the future, in our humble way, we shall stand by you with a devotion that no foreigner can approach, ready to lay down our lives, if need be, in defence of yours, interlacing our industrial, commercial, civil, and religious life with yours in a way that shall make the interests of both races one. In all things that are purely social we can be as separate as the fingers, yet one as the hand in all things essential to mutual progress.

There is no defence or security for any of us except in the highest intelligence and development of all. If anywhere there are efforts tending to curtail the fullest growth of the Negro, let these efforts be turned into stimulating, encouraging, and making him the most useful and intelligent citizen. Effort or means so invested will pay a thousand per cent interest. These efforts will be twice blessed—"blessing him that gives and him that takes."[7]

There is no escape through law of man or God from the inevitable:—

> *"The laws of changeless justice bind*
>   *Oppressor with oppressed;*
> *And close as sin and suffering joined*
>   *We march to fate abreast."*[8]

Nearly sixteen millions of hands will aid you in pulling the load upward, or they will pull against you the load downward. We shall constitute one-third and more of the ignorance and crime of the South, or one-third its intelligence and progress; we shall contribute one-third to the business and industrial prosperity of the South, or we shall prove a veritable body of death, stagnating, depressing, retarding every effort to advance the body politic.

[7]William Shakespeare, *The Merchant of Venice*, Act IV, scene 1, line 1670.

[8]"Song of the Negro Boatman," by John Greenleaf Whittier (1807–1892).

Gentlemen of the Exposition, as we present to you our humble effort at an exhibition of our progress, you must not expect overmuch. Starting thirty years ago with ownership here and there in a few quilts and pumpkins and chickens (gathered from miscellaneous sources), remember the path that has led from these to the inventions and production of agricultural implements, buggies, steam-engines, newspapers, books, statuary, carving, paintings, the management of drug-stores and banks, has not been trodden without contact with thorns and thistles. While we take pride in what we exhibit as a result of our independent efforts, we do not for a moment forget that our part in this exhibition would fall far short of your expectations but for the constant help that has come to our educational life, not only from the Southern states, but especially from Northern philanthropists, who have made their gifts a constant stream of blessing and encouragement.

The wisest among my race understand that the agitation of questions of social equality is the extremest folly, and that progress in the enjoyment of all the privileges that will come to us must be the result of severe and constant struggle rather than of artificial forcing. No race that has anything to contribute to the markets of the world is long in any degree ostracized. It is important and right that all privileges of the law be ours, but it is vastly more important that we be prepared for the exercise of these privileges. The opportunity to earn a dollar in a factory just now is worth infinitely more than the opportunity to spend a dollar in an opera-house.

In conclusion, may I repeat that nothing in thirty years has given us more hope and encouragement, and drawn us so near to you of the white race, as this opportunity offered by the Exposition; and here bending, as it were, over the altar that represents the results of the struggles of your race and mine, both starting practically empty-handed three decades ago, I pledge that in your effort to work out the great and intricate problem which God has laid at the doors of the South, you shall have at all times the patient, sympathetic help of my race; only let this be constantly in mind, that, while from representations in these buildings of the product of field, of forest, of mine, of factory, letters, and art, much good will come, yet far above and beyond material benefits will be that higher good, that, let us pray God, will come, in a blotting out of sectional differences and racial animosities and suspicions, in a determination to administer absolute justice, in a willing obedience among all classes to the mandates of law. This, coupled with our material prosperity, will bring into our beloved South a new heaven and a new earth.

The first thing that I remember, after I had finished speaking, was that Governor Bullock rushed across the platform and took me by the hand, and that others did the same. I received so many and such hearty congratulations that I found it difficult to get out of the building. I did not appreciate to any degree, however, the impression which my address seemed to have made, until the next morning, when I went into the business part of the city. As soon as I was recognized, I was surprised to find myself pointed out and surrounded by a crowd of men who wished to shake hands with me. This was kept up on every street on to which I went, to an extent which embarrassed me so much that I went back to my boarding-place. The next morning I returned to Tuskegee. At the station in Atlanta, and at almost all of the stations at which the train stopped between that city and Tuskegee, I found a crowd of people anxious to shake hands with me.

The papers in all parts of the United States published the address in full, and for months afterward there were complimentary editorial references to it. Mr. Clark Howell, the editor of the Atlanta *Constitution*, telegraphed to a New York paper, among other words, the following, "I do not exaggerate when I say that Professor Booker T. Washington's address yesterday was one of the most notable speeches, both as to character and as to the warmth of its reception, ever delivered to a Southern audience. The address was a revelation. The whole speech is a platform upon which blacks and whites can stand with full justice to each other."

The Boston *Transcript* said editorially: "The speech of Booker T. Washington at the Atlanta Exposition, this week, seems to have dwarfed all the other proceedings and the Exposition itself. The sensation that it has caused in the press has never been equalled."

I very soon began receiving all kinds of propositions from lecture bureaus, and editors of magazines and papers, to take the lecture platform, and to write articles. One lecture bureau offered me fifty thousand dollars, or two hundred dollars a night and expenses, if I would place my services at its disposal for a given period. To all these communications I replied that my life-work was at Tuskegee; and that whenever I spoke it must be in the interests of the Tuskegee school and my race, and that I would enter into no arrangements that seemed to place a mere commercial value upon my services.

Some days after its delivery I sent a copy of my address to the President of the United States, the Hon. Grover Cleveland. I received from him the following autograph reply:—

Gray Gables
Buzzard's Bay, Mass., October 6, 1895

Booker T. Washington, Esq.:

My Dear Sir: I thank you for sending me a copy of your address delivered at the Atlanta Exposition.

I thank you with much enthusiasm for making the address. I have read it with intense interest, and I think the Exposition would be fully justified if it did not do more than furnish the opportunity for its delivery. Your words cannot fail to delight and encourage all who wish well for your race; and if our coloured fellow-citizens do not from your utterances gather new hope and form new determinations to gain every valuable advantage offered them by their citizenship, it will be strange indeed. Yours very truly,

Grover Cleveland

Later I met Mr. Cleveland, for the first time, when, as President, he visited the Atlanta Exposition. At the request of myself and others he consented to spend an hour in the Negro Building, for the purpose of inspecting the Negro exhibit and of giving the coloured people in attendance an opportunity to shake hands with him. As soon as I met Mr. Cleveland I became impressed with his simplicity, greatness, and rugged honesty. I have met him many times since then, both at public functions and at his private residence in Princeton, and the more I see of him the more I admire him. When he visited the Negro Building in Atlanta he seemed to give himself up wholly, for that hour, to the coloured people. He seemed to be as careful to shake hands with some old coloured "auntie" clad partially in rags, and to take as much pleasure in doing so, as if he were greeting some millionnaire. Many of the coloured people took advantage of the occasion to get him to write his name in a book or on a slip of paper. He was as careful and patient in doing this as if he were putting his signature to some great state document.

Mr. Cleveland has not only shown his friendship for me in many personal ways, but has always consented to do anything I have asked of him for our school. This he has done, whether it was to make a personal donation or to use his influence in securing the donations of others. Judging from my personal acquaintance with Mr. Cleveland, I do not believe that he is conscious of possessing any colour prejudice. He is too great for that. In my contact with people I find that, as a rule, it is only the little, narrow people who live for themselves, who never read good books, who do not travel, who never open up their souls in a way to permit them to come into contact with other souls—with the great outside world. No man whose vision is bounded by colour can come into contact with what is highest and best in the world. In meeting men, in many places, I have found that the happiest people are those who do the most for others; the most miserable are those who do the least. I have also found that few things, if any, are capable of making one so blind and narrow as race prejudice. I often say to our students, in the course of my talks to them on Sunday evenings in the chapel, that the longer I live and the more experience I have of the world, the more I am convinced that, after all, the one thing that is most worth living for— and dying for, if need be—is the opportunity of making some one else more happy and more useful.

The coloured people and the coloured newspapers at first seemed to be greatly pleased with the character of my Atlanta address, as well as with its reception. But after the first burst of enthusiasm began to die away, and the coloured people began reading the speech in cold type, some of them seemed to feel that they had been hypnotized. They seemed to feel that I had been too liberal in my remarks toward the Southern whites, and that I had not spoken out strongly enough for what they termed the "rights" of the race. For a while there was a reaction, so far as a certain element of my own race was concerned, but later these reactionary ones seemed to have been won over to my way of believing and acting.

While speaking of changes in public sentiment, I recall that about ten years after the school at Tuskegee was established, I had an experience that I shall never forget. Dr. Lyman Abbott, then the pastor of Plymouth

Church, and also editor of the *Outlook* (then the *Christian Union*), asked me to write a letter for his paper giving my opinion of the exact condition, mental and moral, of the coloured ministers in the South, as based upon my observations. I wrote the letter, giving the exact facts as I conceived them to be. The picture painted was a rather black one—or, since I am black, shall I say "white"? It could not be otherwise with a race but a few years out of slavery, a race which had not had time or opportunity to produce a competent ministry.

What I said soon reached every Negro minister in the country, I think, and the letters of condemnation which I received from them were not few. I think that for a year after the publication of this article every association and every conference or religious body of any kind, of my race, that met, did not fail before adjourning to pass a resolution condemning me, or calling upon me to retract or modify what I had said. Many of these organizations went so far in their resolutions as to advise parents to cease sending their children to Tuskegee. One association even appointed a "missionary" whose duty it was to warn the people against sending their children to Tuskegee. This missionary had a son in the school, and I noticed that, whatever the "missionary" might have said or done with regard to others, he was careful not to take his son away from the institution. Many of the coloured papers, especially those that were the organs of religious bodies, joined in the general chorus of condemnation or demands for retraction.

During the whole time of the excitement, and through all the criticism, I did not utter a word of explanation or retraction. I knew that I was right, and that time and the sober second thought of the people would vindicate me. It was not long before the bishops and other church leaders began to make a careful investigation of the conditions of the ministry, and they found out that I was right. In fact, the oldest and most influential bishop in one branch of the Methodist Church said that my words were far too mild. Very soon public sentiment began making itself felt, in demanding a purifying of the ministry. While this is not yet complete by any means, I think I may say, without egotism, and I have been told by many of our most influential ministers, that my words had much to do with starting a demand for the placing of a higher type of men in the pulpit. I have had the satisfaction of having many who once condemned me thank me heartily for my frank words.

The change of the attitude of the Negro ministry, so far as regards myself, is so complete that at the present time I have no warmer friends among any class than I have among the clergymen. The improvement in the character and life of the Negro ministers is one of the most gratifying evidences of the progress of the race. My experience with them, as well as other events in my life, convince me that the thing to do, when one feels sure that he has said or done the right thing, and is condemned, is to stand still and keep quiet. If he is right, time will show it.

In the midst of the discussion which was going on concerning my Atlanta speech, I received the letter which I give below, from Dr. Gilman, the President of Johns Hopkins University, who had been made chairman of the judges of award in connection with the Atlanta Exposition:

Johns Hopkins University, Baltimore
President's Office, September 30, 1895

Dear Mr. Washington: Would it be agreeable to you to be one of the Judges of Award in the Department of Education at Atlanta? If so, I shall be glad to place your name upon the list. A line by telegraph will be welcomed. Yours very truly,

D.C. Gilman

I think I was even more surprised to receive this invitation than I had been to receive the invitation to speak at the opening of the Exposition. It was to be a part of my duty, as one of the jurors, to pass not only upon the exhibits of the coloured schools, but also upon those of the white schools. I accepted the position, and spent a month in Atlanta in performance of the duties which it entailed. The board of jurors was a large one, consisting in all of sixty members. It was about equally divided between Southern white people and Northern white people. Among them were college presidents, leading scientists and men of letters, and specialists in many subjects. When the group of jurors to which I was assigned met for organization, Mr. Thomas Nelson Page,[9] who was one of the number, moved that I be made secretary of that division, and the motion was unanimously adopted. Nearly half of our division were Southern people. In performing my duties in the inspection of the exhibits of white schools I was in every case treated with respect, and at the close of our labours I parted from my associates with regret.

I am often asked to express myself more freely than I do upon the political condition and the political future of my race. These recollections of my experience in Atlanta give me the opportunity to do so briefly. My own belief is, although I have never before said so in so many words, that the time will come when the Negro in the South will be accorded all the political rights which his ability, character, and material possessions entitle him to. I think, though, that the opportunity to freely exercise such political rights will not come in any large degree through outside or artificial forcing, but will be accorded to the Negro by the Southern white people themselves, and that they will protect him in the exercise of those rights. Just as soon as the South gets over the old feeling that it is being forced by "foreigners," or "aliens," to do something which it does not want to do, I believe that the change in the direction that I have indicated is going to begin. In fact, there are indications that it is already beginning in a slight degree.

Let me illustrate my meaning. Suppose that some months before the opening of the Atlanta Exposition there had been a general demand from

[9]Thomas Nelson Page, southern writer (1853–1922).

the press and public platform outside the South that a Negro be given a place on the opening programme, and that a Negro be placed upon the board of jurors of award. Would any such recognition of the race have taken place? I do not think so. The Atlanta officials went as far as they did because they felt it to be a pleasure, as well as a duty, to reward what they considered merit in the Negro race. Say what we will, there is something in human nature which we cannot blot out, which makes one man, in the end, recognize and reward merit in another, regardless of colour or race.

I believe it is the duty of the Negro—as the greater part of the race is already doing—to deport himself modestly in regard to political claims, depending upon the slow but sure influences that proceed from the possession of property, intelligence, and high character for the full recognition of his political rights. I think that the according of the full exercise of political rights is going to be a matter of natural, slow growth, not an over-night, gourd-vine affair. I do not believe that the Negro should cease voting, for a man cannot learn the exercise of self-government by ceasing to vote, any more than a boy can learn to swim by keeping out of the water, but I do believe that in his voting he should more and more be influenced by those of intelligence and character who are his next-door neighbours.

I know coloured men who, through the encouragement, help, and advice of Southern white people, have accumulated thousands of dollars' worth of property, but who, at the same time, would never think of going to those same persons for advice concerning the casting of their ballots. This, it seems to me, is unwise and unreasonable, and should cease. In saying this I do not mean that the Negro should truckle, or not vote from principle, for the instant he ceases to vote from principle he loses the confidence and respect of the Southern white man even.

I do not believe that any state should make a law that permits an ignorant and poverty-stricken white man to vote, and prevents a black man in the same condition from voting. Such a law is not only unjust, but it will react, as all unjust laws do, in time; for the effect of such a law is to encourage the Negro to secure education and property, and at the same time it encourages the white man to remain in ignorance and poverty. I believe that in time, through the operation of intelligence and friendly race relations, all cheating at the ballot-box in the South will cease. It will become apparent that the white man who begins by cheating a Negro out of his ballot soon learns to cheat a white man out of his, and that the man who does this ends his career of dishonesty by the theft of property or by some equally serious crime. In my opinion, the time will come when the South will encourage all of its citizens to vote. It will see that it pays better, from every standpoint, to have healthy, vigorous life than to have that political stagnation which always results when one-half of the population has no share and no interest in the Government.

As a rule, I believe in universal, free suffrage, but I believe that in the South we are confronted with peculiar conditions that justify the protection of the ballot in many of the states, for a while at least, either by an educational test, a property test, or by both combined; but whatever tests are required, they should be made to apply with equal and exact justice to both races.

1901

W.E.B. Du Bois
1868–1963

At the turn of the twentieth century, William Edward Burghardt Du Bois, the most outspoken civil rights activist in America, committed himself to a style of political leadership that emphasized that, in order for African Americans to survive the inordinate stress and cruelty of racial discrimination, they had to make a "... determined attempt at self-development, self-realization, in spite of environing discouragement and prejudice." The style called upon African Americans to seek full exercise of civil rights in the United States through militant protest and agitation.

Du Bois's posture met with little popularity, for it was at the time that the nation had witnessed the undermining of the "Reconstruction Amendments"—which had given blacks the legal prerogatives of the vote, access to public facilities and services, and equal rights under the law—by the 1896 Supreme Court decision, *Plessy v. Fergusson*, or the "separate but equal" doctrine. Rayford W. Logan, a noted historian, called the ensuing period of disfranchisement the "nadir" and betrayal of African American citizenship in the United States. Du Bois was undaunted in his conviction that, despite *Plessy v. Fergusson*, the Declaration of Independence and the Constitution of the United States were documents of entitlement and that the struggle of African Americans was a struggle for securing basic human and civil rights for *all* Americans. Hence, for Du Bois, the turn-of-the-century nadir signaled social and political conditions for blacks that made protest an absolute necessity.

Du Bois's political idealism was a product of his childhood observations of and participation in the civic activities of his home town of Great Barrington, Massachusetts, and of his formal education in the nineteenth-century disciplines of history and sociology, both of which held firm to a belief in human progress and the perfectibility of man in society. Born in 1868, Du Bois grew up in a typical New England small-town environment, where social and economic activities were reinforced by strong traditions in "primary democracy": all of its citizens had a right to be heard. Having grown up in such an environment, Du Bois had little direct experience with the social, political, and economic exclusion of blacks before he went south to attend Fisk University in 1885.

After graduating from Fisk University, Du Bois went to Harvard, 1888 to 1892, where he completed a second baccalaureate degree in philosophy and a master's degree in history. He studied philosophy with William James, George

Santayana, and Josiah Royce, whose thoughts on individualism, community, pragmatism, and the use of ideas to promote social change influenced Du Bois's thinking throughout his long career as an activist and writer. His advanced study led to his earning a Ph.D. in history at Harvard and the distinction of having his dissertation, *The Suppression of the Slave Trade in the United States of America*, published as the first volume of the *Harvard Historical Studies* in 1896.

The new social science held that one should seek the "truth" of the human history through an examination of a range of historical documents: the Congressional Record, the census, newspapers, private papers, and so forth. During the initial period of his career, Du Bois utilized the new social science methodology as a researcher and teacher at Wilberforce University (1894–1896), the University of Pennsylvania (1897), and Atlanta University (1897–1910). Between 1896 and 1905, he conducted studies of the urbanization of blacks in the North (*The Philadelphia Negro*) and the social organization of blacks in the rural South (*The Atlanta University Publications*). By 1900, however, having declared that "the problem of the twentieth century is the problem of the color line," he realized that his scholarly work reached a limited audience. He began experimenting with the literary forms in search of containers, as it were, for a kind of literature that portrayed the African American's social and cultural distinctiveness in ways the social sciences did not.

Du Bois created a masterpiece in 1903, *The Souls of Black Folks*. This lyrical book created the possibility of seeing "the Negro" as an object of academic study and esthetic reflection. Nothing quite like it had ever been written, and its structure has been analyzed by many different scholars and critics. Partly because of its hybrid nature—part autobiography, part social science and anthropology, and part cultural criticism—the book repays repeated reading, and it made Du Bois the most famous African American intellectual of his generation and perhaps of the twentieth century.

Du Bois also realized as early as 1900 that organized collective action by black people needed an institutional structure in order to be effective. In 1905, he was the principal founder of the Niagara Movement, a civil rights protest organization, in opposition to Booker T. Washington's conciliatory posture of accommodating racial discrimination. The organization called for direct action against racial discrimination through protest, through the use of the courts, and through education of the American people. Four years later, he was a principal organizer of the National Association for the Advancement of Colored People (NAACP). Its mission was identical to that of the Niagara Movement, but its membership included both blacks and whites. From 1910 to 1934, as the NAACP director of publicity and research and editor of its magazine (the *Crisis*), he combined his experimentation in literature, his understanding of American culture, and the rhetoric of protest. He was, for nearly a quarter century, the undisputed intellectual leader of a new generation of African Americans.

Inevitably, his status drew criticism; Harlem Renaissance writers such as Wallace Thurman parodied Du Bois in *Infants of the Spring* (1929). Satire was one thing. In 1934 he was fired from his post with the NAACP because he advocated use of segregation as a strategy for binding blacks into a cohesive group during the worst of the Great Depression years. Other officials of the organization felt such a strategy was against the NAACP's basic mission: seeking an integrated society. While Du Bois's strategy is little understood, nevertheless it remains the primary reason cited for his departure from the civil rights organization that he helped to found and to which he gave direction.

Although Du Bois returned to the NAACP as director of special research from 1944 to 1948, 1934 marked the end of his influence in the organization and in the affairs of African American letters. Already a world leader by 1900, Du Bois dedicated his post-1934 years almost exclusively to world affairs. For almost two decades, to his death, he was identified as a sympathizer with world peace movements. In 1963, he became a citizen of Ghana, where he died in August of the same year.

Frederick Woodard
University of Iowa

PRIMARY WORKS

The Suppression of the African Slave Trade to the United States of America, 1896; *The Philadelphia Negro: A Social Study,* 1899; *Atlanta University Studies on the American Negro,* 19 volumes published between 1897 and 1915; *The Souls of Black Folk,* 1903; *John Brown,* 1909; *The Quest of the Silver Fleece,* 1911; *The Star of Ethiopia,* 1913; *The Negro,* 1916; *Darkwater,* 1920; *The Gift of the Negro,* 1924; *Dark Princess: Voices from Within the Veil,* 1928; *Black Reconstruction,* 1935; *Dusk of Dawn: An Essay Toward an Autobiography of a Race Concept,* 1940; *Color and Democracy: Colonies and Peace,* 1945; *The World and Africa,* 1947; *The Black Flame—A Trilogy: The Ordeal of Mansart, Mansart Builds a School, and Worlds of Color,* 1957, 1959, and 1961; *The Correspondence of W.E.B. Du Bois,* Vols. 1–3, 1973–1978; *Against Racism, Unpublished Essays, Papers, Addresses,* 1887–1961, 1985.

from **The Souls of Black Folk**

Chapter I. Of Our Spiritual Strivings[1]

O water, voice of my heart, crying in the sand,
  All night long crying with a mournful cry,
  As I lie and listen, and cannot understand

[1]The musical epigraph is taken from the spiritual, "Nobody Know the Trouble I've Seen," whose message of striving and salvation is translated into secular terms in Du Bois's chapter: "Sometimes I'm up, sometimes I'm down,/ Sometimes I'm almost to the ground./ Oh, nobody knows the trouble I've seen ..." The chapter's famous passage on the veil that yields black men and women "no true self consciousness" may also be compared to the song's second verse: "One day when I was walking along, Oh yes, Lord—/ The element opened, and the Love came down, Oh yes Lord." There were numerous collections of spirituals at the turn of the century, but the musicological evidence suggests that Du Bois probably took his examples from J.B.T. Marsh, *The Story of the Jubilee Singers* (1872), and M. F. Armstrong and Helen W. Ludlow, *Hampton and Its Students, with Fifty Cabin and Plantation Songs,* arranged by Thomas P. Fenner (1874). Some of the songs mentioned in Chapter 14, "Of the Sorrow Songs," had been commented on by earlier collectors of spirituals such as William Allen in *Slave Songs in the United States* (1867). The most complete compilation in the early twentieth century was James Weldon Johnson and Rosamond Johnson's two-volume *Book of American Negro Spirituals* (1925, 1926).

The voice of my heart in my side or the voice of the sea,
O water, crying for rest, is it I, is it I?
All night long the water is crying to me.

Unresting water, there never shall be rest
Till the last moon droop and the last tide fail,
And the fire of the end begin to burn in the west;
And the heart shall be weary and wonder and cry like the sea,
All life long crying without avail,
As the water all night long is crying to me.

—Arthur Symons

Between me and the other world there is ever an unasked question: unasked by some through feelings of delicacy; by others through the difficulty of rightly framing it. All, nevertheless, flutter round it. They approach me in a half-hesitant sort of way, eye me curiously or compassionately, and then, instead of saying directly, How does it feel to be a problem? they say, I know an excellent colored man in my town; or, I fought at Mechanicsville; or, Do not these Southern outrages make your blood boil? At these I smile, or am interested, or reduce the boiling to a simmer, as the occasion may require. To the real question, How does it feel to be a problem? I answer seldom a word.

And yet, being a problem is a strange experience,—peculiar even for one who has never been anything else, save perhaps in babyhood and in Europe. It is in the early days of rollicking boyhood that the revelation first bursts upon one, all in a day, as it were. I remember well when the shadow swept across me. I was a little thing, away up in the hills of New England, where the dark Housatonic winds between Hoosac and Taghkanic to the sea. In a wee wooden schoolhouse, something put it into the boys' and girls' heads to buy gorgeous visiting-cards—ten cents a package—and exchange. The exchange was merry, till one girl, a tall newcomer, refused my card,— refused it peremptorily, with a glance. Then it dawned upon me with a certain suddenness that I was different from the others; or like, mayhap, in heart and life and longing, but shut out from their world by a vast veil. I had thereafter no desire to tear down that veil, to creep through; I held all beyond it in common contempt, and lived above it in a region of blue sky and great wandering shadows. That sky was bluest when I could beat my mates at examination time, or beat them at a foot-race, or even beat their stringy heads. Alas, with the years all this fine contempt began to fade; for the worlds I longed for, and all their dazzling opportunities, were theirs, not mine. But they should not keep these prizes, I said; some, all, I would wrest from them. Just how I would do it I could never decide: by reading law, by healing the sick, by telling the wonderful tales that swam in my head,— some way. With other black boys the strife was not so fiercely sunny: their youth shrunk into tasteless sycophancy, or into silent hatred of the pale world about them and mocking distrust of everything white; or wasted itself in a bitter cry, Why did God make me an outcast and a stranger in mine own house? The shades of the prison-house closed round about us all: walls strait and stubborn to the whitest, but relentlessly narrow, tall, and unscalable to sons of night who must plod darkly on in resignation, or beat unavailing palms against the stone, or steadily, half hopelessly, watch the streak of blue above.

After the Egyptian and Indian, the Greek and Roman, the Teuton and Mongolian, the Negro is a sort of seventh son, born with a veil, and gifted with second-sight in this American world,—a world which yields him no true self-consciousness, but only lets him see himself through the revelation of the other world. It is a peculiar sensation, this double-consciousness, this sense of always looking at one's self through the eyes of others, of measuring one's soul by the tape of a world that looks on in amused contempt and pity. One ever feels his two-ness,—an American, a Negro; two souls, two thoughts, two unreconciled strivings; two warring ideals in one dark body, whose dogged strength alone keeps it from being torn asunder.[2]

The history of the American Negro is the history of this strife,—this longing to attain self-conscious manhood, to merge his double self into a better and truer self. In this merging he wishes neither of the older selves to be lost. He would not Africanize America, for America has too much to teach the world and Africa. He would not bleach the Negro soul in a flood of white Americanism, for he knows that Negro blood has a message for the world. He simply wishes to make it possible for a man to be both a Negro and an American, without being cursed and spit upon by his fellows, without having the doors of Opportunity closed roughly in his face.

This, then, is the end of his striving: to be a co-worker in the kingdom of culture, to escape both death and isolation, to husband and use his best powers and his latent genius. These powers of body and mind have in the past been strangely wasted, dispersed, or forgotten. The shadow of a mighty Negro past flits through the tale of Ethiopia the Shadowy and of Egypt the Sphinx. Throughout history, the powers of single black men flash here and there like falling stars, and die sometimes before the world has rightly gauged their brightness. Here in America, in the few days since Emancipation, the black man's turning hither and thither in hesitant and doubtful striving has often made his very strength to lose effectiveness, to seem like absence of power, like weakness. And yet it is not weakness,—it is the contradiction of double aims. The double-aimed struggle of the black artisan—on the one hand to escape white contempt for a nation of mere hewers of wood and drawers of water, and on the other hand to plough and nail and dig for a poverty-stricken horde—could only result in making him a poor craftsman, for he had but half a heart in either cause. By the poverty and

[2]This passage is often referred to as Du Bois's theory of the "double-consciousness." It is a "gift of second-sight" but it is also a curse of ambivalence.

ignorance of his people, the Negro minister or doctor was tempted toward quackery and demagogy; and by the criticism of the other world, toward ideals that made him ashamed of his lowly tasks. The would-be black *savant* was confronted by the paradox that the knowledge his people needed was a twice-told tale to his white neighbors, while the knowledge which would teach the white world was Greek to his own flesh and blood. The innate love of harmony and beauty that set the ruder souls of his people a-dancing and a-singing raised but confusion and doubt in the soul of the black artist; for the beauty revealed to him was the soul-beauty of a race which his larger audience despised, and he could not articulate the message of another people. This waste of double aims, this seeking to satisfy two unreconciled ideals, has wrought sad havoc with the courage and faith and deeds of ten thousand thousand people,—has sent them often wooing false gods and invoking false means of salvation, and at times has even seemed about to make them ashamed of themselves.

Away back in the days of bondage they thought to see in one divine event the end of all doubt and disappointment; few men ever worshipped Freedom with half such unquestioning faith as did the American Negro for two centuries. To him, so far as he thought and dreamed, slavery was indeed the sum of all villainies, the cause of all sorrow, the root of all prejudice; Emancipation was the key to a promised land of sweeter beauty than ever stretched before the eyes of wearied Israelites. In song and exhortation swelled one refrain—Liberty; in his tears and curses the God he implored had Freedom in his right hand. At last it came,—suddenly, fearfully, like a dream. With one wild carnival of blood and passion came the message in his own plaintive cadences:—

> "Shout, O children!
> Shout, you're free!
> For God has bought your liberty!"

Years have passed away since then,—ten, twenty, forty; forty years of national life, forty years of renewal and development, and yet the swarthy spectre sits in its accustomed seat at the Nation's feast. In vain do we cry to this our vastest social problem:—

> "Take any shape but that, and my firm nerves
> Shall never tremble!"

The Nation has not yet found peace from its sins; the freedman has not yet found in freedom his promised land. Whatever of good may have come in these years of change, the shadow of a deep disappointment rests upon the Negro people,—a disappointment all the more bitter because the unattained ideal was unbounded save by the simple ignorance of a lowly people.

The first decade was merely a prolongation of the vain search for freedom, the boon that seemed ever barely to elude their grasp,—like a tantalizing will-of-the-wisp, maddening and misleading the headless host. The holocaust of war, the terrors of the Ku-Klux-Klan, the lies of carpet-baggers, the disorganization of industry, and the contradictory advice of friends and foes, left the bewildered serf with no new watchword beyond the old cry for freedom. As the time flew, however, he began to grasp a new idea. The ideal of liberty demanded for its attainment powerful means, and these the Fifteenth Amendment gave him. The ballot, which before he had looked upon as a visible sign of freedom, he now regarded as the chief means of gaining and perfecting the liberty with which war had partially endowed him. And why not? Had not votes made war and emancipated millions? Had not votes enfranchised the freedmen? Was anything impossible to a power that had done all this? A million black men started with renewed zeal to vote themselves into the kingdom. So the decade flew away, the revolution of 1876 came, and left the half-free serf weary, wondering, but still inspired. Slowly but steadily, in the following years, a new vision began gradually to replace the dream of political power,—a powerful movement, the rise of another ideal to guide the unguided, another pillar of fire by night after a clouded day. It was the ideal of "book-learning"; the curiosity, born of compulsory ignorance, to know and test the power of the cabalistic letters of the white man, the longing to know. Here at last seemed to have been discovered the mountain path to Canaan; longer than the highway of Emancipation and law, steep and ragged, but straight, leading to heights high enough to overlook life.

Up the new path the advance guard toiled, slowly, heavily, doggedly; only those who have watched and guided the faltering feet, the misty minds, the dull understandings, of the dark pupils of those schools know how faithfully, how piteously, this people strove to learn. It was weary work. The cold statistician wrote down the inches of progress here and there, noted also where here and there a foot had slipped or some one had fallen. To the tired climbers, the horizon was ever dark, the mists were often cold, the Canaan was always dim and far away. If, however, the vistas disclosed as yet no goal, no resting-place, little but flattery and criticism, the journey at least gave leisure for reflection and self-examination; it changed the child of Emancipation to the youth with dawning self-consciousness, self-realization, self-respect. In those sombre forests of his striving his own soul rose before him, and he saw himself,—darkly as through a veil; and yet he saw in himself some faint revelation of his power, of his mission. He began to have a dim feeling that, to attain his place in the world, he must be himself, and not another. For the first time he sought to analyze the burden he bore upon his back, that dead weight of social degradation partially masked behind a half-named Negro problem. He felt his poverty; without a cent, without a home, without land, tools, or savings, he had entered into competition with rich, landed, skilled neighbors. To be a poor man is hard, but to be a poor race in a land of dollars is the very bottom of hardships. He felt the weight of his ignorance,—not simply of letters, but of life, of business, of the humanities; the accumulated sloth and shirking and awkwardness of decades and centuries shackled his hands and feet. Nor was his burden all poverty and ignorance. The red stain of bastardy, which two centuries of systematic legal defilement of Negro women had stamped upon his race, meant not only the loss of ancient African chastity, but also the hereditary weight of a mass of corruption from white adulterers, threatening almost the obliteration of the Negro home.

A people thus handicapped ought not to be asked to race with the world, but rather allowed to give all its time and thought to its own social problems. But alas! while sociologists gleefully count his bastards and his prostitutes, the very soul of the toiling, sweating black man is darkened by the shadow of a vast despair. Men call the shadow prejudice, and learnedly explain it as the natural defence of culture against barbarism, learning against ignorance, purity against crime, the "higher" against the "lower" races. To which the Negro cries Amen! and swears that to so much of this strange prejudice as is founded on just homage to civilization, culture, righteousness, and progress, he humbly bows and meekly does obeisance. But before that nameless prejudice that leaps beyond all this he stands helpless, dismayed, and well-nigh speechless; before that personal disrespect and mockery, the ridicule and systematic humiliation, the distortion of fact and wanton license of fancy, the cynical ignoring of the better and the boisterous welcoming of the worse, the all-pervading desire to inculcate disdain for everything black, from Toussaint[3] to the devil,—before this there rises a sickening despair that would disarm and discourage any nation save that black host to whom "discouragement" is an unwritten word.

But the facing of so vast a prejudice could not but bring the inevitable self-questioning, self-disparagement, and lowering of ideals which ever accompany repression and breed in an atmosphere of contempt and hate. Whisperings and portents came borne upon the four winds: Lo! we are diseased and dying, cried the dark hosts; we cannot write, our voting is vain; what need of education, since we must always cook and serve? And the Nation echoed and enforced this self-criticism, saying: Be content to be servants, and nothing more; what need of higher culture for half-men? Away with the black man's ballot, by force or fraud,—and behold the suicide of a race! Nevertheless, out of the evil came something of good,—the more careful adjustment of education to real life, the clearer perception of the Negroes' social responsibilities, and the sobering realization of the meaning of progress.

So dawned the time of *Sturm und Drang:* storm and stress to-day rocks our little boat on the mad waters of the world-sea; there is within and without the sound of conflict, the burning of body and rending of soul; inspiration strives with doubt, and faith with vain questionings. The bright ideals of the past,—physical freedom, political power, the training of brains and the training of hands,—all these in turn have waxed and waned, until even the last grows dim and overcast. Are they all wrong,—all false? No, not that, but each alone was over-simple and incomplete,—the dreams of a credulous race-childhood, or the fond imaginings of the other world which does not

[3]Toussaint L'Overture, a Haitian general who led peasants against the French army in Haiti during time of the French Revolution. Du Bois refers to him as early as in *The* *Suppression of the Slave Trade.* Toussaint is a symbol, in many of Du Bois's works, of the undauntable spirit of black people in the New World.

know and does not want to know our power. To be really true, all these ideals must be melted and welded into one. The training of the schools we need to-day more than ever,—the training of deft hands, quick eyes and ears, and above all the broader, deeper, higher culture of gifted minds and pure hearts. The power of the ballot we need in sheer self-defence,—else what shall save us from a second slavery? Freedom, too, the long-sought, we still seek,—the freedom of life and limb, the freedom to work and think, the freedom to love and aspire. Work, culture, liberty,—all these we need, not singly but together, not successively but together, each growing and aiding each, and all striving toward that vaster ideal that swims before the Negro people, the ideal of human brotherhood, gained through the unifying ideal of Race; the ideal of fostering and developing the traits and talents of the Negro, not in opposition to or contempt for other races, but rather in large conformity to the greater ideals of the American Republic, in order that some day on American soil two world-races may give to each those characteristics both so sadly lack. We the darker ones come even now not altogether empty-handed: there are to-day no truer exponents of the pure human spirit of the Declaration of Independence than the American Negroes; there is no true American music but the wild sweet melodies of the Negro slave; the American fairy tales and folk-lore are Indian and African; and, all in all, we black men seem the sole oasis of simple faith and reverence in a dusty desert of dollars and smartness. Will America be poorer if she replace her brutal dyspeptic blundering with light-hearted but determined Negro humility? or her coarse and cruel wit with loving jovial good-humor? or her vulgar music with the soul of the Sorrow Songs?

Merely a concrete test of the underlying principles of the great republic is the Negro Problem, and the spiritual striving of the freedmen's sons is the travail of souls whose burden is almost beyond the measure of their strength, but who bear it in the name of an historic race, in the name of this the land of their fathers' fathers, and in the name of human opportunity.

And now what I have briefly sketched in large outline let me on coming pages tell again in many ways, with loving emphasis and deeper detail, that men may listen to the striving in the souls of black folk.

Chapter III. Of Mr. Booker T. Washington and Others[4]

From birth till death enslaved; in word, in deed, unmanned!

. . . .

Hereditary bondsmen! Know ye not
Who would be free themselves must strike the blow?

—Byron

---

[4]The musical epigraph in this case comes from the spiritual "A Great Camp-Meeting in the Promised Land," whose message of solidarity stands in contrast to Du Bois's criticism of Washington, though it may also indicate his admiration of his opponent's hard work and achievements: "Oh, walk together, children,/ Don't you get weary,/ Walk together, children,/ Don't you get weary,/ There's a great camp-meeting in the Promised Land."

Easily the most striking thing in the history of the American Negro since 1876 is the ascendancy of Mr. Booker T. Washington. It began at the time when war memories and ideals were rapidly passing; a day of astonishing commercial development was dawning; a sense of doubt and hesitation overtook the freedmen's sons,—then it was that his leading began. Mr. Washington came, with a single definite programme, at the psychological moment when the nation was a little ashamed of having bestowed so much sentiment on Negroes, and was concentrating its energies on Dollars. His programme of industrial education, conciliation of the South, and submission and silence as to civil and political rights, was not wholly original; the Free Negroes from 1830 up to war-time had striven to build industrial schools, and the American Missionary Association had from the first taught various trades; and Price and others had sought a way of honorable alliance with the best of the Southerners. But Mr. Washington first indissolubly linked these things; he put enthusiasm, unlimited energy, and perfect faith into his programme, and changed it from a by-path into a veritable Way of Life. And the tale of the methods by which he did this is a fascinating study of human life.

It startled the nation to hear a Negro advocating such a programme after many decades of bitter complaint; it startled and won the applause of the South, it interested and won the admiration of the North; and after a confused murmur of protest, it silenced if it did not convert the Negroes themselves.

To gain the sympathy and coöperation of the various elements comprising the white South was Mr. Washington's first task; and this, at the time Tuskegee was founded, seemed, for a black man, well-nigh impossible. And yet ten years later it was done in the word spoken at Atlanta: "In all things purely social we can be as separate as the five fingers, and yet one as the hand in all things essential to mutual progress." This "Atlanta Compromise" is by all odds the most notable thing in Mr. Washington's career. The South interpreted it in different ways: the radicals received it as a complete surrender of the demand for civil and political equality; the conservatives, as a generously conceived working basis for mutual understanding. So both approved it, and to-day its author is certainly the most distinguished Southerner since Jefferson Davis, and the one with the largest personal following.

Next to this achievement comes Mr. Washington's work in gaining place and consideration in the North. Others less shrewd and tactful had formerly essayed to sit on these two stools and had fallen between them; but as Mr. Washington knew the heart of the South from birth and training, so by singular insight he intuitively grasped the spirit of the age which was dominating the North. And so thoroughly did he learn the speech and thought of triumphant commercialism, and the ideals of material prosperity, that the picture of a lone black boy poring over a French grammar amid the weeds and dirt of a neglected home soon seemed to him the acme of absurdities. One wonders what Socrates and St. Francis of Assisi would say to this.

And yet this very singleness of vision and thorough oneness with his age is a mark of the successful man. It is as though Nature must needs make men narrow in order to give them force. So Mr. Washington's cult has gained unquestioning followers, his work has wonderfully prospered, his friends are legion, and his enemies are confounded. To-day he stands as the one recognized spokesman of his ten million fellows, and one of the most notable figures in a nation of seventy millions. One hesitates, therefore, to criticise a life which, beginning with so little, has done so much. And yet the time is come when one may speak in all sincerity and utter courtesy of the mistakes and shortcomings of Mr. Washington's career, as well as of his triumphs, without being thought captious or envious, and without forgetting that it is easier to do ill than well in the world.

The criticism that has hitherto met Mr. Washington has not always been of this broad character. In the South especially has he had to walk warily to avoid the harshest judgments,—and naturally so, for he is dealing with the one subject of deepest sensitiveness to that section. Twice—once when at the Chicago celebration of the Spanish-American War he alluded to the color-prejudice that is "eating away the vitals of the South," and once when he dined with President Roosevelt—has the resulting Southern criticism been violent enough to threaten seriously his popularity. In the North the feeling has several times forced itself into words, that Mr. Washington's counsels of submission overlooked certain elements of true manhood, and that his educational programme was unnecessarily narrow. Usually, however, such criticism has not found open expression, although, too, the spiritual sons of the Abolitionists have not been prepared to acknowledge that the schools founded before Tuskegee, by men of broad ideals and self-sacrificing spirit, were wholly failures or worthy of ridicule. While, then, criticism has not failed to follow Mr. Washington, yet the prevailing public opinion of the land has been but too willing to deliver the solution of a wearisome problem into his hands, and say, "If that is all you and your race ask, take it."

Among his own people, however, Mr. Washington has encountered the strongest and most lasting opposition, amounting at times to bitterness, and even today continuing strong and insistent even though largely silenced in outward expression by the public opinion of the nation. Some of this opposition is, of course, mere envy; the disappointment of displaced demagogues and the spite of narrow minds. But aside from this, there is among educated and thoughtful colored men in all parts of the land a feeling of deep regret, sorrow, and apprehension at the wide currency and ascendancy which some of Mr. Washington's theories have gained. These same men admire his sincerity of purpose, and are willing to forgive much to honest endeavor which is doing something worth the doing. They coöperate with Mr. Washington as far as they conscientiously can; and, indeed, it is no ordinary tribute to this man's tact and power that, steering as he must between so many diverse interests and opinions, he so largely retains the respect of all.

But the hushing of the criticism of honest opponents is a dangerous thing. It leads some of the best of the critics to unfortunate silence and paralysis of effort, and others to burst into speech so passionately and intemperately as to lose listeners. Honest and earnest criticism from those whose interests are most nearly touched,—criticism of writers by readers, of government by those governed, of leaders by those led,—this is the soul of democracy and the safeguard of modern society. If the best of the American Negroes receive by outer pressure a leader whom they had not recognized before, manifestly there is here a certain palpable gain. Yet there is also irreparable loss,—a loss of that peculiarly valuable education which a group receives when by search and criticism it finds and commissions its own leaders. The way in which this is done is at once the most elementary and the nicest problem of social growth. History is but the record of such group-leadership; and yet how infinitely changeful is its type and character! And of all types and kinds, what can be more instructive than the leadership of a group within a group?—that curious double movement where real progress may be negative and actual advance be relative retrogression. All this is the social student's inspiration and despair.

Now in the past the American Negro has had instructive experience in the choosing of group leaders, founding thus a peculiar dynasty which in the light of pres-ent conditions is worth while studying. When sticks and stones and beasts form the sole environment of a people, their attitude is largely one of determined opposition to and conquest of natural forces. But when to earth and brute is added an environment of men and ideas, then the attitude of the imprisoned group may take three main forms,—a feeling of revolt and revenge; an attempt to adjust all thought and action to the will of the greater group; or, finally, a determined effort at self-realization and self-development despite environing opinion. The influence of all of these attitudes at various times can be traced in the history of the American Negro, and in the evolution of his successive leaders.

Before 1750, while the fire of African freedom still burned in the veins of the slaves, there was in all leadership or attempted leadership but the one motive of revolt and revenge,—typified in the terrible Maroons, the Danish blacks, and Cato of Stono, and veiling all the Americas in fear of insurrection. The liberalizing tendencies of the latter half of the eighteenth century brought, along with kindlier relations between black and white, thoughts of ultimate adjustment and assimilation. Such aspiration was especially voiced in the earnest songs of Phyllis, in the martyrdom of Attucks, the fighting of Salem and Poor, the intellectual accomplishments of Banneker and Derham, and the political demands of the Cuffes.

Stern financial and social stress after the war cooled much of the previous humanitarian ardor. The disappointment and impatience of the

Negroes at the persistence of slavery and serfdom voiced itself in two movements. The slaves in the South, aroused undoubtedly by vague rumors of the Haytian revolt, made three fierce attempts at insurrection,—in 1800 under Gabriel in Virginia, in 1822 under Vesey in Carolina, and in 1831 again in Virginia under the terrible Nat Turner. In the Free States, on the other hand, a new and curious attempt at self-development was made. In Philadelphia and New York color-prescription led to a withdrawal of Negro communicants from white churches and the formation of a peculiar socio-religious institution among the Negroes known as the African Church,—an organization still living and controlling in its various branches over a million of men.

Walker's wild appeal against the trend of the times showed how the world was changing after the coming of the cotton-gin. By 1830 slavery seemed hopelessly fastened on the South, and the slaves thoroughly cowed into submission. The free Negroes of the North, inspired by the mulatto immigrants from the West Indies, began to change the basis of their demands; they recognized the slavery of slaves, but insisted that they themselves were freemen, and sought assimilation and amalgamation with the nation on the same terms with other men. Thus, Forten and Purvis of Philadelphia, Shad of Wilmington, Du Bois of New Haven, Barbadoes of Boston, and others, strove singly and together as men, they said, not as slaves; as "people of color," not as "Negroes." The trend of the times, however, refused them recognition save in individual and exceptional cases, considered them as one with all the despised blacks, and they soon found themselves striving to keep even the rights they formerly had of voting and working and moving as freemen. Schemes of migration and colonization arose among them; but these they refused to entertain, and they eventually turned to the Abolition movement as a final refuge.

Here, led by Remond, Nell, Wells-Brown, and Douglass, a new period of self-assertion and self-development dawned. To be sure, ultimate freedom and assimilation was the ideal before the leaders, but the assertion of the manhood rights of the Negro by himself was the main reliance, and John Brown's raid was the extreme of its logic. After the war and emancipation, the great form of Frederick Douglass, the greatest of American Negro leaders, still led the host. Self-assertion, especially in political lines, was the main programme, and behind Douglass came Elliot, Bruce, and Langston, and the Reconstruction politicians, and, less conspicuous but of greater social significance, Alexander Crummell and Bishop Daniel Payne.

Then came the Revolution of 1876, the suppression of the Negro votes, the changing and shifting of ideals, and the seeking of new lights in the great night. Douglass, in his old age, still bravely stood for the ideals of his early manhood,—ultimate assimilation *through* self-assertion, and on no other terms. For a time Price arose as a new leader, destined, it seemed, not to give up, but to re-state the old ideals in a form less repugnant to the white South. But he passed away in his prime. Then came the new leader.

Nearly all the former ones had become leaders by the silent suffrage of their fellows, had sought to lead their own people alone, and were usually, save Douglass, little known outside their race. But Booker T. Washington arose as essentially the leader not of one race but of two,—a compromiser between the South, the North, and the Negro. Naturally the Negroes resented, at first bitterly, signs of compromise which surrendered their civil and political rights, even though this was to be exchanged for larger chances of economic development. The rich and dominating North, however, was not only weary of the race problem, but was investing largely in Southern enterprises, and welcomed any method of peaceful coöperation. Thus, by national opinion, the Negroes began to recognize Mr. Washington's leadership; and the voice of criticism was hushed.

Mr. Washington represents in Negro thought the old attitude of adjustment and submission; but adjustment at such a peculiar time as to make his programme unique. This is an age of unusual economic development, and Mr. Washington's programme naturally takes an economic cast, becoming a gospel of Work and Money to such an extent as apparently almost completely to overshadow the higher aims of life. Moreover, this is an age when the more advanced races are coming in closer contact with the less developed races, and the race-feeling is therefore intensified; and Mr. Washington's programme practically accepts the alleged inferiority of the Negro races. Again, in our own land, the reaction from the sentiment of war time has given impetus to race-prejudice against Negroes, and Mr. Washington withdraws many of the high demands of Negroes as men and American citizens. In other periods of intensified prejudice all the Negro's tendency to self-assertion has been called forth; at this period a policy of submission is advocated. In the history of nearly all other races and peoples the doctrine preached at such crises has been that manly self-respect is worth more than lands and houses, and that a people who voluntarily surrender such respect, or cease striving for it, are not worth civilizing.

In answer to this, it has been claimed that the Negro can survive only through submission. Mr. Washington distinctly asks that black people give up, at least for the present, three things,—

First, political power,

Second, insistence on civil rights,

Third, higher education of Negro youth,—

and concentrate all their energies on industrial education, and accumulation of wealth, and the conciliation of the South. This policy has been courageously and insistently advocated for over fifteen years, and has been triumphant for perhaps ten years. As a result of this tender of the palm-branch, what has been the return? In these years there have occurred:

1. The disfranchisement of the Negro.

2. The legal creation of a distinct status of civil inferiority for the Negro.

3. The steady withdrawal of aid from institutions for the higher training of the Negro.

These movements are not, to be sure, direct results of Mr. Washington's teachings; but his propaganda has, without a shadow of doubt, helped their speedier accomplishment. The question then comes: Is it possible, and probable, that nine millions of men can make effective progress in economic lines if they are deprived of political rights, made a servile caste, and allowed only the most meagre chance for developing their exceptional men? If history and reason give any distinct answer to these questions, it is an emphatic *No*. And Mr. Washington thus faces the triple paradox of his career:

1. He is striving nobly to make Negro artisans business men and property-owners; but it is utterly impossible, under modern competitive methods, for workingmen and property-owners to defend their rights and exist without the right of suffrage.

2. He insists on thrift and self-respect, but at the same time counsels a silent submission to civic inferiority such as is bound to sap the manhood of any race in the long run.

3. He advocates common-school and industrial training, and depreciates institutions of higher learning; but neither the Negro common-schools, nor Tuskegee itself, could remain open a day were it not for teachers trained in Negro colleges, or trained by their graduates.

This triple paradox in Mr. Washington's position is the object of criticism by two classes of colored Americans. One class is spiritually descended from Toussaint the Savior, through Gabriel, Vesey, and Turner, and they represent the attitude of revolt and revenge; they hate the white South blindly and distrust the white race generally, and so far as they agree on definite action, think that the Negro's only hope lies in emigration beyond the borders of the United States. And yet, by the irony of fate, nothing has more effectually made this programme seem hopeless than the recent course of the United States toward weaker and darker peoples in the West Indies, Hawaii, and the Philippines,—for where in the world may we go and be safe from lying and brute force?

The other class of Negroes who cannot agree with Mr. Washington has hitherto said little aloud. They deprecate the sight of scattered counsels, of internal disagreement; and especially they dislike making their just criticism of a useful and earnest man an excuse for a general discharge of venom from small-minded opponents. Nevertheless, the questions involved are so fundamental and serious that it is difficult to see how men like Archibald Grimké, Kelly Miller, J. W. E. Bowen, and other representatives of this group, can much longer be silent. Such men feel in conscience bound to ask of this nation three things:

1. The right to vote.
2. Civic equality.
3. The education of youth according to ability.

They acknowledge Mr. Washington's invaluable service in counselling patience and courtesy in such demands; they do not ask that ignorant black men vote when ignorant whites are debarred, or that any reasonable restrictions in the suffrage should not be applied; they know that the low social level of the mass of the race is responsible for much discrimination against it, but they also know, and the nation knows, that relentless color-prejudice is more often a cause than a result of the Negro's degradation; they seek the abatement of this relic of barbarism, and not its systematic encouragement and pampering by all agencies of social power from the Associated Press to the Church of Christ. They advocate, with Mr. Washington, a broad system of Negro common schools supplemented by thorough industrial training; but they are surprised that a man of Mr. Washington's insight cannot see that no such educational system ever has rested or can rest on any other basis than that of the well-equipped college and university, and they insist that there is a demand for a few such institutions throughout the South to train the best of the Negro youth as teachers, professional men, and leaders.

This group of men honor Mr. Washington for his attitude of conciliation toward the white South; they accept the "Atlanta Compromise" in its broadest interpretation; they recognize, with him, many signs of promise, many men of high purpose and fair judgment, in this section; they know that no easy task has been laid upon a region already tottering under heavy burdens. But, nevertheless, they insist that the way to truth and right lies in straightforward honesty, not in indiscriminate flattery; in praising those of the South who do well and criticising uncompromisingly those who do ill; in taking advantage of the opportunities at hand and urging their fellows to do the same, but at the same time in remembering that only a firm adherence to their higher ideals and aspirations will ever keep those ideals within the realm of possibility. They do not expect that the free right to vote, to enjoy civic rights, and to be educated, will come in a moment; they do not expect to see the bias and prejudices of years disappear at the blast of a trumpet; but they are absolutely certain that the way for a people to gain their reasonable rights is not by voluntarily throwing them away and insisting that they do not want them; that the way for a people to gain respect is not by continually belittling and ridiculing themselves; that, on the contrary, Negroes must insist continually, in season and out of season, that voting is necessary to modern manhood, that color discrimination is barbarism, and that black boys need education as well as white boys.

In failing thus to state plainly and unequivocally the legitimate demands of their people, even at the cost of opposing an honored leader, the thinking classes of American Negroes would shirk a heavy responsibility,—a responsibility to themselves, a responsibility to the struggling masses, a responsibility to the darker races of men whose future depends so largely on this American experiment, but especially a responsibility to this nation,—this common Fatherland. It is wrong to encourage a man or a people in evildoing; it is wrong to aid and abet a national crime simply because it is unpopular not to do so. The growing spirit of kindliness and reconciliation between the North and South after the frightful difference of a generation ago ought to be a source of deep congratulation to all, and especially to those whose mistreatment caused the war; but if that reconciliation is to be marked by the industrial slavery and civic death of those same black men, with permanent legislation into a position of inferiority, then those black men, if they are really men, are called upon by every consideration of patriotism and loyalty to oppose such a course by all civilized methods, even though such opposition involves disagreement with Mr. Booker T. Washington. We have no right to sit silently by while the inevitable seeds are sown for a harvest of disaster to our children, black and white.

First, it is the duty of black men to judge the South discriminatingly. The present generation of Southerners are not responsible for the past, and they should not be blindly hated or blamed for it. Furthermore, to no class is the indiscriminate endorsement of the recent course of the South toward Negroes more nauseating than to the best thought of the South. The South is not "solid"; it is a land in the ferment of social change, wherein forces of all kinds are fighting for supremacy; and to praise the ill the South is today perpetrating is just as wrong as to condemn the good. Discriminating and broad-minded criticism is what the South needs,—needs it for the sake of her own white sons and daughters, and for the insurance of robust, healthy mental and moral development.

To-day even the attitude of the Southern whites toward the blacks is not, as so many assume, in all cases the same; the ignorant Southerner hates the Negro, the workingmen fear his competition, the money-makers wish to use him as a laborer, some of the educated see a menace in his upward development, while others—usually the sons of the masters—wish to help him to rise. National opinion has enabled this last class to maintain the Negro common schools, and to protect the Negro partially in property, life, and limb. Through the pressure of the money-makers, the Negro is in danger of being reduced to semi-slavery, especially in the country districts; the workingmen, and those of the educated who fear the Negro, have united to disfranchise him, and some have urged his deportation; while the passions of the ignorant are easily aroused to lynch and abuse any black man. To praise this intricate whirl of thought and prejudice is nonsense; to inveigh indiscriminately against "the South" is unjust; but to use the same breath in praising Governor Aycock, exposing Senator Morgan, arguing with Mr. Thomas Nelson Page, and denouncing Senator Ben Tillman, is not only sane, but the imperative duty of thinking black men.

It would be unjust to Mr. Washington not to acknowledge that in several instances he has opposed movements in the South which were unjust to the Negro; he sent memorials to the Louisiana and Alabama constitutional conventions, he has spoken against lynching, and in other ways has openly or silently set his influence against sinister schemes and unfortunate happenings. Notwithstanding this, it is equally true to assert that on the whole the distinct impression left by Mr. Washington's propaganda is, first, that the South is justified in its present attitude toward the Negro because of the Negro's degradation; secondly, that the prime cause of the Negro's failure to rise more quickly is his wrong education in the past; and, thirdly, that his future rise depends primarily on his own efforts. Each of these propositions is a dangerous half-truth. The supplementary truths must never be lost sight of: first, slavery and race-prejudice are potent if not sufficient causes of the Negro's position; second, industrial and common-school training were necessarily slow in planting because they had to await the black teachers trained by higher institutions,—it being extremely doubtful if any essentially different development was possible, and certainly a Tuskegee was unthinkable before 1880; and, third, while it is a great truth to say that the Negro must strive and strive mightily to help himself, it is equally true that unless his striving be not simply seconded, but rather aroused and encouraged, by the initiative of the richer and wiser environing group, he cannot hope for great success.

In his failure to realize and impress this last point, Mr. Washington is especially to be criticised. His doctrine has tended to make the whites, North and South, shift the burden of the Negro problem to the Negro's shoulders and stand aside as critical and rather pessimistic spectators; when in fact the burden belongs to the nation, and the hands of none of us are clean if we bend not our energies to righting these great wrongs.

The South ought to be led, by candid and honest criticism, to assert her better self and do her full duty to the race she has cruelly wronged and is still wronging. The North—her co-partner in guilt—cannot salve her conscience by plastering it with gold. We cannot settle this problem by diplomacy and suaveness, by "policy" alone. If worse come to worst, can the moral fibre of this country survive the slow throttling and murder of nine millions of men?

The black men of America have a duty to perform, a duty stern and delicate,—a forward movement to oppose a part of the work of their greatest leader. So far as Mr. Washington preaches Thrift, Patience, and Industrial Training for the masses, we must hold up his hands and strive with him, rejoicing in his honors and glorying in the strength of this Joshua called of God and of man to lead the headless host. But so far as Mr. Washington apologizes for injustice, North or South, does not rightly value the privilege and duty of voting, belittles the emasculating effects of caste distinctions, and opposes the higher training and ambition of our brighter minds,—so far as he, the South, or the Nation, does this,—we must unceasingly and firmly oppose them. By every civilized and peaceful method we must strive for the rights which the world accords to men, clinging unwaveringly to those great words which the sons of the Fathers would fain forget: "We hold these truths to be self-evident: That all men are created equal; that they are endowed by their Creator with certain unalienable rights; that among these are life, liberty, and the pursuit of happiness."

Chapter XIV. Of the Sorrow Songs[5]

I walk through the churchyard
  To lay this body down;
I know moon-rise, I know star-rise;
I walk in the moonlight, I walk in the starlight;
I'll lie in the grave and stretch out my arms,
I'll go to judgment in the evening of the day,
And my soul and thy soul shall meet that day,
  When I lay this body down.

—*Negro Song*

They that walked in darkness sang songs in the olden days—Sorrow Songs—for they were weary at heart. And so before each thought that I have written in this book I have set a phrase, a haunting echo of these weird old songs in which the soul of the black slave spoke to men. Ever since I was a child these songs have stirred me strangely. They came out of the South unknown to me, one by one, and yet at once I knew them as of me and of mine. Then in after years when I came to Nashville I saw the great temple builded of these songs towering over the pale city. To me Jubilee Hall seemed ever made of the songs themselves, and its bricks were red with the blood and dust of toil. Out of them rose for me morning, noon, and night, bursts of wonderful melody, full of the voices of my brothers and sisters, full of the voices of the past.

Little of beauty has America given the world save the rude grandeur God himself stamped on her bosom; the human spirit in this new world has expressed itself in vigor and ingenuity rather than in beauty. And so by fateful chance the Negro folk-song—the rhythmic cry of the slave—stands today not simply as the sole American music, but as the most beautiful expression of human experience born this side the seas. It has been neglected, it has been, and is, half despised, and above all it has been persistently mistaken and misunderstood; but notwithstanding, it still remains as the singular spiritual heritage of the nation and the greatest gift of the Negro people.

---

[5]The musical epigraph in Du Bois's final chapter comes from "Wrestling Jacob": "Wrestling Jacob, Jacob, day is a-breaking,/ Wrestling Jacob, Jacob, I will not let thee go ... Until thou bless me." The spiritual speaks of Jacob's wrestling with the angel in Genesis 32, which signifies the triumph and reconciliation that make him a patriarch of Israel. In this chapter, which is saturated with the songs of the African American past, Du Bois likewise suggests that he has struggled with the patriarchs of his own tradition in order to become a leader and to create a new cultural language that combines music and oratory.

Away back in the thirties the melody of these slave songs stirred the nation, but the songs were soon half forgotten. Some, like "Near the lake where drooped the willow," passed into current airs and their source was forgotten; others were caricatured on the "minstrel" stage and their memory died away. Then in war-time came the singular Port Royal experiment after the capture of Hilton Head, and perhaps for the first time the North met the Southern slave face to face and heart to heart with no third witness. The Sea Islands of the Carolinas, where they met, were filled with a black folk of primitive type, touched and moulded less by the world about them than any others outside the Black Belt. Their appearance was uncouth, their language funny, but their hearts were human and their singing stirred men with a mighty power. Thomas Wentworth Higginson hastened to tell of these songs, and Miss McKim and others urged upon the world their rare beauty. But the world listened only half credulously until the Fisk Jubilee Singers sang the slave songs so deeply into the world's heart that it can never wholly forget them again.

There was once a blacksmith's son born at Cadiz, New York, who in the changes of time taught school in Ohio and helped defend Cincinnati from Kirby Smith. Then he fought at Chancellorsville and Gettysburg and finally served in the Freedman's Bureau at Nashville. Here he formed a Sunday-school class of black children in 1866, and sang with them and taught them to sing. And then they taught him to sing, and when once the glory of the Jubilee songs passed into the soul of George L. White, he knew his life-work was to let those Negroes sing to the world as they had sung to him. So in 1871 the pilgrimage of the Fisk Jubilee Singers began. North to Cincinnati they rode,—four half-clothed black boys and five girl-women,—led by a man with a cause and a purpose. They stopped at Wilberforce, the oldest of Negro schools, where a black bishop blessed them. Then they went, fighting cold and starvation, shut out of hotels, and cheerfully sneered at, ever northward; and ever the magic of their song kept thrilling hearts, until a burst of applause in the Congregational Council at Oberlin revealed them to the world. They came to New York and Henry Ward Beecher dared to welcome them, even though the metropolitan dailies sneered at his "Nigger Minstrels." So their songs conquered till they sang across the land and across the sea, before Queen and Kaiser, in Scotland and Ireland, Holland and Switzerland. Seven years they sang, and brought back a hundred and fifty thousand dollars to found Fisk University.

Since their day they have been imitated—sometimes well, by the singers of Hampton and Atlanta, sometimes ill, by straggling quartettes. Caricature has sought again to spoil the quaint beauty of the music, and has filled the air with many debased melodies which vulgar ears scarce know from the real. But the true Negro folk-song still lives in the hearts of those who have heard them truly sung and in the hearts of the Negro people.

What are these songs, and what do they mean? I know little of music and can say nothing in technical phrase, but I know something of men, and knowing them, I know that these songs are the articulate message of the slave to the world. They tell us in these eager days that life was joyous to the black slave, careless and happy. I can easily believe this of some, of many. But not all the past South, though it rose from the dead, can gainsay the heart-touching witness of these songs. They are the music of an unhappy people, of the children of disappointment; they tell of death and suffering and unvoiced longing toward a truer world, of misty wanderings and hidden ways.

The songs are indeed the siftings of centuries; the music is far more ancient than the words, and in it we can trace here and there signs of development. My grandfather's grandmother was seized by an evil Dutch trader two centuries ago; and coming to the valleys of the Hudson and Housatonic, black, little, and lithe, she shivered and shrank in the harsh north winds, looked longingly at the hills, and often crooned a heathen melody to the child between her knees, thus:

Do ba-na co-ba, ge-ne me, ge-ne me!
Do ba-na co-ba, ge-ne me, ge-ne me!
Ben d'nu-li, nu-li, nu-li, nu-li, ben d'le.

The child sang it to his children and they to their children's children, and so two hundred years it has travelled down to us and we sing it to our children, knowing as little as our fathers what its words may mean, but knowing well the meaning of its music.

This was primitive African music; it may be seen in larger form in the strange chant which heralds "The Coming of John":

"You may bury me in the East,
You may bury me in the West,
But I'll hear the trumpet sound in that morning."

—the voice of exile.

Ten master songs, more or less, one may pluck from this forest of melody—songs of undoubted Negro origin and wide popular currency, and songs peculiarly characteristic of the slave. One of these I have just mentioned. Another whose strains begin this book is "Nobody knows the trouble I've seen." When, struck with a sudden poverty, the United States refused to fulfill its promises of land to the freedmen, a brigadier-general went down to the Sea Islands to carry the news. An old woman on the outskirts of the throng began singing this song; all the mass joined with her, swaying. And the soldier wept.

The third song is the cradle-song of death which all men know,—"Swing low, sweet chariot,"—whose bars begin the life story of "Alexander Crummell." Then there is the song of many waters, "Roll, Jordan, roll," a mighty chorus with minor cadences. There were many songs of the fugitive like that which opens "The Wings of Atalanta," and the more familiar "Been a-listening." The seventh is the song of the End and the Beginning—"My Lord, what a mourning! when the stars begin to fall"; a strain of this is placed before "The Dawn of Freedom." The song of groping—"My way's cloudy"—begins "The Meaning of Progress"; the ninth is the song of this chapter—"Wrestlin' Jacob, the day is a-breaking,"—a paean of hopeful strife. The last master song is the song of songs—"Steal away,"—sprung from "The Faith of the Fathers."

There are many others of the Negro folk-songs as striking and character-istic as these, as, for instance, the three strains in the third, eighth, and ninth chapters; and others I am sure could easily make a selection on more scientific principles. There are, too, songs that seem to be a step removed from the more primitive types: there is the maze-like medley, "Bright spar-kles," one phrase of which heads "The Black Belt"; the Easter carol, "Dust, dust and ashes"; the dirge, "My mother's took her flight and gone home"; and that burst of melody hovering over "The Passing of the First-Born"—"I hope my mother will be there in that beautiful world on high."

These represent a third step in the development of the slave song, of which "You may bury me in the East" is the first, and songs like "March on" (chapter six) and "Steal away" are the second. The first is African music, the second Afro-American, while the third is a blending of Negro music with the music heard in the foster land. The result is still distinctively Negro and the method of blending original, but the elements are both Negro and Cau-casian. One might go further and find a fourth step in this development, where the songs of white America have been distinctively influenced by the slave songs or have incorporated whole phrases of Negro melody, as "Swa-nee River" and "Old Black Joe." Side by side, too, with the growth has gone the debasements and imitations—the Negro "minstrel" songs, many of the "gospel" hymns, and some of the contemporary "coon" songs,—a mass of music in which the novice may easily lose himself and never find the real Negro melodies.

In these songs, I have said, the slave spoke to the world. Such a message is naturally veiled and half articulate. Words and music have lost each other and new and cant phrases of a dimly understood theology have displaced the older sentiment. Once in a while we catch a strange word of an unknown tongue, as the "Mighty Myo," which figures as a river of death; more often slight words or mere doggerel are joined to music of singular sweetness. Purely secular songs are few in number, partly because many of them were turned into hymns by a change of words, partly because the frolics were seldom heard by the stranger, and the music less often caught. Of nearly all the songs, however, the music is distinctly sorrowful. The ten master songs I have mentioned tell in word and music of trouble and exile, of strife and hiding; they grope toward some unseen power and sigh for rest in the End.

The words that are left to us are not without interest, and, cleared of evident dross, they conceal much of real poetry and meaning beneath con-ventional theology and unmeaning rhapsody. Like all primitive folk, the slave stood near to Nature's heart. Life was a "rough and rolling sea" like the brown Atlantic of the Sea Islands; the "Wilderness" was the home of God, and the "lonesome valley" led to the way of life. "Winter'll soon be over," was the picture of life and death to a tropical imagination. The sudden wild thunder-storms of the South awed and impressed the Negroes,—at times the rumbling seemed to them "mournful," at times imperious:

"My Lord calls me,
He calls me by the thunder,
The trumpet sounds it in my soul."

The monotonous toil and exposure is painted in many words. One sees the ploughmen in the hot, moist furrow, singing:

"Dere's no rain to wet you,
Dere's no sun to burn you,
Oh, push along, believer,
I want to go home."

The bowed and bent old man cries, with thrice-repeated wail:

"O Lord, keep me from sinking down,"

and he rebukes the devil of doubt who can whisper:

"Jesus is dead and God's gone away."

Yet the soul-hunger is there, the restlessness of the savage, the wail of the wanderer, and the plaint is put in one little phrase:

My soul wants something that's new, that's new

Over the inner thoughts of the slaves and their relations one with another the shadow of fear ever hung, so that we get but glimpses here and there, and also with them, eloquent omissions and silences. Mother and child are sung, but seldom father; fugitive and weary wanderer call for pity and affection, but there is little of wooing and wedding; the rocks and the mountains are well known, but home is unknown. Strange blending of love and helplessness signs through the refrain:

"Yonder's my ole mudder,
Been waggin' at de hill so long;
'Bout time she cross over,
Git home bime-by."

Elsewhere comes the cry of the "motherless" and the "Farewell, farewell, my only child."

Love-songs are scarce and fall into two categories—the frivolous and light, and the sad. Of deep successful love there is ominous silence, and in one of the oldest of these songs there is a depth of history and meaning:

Poor Ro-sy, poor gal; Poor Ro-sy,
    poor gal; Ro-sy break my poor heart,
Heav'n shall-a-be my home.

A black woman said of the song, "It can't be sung without a full heart and a troubled sperrit." The same voice sings here that sings in the German folk-song:

"Jetz Geh i' an's brunele, trink' aber net."

Of death the Negro showed little fear, but talked of it familiarly and even fondly as simply a crossing of the waters, perhaps—who knows?—back to his ancient forests again. Later days transfigured his fatalism, and amid the dust and dirt the toiler sang:

"Dust, dust and ashes, fly over my grave,
But the Lord shall bear my spirit home."

The things evidently borrowed from the surrounding world undergo characteristic change when they enter the mouth of the slave. Especially is this true of Bible phrases. "Weep, O captive daughter of Zion," is quaintly turned into "Zion, weep-a-low," and the wheels of Ezekiel are turned every way in the mystic dreaming of the slave, till he says:

"There's a little wheel a-turnin' in-a-my heart."

As in olden time, the words of these hymns were improvised by some leading minstrel of the religious band. The circumstances of the gathering, however, the rhythm of the songs, and the limitations of allowable thought, confined the poetry for the most part to single or double lines, and they seldom were expanded to quatrains or longer tales, although there are some few examples of sustained efforts, chiefly paraphrases of the Bible. Three short series of verses have always attracted me,—the one that heads this chapter, of one line of which Thomas Wentworth Higginson has fittingly said, "Never, it seems to me, since man first lived and suffered was his infinite longing for peace uttered more plaintively." The second and third are descriptions of the Last Judgment,—the one a late improvisation, with some traces of outside influence:

"Oh, the stars in the elements are falling,
And the moon drips away into blood,
And the ransomed of the Lord are returning unto God,
Blessed be the name of the Lord."

And the other earlier and homelier picture from the low coast lands:

"Michael, haul the boat ashore,
Then you'll hear the horn they blow,
Then you'll hear the trumpet sound,
    Trumpet sound the world around,
    Trumpet sound for rich and poor,
    Trumpet sound for Jubilee,
    Trumpet sound for you and me."

Through all the sorrow of the Sorrow Songs there breathes a hope—a faith in the ultimate justice of things. The minor cadences of despair change often to triumph and calm confidence. Sometimes it is faith in life, sometimes a faith in death, sometimes assurance of boundless justice in some fair world beyond. But whichever it is, the meaning is always clear: that sometime, somewhere, men will judge men by their souls and not by their skins. Is such a hope justified? Do the Sorrow Songs sing true?

The silently growing assumption of this age is that the probation of races is past, and that the backward races of to-day are of proven inefficiency and not worth the saving. Such an assumption is the arrogance of peoples irreverent toward Time and ignorant of the deeds of men. A thousand years ago such an assumption, easily possible, would have made it difficult for the Teuton to prove his right to life. Two thousand years ago such dogmatism, readily welcome, would have scouted the idea of blond races ever leading civilization. So wofully unorganized is sociological knowledge that the meaning of progress, the meaning of "swift" and "slow" in human doing, and the limits of human perfectability, are veiled, unanswered sphinxes on the shores of science. Why should Æschylus have sung two thousand years before Shakespeare was born? Why has civilization flourished in Europe, and flickered, flamed, and died in Africa? So long as the world stands meekly dumb before such questions, shall this nation proclaim its ignorance and unhallowed prejudices by denying freedom of opportunity to those who brought the Sorrow Songs to the Seats of the Mighty?

Your country? How came it yours? Before the Pilgrims landed we were here. Here we have brought our three gifts and mingled them with yours: a gift of story and song—soft, stirring melody in an ill-harmonized and unmelodious land; the gift of sweat and brawn to beat back the wilderness, conquer the soil, and lay the foundations of this vast economic empire two hundred years earlier than your weak hands could have done it; the third, a gift of the Spirit. Around us the history of the land has centred for thrice a hundred years; out of the nation's heart we have called all that was best to throttle and subdue all that was worst; fire and blood, prayer and sacrifice, have billowed over this people, and they have found peace only in the altars of the God of Right. Nor has our gift of the Spirit been merely passive. Actively we have woven ourselves with the very warp and woof of this nation,—we fought their battles, shared their sorrow, mingled our blood with theirs, and generation after generation have pleaded with a headstrong, careless people to despise not Justice, Mercy, and Truth, lest the nation be smitten with a curse. Our song, our toil, our cheer, and warning have been given to this nation in blood-brotherhood. Are not these gifts worth the giving? Is not this work and striving? Would America have been America without her Negro people?

Even so is the hope that sang in the songs of my fathers well sung. If somewhere in this whirl and chaos of things there dwells Eternal Good, pitiful yet masterful, then anon in His good time America shall rend the Veil and the prisoned shall be free. Free, free as the sunshine trickling down the morning into these high windows of mine, free as yonder fresh young voices welling up to me from the caverns of brick and mortar below—welling with song, instinct with life, tremulous treble and darkening bass. My children, my little children, are singing to the sunshine, and thus they sing:

> Let us cheer the weary traveller,
> Cheer the weary traveller,
> Let us cheer the weary traveller
> Along the heavenly way.

And the traveller girds himself, and sets his face toward the Morning, and goes his way.

1903

The Song of the Smoke

I am the smoke king,
I am black.
I am swinging in the sky.
I am ringing worlds on high:
I am the thought of the throbbing mills,   5
I am the soul of the soul toil kills,
I am the ripple of trading rills,

Up I'm curling from the sod,
I am whirling home to God.
I am the smoke king,   10
I am black.

I am the smoke king,
I am black.

I am wreathing broken hearts,
I am sheathing devils' darts;   15
Dark inspiration of iron times,
Wedding the toil of toiling climes
Shedding the blood of bloodless crimes,

Down I lower in the blue,
Up I tower toward the true,   20
I am the smoke king,
I am black.

I am the smoke king,
I am black.

I am darkening with song,   25
I am hearkening to wrong;
I will be as black as blackness can,
The blacker the mantle the mightier the man,
My purpl'ing midnights no day dawn may ban.

I am carving God in night,   30
I am painting hell in white.
I am the smoke king,
I am black.

I am the smoke king,
I am black.   35

I am cursing ruddy morn,
I am nursing hearts unborn;
Souls unto me are as mists in the night,
I whiten my blackmen, I beckon my white,
What's the hue of a hide to a man in his might!   40

Hail, then, grilly, grimy hands,
Sweet Christ, pity toiling lands!
Hail to the smoke king,
Hail to the black!

                                                             1907

JAMES WELDON JOHNSON
1871–1938

James Weldon Johnson was Harlem's Renaissance Man—gifted with talent and aplomb. He had the ability to deal with the struggles of life as he worked to develop his intellectual and artistic powers in a dual society. Rather than being devastated by the Du Boisian divided consciousness that drove some black leaders to extremes and others to annihilation, he subverted the marginality strain to a victorious stance. His contributions to American culture help to support the premise that marginality may be a requisite for creativity and innovation. So the imperative in his poem "The Creation," "I'll make me a world," bears some relevance to the line of his own destiny in the Western world.

Johnson was born in Jacksonville, Florida, where he attended school at Stanton. His immediate family and acquaintances provided a cultural background and economic security that gave him the chance to pursue his career.

These advantages, with his ability to learn, served him well as an Atlanta University student. The professors who taught the classics exerted every effort to make students nobler and higher beings. Johnson worked to become an "all-sided man," *l'homo universale*.

Johnson received a B.A. degree at Atlanta University in 1894, his M.A. in 1904. Immediately after graduation, he taught at Stanton, but he moved up to the level of high school and became principal. In order to hasten the advancement of racial uplift, he helped to found the *Daily American* in 1895 as the first black daily paper in America. He made his mark as a journalist, however, when he became a contributing editor of the *New York Age*, 1914–1916, where he used his column as a "strong weapon" in the fight against inequality and injustice.

From 1916 through 1930, Johnson served as an official for the National Association for the Advancement of Colored People and was responsible for building support for the organization in the South and the West. In addition, he investigated America's misrule in Haiti in 1920, and he successfully lobbied Congress in 1921–1922 for passage of the Dyer-Lynching Bill. It was his finest hour as a race leader. However, Johnson likewise won acclaim in the diplomatic service. From 1906–1920 he served as Consul to Venezuela and Nicaragua. In 1929, he was a representative to the Institute on Pacific Relations held in Kyoto, Japan.

Somehow Johnson's more ardent pursuits led to his early orientation in school life and the arts. Fisk University named Johnson as Adam K. Spence Professor of Creative Writing, a position he filled from 1930 to 1938. At the same time (1934), he became Visiting Professor at New York University. On the day of his death in an automobile accident, June 26, 1938, in Wiscasset, Maine, he had just been appointed Extension Professor of Black Literature at New York University.

Johnson believed that the creation of "pure literature" by a people is their mark of civilization. His first "pure" literary offering is "Sence You Went Away," a dialect poem in the style of Paul L. Dunbar. His second poem, the standard English lyric "Lift Ev'ry Voice and Sing," was set to music by his brother, J. Rosamond, in 1900, and is still his hallmark as "The Black National Anthem."

When he joined Bob Cole and his brother in 1901 in New York, where they became successful writers of "Coon songs" and black musical reviews, they (along with Will Marion Cook and others) knew that something was lacking. Their art failed to tap the source-stream of black folk culture and folk art. James Weldon erected a frame: the super-structure of conscious black art must be built on the cultural background of the black folk.

As a writer, Johnson was a novelist, poet, literary critic, biographer, cultural historian, revolutionary philosopher, and more. Published anonymously in 1912, signed in 1927, *Autobiography of an Ex-Colored Man* is a sociological treatise as well as a fictive narrative. Johnson's boyhood friend, Judson Douglass Wetmore, was the model for the hero of the book. The theme of this important novel is "passing," but the hero's exploits reflect all of the author's rich experiences up to the year 1912. Of his three volumes of poetry—*Fifty Years and Other Poems* (1917), *God's Trombones* (1927), and *St. Peter Relates an Incident* (1930)—*Trombones* is the most innovative. In it he recorded the "sermon sagas" of his people, thus helping to perpetuate the oral tradition.

Five essays play a major role in establishing Johnson as a literary critic: prefaces to the two editions of *The Book of American Negro Poetry* (1922, 1931); to *The First Book of American Negro Spirituals* (1925); to *The Second Book of American Negro Spirituals* (1926); and to *God's Trombones*. In them he praises the "creative genius of blacks," analyzes song-poems as poetry, and isolates the folk sermon as a genre.

Along This Way (1933) is an autobiography that helps to establish Johnson as a precursor to and participant in the Harlem Renaissance. *Black Manhattan* is a cultural history of Harlem itself with an accurate history of the New York Theatrical Stage. *Negro Americans, What Now?* (1934) is considered by at least one scholar as a blueprint of the general philosophy of the Black Revolution of the sixties.

Mayor Fiorello La Guardia's New York eulogy is the proper assessment of Johnson's life and works: "Greatness in a man is a quality that does not know the boundaries of race or creed."

Arthenia J. Bates Millican
Southern University

PRIMARY WORKS

The Autobiography of an Ex-Colored Man, 1912; *Fifty Years and Other Poems*, 1917; *God's Trombones*, 1927; *Black Manhattan*, 1930; *Along This Way*, 1933; *Negro Americans, What Now?*, 1934; *St. Peter Relates an Incident: Selected Poems*, 1935; *The Creation*, 1994; *Writings*, 2004.

Lift Every Voice and Sing

Lift every voice and sing
Till earth and heaven ring,
Ring with the harmonies of Liberty;
Let our rejoicing rise
High as the listening skies,   5
Let it resound loud as the rolling sea.
Sing a song full of the faith that the dark past has taught us,
Sing a song full of the hope that the present has brought us.
Facing the rising sun of our new day begun,
Let us march on till victory is won.   10

Stony the road we trod,
Bitter the chastening rod,
Felt in the days when hope unborn had died;
Yet with a steady beat
Have not our weary feet   15
Come to the place for which our fathers sighed?
We have come over a way that with tears has been watered,
We have come, treading our path through the blood of the
        slaughtered,
Out from the gloomy past,   20

Till now we stand at last
Where the white gleam of our bright star is cast.

God of our weary years,
God of our silent tears,
Thou who hast brought us thus far on the way;   25
Thou who hast by Thy might
Led us into the light,
Keep us forever in the path, we pray.
Lest our feet stray from the places, our God, where we met Thee,
Lest, our hearts drunk with the wine of the world, we forget Thee,   30
Shadowed beneath Thy hand,
May we forever stand.
True to our God,
True to our native land.

                                                              1900

O Black and Unknown Bards

O black and unknown bards of long ago,
How came your lips to touch the sacred fire?
How, in your darkness, did you come to know
The power and beauty of the minstrel's lyre?
Who first from midst his bonds lifted his eyes?   5
Who first from out the still watch, lone and long,
Feeling the ancient faith of prophets rise
Within his dark-kept soul, burst into song?

Heart of what slave poured out such melody
As "Steal Away to Jesus"? On its strains   10
His spirit must have nightly floated free,
Though still about his hands he felt his chains.
Who heard great "Jordan roll"? Whose starward eye
Saw chariot "swing low"? And who was he
That breathed that comforting, melodic sigh,   15
"Nobody Knows de Trouble I See"?

What merely living clod, what captive thing,
Could up toward God through all its darkness grope,
And find within its deadened heart to sing
These songs of sorrow, love, and faith, and hope?   20
How did it catch that subtle undertone,
That note in music heard not with the ears?
How sound the elusive reed so seldom blown,
Which stirs the soul or melts the heart to tears?

Not that great German master in his dream   25
Of harmonies that thundered amongst the stars
At the creation, ever heard a theme
Nobler than "Go Down, Moses." Mark its bars,
How like a mighty trumpet-call they stir
The blood. Such are the notes that men have sung   30
Going to valorous deeds; such tones there were
That helped make history when Time was young.

There is a wide, wide wonder in it all,
That from degraded rest and servile toil
The fiery spirit of the seer should call   35
These simple children of the sun and soil.
O black slave singers, gone, forgot, unfamed,
You—you alone, of all the long, long line
Of those who've sung untaught, unknown, unnamed,
Have stretched out upward, seeking the divine.   40

You sang not deeds of heroes or of kings;
No chant of bloody war, no exulting paean
Of arms-won triumphs; but your humble strings
You touched in chord with music empyrean.
You sang far better than you knew; the songs   45
That for your listeners' hungry hearts sufficed
Still live—but more than this to you belongs;
You sang a race from wood and stone to Christ.

                                                                              1908

from **Autobiography of an Ex-Colored Man**

Chapter X

[This chapter is the second-to-last in the book and tells of the narrator's
return to America and the deep South after several years overseas. The final
chapter traces his move to New York City, where he finds financial success
as a "white man."]

Among the first of my fellow-passengers of whom I took any particular
notice was a tall, broad-shouldered, almost gigantic, colored man. His dark-
brown face was clean-shaven; he was well-dressed and bore a decidedly distinguished air. In fact, if he was not handsome, he at least compelled admiration for his fine physical proportions. He attracted general attention as he
strode the deck in a sort of majestic loneliness. I became curious to know
who he was and determined to strike up an acquaintance with him at the
first opportune moment. The chance came a day or two later. He was sitting
in the smoking-room, with a cigar, which had gone out, in his mouth,

reading a novel. I sat down beside him and, offering him a fresh cigar, said: "You don't mind my telling you something unpleasant, do you?" He looked at me with a smile, accepted the proffered cigar, and replied in a voice which comported perfectly with his size and appearance: "I think my curiosity overcomes any objections I might have." "Well," I said, "have you noticed that the man who sat at your right in the saloon during the first meal has not sat there since?" He frowned slightly without answering my question. "Well," I continued, "he asked the steward to remove him; and not only that, he attempted to persuade a number of the passengers to protest against your presence in the dining-saloon." The big man at my side took a long draw from his cigar, threw his head back, and slowly blew a great cloud of smoke toward the ceiling. Then turning to me he said: "Do you know, I don't object to anyone's having prejudices so long as those prejudices don't interfere with my personal liberty. Now, the man you are speaking of had a perfect right to change his seat if I in any way interfered with his appetite or his digestion. I should have no reason to complain if he removed to the farthest corner of the saloon, or even if he got off the ship; but when his prejudice attempts to move *me* one foot, one inch, out of the place where I am comfortably located, then I object." On the word "object" he brought his great fist down on the table in front of us with such a crash that everyone in the room turned to look. We both covered up the slight embarrassment with a laugh and strolled out on the deck.

We walked the deck for an hour or more, discussing different phases of the Negro question. In referring to the race I used the personal pronoun "we"; my companion made no comment about it, nor evinced any surprise, except to raise his eyebrows slightly the first time he caught the significance of the word. He was the broadest-minded colored man I have ever talked with on the Negro question. He even went so far as to sympathize with and offer excuses for some white Southern points of view. I asked him what were his main reasons for being so hopeful. He replied: "In spite of all that is written, said, and done, this great, big, incontrovertible fact stands out— the Negro is progressing, and that disproves all the arguments in the world that he is incapable of progress. I was born in slavery, and at emancipation was set adrift a ragged, penniless bit of humanity. I have seen the Negro in every grade, and I know what I am talking about. Our detractors point to the increase of crime as evidence against us; certainly we have progressed in crime as in other things; what less could be expected? And yet, in this respect, we are far from the point which has been reached by the more highly civilized white race. As we continue to progress, crime among us will gradually lose much of its brutal, vulgar, I might say healthy, aspect, and become more delicate, refined, and subtle. Then it will be less shocking and noticeable, although more dangerous to society." Then dropping his tone of irony, he continued with some show of eloquence: "But, above all, when I am discouraged and disheartened, I have this to fall back on: if there is a principle of right in the world, which finally prevails, and I believe that there is; if there is a merciful but justice-loving God in heaven, and I believe that there is, we shall win; for we have right on our side, while those who oppose us can defend themselves by nothing in the moral law, nor even by anything in the enlightened thought of the present age."

For several days, together with other topics, we discussed the race problem, not only of the United States, but as it affected native Africans and Jews. Finally, before we reached Boston, our conversation had grown familiar and personal. I had told him something of my past and much about my intentions for the future. I learned that he was a physician, a graduate of Howard University, Washington, and had done post-graduate work in Philadelphia; and this was his second trip abroad to attend professional courses. He had practiced for some years in the city of Washington, and though he did not say so, I gathered that his practice was a lucrative one. Before we left the ship, he had made me promise that I would stop two or three days in Washington before going on south.

We put up at a hotel in Boston for a couple of days and visited several of my new friend's acquaintances; they were all people of education and culture and, apparently, of means. I could not help being struck by the great difference between them and the same class of colored people in the South. In speech and thought they were genuine Yankees. The difference was especially noticeable in their speech. There was none of that heavy-tongued enunciation which characterizes even the best-educated colored people of the South. It is remarkable, after all, what an adaptable creature the Negro is. I have seen the black West Indian gentleman in London, and he is in speech and manners a perfect Englishman. I have seen natives of Haiti and Martinique in Paris, and they are more Frenchy than a Frenchman. I have no doubt that the Negro would make a good Chinaman, with exception of the pigtail.

My stay in Washington, instead of being two or three days, was two or three weeks. This was my first visit to the national capital, and I was, of course, interested in seeing the public buildings and something of the working of the government; but most of my time I spent with the doctor among his friends and acquaintances. The social phase of life among colored people is more developed in Washington than in any other city in the country. This is on account of the large number of individuals earning good salaries and having a reasonable amount of leisure time to draw from. There are dozens of physicians and lawyers, scores of school teachers, and hundreds of clerks in the departments. As to the colored department clerks, I think it fair to say that in educational equipment they average above the white clerks of the same grade; for, whereas a colored college graduate will seek such a job, the white university man goes into one of the many higher vocations which are open to him.

In a previous chapter I spoke of social life among colored people; so there is no need to take it up again here. But there is one thing I did not mention: among Negroes themselves there is the peculiar inconsistency of a color question. Its existence is rarely admitted and hardly ever mentioned; it may not be too strong a statement to say that the greater portion of the race is unconscious of its influence; yet this influence, though silent, is constant. It is evidenced most plainly in marriage selection; thus the black men generally marry women fairer than themselves; while, on the other hand, the dark women of stronger mental endowment are very often married to light-complexioned men; the effect is a tendency toward lighter complexions, especially among the more active elements in the race. Some might claim that this is a tacit admission of colored people among themselves of their own inferiority judged by the color line. I do not think so. What I have termed an inconsistency is, after all, most natural; it is, in fact, a tendency in accordance with what might be called an economic necessity. So far as racial differences go, the United States puts a greater premium on color, or, better, lack of color, than upon anything else in the world. To paraphrase, "Have a white skin, and all things else may be added unto you." I have seen advertisements in newspapers for waiters, bell-boys, or elevator men, which read: "Light-colored man wanted." It is this tremendous pressure which the sentiment of the country exerts that is operating on the race. There is involved not only the question of higher opportunity, but often the question of earning a livelihood; and so I say it is not strange, but a natural tendency. Nor is it any more a sacrifice of self-respect that a black man should give to his children every advantage he can which complexion of the skin carries than that the new or vulgar rich should purchase for their children the advantages which ancestry, aristocracy, and social position carry. I once heard a colored man sum it up in these words: "It's no disgrace to be black, but it's often very inconvenient."

Washington shows the Negro not only at his best, but also at his worst. As I drove around with the doctor, he commented rather harshly on those of the latter class which we saw. He remarked: "You see those lazy, loafing, good-for-nothing darkies; they're not worth digging graves for; yet they are the ones who create impressions of the race for the casual observer. It's because they are always in evidence on the street corners, while the rest of us are hard at work, and you know a dozen loafing darkies make a bigger crowd and a worse impression in this country than fifty white men of the same class. But they ought not to represent the race. We are the race, and the race ought to be judged by us, not by them. Every race and every nation should be judged by the best it has been able to produce, not by the worst."

The recollection of my stay in Washington is a pleasure to me now. In company with the doctor I visited Howard University, the public schools, the excellent colored hospital, with which he was in some way connected, if I remember correctly, and many comfortable and even elegant homes. It was with some reluctance that I continued my journey south. The doctor was very kind in giving me letters to people in Richmond and Nashville when I told him that I intended to stop in both of these cities. In Richmond a man who was then editing a very creditable colored newspaper gave me a great deal of his time and made my stay there of three or four days very pleasant. In Nashville I spent a whole day at Fisk University, the home of the "Jubilee Singers," and was more than repaid for my time. Among my letters of introduction was one to a very prosperous physician. He drove me about the city and introduced me to a number of people. From Nashville I went to Atlanta, where I stayed long enough to gratify an old desire to see Atlanta University again. I then continued my journey to Macon.

During the trip from Nashville to Atlanta I went into the smoking-compartment of the car to smoke a cigar. I was traveling in a Pullman, not because of an abundance of funds, but because through my experience with my millionaire a certain amount of comfort and luxury had become a necessity to me whenever it was obtainable. When I entered the car, I found only a couple of men there; but in a half-hour there were half a dozen or more. From the general conversation I learned that a fat Jewish-looking man was a cigar manufacturer, and was experimenting in growing Havana tobacco in Florida; that a slender bespectacled young man was from Ohio and a professor in some State institution in Alabama; that a white-mustached, well-dressed man was an old Union soldier who had fought through the Civil War; and that a tall, raw-boned, red-faced man, who seemed bent on leaving nobody in ignorance of the fact that he was from Texas, was a cotton planter.

In the North men may ride together for hours in a "smoker" and unless they are acquainted with each other never exchange a word; in the South men thrown together in such manner are friends in fifteen minutes. There is always present a warmhearted cordiality which will melt down the most frigid reserve. It may be because Southerners are very much like Frenchmen in that they must talk; and not only must they talk, but they must express their opinions.

The talk in the car was for a while miscellaneous—on the weather, crops, business prospects; the old Union soldier had invested capital in Atlanta, and he predicted that that city would soon be one of the greatest in the country. Finally the conversation drifted to politics; then, as a natural sequence, turned upon the Negro question.

In the discussion of the race question the diplomacy of the Jew was something to be admired; he had the faculty of agreeing with everybody without losing his allegiance to any side. He knew that to sanction Negro oppression would be to sanction Jewish oppression and would expose him to a shot along that line from the old soldier, who stood firmly on the ground of equal rights and opportunity to all men; long traditions and business instincts told him when in Rome to act as a Roman. Altogether his position was a delicate one, and I gave him credit for the skill he displayed in maintaining it. The young professor was apologetic. He had had the same views as the G.A.R. man; but a year in the South had opened his eyes, and he had to confess that the problem could hardly be handled any better than it was being handled by the Southern whites. To which the G.A.R. man responded somewhat rudely that he had spent ten times as many years in the South as his young friend and that he could easily understand how holding a position in a State institution in Alabama would bring about a change of views. The professor turned very red and had very little more to say. The

Texan was fierce, eloquent, and profane in his argument, and, in a lower sense, there was a direct logic in what he said, which was convincing; it was only by taking higher ground, by dealing in what Southerners call "theories," that he could be combated. Occasionally some one of the several other men in the "smoker" would throw in a remark to reinforce what he said, but he really didn't need any help; he was sufficient in himself.

In the course of a short time the controversy narrowed itself down to an argument between the old soldier and the Texan. The latter maintained hotly that the Civil War was a criminal mistake on the part of the North and that the humiliation which the South suffered during Reconstruction could never be forgotten. The Union man retorted just as hotly that the South was responsible for the war and that the spirit of unforgetfulness on its part was the greatest cause of present friction; that it seemed to be the one great aim of the South to convince the North that the latter made a mistake in fighting to preserve the Union and liberate the slaves. "Can you imagine," he went on to say, "what would have been the condition of things eventually if there had been no war, and the South had been allowed to follow its course? Instead of one great, prosperous country with nothing before it but the conquests of peace, a score of petty republics, as in Central and South America, wasting their energies in war with each other or in revolutions."

"Well," replied the Texan, "anything—no country at all—is better than having niggers over you. But anyhow, the war was fought and the niggers were freed; for it's no use beating around the bush, the niggers, and not the Union, was the cause of it; and now do you believe that all the niggers on earth are worth the good white blood that was spilt? You freed the nigger and you gave him the ballot, but you couldn't make a citizen out of him. He don't know what he's voting for, and we buy 'em like so many hogs. You're giving 'em education, but that only makes slick rascals out of 'em."

"Don't fancy for a moment," said the Northern man, "that you have any monopoly in buying ignorant votes. The same thing is done on a larger scale in New York and Boston, and in Chicago and San Francisco; and they are not black votes either. As to education's making the Negro worse, you might just as well tell me that religion does the same thing. And, by the way, how many educated colored men do you know personally?"

The Texan admitted that he knew only one, and added that he was in the penitentiary. "But," he said, "do you mean to claim, ballot or no ballot, education or no education, that niggers are the equals of white men?"

"That's not the question," answered the other, "but if the Negro is so distinctly inferior, it is a strange thing to me that it takes such tremendous effort on the part of the white man to make him realize it, and to keep him in the same place into which inferior men naturally fall. However, let us grant for sake of argument that the Negro is inferior in every respect to the white man; that fact only increases our moral responsibility in regard to our actions toward him. Inequalities of numbers, wealth, and power, even of intelligence and morals, should make no difference in the essential rights of men."

"If he's inferior and weaker, and is shoved to the wall, that's his own look-out," said the Texan. "That's the law of nature; and he's bound to go to the wall; for no race in the world has ever been able to stand competition with the Anglo-Saxon. The Anglo-Saxon race has always been and always will be the masters of the world, and the niggers in the South ain't going to change all the records of history."

"My friend," said the old soldier slowly, "if you have studied history, will you tell me, as confidentially between white men, what the Anglo-Saxon has ever done?"

The Texan was too much astonished by the question to venture any reply.

His opponent continued: "Can you name a single one of the great fundamental and original intellectual achievements which have raised man in the scale of civilization that may be credited to the Anglo-Saxon? The art of letters, of poetry, of music, of sculpture, of painting, of the drama, of architecture; the science of mathematics, of astronomy, of philosophy, of logic, of physics, of chemistry, the use of the metals, and the principles of mechanics, were all invented or discovered by darker and what we now call inferior races and nations. We have carried many of these to their highest point of perfection, but the foundation was laid by others. Do you know the only original contribution to civilization we can claim is what we have done in steam and electricity and in making implements of war more deadly? And there we worked largely on principles which we did not discover. Why, we didn't even originate the religion we use. We are a great race, the greatest in the world today, but we ought to remember that we are standing on a pile of past races, and enjoy our position with a little less show of arrogance. We are simply having our turn at the game, and we were a long time getting to it. After all, racial supremacy is merely a matter of dates in history. The man here who belongs to what is, all in all, the greatest race the world ever produced, is almost ashamed to own it. If the Anglo-Saxon is the source of everything good and great in the human race from the beginning, why wasn't the German forest the birthplace of civilization, rather than the valley of the Nile?"

The Texan was somewhat disconcerted, for the argument had passed a little beyond his limits, but he swung it back to where he was sure of his ground by saying: "All that may be true, but it hasn't got much to do with us and the niggers here in the South. We've got 'em here, and we've got 'em to live with, and it's a question of white man or nigger, no middle ground. You want us to treat niggers as equals. Do you want to see 'em sitting around in our parlors? Do you want to see a mulatto South? To bring it right home to you, would you let your daughter marry a nigger?"

"No, I wouldn't consent to my daughter's marrying a nigger, but that doesn't prevent my treating a black man fairly. And I don't see what fair treatment has to do with niggers sitting around in your parlors; they can't come there unless they're invited. Out of all the white men I know, only a hundred or so have the privilege of sitting around in my parlor. As to the mulatto South, if you Southerners have one boast that is stronger than another, it is your women; you put them on a pinnacle of purity and virtue and bow down in a chivalric worship before them; yet you talk and act as though, should you treat the Negro fairly and take the anti-inter-marriage laws off your statute books, these same women would rush into the arms of black lovers and husbands. It's a wonder to me that they don't rise up and resent the insult."

"Colonel," said the Texan, as he reached into his handbag and brought out a large flask of whisky, "you might argue from now until hell freezes over, and you might convince me that you're right, but you'll never convince me that I'm wrong. All you say sounds very good, but it's got nothing to do with facts. You can say what men ought to be, but they ain't that; so there you are. Down here in the South we're up against facts, and we're meeting 'em like facts. We don't believe the nigger is or ever will be the equal of the white man, and we ain't going to treat him as an equal; I'll be damned if we will. Have a drink." Everybody except the professor partook of the generous Texan's flask, and the argument closed in a general laugh and good feeling.

I went back into the main part of the car with the conversation on my mind. Here I had before me the bald, raw, naked aspects of the race question in the South; and, in consideration of the step I was just taking, it was far from encouraging. The sentiments of the Texan—and he expressed the sentiments of the South—fell upon me like a chill. I was sick at heart. Yet I must confess that underneath it all I felt a certain sort of admiration for the man who could not be swayed from what he held as his principles. Contrasted with him, the young Ohio professor was indeed a pitiable character. And all along, in spite of myself, I have been compelled to accord the same kind of admiration to the Southern white man for the manner in which he defends not only his virtues, but his vices. He knows that, judged by a high standard, he is narrow and prejudiced, that he is guilty of unfairness, oppression, and cruelty, but this he defends as stoutly as he would his better qualities. This same spirit obtains in a great degree among the blacks; they, too, defend their faults and failings. This they generally do whenever white people are concerned. And yet among themselves they are their own most merciless critics. I have never heard the race so terribly arraigned as I have by colored speakers to strictly colored audiences. It is the spirit of the South to defend everything belonging to it. The North is too cosmopolitan and tolerant for such a spirit. If you should say to an Easterner that Paris is a gayer city than New York, he would be likely to agree with you, or at least to let you have your own way; but to suggest to a South Carolinian that Boston is a nicer city to live in than Charleston would be to stir his greatest depths of argument and eloquence.

But to-day, as I think over that smoking-car argument, I can see it in a different light. The Texan's position does not render things so hopeless, for it indicates that the main difficulty of the race question does not lie so much in the actual condition of the blacks as it does in the mental attitude of the whites; and a mental attitude, especially one not based on truth, can be changed more easily than actual conditions. That is to say, the burden of the question is not that the whites are struggling to save ten million despondent and moribund people from sinking into a hopeless slough of ignorance, poverty, and barbarity in their very midst, but that they are unwilling to open certain doors of opportunity and to accord certain treatment to ten million aspiring, education-and-property-acquiring people. In a word, the difficulty of the problem is not so much due to the facts presented as to the hypothesis assumed for its solution. In this it is similar to the problem of the solar system. By a complex, confusing, and almost contradictory mathematical process, by the use of zigzags instead of straight lines, the earth can be proved to be the center of things celestial; but by an operation so simple that it can be comprehended by a schoolboy, its position can be verified among the other worlds which revolve about the sun, and its movements harmonized with the laws of the universe. So, when the white race assumes as a hypothesis that it is the main object of creation and that all things else are merely subsidiary to its well-being, sophism, subterfuge, perversion of conscience, arrogance, injustice, oppression, cruelty, sacrifice of human blood, all are required to maintain the position, and its dealings with other races become indeed a problem, a problem which, if based on a hypothesis of common humanity, could be solved by the simple rules of justice.

When I reached Macon, I decided to leave my trunk and all my surplus belongings, to pack my bag, and strike out into the interior. This I did; and by train, by mule and ox-cart, I traveled through many counties. This was my first real experience among rural colored people, and all that I saw was interesting to me; but there was a great deal which does not require description at my hands; for log cabins and plantations and dialect-speaking "darkies" are perhaps better known in American literature than any other single picture of our national life. Indeed, they form an ideal and exclusive literary concept of the American Negro to such an extent that it is almost impossible to get the reading public to recognize him in any other setting; so I shall endeavor to avoid giving the reader any already overworked and hackneyed descriptions. This generally accepted literary ideal of the American Negro constitutes what is really an obstacle in the way of the thoughtful and progressive element of the race. His character has been established as a happy-go-lucky, laughing, shuffling, banjo-picking being, and the reading public has not yet been prevailed upon to take him seriously. His efforts to elevate himself socially are looked upon as a sort of absurd caricature of "white civilization." A novel dealing with colored people who lived in respectable homes and amidst a fair degree of culture and who naturally acted "just like white folks" would be taken in a comic-opera sense. In this respect the Negro is much in the position of a great comedian who gives up the lighter roles to play tragedy. No matter how well he may portray the deeper passions, the public is loath to give him up in his old character; they even conspire to make him a failure in serious work, in order to force him back into comedy. In the same respect, the public is not too much to be blamed, for great comedians are far more scarce than mediocre tragedians; every amateur actor is a tragedian. However, this very fact constitutes the opportunity of the future Negro novelist and poet to give the country something new and unknown, in depicting the life, the ambitions, the struggles, and the passions of those of their race who are striving to break the narrow limits of traditions. A beginning has already been made in that remarkable book by Dr. Du Bois' *The Souls of Black Folk*.

Much, too, that I saw while on this trip, in spite of my enthusiasm, was disheartening. Often I thought of what my millionaire had said to me, and wished myself back in Europe. The houses in which I had to stay were generally uncomfortable, sometimes worse. I often had to sleep in a division or compartment with several other people. Once or twice I was not so fortunate as to find divisions; everybody slept on pallets on the floor. Frequently I was able to lie down and contemplate the stars which were in their zenith. The food was at times so distasteful and poorly cooked that I could not eat it. I remember that once I lived for a week or more on buttermilk, on account of not being able to stomach the fat bacon, the rank turniptops, and the heavy damp mixture of meal, salt, and water which was called corn bread. It was only my ambition to do the work which I had planned that kept me steadfast to my purpose. Occasionally I would meet with some signs of progress and uplift in even one of these back-wood settlements—houses built of boards, with windows, and divided into rooms; decent food, and a fair standard of living. This condition was due to the fact that there was in the community some exceptionally capable Negro farmer whose thrift served as an example. As I went about among these dull, simple people—the great majority of them hard working, in their relations with the whites submissive, faithful, and often affectionate, negatively content with their lot—and contrasted them with those of the race who had been quickened by the forces of thought, I could not but appreciate the logic of the position held by those Southern leaders who have been bold enough to proclaim against the education of the Negro. They are consistent in their public speech with Southern sentiment and desires. Those public men of the South who have not been daring or heedless enough to defy the ideals of twentieth-century civilization and of modern humanitarianism and philanthropy, find themselves in the embarrassing situation of preaching one thing and praying for another. They are in the position of the fashionable woman who is compelled by the laws of polite society to say to her dearest enemy: "How happy I am to see you!"

And yet in this respect how perplexing is Southern character; for, in opposition to the above, it may be said that the claim of the Southern whites that they love the Negro better than the Northern whites do is in a manner true. Northern white people love the Negro in a sort of abstract way, as a race; through a sense of justice, charity, and philanthropy, they will liberally assist in his elevation. A number of them have heroically spent their lives in this effort (and just here I wish to say that when the colored people reach the monument-building stage, they should not forget the men and women who went South after the war and founded schools for them).

Yet, generally speaking, they have no particular liking for individuals of the race. Southern white people despise the Negro as a race, and will do nothing to aid in his elevation as such; but for certain individuals they have a strong affection, and are helpful to them in many ways. With these individual members of the race they live on terms of the greatest intimacy; they entrust to them their children, their family treasures, and their family secrets; in trouble they often go to them for comfort and counsel; in sickness they often rely upon their care. This affectionate relation between the Southern whites and those blacks who come into close touch with them has not been overdrawn even in fiction.

This perplexity of Southern character extends even to the intermixture of the races. That is spoken of as though it were dreaded worse than small-pox, leprosy, or the plague. Yet, when I was in Jacksonville, I knew several prominent families there with large colored branches, which went by the same name and were known and acknowledged as blood relatives. And what is more, there seemed to exist between these black brothers and sisters and uncles and aunts a decidedly friendly feeling.

I said above that Southern whites would do nothing for the Negro as a race. I know the South claims that it has spent millions for the education of the blacks, and that it has of its own free will shouldered this awful burden. It seems to be forgetful of the fact that these millions have been taken from the public tax funds for education, and that the law of political economy which recognizes the land owner as the one who really pays the taxes is not tenable. It would be just as reasonable for the relatively few land owners of Manhattan to complain that they had to stand the financial burden of the education of the thousands and thousands of children whose parents pay rent for tenements and flats. Let the millions of producing and consuming Negroes be taken out of the South, and it would be quickly seen how much less of public funds there would be to appropriate for education or any other purpose.

In thus traveling about through the country I was sometimes amused on arriving at some little railroad-station town to be taken for and treated as a white man, and six hours later, when it was learned that I was stopping at the house of the colored preacher or school teacher, to note the attitude of the whole town change. At times this led even to embarrassment. Yet it cannot be so embarrassing for a colored man to be taken for white as for a white man to be taken for colored; and I have heard of several cases of the latter kind.

All this while I was gathering material for work, jotting down in my note-book themes and melodies, and trying to catch the spirit of the Negro in his relatively primitive state. I began to feel the necessity of hurrying so that I might get back to some city like Nashville to begin my compositions and at the same time earn at least a living by teaching and performing before my funds gave out. At the last settlement in which I stopped I found a mine of material. This was due to the fact that "big meeting" was in progress. "Big meeting" is an institution something like camp-meeting, the difference being that it is held in a permanent church, and not in a temporary structure. All the churches of some one denomination—of course, either Methodist or Baptist—in a county, or, perhaps, in several adjoining counties, are closed, and the congregations unite at some centrally located church for a series of meetings lasting a week. It is really a social as well as a religious function. The people come in great numbers, making the trip, according to their financial status, in buggies drawn by sleek, fleet-footed mules, in ox-carts, or on foot. It was amusing to see some of the latter class trudging down the hot and dusty road, with their shoes, which were brand-new, strung across their shoulders. When they got near the church, they sat on the side of the road and, with many grimaces, tenderly packed their feet into those instruments of torture. This furnished, indeed, a trying test of their religion. The famous preachers come from near and far and take turns in warning sinners of the day of wrath. Food, in the form of those two Southern luxuries, fried chicken and roast pork, is plentiful, and no one need go hungry. On the opening Sunday the women are immaculate in starched stiff white dresses adorned with ribbons, either red or blue. Even a great many of the men wear streamers of vari-colored ribbons in the button-holes of their coats. A few of them carefully cultivate a forelock of hair by wrapping it in twine, and on such festive occasions decorate it with a narrow ribbon streamer. Big meetings afford a fine opportunity to the younger people to meet each other dressed in their Sunday clothes, and much rustic courting, which is as enjoyable as any other kind, is indulged in.

This big meeting which I was lucky enough to catch was particularly well attended; the extra large attendance was due principally to two attractions, a man by the name of John Brown, who was renowned as the most powerful preacher for miles around; and a wonderful leader of singing, who was known as "Singing Johnson." These two men were a study and a revelation to me. They caused me to reflect upon how great an influence their types have been in the development of the Negro in America. Both these types are now looked upon generally with condescension or contempt by the progressive element among the colored people; but it should never be forgotten that it was they who led the race from paganism and kept it steadfast to Christianity through all the long, dark years of slavery.

John Brown was a jet-black man of medium size, with a strikingly intelligent head and face, and a voice like an organ peal. He preached each night after several lesser lights had successively held the pulpit during an hour or so. As far as subject-matter is concerned, all of the sermons were alike: each began with the fall of man, ran through various trials and tribulations of the Hebrew children, on to the redemption by Christ, and ended with a fervid picture of the judgment day and the fate of the damned. But John Brown possessed magnetism and an imagination so free and daring that he was able to carry through what the other preachers would not attempt. He knew all the arts and tricks of oratory, the modulation of the voice to almost a whisper, the pause for effect, the rise through light, rapid-fire sentences to the terrific, thundering outburst of an electrifying climax. In addition, he had the intuition of a born theatrical manager. Night after night this man held me fascinated. He convinced me that, after all, eloquence consists more in the manner of saying than in what is said. It is largely a matter of tone pictures.

The most striking example of John Brown's magnetism and imagination was his "heavenly march"; I shall never forget how it impressed me when I heard it. He opened his sermon in the usual way; then, proclaiming to his listeners that he was going to take them on the heavenly march, he seized the Bible under his arm and began to pace up and down the pulpit platform. The congregation immediately began with their feet a tramp, tramp, tramp, in time with the preacher's march in the pulpit, all the while singing in an undertone a hymn about marching to Zion. Suddenly he cried: "Halt!" Every foot stopped with the precision of a company of well-drilled soldiers, and the singing ceased. The morning star had been reached. Here the preacher described the beauties of that celestial body. Then the march, the tramp, tramp, tramp, and the singing were again taken up. Another "Halt!" They had reached the evening star. And so on, past the sun and moon—the intensity of religious emotion all the time increasing—along the milky way, on up to the gates of heaven. Here the halt was longer, and the preacher described at length the gates and walls of the New Jerusalem. Then he took his hearers through the pearly gates, along the golden streets, pointing out the glories of the city, pausing occasionally to greet some patriarchal members of the church, well-known to most of his listeners in life, who had had "the tears wiped from their eyes, were clad in robes of spotless white, with crowns of gold upon their heads and harps within their hands," and ended his march before the great white throne. To the reader this may sound ridiculous, but listened to under the circumstances, it was highly and effectively dramatic. I was a more or less sophisticated and non-religious man of the world, but the torrent of the preacher's words, moving with the rhythm and glowing with the eloquence of primitive poetry, swept me along, and I, too, felt like joining in the shouts of "Amen! Hallelujah!"

John Brown's powers in describing the delights of heaven were no greater than those in depicting the horrors of hell. I saw great, strapping fellows trembling and weeping like children at the "mourners' bench." His warnings to sinners were truly terrible. I shall never forget one expression that he used, which for originality and aptness could not be excelled. In my opinion, it is more graphic and, for us, far more expressive than St. Paul's "It is hard to kick against the pricks." He struck the attitude of a pugilist and thundered out: "Young man, your arm's too short to box with God!"

Interesting as was John Brown to me, the other man, "Singing Johnson," was more so. He was a small, dark-brown, one-eyed man, with a clear, strong, high-pitched voice, a leader of singing, a maker of songs, a man who could improvise at the moment lines to fit the occasion. Not so striking a figure as John Brown, but, at "big meetings," equally important. It is indispensable to the success of the singing, when the congregation is a large one made up of people from different communities, to have someone with a strong voice who knows just what hymn to sing and when to sing it, who can pitch it in the right key, and who has all the leading lines committed to memory. Sometimes it devolves upon the leader to "sing down" a long-winded or uninteresting speaker. Committing to memory the leading lines of all the Negro spiritual songs is no easy task, for they run up into the hundreds. But the accomplished leader must know them all, because the congregation sings only the refrains and repeats; every ear in the church is fixed upon him, and if he becomes mixed in his lines or forgets them, the responsibility falls directly on his shoulders.

For example, most of these hymns are constructed to be sung in the following manner:

> *Leader*. Swing low, sweet chariot.
> *Congregation*. Coming for to carry me home.
> *Leader*. Swing low, sweet chariot.
> *Congregation*. Coming for to carry me home.
> *Leader*. I look over yonder, what do I see?
> *Congregation*. Coming for to carry me home.
> *Leader*. Two little angels coming after me.
> *Congregation*. Coming for to carry me home. . . .

The solitary and plaintive voice of the leader is answered by a sound like the roll of the sea, producing a most curious effect.

In only a few of these songs do the leader and the congregation start off together. Such a song is the well-known "Steal away to Jesus."

The leader and the congregation begin with part-singing:

> Steal away, steal away,
> Steal away to Jesus;
> Steal away, steal away home,
> I ain't got long to stay here.

Then the leader alone or the congregation in unison:

> My Lord he calls me,
> He calls me by the thunder,
> The trumpet sounds within-a my soul.

Then all together:

> I ain't got long to stay here.

The leader and the congregation again take up the opening refrain; then the leader sings three more leading lines alone, and so on almost *ad infinitum*. It will be seen that even here most of the work falls upon the leader, for the congregation sings the same lines over and over, while his memory and ingenuity are taxed to keep the songs going.

Generally the parts taken up by the congregation are sung in a three-part harmony, the women singing the soprano and a transposed tenor, the men with high voices singing the melody, and those with low voices a thundering bass. In a few of these songs, however, the leading part is sung in unison by the whole congregation, down to the last line, which is harmonized. The effect of this is intensely thrilling. Such a hymn is "Go down, Moses." It stirs the heart like a trumpet call.

"Singing Johnson" was an ideal leader, and his services were in great demand. He spent his time going about the country from one church to another. He received his support in much the same way as the preachers— part of a collection, food and lodging. All of his leisure time he devoted to originating new words and melodies and new lines for old songs. He always sang with his eyes—or, to be more exact, his eye—closed, indicating the *tempo* by swinging his head to and fro. He was a great judge of the proper hymn to sing at a particular moment; and I noticed several times, when the preacher reached a certain climax, or expressed a certain sentiment, that Johnson broke in with a line or two of some appropriate hymn. The speaker understood and would pause until the singing ceased.

As I listened to the singing of these songs, the wonder of their production grew upon me more and more. How did the men who originated them manage to do it? The sentiments are easily accounted for; they are mostly taken from the Bible; but the melodies, where did they come from? Some of them so weirdly sweet, and others so wonderfully strong. Take, for instance, "Go down, Moses." I doubt that there is a stronger theme in the whole musical literature of the world. And so many of these songs contain more than mere melody; there is sounded in them that elusive undertone, the note in music which is not heard with the ears. I sat often with the tears rolling down my cheeks and my heart melted within me. Any musical person who has never heard a Negro congregation under the spell of religious fervor sing these old songs has missed one of the most thrilling emotions which the human heart may experience. Anyone who without shedding tears can listen to Negroes sing "Nobody knows de trouble I see, Nobody knows but Jesus" must indeed have a heart of stone.

As yet, the Negroes themselves do not fully appreciate these old slave songs. The educated classes are rather ashamed of them and prefer to sing hymns from books. This feeling is natural; they are still too close to the conditions under which the songs were produced; but the day will come when this slave music will be the most treasured heritage of the American Negro.

At the close of the "big meeting" I left the settlement where it was being held, full of enthusiasm. I was in that frame of mind which, in the artistic temperament, amounts to inspiration. I was now ready and anxious to get to some place where I might settle down to work, and give expression to the ideas which were teeming in my head; but I strayed into another deviation from my path of life as I had it marked out, which led me upon an entirely different road. Instead of going to the nearest and most convenient railroad station, I accepted the invitation of a young man who had been present the closing Sunday at the meeting to drive with him some miles farther to the town in which he taught school, and there take the train. My conversation with this young man as we drove along through the country was extremely interesting. He had been a student in one of the Negro colleges—strange coincidence, in the very college, as I learned through him, in which "Shiny" was now a professor. I was, of course, curious to hear about my boyhood friend; and had it not been vacation time, and that I was not sure that I should find him, I should have gone out of my way to pay him a visit; but I determined to write to him as soon as the school opened. My companion talked to me about his work among the people, of his hopes and his discouragements. He was tremendously in earnest; I might say, too much so. In fact, it may be said that the majority of intelligent colored people are, in some degree, too much in earnest over the race question. They assume and carry so much that their progress is at times impeded and they are unable to see things in their proper proportions. In many instances a slight exercise of the sense of humor would save much anxiety of soul. Anyone who marks the general tone of editorials in colored newspapers is apt to be impressed with this idea. If the mass of Negroes took their present and future as seriously as do the most of their leaders, the race would be in no mental condition to sustain the terrible pressure which it undergoes; it would sink of its own weight. Yet it must be acknowledged that in the making of a race over-seriousness is a far lesser failing than its reverse, and even the faults resulting from it lean toward the right.

We drove into the town just before dark. As we passed a large, unpainted church, my companion pointed it out as the place where he held his school. I promised that I would go there with him the next morning and visit awhile. The town was of that kind which hardly requires or deserves description; a straggling line of brick and wooden stores on one side of the railroad track and some cottages of various sizes on the other side constituted about the whole of it. The young school teacher boarded at the best house in the place owned by a colored man. It was painted, had glass windows, contained "store bought" furniture, an organ, and lamps with chimneys. The owner held a job of some kind on the railroad. After supper it was not long before everybody was sleepy. I occupied the room with the school teacher. In a few minutes after we got into the room he was in bed and asleep; but I took advantage of the unusual luxury of a lamp which gave light, and sat looking over my notes and jotting down some ideas which were still fresh in my mind. Suddenly I became conscious of that sense of alarm which is always aroused by the sound of hurrying footsteps on the silence of the night. I stopped work and looked at my watch. It was after eleven. I listened, straining every nerve to hear above the tumult of my quickening pulse. I caught the murmur of voices, then the gallop of a horse, then of another and another. Now thoroughly alarmed, I woke my companion, and together we both listened. After a moment he put out the light and softly opened the window-blind, and we cautiously peeped out. We saw men moving in one direction, and from the mutterings we vaguely caught the rumor that some terrible crime had been committed. I put on my coat and hat. My friend did all in his power to dissuade me from venturing out, but it was impossible for me to remain in the house under such tense excitement. My nerves would not have stood it. Perhaps what bravery I exercised in going out was due to the fact that I felt sure my identity as a colored man had not yet become known in the town.

I went out and, following the drift, reached the railroad station. There was gathered there a crowd of men, all white, and others were steadily arriving, seemingly from all the surrounding country. How did the news spread so quickly? I watched these men moving under the yellow glare of the kerosene lamps about the station, stern, comparatively silent, all of them armed, some of them in boots and spurs; fierce, determined men. I had come to know the type well, blond, tall, and lean, with ragged mustache and beard, and glittering gray eyes. At the first suggestion of daylight they began to disperse in groups, going in several directions. There was no extra noise or excitement, no loud talking, only swift, sharp words of command given by those who seemed to be accepted as leaders by mutual understanding. In fact, the impression made upon me was that everything was being done in quite an orderly manner. In spite of so many leaving, the crowd around the station continued to grow; at sunrise there were a great many women and children. By this time I also noticed some colored people; a few seemed to be going about customary tasks; several were standing on the outskirts of the crowd; but the gathering of Negroes usually seen in such towns was missing.

Before noon they brought him in. Two horsemen rode abreast; between them, half dragged, the poor wretch made his way through the dust. His hands were tied behind him, and ropes around his body were fastened to the saddle horns of his double guard. The men who at midnight had been stern and silent were now emitting that terror-instilling sound known as the "rebel yell." A space was quickly cleared in the crowd, and a rope placed about his neck, when from somewhere came the suggestion, "Burn him!" It ran like an electric current. Have you ever witnessed the transformation of human beings into savage beasts? Nothing can be more terrible. A railroad tie was sunk into the ground, the rope was removed, and a chain brought and securely coiled around the victim and the stake. There he stood, a man only in form and stature, every sign of degeneracy stamped upon his countenance. His eyes were dull and vacant, indicating not a single ray of thought. Evidently the realization of his fearful fate had robbed him of whatever reasoning power he had ever possessed. He was too stunned and stupefied even to tremble. Fuel was brought from everywhere, oil, the torch; the flames crouched for an instant as though to gather strength, then leaped up as high as their victim's head. He squirmed, he writhed, strained at his chains, then gave out cries and groans that I shall always hear. The cries and groans were choked off by the fire and smoke; but his eyes, bulging from their sockets, rolled from side to side, appealing in vain for help. Some of the crowd yelled and cheered, others seemed appalled at what they had done, and there were those who turned away sickened at the sight. I was fixed to the spot where I stood, powerless to take my eyes from what I did not want to see.

It was over before I realized that time had elapsed. Before I could make myself believe that what I saw was really happening, I was looking at a scorched post, a smoldering fire, blackened bones, charred fragments sifting down through coils of chain; and the smell of burnt flesh—human flesh— was in my nostrils.

I walked a short distance away and sat down in order to clear my dazed mind. A great wave of humiliation and shame swept over me. Shame that I belonged to a race that could be so dealt with; and shame for my country, that it, the great example of democracy to the world, should be the only civilized, if not the only state on earth, where a human being would be burned alive. My heart turned bitter within me. I could understand why Negroes are led to sympathize with even their worst criminals and to protect them when possible. By all the impulses of normal human nature they can and should do nothing less.

Whenever I hear protests from the South that it should be left alone to deal with the Negro question, my thoughts go back to that scene of brutality and savagery. I do not see how a people that can find in its conscience any excuse whatever for slowly burning to death a human being, or for tolerating such an act, can be entrusted with the salvation of a race. Of course, there are in the South men of liberal thought who do not approve lynching, but I wonder how long they will endure the limits which are placed upon free speech. They still cower and tremble before "Southern opinion." Even so late as the recent Atlanta riot those men who were brave enough to speak a word in behalf of justice and humanity felt called upon, by way of apology, to preface what they said with a glowing rhetorical tribute to the Anglo-Saxon's superiority and to refer to the "great and impassable gulf" between the races "fixed by the Creator at the foundation of the world." The question of the relative qualities of the two races is still an open one. The reference to the "great gulf" loses force in face of the fact that there are in this country perhaps three or four million people with the blood of both races in their veins; but I fail to see the pertinency of either statement subsequent to the beating and murdering of scores of innocent people in the streets of a civilized and Christian city.

The Southern whites are in many respects a great people. Looked at from a certain point of view, they are picturesque. If one will put oneself in a romantic frame of mind, one can admire their notions of chivalry and bravery and justice. In this same frame of mind an intelligent man can go to the theatre and applaud the impossible hero, who with his single sword slays everybody in the play except the equally impossible heroine. So can an ordinary peace-loving citizen sit by a comfortable fire and read with enjoyment of the bloody deeds of pirates and the fierce brutality of Vikings. This is the way in which we gratify the old, underlying animal instincts and passions; but we should shudder with horror at the mere idea of such practices being realities in this day of enlightened and humanitarianized thought. The Southern whites are not yet living quite in the present age; many of their general ideas hark back to a former century, some of them to the Dark Ages.

In the light of other days they are sometimes magnificent. Today they are often cruel and ludicrous.

How long I sat with bitter thoughts running through my mind I do not know; perhaps an hour or more. When I decided to get up and go back to the house, I found that I could hardly stand on my feet. I was as weak as a man who had lost blood. However, I dragged myself along, with the central idea of a general plan well fixed in my mind. I did not find my school teacher friend at home, so I did not see him again. I swallowed a few mouthfuls of food, packed my bag, and caught the afternoon train.

When I reached Macon, I stopped only long enough to get the main part of my luggage and to buy a ticket for New York. All along the journey I was occupied in debating with myself the step which I had decided to take. I argued that to forsake one's race to better one's condition was no less worthy an action than to forsake one's country for the same purpose. I finally made up my mind that I would neither disclaim the black race nor claim the white race; but that I would change my name, raise a mustache, and let the world take me for what it would; that it was not necessary for me to go about with a label of inferiority pasted across my forehead. All the while I understood that it was not discouragement or fear or search for a larger field of action and opportunity that was driving me out of the Negro race. I knew that it was shame, unbearable shame. Shame at being identified with a people that could with impunity be treated worse than animals. For certainly the law would restrain and punish the malicious burning alive of animals.

So once again I found myself gazing at the towers of New York and wondering what future that city held in store for me.

1912

The Creation

And God stepped out on space,
And he looked around and said:
I'm lonely—
I'll make me a world.

And far as the eye of God could see   5
Darkness covered everything,
Blacker than a hundred midnights
Down in a cypress swamp.

Then God smiled,
And the light broke,   10
And the darkness rolled up on one side,
And the light stood shining on the other,
And God said: That's good!

Then God reached out and took the light in his hands,
And God rolled the light around in his hands   15
Until he made the sun;
And he set that sun a-blazing in the heavens.
And the light that was left from making the sun
God gathered it up in a shining ball
And flung it against the darkness,   20
Spangling the night with the moon and stars.
Then down between
The darkness and the light
He hurled the world;
And God said: That's good!   25

Then God himself stepped down—
And the sun was on his right hand,
And the moon was on his left;
The stars were clustered about his head,
And the earth was under his feet.   30
And God walked, and where he trod
His footsteps hollowed the valleys out
And bulged the mountains up.

Then he stopped and looked and saw
That the earth was hot and barren.   35
So God stepped over to the edge of the world
And he spat out the seven seas—
He batted his eyes, and the lightnings flashed—
He clapped his hands, and the thunders rolled—
And the waters above the earth came down,   40
The cooling waters came down.

Then the green grass sprouted,
And the little red flowers blossomed,
The pine tree pointed his finger to the sky,
And the oak spread out his arms,   45
The lakes cuddled down in the hollows of the ground,
And the rivers ran down to the sea;
And God smiled again,
And the rainbow appeared,
And curled itself around his shoulder.   50

Then God raised his arm and he waved his hand
Over the sea and over the land,
And he said: Bring forth! Bring forth!
And quicker than God could drop his hand,
Fishes and fowls   55

And beasts and birds
Swam the rivers and the seas,
Roamed the forests and the woods,
And split the air with their wings.
And God said: That's good!   60

Then God walked around,
And God looked around
On all that he had made.
He looked at his sun,
And he looked at his moon,   65
And he looked at his little stars;
He looked on his world
With all its living things,
And God said: I'm lonely still.

Then God sat down—   70
On the side of a hill where he could think;
By a deep, wide river he sat down;
With his head in his hands,
God thought and thought,
Till he thought: I'll make me a man!   75

Up from the bed of the river
God scooped the clay;
And by the bank of the river
He kneeled him down;
And there the great God Almighty   80
Who lit the sun and fixed it in the sky,

Who flung the stars to the most far corner of the night,
Who rounded the earth in the middle of his hand;
This Great God,
Like a mammy bending over her baby,   85
Kneeled down in the dust
Toiling over a lump of clay
Till he shaped it in his own image;

Then into it he blew the breath of life,
And man became a living soul.   90
Amen. Amen.

                                                           1927

Nature and Religion—Efficiency, Entrepreneurial Christianity, and the Rise of the Machine Culture

THIS IN FOCUS SUGGESTS HOW MODERNITY RESHAPED NOTIONS OF NATURE AND the body through technology by depicting natural processes as inherently mechanical rather than organic. Thanks to new movements such as the efficiency craze of the 1910s, the natural world became a form whose energies could be imitated to maximize one's innate vitality and realize the ideal self. Enabling this urge toward self-perfection was the new explosion of consumerism, which promised betterment through buying power.

Of course, not all commentators were so optimistic. For every Bernarr Macfadden who evangelized on the vim and vigor attainable by mimicking nature's own well-being, there was Edward J. O'Brien, who insisted that machine culture routinized modern life. And for every optimist who believed that the new consumerism elevated civilization, there was Thorstein Veblen, who, in introducing the term *conspicuous consumption* into the vernacular, cautioned against the disempowerment of inculcated purchasing patterns. The essential question of the plasticity of the self—to what degree did people have the power to define their identities?—likewise dominated religion. Bruce Barton's immensely popular *The Man Nobody Knows* promoted a new vision of Jesus Christ as the ultimate entrepreneur who popularized Christianity through savvy salesmanship. The unabashed theatricality that Barton attributed to Christ was typical of the era's new evangelists, including, most famously, Billy Sunday and Amee Semple McPherson. For every skeptic who criticized this performativity as pure vaudeville, there were critics who recognized that the stereotype it perpetuated—emblematized by Sinclair Lewis's Elmer Gantry—did a disservice to the faith of many Americans. The selections excerpted here reveal the polar extremes to which observers both welcomed and feared the new possibilities of self-definition that modern technologies gave to people. They also dramatize the concomitant degrees to which observers attempted to label these possibilities as either natural or unnatural.

Kirk Curnutt,
Troy University–Montgomery, Alabama

FREDERICK W. TAYLOR
1856–1915

Introduction to
The Principles of Scientific Management[1]

President Roosevelt in his address to the Governors at the White House, prophetically remarked that "The conservation of our national resources is only preliminary to the larger question of national efficiency."[2]

The whole country at once recognized the importance of conserving our material resources and a large movement has been started which will be effective in accomplishing this object. As yet, however, we have but vaguely appreciated the importance of "the larger question of increasing our national efficiency."

We can see our forests vanishing, our water-powers going to waste, our soil being carried by floods into the sea; and the end of our coal and our iron is in sight. But our larger wastes of human effort, which go on every day through such of our acts as are blundering, ill-directed, or inefficient, and which Mr. Roosevelt refers to as a lack of "national efficiency," are less visible, less tangible, and are but vaguely appreciated.

We can see and feel the waste of material things. Awkward, inefficient, or ill-directed movements of men, however, leave nothing visible or tangible behind them. Their appreciation calls for an act of memory, an effort of the imagination. And for this reason, even though our daily loss from this source is greater than from our waste of material things, the one has stirred us deeply, while the other has moved us but little.

As yet there has been no public agitation for "greater national efficiency," no meetings have been called to consider how this is to be brought about. And still there are signs that the need for greater efficiency is widely felt.

The search for better, for more competent men, from the presidents of our great companies down to our household servants, was never more vigorous than it is now. And more than ever before is the demand for competent men in excess of the supply.

What we are all looking for, however, is the ready-made, competent man; the man whom some one else has trained. It is only when we fully realize that our duty, as well as our opportunity, lies in systematically cooperating to train and to make this competent man, instead of in hunting for a

---

[1] Frederick W. Taylor, introduction to *The Principles of Scientific Management* (New York: Harper & Row, 1911), www.fordham.edu/halsall/mod/1911taylor.html.

[2] Theodore Roosevelt (1858–1919) served as president from 1901 (following the assassination of William McKinley) until 1909.

man whom some one else has trained, that we shall be on the road to national efficiency.

In the past the prevailing idea has been well expressed in the saying that "Captains of industry are born, not made" and the theory has been that if one could get the right man, methods could be safely left to him. In the future it will be appreciated that our leaders must be trained right as well as born right, and that no great man can (with the old system of personal management) hope to compete with a number of ordinary men who have been properly organized so as efficiently to cooperate.

In the past the man has been first; in the future the system must be first. This in no sense, however, implies that great men are not needed. On the contrary, the first object of any good system must be that of developing first-class men; and under systematic management the best man rises to the top more certainly and more rapidly than ever before.

This paper has been written:

First. To point out, through a series of simple illustrations, the great loss which the whole country is suffering through inefficiency in almost all of our daily acts.

Second. To try to convince the reader that the remedy for this inefficiency lies in systematic management, rather than in searching for some unusual or extraordinary man.

Third. To prove that the best management is a true science, resting upon clearly defined laws, rules, and principles, as a foundation. And further to show that the fundamental principles of scientific management are applicable to all kinds of human activities, from our simplest individual acts to the work of our great corporations, which call for the most elaborate cooperation. And, briefly, through a series of illustrations, to convince the reader that whenever these principles are correctly applied, results must follow which are truly astounding.

This paper was originally prepared for presentation to The American Society of Mechanical Engineers. The illustrations chosen are such as, it is believed, will especially appeal to engineers and to managers of industrial and manufacturing establishments, and also quite as much to all of the men who are working in these establishments. It is hoped, however, that it will be clear to other readers that the same principles can be applied with equal force to all social activities: to the management of our homes; the management of our farms; the management of the business of our tradesmen, large and small; of our churches, our philanthropic institutions, our universities, and our governmental departments.

1911

■   # BERNARR MACFADDEN
1868–1955   ■

from Vitality Supreme[1]

The war cry of to-day in peace no less than in war is for efficiency. We need stronger, more capable men; healthier, superior women. Force is supreme—the king of all mankind. And it is force that stands back of efficiency, for efficiency, first of all, means power. It comes from power, and power either comes directly from inheritance or it is developed by an intelligent application of the laws that control the culture of the physique. The value of efficiency is everywhere recognized. The great prizes of life come to those who are efficient. Those who desire capacities of this sort must recognize the importance of a strong, enduring physique. The body must be developed completely, splendidly. The buoyancy, vivacity, energy, enthusiasm and ambition ordinarily associated with youth can be maintained through middle age and in some cases even to old age. If your efforts are to be crowned with the halo of success, they must be spurred on by the pulsating throbbing powers that accompany physical excellence. These truly extraordinary characteristics come without effort to but few of us, but they can be developed, attained and maintained.

Why not throb with superior vitality! Why not possess the physical energy of a young lion? For then you will compel success. You will stand like a wall if need be, or rush with the force of a charging bison toward the desired achievements....

from Chapter 1, Vitality: What Is It?

Vitality first of all means endurance and the ability to live long. It naturally indicates functional and organic vigor. You cannot be vital unless the organs of the body are possessed of at least a normal degree of strength and are performing their functions harmoniously and satisfactorily. To be vital means you are full of vim and energy, that you possess that enviable characteristic known as vivacity. It means that you are vibrating, pulsating with life in all its most attractive forms. For life, energy, vitality—call it what you wish—in all its normal manifestations, will always be found attractive.

A vital man is at all times thoroughly alive. The forces of life seem to imbue every part of his organism with energy, activity and all characteristics opposed to things inanimate. A vital man is naturally enthusiastic. He can

[1]Bernarr Macfadden, *Vitality Supreme* (New York: Physical Culture Publishing, 1922), xi–xii, 1–3.

hardly avoid being ambitious. And consequently success, with all its splendid rewards, comes to such a man in abundance. Life to such a man should be resplendent with worthy achievements.

No one belittles the importance of success. Everyone is guided to a large extent by the desire to succeed. When a child toddles off to school the training which he secures there is given for the single purpose of bringing success, but this purpose cannot possibly be reached without throbbing vitality. In fact, you are not yourself in every sense unless you possess vitality of this sort. The emotions and instincts that come to one when thoroughly developed, with the vital forces surging within, are decidedly different from those which influence one when lacking in stamina. Many who have grown beyond adult age are still undeveloped, so far as physical condition and vigor is concerned, and this lack of physical development means immaturity—incompleteness. It means that one is short on manhood or womanhood. This statement, that one's personality, under such circumstances, is not completely brought out, may seem strange to some; but careful reasoning will soon verify its accuracy. Success of the right sort, therefore, depends first of all upon intelligent efforts that are guided day after day, with a view, first of all, of developing the physical organism to the highest possible standard, and maintaining it there.

In other words, it is our first duty to be men, strong and splendid, or women, healthy and perfect, if we are desirous of securing life's most gratifying prizes. . . .

1922

Edward J. O'Brien
1890–1941

from **The Dance of the Machines**[1]

American life has been chiefly shaped for our generation by the spiritual dictatorship of machinery, warfare, and magazines and newspapers of large circulation. To these shaping influences are now to be added the motion picture, the radio, the gramophone, the automobile, the corporation, queen-bee finance, and all forms of national and international advertising and propaganda. . . .

[1]Edward J. O'Brien, *The Dance of the Machines*
(New York: Macaulay, 1929), 15, 213–16.

The machine, in order to reduce humanity to the point of subservience necessary for it to assert its supposed supermanhood[2] successfully, finds it convenient to begin with a country which has the oldest and most deeply rooted industrial tradition, and in which any other tradition is either young and weak, moribund, dead, or non-existent. That country, needless to say, is the United States of America....

So far as I can perceive, apart form the ordinary powerful means of social pressure and the sheer conscription of labor which industrialism now compels, the machine has discovered ten influential media to assist it in its purpose.

1. The standardized motion picture.

2. The standardized radio.

3. The standardized newspaper and magazine with their standardized advertising.

4. The standardized automobile.

5. The standardized theater.

6. The standardized corporation.

7. The crossword puzzle and its cousins.

8. Philosophy in its descent through pragmatism to behaviorism, applied psychology, and the "science of advertising." The last revels in "conditioned reflexes."

9. Welfare work and all forms of organized charity.

10. The standardized American short story.

The manner in which the cinema, the radio, the newspaper, the automobile, the theater, the corporation, the crossword puzzle, and American welfare work contribute to the necessary leveling down of mind and soul into moron-like conformity is transparently obvious.... The drift of the whole process has been summed up briefly by Graham Wallas in his comment on Taylorism. "Mr. F. W. Taylor assumes that men can be found to handle pig-iron, each of whom 'more nearly resembles in his mental make-up the ox than any other type.'[3] But the Chinese experiment of building the Great Wall by the labor of six hundred thousand prisoners, who had been surgically reduced to the condition of oxen, has not been repeated."[4]

Nevertheless, I seem to have heard rumors among American intellectuals that scientists and engineers are clamoring already for the sterilization of the unfit. Those who are most unfit to adapt themselves to a machine civilization are the nation's artists, and I daresay that before long there will be an agitation for the sterilization of artists. Every attempt to sterilize their minds has been made already with tolerably successful results.

1929

---

[2]An ironic reference to Friedrich Nietzsche's concept of the Übermensch, or "Overman," the evolutionary epitome of human supremeness, as defined in *Thus Spoke Zarathustra* (1883).

[3]Frederick W. Taylor, *The Principles of Scientific Management* (New York: Harper & Row, 1911), 59. [O'Brien's footnote]

[4]Graham Wallas, *The Great Society* (New York: Macmillan, 1914), 339. [O'Brien's footnote]

THORSTEIN VEBLEN
1857–1929

from The Theory of the Leisure Class: A Study of Economic Institutions[1]

The quasi-peaceable gentleman of leisure … not only consumes of the staff of life beyond the minimum required for subsistence and physical efficiency, but his consumption also undergoes a specialization as regards the quality of the goods consumed. He consumes freely and of the best, in food, drink, narcotics, shelter, services, ornaments, apparel, weapons and accoutrements, amusements, amulets, and idols or divinities. In the process of gradual amelioration which takes place in the articles of his consumption, the motive principle and proximate aim of innovation is no doubt the higher efficiency of the improved and more elaborate products for personal comfort and well-being. But that does not remain the sole purpose of their consumption. The canon of reputability is at hand and seizes upon such innovations as are, according to its standard, fit to survive. Since the consumption of these more excellent goods is an evidence of wealth, it becomes honorific; and conversely, the failure to consume in due quantity and quality becomes a mark of inferiority and demerit.

This growth of punctilious discrimination as to qualitative excellence in eating, drinking, etc. presently affects not only the manner of life, but also the training and intellectual activity of the gentleman of leisure. He is no longer simply the successful, aggressive male—the man of strength, resource, and intrepidity. In order to avoid stultification he must also cultivate his tastes, for it now becomes incumbent on him to discriminate with some nicety between the noble and the ignoble in consumable goods. He becomes a connoisseur in creditable viands of various degrees of merit, in manly beverages and trinkets, in seemly apparel and architecture, in weapons, games, dancers, and the narcotics. This cultivation of aesthetic faculty requires time and application, and the demands made upon the gentleman in this direction therefore tend to change his life of leisure into a more or less arduous application to the business of learning how to live a life of ostensible leisure in a becoming way. Closely related to the requirement that the gentleman must consume freely and of the right kind of goods, there is the requirement that he must know how to consume them in a seemly manner. His life of leisure must be conducted in due form. Hence arise good manners…. High-bred manners and ways of living are items of conformity to the norm of conspicuous leisure and conspicuous consumption.

[1]Thorstein Veblen, *The Theory of the Leisure Class: A Study of Economic Institutions* (New York: Huebsch, 1912), 73–76.

Conspicuous consumption of valuable goods is a means of reputability to the gentleman of leisure. As wealth accumulates on his hands, his own unaided effort will not avail to sufficiently put his opulence in evidence by this method. The aid of friends and competitors is therefore brought in by resorting to the giving of valuable presents and expensive feasts and entertainments. Presents and feasts had probably another origin than that of naive ostentation, but they required their utility for this purpose very early, and they have retained that character to the present; so that their utility in this respect has now long been the substantial ground on which these usages rest. Costly entertainments, such as the potlatch or the ball, are peculiarly adapted to serve this end. The competitor with whom the entertainer wishes to institute a comparison is, by this method, made to serve as a means to the end. He consumes vicariously for his host at the same time that he is witness to the consumption of that excess of good things which his host is unable to dispose of single-handed, and he is also made to witness his host's facility in etiquette.

1912

BRUCE BARTON
1886–1967

from **The Man Nobody Knows: A Discovery of the Real Jesus**[1]

> *How is it that ye sought me? Wist ye that I must be about my father's business?*

—JESUS

What interests us most in this one recorded incident of [Jesus's] boyhood is the fact that for the first time he defined the purpose of his career. He did not say, 'Wist ye not that I must practice preaching?' or 'Wist ye not that I must get ready to meet the arguments of men like these?' The language was quite different, and well worth remembering. 'Wist ye not that I must be about my father's *business?*" he said. He thought of his life as *business*. What did he mean by business? To what extent are the principles by which he conducted his business applicable to ours? And if he were among us again, in our highly competitive world, would his business philosophy work?

On one occasion, you recall, he stated his recipe for success. It was on the afternoon when James and John came to ask him what promotion they might expect. They were two of the most energetic of the lot, called "Sons

---

[1]Bruce Barton, *The Man Nobody Knows: A Discovery of the Real Jesus* (Indianapolis: Bobbs-Merrill, 1925), 161ff.

of Thunder" by the rest, being noisy and always in the midst of some sort of storm. They had joined the ranks because they liked him, but with no definite idea of what it was all about; and now they wanted to know where the enterprise was heading, and just what there would be in it for them.

"Master," they said, "we want to ask what plans you have in mind for us. You're going to need big men around you when you establish your kingdom; our ambition is to sit on either side of you, one on your right hand and the other on your left."

Who can object to that attitude? If a man fails to look after himself, certainly no one will look after him. If you want a big place, go ask for it. That's the way to get ahead.

Jesus answered with a sentence that sounds poetically absurd.

"Whosoever will be great among you, shall be your minister," he said, "and whosoever of you will be the chiefest, shall be servant of all."

A fine piece of rhetoric, now isn't it? Be a good servant and you will be great; be the best possible servant and you will occupy the highest possible place. Nice idealistic talk but utterly impractical; nothing to take seriously in a common sense world. That is just what men thought for some hundreds of years; and then, quite suddenly, Business woke up to a great discovery. You will hear that discovery proclaimed in every sales convention as something distinctly modern and up to date. It is emblazoned in the advertising pages of every magazine.

Look through those pages.

Here is the advertisement of an automobile company, one of the greatest in the world. And why is it the greatest? On what does it base its claim to leadership? On its huge factories and financial strength? They are never mentioned. On its army of workmen or its high salaried executives? You might read its advertisements for years without suspecting that it had either. No. "We are great because of our service," the advertisements cry. "We will crawl under your car oftener and get our backs dirtier than any of our competitors. Drive up to our service stations and ask for anything at all—it will be granted cheerfully. We serve; therefore we grow."

A manufacturer of shoes makes the same boast in other terms. "We put ourselves at your feet and give you everything that you can possibly demand." Manufacturers of building equipment, of clothes, of food; presidents of railroads and steamship companies; the heads of banks and investment houses—*all* of them tell the same story. "Service is what we are here for," they exclaim. They call it the "spirit of modern business"; they suppose, most of them, that it is something very new. But Jesus preached it more than nineteen hundred years ago. . . .

So we have the main points of [Jesus's] business philosophy:

1. Whosoever will be great must render great service.

2. Whosoever will find himself at the top must be willing to lose himself at the bottom.

3. The big rewards come to those who travel the second, undemanded mile.

1925

■ EDWIN ARLINGTON ROBINSON ■
1869–1935

America's first important poet of the twentieth century, Edwin Arlington Robinson is also the most prolific. Unlike his more prominent contemporaries—Frost, Stevens, Eliot, and Williams—Robinson devoted his energies exclusively to the writing of poetry. For that reason, his life is markedly unremarkable, but he published an astonishing twenty volumes of poems that were eventually combined into *Collected Poems*, a volume of nearly 1500 pages. It is a Robinsonian irony that today he is known for only a handful of poems of the sort he once complained were "pickled in anthological brine."

He grew up in Gardiner, Maine, the "Tilbury Town" of his poetry, spent two years at Harvard, and went home to Maine, where he published privately his first volume, *The Torrent and The Night Before*, in 1896. On his mother's side he was descended from Anne Bradstreet, one of America's first poets. From 1911 onward he established a routine of spending the winters in New York City and the summers in New Hampshire at the MacDowell Colony, where he did most of his writing. The first of his three Pulitzer Prizes was won for *Collected Poems* in 1921. He died in New York in 1935, literally hours after he had completed reading the galley proofs of *King Jasper*.

In his preface to *King Jasper*, Robert Frost said aptly that Robinson was "content with the old-fashioned way to be new." He was a strict traditionalist in his use of verse forms, experimenting in his early years with elaborate French forms, showing great proficiency with the sonnet, and turning to blank verse for his book-length narratives. In both subject matter and attitude, however, Robinson was an innovator. Frequently compared to Robert Browning and Henry James, he has been called variously realistic, romantic, naturalistic, and existential. His attitudes range from satire to understatement, from pessimism to compassion. Most pervasive is his sensitivity to the struggle in the human condition between the mundane and the mystical.

Rather than being simply a recorder of the failed life, as he has often been perceived, Robinson is actually a poet fascinated by how the unsuccessful cope. This celebration of the human spirit in spite of the disappointments of life is connected to an element of his poetry that has generally gone unnoticed: its autobiographical qualities. In 1965 Chard Powers Smith took as a thesis for his biography of Robinson, *Where the Light Falls*, that the preponderance of triangular love situations in the poetry is a direct result of E. A.'s having lost his fiancée, Emma Shepherd, to his brother Herman.

The selections in this anthology give only a partial indication of Robinson's range and variety. "The Clerks" represents one of his brief Tilbury Town portraits of ordinary individuals, but it also includes a reference to the life of a poet and thus combines two of his most prevalent themes. "Aunt Imogen" illustrates a medium-length character sketch of a woman who was basically in the same situation as Robinson in his relationship with his three nieces. The famous "Mr. Hood's Party" (which Robinson claimed was his favorite poem) transforms a boyhood prank in Gardiner. The infrequently anthologized "Momus" illustrates not only Robinson's playfulness, but also his consciousness of the uncertain lot of a poet. "Eros Turannos" and "The Tree in Pamela's Garden" deal in contrasting ways with relationships between women and men.

Robinson wrote poetry that is contrivedly unspectacular, a characteristic that has cost him readers in the second half of the twentieth century. Nevertheless, as Scott Donaldson's 2006 biography convincingly demonstrates, the precision and skill with which Robinson wrote and the human quality of his themes promise his work an enduring place in the American canon.

Nancy Carol Joyner
Western Carolina University

PRIMARY WORKS

Collected Poems, 1937; *Selected Letters*, 1940; *Uncollected Poems and Prose*, 1975.

The Clerks

I did not think that I should find them there
When I came back again; but there they stood,
As in the days they dreamed of when young blood
Was in their cheeks and women called them fair.
Be sure, they met me with an ancient air,—   5
And yes, there was a shop-worn brotherhood
About them; but the men were just as good,
And just as human as they ever were.

And you that ache so much to be sublime,
And you that feed yourselves with your descent,   10
What comes of all your visions and your fears?
Poets and kings are but the clerks of Time,
Tiering the same dull webs of discontent,
Clipping the same sad alnage[1] of the years.

1897

Aunt Imogen

Aunt Imogen was coming, and therefore
The children—Jane, Sylvester, and Young George—
Were eyes and ears; for there was only one
Aunt Imogen to them in the whole world,
And she was in it only for four weeks   5
In fifty-two. But those great bites of time
Made all September a Queen's Festival;

[1]A measure of cloth.

And they would strive, informally, to make
The most of them.—The mother understood,
And wisely stepped away. Aunt Imogen   10
Was there for only one month in the year,
While she, the mother,—she was always there;
And that was what made all the difference.
She knew it must be so, for Jane had once
Expounded it to her so learnedly   15
That she had looked away from the child's eyes
And thought; and she had thought of many things.

There was a demonstration every time
Aunt Imogen appeared, and there was more
Than one this time. And she was at a loss   20
Just how to name the meaning of it all:
It puzzled her to think that she could be
So much to any crazy thing alive—
Even to her sister's little savages
Who knew no better than to be themselves;   25
But in the midst of her glad wonderment
She found herself besieged and overcome
By two tight arms and one tumultuous head,
And therewith half bewildered and half pained
By the joy she felt and by the sudden love   30
That proved itself in childhood's honest noise.
Jane, by the wings of sex, had reached her first;
And while she strangled her, approvingly,
Sylvester thumped his drum and Young George howled.
But finally, when all was rectified,   35
And she had stilled the clamor of Young George
By giving him a long ride on her shoulders,
They went together into the old room
That looked across the fields; and Imogen
Gazed out with a girl's gladness in her eyes,   40
Happy to know that she was back once more
Where there were those who knew her, and at last
Had gloriously got away again
From cabs and clattered asphalt for a while;
And there she sat and talked and looked and laughed   45
And made the mother and the children laugh.
Aunt Imogen made everybody laugh.

There was the feminine paradox—that she
Who had so little sunshine for herself
Should have so much for others. How it was   50

That she could make, and feel for making it,
So much of joy for them, and all along
Be covering, like a scar, and while she smiled,
That hungering incompleteness and regret—
That passionate ache for something of her own,   55
For something of herself—she never knew.
She knew that she could seem to make them all
Believe there was no other part of her
Than her persistent happiness; but the why
And how she did not know. Still none of them   60
Could have a thought that she was living down—
Almost as if regret were criminal,
So proud it was and yet so profitless—
The penance of a dream, and that was good.
Her sister Jane—the mother of little Jane,   65
Sylvester, and Young George—might make herself
Believe she knew, for she—well, she was Jane.

Young George, however, did not yield himself
To nourish the false hunger of a ghost
That made no good return. He saw too much: 70
The accumulated wisdom of his years
Had so conclusively made plain to him
The permanent profusion of a world
Where everybody might have everything
To do, and almost everything to eat,   75
That he was jubilantly satisfied
And all unthwarted by adversity.
Young George knew things. The world, he had found out,
Was a good place, and life was a good game—
Particularly when Aunt Imogen   80
Was in it. And one day it came to pass—
One rainy day when she was holding him
And rocking him—that he, in his own right,
Took it upon himself to tell her so;
And something in his way of telling it—   85
The language, or the tone, or something else—
Gripped like insidious fingers on her throat,
And then went foraging as if to make
A plaything of her heart. Such undeserved
And unsophisticated confidence   90
Went mercilessly home; and had she sat
Before a looking glass, the deeps of it
Could not have shown more clearly to her then
Than one thought-mirrored little glimpse had shown,
The pang that wrenched her face and filled her eyes   95

With anguish and intolerable mist.
The blow that she had vaguely thrust aside
Like fright so many times had found her now:
Clean-thrust and final it had come to her
From a child's lips at last, as it had come   100
Never before, and as it might be felt
Never again. Some grief, like some delight,
Stings hard but once: to custom after that
The rapture or the pain submits itself,
And we are wiser than we were before.   105
And Imogen was wiser; though at first
Her dream-defeating wisdom was indeed
A thankless heritage: there was no sweet,
No bitter now; nor was there anything
To make a daily meaning for her life—   110
Till truth, like Harlequin,[1] leapt out somehow
From ambush and threw sudden savor to it—
But the blank taste of time. There were no dreams,
No phantoms in her future any more:
One clinching revelation of what was   115
One by-flash of irrevocable chance,
Had acridly but honestly foretold
The mystical fulfilment of a life
That might have once ... But that was all gone by:
There was no need of reaching back for that: 120
The triumph was not hers: there was no love
Save borrowed love: there was no might have been.

But there was yet Young George—and he had gone
Conveniently to sleep, like a good boy;
And there was yet Sylvester with his drum,   125
And there was frowzle-headed little Jane;
And there was Jane the sister, and the mother,—
Her sister, and the mother of them all.
They were not hers, not even one of them:
She was not born to be so much as that,   130
For she was born to be Aunt Imogen.
Now she could see the truth and look at it;
Now she could make stars out where once had palled
A future's emptiness; now she could share
With others—ah, the others!—to the end   135
The largess of a woman who could smile;
Now it was hers to dance the folly down,
And all the murmuring; now it was hers

[1] A traditional buffoon of Italian comedy.

To be Aunt Imogen.—So, when Young George
Woke up and blinked at her with his big eyes,   140
And smiled to see the way she blinked at him,
'T was only in old concord with the stars
That she took hold of him and held him close,
Close to herself, and crushed him till he laughed.

1902

Momus[1]

"Where's the need of singing now?"—
Smooth your brow,
Momus, and be reconciled,
For King Kronos[2] is a child—
Child and father,   5
Or god rather,
And all gods are wild.

"Who reads Byron[3] any more?"—
Shut the door,
Momus, for I feel a draught;   10
Shut it quick, for some one laughed.—
"What's become of
Browning? Some of
Wordsworth[4] lumbers like a raft?
"What are poets to find here?"—   15
Have no fear:
When the stars are shining blue
There will yet be left a few
Themes availing—
And these failing,   20
Momus, there'll be you.

1910

Eros Turannos[1']

She fears him, and will always ask
    What fated her to choose him;

---

[1]Minor Greek deity, god of blame and ridicule.
[2]In Greek mythology, a Titan who ruled the universe until dethroned by his son, Zeus.
[3]Prominent 19th-century British poet who made satirical attacks on critics in "English Bards and Scottish Reviewers" and "Who Killed John Keats?"

[4]Robert Browning (1812–1889) and William Wordsworth (1770–1850), two prominent British poets of the 19th century, both of whom share Robinson's penchant for long narrative poems.
[1']Greek: "Love, the Tyrant."

She meets in his engaging mask
   All reasons to refuse him;
But what she meets and what she fears   5
Are less than are the downward years,
Drawn slowly to the foamless weirs
   Of age, were she to lose him.

Between a blurred sagacity
   That once had power to sound him,   10
And Love, that will not let him be
   The Judas[2] that she found him,
Her pride assuages her almost,
As if it were alone the cost.—
He sees that he will not be lost,   15
   And waits and looks around him.

A sense of ocean and old trees
   Envelops and allures him;
Tradition, touching all he sees,
   Beguiles and reassures him;   20
And all her doubts of what he says
Are dimmed with what she knows of days—
Till even prejudice delays
   And fades, and she secures him.

The falling leaf inaugurates   25
   The reign of her confusion;
The pounding wave reverberates
   The dirge of her illusion;
And home, where passion lived and died,
Becomes a place where she can hide,   30
While all the town and harbor side
   Vibrate with her seclusion.

We tell you, tapping on our brows,
   The story as it should be,—
As if the story of a house   35
   Were told, or ever could be;
We'll have no kindly veil between
Her visions and those we have seen,—
As if we guessed what hers have been,
   Or what they are or would be.   40

[2]See Matthew 26:47–49.

Meanwhile we do no harm; for they
 That with a god have striven,
Not hearing much of what we say,
 Take what the god has given;
Though like waves breaking it may be,   45
Or like a changed familiar tree,
Or like a stairway to the sea
 Where down the blind are driven.

                  1916

The Tree in Pamela's Garden

Pamela was too gentle to deceive
Her roses. "Let the men stay where they are,"
She said, "and if Apollo's avatar[1]
Be one of them, I shall not have to grieve."
And so she made all Tilbury Town[2] believe   5
She sighed a little more for the North Star
Than over men, and only in so far
As she was in a garden was like Eve.

Her neighbors—doing all that neighbors can
To make romance of reticence meanwhile—   10
Seeing that she had never loved a man,
Wished Pamela had a cat, or a small bird,
And only would have wondered at her smile
Could they have seen that she had overheard.

                  1921

Mr. Flood's Party

Old Eben Flood, climbing alone one night
Over the hill between the town below
And the forsaken upland hermitage
That held as much as he should ever know
On earth again of home, paused warily.   5
The road was his with not a native near;
And Eben, having leisure, said aloud,
For no man else in Tilbury Town to hear:

---

[1]Embodiment. Apollo, unlucky in love, has been called "the most Greek of the Greek gods."

[2]Robinson's fictional name for his home town, Gardiner, Maine.

"Well, Mr. Flood, we have the harvest moon
Again, and we may not have many more;   10
The bird is on the wing, the poet says[1]
And you and I have said it here before.
Drink to the bird." He raised up to the light
The jug that he had gone so far to fill,
And answered huskily: "Well, Mr. Flood,   15
Since you propose it, I believe I will."

Alone, as if enduring to the end
A valiant armor of scarred hopes outworn,
He stood there in the middle of the road
Like Roland's ghost winding a silent horn.[2]   20
Below him, in the town among the trees,
Where friends of other days had honored him,
A phantom salutation of the dead
Rang thinly till old Eben's eyes were dim.

Then, as a mother lays her sleeping child   25
Down tenderly, fearing it may awake,
He set the jug down slowly at his feet
With trembling care, knowing that most things break;
And only when assured that on firm earth
It stood, as the uncertain lives of men   30
Assuredly did not, he paced away,
And with his hand extended paused again:

"Well, Mr. Flood, we have not met like this
In a long time; and many a change has come
To both of us, I fear, since last it was   35
We had a drop together. Welcome home!"
Convivially returning with himself,
Again he raised the jug up to the light;
And with an acquiescent quaver said:
"Well, Mr. Flood, if you insist, I might.   40

"Only a very little, Mr. Flood—
For auld lang syne.[3] No more, sir; that will do."
So, for the time, apparently it did,
And Eben evidently thought so too;
For soon amid the silver loneliness   45
Of night he lifted up his voice and sang,

[1]See Edward Fitzgerald, *The Rubaiyat of Omar Khayyam*, 11.27–28.
[2]In *Song of Roland*, Roland died after he had blown his horn to warn Charlemagne.
[3]Scottish dialect for "days long gone." The song is attributed to Robert Burns.

Secure, with only two moons listening,
Until the whole harmonious landscape rang—

"For auld lang syne." The weary throat gave out,
The last word wavered, and the song was done;   50
He raised again the jug regretfully
And shook his head, and was again alone.
There was not much that was ahead of him,
And there was nothing in the town below—
Where strangers would have shut the many doors   55
That many friends had opened long ago.

1920

ELLEN GLASGOW ■
1873–1945

Southern literature was romantic when Ellen Glasgow began writing. She saw herself as a realist bringing "blood and irony" to a society based on pretense. The vantage from which most of her nineteen novels were written was the family home at One West Main Street in Richmond. As a child she watched her gentle mother, a lady of the Virginia aristocracy, decline to nervous invalidism after bearing ten children. Her father, manager of an ironworks, appeared self-righteous and unfeeling to a daughter who would, nevertheless, give some of her more admirable characters a Scots-Calvinist background like his and a similar "vein of iron."

As a young woman, Ellen Glasgow refused to attend church with her father, an act of intellectual rebellion. Without much formal schooling, she read, on her own, advanced thinkers of the time and was particularly influenced by Social Darwinism, a philosophy that hardly consoled her for what she saw as life's cruelty. Poor health and loss of hearing that sent her to many doctors over the years increased the pessimism.

The hero of Glasgow's first novel is an "illegitimate" outcast from a southern town who becomes, briefly, a radical journalist. Written in secret and published anonymously, *The Descendant* (1897) was intended to shock. The author, who later provided newspapers with a photograph of herself in white ruffles, was aware of the incongruity of her writing on matters about which a young lady was supposed to know nothing. Yet Glasgow did not at first make women's roles her major theme, and she was slow to place heroines rather than heroes at the centers of the stories.

In *Virginia* (1913), the protagonist is a woman, though not a rebel. Virginia Pendleton, based on Glasgow's mother, is an old-fashioned southern lady raised on "the simple theory that the less a girl knew about life, the better prepared she would be to contend with it." The author was capable of irony about such figures, sustained by illusion, at times controlling through weakness. Blind Mrs. Blake in *The Deliverance* (1904) is protected by her family from knowing the Civil War is lost and the slaves freed. But Virginia is treated sympathetically, even idealized, as Glasgow tended to idealize all her heroines.

The author depicted a new kind of woman that feminism and confidence in evolution made her believe possible. She had difficulty, though, imagining a woman's life that combined love and work. The feminine quality of sympathy, which made a heroine worthy of interest, would lead her, like Judith Campbell in "The Professional Instinct," to choose love over ambition. In *The Woman Within* (1954), an autobiography written for posthumous publication, Glasgow tells of a long, secret affair with a married man she had met in New York. Later she was engaged twice, even collaborating on novels with one fiancé, but did not marry. Her best work was done when love was over, she said.

The novel of greatest personal importance to the author was *Barren Ground* (1925), in which she felt she had reversed the traditional seduction plot. When Glasgow's heroines are strong, they are so only because men are weak, and the women's victories are sad triumphs. She thought that writing *Barren Ground*, a "tragedy," freed her for the comedies of manners: *The Romantic Comedians* (1926), *They Stooped to Folly* (1929), and *The Sheltered Life* (1932). These late works are the most artful criticism of romantic illusion in all her long career.

Linda Pannill
Transylvania University

PRIMARY WORKS

Virginia, 1913; *Barren Ground*, 1925; *The Romantic Comedians*, 1926; *They Stooped to Folly*, 1929; *The Sheltered Life*, 1932; *Vein of Iron*, 1935; *A Certain Measure: An Interpretation of Prose Fiction*, 1943; *The Woman Within*, 1954; *Letters*, ed. Blair Rouse, 1958; *The Collected Stories of Ellen Glasgow*, ed. Richard K. Meeker, 1963.

The Professional Instinct[1]

As he unfolded his napkin and broke his toast with the precise touch of fingers that think, Doctor John Estbridge concluded that holidays were becoming unbearable. Christmas again, he reflected gloomily, and Christmas in New York, with a heavy snowstorm that meant weeks of dirt and slush and back-breaking epidemics of influenza and pneumonia! Beyond the curtains of rose-colored damask the storm rocked the boughs of an ailanthus tree[2] which grew midway of the high-fenced backyard. Long ago, in the days of his youth and mania for reform, Estbridge remembered that he had once tried to convert the backyard into an Italian garden. For a brief season box[3]

---

[1]Left in manuscript, this story was not published until 1962, when William W. Kelly edited it for *Western Humanities Review*. Kelly, whose text is reproduced here, dates composition between 1916 and 1924. The manuscript is housed at Alderman Library, University of Virginia.

[2]Tree of Heaven, a Chinese import much used in urban gardens.

[3]Boxwood, the evergreen shrub.

had survived, if it had not actually flourished there, and a cypress tree, sent by an ex-patient from Northern Italy, had lived through a single summer and had died with the first frost of winter. That was nearly twenty years ago, for Estbridge had relinquished his garden with the other dreams of his youth, and to-day the brawny ailanthus stood there as a symbol of the prosperous failure of his career.

"What's to be got out of this business of living anyhow?" he enquired, gazing over his breakfast at a portrait of Savonarola[4] which hung above the French clock on the mantelpiece. With a laugh he recalled that it had been his business for twenty years to answer this immemorial question for the satisfaction of the unsound or the dejected. "To have stuffed all those poor devils with sawdust," he added, and a minute later: "By Jove, if happiness were only as cheap as philosophy!"

Within the last few weeks several cases of changed personalities had passed through his hands. They concerned men and women, not far from his own age, who had undergone curious psychological crises that emerged quite new personalities and the thought flashed through his mind that he was in something of the same mental state at this moment. "What if I should cut it good and begin over again?" he asked suddenly. "What if I should take the only way out and cut it for good?"

Over the trivial French clock the eyes of the great Italian reformer looked down on him. "You were right, Monk, as far as you went," murmured Estbridge ironically, "but the primal force got beyond you: the trouble was that man wanted his little happiness in Florence just as badly as he wants it here to-day in New York."

For a blank instant, while his gaze still hung on the portrait, he tried to evoke the impression of that day, more than twenty years ago, when he had bought the picture and hung it with his own hands over his mantel. Even after the crucial scene of last night he had never forgotten the curious episode. It was the morning after he had seen Tilly Pratt in a graduating play; and though the girl had laid aside her religious fervor as easily as she had the flowing robes and cowl of the Florentine Friar, she had still impersonated the militant idealism of Estbridge's youth. For he had loved Tilly, not for herself, but because she had shown him his own image. Like most men, according to the analytical psychologists, he had identified his own dreams with the shape of a woman. "Yes, it was not you, Tilly. You were not Savonarola," he said.

For a grey quarter of a century hung now like a fog between the ample figure of the present Mrs. Estbridge and the girl who had bewitched him during his internship at Christ's Hospital. It was impossible for the most active imagination to create an illusion about the wife who invariably ruffled his contentment and devoured his time. Florid, robust, and bristling with

---

[4]Savonarola (1452–1498), Dominican friar. Preached moral reform in Florence and briefly gained political power there. Remembered for "burning of the vanities," including some books. Falling to his enemies, he was hanged and burned.

activity, she had triumphantly checkmated him during the twenty years of their marriage. So relentless had been her rule, that her victim, though still at bay, had been forced to accord a critical admiration to her performance. But for her amazing perseverance, he thought now, his whole life might have been different, and instead of missing the coveted chair of physiology at the University, he might have watched some of his early dreams acquire the outlines and substance of reality. But for her he might have abandoned his profession as a means, no longer necessary, of breadwinning; and but for her, he added bitterly after a minute, he might have used his great experience and his undoubted gift to raise the vision and standards of accomplishment in the schools where doctors were formed. Yes, she had always been at his elbow, holding him back. It was incredible; it was diabolical; but she had done it for twenty years, and she was doing it still!

A convenient neurosis, cured now and then, but intermittently subject to relapse in favor of some new doctor, kept Mrs. Estbridge in bed for breakfast; and Estbridge had come to grasp eagerly this one rich hour of solitude. Between eight and nine o'clock, no one invaded the dining-room where he sat at his simple breakfast which had been left by some servant who had vanished. If the telephone rang he did not answer it. If patients chose that hour to die, they died without his attentions. There was no rustling of newspapers, no slitting of fresh correspondence. The only sound in the room was the bubbling of the coffee percolator, and while this morning he brooded over the meal, he was thankfully aware of the restful hush of the place—of the mute service of inanimate things which surrounded him.

"That's the last straw—to miss that appointment," he thought. "To have worked for twenty years, and then to see the chair go to Adamson—to Adamson who was my assistant when he began." With the words he rose hurriedly from the table, and crossing to the window, looked out on the swaying ailanthus tree. "There's but one way out, and no one could blame me for taking it," he added under his breath.

The sound of the opening door made him wheel quickly about, and he shivered with a nervous movement of protest as he found himself facing the commanding form of his wife.

"Doctor Railston says I may begin to get up for breakfast," she remarked affably, as she passed to the head of the table, and took her place behind the archaic silver service she had inherited from some Pratt who had figured in history. "So I planned a little surprise for you."

While she smiled benignly upon him, Estbridge realized that she had become, by the authority of metaphor and fact, an immovable body. Though he had longed for years to forbid her the room, he knew that he was morally powerless to do so. Her presence now was merely part of the whole plan; and in the very instant that he perceived her design, he understood that he was incapable of making an effort to thwart it. Just as she had victoriously substituted herself for his profession and for the few free hours at the end of his day, she meant now, he saw, to devour the one brief interval of time he could call his own. Not content with destroying his happiness, she was opening, with the best possible intentions, an attack upon the intellectual side of his work.

"You drink too much strong coffee," she said as her competent glance swept the table. "Bates tells me you sometimes fill the percolator twice."

He had fallen back into his chair, and while his lip tightened with exasperation, he watched her ring the bell and order bacon and eggs. From the moment when she had entered, she had become the dominant figure. She was a woman, and by virtue of her womanhood she had made the breakfast table her ally. By every law, by every custom she was fulfilling the domestic tradition; and without disturbing a convention, without disobeying a religious behest, she was ruining his life. Society was on her side—God, he felt for one bitter moment, was on her side. Had she been violent or vicious, he might have withstood her; but her authority was rooted in virtue, and before the tyranny of virtue he was helpless.

While she sat there, calmly waiting for her breakfast, he surveyed her large handsome face with a resentful gaze. From her stiff iron grey hair to her firm and massive figure, she presented a picture of matronly rectitude. The very perfection of her type was the thing he found it hardest to forgive in her. She was born to be "a good manager," and it was not to be expected that her inherited talent should stop short before the man whom fate, or his own folly, had delivered into her hands. With children to occupy her, she might have found, he realized, other outlets for her benevolent impulses; but there were no children, and as the years went by he had ceased his early rejoicing that his wife lacked the inclination for public reforms. From a firmly efficient management of her household, she had passed, without perceptible loss of either firmness or efficiency, to the management of his clothes, his diet, his exercise, and the number and the brands of his cigarettes. With an unholy dread he saw that it was only a question of time—perhaps days—before she would begin to "manage" his hospital.

"I want you to eat more breakfast, John." She was pouring a plentiful supply of hot milk into her coffee. "And it is really absurd of you to fancy that you can think while you eat."

From the oblong mirror over the sideboard the reflection of his own features flashed back at him, and he stared at his distinguished face as if it had been the face of a stranger. Although they were exactly the same age, he became suddenly aware that he looked at least ten years younger than the capable lady whom he had married. Science had kept him young in return for the passion he had lavished upon her. In his bright blue eyes, which grew hard enough on occasions, still glistened the eternal enquiring spirit of youth. His dark hair had silvered, but it was still thick, and his compact and muscular figure had escaped the increasing weight which sent most of his contemporaries into belated training.

"Thank heaven for this holiday." She was beginning to ramble. "There won't be any need for you to rush off this morning. If it's Christmas, it might as well be a merry one."

She was in an amiable mood, and it was plain to him, after the first moment or two, that the scene of last night had barely ruffled the surface of her composure. Well, of course, if a thing like that didn't ruffle one! A smile, half of humor, half of irony, twisted his lip, while there floated through his mind a sentence from one of his lectures on mental deficiency: *"To be unable to recall experience and to profit by it is a common characteristic of the morons."*

When she had skewered the last bit of bacon on her fork, and not before, Mrs. Estbridge raised her eyes again to her husband.

"Have you heard that the chair of physiology has been given to Adamson?"

"Yes, I heard." A flush rose to Estbridge's face, staining his scholarly brow under the silver hair. The board of trustees had not only passed him over—they had passed him over for Adamson, a young fellow with merely a fair record and, as Estbridge told himself now, with a hopelessly limited horizon. If not Estbridge, it must, of course, have been Adamson—but by all that was fair and honest, it should have been Estbridge! What other man in New York combined his venturesome imagination with his sound knowledge and understanding of modern achievement?

"How did you get the news?" he asked after a minute. Was it possible that here also she had helped to defeat him? In the old days when he had tried to make her share in his ambition to be a leader of young men, he remembered she had laughingly said to him more than once: "But that sounds very foolish to me. What's the use of standing up before a lot of Jews and telling them things that are all in the books anyhow?"

"Aunt Clara came in last evening," she replied, and added with a scarcely perceptible emphasis: "after you went out. Uncle Timothy rushed the appointment through, and would hear of no one but Adamson. He insisted on having a practical man. . . ."

So it was out at last! Old Timothy Pratt, his wife's uncle, had won over the board of trustees to Adamson . . . old Timothy Pratt, who had trebled in inherited fortune though he never got up before mid-day.

"Of course I know that your uncle was opposed to me," said Estbridge, "but I had counted on Jim." Until that instant he had not realized how much he had counted on Jim Hoadly.

"Poor old Jim." Mrs. Estbridge's voice was faintly patronizing. "He did his best, but he is hardly a match for Uncle Timothy. I wonder why he doesn't come here any more?" As she paused she reached for the jar of marmalade and (helped) herself to an even spoonful. It was Mrs. Estbridge's proudest boast that she let nothing impair her appetite.

"I trust that Aunt Clara at least is pleased." Estbridge had recovered his humor, if not his temper.

"Not at all. On the contrary she asked me several weeks ago about the advisability of her speaking to Uncle Timothy. She seemed to feel, and quite naturally, I think, that Uncle Timothy ought not to . . . at least that he ought not to appear to be leading a fight against you. . . ."

"Indeed!"

"But, of course, when she asked me frankly, I was obliged to tell her what I thought...."

His nerves jerked, and pushing back his chair, he walked quickly to the door.

"Yes, John, when she asked me for the truth, I was obliged to speak it. Even as things are now, I was forced to tell her that I rarely see you, that you show signs of irritability—you know you do, John—that you are over-worked, and that any well-wisher...."

The volume of sound was interrupted by the sudden entrance of Bates, who felt, doubtless, that if the doctor had taken to entertaining at breakfast, the butler was entitled to be present. But even if the sombre Englishman, compressed to silence by generations of servitude, had miraculously acquired the gift of fluent speech, it would have availed him little against the torrential overflow of directions which followed Estbridge into the hall.

"John, it is snowing hard." The voice pursued him with the imperious accents of destiny. "If you *will* go out, don't forget to put on your overshoes."

One overshoe was already half on, but prying it off, Estbridge kicked it furiously under the hat-rack. "It would be an interesting experience," he muttered to himself as he slammed the door behind him, "if some rainy day she should remind me to put on my hat. I wonder what the devil I should do if she did?"

As he plunged through the storm in the direction of Fifth Avenue, he felt that his body vibrated in every cell and fibre with rebellion. It was a revolt not only against his wife, but against the whole world of women. At the instant he saw all women as victorious over the lives and destinies of men. As for his wife, he knew now, as he had known for years, that he had never perhaps loved any woman. He was passing the mansion of Mr. Pratt, just a few blocks south of the Park, and as he glanced up at the high windows, framed in snow, he felt that he wanted to curse the pompous old mandarin still asleep in his bed.

"Why shouldn't I cut it for good?" he asked again as he had asked an hour before. "By God, I will cut it for good! I'll take the post that is still open at Shanghai!" The wish which had created the thought evolved from a simple impulse into a practical idea. He saw before him a definite vision of freedom, and he saw the ten vigorous years ahead of him crowded, not with vain attempts, not with frustrated efforts, but with adventure, accomplishment, and reward.

The door of his office swung back into emptiness, and he rejoiced for the first time in the holiday which had relieved him of his usual staff of helpers. As he turned, still with the thought of Shanghai in his mind, to an atlas on the table of his waiting-room, he saw a woman's figure dimly outlined against the glass of the door. "Can it be Judith Campbell?" he thought while a tremor passed over him. Then, flinging the door open, he fell back a step, and stood waiting for her to cross the threshold. "What an angel you are to come to me through the storm!"

She entered slowly, wrapped in dark furs to the chin, and he had an impression even before she spoke, of the softness and grace of her manner.

"I felt that you would be here, and I couldn't let Christmas go by without seeing you for a minute." Stopping beside the table, with its litter of last year's magazines, she gazed up at him with the strange gentleness which had first drawn him to her—that rare gentleness, he found himself thinking now, which alone can make a woman the equal of men.

"I wanted to bring my little gift," she said. "Last year I should hardly have dared." While he watched her take from her muff the white package, with its red ribbon and spray of holly, he became aware that her body like her mind was compacted of delicate graces, of exquisite surprises. Though she had been for years the professor of philosophy in a college for women, she was as feminine in appearance as any early Victorian heroine of fiction. She was, he realized forcibly at the instant, everything that his wife was not and could never become. His wife was a dull woman with an instinct to dominate; but Judith Campbell—he felt this as he had never felt it before—was a clever woman with an instinct to yield.

"Your coming begins my Christmas," he said, and the words sounded so inadequate as he uttered them that he went on more rapidly: "I am so glad. It is your book. May I open it?"

She shook her head with a little laugh that had a yielding and tremulous grace. "After I go, I can stay only a minute."

The slender figure in the heavy furs had the look of a cypress-tree that sways and bends under the storm. Through the veil of dotted net her large grey eyes still gazed at him with an enigmatical softness. Even her intellect, in spite of its flashing brilliance, gave him this impression of softness and grace, as if its strength were tempered by sympathy. Though she had always appeared in her spiritual detachment to stand above the more commonplace aspects of passion, he had sometimes wondered if her perfect response to his moods meant a gradual change in her friendship. Could her delicate intuitions remain insensible to the inevitable course such things take?

And yet only at this moment did he realize that his will was drawing him to her. Against his judgment, against his ideals, against his teaching and his habits, the will to live was driving him away from his work to the love of a woman. To his profession, and his conception of what it might some day become, he had dedicated both his intellect and his passion. For twenty years his marriage had been sufficient to keep him out of casual temptation; and his friendship for Jim Hoadly had supplied him, as he blindly supposed, with all that he required of sympathy and understanding. But at this instant, looking back on his association with Judith Campbell— on their first rare meetings at joint boards, on their occasional walks in the Park, on an evening now and then at some waterside restaurant during the summer, on the substantial help he had been able to give her in her work, and more than all on the ready comprehension with which she had met him from the start—looking back on all these things, he saw, with a luminous flash of understanding, that the miracle of renewed youth had occurred.

While he stood there he felt like a man who had gone shivering to sleep in the winter, and had awakened to find the scented air of spring blowing in his window.

"There is something else I must tell you." Her soft voice quivered for an instant. "I had this morning the offer of the presidency of Hartwell College."

He breathed hard with suspense, yet he could think of nothing to say except the obvious: "But that's in St. Louis."

"Yes."

"And you will accept it?"

"Yes, I shall accept it."

"That means you will live in St. Louis?"

"That means I shall live in St. Louis."

The parrying had restored his composure. "You have always wanted something like that more than anything else in the world."

"I told myself this morning that I had always wanted such a place more than anything in the world."

The note of hesitation in her voice made him look at her quickly. He had always supposed that her face was too strong, too intelligent, to conform to any standard of beauty, but he recognized now, with a start, that she embodied the complete and absolute perfection of womanhood. And he felt that he wanted her as from his youth up he had wanted the unattainable—as an hour ago he had wanted the chair of physiology that went to Adamson.

"You deserve it," he said after a pause. "It is the outcome of your work, and the crowning of your ambition."

"Yes," the word faltered on her lips. "I suppose it is the crowning of my ambition." Though her age was thirty-eight there was the shyness of a girl in her eyes, and by her shyness and the quiver of her lashes as he looked at her, he knew that she loved him.

"I wish," she pursued slowly, "that I had no ambition."

"But would you give it up?" It was a simple enough question, and yet after he had put it, he stood watching her as if he were in a laboratory awaiting the result of some physiological experiment.

"Crowning a woman's ambition often makes her a beggar," she answered quietly, adding after a minute, "What a shame it is about Adamson!"

He laughed grimly. "Yes, I did want that; more, perhaps, than you wanted Hartwell. But that's over now. Who knows, after all, if it wasn't something else that I wanted?"

Her look touched him like a caress. "If I could only give you what I have."

"And yet it is the highest honor that could come to you."

She smiled, a little wearily he thought, as she answered:

"That is why I would give it to you."

"Judith!"

She had moved a step nearer the door, and stopping there at his call, she looked back with a startled glow in her face.

"Judith, would you give it up if I asked you?"

"If you asked me?"

"Would you stay—would you give it up if I asked you?" The glow in her face seemed to pervade her whole body while she stood before him transfigured.

"I would give up the whole world if you asked me."

"You would sacrifice your ambition—your future?"

A laugh broke from her lips. "I haven't any ambition—any future—except yours." It was as if the passive substance of her nature had flamed into energy.

He walked to the window, gazing down on the city, which loomed in bizarre outlines through the storm. "It's this way with me," he began impersonally, as if to the street. "An hour ago I made up my mind to quit New York for good. You know most of the reasons. All of them now since you know about Adamson. I have made up my mind to begin over again, and for once to get down to some real work—something genuine—in China. I told you about the post in Shanghai. Well, I am going to take it."

She drew her breath sharply, and though he still looked away from her, he felt her very will had passed into the flame and fervor of his.

"For twenty years I have thought that my hour would come," he said in a voice which he tried in vain to make as guarded as his manner. "It has come now."

"It has come now?" Her words were scarcely more than a sigh faintly drawn.

"It is here, and I want to grasp it while I have still the courage. I want to grasp it before it escapes me."

Though she looked as if she would yield—as if she would dissolve at a touch, he did not stretch out his hand to her. He had made his appeal and she had answered it.

"Yes, if I go, I must go while I have the courage. I must go now—to-day," he went on, gaining confidence while he watched her drooping under the weight of her furs. "I must go while you will go with me."

As he moved a step nearer, she swayed towards him, and for a moment he held her close with a gentleness that was strangely sacramental for a lover. Neither spoke until she released herself, and threw back her veil with the gesture of one who is casting aside the burden of years.

"Wherever you go, I will go with you," she said.

"You will go with me to-day?"

She glanced with brightly questioning eyes at the clock. "Is there a boat on Christmas day?"

He laughed, and with the sound he looked suddenly boyish. "Oh, enchanting professor of philosophy! No, there isn't a boat, but we'll catch the noon train to Chicago. To-morrow we'll go on to San Francisco, and after that the way will be easy. You have an hour. Will you be ready?"

"It will not take me an hour. I can get what I need in San Francisco."

He was allowing her only an hour, she knew, because to go at all they must go without thinking. They must act at once as each had dreamed so often of acting, in obedience to the divine indomitable impulse. They must follow with bandaged eyes the spirit of adventure.

"And I'll go after burning my boats. I shan't even look over my papers. There must be no compromises." Then, as if craving movement, action, certainty, he glanced at the clock. "I'll telephone my man to send my things to the train. There will be a sudden call to Chicago. In exactly fifty-five minutes will you meet me in the Pennsylvania Station—by the gate?"

"I shall not fail you. I shall never fail you."

With the promise she had gone; and crossing to the window of the outer office, he looked down on her figure making its way through the storm. In the midst of thronging pedestrians, of noisy motors, of newsboys frantically crying the extras, he watched her press evenly forward until at last the whirling snowflakes gathered her in.

Well, that was over! He had made his decision; he had burned his boats; and no good could come from looking back over his shoulder. While he stood there gazing down into the street, he felt that the flame and glory of his hour was still with him. His nerves no longer reacted jarringly to his surroundings. He was aware of a complete, harmonious adjustment to the circumstances of his life. Destiny for once moved in obedience to his will. It was all so easy—this quick shedding of the husks of the past, this putting forth, with renewed growth and vigor, in a strange soil amid an alien people. What fools men were to talk of convention and experience! All one needed was the will to choose, the courage to act promptly.

Turning to his desk, he mechanically rang for his secretary, before he remembered that the day was Christmas. Then, reflecting with a smile that he couldn't very well use her for the business on hand, he began hurriedly filling his black portfolio with check-books, manuscripts, and letters which required personal answers. While he sorted his papers, littering the floor with what was not needed, and lighting a fire in the grate in order to burn certain documents which he wished to destroy, he found himself thinking, not of the post at Shanghai, not of the future with Judith Campbell, but of the chair of physiology which had been given to Adamson. The hurt had not healed. Though he told himself passionately that life without Judith would not be worth living, he was aware that beneath his happiness the wound to his ambition still throbbed.

He had been barely ten minutes at his task when an imperative knock on the door forced him to open it.

"I might have known who it was," he thought moodily as he turned the knob. "What an ass I was not to hide where he couldn't find me."

Jim Hoadly was a big man—so big that he seemed to fill the space in the doorway, and his mere physical bulk had always possessed a curious fascination for his classmate. To-day, however, Estbridge was conscious of a latent antagonism, of a secret revolt against all the qualities he had once admired in his friend. It was as if the demon of the inopportune had suddenly entered.

"I knew I'd find you here," began the caller, while he shook the snow from his shoulders with a vigorous movement. "No," he went on gaily in reply to the question in Estbridge's eyes, "I didn't even try at the house." A minute afterwards, as he passed through the doorway of the inner office, he broke into a low whistle of astonishment. "Whew! Quite a wind blowing, isn't there? and a conflagration on top of it!"

"I lit a fire, that's all." Estbridge was trying to smile unconcernedly.

"If I remember rightly it isn't your first fire either," retorted Hoadly, drying his sandy beard with his fingers. "You know, Jack, I always said you could act when your hour caught you."

"My hour?" Estbridge's glance flew to the clock. "Well you were right, Jim, my hour has caught me, and I am acting. I am leaving at twelve o'clock—for the future."

A grey light, as if from the sombre sky outside, sobered Jim's merry features. "Do you mean to kill yourself, Jack?"

"Kill myself?" Estbridge laughed with joy. "No, I am going to live. For the first time in my life, I am going to live!"

Though Hoadly had led a life of singular detachment, twenty-five years of journalism had made him a shrewd interpreter of the emotions of others. "Shall I go through the form of enquiring," he asked airily, "if you intend to begin this new existence alone?"

"Alone? No."

"You won't mind my asking, I suppose, if Judith Campbell goes with you?"

For a moment Estbridge looked as if he were about to show resentment. Then his manner grew flippant, and he replied carelessly: "Well, why shouldn't you know? I want you to know before anyone else. You won't have a start of more than twenty-four hours over the papers at that."

"So it's the famous professor of philosophy!" Jim's tone was measured in its calmness. "I must say I find it hard to follow these feminists. But, Jack, you can't do it!"

"Who's to stop me?" Estbridge's voice was sharp with defiance.

"I am."

The thought of physical violence shot through Estbridge's mind, and he retorted angrily, "Don't try that game, it is dangerous."

"Oh, I don't know," responded Jim drily. "I've tried it before now, and I'm still living. But, come, Jack, you can't toss aside an old friend so easily. At least you can't do it until you have offered him a chair," he added, flinging himself into the worn leather chair facing the window. "I may sit down, I suppose, while I argue. Great Jove! How many poor devils, I wonder, have sat here before me?"

"You may sit down and you may argue," replied Estbridge, "but you won't mind my not listening to you, I hope. My train goes at twelve o'clock."

"Has it ever occurred to you to make an inventory, mainly in the interest of science, of what you are leaving behind?"

"It has. I am leaving behind a life that gets nowhere, and one that bores me to death."

"And to ask yourself what the lady is giving up in return for the doubtful constancy you offer her. By George, Jack, have you thought to tell her that the only thing you ever loved in any woman was your own reflection?"

"If that's all you know about it?"

"It isn't all, perhaps, but it's a good bit. You aren't the first analytical psychologist who has identified the world with himself, and, God permitting, you probably won't be the last."

"If that's your game, my boy, you are wasting time."

"Well, after all, you are dodging my question about the lady."

"Have you read her book on 'Marriage and Individuality'?" Estbridge glanced at the package on the table.

"No, I haven't, but I can make a good guess as to what it is all about. There is not much to be said on that subject, I fancy. It is take it or leave it—that's all. But, granting that she doesn't lose much as she sees it, she doesn't stand to win very big stakes either, does she? Does she, now, really? Come, Jack, as a married man, nearing fifty, don't you agree with me?"

"If I do, how is the case altered? Of course I am not worthy of her, but what, in heaven's name, has that got to do with it?"

"You realize that your wife will never divorce you?"

With a shrug Estbridge went back to his papers. "Have I lived with her for twenty years without discovering that?"

"And the end will be, I suppose," Hoadly's voice had grown rasping, "that you will feel yourself bound to Judith Campbell until—until she comes between you and something that you want more than any woman. There is an instinct in you stronger than love, Jack, and God pity her when she crosses it. I have always said that your Grand Inquisitor[5] was a humanitarian crossed in his purpose."

Estbridge's face darkened. "There are barely fifteen minutes left, and I've as much as I can attend to."

"Don't let me delay you." Rising from his chair, Hoadly held out his hand with the casual manner of an attorney who continues to smile pleasantly in the face of defeat. "You aren't allowing yourself a great deal of time, are you?" As he reached the door he glanced back, and said carelessly, "By the way, I forgot to tell you about Adamson. But I suppose you have heard?"

"I heard this morning," replied Estbridge sharply, "I wish the University well of him."

"Then you haven't seen the extras?" The door closed with a slam, and Hoadly turned back into the room. "He's dead, you know—run over this morning in West Fifty-ninth Street. I heard it two hours ago." For a moment he hesitated, and then added maliciously, "I suppose we'll have a hard time now to replace him."

"Adamson!" The portfolio he had picked up slipped from Estbridge's grasp, and he stood staring incredulously into the face of his friend. "Why hadn't you told me?"

"I came down for that, not just to wish you a Merry Christmas—but the news went quite out of my mind when I found myself in the midst of this romantic episode. After all, life is so much more engrossing than death, isn't it?"

[5]Most famous was Torquemada (1420–1498), first head of the Spanish Inquisition, who is said to have put thousands to death at the stake.

"Adamson?" Estbridge was repeating the name blankly. As if awakening from the effects of a narcotic, he stretched out his hand with a groping uncertain gesture. Not only his tone, but his face, his look, even his figure, appeared to have altered. It was as if an entirely different set of nerve cells had begun acting at the instant—as if the molecular rhythm of his brain had run down, and then started feverishly with fresh waves of energy. He was like a man who had died and been born anew in an instant; and, watching him, Hoadly realized that his friend was now living with a different side of his nature—with other impulses, with other vibrations of memory, with other automatic reactions.

"So Adamson is dead, and the place at the University is vacant!"

Over Jim Hoadly's impassive features a smile that was slightly sardonic in its humor flickered for an instant. "You have just time to catch your train," he said, and added gravely, with a vague movement toward the portfolio, "the snow makes traffic difficult."

At the reminder the exultation faded from Estbridge's look, while his anxious gaze sought the face of the clock, and hung there as if drawn and held by an irresistible magnet.

"Yes, there is just time," he repeated; but he did not turn, and his shoulders did not stoop for the overcoat which Hoadly held waiting behind him.

"You had better start or you miss it," said Hoadly again, after three minutes in which he had watched the struggle with his smile of flickering irony—like the smile of some inscrutable image of wisdom. "It would be a pity to miss that train, wouldn't it?"

But the clock ticked slowly on, while Estbridge stood transfixed, bewildered, brooding, with his eyes on the hands which travelled inevitably toward the appointed hour.

1962

EDITH WHARTON
1862–1937

Edith Newbold Jones was the third child and only daughter in an elite, conservative, old New York family. Tracing their lineage to pre-Revolutionary settlers, her parents, George Frederic and Lucretia Stevens Rhinelander Jones, belonged to a class that prided itself on its avoidance of ostentation, intellectualism, publicity, and, according to the author as a grown woman, emotion. That Wharton was to become a famous, brilliantly accomplished author in no way fulfilled her family's program for her.

During her childhood, the Joneses divided their time between New York and Europe, with summers in Newport, Rhode Island. Because her two brothers were already in their teens when she was born, she grew up as if she were an only child, and, as with other girls of her time and class, her life was sheltered. She was tutored at home and, making her debut at the age of seventeen, she was expected thereafter simply to marry. When she did, accepting in 1885 Edward ("Teddy") Wharton, a good-natured man thirteen years her senior, she made a match that was conventional and, ultimately, unhappy. As a leisure-class wife, she traveled and visited, entertained, supervised servants, and built and decorated homes. Some of these activities appealed to Wharton. Increasingly, however, she found this existence suffocating and, on the advice of doctors treating her for depression, turned to writing as an outlet.

Publishing short stories in the 1890s and then long fiction at the turn of the century, Wharton grew in strength as her husband's mental health deteriorated. The couple had no children, and their lives steadily diverged. In the early 1900s, Wharton had a secret love affair with a younger man, Morton Fullerton, and in 1913 pursued a divorce. The divorce pained and shocked family members.

The publication of *The House of Mirth* in 1905 launched Wharton as America's most acclaimed twentieth-century fiction writer in the decades preceding the 1920s. During her major period, the years from 1905 to 1920, she published novels prolifically: *The House of Mirth, Madame de Treymes, Ethan Frome, The Reef, The Custom of the Country, Summer,* and *The Age of Innocence.* Her work is distinguished by her brilliance as a stylist, her urbane intelligence, and her acuity as a social observer and critic, particularly of the leisure class.

Wharton wrote about the rapaciousness and vulgarity of the *nouveaux riches,* the timidity and repression of the upper class, the contrast between European and American customs and values, and the inequality and repression of women, which often showed up in patriarchal culture—by design, of course—in hostility and rivalry among women. As both "The Valley of Childish Things" and "Roman Fever" show, issues of female sexual freedom, frustrated artistic ambition, and severely limited status in the public realm interested her. Poverty also arrested her imagination and stimulated some of her best work, such as *Ethan Frome* and *Summer.* Not surprisingly, given her personal experience, she also focused on marriage, which she usually portrayed as incarcerating, especially for women. At the same time, as "Souls Belated" illustrates, she was keenly aware of how psychologically important the conventional relationship of marriage and its attendant responsibility could be. The private love diary she wrote during her affair with Morton Fullerton, "The Life Apart," which was never published during her lifetime, shows yet another side of Wharton—anxious, at times insecure, bold, sensual. "The Eyes," meanwhile, demonstrates her skill in projecting these concerns into popular forms such as the horror story.

The contribution of Edith Wharton to American literature is major. Often compared with Henry James, a close friend, she is recognized along with other women writers at the turn into the twentieth century—Kate Chopin, Alice Dunbar-Nelson, Ellen Glasgow, Willa Cather—for moving nineteenth-century women's literary tradition into a new phase of artistic ambitiousness and excellence. In her lifetime she published nineteen novels and novellas, eleven

volumes of short stories, a number of book-length discursive works, some poetry, and many essays, reviews, and articles. Perceived in her own time as an
extraordinary writer, she received the Pulitzer Prize in 1921 and in 1923 was
the first woman to be honored by Yale University with the degree of doctor of
letters. Wharton died of a stroke at the age of seventy-five and is buried in
France, where she made her home for the last twenty-five years of her life. Her
grave is in the Cimetière des Gonards at Versailles.

Elizabeth Ammons
Tufts University

PRIMARY WORKS

The House of Mirth, 1905; *Madame de Treymes,* 1907; *Ethan Frome,* 1911; *The Reef,*
1912; *The Custom of the Country,* 1913; *Summer,* 1917; *The Age of Innocence,* 1920;
Old New York, 1924; *The Mother's Recompense,* 1925; *A Backward Glance,* 1934 (memoir); *Collected Short Stories,* ed. R. W. B. Lewis, 1968; *Letters,* ed. R. W. B. Lewis,
1988.

The Valley of Childish Things

Once upon a time a number of children lived together in the Valley of Childish Things, playing all manner of delightful games, and studying the same
lesson books. But one day a little girl, one of their number, decided that it
was time to see something of the world about which the lesson books had
taught her; and as none of the other children cared to leave their games, she
set out alone to climb the pass which led out of the valley.

It was a hard climb, but at length she reached a cold, bleak tableland
beyond the mountains. Here she saw cities and men, and learned many useful arts, and in so doing grew to be a woman. But the tableland was bleak
and cold, and when she had served her apprenticeship she decided to return
to her old companions in the Valley of Childish Things, and work with them
instead of with strangers.

It was a weary way back, and her feet were bruised by the stones, and
her face was beaten by the weather; but halfway down the pass she met a
man, who kindly helped her over the roughest places. Like herself, he was
lame and weather-beaten; but as soon as he spoke she recognized him as
one of her old playmates. He too had been out in the world, and was going
back to the valley; and on the way they talked together of the work they
meant to do there. He had been a dull boy, and she had never taken much
notice of him; but as she listened to his plans for building bridges and draining swamps and cutting roads through the jungle, she thought to herself,
"Since he has grown into such a fine fellow, what splendid men and women
my other playmates must have become!"

But what was her surprise to find, on reaching the valley, that her former companions, instead of growing into men and women, had all remained
little children. Most of them were playing the same old games, and the few
who affected to be working were engaged in such strenuous occupations as

building mudpies and sailing paper boats in basins. As for the lad who had been the favorite companion of her studies, he was playing marbles with all the youngest boys in the valley.

At first the children seemed glad to have her back, but soon she saw that her presence interfered with their games; and when she tried to tell them of the great things that were being done on the tableland beyond the mountains, they picked up their toys and went farther down the valley to play.

Then she turned to her fellow traveler, who was the only grown man in the valley; but he was on his knees before a dear little girl with blue eyes and a coral necklace, for whom he was making a garden out of cockleshells and bits of glass and broken flowers stuck in sand.

The little girl was clapping her hands and crowing (she was too young to speak articulately); and when she who had grown to be a woman laid her hand on the man's shoulder, and asked him if he did not want to set to work with her building bridges, draining swamps, and cutting roads through the jungle, he replied that at that particular moment he was too busy.

And as she turned away, he added in the kindest possible way, "Really, my dear, you ought to have taken better care of your complexion."

1896

Souls Belated

Their railway carriage had been full when the train left Bologna; but at the first station beyond Milan their only remaining companion—a courtly person who ate garlic out of a carpetbag—had left his crumb-strewn seat with a bow.

Lydia's eye regretfully followed the shiny broadcloth of his retreating back till it lost itself in the cloud of touts and cab drivers hanging about the station; then she glanced across at Gannett and caught the same regret in his look. They were both sorry to be alone.

"*Par-ten-za!*"[1] shouted the guard. The train vibrated to a sudden slamming of doors; a waiter ran along the platform with a tray of fossilized sandwiches; a belated porter flung a bundle of shawls and bandboxes into a third-class carriage; the guard snapped out a brief *Partenza!* which indicated the purely ornamental nature of his first shout; and the train swung out of the station.

The direction of the road had changed, and a shaft of sunlight struck across the dusty red-velvet seats into Lydia's corner. Gannett did not notice it. He had returned to his *Revue de Paris*, and she had to rise and lower the shade of the farther window. Against the vast horizon of their leisure such incidents stood out sharply.

---

[1]Italian: "departing" (i.e., "all aboard").

Having lowered the shade, Lydia sat down, leaving the length of the carriage between herself and Gannett. At length he missed her and looked up.

"I moved out of the sun," she hastily explained.

He looked at her curiously: the sun was beating on her through the shade.

"Very well," he said pleasantly; adding, "You don't mind?" as he drew a cigarette case from his pocket.

It was a refreshing touch, relieving the tension of her spirit with the suggestion that, after all, he could *smoke*—! The relief was only momentary. Her experience of smokers was limited (her husband had disapproved of the use of tobacco) but she knew from hearsay that men sometimes smoked to get away from things; that a cigar might be the masculine equivalent of darkened windows and a headache. Gannett, after a puff or two, returned to his review.

It was just as she had foreseen; he feared to speak as much as she did. It was one of the misfortunes of their situation that they were never busy enough to necessitate, or even to justify, the postponement of unpleasant discussions. If they avoided a question it was obviously, unconcealably because the question was disagreeable. They had unlimited leisure and an accumulation of mental energy to devote to any subject that presented itself; new topics were in fact at a premium. Lydia sometimes had premonitions of a famine-stricken period when there would be nothing left to talk about, and she had already caught herself doling out piecemeal what, in the first prodigality of their confidences, she would have flung to him in a breath. Their silence therefore might simply mean that they had nothing to say; but it was another disadvantage of their position that it allowed infinite opportunity for the classification of minute differences. Lydia had learned to distinguish between real and factitious silences; and under Gannett's she now detected a hum of speech to which her own thoughts made breathless answer.

How could it be otherwise, with that thing between them? She glanced up at the rack overhead. The *thing* was there, in her dressing bag, symbolically suspended over her head and his. He was thinking of it now, just as she was; they had been thinking of it in unison ever since they had entered the train. While the carriage had held other travelers they had screened her from his thoughts; but now that he and she were alone she knew exactly what was passing through his mind; she could almost hear him asking himself what he should say to her.

The thing had come that morning, brought up to her in an innocent-looking envelope with the rest of their letters, as they were leaving the hotel at Bologna. As she tore it open, she and Gannett were laughing over some ineptitude of the local guidebook—they had been driven, of late, to make the most of such incidental humors of travel. Even when she had unfolded the document she took it for some unimportant business paper sent abroad for her signature, and her eye traveled inattentively over the curly *Whereases* of the preamble until a word arrested her: Divorce. There it stood, an impassable barrier, between her husband's name and hers.

She had been prepared for it, of course, as healthy people are said to be prepared for death, in the sense of knowing it must come without in the least expecting that it will. She had known from the first that Tillotson meant to divorce her—but what did it matter? Nothing mattered, in those first days of supreme deliverance, but the fact that she was free; and not so much (she had begun to be aware) that freedom had released her from Tillotson as that it had given her to Gannett. This discovery had not been agreeable to her self-esteem. She had preferred to think that Tillotson had himself embodied all her reasons for leaving him; and those he represented had seemed cogent enough to stand in no need of reinforcement. Yet she had not left him till she met Gannett. It was her love for Gannett that had made life with Tillotson so poor and incomplete a business. If she had never, from the first, regarded her marriage as a full canceling of her claims upon life, she had at least, for a number of years, accepted it as a provisional compensation,—she had made it "do." Existence in the commodious Tillotson mansion in Fifth Avenue—with Mrs. Tillotson senior commanding the approaches from the second-story front windows—had been reduced to a series of purely automatic acts. The moral atmosphere of the Tillotson interior was as carefully screened and curtained as the house itself: Mrs. Tillotson senior dreaded ideas as much as a draft in her back. Prudent people liked an even temperature; and to do anything unexpected was as foolish as going out in the rain. One of the chief advantages of being rich was that one need not be exposed to unforeseen contingencies: by the use of ordinary firmness and common sense one could make sure of doing exactly the same thing every day at the same hour. These doctrines, reverentially imbibed with his mother's milk, Tillotson (a model son who had never given his parents an hour's anxiety) complacently expounded to his wife, testifying to his sense of their importance by the regularity with which he wore galoshes on damp days, his punctuality at meals, and his elaborate precautions against burglars and contagious diseases. Lydia, coming from a smaller town, and entering New York life through the portals of the Tillotson mansion, had mechanically accepted this point of view as inseparable from having a front pew in church and a parterre box at the opera. All the people who came to the house revolved in the same small circle of prejudices. It was the kind of society in which, after dinner, the ladies compared the exorbitant charges of their children's teachers, and agreed that, even with the new duties on French clothes, it was cheaper in the end to get everything from Worth; while the husbands, over their cigars, lamented municipal corruption, and decided that the men to start a reform were those who had no private interests at stake.

To Lydia this view of life had become a matter of course, just as lumbering about in her mother-in-law's landau had come to seem the only possible means of locomotion, and listening every Sunday to a fashionable Presbyterian divine the inevitable atonement for having thought oneself bored on the other six days of the week. Before she met Gannett her life had seemed merely dull; his coming made it appear like one of those dismal Cruikshank prints in which the people are all ugly and all engaged in occupations that are either vulgar or stupid.

It was natural that Tillotson should be the chief sufferer from this readjustment of focus. Gannett's nearness had made her husband ridiculous, and a part of the ridicule had been reflected on herself. Her tolerance laid her open to a suspicion of obtuseness from which she must, at all costs, clear herself in Gannett's eyes.

She did not understand this until afterwards. At the time she fancied that she had merely reached the limits of endurance. In so large a charter of liberties as the mere act of leaving Tillotson seemed to confer, the small question of divorce or no divorce did not count. It was when she saw that she had left her husband only to be with Gannett that she perceived the significance of anything affecting their relations. Her husband, in casting her off, had virtually flung her at Gannett: it was thus that the world viewed it. The measure of alacrity with which Gannett would receive her would be the subject of curious speculation over afternoon tea tables and in club corners. She knew what would be said—she had heard it so often of others! The recollection bathed her in misery. The men would probably back Gannett to "do the decent thing"; but the ladies' eyebrows would emphasize the worthlessness of such enforced fidelity; and after all, they would be right. She had put herself in a position where Gannett "owed" her something; where, as a gentleman, he was bound to "stand the damage." The idea of accepting such compensation had never crossed her mind; the so-called rehabilitation of such a marriage had always seemed to her the only real disgrace. What she dreaded was the necessity of having to explain herself; of having to combat his arguments; of calculating, in spite of herself, the exact measure of insistence with which he pressed them. She knew not whether she most shrank from his insisting too much or too little. In such a case the nicest sense of proportion might be at fault; and how easily to fall into the error of taking her resistance for a test of his sincerity! Whichever way she turned, an ironical implication confronted her: she had the exasperated sense of having walked into the trap of some stupid practical joke.

Beneath all these preoccupations lurked the dread of what he was thinking. Sooner or later, of course, he would have to speak; but that, in the meantime, he should think, even for a moment, that there was any use in speaking, seemed to her simply unendurable. Her sensitiveness on this point was aggravated by another fear, as yet barely on the level of consciousness; the fear of unwillingly involving Gannett in the trammels of her dependence. To look upon him as the instrument of her liberation; to resist in herself the least tendency to a wifely taking possession of his future; had seemed to Lydia the one way of maintaining the dignity of their relation. Her view had not changed, but she was aware of a growing inability to keep her thoughts fixed on the essential point—the point of parting with Gannett. It was easy to face as long as she kept it sufficiently far off: but what was this act of mental postponement but a gradual encroachment on his future? What was needful was the courage to recognize the moment when, by some word or look, their voluntary fellowship should be transformed into a bondage the more wearing that it was based on none of those common obligations which make the most imperfect marriage in some sort a center of gravity.

When the porter, at the next station, threw the door open, Lydia drew back, making way for the hoped-for intruder; but none came, and the train took up its leisurely progress through the spring wheat fields and budding copses. She now began to hope that Gannett would speak before the next station. She watched him furtively, half-disposed to return to the seat opposite his, but there was an artificiality about his absorption that restrained her. She had never before seen him read with so conspicuous an air of warding off interruption. What could he be thinking of? Why should he be afraid to speak? Or was it her answer that he dreaded?

The train paused for the passing of an express, and he put down his book and leaned out of the window. Presently he turned to her with a smile.

"There's a jolly old villa out here," he said.

His easy tone relieved her, and she smiled back at him as she crossed over to his corner.

Beyond the embankment, through the opening in a mossy wall, she caught sight of the villa, with its broken balustrades, its stagnant fountains, and the stone satyr closing the perspective of a dusky grass walk.

"How should you like to live there?" he asked as the train moved on.

"There?"

"In some such place, I mean. One might do worse, don't you think so? There must be at least two centuries of solitude under those yew trees. Shouldn't you like it?"

"I—I don't know," she faltered. She knew now that he meant to speak.

He lit another cigarette. "We shall have to live somewhere, you know," he said as he bent above the match.

Lydia tried to speak carelessly. "*Je n'en vois pas la nécessité!*[2] Why not live everywhere, as we have been doing?"

"But we can't travel forever, can we?"

"Oh, forever's a long word," she objected, picking up the review he had thrown aside.

"For the rest of our lives then," he said, moving nearer.

She made a slight gesture which caused his hand to slip from hers.

"Why should we make plans? I thought you agreed with me that it's pleasanter to drift."

He looked at her hesitatingly. "It's been pleasant, certainly; but I suppose I shall have to get at my work again some day. You know I haven't written a line since—all this time," he hastily amended.

She flamed with sympathy and self-reproach. "Oh, if you mean *that*—if you want to write—of course we must settle down. How stupid of me not

---

[2]French: "I don't see the need!"

to have thought of it sooner! Where shall we go? Where do you think you could work best? We oughtn't to lose any more time."

He hesitated again. "I had thought of a villa in these parts. It's quiet; we shouldn't be bothered. Should you like it?"

"Of course I should like it." She paused and looked away. "But I thought—I remember your telling me once that your best work had been done in a crowd—in big cities. Why should you shut yourself up in a desert?"

Gannett, for a moment, made no reply. At length he said, avoiding her eye as carefully as she avoided his: "It might be different now; I can't tell, of course, till I try. A writer ought not to be dependent on his *milieu*; it's a mistake to humor oneself in that way; and I thought that just at first you might prefer to be—"

She faced him. "To be what?"

"Well—quiet. I mean—"

"What do you mean by 'at first'?" she interrupted.

He paused again. "I mean after we are married."

She thrust up her chin and turned toward the window. "Thank you!" she tossed back at him.

"Lydia!" he exclaimed blankly; and she felt in every fiber of her averted person that he had made the inconceivable, the unpardonable mistake of anticipating her acquiescence.

The train rattled on and he groped for a third cigarette. Lydia remained silent.

"I haven't offended you?" he ventured at length, in the tone of a man who feels his way.

She shook her head with a sigh. "I thought you understood," she moaned. Their eyes met and she moved back to his side.

"Do you want to know how not to offend me? By taking it for granted, once for all, that you've said your say on the odious question and that I've said mine, and that we stand just where we did this morning before that—that hateful paper came to spoil everything between us!"

"To spoil everything between us? What on earth do you mean? Aren't you glad to be free?"

"I was free before."

"Not to marry me," he suggested.

"But I don't *want* to marry you!" she cried.

She saw that he turned pale. "I'm obtuse, I suppose," he said slowly. "I confess I don't see what you're driving at. Are you tired of the whole business? Or was I simply a—an excuse for getting away? Perhaps you didn't care to travel alone? Was that it? And now you want to chuck me?" His voice had grown harsh. "You owe me a straight answer, you know; don't be tenderhearted!"

Her eyes swam as she leaned to him. "Don't you see it's because I care—because I care so much? Oh, Ralph! Can't you see how it would humiliate me? Try to feel it as a woman would! Don't you see the misery of being made your wife in this way? If I'd known you as a girl—that would have been a real marriage! But now—this vulgar fraud upon society—and upon a society we despised and laughed at—this sneaking back into a position that we've voluntarily forfeited: don't you see what a cheap compromise it is? We neither of us believe in the abstract 'sacredness' of marriage; we both know that no ceremony is needed to consecrate our love for each other; what object can we have in marrying, except the secret fear of each that the other may escape, or the secret longing to work our way back gradually—oh, very gradually—into the esteem of the people whose conventional morality we have always ridiculed and hated? And the very fact that, after a decent interval, these same people would come and dine with us—the women who talk about the indissolubility of marriage, and who would let me die in a gutter today because I am 'leading a life of sin'—doesn't that disgust you more than their turning their backs on us now? I can stand being cut by them, but I couldn't stand their coming to call and asking what I meant to do about visiting that unfortunate Mrs. So-and-so!"

She paused, and Gannett maintained a perplexed silence.

"You judge things too theoretically," he said at length, slowly. "Life is made up of compromises."

"The life we ran away from—yes! If we had been willing to accept them"—she flushed—"we might have gone on meeting each other at Mrs. Tillotson's dinners."

He smiled slightly. "I didn't know that we ran away to found a new system of ethics. I supposed it was because we loved each other."

"Life is complex, of course; isn't it the very recognition of that fact that separates us from the people who see it *tout d'une pièce*?[3] If *they* are right— if marriage is sacred in itself and the individual must always be sacrificed to the family—then there can be no real marriage between us, since our—our being together is a protest against the sacrifice of the individual to the family." She interrupted herself with a laugh. "You'll say now that I'm giving you a lecture on sociology! Of course one acts as one can—as one must, perhaps—pulled by all sorts of invisible threads; but at least one needn't pretend, for social advantages, to subscribe to a creed that ignores the complexity of human motives—that classifies people by arbitrary signs, and puts it in everybody's reach to be on Mrs. Tillotson's visiting list. It may be necessary that the world should be ruled by conventions—but if we believed in them, why did we break through them? And if we don't believe in them, is it honest to take advantage of the protection they afford?"

Gannett hesitated. "One may believe in them or not; but as long as they do rule the world it is only by taking advantage of their protection that one can find a *modus vivendi*."

"Do outlaws need a *modus vivendi*?"

He looked at her hopelessly. Nothing is more perplexing to man than the mental process of a woman who reasons her emotions.

[3]French: "all as a piece."

She thought she had scored a point and followed it up passionately. "You do understand, don't you? You see how the very thought of the thing humiliates me! We are together today because we choose to be—don't let us look any farther than that!" She caught his hands. "*Promise* me you'll never speak of it again; promise me you'll never *think* of it even," she implored, with a tearful prodigality of italics.

Through what followed—his protests, his arguments, his final unconvinced submission to her wishes—she had a sense of his but half-discerning all that, for her, had made the moment so tumultuous. They had reached that memorable point in every heart history when, for the first time, the man seems obtuse and the woman irrational. It was the abundance of his intentions that consoled her, on reflection, for what they lacked in quality. After all, it would have been worse, incalculably worse, to have detected any overreadiness to understand her.

II

When the train at nightfall brought them to their journey's end at the edge of one of the lakes, Lydia was glad that they were not, as usual, to pass from one solitude to another. Their wanderings during the year had indeed been like the flight of outlaws: through Sicily, Dalmatia, Transylvania and Southern Italy they had persisted in their tacit avoidance of their kind. Isolation, at first, had deepened the flavor of their happiness, as night intensifies the scent of certain flowers; but in the new phase on which they were entering, Lydia's chief wish was that they should be less abnormally exposed to the action of each other's thoughts.

She shrank, nevertheless, as the brightly-looming bulk of the fashionable Anglo-American hotel on the water's brink began to radiate toward their advancing boat its vivid suggestion of social order, visitors' lists, Church services, and the bland inquisition of the *table d'hôte*. The mere fact that in a moment or two she must take her place on the hotel register as Mrs. Gannett seemed to weaken the springs of her resistance.

They had meant to stay for a night only, on their way to a lofty village among the glaciers of Monte Rosa; but after the first plunge into publicity, when they entered the dining room, Lydia felt the relief of being lost in a crowd, of ceasing for a moment to be the center of Gannett's scrutiny; and in his face she caught the reflection of her feeling. After dinner, when she went upstairs, he strolled into the smoking room, and an hour or two later, sitting in the darkness of her window, she heard his voice below and saw him walking up and down the terrace with a companion cigar at his side. When he came up he told her he had been talking to the hotel chaplain—a very good sort of fellow.

"Queer little microcosms, these hotels! Most of these people live here all summer and then migrate to Italy or the Riviera. The English are the only people who can lead that kind of life with dignity—those soft-voiced old ladies in Shetland shawls somehow carry the British Empire under their caps. *Civis Romanus sum.*[4] It's a curious study—there might be some good things to work up here."

He stood before her with the vivid preoccupied stare of the novelist on the trail of a "subject." With a relief that was half painful she noticed that, for the first time since they had been together, he was hardly aware of her presence.

"Do you think you could write here?"

"Here? I don't know." His stare dropped. "After being out of things so long one's first impressions are bound to be tremendously vivid, you know. I see a dozen threads already that one might follow—"

He broke off with a touch of embarrassment.

"Then follow them. We'll stay," she said with sudden decision.

"Stay here?" He glanced at her in surprise, and then, walking to the window, looked out upon the dusky slumber of the garden.

"Why not?" she said at length, in a tone of veiled irritation.

"The place is full of old cats in caps who gossip with the chaplain. Shall you like—I mean, it would be different if—"

She flamed up.

"Do you suppose I care? It's none of their business."

"Of course not; but you won't get them to think so."

"They may think what they please."

He looked at her doubtfully.

"It's for you to decide."

"We'll stay," she repeated.

Gannett, before they met, had made himself known as a successful writer of short stories and of a novel which had achieved the distinction of being widely discussed. The reviewers called him "promising," and Lydia now accused herself of having too long interfered with the fulfillment of his promise. There was a special irony in the fact, since his passionate assurances that only the stimulus of her companionship could bring out his latent faculty had almost given the dignity of a "vocation" to her course: there had been moments when she had felt unable to assume, before posterity, the responsibility of thwarting his career. And, after all, he had not written a line since they had been together: his first desire to write had come from renewed contact with the world! Was it all a mistake then? Must the most intelligent choice work more disastrously than the blundering combinations of chance? Or was there a still more humiliating answer to her perplexities? His sudden impulse of activity so exactly coincided with her own wish to withdraw, for a time, from the range of his observation, that she wondered if he too were not seeking sanctuary from intolerable problems.

"You must begin tomorrow!" she cried, hiding a tremor under the laugh with which she added, "I wonder if there's any ink in the inkstand?"

* * *

[4]Latin: "I am a Roman citizen."

Whatever else they had at the Hotel Bellosguardo, they had, as Miss Pinsent said, "a certain tone." It was to Lady Susan Condit that they owed this inestimable benefit; an advantage ranking in Miss Pinsent's opinion above even the lawn tennis courts and the resident chaplain. It was the fact of Lady Susan's annual visit that made the hotel what it was. Miss Pinsent was certainly the last to underrate such a privilege: "It's so important, my dear, forming as we do a little family, that there should be someone to give *the tone*; and no one could do it better than Lady Susan—an earl's daughter and a person of such determination. Dear Mrs. Ainger now—who really *ought*, you know, when Lady Susan's away—absolutely refuses to assert herself." Miss Pinsent sniffed derisively. "A bishop's niece!—my dear, I saw her once actually give in to some South Americans—and before us all. She gave up her seat at table to oblige them—such a lack of dignity! Lady Susan spoke to her very plainly about it afterwards."

Miss Pinsent glanced across the lake and adjusted her auburn front.

"But of course I don't deny that the stand Lady Susan takes is not always easy to live up to—for the rest of us, I mean. Monsieur Grossart, our good proprietor, finds it trying at times, I know—he has said as much, privately, to Mrs. Ainger and me. After all, the poor man is not to blame for wanting to fill his hotel, is he? And Lady Susan is so difficult—so very difficult—about new people. One might almost say that she disapproves of them beforehand, on principle. And yet she's had warnings—she very nearly made a dreadful mistake once with the Duchess of Levens, who dyed her hair and—well, swore and smoked. One would have thought that might have been a lesson to Lady Susan." Miss Pinsent resumed her knitting with a sigh. "There are exceptions, of course. She took at once to you and Mr. Gannett—it was quite remarkable, really. Oh, I don't mean that either—of course not! It was perfectly natural—we *all* thought you so charming and interesting from the first day—we knew at once that Mr. Gannett was intellectual, by the magazines you took in; but you know what I mean. Lady Susan is so very—well, I won't say prejudiced, as Mrs. Ainger does—but so prepared *not* to like new people, that her taking to you in that way was a surprise to us all, I confess."

Miss Pinsent sent a significant glance down the long laurustinus alley from the other end of which two people—a lady and gentleman—were strolling toward them through the smiling neglect of the garden.

"In this case, of course, it's very different; that I'm willing to admit. Their looks are against them; but, as Mrs. Ainger says, one can't exactly tell them so."

"She's very handsome," Lydia ventured, with her eyes on the lady, who showed, under the dome of a vivid sunshade, the hourglass figure and superlative coloring of a Christmas chromo.

"That's the worst of it. She's too handsome."

"Well, after all, she can't help that."

"Other people manage to," said Miss Pinsent skeptically.

"But isn't it rather unfair of Lady Susan—considering that nothing is known about them?"

"But, my dear, that's the very thing that's against them. It's infinitely worse than any actual knowledge."

Lydia mentally agreed that, in the case of Mrs. Linton, it possibly might be.

"I wonder why they came here?" she mused.

"That's against them too. It's always a bad sign when loud people come to a quiet place. And they've brought van loads of boxes—her maid told Mrs. Ainger's that they meant to stop indefinitely."

"And Lady Susan actually turned her back on her in the salon?"

"My dear, she said it was for our sakes: that makes it so unanswerable! But poor Grossart *is* in a way! The Lintons have taken his most expensive suite, you know—the yellow damask drawing room above the portico—and they have champagne with every meal!"

They were silent as Mr. and Mrs. Linton sauntered by; the lady with tempestuous brows and challenging chin; the gentleman, a blond stripling, trailing after her, head downward, like a reluctant child dragged by his nurse.

"What does your husband think of them, my dear?" Miss Pinsent whispered as they passed out of earshot.

Lydia stooped to pick a violet in the border.

"He hasn't told me."

"Of your speaking to them, I mean. Would he approve of that? I know how very particular nice Americans are. I think your action might make a difference; it would certainly carry weight with Lady Susan."

"Dear Miss Pinsent, you flatter me!"

Lydia rose and gathered up her book and sunshade.

"Well, if you're asked for an opinion—if Lady Susan asks you for one—I think you ought to be prepared," Miss Pinsent admonished her as she moved away.

III

Lady Susan held her own. She ignored the Lintons, and her little family, as Miss Pinsent phrased it, followed suit. Even Mrs. Ainger agreed that it was obligatory. If Lady Susan owed it to the others not to speak to the Lintons, the others clearly owed it to Lady Susan to back her up. It was generally found expedient, at the Hotel Bellosguardo, to adopt this form of reasoning.

Whatever effect this combined action may have had upon the Lintons, it did not at least have that of driving them away. Monsieur Grossart, after a few days of suspense, had the satisfaction of seeing them settle down in his yellow damask *premier* with what looked like a permanent installation of palm trees and silk cushions, and a gratifying continuance in the consumption of champagne. Mrs. Linton trailed her Doucet draperies up and down the garden with the same challenging air, while her husband, smoking innumerable cigarettes, dragged himself dejectedly in her wake; but neither of them, after the first encounter with Lady Susan, made any attempt to extend their acquaintance. They simply ignored their ignorers. As Miss Pinsent resentfully observed, they behaved exactly as though the hotel were empty.

It was therefore a matter of surprise, as well as of displeasure, to Lydia, to find, on glancing up one day from her seat in the garden, that the shadow which had fallen across her book was that of the enigmatic Mrs. Linton.

"I want to speak to you," that lady said, in a rich hard voice that seemed the audible expression of her gown and her complexion.

Lydia stared. She certainly did not want to speak to Mrs. Linton.

"Shall I sit down here?" the latter continued, fixing her intensely-shaded eyes on Lydia's face, "or are you afraid of being seen with me?"

"Afraid?" Lydia colored. "Sit down, please. What is it that you wish to say?"

Mrs. Linton, with a smile, drew up a garden chair and crossed one openwork ankle above the other.

"I want you to tell me what my husband said to your husband last night."

Lydia turned pale.

"My husband—to yours?" she faltered, staring at the other.

"Didn't you know they were closeted together for hours in the smoking room after you went upstairs? My man didn't get to bed until nearly two o'clock and when he did I couldn't get a word out of him. When he wants to be aggravating I'll back him against anybody living!" Her teeth and eyes flashed persuasively upon Lydia. "But you'll tell me what they were talking about, won't you? I know I can trust you—you look so awfully kind. And it's for his own good. He's such a precious donkey and I'm so afraid he's got into some beastly scrape or other. If he'd only trust his own old woman! But they're always writing to him and setting him against me. And I've got nobody to turn to." She laid her hand on Lydia's with a rattle of bracelets. "You'll help me, won't you?"

Lydia drew back from the smiling fierceness of her brows.

"I'm sorry—but I don't think I understand. My husband has said nothing to me of—of yours."

The great black crescents above Mrs. Linton's eyes met angrily.

"I say—is that true?" she demanded.

Lydia rose from her seat.

"Oh, look here, I didn't mean that, you know—you mustn't take one up so! Can't you see how rattled I am?"

Lydia saw that, in fact, her beautiful mouth was quivering beneath softened eyes.

"I'm beside myself!" the splendid creature wailed, dropping into her seat.

"I'm so sorry," Lydia repeated, forcing herself to speak kindly; "but how can I help you?"

Mrs. Linton raised her head sharply.

"By finding out—there's a darling!"

"Finding what out?"

"What Trevenna told him."

"Trevenna—?" Lydia echoed in bewilderment.

Mrs. Linton clapped her hand to her mouth.

"Oh, Lord—there, it's out! What a fool I am! But I supposed of course you knew; I supposed everybody knew." She dried her eyes and bridled. "Didn't you know that he's Lord Trevenna? I'm Mrs. Cope."

Lydia recognized the names. They had figured in a flamboyant elopement which had thrilled fashionable London some six months earlier.

"Now you see how it is—you understand, don't you?" Mrs. Cope continued on a note of appeal. "I knew you would—that's the reason I came to you. I suppose *he* felt the same thing about your husband; he's not spoken to another soul in the place." Her face grew anxious again. "He's awfully sensitive, generally—he feels our position, he says—as if it wasn't *my* place to feel that! But when he does get talking there's no knowing what he'll say. I know he's been brooding over something lately, and I *must* find out what it is—it's to his interest that I should. I always tell him that I think only of his interest; if he'd only trust me! But he's been so odd lately—I can't think what he's plotting. You will help me, dear?"

Lydia, who had remained standing, looked away uncomfortably.

"If you mean by finding out what Lord Trevenna has told my husband, I'm afraid it's impossible."

"Why impossible?"

"Because I infer that it was told in confidence."

Mrs. Cope stared incredulously.

"Well, what of that? Your husband looks such a dear—anyone can see he's awfully gone on you. What's to prevent your getting it out of him?"

Lydia flushed.

"I'm not a spy!" she exclaimed.

"A spy—a spy? How dare you?" Mrs. Cope flamed out. "Oh, I don't mean that either! Don't be angry with me—I'm so miserable." She essayed a softer note. "Do you call that spying—for one woman to help out another? I do need help so dreadfully! I'm at my wits' end with Trevenna, I am indeed. He's such a boy—a mere baby, you know; he's only two-and-twenty." She dropped her orbed lids. "He's younger than me—only fancy, a few months younger. I tell him he ought to listen to me as if I was his mother; oughtn't he now? But he won't, he won't! All his people are at him, you see—oh, I know *their* little game! Trying to get him away from me before I can get my divorce—that's what they're up to. At first he wouldn't listen to them; he used to toss their letters over to me to read; but now he reads them himself, and answers 'em too, I fancy; he's always shut up in his room, writing. If I only knew what his plan is I could stop him fast enough—he's such a simpleton. But he's dreadfully deep too—at times I can't make him out. But I know he's told your husband everything—I knew that last night the minute I laid eyes on him. And I *must* find out—you must help me—I've got no one else to turn to!"

She caught Lydia's fingers in a stormy pressure.

"Say you'll help me—you and your husband."

Lydia tried to free herself.

"What you ask is impossible; you must see that it is. No one could interfere in—in the way you ask."

Mrs. Cope's clutch tightened.

"You won't, then? You won't?"

"Certainly not. Let me go, please."

Mrs. Cope released her with a laugh.

"Oh, go by all means—pray don't let me detain you! Shall you go and tell Lady Susan Condit that there's a pair of us—or shall I save you the trouble of enlightening her?"

Lydia stood still in the middle of the path, seeing her antagonist through a mist of terror. Mrs. Cope was still laughing.

"Oh, I'm not spiteful by nature, my dear; but you're a little more than flesh and blood can stand! It's impossible, is it? Let you go, indeed! You're too good to be mixed up in my affairs, are you? Why, you little fool, the first day I laid eyes on you I saw that you and I were both in the same box— that's the reason I spoke to you."

She stepped nearer, her smile dilating on Lydia like a lamp through a fog.

"You can take your choice, you know; I always play fair. If you'll tell I'll promise not to. Now then, which is it to be?"

Lydia, involuntarily, had begun to move away from the pelting storm of words; but at this she turned and sat down again.

"You may go," she said simply. "I shall stay here."

IV

She stayed there for a long time, in the hypnotized contemplation, not of Mrs. Cope's present, but of her own past. Gannett, early that morning, had gone off on a long walk—he had fallen into the habit of taking these mountain tramps with various fellow lodgers; but even had he been within reach she could not have gone to him just then. She had to deal with herself first. She was surprised to find how, in the last months, she had lost the habit of introspection. Since their coming to the Hotel Bellosguardo she and Gannett had tacitly avoided themselves and each other.

She was aroused by the whistle of the three o'clock steamboat as it neared the landing just beyond the hotel gates. Three o'clock! Then Gannett would soon be back—he had told her to expect him before four. She rose hurriedly, her face averted from the inquisitorial façade of the hotel. She could not see him just yet; she could not go indoors. She slipped through one of the overgrown garden alleys and climbed a steep path to the hills.

It was dark when she opened their sitting-room door. Gannett was sitting on the window ledge smoking a cigarette. Cigarettes were now his chief resource: he had not written a line during the two months they had spent at the Hotel Bellosguardo. In that respect, it had turned out not to be the right *milieu* after all.

He started up at Lydia's entrance.

"Where have you been? I was getting anxious."

She sat down in a chair near the door.

"Up the mountain," she said wearily.

"Alone?"

"Yes."

Gannett threw away his cigarette: the sound of her voice made him want to see her face.

"Shall we have a little light?" he suggested.

She made no answer and he lifted the globe from the lamp and put a match to the wick. Then he looked at her.

"Anything wrong? You look done up."

She sat glancing vaguely about the little sitting room, dimly lit by the pallid-globed lamp, which left in twilight the outlines of the furniture, of his writing table heaped with books and papers, of the tea roses and jasmine drooping on the mantelpiece. How like home it had all grown—how like home!

"Lydia, what is wrong?" he repeated.

She moved away from him, feeling for her hatpins and turning to lay her hat and sunshade on the table.

Suddenly she said: "That woman has been talking to me."

Gannett stared.

"That woman? What woman?"

"Mrs. Linton—Mrs. Cope."

He gave a start of annoyance, still, as she perceived, not grasping the full import of her words.

"The deuce! She told you—?"

"She told me everything."

Gannett looked at her anxiously.

"What impudence! I'm so sorry that you should have been exposed to this, dear."

"Exposed!" Lydia laughed.

Gannett's brow clouded and they looked away from each other.

"Do you know *why* she told me? She had the best of reasons. The first time she laid eyes on me she saw that we were both in the same box."

"Lydia!"

"So it was natural, of course, that she should turn to me in a difficulty."

"What difficulty?"

"It seems she has reason to think that Lord Trevenna's people are trying to get him away from her before she gets her divorce—"

"Well?"

"And she fancied he had been consulting with you last night as to—as to the best way of escaping from her."

Gannett stood up with an angry forehead.

"Well—what concern of yours was all this dirty business? Why should she go to you?"

"Don't you see? It's so simple. I was to wheedle his secret out of you."

"To oblige that woman?"

"Yes; or, if I was unwilling to oblige her, then to protect myself."

"To protect yourself? Against whom?"

"Against her telling everyone in the hotel that she and I are in the same box."

"She threatened that?"

"She left me the choice of telling it myself or of doing it for me."

"The beast!"

There was a long silence. Lydia had seated herself on the sofa, beyond the radius of the lamp, and he leaned against the window. His next question surprised her.

"When did this happen? At what time, I mean?"

She looked at him vaguely.

"I don't know—after luncheon, I think. Yes, I remember; it must have been at about three o'clock."

He stepped into the middle of the room and as he approached the light she saw that his brow had cleared.

"Why do you ask?" she said.

"Because when I came in, at about half-past three, the mail was just being distributed, and Mrs. Cope was waiting as usual to pounce on her letters; you know she was always watching for the postman. She was standing so close to me that I couldn't help seeing a big official-looking envelope that was handed to her. She tore it open, gave one look at the inside, and rushed off upstairs like a whirlwind, with the director shouting after her that she had left all her other letters behind. I don't believe she ever thought of you again after that paper was put into her hand."

"Why?"

"Because she was too busy. I was sitting in the window, watching for you, when the five o'clock boat left, and who should go on board, bag and baggage, valet and maid, dressing bags and poodle, but Mrs. Cope and Trevenna. Just an hour and a half to pack up in! And you should have seen her when they started. She was radiant—shaking hands with everybody—waving her handkerchief from the deck—distributing bows and smiles like an empress. If ever a woman got what she wanted just in the nick of time that woman did. She'll be Lady Trevenna within a week, I'll wager."

"You think she has her divorce?"

"I'm sure of it. And she must have got it just after her talk with you."

Lydia was silent.

At length she said, with a kind of reluctance, "She was horribly angry when she left me. It wouldn't have taken long to tell Lady Susan Condit."

"Lady Susan Condit has not been told."

"How do you know?"

"Because when I went downstairs half an hour ago I met Lady Susan on the way—"

He stopped, half smiling.

"Well?"

"And she stopped to ask if I thought you would act as patroness to a charity concert she is getting up."

In spite of themselves they both broke into a laugh. Lydia's ended in sobs and she sank down with her face hidden. Gannett bent over her, seeking her hands.

"That vile woman—I ought to have warned you to keep away from her; I can't forgive myself! But he spoke to me in confidence; and I never dreamed—well, it's all over now."

Lydia lifted her head.

"Not for me. It's only just beginning."

"What do you mean?"

She put him gently aside and moved in her turn to the window. Then she went on, with her face turned toward the shimmering blackness of the lake, "You see of course that it might happen again at any moment."

"What?"

"This—this risk of being found out. And we could hardly count again on such a lucky combination of chances, could we?"

He sat down with a groan.

Still keeping her face toward the darkness, she said, "I want you to go and tell Lady Susan—and the others."

Gannett, who had moved towards her, paused a few feet off.

"Why do you wish me to do this?" he said at length, with less surprise in his voice than she had been prepared for.

"Because I've behaved basely, abominably, since we came here: letting these people believe we were married—lying with every breath I drew—"

"Yes, I've felt that too," Gannett exclaimed with sudden energy.

The words shook her like a tempest: all her thoughts seemed to fall about her in ruins.

"You—you've felt so?"

"Of course I have." He spoke with low-voiced vehemence. "Do you suppose I like playing the sneak any better than you do? It's damnable."

He had dropped on the arm of a chair, and they stared at each other like blind people who suddenly see.

"But you have liked it here," she faltered.

"Oh, I've liked it—I've liked it." He moved impatiently. "Haven't you?"

"Yes," she burst out; "that's the worst of it—that's what I can't bear. I fancied it was for your sake that I insisted on staying—because you thought you could write here; and perhaps just at first that really was the reason. But afterwards I wanted to stay myself—I loved it." She broke into a laugh. "Oh, do you see the full derision of it? These people—the very prototypes of the bores you took me away from, with the same fenced-in view of life, the same keep-off-the-grass morality, the same little cautious virtues and the same little frightened vices—well, I've clung to them, I've delighted in them, I've done my best to please them. I've toadied Lady Susan, I've gossiped with Miss Pinsent, I've pretended to be shocked with Mrs. Ainger.

Respectability! It was the one thing in life that I was sure I didn't care about, and it's grown so precious to me that I've stolen it because I couldn't get it in any other way."

She moved across the room and returned to his side with another laugh.

"I who used to fancy myself unconventional! I must have been born with a cardcase in my hand. You should have seen me with that poor woman in the garden. She came to me for help, poor creature, because she fancied that, having 'sinned,' as they call it, I might feel some pity for others who had been tempted in the same way. Not I! She didn't know me. Lady Susan would have been kinder, because Lady Susan wouldn't have been afraid. I hated the woman—my one thought was not to be seen with her—I could have killed her for guessing my secret. The one thing that mattered to me at that moment was my standing with Lady Susan!"

Gannett did not speak.

"And you—you've felt it too!" she broke out accusingly. "You've enjoyed being with these people as much as I have; you've let the chaplain talk to you by the hour about The Reign of Law and Professor Drummond. When they asked you to hand the plate in church I was watching you—*you wanted to accept.*"

She stepped close, laying her hand on his arm.

"Do you know, I begin to see what marriage is for. It's to keep people away from each other. Sometimes I think that two people who love each other can be saved from madness only by the things that come between them—children, duties, visits, bores, relations—the things that protect married people from each other. We've been too close together—that has been our sin. We've seen the nakedness of each other's souls."

She sank again on the sofa, hiding her face in her hands.

Gannett stood above her perplexedly: he felt as though she were being swept away by some implacable current while he stood helpless on its bank.

At length he said, "Lydia, don't think me a brute—but don't you see yourself that it won't do?"

"Yes, I see it won't do," she said without raising her head.

His face cleared.

"Then we'll go tomorrow."

"Go—where?"

"To Paris; to be married."

For a long time she made no answer; then she asked slowly, "Would they have us here if we were married?"

"Have us here?"

"I mean Lady Susan—and the others."

"Have us here? Of course they would."

"Not if they knew—at least, not unless they could pretend not to know."

He made an impatient gesture.

"We shouldn't come back here, of course; and other people needn't know—no one need know."

She sighed. "Then it's only another form of deception and a meaner one. Don't you see that?"

"I see that we're not accountable to any Lady Susans on earth!"

"Then why are you ashamed of what we are doing here?"

"Because I'm sick of pretending that you're my wife when you're not— when you won't be."

She looked at him sadly.

"If I were your wife you'd have to go on pretending. You'd have to pretend that I'd never been—anything else. And our friends would have to pretend that they believed what you pretended."

Gannett pulled off the sofa tassel and flung it away.

"You're impossible," he groaned.

"It's not I—it's our being together that's impossible. I only want you to see that marriage won't help it."

"What will help it then?"

She raised her head.

"My leaving you."

"Your leaving me?" He sat motionless, staring at the tassel which lay at the other end of the room. At length some impulse of retaliation for the pain she was inflicting made him say deliberately:

"And where would you go if you left me?"

"Oh!" she cried.

He was at her side in an instant.

"Lydia—Lydia—you know I didn't mean it; I couldn't mean it! But you've driven me out of my senses; I don't know what I'm saying. Can't you get out of this labyrinth of self-torture? It's destroying us both."

"That's why I must leave you."

"How easily you say it!" He drew her hands down and made her face him. "You're very scrupulous about yourself—and others. But have you thought of me? You have no right to leave me unless you've ceased to care—"

"It's because I care—"

"Then I have a right to be heard. If you love me you can't leave me."

Her eyes defied him.

"Why not?"

He dropped her hands and rose from her side.

"Can you?" he said sadly.

The hour was late and the lamp flickered and sank. She stood up with a shiver and turned toward the door of her room.

V

At daylight a sound in Lydia's room woke Gannett from a troubled sleep. He sat up and listened. She was moving about softly, as though fearful of disturbing him. He heard her push back one of the creaking shutters; then there was a moment's silence, which seemed to indicate that she was waiting to see if the noise had roused him.

Presently she began to move again. She had spent a sleepless night, probably, and was dressing to go down to the garden for a breath of air. Gannett rose also; but some undefinable instinct made his movements as cautious as hers. He stole to his window and looked out through the slats of the shutter.

It had rained in the night and the dawn was gray and lifeless. The cloud-muffled hills across the lake were reflected in its surface as in a tarnished mirror. In the garden, the birds were beginning to shake the drops from the motionless laurustinus boughs.

An immense pity for Lydia filled Gannett's soul. Her seeming intellectual independence had blinded him for a time to the feminine cast of her mind. He had never thought of her as a woman who wept and clung: there was a lucidity in her intuitions that made them appear to be the result of reasoning. Now he saw the cruelty he had committed in detaching her from the normal conditions of life; he felt, too, the insight with which she had hit upon the real cause of their suffering. Their life was "impossible," as she had said—and its worst penalty was that it had made any other life impossible for them. Even had his love lessened, he was bound to her now by a hundred ties of pity and self-reproach; and she, poor child, must turn back to him as Latude returned to his cell.

A new sound startled him: it was the stealthy closing of Lydia's door. He crept to his own and heard her footsteps passing down the corridor. Then he went back to the window and looked out.

A minute or two later he saw her go down the steps of the porch and enter the garden. From his post of observation her face was invisible, but something about her appearance struck him. She wore a long traveling cloak and under its folds he detected the outline of a bag or bundle. He drew a deep breath and stood watching her.

She walked quickly down the laurustinus alley toward the gate; there she paused a moment, glancing about the little shady square. The stone benches under the trees were empty, and she seemed to gather resolution from the solitude about her, for she crossed the square to the steamboat landing, and he saw her pause before the ticket office at the head of the wharf. Now she was buying her ticket. Gannett turned his head a moment to look at the clock: the boat was due in five minutes. He had time to jump into his clothes and overtake her—

He made no attempt to move; an obscure reluctance restrained him. If any thought emerged from the tumult of his sensations, it was that he must let her go if she wished it. He had spoken last night of his rights: what were they? At the last issue, he and she were two separate beings, not made one by the miracle of common forbearances, duties, abnegations, but bound together in a *noyade*[5] of passion that left them resisting yet clinging as they went down.

After buying her ticket, Lydia had stood for a moment looking out across the lake; then he saw her seat herself on one of the benches near the

[5]French: "drowning."

landing. He and she, at that moment, were both listening for the same sound: the whistle of the boat as it rounded the nearest promontory. Gannett turned again to glance at the clock: the boat was due now.

Where would she go? What would her life be when she had left him? She had no near relations and few friends. There was money enough . . . but she asked so much of life, in ways so complex and immaterial. He thought of her as walking barefooted through a stony waste. No one would understand her—no one would pity her—and he, who did both, was powerless to come to her aid.

He saw that she had risen from the bench and walked toward the edge of the lake. She stood looking in the direction from which the steamboat was to come; then she turned to the ticket office, doubtless to ask the cause of the delay. After that she went back to the beach and sat down with bent head. What was she thinking of?

The whistle sounded; she started up, and Gannett involuntarily made a movement toward the door. But he turned back and continued to watch her. She stood motionless, her eyes on the trail of smoke that preceded the appearance of the boat. Then the little craft rounded the point, a dead white object on the leaden water: a minute later it was puffing and backing at the wharf.

The few passengers who were waiting—two or three peasants and a snuffy priest—were clustered near the ticket office. Lydia stood apart under the trees.

The boat lay alongside now; the gangplank was run out and the peasants went on board with their baskets of vegetables, followed by the priest. Still Lydia did not move. A bell began to ring querulously; there was a shriek of steam, and someone must have called to her that she would be late, for she started forward, as though in answer to a summons. She moved waveringly, and at the edge of the wharf she paused. Gannett saw a sailor beckon to her; the bell rang again and she stepped upon the gangplank.

Halfway down the short incline to the deck she stopped again; then she turned and ran back to the land. The gangplank was drawn in, the bell ceased to ring, and the boat backed out into the lake. Lydia, with slow steps, was walking toward the garden.

As she approached the hotel she looked up furtively and Gannett drew back into the room. He sat down beside a table; a Bradshaw lay at his elbow, and mechanically, without knowing what he did, he began looking out at the trains to Paris.

1899

The Other Two

Waythorn, on the drawing-room hearth, waited for his wife to come down to dinner.

It was their first night under his own roof, and he was surprised at his thrill of boyish agitation. He was not so old, to be sure—his glass gave him little more than the five-and-thirty years to which his wife confessed—but he had fancied himself already in the temperate zone; yet here he was listening for her step with a tender sense of all it symbolized, with some old trail of verse about the garlanded nuptial doorposts floating through his enjoyment of the pleasant room and the good dinner just beyond it.

They had been hastily recalled from their honeymoon by the illness of Lily Haskett, the child of Mrs. Waythorn's first marriage. The little girl, at Waythorn's desire, had been transferred to his house on the day of her mother's wedding, and the doctor, on their arrival, broke the news that she was ill with typhoid, but declared that all the symptoms were favorable. Lily could show twelve years of unblemished health, and the case promised to be a light one. The nurse spoke as reassuringly, and after a moment of alarm Mrs. Waythorn had adjusted herself to the situation. She was very fond of Lily—her affection for the child had perhaps been her decisive charm in Waythorn's eyes—but she had the perfectly balanced nerves which her little girl had inherited, and no woman ever wasted less tissue in unproductive worry. Waythorn was therefore quite prepared to see her come in presently, a little late because of a last look at Lily, but as serene and well-appointed as if her goodnight kiss had been laid on the brow of health. Her composure was restful to him; it acted as ballast to his somewhat unstable sensibilities. As he pictured her bending over the child's bed he thought how soothing her presence must be in illness: her very step would prognosticate recovery.

His own life had been a gray one, from temperament rather than circumstance, and he had been drawn to her by the unperturbed gaiety which kept her fresh and elastic at an age when most women's activities are growing either slack or febrile. He knew what was said about her; for, popular as she was, there had always been a faint undercurrent of detraction. When she had appeared in New York, nine or ten years earlier, as the pretty Mrs. Haskett whom Gus Varick had unearthed somewhere—was it in Pittsburgh or Utica?—society, while promptly accepting her, had reserved the right to cast a doubt on its own indiscrimination. Inquiry, however, established her undoubted connection with a socially reigning family, and explained her recent divorce as the natural result of a runaway match at seventeen; and as nothing was known of Mr. Haskett it was easy to believe the worst of him.

Alice Haskett's remarriage with Gus Varick was a passport to the set whose recognition she coveted, and for a few years the Varicks were the most popular couple in town. Unfortunately the alliance was brief and stormy, and this time the husband had his champions. Still, even Varick's stanchest supporters admitted that he was not meant for matrimony, and Mrs. Varick's grievances were of a nature to bear the inspection of the New York courts. A New York divorce is in itself a diploma of virtue, and in the semiwidowhood of this second separation Mrs. Varick took on an air of sanctity, and was allowed to confide her wrongs to some of the most scrupulous ears in town. But when it was known that she was to marry Waythorn there was a momentary reaction. Her best friends would have preferred to see her remain in the role of the injured wife, which was as becoming to her as crepe to a rosy complexion. True, a decent time had elapsed, and it was not even suggested that Waythorn had supplanted his predecessor. People shook their heads over him, however, and one grudging friend, to whom he affirmed that he took the step with his eyes open, replied oracularly: "Yes—and with your ears shut."

Waythorn could afford to smile at these innuendoes. In the Wall Street phrase, he had "discounted" them. He knew that society has not yet adapted itself to the consequences of divorce, and that till the adaptation takes place every woman who uses the freedom the law accords her must be her own social justification. Waythorn had an amused confidence in his wife's ability to justify herself. His expectations were fulfilled, and before the wedding took place Alice Varick's group had rallied openly to her support. She took it all imperturbably: she had a way of surmounting obstacles without seeming to be aware of them, and Waythorn looked back with wonder at the trivialities over which he had worn his nerves thin. He had the sense of having found refuge in a richer, warmer nature than his own, and his satisfaction, at the moment, was humorously summed up in the thought that his wife, when she had done all she could for Lily, would not be ashamed to come down and enjoy a good dinner.

The anticipation of such enjoyment was not, however, the sentiment expressed by Mrs. Waythorn's charming face when she presently joined him. Though she had put on her most engaging tea gown she had neglected to assume the smile that went with it, and Waythorn thought he had never seen her look so nearly worried.

"What is it?" he asked. "Is anything wrong with Lily?"

"No; I've just been in and she's still sleeping." Mrs. Waythorn hesitated. "But something tiresome has happened."

He had taken her two hands, and now perceived that he was crushing a paper between them.

"This letter?"

"Yes—Mr. Haskett has written—I mean his lawyer has written."

Waythorn felt himself flush uncomfortably. He dropped his wife's hands.

"What about?"

"About seeing Lily. You know the courts—"

"Yes, yes," he interrupted nervously.

Nothing was known about Haskett in New York. He was vaguely supposed to have remained in the outer darkness from which his wife had been rescued, and Waythorn was one of the few who were aware that he had given up his business in Utica and followed her to New York in order to be near his little girl. In the days of his wooing, Waythorn had often met Lily on the doorstep, rosy and smiling, on her way "to see papa."

"I am so sorry," Mrs. Waythorn murmured.

He roused himself. "What does he want?"

"He wants to see her. You know she goes to him once a week."

"Well—he doesn't expect her to go to him now, does he?"

"No—he has heard of her illness; but he expects to come here."

"Here?"

Mrs. Waythorn reddened under his gaze. They looked away from each other.

"I'm afraid he has the right.... You'll see...." She made a proffer of the letter.

Waythorn moved away with a gesture of refusal. He stood staring about the softly-lighted room, which a moment before had seemed so full of bridal intimacy.

"I'm so sorry," she repeated. "If Lily could have been moved—"

"That's out of the question," he returned impatiently.

"I suppose so."

Her lip was beginning to tremble, and he felt himself a brute.

"He must come, of course," he said. "When is—his day?"

"I'm afraid—tomorrow."

"Very well. Send a note in the morning."

The butler entered to announce dinner.

Waythorn turned to his wife. "Come—you must be tired. It's beastly, but try to forget about it," he said, drawing her hand through his arm.

"You're so good, dear. I'll try," she whispered back.

Her face cleared at once, and as she looked at him across the flowers, between the rosy candleshades, he saw her lips waver back into a smile.

"How pretty everything is!" she sighed luxuriously.

He turned to the butler. "The champagne at once, please. Mrs. Waythorn is tired."

In a moment or two their eyes met above the sparkling glasses. Her own were quite clear and untroubled: he saw that she had obeyed his injunction and forgotten.

II

Waythorn, the next morning, went downtown earlier than usual. Haskett was not likely to come till the afternoon, but the instinct of flight drove him forth. He meant to stay away all day—he had thoughts of dining at his club. As his door closed behind him he reflected that before he opened it again it would have admitted another man who had as much right to enter it as himself, and the thought filled him with a physical repugnance.

He caught the elevated at the employees' hour, and found himself crushed between two layers of pendulous humanity. At Eighth Street the man facing him wriggled out, and another took his place. Waythorn glanced up and saw that it was Gus Varick. The men were so close together that it was impossible to ignore the smile of recognition on Varick's handsome overblown face. And after all—why not? They had always been on good terms, and Varick had been divorced before Waythorn's attentions to his wife began. The two exchanged a word on the perennial grievance of the congested trains, and when a seat at their side was miraculously left empty the instinct of self-preservation made Waythorn slip into it after Varick.

The latter drew the stout man's breath of relief. "Lord—I was beginning to feel like a pressed flower." He leaned back, looking unconcernedly at Waythorn. "Sorry to hear that Sellers is knocked out again."

"Sellers?" echoed Waythorn, starting at his partner's name.

Varick looked surprised. "You didn't know he was laid up with the gout?"

"No. I've been away—I only got back last night." Waythorn felt himself reddenly in anticipation of the other's smile.

"Ah—yes; to be sure. And Sellers' attack came on two days ago. I'm afraid he's pretty bad. Very awkward for me, as it happens, because he was just putting through a rather important thing for me."

"Ah?" Waythorn wondered vaguely since when Varick had been dealing in "important things." Hitherto he had dabbled only in the shallow pools of speculation, with which Waythorn's office did not usually concern itself.

It occurred to him that Varick might be talking at random, to relieve the strain of their propinquity. That strain was becoming momentarily more apparent to Waythorn, and when, at Cortlandt Street, he caught sight of an acquaintance and had a sudden vision of the picture he and Varick must present to an initiated eye, he jumped up with a muttered excuse.

"I hope you'll find Sellers better," said Varick civilly, and he stammered back: "If I can be of any use to you—" and let the departing crowd sweep him to the platform.

At his office he heard that Sellers was in fact ill with the gout, and would probably not be able to leave the house for some weeks.

"I'm sorry it should have happened so, Mr. Waythorn," the senior clerk said with affable significance. "Mr. Sellers was very much upset at the idea of giving you such a lot of extra work just now."

"Oh, that's no matter," said Waythorn hastily. He secretly welcomed the pressure of additional business, and was glad to think that, when the day's work was over, he would have to call at his partner's on the way home.

He was late for luncheon, and turned in at the nearest restaurant instead of going to his club. The place was full, and the waiter hurried him to the back of the room to capture the only vacant table. In the cloud of cigar smoke Waythorn did not at once distinguish his neighbors: but presently, looking about him, he saw Varick seated a few feet off. This time, luckily, they were too far apart for conversation, and Varick, who faced another way, had probably not even seen him; but there was an irony in their renewed nearness.

Varick was said to be fond of good living, and as Waythorn sat dispatching his hurried luncheon he looked across half enviously at the other's leisurely degustation of his meal. When Waythorn first saw him he had been helping himself with critical deliberation to a bit of Camembert at the ideal point of liquefaction, and now, the cheese removed, he was just pouring his *café double* from its little two-storied earthen pot. He poured slowly, his ruddy profile bent over the task, and one beringed white hand steadying the lid of the coffeepot; then he stretched his other hand to the decanter of cognac at his elbow, filled a liqueur glass, took a tentative sip, and poured the brandy into his coffee cup.

Waythorn watched him in a kind of fascination. What was he thinking of—only of the flavor of the coffee and the liqueur? Had the morning's meeting left no more trace in his thoughts than on his face? Had his wife so completely passed out of his life that even this odd encounter with her present husband, within a week after her remarriage, was no more than an incident in his day? And as Waythorn mused, another idea struck him: had Haskett ever met Varick as Varick and he had just met? The recollection of Haskett perturbed him, and he rose and left the restaurant, taking a circuitous way out to escape the placid irony of Varick's nod.

It was after seven when Waythorn reached home. He thought the footman who opened the door looked at him oddly.

"How is Miss Lily?" he asked in haste.

"Doing very well, sir. A gentleman—"

"Tell Barlow to put off dinner for half an hour," Waythorn cut him off, hurrying upstairs.

He went straight to his room and dressed without seeing his wife. When he reached the drawing room she was there, fresh and radiant. Lily's day had been good; the doctor was not coming back that evening.

At dinner Waythorn told her of Sellers's illness and of the resulting complications. She listened sympathetically, adjuring him not to let himself be overworked, and asking vague feminine questions about the routine of the office. Then she gave him the chronicle of Lily's day; quoted the nurse and doctor, and told him who had called to inquire. He had never seen her more serene and unruffled. It struck him, with a curious pang, that she was very happy in being with him, so happy that she found a childish pleasure in rehearsing the trivial incidents of her day.

After dinner they went to the library, and the servant put the coffee and liqueurs on a low table before her and left the room. She looked singularly soft and girlish in her rosy-pale dress, against the dark leather of one of his bachelor armchairs. A day earlier the contrast would have charmed him.

He turned away now, choosing a cigar with affected deliberation.

"Did Haskett come?" he asked, with his back to her.

"Oh, yes—he came."

"You didn't see him, of course?"

She hesitated a moment. "I let the nurse see him."

That was all. There was nothing more to ask. He swung round toward her, applying a match to his cigar. Well, the thing was over for a week, at any rate. He would try not to think of it. She looked up at him, a trifle rosier than usual, with a smile in her eyes.

"Ready for your coffee, dear?"

He leaned against the mantelpiece, watching her as she lifted the coffee-pot. The lamplight struck a gleam from her bracelets and tipped her soft hair with brightness. How light and slender she was, and how each gesture flowed into the next! She seemed a creature all compact of harmonies. As the thought of Haskett receded, Waythorn felt himself yielding again to the joy of possessorship. They were his, those white hands with their flitting motions, his the light haze of hair, the lips and eyes. . . .

She set down the coffeepot, and reaching for the decanter of cognac, measured off a liqueur glass and poured it into his cup.

Waythorn uttered a sudden exclamation.

"What is the matter?" she said, startled.

"Nothing; only—I don't take cognac in my coffee."

"Oh, how stupid of me," she cried.

Their eyes met, and she blushed a sudden agonized red.

III

Ten days later, Mr. Sellers, still housebound, asked Waythorn to call on his way downtown.

The senior partner, with his swaddled foot propped up by the fire, greeted his associate with an air of embarrassment.

"I'm sorry, my dear fellow; I've got to ask you to do an awkward thing for me."

Waythorn waited, and the other went on, after a pause apparently given to the arrangement of his phrases: "The fact is, when I was knocked out I had just gone into a rather complicated piece of business for—Gus Varick."

"Well?" said Waythorn, with an attempt to put him at his ease.

"Well—it's this way: Varick came to me the day before my attack. He had evidently had an inside tip from somebody, and had made about a hundred thousand. He came to me for advice, and I suggested his going in with Vanderlyn."

"Oh, the deuce!" Waythorn exclaimed. He saw in a flash what had happened. The investment was an alluring one, but required negotiation. He listened quietly while Sellers put the case before him, and, the statement ended, he said: "You think I ought to see Varick?"

"I'm afraid I can't as yet. The doctor is obdurate. And this thing can't wait. I hate to ask you, but no one else in the office knows the ins and outs of it."

Waythorn stood silent. He did not care a farthing for the success of Varick's venture, but the honor of the office was to be considered, and he could hardly refuse to oblige his partner.

"Very well," he said, "I'll do it."

That afternoon, apprised by telephone, Varick called at the office. Waythorn, waiting in his private room, wondered what the others thought of it. The newspapers, at the time of Mrs. Waythorn's marriage, had acquainted their readers with every detail of her previous matrimonial ventures, and Waythorn could fancy the clerks smiling behind Varick's back as he was ushered in.

Varick bore himself admirably. He was easy without being undignified, and Waythorn was conscious of cutting a much less impressive figure. Varick had no experience of business, and the talk prolonged itself for nearly an hour while Waythorn set forth with scrupulous precision the details of the proposed transaction.

"I'm awfully obliged to you," Varick said as he rose. "The fact is I'm not used to having much money to look after, and I don't want to make an ass of myself—" He smiled, and Waythorn could not help noticing that there was something pleasant about his smile. "It feels uncommonly queer to have enough cash to pay one's bills. I'd have sold my soul for it a few years ago!"

Waythorn winced at the allusion. He had heard it rumored that a lack of funds had been one of the determining causes of the Varick separation, but it did not occur to him that Varick's words were intentional. It seemed more likely that the desire to keep clear of embarrassing topics had fatally drawn him into one. Waythorn did not wish to be outdone in civility.

"We'll do the best we can for you," he said. "I think this is a good thing you're in."

"Oh, I'm sure it's immense. It's awfully good of you—" Varick broke off, embarrassed. "I suppose the thing's settled now—but if—"

"If anything happens before Sellers is about, I'll see you again," said Waythorn quietly. He was glad, in the end, to appear the more selfpossessed of the two.

The course of Lily's illness ran smooth, and as the days passed Waythorn grew used to the idea of Haskett's weekly visit. The first time the day came round, he stayed out late, and questioned his wife as to the visit on his return. She replied at once that Haskett had merely seen the nurse downstairs, as the doctor did not wish anyone in the child's sickroom till after the crisis.

The following week Waythorn was again conscious of the recurrence of the day, but had forgotten it by the time he came home to dinner. The crisis of the disease came a few days later, with a rapid decline of fever, and the little girl was pronounced out of danger. In the rejoicing which ensued the thought of Haskett passed out of Waythorn's mind, and one afternoon, letting himself into the house with a latchkey, he went straight to his library without noticing a shabby hat and umbrella in the hall.

In the library he found a small effaced-looking man with a thinnish gray beard sitting on the edge of a chair. The stranger might have been a piano tuner, or one of those mysteriously efficient persons who are summoned in emergencies to adjust some detail of domestic machinery. He blinked at Waythorn through a pair of gold-rimmed spectacles and said mildly: "Mr. Waythorn, I presume? I am Lily's father."

Waythorn flushed. "Oh—" he stammered uncomfortably. He broke off, disliking to appear rude. Inwardly he was trying to adjust the actual Haskett to the image of him projected by his wife's reminiscences. Waythorn had been allowed to infer that Alice's first husband was a brute.

"I am sorry to intrude," said Haskett, with his over-the-counter politeness.

"Don't mention it," returned Waythorn, collecting himself. "I suppose the nurse has been told?"

"I presume so. I can wait," said Haskett. He had a resigned way of speaking, as though life had worn down his natural powers of resistance.

Waythorn stood on the threshold, nervously pulling off his gloves.

"I'm sorry you've been detained. I will send for the nurse," he said; and as he opened the door he added with an effort: "I'm glad we can give you a good report of Lily." He winced as the *we* slipped out, but Haskett seemed not to notice it.

"Thank you, Mr. Waythorn, it's been an anxious time for me."

"Ah, well, that's past. Soon she'll be able to go to you." Waythorn nodded and passed out.

In his own room he flung himself down with a groan. He hated the womanish sensibility which made him suffer so acutely from the grotesque chances of life. He had known when he married that his wife's former husbands were both living, and that amid the multiplied contacts of modern existence there were a thousand chances to one that he would run against one or the other, yet he found himself as much disturbed by his brief encounter with Haskett as though the law had not obligingly removed all difficulties in the way of their meeting.

Waythorn sprang up and began to pace the room nervously. He had not suffered half as much from his two meetings with Varick. It was Haskett's presence in his own house that made the situation so intolerable. He stood still, hearing steps in the passage.

"This way, please," he heard the nurse say. Haskett was being taken upstairs, then: not a corner of the house but was open to him. Waythorn dropped into another chair, staring vaguely ahead of him. On his dressing table stood a photograph of Alice, taken when he had first known her. She was Alice Varick then—how fine and exquisite he had thought her! Those were Varick's pearls about her neck. At Waythorn's instance they had been returned before her marriage. Had Haskett ever given her any trinkets— and what had become of them, Waythorn wondered? He realized suddenly that he knew very little of Haskett's past or present situation; but from the man's appearance and manner of speech he could reconstruct with curious precision the surroundings of Alice's first marriage. And it startled him to think that she had, in the background of her life, a phase of existence so different from anything with which he had connected her. Varick, whatever his faults, was a gentleman, in the conventional, traditional sense of the term: the sense which at that moment seemed, oddly enough, to have most meaning to Waythorn. He and Varick had the same social habits, spoke the same language, understood the same allusions. But this other man ... it was grotesquely uppermost in Waythorn's mind that Haskett had worn a made-up tie attached with an elastic. Why should that ridiculous detail symbolize the whole man? Waythorn was exasperated by his own paltriness, but the fact of the tie expanded, forced itself on him, became as it were the key to Alice's past. He could see her, as Mrs. Haskett, sitting in a "front parlor" furnished in plush, with a pianola, and copy of *Ben Hur* on the center table. He could see her going to the theater with Haskett—or perhaps even to a "Church

Sociable"—she in a "picture hat" and Haskett in a black frock coat, a little creased, with the made-up tie on an elastic. On the way home they would stop and look at the illuminated shop windows, lingering over the photographs of New York actresses. On Sunday afternoons Haskett would take her for a walk, pushing Lily ahead of them in a white enameled perambulator, and Waythorn had a vision of the people they would stop and talk to. He could fancy how pretty Alice must have looked, in a dress adroitly constructed from the hints of a New York fashion paper, and how she must have looked down on the other women, chafing at her life, and secretly feeling that she belonged in a bigger place.

For the moment his foremost thought was one of wonder at the way in which she had shed the phase of existence which her marriage with Haskett implied. It was as if her whole aspect, every gesture, every inflection, every allusion, were a studied negation of that period of her life. If she had denied being married to Haskett she could hardly have stood more convicted of duplicity than in this obliteration of the self which had been his wife.

Waythorn started up, checking himself in the analysis of her motives. What right had he to create a fantastic effigy of her and then pass judgment on it? She had spoken vaguely of her first marriage as unhappy, had hinted, with becoming reticence, that Haskett had wrought havoc among her young illusions.... It was a pity for Waythorn's peace of mind that Haskett's very inoffensiveness shed a new light on the nature of those illusions. A man would rather think that his wife has been brutalized by her first husband than that the process has been reversed.

IV

"Mr. Waythorn, I don't like that French governess of Lily's."

Haskett, subdued and apologetic, stood before Waythorn in the library, revolving his shabby hat in his hand.

Waythorn, surprised in his armchair over the evening paper, stared back perplexedly at his visitor.

"You'll excuse my asking to see you," Haskett continued. "But this is my last visit, and I thought if I could have a word with you it would be a better way than writing to Mrs. Waythorn's lawyer."

Waythorn rose uneasily. He did not like the French governess either; but that was irrelevant.

"I am not so sure of that," he returned stiffly; "but since you wish it I will give your message to—my wife." He always hesitated over the possessive pronoun in addressing Haskett.

The latter sighed. "I don't know as that will help much. She didn't like it when I spoke to her."

Waythorn turned red. "When did you see her?" he asked.

"Not since the first day I came to see Lily—right after she was taken sick. I remarked to her then that I didn't like the governess."

Waythorn made no answer. He remembered distinctly that, after that first visit, he had asked his wife if she had seen Haskett. She had lied to him then, but she had respected his wishes since; and the incident cast a curious light on her character. He was sure she would not have seen Haskett that first day if she had divined that Waythorn would object, and the fact that she did not divine it was almost as disagreeable to the latter as the discovery that she had lied to him.

"I don't like the woman," Haskett was repeating with mild persistency. "She ain't straight, Mr. Waythorn—she'll teach the child to be underhand. I've noticed a change in Lily—she's too anxious to please—and she don't always tell the truth. She used to be the straightest child, Mr. Waythorn—" He broke off, his voice a little thick. "Not but what I want her to have a stylish education," he ended.

Waythorn was touched. "I'm sorry, Mr. Haskett; but frankly, I don't quite see what I can do."

Haskett hesitated. Then he laid his hat on the table, and advanced to the hearthrug, on which Waythorn was standing. There was nothing aggressive in his manner, but he had the solemnity of a timid man resolved on a decisive measure.

"There's just one thing you can do, Mr. Waythorn," he said. "You can remind Mrs. Waythorn that, by the decree of the courts, I am entitled to have a voice in Lily's bringing-up." He paused, and went on more deprecatingly: "I'm not the kind to talk about enforcing my rights, Mr. Waythorn. I don't know as I think a man is entitled to rights he hasn't known how to hold on to; but this business of the child is different. I've never let go there—and I never mean to."

The scene left Waythorn deeply shaken. Shamefacedly, in indirect ways, he had been finding out about Haskett; and all that he had learned was favorable. The little man, in order to be near his daughter, had sold out his share in a profitable business in Utica, and accepted a modest clerkship in a New York manufacturing house. He boarded in a shabby street and had few acquaintances. His passion for Lily filled his life. Waythorn felt that this exploration of Haskett was like groping about with a dark lantern in his wife's past; but he saw now that there were recesses his lantern had not explored. He had never inquired into the exact circumstances of his wife's first matrimonial rupture. On the surface all had been fair. It was she who had obtained the divorce, and the court had given her the child. But Waythorn knew how many ambiguities such a verdict might cover. The mere fact that Haskett retained a right over his daughter implied an unsuspected compromise. Waythorn was an idealist. He always refused to recognize unpleasant contingencies till he found himself confronted with them, and then he saw them followed by a spectral train of consequences. His next days were thus haunted, and he determined to try to lay the ghosts by conjuring them up in his wife's presence.

When he repeated Haskett's request a flame of anger passed over her face; but she subdued it instantly and spoke with a slight quiver of outraged motherhood.

"It is very ungentlemanly of him," she said.

The word grated on Waythorn. "That is neither here nor there. It's a bare question of rights."

She murmured: "It's not as if he could ever be a help to Lily—"

Waythorn flushed. This was even less to his taste. "The question is," he repeated, "what authority has he over her?"

She looked downward, twisting herself a little in her seat. "I am willing to see him—I thought you objected," she faltered.

In a flash he understood that she knew the extent of Haskett's claims. Perhaps it was not the first time she had resisted them.

"My objecting has nothing to do with it," he said coldly; "if Haskett has a right to be consulted you must consult him."

She burst into tears, and he saw that she expected him to regard her as a victim.

Haskett did not abuse his rights. Waythorn had felt miserably sure that he would not. But the governess was dismissed, and from time to time the little man demanded an interview with Alice. After the first outburst she accepted the situation with her usual adaptability. Haskett had once reminded Waythorn of the piano tuner, and Mrs. Waythorn, after a month or two, appeared to class him with that domestic familiar. Waythorn could not but respect the father's tenacity. At first he had tried to cultivate the suspicion that Haskett might be "up to" something, that he had an object in securing a foothold in the house. But in his heart Waythorn was sure of Haskett's single-mindedness; he even guessed in the latter a mild contempt for such advantages as his relation with the Waythorns might offer. Haskett's sincerity of purpose made him invulnerable, and his successor had to accept him as a lien on the property.

Mr. Sellers was sent to Europe to recover from his gout, and Varick's affairs hung on Waythorn's hands. The negotiations were prolonged and complicated; they necessitated frequent conferences between the two men, and the interests of the firm forbade Waythorn's suggesting that his client should transfer his business to another office.

Varick appeared well in the transaction. In moments of relaxation his coarse streak appeared, and Waythorn dreaded his geniality; but in the office he was concise and clear-headed, with a flattering deference to Waythorn's judgment. Their business relations being so affably established, it would have been absurd for the two men to ignore each other in society. The first time they met in a drawing room, Varick took up their intercourse in the same easy key, and his hostess' grateful glance obliged Waythorn to respond to it. After that they ran across each other frequently, and one evening at a ball Waythorn, wandering through the remoter rooms, came upon Varick seated beside his wife. She colored a little, and faltered in what she was saying; but Varick nodded to Waythorn without rising, and the latter strolled on.

In the carriage, on the way home, he broke out nervously: "I didn't know you spoke to Varick."

Her voice trembled a little. "It's the first time—he happened to be standing near me; I didn't know what to do. It's so awkward, meeting everywhere—and he said you had been very kind about some business."

"That's different," said Waythorn.

She paused a moment. "I'll do just as you wish," she returned pliantly. "I thought it would be less awkward to speak to him when we meet."

Her pliancy was beginning to sicken him. Had she really no will of her own—no theory about her relation to these men? She had accepted Haskett—did she mean to accept Varick? It was "less awkward," as she had said, and her instinct was to evade difficulties or to circumvent them. With sudden vividness Waythorn saw how the instinct had developed. She was "as easy as an old shoe"—a shoe that too many feet had worn. Her elasticity was the result of tension in too many different directions. Alice Haskett— Alice Varick—Alice Waythorn—she had been each in turn, and had left hanging to each name a little of her privacy, a little of her personality, a little of the inmost self where the unknown god abides.

"Yes—it's better to speak to Varick," said Waythorn wearily.

V

The winter wore on, and society took advantage of the Waythorns' acceptance of Varick. Harassed hostesses were grateful to them for bridging over a social difficulty, and Mrs. Waythorn was held up as a miracle of good taste. Some experimental spirits could not resist the diversion of throwing Varick and his former wife together, and there were those who thought he found a zest in the propinquity. But Mrs. Waythorn's conduct remained irreproachable. She neither avoided Varick nor sought him out. Even Waythorn could not but admit that she had discovered the solution of the newest social problem.

He had married her without giving much thought to that problem. He had fancied that a woman can shed her past like a man. But now he saw that Alice was bound to hers both by the circumstances which forced her into continued relation with it, and by the traces it had left on her nature. With grim irony Waythorn compared himself to a member of a syndicate. He held so many shares in his wife's personality and his predecessors were his partners in the business. If there had been any element of passion in the transaction he would have felt less deteriorated by it. The fact that Alice took her change of husbands like a change of weather reduced the situation to mediocrity. He could have forgiven her for blunders, for excesses; for resisting Haskett, for yielding to Varick; for anything but her acquiescence and her tact. She reminded him of a juggler tossing knives; but the knives were blunt and she knew they would never cut her.

And then, gradually, habit formed a protecting surface for his sensibilities. If he paid for each day's comfort with the small change of his illusions, he grew daily to value the comfort more and set less store upon the coin. He had drifted into a dulling propinquity with Haskett and Varick and he took refuge in the cheap revenge of satirizing the situation. He even began to reckon up the advantages which accrued from it, to ask himself if it were not better to own a third of a wife who knew how to make a man happy than a whole one who had lacked opportunity to acquire the art. For it *was* an art, and made up, like all others, of concessions, eliminations and embellishments; of lights judiciously thrown and shadows skillfully softened. His wife knew exactly how to manage the lights, and he knew exactly to what training she owed her skill. He even tried to trace the source of his obligations, to discriminate between the influences which had combined to produce his domestic happiness: he perceived that Haskett's commonness had made Alice worship good breeding, while Varick's liberal construction of the marriage bond had taught her to value the conjugal virtues; so that he was directly indebted to his predecessors for the devotion which made his life easy if not inspiring.

From this phase he passed into that of complete acceptance. He ceased to satirize himself because time dulled the irony of the situation and the joke lost its humor with its sting. Even the sight of Haskett's hat on the hall table had ceased to touch the springs of epigram. The hat was often seen there now, for it had been decided that it was better for Lily's father to visit her than for the little girl to go to his boardinghouse. Waythorn, having acquiesced in this arrangement, had been surprised to find how little difference it made. Haskett was never obtrusive, and the few visitors who met him on the stairs were unaware of his identity. Waythorn did not know how often he saw Alice, but with himself Haskett was seldom in contact.

One afternoon, however, he learned on entering that Lily's father was waiting to see him. In the library he found Haskett occupying a chair in his usual provisional way. Waythorn always felt grateful to him for not leaning back.

"I hope you'll excuse me, Mr. Waythorn," he said rising. "I wanted to see Mrs. Waythorn about Lily, and your man asked me to wait here till she came in."

"Of course," said Waythorn, remembering that a sudden leak had that morning given over the drawing room to the plumbers.

He opened his cigar case and held it out to his visitor, and Haskett's acceptance seemed to mark a fresh stage in their intercourse. The spring evening was chilly, and Waythorn invited his guest to draw up his chair to the fire. He meant to find an excuse to leave Haskett in a moment; but he was tired and cold, and after all the little man no longer jarred on him.

The two were enclosed in the intimacy of their blended cigar smoke when the door opened and Varick walked into the room. Waythorn rose abruptly. It was the first time that Varick had come to the house, and the surprise of seeing him, combined with the singular inopportuneness of his arrival, gave a new edge to Waythorn's blunted sensibilities. He stared at his visitor without speaking.

Varick seemed too preoccupied to notice his host's embarrassment.

"My dear fellow," he exclaimed in his most expansive tone, "I must apologize for tumbling in on you in this way, but I was too late to catch you downtown, and so I thought—"

He stopped short, catching sight of Haskett, and his sanguine color deepened to a flush which spread vividly under his scant blond hair. But in a moment he recovered himself and nodded slightly. Haskett returned the bow in silence, and Waythorn was still groping for speech when the footman came in carrying a tea table.

The intrusion offered a welcome vent to Waythorn's nerves. "What the deuce are you bringing this here for?" he said sharply.

"I beg your pardon, sir, but the plumbers are still in the drawing room, and Mrs. Waythorn said she would have tea in the library." The footman's perfectly respectful tone implied a reflection on Waythorn's reasonableness.

"Oh, very well," said the latter resignedly, and the footman proceeded to open the folding tea table and set out its complicated appointments. While this interminable process continued the three men stood motionless, watching it with a fascinated stare, till Waythorn, to break the silence, said to Varick, "Won't you have a cigar?"

He held out the case he had just tendered to Haskett, and Varick helped himself with a smile. Waythorn looked about for a match, and finding none, proffered a light from his own cigar. Haskett, in the background held his ground mildly, examining his cigar tip now and then, and stepping forward at the right moment to knock its ashes into the fire.

The footman at last withdrew, and Varick immediately began: "If I could just say half a word to you about this business—"

"Certainly," stammered Waythorn; "in the dining room—"

But as he placed his hand on the door it opened from without, and his wife appeared on the threshold.

She came in fresh and smiling, in her street dress and hat, shedding a fragrance from the boa which she loosened in advancing.

"Shall we have tea in here, dear?" she began; and then she caught sight of Varick. Her smile deepened, veiling a slight tremor of surprise.

"Why, how do you do?" she said with a distinct note of pleasure.

As she shook hands with Varick she saw Haskett standing behind him. Her smile faded for a moment, but she recalled it quickly, with a scarcely perceptible side glance at Waythorn.

"How do you do, Mr. Haskett?" she said, and shook hands with him a shade less cordially.

The three men stood awkwardly before her, till Varick, always the most self-possessed, dashed into an explanatory phrase.

"We—I had to see Waythorn a moment on business," he stammered, brick-red from chin to nape.

Haskett stepped forward with his air of mild obstinacy. "I am sorry to intrude; but you appointed five o'clock—" he directed his resigned glance to the timepiece on the mantel.

She swept aside their embarrassment with a charming gesture of hospitality.

"I'm so sorry—I'm always late; but the afternoon was so lovely." She stood drawing off her gloves, propitiatory and graceful, diffusing about her a sense of ease and familiarity in which the situation lost its grotesqueness. "But before talking business," she added brightly, "I'm sure everyone wants a cup of tea."

She dropped into her low chair by the tea table, and the two visitors, as if drawn by her smile, advanced to receive the cups she held out.

She glanced about for Waythorn, and he took the third cup with a laugh.

1904

The Life Apart (*L'âme close*)[1]

The Mount.[2] Oct 29th 1907.

If you had not enclosed that sprig of wych-hazel in your note I should not have opened this long-abandoned book; for the note in itself might have meant nothing—would have meant nothing to me—beyond the inference that you had a more "personal" accent than week-end visitors usually put into their leave-takings. But you sent the wych-hazel—& sent it without a word—thus telling me (as I choose to think!) that you knew what was in my mind when I found it blooming on that wet bank in the woods, where we sat together & smoked a cigarette while the chains were put on the wheels of the motor.

And so it happens that, finding myself—after so long!—with some one to talk to, I take up this empty volume, in which, long ago, I made one or two spasmodic attempts to keep a diary. For I had no one but myself to talk to, & it is absurd to write down what one says of to one's self; but now I shall have the illusion that I am talking to you, & that—as when I picked the wych-hazel—something of what I say will somehow reach you. . . .

Your evening here the other day was marked by curious symbols; for the day before you arrived we had our first autumn snow-storm (we have October snow in these hills); & on the bank where you & I sat we found the first sprig of the "old woman's flower"—the flower that blooms in the autumn!

Nov. 27th Your letter from Paris . . .

* * *

[1]French: the enclosed soul. "The Life Apart" is published with the permission of both the Lilly Library, Indiana University, Bloomington, Indiana, and the Watkins/Loomis Agency, agents for the estate of Edith Wharton. It was first published in full in *American Literature* 66 (December 1994): 663–88, edited by Kenneth M. Price and Phyllis McBride. The editors of *The Heath Anthology* wish to thank them for sharing the fruits of their labor with us and with our students.

Ellipses and revisions are Wharton's; brackets indicate material that is unclear in the original manuscript.

[2]Wharton's home in Lenox, Massachusetts.

February 21ˢᵗ.

All these months I thought after all I had been mistaken; & my poor "âme close" barred its shutters & bolted its doors again, & the dust gathered & the cobwebs thickened in the empty rooms, where for a moment I had heard an echo. . . .

Then we went to Herblay. Such a cold, sad winter day, with the wind beating the bare trees, & a leaden sieve between brown banks! In the church it was still & dim, & in the shadowy corner where I sat while you talked with the curé, a veiled figure stole up & looked at me a moment. Was its name Happiness? I dared not lift the veil . . .

When you came to dine, two nights afterward, you said things that distressed me. At first it was exquisite. I had my work, & you sat near the lamp, & read me a page of Chevrillon's article in the Revue de Paris—the article on Meredith that I had told you about.[3] And as I followed you, seeing your mind leap ahead, as it always does, noting how you instantly singled out the finer values I had missed—discriminated, classified, with that flashing, illuminating sense of differences & relations that so exquisitely distinguishes your thought—ah, the illusion I had, of a life in which such evenings might be a dear, accepted habit! At that moment indeed, "the hour became her husband . . ."[4]

Why did you spoil it? Because men & women are different, because—in that respect—w in the way of mental companionship—what I can give you is so much less interesting, less arresting, than what I receive from you? It was as if there stood between us at that moment a the frailest of glass cups, filled with a rare colourless liquid wine—& with a gesture you broke the glass & spilled the drops.

You hurt me—you disillusionized me—& when you left me I was more deeply yours . . . Ah, the confused processes within us!

Feb. 22ᵈ.

How can I ever dream that life has in store for me a single moment of happiness? . . . This is the day on which we were to have gone together to M . . . l'A[5] . . . a whole day together in the country!—I said to myself all the week: "I have never in my life known what it was to be happy (as a woman understands happiness) even for a single hour—now at last I shall be happy for a whole day, talking à coeur ouvert,[6] saying for once what I feel, and *all that I feel*, as other women do . . . Ah, pauvre âme close! Y ai-je vraiment cru un seul instant? Non, je savais trop bien que quand il s'agit de moi les Erynnies de dorment jamais, hélas.[7] . . .

---

[3]André Chevrillon was a nephew of the historian Hippolite Taine and wrote about English literature.
[4]The line comes from sonnet forty-seven of George Meredith's "Modern Love."
[5]Montfort l'Amaury.

[6]French: with open heart.
[7]French: Oh, poor enclosed soul! Did I truly believe it for even a single moment? No, I know too well that when it is a question of myself, the Furies never sleep.

~~Un retour inattendu changed everything; I am back in the tread mill
again~~ ...[8] I had to put you off, by a vague note, not daring to be explicit—&
you were hurt, you didn't understand—& the sky is all dark again ...

And here is the day—soft & sunny, with spring in the air ... Some other
woman's day, not mine ...

Ame close.[9]

My soul is like a house that dwellers nigh
Can see no light in. "Ah, poor house," they say,
"Long since its owners died or went their way.
Thick ivy loops the rusted door-latch tie,
The chimney rises cold against the sky,
And flowers turned weed down the bare paths ~~in the dry
cold earth~~ decay" ...
Yet one stray passer, at the shut of day,
Sees a light tremble in a casement high.

Even so, my soul would set a light for you,
A light invisible to all beside,
As though a lover's ghost should yearn & glide
From pane to pane, to let the flame shine through.
Yet enter not, lest, as it flits ahead,
You see the hand that carries it is dead.
Feb. 21st.

March 3^{d}

The other night at the theatre, when you came into the box—that little, dim
baignoire (no. 13, I shall always remember!) I felt for the first time that indescribable current of communication flowing between myself & some one else—
felt it, I mean, uninterruptedly, securely, so that it penetrated every sense &
every thought ... & said to myself: "This must be what happy women feel....."

(The theatre was the Renaissance.)

And we had another dear half-hour, coming back from St C—last Sunday in the motor. It was snowing—the first snow of the winter!—& the
flakes froze on the windows, shutting us in, shutting everything else out ...
I felt your *dearest* side then, the side that is simple & sensitive & true ... &
I felt that all that must have been, at first, so unintelligible to you in me &
in my life, was clear at last, & that our hearts & our minds met ...

I should like to be to you, friend of my heart, like a touch of wings
brushing by you in the darkness, or like the scent of an ~~unseen~~ invisible garden, that one passes on an unknown road at night ...

* * *

[8]French: an unexpected return.   [9]This poem is by Wharton.

April 20th.

I haven't written for six weeks or more. I have been afraid to write … Since then I have had my "day"—two "days" … one at Montfort, one at Provins. I have known "what happy women feel"…. with the pang, all through, every moment, of what heart-broken women feel! Ah, comme j'avais raison de vous ecrire[10]: "I didn't know what it would be like."—

For a month now I have been here alone—in another month I shall be gone. *It will be over.* Those four words are always before me, day & night; & yet I don't understand them, they mean nothing to me … What! I shall be gone, I shan't see you, I shan't hear your voice, I shan't wake up to think: "In so many hours we shall meet, my hand will be in his, my eyes will be in his." . . ? But what shall I *be* then? Nothing else lives in me now but *you*— I have no conscious existence outside the thought of you, the feeling of you. I, who dominated life, stood aside from it so, how I am humbled, absorbed, without a shred of will or identity left! All I want is to be near you, to feel my hands in yours. Ah, if you ever read these pages you will know you have been loved!

Sometimes I am calm, exalted almost, so enclosed & satisfied in the thought of you, that I could say to you truly, as I did yesterday: "I never wonder what you are doing when you are not with me." At such moments I feel as though all the mysticism in me—the transcendentalism that in other women turns to religion—were poured into my feeling for you, giving me a sense of *immanence*, of inseparableness from you.—In one of these moods, the other day, when you were reproaching me for never giving you any sign of my love for you, I felt like answering: "But there is a contact of thoughts that seems so much closer than a kiss" …

Then there are other days, tormented days—this is one of them—when that sense of mystic nearness fails me, when in your absence I long, I ache for you, I feel that what I want is to be in your arms, to be held fast there— "like other women!" And then comes the terrible realization of the fugitiveness of it all, the weariness of the struggle, the à quoi bon?,[11] the failing courage, the mortal weakness—the blind cry: "I want you! I want you!" that bears down everything else …

And sometimes you say to me: "Ah, *si* vous m'aimiez d'amour"—Si je vous aimais, mon amour![12]

April 25th.

Less than a month now! Sursum corda![13] Let us not think of such things, when there is so much gained of exquisite & imperishable, "beyond the reach of accident" …

---

[10]French: Oh, how right I was to write to you.
[11]French: what's the use?
[12]French: "Oh, *if* you truly loved me"—if I loved you, my love!

[13]Heart on high! From *The Episcopal Book of Common Prayer*.

The day before yesterday, when I made you some answer that surprised & amused you, & you exclaimed: "Oh, the joy of *seeing around things together!*," I felt for the first time that you understood what I mean by the thoughts that are closer than a kiss.—And yet *I* understand now, for the first time, how thought may be dissolved in feeling, & what Dante meant when he {???} said: "Donne che avete l'intelletto d'amore"....[14]

Malgrè moi,[15] I am a little humbled, a little ashamed, to find how poor a thing I am, how the personality I had moulded into such strong firm lines has crumbled to a pinch of ashes in this flame! For the first time in my life *I can't read* ... I hold the book in my hand, & {???} see your name all over the page!—I always thought I should know how to bear suffering better than happiness, & so it is ... I am stupified, anéantie[16] ... There lies the profound difference between man & woman. What enlarges & enriches life for the one, eliminates everything but itself for the other.—Now & then I say to myself: "Je vais me ressaisir"—mais saisir quoi?[17] This pinch of ashes that slips through my fingers? Oh, my free, proud, secure soul, where are you? *What were you*, to escape me like this? . . . .

It is curious how the scraps of verses I wrote from time to time in the past, when a wave of Beauty rushed over me, & felt *I must tell some one!*—it is curious how they express what I am feeling now, how they say more than I then understood, & how they go straight to you, like homing birds released long long ago by a hand that knew not whence they came!

April 27ᵗʰ

A note comes almost every morning now. It is brought in on my breakfast-tray, with the other letters, & there is the delicious moment of postponement, when one leaves it unopened while one pours the tea, just in order to "savourer"[18] longer the joy that is coming!—Ah, how I see in all this the instinctive longing to pack every moment of my present with all the wasted, driven-in feeling of the past! One should be happy in one's youth to be happy freely, carelessly, *extravagantly*! How I hoard & tremble over each incident & sign! I am like a hungry beggar who crumbles up the crust he has found in order to make it last longer! ... And then comes the opening of the letter, the slipping of the little silver knife under the flap (which one would never tear!), the first glance to see how many pages there are, the second to see how it ends, & then the return to the beginning, the breathless first reading, & the slow lingering again over each phrase & each word, the taking possession, the absorbing of them one by one, & finally the choosing of the one that will be carried in one's thoughts all day, making an exquisite accompaniment to all the dull prose of life ... Sometimes I think the moment of reading the letter is the best of all—I think that till I see you again, &

---

[14]Italian: "Women who have the intellect of love."

[15]French: in spite of myself.

[16]French: crushed.

[17]French: "I go to capture myself"—but to capture what?

[18]French: savor.

then, when you are *there*, & my hands are in yours, & *my soul is in my hands*, then what grey ghosts the letters all become!.....

May 3ᵈ.

Yesterday at Beauvais.—a memory bathed with ~~the~~ light. . . . You did not want to go, objecting that with H.J.[19] it would not be like our excursions à deux.[20] But I could not make up my mind to go without you, & I *begged* (so against my usual habit!), & you yielded.

You write me this morning that ~~your~~ you want me to know "how delicious" it all was . . . I think you really found it so . . . Alone with you I am often shy & awkward, tormented by the fear that I may not please you—but with our dear H.J. I felt at my ease, & full of the "motor nonsense" that always seizes me after one of these long flights through the air. And what a flight it was! History & romance & natural loveliness every mile of the way—across the windings of Seine & Oise, through the grey old towns piled up above their rivers, through the melting spring landscape, all tender green & snowy fruit-blossoms, against black slopes of fir—till a last climb brought us out above the shimmering plain, with Beauvais choir rising "like a white Albi" on its ledge . . .

Then the lazy, happy luncheon in the warm court-yard of the Hôtel d'Angleterre, with dogs & children playing, canaries singing, flowers blooming about the little fountain—the coffee & cigarettes in the sunshine, & the slow stroll through the narrow streets first to St Etienne, then through the bright variegated fair which filled the Grande Place—till, guided by you, we reached the little lane behind the ~~choir~~ cathedral, & saw, far up against the blue, the soaring, wheeling choir—"saw it turn", as you put it, "cosmically spin through space . . ."

Then, inside, the sense of ~~immense~~ glad upward rush of all these converging lives—"gladness," as H.J. said, is the dominant note within the church—The mystic impression of something swung aloft, suspended, "qui plane"[21] in supernatural levitation—&, while H.J. made the tour of the ambulatory, ~~[your]~~ our little minute, sitting outside on the steps in the sunshine; with the "*Dear, are you happy?*" that made it all yours & mine, that drew the great miracle down into the compass of our two hearts—our one heart . . . . . .

May 3ᵈ. Only, after such days, the blankness, the intolerableness of the morrow—the day when one does not see you! What a pity that one cannot live longer in the memory of such hours—that the eager heart must always reach out for more, & more! I used to think: "If I could be happy for a week—an hour!" And now I am asking to be happy all the rest of my life . . .

Sometimes I think that if I could go off with you for twenty-four hours to a little inn in the country, in the depths of a green wood, I should ask no

[19]Henry James. [21]French: that soars.
[20]French: together.

more. Just to have one long day & quiet evening with you, & the next morning to be still together—oh, how I ache for it sometimes! But how I should ache for it again when it was over—& oh, the sweet, vain impossible pictures it would evoke! Poor hearts, in this shifting stream of life, so hungry for permanence & security!—As I wrote these lines I suddenly said to myself: "*I will go with him once before we separate.*"

How strange to feel one's self all at once "Jenseits von Gut und Böse"[22] ... It would hurt no one—it would give me my first, last, draught of life ... Why not? I have always laughed at the "mala prohibita"[23]—"bugbears to frighten children." The anti-social act is the only one that is harmful "per se". And, as you told me the other day—*and as I needed no telling!*—what I have given already is far, far more.......

May 5th. How I love the queer letter paper with ~~ruled~~ criss-cross rulings on which you write me at night, chez le restaurateur du coin,[24] on your way home! There seems to ~~me~~ be more feeling in what you say on that humble poor paper, on which the fashionable & the conventional are never expressed!

You say in your note of last night: "We are behind the scenes together— *on the hither side*" ... Just a few hours after I had written that "*Jenseits*" above there ... Such coincidences make it seem true, don't they?

May 7th. The night before last you dined with me alone. Yesterday evening we had planned to go to Versailles & dine. But the weather was doubtful, you were likely to be detained late at yr work, & I was afraid of appearing eager to go when you were less so. (By note & telephone, one can explain nothing.) So we missed our dear, dear evening, & this morning you write: "Instead of being stupidly sundered, we might have been happy together."—Let us not lose one of the few remaining chances to "be happy together" ... Strange words!—that I never spoke, or heard spoken to me, before ... I appear to myself like a new creature opening dazzled eyes on a new world. C'est l'aube![25]

May 9th   La Châtaignerie.
                                                                      Montmorency.

[A flower is pressed onto this page.]

May 13th.

Something gave me the impression the other day that we were watched in this house ... commented on.—Ah, how a great love needs to be a happy & open love! How degraded I feel by other people's degrading thoughts ...

*   *   *

---

[22]German: beyond good and evil. Wharton was reading Nietzsche at the time.
[23]"Forbidden evils."

[24]French: at the corner restaurant.
[25]French: It is dawn!

We met the other day at the Louvre, & walked to St. Germain l'Auxerrois. Then we took a motor, & went over to "Les Arènes de Lutéce," & then to St Etienne du Mont . . . Then we walked to the Luxembourg, & sat for a long time in a quiet corner under the trees. But what I long for, these last days, is to be with you alone, far off, in quietness—held fast, peacefully, "while close as lips lean, lean the thoughts between."[26] . . . There is no use in trying to look at things together. We don't see them any longer . . .

Senlis. May 16th

Hung high against the perfect blue,
Like flame the belfry trembled higher,
Like leafage let the bird-flights through,
Like incense wreathed its melting spire.

From the dim vantage, lilacs hung,
Niched in the Roman rampart's strength,
We watched the foaming clouds that swung
Against the church's island-length;

~~The sheet of emerald foliage spread~~
~~Like some deep inlet's inmost reach~~
~~Between the cliff like towers o'erhead,~~
~~The low slate roof that [framed] their beach~~

We watched, & felt the tides of time
Coil round our hidden leafy place,
Sweep on through changing race & clime,
And leave us at the heart of space,

In some divine transcendent hush
Where light & darkness melt & cease,
Staying the awful cosmic rush
To give two hearts an hour of peace.....

So deep the peace, so h ours the hour,
When night-fall & the fiery train
Had swept us from our high-built bower,
And out across the dreaming plain,

Stillness yet brooded in our souls,
And even our rushing chariot stayed,
Loitering through aisles of silvery boles,
In some remote & star-laced glade,

[26]The line is from "Ogrin the Hermit," a poem
    Wharton was composing.

Where through the pale & secret night,
Past gleams of water, depths of shade,
Under a low moon's golden light
I felt the quiet fields outspread—

And there, on the calm air afloat,
While silence held the throbbing train,
Some thrush from immemorial throat
Poured all the sweetness, all the pain.

May 19th

I didn't suppose that, to a creature as exacting, scrutinizing, analytical as I am, life could hold an absolutely perfect day—but it came to me last week at Senlis ... I see you still, meeting me at the station when I drove up at 11.20.—We were together from then till 9.15 in the evening.—The sense of peace those long hours gave! And yet how they rushed & swept us with them!—But there came a moment of divine, deep calm, when, alone in the train returning to Paris, we watched the full moon rise, & heard the thrush on the lisière des bois[27] filling the night with what was in our hearts.—I knew then, dearest dear, all that I had never known before—the interfusion of spirit & sense, the double nearness, the [blest] the mingled communion of touch & thought ... One such hour ought to irradiate a whole life—

Yesterday I went with you to see the répétition générale of Polyphème[28].... I don't suppose you knew—since it is more of my sex than yours—the quiet ecstasy I feel in sitting next you in a public place, looking now & then at the way the hair grows on your forehead, at the line of your profile turned to the stage, your attitude, your expression—while every drop of blood in my body whispers: "Mine—mine—mine!"....

Then we went to the Tuileries, & found a quiet seat under the trees, on the terrace above the Seine ... I am always glad to go with you to some new place, so that in the empty future years I may say, going there alone: "We were here together once". It will make the world less empty. And I shall always remember now that, sitting under that tree, you said to me: "My love! my darling!" while people walked up & down before us, not knowing— not knowing *that it was not worth their while to be alive.*.......

May 21st.

My two months, my incredible two months, are almost over! ... I have drunk of the wine of life at last, I have known the thing best worth knowing, I have been warmed through & through, never to grow quite cold again till the end....

---

[27]French: edge of the woods.   [28]Dress rehearsal of Samain's play *Polyphème*.

Oh, Life, Life, how I give thanks to you for this! How right I was to trust you, to know that my day would come, & to be too proud, & too confident of my fate, to take for a moment any lesser gift, any smaller happiness than this that you had in store for me!

How often I used to say to myself: "No one can love life as I do, love the beauty & the splendour & the ardour, & find words for them as I can, without having a share in them some day"—I mean the dear intimate share that one guessed at, always, beyond & behind their universal thrill!—And the day came—the day has *been*—& I have poured into it all my stored-up joy of living, all my sense of the beauty & mystery of the world, every impression of joy & loveliness, in sight or sound or touch, that I ever figured to myself in all the lovely days when I used to weave such sensations into a [perf] veil of colour to hide the great blank behind. . . . .

May 22^d. The last Day.

My room is full of the traces of packing for tomorrow's departure . . . On the bed, the sofa, every chair, the dresses, cloaks, hats, tea-gowns, I have worn these last six months . . . There is the black dress I had on the first time we went to the Sorbonne, to hear B.—[29]lecture last December. I remember thinking: "Will he like me in it?" And of how many of the others, afterward, I had the same thought! And when you noticed one of my dresses, & praised it, quelle joie![30] I used to say to myself: "It must be becoming, or I or he never would have thought it pretty." . . . .

There is the dress teagown I wore the first night you dined with me alone . . . You liked it, you said. . . . And here is the one dress I wore the day we went to Herblay, when, in the church, for a moment, the Veiled Happiness stole up to me. . . . . Here is the grey dress, with Irish lace,

May 24th At sea—on the way home.
10. a.m.

Yesterday morning you wrote those lines on the opposite page . . . Just twenty four hours ago, you handed me this book, which I had lent you overnight, & sat beside me in the compartment of the Hâvre train. How far away we seemed from each other already, while we waited for the train to start! With people coming & going, & the good gay L.R.K.,[31] all unconscious, & lingering between us to the last, how futile it seemed to be together! Yet we *were* together, at least—our eyes could meet, I saw your forehead, & the way the hair lies on it—when shall I see that again?—Through the window, when the train started, I saw you lingering to wave a goodbye; & I had to wave & smile at you—to smile at that moment!

[29]Frank Baker, an American professor who lectured on Elizabethan playwrights.
[30]French: what joy!
[31]Le Roy King, Wharton's younger second cousin.

And now the sea is between us, & silence, & the long days, & the inexorable fate that binds me here & you there.

It is over, my Heart, all over!—

Et on ~~en~~ n'en meurt pas, hélas!³²

May 25th. At sea.

> When I am gone, recall my hair,
> Not for the light it used to hold,
> But that your touch~~ed~~ enmeshèd there,
> Has turned it to a younger gold.
>
> Recall my hands, that were not soft
> Or white or fine beyond expressing,
> Till they had slept so long & oft,
> So warm & close, in your possessing.
>
> Recall my eyes, that used to lie
> Blind pools with summer's wreckage strewn.
> You cleared the drifts, but in their sky
> You hung no image but your own.
>
> Recall my mouth, that knew not how
> A kiss is cradled & takes wing,
> ~~But~~ Yet fluttered like a nest-hung bough
> When you had touched it like the spring ...

At Sea
May 26th

Herblay ... Montfort l'Amaury ... Provins ... Beauvais ... Montmorency ... Senlis ... Meudon ...

What dear, sweet, crowding memories! What wealth for a heart that was empty this time last year. How the wych-hazel has kept its promise, since it flowered in our hands last October!—Bring me, magic flower, one more day such as those—but dearer, nearer, by all these death-pangs of separation with which my heart is torn!

The Mount. May [31st].

Arrived yesterday.—
At sea I could bear it. Ici j'étouffe ...³³
In the train yesterday I was reading Lock's Heredity & Variation, & struck by a curious & rather amusing passage, held it out & said: "Read that."

---

³²French: And we die not (of heartbreak), alas!   ³³French: Here, I am suffocating.

The answer was: "Does that sort of thing really amuse you?"—I heard the key turn in my prison-lock.—That is the answer to everything worth while!

Oh, Gods of derision! And you've given me over twenty years of it! Je n'en peut plus ...[34]

And yet I must be just. I have stood it all these years, & hardly felt it, because I had created a world of ~~mine~~ my own, in which I ~~lif~~ lived without heeding what went on outside. But since I have known what it was to have some one enter into that world & live there with me, the mortal solitude I came back to has become terrible ...

June 12th

I have not written again in this book since my return, because I have written to you instead, my own dear Love, answering the letters you have sent me by every steamer ...

But yesterday your letter of June 2[d] came, & I learned from it that you will certainly not come here till the autumn, & that all your future is in doubt. You don't even know where you will be next winter—at the ends of the Earth, perhaps!—Leagues beyond leagues of distance seems to have widened between us since I read that letter—all hope forsook me, & I sent you back a desperate word: "Don't write to me again! Let me face at once the fact *that it is over*. Without a date to look to, I can't bear to go on, & it will be easier to make the break now, voluntarily, than to see it slowly, agonizingly made by time & circumstance."—

So I felt ~~now~~ then, so I still feel—but, oh, my adored, my own Love, you who have given me the only moments of real life I have ever known, how am I to face the long hours & days before I learn again the old hard lesson of "how existence may be cherished, strengthened & fed, without the aid of joy"?—

I knew that lesson once, but I have unlearned it—you have kissed away the memory of it.... If you knew how I repeat to myself: "I have had my hour, & I am grateful for it!" Yes—but the human heart is insatiable, & I didn't know, my own, I didn't know!—

I wrote of Senlis:—"One such hour ought to irradiate a whole life."—Eh bien, non—ce n'est pas assez![35]

The Eyes

We had been put in the mood for ghosts, that evening, after an excellent dinner at our old friend Culwin's, by a tale of Fred Murchard's—the narrative of a strange personal invitation.

Seen through the haze of our cigars, and by the drowsy gleam of a coal fire, Culwin's library, with its oak walls and dark old bindings, made a good setting for such evocations; and ghostly experiences at first hand

[34]French: I can stand it no longer.　　　[35]French: Very well; no, it is not enough!

being, after Murchard's opening, the only kind acceptable to us, we proceeded to take stock of our group and tax each member for a contribution. There were eight of us, and seven contrived, in a manner more or less adequate, to fulfill the condition imposed. It surprised us all to find that we could muster such a show of supernatural impressions, for none of us, excepting Murchard himself and young Phil Frenham—whose story was the slightest of the lot—had the habit of sending our souls into the invisible. So that, on the whole, we had every reason to be proud of our seven "exhibits," and none of us would have dreamed of expecting an eighth from our host.

Our old friend, Mr. Andrew Culwin, who had sat back in his armchair, listening and blinking through the smoke circles with the cheerful tolerance of a wise old idol, was not the kind of man likely to be favored with such contacts, though he had imagination enough to enjoy, without envying, the superior privileges of his guests. By age and by education he belonged to the stout Positivist tradition, and his habit of thought had been formed in the days of the epic struggle between physics and metaphysics. But he had been, then and always, essentially a spectator, a humorous detached observer of the immense muddled variety show of life, slipping out of his seat now and then for a brief dip into the convivialities at the back of the house, but never, as far as one knew, showing the least desire to jump on the stage and do a "turn."

Among his contemporaries there lingered a vague tradition of his having, at a remote period, and in a romantic clime, been wounded in a duel; but his legend no more tallied with what we younger men knew of his character than my mother's assertion that he had once been "a charming little man with nice eyes" corresponded to any possible reconstitution of his physiognomy.

"He never can have looked like anything but a bundle of sticks," Murchard had once said of him. "Or a phosphorescent log, rather," some one else amended; and we recognized the happiness of this description of his small squat trunk, with the red blink of the eyes in a face like mottled bark. He had always been possessed of a leisure which he had nursed and protected, instead of squandering it in vain activities. His carefully guarded hours had been devoted to the cultivation of a fine intelligence and a few judiciously chosen habits; and none of the disturbances common to human experience seemed to have crossed his sky. Nevertheless, his dispassionate survey of the universe had not raised his opinion of that costly experiment, and his study of the human race seemed to have resulted in the conclusion that all men were superfluous, and women necessary only because someone had to do the cooking. On the importance of this point his convictions were absolute, and gastronomy was the only science which he revered as a dogma. It must be owned that his little dinners were a strong argument in favor of this view, besides being a reason—though not the main one—for the fidelity of his friends.

Mentally he exercised a hospitality less seductive but no less stimulating. His mind was like a forum, or some open meeting place for the exchange of ideas: somewhat cold and drafty, but light, spacious and orderly—a kind of academic grove from which all the leaves have fallen. In this privileged area a dozen of us were wont to stretch our muscles and expand our lungs; and, as if to prolong as much as possible the tradition of what we felt to be a vanishing institution, one or two neophytes were now and then added to our band.

Young Phil Frenham was the last, and the most interesting, of these recruits, and a good example of Murchard's somewhat morbid assertion that our old friend "liked 'em juicy." It was indeed a fact that Culwin, for all his dryness, specially tasted the lyric qualities in youth. As he was far too good an Epicurean to nip the flowers of soul which he gathered for his garden, his friendship was not a disintegrating influence: on the contrary, it forced the young idea to robuster bloom. And in Phil Frenham he had a good subject for experimentation. The boy was really intelligent, and the soundness of his nature was like the pure paste under a fine glaze. Culwin had fished him out of a fog of family dullness, and pulled him up to a peak in Darien; and the adventure hadn't hurt him a bit. Indeed, the skill with which Culwin had contrived to stimulate his curiosities without robbing them of their bloom of awe seemed to me a sufficient answer to Murchard's ogreish metaphor. There was nothing hectic in Frenham's efflorescence, and his old friend had not laid even a finger tip on the sacred stupidities. One wanted no better proof of that than the fact that Frenham still reverenced them in Culwin.

"There's a side of him you fellows don't see. I believe that story about the duel!" he declared; and it was of the very essence of this belief that it should impel him—just as our little party was dispersing—to turn back to our host with the joking demand: "And now you've got to tell us about *your* ghost!"

The outer door had closed on Murchard and the others; only Frenham and I remained; and the devoted servant who presided over Culwin's destinies, having brought a fresh supply of soda water, had been laconically ordered to bed.

Culwin's sociability was a night-blooming flower, and we knew that he expected the nucleus of his group to tighten around him after midnight. But Frenham's appeal seemed to disconcert him comically, and he rose from the chair in which he had just reseated himself after his farewells in the hall.

"*My* ghost? Do you suppose I'm fool enough to go to the expense of keeping one of my own, when there are so many charming ones in my friends' closets? Take another cigar," he said, revolving toward me with a laugh.

Frenham laughed too, pulling up his slender height before the chimney piece as he turned to face his short bristling friend.

"Oh," he said, "you'd never be content to share if you met one you really liked."

Culwin had dropped back into his armchair, his shock head embedded in the hollow of worn leather, his little eyes glimmering over a fresh cigar.

"Liked—*liked?* Good Lord!" he growled.

"Ah, you *have*, then!" Frenham pounced on him in the same instant, with a side glance of victory at me; but Culwin cowered gnomelike among his cushions, dissembling himself in a protective cloud of smoke.

"What's the use of denying it? You've seen everything, so of course you've seen a ghost!" his young friend persisted, talking intrepidly into the cloud. "Or, if you haven't seen one, it's only because you've seen two!"

The form of the challenge seemed to strike our host. He shot his head out of the mist with a queer tortoise-like motion he sometimes had, and blinked approvingly at Frenham.

"That's it," he flung at us on a shrill jerk of laughter; "it's only because I've seen two!"

The words were so unexpected that they dropped down and down into a deep silence, while we continued to stare at each other over Culwin's head, and Culwin stared at his ghosts. At length Frenham, without speaking, threw himself into the chair on the other side of the hearth, and leaned forward with his listening smile. . . .

II

"Oh, of course they're not show ghosts—a collector wouldn't think anything of them. . . . Don't let me raise your hopes . . . their one merit is their numerical strength: the exceptional fact of there being *two*. But, as against this, I'm bound to admit that at any moment I could probably have exorcised them both by asking my doctor for a prescription, or my oculist for a pair of spectacles. Only, as I never could make up my mind whether to go to the doctor or the oculist—whether I was afflicted by an optical or a digestive delusion—I left them to pursue their interesting double life, though at times they made mine exceedingly uncomfortable. . . .

"Yes—uncomfortable; and you know how I hate to be uncomfortable! But it was part of my stupid pride, when the thing began, not to admit that I could be disturbed by the trifling matter of seeing two.

"And then I'd no reason, really, to suppose I was ill. As far as I knew I was simply bored—horribly bored. But it was part of my boredom—I remember—that I was feeling so uncommonly well, and didn't know how on earth to work off my surplus energy. I had come back from a long journey—down in South America and Mexico—and had settled down for the winter near New York with an old aunt who had known Washington Irving and corresponded with N. P. Willis. She lived, not far from Irvington, in a damp Gothic villa overhung by Norway spruces and looking exactly like a memorial emblem done in hair. Her personal appearance was in keeping with this image, and her own hair—of which there was little left—might have been sacrificed to the manufacture of the emblem.

"I had just reached the end of an agitated year, with considerable arrears to make up in money and emotion; and theoretically it seemed as though my aunt's mild hospitality would be as beneficial to my nerves as to my purse. But the deuce of it was that as soon as I felt myself safe and sheltered my energy began to revive; and how was I to work it off inside of a memorial emblem? I had, at that time, the illusion that sustained intellectual effort could engage a man's whole activity; and I decided to write a great book—I forget about what. My aunt, impressed by my plan, gave up to me her Gothic library, filled with classics bound in black cloth and daguerreotypes of faded celebrities; and I sat down at my desk to win myself a place among their number. And to facilitate my task she lent me a cousin to copy my manuscript.

"The cousin was a nice girl, and I had an idea that a nice girl was just what I needed to restore my faith in human nature, and principally in myself. She was neither beautiful nor intelligent—poor Alice Nowell!—but it interested me to see any woman content to be so uninteresting, and I wanted to find out the secret of her content. In doing this I handled it rather rashly, and put it out of joint—oh, just for a moment! There's no fatuity in telling you this, for the poor girl had never seen anyone but cousins. . . .

"Well, I was sorry for what I'd done, of course, and confoundedly bothered as to how I should put it straight. She was staying in the house, and one evening, after my aunt had gone to bed, she came down to the library to fetch a book she'd mislaid, like any artless heroine, on the shelves behind us. She was pink-nosed and flustered, and it suddenly occurred to me that her hair, though it was fairly thick and pretty, would look exactly like my aunt's when she grew older. I was glad I had noticed this, for it made it easier for me to decide to do what was right; and when I had found the book she hadn't lost I told her I was leaving for Europe that week.

"Europe was terribly far off in those days, and Alice knew at once what I meant. She didn't take it in the least as I'd expected—it would have been easier if she had. She held her book very tight, and turned away a moment to wind up the lamp on my desk—it had a ground-glass shade with vine leaves, and glass drops around the edge, I remember. Then she came back, held out her hand, and said: 'Good-bye.' And as she said it she looked straight at me and kissed me. I had never felt anything as fresh and shy and brave as her kiss. It was worse than any reproach, and it made me ashamed to deserve a reproach from her. I said to myself: 'I'll marry her, and when my aunt dies she'll leave us this house, and I'll sit here at the desk and go on with my book; and Alice will sit over there with her embroidery and look at me as she's looking now. And life will go on like that for any number of years.' The prospect frightened me a little, but at the time it didn't frighten me as much as doing anything to hurt her; and ten minutes later she had my seal ring on her finger, and my promise that when I went abroad she should go with me.

"You'll wonder why I'm enlarging on this incident. It's because the evening on which it took place was the very evening on which I first saw the queer sight I've spoken of. Being at that time an ardent believer in a necessary sequence between cause and effect, I naturally tried to trace some kind of link between what had just happened to me in my aunt's library, and what was to happen a few hours later on the same night; and so the coincidence between the two events always remained in my mind.

"I went up to bed with rather a heavy heart, for I was bowed under the weight of the first good action I had ever consciously committed; and young as I was, I saw the gravity of my situation. Don't imagine from this that I had hitherto been an instrument of destruction. I had been merely a harmless young man, who had followed his bent and declined all collaboration with Providence. Now I had suddenly undertaken to promote the moral order of the world, and I felt a good deal like the trustful spectator who has given his gold watch to the conjurer, and doesn't know in what shape he'll get it back when the trick is over.... Still, a glow of self-righteousness tempered my fears, and I said to myself as I undressed that when I'd got used to being good it probably wouldn't make me as nervous as it did at the start. And by the time I was in bed, and had blown out my candle, I felt that I really *was* getting used to it, and that, as far as I'd got, it was not unlike sinking down into one of my aunt's very softest wool mattresses.

"I closed my eyes on this image, and when I opened them it must have been a good deal later, for my room had grown cold, and intensely still. I was waked by the queer feeling we all know—the feeling that there was something in the room that hadn't been there when I fell asleep. I sat up and strained my eyes into the darkness. The room was pitch black, and at first I saw nothing; but gradually a vague glimmer at the foot of the bed turned into two eyes staring back at me. I couldn't distinguish the features attached to them, but as I looked the eyes grew more and more distinct: they gave out a light of their own.

"The sensation of being thus gazed at was far from pleasant, and you might suppose that my first impulse would have been to jump out of bed and hurl myself on the invisible figure attached to the eyes. But it wasn't— my impulse was simply to lie still.... I can't say whether this was due to an immediate sense of the uncanny nature of the apparition—to the certainty that if I did jump out of bed I should hurl myself on nothing—or merely to the benumbing effect of the eyes themselves. They were the very worst eyes I've ever seen: a man's eyes—but what a man! My first thought was that he must be frightfully old. The orbits were sunk, and the thick red-lined lids hung over the eyeballs like blinds of which the cords are broken. One lid drooped a little lower than the other, with the effect of a crooked leer; and between these folds of flesh, with their scant bristle of lashes, the eyes themselves, small glassy disks with an agate-like rim, looked like sea pebbles in the grip of a starfish.

"But the age of the eyes was not the most unpleasant thing about them. What turned me sick was their expression of vicious security. I don't know how else to describe the fact that they seemed to belong to a man who had done a lot of harm in his life, but had always kept just inside the danger lines. They were not the eyes of a coward, but of someone much too clever to take risks; and my gorge rose at their look of base astuteness. Yet even that wasn't the worst; for as we continued to scan each other I saw in them a tinge of derision, and felt myself to be its object.

"At that I was seized by an impulse of rage that jerked me to my feet and pitched me straight at the unseen figure. But of course there wasn't any figure there, and my fists struck at emptiness. Ashamed and cold, I groped about for a match and lit the candles. The room looked just as usual—as I had known it would; and I crawled back to bed, and blew out the lights.

"As soon as the room was dark again the eyes reappeared; and I now applied myself to explaining them on scientific principles. At first I thought the illusion might have been caused by the glow of the last embers in the chimney; but the fireplace was on the other side of my bed, and so placed that the fire could not be reflected in my toilet glass, which was the only mirror in the room. Then it struck me that I might have been tricked by the reflection of the embers in some polished bit of wood or metal; and though I couldn't discover any object of the sort in my line of vision, I got up again, groped my way to the hearth, and covered what was left of the fire. But as soon as I was back in bed the eyes were back at its foot.

"They were an hallucination, then: that was plain. But the fact that they were not due to any external dupery didn't make them a bit pleasanter. For if they were a projection of my inner consciousness, what the deuce was the matter with that organ? I had gone deeply enough into the mystery of morbid pathological states to picture the conditions under which an exploring mind might lay itself open to such a midnight admonition; but I couldn't fit it to my present case. I had never felt more normal, mentally and physically; and the only unusual fact in my situation—that of having assured the happiness of an amiable girl—did not seem of a kind to summon unclean spirits about my pillow. But there were the eyes still looking at me.

"I shut mine, and tried to evoke a vision of Alice Nowell's. They were not remarkable eyes, but they were as wholesome as fresh water, and if she had had more imagination—or longer lashes—their expression might have been interesting. As it was, they did not prove very efficacious, and in a few moments I perceived that they had mysteriously changed into the eyes at the foot of the bed. It exasperated me more to feel these glaring at me through my shut lids than to see them, and I opened my eyes again and looked straight into their hateful stare. . . .

"And so it went on all night. I can't tell you what that night was like, nor how long it lasted. Have you ever lain in bed, hopelessly wide awake, and tried to keep your eyes shut, knowing that if you opened 'em you'd see something you dreaded and loathed? It sounds easy, but it's devilishly hard. Those eyes hung there and drew me. I had the *vertige de l'abîme*,[1] and their red lids were the edge of my abyss. . . . I had known nervous hours before: hours when I'd felt the wind of danger in my neck; but never this kind of strain. It wasn't that the eyes were awful; they hadn't the majesty of the powers of darkness. But they had—how shall I say?—a physical effect that

[1]French: vertigo, dizziness.

was the equivalent of a bad smell: their look left a smear like a snail's. And I didn't see what business they had with me, anyhow—and I stared and stared, trying to find out.

"I don't know what effect they were trying to produce; but the effect they *did* produce was that of making me pack my portmanteau and bolt to town early the next morning. I left a note for my aunt, explaining that I was ill and had gone to see my doctor; and as a matter of fact I did feel uncommonly ill—the night seemed to have pumped all the blood out of me. But when I reached town I didn't go to the doctor's. I went to a friend's rooms, and threw myself on a bed, and slept for ten heavenly hours. When I woke it was the middle of the night, and I turned cold at the thought of what might be waiting for me. I sat up, shaking, and stared into the darkness; but there wasn't a break in its blessed surface, and when I saw that the eyes were not there I dropped back into another long sleep.

"I had left no word for Alice when I fled, because I meant to go back the next morning. But the next morning I was too exhausted to stir. As the day went on the exhaustion increased, instead of wearing off like the fatigue left by an ordinary night of insomnia: the effect of the eyes seemed to be cumulative, and the thought of seeing them again grew intolerable. For two days I fought my dread; and on the third evening I pulled myself together and decided to go back the next morning. I felt a good deal happier as soon as I'd decided, for I knew that my abrupt disappearance, and the strangeness of my not writing, must have been very distressing to poor Alice. I went to bed with an easy mind, and fell asleep at once; but in the middle of the night I woke, and there were the eyes. . . .

"Well, I simply couldn't face them; and instead of going back to my aunt's I bundled a few things into a trunk and jumped aboard the first steamer for England. I was so dead tired when I got on board that I crawled straight into my berth, and slept most of the way over; and I can't tell you the bliss it was to wake from those long dreamless stretches and look fearlessly into the dark, *knowing* that I shouldn't see the eyes. . . .

"I stayed abroad for a year, and then I stayed for another; and during that time I never had a glimpse of them. That was enough reason for prolonging my stay if I'd been on a desert island. Another was, of course, that I had perfectly come to see, on the voyage over, the complete impossibility of my marrying Alice Nowell. The fact that I had been so slow in making this discovery annoyed me, and made me want to avoid explanations. The bliss of escaping at one stroke from the eyes, and from this other embarrassment, gave my freedom an extraordinary zest; and the longer I savored it the better I liked its taste.

"The eyes had burned such a hole in my consciousness that for a long time I went on puzzling over the nature of the apparition, and wondering if it would ever come back. But as time passed I lost this dread, and retained only the precision of the image. Then that faded in its turn.

"The second year found me settled in Rome, where I was planning, I believe, to write another great book—a definitive work on Etruscan influences in Italian art. At any rate, I'd found some pretext of the kind for taking a sunny apartment in the Piazza di Spagna and dabbling about in the Forum; and there, one morning, a charming youth came to me. As he stood there in the warm light, slender and smooth and hyacinthine, he might have stepped from a ruined altar—one to Antinous, say; but he'd come instead from New York, with a letter from (of all people) Alice Nowell. The letter—the first I'd had from her since our break—was simply a line introducing her young cousin, Gilbert Noyes, and appealing to me to befriend him. It appeared, poor lad, that he 'had talent,' and 'wanted to write'; and, an obdurate family having insisted that his calligraphy should take the form of double entry, Alice had intervened to win him six months' respite, during which he was to travel abroad on a meager pittance, and somehow prove his ability to increase it by his pen. The quaint conditions of the test struck me first: it seemed about as conclusive as a medieval 'ordeal.' Then I was touched by her having sent him to me. I had always wanted to do her some service, to justify myself in my own eyes rather than hers; and here was a beautiful occasion.

"I imagine it's safe to lay down the general principle that predestined geniuses don't, as a rule, appear before one in the spring sunshine of the Forum looking like one of its banished gods. At any rate, poor Noyes wasn't a predestined genius. But he *was* beautiful to see, and charming as a comrade. It was only when he began to talk literature that my heart failed me. I knew all the symptoms so well—the things he had 'in him,' and the things outside him that impinged! There's the real test, after all. It was always—punctually, inevitably, with the inexorableness of a mechnical law—it was *always* the wrong thing that struck him. I grew to find a certain fascination in deciding in advance exactly which wrong thing he'd select; and I acquired an astonishing skill at the game....

"The worst of it was that his *bêtise*[2] wasn't of the too obvious sort. Ladies who met him at picnics thought him intellectual; and even at dinners he passed for clever. I, who had him under the microscope, fancied now and then that he might develop some kind of a slim talent, something that he could make 'do' and be happy on; and wasn't that, after all, what I was concerned with? He was so charming—he continued to be so charming—that he called forth all my charity in support of this argument; and for the first few months I really believed there was a chance for him....

"Those months were delightful. Noyes was constantly with me, and the more I saw of him, the better I liked him. His stupidity was a natural grace—it was as beautiful, really, as his eyelashes. And he was so gay, so affectionate, and so happy with me, that telling him the truth would have been about as pleasant as slitting the throat of some gentle animal. At first I used to wonder what had put into that radiant head the detestable delusion that it held a brain. Then I began to see that it was simply protective mimicry—an instinctive ruse to get away from family life and an office desk. Not that Gilbert didn't—dear lad!—believe in himself. There wasn't a trace of hypocrisy in

[2]French: stupidity, foolishness.

him. He was sure that his 'call' was irresistible, while to me it was the saving grace of his situation that it *wasn't*, and that a little money, a little leisure, a little pleasure would have turned him into an inoffensive idler. Unluckily, however, there was no hope of money, and with the alternative of the office desk before him he couldn't postpone his attempt at literature. The stuff he turned out was deplorable, and I see now that I knew it from the first. Still, the absurdity of deciding a man's whole future on a first trial seemed to justify me in withholding my verdict, and perhaps even in encouraging him a little, on the ground that the human plant generally needs warmth to flower.

"At any rate, I proceeded on that principle, and carried it to the point of getting his term of probation extended. When I left Rome he went with me, and we idled away a delicious summer between Capri and Venice. I said to myself: 'If he has anything in him, it will come out now,' and it *did*. He was never more enchanting and enchanted. There were moments of our pilgrimage when beauty born of murmuring sound seemed actually to pass into his face—but only to issue forth in a flood of the palest ink. . . .

"Well, the time came to turn off the tap; and I knew there was no hand but mine to do it. We were back in Rome, and I had taken him to stay with me, not wanting him to be alone in his *pension* when he had to face the necessity of renouncing his ambition. I hadn't, of course, relied solely on my own judgment in deciding to advise him to drop literature. I had sent his stuff to various people—editors and critics—and they had always sent it back with the same chilling lack of comment. Really there was nothing on earth to say.

"I confess I never felt more shabby than I did on the day when I decided to have it out with Gilbert. It was well enough to tell myself that it was my duty to knock the poor boy's hopes into splinters—but I'd like to know what act of gratuitous cruelty hasn't been justified on that plea? I've always shrunk from usurping the functions of Providence, and when I have to exercise them I decidely prefer that it shouldn't be on an errand of destruction. Besides, in the last issue, who was I to decide, even after a year's trial, if poor Gilbert had it in him or not?

"The more I looked at the part I'd resolved to play, the less I liked it; and I liked it still less when Gilbert sat opposite me, with his head thrown back in the lamplight, just as Phil's is now. . . . I'd been going over his last manuscript, and he knew it, and he knew that his future hung on my verdict—we'd tacitly agreed to that. The manuscript lay between us, on my table—a novel, his first novel, if you please!—and he reached over and laid his hand on it, and looked up at me with all his life in the look.

"I stood up and cleared my throat, trying to keep my eyes away from his face and on the manuscript.

"'The fact is, my dear Gilbert,' I began—

"I saw him turn pale, but he was up and facing me in an instant.

"'Oh, look here, don't take on so, my dear fellow! I'm not so awfully cut up as all that!' His hands were on my shoulders, and he was laughing down on me from his full height, with a kind of mortally stricken gaiety that drove the knife into my side.

"He was too beautifully brave for me to keep up any humbug about my duty. And it came over me suddenly how I should hurt others in hurting him: myself first, since sending him home meant losing him; but more particularly poor Alice Nowell, to whom I had so longed to prove my good faith and my desire to serve her. It really seemed like failing her twice to fail Gilbert.

"But my intuition was like one of those lightning flashes that encircle the whole horizon, and in the same instant I saw what I might be letting myself in for if I didn't tell the truth. I said to myself: 'I shall have him for life'—and I'd never yet seen anyone, man or woman, whom I was quite sure of wanting on those terms. Well, this impulse of egotism decided me. I was ashamed of it, and to get away from it I took a leap that landed me straight in Gilbert's arms.

"'The thing's all right, and you're all wrong!' I shouted up at him; and as he hugged me, and I laughed and shook in his clutch, I had for a minute the sense of self-complacency that is supposed to attend the footsteps of the just. Hang it all, making people happy *has* its charms.

"Gilbert, of course, was for celebrating his emancipation in some spectacular manner; but I sent him away alone to explode his emotions, and went to bed to sleep off mine. As I undressed I began to wonder what their aftertaste would be—so many of the finest don't keep! Still, I wasn't sorry, and I meant to empty the bottle, even if it *did* turn a trifle flat.

"After I got into bed I lay for a long time smiling at the memory of his eyes—his blissful eyes.... Then I fell asleep, and when I woke the room was deathly cold, and I sat up with a jerk—and there were *the other eyes*....

"It was three years since I'd seen them, but I'd thought of them so often that I fancied they could never take me unawares again. Now, with their red sneer on me, I knew that I had never really believed they would come back, and that I was as defenceless as ever against them.... As before, it was the insane irrelevance of their coming that made it so horrible. What the deuce were they after, to leap out at me at such a time? I had lived more or less carelessly in the years since I'd seen them, though my worst indiscretions were not dark enough to invite the searchings of their infernal glare; but at this particular moment I was really in what might have been called a state of grace; and I can't tell you how the fact added to their horror....

"But it's not enough to say they were as bad as before: they were worse. Worse by just so much as I'd learned of life in the interval; by all the damnable implications my wider experience read into them. I saw now what I hadn't seen before: that they were eyes which had grown hideous gradually, which had built up their baseness coral-wise, bit by bit, out of a series of small turpitudes slowly accumulated through the industrious years. Yes—it came to me that what made them so bad was that they'd grown bad so slowly....

"There they hung in the darkness, their swollen lids dropped across the little watery bulbs rolling loose in the orbits, and the puff of flesh making a muddy shadow underneath—and as their stare moved with my movements, there came over me a sense of their tacit complicity, of a deep hidden under-standing between us that was worse than the first shock of their strange-ness. Not that I understood them; but that they made it so clear that someday I should.... Yes, that was the worst part of it, decidedly; and it was the feeling that became stronger each time they came back....

"For they got into the damnable habit of coming back. They reminded me of vampires with a taste for young flesh, they seemed so to gloat over the taste of a good conscience. Every night for a month they came to claim their morsel of mine: since I'd made Gilbert happy they simply wouldn't loosen their fangs. The coincidence almost made me hate him, poor lad, for-tuitous as I felt it to be. I puzzled over it a good deal, but couldn't find any hint of an explanation except in the chance of his association with Alice Nowell. But then the eyes had let up on me the moment I had abandoned her, so they could hardly be the emissaries of a woman scorned, even if one could have pictured poor Alice charging such spirits to avenge her. That set me thinking, and I began to wonder if they would let up on me if I aban-doned Gilbert. The temptation was insidious, and I had to stiffen myself against it; but really, dear boy! he was too charming to be sacrificed to such demons. And so, after all, I never found out what they wanted...."

III

The fire crumbled, sending up a flash which threw into relief the narrator's gnarled face under its grey-black stubble. Pressed into the hollow of the chair back, it stood out an instant like an intaglio of yellowish red-veined stone, with spots of enamel for the eyes; then the fire sank and it became once more a dim Rembrandtish blur.

Phil Frenham, sitting in a low chair on the opposite side of the hearth, one long arm propped on the table behind him, one hand supporting his thrown-back head, and his eyes fixed on his old friend's face, had not moved since the tale began. He continued to maintain his silent immobility after Culwin had ceased to speak, and it was I who, with a vague sense of disap-pointment at the sudden drop of the story, finally asked: "But how long did you keep on seeing them?"

Culwin, so sunk into his chair that he seemed like a heap of his own empty clothes, stirred a little, as if in surprise at my question. He appeared to have half-forgotten what he had been telling us.

"How long? Oh, off and on all that winter. It was infernal. I never got used to them. I grew really ill."

Frenham shifted his attitude, and as he did so his elbow struck against a small mirror in a bronze frame standing on the table behind him. He turned and changed its angle slightly; then he resumed his former attitude, his dark head thrown back on his lifted palm, his eyes intent on Culwin's face. Some-thing in his silent gaze embarrassed me, and as if to divert attention from it I pressed on with another question:

"And you never tried sacrificing Noyes?"

"Oh, no. The fact is I didn't have to. He did it for me, poor boy!"

"Did it for you? How do you mean?"

"He wore me out—wore everybody out. He kept on pouring out his lamentable twaddle, and hawking it up and down the place till he became a thing of terror. I tried to wean him from writing—oh, ever so gently, you understand, by throwing him with agreeable people, giving him a chance to make himself felt, to come to a sense of what he *really* had to give. I'd foreseen this solution from the beginning—felt sure that, once the first ardor of authorship was quenched, he'd drop into his place as a charming parasitic thing, the kind of chronic Cherubino for whom, in old societies, there's always a seat at table, and a shelter behind the ladies' skirts. I saw him take his place as 'the poet': the poet who doesn't write. One knows the type in every drawing room. Living in that way doesn't cost much—I'd worked it all out in my mind, and felt sure that, with a little help, he could manage it for the next few years; and meanwhile he'd be sure to marry. I saw him married to a widow, rather older, with a good cook and a well-run house. And I actually had my eye on the widow. . . . Meanwhile I did everything to help the transition—lent him money to ease his conscience, introduced him to pretty women to make him forget his vows. But nothing would do him: he had but one idea in his beautiful obstinate head. He wanted the laurel and not the rose, and he kept on repeating Gautier's axiom, and battering and filing at his limp prose till he'd spread it out over Lord knows how many hundred pages. Now and then he would send a barrelful to a publisher, and of course it would always come back.

"At first it didn't matter—he thought he was 'misunderstood.' He took the attitudes of genius, and whenever an opus came home he wrote another to keep it company. Then he had a reaction of despair, and accused me of deceiving him, and Lord knows what. I got angry at that, and told him it was he who had deceived himself. He'd come to me determined to write, and I'd done my best to help him. That was the extent of my offence, and I'd done it for his cousin's sake, not his.

"That seemed to strike home, and he didn't answer for a minute. Then he said: 'My time's up and my money's up. What do you think I'd better do?'

"'I think you'd better not be an ass,' I said.

"'What do you mean by being an ass?' he asked.

"I took a letter from my desk and held it out to him.

"'I mean refusing this offer of Mrs. Ellinger's: to be her secretary at a salary of five thousand dollars. There may be a lot more in it than that.'

"He flung out his hand with a violence that struck the letter from mine. 'Oh, I know well enough what's in it!' he said, red to the roots of his hair.

"'And what's the answer, if you know?' I asked.

"He made none at the minute, but turned away slowly to the door. There, with his hand on the threshold, he stopped to say, almost under his breath: 'Then you really think my stuff's no good?'

"I was tired and exasperated, and I laughed. I don't defend my laugh—it was in wretched taste. But I must plead in extenuation that the boy was a fool, and that I'd done my best for him—I really had.

"He went out of the room, shutting the door quietly after him. That afternoon I left for Frascati, where I'd promised to spend the Sunday with some friends. I was glad to escape from Gilbert, and by the same token, as I learned that night, I had also escaped from the eyes. I dropped into the same lethargic sleep that had come to me before when I left off seeing them; and when I woke the next morning in my peaceful room above the ilexes, I felt the utter weariness and deep relief that always followed on that sleep. I put in two blessed nights at Frascati, and when I got back to my rooms in Rome I found that Gilbert had gone.... Oh, nothing tragic had happened—the episode never rose to *that*. He'd simply packed his manuscripts and left for America—for his family and the Wall Street desk. He left a decent enough note to tell me of his decision, and behaved altogether, in the circumstances, as little like a fool as it's possible for a fool to behave...."

<h1 style="text-align:center">IV</h1>

Culwin paused again, and Frenham still sat motionless, the dusky contour of his young head reflected in the mirror at his back.

"And what became of Noyes afterward?" I finally asked, still disquieted by a sense of incompleteness, by the need of some connecting thread between the parallel lines of the tale.

Culwin twitched his shoulders. "Oh, nothing became of him—because he became nothing. There could be no question of 'becoming' about it. He vegetated in an office, I believe, and finally got a clerkship in a consulate, and married drearily in China. I saw him once in Hong Kong, years afterward. He was fat and hadn't shaved. I was told he drank. He didn't recognize me."

"And the eyes?" I asked, after another pause which Frenham's continued silence made oppressive.

Culwin, stroking his chin, blinked at me meditatively through the shadows. "I never saw them after my last talk with Gilbert. Put two and two together if you can. For my part, I haven't found the link."

He rose, his hands in his pockets, and walked stiffly over to the table on which reviving drinks had been set out.

"You must be parched after this dry tale. Here, help yourself, my dear fellow. Here, Phil—" He turned back to the hearth.

Frenham made no response to his host's hospitable summons. He still sat in his low chair without moving, but as Culwin advanced toward him, their eyes met in a long look; after which the young man, turning suddenly, flung his arms across the table behind him, and dropped his face upon them.

Culwin, at the unexpected gesture, stopped short, a flush on his face.

"Phil—what the deuce? Why, have the eyes scared *you*? My dear boy— my dear fellow—I never had such a tribute to my literary ability, never!"

He broke into a chuckle at the thought, and halted on the hearthrug, his hands still in his pockets, gazing down at the youth's bowed head. Then, as Frenham still made no answer, he moved a step or two nearer.

"Cheer up, my dear Phil! It's years since I've seen them—apparently I've done nothing lately bad enough to call them out of chaos. Unless my present evocation of them has made *you* see them; which would be their worst stroke yet!"

His bantering appeal quivered off into an uneasy laugh, and he moved still nearer, bending over Frenham, and laying his gouty hands on the lad's shoulders.

"Phil, my dear boy, really—what's the matter? Why don't you answer? *Have* you seen the eyes?"

Frenham's face was still hidden, and from where I stood behind Culwin I saw the latter, as if under the rebuff of this unaccountable attitude, draw back slowly from his friend. As he did so, the light of the lamp on the table fell full on his congested face, and I caught its reflection in the mirror behind Frenham's head.

Culwin saw the reflection also. He paused, his face level with the mirror, as if scarcely recognizing the countenance in it as his own. But as he looked his expression gradually changed, and for an appreciable space of time he and the image in the glass confronted each other with a glare of slowly gathering hate. Then Culwin let go of Frenham's shoulders, and drew back a step....

Frenham, his face still hidden, did not stir.

1910

Roman Fever

From the table at which they had been lunching two American ladies of ripe but well-cared-for middle age moved across the lofty terrace of the Roman restaurant and, leaning on its parapet, looked first at each other, and then down on the outspread glories of the Palatine and the Forum, with the same expression of vague but benevolent approval.

As they leaned there a girlish voice echoed up gaily from the stairs leading to the court below. "Well, come along, then," it cried, not to them but to an invisible companion, "and let's leave the young things to their knitting"; and a voice as fresh laughed back: "Oh, look here, Babs, not actually *knitting*—" "Well, I mean figuratively," rejoined the first. "After all, we haven't left our poor parents much else to do...." and at that point the turn of the stairs engulfed the dialogue.

The two ladies looked at each other again, this time with a tinge of smiling embarrassment, and the smaller and paler one shook her head and colored slightly.

"Barbara!" she murmured, sending an unheard rebuke after the mocking voice in the stairway.

The other lady, who was fuller, and higher in color, with a small determined nose supported by vigorous black eyebrows, gave a good-humored laugh. "That's what our daughters think of us!"

Her companion replied by a deprecating gesture. "Not of us individually. We must remember that. It's just the collective modern idea of Mothers. And you see—" Half-guiltily she drew from her handsomely mounted black handbag a twist of crimson silk run through by two fine knitting needles. "One never knows," she murmured. "The new system has certainly given us a good deal of time to kill; and sometimes I get tired just looking—even at this." Her gesture was now addressed to the stupendous scene at their feet.

The dark lady laughed again, and they both relapsed upon the view, contemplating it in silence, with a sort of diffused serenity which might have been borrowed from the spring effulgence of the Roman skies. The luncheon hour was long past, and the two had their end of the vast terrace to themselves. At its opposite extremity a few groups, detained by a lingering look at the outspread city, were gathering up guidebooks and fumbling for tips. The last of them scattered, and the two ladies were alone on the air-washed height.

"Well, I don't see why we shouldn't just stay here," said Mrs. Slade, the lady of the high color and energetic brows. Two derelict basket chairs stood near, and she pushed them into the angle of the parapet, and settled herself in one, her gaze upon the Palatine. "After all, it's still the most beautiful view in the world."

"It always will be, to me," assented her friend Mrs. Ansley, with so slight a stress on the "me" that Mrs. Slade, though she noticed it, wondered if it were not merely accidental, like the random underlinings of old-fashioned letter writers.

"Grace Ansley was always old-fashioned," she thought; and added aloud, with a retrospective smile: "It's a view we've both been familiar with for a good many years. When we first met here we were younger than our girls are now. You remember?"

"Oh, yes, I remember," murmured Mrs. Ansley, with the same undefinable stress. "There's that headwaiter wondering," she interpolated. She was evidently far less sure than her companion of herself and of her rights in the world.

"I'll cure him of wondering," said Mrs. Slade, stretching her hand toward a bag as discreetly opulent-looking as Mrs. Ansley's. Signing to the headwaiter, she explained that she and her friend were old lovers of Rome, and would like to spend the end of the afternoon looking down on the view— that is, if it did not disturb the service? The headwaiter, bowing over her gratuity, assured her that the ladies were most welcome, and would be still more so if they would condescend to remain for dinner. A full-moon night, they would remember. . . .

Mrs. Slade's black brows drew together, as though references to the moon were out of place and even unwelcome. But she smiled away her frown as the headwaiter retreated. "Well, why not? We might do worse. There's no knowing, I suppose, when the girls will be back. Do you even know back from *where?* I don't!"

Mrs. Ansley again colored slightly. "I think those young Italian aviators we met at the Embassy invited them to fly to Tarquinia for tea. I suppose they'll want to wait and fly back by moonlight."

"Moonlight—moonlight! What a part it still plays. Do you suppose they're as sentimental as we were?"

"I've come to the conclusion that I don't in the least know what they are," said Mrs. Ansley. "And perhaps we didn't know much more about each other."

"No; perhaps we didn't."

Her friend gave her a shy glance. "I never should have supposed you were sentimental, Alida."

"Well, perhaps I wasn't." Mrs. Slade drew her lids together in retrospect; and for a few moments the two ladies, who had been intimate since childhood, reflected how little they knew each other. Each one, of course, had a label ready to attach to the other's name; Mrs. Delphin Slade, for instance, would have told herself, or anyone who asked her, that Mrs. Horace Ansley, twenty-five years ago, had been exquisitely lovely—no, you wouldn't believe it, would you? ... though, of course, still charming, distinguished.... Well, as a girl she had been exquisite; far more beautiful than her daughter Barbara, though certainly Babs, according to the new standards at any rate, was more effective—had more *edge*, as they say. Funny where she got it, with those two nullities as parents. Yes; Horace Ansley was—well, just the duplicate of his wife. Museum specimens of old New York. Good-looking, irreproachable, exemplary. Mrs. Slade and Mrs. Ansley had lived opposite each other—actually as well as figuratively—for years. When the drawing-room curtains in No. 20 East 73rd Street were renewed, No. 23, across the way, was always aware of it. And of all the movings, buyings, travels, anniversaries, illnesses—the tame chronicle of an estimable pair. Little of it escaped Mrs. Slade. But she had grown bored with it by the time her husband made his big *coup* in Wall Street, and when they bought in upper Park Avenue had already begun to think: "I'd rather live opposite a speakeasy for a change; at least one might see it raided." The idea of seeing Grace raided was so amusing that (before the move) she launched it at a woman's lunch. It made a hit, and went the rounds—she sometimes wondered if it had crossed the street, and reached Mrs. Ansley. She hoped not, but didn't much mind. Those were the days when respectability was at a discount, and it did the irreproachable no harm to laugh at them a little.

A few years later, and not many months apart, both ladies lost their husbands. There was an appropriate exchange of wreaths and condolences, and a brief renewal of intimacy in the half-shadow of their mourning; and now, after another interval, they had run across each other in Rome, at the same hotel, each of them the modest appendage of a salient daughter. The similarity of their lot had again drawn them together, lending itself to mild jokes, and the mutual confession that, if in old days it must have been tiring to "keep up" with daughters, it was now, at times, a little dull not to.

No doubt, Mrs. Slade reflected, she felt her unemployment more than poor Grace ever would. It was a big drop from being the wife of Delphin

Slade to being his widow. She had always regarded herself (with a certain conjugal pride) as his equal in social gifts, as contributing her full share to the making of the exceptional couple they were: but the difference after his death was irremediable. As the wife of the famous corporation lawyer, always with an international case or two on hand, every day brought its exciting and unexpected obligation: the impromptu entertaining of eminent colleagues from abroad, the hurried dashes on legal business to London, Paris or Rome, where the entertaining was so handsomely reciprocated; the amusement of hearing in her wake: "What, that handsome woman with the good clothes and the eyes is Mrs. Slade—*the* Slade's wife? Really? Generally the wives of celebrities are such frumps."

Yes; being *the* Slade's widow was a dullish business after that. In living up to such a husband all her faculties had been engaged; now she had only her daughter to live up to, for the son who seemed to have inherited his father's gifts had died suddenly in boyhood. She had fought through that agony because her husband was there, to be helped and to help; now, after the father's death, the thought of the boy had become unbearable. There was nothing left but to mother her daughter; and dear Jenny was such a perfect daughter that she needed no excessive mothering. "Now with Babs Ansley I don't know that I *should* be so quiet," Mrs. Slade sometimes half-enviously reflected; but Jenny, who was younger than her brilliant friend, was that rare accident, an extremely pretty girl who somehow made youth and prettiness seem as safe as their absence. It was all perplexing—and to Mrs. Slade a little boring. She wished that Jenny would fall in love—with the wrong man, even; that she might have to be watched, out-maneuvered, rescued. And instead, it was Jenny who watched her mother, kept her out of drafts, made sure that she had taken her tonic....

Mrs. Ansley was much less articulate than her friend, and her mental portrait of Mrs. Slade was slighter, and drawn with fainter touches. "Alida Slade's awfully brilliant; but not as brilliant as she thinks," would have summed it up; though she would have added, for the enlightenment of strangers, that Mrs. Slade had been an extremely dashing girl; much more so than her daughter, who was pretty, of course, and clever in a way, but had none of her mother's—well, "vividness," someone had once called it. Mrs. Ansley would take up current words like this, and cite them in quotation marks, as unheard-of audacities. No; Jenny was not like her mother. Sometimes Mrs. Ansley thought Alida Slade was disappointed; on the whole she had had a sad life. Full of failures and mistakes; Mrs. Ansley had always been rather sorry for her....

So these two ladies visualized each other, each through the wrong end of her little telescope.

II

For a long time they continued to sit side by side without speaking. It seemed as though, to both, there was a relief in laying down their somewhat futile activities in the presence of the vast Memento Mori which faced them. Mrs. Slade sat quite still, her eyes fixed on the golden slope of the Palace of the Caesars, and after a while Mrs. Ansley ceased to fidget with her bag, and she too sank into meditation. Like many intimate friends, the two ladies had never before had occasion to be silent together, and Mrs. Ansley was slightly embarrassed by what seemed, after so many years, a new stage in their intimacy, and one with which she did not yet know how to deal.

Suddenly the air was full of that deep clangor of bells which periodically covers Rome with a roof of silver. Mrs. Slade glanced at her wristwatch. "Five o'clock already," she said, as though surprised.

Mrs. Ansley suggested interrogatively: "There's bridge at the Embassy at five." For a long time Mrs. Slade did not answer. She appeared to be lost in contemplation, and Mrs. Ansley thought the remark had escaped her. But after a while she said, as if speaking out of a dream: "Bridge, did you say? Not unless you want to.... But I don't think I will, you know."

"Oh, no," Mrs. Ansley hastened to assure her. "I don't care to at all. It's so lovely here; and so full of old memories, as you say." She settled herself in her chair, and almost furtively drew forth her knitting. Mrs. Slade took sideway note of this activity, but her own beautifully cared-for hands remained motionless on her knee.

"I was just thinking," she said slowly, "what different things Rome stands for to each generation of travelers. To our grandmothers, Roman fever; to our mothers, sentimental dangers—how we used to be guarded!—to our daughters, no more dangers than the middle of Main Street. They don't know it—but how much they're missing!"

The long golden light was beginning to pale, and Mrs. Ansley lifted her knitting a little closer to her eyes. "Yes; how we were guarded!"

"I always used to think," Mrs. Slade continued, "that our mothers had a much more difficult job than our grandmothers. When Roman fever stalked the streets it must have been comparatively easy to gather in the girls at the danger hour; but when you and I were young, with such beauty calling us, and the spice of disobedience thrown in, and no worse risk than catching cold during the cool hour after sunset, the mothers used to be put to it to keep us in—didn't they?"

She turned again toward Mrs. Ansley, but the latter had reached a delicate point in her knitting. "One, two, three—slip two; yes, they must have been," she assented, without looking up.

Mrs. Slade's eyes rested on her with a deepened attention. "She can knit—in the face of *this*! How like her...."

Mrs. Slade leaned back, brooding, her eyes ranging from the ruins which faced her to the long green hollow of the Forum, the fading flow of the church fronts beyond it, and the outlying immensity of the Colosseum. Suddenly she thought: "It's all very well to say that our girls have done away with sentiment and moonlight. But if Babs Ansley isn't out to catch that young aviator—the one who's a Marchese—then I don't know anything. And Jenny has no chance beside her. I know that too. I wonder if that's why

Grace Ansley likes the two girls to go everywhere together? My poor Jenny as a foil—!" Mrs. Slade gave a hardly audible laugh, and at the sound Mrs. Ansley dropped her knitting.

"Yes—?"

"I—oh, nothing. I was only thinking how your Babs carries everything before her. That Campolieri boy is one of the best matches in Rome. Don't look so innocent, my dear—you know he is. And I was wondering, ever so respectfully, you understand ... wondering how two such exemplary characters as you and Horace had managed to produce anything quite so dynamic." Mrs. Slade laughed again, with a touch of asperity.

Mrs. Ansley's hands lay inert across her needles. She looked straight out at the great accumulated wreckage of passion and splendor at her feet. But her small profile was almost expressionless. At length she said: "I think you overrate Babs, my dear."

Mrs. Slade's tone grew easier. "No; I don't. I appreciate her. And perhaps envy you. Oh, my girl's perfect; if I were a chronic invalid I'd—well, I think I'd rather be in Jenny's hands. There must be times ... but there! I always wanted a brilliant daughter ... and never quite understood why I got an angel instead."

Mrs. Ansley echoed her laugh in a faint murmur. "Babs is an angel too."

"Of course—of course! But she's got rainbow wings. Well, they're wandering by the sea with their young men; and here we sit ... and it all brings back the past a little too acutely."

Mrs. Ansley had resumed her knitting. One might almost have imagined (if one had known her less well, Mrs. Slade reflected) that, for her also, too many memories rose from the lengthening shadows of those august ruins. But no; she was simply absorbed in her work. What was there for her to worry about? She knew that Babs would almost certainly come back engaged to the extremely eligible Campolieri. "And she'll sell the New York house, and settle down near them in Rome, and never be in their way ... she's much too tactful. But she'll have an excellent cook, and just the right people in for bridge and cocktails ... and a perfectly peaceful old age among her grandchildren."

Mrs. Slade broke off this prophetic flight with a recoil of self-disgust. There was no one of whom she had less right to think unkindly than of Grace Ansley. Would she never cure herself of envying her? Perhaps she had begun too long ago.

She stood up and leaned against the parapet, filling her troubled eyes with the tranquilizing magic of the hour. But instead of tranquilizing her the sight seemed to increase her exasperation. Her gaze turned toward the Colosseum. Already its golden flank was downed in purple shadow, and above it the sky curved crystal clear, without light or color. It was the moment when afternoon and evening hang balanced in midheaven.

Mrs. Slade turned back and laid her hand on her friend's arm. The gesture was so abrupt that Mrs. Ansley looked up, startled.

"The sun's set. You're not afraid, my dear?"

"Afraid—?"

"Of Roman fever or pneumonia? I remember how ill you were that winter. As a girl you had a very delicate throat, hadn't you?"

"Oh, we're all right up here. Down below, in the Forum, it does get deathly cold, all of a sudden ... but not here."

"Ah, of course you know because you had to be so careful." Mrs. Slade turned back to the parapet. She thought: "I must make one more effort not to hate her." Aloud she said: "Whenever I look at the Forum from up here, I remember that story about a great-aunt of yours, wasn't she? A dreadfully wicked great-aunt?"

"Oh, yes; great-aunt Harriet. The one who was supposed to have sent her young sister out to the Forum after sunset to gather a nightblooming flower for her album. All our great-aunts and grandmothers used to have albums of dried flowers."

Mrs. Slade nodded. "But she really sent her because they were in love with the same man—"

"Well, that was the family tradition. They said Aunt Harriet confessed it years afterward. At any rate, the poor little sister caught the fever and died. Mother used to frighten us with the story when we were children."

"And you frightened *me* with it, that winter when you and I were here as girls. The winter I was engaged to Delphin."

Mrs. Ansley gave a faint laugh. "Oh, did I? Really frightened you? I don't believe you're easily frightened."

"Not often; but I was then. I was easily frightened because I was too happy. I wonder if you know what that means?"

"I—yes ..." Mrs. Ansley faltered.

"Well, I suppose that was why the story of your wicked aunt made such an impression on me. And I thought: 'There's no more Roman fever, but the Forum is deathly cold after sunset—especially after a hot day. And the Colosseum's even colder and damper'."

"The Colosseum—?"

"Yes. It wasn't easy to get in, after the gates were locked for the night. Far from easy. Still, in those days it could be managed; it *was* managed, often. Lovers met there who couldn't meet elsewhere. You knew that?"

"I—I dare say. I don't remember."

"You don't remember? You don't remember going to visit some ruins or other one evening, just after dark, and catching a bad chill? You were supposed to have gone to see the moon rise. People always said that expedition was what caused your illness."

There was a moment's silence; then Mrs. Ansley rejoined: "Did they? It was all so long ago."

"Yes. And you got well again—so it didn't matter. But I suppose it struck your friends—the reason given for your illness, I mean—because everybody knew you were so prudent on account of your throat, and your mother took such care of you. ... You *had* been out late sight-seeing, hadn't you, that night?"

"Perhaps I had. The most prudent girls aren't always prudent. What made you think of it now?"

Mrs. Slade seemed to have no answer ready. But after a moment she broke out: "Because I simply can't bear it any longer—!"

Mrs. Ansley lifted her head quickly. Her eyes were wide and very pale. "Can't bear what?"

"Why—your not knowing that I've always known why you went."

"Why I went—?"

"Yes. You think I'm bluffing, don't you? Well, you went to meet the man I was engaged to—and I can repeat every word of the letter that took you there."

While Mrs. Slade spoke Mrs. Ansley had risen unsteadily to her feet. Her bag, her knitting and gloves, slid in a panic-stricken heap to the ground. She looked at Mrs. Slade as though she were looking at a ghost.

"No, no—don't," she faltered out.

"Why not? Listen, if you don't believe me. 'My one darling, things can't go on like this. I must see you alone. Come to the Colosseum immediately after dark tomorrow. There will be somebody to let you in. No one whom you need fear will suspect'—but perhaps you've forgotten what the letter said?"

Mrs. Ansley met the challenge with an unexpected composure. Steadying herself against the chair she looked at her friend, and replied: "No; I know it by heart too."

"And the signature? 'Only *your* D.S.' Was that it? I'm right, am I? That was the letter that took you out that evening after dark?"

Mrs. Ansley was still looking at her. It seemed to Mrs. Slade that a slow struggle was going on behind the voluntarily controlled mask of her small quiet face. "I shouldn't have thought she had herself so well in hand," Mrs. Slade reflected, almost resentfully. But at this moment Mrs. Ansley spoke. "I don't know how you knew. I burnt the letter at once."

"Yes; you would, naturally—you're so prudent!" The sneer was open now. "And if you burnt the letter you're wondering how on earth I know what was in it. That's it, isn't it?"

Mrs. Slade waited, but Mrs. Ansley did not speak.

"Well, my dear, I know what was in that letter because I wrote it!"

"You wrote it?"

"Yes."

The two women stood for a minute staring at each other in the last golden light. Then Mrs. Ansley dropped back into her chair. "Oh," she murmured, and covered her face with her hands.

Mrs. Slade waited nervously for another word or movement. None came, and at length she broke out: "I horrify you."

Mrs. Ansley's hands dropped to her knee. The face they uncovered was streaked with tears. "I wasn't thinking of you. I was thinking—it was the only letter I ever had from him!"

"And I wrote it. Yes; I wrote it! But I was the girl he was engaged to. Did you happen to remember that?"

Mrs. Ansley's head drooped again. "I'm not trying to excuse myself . . . I remembered. . . ."

"And still you went?"

"Still I went."

Mrs. Slade stood looking down on the small bowed figure at her side. The flame of her wrath had already sunk, and she wondered why she had ever thought there would be any satisfaction in inflicting so purposeless a wound on her friend. But she had to justify herself.

"You do understand? I'd found out—and I hated you, hated you. I knew you were in love with Delphin—and I was afraid; afraid of you, of your quiet ways, your sweetness . . . your . . . well, I wanted you out of the way, that's all. Just for a few weeks; just till I was sure of him. So in a blind fury I wrote that letter . . . I don't know why I'm telling you now."

"I suppose," said Mrs. Ansley slowly, "it's because you've always gone on hating me."

"Perhaps. Or because I wanted to get the whole thing off my mind." She paused. "I'm glad you destroyed the letter. Of course I never thought you'd die."

Mrs. Ansley relapsed into silence, and Mrs. Slade, leaning above her, was conscious of a strange sense of isolation, of being cut off from the warm current of human communion. "You think me a monster!"

"I don't know. . . . It was the only letter I had, and you say he didn't write it?"

"Ah, how you care for him still!"

"I cared for that memory," said Mrs. Ansley.

Mrs. Slade continued to look down on her. She seemed physically reduced by the blow—as if, when she got up, the wind might scatter her like a puff of dust. Mrs. Slade's jealousy suddenly leapt up again at the sight. All these years the woman had been living on that letter. How she must have loved him, to treasure the mere memory of its ashes! The letter of the man her friend was engaged to. Wasn't it she who was the monster?

"You tried your best to get him away from me, didn't you? But you failed; and I kept him. That's all."

"Yes. That's all."

"I wish now I hadn't told you. I'd no idea you'd feel about it as you do; I thought you'd be amused. It all happened so long ago, as you say; and you must do me the justice to remember that I had no reason to think you'd ever taken it seriously. How could I, when you were married to Horace Ansley two months afterward? As soon as you could get out of bed your mother rushed you off to Florence and married you. People were rather surprised—they wondered at its being done so quickly; but I thought I knew. I had an idea you did it out of *pique*—to be able to say you'd got ahead of Delphin and me. Girls have such silly reasons for doing the most serious things. And your marrying so soon convinced me that you'd never really cared."

"Yes. I suppose it would," Mrs. Ansley assented.

The clear heaven overhead was emptied of all its gold. Dusk spread over it, abruptly darkening the Seven Hills. Here and there lights began to twinkle through the foliage at their feet. Steps were coming and going on the deserted terrace—waiters looking out of the doorway at the head of the stairs, then reappearing with trays and napkins and flasks of wine. Tables were moved, chairs straightened. A feeble string of electric lights flickered out. Some vases of faded flowers were carried away, and brought back replenished. A stout lady in a dust coat suddenly appeared, asking in broken Italian if anyone had seen the elastic band which held together her tattered Baedeker. She poked with her stick under the table at which she had lunched, the waiters assisting.

The corner where Mrs. Slade and Mrs. Ansley sat was still shadowy and deserted. For a long time neither of them spoke. At length Mrs. Slade began again: "I suppose I did it as a sort of joke—"

"A joke?"

"Well, girls are ferocious sometimes, you know. Girls in love especially. And I remember laughing to myself all that evening at the idea that you were waiting around there in the dark, dodging out of sight, listening for every sound, trying to get in—Of course I was upset when I heard you were so ill afterward."

Mrs. Ansley had not moved for a long time. But now she turned slowly toward her companion. "But I didn't wait. He'd arranged everything. He was there. We were let in at once," she said.

Mrs. Slade sprang up from her leaning position. "Delphin there? They let you in?—Ah, now you're lying!" she burst out with violence.

Mrs. Ansley's voice grew clearer, and full of surprise. "But of course he was there. Naturally he came—"

"Came? How did he know he'd find you there? You must be raving!"

Mrs. Ansley hesitated, as though reflecting. "But I answered the letter. I told him I'd be there. So he came."

Mrs. Slade flung her hands up to her face. "Oh, God—you answered! I never thought of your answering...."

"It's odd you never thought of it, if you wrote the letter."

"Yes. I was blind with rage."

Mrs. Ansley rose, and drew her fur scarf about her. "It is cold here. We'd better go ... I'm sorry for you," she said, as she clasped the fur about her throat.

The unexpected words sent a pang through Mrs. Slade. "Yes; we'd better go." She gathered up her bag and cloak. "I don't know why you should be sorry for me," she muttered.

Mrs. Ansley stood looking away from her toward the dusky secret mass of the Colosseum. "Well—because I didn't have to wait that night."

Mrs. Slade gave an unquiet laugh. "Yes; I was beaten there. But I oughtn't to begrudge it to you, I suppose. At the end of all these years. After all, I had everything; I had him for twenty-five years. And you had nothing but that one letter that he didn't write."

Mrs. Ansley was again silent. At length she turned toward the door of the terrace. She took a step, and turned back, facing her companion.

"I had Barbara," she said, and began to move ahead of Mrs. Slade toward the stairway.

1936

EDGAR LEE MASTERS
1869–1950

Edgar Lee Masters is best known for his internationally acclaimed *Spoon River Anthology* (1915), a book that prompted Ezra Pound to conclude that "at last America has discovered a poet" and British critic John Cowper Powys to call Masters "the natural child of Walt Whitman." The *Spoon River* graveyard epitaphs spoke not only to the heart of America but to the anxieties and triumphs of humanity everywhere. Masters's later works have not received the critical acclaim they deserve. In spite of his popularity with the public, his poetry and fiction have been slighted by many critics who complain that he wrote too much too quickly.

Masters was raised in Petersburg in western Illinois—an area he celebrated often in his hymns to the eternal energy of the midwestern prairies. A lawyer by profession, he admitted to having read Shelley and Browning on the side camouflaged by law books in his office. His poetry was influenced by the tightness of the *Greek Anthology* and the expanse of Beethoven. He felt "lifted and strengthened" by Emerson; he was influenced by Whitman's native genius, Browning's dramatic monologues, Goethe's epic yearnings, Shelley's liberating imagery. Masters was also an astute critic of American culture. Sherwood Anderson and Masters were the most renowned of the Chicago Renaissance writers in the 1920s.

The variety of Masters's writing is impressive. Over four decades, he published fiction and critical essays as well as an autobiography, *Across Spoon River* (1936); critical biographies on Vachel Lindsay (1935), Whitman (1937), and Mark Twain (1938); and a wide range of poetry. *The New Spoon River* (1924) captured some of the nuances of the original, and several volumes from *Songs and Satires* (1916) to *Along the Illinois* (1942) featured short pieces. He paid tribute to the accomplishments of natural heroes and ordinary folks in the lyrical ballads of *Toward the Gulf* (1918) and *The Open Sea* (1921) and particularly in *Poems of People* (1936) and *More People* (1939). He experimented with innovative verse patterns and long narrative forms in *Lichee Nuts* (1930) and *The Serpent in the Wilderness* (1933) and drew upon his legal expertise in the courtroom suspense drama of *Domesday Book* (1920) and its sequel, *The Fate of the Jury* (1929). Though he spent his later years in the East, Masters's last volumes sang the praises of his native Midwest—in *Illinois Poems* (1941), *The Sangamon* (1942), and *The Harmony of Deeper Music*, (1976) edited by Frank K. Robinson, published after his death.

Masters heeded Emerson's warning that Americans had for too long listened to "the courtly Muses of Europe." He wrote about ordinary people and their everyday experiences. He saw small-town America as a microcosm of the universe and worked the rhythms of daily experience into his poems. He felt that poets in his time had largely avoided the challenges Whitman had issued to sing in the American idiom and to develop an American mythos. At a time when it wasn't popular to do so, he called for "American poetry, plain as the prairies, level as the quiet sea."

Ronald Primeau
Central Michigan University

PRIMARY WORKS

Spoon River Anthology, 1915; *Songs and Satires*, 1916; *Toward the Gulf*, 1918; *Domesday Book*, 1920; *The Open Sea*, 1921; *The New Spoon River*, 1924; *The Fate of the Jury*, 1929; *Lichee Nuts*, 1930; *The Serpent in the Wilderness*, 1933; *Across Spoon River*, 1936, 1991; *Poems of People*, 1936; *More People*, 1939; *Illinois Poems*, 1941; *Along the Illinois*, 1942; *The Sangamon*, 1942; *The Harmony of Deeper Music: Posthumous Poems of Edgar Lee Masters*, 1976, ed. by Frank K. Robinson; *The Enduring River: Edgar Lee Masters's Uncollected Spoon River Poems*, 1991; *Spoon River Anthology: An Annotated Edition*, 1992.

from Spoon River Anthology

Petit, the Poet

Seeds in a dry pod, tick, tick, tick,
Tick, tick, tick, like mites in a quarrel—
Faint iambics that the full breeze wakens—
But the pine tree makes a symphony thereof.
Triolets, villanelles, rondels, rondeaus,   5
Ballades by the score with the same old thought:
The snows and the roses of yesterday are vanished;
And what is love but a rose that fades?
Life all around me here in the village:
Tragedy, comedy, valor and truth,   10
Courage, constancy, heroism, failure—
All in the loom, and oh what patterns!
Woodlands, meadows, streams and rivers—
Blind to all of it all my life long.
Triolets, villanelles, rondels, rondeaus,   15
Seeds in a dry pod, tick, tick, tick,
Tick, tick, tick, what little iambics,
While Homer and Whitman roared in the pines?

Seth Compton

When I died, the circulating library
Which I built up for Spoon River,
And managed for the good of inquiring minds,
Was sold at auction on the public square,
As if to destroy the last vestige   5
Of my memory and influence.
For those of you who could not see the virtue
Of knowing Volney's "Ruins" as well as Butler's "Analogy"
And "Faust" as well as "Evangeline,"
Were really the power in the village,   10
And often you asked me,
"What is the use of knowing the evil in the world?"
I am out of your way now, Spoon River,
Choose your own good and call it good.
For I could never make you see   15
That no one knows what is good
Who knows not what is evil;
And no one knows what is true
Who knows not what is false.

Lucinda Matlock

I went to the dances at Chandlerville,
And played snap-out at Winchester.
One time we changed partners,
Driving home in the moonlight of middle June,
And then I found Davis.   5
We were married and lived together for seventy years,
Enjoying, working, raising the twelve children,
Eight of whom we lost
Ere I had reached the age of sixty.
I spun, I wove, I kept the house, I nursed the sick,   10
I made the garden, and for holiday
Rambled over the fields where sang the larks,
And by Spoon River gathering many a shell,
And many a flower and medicinal weed—
Shouting to the wooded hills, singing to the green valleys.   15
At ninety-six I had lived enough, that is all,
And passed to a sweet repose.
What is this I hear of sorrow and weariness,
Anger, discontent and drooping hopes?
Degenerate sons and daughters,   20
Life is too strong for you—
It takes life to love Life.

The Village Atheist

Ye young debaters over the doctrine
Of the soul's immortality,
I who lie here was the village atheist,
Talkative, contentious, versed in the arguments
Of the infidels.   5
But through a long sickness
Coughing myself to death
I read the *Upanishads*[1] and the poetry of Jesus.
And they lighted a torch of hope and intuition
And desire which the Shadow,   10
Leading me swiftly through the caverns of darkness,
Could not extinguish.
Listen to me, ye who live in the senses
And think through the senses only:
Immortality is not a gift,   15
Immortality is an achievement;
And only those who strive mightily
Shall possess it.

1915

■   WILLA CATHER   ■
1873–1947

Willa Cather was 38 in 1912 when her first novel, *Alexander's Bridge*, appeared
and 67 when her thirteenth and last novel, *Sapphira and the Slave Girl*, was published in 1940. Today she is compared with the most widely acclaimed American
novelists of the twentieth century—Ernest Hemingway, F. Scott Fitzgerald, and
William Faulkner—all of whom were a full generation younger than she. She
grew to maturity at the end of the nineteenth century and became an eloquent
spokeswoman for the values that shaped her to a twentieth-century world so
different from the one into which she was born. Her new subject for American
readers in the teens was the life of immigrant populations and transplanted
Americans living on the high prairies of Nebraska, Kansas, and Colorado, but
her subtle prose style and careful handling of narrative grew from her admiration for the work of American, British, and European writers such as Hawthorne, Flaubert, Stevenson, and James.

[1]Hindu metaphysical treatises dealing with
man in relation to the universe.

A recurring situation in much of Cather's best fiction is one that ties her work to a characteristic American experience—that of starting over. Willa Cather herself was born in the Upper Shenandoah Valley in western Virginia, near Winchester, the oldest of seven children of Charles and Virginia Cather. When she was nine, her parents moved west to join her paternal grandparents on the open plains of Nebraska, taking a large and varied household with them. At first the newcomers lived on the grandfather's farm in the Catherton precinct of Webster County, an area so populated with southerners that its school was called the New Virginia School. Within two years, however, Charles Cather moved the large household into the town of Red Cloud, where he opened a real estate office.

Red Cloud was no stereotypical isolated country town; a main spur of the Burlington railroad passed through it, and the Cathers saw performances in the local opera house of the most popular plays of the day produced by major traveling companies. Just as her months in the country had introduced her to the immigrant farmers from Sweden, France, and Bohemia, in Red Cloud Willa Cather discovered a cast of small-town characters rich in cultural diversity. Settlers in this small western town were from Europe, the American South, New England, northeastern cities, and the farms surrounding the small town.

A tomboy who fought the restrictions placed on "young ladies" in the American version of the Victorian era in which she grew up, Cather began signing her name on school papers as "William Cather, M.D." when she was 15. Her closely cropped hair and masculine dress made her stand out when she left home to prepare to enter the new state university in Lincoln. By the time she graduated from the University of Nebraska in 1895, she had modified her appearance and behavior to be more in keeping with the "New Women" of the 1890s that she encountered there. Her biographer Sharon O'Brien finds her early rebellion against conventional behavior in dress and demeanor a sign of the assertiveness that gave Cather the confidence she needed to succeed in a culture that was so repressive to women who did not accept their culturally assigned roles.

While in college, Cather began writing reviews for campus and Lincoln newspapers that led to her first job in Pittsburgh as an editor of a ladies' magazine. There she taught high school English and Latin for a few years before joining *McClure's Magazine* in New York City after publishing her first collection of short stories in 1905. (It includes "Paul's Case," her most anthologized work.) For the next forty years, she would live and write in New York, but rarely would that city appear in her fiction. Instead, the memories of her early years in Virginia and Nebraska, her trips to the American Southwest, New England, Europe, and Canada tantalized her mind. Midway through her career as a novelist, she broadened her attention from the worlds of her personal past to include the history of the settlement of North America in novels such as *Death Comes for the Archbishop* and *Shadows on the Rock*, which treat European immigration to New Mexico and Quebec.

Cather left no diaries, journals, or autobiography behind her when she died. Nor did she permit the publication or quotation of the many letters she wrote to friends that help biographers to explain the relationship she had to the subjects of her work. Yet clearly she found much of the power of her lifelong subjects from her own experience. Several recent biographers and critics see evidence of a lesbianism in Cather's life that she never openly proclaimed. Her strongest ties were clearly to women—her friend and traveling companion Isabelle McClung with whom Cather roomed during her years of high school teaching in Pittsburgh, her mentor Sarah Orne Jewett whom she met while working as a journalist for *McClure's Magazine*, and Edith Lewis, with whom Cather lived for almost forty years in New York. With no definitive evidence of Cather's sexual preference available, biographer James Woodress sees her as conscientiously avoiding binding romantic entanglements with either the men or the women in her life in order to devote all her energies to her writing.

Margaret Anne O'Connor
University of North Carolina at Chapel Hill

PRIMARY WORKS

April Twilights (poetry), 1903, 1923; *The Troll Garden* (stories), 1905; *Alexander's Bridge*, 1912; *O Pioneers!*, 1913; *The Song of the Lark*, 1915; *My Ántonia*, 1918; *Youth and the Bright Medusa* (stories), 1920; *One of Ours*, 1922; *A Lost Lady*, 1923; *The Professor's House*, 1925; *My Mortal Enemy*, 1926; *Death Comes for the Archbishop*, 1927; *Shadows on the Rock*, 1931; *Obscure Destinies* (stories), 1932; *Lucy Gayheart*, 1935; *Not Under Forty* (essays retitled *Literary Excursions* in the Autograph Edition of Cather's collected works, 1937–1941), 1936; *Sapphira and the Slave Girl*, 1940; *The Old Beauty and Others*, 1948; *Willa Cather on Writing*, 1949; *Uncle Valentine and Other Stories: 1915–1929*, 1973; *Collected Stories, 1892–1912*, ed. Mildred R. Bennett, 1965; *Willa Cather in Person: Interviews, Speeches, and Letters*, 1986.

Coming, Aphrodite!

I

Don Hedger had lived for four years on the top floor of an old house on the south side of Washington Square, and nobody had ever disturbed him. He occupied one big room with no outside exposure except on the north, where he had built in a many-paned studio window that looked upon a court and upon the roofs and walls of other buildings. His room was very cheerless, since he never got a ray of direct sunlight; the south corners were always in shadow. In one of the corners was a clothes closet, built against the partition, in another a wide divan, serving as a seat by day and a bed by night. In the front corner, the one farther from the window, was a sink, and a table with two gas burners where he sometimes cooked his food. There, too, in the perpetual dusk, was the dog's bed, and often a bone or two for his comfort.

The dog was a Boston bull terrier, and Hedger explained his surly disposition by the fact that he had been bred to the point where it told on his nerves. His name was Caesar III, and he had taken prizes at very exclusive dog shows. When he and his master went out to prowl about University Place or to promenade along West Street, Caesar III was invariably fresh and shining. His pink skin showed through his mottled coat, which glistened as if it had just been rubbed with olive oil, and he wore a brass-studded collar, bought at the smartest saddler's. Hedger, as often as not, was hunched up in an old striped blanket coat, with a shapeless felt hat pulled over his bushy hair, wearing black shoes that had become grey, or brown ones that had become black, and he never put on gloves unless the day was biting cold.

Early in May, Hedger learned that he was to have a new neighbour in the rear apartment—two rooms, one large and one small, that faced the west. His studio was shut off from the larger of these rooms by double doors, which, though they were fairly tight, left him a good deal at the mercy of the occupant. The rooms had been leased, long before he came there, by a trained nurse who considered herself knowing in old furniture. She went to auction sales and bought up mahogany and dirty brass and stored it away here, where she meant to live when she retired from nursing. Meanwhile, she sub-let her rooms, with their precious furniture, to young people who came to New York to "write" or to "paint"—who proposed to live by the sweat of the brow rather than of the hand, and who desired artistic surroundings.

When Hedger first moved in, these rooms were occupied by a young man who tried to write plays,—and who kept on trying until a week ago, when the nurse had put him out for unpaid rent.

A few days after the playwright left, Hedger heard an ominous murmur of voices through the bolted double doors: the lady-like intonation of the nurse—doubtless exhibiting her treasures—and another voice, also a woman's, but very different; young, fresh, unguarded, confident. All the same, it would be very annoying to have a woman in there. The only bath-room on the floor was at the top of the stairs in the front hall, and he would always be running into her as he came or went from his bath. He would have to be more careful to see that Caesar didn't leave bones about the hall, too; and she might object when he cooked steak and onions on his gas burner.

As soon as the talking ceased and the women left, he forgot them. He was absorbed in a study of paradise fish at the Aquarium, staring out at people through the glass and green water of their tank. It was a highly gratifying idea; the incommunicability of one stratum of animal life with another,—though Hedger pretended it was only an experiment in unusual lighting. When he heard trunks knocking against the sides of the narrow hall, then he realized that she was moving in at once. Toward noon, groans and deep gasps and the creaking of ropes, made him aware that a piano was arriving. After the tramp of the movers died away down the stairs, somebody touched off a few scales and chords on the instrument, and then there was peace. Presently he heard her lock her door and go down the hall humming something; going out to lunch, probably. He stuck his brushes in a can of turpentine and put on his hat, not stopping to wash his hands. Caesar was smelling along the crack under the bolted doors; his bony tail stuck out hard as a hickory withe, and the hair was standing up about his elegant collar.

Hedger encouraged him. "Come along, Caesar. You'll soon get used to a new smell."

In the hall stood an enormous trunk, behind the ladder that led to the roof, just opposite Hedger's door. The dog flew at it with a growl of hurt amazement. They went down three flights of stairs and out into the brilliant May afternoon.

Behind the Square, Hedger and his dog descended into a basement oyster house where there were no tablecloths on the tables and no handles on the coffee cups, and the floor was covered with sawdust, and Caesar was always welcome,—not that he needed any such precautionary flooring. All the carpets of Persia would have been safe for him. Hedger ordered steak and onions absentmindedly, not realizing why he had an apprehension that this dish might be less readily at hand hereafter. While he ate, Caesar sat beside his chair, gravely disturbing the sawdust with his tail.

After lunch Hedger strolled about the Square for the dog's health and watched the stages pull out;—that was almost the very last summer of the old horse stages on Fifth Avenue. The fountain had but lately begun operations for the season and was throwing up a mist of rainbow water which now and then blew south and sprayed a bunch of Italian babies that were being supported on the outer rim by older, very little older, brothers and sisters. Plump robins were hopping about on the soil; the grass was newly cut and blindingly green. Looking up the Avenue through the Arch, one could see the young poplars with their bright, sticky leaves, and the Brevoort glistening in its spring coat of paint, and shining horses and carriages,—occasionally an automobile, misshapen and sullen, like an ugly threat in a stream of things that were bright and beautiful and alive.

While Caesar and his master were standing by the fountain, a girl approached them, crossing the Square. Hedger noticed her because she wore a lavender cloth suit and carried in her arms a big bunch of fresh lilacs. He saw that she was young and handsome,—beautiful, in fact, with a splendid figure and good action. She, too, paused by the fountain and looked back through the Arch up the Avenue. She smiled rather patronizingly as she looked, and at the same time seemed delighted. Her slowly curving upper lip and half-closed eyes seemed to say: "You're gay, you're exciting, you are quite the right sort of thing; but you're none too fine for me!"

In the moment she tarried, Caesar stealthily approached her and sniffed at the hem of her lavender skirt, then, when she went south like an arrow, he ran back to his master and lifted a face full of emotion and alarm, his lower lip twitching under his sharp white teeth and his hazel eyes pointed with a very definite discovery. He stood thus, motionless, while Hedger watched the lavender girl go up the steps and through the door of the house in which he lived.

"You're right, my boy, it's she! She might be worse looking, you know."

When they mounted to the studio, the new lodger's door, at the back of the hall, was a little ajar, and Hedger caught the warm perfume of lilacs just brought in out of the sun. He was used to the musty smell of the old hall carpet. (The nurse-lessee had once knocked at his studio door and complained that Caesar must be somewhat responsible for the particular flavour of that mustiness, and Hedger had never spoken to her since.) He was used to the old smell, and he preferred it to that of the lilacs, and so did his companion, whose nose was so much more discriminating. Hedger shut his door vehemently, and fell to work.

Most young men who dwell in obscure studios in New York have had a beginning, come out of something, have somewhere a home town, a family, a paternal roof. But Don Hedger had no such background. He was a foundling, and had grown up in a school for homeless boys, where book-learning was a negligible part of the curriculum. When he was sixteen, a Catholic priest took him to Greensburg, Pennsylvania, to keep house for him. The priest did something to fill in the large gaps in the boy's education,—taught him to like "Don Quixote" and "The Golden Legend," and encouraged him to mess with paints and crayons in his room up under the slope of the mansard. When Don wanted to go to New York to study at the Art League, the priest got him a night job as packer in one of the big department stores. Since then, Hedger had taken care of himself; that was his only responsibility. He was singularly unencumbered; had no family duties, no social ties, no obligations toward any one but his landlord. Since he travelled light, he had travelled rather far. He had got over a good deal of the earth's surface, in spite of the fact that he never in his life had more than three hundred dollars ahead at any one time, and he had already outlived a succession of convictions and revelations about his art.

Though he was now but twenty-six years old, he had twice been on the verge of becoming a marketable product; once through some studies of New York streets he did for a magazine, and once through a collection of pastels he brought home from New Mexico, which Remington, then at the height of his popularity, happened to see, and generously tried to push. But on both occasions Hedger decided that this was something he didn't wish to carry further,—simply the old thing over again and got nowhere,—so he took enquiring dealers experiments in a "later manner," that made them put him out of the shop. When he ran short of money, he could always get any amount of commercial work; he was an expert draughtsman and worked with lightning speed. The rest of his time he spent in groping his way from one kind of painting into another, or travelling about without luggage, like a tramp, and he was chiefly occupied with getting rid of ideas he had once thought very fine.

Hedger's circumstances, since he had moved to Washington Square, were affluent compared to anything he had ever known before. He was now able to pay advance rent and turn the key on his studio when he went away for four months at a stretch. It didn't occur to him to wish to be richer than this. To be sure, he did without a great many things other people think necessary, but he didn't miss them, because he had never had them. He belonged to no clubs, visited no houses, had no studio friends, and he ate his dinner alone in some decent little restaurant, even on Christmas and New Year's. For days together he talked to nobody but his dog and the janitress and the lame oysterman.

After he shut the door and settled down to his paradise fish on that first Tuesday in May, Hedger forgot all about his new neighbour. When the light failed, he took Caesar out for a walk. On the way home he did his marketing on West Houston Street, with a one-eyed Italian woman who always cheated him. After he had cooked his beans and scallopini, and drunk half a bottle of Chianti, he put his dishes in the sink and went up on the roof to smoke. He was the only person in the house who ever went to the roof, and he had a secret understanding with the janitress about it. He was to have "the privilege of the roof," as she said, if he opened the heavy trapdoor on sunny days to air out the upper hall, and was watchful to close it when rain threatened. Mrs. Foley was fat and dirty and hated to climb stairs,—besides, the roof was reached by a perpendicular iron ladder, definitely inaccessible to a woman of her bulk, and the iron door at the top of it was too heavy for any but Hedger's strong arm to lift. Hedger was not above medium height, but he practised with weights and dumb-bells, and in the shoulders he was as strong as a gorilla.

So Hedger had the roof to himself. He and Caesar often slept up there on hot nights, rolled in blankets he had brought home from Arizona. He mounted with Caesar under his left arm. The dog had never learned to climb a perpendicular ladder, and never did he feel so much his master's greatness and his own dependence upon him, as when he crept under his arm for this perilous ascent. Up there was even gravel to scratch in, and a dog could do whatever he liked, so long as he did not bark. It was a kind of Heaven, which no one was strong enough to reach but his great, paint-smelling master.

On this blue May night there was a slender, girlish looking young moon in the west, playing with a whole company of silver stars. Now and then one of them darted away from the group and shot off into the gauzy blue with a soft little trail of light, like laughter. Hedger and his dog were delighted when a star did this. They were quite lost in watching the glittering game, when they were suddenly diverted by a sound,—not from the stars, though it was music. It was not the Prologue to Pagliacci, which rose ever and anon on hot evenings from an Italian tenement on Thompson Street, with the gasps of the corpulent baritone who got behind it; nor was it the hurdygurdy man, who often played at the corner in the balmy twilight. No, this was a woman's voice, singing the tempestuous, over-lapping phrases of Signor Puccini, then comparatively new in the world, but already so popular that even Hedger recognized his unmistakable gusts of breath. He looked about over the roofs; all was blue and still, with the well-built chimneys that were never used now standing up dark and mournful. He moved softly toward the yellow quadrangle where the gas from the hall shone up through the half-lifted trapdoor. Oh yes! It came up through the hole like a strong draught, a big, beautiful voice, and it sounded rather like a professional's. A piano had arrived in the morning, Hedger remembered. This might be a very great nuisance. It would be pleasant enough to listen to, if you could turn it on and off as you wished; but you couldn't. Caesar, with the gas light shining on his collar and his ugly but sensitive face, panted and looked up for information. Hedger put down a reassuring hand.

"I don't know. We can't tell yet. It may not be so bad."

He stayed on the roof until all was still below, and finally descended, with quite a new feeling about his neighbour. Her voice, like her figure, inspired respect,—if one did not choose to call it admiration. Her door was shut, the transom was dark; nothing remained of her but the obtrusive trunk, unrightfully taking up room in the narrow hall.

II

For two days Hedger didn't see her. He was painting eight hours a day just then, and only went out to hunt for food. He noticed that she practised scales and exercises for about an hour in the morning; then she locked her door, went humming down the hall, and left him in peace. He heard her getting her coffee ready at about the same time he got his. Earlier still, she passed his room on her way to her bath. In the evening she sometimes sang, but on the whole she didn't bother him. When he was working well he did not notice anything much. The morning paper lay before his door until he reached out for his milk bottle, then he kicked the sheet inside and it lay on the floor until evening. Sometimes he read it and sometimes he did not. He forgot there was anything of importance going on in the world outside of his third floor studio. Nobody had ever taught him that he ought to be interested in other people; in the Pittsburgh steel strike, in the Fresh Air Fund, in the scandal about the Babies' Hospital. A grey wolf, living in a Wyoming canyon, would hardly have been less concerned about these things than was Don Hedger.

One morning he was coming out of the bathroom at the front end of the hall, having just given Caesar his bath and rubbed him into a glow with a heavy towel. Before the door, lying in wait for him, as it were, stood a tall figure in a flowing blue silk dressing gown that fell away from her marble arms. In her hands she carried various accessories of the bath.

"I wish," she said distinctly, standing in his way, "I wish you wouldn't wash your dog in the tub. I never heard of such a thing! I've found his hair in the tub, and I've smelled a doggy smell, and now I've caught you at it. It's an outrage!"

Hedger was badly frightened. She was so tall and positive, and was fairly blazing with beauty and anger. He stood blinking, holding on to his sponge and dog-soap, feeling that he ought to bow very low to her. But what he actually said was:

"Nobody has ever objected before. I always wash the tub,—and, anyhow, he's cleaner than most people."

"Cleaner than me?" her eyebrows went up, her white arms and neck and her fragrant person seemed to scream at him like a band of outraged nymphs. Something flashed through his mind about a man who was turned into a dog, or was pursued by dogs, because he unwittingly intruded upon the bath of beauty.

"No, I didn't mean that," he muttered, turning scarlet under the bluish stubble of his muscular jaws. "But I know he's cleaner than I am."

"That I don't doubt!" Her voice sounded like a soft shivering of crystal, and with a smile of pity she drew the folds of her voluminous blue robe close about her and allowed the wretched man to pass. Even Caesar was frightened; he darted like a streak down the hall, through the door and to his own bed in the corner among the bones.

Hedger stood still in the doorway, listening to indignant sniffs and coughs and a great swishing of water about the sides of the tub. He had washed it; but as he had washed it with Caesar's sponge, it was quite possible that a few bristles remained; the dog was shedding now. The playwright had never objected, nor had the jovial illustrator who occupied the front apartment,—but he, as he admitted, "was usually pye-eyed, when he wasn't in Buffalo." He went home to Buffalo sometimes to rest his nerves.

It had never occurred to Hedger that any one would mind using the tub after Caesar;—but then, he had never seen a beautiful girl caparisoned for the bath before. As soon as he beheld her standing there, he realized the unfitness of it. For that matter, she ought not to step into a tub that any other mortal had bathed in; the illustrator was sloppy and left cigarette ends on the moulding.

All morning as he worked he was gnawed by a spiteful desire to get back at her. It rankled that he had been so vanquished by her disdain. When he heard her locking her door to go out for lunch, he stepped quickly into the hall in his messy painting coat, and addressed her.

"I don't wish to be exigent, Miss,"—he had certain grand words that he used upon occasion—"but if this is your trunk, it's rather in the way here."

"Oh, very well!" she exclaimed carelessly, dropping her keys into her handbag. "I'll have it moved when I can get a man to do it," and she went down the hall with her free, roving stride.

Her name, Hedger discovered from her letters, which the postman left on the table in the lower hall, was Eden Bower.

III

In the closet that was built against the partition separating his room from Miss Bower's, Hedger kept all his wearing apparel, some of it on hooks and hangers, some of it on the floor. When he opened his closet door now-a-days, little dust-coloured insects flew out on downy wing, and he suspected that a brood of moths were hatching in his winter overcoat. Mrs. Foley, the janitress, told him to bring down all his heavy clothes and she would give them a beating and hang them in the court. The closet was in such disorder that he shunned the encounter, but one hot afternoon he set himself to the task. First he threw out a pile of forgotten laundry and tied it up in a sheet. The bundle stood as high as his middle when he had knotted the corners. Then he got his shoes and overshoes together. When he took his overcoat from its place against the partition, a long ray of yellow light shot across the dark enclosure,—a knot hole, evidently, in the high wainscoting of the west room. He had never noticed it before, and without realizing what he was doing, he stooped and squinted through it.

Yonder, in a pool of sunlight, stood his new neighbour, wholly unclad, doing exercises of some sort before a long gilt mirror. Hedger did not happen to think how unpardonable it was of him to watch her. Nudity was not improper to any one who had worked so much from the figure, and he continued to look, simply because he had never seen a woman's body so beautiful as this one,—positively glorious in action. As she swung her arms and changed from one pivot of motion to another, muscular energy seemed to flow through her from her toes to her finger-tips. The soft flush of exercise and the gold of afternoon sun played over her flesh together, enveloped her in a luminous mist which, as she turned and twisted, made now an arm, now a shoulder, now a thigh, dissolve in pure light and instantly recover its outline with the next gesture. Hedger's fingers curved as if he were holding a crayon; mentally he was doing the whole figure in a single running line, and the charcoal seemed to explode in his hand at the point where the energy of each gesture was discharged into the whirling disc of light, from a foot or shoulder, from the up-thrust chin or the lifted breasts.

He could not have told whether he watched her for six minutes or sixteen. When her gymnastics were over, she paused to catch up a lock of hair that had come down, and examined with solicitude a little reddish mole that grew under her left arm-pit. Then, with her hand on her hip, she walked unconcernedly across the room and disappeared through the door into her bedchamber.

Disappeared—Don Hedger was crouching on his knees, staring at the golden shower which poured in through the west windows, at the lake of gold sleeping on the faded Turkish carpet. The spot was enchanted; a vision out of Alexandria, out of the remote pagan past, had bathed itself there in Helianthine fire.

When he crawled out of his closet, he stood blinking at the grey sheet stuffed with laundry, not knowing what had happened to him. He felt a little sick as he contemplated the bundle. Everything here was different; he hated the disorder of the place, the grey prison light, his old shoes and himself and all his slovenly habits. The black calico curtains that ran on wires over his big window were white with dust. There were three greasy frying pans in the sink, and the sink itself—He felt desperate. He couldn't stand this another minute. He took up an armful of winter clothes and ran down four flights into the basement.

"Mrs. Foley," he began, "I want my room cleaned this afternoon, thoroughly cleaned. Can you get a woman for me right away?"

"Is it company you're having?" the fat, dirty janitress enquired. Mrs. Foley was the widow of a useful Tammany man, and she owned real estate in Flatbush. She was huge and soft as a feather bed. Her face and arms were permanently coated with dust, grained like wood where the sweat had trickled.

"Yes, company. That's it."

"Well, this is a queer time of the day to be asking for a cleaning woman. It's likely I can get you old Lizzie, if she's not drunk. I'll send Willy round to see."

Willy, the son of fourteen, roused from the stupor and stain of his fifth box of cigarettes by the gleam of a quarter, went out. In five minutes he returned with old Lizzie,—she smelling strong of spirits and wearing several jackets which she had put on one over the other, and a number of skirts, long and short, which made her resemble an animated dish-clout. She had, of course, to borrow her equipment from Mrs. Foley, and toiled up the long flights, dragging mop and pail and broom. She told Hedger to be of good cheer, for he had got the right woman for the job, and showed him a great leather strap she wore about her wrist to prevent dislocation of tendons. She swished about the place, scattering dust and splashing soapsuds, while he watched her in nervous despair. He stood over Lizzie and made her scour the sink, directing her roughly, then paid her and got rid of her. Shutting the door on his failure, he hurried off with his dog to lose himself among the stevedores and dock labourers on West Street.

A strange chapter began for Don Hedger. Day after day, at that hour in the afternoon, the hour before his neighbour dressed for dinner, he crouched down in his closet to watch her go through her mysterious exercises. It did not occur to him that his conduct was detestable; there was nothing shy or retreating about this unclad girl,—a bold body, studying itself quite coolly and evidently well pleased with itself, doing all this for a purpose. Hedger scarcely regarded his action as conduct at all; it was something that had happened to him. More than once he went out and tried to stay away for the whole afternoon, but at about five o'clock he was sure to find himself among his old shoes in the dark. The pull of that aperture was stronger than his will,—and he had always considered his will the strongest thing about him. When she threw herself upon the divan and lay resting, he still stared, holding his breath. His nerves were so on edge that a sudden noise made him start and brought out the sweat on his forehead. The dog would come and tug at his sleeve, knowing that something was wrong with his master. If he attempted a mournful whine, those strong hands closed about his throat.

When Hedger came slinking out of his closet, he sat down on the edge of the couch, sat for hours without moving. He was not painting at all now. This thing, whatever it was, drank him up as ideas had sometimes done, and he sank into a stupor of idleness as deep and dark as the stupor of work. He could not understand it; he was no boy, he had worked from models for years, and a woman's body was no mystery to him. Yet now he did nothing but sit and think about one. He slept very little, and with the first light of morning he awoke as completely possessed by this woman as if he had been with her all the night before. The unconscious operations of life went on in him only to perpetuate this excitement. His brain held but one image now—vibrated, burned with it. It was a heathenish feeling; without friendliness, almost without tenderness.

Women had come and gone in Hedger's life. Not having had a mother to begin with, his relations with them, whether amorous or friendly, had been casual. He got on well with janitresses and wash-women, with Indians and with the peasant women of foreign countries. He had friends among the silk-skirt factory girls who came to eat their lunch in Washington Square, and he sometimes took a model for a day in the country. He felt an unreasoning antipathy toward the well-dressed women he saw coming out of big shops, or driving in the Park. If, on his way to the Art Museum, he noticed a pretty girl standing on the steps of one of the houses on upper Fifth Avenue, he frowned at her and went by with his shoulders hunched up as if he were cold. He had never known such girls, or heard them talk, or seen the inside of the houses in which they lived; but he believed them all to be artificial and, in an aesthetic sense, perverted. He saw them enslaved by desire of merchandise and manufactured articles, effective only in making life complicated and insincere and in embroidering it with ugly and meaningless trivialities. They were enough, he thought, to make one almost forget woman as she existed in art, in thought, and in the universe.

He had no desire to know the woman who had, for the time at least, so broken up his life,—no curiosity about her every-day personality. He shunned any revelation of it, and he listened for Miss Bower's coming and going, not to encounter, but to avoid her. He wished that the girl who wore shirt-waists and got letters from Chicago would keep out of his way, that she did not exist. With her he had naught to make. But in a room full of sun, before an old mirror, on a little enchanted rug of sleeping colours, he had seen a woman who emerged naked through a door, and disappeared naked. He thought of that body as never having been clad, or as having worn the stuffs and dyes of all the centuries but his own. And for him she had no geographical associations; unless with Crete, or Alexandria, or Veronese's Venice. She was the immortal conception, the perennial theme.

The first break in Hedger's lethargy occurred one afternoon when two young men came to take Eden Bower out to dine. They went into her music room, laughed and talked for a few minutes, and then took her away with them. They were gone a long while, but he did not go out for food himself; he waited for them to come back. At last he heard them coming down the hall, gayer and more talkative than when they left. One of them sat down at the piano, and they all began to sing. This Hedger found absolutely unendurable. He snatched up his hat and went running down the stairs. Caesar leaped beside him, hoping that old times were coming back. They had supper in the oysterman's basement and then sat down in front of their own doorway. The moon stood full over the Square, a thing of regal glory; but Hedger did not see the moon; he was looking, murderously, for men. Presently two, wearing straw hats and white trousers and carrying canes, came down the steps from his house. He rose and dogged them across the Square. They were laughing and seemed very much elated about something. As one stopped to light a cigarette, Hedger caught from the other:

"Don't you think she has a beautiful talent?"

His companion threw away his match. "She has a beautiful figure." They both ran to catch the stage.

Hedger went back to his studio. The light was shining from her transom. For the first time he violated her privacy at night, and peered through that fatal aperture. She was sitting, fully dressed, in the window, smoking a cigarette and looking out over the housetops. He watched her until she rose, looked about her with a disdainful, crafty smile, and turned out the light.

The next morning, when Miss Bower went out, Hedger followed her. Her white skirt gleamed ahead of him as she sauntered about the Square. She sat down behind the Garibaldi statue and opened a music book she carried. She turned the leaves carelessly, and several times glanced in his direction. He was on the point of going over to her, when she rose quickly and looked up at the sky. A flock of pigeons had risen from somewhere in the crowded Italian quarter to the south, and were wheeling rapidly up through the morning air, soaring and dropping, scattering and coming together, now grey, now white as silver, as they caught or intercepted the sunlight. She put up her hand to shade her eyes and followed them with a kind of defiant delight in her face.

Hedger came and stood beside her. "You've surely seen them before?"

"Oh, yes," she replied, still looking up. "I see them every day from my windows. They always come home about five o'clock. Where do they live?"

"I don't know. Probably some Italian raises them for the market. They were here long before I came, and I've been here four years."

"In that same gloomy room? Why didn't you take mine when it was vacant?"

"It isn't gloomy. That's the best light for painting."

"Oh, is it? I don't know anything about painting. I'd like to see your pictures sometime. You have such a lot in there. Don't they get dusty, piled up against the wall like that?"

"Not very. I'd be glad to show them to you. Is your name really Eden Bower? I've seen your letters on the table."

"Well, it's the name I'm going to sing under. My father's name is Bowers, but my friend Mr. Jones, a Chicago newspaper man who writes about music, told me to drop the 's.' He's crazy about my voice."

Miss Bower didn't usually tell the whole story,—about anything. Her first name, when she lived in Huntington, Illinois, was Edna, but Mr. Jones had persuaded her to change it to one which he felt would be worthy of her future. She was quick to take suggestions, though she told him she "didn't see what was the matter with 'Edna.'"

She explained to Hedger that she was going to Paris to study. She was waiting in New York for Chicago friends who were to take her over, but who had been detained. "Did you study in Paris?" she asked.

"No, I've never been in Paris. But I was in the south of France all last summer, studying with C——. He's the biggest man among the moderns,— at least I think so."

Miss Bower sat down and made room for him on the bench. "Do tell me about it. I expected to be there by this time, and I can't wait to find out what it's like."

Hedger began to relate how he had seen some of this Frenchman's work in an exhibition, and deciding at once that this was the man for him, he had taken a boat for Marseilles the next week, going over steerage. He proceeded at once to the little town on the coast where his painter lived, and presented himself. The man never took pupils, but because Hedger had come so far, he let him stay. Hedger lived at the master's house and every day they went out together to paint, sometimes on the blazing rocks down by the sea. They wrapped themselves in light woollen blankets and didn't feel the heat. Being there and working with C____ was being in Paradise, Hedger concluded; he learned more in three months than in all his life before.

Eden Bower laughed. "You're a funny fellow. Didn't you do anything but work? Are the women very beautiful? Did you have awfully good things to eat and drink?"

Hedger said some of the women were fine looking, especially one girl who went about selling fish and lobsters. About the food there was nothing remarkable,—except the ripe figs, he liked those. They drank sour wine, and used goat-butter, which was strong and full of hair, as it was churned in a goat skin.

"But don't they have parties or banquets? Aren't there any fine hotels down there?"

"Yes, but they are all closed in summer, and the country people are poor. It's a beautiful country, though."

"How, beautiful?" she persisted.

"If you want to go in, I'll show you some sketches, and you'll see."

Miss Bower rose. "All right. I won't go to my fencing lesson this morning. Do you fence? Here comes your dog. You can't move but he's after you. He always makes a face at me when I meet him in the hall, and shows his nasty little teeth as if he wanted to bite me."

In the studio Hedger got out his sketches, but to Miss Bower, whose favourite pictures were Christ Before Pilate and a redhaired Magdalen of Henner, these landscapes were not at all beautiful, and they gave her no idea of any country whatsoever. She was careful not to commit herself, however. Her vocal teacher had already convinced her that she had a great deal to learn about many things.

"Why don't we go out to lunch somewhere?" Hedger asked, and began to dust his fingers with a handkerchief—which he got out of sight as swiftly as possible.

"All right, the Brevoort," she said carelessly. "I think that's a good place, and they have good wine. I don't care for cocktails."

Hedger felt his chin uneasily. "I'm afraid I haven't shaved this morning. If you could wait for me in the Square? It won't take me ten minutes."

Left alone, he found a clean collar and handkerchief, brushed his coat and blacked his shoes, and last of all dug up ten dollars from the bottom of an old copper kettle he had brought from Spain. His winter hat was of such a complexion that the Brevoort hall boy winked at the porter as he took it and placed it on the rack in a row of fresh straw ones.

IV

That afternoon Eden Bower was lying on the couch in her music room, her face turned to the window, watching the pigeons. Reclining thus she could see none of the neighbouring roofs, only the sky itself and the birds that crossed and recrossed her field of vision, white as scraps of paper blowing in the wind. She was thinking that she was young and handsome and had had a good lunch, that a very easy-going, light-hearted city lay in the streets below her; and she was wondering why she found this queer painter chap, with his lean, bluish cheeks and heavy black eyebrows, more interesting than the smart young men she met at her teacher's studio.

Eden Bower was, at twenty, very much the same person that we all know her to be at forty, except that she knew a great deal less. But one thing she knew: that she was to be Eden Bower. She was like some one standing before a great show window full of beautiful and costly things, deciding which she will order. She understands that they will not all be delivered immediately, but one by one they will arrive at her door. She already knew some of the many things that were to happen to her; for instance, that the Chicago millionaire who was going to take her abroad with his sister as chaperone, would eventually press his claim in quite another manner. He was the most circumspect of bachelors, afraid of everything obvious, even of women who were too flagrantly handsome. He was a nervous collector of pictures and furniture, a nervous patron of music, and a nervous host; very cautious about his health, and about any course of conduct that might make him ridiculous. But she knew that he would at last throw all his precautions to the winds.

People like Eden Bower are inexplicable. Her father sold farming machinery in Huntington, Illinois, and she had grown up with no acquaintances or experiences outside of that prairie town. Yet from her earliest childhood she had not one conviction or opinion in common with the people about her,— the only people she knew. Before she was out of short dresses she had made up her mind that she was going to be an actress, that she would live far away in great cities, that she would be much admired by men and would have everything she wanted. When she was thirteen, and was already singing and reciting for church entertainments, she read in some illustrated magazine a long article about the late Czar of Russia, then just come to the throne or about to come to it. After that, lying in the hammock on the front porch on summer evenings, or sitting through a long sermon in the family pew, she amused herself by trying to make up her mind whether she would or would not be the Czar's mistress when she played in his Capital. Now Edna had met this fascinating word only in the novels of Ouida,—her hard-worked little mother kept a long row of them in the upstairs storeroom, behind the linen chest. In Huntington, women who bore that relation to men were called by a very different name, and their lot was not an enviable one; of all the shabby and poor, they were the shabbiest. But then, Edna had never lived in Huntington, not even before she began to find books like "Sapho" and "Mademoiselle de Maupin," secretly sold in paper covers throughout

Illinois. It was as if she had come into Huntington, into the Bowers family, on one of the trains that puffed over the marshes behind their back fence all day long, and was waiting for another train to take her out.

As she grew older and handsomer, she had many beaux, but these small-town boys didn't interest her. If a lad kissed her when he brought her home from a dance, she was indulgent and she rather liked it. But if he pressed her further, she slipped away from him, laughing. After she began to sing in Chicago, she was consistently discreet. She stayed as a guest in rich people's houses, and she knew that she was being watched like a rabbit in a laboratory. Covered up in bed, with the lights out, she thought her own thoughts, and laughed.

This summer in New York was her first taste of freedom. The Chicago capitalist, after all his arrangements were made for sailing, had been compelled to go to Mexico to look after oil interests. His sister knew an excellent singing master in New York. Why should not a discreet, well-balanced girl like Miss Bower spend the summer there, studying quietly? The capitalist suggested that his sister might enjoy a summer on Long Island; he would rent the Griffith's place for her, with all the servants, and Eden could stay there. But his sister met this proposal with a cold stare. So it fell out, that between selfishness and greed, Eden got a summer all her own,—which really did a great deal toward making her an artist and whatever else she was afterward to become. She had time to look about, to watch without being watched; to select diamonds in one window and furs in another, to select shoulders and moustaches in the big hotels where she went to lunch. She had the easy freedom of obscurity and the consciousness of power. She enjoyed both. She was in no hurry.

While Eden Bower watched the pigeons, Don Hedger sat on the other side of the bolted doors, looking into a pool of dark turpentine, at his idle brushes, wondering why a woman could do this to him. He, too, was sure of his future and knew that he was a chosen man. He could not know, of course, that he was merely the first to fall under a fascination which was to be disastrous to a few men and pleasantly stimulating to many thousands. Each of these two young people sensed the future, but not completely. Don Hedger knew that nothing much would ever happen to him. Eden Bower understood that to her a great deal would happen. But she did not guess that her neighbour would have more tempestuous adventures sitting in his dark studio than she would find in all the capitals of Europe, or in all the latitude of conduct she was prepared to permit herself.

V

One Sunday morning Eden was crossing the Square with a spruce young man in a white flannel suit and a panama hat. They had been breakfasting at the Brevoort and he was coaxing her to let him come up to her rooms and sing for an hour.

"No, I've got to write letters. You must run along now. I see a friend of mine over there, and I want to ask him about something before I go up."

"That fellow with the dog? Where did you pick him up?" the young man glanced toward the seat under a sycamore where Hedger was reading the morning paper.

"Oh, he's an old friend from the West," said Eden easily. "I won't introduce you, because he doesn't like people. He's a recluse. Good-bye. I can't be sure about Tuesday. I'll go with you if I have time after my lesson." She nodded, left him, and went over to the seat littered with newspapers. The young man went up the Avenue without looking back.

"Well, what are you going to do today? Shampoo this animal all morning?" Eden enquired teasingly.

Hedger made room for her on the seat. "No, at twelve o'clock I'm going out to Coney Island. One of my models is going up in a balloon this afternoon. I've often promised to go and see her, and now I'm going."

Eden asked if models usually did such stunts. No, Hedger told her, but Molly Welch added to her earnings in that way. "I believe," he added, "she likes the excitement of it. She's got a good deal of spirit. That's why I like to paint her. So many models have flaccid bodies."

"And she hasn't, eh? Is she the one who comes to see you? I can't help hearing her, she talks so loud."

"Yes, she has a rough voice, but she's a fine girl. I don't suppose you'd be interested in going?"

"I don't know," Eden sat tracing patterns on the asphalt with the end of her parasol. "Is it any fun? I got up feeling I'd like to do something different today. It's the first Sunday I've not had to sing in church. I had that engagement for breakfast at the Brevoort, but it wasn't very exciting. That chap can't talk about anything but himself."

Hedger warmed a little. "If you've never been to Coney Island, you ought to go. It's nice to see all the people; tailors and bar-tenders and prize-fighters with their best girls, and all sorts of folks taking a holiday."

Eden looked sidewise at him. So one ought to be interested in people of that kind, ought one? He was certainly a funny fellow. Yet he was never, somehow, tiresome. She had seen a good deal of him lately, but she kept wanting to know him better, to find out what made him different from men like the one she had just left—whether he really was as different as he seemed. "I'll go with you," she said at last, "if you'll leave that at home." She pointed to Caesar's flickering ears with her sunshade.

"But he's half the fun. You'd like to hear him bark at the waves when they come in."

"No, I wouldn't. He's jealous and disagreeable if he sees you talking to any one else. Look at him now."

"Of course, if you make a face at him. He knows what that means, and he makes a worse face. He likes Molly Welch, and she'll be disappointed if I don't bring him."

Eden said decidedly that he couldn't take both of them. So at twelve o'clock when she and Hedger got on the boat at Desbrosses street, Caesar was lying on his pallet, with a bone.

Eden enjoyed the boat-ride. It was the first time she had been on the water, and she felt as if she were embarking for France. The light warm breeze and the plunge of the waves made her very wide awake, and she liked crowds of any kind. They went to the balcony of a big, noisy restaurant and had a shore dinner, with tall steins of beer. Hedger had got a big advance from his advertising firm since he first lunched with Miss Bower ten days ago, and he was ready for anything.

After dinner they went to the tent behind the bathing beach, where the tops of two balloons bulged out over the canvas. A red-faced man in a linen suit stood in front of the tent, shouting in a hoarse voice and telling the people that if the crowd was good for five dollars more, a beautiful young woman would risk her life for their entertainment. Four little boys in dirty red uniforms ran about taking contributions in their pillbox hats. One of the balloons was bobbing up and down in its tether and people were shoving forward to get nearer the tent.

"Is it dangerous, as he pretends?" Eden asked.

"Molly says it's simple enough if nothing goes wrong with the balloon. Then it would be all over, I suppose."

"Wouldn't you like to go up with her?"

"I? Of course not. I'm not fond of taking foolish risks."

Eden sniffed. "I shouldn't think sensible risks would be very much fun."

Hedger did not answer, for just then every one began to shove the other way and shout, "Look out. There she goes!" and a band of six pieces commenced playing furiously.

As the balloon rose from its tent enclosure, they saw a girl in green tights standing in the basket, holding carelessly to one of the ropes with one hand and with the other waving to the spectators. A long rope trailed behind to keep the balloon from blowing out to sea.

As it soared, the figure in green tights in the basket diminished to a mere spot, and the balloon itself, in the brilliant light, looked like a big silver-grey bat, with its wings folded. When it began to sink, the girl stepped through the hole in the basket to a trapeze that hung below, and gracefully descended through the air, holding to the rod with both hands, keeping her body taut and her feet close together. The crowd, which had grown very large by this time, cheered vociferously. The men took off their hats and waved, little boys shouted, and fat old women, shining with the heat and a beer lunch, murmured admiring comments upon the balloonist's figure. "Beautiful legs, she has!"

"That's so," Hedger whispered. "Not many girls would look well in that position." Then, for some reason, he blushed a slow, dark, painful crimson.

The balloon descended slowly, a little way from the tent, and the red-faced man in the linen suit caught Molly Welch before her feet touched the ground, and pulled her to one side. The band struck up "Blue Bell" by way of welcome, and one of the sweaty pages ran forward and presented the balloonist with a large bouquet of artificial flowers. She smiled and thanked him, and ran back across the sand to the tent.

"Can't we go inside and see her?" Eden asked. "You can explain to the door man. I want to meet her." Edging forward, she herself addressed the man in the linen suit and slipped something from her purse into his hand.

They found Molly seated before a trunk that had a mirror in the lid and a "make-up" outfit spread upon the tray. She was wiping the cold cream and powder from her neck with a discarded chemise.

"Hello, Don," she said cordially. "Brought a friend?"

Eden liked her. She had an easy, friendly manner, and there was something boyish and devil-may-care about her.

"Yes, it's fun. I'm mad about it," she said in reply to Eden's questions. "I always want to let go, when I come down on the bar. You don't feel your weight at all, as you would on a stationary trapeze."

The big drum boomed outside, and the publicity man began shouting to newly arrived boatloads. Miss Welch took a last pull at her cigarette. "Now you'll have to get out, Don. I change for the next act. This time I go up in a black evening dress, and lose the skirt in the basket before I start down."

"Yes, go along," said Eden. "Wait for me outside the door. I'll stay and help her dress."

Hedger waited and waited, while women of every build bumped into him and begged his pardon, and the red pages ran about holding out their caps for coins, and the people ate and perspired and shifted parasols against the sun. When the band began to play a two-step, all the bathers ran up out of the surf to watch the ascent. The second balloon bumped and rose, and the crowd began shouting to the girl in a black evening dress who stood leaning against the ropes and smiling. "It's a new girl," they called. "It ain't the Countess this time. You're a peach, girlie!"

The balloonist acknowledged these compliments, bowing and looking down over the sea of upturned faces,—but Hedger was determined she should not see him, and he darted behind the tent-fly. He was suddenly dripping with cold sweat, his mouth was full of the bitter taste of anger and his tongue felt stiff behind his teeth. Molly Welch, in a shirt-waist and a white tam-o'-shanter cap, slipped out from the tent under his arm and laughed up in his face. "She's a crazy one you brought along. She'll get what she wants!"

"Oh, I'll settle with you, all right!" Hedger brought out with difficulty.

"It's not my fault, Donnie. I couldn't do anything with her. She bought me off. What's the matter with you? Are you soft on her? She's safe enough. It's as easy as rolling off a log, if you keep cool." Molly Welch was rather excited herself, and she was chewing gum at a high speed as she stood beside him, looking up at the floating silver cone. "Now watch," she exclaimed suddenly. "She's coming down on the bar. I advised her to cut that out, but you see she does it first-rate. And she got rid of the skirt, too. Those black tights show off her legs very well. She keeps her feet together like I told her, and makes a good line along the back. See the light on those silver slippers,—that was a good idea I had. Come along to meet her. Don't be a grouch; she's done it fine!"

Molly tweaked his elbow, and then left him standing like a stump, while she ran down the beach with the crowd.

Though Hedger was sulking, his eye could not help seeing the low blue welter of the sea, the arrested bathers, standing in the surf, their arms and legs stained red by the dropping sun, all shading their eyes and gazing upward at the slowly falling silver star.

Molly Welch and the manager caught Eden under the arms and lifted her aside, a red page dashed up with a bouquet, and the band struck up "Blue Bell." Eden laughed and bowed, took Molly's arm, and ran up the sand in her black tights and silver slippers, dodging the friendly old women, and the gallant sports who wanted to offer their homage on the spot.

When she emerged from the tent, dressed in her own clothes, that part of the beach was almost deserted. She stepped to her companion's side and said carelessly: "Hadn't we better try to catch this boat? I hope you're not sore at me. Really, it was lots of fun."

Hedger looked at his watch. "Yes, we have fifteen minutes to get to the boat," he said politely.

As they walked toward the pier, one of the pages ran up panting. "Lady, you're carrying off the bouquet," he said, aggrievedly.

Eden stopped and looked at the bunch of spotty cotton roses in her hand. "Of course. I want them for a souvenir. You gave them to me yourself."

"I give 'em to you for looks, but you can't take 'em away. They belong to the show."

"Oh, you always use the same bunch?"

"Sure we do. There ain't too much money in this business."

She laughed and tossed them back to him. "Why are you angry?" she asked Hedger. "I wouldn't have done it if I'd been with some fellows, but I thought you were the sort who wouldn't mind. Molly didn't for a minute think you would."

"What possessed you to do such a fool thing?" he asked roughly.

"I don't know. When I saw her coming down, I wanted to try it. It looked exciting. Didn't I hold myself as well as she did?"

Hedger shrugged his shoulders, but in his heart he forgave her.

The return boat was not crowded, though the boats that passed them, going out, were packed to the rails. The sun was setting. Boys and girls sat on the long benches with their arms about each other, singing. Eden felt a strong wish to propitiate her companion, to be alone with him. She had been curiously wrought up by her balloon trip; it was a lark, but not very satisfying unless one came back to something after the flight. She wanted to be admired and adored. Though Eden said nothing, and sat with her arms limp on the rail in front of her, looking languidly at the rising silhouette of the city and the bright path of the sun, Hedger felt a strange drawing near to her. If he but brushed her white skirt with his knee, there was an instant communication between them, such as there had never been before. They did not talk at all, but when they went over the gang-plank she took his arm and kept her shoulder close to his. He felt as if they were enveloped in a highly charged atmosphere, an invisible network of subtle, almost painful sensibility. They had somehow taken hold of each other.

An hour later, they were dining in the back garden of a little French hotel on Ninth Street, long since passed away. It was cool and leafy there, and the mosquitoes were not very numerous. A party of South Americans at another table were drinking champagne, and Eden murmured that she thought she would like some, if it were not too expensive. "Perhaps it will make me think I am in the balloon again. That was a very nice feeling. You've forgiven me, haven't you?"

Hedger gave her a quick straight look from under his black eyebrows, and something went over her that was like a chill, except that it was warm and feathery. She drank most of the wine; her companion was indifferent to it. He was talking more to her tonight than he had ever done before. She asked him about a new picture she had seen in his room; a queer thing full of stiff, supplicating female figures. "It's Indian, isn't it?"

"Yes. I call it Rain Spirits, or maybe, Indian Rain. In the Southwest, where I've been a good deal, the Indian traditions make women have to do with the rain-fall. They were supposed to control it, somehow, and to be able to find springs, and make moisture come out of the earth. You see I'm trying to learn to paint what people think and feel; to get away from all that photographic stuff. When I look at you, I don't see what a camera would see, do I?"

"How can I tell?"

"Well, if I should paint you, I could make you understand what I see." For the second time that day Hedger crimsoned unexpectedly, and his eyes fell and steadily contemplated a dish of little radishes. "That particular picture I got from a story a Mexican priest told me; he said he found it in an old manuscript book in a monastery down there, written by some Spanish Missionary, who got his stories from the Aztecs. This one he called 'The Forty Lovers of the Queen,' and it was more or less about rain-making."

"Aren't you going to tell it to me?" Eden asked.

Hedger fumbled among the radishes. "I don't know if it's the proper kind of story to tell a girl."

She smiled; "Oh, forget about that! I've been balloon riding today. I like to hear you talk."

Her low voice was flattering. She had seemed like clay in his hands ever since they got on the boat to come home. He leaned back in his chair, forgot his food, and, looking at her intently, began to tell his story, the theme of which he somehow felt was dangerous tonight.

The tale began, he said, somewhere in Ancient Mexico, and concerned the daughter of a king. The birth of this Princess was preceded by unusual portents. Three times her mother dreamed that she was delivered of serpents, which betokened that the child she carried would have power with the rain gods. The serpent was the symbol of water. The Princess grew up dedicated to the gods, and wise men taught her the rain-making mysteries.

She was with difficulty restrained from men and was guarded at all times, for it was the law of the Thunder that she be maiden until her marriage. In the years of her adolescence, rain was abundant with her people. The oldest man could not remember such fertility. When the Princess had counted eighteen summers, her father went to drive out a war party that harried his borders on the north and troubled his prosperity. The King destroyed the invaders and brought home many prisoners. Among the prisoners was a young chief, taller than any of his captors, of such strength and ferocity that the King's people came a day's journey to look at him. When the Princess beheld his great stature, and saw that his arms and breast were covered with the figures of wild animals, bitten into the skin and coloured, she begged his life from her father. She desired that he should practise his art upon her, and prick upon her skin the signs of Rain and Lightning and Thunder, and stain the wounds with herb-juices, as they were upon his own body. For many days, upon the roof of the King's house, the Princess submitted herself to the bone needle, and the women with her marvelled at her fortitude. But the Princess was without shame before the Captive, and it came about that he threw from him his needles and his stains, and fell upon the Princess to violate her honour; and her women ran down from the roof screaming, to call the guard which stood at the gateway of the King's house, and none stayed to protect their mistress.

When the guard came, the Captive was thrown into bonds, and he was gelded, and his tongue was torn out, and he was given for a slave to the Rain Princess.

The country of the Aztecs to the east was tormented by thirst, and their king, hearing much of the rain-making arts of the Princess, sent an embassy to her father, with presents and an offer of marriage. So the Princess went from her father to be the Queen of the Aztecs, and she took with her the Captive, who served her in everything with entire fidelity and slept upon a mat before her door.

The King gave his bride a fortress on the outskirts of the city, whither she retired to entreat the rain gods. This fortress was called the Queen's House, and on the night of the new moon the Queen came to it from the palace. But when the moon waxed and grew toward the round, because the god of Thunder had had his will of her, then the Queen returned to the King. Drought abated in the country and rain fell abundantly by reason of the Queen's power with the stars.

When the Queen went to her own house she took with her no servant but the Captive, and he slept outside her door and brought her food after she had fasted. The Queen had a jewel of great value, a turquoise that had fallen from the sun, and had the image of the sun upon it. And when she desired a young man whom she had seen in the army or among the slaves, she sent the Captive to him with the jewel, for a sign that he should come to her secretly at the Queen's House upon business concerning the welfare of all. And some, after she had talked with them, she sent away with rewards; and some she took into her chamber and kept them by her for one night or two. Afterward she called the Captive and bade him conduct the youth by the secret way he had come, underneath the chambers of the fortress. But for the going away of the Queen's lovers the Captive took out the bar that was beneath a stone in the floor of the passage, and put in its stead a rush-reed, and the youth stepped upon it and fell through into a cavern that was the bed of an underground river, and whatever was thrown into it was not seen again. In this service nor in any other did the Captive fail the Queen.

But when the Queen sent for the Captain of the Archers, she detained him four days in her chamber, calling often for food and wine, and was greatly content with him. On the fourth day she went to the Captive outside her door and said: "Tomorrow take this man up by the sure way, by which the King comes, and let him live."

In the Queen's door were arrows, purple and white. When she desired the King to come to her publicly, with his guard, she sent him a white arrow; but when she sent the purple, he came secretly, and covered himself with his mantle to be hidden from the stone gods at the gate. On the fifth night that the Queen was with her lover, the Captive took a purple arrow to the King, and the King came secretly and found them together. He killed the Captain with his own hand, but the Queen he brought to public trial. The Captive, when he was put to the question, told on his fingers forty men that he had let through the underground passage into the river. The Captive and the Queen were put to death by fire, both on the same day, and afterward there was scarcity of rain.

Eden Bower sat shivering a little as she listened. Hedger was not trying to please her, she thought, but to antagonize and frighten her by his brutal story. She had often told herself that his lean, big-boned lower jaw was like his bull-dog's, but tonight his face made Caesar's most savage and determined expression seem an affectation. Now she was looking at the man he really was. Nobody's eyes had ever defied her like this. They were searching her and seeing everything; all she had concealed from Livingston, and from the millionaire and his friends, and from the newspaper men. He was testing her, trying her out, and she was more ill at ease than she wished to show.

"That's quite a thrilling story," she said at last, rising and winding her scarf about her throat. "It must be getting late. Almost every one has gone."

They walked down the Avenue like people who have quarrelled, or who wish to get rid of each other. Hedger did not take her arm at the street crossings, and they did not linger in the Square. At her door he tried none of the old devices of the Livingston boys. He stood like a post, having forgotten to take off his hat, gave her a harsh, threatening glance, muttered "goodnight," and shut his own door noisily.

There was no question of sleep for Eden Bower. Her brain was working like a machine that would never stop. After she undressed, she tried to calm her nerves by smoking a cigarette, lying on the divan by the open window. But she grew wider and wider awake, combating the challenge that had flamed all evening in Hedger's eyes. The balloon had been one kind of excitement, the wine another; but the thing that had roused her, as a blow rouses a proud man, was the doubt, the contempt, the sneering hostility with which the painter had looked at her when he told his savage story. Crowds and balloons were all very well, she reflected, but woman's chief adventure is man. With a mind over active and a sense of life over strong, she wanted to walk across the roofs in the starlight, to sail over the sea and face at once a world of which she had never been afraid.

Hedger must be asleep; his dog had stopped sniffing under the double doors. Eden put on her wrapper and slippers and stole softly down the hall over the old carpet; one loose board creaked just as she reached the ladder. The trap-door was open, as always on hot nights. When she stepped out on the roof she drew a long breath and walked across it, looking up at the sky. Her foot touched something soft; she heard a low growl, and on the instant Caesar's sharp little teeth caught her ankle and waited. His breath was like steam on her leg. Nobody had ever intruded upon his roof before, and he panted for the movement or the word that would let him spring his jaw. Instead, Hedger's hand seized his throat.

"Wait a minute. I'll settle with him," he said grimly. He dragged the dog toward the manhole and disappeared. When he came back, he found Eden standing over by the dark chimney, looking away in an offended attitude.

"I caned him unmercifully," he panted. "Of course you didn't hear anything; he never whines when I beat him. He didn't nip you, did he?"

"I don't know whether he broke the skin or not," she answered aggrievedly, still looking off into the west.

"If I were one of your friends in white pants, I'd strike a match to find whether you were hurt, though I know you are not, and then I'd see your ankle, wouldn't I?"

"I suppose so."

He shook his head and stood with his hands in the pockets of his old painting jacket. "I'm not up to such boy-tricks. If you want the place to yourself, I'll clear out. There are plenty of places where I can spend the night, what's left of it. But if you stay here and I stay here—" He shrugged his shoulders.

Eden did not stir, and she made no reply. Her head drooped slightly, as if she were considering. But the moment he put his arms about her they began to talk, both at once, as people do in an opera. The instant avowal brought out a flood of trivial admissions. Hedger confessed his crime, was reproached and forgiven, and now Eden knew what it was in his look that she had found so disturbing of late.

Standing against the black chimney, with the sky behind and blue shadows before, they looked like one of Hedger's own paintings of that period;

two figures, one white and one dark, and nothing whatever distinguishable about them but that they were male and female. The faces were lost, the contours blurred in shadow, but the figures were a man and a woman, and that was their whole concern and their mysterious beauty,—it was the rhythm in which they moved, at last, along the roof and down into the dark hole; he first, drawing her gently after him. She came down very slowly. The excitement and bravado and uncertainty of that long day and night seemed all at once to tell upon her. When his feet were on the carpet and he reached up to lift her down, she twined her arms about his neck as after a long separation, and turned her face to him, and her lips, with their perfume of youth and passion.

One Saturday afternoon Hedger was sitting in the window of Eden's music room. They had been watching the pigeons come wheeling over the roofs from their unknown feeding grounds.

"Why," said Eden suddenly, "don't we fix those big doors into your studio so they will open? Then, if I want you, I won't have to go through the hall. That illustrator is loafing about a good deal of late."

"I'll open them, if you wish. The bolt is on your side."

"Isn't there one on yours, too?"

"No. I believe a man lived there for years before I came in, and the nurse used to have these rooms herself. Naturally, the lock was on the lady's side."

Eden laughed and began to examine the bolt. "It's all stuck up with paint." Looking about, her eye lighted upon a bronze Buddah which was one of the nurse's treasures. Taking him by his head, she struck the bolt a blow with his squatting posteriors. The two doors creaked, sagged, and swung weakly inward a little way, as if they were too old for such escapades. Eden tossed the heavy idol into a stuffed chair. "That's better," she exclaimed exultantly. "So the bolts are always on the lady's side? What a lot society takes for granted!"

Hedger laughed, sprang up and caught her arms roughly. "Whoever takes you for granted—Did anybody, ever?"

"Everybody does. That's why I'm here. You are the only one who knows anything about me. Now I'll have to dress if we're going out for dinner."

He lingered, keeping his hold on her. "But I won't always be the only one, Eden Bower. I won't be the last."

"No, I suppose not," she said carelessly. "But what does that matter? You are the first."

As a long, despairing whine broke in the warm stillness, they drew apart. Caesar, lying on his bed in the dark corner, had lifted his head at this invasion of sunlight, and realized that the side of his room was broken open, and his whole world shattered by change. There stood his master and this woman, laughing at him! The woman was pulling the long black hair of this mightiest of men, who bowed his head and permitted it.

VI

In time they quarrelled, of course, and about an abstraction,—as young people often do, as mature people almost never do. Eden came in late one afternoon. She had been with some of her musical friends to lunch at Burton Ives' studio, and she began telling Hedger about its splendours. He listened a moment and then threw down his brushes. "I know exactly what it's like," he said impatiently. "A very good department-store conception of a studio. It's one of the show places."

"Well, it's gorgeous, and he said I could bring you to see him. The boys tell me he's awfully kind about giving people a lift, and you might get something out of it."

Hedger started up and pushed his canvas out of the way. "What could I possibly get from Burton Ives? He's almost the worst painter in the world; the stupidest, I mean."

Eden was annoyed. Burton Ives had been very nice to her and had begged her to sit for him. "You must admit that he's a very successful one," she said coldly.

"Of course he is! Anybody can be successful who will do that sort of thing. I wouldn't paint his pictures for all the money in New York."

"Well, I saw a lot of them, and I think they are beautiful."

Hedger bowed stiffly.

"What's the use of being a great painter if nobody knows about you?" Eden went on persuasively. "Why don't you paint the kind of pictures people can understand, and then, after you're successful, do whatever you like?"

"As I look at it," said Hedger brusquely, "I am successful."

Eden glanced about. "Well, I don't see any evidences of it," she said, biting her lip. "He has a Japanese servant and a wine cellar, and keeps a riding horse."

Hedger melted a little. "My dear, I have the most expensive luxury in the world, and I am much more extravagant than Burton Ives, for I work to please nobody but myself."

"You mean you could make money and don't? That you don't try to get a public?"

"Exactly. A public only wants what has been done over and over. I'm painting for painters,—who haven't been born."

"What would you do if I brought Mr. Ives down here to see your things?"

"Well, for God's sake, don't! Before he left I'd probably tell him what I thought of him."

Eden rose. "I give you up. You know very well there's only one kind of success that's real."

"Yes, but it's not the kind you mean. So you've been thinking me a scrub painter, who needs a helping hand from some fashionable studio man? What the devil have you had anything to do with me for, then?"

"There's no use talking to you," said Eden walking slowly toward the door. "I've been trying to pull wires for you all afternoon, and this is what it comes to." She had expected that the tidings of a prospective call from the great man would be received very differently, and had been thinking as she came home in the stage how, as with a magic wand, she might gild Hedger's future, float him out of his dark hole on a tide of prosperity, see his name in the papers and his pictures in the windows on Fifth Avenue.

Hedger mechanically snapped the midsummer leash on Caesar's collar and they ran downstairs and hurried through Sullivan Street off toward the river. He wanted to be among rough, honest people, to get down where the big drays bumped over stone paving blocks and the men wore corduroy trowsers and kept their shirts open at the neck. He stopped for a drink in one of the sagging bar-rooms on the water front. He had never in his life been so deeply wounded; he did not know he could be so hurt. He had told this girl all his secrets. On the roof, in these warm, heavy summer nights, with her hands locked in his, he had been able to explain all his misty ideas about an unborn art the world was waiting for; had been able to explain them better than he had ever done to himself. And she had looked away to the chattels of this uptown studio and coveted them for him! To her he was only an unsuccessful Burton Ives.

Then why, as he had put it to her, did she take up with him? Young, beautiful, talented as she was, why had she wasted herself on a scrub? Pity? Hardly; she wasn't sentimental. There was no explaining her. But in this passion that had seemed so fearless and so fated to be, his own position now looked to him ridiculous; a poor dauber without money or fame,—it was her caprice to load him with favours. Hedger ground his teeth so loud that his dog, trotting beside him, heard him and looked up.

While they were having supper at the oyster-man's, he planned his escape. Whenever he saw her again, everything he had told her, that he should never have told any one, would come back to him; ideas he had never whispered even to the painter whom he worshipped and had gone all the way to France to see. To her they must seem his apology for not having horses and a valet, or merely the puerile boastfulness of a weak man. Yet if she slipped the bolt tonight and came through the doors and said, "Oh, weak man, I belong to you!" what could he do? That was the danger. He would catch the train out to Long Beach tonight, and tomorrow he would go on to the north end of Long Island, where an old friend of his had a summer studio among the sand dunes. He would stay until things came right in his mind. And she could find a smart painter, or take her punishment.

When he went home, Eden's room was dark; she was dining out somewhere. He threw his things into a hold-all he had carried about the world with him, strapped up some colours and canvases, and ran downstairs.

VII

Five days later Hedger was a restless passenger on a dirty, crowded Sunday train, coming back to town. Of course he saw now how unreasonable he had been in expecting a Huntington girl to know anything about pictures; here was a whole continent full of people who knew nothing about pictures and he didn't hold it against them. What had such things to do with him and Eden Bower? When he lay out on the dunes, watching the moon come up out of the sea, it had seemed to him that there was no wonder in the world like the wonder of Eden Bower. He was going back to her because she was older than art, because she was the most overwhelming thing that had ever come into his life.

He had written her yesterday, begging her to be at home this evening, telling her that he was contrite, and wretched enough.

Now that he was on his way to her, his stronger feeling unaccountably changed to a mood that was playful and tender. He wanted to share everything with her, even the most trivial things. He wanted to tell her about the people on the train, coming back tired from their holiday with bunches of wilted flowers and dirty daisies; to tell her that the fish-man, to whom she had often sent him for lobsters, was among the passengers, disguised in a silk shirt and a spotted tie, and how his wife looked exactly like a fish, even to her eyes, on which cataracts were forming. He could tell her, too, that he hadn't as much as unstrapped his canvases,—that ought to convince her.

In those days passengers from Long Island came into New York by ferry. Hedger had to be quick about getting his dog out of the express car in order to catch the first boat. The East River, and the bridges, and the city to the west, were burning in the conflagration of the sunset; there was that great home-coming reach of evening in the air.

The car changes from Thirty-fourth Street were too many and too perplexing; for the first time in his life Hedger took a hansom cab for Washington Square. Caesar sat bolt upright on the worn leather cushion beside him, and they jogged off, looking down on the rest of the world.

It was twilight when they drove down lower Fifth Avenue into the Square, and through the Arch behind them were the two long rows of pale violet lights that used to bloom so beautifully against the grey stone and asphalt. Here and yonder about the Square hung globes that shed a radiance not unlike the blue mists of evening, emerging softly when daylight died, as the stars emerged in the thin blue sky. Under them the sharp shadows of the trees fell on the cracked pavement and the sleeping grass. The first stars and the first lights were growing silver against the gradual darkening, when Hedger paid his driver and went into the house,—which, thank God, was still there! On the hall table lay his letter of yesterday, unopened.

He went upstairs with every sort of fear and every sort of hope clutching at his heart; it was as if tigers were tearing him. Why was there no gas burning in the top hall? He found matches and the gas bracket. He knocked, but got no answer; nobody was there. Before his own door were exactly five bottles of milk, standing in a row. The milk-boy had taken spiteful pleasure in thus reminding him that he forgot to stop his order.

Hedger went down to the basement; it, too, was dark. The janitress was taking her evening airing on the basement steps. She sat waving a palm-leaf fan majestically, her dirty calico dress open at the neck. She told him at once that there had been "changes." Miss Bower's room was to let again, and the piano would go tomorrow. Yes, she left yesterday, she sailed for Europe with friends from Chicago. They arrived on Friday, heralded by many telegrams. Very rich people they were said to be, though the man had refused to pay the nurse a month's rent in lieu of notice,—which would have been only right, as the young lady had agreed to take the rooms until October. Mrs. Foley had observed, too, that he didn't overpay her or Willy for their trouble, and a great deal of trouble they had been put to, certainly. Yes, the young lady was very pleasant, but the nurse said there were rings on the mahogany table where she had put tumblers and wine glasses. It was just as well she was gone. The Chicago man was uppish in his ways, but not much to look at. She supposed he had poor health, for there was nothing to him inside his clothes.

Hedger went slowly up the stairs—never had they seemed so long, or his legs so heavy. The upper floor was emptiness and silence. He unlocked his room, lit the gas, and opened the windows. When he went to put his coat in the closet, he found, hanging among his clothes, a pale, flesh-tinted dressing gown he had liked to see her wear, with a perfume—oh, a perfume that was still Eden Bower! He shut the door behind him and there, in the dark, for a moment he lost his manliness. It was when he held this garment to him that he found a letter in the pocket.

The note was written with a lead pencil, in haste: She was sorry that he was angry, but she still didn't know just what she had done. She had thought Mr. Ives would be useful to him; she guessed he was too proud. She wanted awfully to see him again, but Fate came knocking at her door after he had left her. She believed in Fate. She would never forget him, and she knew he would become the greatest painter in the world. Now she must pack. She hoped he wouldn't mind her leaving the dressing gown; somehow, she could never wear it again.

After Hedger read this, standing under the gas, he went back into the closet and knelt down before the wall; the knot hole had been plugged up with a ball of wet paper,—the same blue note-paper on which her letter was written.

He was hard hit. Tonight he had to bear the loneliness of a whole lifetime. Knowing himself so well, he could hardly believe that such a thing had ever happened to him, that such a woman had lain happy and contented in his arms. And now it was over. He turned out the light and sat down on his painter's stool before the big window. Caesar, on the floor beside him, rested his head on his master's knee. We must leave Hedger thus, sitting in his tank with his dog, looking up at the stars.

COMING, APHRODITE! This legend, in electric lights over the Lexington Opera House, had long announced the return of Eden Bower to New York after years of spectacular success in Paris. She came at last, under the management of an American Opera Company, but bringing her own *chef d'orchestre*.

One bright December afternoon Eden Bower was going down Fifth Avenue in her car, on the way to her broker, in Williams Street. Her thoughts were entirely upon stocks,—Cerro de Pasco, and how much she should buy of it,—when she suddenly looked up and realized that she was skirting Washington Square. She had not seen the place since she rolled out of it in an old-fashioned four-wheeler to seek her fortune, eighteen years ago.

"*Arretez, Alphonse. Attendez moi*," she called, and opened the door before he could reach it. The children who were streaking over the asphalt on roller skates saw a lady in a long fur coat, and short, high-heeled shoes, alight from a French car and pace slowly about the Square, holding her muff to her chin. This spot, at least, had changed very little, she reflected; the same trees, the same fountain, the white arch, and over yonder, Garibaldi, drawing the sword for freedom. There, just opposite her, was the old red brick house.

"Yes, that is the place," she was thinking. "I can smell the carpets now, and the dog,—what was his name? That grubby bathroom at the end of the hall, and that dreadful Hedger—still, there was something about him, you know—" She glanced up and blinked against the sun. From somewhere in the crowded quarter south of the Square a flock of pigeons rose, wheeling quickly upward into the brilliant blue sky. She threw back her head, pressed her muff closer to her chin, and watched them with a smile of amazement and delight. So they still rose, out of all that dirt and noise and squalor, fleet and silvery, just as they used to rise that summer when she was twenty and went up in a balloon on Coney Island!

Alphonse opened the door and tucked her robes about her. All the way down town her mind wandered from Cerro de Pasco, and she kept smiling and looking up at the sky.

When she had finished her business with the broker, she asked him to look in the telephone book for the address of M. Gaston Jules, the picture dealer, and slipped the paper on which he wrote it into her glove. It was five o'clock when she reached the French Galleries, as they were called. On entering she gave the attendant her card, asking him to take it to M. Jules. The dealer appeared very promptly and begged her to come into his private office, where he pushed a great chair toward his desk for her and signalled his secretary to leave the room.

"How good your lighting is in here," she observed, glancing about. "I met you at Simon's studio, didn't I? Oh, no! I never forget anybody who interests me." She threw her muff on his writing table and sank into the deep chair. "I have come to you for some information that's not in my line. Do you know anything about an American painter named Hedger?"

He took the seat opposite her. "Don Hedger? But, certainly! There are some very interesting things of his in an exhibition at V—'s. If you would care to—"

She held up her hand. "No, no. I've no time to go to exhibitions. Is he a man of any importance?"

"Certainly. He is one of the first men among the moderns. That is to say, among the very moderns. He is always coming up with something different. He often exhibits in Paris, you must have seen—"

"No, I tell you I don't go to exhibitions. Has he had great success? That is what I want to know."

M. Jules pulled at his short grey moustache. "But, Madame, there are many kinds of success," he began cautiously.

Madame gave a dry laugh. "Yes, so he used to say. We once quarrelled on that issue. And how would you define his particular kind?"

M. Jules grew thoughtful. "He is a great name with all the young men, and he is decidedly an influence in art. But one can't definitely place a man who is original, erratic, and who is changing all the time."

She cut him short. "Is he much talked about at home? In Paris, I mean? Thanks. That's all I want to know." She rose and began buttoning her coat. "One doesn't like to have been an utter fool, even at twenty."

"Mais, non!" M. Jules handed her her muff with a quick, sympathetic glance. He followed her out through the carpeted show-room, now closed to the public and draped in cheesecloth, and put her into her car with words appreciative of the honour she had done him in calling.

Leaning back in the cushions, Eden Bower closed her eyes, and her face, as the street lamps flashed their ugly orange light upon it, became hard and settled, like a plaster cast; so a sail, that has been filled by a strong breeze, behaves when the wind suddenly dies. Tomorrow night the wind would blow again, and this mask would be the golden face of Aphrodite. But a "big" career takes its toll, even with the best of luck.

SUSAN GLASPELL
1876–1948

Susan Glaspell was born in Davenport, Iowa. Her father's family was among the first settlers of that region, and from him she learned to cherish the independence, integrity, idealism, and practicality of her pioneer ancestry and to emphasize these values in her art. After graduating from Drake University in 1899, she worked for two years as a reporter for the *Des Moines Daily News*, finding in the everyday details of midwestern life the materials for the short stories she began to publish in the ladies' magazines of the period. Her early stories were in the local color tradition. Like other local colorists, such as Zona Gale and Mary French, Susan Glaspell wanted to preserve in her art those special qualities of place, speech, and thought that made her region unique. Resisting the homogenization of American life brought on by the railroad and the growing urbanindustrial expansion, these writers depicted a native son or daughter renewed by an association with the land, finding a bond between man and nature that echoed the earlier pastoral dream of the nineteenth century.

In 1907 Susan Glaspell met George Cram Cook, who was also born and raised in Davenport, but, unlike her, Cook revolted against the provincialism he saw in Davenport and against the "medieval-romantic" views of writers like Glaspell. Cook helped her discover a literary tradition that treated contemporary issues in realistic terms. At the same time, he strengthened her own idealism with his vision of a classical revival in America, where, especially in the theater, all the arts would come together in a single creative totality. In her full-length plays, a few short stories, and the novels she wrote in the 1930s and 1940s, she creates modern "pioneers" who make for themselves new frontiers of feeling, thinking, and living, often at considerable cost, both financial and psychological, to themselves.

Susan Glaspell married Cook in 1913 and moved to Provincetown, Massachusetts, where in 1915 they put on a few one-act plays in a makeshift theater. Under "Jig" Cook's inspired leadership, they continued to write and produce plays that winter in New York and soon established the Playwright's Theatre, or, as they came to be called, the Provincetown Players. Between 1916 and 1922, the Provincetown Players was the leading force in causing a revolution in American theater. In contrast to other little theaters in New York at that time, Cook insisted that the Provincetown produce only original plays written by American playwrights, and, in time, they proved that a tiny, experimental theater, dedicated to native dramatists, could succeed and that the theater audience was ready for serious plays of ideas. Along with Eugene O'Neill, Susan Glaspell was the Provincetown's most important and prolific playwright. She wrote about the new woman striving to fulfill her dreams in a hostile and insensitive world; she treated psychoanalysis when it was still new in this country; she depicted the little magazine, the bohemian, the war's effect on minorities, and the tragedy of the isolated midwestern farm-wife. She brought together European expressionism with American realism, showing an extraordinary diversity of dramatic techniques. In the seven one-acts and three full-length plays she wrote for the Provincetown, she created an original dramatic voice that spoke to the American audience in a new way about contemporary concerns.

After Cook's death in Greece in 1922, Susan Glaspell returned to Cape Cod, where she lived until her death in 1948. In 1930 she wrote *Alison's House*, a play based on the life of Emily Dickinson, which won the Pulitzer Prize for drama in 1931. Whereas the fiction she wrote before and after the Provincetown years exemplifies an established and conservative literary tradition, her plays fostered new forms of dramatic expression and helped bring about a radical shift in the direction of American drama. Thus, her novels are rarely read today, but her plays still speak to audiences the world over.

Arthur Waterman
Georgia State University

PRIMARY WORKS

Plays, 1920; *Plays by Susan Glaspell,* ed. C. W. E. Bigsby, 1987; *Inheritors,* 1921; *The Verge,* 1922; *Alison's House,* 1930; *Ambrose Holt and Family,* 1931; *Judd Rankin's Daughter,* 1945; *Plays,* ed. C. W. E. Bigsby and Christine Dymkowski, 1987.

Trifles[1]

SCENE. *The kitchen in the now abandoned farmhouse of* JOHN WRIGHT, *a gloomy kitchen, and left without having been put in order—unwashed pans under the sink, a loaf of bread outside the bread-box, a dish-towel on the table—other signs of incompleted work. At the rear the outer door opens and the* SHERIFF *comes in followed by the* COUNTY ATTORNEY *and* HALE. *The* SHERIFF *and* HALE *are men in middle life, the* COUNTY ATTORNEY *is a young man; all are much bundled up and go at once to the stove. They are followed by the two women—the* SHERIFF'S *wife first; she is a slight wiry woman, a thin nervous face.* MRS. HALE *is larger and would ordinarily be called more comfortable looking, but she is disturbed now and looks fearfully about as she enters. The women have come in slowly, and stand close together near the door.*

COUNTY ATTORNEY: [*Rubbing his hands.*] This feels good. Come up to the fire, ladies.

MRS. PETERS: [*After taking a step forward.*] I'm not—cold.

SHERIFF: [*Unbuttoning his overcoat and stepping away from the stove as if to mark the beginning of official business.*] Now, Mr. Hale, before we move things about, you explain to Mr. Henderson just what you saw when you came here yesterday morning.

COUNTY ATTORNEY: By the way, has anything been moved? Are things just as you left them yesterday?

SHERIFF: [*Looking about.*] It's just the same. When it dropped below zero last night I thought I'd better send Frank out this morning to make a fire for us—no use getting pneumonia with a big case on, but I told him not to touch anything except the stove—and you know Frank.

COUNTY ATTORNEY: Somebody should have been left here yesterday.

SHERIFF: Oh—yesterday. When I had to send Frank to Morris Center for that man who went crazy—I want you to know I had my hands full yesterday. I knew you could get back from Omaha by today and as long as I went over everything here myself—

COUNTY ATTORNEY: Well, Mr. Hale, tell just what happened when you came here yesterday morning.

HALE: Harry and I had started to town with a load of potatoes. We came along the road from my place and as I got here I said, "I'm going to see if I can't get John Wright to go in with me on a party telephone." I spoke to Wright about it once before and he put me off, saying folks talked too much anyway, and all he asked was peace and quiet—I guess you know about how much he talked himself; but I thought maybe if I went to the house and talked about it before his wife, though I said to Harry that I didn't know as what his wife wanted made much difference to John—

---

[1]First performed by the Provincetown Players in Provincetown, Mass., August 8, 1916. Rewritten as a short story, "Jury of Her Peers," and first published in *Everyweek*, March 5, 1917.

COUNTY ATTORNEY: Let's talk about that later, Mr. Hale. I do want to talk about that, but tell now just what happened when you got to the house.

HALE: I didn't hear or see anything; I knocked at the door, and still it was all quiet inside. I knew they must be up, it was past eight o'clock. So I knocked again, and I thought I heard somebody say, "Come in." I wasn't sure, I'm not sure yet, but I opened the door—this door [*indicating the door by which the two women are still standing*] and there in that rocker— [*pointing to it*] sat Mrs. Wright.

[*They all look at the rocker.*]

COUNTY ATTORNEY: What—was she doing?

HALE: She was rockin' back and forth. She had her apron in her hand and was kind of—pleating it.

COUNTY ATTORNEY: And how did she—look?

HALE: Well, she looked queer.

COUNTY ATTORNEY: How do you mean—queer?

HALE: Well, as if she didn't know what she was going to do next. And kind of done up.

COUNTY ATTORNEY: How did she seem to feel about your coming?

HALE: Why, I don't think she minded—one way or other. She didn't pay much attention. I said, "How do, Mrs. Wright, it's cold, ain't it?" And she said, "Is it?"—and went on kind of pleating at her apron. Well, I was surprised; she didn't ask me to come up to the stove, or to set down, but just sat there, not even looking at me, so I said, "I want to see John." And then she—laughed. I guess you would call it a laugh. I thought of Harry and the team outside, so I said a little sharp: "Can't I see John?" "No," she says, kind o' dull like. "Ain't he home?" says I. "Yes," says she, "he's home." "Then why can't I see him?" I asked her, out of patience. "'Cause he's dead," says she. "*Dead?*" says I. She just nodded her head, not getting a bit excited, but rockin' back and forth. "Why—where is he?" says I, not knowing what to say. She just pointed upstairs—like that [*himself pointing to the room above*]. I got up, with the idea of going up there. I walked from there to here—then I says, "Why, what did he die of?" "He died of a rope round his neck," says she, and just went on pleatin' at her apron. Well, I went out and called Harry. I thought I might—need help. We went upstairs and there he was lyin'—

COUNTY ATTORNEY: I think I'd rather have you go into that upstairs, where you can point it all out. Just go on now with the rest of the story.

HALE: Well, my first thought was to get that rope off. It looked ... [*Stops, his face twitches*] ... but Harry, he went up to him, and he said, "No, he's dead all right, and we'd better not touch anything." So we went back downstairs. She was still sitting that same way. "Has anybody been notified?" I asked. "No," says she, unconcerned. "Who did this, Mrs. Wright?" said Harry. He said it business-like—and she stopped pleatin' of her apron. "I don't know," she says. "You don't *know?*" says Harry. "No," says she. "Weren't you sleepin' in the bed with him?" says Harry. "Yes," says she, "but I was on the inside." "Somebody slipped a rope round his neck and strangled him and you didn't wake up?" says Harry. "I didn't wake up," she said after him. We must 'a looked as if we didn't see how that could be, for after a minute she said, "I sleep sound." Harry was going to ask her more questions but I said maybe we ought to let her tell her story first to the coroner, or the sheriff, so Harry went fast as he could to Rivers' place, where there's a telephone.

COUNTY ATTORNEY: And what did Mrs. Wright do when she knew that you had gone for the coroner?

HALE: She moved from that chair to this one over here [*Pointing to a small chair in the corner*] and just sat there with her hands held together and looking down. I got a feeling that I ought to make some conversation, so I said I had come in to see if John wanted to put in a telephone, and at that she started to laugh, and then she stopped and looked at me— scared. [*The* County Attorney, *who has had his notebook out, makes a note.*] I dunno, maybe it wasn't scared. I wouldn't like to say it was. Soon Harry got back, and then Dr. Lloyd came, and you, Mr. Peters, and so I guess that's all I know that you don't.

COUNTY ATTORNEY: [*Looking around.*] I guess we'll go upstairs first—and then out to the barn and around there. [*To the Sheriff.*] You're convinced that there was nothing important here—nothing that would point to any motive.

SHERIFF: Nothing here but kitchen things.

[*The* COUNTY ATTORNEY, *after again looking around the kitchen, opens the door of a cupboard closet. He gets up on a chair and looks on a shelf. Pulls his hand away, sticky.*]

COUNTY ATTORNEY: Here's a nice mess.

[*The women draw nearer.*]

MRS. PETERS: [*To the other woman.*] Oh, her fruit; it did freeze. [*To the Lawyer.*] She worried about that when it turned so cold. She said the fire'd go out and her jars would break.

SHERIFF: Well, can you beat the women! Held for murder and worryin' about her preserves.

COUNTY ATTORNEY: I guess before we're through she may have something more serious than preserves to worry about.

HALE: Well, women are used to worrying over trifles.

[*The two women move a little closer together.*]

COUNTY ATTORNEY: [*With the gallantry of a young politician.*] And yet, for all their worries, what would we do without the ladies? [*The women do not unbend. He goes to the sink, takes a dipperful of water from the pail and pouring it into a basin, washes his hands. Starts to wipe them on the roller-towel, turns it for a cleaner place.*] Dirty towels! [*Kicks his foot against the pans under the sink.*] Not much of a housekeeper, would you say, ladies?

MRS. HALE: [*Stiffly.*] There's a great deal of work to be done on a farm.

COUNTY ATTORNEY: To be sure. And yet [*With a little bow to her*] I know there are some Dickson county farmhouses which do not have such roller towels.

[*He gives it a pull to expose its full length again.*]

MRS. HALE: Those towels get dirty awful quick. Men's hands aren't always as clean as they might be.

COUNTY ATTORNEY: Ah, loyal to your sex, I see. But you and Mrs. Wright were neighbors. I suppose you were friends, too.

MRS. HALE: [*Shaking her head.*] I've not seen much of her of late years. I've not been in this house—it's more than a year.

COUNTY ATTORNEY: And why was that? You didn't like her?

MRS. HALE: I liked her all well enough. Farmers' wives have their hands full, Mr. Henderson. And then—

COUNTY ATTORNEY: Yes—?

MRS. HALE: [*Looking about.*] It never seemed a very cheerful place.

COUNTY ATTORNEY: No—it's not cheerful. I shouldn't say she had the home-making instinct.

MRS. HALE: Well, I don't know as Wright had, either.

COUNTY ATTORNEY: You mean that they didn't get on very well?

MRS. HALE: No, I don't mean anything. But I don't think a place'd be any cheerfuller for John Wright's being in it.

COUNTY ATTORNEY: I'd like to talk more of that a little later. I want to get the lay of things upstairs now.

[*He goes to the left, where three steps lead to a stair door.*]

SHERIFF: I suppose anything Mrs. Peters does'll be all right. She was to take in some clothes for her, you know, and a few little things. We left in such a hurry yesterday.

COUNTY ATTORNEY: Yes, but I would like to see what you take, Mrs. Peters, and keep an eye out for anything that might be of use to us.

MRS. PETERS: Yes, Mr. Henderson.

[*The women listen to the men's steps on the stairs, then look about the kitchen.*]

MRS. HALE: I'd hate to have men coming into my kitchen, snooping around and criticising.

[*She arranges the pans under sink which the Lawyer had shoved out of place.*]

MRS. PETERS: Of course it's no more than their duty.

MRS. HALE: Duty's all right, but I guess that deputy sheriff that came out to make the fire might have got a little of this on. [*Gives the roller towel a pull.*] Wish I'd thought of that sooner. Seems mean to talk about her for not having things slicked up when she had to come away in such a hurry.

MRS. PETERS: [*Who has gone to a small table in the left rear corner of the room, and lifted one end of a towel that covers a pan.*] She had bread set.

[*Stands still.*]

MRS. HALE: [*Eyes fixed on a loaf of bread beside the breadbox, which is on a low shelf at the other side of the room. Moves slowly toward it.*] She was going to put this in there. [*Picks up loaf, then abruptly drops it. In a manner of returning to familiar things.*] It's a shame about her fruit. I wonder if it's all gone. [*Gets up on the chair and looks.*] I think there's some here that's all right, Mrs. Peters. Yes—here; [*Holding it toward the window*] this is cherries, too. [*Looking again.*] I declare I believe that's the only one. [*Gets down, bottle in her hand. Goes to the sink and wipes it off on the outside.*] She'll feel awful bad after all her hard work in the hot weather. I remember the afternoon I put up my cherries last summer.

[*She puts the bottle on the big kitchen table, center of the room. With a sigh, is about to sit down in the rocking-chair. Before she is seated realizes what chair it is; with a slow look at it, steps back. The chair which she has touched rocks back and forth.*]

MRS. PETERS: Well, I must get those things from the front room closet. [*She goes to the door at the right, but after looking into the other room, steps back.*] You coming with me, Mrs. Hale? You could help me carry them.

[*They go in the other room; reappear,* MRS. PETERS *carrying a dress and skirt,* MRS. HALE *following with a pair of shoes.*]

MRS. PETERS: My, it's cold in there.

[*She puts the clothes on the big table, and hurries to the stove.*]

MRS. HALE: [*Examining the skirt.*] Wright was close.[2] I think maybe that's why she kept so much to herself. She didn't even belong to the Ladies Aid. I suppose she felt she couldn't do her part, and then you don't enjoy things when you feel shabby. She used to wear pretty clothes and be lively, when she was Minnie Foster, one of the town girls singing in the choir. But that—oh, that was thirty years ago. This all you was to take in?

MRS. PETERS: She said she wanted an apron. Funny thing to want, for there isn't much to get you dirty in jail, goodness knows. But I suppose just to make her feel more natural. She said they was in the top drawer in this cupboard. Yes, here. And then her little shawl that always hung behind the door. [*Opens stair door and looks.*] Yes, here it is.

[*Quickly shuts door leading upstairs.*]

MRS. HALE: [*Abruptly moving toward her.*] Mrs. Peters?
MRS. PETERS: Yes, Mrs. Hale?
MRS. HALE: Do you think she did it?
MRS. PETERS: [*In a frightened voice.*] Oh, I don't know.

---

[2]Not sociable, kept close to himself.

MRS. HALE: Well, I don't think she did. Asking for an apron and her little shawl. Worrying about her fruit.

MRS. PETERS: [*Starts to speak, glances up, where footsteps are heard in the room above. In a low voice.*] Mr. Peters says it looks bad for her. Mr. Henderson is awful sarcastic in a speech and he'll make fun of her sayin' she didn't wake up.

MRS. HALE: Well, I guess John Wright didn't wake when they was slipping that rope under his neck.

MRS. PETERS: No, it's strange. It must have been done awful crafty and still. They say it was such a—funny way to kill a man, rigging it all up like that.

MRS. HALE: That's just what Mr. Hale said. There was a gun in the house. He says that's what he can't understand.

MRS. PETERS: Mr. Henderson said coming out that what was needed for the case was a motive; something to show anger, or—sudden feeling.

MRS. HALE: [*Who is standing by the table.*] Well, I don't see any signs of anger around here. [*She puts her hand on the dish towel which lies on the table, stands looking down at table, one half of which is clean, the other half messy.*] It's wiped to here. [*Makes a move as if to finish work, then turns and looks at loaf of bread outside the breadbox. Drops towel. In that voice of coming back to familiar things.*] Wonder how they are finding things upstairs. I hope she had it a little more red-up[3] up there. You know, it seems kind of *sneaking.* Locking her up in town and then coming out here and trying to get her own house to turn against her!

MRS. PETERS: But Mrs. Hale, the law is the law.

MRS. HALE: I s'pose 'tis. [*Unbuttoning her coat.*] Better loosen up your things, Mrs. Peters. You won't feel them when you go out.

[MRS. PETERS *takes off her fur tippet, goes to hang it on hook at back of room, stands looking at the under part of the small corner table.*]

MRS. PETERS: She was piecing a quilt.

[*She brings the large sewing basket and they look at the bright pieces.*]

MRS. HALE: It's log cabin pattern. Pretty, isn't it? I wonder if she was goin' to quilt it or just knot it?[4]

[*Footsteps have been heard coming down the stairs. The* SHERIFF *enters followed by* HALE *and the* COUNTY ATTORNEY.]

SHERIFF: They wonder if she was going to quilt it or just knot it!

[*The men laugh, the women look abashed.*]

COUNTY ATTORNEY: [*Rubbing his hands over the stove.*] Frank's fire didn't do much up there, did it? Well, let's go out to the barn and get that cleared up.

---

[3]Gotten ready, made-up.
[4]Different methods of connecting the parts of
a quilt.

[*The men go outside.*]

MRS. HALE: [*Resentfully.*] I don't know as there's anything so strange, our takin' up our time with little things while we're waiting for them to get the evidence. [*She sits down at the big table smoothing out a block with decision.*] I don't see as it's anything to laugh about.

MRS. PETERS: [*Apologetically.*] Of course they've got awful important things on their minds.

[*Pulls up a chair and joins* MRS. HALE *at the table.*]

MRS. HALE: [*Examining another block.*] Mrs. Peters, look at this one. Here, this is the one she was working on, and look at the sewing! All the rest of it has been so nice and even. And look at this! It's all over the place! Why, it looks as if she didn't know what she was about!

[*After she had said this they look at each other, then start to glance back at the door. After an instant* MRS. HALE *has pulled at a knot and ripped the sewing.*]

MRS. PETERS: Oh, what are you doing, Mrs. Hale?

MRS. HALE: [*Mildly.*] Just pulling out a stitch or two that's not sewed very good. [*Threading a needle.*] Bad sewing always made me fidgety.

MRS. PETERS: [*Nervously.*] I don't think we ought to touch things.

MRS. HALE: I'll just finish up this end. [*Suddenly stopping and leaning forward.*] Mrs. Peters?

MRS. PETERS: Yes, Mrs. Hale?

MRS. HALE: What do you suppose she was so nervous about?

MRS. PETERS: Oh—I don't know. I don't know as she was nervous. I sometimes sew awful queer when I'm just tired. [*Mrs. Hale starts to say something, looks at Mrs. Peters, then goes on sewing.*] Well I must get these things wrapped up. They may be through sooner than we think. [*Putting apron and other things together.*] I wonder where I can find a piece of paper, and string.

MRS. HALE: In that cupboard, maybe.

MRS. PETERS: [*Looking in cupboard.*] Why, here's a bird-cage. [*Holds it up.*] Did she have a bird, Mrs. Hale?

MRS. HALE: Why, I don't know whether she did or not—I've not been here for so long. There was a man around last year selling canaries cheap, but I don't know as she took one; maybe she did. She used to sing real pretty herself.

MRS. PETERS: [*Glancing around.*] Seems funny to think of a bird here. But she must have had one, or why would she have a cage? I wonder what happened to it.

MRS. HALE: I s'pose maybe the cat got it.

MRS. PETERS: No, she didn't have a cat. She's got that feeling some people have about cats—being afraid of them. My cat got in her room and she was real upset and asked me to take it out.

MRS. HALE: My sister Bessie was like that. Queer, ain't it?

MRS. PETERS: [*Examining the cage.*] Why, look at this door. It's broke. One hinge is pulled apart.

MRS. HALE: [*Looking too.*] Looks as if someone must have been rough with it.

MRS. PETERS: Why, yes.

[*She brings the cage forward and puts it on the table.*]

MRS. HALE: I wish if they're going to find any evidence they'd be about it. I don't like this place.

MRS. PETERS: But I'm awful glad you came with me, Mrs. Hale. It would be lonesome for me sitting here alone.

MRS. HALE: It would, wouldn't it? [*Dropping her sewing.*] But I tell you what I do wish, Mrs. Peters. I wish I had come over sometimes when *she* was here. I—[*Looking around the room*]—wish I had.

MRS. PETERS: But of course you were awful busy, Mrs. Hale—your house and your children.

MRS. HALE: I could've come. I stayed away because it weren't cheerful—and that's why I ought to have come. I—I've never liked this place. Maybe because it's down in a hollow and you don't see the road. I dunno what it is, but it's a lonesome place and always was. I wish I had come over to see Minnie Foster sometimes. I can see now—

[*Shakes her head.*]

MRS. PETERS: Well, you mustn't reproach yourself, Mrs. Hale. Somehow we just don't see how it is with other folks until—something comes up.

MRS. HALE: Not having children makes less work—but it makes a quiet house, and Wright out to work all day, and no company when he did come in. Did you know John Wright, Mrs. Peters?

MRS. PETERS: Not to know him; I've seen him in town. They say he was a good man.

MRS. HALE: Yes—good; he didn't drink, and kept his word as well as most, I guess, and paid his debts. But he was a hard man, Mrs. Peters. Just to pass the time of day with him—[*Shivers.*] Like a raw wind that gets to the bone. [*Pauses, her eye falling on the cage.*] I should think she would 'a wanted a bird. But what do you suppose went with it?

MRS. PETERS: I don't know, unless it got sick and died.

[*She reaches over and swings the broken door, swings it again, both women watch it.*]

MRS. HALE: You weren't raised round here, were you? [*Mrs. Peters shakes her head.*] You didn't know—her?

MRS. PETERS: Not till they brought her yesterday.

MRS. HALE: She—come to think of it, she was kind of like a bird herself—real sweet and pretty, but kind of timid and—fluttery. How—she—did—change. [*Silence; then as if struck by a happy thought and relieved to get back to every day things.*] Tell you what, Mrs. Peters, why don't you take the quilt in with you? It might take up her mind.

MRS. PETERS: Why, I think that's a real nice idea, Mrs. Hale. There couldn't possibly be any objection to it, could there? Now, just what would I take? I wonder if her patches are in here—and her things.

[*They look in the sewing basket.*]

MRS. HALE: Here's some red. I expect this has got sewing things in it. [*Brings out a fancy box.*] What a pretty box. Looks like something somebody would give you. Maybe her scissors are in here. [*Opens box. Suddenly puts her hand to her nose.*] Why—[Mrs. Peters *bends nearer, then turns her face away.*] There's something wrapped up in this piece of silk.

MRS. PETERS: Why, this isn't her scissors.

MRS. HALE: [*Lifting the silk.*] Oh, Mrs. Peters—its—

[MRS. PETERS *bends closer.*]

MRS. PETERS: It's the bird.

MRS. HALE: [*Jumping up.*] But, Mrs. Peters—look at it! It's [sic] neck! Look at its neck! It's all—other side *to*.

MRS. PETERS: Somebody—wrung—its—neck.

[*Their eyes meet. A look of growing comprehension, of horror. Steps are heard outside.* MRS. HALE *slips box under quilt pieces, and sinks into her chair. Enter* SHERIFF *and* COUNTY ATTORNEY. MRS. PETERS *rises.*]

COUNTY ATTORNEY: [*As one turning from serious things to little pleasantries.*] Well, ladies, have you decided whether she was going to quilt it or knot it?

MRS. PETERS: We think she was going to—knot it.

COUNTY ATTORNEY: Well, that's interesting, I'm sure. [*Seeing the birdcage.*] Has the bird flown?

MRS. HALE: [*Putting more quilt pieces over the box.*] We think the—cat got it.

COUNTY ATTORNEY: [*Preoccupied.*] Is there a cat?

[MRS. HALE *glances in a quick covert way at* MRS. PETERS.]

MRS. PETERS: Well, not *now*. They're superstitious, you know. They leave.

COUNTY ATTORNEY: [*To Sheriff Peters, continuing an interrupted conversation.*] No sign at all of anyone having come from the outside. Their own rope. Now let's go up again and go over it piece by piece. [*They start upstairs.*] It would have to have been someone who knew just the—

[MRS. PETERS *sits down. The two women sit there not looking at one another, but as if peering into something and at the same time holding back. When they talk now it is in the manner of feeling their way over strange ground, as if afraid of what they are saying, but as if they can not help saying it.*]

MRS. HALE: She liked the bird. She was going to bury it in that pretty box.

MRS. PETERS: [*In a whisper.*] When I was a girl—my kitten—there was a boy took a hatchet, and before my eyes—and before I could get there—[*Covers her face an instant.*] If they hadn't held me back I would have—[*Catches herself, looks upstairs where steps are heard, falters weakly*]—hurt him.

MRS. HALE: [*With a slow look around her.*] I wonder how it would seem never to have had any children around. [*Pause.*] No, Wright wouldn't like the bird—a thing that sang. She used to sing. He killed that, too.

MRS. PETERS: [*Moving uneasily.*] We don't know who killed the bird.

MRS. HALE: I knew John Wright.

MRS. PETERS: It was an awful thing was done in this house that night, Mrs. Hale. Killing a man while he slept, slipping a rope around his neck that choked the life out of him.

MRS. HALE: His neck. Choked the life out of him.

[*Her hand goes out and rests on the bird-cage.*]

MRS. PETERS: [*With rising voice.*] We don't know who killed him. We don't know.

MRS. HALE: [*Her own feeling not interrupted.*] If there'd been years and years of nothing, then a bird to sing to you, it would be awful—still, after the bird was still.

MRS. PETERS: [*Something within her speaking.*] I know what stillness is. When we homesteaded in Dakota, and my first baby died—after he was two years old, and me with no other then—

MRS. HALE: [*Moving.*] How soon do you suppose they'll be through, looking for the evidence?

MRS. PETERS: I know what stillness is. [*Pulling herself back.*] The law has got to punish crime, Mrs. Hale.

MRS. HALE: [*Not as if answering that.*] I wish you'd seen Minnie Foster when she wore a white dress with blue ribbons and stood up there in the choir and sang. [*A look around the room.*] Oh, I *wish* I'd come over here once in a while! That was a crime! That was a crime! Who's going to punish that?

MRS. PETERS: [*Looking upstairs.*] We mustn't—take on.

MRS. HALE: I might have known she needed help! I know how things can be—for women. I tell you, it's queer, Mrs. Peters. We live close together and we live far apart. We all go through the same things—it's all just a different kind of the same thing. [*Brushes her eyes, noticing the bottle of fruit, reaches out for it.*] If I was you I wouldn't tell her her fruit was gone. Tell her it *ain't*. Tell her it's all right. Take this in to prove it to her. She—she may never know whether it was broke or not.

MRS. PETERS: [*Takes the bottle, looks about for something to wrap it in; takes petticoat from the clothes brought from the other room, very nervously begins winding this around the bottle. In a false voice.*] My, it's a good thing the men couldn't hear us. Wouldn't they just laugh! Getting all stirred up over a little thing like a—dead canary. As if that could have anything to do with—with—wouldn't they *laugh!*

[*The men are heard coming down stairs.*]

MRS. HALE: [*Under her breath.*] Maybe they would—maybe they wouldn't.

COUNTY ATTORNEY: No, Peters, it's all perfectly clear except a reason for doing it. But you know juries when it comes to women. If there was some definite thing. Something to show—something to make a story about—a thing that would connect up with this strange way of doing it—

[*The women's eyes meet for an instant. Enter* HALE *from outer door.*]

HALE: Well, I've got the team around. Pretty cold out there.

COUNTY ATTORNEY: I'm going to stay here a while by myself. [*To the* Sheriff.] You can send Frank out for me, can't you? I want to go over everything. I'm not satisfied that we can't do better.

SHERIFF: Do you want to see what Mrs. Peters is going to take in?

[The LAWYER *goes to the table, picks up the apron, laughs.*]

COUNTY ATTORNEY: Oh, I guess they're not very dangerous things the ladies have picked out. [*Moves a few things about, disturbing the quilt pieces which cover the box. Steps back.*] No, Mrs. Peters doesn't need supervising. For that matter, a sheriff's wife is married to the law. Ever think of it that way, Mrs. Peters?

MRS. PETERS: Not—just that way.

SHERIFF: [*Chuckling.*] Married to the law. [*Moves toward the other room.*] I just want you to come in here a minute, George. We ought to take a look at these windows.

COUNTY ATTORNEY: [*Scoffingly.*] Oh, windows!

SHERIFF: We'll be right out, Mr. Hale.

[HALE *goes outside. The* SHERIFF *follows the* COUNTY ATTORNEY *into the other room. Then* MRS. HALE *rises, hands tight together, looking intensely at* MRS. PETERS, *whose eyes make a slow turn, finally meeting* MRS. HALE's. *A moment* MRS. HALE *holds her, then her own eyes point the way to where the box is concealed. Suddenly* MRS. PETERS *throws back quilt pieces and tries to put the box in the bag she is wearing. It is too big. She opens box, starts to take bird out, cannot touch it, goes to pieces, stands there helpless. Sound of a knob turning in the other room. Mrs. Hale snatches the box and puts it in the pocket of her big coat. Enter* COUNTY ATTORNEY *and* SHERIFF.]

COUNTY ATTORNEY: [*Facetiously.*] Well, Henry, at least we found out that she was not going to quilt it. She was going to—what is it you call it, ladies?

MRS. HALE: [*Her hand against her pocket.*] We call it—knot it, Mr. Henderson.

(CURTAIN)

1917

Literary Engagements with the Mexican Revolution

The Mexican Revolution (1910–1920), the first major revolution of the twentieth century, was a seismic event that transformed not only Mexico, but also the United States. Initially, it was characterized by a diverse group of socialist, liberal, anarchist, and agrarian movements. These groups briefly coalesced under the leadership of the politically moderate and wealthy landowner, Francisco Madero, to revolt against longtime dictator Porfirio Díaz. Over time this tenuous coalition disintegrated, and the Revolution changed from a revolt against the established order to a multisided civil war that would transform Mexican society and influence the country's politics and culture for the rest of the century.

Numerous segments of the U.S. population watched as events unfolded south of the border, and the Revolution became a flashpoint for some of the major debates and cultural currents of the day. Nativists such as Madison Grant warned that the chaos engulfing Mexico through its revolution showed that mixed-race peoples were incapable of self-government (the prevailing view was that Mexicans were a "mongrel" people, made up of Spanish, Indian, and African blood), and that the United States should be vigilant in guarding the racial composition of the national body. Conversely, leftists such as John Reed lauded the Revolution as a war for peasant social justice. They found inspiration in the "cult of the Indian," a central theme of Mexican revolutionary rhetoric that (problematically) romanticized the country's indigenous people, understanding them to embody a spiritually incorruptible and premodern essence that would be the symbolic basis for postrevolutionary Mexican national identity. The burgeoning Hollywood film industry seized on the war for its potential as an exotic and titillating event that would draw audiences. Swarms of Anglo-Americans went to the United States–Mexico border to view firsthand some of the ferocious battles taking place just on the other side of the Rio Grande. In short, the Revolution catapulted Mexico into the U.S. national imagination for the first time since the United States–Mexico War (1846–1848), influencing U.S. politics and culture on a number of levels.

For Mexicans living in the United States, especially those who lived in the border region, the Revolution was much more than an opportunity for abstract debate or cultural invigoration. Mexicans who lived on either side of the United States–Mexico borderline had functioned as a cohesive community for decades, moving freely back and forth across the border well into the twentieth century. When the Revolution began, the international boundary did little to stop Mexicans north of the Rio Grande from participating. On the contrary, significant groundwork for the war was laid in the United States, with Mexican expatriates, Mexican Americans, and proto Mexican Americans working together to plan the overthrow of the Díaz regime. It is important to note that support for the war was by no means universal among Mexicans in the United States. They were not a homogeneous group, and many political refugees who became influential north of the border were staunch counterrevolutionaries.

At the same time, many felt deeply committed to the Revolution for several interrelated reasons. First, a large number continued to consider Mexico their homeland long after they had settled in the United States; for them, it was wholly natural, even essential, that they participate in and influence a Mexican event of such magnitude. Second, *Tejanos* (Texans of Mexican descent) in partic- ular saw parallels between their situation as an embattled ethnic group in the United States and that of the economically and politically oppressed Mexican insurgents. Américo Paredes explained that Mexicans on both sides of the river existed under similar conditions for many decades, with "those on the north bank exploited by Anglos, whose power was backed by the Texas Rangers" (a ru- ral constabulary), whereas those to the south were "exploited by a creole elite, with Díaz's *rurales* [similar to the Rangers] as the strong-arm unit." Part of the reason, then, that the Revolution resonated with so many *Tejanos* was that they felt they were in the midst of a similar war with the Texas Rangers, one that was analogous and in some ways directly related to the war south of the border and that they hoped would spark a similar revolt among Mexicans in the United States. Third, Richard Griswold del Castillo noted the deep concern felt by Mexi- cans north of the border regarding the possibility of U.S. intervention and their conviction that such an outcome would lead to the enslavement of all Mexicans by an opportunistic U.S. government that had no respect for Mexican territorial sovereignty. Their sense was that U.S. disrespect for the Mexican nation fed dis- crimination and violence against Mexicans living north of the border and that peace for the latter was predicated upon respect in the international arena for the former.

Such issues are manifest in the rich expressive culture produced by Mexi- cans in the U.S. *Corridos*—narrative ballads composed anonymously and trans- mitted by word of mouth to commemorate events and experiences—were the most important forms of cultural expression for border Mexicans, and they pro- duced hundreds in response to the Revolution. Although *corridos* about the war appeared throughout Mexico, those from the border subtly include references to the climate of cultural conflict that marked the region, thus inscribing the expe- riences of border Mexicans as an embattled ethnic group in the United States into the story of the Revolution. In "La Persecución de Villa," for example, a *cor- rido* that proudly chronicles the great revolutionary general Pancho Villa's ability to elude a U.S. army contingent charged with capturing him, the U.S. soldiers are referred to as "rinches." This was a pejorative nickname bestowed upon the Texas Rangers by border Mexicans; its inclusion in the *corrido* indicates the con- nections border Mexicans made between the war they were waging with the Rangers north of the border and the revolutionary war to the south.

There were close to 200 Spanish-language newspapers published in the U.S. Southwest during the Revolution. They encompassed the entire political spec- trum and were also vocal about the events occurring south of the border.

Conservative newspapers, such as San Antonio's *La Prensa*, opposed the Revolution. They were often run by political refugees who considered their stay in the United States to be temporary because they planned to return to Mexico once the Porfirian order was restored. On the other end of the spectrum were a significant number of anarchist newspapers, the most influential being Los Angeles's *Regeneración*, published by Ricardo Flores Magón. Magón was one of the first to call for revolution in Mexico. Due to the resulting threats to his life, he was forced into exile in the United States in 1903. His newspapers promoted an anarchist position dedicated to proletarian social justice through the total destruction of the existing order. One indication of Magón's influence in Mexico is that his 1910 anarchist manifesto, "Land and Liberty," became the unofficial platform for Emiliano Zapata's indigenous-based insurgency during the Revolution. At the same time, Magón produced articles denouncing the escalating violence perpetrated against border Mexicans, while also voicing vehement opposition to the possibility of U.S. intervention in the Mexican civil war. As Griswold del Castillo argues, Magón believed that Mexicans struggling against political tyranny and economic exploitation in Mexico were leading the way for the liberation of working-class Mexicans in the United States. Furthermore, although he had little interest in championing nationalist causes, he suggested that U.S. disrespect for the Mexican nation ultimately would lead to negative consequences for Mexicans in the United States.

Many Mexicans north of the border were political moderates who were ambivalent about their national identity. Rather than choosing to be "Mexican" or "American," they demanded recognition of their rights as citizens of the United States while simultaneously participating in Mexican politics and culture. Leonor Villegas de Magnón, an affluent Mexican emigre, was one such moderate. She was remarkably active in the Revolution, housing political exiles, founding a female nursing corps, and rubbing shoulders with the likes of Pancho Villa and Emiliano Zapata. She published articles of political and social criticism that appeared in numerous newspapers, including *La Crónica*, and wrote her memoirs in the hope that they would immortalize the contributions of border Mexicans—both men *and* women—to the revolutionary cause. As Clara Lomas explained, the mainstream cultures of Mexico and the United States either held border Mexicans in contempt or ignored them altogether. Magnón's memoir is one of very few documents written between 1910 and 1920 that challenge negative stereotypes of *Tejanos*.

Mexicans in the United States continued to engage the Revolution and its legacies long after the last shot had been fired. One could argue that Magnón's memoir, along with other literary engagements with the Revolution written by Mexicans in the United States, belong to the preeminent Mexican narrative tradition, that of the novel of the Revolution. These Mexican American narratives share many of the key concerns of the Mexican tradition, including an emphasis on the betrayal of the Revolution. However, whereas narratives written south of the border express a national orientation, those written to the north express a transnational orientation, one that asserts the centrality of Mexican Americans to the Revolution and insists that Mexicans in the United States be accounted for in the Mexican national project. In so doing, they emplot issues in the Mexican tradition that reflect their local conditions as members of an emerging and embattled ethnic group, including territorial dispossession, racial and ethnic conflict, and cultural integrity.

Josefina Niggli's 1945 novel, *Mexican Village*, exemplifies such narrative concerns. Niggli was born in northern Mexico in 1910, the year of the Revolution's outbreak. She embarked on an extraordinarily successful career as a playwright and novelist, and *Mexican Village* marks the apex of her writing career. Like many novels of the Revolution, *Mexican Village* explores the betrayal of the war's principles, the relationship between race and national identity, and the related interplay between the primitive and the modern. What makes Niggli's narrative distinctive, however, is its examination of issues facing postrevolutionary Mexico through the eyes of a Mexican American protagonist. In so doing, it examines the legacies of the Revolution for Mexican Americans and proto Mexican Americans, foregrounds the racial conflict that plagues Mexicans north of the border while considering the potential place they might have in the *mestizo* society that the Mexican government was promoting as the national ideal, and consequently elucidates the deep interlocking histories that underlie the neocolonial relationship between Mexico and the United States.

ANONYMOUS

The Pursuit of Villa

Our Mexico, on the twenty-third of February,
Carranza let Americans cross the border,
ten thousand soldiers, six hundred airplanes,
looking for Villa, wanting to kill him.

Don Venustiano tells them, "You may advance.
If you are brave and want to pursue him,
I give you permission to move forward
so that you too will learn how to die."

They began sending out expeditions,
and Pancho Villa then disguised himself;
fully dressed like an American soldier,
he laughed right in Pershing's face.

When they saw the raising of the American flag
and the stars that Villa painted for them,
the airplanes came down to earth,
and Pancho Villa took them prisoner.

When these Gringos arrived in Mexico,
they were looking for bread and crackers with ham;
but *la raza*, who were very angry,
gave them nothing but cannonballs.

Oh, those poor Americans,
they burst out sobbing and crying;
they had only been in battle for two hours,
and they were ready to go back to their country.

Those on horseback no longer could sit down,
and those on foot could no longer walk,
while Pancho Villa flew over them in his airplane,
and from up there he said to them, "Goodbye!"

Pancho Villa no longer rides a horse,
for that is no longer the custom over there;
Francisco Villa is the owner of airplanes,
and he rents them out at very reasonable rates.

All the people in Ciudad Juárez,
all the people were greatly surprised
to see so many American soldiers
that Pancho Villa hanged from telegraph poles.

And then Pershing received the message
that he had lost two hundred dead at Carrizales;
let him also be grateful to Carranza
about the prisoners, for it was Carranza who saved them.

What did these cowardly *rinches* think,
that making war was like a fancy ball?
With their faces all full of shame
they returned once more to their country.
Didn't these bigfooted Gringos know
that they were no match for Pancho Villa?
Francisco Villa is now in Carrizales;
if you so please, you can go see him there.

1976

RICARDO FLORES MAGÓN
1874–1922

Land and Liberty

The fruit, well-ripened by ardent revolt, is about to fall—fruit bitter to all who have become flushed with pride, thanks to a situation which brings honour, wealth and distinction to those who make the sorrows and slavery of humanity the foundation of their pleasures; but fruit sweet and pleasant to all who have regarded as beneath their dignity the filthinesses of the beasts who, through a night that has lasted thirty-four years, have robbed, violated, slain, cheated and played the traitor, while hiding their crimes beneath the mantle of the law and using official position to shield them from punishment.

Who are they that fear the Revolution? They who have provoked it; they who, by oppression and exploitation of the masses, have sought to bring the victims of their infamies despairingly into their power; they who, by injustice and rapine, have awakened sleeping consciences and made honourable men throughout the world turn pale with indignation.

The Revolution is now about to break out at any moment. We, who during so many years have followed attentively the social and political life of Mexico, cannot deceive ourselves. The symptoms of a formidable cataclysm leave no room for doubt that we are on the eve of an uplift and a crash, a rising and a fall. At last, after four and thirty years of shame, the Mexican people is about to raise its head, and at last, after this long night the black edifice, which has been strangling us beneath its weight, is about to crumble into dust.

It is timely that we should here repeat what already we have said so often; that this movement, springing from despair, must not be a blind effort to free ourselves from an enormous burden, but a movement in which instinct must be dominated almost completely by reason. We [Liberals] must try to bring it about that this movement shall be guided by the light of Science. If we fail to do this, the Revolution now on the point of coming to the surface will serve merely to substitute one President for another, one master for another. We must bear in mind that the necessary thing is that the people shall have bread, shelter, land to cultivate; we must bear in mind that no government, however honourable, can decree the abolition of misery. The people themselves—the hungry and disinherited—are they who must abolish misery, by taking into their possession, as the very first step, the land which by natural right should not be monopolized by a few but must be the property of every human being.

No one can foretell the lengths to which the impending Revolution's task of recovery will go; but, if we fighters undertake in good faith [to help] it as far as possible along the road; if, when we pick up the Winchester, we go forth decided not to elevate to power another master but redeem the proletariat's rights; if we take the field pledged to conquer that economic liberty which is the foundation on which all liberties rest, and the condition without which no liberties can exist; if we make this our purpose, we shall start it on a road worthy of this epoch. But if we are carried away by the desire for easy triumph; if, seeking to make the struggle shorter, we desert our own radicalism and aims, so incompatible with those of the purely bourgeois and conservative parties—then we shall have done only the work of bandits and assassins; for the blood spilled will serve merely to increase the power of the bourgeoisie and the caste that today possesses wealth, and, after the triumph, that caste will fasten anew on the proletariat the chain forged with the proletariat's own blood, its own sacrifices, its own martyrdom, which will have conquered power for the bourgeoisie.

It is necessary, therefore, proletarians; it is necessary therefore, disinherited, that your thought be not confused. The conservative and bourgeois parties speak to you of liberty, of justice, of law, of honourable government; and they tell you that when you replace with others those who are now in power, you will have that liberty, justice, law and honourable government. Be not deceived! What you need is to secure the well-being of your families—their daily bread—and this no government can give you. You yourselves must conquer these good things, and you must do it by taking immediate possession of the land, which is the original source of all wealth. Understand this well; no government will be able to give you that, for the law defends the "right" of those who are withholding wealth. You yourselves must take it, despite the law, despite the government, despite the pretended right of property. You yourselves must take it in the name of natural justice; in the name of the right of every human being to life and the development of his physical and intellectual powers.

When you are in possession of the land you will have liberty and justice, for Liberty and justice are not decreed but are the result of economic independence. They spring from the fact that the individual is able to live without depending on a master, and to enjoy, for himself and his family, the product of his toil.

Take, then, the land! The law tells you that you must not take it, since it is private property; but the law which so instructs you was a law written by those who are holding you in slavery and a law that needs to be supported by force is a law that does not respond to general needs. If the law were the result of general agreement it would not need upholding by the policeman, the jailer, the judge, the hangman, the soldier and the official. The law has been imposed on you, and these arbitrary impositions we, as men of dignity, must answer with rebellion.

Therefore, to the struggle! Imperious, unrestrainable, the Revolution will not tarry. If you would be really free, group yourselves beneath the [Liberal] Party's banner of freedom; but, if you merely want the strange pleasure of shedding blood, and shedding your own by "playing at soldiers," group yourselves under other banners—that of the Anti-reelectionists, for example, which, after you have done "playing at soldiers," will put you anew under the yoke of the employer and government. In that case you will enjoy the great pleasure of changing the old President, with whom already you were becoming disgusted, for a spick and span new one, fresh from the mint.

Comrades, the question is a grave one. I understand that you are ready for the fight; but fight so that it shall be of benefit to the poor. Hitherto all your revolutions have profited the classes in power, because you have no clear conception of your rights and interests, which, as you now know, are completely opposed to the rights and interests of the intellectual and wealthy classes. It is to the interest of the rich that the poor shall be poor eternally, for the poverty of the masses guarantees their wealth. If there were not men who found themselves compelled to work for other men, the rich would be under the necessity of doing something useful, of producing something of general utility, that they might be able to exist. No longer would there be slaves they could exploit.

I repeat, it is not possible to foretell the lengths in which the approaching Revolution's task of recovery will go; what we must do is to endeavour to get all we can. It would be a great step in advance if the land were to become the property of all; and if among the revolutionists there should ... be the strength, the conscious strength, sufficient to gain more than that, the basis would be laid for further recoveries which the proletariat by force of circumstances would conquer.

Forward, comrades! Soon you will hear the first shots; soon the shout of rebellion will thunder from the throats of the oppressed. Let not a single one of you fail to second this movement, launching, with all the power of conviction, that supremest of cries, Land and Liberty!

1910

from Intervention on Behalf of Texas Prisoners[1]

Comrades:

Man is free, truly free, only when he is liberated from the need to sell his labor for the sake of a piece of bread, and this liberty can only be achieved in one way: by resolutely, and fearlessly, taking the land, the machinery and the means of transportation so that they can be the property of everyone, men and women.

This cannot be achieved by simply electing someone to the presidency; since the State, whatever its form—republic or monarchy—cannot be on the side of the people. The mission of the State is to protect the interests of the rich. In a thousand years of history, there has not been a single case in which the State has taken from the property/goods of the rich and given them to the poor. On the contrary, we have witnessed the State continually

[1]Translated by Omar Figueredo.

using its force to repress any attempt made by the poor to better their own condition. Recall the case of Río Blanco[2], remember Cananea[3], where the bullets of the State's soldiers drowned out the voices of the proletariat begging for bread: remember Papantla[4], remember Juchitán[5], remember the Yaqui[6], where the State's machine guns and artillery decimated the valiant residents that refused to give up the lands that sustained them to the rich.

This should serve as an example to you all that efforts for your own liberty and well-being cannot be entrusted to anyone else. Learn from the noble proletariat of southern Mexico. They know better than to wait for a new tyrant to satisfy their hunger. Proud and brave, they don't ask: they take. Taking into consideration the woman and the child that beg for bread, they don't wait for a Carranza[7] or a Villa[8] to rise to the presidency and deliver what they need; proudly and bravely, with a pistol in their hand, between the roar of battle and the radiance of the blaze, they take the proud bourgeoisie's life and money.

They don't wait for a strongman to rise so that they can feed them: intelligent and honorable, they destroy property titles, remove fences and place their fruitful/fecund hands over the freed land. Begging is for cowards; real men take. One gets closer to death by kneeling, not to life. Rise up!

Rise up and with the same shovel that you presently use to pile our boss' gold, let's break his skull in two, and with the sickle we use to reap the wheat let us cut the heads off of the tyrants and the bourgeoisie. Over the debris of a heinous system, we'll raise our flag, the flag of the poor, chanting "Land and Liberty!"

We'll no longer raise anyone; everyone rise! No longer will we hang medals nor crosses across our leaders' chests: if they want decorations, we'll decorate them with stabs/piercings/punctures. Whoever shall rise even an inch

---

[2]A French-owned textile factory in the city of Veracruz (in the state of Veracruz), site of labor unrest since 1901. Clashes between management workers intensified throughout 1906, with the Díaz government siding with the owners. On January 8, 1907, the Mexican army shot close to 200 workers and imprisoned another 400; workers killed two dozen soldiers. The government quickly attributed the bloodshed to anarchist influences.

[3]When a 1906 strike at the Cananea Consolidated Copper Company mine in Chihuahua resulted in fights between workers and security guards, the American owner, William Greene, organized a civilian force of 300 American fighters known as the Arizona Rangers. The band crossed the border in violation of Mexican sovereignty. After more than a hundred deaths, the mine workers returned to work without winning any concessions from Greene.

[4]Another city in the state of Veracruz, site of a 1896 uprising by campesinos rebelling against land grabs by outside "investors" seeking to develop the area's industrial output.

[5]City in the state of Oaxaca where the popular José Fructuoso Gómez ("Che Gómez") fought for independence from the national government. Gómez was murdered under mysterious circumstances on December 5, 1911.

[6]A tribe of some 30,000 Native Americans from the Northern Mexican state of Sonora. The Díaz regime enslaved and forcibly relocated the Yaqui to the Yucatán.

[7]Venustiano Carranza de la Garza (1859–1920), the Revolution leader who replaced Victoriano Huerta as Mexican president on August 15, 1914.

[8]José Doroteo Arango Arámbula (1878–1913), better known as Pancho Villa, commander of the División del Norte during the Revolution.

above the rest is a tyrant: overthrow him! The time has come for justice. And instead of the old line, threat to the bourgeois, of "your money or your life," we'll replace it with: "your money and your life!" Because, if we leave even one bourgeois with his life, sooner or later he'll figure out a way to put us under his boot.

Putting into practice the ideals of supreme justice, the same ideals of the Liberal Mexican Party, a group of workers organized a march one day in September of last year in Texas. Those men were on a great mission. They went equipped with great ideas in order to inject new blood into the spirit of rebellion in that region, which is rapidly degenerating into a state of discipline and subordination. Those men went to establish a link between the revolutionary forces of the south and central Mexico, and those that have remained loyal in the north. You must already be aware about the fate of these men: two of them, Juan Rincón and Silvestre Lomas, were shot dead by the state of Texas's henchmen, before they could return to Mexico.[9] The rest, Rangel, Alzalde, Cisneros and eleven others, are currently being held prisoners in that state, some of them serving long sentences, others sentenced to life in prison, while Rangel, Alzalde, Cisneros and others have been sentenced to death. All of these noble workers are innocent of the crime of which they've been accused. One night, during their pilgrimage back to Mexico, a Texan "sheriff" named Candelario Ortiz happened to be killed, and the blame was immediately laid on these fourteen revolutionaries. And who witnessed the crime? No one! Our friends weren't even anywhere near the scene of the crime. And yet, they are the ones being held responsible for the death of one of Capital's dogs, for the simple reason that our imprisoned brothers are both poor and rebels. All they needed was to be members of the working class, and to have the intention of crossing the border in order to fight for their class interests, for American capitalism to come down against them over the loss of its business in Mexico. If they had been Carrancistas or Villistas; if they had been going to Mexico with the intention of placing Villa or Carranza in the presidency, so that these could give away business to the Americans, nothing would have happened to them. What's more, the American authorities probably would have protected them. But since they are honest men, fighting for the liberation of the Mexican worker, the American bourgeoisie releases its fury on them and asks for the death penalty, as due compensation for the losses its business has experienced because of the proletarian revolution.

Meanwhile, Rincón and Lomas's murderers roam free. The same American bourgeoisie that demands the death penalty for Rangel and company, showers the criminals that took the lives of two innocent men with honors and distinctions. Witness here, proletariat, the so-called bourgeois justice. The worker can die like a dog, but don't dare touch a cop! Here and

[9]On September 13, 1913, Rincon, Lomas, Jesus M. Rangel, and the other men attempted to cross the border to fight Huerta forces. Candelario Ortiz, the Texas "sheriff," died during a shoot-out with the men. As a result, Rangel was sentenced to 99 years.

elsewhere, the worker is worth nothing; the only ones that are worth anything are the ones that do nothing! In the hive, the bees kill the drone bees that eat without producing; humans, less intelligent than the bees, kill the workers—the ones that produce everything—so that the bourgeois, the politicians, the policemen and the soldiers, those drone bees of the social hive, can continue living in complete comfort, without producing anything useful.

That's what is called bourgeois justice; that is the evil justice that we revolutionaries must destroy, no matter the cost.

Mexican brothers: this is a solemn moment. The time has come to take stock of ourselves: we number in the millions, while our executioners are only a few. Let's reclaim our imprisoned brothers in Texas from the hands of capitalist justice. We cannot allow the executioner's hand to place the noose around their honest necks. Let's contribute to the defense fund of these martyrs; we'll rally public support for them.

No more crimes against our race. Antonio Rodriguez's ashes[10] have not yet dissipated with the winds; the Texas plains are fresh with the scent of blood of Mexicans murdered at the hands of white savages. Let us raise our arm against the new crime that the American bourgeoisie secretly prepares against Rangel and company.

Mexican brothers: if you have blood in your arteries, join us to save our imprisoned brothers in Texas. You won't just be saving Rangel, Alzalde, Cisenos and the rest of the workers: you will be saving yourselves, because your action will serve to demand respect. How many of you have ever been the victim of some insult in this country, solely for being Mexican? How many times have you heard stories of crimes that are daily committed against people of our race? Did you know that in the American south, it is illegal for a Mexican to sit next to an American in a restaurant? Have you ever walked into a barbershop, been inspected up and down and told: "we don't serve Mexicans here"? Did you know that the United States prisons are filled with Mexicans? Do you have any idea how many Mexicans have been lynched or burned by brutal mobs of whites?

If you know all of this, help to save your fellow Mexican brothers imprisoned in Texas. Let us contribute with our money and our intelligence to save them; let us campaign for their sake; let us declare a general strike for one day as a sign of protest against the persecution of those martyrs. And if neither our protests nor our legal defenses are worth anything; if neither mobilizations nor a strike produce the desired effect of fully liberating these fourteen prisoners, then we must rise up in arms and respond to the injustice with the barricade and with dynamite. Rise up: we are millions!

Long live land and liberty!

May 31, 1914

[10]A twenty-year old Mexican burned at the stake in Rocksprings, Texas, on November 4, 1910, after his arrest for the rape and murder of the wife of local rancher Lem Henderson. The ugly incident was a major diplomatic crisis, fomenting anti-American sentiment and encouraging the revolutionary fervor. No one was ever arrested for Rodriguez's killing.

ANONYMOUS

End the Fratricidal Conflict[1,2]

No more bloodshed
An appeal to the patriotism of General Díaz

It's been more than three months since the current revolutionary movement began with the discovery of the unsuccessful Serdán conspiracy in Puebla.[3] It has cost and continues costing many lives, not to mention the numerous disinvestments from the Mexican treasury and the debilitation of national body.

The conflict is in no way necessary for the consolidation of Mexico's future stability, as a free and independent nation, and could very well end in contrary results, burying the country in anarchy and making way for the most unscrupulous characters, which unfortunately exist in every country on earth.

The fight pits brother against brother; the blood that is shed is only Mexican blood; the widows and orphans that shiver in helplessly over the disappearance of the father and the husband, whether he is from the forces of the state or the insurgency, are only Mexican orphans and widows, that only increase the number of heartbreaking scenes in the insurgent regions; the losses that the war causes for foreign interests will be compensated by the national treasury; the losses caused for the nation's own private interests, for the nation's children, those cannot be repaid by anyone, and the final result will be a giant step backward in the nation's progress, of at least fifty years, that will necessitate several years of tireless work in order to recuperate what has been lost and to continue the march of progress in which Mexico was previously engaged.

So long as the insurgents' numbers remain low there will be no significant battle. And the chain of fatalities and disasters that only affect the Mexican Republic—which continue to place the nation's sovereignty in danger, threatened with the intervention of a pacifying government—will be prolonged for much more time, if the stronger party does not extend a sincere and frank peaceful handshake, so as to end this terrible state of affairs. And in this case, the state is that stronger party, although it is not strong enough to squash the revolution purely through military means, mostly because it can't afford mobilizing a sufficient number of troops to one region at the risk of new insurgencies growing elsewhere.

---

[1]*La Crónica*, 2 March, 1911.
[2]Translated by Omar Figueredo.
[3]Aquiles Serdán Alatriste (1876–1910), a leading Madero supporter, killed November 18, 1910, in a shootout with police at his Puebla home at 4 Santa Clara Street, where his family stockpiled weapons for the anti-Díaz revolutionaries. 4 Santa Clara Street has been a popular museum in Puebla since 1960, with the bullet holes preserved in the facade; it operates under the name Casa de los Hermanos Serdan (Serdan Siblings' House).

Amongst the educated Mexicans that have sought political exile in the United States, there is surely more than one that is not inspired by an immaculate and pure nationalism. But it is nevertheless unfair to judge them all by the same standard. Without a doubt, there are countless amongst those Mexicans that would bring their homeland great honor and prestige were their rights not trampled upon and were they free of humiliating persecutions. We thought about naming some of those Mexicans in the present writing, but for fear of leaving anyone out and causing greater vulnerability, we decided against it.

Since General Díaz is the only Mexican statesman we deem to have the sufficient power and prestige to end these anomalous conditions that afflict the republic, it is to him that we direct our call, appealing to his patriotism so that he calls an end to the fratricidal conflict, granting the following concessions to the nation:

FIRST: That Mr. Ramón Corral[4] be granted free license to remove himself from his investitures as the vice president and interior minister, so that he can attend completely to the full recovery of his health abroad, where he may be entrusted to the care of some special mission close to the European monarchs; and that Benito Juárez[5] be designated as his immediate substitute.

SECOND: That the residents living in the states of Puebla, Veracruz, Tlaxcala, Michoacán, etc., whose administrations have been governing for longer than two terms, be granted full liberty so that they may hold a popular election in which no current administrator can run as candidates, nor any military authority be sent from the capital for such purposes.

THIRD: That all citizens of the republic be immediately granted full liberty of suffrage to vote for their local authorities, such as governors, municipal presidents, and in general all posts that may be eligible according to the law.

FOURTH: That General Díaz pledge, under oath and signed document to inform the nation through the public record, to not designate any candidate for state governor in the following elections, as they come to take place, according to whatever other particular restrictions established by each state's legislature.

FIFTH: That amnesty be granted to any and all men bearing arms without any particular distinction, encouraging them to put down their arms, guaranteeing the protection of their lives and that all of the republic's courts will hear their claims for small holdings lost to powerful landowners or any other relevant claims they may have. This amnesty shall also be extended to all political prisoners held in all Mexican prisons and penitentiaries, granting them absolute liberty. Those political exiles should also be welcomed to

---

[4]Corral (1854–1912) was Díaz's unpopular vice president from 1904 to 1911.

[5]Benito Juárez Maza was the son of national hero Benito Juárez, five-term president of Mexico from 1858 to 1872.

return to the country with the guarantee of freedom from unjust persecution.

SIXTH: That General Díaz pledge, again under oath and through signed affidavit to be published in the public record and the general press, to not seek the presidency in the upcoming election set to begin in December 1916, nor to accept the candidacy for such a post, no matter the pressure from his close allies. That he should solely be concerned with ensuring that the elections be carried out according to the Constitution's provisions and any other corresponding laws.

SEVENTH: That the sovereignty and independence of the federation's states be made effective, and that the municipalities, departments, parties and districts be granted the full independence needed for their own interior governance, and the same be granted to the election of local authorities so that there may be no interference nor pressure whatsoever from either the state or federal government.

Though we wished it could have come from more authoritative and capable hands than our own, we feel compelled to direct these lines to General Díaz by a general commiseration with the poor souls who do not bear the slightest responsibility for the state of things and yet find themselves suffering through hunger and misery without any help.

Surely there are many other important points that we must have escaped our attention here. But if we merit the necessary attention from the president, he shall know how to interpret with greater skill the general sentiment of the nation and how to solve this serious problem, without creating damaging impositions for anyone, ensuring once and for all the end to the terror of political persecution so that the republic can enter fully into an era of civilization worthy of the North American tradition exhibited by Canada and the United States. Let the politician that oversteps his boundaries be punished according to the rule of law and nothing more, still granting him all the necessary privileges for his defense; but not openly attacking him through extra-legal means, forcing him to seek exile abroad in order to guarantee his own life. Mexico cannot be the Russia of North America, nor can it allow the formation of a new class of nihilism through the despotic dealings of inferior leaders, for this would constitute a serious affront and dishonor to the Mexican people.

We call on the Mexican and American press to support, for the sake of humanity and national allegiance, or to critique with sincerity and full liberty this initiative, with whatever modifications, amendments or additions deemed necessary.

March 2, 1911

LEONOR VILLEGAS DE MAGNON
1876–1955

Laredo and the Constitutionalists[1]

With the Maderista revolution reaching its apogee, the Rebel and her children were unable to return to Mexico. Neither could she have gone without first arranging the execution of her father's last will and testament. By an unexpected coincidence, her husband had remained in the Mexican capital, and they were unable to communicate with each other. Her husband worked with an American company, the American Goodyear Rubber Co. His boss Mr. Fuller and the rest of the employees took refuge at the American Club, where they spent the Ten Tragic Days.[2]

Through documents located at the State Department, and others that the Rebel still has in her possession, her husband knew that she had aligned herself with the Revolutionary Council operating on the border. The Council had to distance itself from the border region due to the danger, but it continued its crusade for the Revolution's well-known ideals from afar.

At the same time, on both sides of the border, Reyista groups were forming, the Maderistas alert and silent like shadows observed these activities and mysteriously made such well organized machinations fall to the ground. The fighting in Laredo, Texas stopped the supporters of General Reyes[3] from greater activity and intensity. The Hicks & Hicks law firm, Reyes defenders, was there; as well as Sandoval, Adolfo Reyes and a great number of his powerful sympathizers.

The Rebel found a great reception with the Revolutionary Council, headed by don Melquiades García, don Emeterio Flores, don Manual Amaya, don Nicéforo Zambrano, don Alberto Guimbarda, don Carlos Fierros, don Manuel Cavazos, the elder Castro, Mr. Lozano, don Clemente Idar, and Mr. Donaciano Lassaulx, all of whom were so united that it seemed like it was just one person, confirming the uniformity of idea that facilitated the quick triumph and coordination culminating in perfect harmony and long friendship.

Those opponents of Madero who arrived in Laredo awoke in jail— though in cells of distinction, of course, because they were still Mexicans,

---

[1]Translated by Omar Figueredo and Yolanda Padilla.

[2]"La decena trágica" (February 9–19, 1913) is the name for the military coup d'état that ended the brief presidency of the democratically elected Francisco I. Madero (1873–1913), who had unseated the aged autocrat Porfio Díaz (1830–1915) in 1911. Madero's overthrow was abetted by the American ambassador to Mexico, Henry Lane Wilson (1857–1932), who considered Madero a leftist and a "lunatic." Madero was assassinated on February 22, 1913, by forces loyal to General Victoriano Huerto (1850–1916).

[3]Bernado Reyes (1850–1913), a Díaz supporter who led the first failed revolt against Madero in late 1911.

after all. But we needed to clip their wings at the same time that we lavished them with attention.[4]

Don Emeterio Flores, don Melquiades García, and the Rebel created for themselves a vast network of power and controlled the Laredo area; soon the Rebel, who had the support of the most distinguished families in town—many of whom were affiliated with Madero—organized those same families into auxiliary groups. Madero's supporters from the border region were instrumental in his triumphant march to the National Palace where he was declared Mexico's president. History takes upon itself the responsibility of relating events, but it has forgotten the important role of Laredo, Texas, Nuevo Laredo, Tamaulipas, and other border towns that united during the Revolution in a fraternal agreement.

General Bernardo Reyes's rebellion did not resonate, to the surprise of his supporters. The noble warrior soon surrendered and was imprisoned in Santiago Tlatelolco.[5]

The Revolutionary Council was composed of two factions: the older people with greater experience and level heads, and the youths of action and ardent aspirations. The Rebel was able to function between the two so well that she was able to obtain the friendship of both the elders and the youth. Sincere and loyal friendship, free of any malice or perversion, with whom she could command like brothers without any particular distinction.

Clemente M. Idar[6], a vigorous journalist and orator, possessing a strong moral character that distinguished all of his acts, achieved international fame at a young age for his work defending Mexican workers in the United States. At the time he was a tireless supporter of the Maderismo movement and later of the Constitutionalism, to which he gave the fire and first fruits of his own youth. He went on to become the only Latino leader in labor organizing to achieve distinction in the United States for these efforts.

As the general organizer of the American Federation of Labor, Clemente Idar elevated Latino labor organization like no other. His magnetic oratory and his distinguished organization gained him the friendship of Samuel Gompers, president of the AFL, and William Green, secretary-treasurer and Gompers's successor in the AFL, both of whom Idar represented during important labor efforts. So great was his fervor that his dying words were an invocation of his beliefs in civic duty and brotherhood. At his wake,

[4]Laredo was a central site of reyista support, with the local sheriff, Amador Sánchez, stockpiling weapons at the Webb County jail. On November 16, 1911, a federal grand jury handed down indictments on Reyes, Sánchez, and several other prominent reyistas for violating American neutrality.
[5]After his rebellion failed to gather much support, Reyes surrendered on December 25, 1911, and was imprisoned in the Santiago Tlatelolco Military Prison until February 1913.
[6]Idar (1883–1934) was the first Mexican American labor leader to achieve mainstream recog-

nition. Brother Frederico (1893–1938) was a railroad union organizer who went on to become one of the most celebrated working-class politicians elected to the Mexican Senate. He was murdered in Mexico City on March 12, 1938, probably for political reasons: his reputed killer was a former employee of Emilio Portes Gil, president of Mexico from 1928 to 1930. Like Leonor Villegas de Magnón herself, sister Jovita Idar (1885–1946) has been rediscovered in recent years as a significant feminist figure.

thousands of workers with their heads bowed lined up to pay their respects and shed tears as they said goodbye to their champion for the sake of brotherhood.

Years later, his brother Federico, who had traveled as a senator throughout Latin America promoting the same ideas, was assassinated in the Mexican capital as he defended the rights of railroad workers.

For the Rebel, the Idar family—in particular Clemente, Federico and Jovita—reflected the exemplary heroism that had been previously demonstrated by the Serdán brothers and their sister Carmelita in Puebla; the Idars were the Serdán of Tamaulipas. Carmelita Serdán deserves to receive the highest honor that can be bestowed upon a Mexican woman for her efforts in the Revolution of 1910.

Another fighter who deserves to be honored was the young Carlos S. Fierros, who achieved the rank of general through leaps and bounds at a very young age and whose memory continues to live on in Laredo society where he was highly esteemed. Carlos S. Fierros and Clemente M. Idar were two champions responsible for much of the revolutionary enthusiasm that arose on the border. These early Constitutionalists, Idar and Fierros, began meeting in January 1910, at the Idar press shop on Flores Avenue, attracting ambitious youth to join and discuss the first revolutionary plans. It was there that the Rebel, Jovita and Elvira Idar experienced the spark that ignited the passion in their hearts for the just cause. It was also the site for the idea to organize the Latina women of that border city into a strong association that in a propitious moment would help collaborate with the efforts of the revolution's great leaders.

Clemente and Carlos soon incorporated themselves with Mr. Adrián Aguirre Benavides to organize the first Maderista committee, galvanizing many other residents and patriots that were anxious to support their efforts. They worked with extreme caution because they weren't sure about the American public's reaction and in a foreign land it was not easy to engage in politics.

Let us briefly recall Carlos Dalrymple, a railroad worker, son-in-law of the famous don Ramón Llerena, proprietor of half of Veracruz by way of his Spanish ancestors. He took with him to the grave two authentic documents that would have made him heir to a vast fortune that he never wanted to even share with in any lawyer. Carlos would say: "at least we'll let the poor live in peace without claiming anything."

These are examples of the so-called "Pochos" that are so despised in the capital, but that maintain their honor and international decorum within their tightly bound fists and bearers of a grand and indecipherable intelligence/consciousness. The Rebel received much help from them and they were her inspiration.

This nucleus of effervescent democratic and liberal ideas would meet in the offices of the weekly paper *La Crónica* until the early hours of the morning. It was the principal artery for disseminating the community's sentiments through seemingly wireless threads.

It was that Revolution, one man's will to which all of the Mexican souls, both in Mexico and in the United States, united themselves, that soon resulted in the unanimous election of the people's idol, who on the 7th of June made his triumphant and glorious entry into the capital; Mr. Francisco I. Madero assumed the presidency on the 6th of November 1911.

As a result of those activities, in Laredo, Texas there remained a standing force of 100 of the most select women of that great, hospitable and civilized town. These were women who were destined to later figure in the counterrevolution of 1913, headed by the *Primer Jefe* don Venustiano Carranzo against the usurper General Victoriano Huerta.

The Rebel served as president of the organization, having astutely woven the group's destinies by making sure that at a given moment the organization could, without violating international laws, pass from a civic group as its name indicated, Group for Progress and Charity, to a supportive one that could attend to the injured soldiers in case of emergencies on either sides of the border.

A compassionate and caring woman emerged from the Maderista Revolution: the young and lovely Elena Arizmendi founded a Neutral White Cross. Mexico should honor that beautiful woman for it owes her for so much beneficent work. The Rebel greatly admired that angel of charity but could never put up with the characterization of that beneficent institution as neutral. It was called the Neutral White Cross. It was only explicable by the fact that it was founded in the dangerous zone where both Porfiristas and Huertistas operated. "But there can be no danger where there is right"; The Rebel hated the adjective *neutral*.

The work of the Maderistas in Laredo had been entirely selfless and loyal. It didn't occur to anyone to go to Mexico after the campaign's triumph in order to ask for a post or claim some compensation. The community went on with its quiet, everyday life just like the Río Grande. Great for its peace and great for its justified indignation. The newspaper *El Progreso* was also born of the political turmoil of that time.

The Rebel's friend Santiago Paz informed her of the need for an official Spanish instrument of communication/propaganda. The Rebel, who was always fond of journalists, promised to help them. She was in touch with the best people in Laredo. She first suggested her brother Leopoldo Villegas, to whom, because of his power, they offered the presidency. He purchased half of the stocks, while the other half were divided between the rich cattleman Emeterio Flores and the reputable businessman Melquiades García. And that's how they did it, naming don Santiago Paz as the director and Andrés Patiño as the administrator. That was the front-page that served the Maderista propaganda and later for the 1913 Revolution.

Since the days of Porfirio, there already existed the newspaper *La Crónica*, directed by the liberal Maderista don Nicasio Idar, wherein great articles were penned and the lives of exiled Mexicans were defended. The newspaper accommodated the opinions of noted Maderistas. Rafael Martínez (Rip Rip) guided the opinions of all *fronterizos* or border residents; the paper often distinguished the Rebel, given that she was the favorite of the paper thanks to her social activities that often easily translated into revolutionary efforts.

Jovita Idar, intimate and inseparable friend of the Rebel, was in charge of typing and advertisement/propaganda. Not to underestimate the tireless fighter of so many years, his paper *La Crónica*, which was only a weekly paper, was respected even as *El Progreso* was established, which enjoyed a tremendous success from its first day.

The Rebel organized a group of select and pretty women to collect donations for the victims in Oaxaca and other disasters that were already beginning to appear in Mexico's turbulent situation.

Three tireless, amazing writers dedicated their lives to the triumph of the revolution: Manuel García Vigil, Carlos Samper and José Ugarte gave emphasis and praise to those columns that would later serve as the most powerful weapon in the fight for democracy and liberty.

The history books have already related the tenure of the martyr president Francisco I. Madero. About the Tragic Ten Days, as well as General Felipe Ángeles's loyalty towards Madero, and of the shameful assassination of the president and vice-president Pino Suárez. For those who were in the capital, at first rejoicing over the new leaders and later terrified by the assassination. What must it have felt like for those that left at the hour of victory, satisfied with a sense of completed responsibility, without a single sin of personal gain or interest, thinking that Mexico's problems had been resolved?

For humble, noble towns, like those on the border, where life is organized around the home, the fields and farms, those towns where politics does not penetrate their modest way of life, these were some truly horrible times. But in the capital, the heart of the nation, it was a hotbed of hate and betrayal; such tragic betrayal was to be expected, but perhaps not the sheer magnitude that developed. Mexico should be the golden chalice where Christ's wine and water mix to purify the native Eden that God himself placed in the hands of each and every Mexican. History will go on, even after so much time.

The life of the martyr Madero was a holocaust that shed the blood necessary to redeem us and his work shall not be in vain. On the 22nd of February, 1913 President Francisco I. Madero and Vice-President Pino Suárez were assassinated. Miguel Alessio Robles states:

"In their minds, an entire people opened their hearts like a great temple so that he may live there eternally amongst the clouds ignited with applause and admiration, and to teach all generations how a man that sacrifices himself for the sake of liberty and country lives an immortal and glorious life."

Echoing Miguel Alessio Robles's divine words, the unbreakable warrior, General Francisco L. Urquizo says: "Huerta and his supporters drowned in blood the noble aspirations of a people, aspirations that were just beginning to breathe their first breath."

Peace reigned in the silent, impenetrable tomb of dead things. But the dead live ... so meditated the Rebel ... that's how it was. Moments later, the man from Cuatro Ciénegas's soul was stirred up with just indignation.

He didn't dream about enriching himself, but rather about defending the justice that was unjustly robbed of a people that dreamt of enjoying an until-then unknown liberty.

The loyalists living on the banks of the Río Bravo felt the influx of those furious waters that threatened to avenge and displace the traitors like a righteous whirlwind. The great and generous state of Texas, whose land was once fertilized by Mexican blood, erupted at their sons' calling. They sensed the crime and heard the voice that said: "Cain, what have you done to your brother?"

Those small towns were stirred up. For a time, the rebellion in their hearts grew. The Rebel announced it so to the Revolutionary Committee in Laredo, Texas after a 26-hour car route across the entire border, including Brownsville, Laredo, Eagle Pass, El Paso and Mexicali, while at the same time the loyalists were mobilizing in the cities of Sonora, Chihuahua, Coahuila, Nuevo León, Tamaulipas and the heroic city of Matamoros. Together they formed an invincible fortress along the banks of the historic Río Bravo, boundary between two powerful countries that love justice and respect the rights of others.

The Rebel took possession of a beautiful Mexican flag that previously belonged to don Melquiades García, who with teary eyes instructed her: "Guard it well!"

"Don't worry," she replied and quickly went out to the street where she was awaited by a loyal patriot mounted on a spirited horse, telling her: "Take it through all the streets of Laredo." (This was the first Mexican flag to be raised on American soil.)

More than 5,000 of our brothers beyond the Río Bravo mobilized in silent protest, respectfully supporting the painful demonstration. They were historic moments for the two Laredos and especially for the two sister nations; while the Mexican side armed itself over the unjust murder of Francisco I. Madero, the loyalists in Laredo, Texas experienced an even greater sense of indignation.

When the constituents signed the Plan de Guadalupe, surrounding the Governor Venustiano Carranza, the residents of Laredo were also gathering with equal fervor (although to this day it has not been recognized). They gathered at the entrance of the newspaper El Progreso, recognizing Mr. Venustiano Carranza as the leader of the new revolutionary movement and Melquiades García as the leader of the border. They quickly formed a powerful block to counteract the activities of the Huertistas, whose name is not worthy of mentioning so as to not sully the pages of this work.

Don Melquiades García received some powerful collaboration along his side from Nicéforo Zambrano, don Manuel Amaya, Mr. Ávila, don Alberto Guimbarda, don Emeterio Flores, don Clemente Idar, don Carlos Fierros and the Rebel.

We're all familiar with the Ten Tragic Days. We the revolutionaries have experienced minute by minute those anguishing moments. We use it to call people of conscience to action, to their duty towards their country, to protect the well being of their flag and their land, rejecting the government born out of treason and naming don Venustiano Carranza, governor of Coahuila, the commander-in-chief of the Revolutionary Army.

On the 22 of February, George Washington's birthday, was the date worthy of greatest remembrance on Mexican soil. It was chosen to ignite the spirits of both sister countries. It was a day of celebration in the United States, while Mexico mourned the death of the apostle of the Mexican Revolution.

The treacherous plans of Huerta and the U.S. ambassador, Lane Wilson (two traitors), toasted that same night to Mexico's happiness. They rushed to fill the cups with which they were to toast with bitterness, but the day was bound to arrive when hate would be destroyed by love. The flags of both powerful nations would later sail together at the global call of duty. Casting shadows on the face of the earth, the two nations mobilized in allegiance to their governments.

2004; translation, 2012

■   JOSEPHINA NIGGLI   ■
                        1910–1983

from **Mexican Village**

Rivers rise in flood and destroy,
Brooks water the land and sing.

—MEXICAN PROVERB

The engine swung around the sharp curve between walls of packed yellow earth, travelled into open country long enough to free the rattling cars behind it, and then came to a jerking pause beside the tall wooden supports of the water tower.

A young man swung down from the last coach, his snap-brimmed felt hat pulled low over his eyes, the collar of his shabby tan raincoat standing up at the back. In one hand he held a heavy, battered suitcase that had seen hard wear in many countries. In the other was a cigarette caught between thumb and forefinger, the glowing tip protected by the cup of the narrow palm, an unconscious gesture, for there was no wind blowing.

He looked about him at the stretching fields hot under the clear yellow sun, bare of houses, with the line of mountains blue in the distance.

The conductor thrust his head through one of the open train windows and spoke jovially. "Do not be alarmed, friend. Under the slope of the hill lies the town of Hidalgo. I, personally, assure you of this."

The train, no longer thirsty, shook itself, tottered, gained speed, fled forward to meet another curve and so disappear. Its movements revealed another line of mountains, etched in gray against the dark blue sky, more cactus-studded fields, and, by the water tower, an old man standing between two saddled horses. He was slender, with a dirty blue shirt and gray trousers belted with rope. His broad-brimmed straw hat had a ragged edge, and a bushy gray mustache neatly bisected his brown face.

The stranger in the raincoat walked up to him. "Are you from the quarry?" he asked pleasantly in a deep, hard voice that clipped the words like scissors.

"As you say," the old man answered politely, but the black eyes were investigating the stranger without friendliness. "The letter that came yesterday by train, and it was read to me by Don Nacho, the alcalde, himself, said that you were a *Yanqui* with a most unpronounceable name. And yet you speak Spanish. I do not understand this. Pepe Gonzales, without doubt a boy of little worth, but with two years' schooling in Texas, taught me to say, 'Follow me, please.' It now appears that the lesson was of no necessity."

The stranger laughed, flicked his cigarette to the ground, stepped on it with the toe of his worn black shoe, grinding it to powder in the sand.

"It would also appear," continued the old man tranquilly, "that you were raised in the country, knowing well the danger of fire. That is a good thing."

"One learns."

"Yes. It is also possible that your grace knows how to mount a horse?"

"That also. Not so well, doubtless, as yourself, but that, too, can be learned. What does one do with the valise?"

The old man took the bag from him and placed it between the struts of the water tower. "Here it will be safe. You have papers in it?"

The stranger's mouth twitched in annoyance at this personal question. He answered stiffly, "No. My papers are in my pocket."

"That is good. Papers are better kept in safety. To me all papers are mysterious things, for I cannot read them, but my daughter Candelaria can read; she can also write. It is not good for a child to know more than the parent." He jerked the reins he held in his right hand. "The black horse is for you. It is one of the Castillo blacks, and the foreman of the Rancho Santo Tomás, may the good God take pity on his stupidity for he is in all things stupid save in the knowledge of horses, has assured me that it is of a complete gentleness. You understand," he added anxiously "that the letter did not state that you were learned in the matter of horses."

"I understand." The young man swung easily into the saddle, allowing his body to settle against its hardness, resting his arm across the broad pommel while the old man adjusted the stirrups.

"You are not so tall as we expected. Pepe Gonzales, who is truly a fool but has had two years' schooling in Austin, Texas, assured me that all *Yanquis* are tall, even as tall as Joaquín Castillo, may the saints watch over his soul in Paradise."

The stranger allowed the old man's chatter to flow over him like water. He reached up with a sudden gesture and pulled off his hat so that the soft, scented air could stir against his long square-chinned face. He thought, One year of this. Is it worth it for twelve God-forsaken months?

The old man had mounted the sorrel horse and was watching him, patiently waiting for the signal to move forward. But the stranger did not give it. He was looking up and down the narrow, mountain-walled valley, seeing the yellow sand broken by gray-green cactus, each leaf flaunting its crown of purple fruit, the small flowering thorn bushes covered with tiny yellow blossoms that distilled a too-sweet fragrance, and the tall *yuca* palms bent under the weight of long, purple-tipped white blossoms. Through this desolation ran the silver tracks, reflecting the sun in angry stabs of light, and curving indolently around a cement platform, which had originally been walled with red brick but was now a blackened ruin, obviously once gutted by fire. He pointed toward it.

"What was that?"

"The railroad station, and a fine building it was, presented to Hidalgo by that great good man Don Saturnino Castillo. But who is there to give buildings now that he is gone in exile from the valley? The Great Revolution was a grand thing. Don Nacho, who is alcalde, says so. Also Don Rosalío and the little Doctor, and even the priest, say so. They are all very wise. But me, I stayed safe from the battles in the hills, and now that the fighting is two years done, I say to them, 'Of what good is the Great Revolution save to hang people and to burn buildings? If it was so fine, why do they not bring people back to life and give us new buildings?" They answer me with pretty words that mean nothing. Your grace is ready?"

The stranger nodded and let the reins go lax against the silky arched neck of the black horse.

With the old man in the lead, they trotted through the fields and found a trail that led them through still more fields to the line of eastern mountains. Then they came into a cañon, and the trail mounted upwards into air that grew sharper and colder. The vegetation changed, the cactus and flowering thorn disappeared, but the *yuca* remained, and lichens curved their feathery gray softness over the massive rocks. At last they reached a high mesa that hung out in space, the mountain supporting it like a placid woman carrying a tray.

In front of them was a tin-roofed wooden shack, the unpainted door fastened with a heavy chain and padlock. The old man found a key after much searching in his pockets, and with many requests for aid to various saints opened the lock and flung the door wide. "This," he said proudly, "is the office. Here much work can be done with papers."

But the stranger was paying him no attention. He had strolled to the mesa edge and was staring across the great cut in space that was the valley. The old man came to his shoulder and pointed with one gray-dirt hand toward the northeast. "There lies Monterrey."

You can see the smoke from the smelters. It is a very great city. Don Nacho, who is the alcalde and should know, says it is the third largest in all the Republic. This I do not believe. Monterrey is very great. I believe it is the largest. No city could be larger. That is an impossibility. Ay, the cloud has moved. That is a good omen. The cloud wants you to see Saddle Mountain— the mountain of Monterrey. Do you not consider it beautiful?"

The young man nodded, looking at the distant purple smudge of rock with the double peak that characterized it. For a moment he was a little boy again, and a woman's voice was recounting softly in Spanish, "So the great god of winds, Hurikán, transformed his horse into a mountain to guard his favorite valley. He smoothed down the trembling limbs. The tail he smoothed down, the fine arching neck and the proud head. But in his haste he forgot the saddle..." The stranger moved his shoulders under the shabby raincoat. "Very beautiful," he agreed politely.

"And there," the old veined hand swept in a wide half circle to the southwest, "is the Peak of the Prow. Like a ship it sails the air, not so?"

"As you say. And the town at its base, that is Hidalgo?"

"No, señor, that is Mina. My daughter Candelaria, who has had, you understand, a certain schooling, says that it was named for a hero of the Revolution of 1810, one Ignacio Mina. This I do not know for truth, but only as she says. We have five towns in the Sabinas. It is a very rich valley. And there they are spread out before you."

Like toys, thought the young man. Like toys a giant has thrown down and forgotten.

The old man was saying, "Close to Saddle Mountain is Topo Grande. There is no need for you to remember the name. A collection of mud huts, a small thing of no importance. But the next town, the one with many houses and streets, that is El Carmen. The people there raise cows and sell the milk in Monterrey. Don Nacho says that many people there prefer the milk of cows to the milk of the she-goats, but this is a matter of great amazement, and I do not know it of my own knowledge."

The stranger nodded to the next town. "That one looks like a seashell, one street spiraled around to a center."

"A curious thing," agreed the old man. "My daughter Candelaria says that it is named for another hero of 1810, one Abasolo. A hero he may have been, but the name is stupid: the lonely bean!" For the first time the old man laughed, his face crinkling with mirth, like worn brown leather tortured into creases.

Another town stretched out far below them. It was oblong-shaped, with a church thrusting its belfry up from the center. The buildings were of all colors, and standing aloof was a single great house, the walls white, the roof of red tiles. This house seemed to rise out of a sea of glossy green trees, and beyond it were the sheer cliffs on which the town was built, swung out over a river that twisted through the entire length of the valley like a lazily curving shiny blue serpent. Across the river was a checkerboard of green and yellow, which the old man said were farms, and farther still was the wall of western mountains, small buildings tucked like colored dots into the folding flanks.

Looking at all this, the stranger raised his head slightly, his hazel eyes under the triangular brows filled with an almost passionate sadness. But the mouth, with the sharply cut corners jutting upwards, believed the eyes, as though the body wanted to laugh but the spirit refused the laughter. "So that's the hole I have to live in for a year," he said in English.

The old man grinned again, finding the incomprehensible sounds amusing. "If your grace will go into the office I can show you many papers. When the last *jefe* went away, he said to me, 'Anselmo'—for your grace understands that is my name, Anselmo Carvajal, your servant." He carefully wiped his palm on his trouser leg and extended it. When the stranger shook it without comment the old man seemed disappointed, as though he had expected words which had not been said. After a moment he continued, "The *jefe* said, 'Soon this Revolution will be over, and if I do not come back, another *jefe* will come, and he will want the papers; so guard them well' That was in 1913. For seven years I have guarded the papers, and they are all in the office."

"That is a fine thing," said the young man. "I will now go and admire the papers."

Don Anselmo pattered after him into the shack. "Seven years is a long time. To God, of course, it is not even a moment, but to me, who am old, it is a long time. This office is even as the other *jefe* left it. He was a good *jefe*, not a *Yanqui* like your grace, but an Italian. He stayed here two years. He had a fine house in Hidalgo but he would not live in it. He slept on the office floor, sometimes alone but generally with one of the cave women. My woman was too old for him, and my daughter Candelaria, too young. She is, you understand, the child of my age. But many of the cave women rolled the eye at him, and then he would sleep with them. It was strange, for there were never any children. He had not in him the richness of seed. You are perhaps different, señor?"

The question was so politely put that it caught the stranger off guard. He was hardly listening to the interminable chatter while he surveyed the battered oak desk, a gaudy calendar showing a harshly colored picture of the cement plant in Monterrey, and the date, 1913, the scarred wooden filing cabinet, and the empty liquor bottles powdered with dust and linked together with strong cables of spider webs.

"How the hell should I know," he muttered with a curious sense of embarrassment.

"Precisely, señor. But then you are still young. You are perhaps twenty-four?"

The stranger's narrow face betrayed no hint of his resentment at this second invasion of his privacy. "Twenty-six," he said curtly. "Now that we have seen the office, where is the quarry?"

"But the papers, señor—all the beautiful papers in the cabinet. You do not wish to see the papers?"

To humor the old man, he pulled out a drawer of the filing case. For a moment his lips slid into a long sideways smile. The drawer was filled with French magazines devoted to displaying the beauty of nude women. "This Italian—what became of him?"

"It was a sad thing. The morning he chose to leave the safety of the mountains was the same morning that *El Rubio* captured Hidalgo and started to hang people. That blond one was very angry at not finding Don Saturnino Castillo. He would say, 'Where is Don Saturnino?' and if a man could not answer him, zas! he was hanged. Lucky for Hidalgo, all the good men were away fighting. This *Rubio* caught the Italian, and because he could not answer the question—for who was the Italian to know the secrets of such a great one as Don Saturnino—the *Rubio* hanged him. I personally went down and protested, but the *Rubio* paid me no more mind than if I had been the husband of an actress. It was a very sad thing."

The stranger shut the drawer with a quick gesture of finality. "And the quarry?"

"If you grace will follow me. It is around the slope of the mountain."

1945

MARÍA CRISTINA MENA
1893–1965

María Cristina Mena was the first Mexican American author to publish short fiction in English in major U.S. literary magazines, including *The Century*, *American*, *Cosmopolitan*, and *Household*, where she was named "the foremost interpreter of Mexican life." Born in Mexico City in 1893 to "a Spanish mother and Yucatecan father of European descent," she received an elite, multilingual education, then emigrated to the United States at the age of fourteen, before the Mexican Revolution. She was commissioned to publish a series of short stories set in Mexico for *Century* beginning in 1913, with the publication of "John of God, the Water-Carrier," later published in *The Monthly Criterion* in 1927, edited by T. S. Eliot, and selected for *The Best Short Stories of 1928*. Speculating on the possibilities of turning her life into fiction in a letter to her *Century* editors, she describes a "family of wealthy refugees from Mexico" and "the gradual emancipation of their daughter" who "takes to American freedom like a duck to water." Rather than her personal story, her fiction offers diverse perspectives on Mexican culture, with detailed depictions of the class, ethnic, and gender hierarchies of the period. Her stories include indigenous characters, such as the protagonist in "John of God," and upper-class families, as in "The Education of Popo," adjusting to a society and economy in transition to modernization.

Along with her nuanced social criticism, her references to Mexican history, folklore, and religion suggest her role as cultural translator. As aesthetic interests turned to Mexico, her fiction earned the attention of prominent literary modernists. She developed a correspondence with D. H. Lawrence after the 1927 republication of "John of God, the Water-Carrier." She visited the Lawrences in 1929, which she recalls in a final essay, "Afternoons in Italy with D. H. Lawrence." Her personal papers also reveal her admiration of authors José Juan Tablada, a poet from Mexico City who lived in New York City; Indian philosopher and writer Rabindranath Tagore; and William Butler Yeats. She married playwright and journalist Henry Kellett Chambers in 1916 and returned to publishing after his death in 1935. She published young adult fiction, including *The Water-Carrier's Secrets* (1942), an expanded, more thematically explicit version of her short story "John of God, the Water-Carrier," *The Two Eagles* (1943), *The Bullfighter's Son* (1944), *The Three Kings* (1946), and *Boy Heroes of Chapultepec: A Story of the Mexican War* (1953). In "My Protocol for Our Sister Americas," an essay sent to *Pan-American Magazine* on August 18, 1943, she argues for greater knowledge of and compassion for "our fellow-Americans in the Southern Republics." In 1964, the last year of her life, she published "In Memoriam: President John F. Kennedy" in *The Brooklyn Heights Press*, and a personal essay, "Easter in Mexico," in *The Texas Observer* and *Mexico City Times*. She died in 1965 at the age of seventy-two. Her *New York Times* obituary states that she "dedicated her work 'to bringing to the American public the life of the Mexican people.'"

Her narratives provide insight into Mexican American relations in the early twentieth century, including the imperialistic influence of the United States, demonstrated in forms of industrialization, tourism, and consumerism. Published as magazine fiction, her work also evokes the genres of regionalism, mystery, and romance. However, with humor and dramatic irony, these texts not only counter more voyeuristic portrayals of Mexico, but also inspire readings of resistance, as she casts a critical eye on modernization and builds toward narratives of the Mexican Revolution.

The literary recovery of Mena's work occurred with the support of the Recovering the U.S. Hispanic Literary Heritage Project, resulting in the publication of her short fiction by Arte Público Press.

Amy Doherty Mohr
Ludwig-Maximilians-Universität in Munich

PRIMARY WORKS

The Water-Carrier's Secrets, 1942; *The Two Eagles*, 1943; *The Bullfighter's Son*, 1944; *The Three Kings*, 1946; *Boy Heroes of Chapultepec, A Story of the Mexican War*, 1953; *The Collected Stories of María Cristina Mena*, 1997.

John of God, the Water-Carrier

Most of the inhabitants were still on their knees in the middle of the street, praying that there might be no repetition of the trembler. Others were searching anxiously for divine symbolism in the earthquake's handwriting of crossed and zigzagged crackings in adobe walls. It had come without warning. Through the ground had passed a series of shudders, like those of a dying animal, with a twitching of houses, a spilling of fountains, and a quick sickness to people's brains.

Several horses from a burning stable were running wild through the streets. An Indian boy who had just risen from his knees unslung his *lazo*[1] and tried to catch one that galloped past him, but it swerved from the flung noose and charged through an open cabin, striking down a kneeling woman in the doorway. The boy ran to her and lifted her head, then lowered it quickly and crossed himself. Beneath the wetted hair, where a hoof had struck, he had felt the grate of a fractured edge of bone.

Suddenly he was driven at one bound into the street by a thin cry inside the hut.

"*Mamá!*" said the voice, and then, "*Mamacíta!*"[2] with a drawling petulance on the diminutive.

The boy moved a little nearer, calling: "Come out, *muchachita!*"

But the unseen raised her voice and replied that she could not come out without her *mamá*, being a little bad with fever. Also, her name was Dolores and she did not desire to be called "*muchachita*," and she was thirsty, and where was her *mamá*?

"I will come to thee, Dolores," the boy replied in a shaking voice.

[1]Lasso.

[2]Mommy.

As he stepped past the dead woman he turned his head aside with a prayer. There in a corner was the child, swaddled in coarse cloth, lying on a straw mat. Her head was tied up with fresh leaves of rosemary and mallow, which are sovereign for fever if allowed to wither on the skin. He gave her drink from a water-jug, and then she sucked her lips and looked at him searchingly from eyes like balls of black onyx.

"Who art thou?" she demanded.

"I am Juan de Dios, son of Pancho the *aguador*."[3]

Baptismal names of sacred meaning are in high favor with the *Inditos*,[4] and in "John of God" there was nothing uncommon except the solemnity of the youth's tone as he announced himself to the wondering child.

"And thou," she replied impatiently, "Where is my *mamá*?"

"Five Aprils," she replied impatiently, "where is my *mamá*?"

"Perhaps with thy *papá*."

"That cannot be. My *papá* is dead." And then, raising herself on one elbow to see him better, "Why dost thou weep?"

"There is dust in my eyes," said Juan de Dios. "Tell me—thou hast brothers and sisters?"

"I have none."

"Grandparents?"

"*¿Quién sabe?*"[5]

"How '*¿quién sabe?*' Hast thou no one?"

"Foolish one! My *mamá* is enough. Where is my *mamá*?"

"Perhaps at the church. We have had a trembler.

"*Santa Bárbara bendita!*[6] Then it woke me!"

"It was a very strong trembler, and if we should have another—"

"Take me out, Juan de Dios!" she cried, holding out her arms to be lifted.

He wrapped her in a blanket, covering her face so that she might not see her mother, and carried her out unnoticed figure in that agitated hour, he walked, he stopped, he ran a few steps, he looked around wildly. At last, discerning a closed carriage approaching soberly, he dropped to his knees, uncovering the child's head and his own. The black curtains over the carriage windows were partly drawn, but not sufficiently to hide from view the gold chalice[7] covered with an embroidered cloth which an acolyte in red and white held steadily before a black-robed ecclesiastic. Poor and rich, old and young, kneeled in the dust as it passed, for this was the carriage of Our Master— "*Nuestsro Amo*"—and the whole *pueblo* felt blessed, comforted, and protected by the divine Mystery which it bore among the people. The boy after its passing rose with a light heart and continued on his way, uplifted by what seemed to him a personal message of pardon and peace. The little girl, who a few moments earlier had said, "Why dost thou weep, Juan de Dios?" now said,

---

[3]Water-carrier.
[4]Diminutive of *Indian*.
[5]Who knows?

[6]Blessed, holy.
[7]A wine cup used in Communion service.

"Why dost thou smile. Juan de Dios?" He only replied, "*Nuestro Amo* has passed." And she fell asleep, and the warmth of her little body filled him with a troubled tenderness.

His parents ran to meet him, thanking the saints for having preserved their first-born.

"But what thing bringest thou?" said his father, looking at the bundle in his arms.

"A little sick one," said Juan de Dios, displaying the green herbs that crowned his protégé and permitting her sleeping face to make its own appeal. It was the face of a toast-colored cherub.

"¡*Qué bonita!*"[8] exclaimed his mother, admiringly. "But of whom is she, son of mine?"

And he told them in a whisper how the child's mother had been killed, not mentioning the unluckily thrown *lazo* and his own blood-remorse, but adding simply that *Nuestro Amo* had sent him the thought to take care of the little orphan.

"Be it so, son of ours!" exclaimed the water-carrier and his wife in one voice; and Juan de Dios, who still looked at the face of the sleeping child, added:

"The *chiquita*[9] will grow fat and strong for helping, and when she has taken her first communion I will marry her,"

And so it was settled. No one else claimed the orphan, and the priest saw no reason why Pancho, the water-carrier, should not add a ninth young mouth to the eight that already busied themselves at feeding-time beneath the flat roof of his adobe cabin. After Juan de Dios. who was twelve, came Tiburcio, two years younger, and then a mixed rabble of barefooted infancy, in which the new-comer took a middle place and proved able to hold her own. The new home was a counterpart of the old one, except that it was more populous and amusing. The *tortillas* were just as warm and as grateful to little stomachs; there wasn't a pin to choose between the niceness of the beans, black and red, or of the sauces that would sometimes bite little tongues; and as for the *chilitos verdes*—little green peppers just the size of her fingers—Juan de Dios would bring them to her in handfuls, knowing that she adored to crunch them between her sharp little teeth. She developed a strong affection for the household altar which stood in one comer and was touched by no one but Juan de Dios. It consisted of an image of the Virgin of Guadalupe stamped on a large piece of leather and decorated with delicate white plumes, at its feet an earthen dish of oil in which a butterfly was always burning—not a real butterfly, of course, but one of those little contrivances of a short wick stuck in a float called by the same name, *mariposa*.

A month after his adoption of Dolores, Juan de Dios was a different person. By parting with certain property, to wit, one carved leather belt, one

---

[8] How pretty!   [9] Young girl.

knife, one *lazo*, fashioned in a superior manner with fancy knots and stained in bright colors, one flute, which he had made from a piece of sugar-cane, and one veteran fighting-cock with a bamboo leg, he had raised enough money to buy an income-earning equipment consisting of two water-jugs suspended at either end of a long pole which he balanced on his shoulder. So burdened, he embarked in business in a small way, delivering water to households of the humbler sort, and earning about three *reales*[10] a week. And he was soon rich enough to buy Dolores three white shirts, three skirts of gaily striped and figured baize, much green cotton ribbon for her hair, a medal of their Mother the Virgin of Guadalupe, and scapularies[11] of Santa Barbara, who protects from thunder, the Virgin of the Conception, who defends chastity, and the Archangel Gabriel, who watches over little children.

When his day's work was over Dolores would beg for a story, and sitting cross-legged, with their backs against the sun-warmed cabin wall, he would tell her stories of the miracles and apparitions of saints, and she would catch her breath and stretch the rims of her eyes at the exciting parts, just as children of the northern land do over the deeds of giants and fairies.

And she would tell him the events of her day. She had spread the clothes on the rocks to dry for the *mamacita* washing at the brook; she had fetched holy water from the church; she had gathered wild jasmine, pink and white, and made a basket of posies which she had taken to the station with Tiburcio and some of the sisters, and the passengers in the trains had given her many *centavos*, which she had tied in a corner of her *rebozo*[12] to keep them from Tiburcio, who was as full of tricks as a monkey.

Sometimes Juan de Dios would remonstrate with Tiburcio for teasing the little motherless one; and then Tiburcio, taking the scolding in good part, would make Dolores laugh with his comical grimaces. He had bright, impudent eyes and a mole under his mouth which gave him a laughing look and earned him many gracious glances from the *señores* on the trains when they bought his pomegranates or purple passion-fruit.

Juan de Dios saved enough money in the course of a year to discard his long pole, which caused the *porteros*[13] of the better residences to exclude him from their patios, and provide himself with a mature *aguador's* outfit like his father's. Thenceforward he bore a very large jug on his back, balanced by a smaller one on his breast, and his knees bent more than ever, and he was very proud. No other Indito was so alert in undertaking small errands or so faithful in performing them. And at last it fell out that some of the oldest families in the *pueblo*, lifelong patrons of the deliberate Pancho, would ask him in emergencies for the services of his son. Now, Pancho loved his son, but he also had

[10]One-quarter of a peso.
[11]Symbol of affiliation to an ecclesiastical order consisting of two strips of cloth hanging down the breast and back and joined across the shoulder.
[12]Cloak.
[13]Doormen.

his proper pride, and one day he said to Juan de Dios: "Son of my life, comfort of my soul, thou art now a man and mayest choose thine occupation."

"Choose my occupation?" stammered the astonished youth. "But your honor knows that I have chosen it these four years."

"Not so," replied Pancho, positively. "Of *aguador*, sufficient with thy father. Better that thou be a donkey-driver. It is my wish, thou consolation of my miseries; and the day of thy saint I will give thee a burro—and may God accompany thee!"

Juan de Dios was silent. The thought of changing his occupation filled his heart with anguish. Was he not sixteen, and long settled in life? Did not all the world know him as Juan de Dios, the *aguador*?

That evening at twilight, as he and Dolores squatted against the wall, he said to her: "To-morrow we will go to early mass, and after we will speak to the padre about thy confirmation. I have to leave thee, Dolores."

"To leave me!" Incredulity and indignant protest struggled with a very lively curiosity.

"Even as I say. I have a weight in my heart, Dolores, but all is for the best. I am going to work for thee a few years in the capital."

She looked at him with mingled terror and admiration, for in the imagination of the Indian of the *pueblos* the City of Mexico is enveloped in formidable and sinister mystery. With the same feeling in his heart, and a sudden surge of loneliness, Juan de Dios wept. She tried to comfort him, begging him not to go, but he stammered: "The road of the glory is sown with thorns. I will go. Resign thyself, little daughter. When I return we shall receive the benediction of the padre, and thou shalt be my little wife."

"Yes, yes, Juan de Dios!" She joined her bronze hands flatly as in prayer, bowed her forehead on the finger-tips, and then threw back her head with a heavenward glance of mild ecstasy. "Yes, yes! I shall be very big when thou comest back, and thou wilt take me to my own little cabin—oh, what enchantment!"

She kissed his hand reverentially, and her heart was filled with the great calm that assurance of protection gives to the weak and ignorant.

And so a morning arrived when Juan de Dios departed from his birthplace, accompanying a party of donkey-drivers who were taking various wares to sell in the capital. It was a morning of farewells, promises, benedictions, and tears. The capital was only two days' easy march distant, but it seemed to all that Juan de Dios, the confidant and comforter, whose daily blessing of the hut had carried an unnameable gentle charm, was embarking into dark distances full of dangers.

The capital, as sensitive of its reputation as an elegant woman, has a code of manners for *Inditos* and enforces it in times of peace, peremptorily though kindly. Juan de Dios learned that in the City of Mexico one may no longer enjoy the comfort of going barefoot, and dutifully he taught his feet to endure the encumbrance of leather sandals. He learned that the city *aguador* may not blow his whistle to halt the traffic while he gravely crosses the

street, but must wait for the passing of many vehicles, some with horses
and some outlandishly without. From early morn to the fall of the afternoon
he would go from fountain to fountain and from portal to portal, his lean
body so accustomed to bending that he never thought of straightening it,
his head bowed as if in prayer.

On the first day of each month he visited a little shop in the street of
San Felipe Neri, where a good old widow sold tobacco and snuff, candles for
the poor, for the rich, and for the church; flags of silver and gold paper
stuck in dry oranges to adorn altars; toys, candies, lottery-tickets, and many
other necessaries. With her Juan de Dios understood himself very well. She
would change his mountain of centavos into silver pesos, and from her he
would buy his meager supplies for the month, including his lottery-ticket,
with which he never won a prize although he never neglected to have it
blessed by holding it up in church at the moment of benediction. Very
happy, he would jog home, the heavy silver pieces in his leather pockets
making a discreet and dulcet "*tank-trak*" between his jugs and his body. He
lived with a charcoal-seller in one room at the back of a *bodega*,[14] where the
odors of dried fish and vats of wine mingled with the dust of the charcoal
nightly swept into the farthest corner of the soft earth floor to make place
for his sleeping-mat.

When his first jugs had worn out—the sweet-scented, porous red clay
becomes perforated in time—he had buried them to their necks in the corner where he slept, and they were now his treasury. On returning home
from the widow's he would uncover them and drop his coins one by one
into their depths, receiving a separate thrill of satisfaction at the piquant
echo of each one from the hollow of its prison.

Once in a year or so he received word from his family by the mouth of
some donkey-driver or pilgrim. They were well. They sent him benedictions.
And he, as opportunity offered, sent them gifts for their saint-days.

It was the month of June, which always makes the heart restless. During
his five years in the capital Juan de Dios had treated himself to fewer holidays than most *peons*[15]—not celebrating the days of more than ten or a
dozen favorite saints each year—and now his spirit rebelled at many things.
The rainy season was, as usual, depriving him of the *centavos* which at other
times accrued from the sprinkling of the streets in front of his customers'
houses, as ordained by law. And then there was a new and mischievous spirit in the air, a spirit named "modern improvement," and it now possessed
and agitated one of the houses on his route, a three-patio building inhabited
by fifteen families of the middle class. The plumber—worker of evil and
oppressor of God's poor—had been exercising his malign spells. Was it the
will of God that water should run upstairs, except in jugs sustained by the

[14]Cellar or shop selling wine and food.
[15]Members of the landless laboring class, or
persons in compulsory servitude.

proper legs of a man? Was the roof of a building a fit place for a large and unsightly tank? Was it reasonable to suppose that a man could fill such a reservoir with water by see-sawing laboriously an erect stake of painted iron, as tall as his breast, which had sprouted diabolically in a patio at the margin of the fountain? Or that the tenants could supply themselves with water by no more than turning a stick of brass not as an honest man's finger? Was it for him, Juan de Dios, to become a confederate in these mysteries by hauling and thrusting that painted stake, instead of making many sociable trips between the fountain and the kitchens of his customers? No! He would not so endanger his soul. With firmness he had refused to serve the strange gods of the plumber. And the owner and tenants of the building, liking well their patient and apostolic-looking *aguador*, and understanding perfectly his prejudices, and murmured "*¡Mannana!*"[16] and allowed the highly painted and patented American force-pumps in the three patios to rust in unlovely idleness.

But the incident had given Juan de Dios a shock, and turned his heart toward the simplicity and piety of the *pueblo*. His Dolores was fourteen now, and ready for marriage. He had saved enough money. He could build a little hut and buy a *burro*, and lead an easy and blessed existence with his chattering little squirrel of a wife, and the babies that would crawl in the sunshine at their cabin door.

Meanwhile the excellent business which he had built up in the capital should not be lost to the family, for Tiburcio should succeed to it. That part of it had already been arranged; it only remained to send him word that the time had come.

Then came many days of patient waiting and of serious preparation— days, too, of fasting and prayer—until one afternoon there dawned upon his vision at the public fountain which he had appointed as their meeting-place a radiant young spark whom he would not have identified as the weeping boy he had left in the road except for the eloquent mole under the still-laughing mouth. He wore leather trousers, wondrously tight-fitting, and laced up the sides from foot to hip between double rows of brass buttons; a white shirt, without a collar, but with a large, flowing scarlet bow sewed to the middle of the bosom; a leather belt hung with a fancy knife, a plain knife, and other decorative items; from his neck a religious medal which clashed cheerfully against the metal of the knives; on his feet heavy shoes of wine-colored leather, much overlaid and ornamented in punctured designs; on his head a cheap straw *sombrero* heavily bound to its very apex with silver rope, richly knotted.

Tiburcio saw his brother trotting along with head bended as of old, and moved to meet him; and with many simple ejaculations of joy and affection they placed each his hands on the other's shoulders, with smiles and graceful bendings of heads, and strokings and partings, like a pair of friendly ants. Thus they remained, regardless of the disorganized traffic, until a

[16]Tomorrow!

gendarme,[17] himself an *Indito*, ran to them and in a friendly fashion moved them on. And at length Juan de Dios permitted himself to take cognizance of Tiburcio's elegance.

"But, brother of my soul," he protested, "thou appearest a Judas!"

Tiburcio hung his head in shame at this allusion to the garishly bedizened effigies of Judas which are hanged in the streets and plazas on Saturday of Glory and burned amid festive mockery and the sputtering of firecrackers. Fortunately he had working garments tied up in his blanket, and the *portero* of a neighboring house where June de Dios was known allowed him to change there and emerge in the simple habit that God had undoubtedly ordained for water-carriers. And not until then did he remember to impart to his brother a piece of important news. Laughing, he said:

"Brother, with all thy scoldings thou didst put it away from my memory to tell thee that Lola is here."

"Lola?" repeated Juan de Dios, not understanding.

"Dolores—she came with me."

"Protect me, Saint of my name! Dolores here—but for what? And where is she?

"While I found thee I left her at the cathedral."

"Well chosen the place! But I beat my brains to comprehend. Did I not tell her to wait for me in the *pueblo*? And now—¡Ay! ¡Ay! What sinful impatience that she must come to meet me here! What sad fortune that I could not have embraced her as I always wished, in the cabin where I left her!" He wagged his bended head with a heavy sigh at this upsetting of his plans. Tiburcio looked uncomfortable and opened his pique, began to rejoice: "But since God wishes it to come sooner, the pleasure, so much better. She is here, my young woman! What little moments we will pass! ¡Uy, újule!"

And with that liquid cry of joy he unharnessed himself, pulling over his head the shoulder-straps, with the leather breast-and-back plates and head-piece, and the heavy jugs, and proceeded to harness his brother, saying: "Do me this service, Tiburcio. Carry on this street five journeys to number fourteen, six to number eighteen, three to number twenty, and eight to the principal patio in number twenty-two. Take care not to touch the pots of flowers in the corridors, and where the cages of birds hang be sure to bend lest thou knock them down. If the parrots speak to thee, answer them not, for *señoras* like them not to learn our manner of expressing ourselves. If thou seest a melon or a bunch of flowers swimming in a patron's water-jar, touch them not, for after thou hast poured the water they will but dance a little and come up again. Here are my colorines." He passed over a leather bag filled with scarlet beans. "With these count thy journeys, leaving one each time with the servant of the house. Conduct thyself well, and that God may accompany thee. I go to the cathedral to find my Dolores. ¡Adios! ¡Adios!"

[17]Soldier employed in police duties.

The new *aguador* attracted the attention of a lady and gentleman sitting in the principal patio, and they asked him about Juan de Dios. Tiburcio explained everything with great care, and added in a confident and winning manner that he expected to give just as good service as his brother, if not a little bit better. And the lady in some excitement whispered to her husband: "Perhaps this youth will agitate the pump, and by the grace of God we can utilize at last our porcelain bath!"

The lady's husband, who was the owner of the house, jumped at the idea, and Tiburcio was conducted to the pump. He rolled his eyes at it distrustfully, and seemed to regard the *señor's* explanation of its *raison d'être* as a rather lame one; but when the *señor* himself grasped the lever and moved it sturdily back and forth without suffering any other penalty than a shortness of breath—for he was a fat and not younger *señor*—the youth recovered his courage.

"Lend here, *Patrón*," he said; and getting free of his jugs and rolling up his trousers he attacked the business with confidence. The proprietor and his wife put heart into him at intervals by remarking what a strong fellow he was and how the capital was the proper place for him; and although Tiburcio's muscles were not hardened to such labor he kept at it, his spirit swimming in the ether of pride and praise, for half an hour. Meanwhile the news that an *aguador* who would pump was on the premises had spread to the second and third patios, and so flattering were the overtures made to him that Tiburcio, concealing his fatigue, addressed himself with zeal to the other two force-pumps. When his arms failed him he continued by employing the weight of his body, the forward plunge pulling a quart of water from the fountain and the backward fall projecting it toward the roof—for it is the ungracious nature of a force-pump to work equally hard both ways. On abandoning the third pump Tiburcio felt a weight in his chest, and his legs bent under him like green twigs; but he was wonderfully happy as he took the silver pieces that he had earned by the sweat of his body, and with them made the sign of the cross on his brow, his eyes, his mouth and his breast. After which he rolled himself in a straw mat in a shady corner, and abandoned himself like a tired child to his well-earned *siesta*.[18]

Juan de Dios and Dolores met under the trees of the plaza in front of the cathedral—a new Dolores, almost as tall as himself, with dove's eyes and a sad little voice, very desirable—and they embraced just as he and Tiburcio had embraced, hands on shoulders with the same little glances and bendings and soft ejaculations. And she called him "*Padrino*,"[19] as of old, at which he protested playfully, "*¿Que padrino ni qué calabazas?*"

"What godfather nor what pumpkins? Not thy *padrino*, but thy husband, who forgives thee for coming to him."

At that she was troubled, and abruptly withdrew her hands from his shoulders, averting her face. That gesture smote him with the knowledge

---

[18]Afternoon nap.   [19]Godfather.

that an evil had come between them. Trembling with anger, he exclaimed: "What thing is this I see? What thing? What thing?"

His voice pitched higher and higher. Her hands flew to her downcast face. He seized her wrists and shook them, making her whole body reel like a palm in a hurricane.

"Don't beat me, don't beat me!" she sobbed. "Where is Bucho?"

The endearing diminutive of his brother's name, or the tone of instinct in which it was uttered, told him all. He fetched a great sobbing breath and struck her in the face with the back of his hand, and then again with the palm, and then rained blows on her head and shoulders; and she, being a woman and born of blood impressed with the proverb "Who well loves thee will make thee weep," snuggled against him, whimpering. While beating her he swore many oaths, such as "Lightnings and chains of fire!" and spoke bitter reproaches of ingratitude and perfidy, weeping all the while They were near the central terminus of trolley-lines, and a crowd gathered about them, and there were calls for a gendarme. Hearing that, Juan de Dios turned her about and gave her a push to make her walk in front of him.

Tiburcio had not been seen at number fourteen, nor eighteen nor twenty, but in the principal patio of twenty-two Dolores heard snores which she recognized, and they found Tiburcio curled in slumber.

Deeply curled, for it required several kicks from his brother to awaken him, and even then his fatigue pressed upon him so heavily that he stared up at them with a vague smile, unconscious of the fury in one face and the fear in the other. Soon, however, it dawned on his sluggish senses that Juan de Dios was declaiming angrily, then that Lola was weeping, then that her love and his own was the cause of the outburst, and then that the girl had thrown herself between them with upraised arms, crying to Juan de Dios: "Don't curse him! Don't curse Bucho! Bucho, speak to him!"

"Lightnings!" shouted Juan de Dios, his voice muffled with foam. "For his sorceries with which he hath bewitched thee, that God may cripple him!"

Dolores gave a gasp of horror. Tiburcio, his face suddenly bleaching to a waxen yellow, tried to rise to his knees for prayer, but at the first movement an intense pain shot through his back between the shoulders and he tumbled over on his face, howling: "Crippled! God favor me, miserable sinner that I am! Brother, brother, thy words have fallen over me! I am crippled truly! I cannot move! ¡Ay-ay-ay¡"

In a series of shrieks he described the progress of his affliction, which extended to all the muscles that he had brought into unwonted action during his intemperate exertions with the force-pumps. Dolores screamed for help, sputtered incoherencies at the *portero* and ran round the patio like a wild animal, kneeling at intervals to pray but not daring to go near Tiburcio from fear of the demon that possessed him. Shudder after shudder convulsed him as he sprawled with his forehead on the pavement, the poison of terror augmenting that of fatigue. From the house emerged many servants, male and female, asking questions, offering advice, chattering and crossing themselves, afraid to approach.

It was important to get Tiburcio away. Juan de Dios lifted him to his feet at last, despite his piteous moans. It appeared that he could use his legs, although feebly, but from loins to neck he seemed paralyzed. Supported by his brother and Dolores, and uttering cries at each step, he traversed the streets to the charcoal-seller's and was laid on a mat. Juan de Dios rubbed his body with holy water, sprinkling what was left of it all over the room to frighten away evil spirits.

Night fell over the anguish of the three, but without abating it. Toward Juan de Dios and his prayers the other two deferred in a spirit of humility and anxious expectancy, while he performed such prodigies of spiritual concentration that he shook as with an ague and his tears lost their identity among the drops of sweat that rolled down his contorted visage. They would not believe that he could pray in vain—he, the blessed one, he at whose curse that punishment had fallen! And yet, soon after the great clock of the palace had boomed out eleven, Tiburcio reported to Dolores in whisper that he seemed to be breaking into two pieces. She wailed loudly, and in desperation demanded of Juan de Dios what thing she could do, or he and she together, that would incline the good God to show mercy to Bucho. Since He was angry at the broken troth, might it not appease Him if she renounced her love of Tiburcio and become the little wife of Juan de Dios? Tiburcio from his mat begged that the efficacy of that method of cure might be tested. Juan de Dios said nothing, but his eyes burned as he looked at Dolores, and shortly afterward abruptly went our into the rain. From the door she could see him dimly, by the light of a distant street lamp, sitting motionless under the sky with his knees to his breast, his face upturned in submission and inquiry.

Hours passed before he returned, and then he was alight with resolve. Making a sign to Dolores that she should help him, he uncovered the buried jugs and removed by handfuls all his savings, which they packed in two leather bags. Soon afterward the three set forth into the dark and rain-swept night, Tiburcio traveling as a passenger on his brother's back, partly sustained by a leather band which passed across the other's forehead, and inadequately counterpoised by the two bags of silver pesos which alternately patted Juan de Dios's chest as he trotted. They traversed unfrequented streets until they reached the outskirts, and then struck the road along which a trolley-line runs to the Villa de Guadalupe,[20] the Mecca of the Mexicans. Tiburcio suffered severely from the jolting and straining of sore muscles; but the knowledge of his destinations so filled him with hope that he suppressed his groans.

---

[20]Site where the Virgin of Guadalupe first appeared to the Indio Juan Diego on December 9, 1531.

The sun was rising when they reached the Villa de Guadalupe. Juan de Dios stretched his brother on one of the heavy iron benches in the plaza at the foot of the hill. Tiburcio seemed a little easier which was not to be wondered at, for many miracles had been known to follow the mere arrival of the sufferer within the precincts of the sacred *pueblo*. To Juan de Dios the very air was sensibly impregnated with sanctity, and he breathed it with rapture. Faint incense instilled it, bells trembled in it, some as remote voices imploring faith, others strong and impatient mandates to repentance. *Padres*[21] in long black cassocks flitted hither and thither from church to church and from chapel to chapel. Their houses loomed somberly above gardens which seemed thronging congregations of flowers. Even the rag awnings fluttering here and there under the old trees of the plaza played their part in the enchantment, for beneath them were exposed for sale every imaginable aid to devotion—rosaries, images, ribbons of saints, and many other objects, even to little dark papers of blessed earth, the virtue of which is notorious all over Mexico. Juan de Dios bought some of the earth and all three devoured it, as is the way of the faithful, Tiburcio receiving the largest share. It was a natural transition to blessed water. This they obtained from the sacred well at the foot of the hill in the center of a little ancient domed temple, by casting into its rocky depths a heavy, conical cup of iron attached to a chain. Tiburcio drank of the water as much as he could, its abominable flavor strengthening his faith in its miraculous powers. Also his brother poured a cup of it over him.

And now Juan de Dios was ready for the pilgrimage proper. Shading his eyes with his hand, he traced the course of the stone stairway mounting heavenward from his feet, flight after flight, at first shaded by great trees and at last almost lost amid wild creepers as it aspired in curves like those of a snail's shell to the lofty summit, with its coronet of churches and chapels now ethereal with the golden light of the young morning. With an eagle glance which seemed to perceive in that radiance an authentic sign from the Virgin of Guadalupe, whom he had adored from childhood, he exclaimed: "If yonder thou art, Mother of mine, unto thee I bear a sinner. He is my brother. Make me the road hard, dangerous. Put me obstacles; all that may be necessary to make merit for my presentation before thee with Tiburcio— that is his name."

He wiped the sweat from his forehead with one finger, and continued in a tone of exaltation which thrilled the others.

"I will carry him to thee on my knees, over all those steps, unto thine altar! This act of devotion, I offer it to thee for the health of my sinner brother, that thou wilt permit him to move the body again, if thou thinkest he merits it."

And having signed himself, he dropped to his knees and with much difficulty, Dolores assisting, hoisted Tiburcio to his shoulders with feet hanging down in front and hands clasping his brother's brow. Juan de Dios held his

---

[21]Priests.

body upright, balancing carefully as he felt his way upward, one knee after another, slowly—always slowly. Dolores followed, marveling at his sanctity It being the rainy season, there was no great throng of pilgrims, but the few who were ascending to the shrine—some women carrying wax candles decorated with gold paper, others with plates or sprouting wheat of a delicate pallor from having been grown in the dark and a few *Inditos* with bamboo cages containing fighting-cock's to be blessed in church that they might have fortune in battle—these remarked the superior zeal of Juan de Dios, and regarded him respectfully as a holy person, one whom it was fortunate to have seen. The same spirit was manifested by the sellers of blessed articles on the landings of the stair. While he rested Juan de Dios caused Dolores to buy the largest and most beautiful candle obtainable, and thereafter she carried it, unlighted, in front of them Also, for refreshment and edification of them all, they bought blessed fruit, blessed *tortillas* fried in chile sauce, and *tortillas* of the Virgin, which are made sweet and very small and dyed in different colors.

As he climbed, Juan de Dios prayed, and the more he suffered the more he thanked God. His white cotton trousers gave but the scantiest protection to his knees, and that not for long, yet he did not look for smooth places, and Tiburcio groaned more than he. Once he slipped on a rolling pebble, and after that he mounted every step with the same knee, lifting the hurt one after it. The time came when even his strength of *aguador* wore out, and he clawed the stone balustrade to raise himself and stopped on each step, his breath hissing between his locked teeth from which the lips were stiffly peeled; and still his eyes pleaded for martyrdom. Dolores at every opportunity would wipe Tiburcio's face where the thorns had scratched it.

When Juan de Dios reached the top he signed to Dolores to light the candle, and he held it at arm's-length as he continued his march into the ancient church of the hill, his knees leaving prints of red on the white marble pavement. Into the depth of the church straight to the blazing shrine he went, and Dolores saw his face working frightfully as he unlocked his teeth to proclaim that he had kept his word; but no sound came from his throat, and he suddenly fell forward in a swoon, spilling Tiburcio, who executed a series of instinctive movements, too quick for eye to follow, which landed him on his feet, supple and free from pain; and he and Dolores threw themselves on their knees beside the unconscious one at the shrine, to recite a multitude of "*gracias*" for the miracle.

Dolores fully expected to become the little wife of Juan de Dios. He had come from the confessional when he said to them: "I now comprehend that I do not serve for this world. The love of woman confounds me too much. God will free me from committing more barbarities. I will remain in this saintly place, for which it seemeth to me I was ordained before my mother bore me. Thou, Dolores, and thou, Tiburcio, serve for this earth. Go, and may the good God accompany you always. Take this bag of money, that it may help you to marry and live justly as good Christians. The other bag I have given to the good padre, who will manage it so that I shall have enough prayers and masses said for the guidance of my steps while I live."

Much more he said to them in the same peaceful strain, and laid an obligation upon them to make pilgrimage every year for the feast of the Virgin of Guadalupe in remembrance of the miracle she had performed for Tiburcio.

They left him, and he continued to be an *aguador*, carrying water from the sacred well to the top of the sacred hill with which to refresh pilgrims, especially the sick and crippled, after the ascent. He himself was crippled, never recovering from a stiffness of one knee, which remained bent. And in this manner Juan de Dios became veritably John of God.

November 1913

The Education of Popo

Governor Fernando Arriola and his amiable *señora* were confronted with a critical problem in hospitality: it was nothing less than the entertaining of American ladies, who by all means must be given the most favorable impressions of Mexican civilization.

Hence some unusual preparations. On the backs of men and beasts were arriving magnificent quantities, requisitioned from afar, of American canned soups, fish, meats, sweets, *hors d'oeuvres*, and nondescripts; ready-to-serve cereals, ready-to-drink cocktails, a great variety of pickles, and much other cheer of American manufacture. Even an assortment of can-openers had not been forgotten. Above all, an imperial had gone out for ice, and precious consignments of that exotic commodity were now being delivered in various stages of dissolution, to be installed with solicitude in cool places, and kept refreshed with a continual agitation of fans in the hands of superfluous servants. By such amiable extremities it was designed to insure the ladies Cherry against all danger of going hungry or thirsty for lack of conformable aliment or sufficiently frigid liquids.

The wife and daughter of that admirable *Señor* Montague Cherry of the United States, who was manipulating the extension of certain important concessions in the State of which Don Fernando was governor, and with whose operations his Excellency found his own private interests to be pleasantly involved, their visit was well-timed in a social way, for they would be present on the occasion of a great ball to be given by the governor. For other entertainment of the Arriola family would provide as God might permit. Leonor, the only unmarried daughter, was practicing several new selections on the harp, her mama sagaciously conceiving that an abundance of music might ease the strain of conversation in the event of the visitors having no Spanish. And now Próspero, the only son, aged fourteen, generally known as Popo, blossomed suddenly as the man of the hour; for, thanks to divine Providence, he had been studying English, and could say prettily, although slowly, "What o'clock it is?" and "Please you this," and "Please you that," and doubtless much more if he were put to it.

Separately and in council the rest of the family impressed upon Popo that the honor of the house of Arriola, not to mention that of his native land, reposed in his hands, and he was conjured to comport himself as a true-born *caballero*.[1] With a heavy sense of responsibility upon him, he bought some very high collars, burned much midnight oil over his English "method," and became suddenly censorious of his stockinged legs, which, accompanying him everywhere, decoyed his down-sweeping eyes and defied concealment or palliation. After anxious consideration, he put the case to his mama.

"Thou amiable companion of all my anguishes," he said tenderly, "thou knowest my anxiety to comport myself with credit in the view of the honored Meesees Cherry. Much English I have already, with immobile delivery the most authentic and distinguished. So far I feel myself modestly secure. But these legs, Mama—these legs of my nightmares—"

"¡Chist, chist![2] Thou hadst ever a symmetrical leg, Popo mine," expostulated Doña Elvira, whose soul of a young matron dreaded her boy's final plunge into manhood.

"But consider, little Mama," he cried, "that very soon I shall have fifteen years. Since the last day of my saint I have shaved the face scrupulously on alternate mornings; but that no longer suffices, for my maturing beard now asks for the razor every day, laughing to scorn these legs, which continue to lack the investment of dignity. Mother of my soul, for the honor of our family in the eyes of the foreign ladies, I supplicate thy consent that I should be of long pantaloons!"

Touched on the side of her obligations as an international hostess, Doña Elvira pondered deeply, and at length confessed with a sigh:

"It is unfortunately true, thou repose of my fatigues, that in long pantaloons thou wouldst represent more."

And it followed, as a crowning graciousness toward Mrs. Montague Cherry and her daughter, that Popo was promoted to trousers.

When the visitors arrived, he essayed gallantly to dedicate himself to the service of the elder lady, in accordance with Mexican theories of propriety, but found his well-meaning efforts frustrated by the younger one, who, seeing no other young man thereabout, proceeded methodically to attach the governor's handsome little son to herself.

Popo found it almost impossible to believe that they were mother and daughter. By some magic peculiar to the highly original country of the *Yanquis*,[3] their relation appeared to be that of an indifferent sisterliness, with a balance of authority in favor of the younger. That revolutionary

[1]Gentleman.
[2]Ssh! Hush!

[3]Yankees, natives of the United States.

arrangement would have scandalized Popo had he not perceived from the first that Alicia Cherry was entitled to extraordinary consideration. Never before had he seen a living woman with hair like daffodils, eyes like violets, and a complexion of coral and porcelain. It seemed to him that some precious image of the Virgin had been changed into a creature of sweet flesh and capricious impulses, animate with a fearless urbanity far beyond the dreams of the dark-eyed, demure, and now despised damsels of his own race. His delicious bewilderment was completed when Miss Cherry, after staring him in the face with a frank and inviting smile, turned to her mother, and drawled laconically:

"He just simply talks with those eyes!"

There was a moon on the night of the day that the Cherrys arrived. There was also music, the bi-weekly *serenata*[4] in the plaza fronting the governor's residence. The band swept sweetly into its opening number at the moment when Don Fernando, with Mrs. Cherry on his arm, stepped out upon his long balcony, and all the town began to move down there among the palms. Miss Cherry, who followed with Popo, exclaimed at the romantic strangeness the scene, and you may be sure that a stir and buzzing passed through the crowd as it gazed up at the glittering coiffure and snowy shoulders of that angelic *señorita* from the United States.

Popo got her seated advantageously, and leaned with somewhat exaggerated gallantry over her chair, answering her vivacious questions, and feeling as one translated to another and far superior planet. He explained as well as he could the social conventions of the *serenata* as unfolded before their eyes in a concerted coil of languid movement—how the ladies, when the music begins rise and promenade slowly around the kiosk of the band, and how the gentlemen form an outer wheel revolving in the reverse direction, with constant interplay of salutations, compliments, seekings' avoidings, coquetries, intrigues, and a thousand other manifestations of the mysterious forces of attraction and repulsion.

Miss Cherry conceived a strong desire to go down and become merged in that moving coil. No, she would not dream of dragging Doña Elvira or Leonor or mama from the dignified repose of the balcony; but she did beg the privilege, however unprecedented, of promenading with a young gentleman at her side, and showing the inhabitants how such things were managed in America—beg pardon, the United States.

So they walked, together under the palms, Alicia Cherry and Próspero Arriola, and although the youth's hat was in the air most of the time in acknowledgment of salutes, he did not really recognize those familiar and astonished faces, for his head was up somewhere near the moon, while his legs, in the proud shelter of their first trousers, were pleasantly afflicted with pins and needles as he moved on tiptoe beside the blonde *Americana*, a page beside a princess.

[4]Serenade.

Miss Cherry was captivated by the native courtliness of his manners. She thought of a certain junior brother of her own, to whom the business of "tipping his hat," as he called it, to a lady occasioned such extreme anguish of mind that he would resort to the most laborious maneuvers to avoid occasions when the performance of that rite would be expected of him. As for Próspero, he had held tips of her fingers lightly as they had descended the marble steps of his father's house, and then with a charming little bow had offered her his arm, which she with laughing independence had declined. And now she perused with sidelong glances the infantile curve of his chin, the April fluctuations of his lips, the occasional quiver of his thick lashes, and decided that he was an amazingly cute little cavalier.

With a deep breath she expelled everything disagreeable from her mind, and gave up her spirit to the enjoyment of finding herself for a little while among a warmer, wilder people, with gallant gestures and languorous smiles. And the aromatic air, the tantalizing music, the watchful fire that glanced from under the *sombreros* of the *peons* squatting in colorful lines between the benches—all the ardor and mystery of that unknown life caused a sudden fluttering in her breast, and almost unconsciously she took her escort's arm, pressing it impulsively to her side. His dark eyes flashed to hers, and for the first time failed to flutter and droop at the encounter; this time it was her own that lost courage and hastily veiled themselves.

"That waltz," she stammered, "isn't it delicious?"

He told her the name of the composer, and begged her to promise him the privilege of dancing that waltz with her at the ball, in two weeks' time. As she gave the promise, she perceived with amusement, and not without delight, that he trembled exceedingly.

Mrs. Cherry was a little rebellious when she and Alicia had retired to their rooms that night.

"Yes, I suppose it's all very beautiful and romantic," she responded fretfully to her daughter's panegyrics, "but I'm bound to confess that I could do with a little less moonlight for the sake of a few words of intelligible speech."

"One always feels that way at first in a foreign country," said Alicia, soothingly, "and it certainly is splendid incentive to learn the language. You ought to adopt my plan, which is to study Spanish very hard every moment we're here."

"If you continue studying the language," her mother retorted, as industriously as you have been doing to-night, my dear, you will soon be speaking it like a native."

Alicia was impervious to irony. Critically inspecting her own pink-and-gold effulgence in the mirror, she went on:

"Of course this is also a splendid opportunity for Próspero to learn some real English, which will please the family very much, as they've decided to send him to an American college. I do hope it won't spoil him. Isn't he a perfect darling?"

"I don't know, not having been given a chance to exchange three words with—Sh-h! Did you hear a noise?"

It had sounded like a sigh, followed by a stealthy shuffle. Alicia went to the door, which had been left ajar, and looked out upon the moonlit gallery just in time to catch a glimpse of a fleeting figure, as Próspero raced for his English dictionary, to look up the strange word "darling."

"The little rascal!" she murmured to herself. "What a baby, after all!" But to her mother she only said, as she closed the door, "It was nothing, dear; just one of those biblical-looking servants covering a parrot's cage."

"Even the parrots here speak nothing but Spanish," Mrs. Cherry pursued fretfully. "Of course I am glad to sacrifice my own comfort to any extent to help your dear father in his schemes, although I do think the syndicate might make some graceful little acknowledgment of my social services; but I'm sure that papa never dreamed of your monopolizing the only member of this household to whom it is possible to communicate the most primitive idea without screaming one's head off. I am too old to learn to gesticulate, and I refuse to dislodge all my hairpins in the attempt. And as for your studies in Spanish," she continued warmly, as Alicia laughed, "I'd like to know how you reconcile that pretext with the fact that I distinctly heard you and that infant Lord Chesterfield[5] chattering away together in French."

"French does come in handy at times," Alicia purred, "and if you were not so shy about your accent, Mama dear, you could have a really good time with Doña Elvira. I must ask her to encourage you."

"Don't do anything of the kind!" Mrs. Cherry exclaimed. "You know perfectly well that my French is not fit for foreign ears. And I do think, Alicia, that you might try to make things as easy as possible for me, after my giving way to you in everything, even introducing you here under false pretenses, so to speak."

"It isn't a case of false pretenses, Mama. I've decided to resume my maiden name, and there was no necessity to enter into long explanations to these dear people, who, living as they do in a Catholic-country, naturally know nothing about the blessings of divorce."

"So much the better for them!" retorted Mrs. Cherry. "However much of a blessing divorce may be, I've noticed that since you got your decree your face has not had one atom of real enjoyment in it until to-night."

"Until to-night!" Alicia echoed with a stoical smile. "And tonight, because you see a spark of reviving interest in my face, you try to extinguish it with reproaches!"

"No, no, my darling. Forgive me, I'm a little tired and nervous. And I can't help being anxious about you. It's a very trying position for a woman

[5]Title of Philip Domer Stanhope (1694–1773), English earl and diplomat known for his "honeyed words" (James Boswell).

to be in at your age. It's trying for your mother, too. I could box that wretched Edward's ears."

"Not very hard, I'm thinking. You wanted me to forgive him."

"No, my dear, only to take him back on probation. We can punish men for their favorite sins much more effectually by not giving them their freedom."

"I couldn't be guilty of that meanness, and I shall never regret having shown some dignity. And I think that closes the subject, doesn't it, dearest?" Alicia yawned.

"Poor Edward!" her mother persisted. "How he would have enjoyed this picturesque atmosphere with you!"

Alicia calmly creamed her face.

Próspero spent a great part of the night over his English dictionary. Again and again he conned the Spanish equivalents listed against that word "darling." A significant word, it seemed, heart-agitating, sky-transporting. He had not dreamed that the harsh, baffling English language could contain in seven letters a treasure so rare. *Predilecto, querido, favorito, amado*[6]— which translation should he accept as defining his relation to Mees Cherry, avowed by her own lips? The patient compiler of that useful book could never have foreseen the ecstasy it would one day bring to a Mexican boy's heart.

He was living in a realm of enchantment. To think that already, on the very day of their meeting, he and his blonde Venus should have arrived at intimacies far transcending any that are possible in Mexico except between the wedded or the wicked! In stark freedom, miraculously unchaperoned, they had talked together, walked together, boldly linked their very arms! In his ribs he still treasured the warmth of her; in his fingers throbbed the memory that for one electric instant their hands had fluttered, dove-like, each to each. Small enough, those tender contacts; yet by such is the life force unchained: Popo found himself looking into a seething volcano which was his own manhood. That discovery, conflicting as it did with the religious quality of his love, disturbed him mightily. Sublimely he invoked all his spiritual strength to subdue the volcano. And his travail was richly rewarded. The volcano became transformed magically into a fount of pellucid purity in which, bathing his exhausted soul, young Popo became a saint.

In that interesting but arduous capacity he labored for many days, during which Miss Cherry created no further occasion for their being alone together, but seemed to throw him in the way of her mama, a trial which he endured with fiery fortitude. He was living the spiritual life with rigorous intensity, a victim of the eternal mandate that those fountains of purity into which idealism has power to transform the most troublesome of volcanoes should be of a temperature little short of the boiling-point.

[6]Synonyms: preferred; loved, darling; favorite;
 dear, beloved, sweetheart.

His dark eyes kept his divinity faithfully informed of his anguish and his worship, and her blue ones discreetly accepted the offering. Once or twice their hands met lightly, and it seemed that the shock might have given birth to flaming worlds. When alone with her mama, Alicia showed signs of an irritable ardor which Mrs. Cherry, with secret complacency, set down to regrets for the too hastily renounced blessings of matrimony.

"Poor old Ned!" the mother sighed one night. "Your father has seen him, and tells me that he looks dreadful."

On the morning of the night of the ball the entire party, to escape from the majordomo[7] and his gang of hammering decorators, motored into the country on a visit to Popo's grandmother, whose house sheltered three priests and a score of orphan girls, and was noted for its florid magnificence of the Maximilian period.[8]

Popo hoped that some mention might be made in Alicia's hearing of his grandmother's oft-expressed intention to bequeath the place to him, and he was much gratified when the saintly old lady, who wore a mustache *á la española*,[9] brought up the subject, and dilated upon it at some length, telling Popo that he must continue to make the house blessed by the presence of the three padres, but that she would make provision for the orphans to be taken elsewhere, out of his way, a precaution she mentioned to an accompaniment of winks and innuendoes which greatly amused all the company, including the padres, only Alicia and Popo showing signs of distress.

After dinner, which occurred early in the afternoon, Popo maneuvered Alicia apart from the others in the garden. His eyes telegraphed a desperate plea, to which hers consented, and he took her by the hand, and they ran through a green archway into a terraced Italian garden peopled with marble nymphs and fauns, from which they escaped by a little side gate into an avenue of orange-blossoms. Presently they were laboring over rougher ground, where their feet crushed the fat stems of lilies, and then they turned and descended a roughly cut pat winding down the scarred, dripping face of a cliff into the green depth of a little *cañón*,[10] at the upper end of which a cascade resembling a scarf flung over a wall sang a song of eternity, and baptized the tall tree-ferns that climbed in disorderly rivalry for its kisses.

Alicia breathed deeply the cool, moss-scented air. The trembling boy, suddenly appalled at the bounty of life in presenting him with his sovereign concatenation of the hour, the place, and the woman, could only stammer irrelevantly, as he switched at the leaves with his cane:

"There is a cave in there behind the waterfall. One looks through the moving water as through a thick window, but one gets wet. Sometimes I come here alone, all alone, without going to the house, and *mamagrande*[11]

---

[7]Head servant of a wealthy household.

[8]Maximilian, Archduke of Austria, was declared the emperor of Mexico by France's Napoleon III in 1863. He was executed by Mexican troops in 1867.

[9]In the Spanish style.

[10]Canyon. *Cañoncito*: little canyon.

[11]Grandmother.

never knows. The road we came by passes just below, crossing this little stream, where thou didst remark the tall bamboos before we saw the porter's lodge. The mud wall is low, and I tie my horse in the bamboo thicket."

"Why do you come here?" she asked, her eyes tracing the Indian character in the clear line of his profile and the dusky undertone of his cheek.

"It is my caprice to meditate here. From my childhood I have loved the *cañoncito* in a peculiar way. Thou wilt laugh at me—no? Well, I have always felt a presence here, unseen, a very quiet spirit that seemed to speak to me of—¿*quién sabe?*[12] I never knew—never until now."

His voice thrilled, and his eyes lifted themselves to hers, as if for permission, before he continued in ringing exaltation:

"Now that thou hast come, now that thou appearest here in all thy lovely splendor, now I know that the spirit I once felt and loved in secret was a prophecy of thee. Yes, Alicia mine, for thee this place has waited long—for thee, thou adored image of all beauty, queen of my heart, object of my prayers, whose purity has sanctified my life."

Alicia, a confirmed matinée girl, wished that all her woman friends might have seen her at that moment (she had on a sweet frock and a perfectly darling hat), and that they might have heard the speech that had just been addressed to her by the leading man. He was a thorough juvenile, to be sure, but he had lovely, adoring eyes and delightfully passionate tones in his voice; and, anyhow, it was simply delicious to be made love to in a foreign language.

She was extremely pleased, too, to note that her own heart was going pitapat in a fashion quite uncomfortable and sweet and girly. She wouldn't have missed that sensation for a good deal. What a comfort to a bruised heart to be loved like this! He was calling her his saint. If that Edward could only hear him! Perhaps, after all, she *was* a saint. Yes, she felt that she certainly was, or could be if she tried. Now he was repeating some verses that he had made to her in Spanish. Such musical words! One had to come to the hot countries to discover what emotion was; and as for love-making! How the child had suffered!

As he bowed his bared head before her she laid her hands, as in benediction, where a bronze light glanced upon the glossy, black waves of his hair; and that touch, so tender, felled Popo to the earth, where he groveled with tears and broken words and kisses for her little shoes, damp from the spongy soil. And she suddenly dropped her posings and her parasol, and forgot her complexion and her whalebones,[13] and huddled down beside him in the bracken, hushing his sobs and wiping his face, with sweet epithets and sweeter assurances, finding a strange, wild comfort in mothering him recklessly, straight from the soul. At the height of which really promising situation she was startled by a familiar falsetto hail from her mama as the rest of the party descended into the *cañoncito*, whither it had been surmised that Popo had conducted Miss Cherry.

---

[12]Who knows?

[13]Plates from the upper jaw of some whales, used to corset women's dresses.

After flinging an artless yodel in response to the maternal signal, and while composing Popo and herself into lifelike attitudes suggestive of a mild absorption in the beauties of nature, she whispered in his ear:

"The next time you come here you shall have two horses to tie in the bamboos."

"*¡Ay Dios!* All blessings on thee! But when?" he pleaded. "Tell me when!"

"Well, to-morrow," she replied after quick thought; "as you would say, my dear, *mañana*. Yes, I'll manage it. I'm dying for a horseback ride, and I've had such a lovely time today."

To be the only blonde at a Mexican ball is to be reconciled for a few hours to the fate of being a woman. Alicia, her full-blown figure habited in the palest of pink, which seemed of the living texture of her skin, with a generous measure of diamonds winking in effective constellations upon her golden head and dazzling bosom, absorbed through every pore the enravished admiration of the beholders, and beneficently poured it forth again in magnetic waves of the happiness with which triumph enhances beauty. Popo almost swooned with rapture at this apotheosis of the being who, a few hours earlier, had actually hugged him in the arms now revealed as those of a goddess. And to-morrow! With swimming brain he repeated over and over, as if to convince himself of the incredible, "*¡Mañana!*"

Almost as acute as the emotions of Popo, in a different way, were those of a foreign gentleman who had just been presented to the governor by the newly arrived Mr. Montague Cherry. So palpably moved was the stranger at the sight of Alicia that Mrs. Cherry laid a soothing hand on his arm and whispered a conspirator's caution. Presently he and Alicia stood face to face. Had they been Mexican, there would have ensued an emotional and edifying scene. But all that Alicia said, after one sharp inspiration of surprise, was, with an equivocal half-smile:

"Why, Edward! Of all people!"

And the gentleman addressed as Edward, finding his voice with difficulty, blurted out hoarsely:

"How are you, Alicia?"

At which Alicia turned smilingly to compliment Doña Elvira on the decorations.

Mr. Edward P. Winterbottom was one of those fortunate persons who seem to prefigure the ideal toward which their race is striving. A thousand conscientious draftsmen, with that national ideal in their subconsciousness, were always hard at work portraying his particular type in various romantic capacities, as those of foot-ball hero, triumphant engineer, "well-known clubman," and pleased patron of the latest collar, cigarette, sauce, or mineral water. Hence he would give you the impression of having seen him before somewhere under very admirable auspices. Extremely good-looking, with long legs, a magnificent chin, and an expression of concentrated manhood, he had every claim to be classed as "wholesome," cherishing a set of opinions suitable to his excellent station in life, a proper reverence for the female of the species, and an adequate working assortment of simple emotions easily predicable by a reasonably clever woman. Of the weaknesses common to humanity he had fewer than the majority, and in the prostration of remorse and desire in which he now presented himself to Alicia he seemed to offer timber capable of being made over into a prince of lifelong protectors.

Alicia had come to feel that she needed a protector, chiefly from herself. Presently, without committing herself, however, she favored him with a waltz. As they started off, she saw the agonized face of Popo, who had been trying to reach her. She threw him a smile, which he lamentably failed to return. Not until then did she identify the music as that of the waltz she had promised him on the night of that first *serenata*. After it was over she good-naturedly missed a dance or two in search of him, meaning to make amends; but he was nowhere to be found.

With many apologies, Doña Elvira mentioned to Alicia, when he appeared the following morning, that the household was some-what per-turbed over the disappearance of Próspero. No one could remember having seen him since early in the progress of the ball. He had not slept in his bed, and his favorite horse was missing from the stable. Don Fernando had set the police in motion. Moreover, *la mamagrande*, informed by telephone, was causing masses to be said for the safety of her favorite. God would undoubt-edly protect him, and meanwhile the honored *señorita* and her mama would be so very gracious as to attribute any apparent neglect of the canons of hospitality to the anxieties of an unduly affectionate mother.

Alicia opened her mouth to reply to that tremulous speech, but finding no voice, turned and bolted to her room, trying to shut out a vision of a slender boy lying self-slain among the ferns where he had received caresses and whispers of love from a goddess of light fancy and lighter faith. She had no doubt that he was there in his *cañoncito*. But perhaps he yet lived, wait-ing for her! She would go at once. Old Ned should escort her as far as the bamboos, to be within call in case of the worst.

Old Ned was so grateful for the privilege of riding into the blossoming country with his Alicia that she rewarded him with a full narration of the Popo episode; and he received the confidence with discreet respect, swallow-ing any qualms of jealousy, and extolling her for the high-minded sense of responsibility which now possessed her to the point of tears.

"It's all your fault, anyway," she declared as they walked their horses up a long hill.

He accepted the blame with alacrity as a breath of the dear connubial days.

"One thing I've demonstrated," she continued fretfully, "and that is that the summer flirtation of our happy land simply cannot be acclimated south of the Rio Grande.[14] These people lack the necessary imperturbability of mind, which may be one good reason why they're not permitted to hold hands before the marriage ceremony. To complicate matters, it seems that

[14]River forming the natural border between Texas and Mexico.

I'm the first blonde with the slightest claim to respectability that ever invaded this part of Mexico, and although the inhabitants have a deluded idea that blue eyes are intensely spiritual, they get exactly the same Adam-and-Eve palpitations from them that we do from the lustrous black orbs of the languishing tropics."

"Did you—ah—did you get as far as—um—kissing?" Mr. Winterbottom inquired, with an admirable air of detachment.

"Not quite, Edward; that was where the rest of the folks came tagging along. But I promise you this: if I find that Popo alive, I'm going to kiss him for all I'm worth. The unfortunate child is entitled to nothing less."

"But wouldn't that—hum—add fuel to the flame?" he asked anxiously.

"It would give him back his self-respect," she declared. "It isn't healthy for a high-spirited boy to feel like a worm."

Mr. Winterbottom, while waiting among the bamboos in company with three sociable horses—Popo's was in possession when they arrived—smoked one very long cigar and chewed another into pulpy remains. Alicia not having yodeled, he understood that he had found the boy alive, and he tried to derive comfort from that reflection. He had promised to preserve patience and silence, and such was his anxiety to propitiate Alicia that he managed to subjugate his native energy, although the process involved the kicking up of a good deal of soil. She reflected, when she noted on her return his carefully cheerful expression, that a long course of such discipline would go far toward regenerating him as a man and a husband.

"Well, how is our little patient today?" he inquired with gentle jocosity as he held the stirrup for her.

"I believe he'll pull through now," Alicia responded gravely, "I've sent him up to his grandmother's to be fed, and he's going to telephone his mother right away."

"That's bully," Mr. Winterbottom pronounced heartily; and for some moments, as they gained the road, nothing more was said. Alicia seemed thoughtful. Mr. Winterbottom was the first to speak.

"Poor little beggar must have been hungry," he hazarded.

"He had eaten a few bananas, but as they're not recognized as food here, they only increased his humiliation. You know, banana-trees are just grown to shade the coffee-plants, which are delicate."

Mr Winterbottom signified a proper interest in that phase of coffee culture, and Alicia took advantage of a level stretch of road to put her horse to the gallop. When he regained her side, half a mile farther on, he was agitated.

"Alicia, would you mind enlightening me on one point?" he asked. "Did you—give him back his self-respect?"

"Perhaps I'd better tell you all that happened, Edward."

"By Jove! I wish you would!" he cried earnestly.

"Well, Popo wasn't a bit surprised to see me. In face, he was expecting me."

"Indeed? Hadn't lost his assurance, then.

"He had simply worked out my probable actions, just as I had worked out his. Of course he looked like a wild thing, hair on end, eyes like a panther, regular young bandit. Well, I rag-timed up in my best tra-la-la style, but he halted me with a splendid gesture, and started a speech. You know what a command of language foreigners have, even the babies. He never fumbled for a word, and all his nouns had verbs waiting, and the climaxes just rolled over one another like waves. It was beautiful."

"But what was it about?"

"Me of course: my iniquity, the treacherous falseness residing as ashes in the Dead Sea fruit of my beauty, with a lurid picture of the ruin I had made of his belief in woman, his capacity for happiness and all that. And he wound up with a burst of denunciation in which he called me by a name which ought not to be applied to any lady in any language."

"Alicia!"

"Oh I deserved it, Edward, and I told him so. I didn't care how badly he thought of me if I could only give him back his faith in love. It's such a wonderful thing to get *that* back! So I sang pretty small about myself; and when I revealed my exact status as an ex-wife in process of being courted by her divorced husband, his eyes nearly dropped out of his head. You see, they don't play 'Tag' You're it!' with marriage down here. That boy actually began to hand me out a line of missionary talk. He thinks I ought to remarry you, Ned."

"He must have splendid instincts, after all. So of course you didn't kiss him?"

"Wait a minute. After mentioning that I was eleven years older than he, and that my hair had been an elegant mouse-drab before I started touching it up—"

"Not at all. I liked its color—a very pretty shade of—"

"After that, I told him that he could thank his stars for the education I had given him, in view of the fact that he's going to be sent to college in the U.S.A., and I gave him a few first-rate pointers on the college widow breed. And finally, Ned, I put it to him that I was anxious to do the square thing, and if he considered himself entitled to a few kisses while you were waiting, he could help himself."

"And he?" Mr. Winterbottom inquired with a pinched look.

"He looked so cute that I could have hugged him. But he nobly declined."

"That young fellow," said Mr. Winterbottom, taking off his hat and wiping his brow, "is worthy of being an American."

"Why, that was his Indian revenge, the little monkey! But he was tempted, Ned."

"Of course he was. If you'd only tempt *me*! O Alicia, you're a saint!"

"That's what Popo called me yesterday, and it was neither more nor less true than what he called me today. I suppose we're all mixtures of one kind and another. And I've discovered, Ned, that it's the healthiest kind of fun to be perfectly frank with—with an old pal. Let's try it that way next time, shall we, dear?"

She offered her lips for the second time that day, and—

March 1914

ROBERT FROST
1874–1963

Throughout his career, Robert Frost skillfully assumed the persona of a New England farmer-poet. Actually, however, Frost was born in San Francisco; he did not move East with his widowed mother until he was eleven, and he spent most of his adolescence in Lawrence, an industrialized Massachusetts mill town. Between 1892 and 1900, he married Elinor Miriam White and began raising his family while he worked in mills, taught school, and attended Dartmouth College and Harvard University. In 1900 he moved to a farm in Derry, New Hampshire, which was purchased for him by his grandfather. He taught English at a private school, the Pinkerton Academy, from 1906 to 1911, and he taught English and psychology at a teacher's college in Plymouth, New Hampshire, for a year in 1911–1912. He sold the Derry farm in 1911 and moved with his family to England the following year, where he met the English Georgian poets Wilfred Gibson, Lascelles Abercrombie, and Edward Thomas and began writing poetry full time. Although Frost had adopted rural New England life as his special subject matter, his first two books, *A Boy's Will* (1913) and *North of Boston* (1914), were published in London before they appeared in the United States.

After returning to America in 1915, Frost became popular, particularly with English teachers and academic audiences. He taught or was a "Poet in Residence" at Amherst, the University of Michigan, and other colleges, and he spent many summers at the Bread Loaf Writers' Conference in Vermont. Frost was awarded the Pulitzer Prize for Poetry in 1924, 1931, 1937, and 1943. The United States Senate extended its felicitations to him on his birthday in 1950; a mountain in Vermont was named after him in 1955; the State Department sent him to South America, England, and Russia on "good-will missions" in 1954, 1957, and 1962; and in 1961 he was invited to read a poem at John F. Kennedy's inaugural ceremonies. Frost's admirers were upset by Lawrance Thompson's definitive, three-volume biography, published between 1966 and 1976, which revealed that the poet had been a vain, vindictive, inordinately ambitious, and frequently cruel man in his private life who had caused great suffering to his family and friends. Thompson also emphasized that Frost's public and poetic stoicism had sometimes masked acute depression, self-doubt, and guilt and that he had suffered many personal miseries and tragedies—the insanity of his sister Jeanie, the deaths of his daughter Marjorie and his wife in 1934 and 1938, and the suicide of his only son in 1940. (Jay Parini's 2000 biography attempts to redeem Frost from Thompson's charges, though not entirely successfully.)

The time Frost spent in back-country New England gave him the opportunity to encounter farmers. For these New Englanders, like the old farmer in "Mending Wall," isolation could have certain advantages, and it is significant that in "The Line-Gang" Frost describes the arrival of the telephone—that very modern means of communication—in a distinctly ambivalent manner. In *North of Boston, Mountain Interval* (1916), and *New Hampshire* (1923), he was able to communicate both the limitations and the virtues of this rural, isolated, older America to the urban and academic Americans who read his poems and attended his readings.

Poetically, Frost can be considered a link between an older era and modern culture, and his relationship to literary modernism was equivocal. His early poems are similar to those of nineteenth-century American fireside poets such as Longfellow and English Georgians such as Thomas and Gibson. And many of his mature poems have more in common with the works of William Wordsworth or Robert Browning than they do with those of his contemporaries T. S. Eliot, Wallace Stevens, or William Carlos Williams. Frost eschewed free verse and wrote his poems in traditional rhymes and metrical forms like blank verse. Moreover, like his popular New England contemporary, Edward Arlington Robinson, Frost wrote many poems that are dramatic narratives and can be appreciated, like prose fiction, for their characterizations and plot development.

Intellectually, Frost was the heir of the nineteenth-century romantic individualism exemplified by Emerson and Thoreau. He assumed the lone individual could question and work out his or her own relationships to God and existence—preferably in a natural setting and with a few discrete references to Christianity and Transcendentalism. Unlike Thoreau, however, Frost was never daring enough to challenge the social order boldly in his writings—though he was capable of the conservative cynicism of "Provide, Provide." Nor was he able to express the romantic affirmations that characterize many of Emerson's works. The poet, to Emerson, was a seer whose poems should contain truths analogous to religious revelations. Frost's view of the poet was more modest. In his essay "The Figure a Poem Makes," which he published as a preface to his *Collected Poems*, he emphasized that a poem "begins in delight and ends in wisdom.... it runs a course of lucky events, and ends in a clarification of life—not necessarily a great clarification, such as sects and cults are founded on, but in a momentary stay against confusion."

James Guimond
Rider College

PRIMARY WORKS

Complete Poems of Robert Frost, 1949; *In the Clearing,* 1962; Lawrance Thompson, ed., *Selected Letters of Robert Frost,* 1964; *Collected Poems, Prose and Plays,* 1995.

The Pasture

I'm going out to clean the pasture spring;
I'll only stop to rake the leaves away
(And wait to watch the water clear, I may):
I sha'n't be gone long.—You come too.

I'm going out to fetch the little calf   5
That's standing by the mother. It's so young
It totters when she licks it with her tongue.
I sha'n't be gone long.—You come too.

1913

Mending Wall

Something there is that doesn't love a wall,
That sends the frozen-ground-swell under it,
And spills the upper boulders in the sun;
And makes gaps even two can pass abreast.
The work of hunters is another thing: 5
I have come after them and made repair
Where they have left not one stone on a stone,
But they would have the rabbit out of hiding,
To please the yelping dogs. The gaps I mean,
No one has seen them made or heard them made,   10
But at spring mending-time we find them there.
I let my neighbor know beyond the hill;
And on a day we meet to walk the line
And set the wall between us once again.
We keep the wall between us as we go.   15
To each the boulders that have fallen to each.
And some are loaves and some so nearly balls
We have to use a spell to make them balance:
"Stay where you are until our backs are turned!"
We wear our fingers rough with handling them.   20
Oh, just another kind of outdoor game,
One on a side. It comes to little more:
There where it is we do not need the wall:
He is all pine and I am apple orchard.
My apple trees will never get across   25
And eat the cones under his pines, I tell him.
He only says, "Good fences make good neighbors."
Spring is the mischief in me, and I wonder
If I could put a notion in his head:
"*Why* do they make good neighbors? isn't it   30
Where there are cows? But here there are no cows.
Before I built a wall I'd ask to know
What I was walling in or walling out,
And to whom I was like to give offense.
Something there is that doesn't love a wall,   35
That wants it down." I could say "Elves" to him,
But it's not elves exactly, and I'd rather
He said it for himself. I see him there
Bringing a stone grasped firmly by the top
In each hand, like an old-stone savage armed.   40
He moves in darkness as it seems to me,
Not of woods only and the shade of trees
He will not go behind his father's saying,

And he likes having thought of it so well
He says again, "Good fences make good neighbors."   45

                                                                                       1914

After Apple-Picking

My long two-pointed ladder's sticking through a tree
Toward heaven still,
And there's a barrel that I didn't fill
Beside it, and there may be two or three
Apples I didn't pick upon some bough.   5
But I am done with apple-picking now.
Essence of winter sleep is on the night,
The scent of apples: I am drowsing off.
I cannot rub the strangeness from my sight
I got from looking through a pane of glass   10
I skimmed this morning from the drinking trough
And held against the world of hoary grass.
It melted, and I let it fall and break.
But I was well
Upon my way to sleep before it fell,   15
And I could tell
What form my dreaming was about to take.
Magnified apples appear and disappear,
Stem end and blossom end,
And every fleck of russet showing clear.   20
My instep arch not only keeps the ache,
It keeps the pressure of a ladder-round.
I feel the ladder sway as the boughs bend.
And I keep hearing from the cellar bin
The rumbling sound   25
Of load on load of apples coming in.
For I have had too much
Of apple-picking: I am overtired
Of the great harvest I myself desired.
There were ten thousand thousand fruit to touch,   30
Cherish in hand, lift down, and not let fall.
For all
That struck the earth,
No matter if not bruised or spiked with stubble,
Went surely to the cider-apple heap   35
As of no worth.
One can see what will trouble
This sleep of mine, whatever sleep it is.
Were he not gone,

The woodchuck could say whether it's like his   40
Long sleep, as I describe its coming on,
Or just some human sleep.

                                                        1915

The Wood-Pile

Out walking in the frozen swamp one gray day,
I paused and said, "I will turn back from here.
No, I will go on farther—and we shall see."
The hard snow held me, save where now and then
One foot went through. The view was all in lines   5
Straight up and down of tall slim trees
Too much alike to mark or name a place by
So as to say for certain I was here
Or somewhere else: I was just far from home.   10
A small bird flew before me. He was careful
To put a tree between us when he lighted,
And say no word to tell me who he was
Who was so foolish as to think what *he* thought.
He thought that I was after him for a feather—
The white one in his tail; like one who takes   15
Everything said as personal to himself.
One flight out sideways would have undeceived him.
And then there was a pile of wood for which
I forgot him and let his little fear
Carry him off the way I might have gone,   20
Without so much as wishing him good-night.
He went behind it to make his last stand.
It was a cord of maple, cut and split
And piled—and measured, four by four by eight.
And not another like it could I see.   25
No runner tracks in this year's snow looped near it.
And it was older sure than this year's cutting,
Or even last year's or the year's before.
The wood was gray and the bark warping off it
And the pile somewhat sunken. Clematis   30
Had wound strings round and round it like a bundle.
What held it though on one side was a tree
Still growing, and on one a stake and prop,
These latter about to fall. I thought that only
Someone who lived in turning to fresh tasks   35
Could so forget his handiwork on which
He spent himself, the labor of his ax,
And leave it there far from a useful fireplace

To warm the frozen swamp as best it could
With the slow smokeless burning of decay.   40

                                                                         1915

The Road Not Taken

Two roads diverged in a yellow wood,
And sorry I could not travel both
And be one traveler, long I stood
And looked down one as far as I could
To where it bent in the undergrowth;   5

Then took the other, as just as fair,
And having perhaps the better claim,
Because it was grassy and wanted wear;
Though as for that the passing there
Had worn them really about the same,   10

And both that morning equally lay
In leaves no step had trodden black.
Oh, I kept the first for another day!
Yet knowing how way leads on to way,
I doubted if i should ever come back.   15

I shall be telling this with a sigh
Somewhere ages and ages hence:
Two roads diverged in a wood, and I—
I took the one less traveled by,
And that has made all the difference.   20

                                                                         1916

An Old Man's Winter Night

All out-of-doors looked darkly in at him
Through the thin frost, almost in separate stars,
That gathers on the pane in empty rooms.
What kept his eyes from giving back the gaze
Was the lamp tilted near them in his hand.   5
What kept him from remembering what it was
That brought him to that creaking room was age.
He stood with barrels round him—at a loss.
And having scared the cellar under him
In clomping here, he scared it once again   10
In clomping off;—and scared the outer night,
Which has its sounds, familiar, like the roar

Of trees and crack of branches, common things,
But nothing so like beating on a box.
A light he was to no one but himself   15
Where now he sat, concerned with he knew what,
A quiet light, and then not even that.
He consigned to the moon, such as she was,
So late-arising, to the broken moon
As better than the sun in any case   20
For such a charge, his snow upon the roof,
His icicles along the wall to keep;
And slept. The log that shifted with a jolt
Once in the stove, disturbed him and he shifted,
And eased his heavy breathing, but still slept.   25
One aged man—one man—can't keep a house,
A farm, a countryside, or if he can,
It's thus he does it of a winter night.

                                                                 1916

The Oven Bird[1]

There is a singer everyone has heard,
Loud, a mid-summer and a mid-wood bird,
Who makes the solid tree trunks sound again.
He says that leaves are old and that for flowers
Mid-summer is to spring as one to ten.   5
He says the early petal-fall is past
When pear and cherry bloom went down in showers
On sunny days a moment overcast;
And comes that other fall we name the fall.[2]
He says the highway dust is over all.   10
The bird would cease and be as other birds
But that he knows in singing not to sing.
The question that he frames in all but words
Is what to make of a diminished thing.

                                                                 1916

"Out, Out—"[1']

The buzz saw snarled and rattled in the yard
And made dust and dropped stove-length sticks of wood,

---

[1]American warbler that builds a dome-shaped nest on the ground.
[2]"The fall" may allude to the biblical account of the disobedience of Adam and Eve (Genesis 3) and their expulsion from the Garden of Eden.
[1']Macbeth, V, v.

Sweet-scented stuff when the breeze drew across it.
And from there those that lifted eyes could count
Five mountain ranges one behind the other   5
Under the sunset far into Vermont.
And the saw snarled and rattled, snarled and rattled,
As it ran light, or had to bear a load.
And nothing happened: day was all but done.
Call it a day, I wish they might have said   10
To please the boy by giving him the half hour
That a boy counts so much when saved from work.
His sister stood beside them in her apron
To tell them "Supper." At the word, the saw,
As if to prove saws knew what supper meant,   15
Leaped out at the boy's hand, or seemed to leap—
He must have given the hand. However it was,
Neither refused the meeting. But the hand!
The boy's first outcry was a rueful laugh,
As he swung toward them holding up the hand,   20
Half in appeal, but half as if to keep
The life from spilling. Then the boy saw all—
Since he was old enough to know, big boy
Doing a man's work, though a child at heart—
He saw all spoiled. "Don't let him cut my hand off—   25
The doctor, when he comes. Don't let him, sister!"
So. But the hand was gone already.
The doctor put him in the dark of ether.
He lay and puffed his lips out with his breath.
And then—the watcher at his pulse took fright.   30
No one believed. They listened at his heart.
Little—less—nothing!—and that ended it.
No more to build on there. And they, since they
Were not the one dead, turned to their affairs.

                                                                        1916

The Line-Gang

Here come the line-gang pioneering by.
They throw a forest down less cut than broken.
They plant dead trees for living, and the dead
They string together with a living thread.
They string an instrument against the sky   5
Wherein words whether beaten out or spoken
Will run as hushed as when they were a thought
But in no hush they string it: they go past
With shouts afar to pull the cable taut,

To hold it hard until they make it fast,   10
To ease away—they have it. With a laugh,
An oath of towns that set the wild at naught
They bring the telephone and telegraph.

                                                                      1916

The Ax-Helve

I've known ere now an interfering branch
Of alder catch my lifted ax behind me.
But that was in the woods, to hold my hand
From striking at another alder's roots,
And that was, as I say, an alder branch.   5
This was a man, Baptiste, who stole one day
Behind me on the snow in my own yard
Where I was working at the chopping block,
And cutting nothing not cut down already.
He caught my ax expertly on the rise,   10
When all my strength put forth was in his favor,
Held it a moment where it was, to calm me,
Then took it from me—and I let him take it.
I didn't know him well enough to know
What it was all about. There might be something   15
He had in mind to say to a bad neighbor
He might prefer to say to him disarmed.
But all he had to tell me in French-English
Was what he thought of—not me, but my ax,
Me only as I took my ax to heart.   20
It was the bad ax-helve someone had sold me—
"Made on machine," he said, plowing the grain
With a thick thumbnail to show how it ran
Across the handle's long-drawn serpentine,
Like the two strokes across a dollar sign.   25
"You give her one good crack, she's snap raght off.
Den where's your hax-ead flying t'rough de hair?"
Admitted; and yet, what was that to him?

"Come on my house and I put you one in
What's las' awhile—good hick'ry what's grow crooked,   30
De second growt'[1] I cut myself—tough, tough!"

Something to sell? That wasn't how it sounded.

---

[1]Second growth, trees which grow up after
the virgin forest is logged.

"Den when you say you come? It's cost you nothing.
Tonaght?"

        As well tonight as any night.   35

Beyond an over-warmth of kitchen stove
My welcome differed from no other welcome.
Baptiste knew best why I was where I was.
So long as he would leave enough unsaid,
I shouldn't mind his being overjoyed   40
(If overjoyed he was) at having got me
Where I must judge if what he knew about an ax
That not everybody else knew was to count
For nothing in the measure of a neighbor.
Hard if, though cast away for life with Yankees,   45
A Frenchman couldn't get his human rating!

Mrs. Baptiste came in and rocked a chair
That had as many motions as the world:
One back and forward, in and out of shadow,
That got her nowhere; one more gradual,   50
Sideways, that would have run her on the stove
In time, had she not realized her danger
And caught herself up bodily, chair and all,
And set herself back where she started from.
"She ain't spick too much Henglish—dat's too bad."   55
I was afraid, in brightening first on me,
Then on Baptiste, as if she understood
What passed between us, she was only feigning.
Baptiste was anxious for her; but no more
Than for himself, so placed he couldn't hope   60
To keep his bargain of the morning with me
In time to keep me from suspecting him
Of really never having meant to keep it.

Needlessly soon he had his ax-helves out,
A quiverful to choose from, since he wished me   65
To have the best he had, or had to spare—
Not for me to ask which, when what he took
Had beauties he had to point me out at length
To insure their not being wasted on me.
He liked to have it slender as a whipstock,   70
Free from the least knot, equal to the strain
Of bending like a sword across the knee.
He showed me that the lines of a good helve
Were native to the grain before the knife

Expressed them, and its curves were no false curves   75
Put on it from without. And there its strength lay
For the hard work. He chafed its long white body
From end to end with his rough hand shut round it.
He tried it at the eyehole in the ax-head.
"Hahn, hahn," he mused, "don't need much taking down."   80
Baptiste knew how to make a short job long
For love of it, and yet not waste time either.

Do you know, what we talked about was knowledge?
Baptiste on his defense about the children
He kept from school, or did his best to keep—   85
Whatever school and children and our doubts
Of laid-on education had to do
With the curves of his ax-helves and his having
Used these unscrupulously to bring me
To see for once the inside of his house.   90
Was I desired in friendship, partly as someone
To leave it to, whether the right to hold
Such doubts of education should depend
Upon the education of those who held them?

But now he brushed the shavings from his knee   95
And stood the ax there on its horse's hoof,
Erect, but not without its waves, as when
The snake stood up for evil in the Garden—[2]
Top-heavy with a heaviness his short,
Thick hand made light of, steel-blue chin drawn down   100
And in a little—a French touch in that.
Baptiste drew back and squinted at it, pleased:
"See how she's cock her head!"

     1923

Stopping by Woods on a Snowy Evening

Whose woods these are I think I know.
His house is in the village though;
He will not see me stopping here
To watch his woods fill up with snow.

My little horse must think it queer   5
To stop without a farmhouse near

---

[2]Alludes to the serpent in the Garden of Eden
(Genesis 3).

Between the woods and frozen lake
The darkest evening of the year.

He gives his harness bells a shake
To ask if there is some mistake.   10
The only other sound's the sweep
Of easy wind and downy flake.

The woods are lovely, dark and deep,
But I have promises to keep,
And miles to go before I sleep,   15
And miles to go before I sleep.

                                                    1923

Desert Places

Snow falling and night falling fast, oh, fast
In a field I looked into going past,
And the ground almost covered smooth in snow,
But a few weeds and stubble showing last.

The woods around it have it—it is theirs.   5
All animals are smothered in their lairs.
I am too absent-spirited to count;
The loneliness includes me unawares.

And lonely as it is that loneliness
Will be more lonely ere it will be less—   10
A blanker whiteness of benighted snow
With no expression, nothing to express.

They cannot scare me with their empty spaces
Between stars—on stars where no human race is.
I have it in me so much nearer home   15
To scare myself with my own desert places.

                                                    1936

Once by the Pacific

The shattered water made a misty din.
Great waves looked over others coming in,
And thought of doing something to the shore
That water never did to land before.
The clouds were low and hairy in the skies,   5

Like locks blown forward in the gleam of eyes.
You could not tell, and yet it looked as if
The shore was lucky in being backed by cliff,
The cliff in being backed by continent;
It looked as if a night of dark intent   10
Was coming, and not only a night, an age.
Someone had better be prepared for rage.
There would be more than ocean-water broken
Before God's last *Put out the Light* was spoken.

                                                          1928

Design

I found a dimpled spider, fat and white,
On a white heal-all,[1] holding up a moth
Like a white piece of rigid satin cloth—
Assorted characters of death and blight
Mixed ready to begin the morning right,   5
Like the ingredients of a witches' broth—
A snow-drop spider, a flower like a froth,
And dead wings carried like a paper kite.

What had that flower to do with being white,
The wayside blue and innocent heal-all?   10
What brought the kindred spider to that height,
Then steered the white moth thither in the night?
What but design of darkness to appall?—
If design govern in a thing so small.

                                                          1936

Provide, Provide

The witch that came (the withered hag)
To wash the steps with pail and rag,
Was once the beauty Abishag,[1']

The picture pride of Hollywood.
Too many fall from great and good   5
For you to doubt the likelihood.

Die early and avoid the fate.
Or if predestined to die late,
Make up your mind to die in state.

---

[1]Flower thought to have medicinal qualities; its leaves were applied to slight cuts.

[1']A beautiful young woman mentioned in the Bible (I Kings 1:3).

Make the whole stock exchange your own!   10
If need be occupy a throne,
Where nobody can call *you* crone.

Some have relied on what they knew;
Others on being simply true.
What worked for them might work for you.   15

No memory of having starred
Atones for later disregard,
Or keeps the end from being hard.

Better to go down dignified
With boughten friendship at your side   20
Than none at all. Provide, provide!

           1936

Directive

Back out of all this now too much for us,
Back in a time made simple by the loss
Of detail, burned, dissolved, and broken off
Like graveyard marble sculpture in the weather,
There is a house that is no more a house   5
Upon a farm that is no more a farm
And in a town that is no more a town.
The road there, if you'll let a guide direct you
Who only has at heart your getting lost,
May seem as if it should have been a quarry—   10
Great monolithic knees the former town
Long since gave up pretense of keeping covered.
And there's a story in a book about it:
Besides the wear of iron wagon wheels
The ledges show lines ruled southeast northwest,   15
The chisel work of an enormous Glacier
That braced his feet against the Arctic Pole.
You must not mind a certain coolness from him
Still said to haunt this side of Panther Mountain.
Nor need you mind the serial ordeal   20
Of being watched from forty cellar holes
As if by eye pairs out of forty firkins.[1]
As for the woods' excitement over you
That sends light rustle rushes to their leaves,

[1] Small wooden casks or vessels used to hold
fish, butter, etc.

Charge that to upstart inexperience.   25
Where were they all not twenty years ago?
They think too much of having shaded out
A few old pecker-fretted[2] apple trees.
Make yourself up a cheering song of how
Someone's road home from work this once was,   30
Who may be just ahead of you on foot
Or creaking with a buggy load of grain.
The height of the adventure is the height
Of country where two village cultures faded
Into each other. Both of them are lost.   35
And if you're lost enough to find yourself
By now, pull in your ladder road behind you
And put a sign up CLOSED to all but me.
Then make yourself at home. The only field
Now left's no bigger than a harness gall.[3]   40
First there's the children's house of make believe,
Some shattered dishes underneath a pine,
The playthings in the playhouse of the children.
Weep for what little things could make them glad.
Then for the house that is no more a house,   45
But only a belilaced cellar hole,
Now slowly closing like a dent in dough.
This was no playhouse but a house in earnest.
Your destination and your destiny's
A brook that was the water of the house,   50
Cold as a spring as yet so near its source,
Too lofty and original to rage.
(We know the valley streams that when aroused
Will leave their tatters hung on barb and thorn.)
I have kept hidden in the instep arch   55
Of an old cedar at the waterside
A broken drinking goblet like the Grail[4]
Under a spell so the wrong ones can't find it,
So can't get saved, as Saint Mark[5] says they mustn't.
(I stole the goblet from the children's playhouse.)   60
Here are your waters and your watering place.
Drink and be whole again beyond confusion.

                                                                      1947

---

[2]Dotted with a pattern of holes made by woodpeckers.
[3]A sore on the back of a horse caused by the rubbing of the saddle or harness.
[4]Cup used by Christ at the Last Supper. According to medieval legends, it was brought to England and sought by King Arthur's knights. It could only be found by persons who were pure in their thoughts, words, and deeds.
[5]Alludes to the Bible (Mark 16:16).

SHERWOOD ANDERSON
1876–1941

Sherwood Anderson was above all a storyteller, and in all of his writings he has left his readers a rich record of his life. Born in Camden, Ohio, he spent his first two decades in small towns of northern Ohio, especially Clyde, which became the setting for *Winesburg, Ohio* (1919), his best-known work. He dedicated *Winesburg* to his mother, "whose keen observations on the life about her first awoke in me the hunger to see beneath the surface of lives."

This hunger to see hidden significance and beauty beneath the surface of lonely, often frustrated lives became Anderson's main preoccupation as a writer, whether the setting is "Winesburg," or "Bidwell," as in his best novel, *Poor White* (1920), or described directly as Clyde in his three autobiographies, *A Story Teller's Story* (1924), *Tar: A Midwest Childhood* (1926), and his posthumous *Memoirs* (1942; critical edition, 1969). In depicting the inhabitants of the small midwestern town at the turn of the century, Anderson depicts the struggles of all of us, especially when we are on the threshold of adulthood.

When his mother died in 1895, Anderson left Clyde, and after a stint in the Army during the Spanish-American War, he embarked on a career in advertising in Chicago in 1900. In 1907 he left advertising to found a roof-paint business in Elyria, Ohio, a business that prospered until Anderson neglected it to spend hours at night writing. A dramatic moment, which he tells and retells in his autobiographical work, came in November 1912, when he suffered a kind of mental collapse, walked out of his office, wandered about in a state of amnesia for four days, and finally was hospitalized in Cleveland. After a period of recuperation and the liquidation of his debt-ridden business, he returned to Chicago in February 1913. Whether or not, as Anderson alleged in numerous writings, his repudiation of business was a conscious choice of the life of the artist over the life of the businessman, the fact remains that, at the age of thirty-six, he radically changed the course of his life.

When Anderson returned to Chicago, he became acquainted with the writers, journalists, and critics of the "Chicago Renaissance" of the 1910s, for example, Edgar Lee Masters, Carl Sandburg, and Ben Hecht. He met the established writer Theodore Dreiser and the aspiring writer Ernest Hemingway. In New Orleans, between 1924 and 1925, he met the young William Faulkner. These younger writers, along with Erskine Caldwell, Gertrude Stein, Jean Toomer, and many others, became indebted to Anderson's new method of storytelling and new structuring of stories into a story cycle. In fact, Faulkner later said of Anderson: "He was the father of my whole generation of writers."

Anderson made his greatest contribution to American literature in the genre of the short story. With the publication of *Winesburg* in 1919, the American reading public was introduced to a volume of stories innovative in two important ways. First, the individual stories break with the tradition of tightly plotted, linear stories in order to tell and retell a significant moment until all its meaning is revealed. Second, *Winesburg* is not a collection of isolated stories but is a story cycle, a grouping of stories that, in Anderson's own words, "belong together." "The Book of the Grotesque" serves as a preface introducing the thematic touchstones cohering the stories, whereas "Hands" typifies Anderson's nonlinear method. In *Winesburg*, in addition to the fact that the individual stories have their own unity and beauty, the cycle itself acquires an artistic integrity because of the relationship of all of the stories to each other. Examples of American story cycles that followed *Winesburg* are Hemingway's *In Our Time*, Toomer's *Cane*, Caldwell's *Georgia Boy*, and Faulkner's *The Unvanquished* and *Go Down, Moses*.

Martha Curry
University of Connecticut

PRIMARY WORKS

Winesburg, Ohio, 1919; *Poor White*, 1920; *The Triumph of the Egg*, 1921; *Horses and Men*, 1923; *A Story Teller's Story*, 1924; *Tar: A Midwest Childhood*, 1926; *Death in the Woods*, 1933; *Sherwood Anderson's Memoirs*, Ray Lewis White, ed., 1969.

The Book of the Grotesque

The writer, an old man with a white mustache, had some difficulty in getting into bed. The windows of the house in which he lived were high and he wanted to look at the trees when he awoke in the morning. A carpenter came to fix the bed so that it would be on a level with the window.

Quite a fuss was made about the matter. The carpenter, who had been a soldier in the Civil War, came into the writer's room and sat down to talk of building a platform for the purpose of raising the bed. The writer had cigars lying about and the carpenter smoked.

For a time the two men talked of the raising of the bed and then they talked of other things. The soldier got on the subject of the war. The writer, in fact, led him to that subject. The carpenter had once been a prisoner in Andersonville prison and had lost a brother. The brother had died of starvation, and whenever the carpenter got upon that subject he cried. He, like the old writer, had a white mustache, and when he cried he puckered up his lips and the mustache bobbed up and down. The weeping old man with the cigar in his mouth was ludicrous. The plan the writer had for the raising of his bed was forgotten and later the carpenter did it in his own way and the writer, who was past sixty, had to help himself with a chair when he went to bed at night.

In his bed the writer rolled over on his side and lay quite still. For years he had been beset with notions concerning his heart. He was a hard smoker and his heart fluttered. The idea had got into his mind that he would some time die unexpectedly and always when he got into bed he thought of that. It did not alarm him. The effect in fact was quite a special thing and not easily explained. It made him more alive, there in bed, than at any other time. Perfectly still he lay and his body was old and not of much use any more, but something inside him was altogether young. He was like a pregnant woman, only that the thing inside him was not a baby but a youth. No, it wasn't a youth, it was a woman, young, and wearing a coat of mail like a knight. It is absurd, you see, to try to tell what was inside the old writer as he lay on his high bed and listened to the fluttering of his heart. The thing to get at is what the writer, or the young thing within the writer, was thinking about.

The old writer, like all of the people in the world, had got, during his long fife, a great many notions in his head. He had once been quite handsome and a number of women had been in love with him. And then, of course, he had known people, many people, known them in a peculiarly intimate way that was different from the way in which you and I know people. At least that is what the writer thought and the thought pleased him. Why quarrel with an old man concerning his thoughts?

In the bed the writer had a dream that was not a dream. As he grew somewhat sleepy but was still conscious, figures began to appear before his eyes. He imagined the young indescribable thing within himself was driving a long procession of figures before his eyes.

You see the interest in all this lies in the figures that went before the eyes of the writer. They were all grotesques. All of the men and women the writer had ever known had become grotesques.

The grotesques were not all horrible. Some were amusing, some almost beautiful, and one, a woman all drawn out of shape, hurt the old man by her grotesqueness. When she passed he made a noise like a small dog whimpering. Had you come into the room you might have supposed the old man had unpleasant dreams or perhaps indigestion.

For an hour the procession of grotesques passed before the eyes of the old man, and then, although it was a painful thing to do, he crept out of bed and began to write. Some one of the grotesques had made a deep impression on his mind and he wanted to describe it.

At his desk the writer worked for an hour. In the end he wrote a book which he called "The Book of the Grotesque." It was never published, but I saw it once and it made an indelible impression on my mind. The book had one central thought that is very strange and has always remained with me. By remembering it I have been able to understand many people and things that I was never able to understand before. The thought was involved but a simple statement of it would be something like this:

That in the beginning when the world was young there were a great many thoughts but no such thing as a truth. Man made the truths himself and each truth was a composite of a great many vague thoughts. All about in the world were the truths and they were all beautiful.

The old man had listed hundreds of the truths in his book. I will not try to tell you of all of them. There was the truth of virginity and the truth of passion, the truth of wealth and of poverty, of thrift and of profligacy, of carelessness and abandon. Hundreds and hundreds were the truths and they were all beautiful.

And then the people came along. Each as he appeared snatched up one of the truths and some who were quite strong snatched up a dozen of them.

It was the truths that made the people grotesques. The old man had quite an elaborate theory concerning the matter. It was his notion that the moment one of the people took one of the truths to himself, called it his truth, and tried to live his life by it, he became a grotesque and the truth he embraced became a falsehood.

You can see for yourself how the old man, who had spent all of his life writing and was filled with words, would write hundreds of pages concerning this matter. The subject would become so big in his mind that he himself would be in danger of becoming a grotesque. He didn't, I suppose, for the same reason that he never published the book. It was the young thing inside him that saved the old man.

Concerning the old carpenter who fixed the bed for the writer, I only mentioned him because he, like many of what are called very common people, became the nearest thing to what is understandable and lovable of all the grotesques in the writer's book.

1919

Hands

Upon the half decayed veranda of a small frame house that stood near the edge of a ravine near the town of Winesburg, Ohio, a fat little old man walked nervously up and down. Across a long field that has been seeded for clover but that had produced only a dense crop of yellow mustard weeds, he could see the public highway along which went a wagon filled with berry pickers returning from the fields. The berry pickers, youths and maidens, laughed and shouted boisterously. A boy clad in a blue shirt leaped from the wagon and attempted to drag after him one of the maidens who screamed and protested shrilly. The feet of the boy in the road kicked up a cloud of dust that floated across the face of the departing sun. Over the long field came a thin girlish voice. "Oh, you Wing Biddlebaum, comb your hair, it's falling into your eyes," commanded the voice to the man, who was bald and whose nervous little hands fiddled about the bare white forehead as though arranging a mass of tangled locks.

Wing Biddlebaum, forever frightened and beset by a ghostly band of doubts, did not think of himself as in any way a part of the life of the town where he had lived for twenty years. Among all the people of Winesburg but one had come close to him. With George Willard, son of Tom Willard, the proprietor of the new Willard House, he had formed something like a friendship. George Willard was the reporter on the *Winesburg Eagle* and sometimes in the evenings he walked out along the highway to Wing Biddlebaum's house. Now as the old man walked up and down on the veranda, his hands moving nervously about, he was hoping that George Willard would come and spend the evening with him. After the wagon containing the berry pickers had passed, he went across the field through the tall mustard weeds and climbing a rail fence peered anxiously along the road to the town. For a moment he stood thus, rubbing his hands together and looking up and down the road, and then, fear overcoming him, ran back to walk again upon the porch on his own house.

In the presence of George Willard, Wing Biddlebaum, who for twenty years had been the town mystery, lost something of his timidity, and his shadowy personality, submerged in a sea of doubts, came forth to look at the world. With the young reporter at his side, he ventured in the light of day into Main Street or strode up and down on the rickety front porch of his own house, talking excitedly. The voice that had been low and trembling became shrill and loud. The bent figure straightened. With a kind of wriggle, like a fish returned to the brook by the fisherman, Biddlebaum the silent began to talk, striving to put into words the ideas that had been accumulated by his mind during long years of silence.

Wing Biddlebaum talked much with his hands. The slender expressive fingers, forever active, forever striving to conceal themselves in his pockets or behind his back, came forth and became the piston rods of his machinery of expression.

The story of Wing Biddlebaum is a story of hands. Their restless activity, like unto the beating of the wings of an imprisoned bird, had given him his name. Some obscure poet of the town had thought of it. The hands alarmed their owner. He wanted to keep them hidden away and looked with amazement at the quiet inexpressive hands of other men who worked beside him in the fields, or passed, driving sleepy teams on country roads.

When he talked to George Willard, Wing Biddlebaum closed his fists and beat with them upon a table or on the walls of his house. The action made him more comfortable. If the desire to talk came to him when the two were walking in the fields, he sought out a stump or the top board of a fence and with his hands pounding busily talked with renewed ease.

The story of Wing Biddlebaum's hands is worth a book in itself. Sympathetically set forth it would tap many strange, beautiful qualities in obscure men. It is a job for a poet. In Winesburg the hands had attracted attention merely because of their activity. With them Wing Biddlebaum had picked as high as a hundred and forty quarts of strawberries in a day. They became his distinguishing feature, the source of his fame. Also they made more grotesque an already grotesque and elusive individuality. Winesburg was proud of the hands of Wing Biddlebaum in the same spirit in which it was proud of Banker White's new stone house and Wesley Moyer's bay stallion, Tony Tip, that had won the two-fifteen trot at the fall races in Cleveland.

As for George Willard, he had many times wanted to ask about the hands. At times an almost overwhelming curiosity had taken hold of him. He felt that there must be a reason for their strange activity and their inclination to keep hidden away and only a growing respect for Wing Biddlebaum kept him from blurting out the questions that were often in his mind.

Once he had been on the point of asking. The two were walking in the fields on a summer afternoon and had stopped to sit upon a grassy bank. All afternoon Wing Biddlebaum had talked as one inspired. By a fence he had stopped and beating like a giant woodpecker upon the top board had shouted at George Willard, condemning his tendency to be too much influenced by the people about him. "You are destroying yourself," he cried. "You have the inclination to be alone and to dream and you are afraid of dreams. You want to be like others in town here. You hear them talk and you try to imitate them."

On the grassy bank Wing Biddlebaum had tried again to drive his point home. His voice became soft and reminiscent, and with a sigh of contentment he launched into a long rambling talk, speaking as one lost in a dream.

Out of the dream Wing Biddlebaum made a picture for George Willard. In the picture men lived again in a kind of pastoral golden age. Across a green open country came clean-limbed young men, some afoot, some mounted upon horses. In crowds the young men came to gather about the feet of an old man who sat beneath a tree in a tiny garden and who talked to them.

Wing Biddlebaum became wholly inspired. For once he forgot the hands. Slowly they stole forth and lay upon George Willard's shoulders. Something new and bold came into the voice that talked. "You must try to forget all you have learned," said the old man. "You must begin to dream. From this time on you must shut your ears to the roaring of the voices."

Pausing in his speech, Wing Biddlebaum looked long and earnestly at George Willard. His eyes glowed. Again he raised the hands to caress the boy and then a look of horror swept over his face.

With a convulsive movement of his body, Wing Biddlebaum sprang to his feet and thrust his hands deep into his trousers pockets. Tears came to his eyes. "I must be getting along home. I can talk no more with you," he said nervously.

Without looking back, the old man had hurried down the hillside and across a meadow, leaving George Willard perplexed and frightened upon the grassy slope. With a shiver of dread the boy arose and went along the road toward town. "I'll not ask him about his hands," he thought, touched by the memory of the terror he had seen in the man's eyes. "There's something wrong, but I don't want to know what it is. His hands have something to do with his fear of me and of everyone."

And George Willard was right. Let us look briefly into the story of the hands. Perhaps our talking of them will arouse the poet who will tell the hidden wonder story of the influence for which the hands were but fluttering pennants of promise.

In his youth Wing Biddlebaum had been a school teacher in a town in Pennsylvania. He was not then known as Wing Biddlebaum, but went by the less euphonic name of Adolph Myers. As Adolph Myers he was much loved by the boys of his school.

Adolph Myers was meant by nature to be a teacher of youth. He was one of those rare, little-understood men who rule by a power so gentle that it passes as a lovable weakness. In their feeling for the boys under their charge such men are not unlike the finer sort of women in their love of men.

And yet that is but crudely stated. It needs the poet there. With the boys of his school, Adolph Myers had walked in the evening or had sat talking until dusk upon the schoolhouse steps lost in a kind of dream. Here and there went his hands, caressing the shoulders of the boys, playing about the tousled heads. As he talked his voice became soft and musical. There was a caress in that also. In a way the voice and the hands, the stroking of the shoulders and the touching of the hair was a part of the schoolmaster's effort to carry a dream into the young minds. By the caress that was in his fingers he expressed himself. He was one of those men in whom the force that creates life is diffused, not centralized. Under the caress of his hands doubt and disbelief went out of the minds of the boys and they began also to dream.

And then the tragedy. A half-witted boy of the school became enamored of the young master. In his bed at night he imagined unspeakable things and in the morning went forth to tell his dreams as facts. Strange, hideous accusations fell from his loose-hung lips. Through the Pennsylvania town went a shiver. Hidden, shadowy doubts that had been in men's minds concerning Adolph Myers were galvanized into beliefs.

The tragedy did not linger. Trembling lads were jerked out of bed and questioned. "He put his arms about me," said one. "His fingers were always playing in my hair," said another.

One afternoon a man of the town, Henry Bradford, who kept a saloon, came to the schoolhouse door. Calling Adolph Myers into the school yard he began to beat him with his fists. As his hard knuckles beat down into the frightened face of the schoolmaster, his wrath became more and more terrible. Screaming with dismay, the children ran here and there like disturbed insects. "I'll teach you to put your hands on my boy, you beast," roared the saloon keeper, who, tired of beating the master, had begun to kick him about the yard.

Adolph Myers was driven from the Pennsylvania town in the night. With lanterns in their hands a dozen men came to the door of the house where he lived alone and commanded that he dress and come forth. It was raining and one of the men had a rope in his hands. They had intended to hang the schoolmaster, but something in his figure, so small, white, and pitiful, touched their hearts and they let him escape. As he ran away into the darkness they repented of their weakness and ran after him, swearing and throwing sticks and great balls of soft mud at the figure that screamed and ran faster and faster into the darkness.

For twenty years Adolph Myers had lived alone in Winesburg. He was but forty but looked sixty-five. The name of Biddlebaum he got from a box of goods seen at a freight station as he hurried through an eastern Ohio town. He had an aunt in Winesburg, a black-toothed old woman who raised chickens, and with her he lived until she died. He had been ill for a year after the experience in Pennsylvania, and after his recovery worked as a day laborer in the fields, going timidly about and striving to conceal his hands. Although he did not understand what had happened he felt that the hands must be to blame. Again and again the fathers of the boys had talked of the hands. "Keep your hands to yourself," the saloon keeper had roared, dancing with fury in the schoolhouse yard.

Upon the veranda of his house by the ravine, Wing Biddlebaum continued to walk up and down until the sun had disappeared and the road beyond the field was lost in the grey shadows. Going into his house he cut slices of bread and spread honey upon them. When the rumble of the evening train that took away the express cars loaded with the day's harvest of berries had passed and restored the silence of the summer night, he went again to walk upon the veranda. In the darkness he could not see the hands and they became quiet. Although he still hungered for the presence of the boy, who was the medium through which he expressed his love of man, the hunger became again a part of his loneliness and his waiting. Lighting a lamp, Wing Biddlebaum washed the few dishes soiled by his simple meal and, setting up a folding cot by the screen door that led to the porch, prepared to undress for the night. A few stray white bread crumbs lay on the cleanly washed floor by the table; putting the lamp upon a low stool he began to pick up the crumbs, carrying them to his mouth one by one with unbelievable rapidity. In the dense blotch of light beneath the table, the kneeling figure looked like a priest engaged in some service of his church. The nervous expressive fingers, flashing in and out of the light, might well have been mistaken for the fingers of the devotee going swiftly through decade after decade of his rosary.

1919

Death in the Woods

She was an old woman and lived on a farm near the town in which I lived. All country and small-town people have seen such old women, but no ones knows much about them. Such an old woman comes into town driving an old worn-out horse or she comes afoot carrying a basket. She may own a few hens and have eggs to sell. She brings them in a basket and takes them to a grocer. There she trades them in. She gets some salt pork and some beans. Then she gets a pound or two of sugar and some flour.

Afterwards she goes to the butcher's and asks for some dog meat. She may spend ten or fifteen cents, but when she does she asks for something. Formerly the butchers gave liver to anyone who wanted to carry it away. In our family we were always having it. Once one of my brothers got a whole cow's liver at the slaughterhouse near the fairgrounds in our town. We had it until we were sick of it. It never cost a cent. I have hated the thought of it ever since.

The old farm woman got some liver and a soupbone. She never visited with anyone, and as soon as she got what she wanted she lit out for home. It made quite a load for such an old body. No one gave her a lift. People drive right down a road and never notice an old woman like that.

There was such an old woman who used to come into town past our house one summer and fall when I was a young boy and was sick with what was called inflammatory rheumatism. She went home later carrying a heavy pack on her back. Two or three large gaunt-looking dogs followed at her heels.

The old woman was nothing special. She was one of the nameless ones that hardly anyone knows, but she got into my thoughts. I have just suddenly now, after all these years, remembered her and what happened. It is a story. Her name was Grimes, and she lived with her husband and son in a small unpainted house on the bank of a small creek four miles from town.

The husband and son were a tough lot. Although the son was but twenty-one, he had already served a term in jail. It was whispered about that the woman's husband stole horses and ran them off to some other county. Now and then, when a horse turned up missing, the man had also disappeared. No one ever caught him. Once, when I was loafing at Tom Whitehead's livery barn, the man came there and sat on the bench in front. Two or three other men were there, but no one spoke to him. He sat for a few minutes and then got up and went away. When he was leaving he turned around and stared at the men. There was a look of defiance in his eyes. "Well, I have tried to be friendly. You don't want to talk to me. It has been so wherever I have gone in this town. If, some day, one of your fine horses turns up missing, well, then what?" He did not say anything actually. "I'd like to bust one of you on the jaw," was about what his eyes said. I remember how the look in his eyes made me shiver.

The old man belonged to a family that had had money once. His name was Jake Grimes. It all comes back clearly now. His father, John Grimes, had owned a sawmill when the country was new, and had made money. Then he got to drinking and running after women. When he died there wasn't much left.

Jake blew the rest. Pretty soon there wasn't any more lumber to cut and his land was nearly all gone.

He got his wife off a German farmer, for whom he went to work one June day in the wheat harvest. She was a young thing then and scared to death. You see, the farmer was up to something with the girl—she was, I think, a bound girl and his wife had her suspicions. She took it out on the girl when the man wasn't around. Then, when the wife had to go off to town for supplies, the farmer got after her. She told young Jake that nothing really ever happened, but he didn't know whether to believe it or not.

He got her pretty easy himself, the first time he was out with her. He wouldn't have married her if the German farmer hadn't tried to tell him where to get off. He got her to go riding with him in his buggy one night when he was threshing on the place, and then he came for her the next Sunday night.

She managed to get out of the house without her employer's seeing, but when she was getting into the buggy he showed up. It was almost dark, and he just popped up suddenly at the horse's head. He grabbed the horse by the bridle and Jake got out his buggy whip.

They had it out all right! The German was a tough one. Maybe he didn't care whether his wife knew or not, Jake hit him over the face and shoulders with the buggy whip, but the horse got to acting up and he had to get out.

Then the two men went for it. The girl didn't see it. The horse started to run away and went nearly a mile down the road before the girl got him stopped. Then she managed to tie him to a tree beside the road. (I wonder how I know all this. It must have stuck in my mind from small-town tales when I was a boy.) Jake found her there after he got through with the German. She was huddled up in the buggy seat, crying, scared to death. She told Jake a lot of stuff, how the German had tried to get her, how he chased her once into the barn, how another time, when they happened to be alone in the house together, he tore her dress open clear down the front. The German, she said, might have got her that time if he hadn't heard his old woman drive in at the gate. She had been off to town for supplies. Well, she would be putting the horse in the barn. The German managed to sneak off to the fields without his wife seeing. He told the girl he would kill her if she told. What could she do? She told a lie about ripping her dress in the barn when she was feeding the stock. I remember now that she was a bound girl and did not know where her father and mother were. Maybe she did not have any father. You know what I mean.

Such bound children were often enough cruelly treated. They were children who had no parents, slaves really. There were very few orphan homes then. They were legally bound into some home. It was a matter of pure luck how it came out.

II

She married Jake and had a son and a daughter, but the daughter died.

Then she settled down to feed stock. That was her job. At the German's place she had cooked the food for the German and his wife. The wife was a strong woman with big hips and worked most of the time in the fields with her husband. She fed them and fed the cows in the barn, fed the pigs, the horses and the chickens. Every moment of every day, as a young girl, was spent feeding something.

Then she married Jake Grimes and he had to be fed. She was a slight thing, and when she had been married for three or four years, and after the two children were born, her slender shoulders became stooped.

Jake always had a lot of big dogs around the house, that stood near the unused sawmill near the creek. He was always trading horses when he wasn't stealing something and had a lot of poor bony ones about. Also he kept three or four pigs and a cow. They were all pastured in the few acres left of the Grimes place and Jake did little enough work.

He went into debt for a threshing outfit and ran it for several years, but it did not pay. People did not trust him. They were afraid he would steal the grain at night. He had to go a long way off to get work and it cost too much to get there. In the winter he hunted and cut a little firewood, to be sold in some nearby town. When the son grew up he was just like the father. They got drunk together. If there wasn't anything to eat in the house when they came home the old man gave his old woman a cut over the head. She had a few chickens of her own and had to kill one of them in a hurry. When they were all killed she wouldn't have any eggs to sell when she went to town, and then what would she do?

She had to scheme all her life about getting things fed, getting the pigs fed so they would grow fat and could be butchered in the fall. When they were butchered her husband took most of the meat off to town and sold it. If he did not do it first, the boy did. They fought sometimes and when they fought the old woman stood aside trembling.

She had got the habit of silence anyway—that was fixed. Sometimes, when she began to look old—she wasn't forty yet—and when the husband and son were both off, trading horses or drinking or hunting or stealing, she went around the house and the barnyard muttering to herself.

How was she going to get everything fed?—that was her problem. The dogs had to be fed. There wasn't enough hay in the barn for the horses and the cow. If she didn't feed the chickens how could they lay eggs? Without eggs to sell how could she get things in town, things she had to have to keep the life of the farm going? Thank heaven, she did not have to feed her husband—in a certain way. That hadn't lasted long after their marriage and after the babies came. Where he went on his long trips she did not know. Sometimes he was gone from home for weeks, and after the boy grew up they went off together.

They left everything at home for her to manage and she had no money. She knew no one. No one ever talked to her in town. When it was winter she had to gather sticks of wood for her fire, had to try to keep the stock fed with very little grain.

The stock in the barn cried to her hungrily, the dogs followed her about. In the winter the hens laid few enough eggs. They huddled in the corners of the barn and she kept watching them. If a hen lays an egg in the barn in the winter and you do not find it, it freezes and breaks.

One day in winter the old woman went off to town with a few eggs and the dogs followed her. She did not get started until nearly three o'clock and the snow was heavy. She hadn't been feeling very well for several days and so she went muttering along, scantily clad, her shoulders stooped. She had an old grain bag in which she carried her eggs, tucked away down in the bottom. There weren't many of them, but in winter the price of eggs is up. She would get a little meat in exchange for the eggs, some salt pork, a little sugar, and some coffee perhaps. It might be the butcher would give her a piece of liver.

When she had got to town and was trading in her eggs the dogs lay by the door outside. She did pretty well, got the things she needed, more than she had hoped. Then she went to the butcher and he gave her some liver and some dog meat.

It was the first time anyone had spoken to her in a friendly way for a long time. The butcher was alone in his shop when she came in and was annoyed by the thought of such a sick-looking old woman out on such a day. It was bitter cold and the snow, that had let up during the afternoon, was falling again. The butcher said something about her husband and her son, swore at them, and the old woman stared at him, a look of mild surprise in her eyes as he talked. He said that if either the husband or the son were going to get any of the liver or the heavy bones with scraps of meat hanging to them that he had put into the grain bag, he'd see him starve first.

Starve, eh? Well, things had to be fed. Men had to be fed, and the horses that weren't any good but maybe could be traded off, and the poor thin cow that hadn't given any milk for three months.

Horses, cows, pigs, dogs, men.

III

The old woman had to get back before darkness came if she could. The dogs followed at her heels, sniffing at the heavy grain bag she had fastened on her back. When she got to the edge of town she stopped by a fence and tied the bag on her back with a piece of rope she had carried in her dress pocket for just that purpose. That was an easier way to carry it. Her arms ached. It was hard when she had to crawl over fences and once she fell over and landed in the snow. The dogs went frisking about. She had to struggle to get to her feet again, but she made it. The point of climbing over the fences was that there was a short cut over a hill and through a woods. She might have gone around by the road, but it was a mile farther that way. She was afraid she couldn't make it. And then, besides, the stock had to be fed. There was a little hay left and a little corn. Perhaps her husband and son would bring some home when they came. They had driven off in the only buggy the Grimes family had, a rickety thing, a rickety horse hitched to the buggy, two other rickety horses led by halters. They were going to trade horses, get a little money if they could. They might come home drunk. It would be well to have something in the house when they came back.

The son had an affair on with a woman at the county seat, fifteen miles away. She was a rough enough woman, a tough one. Once, in the summer, the son had brought her to the house. Both she and the son had been drinking. Jake Grimes was away and the son and his woman ordered the old woman about like a servant. She didn't mind much; she was used to it. Whatever happened she never said anything. That was her way of getting along. She had managed that way when she was a young girl at the German's and ever since she had married Jake. That time her son brought his woman to the house they stayed all night, sleeping together just as though they were married. It hadn't shocked the old woman, not much. She had got past being shocked early in life.

With the pack on her back she went painfully along across an open field, wading in the deep snow, and got into the woods.

There was a path, but it was hard to follow. Just beyond the top of the hill, where the woods was thickest, there was a small clearing. Had someone once thought of building a house there? The clearing was as large as a building lot in town, large enough for a house and a garden. The path ran along the side of the clearing, and when she got there the old woman sat down to rest at the foot of a tree.

It was a foolish thing to do. When she got herself placed, the pack against the tree's trunk, it was nice, but what about getting up again? She worried about that for a moment and then quietly closed her eyes.

She must have slept for a time. When you are about so cold you can't get any colder. The afternoon grew a little warmer and the snow came thicker than ever. Then after a time the weather cleared. The moon even came out.

There were four Grimes dogs that had followed Mrs. Grimes into town, all tall gaunt fellows. Such men as Jake Grimes and his son always keep just such dogs. They kick and abuse them, but they stay. The Grimes dogs, in order to keep from starving, had to do a lot of foraging for themselves, and they had been at it while the old woman slept with her back to the tree at the side of the clearing. They had been chasing rabbits in the woods and in adjoining fields and in their ranging had picked up three other farm dogs.

After a time all the dogs came back to the clearing. They were excited about something. Such nights, cold and clear and with a moon, do things to dogs. It may be that some old instinct, come down from the time when they were wolves and ranged the woods in packs on winter nights, comes back into them.

The dogs in the clearing, before the old woman, had caught two or three rabbits and their immediate hunger had been satisfied. They began to play, running in circles in the clearing. Round and round they ran, each dog's nose at the tail of the next dog. In the clearing, under the snow-laden trees and under the wintry moon they made a strange picture, running thus silently, in a circle their running had beaten in the soft snow. The dogs made no sound. They ran around and around in the circle.

It may have been that the old woman saw them doing that before she died. She may have awakened once or twice and looked at the strange sight with dim old eyes.

She wouldn't be very cold now, just drowsy. Life hangs on a long time. Perhaps the old woman was out of her head. She may have dreamed of her girlhood, at the German's, and before that, when she was a child and before her mother lit out and left her.

Her dreams couldn't have been very pleasant. Not many pleasant things have happened to her. Now and then one of the Grimes dogs left the running circle and came to stand before her. The dog thrust his face close to her face. His red tongue was hanging out.

The running of the dogs may have been a kind of death ceremony. It may have been that the primitive instinct of the wolf, having been aroused in the dogs by the night and the running, made them somehow afraid.

"Now we are no longer wolves. We are dogs, the servants of men. Keep alive, man! When man dies we become wolves again."

When one of the dogs came to where the old woman sat with her back against the tree and thrust his nose close to her face he seemed satisfied and went back to run with the pack. All the Grimes dogs did it at some time during the evening, before she died. I knew all about it afterward, when I grew to be a man, because once in a woods in Illinois, on another winter night, I saw a pack of dogs act just like that. The dogs were waiting for me to die as they had waited for the old woman that night when I was a child, but when it happened to me I was a young man and had no intention whatever of dying.

The old woman died softly and quietly. When she was dead and when one of the Grimes dogs had come to her and had found her dead all the dogs stopped running.

They gathered about her.

Well, she was dead now. She had fed the Grimes dogs when she was alive, what about now?

There was the pack on her back, the grain bag containing the piece of salt pork, the liver the butcher had given her, the dog meat, the soupbones. The butcher in town, having been suddenly overcome with a feeling of pity, had loaded her grain bag heavily. It had been a big haul for the old woman.

It was a big haul for the dogs now.

IV

One of the Grimes dogs sprang suddenly out from among the others and began worrying the pack on the old woman's back. Had the dogs really been wolves, that one would have been the leader of the pack. What he did, all the others did.

All of them sank their teeth into the grain bag the old woman had fastened with ropes to her back.

They dragged the old woman's body out into the open clearing. The worn-out dress was quickly torn from her shoulders. When she was found, a day or two later, the dress had been torn from her body clear to the hips, but the dogs had not touched her body. They had got the meat out of the grain bag, that was all. Her body was frozen stiff when it was found, and the shoulders were so narrow and the body so slight that in death it looked like the body of some charming young girl.

Such things happened in towns of the Middle West, on farms near town, when I was a boy. A hunter out after rabbits found the old woman's body and did not touch it. Something, the beaten round path in the little snow-covered clearing, the silence of the place, the place where the dogs had worried the body trying to pull the grain bag away or tear it open—something startled the man and he hurried off to town.

I was in Main Street with one of my brothers who was town newsboy and who was taking the afternoon papers to the stores. It was almost night.

The hunter came into a grocery and told his story. Then he went to a hardware shop and into a drugstore. Men began to gather on the sidewalks. Then they started out along the road to the place in the woods.

My brother should have gone on about his business of distributing papers but he didn't. Everyone was going to the woods. The undertaker went and the town marshal. Several men got on a dray and rode out to where the path left the road and went into the woods, but the horses weren't very sharply shod and slid about on the slippery roads. They made no better time than those of us who walked.

The town marshal was a large man whose leg had been injured in the Civil War. He carried a heavy cane and limped rapidly along the road. My brother and I followed at his heels, and as we went other men and boys joined the crowd.

It had grown dark by the time we got to where the old woman had left the road, but the moon had come out. The marshal was thinking there might have been a murder. He kept asking the hunter questions. The hunter went along with his gun across his shoulders, a dog following at his heels. It isn't often a rabbit hunter has a chance to be so conspicuous. He was taking full advantage of it, leading the procession with the town marshal. "I didn't see any wounds. She was a beautiful young girl. Her face was buried in the snow. No, I didn't know her." As a matter of fact, the hunter had not looked closely at the body. He had been frightened. She might have been murdered and someone might spring out from behind a tree and murder him. In a woods, in the late afternoon, when the trees are all bare and there is white snow on the ground, when all is silent, something creepy steals over the mind and body. If something strange or uncanny has happened in the neighborhood all you think about is getting away from there as fast as you can.

The crowd of men and boys had got to where the old woman had crossed the field and went, following the marshal and the hunter, up the slight incline and into the woods.

My brother and I were silent. He had his bundle of papers in a bag slung across his shoulder. When he got back to town he would have to go on distributing his papers before he went home to supper. If I went along, as he had no doubt already determined I should, we would both be late. Either Mother or our older sister would have to warm our supper.

Well, we would have something to tell. A boy did not get such a chance very often. It was lucky we just happened to go into the grocery when the hunter came in. The hunter was a country fellow. Neither of us had ever seen him before.

Now the crowd of men and boys had got to the clearing. Darkness comes quickly on such winter nights, but the full moon made everything clear. My brother and I stood near the tree beneath which the old woman had died.

She did not look old, lying there in that light, frozen and still. One of the men turned her over in the snow and I saw everything. My body trembled with some strange mystical feeling and so did my brother's. It might have been the cold.

Neither of us had ever seen a woman's body before. It may have been the snow, clinging to the frozen flesh, that made it look so white and lovely, so like marble. No woman had come with the party from town; but one of the men, he was the town blacksmith, took off his overcoat and spread it over her. Then he gathered her into his arms and started off to town, all the others following silently. At that time no one knew who she was.

V

I had seen everything, had seen the oval in the snow, like a miniature race track, where the dogs had run, had seen how the men were mystified, had seen the white bare young-looking shoulders, had heard the whispered comments of the men.

The men were simply mystified. They took the body to the undertaker's, and when the blacksmith, the hunter, the marshal and several others had got inside they closed the door. If Father had been there perhaps he could have got in, but we boys couldn't.

I went with my brother to distribute the rest of his papers and when we got home it was my brother who told the story.

I kept silent and went to bed early. It may have been I was not satisfied with the way he told it.

Later, in the town, I must have heard other fragments of the old woman's story. She was recognized the next day and there was an investigation.

The husband and son were found somewhere and brought to town and there was an attempt to connect them with the woman's death, but it did not work. They had perfect enough alibis.

However, the town was against them. They had to get out. Where they went I never heard.

I remember only the picture there in the forest, the men standing about, the naked girlish-looking figure, face down in the snow, the tracks made by the running dogs and the clear cold winter sky above. White fragments of clouds were drifting across the sky. They went racing across the little open space among the trees.

The scene in the forest had become for me, without my knowing it, the foundation for the real story I am now trying to tell. The fragments, you see, had to be picked up slowly, long afterward.

Things happened. When I was a young man I worked on the farm of a German. The hired girl was afraid of her employer. The farmer's wife hated her.

I saw things at that place. Once later, I had a half-uncanny, mystical adventure with dogs in an Illinois forest on a clear, moonlit winter night. When I was a schoolboy, and on a summer day, I went with a boy friend out along a creek some miles from town and came to the house where the old woman had lived. No one had lived in the house since her death. The doors were broken from the hinges; the window lights were all broken. As the boy and I stood in the road outside, two dogs, just roving farm dogs no doubt, came running around the corner of the house. The dogs were tall, gaunt fellows and came down to the fence and glared through at us, standing in the road.

The whole thing, the story of the old woman's death, was to me as I grew older like music heard from far off. The notes had to be picked up slowly one at a time. Something had to be understood.

The woman who died was one destined to feed animal life. Anyway, that is all she ever did. She was feeding animal life before she was born, as a child, as a young woman working on the farm of the German, after she married, when she grew old, and when she died. She fed animal life in cows, in chickens, in pigs, in horses, in dogs, in men. Her daughter had died in childhood and with her one son she had no articulate relations. On the night when she died she was hurrying homeward, bearing on her body food for animal life.

She died in the clearing in the woods and even after her death continued feeding animal life.

You see, it is likely that when my brother told the story that night when we got home and my mother and sister sat listening I did not think he got the point. He was too young and so was I. A thing so complete has its own beauty.

I shall not try to emphasize the point. I am only explaining why I was dissatisfied then and have been ever since. I speak of that only that you may understand why I have been impelled to try to tell the simple story over again.

1933

EDNA ST. VINCENT MILLAY
1892–1950

Born in Rockland, Maine, Edna St. Vincent Millay was the eldest of three children of Henry Tolman Millay, a school superintendent, and Cora Buzzelle Millay, a practical nurse. Mrs. Millay provided a home environment rich in literature and music. Evidently a gifted child, Millay wrote her first poem at the age of five. When she was twelve, her poems first appeared in *St. Nicholas Magazine*, which two years later awarded her a gold badge for poetry. She contributed poems and playlets to her high school magazine and appeared in high school plays and in local productions by touring acting companies.

When at the age of twenty she recited her poem "Renascence" as entertainment at a local hotel resort, she was "discovered" by a visiting official of the New York City YWCA, who sponsored Millay's entrance into college. While at Vassar College, she wrote poetry and plays for the campus magazine, composed her class's baccalaureate hymn, and drew considerable attention when she acted in college plays. Millay lived for eight years in Greenwich Village, during which time she appeared as an actress at the Provincetown Playhouse, where her popular one-act play *Aria da Capo* was first produced, and devoted herself to writing. After marrying Eugene Boissevain, a Dutch American importer, in 1923, she resided permanently at her estate, Steepletop, in eastern New York State. In addition to being the first woman poet to receive the Pulitzer Prize (1923), Millay was the recipient of five honorary degrees and numerous awards for poetry. She was hailed in the 1940s as "one of the ten greatest living women."

Edmund Wilson, the famous critic, characterized her as a female intellectual. Early reviews ran the gamut, calling her "a romantic idealist" and "an urban pagan." Although at first a few critics were inclined to treat her too lightly, most recognized her as a truly gifted poet who wrote artistically crafted verse about serious matters of the human heart and mind. She was taken to task for being flippant and self-indulgent with her second book, *A Few Figs from Thistles*, which includes her short poem "First Fig," perhaps the most recited quatrain of the 1920s for its jazzy, carpe diem attitude. *Second April* was generally well received. This volume also contains twelve sonnets, a form in which Millay was to work with much distinction. She is arguably one of the great sonnet writers in English and without peer in the sonnet form among all American poets. Subsequent volumes saw her called uneven, lacking in intellectual force, and ill disciplined, but at the same time she was named "America's finest living lyric poet" and "among our foremost twentieth-century poets."

Although many poems in earlier volumes are touched with humor and satire, the mood of the later poetry darkens and deepens as Millay's artistry grows more complex and the ideas more profound. Her treatment of romantic love, for example, grows graver and more reflective. She became a writer very much involved in social issues, an activist and feminist long before these terms were popular. She was outspoken about personal integrity and freedom, which is really the major theme of her work. For a brief time, she also wrote of subjects related to the ongoing war. She is a memorable nature poet, rivaling her contemporary Robert Frost in a fine delineation of natural detail. Millay's range as an author is demonstrated by her periodical short stories, her volume of prose "dialogues," a libretto for a distinguished American opera, and half a dozen dramatic works.

Although Millay published nothing in the last ten years of her life, she wrote constantly. Much of this work appears in the posthumous *Mine the Harvest*. The past thirty years have witnessed a resurgence of interest in Millay, with academic symposia, a growing number of articles, several dissertations, and ten books in whole or in part about her. An artists' colony and a literary society have been established in her name. Two recent biographies, by Daniel Mark Epstein and by Nancy Milford, have generated renewed interest in Millay's life and work.

John J. Patton
Atlantic-Cape Community College

PRIMARY WORKS

Renascence and Other Poems, 1917; *A Few Figs from Thistles, Aria da Capo*, 1920; *Two Slatterns and a King, The Lamp and the Bell, Second April*, 1921; *The Harp Weaver and Other Poems*, 1923; *Distressing Dialogues* (published under "Nancy Boyd"), 1924; *Three Plays*, 1926; *The King's Henchman*, 1927; *The Buck in the Snow*, 1928; *Poems*

Selected for Young People, 1929; *Fatal Interview*, 1931; *The Princess Marries the Page*, 1932; *Wine from These Grapes*, 1934; *Conversation at Midnight*, 1937; *Collected Sonnets*, 1941; *Murder of Lidice*, 1942; *Collected Lyrics*, 1943; *Letters of Edna St. Vincent Millay*, 1952; *Mine the Harvest*, 1954; *Collected Poems*, 1956; *Collected Sonnets, Revised & Expanded ed.*, 1988; *Selected Poems: The Centenary Edition*, 1991.

First Fig

My candle burns at both ends;
It will not last the night;
But ah, my foes, and oh, my friends—
It gives a lovely light!

1918

Spring

To what purpose, April, do you return again?
Beauty is not enough.
You can no longer quiet me with the redness
Of little leaves opening stickily.
I know what I know.   5
The sun is hot on my neck as I observe
The spikes of the crocus.
The smell of the earth is good.
It is apparent that there is no death.
But what does that signify?   10
Not only under ground are the brains of men
Eaten by maggots.
Life in itself
Is nothing,
An empty cup, a flight of uncarpeted stairs.   15
It is not enough that yearly, down this hill,
April
Comes like an idiot, babbling and strewing flowers.

1921

The Spring and the Fall

In the spring of the year, in the spring of the year,
I walked the road beside my dear.
The trees were black where the bark was wet.
I see them yet, in the spring of the year.
He broke me a bough of the blossoming peach   5
That was out of the way and hard to reach.

In the fall of the year, in the fall of the year,
I walked the road beside my dear.
The rooks went up with a raucous trill.
I hear them still, in the fall of the year.   10
He laughed at all I dared to praise,
And broke my heart, in little ways.

Year be springing or year be falling,
The bark will drip and the birds be calling.
There's much that's fine to see and hear   15
In the spring of a year, in the fall of a year.
'Tis not love's going hurts my days,
But that it went in little ways.

         1923

[Euclid alone has looked on Beauty bare]

Euclid[1] alone has looked on Beauty bare.
Let all who prate of Beauty hold their peace,
And lay them prone upon the earth and cease
To ponder on themselves, the while they stare
At nothing, intricately drawn nowhere   5
In shapes of shifting lineage; let geese
Gabble and hiss, but heroes seek release
From dusty bondage into luminous air.
O blinding hour, O holy, terrible day,
When first the shaft into his vision shone   10
Of light anatomized! Euclid alone
Has looked on Beauty bare. Fortunate they
Who, though once only and then but far away,
Have heard her massive sandal set on stone.

         1923

Dirge Without Music

I am not resigned to the shutting away of loving hearts in the hard
     ground.
So it is, and so it will be, for so it has been, time out of mind:
Into the darkness they go, the wise and the lovely. Crowned
With lilies and with laurel they go; but I am not resigned.   5

[1]Third-century B.C. Greek mathematician, the founder of geometry. Millay here considers mathematics a form of pure beauty.

Lovers and thinkers, into the earth with you.
Be one with the dull, the indiscriminate dust.
A fragment of what you felt, of what you knew,
A formula, a phrase remains,—but the best is lost.

The answers quick and keen, the honest look, the laughter, the   10
    love,—
They are gone. They are gone to feed the roses. Elegant and
    curled
Is the blossom. Fragrant is the blossom. I know. But I do not
    approve.   15
More precious was the light in your eyes than all the roses in the
    world.

Down, down, down into the darkness of the grave
Gently they go, the beautiful, the tender, the kind;
Quietly they go, the intelligent, the witty, the brave.   20
I know. But I do not approve. And I am not resigned.

                                              1928

[Love is not all: it is not meat nor drink]

Love is not all: it is not meat nor drink
Nor slumber nor a roof against the rain;
Nor yet a floating spar to men that sink
And rise and sink and rise and sink again;
Love can not fill the thickened lung with breath,   5
Nor clean the blood, nor set the fractured bone;
Yet many a man is making friends with death
Even as I speak, for lack of love alone.
It well may be that in a difficult hour,
Pinned down by pain and moaning for release,   10
Or nagged by want past resolution's power,
I might be driven to sell your love for peace,
Or trade the memory of this night for food.
It well may be. I do not think I would.

                                              1931

The Return

Earth does not understand her child,
    Who from the loud gregarious town

Returns, depleted and defiled,
  To the still woods, to fling him down.

Earth can not count the sons she bore: 5
  The wounded lynx, the wounded man
Come trailing blood unto her door;
  She shelters both as best she can.

But she is early up and out,
  To trim the year or strip its bones;   10
She has no time to stand about
  Talking of him in undertones

Who has no aim but to forget,
  Be left in peace, be lying thus
For days, for years, for centuries yet,   15
  Unshaven and anonymous;

Who, marked for failure, dulled by grief,
  Has traded in his wife and friend
For this warm ledge, this alder leaf:
  Comfort that does not comprehend.   20

                           1934

[Here lies, and none to mourn him but the sea]

Here lies, and none to mourn him but the sea,
That falls incessant on the empty shore,
Most various Man, cut down to spring no more;
Before his prime, even in his infancy
Cut down, and all the clamour that was he,   5
Silenced; and all the riveted pride he wore,
A rusted iron column whose tall core
The rains have tunnelled like an aspen tree.
Man, doughty Man, what power has brought you low,
That heaven itself in arms could not persuade   10
To lay aside the lever and the spade
And be as dust among the dusts that blow?
Whence, whence the broadside? whose the heavy blade? . . .
Strive not to speak, poor scattered mouth; I know.

                           1934

[His stalk the dark delphinium]

His stalk the dark delphinium[1]
Unthorned into the tending hand
Releases ... yet that hour will come ...
And must, in such a spiny land.
The silky, powdery mignonette   5
Before these gathering dews are gone
May pierce me—does the rose regret
The day she did her armour on?
In that the foul supplants the fair,
The coarse defeats the twice-refined,   10
Is food for thought, but not despair:
All will be easier when the mind
To meet the brutal age has grown
An iron cortex of its own.

                                                                1939

Sonnet xli

I, being born a woman and distressed
By all the needs and notions of my kind,
Am urged by your propinquity to find
Your person fair, and feel a certain zest
To bear your body's weight upon my breast: 5
So subtly is the fume of life designed,
To clarify the pulse and cloud the mind,
And leave me once again undone, possessed.
Think not for this, however, the poor treason
Of my stout blood against my staggering brain,   10
I shall remember you with love, or season
My scorn with pity,—let me make it plain:
I find this frenzy insufficient reason
For conversation when we meet again.

                                                                1923

Sonnet xcv

Women have loved before as I love now;
At least, in lively chronicles of the past—
Of Irish waters by a Cornish prow

[1]The delphinium has spurred flowers, the rose has thorns, and mignonette's clusters of tiny flowers are almost hidden. All three flowers are therefore hard to get at because of their natural defenses.

Or Trojan waters by a Spartan mast
Much to their cost invaded—here and there,   5
Hunting the amorous line, skimming the rest,
I find some woman bearing as I bear
Love like a burning city in the breast.
I think however that of all alive
I only in such utter, ancient way   10
Do suffer love; in me alone survive
The unregenerate passions of a day
When treacherous queens, with death upon the tread,
Heedless and wilful, took their knights to bed.

                                                                                   1931

Justice Denied in Massachusetts[1]

Let us abandon then our gardens and go home
And sit in the sitting-room.
Shall the larkspur blossom or the corn grow under this cloud?
Sour to the fruitful seed
Is the cold earth under this cloud,   5
Fostering quack and weed, we have marched upon but cannot
    conquer;
We have bent the blades of our hoes against the stalks of them.

Let us go home, and sit in the sitting-room.
Not in our day   10
Shall the cloud go over and the sun rise as before,
Beneficent upon us
Out of the glittering bay,
And the warm winds be blown inward from the sea
Moving the blades of corn   15
With a peaceful sound.
Forlorn, forlorn,
Stands the blue hay-rack by the empty mow.
And the petals drop to the ground,
Leaving the tree unfruited.   20
The sun that warmed our stooping backs and withered the weed
    uprooted—
We shall not feel it again.
We shall die in darkness, and be buried in the rain.
What from the splendid dead   25

[1]Refers to the case of Nicola Sacco and Bartolomeo Vanzetti, who, believed by many to be
political victims, were self-professed anarchists convicted of robbery and murder and
were executed at Boston in 1927. Despite an
outpouring of appeals for clemency, including a personal plea from Millay, the governor
refused to commute the sentence.

We have inherited—
Furrows sweet to the grain, and the weed subdued—
See now the slug and the mildew plunder.
Evil does overwhelm
The larkspur and the corn;   30
We have seen them go under.

Let us sit here, sit still,
Here in the sitting-room until we die;
At the step of Death on the walk, rise and go;
Leaving to our children's children this beautiful doorway,   35
And this elm,
And a blighted earth to till
With a broken hoe.

1928

Aesthetics—High Art, Popular Culture, and Politics

This In Focus section aims to demonstrate the confluences of modernist ideals of experimentation and the practices of popular-culture arts and advertising. Whereas conventional wisdom once argued that artists were hostile to any medium that was enjoyed by the masses, insisting that true aesthetics must be insulated from the whims of common taste, we now recognize that the borders between "high" and "low" culture were much more fluid and porous, with both sides borrowing theories and motifs from the other.

The excerpt from Gilbert Seldes's *The Seven Lively Arts* offers an illuminating statement on this interchange, insisting that popular media (whether the silent films of Charlie Chaplin or "Krazy Kat" newspaper cartoons) are as innovative as the "elevated" arts. The real villain, Seldes insists, are the stodgy guardians of high culture whose wrongheaded reverence for the "seriousness" of art saps the unruly energies it should express.

Subsequent selections from Edmund Wilson and business theorist Earnest Elmo Calkins reveal how artists and advertisers could envy each others' innovations. Wilson admires the poetic variety of the names of new colors in women's fashion, and Calkins argues that borrowing from modern art allows producers to establish novel ideas of beauty as a selling point. An excerpt from public relations expert Edward Bernays rather disturbingly demonstrates that, as many commentators were complaining, at least some in the business world did indeed view advertising as propaganda with the power to engineer new standards of taste and habits of spending.

By the 1930s, with the turn toward proletarian literature, questions of aesthetics shifted from business to revolution. The main debate among leftists was whether any attention to the aesthetics of radical art compromised its power to reach a mass audience and ignite social change. An example of a *New Masses* call for submissions to the *New Masses* Novel Contest suggests the aversion to any literary style that smacked of "aesthetics," whereas an excerpt from James T. Farrell's *A Note on Literary Criticism* outlines several pragmatic reasons why literature is not an optimum vehicle for propaganda.

Kirk Curnutt
Troy University–Montgomery, Alabama

■   GILBERT SELDES   ■
1893–1970

from **The Seven Lively Arts**[1]

If there were an Academy I should nail upon its doors the following beliefs:

That Al Jolson is more interesting to the intelligent mind than John Barrymore and Fanny Brice than Ethel[2];

That Ring Lardner and Mr. Dooley in their best work are more entertaining and more important than James B. Cabell and Joseph Hergesheimer in their best[3];

That the daily comic strip of George Herriman (Krazy Kat) is easily the most amusing and fantastic and satisfactory work of art produced in America to-day[4];

That Florenz Ziegfeld is a better producer than David Belasco[5];

That one film by Mack Sennett or Charlie Chaplin is worth the entire *oeuvre* of Cecil de Mille[6];

That *Alexander's Ragtime Band* and *I Love a Piano* are musically and emotionally sounder pieces of work than *Indian Love Lyrics* and *The Rosary*;

That the circus can be and often is more artistic than the Metropolitan Opera House in New York;

That Irene Castle is worth all the pseudo-classic dancing ever seen on the American stage[7]; and

That the civic masque is not perceptibly superior to the Elks' Parade in Atlantic City.

Only about half of these are heresies, and I am quite ready to stand by them as I would stand by my opinion of Dean Swift or Picasso or Henry James or James Joyce or Johann Sebastian Bach. But I recognize that they are expressions of personal preference, and possibly valueless unless related

---

[1]Gilbert Seldes, "The Great God Bogus," in *The Seven Lively Arts* (New York: Harper, 1924), 309–12, 318–20.

[2]Al Jolson (1886–1950) was a vaudeville performer best known as the star of the 1927 movie *The Jazz Singer*, the first nationally distributed "talkie." Fanny Brice (1891–1951) was a popular singer and movie star. John (1882–1942) and Ethel (1879–1959) Barrymore were highly acclaimed stage actors.

[3]Ring Lardner (1885–1933) was a popular humorist and newspaper columnist. Mr. Dooley was a fictional bartender created by columnist Finley Peter Dunne (1867–1936). James Brach Cabell (1879–1958) and Joseph Hergesheimer (1880–1954) were prominent novelists.

[4]George Herriman (1880–1944) was a cartoonist and the creator of "Krazy Kat," a popular comic strip that ran from 1913 to 1944.

[5]Florenz Ziegfeld (1867–1932) was a Broadway producer and created the musical revue the *Ziegfeld Follies* (1907–1931). David Belasco (1853–1931) was a Broadway producer and an innovator in theatrical naturalism.

[6]Mack Sennett (1880–1960) and Charlie Chaplin (1889–1977) were known for their slapstick comedies. Director Cecil B. DeMille (1881–1959) was known for his historical epics.

[7]Irene Castle (1893–1969) helped popularize ballroom dancing in the 1920s.

to some general principles. It appears that what I care for in the catalogue above falls in the field of the lively arts; and that the things to which I compare them (for emphasis, not for measurement) are either second-rate instances of the major arts or first-rate examples of the peculiarly disagreeable thing for which I find no other name than the bogus. I shall arrive presently at the general principles of the lively arts and their relation to the major. The bogus is a lion in the path.

Bogus is counterfeit and counterfeit is bad money and bad money is better—or at least more effective—than good money. This is not a private paradox, but a plain statement of a law in economics (Gresham's, I think)[8] that unless it is discovered, bad money will drive out good. Another characteristic of counterfeit is that, once we have accepted it, we try to pass it off on someone else; banks and critics are the only institutions which don't—or ought not to—continue the circulation. In the arts, counterfeit is known as the *faux bon*—the apparently good, essentially bad, which is the enemy of the good. The existence of the bogus is not a serious threat against the great arts, for they have an obstinate vitality and in the end—but only in the end—they prevail. It is the lively arts which are continually jeopardized by the bogus, and it is for their sake that I should like to see the bogus go sullenly down into oblivion.

Namely: vocal concerts, pseudo-classic dancing, the serious intellectual drama, the civic masque, the high-toned moving picture, and grand opera.

The first thing about them is that a very small percentage of those who make the bogus arts prosperous really enjoy them. I recall my own complete stultification after hearing my first concert; and the casual way in which I made it evident to all my companions that I had been to a concert is my only clue to the mystery. For at bottom there is a vast snobbery of the intellect which repays the deadly hours of boredom we spend in the pursuit of art. We are the inheritors of a tradition that what is worth while must be dull; and as often as not we invert the maxim and pretend that what is dull is higher in quality, more serious, "greater art" in short than whatever is light and easy and gay. We suffer fools gladly if we can pretend they are mystics. And the fact that audiences at concerts and opera, spectators at classic dances and masques, are suffering, is the final damnation, for it means that these arts are failures. I do not found my belief on any theory that all the arts ought to be appreciated by all the people. I do mean that most of those who read *Ulysses* or *The Pickwick Papers* do so because they enjoy it, and they stop the moment they are bored. There is no superiority in having read a book. The lively anticipation of delights which one senses in those going to the [*Ziegfeld*] *Follies* or to a circus is wholly absent in the lobby of the Metropolitan or at a performance of *Jane Clegg*.[9] And the art which communicates no ecstasy but that of snobbism is irretrievably bogus. . . .

[8]Gresham's Law, formulated by Sir Thomas Gresham (1519–1579), claims that overvalued currency (currency whose exchange value least resembles its commodity value) will always dominate the undervalued (currency whose exchange and commodity values are roughly equal).
[9]A drama by Irish playwright St. John Greer Ervine (1883–1971).

Our existence is hard, precise, high spirited. There is no nourishment for us in the milk-and-water diet of the bogus arts, and all they accomplish is a genteel corruption, a further thinning out of the blood, a little extra refinement. They are, intellectually, the exact equivalent of a high-toned lady, an elegant dinner or a refined collation served in the saloon, and the contemporary form of the vapours. Everything about them is supposed to be "good taste," including the kiss on the brow which miraculously "ruins" a perfect virgin—and they are in the physical sense of the word utterly taste-less. The great arts and the lively arts have their sources in the strength or in gaiety—and the difference between them is not the degree of intensity, but the degree of intellect. But the bogus arts spring from longing and weak-ness and depression. A happy people creates folk songs or whistles rag; it does not commit the vast atrocity of a "community sing-song"; it goes to Olympic games or to the race track, to *Iphigenia* or to Charlie Chaplin—not to hear a "vocal concert."

The bogus arts are corrupting the lively ones—because an essential defect of the bogus is that they pretend to be better than the popular arts, yet they want desperately to be popular. They borrow and spoil what is good; they persuade people by appealing to their snobbery that they are the real thing. And as the audience watches these arts in action the comforting illusion creeps over them that at last they have achieved art. But they are really watching the manifestations of the Great God Bogus—and what annoys me most is that they might at that very moment be hailing Apollo or Dionysos, or be themselves participating in some of the minor rites of the Great God Pan.

1924

EDMUND WILSON
1895–1972

Current Fashions[1]

The people who make women's hosiery must be employing poets. I quote from an advertisement: Peach—beige—pearl—beach—suede—silver—cin-der—rose taupe—African brown—russet—blonde satin—blush—Aire-dale—cork—shell pink—pebble—skynn—lark—tan—cordovan—mauve—muffin—nude—buck—gold—faun— racquet—sandalwood—oriental pearl—

[1]Edmund Wilson, "Current Fashions," *New Republic* (November 11, 1925), reprinted in *American Earthquake.*

tanbark—log cabin—oakwood—gunmetal. And from another: Mauve gray—rose nutmeg—peach nude—sauterne—orange nude—blush pink—natural.

In the billiard parlors of Waterbury and Scranton, young men are wearing the blue shirts and the white-rimmed gray hats of the Prince of Wales; and in the back streets of Newark and Schenectady, little girls in the green hats of Michael Arlen are dancing the Charleston on the pavement.[2]

1925

EARNEST ELMO CALKINS
1868–1964

from **Beauty: The New Business Tool**[1]

The effect of beauty in distributing goods is interesting from its economic aspect when we consider what is coming to be known as "styling" the goods. When we speak of style, we usually mean a quality which makes a thing popular, with the corollary that popularity will soon cause it to cease to be stylish. Style flourishes best in a civilization in which a small class practices its rites and a large class stands enviously outside, barred by financial considerations and social ignorance from participating. What has happened, apparently, is that many more people have become conscious of style and the style idea has been extended to many more articles than were included in the original indictment.

This means that this new influence on articles of barter and sale is largely used to make people dissatisfied with what they have of the old order, still good and useful and efficient, but lacking the newest touch. In the expressive slang of the day, they "date." People buy a new car, not because the old one is worn out, but because it is no longer modern. It does not satisfy their pride. They refurnish the house, not because the old furniture is unable to perform its duties as furniture, but because it is out of date, out of style, no longer the thing. You cannot produce this state of mind by mere efficiency. You cannot make people substitute a new car that runs well for an old car that runs well unless it has some added quality. The new quality must be borrowed from the realms of good taste—smarter lines, newer design, better color, more luxurious upholstery, more art, or at least more taste.

Within strictly material limits the machine apparently can do anything. It is only a question of time when the most perfect motor car made can be

[2]Waterbury, Connecticut, and Scranton, Pennsylvania. Arlen (1895–1956), born Dikran Kouyoumdjian in Armenia, wrote the popular provocative novel *The Green Hat* (1924).

[1]Earnest Elmo Calkins, "Beauty: The New Business Tool," *Atlantic Monthly* (August 1927): 153–55.

reproduced at a fraction of its present cost. Mechanical knowledge is a tangible thing, easily acquired or imitated; but that intangible something which art gives, that creative, imaginative power, has no appreciable limits.

Much of the art influence which is transforming business is what is described, not very lucidly, as the "new art." The new art is the product of those men who are determined to break with tradition and produce art exactly as was produced that art which is now the tradition. They believe that art should reflect the age, especially an age which has introduced so many new values. The modern school of artists insists that we must have art that grows out of our life, not out of the life of a dead-and-gone era subject to influences so remote from to-day, and they are producing that art. It is logical that business should prove susceptible to these new forms, because, in a way, both are the result of the same set of causes. Both the industrialism and the art are modern. The forces that are making our fast-paced, bright-colored, sharply defined civilization are producing our modern art.

It is also natural that modern art should enter business by the door of advertising. Commercial art began when all art was still subject to the old academic tradition; but, as advertising is the most sensitive and mobile of all business forces, it was the first to feel the innate appropriateness of the new forms to express the spirit of modern industrialism.

When advertising first took up art to help make its message clearer, it was difficult to interest the artist. The artist of that day considered business beneath his contempt. But as time went on better artists became interested because of the greater financial reward, the larger opportunity, the better understanding between manufacturer and artist, the improvement in processes of reproduction; and so a race of artists was developed of remarkable dexterity. At first it was desired only to attain realism, but at length realism as a technique was so mastered that nothing more could be done. The magazines were filled with color pages of honest, sincere, straightforward painting that was, to use a commonplace phrase, lifelike. A dead line was reached, the dead line of excellence. By then the new art had arrived, the school of the more independent artists, trying to shake off bonds of tradition and strike out in new and unknown worlds of imagination, and this impulse was reflected in advertising design. The new art was imaginative rather than realistic. It attempted to suggest rather than to show. And these young men subsidized by business, stimulated by both money and opportunity, have done some very wonderful things, and have gone so far in the advertising creations as to make one wonder whether the public or any great part of the public can follow....

One remembers with what a blare of tom-toms the new art burst on this country a few years before the war. In an armory in New York City about fifteen years ago was held a monster exhibition of the first showings of the new tendencies, largely imported, but with some contributions from the more advanced revels in our own country. That was the time when such names as Picabia, Picasso, Duchamps, Gauguin, Cézanne, Redon, became known on this side of the ocean. The exhibition was a riot. For days that vast armory was crowded with puzzled, giggling, startled, scornful, unbelieving people, who felt, some of them, as if the familiar world were tumbling about them. Shortly after the exhibition closed there appeared in the newspapers of New York a page advertisement announcing the first showing of gowns influenced by the new art to be made at a series of séances in the Wanamaker auditorium. The day was cold and rainy, but the four exhibitions crowded that little theater to its capacity. It was natural that a new art movement should register first in dress fabrics, although it was a little forward-looking to seize so quickly so new an art form. But the astonishing fact is this, that the newer art forms are now being utilized by manufacturers whose goods are remote from those ordinarily influenced by style.

Modern color and design are styling not only products hitherto in the style class—silks, prints, fabrics, textiles, gowns, hats, shoes, and sports clothes—but social stationery, foods, motor cars, building materials, house furnishings, book bindings, interior decoration, furniture, and bric-a-brac.

Some of the new silk designs admirably express the modern spirit. At first glance they appear to be just what they are, sprightly patterns, produced by repeating some simple motif. But the motif, instead of being the old romantic one of a leaf, bird, spray, or scroll, is some bit of our modern life, a map of New York City, a couple dancing the Charleston, *Gentlemen Prefer Blondes*, a graph or statistical chart, the windows of skyscrapers at night, or a group of steam cranes.[2] Beauty may be discerned in unexpected places. It already exists even in our machine-made age. The present ingredients are being assembled in new patterns which will eventually change the aspect of the world around us. Design and color are used to give them modernity.

1927

EDWARD BERNAYS
1891–1995

from **Propaganda**[1]

The conscious and intelligent manipulation of the organized habits and opinions of the masses is an important element in democratic societies. Those who manipulate this unseen mechanism of society constitute an invisible government which is the true ruling power of our country.

We are governed, our minds are molded, our tastes formed, our ideas suggested, largely by men we have never heard of. This is a logical result of

---

[2]*Gentlemen Prefer Blondes*, a popular novel by Anita Loos (1889–1981), now is remembered for the 1953 film starring Marilyn Monroe.

[1]Edward Bernays, *Propaganda* (New York: Liveright, 1928), 9–11, 150–51, 156–59.

the way in which our democratic society is organized. Vast numbers of human beings must cooperate in this manner if they are to live together as a smoothly functioning society.

Our invisible governors are, in many cases, unaware of the identity of their fellow members in the inner cabinet.

They govern us by their qualities of natural leadership, their ability to supply needed ideas and by their key position in the social structure. Whatever attitude one chooses to take toward this condition, it remains a fact that in almost every act of our daily lives, whether in the sphere of politics or business, in our social conduct or our ethical thinking, we are dominated by the relatively small number of persons—a trifling faction of our hundred and twenty million—who understand the mental processes and social patterns of the masses. It is they who pull the wires which control the public mind, who harness old social forces and contrive new ways to bind and guide the world.

It is usually not realized how necessary these invisible governors are to the orderly functioning of our group life. In theory, every citizen may vote for whom he pleases. Our Constitution does not envisage political parties as part of the mechanism of government, and its framers seem not to have pictured to themselves the existence in our national politics of anything like the modern political machine. But the American voters soon found that without organization and direction of their individual votes, cast, perhaps, for dozens or hundreds of candidates, would produce nothing but confusion. Invisible government, in the shape of rudimentary political parties, arose almost overnight. Ever since then we have agreed, for the sake of simplicity and practicality, that party machines should narrow the field of choice to two candidates, or at most three or four.

In theory, every citizen makes up his mind on public questions and matters of private conduct. In practice, if all men had to study for themselves the abstruse economic, political, and ethical data involved in every question, they would find it impossible to come to a conclusion about anything. We have voluntarily agreed to let an invisible government sift the data and high-spot the outstanding issues so that our field of choice shall be narrowed to practical proportions. From our leaders and the media they use to reach the public, we accept evidence and the demarcation of issues bearing upon public questions; from some ethical teacher, be it a minister, a favorite essayist, or merely prevailing opinion, we accept a standardized set of social conduct to which we conform most of the time.

In theory, everybody buys the best and cheapest commodities offered him on the market. In practice, if every one went around pricing, and chemically testing before purchasing, the dozens of soaps or fabrics or brands of bread which are for sale, economic life would become hopelessly jammed. To avoid such confusion, society consents to have its choice narrowed to ideas and objects brought to its attention through propaganda of all kinds. There is consequently a vast and continuous effort going on to capture our minds in the interest of some policy or commodity or idea....

The media by which special pleaders transmit their messages to the public through propaganda include all the means by which people to-day transmit their ideas to one another. There is no means of human communication which may not also be a means of deliberate propaganda, because propaganda is simply the establishing of reciprocal understanding between an individual and a group.

The important point to the propagandist is that the relative value of the various instruments of propaganda, and their relation to the masses, are constantly changing. If he is to get full reach for his message he must take advantage of these shifts of value the instant they occur. Fifty years ago, the public meeting was a propaganda instrument par excellence. To-day it is difficult to get more than a handful of people meeting unless extraordinary attractions are part of the program. The automobile takes them away from home, the radio keeps them in the home, the successive daily editions of the newspaper bring information to them in the office or subway, and also they are sick of the ballyhoo of the rally.

Instead there are numerous other media of communication, some new, others old but so transformed that they have become virtually new. The newspaper, of course, remains always a primary medium for the transmission of opinions and ideas—in other words, for propaganda. . . .

The American motion picture is the greatest unconscious carrier of propaganda in the world to-day. It is a great distributor for ideas and opinions.

The motion picture can standardize the ideas and habits of a nation. Because pictures are made to meet market demands, they reflect, emphasize and even exaggerate broad popular tendencies, rather than stimulate new ideas and opinions. The motion picture avails itself only of ideas and facts which are in vogue. As the newspaper seeks to purvey news, it seeks to purvey entertainment.

Another instrument of propaganda is the personality. Has the device of the exploited personality been pushed too far? President Coolidge photographed on his vacation in full Indian regalia in company with full-blooded chiefs, was the climax of a greatly over-reported vacation.[2] Obviously a public personality can be made absurd by misuse of the very mechanism which helped create it.

Yet the vivid dramatization of personality will always remain one of the functions of the public relations counsel. The public instinctively demands a personality to typify a conspicuous corporation or enterprise.

There is a story that a great financier discharged a partner because he had divorced his wife.

"But what," asked the partner, "have my private affairs to do with the banking business?"

---

[2]Calvin Coolidge (1872–1933) ascended to the presidency after the death of Warren G. Harding in 1923. Coolidge won election in his own right in 1924 but was defeated in 1928 by Herbert Hoover.

"If you are not capable of managing your own wife," was the reply, "the people will certainly believe that you are not capable of managing their money."

The propagandist must treat personality as he would treat any other objective fact within his province.

A personality may create circumstances, as Lindbergh created good will between the United States and Mexico.[3] Events may create a personality, as the Cuban War created the political figure of Roosevelt.[4] It is often difficult to say which creates the other. Once a public figure has decided what ends he wishes to achieve, he must regard himself objectively and present an outward picture of himself which is consistent with his real character and his aims. . . .

Undoubtedly the public is becoming aware of the methods which are being used to mold its opinions and habits. If the public is better informed about the processes of its own life, it will be so much the more receptive to reasonable appeals to its own interests. No matter how sophisticated, how cynical the public may become about publicity methods, it must respond to the basic appeals, because it will always need food, crave amusement, long for beauty, respond to leadership.

If the public becomes more intelligent in its commercial demands, commercial firms will meet the new standards. If it becomes weary of the old methods used to persuade it to accept a given idea or commodity, its leaders will present their appeals more intelligently.

Propaganda will never die out. Intelligent men must realize that propaganda is the modern instrument by which they can fight for productive ends and help bring order out of chaos.

1927

NEW MASSES

from **Novel Contest**[1]

The *New Masses* prize contest for a novel on a proletarian theme, conducted jointly by the *New Masses* and the John Day Company, book publishers, has been won by Clara Weatherwax of Oakland, California, with a novel entitled *Marching, Marching!* . . .

[3]Charles Lindbergh (1902–1974) was the first man to cross the Atlantic Ocean in an airplane.
[4]Theodore Roosevelt (1859–1919) served as president from 1901 (following the assassination of William McKinley) until 1909.

[1]"*New Masses* Novel Contest," *New Masses* (September 3, 1935): 7.

The *New Masses* feels that, if the contest had produced only the winning novel, it would fully have justified itself. In addition, however, it brought forth one novel, Martin Russak's *A Weaver's Son*, that the judges unanimously agreed to recommend for publication and five or six others that, in the opinion of individual judges, deserve to be printed.

It is very significant that most of the novels submitted grew out of the actual experience of the workers. The writing of novels is a craft that requires its own discipline and these worker-writers have had no opportunity to train themselves in this craft. If, however, this contest has stimulated them to begin their training, it has served a valuable purpose. Quite apart from the literary merits of the hundred and more manuscripts submitted, they show that proletarian literature is putting down deep roots into the life of the working class. Out of this will come an abundant growth.

1935

■ JAMES T. FARRELL ■
1904–1979

from **Literature and Propaganda**[1]

In America the word *propaganda* has sometimes been used almost in the sense in which Lenin used *agitation*, except that this latter function was to be performed only by the spoken word.[2] In addition, the word *propaganda* in America has, thanks to the World War and commercial advertising, been given a different meaning from the one given to it in the translations of Lenin's works. I am therefore going to offer, as a basis for this discussion, a definition of the word.

I shall here define propaganda as the scheme or plan or process or technique of propagating a system, a scheme, an idea or set of ideas, a doctrine, or an attitude or attitudes, all with the aim of producing a proposed course of action, or else of producing acquiescence in a proposed course of action. I think that my definition applies to many of the references to propaganda to be found in the reviews and articles of our American revolutionary critics who have discussed the subject. For their emphasis is on action, on not only interpreting the world but also changing the world. When one tries to persuade or convince large masses of people—to propagate ideas among them—one will hardly succeed if one ignores the appropriate methods, or is

---

[1]James T. Farrell, "Literature and Propaganda," in *A Note on Literary Criticism* (London: Constable, 1936), 143–149, 154–56.

[2]Vladimir Ilyich Lenin (1870–1924) led the 1917 October Revolution that installed Communism in Russia.

unaware of certain important facts. One must know how large masses of people are unified, how their attention may be directed toward certain goals, and toward the actions that will enable them to achieve these goals. In propagating an attitude, idea, doctrine, system of ideas, or course of action in the minds of large masses, it is necessary to find common denominators and to eliminate disturbing and contradictory suggestions; otherwise an insufficient unity of will and action will be attained.

One of the instruments of propaganda, in the sense in which I have defined it, is the slogan. The application of propaganda to the solution of social problems is absolutely essential. Propaganda has its definite place, its methods, its values, its necessities. It is, for instance, characteristic of a great leader that the slogans he formulates present a progressive answer to the needs of an objective situation; also that they are part of the program of a long-run policy that is progressive in the Marxian sense; and finally that his slogans contain the potentialities for elaborating policies and methods that will serve as an outline for answering the needs of the objective situation to which they are referred, and of solving, in a progressive Marxian sense, the problems which these needs bring forth.

An illustration here is the slogans which Lenin forged during the days preceding the October Revolution in 1917. He stenciled, in effective slogans, the answer to the problems in Russia at that time and the needs of the Russian masses. These slogans established the basis for achieving the fundamental unity of action necessary in proceeding toward the solution of these problems. Implicit within them were the potentialities for the establishment of the Soviet Government in Russia.

One difference between Lenin's propaganda—his slogans for peace, land, and bread, for the achievement of these ends through the giving of power to the Soviets, etc.—and the propaganda and slogans of a demagogue is apparent. The latter consist in statements or promises that cannot be fulfilled—they are slogans that do not logically contain the necessary potentialities for progressive action in the Marxian sense. A second difference is that Lenin's slogans were a concise description of the ends and the basis of action, carrying policies into effect; whereas the demagogue's slogans are usually the means by which the implementing of effective, progressive policies is prevented. In short, Lenin meant his slogans, and the demagogue does not mean his. Moreover, Lenin's slogans did not degrade thought; on the contrary, they were a precise expression of policies, and thus were the exact opposite of the demagogue's.

Lenin's slogans were effective propaganda in the best sense of the term. However, are we going to interpret the slogan "All art is propaganda" to mean the forging of slogans dealing with political policies? To such a critic as Joseph Freeman, this is not the intended meaning.[3] In others, however,

---

[3]Joseph Freeman (1897–1965) was a leftist poet and author of *An American Testament* (1936).

there is a confusion of meanings, and with this, an evident misconception of functions. To quote a statement by Jack Conroy: "To me a strike or bulleting or an impassioned leaflet are of more moment than three hundred prettily and faultlessly written pages about the private woes of a gigolo or the biological ferment of a society dame as useful to society as the buck brush that infests Missouri cow pastures and takes all the sustenance out of the soil."[4] Though I need hardly say that I favor proper strike bulletins and effective and impassioned leaflets, I see no necessity for counterposing these to works of literature. I agree with Mr. Conroy that the private woes of a gigolo are not particularly interesting, and yet, offhand, it occurs to me that Colette's *Chéri* does describe these private woes with such insight that I was genuinely interested in them; though my liking for *Chéri* certainly would not prevent me from reading a strike bulletin, or an impassioned leaflet, or Lenin's *'Left-Wing' Communism: An Infantile Disorder*.[5] If Mr. Conroy here is referring to Proust—since Proust did write about society dames who were not noted for their usefulness to society—why, my answer is only the more emphatically the same. I assume that there is a unity in society as I have defined it, that there are many manifestations from a given set of objective conditions, and finally that the more deeply one is aware of these manifestations, emotionally as well as intellectually, the better one will succeed in understanding contemporary society.

There seems to be a mixing-up of the tactics required for the roles of agitator, strike leader, political leader, Marxist theoretician, and novelist. One man may be all of these, serve more than one of these valuable functions, but when he does so, he must—if he is to succeed—perform these various functions according to their internal logic and necessities. Politics is obviously concerned with government and with the solution of social problems. It must find answers that are embodied in action. Literature, by contrast, is not so directly concerned with finding answers to social problems that will be immediately embodied in action; and, generally speaking, novelists and poets are not equipped to serve as political leaders. In addition, the process itself of producing literature denies the validity of literature's serving as an effective means of propaganda as I have defined it. Works of literature are, generally, not quickly enough assimilated to become instruments of propaganda leading to the choice of immediate courses of action. The social scene, particularly in unstable times like the present, is too shifting, too changing, to permit literature frequently to act toward the immediate solution of social problems. By the time a writer can assimilate material essential for a novel about a social problem, think through the potentialities of his material, arrange and write it, check his sources, finish it for publication, and correct the proofs—by that time one, two, or three years have elapsed. After this, more time is needed for the distribution of the novel, and for its

[4]Jack Conroy, *The American Writer's Congress*, p. 83. [Farrell's note] In the 1930s, Conroy (1898–1990) was best known for his proletarian novel *The Disinherited* (1933).

[5]Colette was the pen name of French novelist Sidonie-Gabrielle Colette (1873–1954). *Chéri* (1920) is a novel of sexual mores.

assimilation by its readers. And, as likely as not, by that time the social and class relationships will have shifted and altered. For the process of assimilating a novel sometimes takes years. Proust, for instance, is still in the process of being assimilated; so is Joyce. So is Shakespeare for that matter....

There can be no objection to the writer's dealing with politics in his work, or even to his entertaining the field of direct political action, *unless* he attempts either of these without assuming the obligations and the responsibilities that they will inevitably impose on him. If he undertakes to write political slogans, for instance, purporting to express the needs and answer the problems that exist objectively in the field of actual politics, the writer owes it to his art, to his own integrity, and to the masses to whom he addresses himself, to understand these problems, and not merely in terms of a generalized solution, but also in their background and details. And there is a further demand on him: that he utilize his knowledge to forge adequate slogans. Finally, it should be demanded of him—indeed his own integrity demands it of him—that he assume the responsibilities not of politics alone but also of literature. Hence, if he is to write poetry or any other so-called creative literature, he must give his political slogans internal relationship with the other features in his work; his writing as a whole must be marked by intrinsic rather than extrinsic conviction. A writer is not revealing political consciousness, he is not helping humanity or the proletariat, when he merely exposes—perhaps in blatant boldface—a few political slogans that he learned yesterday.

1936

ALIENATION AND LITERARY EXPERIMENTATION

Ezra Pound is generally regarded as the chief spokesperson for experimentation in modern American literature. His famous slogan, "Make it New," was quoted often by many writers who agreed with its premises and aims. For those in agreement, making it new demanded the use of large ideas and specific details in ways that reflected sharp observation and fresh thought. Many who disagreed—other writers as well as readers who were happy to remain conventional—saw in Pound and others a deliberate desire to be obscure. In fact, "The Waste Land," T. S. Eliot's most famous poem and perhaps the most famous poem of the twentieth century, was vociferously rejected by many people as a farce, a trick Eliot was playing on unsuspecting readers. Even Eliot himself, once he converted to the respectability of organized religion, dismissed the poem as nothing but "a grouse against life."

Modernism does, in fact, have a serious argument against many of the features of modern life. Pound objected most to what he called "Victorian slither," by which he meant the tendency to allow one's comfortable and preset attitudes to lead the attention away from what was most pressing or most illusive. Such tendencies were the result of the routinization and increasing bureaucracy in an urbanized and industrial world. Implicit in Pound's polemic blasts against the shop-worn and trite expression was a sense that the artist was, as he put it, the antenna of the race. This claim of an isolated and privileged position for the artist also entailed a separation from normal or "mass" society. Such separation in its severest form was known as alienation, the feeling of being an outsider in one's social environment. Hence, there were many ways in which alienation and experimentation were linked. In fact, the stylistic effects that result from the linking of the two are offered by some critics as the core of modernism.

But alienation and experimentation could be joined on other grounds as well. Many alienated writers argued that their mental and psychological states were simply impossible to record using the traditional or standard forms of expression. Such standard forms had been developed, the argument said, for normal audiences by normal writers. Some writers were aggressively set against everything that acted as a "norm": for example, E. E. Cummings and H.D. not only changed the look of the poem on the page, but also acted out their unconventional beliefs in ways that society found offensively abnormal. However, other writers such as William Carlos Williams and Marianne Moore could retain all the appearances of social propriety, even as their poems were clearly challenging accepted ways of creating meaning and expressing emotion. Alienation was not simply a matter of unconventional behavior, nor was experimentation simply based on a desire to appear different from others.

Some of the writers of the modern period seemed to reflect a belief that society itself was an alienating structure, rather than merely claiming that individual artists "suffered" from a disaffecting situation. F. Scott Fitzgerald and Katherine Anne Porter depicted society in a way that suggested everyone was unhappy in ways that were pervasive and yet largely invisible. Various "solutions" were offered to the problem, though often the proposed solution was itself undercut by irony. Irony was often used in modernism because it makes all foundations of claim and statement less secure; this insecurity appealed to modernists because it reflected their own state and also challenged the security of normal experience. Eugene O'Neill, for example, offers in *The Hairy Ape* a form of primitivism as a solution to alienation, but the problem is far from resolved in any straightforward way.

Even today many readers find that the experimentalism of modernism is too confusing, too needlessly complex, and that the alienation of modern literary thought is too bleak, too utterly empty. Whether or not modernism can be seen as an affirmative cultural tradition, one that challenges and even destroys, but does so in the interest of genuine renewal, remains a much debated question. Disputes about style and attitude are often part of this larger question.

Charles Molesworth
Queens College, City University of New York

■ EZRA POUND ■
1885–1972

No one better symbolizes the course of modern literature—its triumphs and defeats—than Ezra Pound. From the lyric poems of his Edwardian period to the complex allusive style of his epic *Cantos*, Pound marked the path that modern poetry followed. His work in criticism and translation, from his "Imagist Manifesto" and *Guide to Kulchur* to his translations from Provençal and Chinese, signaled new directions in modern literature and criticism. However, it is not only as a major influence on literary modernism that Pound is important.

Pound was born in Hailey, Idaho, and raised in Pennsylvania, where his father worked in the Mint in Philadelphia. His pugnacious spirit is evident in an essay titled "How I Began," in which Pound says that at age fifteen he decided to become a poet and to know by age thirty more about poetry than any living man. Pound was a student at the University of Pennsylvania in 1902, where he met William Carlos Williams, and Hilda Doolittle, who was a student at Bryn Mawr. He received his B.A. from Hamilton College in 1905 and an M.A. in romance languages from the University of Pennsylvania in 1906. After being fired as a teacher at Wabash College for harboring a "lady-gent impersonator" in his room, Pound departed for Europe, where he would remain for most of his life.

In 1908, Pound arrived in Venice, where he arranged to have his first volume of poems, *A Lume Spento*, published at his own expense. Within the next few years, he became a central figure in London literary life. Through his own work and by fostering the work of others, including W. B. Yeats, James Joyce, H.D., Marianne Moore, William Carlos Williams, and T. S. Eliot, Pound sought to bring about a renaissance of the arts in England and America. In "A Few Don'ts by an Imagiste," which appeared in *Poetry* in 1913, he announced the modernist poetics of precision, concision, and metrical freedom that he had formulated in conversation with H.D. and Richard Aldington; this aesthetic was perfectly embodied by the two-line "In a Station of the Metro" (1916).

The poems of *Lustra* (1916) reflect the range of Pound's intellectual interests, the variety of his technical experiments, and the extent of his artistic achievement in his London years. For Pound as for other modernists, the First World War marked a turn away from the aestheticism of his early years toward what he would call "the poem including history." Having entombed the aesthete figure of his early period in "Hugh Selwyn Mauberley," which was published in 1920, Pound departed for Europe and turned his main energies to writing his epic *Cantos*. Under the influence of C. H. Douglas's ideas on Social Credit and, after 1924, the politics of Mussolini in Italy, Pound came to attribute the waste of the war and the malaise of the modern world to the dominance of bankers and munitions manufacturers, usury, and Jews. Insisting on the relationship between good government, good art, and the good life, Pound incorporated his social and economic views into the works he published during the thirties, including *ABC of Economics* (1933), *Eleven New Cantos* (1934), *Social Credit: An Impact* (1935), and *Jefferson and/or Mussolini* (1935).

In 1939 he made a trip to Washington, D.C., where he spoke with members of Congress about his economic policies and about his fear that Roosevelt, the bankers, and the armaments industry were leading America into another war. Unsuccessful with American politicians, he returned to Italy, where in 1941 he began regularly broadcasting his ideas over Rome Radio, in a program aimed at the English-speaking world. Mixing reflections on literature with tirades against Roosevelt, usury, and international finance, Pound continued these broadcasts until July 1943, when he was indicted for treason. After being arrested in May 1945, he was incarcerated for six months in a wire cage in Pisa before he was sent back to America to stand trial. Declared mentally unfit to stand trial by a team of psychologists, Pound was committed in 1946 to St. Elizabeths Hospital in Washington, D.C., where he remained until his release in 1958.

When in February 1949 the Library of Congress awarded the Bollingen Prize for Poetry to the *Pisan Cantos* (1948), Pound became the center of a controversy over the relation of poetry and politics, and modernism and fascism, that raged for several months in the American press. While T. S. Eliot, Allen Tate, and Robert Penn Warren argued for the separation of poetry and politics in the evaluation of Pound's work, others, including Karl Shapiro and Robert Hillyer, argued that Pound's politics ultimately vitiated the artistic value of his poetry.

In his later writings, Pound lost no opportunity to criticize the "mere aesthete," who did not understand the social and regenerative function of his epic "tale of the tribe." In the wake of the Bollingen controversy, however, it was the image of Pound the formalist and aesthete that rose to prominence in the Anglo-American tradition. This emphasis was supported by the increasing obscurity and complexity of Pound's later volumes of Cantos. Since Pound's death, studies of his work have remained split between those who would praise the poet and forget the politician and those who would attack the fascist and forget the poet. But in the final analysis, it may be Pound's Americanism as much as his fascism that pervades his work.

Betsy Erkkila
University of Pennsylvania

PRIMARY WORKS

A Lume Spento, 1908; *Personae,* 1909–1926; *The Spirit of Romance,* 1910; *Cantos,* 1916–1968; *Cathay,* 1915; *Gaudier-Brzeska,* 1916; *Lustra,* 1916; *Hugh Selwyn Mauberley,* 1920; *Make It New,* 1934; *The Letters of Ezra Pound (1907–1941),* ed. D.D. Paige, 1950; *Literary Essays of Ezra Pound,* 1954; *Selected Poems 1908–1959,* 1975; *Poems and Translations,* 2003.

A Virginal[1]

No, no! Go from me, I have left her lately.
I will not spoil my sheath with lesser brightness,
For my surrounding air hath a new lightness;
Slight are her arms, yet they have bound me straitly
And left me cloaked as with a gauze of aether;   5
As with sweet leaves; as with subtle clearness.
Oh, I have picked up magic in her nearness
To sheathe me half in half the things that sheathe her.
No, no! Go from me. I have still the flavour,
Soft as spring wind that's come from birchen bowers.   10
Green come the shoots, aye April in the branches,
As winter's wound with her sleight hand she staunches,
Hath of the trees a likeness of the savour:
As white their bark, so white this lady's hours.

1912

A Pact

I make a pact with you, Walt Whitman—
I have detested you long enough.
I come to you as a grown child
Who has had a pig-headed father;
I am old enough now to make friends.   5
It was you that broke the new wood,
Now is a time for carving.
We have one sap and one root—
Let there be commerce between us.

1916

[1]A virginal is a small harpsichord played in the sixteenth and seventeenth centuries by young girls, virgins.

In a Station of the Metro

The apparition of these faces in the crowd;
Petals on a wet, black bough.

1916

L'art, 1910

Green arsenic smeared on an egg-white cloth,
Crushed strawberries! Come, let us feast our eyes.

1916

A Retrospect[1]

There has been so much scribbling about a new fashion in poetry, that I may perhaps be pardoned this brief recapitulation and retrospect.

In the spring or early summer of 1912, 'H.D.', Richard Aldington and myself decided that we were agreed upon the three principles following:

1. Direct treatment of the 'thing' whether subjective or objective.

2. To use absolutely no word that does not contribute to the presentation.

3. As regarding rhythm: to compose in the sequence of the musical phrase, not in sequence of a metronome.

Upon many points of taste and of predilection we differed, but agreeing upon these three positions we thought we had as much right to a group name, at least as much right, as a number of French 'schools' proclaimed by Mr Flint in the August number of Harold Monro's magazine for 1911.

This school has since been 'joined' or 'followed' by numerous people who, whatever their merits, do not show any signs of agreeing with the second specification. Indeed *vers libre*[2] has become as prolix and as verbose as any of the flaccid varieties that preceded it. It has brought faults of its own. The actual language and phrasing is often as bad as that of our elders without even the excuse that the words are shovelled in to fill a metric pattern or to complete the noise of a rhyme-sound. Whether or no the phrases followed by the followers are musical must be left to the reader's decision. At times I can find a marked metre in 'vers libres', as stale and hackneyed as

[1]A group of early essays that appeared in *Pavannes and Divisions* (1918). "A Few Don'ts by an Imagiste" first appeared in *Poetry*, 1 (March 1913).

[2]*Vers libre* is the French term for free verse.

any pseudo-Swinburnian,[3] at times the writers seem to follow no musical structure whatever. But it is, on the whole, good that the field should be ploughed. Perhaps a few good poems have come from the new method, and if so it is justified.

Criticism is not a circumscription or a set of prohibitions. It provides fixed points of departure. It may startle a dull reader into alertness. That little of it which is good is mostly in stray phrases; or if it be an older artist helping a younger it is in great measure but rules of thumb, cautions gained by experience.

I set together a few phrases on practical working about the time the first remarks on imagisme were published. The first use of the word 'Imagiste' was in my note to T.E. Hulme's five poems, printed at the end of my 'Ripostes' in the autumn of 1912. I reprint my cautions from *Poetry* for March, 1913.

A Few Don'ts

An 'Image' is that which presents an intellectual and emotional complex in an instant of time. I use the term 'complex' rather in the technical sense employed by the newer psychologists, such as Hart, though we might not agree absolutely in our application.

It is the presentation of such a 'complex' instantaneously which gives that sense of sudden liberation; that sense of freedom from time limits and space limits; that sense of sudden growth, which we experience in the presence of the greatest works of art.

It is better to present one Image in a lifetime than to produce voluminous works.

All this, however, some may consider open to debate. The immediate necessity is to tabulate A LIST OF DON'TS for those beginning to write verses. I can not put all of them into Mosaic negative.

To begin with, consider the three propositions (demanding direct treatment, economy of words, and the sequence of the musical phrase), not as dogma—never consider anything as dogma—but as the result of long contemplation, which, even if it is some one else's contemplation, may be worth consideration.

Pay no attention to the criticism of men who have never themselves written a notable work. Consider the discrepancies between the actual writing of the Greek poets and dramatists, and the theories of the Graeco-Roman grammarians, concocted to explain their metres.

1918

---

[3]Algernon Swinburne, a nineteenth-century British poet.

from **Hugh Selwyn Mauberley (Life and Contacts)**[1]

E.P. Ode pour L'election de Son Sepulchre[2]

I

For three years, out of key with his time,
He strove to resuscitate the dead art
Of poetry; to maintain "the sublime"
In the old sense. Wrong from the start—

No, hardly, but seeing he had been born   5
In a half savage country, out of date;
Bent resolutely on wringing lilies from the acorn;
Capaneus[3]; trout for factitious bait;

Ἴδμεν γάρ τοι πάνθ᾽, ὅσ᾽ ἐνὶ Τροίῃ[4]
Caught in the unstopped ear;   10
Giving the rocks small lee-way
The chopped seas held him, therefore, that year.

His true Penelope[5] was Flaubert,[6]
He fished by obstinate isles;
Observed the elegance of Circe's[7] hair   15
Rather than the mottoes on sun-dials.

Unaffected by "the march of events,"
He passed from men's memory in *l'an trentiesme*
De son eage[8]; the case presents
No adjunct to the Muses' diadem.   20

---

[1]"Hugh Selwyn Mauberley" is a kind of farewell to London and the literary culture of Pound's early years. The poem was published in 1920, the same year that Pound left England for France and Italy, where he dedicated himself more fully to the composition of his epic *Cantos*.

[2]"Ode on the Choice of His Tomb," adapted from an ode by Pierre Ronsard (1524–1585), "De l'Election de son sepulchre" ("On the Choice of His Tomb").

[3]One of the seven warriors sent from Argos to attack Thebes. Zeus struck him down with lightning for his boastful defiance.

[4]The siren's song to Odysseus in Homer's *Odyssey* (Book XII): "For we know all that was suffered in Troy."

[5]The faithful wife of Odysseus to whom he returned at the end of his voyage.

[6]Gustave Flaubert (1821–1880), the French novelist and supreme stylist, whom Pound admired for his emphasis on *le mot juste*—the precise word.

[7]The goddess of Aeaea by whom Odysseus and his crew were enchanted for a year in *The Odyssey*.

[8]"The thirtieth year of his age," adapted from the first line of *The Testament* by François Villon (1431–1463?).

II

The age demanded an image
Of its accelerated grimace,
Something for the modern stage,
Not, at any rate, an Attic grace;[9]

Not, not certainly, the obscure reveries   25
Of the inward gaze;
Better mendacities
Than the classics in paraphrase!

The "age demanded" chiefly a mould in plaster,
Made with no loss of time,   30
A prose kinema, not, not assuredly, alabaster
Or the "sculpture" of rhyme.

III

The tea-rose tea-gown, etc.
Supplants the mousseline of Cos,[10]
The pianola "replaces"   35
Sappho's barbitos.[11]

Christ follows Dionysus,[12]
Phallic and ambrosial
Made way for macerations;
Caliban casts out Ariel.[13]   40

All things are a flowing,
Sage Heracleitus[14] says;
But a tawdry cheapness
Shall outlast our days.

Even the Christian beauty   45
Defects—after Samothrace;[15]
We see τὸ καλόν [16]
Decreed in the market place.

[9]A pure style associated with ancient Attica.
[10]Muslin from the Greek island of Cos.
[11]An early form of lyre used by the seventh-century B.C. Greek woman poet Sappho.
[12]Greek god of fertility, wine, and poetic inspiration, associated with orgiastic rites performed in his honor.
[13]In Shakespeare's The Tempest, Caliban is presented as "a savage and deformed Slave," and Ariel is presented as "an airy Spirit."

[14]Greek philosopher (540–480 B.C.) who taught that all things are in a constant flux.
[15]Greek island, associated with the rites of Dionysus and the statue of the "Winged Victory."
[16]Greek word for "the beautiful."

Faun's flesh is not to us,
Nor the saint's vision.   50
We have the press for wafer;
Franchise for circumcision.

All men, in law, are equals.
Free of Pisistratus,[17]
We choose a knave or an eunuch   55
To rule over us.

O bright Apollo,[18]
τίν᾽ ἄνδρα, τίν᾽ ἥρωα, τίνα θεόν,[19]
What god, man, or hero
Shall I place a tin wreath upon!   60

IV

These fought in any case,
and some believing,
                        pro domo[20] in any case ...

Some quick to arm,
some for adventure,   65
some from fear of weakness,
some from fear of censure,
some for love of slaughter, an imagination,
learning later ...
some in fear, learning love of slaughter;   70

Died some, pro patria,
                        non "dulce" non "et decor"[21] ...
walked eye-deep in hell
believing in old men's lies, then unbelieving
came home, home to a lie,   75
home to many deceits,
home to old lies and new infamy;
usury age-old and age-thick
and liars in public places.
Daring as never before, wastage as never before.   80

---

[17]Sixth-century B.C. Athenian tyrant who supported the arts.

[18]Greek god of poetry, prophecy, and civic order.

[19]Greek for "What man, what hero, what god," adapted from Pindar's *Olympian Odes*.

[20]"For the home," from Cicero's *De Domo Sua*.

[21]"For one's country, not sweet and not fitting." From Horace's *Odes:* "Dulce et decorum est pro patria mori" ("It is sweet and fitting to die for one's country").

Young blood and high blood,
fair cheeks, and fine bodies;

fortitude as never before

frankness as never before,
disillusions as never told in the old days,   85
hysterias, trench confessions,
laughter out of dead bellies.

V

There died a myriad,
And of the best, among them,
For an old bitch gone in the teeth,   90
For a botched civilization,

Charm, smiling at the good mouth,
Quick eyes gone under earth's lid,

For two gross of broken statues,
For a few thousand battered books.   95

Yeux Glauques[22]

Gladstone[23] was still respected,
When John Ruskin produced
"King's Treasuries"; Swinburne
And Rossetti still abused.[24]

Fœtid Buchanan[25] lifted up his voice   100
When that faun's head of hers
Became a pastime for
Painters and adulterers.

---

[22]French for "grey eyes." Alludes to a painting by the pre-Raphaelite artist Edward Burne-Jones (1833–1898), "King Cophetua and the Beggar-Maid," in the Tate Gallery in London. Elizabeth Siddal, who later married the poet and painter Dante Gabriel Rossetti (1828–1882), was the model for this and other paintings by the pre-Raphaelites.

[23]William Gladstone, British Chancellor of the Exchequer and Liberal Prime Minister during the period 1859–1894.

[24]John Ruskin (1819–1900) was an art critic who defended the pre-Raphaelites, including Dante Gabriel Rossetti and the poet Algernon Swinburne (1827–1909). In a chapter of Sesame and Lilies (1865) entitled "Kings' Treasuries," he calls for the general diffusion of literature and the arts.

[25]Robert Buchanan (1841–1901), a poet and reviewer who attacked the pre-Raphaelite movement in "The Fleshly School of Poetry" (1871).

The Burne-Jones[26] cartons
Have preserved her eyes;   105
Still, at the Tate, they teach
Cophetua to rhapsodize;

Thin like brook-water,
With a vacant gaze.
The English Rubaiyat[27] was still-born   110
In those days.
The thin, clear gaze, the same
Still darts out faun-like from the half-ruin'd face,
Questing and passive. . . .
"Ah, poor Jenny's case"[28] . . .   115

Bewildered that a world
Shows no surprise
At her last maquero's[29]
Adulteries.

Siena mi fe'; Disfecemi Maremma[30]

Among the pickled fœtuses and bottled bones,   120
Engaged in perfecting the catalogue,
I found the last scion of the
Senatorial families of Strasbourg, Monsieur Verog.[31]

For two hours he talked of Gallifet;[32]
Of Dowson; of the Rhymers' Club;[33]   125
Told me how Johnson (Lionel)[34] died
By falling from a high stool in a pub . . .

But showed no trace of alcohol
At the autopsy, privately performed—

---

[26]Sketches for paintings.
[27]Edward Fitzgerald (1809–1883) translated *The Rubaiyat of Omar Khayyam* in 1859.
[28]"Jenny" is a poem about a prostitute by Dante Gabriel Rossetti.
[29]maquero: pimp.
[30]"Siena made me, Maremma undid me," spoken by "La Pia dei' Tolomei," murdered by her husband in the Maremma marshlands, in Dante's *Purgatoria*.
[31]Fictive name for Victor Plarr (1863–1929), French poet who wrote *In the Dorian Mood*

and later librarian of the Royal College of Surgeons.
[32]Marquis de Galliffet (1830–1909), French general who lost the battle of Sedan during the Franco-Prussian war.
[33]Ernest Dowson (1867–1900), English poet and member of the Rhymers' Club, which was founded by William Butler Yeats and others in 1890–91.
[34]Lionel Johnson (1867–1902), a poet and heavy drinker who was also a member of the Rhymers' Club.

Tissue preserved—the pure mind   130
Arose toward Newman[35] as the whiskey warmed.

Dowson found harlots cheaper than hotels;
Headlam for uplift; Image[36] impartially imbued
With raptures for Bacchus, Terpsichore and the Church.[37]
So spoke the author of "The Dorian Mood,"   135

M. Verog, out of step with the decade,
Detached from his contemporaries,
Neglected by the young,
Because of these reveries.

Brennbaum[38]

The sky-like limpid eyes,   140
The circular infant's face,
The stiffness from spats to collar
Never relaxing into grace;

The heavy memories of Horeb, Sinai and the forty years,[39]
Showed only when the daylight fell   145
Level across the face
Of Brennbaum "The Impeccable."

Mr. Nixon[40]

In the cream gilded cabin of his steam yacht
Mr. Nixon advised me kindly, to advance with fewer
Dangers of delay. "Consider   150
        "Carefully the reviewer.
"I was as poor as you are;
"When I began I got, of course,
"Advance on royalties, fifty at first," said Mr. Nixon,

[35]Cardinal John Henry Newman (1801–1890), Catholic theologian and leader of the Oxford Movement. Johnson and Dowson both converted to Catholicism.

[36]Reverend Stewart D. Headlam (1847–1924), forced to resign his curacy for lecturing on theater and dance to workingmen's clubs. He founded the Church and Stage Guild with Selwyn Image (1849–1930).

[37]Bacchus is the Roman name for Dionysus. Terpsichore is the Greek muse of dance. "The Church" alludes to the Roman Catholic Church.

[38]Portrait suggests Max Beerbohm (1872–1956), an essayist and parodist.

[39]The children of Israel wandered in the wilderness for forty years in search of Canaan. Moses drew water from Horeb; he received the Ten Commandments at Sinai.

[40]Pound said Mr. Nixon was "a fictitious name for a real person." He may be referring to the English journalist and novelist Arnold Bennett (1867–1931).

"Follow me, and take a column,   155
"Even if you have to work free.

"Butter reviewers. From fifty to three hundred
"I rose in eighteen months;
"The hardest nut I had to crack
"Was Dr. Dundas.   160

"I never mentioned a man but with the view
"Of selling my own works.
"The tip's a good one, as for literature
"It gives no man a sinecure.

"And no one knows, at sight, a masterpiece.   165
"And give up verse, my boy,
"There's nothing in it."

Likewise a friend of Bloughram's[41] once advised me:
Don't kick against the pricks,
Accept opinion. The "Nineties" tried your game   170
And died, there's nothing in it.

X

Beneath the sagging roof
The stylist[42] has taken shelter,
Unpaid, uncelebrated,
At last from the world's welter   175

Nature receives him;
With a placid and uneducated mistress
He exercises his talents
And the soil meets his distress.

The haven from sophistications and contentions   180
Leaks through its thatch;
He offers succulent cooking;
The door has a creaking latch.

[41]In Robert Browning's "Bishop Bloughram's Apology," the Bishop rationalizes his sacrifice of sacred principle for worldly comfort.

[42]The stylist Pound has in mind may be James Joyce or Ford Maddox Ford.

XI

"Conservatrix of Milésien"[43]
Habits of mind and feeling,   185
Possibly. But in Ealing[44]
With the most bank-clerkly of Englishmen?

No, "Milésian" is an exaggeration.
No instinct has survived in her
Older than those her grandmother   190
Told her would fit her station.

XII

"Daphne with her thighs in bark
Stretches toward me her leafy hands,"[45]—
Subjectively. In the stuffed-satin drawing-room
I await The Lady Valentine's commands,   195

Knowing my coat has never been
Of precisely the fashion
To stimulate, in her,
A durable passion;

Doubtful, somewhat, of the value   200
Of well-gowned approbation
Of literary effort,
But never of The Lady Valentine's vocation:

Poetry, her border of ideas,
The edge, uncertain, but a means of blending   205
With other strata
Where the lower and higher have ending;
A hook to catch the Lady Jane's attention,
A modulation toward the theatre,
Also, in the case of revolution,   210
A possible friend and comforter.

Conduct, on the other hand, the soul
"Which the highest cultures have nourished"

[43]Adapted from Remy de Gourmont's short story "Stratagèmes": "des femmes ... ces conservatrices des traditions milésiennes" ("women ... these conservers of Milesian traditions").
[44]A suburb of London.

[45]The lines are translated from Théophile Gautier's version of Ovid's story in *Emaux et Camées*). In Ovid's story, Daphne is metamorphosed into a tree in order to escape the embrace of Apollo.

To Fleet St. where
Dr. Johnson[46] flourished;   215

Beside this thoroughfare
The sale of half-hose has
Long since superseded the cultivation
Of Pierian roses.[47]

Envoi (1919)[48]

Go, dumb-born book,   220
Tell her that sang me once that song of Lawes:[49]
Hadst thou but song
As thou hast subjects known,
Then were there cause in thee that should condone
Even my faults that heavy upon me lie,   225
And build her glories their longevity.

Tell her that sheds
Such treasure in the air,
Recking naught else but that her graces give
Life to the moment,   230
I would bid them live
As roses might, in magic amber laid,
Red overwrought with orange and all made
One substance and one colour
Braving time.   235

Tell her that goes
With song upon her lips
But sings not out the song, nor knows
The maker of it, some other mouth,
May be as fair as hers,   240
Might, in new ages, gain her worshippers,
When our two dusts with Waller's shall be laid,
Siftings on siftings in oblivion,
Till change hath broken down
All things save Beauty alone.   245

1920

---

[46]Samuel Johnson (1709–1784), eighteenth-century British journalist, essayist, and critic.
[47]Pieria is the legendary birthplace of the Muses.
[48]An envoi is a writer's parting word. The poem is modeled on Edmund Waller's (1606–1687) "Go, Lovely Rose!"

[49]Henry Lawes (1596–1662), English composer and musician who set Waller's "Go, Lovely Rose!" to music.

from **The Cantos**

I[1]

[And then went down to the ship]

And then went down to the ship,
Set keel to breakers, forth on the godly sea, and
We set up mast and sail on that swart ship,
Bore sheep aboard her, and our bodies also
Heavy with weeping, and winds from sternward   5
Bore us out onward with bellying canvas,
Circe's[2] this craft, the trim-coifed goddess.
Then sat we amidships, wind jamming the tiller,
Thus with stretched sail, we went over sea till day's end.
Sun to his slumber, shadows o'er all the ocean,   10
Came we then to the bounds of deepest water,
To the Kimmerian lands,[3] and peopled cities
Covered with close-webbed mist, unpierced ever
With glitter of sun-rays
Nor with stars stretched, nor looking back from heaven   15
Swartest night stretched over wretched men there.
The ocean flowing backward, came we then to the place
Aforesaid by Circe.
Here did they rites, Perimedes and Eurylochus,[4]
And drawing sword from my hip   20
I dug the ell-square pitkin;
Poured we libations unto each the dead,
First mead and then sweet wine, water mixed with white flour.
Then prayed I many a prayer to the sickly death's-heads;
As set in Ithaca,[5] sterile bulls of the best   25
For sacrifice, heaping the pyre with goods,
A sheep to Tiresias only, black and a bell-sheep.
Dark blood flowed in the fosse,
Souls out of Erebus,[6] cadaverous dead, of brides
Of youths and of the old who had borne much;   30
Souls stained with recent tears, girls tender,
Men many, mauled with bronze lance heads,
Battle spoil, bearing yet dreory arms,
These many crowded about me; with shouting,
Pallor upon me, cried to my men for more beasts;   35

[1]The first canto is an adaptation from Book XI of Homer's *The Odyssey*, which recounts Odysseus' voyage to Hades, the realm of the dead.
[2]Circe, the sorceress of Aeaea who delays Odysseus and his crew for a year. When he requests permission to return home, she directs him to seek prophecy for his journey from Tiresias in the underworld.
[3]Ancient land located at the end of the earth.
[4]Two of Odysseus' companions.
[5]The island home of Odysseus, off the coast of Greece.
[6]Land of the dead.

Slaughtered the herds, sheep slain of bronze;
Poured ointment, cried to the gods,
To Pluto the strong, and praised Proserpine;[7]
Unsheathed the narrow sword,
I sat to keep off the impetuous impotent dead,   40
Till I should hear Tiresias.
But first Elpenor came, our friend Elpenor,[8]
Unburied, cast on the wide earth,
Limbs that we left in the house of Circe,
Unwept, unwrapped in sepulchre, since toils urged other.   45
Pitiful spirit. And I cried in hurried speech:
"Elpenor, how art thou come to this dark coast?
"Cam'st thou afoot, outstripping seamen?"
      And he in heavy speech:
"Ill fate and abundant wine. I slept in Circe's ingle.   50
"Going down the long ladder unguarded,
"I fell against the buttress,
"Shattered the nape-nerve, the soul sought Avernus.[9]
"But thou, O King, I bid remember me, unwept, unburied,
"Heap up mine arms, be tomb by sea-bord, and inscribed: 55
"*A man of no fortune, and with a name to come.*
"And set my oar up, that I swung mid fellows."

And Anticlea[10] came, whom I beat off, and then Tiresias Theban,
Holding his golden wand, knew me, and spoke first:
"A second time? why? man of ill star,   60
"Facing the sunless dead and this joyless region?
"Stand from the fosse, leave me my bloody bever
"For soothsay."
      And I stepped back,
And he strong with the blood, said then: "Odysseus   65
"Shalt return through spiteful Neptune,[11] over dark seas,
"Lose all companions." And then Anticlea came.
Lie quiet Divus. I mean, that is Andreas Divus,[12]
In officina Wecheli,[13] 1538, out of Homer.
And he sailed, by Sirens and thence outward and away   70
And unto Circe.
      Venerandam,[14]

[7]Goddess of fertility abducted by Pluto, the god of the underworld.
[8]Companion of Odysseus who fell to his death from Circe's roof when he awoke from a drunken stupor to hear his friends departing. He was left unburied.
[9]Lake near Naples, the legendary entrance to Hades.
[10]Odysseus' mother, who died in his absence from Ithaca.
[11]God of the sea, who would hinder Odysseus' return home.
[12]Pound acknowledges using the 1538 Latin translation of Homer by Andrea Divus.
[13]"In the printshop of Wechelus," printed on the title page of Divus's *Odyssey*.
[14]"Venerable," from the second Homeric Hymn to Aphrodite as translated by Georgius Dartona Cretensis (the "Cretan") from Greek into Renaissance Latin.

In the Cretan's phrase, with the golden crown, Aphrodite,[15]
Cypri munimenta sortita est,[16] mirthful, orichalchi,[17] with golden
Girdles and breast bands, thou with dark eyelids   75
Bearing the golden bough of Argicida.[18] So that:

                                                                       1917

XIII[1]

[Kung walked]

Kung walked
          by the dynastic temple
and into the cedar grove,
          and then out by the lower river,
And with him Khieu, Tchi   5
          and Tian[2] the low speaking
And "we are unknown," said Kung,
"You will take up charioteering?
          Then you will become known,
"Or perhaps I should take up charioteering, or archery?   10
"Or the practice of public speaking?"
And Tseu-lou said, "I would put the defences in order,"
And Khieu said, "If I were lord of a province
I would put it in better order than this is."
And Tchi said, "I would prefer a small mountain temple,   15
"With order in the observances,
          with a suitable performance of the ritual,"
And Tian said, with his hand on the strings of his lute
The low sounds continuing
          after his hand left the strings,   20
And the sound went up like smoke, under the leaves,
And he looked after the sound:
          "The old swimming hole,
"And the boys flopping off the planks,
"Or sitting in the underbrush playing mandolins."   25
          And Kung smiled upon all of them equally.

---

[15]Aphrodite, the goddess of love and beauty, a recurrent figure in *The Cantos*.

[16]"The citadels of Cyprus were her appointed realm."

[17]Orichalchi—of copper—refers to Aphrodite's earrings.

[18]The golden bough enables Aeneas to gain entrance to the underworld. Here the bough is also associated with Aphrodite, as the goddess of love and slayer of the Greeks ("Argicida").

[1]The first of the "Confucian Cantos," which draws on the teachings of the Chinese philosopher Confucius, or Kung (551–479 B.C.), in three classic texts that Pound translates as *The Great Digest, The Unwobbling Pivot*, and *The Analects*. Pound considered this Canto the "announcement of the backbone moral of the *Cantos*."

[2]Disciples of Confucius.

And Thseng-sie desired to know:
  "Which had answered correctly?"
And Kung said, "They have all answered correctly,
"That is to say, each in his nature."   30
And Kung raised his cane against Yuan Jang,
   Yuan Jang being his elder,
For Yuan Jang sat by the roadside pretending to
    be receiving wisdom.
And Kung said   35
   "You old fool, come out of it,
Get up and do something useful."
   And Kung said
"Respect a child's faculties
"From the moment it inhales the clear air,   40
"But a man of fifty who knows nothing
   Is worthy of no respect."
And "When the prince has gathered about him
"All the savants and artists, his riches will be fully employed."
And Kung said, and wrote on the bo leaves: 45
   If a man have not order within him
He can not spread order about him;
And if a man have not order within him
His family will not act with due order;
   And if the prince have not order within him 50
He can not put order in his dominions.
And Kung gave the words "order"
and "brotherly deference"
And said nothing of the "life after death."
And he said   55
   "Anyone can run to excesses,
It is easy to shoot past the mark,
It is hard to stand firm in the middle."
And they said: If a man commit murder
  Should his father protect him, and hide him? 60
And Kung said:
   He should hide him.

And Kung gave his daughter to Kong-Tch'ang[3]
   Although Kong-Tch'ang was in prison.
And he gave his niece to Nan-Young[4]   65
   although Nan-Young was out of office.
And Kung said "Wang[5] ruled with moderation,
  In his day the State was well kept,

---

[3]Confucius' son-in-law.
[4]Disciple of Confucius.

[5]Wu Wang ruled as the first emperor of the
 Chou dynasty, 1122–1115 B.C.

And even I can remember
A day when the historians left blanks in their writings,   70
I mean for things they didn't know,
But that time seems to be passing."
And Kung said, "Without character you will
        be unable to play on that instrument
Or to execute the music fit for the Odes.   75
The blossoms of the apricot
        blow from the east to the west,
And I have tried to keep them from falling."

1925

XLV

[With usura hath no man a house of good stone]

With Usura[1]

With usura hath no man a house of good stone
each block cut smooth and well fitting
that design might cover their face,
with usura   5
hath no man a painted paradise on his church wall
harpes et luz[2]
or where virgin receiveth message
and halo projects from incision,
with usura   10
seeth no man Gonzaga[3] his heirs and his concubines
no picture is made to endure nor to live with
but it is made to sell and sell quickly
with usura, sin against nature,
is thy bread ever more of stale rags   15
is thy bread dry as paper,
with no mountain wheat, no strong flour
with usura the line grows thick
with usura is no clear demarcation
and no man can find site for his dwelling.   20
Stonecutter is kept from his stone
weaver is kept from his loom

---

[1]Latin for usury. The Catholic Church outlawed the practice of usury up to the time of the Reformation; John Calvin overturned the ban.

[2]Latin for harps and lutes. Pound paraphrases lines from François Villon's "Ballade pour Prier Notre Dame." In *ABC of Reading* he described Villon as the "first voice of man broken by bad economics," representing the "end of the mediaeval dream."

[3]Pound refers to the painting *Gonzaga, His Heirs and His Concubines*, by Andrea Mantegna (1431–1506).

WITH USURA
  wool comes not to market
  sheep bringeth no gain with usura   25
  Usura is a murrain,[4] usura
  blunteth the needle in the maid's hand
  and stoppeth the spinner's cunning. Pietro Lombardo[5]
  came not by usura
  Duccio[6] came not by usura   30
  nor Pier della Francesca; Zuan Bellin'[7] not by usura
  nor was 'La Calunnia'[8] painted.
  Came not by usura Angelico; came not Ambrogio Praedis,[9]
  Came no church of cut stone signed: *Adamo me fecit.*[10]
  Not by usura St Trophime   35
  Not by usura Saint Hilaire,[11]
  Usura rusteth the chisel
  It rusteth the craft and the craftsman
  It gnaweth the thread in the loom
  None learneth to weave gold in her pattern;   40
  Azure hath a canker by usura; cramoisi[12] is unbroidered
  Emerald findeth no Memling[13]
  Usura slayeth the child in the womb
  It stayeth the young man's courting
  It hath brought palsey to bed, lyeth   45
  between the young bride and her bridegroom
                 CONTRA NATURAM[14]
  They have brought whores for Eleusis[15]
  Corpses are set to banquet
  at behest of usura.   50

N.B. Usury: A charge for the use of purchasing power, levied without regard to production; often without regard to the possibilities of production. (Hence the failure of the Medici bank.)[16]

                                      1936

---

[4]Plague.

[5]Pietro Lombardo (1435–1515), Italian architect and sculptor.

[6]Agostino di Duccio (1418?–1481), Italian sculptor.

[7]Pier della Francesca (1420–1492), Italian painter; Giovanni Bellini (1430–1516), Venetian painter.

[8]"La Calunnia" ("Calumny") is a painting by Sandro Botticelli (1444–1510).

[9]Fra Angelico (1387–1455), Florentine painter; Ambrogio Praedis (1455?–1508?), Milanese painter.

[10]Latin for "Adam made me."

[11]St. Trophime is a Church in Arles, France; Saint Hilaire is in Poitiers, France.

[12]French for crimson cloth.

[13]Hans Memling (1430?–1495?), painter of the Flemish school.

[14]Latin for "against nature," a phrase Aristotle uses to describe usury in *Politics*.

[15]Eleusis is the town in ancient Greece where the Eleusinian mysteries were celebrated.

[16]In the year of his death, Pound revised his original formulation on usury to say: "I was out of focus, taking a symptom for a cause. The cause is AVARICE."

LXXXI

[Yet/Ere the season died a-cold]

libretto   Yet
        Ere the season died a-cold
        Borne upon a zephyr's[1] shoulder
  I rose through the aureate sky
                    Lawes and Jenkyns[2] guard thy rest   5
                    Dolmetsch[3] ever be thy guest,
  Has he tempered the viol's wood
  To enforce both the grave and the acute?
  Has he curved us the bowl of the lute?
                    Lawes and Jenkyns guard thy rest   10
                    Dolmetsch ever be thy guest
  Hast 'ou fashioned so airy a mood
    To draw up leaf from the root?
  Hast 'ou found a cloud so light
    As seemed neither mist nor shade?   15

          Then resolve me, tell me aright
          If Waller sang or Dowland[4] played.

      Your eyen two wol sleye me sodenly
      I may the beauté of hem nat susteyne[5]

  And for 180 years almost nothing.   20
  Ed ascoltando al leggier mormorio[6]
    there came new subtlety of eyes into my tent,
  whether of spirit or hypostasis,
    but what the blindfold hides
  or at carneval   25

        nor any pair showed anger
    Saw but the eyes and stance between the eyes,
  colour, diastasis,
    careless or unaware it had not the
    whole tent's room   30
  nor was place for the full Εἰδὼσ[7]
  interpass, penetrate
    casting but shade beyond the other lights

[1]The west wind.
[2]Henry Lawes (1596–1662), English composer; John Jenkins (1592–1678), English composer and musician to Charles I and Charles II.
[3]Arnold Dolmetsch (1858–1940), French musician and instrument maker.
[4]Edmund Waller (1606–1687), English poet; John Dowland (1563–1626), English composer and lute player.
[5]Lines from the poem "Merciles Beaute," attributed to Geoffrey Chaucer.
[6]Italian for "and listening to the light murmur."
[7]Greek for "knowing."

sky's clear
　　night's sea　　　　　　　　　　　　　　　　　　35
green of the mountain pool
shone from the unmasked eyes in half-mask's space.
What thou lovest well remains,
　　　　　　　　　　the rest is dross
What thou lov'st well shall not be reft from thee　　　40
What thou lov'st well is thy true heritage
Whose world, or mine or theirs
　　　　　　　　　or is it of none?
First came the seen, then thus the palpable
　　Elysium,[8] though it were in the halls of hell,　　45
What thou lovest well is thy true heritage
What thou lov'st well shall not be reft from thee

The ant's a centaur in his dragon world.
Pull down thy vanity, it is not man
Made courage, or made order, or made grace,　　　50
　　Pull down thy vanity, I say pull down.
Learn of the green world what can be thy place
In scaled invention or true artistry,
Pull down thy vanity,
　　　　Paquin[9] pull down!　　　　　　　　　　55
The green casque has outdone your elegance.

"Master thyself, then others shall thee beare"[10]
　　Pull down thy vanity
Thou art a beaten dog beneath the hail,
A swollen magpie in a fitful sun,　　　　　　　　60
Half black half white
Nor knowst' ou wing from tail
Pull down thy vanity
　　　　How mean thy hates
Fostered in falsity,　　　　　　　　　　　　　65
　　　　Pull down thy vanity,
Rathe to destroy, niggard in charity,
Pull down thy vanity,
　　　　I say pull down.

But to have done instead of not doing　　　　　70
　　　　this is not vanity
To have, with decency, knocked
That a Blunt[11] should open

---

[8]The Elysian fields of Greek mythology.
[9]A Parisian dressmaker.
[10]An adaptation from Chaucer's "Ballade of Good Counsel."
[11]Wilfred Scawen Blunt (1840–1922), English poet and critic of imperialism.

To have gathered from the air a live tradition
or from a fine old eye the unconquered flame   75
This is not vanity.
    Here error is all in the not done,
all in the diffidence that faltered . . .

                                 1948

CXX

[I have tried to write Paradise]

I have tried to write Paradise

Do not move
    Let the wind speak
        that is paradise.

Let the Gods forgive what I   5
    have made
Let those I love try to forgive
    what I have made.

                                 1969

■   ■

Amy Lowell
1874–1925

Amy Lowell was born in Brookline, Massachusetts, to a family of poets that included James Russell Lowell and, later, Robert Lowell. She grew up on her family estate, Sevenels (named after the seven Lowells—mother, father, and five children), which she ultimately inherited and whose lavish gardens figure prominently in her poetry. A girl of the upper classes was generally not permitted by her family to go off to the university as her brothers did, and so Lowell's education consisted primarily of tutors, access to her father's vast library, and travel in Europe. As she later wrote to the poet Archibald MacLeish in response to his inquiry, her formal education "really did not amount to a hill of beans." She evinced an interest in literature when very young, and her first writing was published when she was eleven years old.

While the diaries she kept as an adolescent suggest an early bisexuality, as she matured she became less interested in men and looked for love and companionship with other women. Her fascination with the theater led to her involvement for a time with the musical starlet Lina Abarbanell. It also led her to her first muse, the tragedian Eleonora Duse, whom she saw on stage for the first time in 1902. Duse's talent and beauty inspired Lowell, already twenty-eight years old, to revive her youthful interest in writing. Lowell later recalled the momentous effect of watching Duse perform: "It loosed a bolt in my brain and I knew where my true function lay." Her first poem since her juvenilia was addressed to the actress and marked the beginning of Lowell's career as a writer, although she did not publish her first book, *A Dome of Many-Coloured Glass*, until 1912, ten years later.

A Dome of Many-Coloured Glass was influenced by nineteenth-century romanticism, and its title comes from a phrase in *Adonais*, Shelley's elegiac tribute to Keats, whose poetry many of the poems echo. Other poems in the volume are more original and show the promise of her later poetry; they are personal poems with brilliant flashes of color, verse about her childhood, her family estate, her quest for love. In the following year, 1913, Lowell discovered several imagist poems by H.D. (Hilda Doolittle) in *Poetry* magazine; these made her recognize that "I, too, am an imagiste." Indeed, before she knew the term "imagism," she had developed her appreciation of Japanese haiku and tanka, her interest in the Orient having been stimulated by her brother Percival, who had lived in Asia. She immediately began to explore the school of imagism of which, she discovered, Ezra Pound was the titular head; in 1913 she traveled to England in order to meet him.

The conflict between them could have been predicted. Lowell was by 1913 a 250-pound woman of vast wealth, a sense of entitlement, and an air of knowing her own mind. Pound found her overbearing and perhaps threatening. Lowell, for her part, would undoubtedly have agreed with Gertrude Stein's description of Pound as a village explainer—which is "fine if you're a village, and if not, not." Despite Pound's hostility, Lowell published three anthologies in 1915, 1916, and 1917, titled *Some Imagist Poets*, which included along with her own work that of H.D., John Gould Fletcher, D. H. Lawrence, and others. When the first volume came out, imagism was still so revolutionary and controversial in the United States that Lowell was denounced by the Poetry Society of America for championing imagist writers. Pound threatened to sue her for stealing his thunder, and Lowell encouraged him, saying that a lawsuit would be "a good advertisement" for *Some Imagist Poets*. However, since neither a title nor a poetic school can be copyrighted, Pound dropped the idea and disassociated himself from American imagism (which he scoffingly called "Amygism"). Lowell adopted the pugilistic posture that she was to use in many of her literary controversies throughout her career.

In her own writing, imagism soon became only one of a panoply of approaches to poetry. She also explored "polyphonic prose," writing that is prose in its typography and poetry in its language, and dense use of imagery. In *Legends* (1921) she adapted folk myths from aboriginal North America, China, Peru, and the Yucatan, as well as Europe. She was also influenced by a broad range of authors, including, as she suggests in "The Sisters," her "spiritual relations," Sappho, Elizabeth Barrett Browning, and Emily Dickinson.

In the thirteen years before she died, Lowell managed to bring out a book of poems every year or two (*East Wind* and *Ballads for Sale* were published in the two years after her death) and several volumes of prose, including a two-volume biography of John Keats (1925).

Although Lowell won the Pulitzer Prize posthumously in 1926 for her volume of poems *What's O'Clock*, the attacks on her reputation became virulent soon after her death. It is difficult to say if her detractors were motivated by homophobia or by a sincere lack of excitement about her poetry. In a particularly scurrilous 1926 book by Clement Wood, *Amy Lowell*, the author was determined to diminish Lowell's reputation at least partly because she was a lesbian. He argued that her poetry did not "word a common cry of many hearts," and he concluded that Lowell may qualify "as an impassioned singer of her own desires; and she may well be laureate also of as many as stand beside her," but nonlesbian readers would find nothing in her verse.

Those who refused to recognize that Lowell was a lesbian but saw her only as an unattractive, overweight woman and an "old maid" were equally unfair in their prejudiced assessments. An article titled "Amy Lowell as a Poet," which appeared in the *Saturday Review of Literature* in 1927, complained that her poetry was bad because she was "cut off from the prime biological experiences of life by her tragic physical predicament." Therefore, the critic goes on to say, erroneously, her poems are decorative rather than expressive of elemental passion "as always happens when the sources of inspiration are literary and secondary rather than primarily the expression of emotional experience." Though some of Lowell's work suffers from prolixity and a tendency to exaggerate, her best work is free from such faults. It is concise, vivid, and honest.

Lillian Faderman
California State University, Fresno

PRIMARY WORKS

John Keats, 1925; *Poetry and Poets: Essays by Amy Lowell*, 1930; *The Complete Poetical Works of Amy Lowell*, 1955.

A Lady

You are beautiful and faded
Like an old opera tune
Played upon a harpsichord;
Or like the sun-flooded silks
Of an eighteenth-century boudoir.   5
In your eyes
Smoulder the fallen roses of out-lived minutes,
And the perfume of your soul
Is vague and suffusing,
With the pungence of sealed spice-jars.   10
Your half-tones delight me,
And I grow mad with gazing
At your blent colours.

My vigour is a new-minted penny,
Which I cast at your feet.   15
Gather it up from the dust,
That its sparkle may amuse you.

1914

Patterns

I walk down the garden paths,
And all the daffodils
Are blowing, and the bright blue squills.
I walk down the patterned garden-paths
In my stiff, brocaded gown.   5
With my powdered hair and jewelled fan,
I too am a rare
Pattern. As I wander down
The garden paths.

My dress is richly figured,   10
And the train
Makes a pink and silver stain
On the gravel, and the thrift
Of the borders.
Just a plate of current fashion   15
Tripping by in high-heeled, ribboned shoes.
Not a softness anywhere about me,
Only whalebone and brocade.
And I sink on a seat in the shade
Of a lime tree. For my passion   20
Wars against the stiff brocade.
The daffodils and squills
Flutter in the breeze
As they please.
And I weep;   25
For the lime-tree is in blossom
And one small flower has dropped upon my bosom.

And the plashing of waterdrops
In the marble fountain
Comes down the garden-paths.   30
The dripping never stops.
Underneath my stiffened gown
Is the softness of a woman bathing in a marble basin,
A basin in the midst of hedges grown
So thick, she cannot see her lover hiding,   35
But she guesses he is near,
And the sliding of the water
Seems the stroking of a dear
Hand upon her.
What is Summer in a fine brocaded gown!   40
I should like to see it lying in a heap upon the ground.
All the pink and silver crumpled up on the ground.

I would be the pink and silver as I ran along the paths,
And he would stumble after,
Bewildered by my laughter.   45
I should see the sun flashing from his sword-hilt and buckles on his
    shoes.
I would choose
To lead him in a maze along the patterned paths,
A bright and laughing maze for my heavy-booted lover.   50
Till he caught me in the shade,
And the buttons of his waistcoat bruised my body as he clasped me,
Aching, melting, unafraid.
With the shadows of the leaves and the sundrops,
And the plopping of the waterdrops,   55
All about us in the open afternoon—
I am very like to swoon
With the weight of this brocade,
For the sun sifts through the shade.
Underneath the fallen blossom   60
In my bosom,
Is a letter I have hid.
It was brought to me this morning by a rider from the Duke.
"Madam, we regret to inform you that Lord Hartwell
Died in action Thursday se'nnight."   65
As I read it in the white, morning sunlight,
The letters squirmed like snakes.
"Any answer, Madam," said my footman.
"No," I told him.
"See that the messenger takes some refreshment.   70
No, no answer."
And I walked into the garden,
Up and down the patterned paths,
In my stiff, correct brocade.
The blue and yellow flowers stood up proudly in the sun,   75
Each one.
I stood upright too,
Held rigid to the pattern
By the stiffness of my gown.
Up and down I walked.   80
Up and down.

In a month he would have been my husband.
In a month, here, underneath this lime,
We would have broken the pattern;
He for me, and I for him,   85
He as Colonel, I as Lady,
On this shady seat.

He had a whim
That sunlight carried blessing.
And I answered, "It shall be as you have said."   90
Now he is dead.
In Summer and in Winter I shall walk
Up and down
The patterned garden-paths
In my stiff, brocaded gown.   95
The squills and daffodils
Will give place to pillared roses, and to asters, and to snow.
I shall go
Up and down,
In my gown.   100
Gorgeously arrayed,
Boned and stayed.
And the softness of my body will be guarded from embrace
By each button, hook, and lace.
For the man who should loose me is dead,   105
Fighting with the Duke in Flanders,
In a pattern called a war.
Christ! What are patterns for?

                                                            1916

The Letter

Little cramped words scrawling all over the paper
Like draggled fly's legs,
What can you tell of the flaring moon
Through the oak leaves?
Or of my uncurtained window and the bare floor   5
Spattered with moonlight?
Your silly quirks and twists have nothing in them
Of blossoming hawthorns,
And this paper is dull, crisp, smooth, virgin of loveliness
Beneath my hand.   10

I am tired, Beloved, of chafing my heart against
The want of you;
Of squeezing it into little inkdrops,
And posting it.
And I scald alone, here, under the fire   15
Of the great moon.

                                                            1919

Summer Rain

All night our room was outer-walled with rain.
Drops fell and flattened on the tin roof,
And rang like little disks of metal.
Ping!—Ping!—and there was not a pinpoint of silence between
    them.   5
The rain rattled and clashed,
And the slats of the shutters danced and glittered.
But to me the darkness was red-gold and crocus-coloured
With your brightness,
And the words you whispered to me   10
Sprang up and flamed—orange torches against the rain.
Torches against the wall of cool, silver rain!

                                                        1919

Venus Transiens[1]

Tell me,
Was Venus more beautiful
Than you are,
When she topped
The crinkled waves,   5
Drifting shoreward
On her plaited shell?
Was Botticelli's vision[2]
Fairer than mine;
And were the painted rosebuds   10
He tossed his lady,
Of better worth
Than the words I blow about you
To cover your too great loveliness
As with a gauze   15
Of misted silver?

For me,
You stand poised
In the blue and buoyant air,
Cinctured by bright winds,   20
Treading the sunlight.

---

[1]Venus is the Roman goddess of love and beauty. The Latin phrase means Venus passing over.

[2]In the painting of Botticelli (1444–1510) called "The Birth of Venus" (c. 1485), the goddess stands on a large scallop shell; small roses are blown about her by the wind.

And the waves which precede you
Ripple and stir
The sands at my feet.

1919

Madonna of the Evening Flowers

All day long I have been working,
Now I am tired.
I call: "Where are you?"
But there is only the oak-tree rustling in the wind.
The house is very quiet,   5
The sun shines in on your books,
On your scissors and thimble just put down,
But you are not there.
Suddenly I am lonely:
Where are you?   10
I go about searching.

Then I see you,
Standing under a spire of pale blue larkspur,
With a basket of roses on your arm.
You are cool, like silver,   15
And you smile.
I think the Canterbury bells[1] are playing little tunes.

You tell me that the peonies need spraying,
That the columbines have overrun all bounds,

That the pyrus japonica should be cut back and rounded.   20
You tell me these things.
But I look at you, heart of silver,
White heart-flame of polished silver,
Burning beneath the blue steeples of the larkspur,
And I long to kneel instantly at your feet,   25
While all about us peal the loud, sweet Te Deums[2] of the
    Canterbury bells.

1919

---

[1]Canterbury bells are cultivated plants with large, bell-like flowers. The poet may also be referring to the bells in Canterbury Cathedral in England.

[2]A Latin hymn beginning "*Te Deum laudamus,*" we praise thee, Lord.

Opal

You are ice and fire,
The touch of you burns my hands like snow.
You are cold and flame.
You are the crimson of amaryllis,
The silver of moon-touched magnolias.   5
When I am with you,
My heart is a frozen pond
Gleaming with agitated torches.

                                                        1919

Wakefulness

Jolt of market-carts;
Steady drip of horses' hoofs on hard pavement;
A black sky lacquered over with blueness,
And the lights of Battersea Bridge
Pricking pale in the dawn.   5
The beautiful hours are passing
And still you sleep!
Tired heart of my joy,
Incurved upon your dreams,
Will the day come before you have opened to me?   10

                                                        1919

Grotesque

Why do the lilies goggle their tongues at me
When I pluck them;
And writhe, and twist,
And strangle themselves against my fingers,
So that I can hardly weave the garland   5
For your hair?
Why do they shriek your name
And spit at me
When I would cluster them?
Must I kill them   10
To make them lie still,
And send you a wreath of lolling corpses
To turn putrid and soft
On your forehead
While you dance?   15

                                                        1919

The Sisters

Taking us by and large, we're a queer lot
We women who write poetry. And when you think
How few of us there've been, it's queerer still.
I wonder what it is that makes us do it,
Singles us out to scribble down, man-wise,   5
The fragments of ourselves. Why are we
Already mother-creatures, double-bearing,
With matrices in body and in brain?
I rather think that there is just the reason
We are so sparse a kind of human being;   10
The strength of forty thousand Atlases
Is needed for our every-day concerns.
There's Sapho, now I wonder what was Sapho.
I know a single slender thing about her:
That, loving, she was like a burning birch tree   15
All tall and glittering fire, and that she wrote
Like the same fire caught up to Heaven and held there,
A frozen blaze before it broke and fell.
Ah, me! I wish I could have talked to Sapho,
Surprised her reticences by flinging mine   20
Into the wind. This tossing off of garments
Which cloud the soul is none too easy doing
With us to-day. But still I think with Sapho
One might accomplish it, were she in the mood
To bare her loveliness of words and tell   25
The reasons, as she possibly conceived them,
Of why they are so lovely. Just to know
How she came at them, just to watch
The crisp sea sunshine playing on her hair,
And listen, thinking all the while 'twas she   30
Who spoke and that we two were sisters
Of a strange, isolated little family.
And she is Sapho—Sapho—not Miss or Mrs.,
A leaping fire we call so for convenience;
But Mrs. Browning—who would ever think   35
Of such presumption as to call her "Ba."
Which draws the perfect line between sea-cliffs
And a close-shuttered room in Wimpole Street.
Sapho could fly her impulses like bright
Balloons tip-tilting to a morning air   40
And write about it. Mrs. Browning's heart
Was squeezed in stiff conventions. So she lay
Stretched out upon a sofa, reading Greek

And speculating, as I must suppose,
In just this way on Sapho; all the need,   45
The huge, imperious need of loving, crushed
Within the body she believed so sick.
And it was sick, poor lady, because words
Are merely simulacra after deeds
Have wrought a pattern; when they take the place   50
Of actions they breed a poisonous miasma
Which, though it leave the brain, eats up the body.
So Mrs. Browning, aloof and delicate,
Lay still upon her sofa, all her strength
Going to uphold her over-topping brain.   55
It seems miraculous, but she escaped
To freedom and another motherhood
Than that of poems. She was a very woman
And needed both.
                          If I had gone to call,   60
Would Wimpole Street have been the kindlier place,
Or Casa Guidi, in which to have met her?
I am a little doubtful of that meeting,
For Queen Victoria was very young and strong
And all-pervading in her apogee   65
At just that time. If we had stuck to poetry,
Sternly refusing to be drawn off by mesmerism
Or Roman revolutions, it might have done.
For, after all, she is another sister,
But always, I rather think, an older sister   70
And not herself so curious a technician
As to admit newfangled modes of writing—
"Except, of course, in Robert, and that is neither
Here nor there for Robert is a genius."
I do not like the turn this dream is taking,   75
Since I am very fond of Mrs. Browning
And very much indeed should like to hear her
Graciously asking me to call her "Ba."
But then the Devil of Verisimilitude
Creeps in and forces me to know she wouldn't.   80
Convention again, and how it chafes my nerves,
For we are such a little family
Of singing sisters, and as if I didn't know
What those years felt like tied down to the sofa.
Confounded Victoria, and the slimy inhibitions   85
She loosed on all us Anglo-Saxon creatures!
Suppose there hadn't been a Robert Browning,
No "Sonnets from the Portuguese" would have been written.
They are the first of all her poems to be,

One might say, fertilized. For, after all,   90
A poet is flesh and blood as well as brain
And Mrs. Browning, as I said before,
Was very, very woman. Well, there are two
Of us, and vastly unlike that's for certain.
Unlike at least until we tear the veils   95
Away which commonly gird souls. I scarcely think
Mrs. Browning would have approved the process
In spite of what had surely been relief;
For speaking souls must always want to speak
Even when bat-eyed, narrow-minded Queens   100
Set prudishness to keep the keys of impulse.
Then do the frowning Gods invent new banes
And make the need of sofas. But Sapho was dead
And I, and others, not yet peeped above
The edge of possibility. So that's an end   105
To speculating over tea-time talks
Beyond the movement of pentameters
With Mrs. Browning.

           But I go dreaming on,
In love with these my spiritual relations.   110
I rather think I see myself walk up
A flight of wooden steps and ring a bell
And send a card in to Miss Dickinson.
Yet that's a very silly way to do.
I should have taken the dream twist-ends about   115
And climbed over the fence and found her deep
Engrossed in the doing of a humming bird
Among nasturtiums. Not having expected strangers,
She might forget to think me one, and holding up
A finger say quite casually: "Take care.   120
Don't frighten him, he's only just begun."
"Now this," I well believe I should have thought,
"Is even better than Sapho. With Emily
You're really here, or never anywhere at all
In range of mind." Wherefore, having begun   125
In the strict centre, we could slowly progress
To various circumferences, as we pleased.
We could, but should we? That would quite depend
On Emily. I think she'd be exacting,
Without intention possibly, and ask   130
A thousand tight-rope tricks of understanding.
But, bless you, I would somersault all day
If by so doing I might stay with her.
I hardly think that we should mention souls

Although they might just round the corner from us   135
In some half-quizzical, half-wistful metaphor.
I'm very sure that I should never seek
To turn her parables to stated fact.
Sapho would speak, I think, quite openly,
And Mrs. Browning guard a careful silence,   140
But Emily would set doors ajar and slam them
And love you for your speed of observation.

Strange trio of my sisters, most diverse,
And how extraordinarily unlike
Each is to me, and which way shall I go?   145
Sapho spent and gained; and Mrs. Browning,
After a miser girlhood, cut the strings
Which tied her money-bags and let them run;
But Emily hoarded—hoarded—only giving
Herself to cold, white paper. Starved and tortured,   150
She cheated her despair with games of patience
And fooled herself by winning. Frail little elf,
The lonely brain-child of a gaunt maturity,
She hung her womanhood upon a bough
And played ball with the stars—too long—too long—   155
The garment of herself hung on a tree
Until at last she lost even the desire
To take it down. Whose fault? Why let us say,
To be consistent, Queen Victoria's.
But really, not to over-rate the queen,   160
I feel obliged to mention Martin Luther,
And behind him the long line of Church Fathers
Who draped their prurience like a dirty cloth
About the naked majesty of God.
Good-bye, my sisters, all of you are great,   165
And all of you are marvellously strange,
And none of you has any word for me.
I cannot write like you, I cannot think
In terms of Pagan or of Christian now.
I only hope that possibly some day   170
Some other woman with an itch for writing
May turn to me as I have turned to you
And chat with me a brief few minutes. How
We lie, we poets! It is three good hours
I have been dreaming. Has it seemed so long   175
To you? And yet I thank you for the time
Although you leave me sad and self-distrustful,
For older sisters are very sobering things.
Put on your cloaks, my dears, the motor's waiting.

No, you have not seemed strange to me, but near,   180
Frightfully near, and rather terrifying.
I understand you all, for in myself—
Is that presumption? Yet indeed it's true—
We are one family. And still my answer
Will not be any one of yours, I see.   185
Well, never mind that now. Good night! Good night!

1925

GERTRUDE STEIN
1874–1946

Gertrude Stein—novelist, poet, essayist and playwright—produced some 571 works during a career that spanned forty-three years. During her lifetime, this quintessentially American writer chose to live in Paris and write from the perspective of a different continent about things American and the American vision of things European. Her interests included art, aesthetics, language, philosophy, history, economics, and human nature. She and her lifelong companion Alice B. Toklas drove for the American Fund for French Wounded during World War I and lived quietly sequestered in the French countryside during the German occupation of France during World War II. As Stein said in 1936, "America is my country and Paris is my home town and it is as it has come to be."

Stein had a gift for doing the uncommon in a commonplace way. Born into a German-Jewish immigrant family in Allegheny, Pennsylvania, at the height of the Victorian era, she lived in Gemunden and Vienna, Austria; Passy, France; Baltimore, Maryland; Oakland and San Francisco, California; Cambridge, Massachusetts; and London, England, before settling in Paris in 1903. The youngest of five children, Stein experienced a comparatively unfettered childhood heavily colored by the companionship of her brother Leo, himself later a critic and writer. In the 1890s she studied philosophy and psychology at Harvard University with William James, George Herbert Palmer, George Santayana, and Hugo Munsterberg, and then went on to medical school at Johns Hopkins University. Within a semester of finishing her M.D. degree, she left the United States to take up residence in Paris so that she might live and write in the comparative freedom afforded to her as an expatriate.

Initially, Gertrude and Leo Stein shared the living and work space at 27 rue de Fleurus, conducting their salon and building their fine collection of Cézanne, Matisse, and Picasso paintings. But Leo had no respect for his sister's work and in time was replaced by Alice B. Toklas, an expatriate Californian who shared Stein's interests and supported her ambitions, and became her lifelong lover and partner. Stein's social and literary networks were as wide and cosmopolitan as the city itself. In the early years she worked, talked, and played with such artists and poets as Pablo Picasso, Guillaume Apollinaire, Natalie Barney, and Renée Vivien, who shared her interests in unconventional literature and art. Stein continued her interest in philosophy, visiting Alfred North Whitehead on the eve of World War I and, in the fifteen years before World War II, writing her own best critical theory and a major philosophical meditation. Her unconventional, experimental work during the early years of the twentieth century brought her to the attention of writers as diverse as Jean Cocteau and Sherwood Anderson, both of whom testified to the liberating impact of *Tender Buttons* (1912) on their own vision.

In the 1920s she mentored Ernest Hemingway, and over the years she entertained and communicated with a number of young writers, artists, and composers. Talented young Americans and artists coming from the United States to Paris carried letters of introduction, and over the years she entertained such persons as Nella Larsen and Paul Robeson. She corresponded with Richard Wright and later encouraged him to live in France. Her Paris circle included Sylvia Beach, Margaret Anderson, Janet Flanner, Djuna Barnes, and H.D. In the mid-1930s, after the unprecedented popular success of her readable *The Autobiography of Alice B. Toklas* (1932), Stein returned with Toklas to the United States for a triumphant coast-to-coast tour. In 1946, at the height of her literary powers and recognition, Stein died quietly of cancer in Paris with Toklas at her side.

Financial success, critical recognition, and popular acclaim did not come easily to Stein, who was as uncompromising in pursuit of her artistic goals as she was in securing her domestic comfort and maintaining her personal integrity. Though formally trained in philosophy and medicine, she was widely read in literature, particularly English prose narrative. Her first major work, *The Making of Americans* (1903, 1906–1911), is a historical record of a German-Jewish immigrant family establishing itself in the new land. *Three Lives* (1905–1906) bears the mark of both Anglo-American naturalism and the psychological probing of Henry James. But already the abstract way in which she defined character in stories such as "The Gentle Lena" and her use of very complex prose rhythms suggested that experimental breakthroughs were to follow.

In *Tender Buttons*, a brilliant prose/poetry meditation on objects, food, and rooms, Stein established once and for all her philosophical interest in the ordinary, her delight in words as an artistic medium, and her willingness to experiment with generic conventions. Her lifelong effort was to show how the human mind perceives, orders, and reflects on the interwoven world of animate and inanimate phenomena.

Through the 1920s, Stein continued to write poetry, portraits, plays, landscapes, novels, and operas—collapsing the aesthetic categories usually reserved for either the visual or the verbal arts. *Four Saints in Three Acts* (1927) explores religion, gender, art, meditation, ritual, and language in a way typical of her mature middle style. *Patriarchal Poetry*, a long poem written the same year, makes it clear that Stein was fully aware of what it meant to be a woman writing in a literary tradition defined by masculine interests, experiences, and values. During the 1930s, Stein wrote in the autobiographies some of her most accessible prose, all the while continuing in the novella and drama to explore the complexity of experience, form, and language. *The Geographical History of America* (1935) states boldly her belief that she—a woman—is doing the major literary thinking of the era. She doubtless felt the need to say this, for her work continued to bewilder common reader and critic alike, much of it remaining unpublished during her lifetime. The attention given to Stein's experiments in form and language during her lifetime long obscured her major contribution to our understanding of domesticity, female culture, myths about women, the social world in which women function, and what it meant in the twentieth century to intentionally create art that is not patriarchal.

Cynthia Secor
University of Denver
Hugh English
Queens College, City University of New York

PRIMARY WORKS

Three Lives, 1909; *Tender Buttons*, 1914; *Geography and Plays*, 1922; *The Making of Americans*, 1925; *Useful Knowledge*, 1929; *Lucy Church Amiably*, 1930; *How to Write*, 1931; *Operas and Plays*, 1932; *The Autobiography of Alice B. Toklas*, 1933; *Four Saints in Three Acts*, 1934; *Lectures in America*, 1935; *Narration*, 1935; *The Geographical History of America, or the Relation of Human Nature to the Human Mind*, 1936; *Everybody's Autobiography*, 1937; *Picasso*, 1938; *The World is Round*, 1939; *Paris France*, 1940; *Ida: A Novel*, 1941; *Wars I Have Seen*, 1945; *Brewsie and Willie*, 1946; *Selected Writings*, 1946; *The Yale Edition of the Unpublished Writings of Gertrude Stein, Vols. 1–8.*, 1951–1958; *Writings 1903–1932*, ed. Catherine R. Stimpson and Harriet Scott Chessman, 1998; *Writings 1932–1946*, ed. Catherine R. Stimpson and Harriet Scott Chessman, 1998.

The Gentle Lena

Lena was patient, gentle, sweet and german. She had been a servant for four years and had liked it very well.

Lena had been brought from Germany to Bridgepoint by a cousin and had been in the same place there for four years.

This place Lena had found very good. There was a pleasant, unexacting mistress and her children, and they all liked Lena very well.

There was a cook there who scolded Lena a great deal but Lena's german patience held no suffering and the good incessant woman really only scolded so for Lena's good.

Lena's german voice when she knocked and called the family in the morning was as awakening, as soothing, and as appealing, as a delicate soft breeze in midday, summer. She stood in the hallway every morning a long time in her unexpectant and unsuffering german patience calling to the young ones to get up. She would call and wait a long time and then call again, always even, gentle, patient, while the young ones fell back often into that precious, tense, last bit of sleeping that gives a strength of joyous vigor in the young, over them that have come to the readiness of middle age, in their awakening.

Lena had good hard work all morning, and on the pleasant, sunny afternoons she was sent out into the park to sit and watch the little two year old girl baby of the family.

The other girls, all them that make the pleasant, lazy crowd, that watch the children in the sunny afternoons out in the park, all liked the simple, gentle, german Lena very well. They all, too, liked very well to tease her, for it was so easy to make her mixed and troubled, and all helpless, for she could never learn to know just what the other quicker girls meant by the queer things they said.

The two or three of these girls, the ones that Lena always sat with, always worked together to confuse her. Still it was pleasant, all this life for Lena.

The little girl fell down sometimes and cried, and then Lena had to soothe her. When the little girl would drop her hat, Lena had to pick it up and hold it. When the little girl was bad and threw away her playthings, Lena told her she could not have them and took them from her to hold until the little girl should need them.

It was all a peaceful life for Lena, almost as peaceful as a pleasant leisure. The other girls, of course, did tease her, but then that only made a gentle stir within her.

Lena was a brown and pleasant creature, brown as blonde races often have them brown, brown, not with the yellow or the red or the chocolate brown of sun burned countries, but brown with the clear color laid flat on the light toned skin beneath, the plain, spare brown that makes it right to have been made with hazel eyes, and not too abundant straight, brown hair, hair that only later deepens itself into brown from the straw yellow of a german childhood.

Lena had the flat chest, straight back and forward falling shoulders of the patient and enduring working woman, though her body was now still in its milder girlhood and work had not yet made these lines too clear.

The rarer feeling that there was with Lena, showed in all the even quiet of her body movements, but in all it was the strongest in the patient, old-world ignorance, and earth made pureness of her brown, flat, soft featured face. Lena had eyebrows that were a wondrous thickness. They were black, and spread, and very cool, with their dark color and their beauty, and beneath them were her hazel eyes, simple and human, with the earth patience of the working, gentle, german woman.

Yes it was all a peaceful life for Lena. The other girls, of course, did tease her, but then that only made a gentle stir within her.

"What you got on your finger Lena," Mary, one of the girls she always sat with, one day asked her. Mary was good natured, quick, intelligent and Irish.

Lena had just picked up the fancy paper made accordion that the little girl had dropped beside her, and was making it squeak sadly as she pulled it with her brown, strong, awkward finger.

"Why, what is it, Mary, paint?" said Lena, putting her finger to her mouth to taste the dirt spot.

"That's awful poison Lena, don't you know?" said Mary, "that green paint that you just tasted."

Lena had sucked a good deal of the green paint from her finger. She stopped and looked hard at the finger. She did not know just how much Mary meant by what she said.

"Ain't it poison, Nellie, that green paint, that Lena sucked just now," said Mary. "Sure it is Lena, its real poison, I ain't foolin' this time anyhow."

Lena was a little troubled. She looked hard at her finger where the paint was, and she wondered if she had really sucked it.

It was still a little wet on the edges and she rubbed it off a long time on the inside of her dress, and in between she wondered and looked at the finger and thought, was it really poison that she had just tasted.

"Ain't it too bad, Nellie, Lena should have sucked that," Mary said.

Nellie smiled and did not answer. Nellie was dark and thin, and looked Italian. She had a big mass of black hair that she wore high up on her head, and that made her face look very fine.

Nellie always smiled and did not say much, and then she would look at Lena to perplex her.

And so they all three sat with their little charges in the pleasant sunshine a long time. And Lena would often look at her finger and wonder if it was really poison that she had just tasted and then she would rub her finger on her dress a little harder.

Mary laughed at her and teased her and Nellie smiled a little and looked queerly at her.

Then it came time, for it was growing cooler, for them to drag together the little ones, who had begun to wander, and to take each one back to its own mother. And Lena never knew for certain whether it was really poison, that green stuff that she had tasted.

During these four years of service, Lena always spent her Sundays out at the house of her aunt, who had brought her four years before to Bridgepoint.

This aunt, who had brought Lena, four years before, to Bridgepoint, was a hard, ambitious, well meaning, german woman. Her husband was a grocer in the town, and they were very well to do. Mrs. Haydon, Lena's aunt, had two daughters who were just beginning as young ladies, and she had a little boy who was not honest and who was very hard to manage.

Mrs. Haydon was a short, stout, hard built, german woman. She always hit the ground very firmly and compactly as she walked. Mrs. Haydon was all a compact and well hardened mass, even to her face, reddish and darkened from its early blonde, with its hearty, shiny cheeks, and doubled chin well covered over with the up roll from her short, square neck.

The two daughters, who were fourteen and fifteen, looked like unkneaded, unformed mounds of flesh beside her.

The elder girl, Mathilda, was blonde, and slow, and simple, and quite fat. The younger, Bertha, who was almost as tall as her sister, was dark, and quicker, and she was heavy, too, but not really fat.

These two girls the mother had brought up very firmly. They were well taught for their position. They were always both well dressed, in the same kinds of hats and dresses, as is becoming in two german sisters. The mother liked to have them dressed in red. Their best clothes were red dresses, made of good heavy cloth, and strongly trimmed with braid of a glistening black. They had stiff, red felt hats, trimmed with black velvet ribbon, and a bird. The mother dressed matronly, in a bonnet and in black, always sat between her two big daughters, firm, directing, and repressed.

The only weak spot in this good german woman's conduct was the way she spoiled her boy, who was not honest and who was very hard to manage.

The father of this family was a decent, quiet, heavy, and uninterfering german man. He tried to cure the boy of his bad ways, and make him honest, but the mother could not make herself let the father manage, and so the boy was brought up very badly.

Mrs. Haydon's girls were now only just beginning as young ladies, and so to get her niece, Lena, married, was just then the most important thing that Mrs. Haydon had to do.

Mrs. Haydon had four years before gone to Germany to see her parents, and had taken the girls with her. This visit had been for Mrs. Haydon most successful, though her children had not liked it very well.

Mrs. Haydon was a good and generous woman, and she patronized her parents grandly, and all the cousins who came from all about to see her. Mrs. Haydon's people were of the middling class of farmers. They were not peasants, and they lived in a town of some pretension, but it all seemed very poor and smelly to Mrs. Haydon's american born daughters.

Mrs. Haydon liked it all. It was familiar, and then here she was so wealthy and important. She listened and decided, and advised all of her relations how to do things better. She arranged their present and their future for them, and showed them how in the past they had been wrong in all their methods.

Mrs. Haydon's only trouble was with her two daughters, whom she could not make behave well to her parents. The two girls were very nasty to all their numerous relations. Their mother could hardly make them kiss their grandparents, and every day the girls would get a scolding. But then Mrs. Haydon was so very busy that she did not have time to really manage her stubborn daughters.

These hard working, earth-rough german cousins were to these American born children, ugly and dirty, and as far below them as were Italian or negro workmen, and they could not see how their mother could ever bear to touch them, and then all the women dressed so funny, and were worked all rough and different.

The two girls stuck up their noses at them all, and always talked in English to each other about how they hated all these people and how they wished their mother would not do so. The girls could talk some German, but they never chose to use it.

It was her eldest brother's family that most interested Mrs. Haydon. Here there were eight children, and out of the eight, five of them were girls.

Mrs. Haydon thought it would be a fine thing to take one of these girls back with her to Bridgepoint and get her well started. Everybody liked that she should do so and they were all willing that it should be Lena.

Lena was the second girl in her large family. She was at this time just seventeen years old. Lena was not an important daughter in the family. She was always sort of dreamy and not there. She worked hard and went very regularly at it, but even good work never seemed to bring her near.

Lena's age just suited Mrs. Haydon's purpose. Lena could first go out to service, and learn how to do things, and then, when she was a little older, Mrs. Haydon could get her a good husband. And then Lena was so still and docile, she would never want to do things her own way. And then, too, Mrs. Haydon, with all her hardness had wisdom, and she could feel the rarer strain there was in Lena.

Lena was willing to go with Mrs. Haydon. Lena did not like her german life very well. It was not the hard work but the roughness that disturbed her. The people were not gentle, and the men when they were glad were very boisterous, and would lay hold of her and roughly tease her. They were good people enough around her, but it was all harsh and dreary for her.

Lena did not really know that she did not like it. She did not know that she was always dreamy and not there. She did not think whether it would be different for her away off there in Bridgepoint. Mrs. Haydon took her and got her different kinds of dresses, and then took her with them to the steamer. Lena did not really know what it was that had happened to her.

Mrs. Haydon, and her daughters, and Lena traveled second class on the steamer. Mrs. Haydon's daughters hated that their mother should take Lena. They hated to have a cousin, who was to them, little better than a nigger, and then everybody on the steamer there would see her. Mrs. Haydon's daughters said things like this to their mother, but she never stopped to hear them, and the girls did not dare to make their meaning very clear. And so they could only go on hating Lena hard, together. They could not stop her from going back with them to Bridgepoint.

Lena was very sick on the voyage. She thought, surely before it was over that she would die. She was so sick she could not even wish that she had not started. She could not eat, she could not moan, she was just blank and scared, and sure that every minute she would die. She could not hold herself in, nor help herself in her trouble. She just staid where she had been put, pale, and scared, and weak, and sick, and sure that she was going to die.

Mathilda and Bertha Haydon had no trouble from having Lena for a cousin on the voyage, until the last day that they were on the ship, and by that time they had made their friends and could explain.

Mrs. Haydon went down every day to Lena, gave her things to make her better, held her head when it was needful, and generally was good and did her duty by her.

Poor Lena had no power to be strong in such trouble. She did not know how to yield to her sickness nor endure. She lost all her little sense of being in her suffering. She was so scared, and then at her best, Lena, who was patient, sweet and quiet, had not self-control, nor any active courage.

Poor Lena was so scared and weak, and every minute she was sure that she would die.

After Lena was on land again a little while, she forgot all her bad suffering. Mrs. Haydon got her the good place, with the pleasant unexacting mistress, and her children, and Lena began to learn some English and soon was very happy and content.

All her Sundays out Lena spent at Mrs. Haydon's house. Lena would have liked much better to spend her Sundays with the girls she always sat with, and who often asked her, and who teased her and made a gentle stir within her, but it never came to Lena's unexpectant and unsuffering german nature to do something different from what was expected of her, just because she would like it that way better. Mrs. Haydon had said that Lena was to come to her house every other Sunday, and so Lena always went there.

Mrs. Haydon was the only one of her family who took any interest in Lena. Mr. Haydon did not think much of her. She was his wife's cousin and he was good to her, but she was for him stupid, and a little simple, and very dull, and sure some day to need help and to be in trouble. All young poor relations, who were brought from Germany to Bridgepoint were sure, before long, to need help and to be in trouble.

The little Haydon boy was always very nasty to her. He was a hard child for any one to manage, and his mother spoiled him very badly. Mrs. Haydon's daughters as they grew older did not learn to like Lena any better. Lena never knew that she did not like them either. She did not know that she was only happy with the other quicker girls, she always sat with in the park, and who laughed at her and always teased her.

Mathilda Haydon, the simple, fat, blonde, older daughter felt very badly that she had to say that this was her cousin Lena, this Lena who was little better for her than a nigger. Mathilda was an overgrown, slow, flabby, blonde, stupid, fat girl, just beginning as a woman; thick in her speech and dull and simple in her mind, and very jealous of all her family and of other girls, and proud that she could have good dresses and new hats and learn music, and hating very badly to have a cousin who was a common servant. And then Mathilda remembered very strongly that dirty nasty place that Lena came from and that Mathilda had so turned up her nose at, and where she had been made so angry because her mother scolded her and liked all those rough cow-smelly people.

Then, too, Mathilda would get very mad when her mother had Lena at their parties, and when she talked about how good Lena was, to certain german mothers in whose sons, perhaps, Mrs. Haydon might find Lena a good husband. All this would make the dull, blonde, fat Mathilda very angry: Sometimes she would get so angry that she would, in her thick, slow way, and with jealous anger blazing in her light blue eyes, tell her mother that she did not see how she could like that nasty Lena; and then her mother would scold Mathilda, and tell her that she knew her cousin Lena was poor and Mathilda must be good to poor people.

Mathilda Haydon did not like relations to be poor. She told all her girl friends what she thought of Lena, and so the girls would never talk to Lena at Mrs. Haydon's parties. But Lena in her unsuffering and unexpectant patience never really knew that she was slighted. When Mathilda was with her girls in the street or in the park and would see Lena, she always turned up her nose and barely nodded to her, and then she would tell her friends how funny her mother was to take care of people like that Lena, and how, back in Germany, all Lena's people lived just like pigs.

The younger daughter, the dark, large, but not fat, Bertha Haydon, who was very quick in her mind, and in her ways, and who was the favorite with her father, did not like Lena, either. She did not like her because for her Lena was a fool and so stupid, and she would let those Irish and Italian girls laugh at her and tease her, and everybody always made fun of Lena, and Lena never got mad, or even had sense enough to know that they were all making an awful fool of her.

Bertha Haydon hated people to be fools. Her father, too, thought Lena was a fool, and so neither the father nor the daughter ever paid any attention to Lena, although she came to their house every other Sunday.

Lena did not know how all the Haydons felt. She came to her aunt's house all her Sunday afternoons that she had out, because Mrs. Haydon had told her she must do so. In the same way Lena always saved all of her wages. She never thought of any way to spend it. The german cook, the good woman who always scolded Lena, helped her to put it in the bank each month, as soon as she got it. Sometimes before it got into the bank to be taken care of, somebody would ask Lena for it. The little Haydon boy sometimes asked and would get it, and sometimes some of the girls, the ones Lena always sat with, needed some more money; but the german cook, who always scolded Lena, saw to it that this did not happen very often. When it did happen she would scold Lena very sharply, and for the next few months she would not let Lena touch her wages, but put it in the bank for her on the same day that Lena got it.

So Lena always saved her wages, for she never thought to spend them, and she always went to her aunt's house for her Sundays because she did not know that she could do anything different.

Mrs. Haydon felt more and more every year that she had done right to bring Lena back with her, for it was all coming out just as she had expected. Lena was good and never wanted her own way, she was learning English, and saving all her wages, and soon Mrs. Haydon would get her a good husband.

All these four years Mrs. Haydon was busy looking around among all the german people that she knew for the right man to be Lena's husband, and now at last she was quite decided.

The man Mrs. Haydon wanted for Lena was a young german-american tailor, who worked with his father. He was good and all the family were very saving, and Mrs. Haydon was sure that this would be just right for Lena, and then too, this young tailor always did whatever his father and his mother wanted.

This old german tailor and his wife, the father and the mother of Herman Kreder, who was to marry Lena Mainz, were very thrifty, careful people. Herman was the only child they had left with them, and he always did everything they wanted. Herman was now twenty-eight years old, but he had never stopped being scolded and directed by his father and his mother. And now they wanted to see him married.

Herman Kreder did not care much to get married. He was a gentle soul and a little fearful. He had a sullen temper, too. He was obedient to his father and his mother. He always did his work well. He often went out on Saturday nights and on Sundays, with other men. He liked it with them but he never became really joyous. He liked to be with men and he hated to have women with them. He was obedient to his mother, but he did not care much to get married.

Mrs. Haydon and the elder Kreders had often talked the marriage over. They all three liked it very well. Lena would do anything that Mrs. Haydon wanted, and Herman was always obedient in everything to his father and his mother. Both Lena and Herman were saving and good workers and neither of them ever wanted their own way.

The elder Kreders, everybody knew, had saved up all their money, and they were hard, good german people, and Mrs. Haydon was sure that with these people Lena would never be in any trouble. Mr. Haydon would not say anything about it. He knew old Kreder had a lot of money and owned some good houses, and he did not care what his wife did with that simple, stupid Lena, so long as she would be sure never to need help or to be in trouble.

Lena did not care much to get married. She liked her life very well where she was working. She did not think much about Herman Kreder. She thought he was a good man and she always found him very quiet. Neither of them ever spoke much to the other. Lena did not care much just then about getting married.

Mrs. Haydon spoke to Lena about it very often. Lena never answered anything at all. Mrs. Haydon thought, perhaps Lena did not like Herman Kreder. Mrs. Haydon could not believe that any girl not even Lena, really had no feeling about getting married.

Mrs. Haydon spoke to Lena very often about Herman. Mrs. Haydon sometimes got very angry with Lena. She was afraid that Lena, for once, was going to be stubborn, now when it was all fixed right for her to be married.

"Why you stand there so stupid, why don't you answer, Lena," said Mrs. Haydon one Sunday, at the end of a long talking that she was giving Lena about Herman Kreder, and about Lena's getting married to him.

"Yes ma'am," said Lena, and then Mrs. Haydon was furious with this stupid Lena. "Why don't you answer with some sense, Lena, when I ask you if you don't like Herman Kreder. You stand there so stupid and don't answer just like you ain't heard a word what I been saying to you. I never see anybody like you, Lena. If you going to burst out at all, why don't you burst out sudden instead of standing there so silly and don't answer. And here I am so good to you, and find you a good husband so you can have a place to live in all your own. Answer me, Lena, don't you like Herman Kreder? He is a fine young fellow, almost too good for you, Lena, when you stand there so stupid and don't make no answer. There ain't many poor girls that get the chance you got now to get married."

"Why, I do anything you say, Aunt Mathilda. Yes, I like him. He don't say much to me, but I guess he is a good man, and I do anything you say for me to do."

"Well then Lena, why you stand there so silly all the time and not answer when I asked you."

"I didn't hear you say you wanted I should say anything to you. I didn't know you wanted me to say nothing. I do whatever you tell me it's right for me to do. I marry Herman Kreder, if you want me."

And so for Lena Mainz the match was made.

Old Mrs. Kreder did not discuss the matter with her Herman. She never thought that she needed to talk such things over with him. She just told him about getting married to Lena Mainz who was a good worker and very saving and never wanted her own way, and Herman made his usual little grunt in answer to her.

Mrs. Kreder and Mrs. Haydon fixed the day and made all the arrangements for the wedding and invited everybody who ought to be there to see them married.

In three months Lena Mainz and Herman Kreder were to be married.

Mrs. Haydon attended to Lena's getting all the things that she needed. Lena had to help a good deal with the sewing. Lena did not sew very well. Mrs. Haydon scolded because Lena did not do it better, but then she was very good to Lena, and she hired a girl to come and help her. Lena still stayed on with her pleasant mistress, but she spent all her evenings and her Sundays with her aunt and all the sewing.

Mrs. Haydon got Lena some nice dresses. Lena liked that very well. Lena liked having new hats even better, and Mrs. Haydon had some made for her by a real milliner who made them very pretty.

Lena was nervous these days, but she did not think much about getting married. She did not know really what it was, that, which was always coming nearer.

Lena liked the place where she was with the pleasant mistress and the good cook, who always scolded, and she liked the girls she always sat with. She did not ask if she would like being married any better. She always did whatever her aunt said and expected, but she was always nervous when she saw the Kreders with their Herman. She was excited and she liked her new hats, and everybody teased her and every day her marrying was coming nearer, and yet she did not really know what it was, this that was about to happen to her.

Herman Kreder knew more what it meant to be married and he did not like it very well. He did not like to see girls and he did not want to have to have one always near him. Herman always did everything that his father and his mother wanted and now they wanted that he should be married.

Herman had a sullen temper; he was gentle and he never said much. He liked to go out with other men, but he never wanted that there should be any women with them. The men all teased him about getting married. Herman did not mind the teasing but he did not like very well the getting married and having a girl always with him.

Three days before the wedding day, Herman went away to the country to be gone over Sunday. He and Lena were to be married Tuesday afternoon. When the day came Herman had not been seen or heard from.

The old Kreder couple had not worried much about it. Herman always did everything they wanted and he would surely come back in time to get married. But when Monday night came, and there was no Herman, they went to Mrs. Haydon to tell her what had happened.

Mrs. Haydon got very much excited. It was hard enough to work so as to get everything all ready, and then to have that silly Herman go off that way, so no one could tell what was going to happen. Here was Lena and everything all ready, and now they would have to make the wedding later so that they would know that Herman would be sure to be there.

Mrs. Haydon was very much excited, and then she could not say much to the old Kreder couple. She did not want to make them angry, for she wanted very badly now that Lena should be married to their Herman.

At last it was decided that the wedding should be put off a week longer. Old Mr. Kreder would go to New York to find Herman, for it was very likely that Herman had gone there to his married sister.

Mrs. Haydon sent word around, about waiting until a week from that Tuesday, to everybody that had been invited, and then Tuesday morning she sent for Lena to come down to see her.

Mrs. Haydon was very angry with poor Lena when she saw her. She scolded her hard because she was so foolish, and now Herman had gone off and nobody could tell where he had gone to, and all because Lena always was so dumb and silly. And Mrs. Haydon was just like a mother to her, and Lena always stood there so stupid and did not answer what anybody asked her, and Herman was so silly too, and now his father had to go and find him. Mrs. Haydon did not think that any old people should be good to their children. Their children always were so thankless, and never paid any attention, and older people were always doing things for their good. Did Lena think it gave Mrs. Haydon any pleasure, to work so hard to make Lena happy, and get her a good husband, and then Lena was so thankless and never did anything that anybody wanted. It was a lesson to poor Mrs. Haydon not to do things any more for anybody. Let everybody take care of themselves and never come to her with any troubles; she knew better now than to meddle to make other people happy. It just made trouble for her and her husband did not like it. He always said she was too good, and nobody ever thanked her for it, and there Lena was always standing stupid and not answering anything anybody wanted. Lena could always talk enough to those silly girls she liked so much, and always sat with, but who never did anything for her except to take away her money, and here was her aunt who tried so hard and was so good to her and treated her just like one of her own children and Lena stood there, and never made any answer and never tried to please her aunt, or to do anything that her aunt wanted. "No, it ain't no use your standin' there and cryin', now, Lena. Its too late now to care about that Herman. You should have cared some before, and then you wouldn't have to stand and cry now, and be a disappointment to me, and then I get scolded by my husband for taking care of everybody, and nobody ever thankful. I am glad you got the sense to feel sorry now, Lena, anyway, and I try to do what I can to help you out in your trouble, only you don't deserve to have anybody take any trouble for you. But perhaps you know better next time. You go home now and take care you don't spoil your clothes and that new hat, you had no business to be wearin' that this morning, but you ain't got no sense at all, Lena. I never in my life see anybody be so stupid."

Mrs. Haydon stopped and poor Lena stood there in her hat, all trimmed with pretty flowers, and the tears coming out of her eyes, and Lena did not know what it was that she had done, only she was not going to be married and it was a disgrace for a girl to be left by a man on the very day she was to be married.

Lena went home all alone, and cried in the street car.

Poor Lena cried very hard all alone in the street car. She almost spoiled her new hat with her hitting it against the window in her crying. Then she remembered that she must not do so.

The conductor was a kind man and he was very sorry when he saw her crying. "Don't feel so bad, you get another feller, you are such a nice girl," he said to make her cheerful. "But Aunt Mathilda said now, I never get married," poor Lena sobbed out for her answer. "Why you really got trouble like that," said the conductor, "I just said that now to josh you. I didn't ever think you really was left by a feller. He must be a stupid feller. But don't you worry, he wasn't much good if he could go away and leave you, lookin' to be such a nice girl. You just tell all your trouble to me, and I help you." The car was empty and the conductor sat down beside her to put his arm around her, and to be a comfort to her. Lena suddenly remembered where she was, and if she did things like that her aunt would scold her. She moved away from the man into the corner. He laughed, "Don't be scared," he said, "I wasn't going to hurt you. But you just keep up your spirit. You are a real nice girl, and you'll be sure to get a real good husband. Don't you let nobody fool you. You're all right and I don't want to scare you."

The conductor went back to his platform to help a passenger get on the car. All the time Lena stayed in the street car, he would come in every little while and reassure her, about her not to feel so bad about a man who hadn't no more sense than to go away and leave her. She'd be sure yet to get a good man, she needn't be so worried, he frequently assured her.

He chatted with the other passenger who had just come in, a very well dressed old man, and then with another who came in later, a good sort of a working man, and then another who came in, a nice lady, and he told them all about Lena's having trouble, and it was too bad there were men who treated a poor girl so badly. And everybody in the car was sorry for poor Lena and the workman tried to cheer her, and the old man looked sharply at her, and said she looked like a good girl, but she ought to be more careful and not to be so careless, and things like that would not happen to her, and the nice lady went and sat beside her and Lena liked it, though she shrank away from being near her.

So Lena was feeling a little better when she got off the car, and the conductor helped her, and he called out to her, "You be sure you keep up a good heart now. He wasn't no good that feller and you were lucky for to lose him. You'll get a real man yet, one that will be better for you. Don't you be worried, you're a real nice girl as I ever see in such trouble," and the conductor shook his head and went back into his car to talk it over with the other passengers he had there.

The german cook, who always scolded Lena, was very angry when she heard the story. She never did think Mrs. Haydon would do so much for Lena, though she was always talking so grand about what she could do for everybody. The good german cook always had been a little distrustful of her. People who always thought they were so much never did really do things right for anybody. Not that Mrs. Haydon wasn't a good woman. Mrs. Haydon was a real, good, german woman, and she did really mean to do well by her niece Lena. The cook knew that very well, and she had always said so, and she always had liked and respected Mrs. Haydon, who always acted very proper to her, and Lena was so backward, when there was a man to talk to, Mrs. Haydon did have hard work when she tried to marry Lena. Mrs. Haydon was a good woman, only she did talk sometimes too grand. Perhaps this trouble would make her see it wasn't always so easy to do, to make everybody do everything just like she wanted. The cook was very sorry now for Mrs. Haydon. All this must be such a disappointment, and such a worry to her, and she really had always been very good to Lena. But Lena had better go and put on her other clothes and stop all that crying. That wouldn't do nothing now to help her, and if Lena would be a good girl, and just be real patient, her aunt would make it all come out right yet for her. "I just tell Mrs. Aldrich, Lena, you stay here yet a little longer. You know she is always so good to you, Lena, and I know she let you, and I tell her all about that stupid Herman Kreder. I got no patience, Lena, with anybody who can be so stupid. You just stop now with your crying, Lena, and take off them good clothes and put them away so you don't spoil them when you need them, and you can help me with the dishes and everything will come off better for you. You see if I ain't right by what I tell you. You just stop crying now Lena quick, or else I scold you."

Lena still choked a little and was very miserable inside her but she did everything just as the cook told her.

The girls Lena always sat with were very sorry to see her look so sad with her trouble. Mary the Irish girl sometimes got very angry with her. Mary was always very hot when she talked to Lena's aunt Mathilda, who thought she was so grand, and had such stupid, stuck up daughters. Mary wouldn't be a fat fool like that ugly tempered Mathilda Haydon, not for anything anybody could ever give her. How Lena could keep on going there so much when they all always acted as if she was just dirt to them, Mary never could see. But Lena never had any sense of how she should make people stand round for her, and that was always all the trouble with her. And poor Lena, she was so stupid to be sorry for losing that gawky fool who didn't ever know what he wanted and just said "ja" to his mamma and his papa, like a baby, and was scared to look at a girl straight, and then sneaked away the last day like as if somebody was going to do something to him. Disgrace, Lena talking about disgrace! It was a disgrace for a girl to be seen with the likes of him, let alone to be married to him. But that poor Lena, she never did know how to show herself off for what she was really. Disgrace to have him go away and leave her. Mary would just like to get a chance to show him. If Lena wasn't worth fifteen like Herman Kreder, Mary would just eat her own head all up. It was a good riddance Lena had of that Herman Kreder and his stingy, dirty parents, and if Lena didn't stop crying about it,—Mary would just naturally despise her.

Poor Lena, she knew very well how Mary meant it all, this she was always saying to her. But Lena was very miserable inside her. She felt the disgrace it was for a decent german girl that a man should go away and leave her. Lena knew very well that her aunt was right when she said the way Herman had acted to her was a disgrace to everyone that knew her. Mary and Nellie and the other girls she always sat with were always very good to Lena but that did not make her trouble any better. It was a disgrace the way Lena had been left, to any decent family, and that could never be made any different to her.

And so the slow days wore on, and Lena never saw her Aunt Mathilda. At last on Sunday she got word by a boy to go and see her aunt Mathilda. Lena's heart beat quick for she was very nervous now with all this that had happened to her. She went just as quickly as she could to see her Aunt Mathilda.

Mrs. Haydon quick, as soon as she saw Lena, began to scold her for keeping her aunt waiting so long for her, and for not coming in all the week to see her, to see if her aunt should need her, and so her aunt had to send a boy to tell her. But it was easy, even for Lena, to see that her aunt was not really angry with her. It wasn't Lena's fault, went on Mrs. Haydon, that everything was going to happen all right for her. Mrs. Haydon was very tired taking all this trouble for her, and when Lena couldn't even take trouble to come and see her aunt, to see if she needed anything to tell her. But Mrs. Haydon really never minded things like that when she could do things for anybody. She was tired now, all the trouble she had been taking to make things right for Lena, but perhaps now Lena heard it she would learn a little to be thankful to her. "You get all ready to be married Tuesday, Lena, you hear me," said Mrs. Haydon to her. "You come here Tuesday morning and I have everything all ready for you. You wear your new dress I got you, and your hat with all them flowers on it, and you be very careful coming you don't get your things all dirty, you so careless all the time, Lena, and not thinking, and you act sometimes you never got no head at all on you. You go home now, and you tell your Mrs. Aldrich that you leave her Tuesday. Don't you go forgetting now, Lena, anything I ever told you what you should do to be careful. You be a good girl, now Lena. You get married Tuesday to Herman Kreder." And that was all Lena ever knew of what had happened all this week to Herman Kreder. Lena forgot there was anything to know about it. She was really to be married Tuesday, and her Aunt Mathilda said she was a good girl, and now there was no disgrace left upon her.

Lena now fell back into the way she always had of being always dreamy and not there, the way she always had been, except for the few days she was so excited, because she had been left by a man the very day she was to have been married. Lena was a little nervous all these last days, but she did not think much about what it meant for her to be married.

Herman Kreder was not so content about it. He was quiet and was sullen and he knew he could not help it. He knew now he just had to let himself get married. It was not that Herman did not like Lena Mainz. She was as good as any other girl could be for him. She was a little better perhaps than other girls he saw, she was so very quiet, but Herman did not like to always have to have a girl around him. Herman had always done everything that his mother and his father wanted. His father had found him in New York, where Herman had gone to be with his married sister.

Herman's father when he had found him coaxed Herman a long time and went on whole days with his complaining to him, always troubled but gentle and quite patient with him, and always he was worrying to Herman about what was the right way his boy Herman should always do, always whatever it was his mother ever wanted from him, and always Herman never made him any answer.

Old Mr. Kreder kept on saying to him, he did not see how Herman could think now, it could be any different. When you make a bargain you just got to stick right to it, that was the only way old Mr. Kreder could ever see it, and saying you would get married to a girl and she got everything all ready, that was a bargain just like one you make in business and Herman he had made it, and now Herman he would just have to do it, old Mr. Kreder didn't see there was any other way a good boy like his Herman had, to do it. And then too that Lena Mainz was such a nice girl and Herman hadn't ought to really give his father so much trouble and make him pay out all that money, to come all the way to New York just to find him, and they both lose all that time from their working, when all Herman had to do was just to stand up, for an hour, and then he would be all right married, and it would be all over for him, and then everything at home would never be any different to him.

And his father went on; there was his poor mother saying always how her Herman always did everything before she ever wanted, and now just because he got notions in him, and wanted to show people how he could be stubborn, he was making all this trouble for her, and making them pay all that money just to run around and find him. "You got no idea Herman, how bad mama is feeling about the way you been acting Herman," said old Mr. Kreder to him. "She says she never can understand how you can be so thankless Herman. It hurts her very much you been so stubborn, and she find you such a nice girl for you, like Lena Mainz who is always just so quiet and always saves up all her wages, and she never wanting her own way at all like some girls are always all the time to have it, and you mama trying so hard, just so you could be comfortable Herman to be married, and then you act so stubborn Herman. You like all young people Herman, you think only about yourself, and what you are just wanting, and your mama she is thinking only what is good for you to have, for you in the future. Do you think your mama wants to have a girl around to be a bother, for herself, Herman. Its just for you Herman she is always thinking, and she talks always about how happy she will be, when she sees her Herman married to a nice girl, and then when she fixed it all up so good for you, so it never would be any bother to you, just the way she wanted you should like it, and you say yes all right, I do it, and then you go away like this and act stubborn, and make all this trouble everybody to take for you, and we spend money, and I got to travel all round to find you. You come home now with me Herman and get married, and I tell your mama she better not say anything to you about how much it cost me to come all the way to look for you—Hey Herman," said his father coaxing, "Hey, you come home now and get married. All you got to do Herman is just to stand up for an hour Herman, and then you don't never to have any more bother to it—Hey Herman!—you come home with me to-morrow and get married. Hey Herman."

Herman's married sister liked her brother Herman, and she had always tried to help him, when there was anything she knew he wanted. She liked it that he was so good and always did everything that their father and their mother wanted, but still she wished it could be that he could have more his own way, if there was anything he ever wanted.

But now she thought Herman with his girl was very funny. She wanted that Herman should be married. She thought it would do him lots of good to get married. She laughed at Herman when she heard the story. Until his father came to find him, she did not know why it was Herman had come just then to New York to see her. When she heard the story she laughed a good deal at her brother Herman and teased him a good deal about his running away, because he didn't want to have a girl to be all the time around him.

Herman's married sister liked her brother Herman, and she did not want him not to like to be with women. He was good, her brother Herman, and it would surely do him good to get married. It would make him stand up for himself stronger. Herman's sister always laughed at him and always she would try to reassure him. "Such a nice man as my brother Herman acting like as if he was afraid of women. Why the girls all like a man like you Herman, if you didn't always run away when you saw them. It do you good really Herman to get married, and then you got somebody you can boss around when you want to. It do you good Herman to get married, you see if you don't like it, when you really done it. You go along home now with papa, Herman and get married to that Lena. You don't know how nice you like it Herman when you try once how you can do it. You just don't be afraid of nothing, Herman. You good enough for any girl to marry, Herman. Any girl be glad to have a man like you to be always with them Herman. You just go along home with papa and try it what I say, Herman. Oh you so funny Herman, when you sit there, and then run away and leave your girl behind you. I know she is crying like anything Herman for to lose you. Don't be bad to her Herman. You go along home with papa now and get married Herman. I'd be awful ashamed Herman, to really have a brother didn't have spirit enough to get married, when a girl is just dying for to have him. You always like me to be with you Herman. I don't see why you say you don't want a girl to be all the time around you. You always been good to me Herman, and I know you always be good to that Lena, and you soon feel just like as if she had always been there with you. Don't act like as if you wasn't a nice strong man, Herman. Really I laugh at you Herman, but you know I like awful well to see you real happy. You go home and get married to that Lena, Herman. She is a real pretty girl and real nice and good and quiet and she make my brother Herman very happy. You just stop your fussing now with Herman, papa. He go with you to-morrow papa, and you see he like it so much to be married, he make everybody laugh just to see him be so happy. Really truly, that's the way it will be with you Herman. You just listen to me what I tell you Herman." And so his sister laughed at him and reassured him, and his father kept on telling what the mother always said about her Herman, and he coaxed him and Herman never said anything in answer, and his sister packed his things up and was very cheerful with him, and she kissed him, and then she laughed and then she kissed him, and his father went and bought the tickets for the train, and at last late on Sunday he brought Herman back to Bridgepoint with him.

It was always very hard to keep Mrs. Kreder from saying what she thought, to her Herman, but her daughter had written her a letter, so as to warn her not to say anything about what he had been doing, to him, and her husband came in with Herman and said, "Here we are come home mama, Herman and me, and we are very tired it was so crowded coming," and then he whispered to her. "You be good to Herman, mama, he didn't mean to make us so much trouble," and so old Mrs. Kreder, held in what she felt was so strong in her to say to her Herman. She just said very stiffly to him, "I'm glad to see you come home to-day, Herman." Then she went to arrange it all with Mrs. Haydon.

Herman was now again just like he always had been, sullen and very good, and very quiet, and always ready to do whatever his mother and his father wanted. Tuesday morning came, Herman got his new clothes on and went with his father and his mother to stand up for an hour and get married. Lena was there in her new dress, and her hat with all the pretty flowers, and she was very nervous for now she knew she was really very soon to be married. Mrs. Haydon had everything all ready. Everybody was there just as they should be and very soon Herman Kreder and Lena Mainz were married.

When everything was really over, they went back to the Kreder house together. They were all now to live together, Lena and Herman and the old father and the old mother, in the house where Mr. Kreder had worked so many years as a tailor, with his son Herman always there to help him.

Irish Mary had often said to Lena she never did see how Lena could ever want to have anything to do with Herman Kreder and his dirty stingy parents. The old Kreders were to an Irish nature, a stingy, dirty couple. They had not the free-hearted, thoughtless, fighting, mud bespattered, ragged, peat-smoked cabin dirt that irish Mary knew and could forgive and love. Theirs was the german dirt of saving, of being dowdy and loose and foul in your clothes so as to save them and yourself in washing, having your hair greasy to save it in the soap and drying, having your clothes dirty, not in freedom, but because so it was cheaper, keeping the house close and smelly because so it cost less to get it heated, living so poorly not only so as to save money but so they should never even know themselves that they had it, working all the time not only because from their nature they just had to and because it made them money but also that they never could be put in any way to make them spend their money.

This was the place Lena now had for her home and to her it was very different than it could be for an irish Mary. She too was german and was thrifty, though she was always so dreamy and not there. Lena was always careful with things and she always saved her money, for that was the only way she knew how to do it. She never had taken care of her own money and she never had thought how to use it.

Lena Mainz had been, before she was Mrs. Herman Kreder, always clean and decent in her clothes and in her person, but it was not because she ever thought about it or really needed so to have it, it was the way her people did in the german country where she came from, and her Aunt Mathilda and the good german cook who always scolded, had kept her on and made her, with their scoldings, always more careful to keep clean and to wash real often. But there was no deep need in all this for Lena and so, though Lena did not like the old Kreders, though she really did not know that, she did not think about their being stingy dirty people.

Herman Kreder was cleaner than the old people, just because it was his nature to keep cleaner, but he was used to his mother and his father, and he never thought that they should keep things cleaner. And Herman too always saved all his money, except for that little beer he drank when he went out with other men of an evening the way he always liked to do it, and he never thought of any other way to spend it. His father had always kept all the money for them and he always was doing business with it. And then too Herman really had no money, for he always had worked for his father, and his father had never thought to pay him.

And so they began all four to live in the Kreder house together, and Lena began soon with it to look careless and a little dirty, and to be more lifeless with it, and nobody ever noticed much what Lena wanted, and she never really knew herself what she needed.

The only real trouble that came to Lena with their living all four there together, was the way old Mrs. Kreder scolded. Lena had always been used to being scolded, but this scolding of old Mrs. Kreder was very different from the way she ever before had had to endure it.

Herman, now he was married to her, really liked Lena very well. He did not care very much about her but she never was a bother to him being there around him, only when his mother worried and was nasty to them because Lena was so careless, and did not know how to save things right for them with their eating, and all the other ways with money, that the old woman had to save it.

Herman Kreder had always done everything his mother and his father wanted but he did not really love his parents very deeply. With Herman it was always only that he hated to have any struggle. It was all always all right with him when he could just go along and do the same thing over every day with his working, and not to hear things, and not to have people make him listen to their anger. And now his marriage, and he just knew it would, was making trouble for him. It made him hear more what his mother was always saying, with her scolding. He had to really hear it now because Lena was there, and she was so scared and dull always when she heard it. Herman knew very well with his mother, it was all right if one ate very little and worked hard all day and did not hear her when she scolded, the way Herman always had done before they were so foolish about his getting married and having a girl there to be all the time around him, and now he had to help her so the girl could learn too, not to hear it when his mother scolded, and not to look so scared, and not to eat much, and always to be sure to save it.

Herman really did not know very well what he could do to help Lena to understand it. He could never answer his mother back to help Lena, that never would make things any better for her, and he never could feel in himself any way to comfort Lena, to make her strong not to hear his mother, in all the awful ways she always scolded. It just worried Herman to have it like that all the time around him. Herman did not know much about how a man could make a struggle with a mother, to do much to keep her quiet, and indeed Herman never knew much how to make a struggle against anyone who really wanted to have anything very badly. Herman all his life never wanted anything so badly, that he would really make a struggle against any one to get it. Herman all his life only wanted to live regular and quiet, and not talk much and to do the same way every day like every other with his working. And now his mother had made him get married to this Lena and now with his mother making all that scolding, he had all this trouble and this worry always on him.

Mrs. Haydon did not see Lena now very often. She had not lost her interest in her niece Lena, but Lena could not come much to her house to see her, it would not be right, now Lena was a married woman. And then too Mrs. Haydon had her hands full just then with her two daughters, for she was getting them ready to find them good husbands, and then too her own husband now worried her very often about her always spoiling that boy of hers, so he would be sure to turn out no good and be a disgrace to a german family, and all because his mother always spoiled him. All these things were very worrying now to Mrs. Haydon, but still she wanted to be good to Lena, though she could not see her very often. She only saw her when Mrs. Haydon went to call on Mrs. Kreder or when Mrs. Kreder came to see Mrs. Haydon, and that never could be very often. Then too these days Mrs. Haydon could not scold Lena, Mrs. Kreder was always there with her, and it would not be right to scold Lena, when Mrs. Kreder was there, who had now the real right to do it. And so her aunt always said nice things now to Lena, and though Mrs. Haydon sometimes was a little worried when she saw Lena looking sad and not careful, she did not have time just then to really worry much about it.

Lena now never any more saw the girls she always used to sit with. She had no way now to see them and it was not in Lena's nature to search out ways to see them, nor did she now ever think much of the days when she had been used to see them. They never any of them had come to the Kreder house to see her. Not even Irish Mary had ever thought to come to see her. Lena had been soon forgotten by them. They had soon passed away from Lena and now Lena never thought any more that she had ever known them.

The only one of her old friends who tried to know what Lena liked and what she needed, and who always made Lena come to see her, was the good german cook who had always scolded. She now scolded Lena hard for letting herself go so, and going out when she was looking so untidy. "I know you going to have a baby Lena, but that's no way for you to be looking. I am ashamed most to see you come and sit here in my kitchen, looking so sloppy and like you never used to Lena. I never see anybody like you Lena. Herman is very good to you, you always say so, and he don't treat you bad even though you don't deserve to have anybody good to you, you so careless all the time, Lena, letting yourself go like you never had anybody tell you what was the right way you should know how to be looking. No, Lena, I don't see no reason you should let yourself go so and look so untidy Lena, so I am ashamed to see you sit there looking so ugly, Lena. No Lena that ain't no way ever I see a woman make things come out better, letting herself go so every way and crying all the time like as if you had real trouble. I never wanted to see you marry Herman Kreder, Lena, I knew what you got to stand with that old woman always, and that old man, he is so stingy too and he don't say things out but he ain't any better in his heart than his wife with her bad ways, I know that Lena, I know they don't hardly give you enough to eat, Lena, I am real sorry for you Lena, you know that Lena, but that ain't any way to be going round so untidy Lena, even if you have got all that trouble. You never see me do like that Lena, though sometimes I got a headache so I can't see to stand to be working hardly, and nothing comes right with all my cooking, but I always see Lena, I look decent. That's the only way a german girl can make things come out right Lena. You hear me what I am saying to you Lena. Now you eat something nice Lena, I got it all ready for you, and you wash up and be careful Lena and the baby will come all right to you, and then I make your Aunt Mathilda see that you live in a house soon all alone with Herman and your baby, and then everything go better for you. You hear me what I say to you Lena. Now don't let me ever see you come looking like this any more Lena, and you just stop with that always crying. You ain't got no reason to be sitting there now with all that crying, I never see anybody have trouble it did them any good to do the way you are doing, Lena. You hear me Lena. You go home now and you be good the way I tell you Lena, and I see what I can do. I make your Aunt Mathilda make old Mrs. Kreder let you be till you get your baby all right. Now don't you be scared and so silly Lena. I don't like to see you act so Lena when really you got a nice man and so many things really any girl should be grateful to be having. Now you go home Lena to-day and you do the way I say, to you, and I see what I can do to help you."

"Yes Mrs. Aldrich" said the good german woman to her mistress later, "Yes Mrs. Aldrich that's the way it is with them girls when they want so to get married. They don't know when they got it good Mrs. Aldrich. They never know what it is they're really wanting when they got it, Mrs. Aldrich. There's that poor Lena, she just been here crying and looking so careless so I scold her, but that was no good that marrying for that poor Lena, Mrs. Aldrich. She do look so pale and sad now Mrs. Aldrich, it just break my heart to see her. She was a good girl was Lena, Mrs. Aldrich, and I never had no trouble with her like I got with so many young girls nowadays, Mrs. Aldrich, and I never see any girl any better to work right than our Lena, and now she got to stand it all the time with that old woman Mrs. Kreder. My! Mrs. Aldrich, she is a bad old woman to her. I never see Mrs. Aldrich how old people can be so bad to young girls and not have no kind of patience with them. If Lena could only live with her Herman, he ain't so bad the way men are, Mrs. Aldrich, but he is just the way always his mother wants him, he ain't got no spirit in him, and so I don't really see no help for that poor Lena. I know her aunt, Mrs. Haydon, meant it all right for her Mrs. Aldrich, but poor Lena, it would be better for her if her Herman had stayed there in New York that time he went away to leave her. I don't like it the way Lena is looking now, Mrs. Aldrich. She looks like as if she don't have no life left in her hardly, Mrs. Aldrich, she just drags around and looks so dirty and after all the pains I always took to teach her and to keep her nice in her ways and looking. It don't do no good to them, for them girls to get married Mrs. Aldrich, they are much better when they only know it, to stay in a good place when they got it, and keep on regular with their working. I don't like it the way Lena looks now Mrs. Aldrich. I wish I knew some way to help that poor Lena, Mrs. Aldrich, but she she is a bad old woman, that old Mrs. Kreder, Herman's mother. I speak to Mrs. Haydon real soon, Mrs. Aldrich, I see what we can do now to help that poor Lena."

These were really bad days for poor Lena. Herman always was real good to her and now he even sometimes tried to stop his mother from scolding Lena. "She ain't well now mama, you let her be now you hear me. You tell me what it is you want she should be doing, I tell her. I see she does it right just the way you want it mama. You let be, I say now mama, with that always scolding Lena. You let be, I say now, you wait till she is feeling better." Herman was getting really strong to struggle, for he could see that

Lena with that baby working hard inside her, really could not stand it any longer with his mother and the awful ways she always scolded.

It was a new feeling Herman now had inside him that made him feel he was strong to make a struggle. It was new for Herman Kreder really to be wanting something, but Herman wanted strongly now to be a father, and he wanted badly that his baby should be a boy and healthy, Herman never had cared really very much about his father and his mother, though always, all his life, he had done everything just as they wanted, and he had never really cared much about his wife, Lena, though he always had been very good to her, and had always tried to keep his mother off her, with the awful way she always scolded, but to be really a father of a little baby, that feeling took hold of Herman very deeply. He was almost ready, so as to save his baby from all trouble, to really make a strong struggle with his mother and with his father, too, if he would not help him to control his mother.

Sometimes Herman even went to Mrs. Haydon to talk all this trouble over. They decided then together, it was better to wait there all four together for the baby, and Herman could make Mrs. Kreder stop a little with her scolding, and then when Lena was a little stronger, Herman should have his own house for her, next door to his father, so he could always be there to help him in his working, but so they could eat and sleep in a house where the old woman could not control them and they could not hear her awful scolding.

And so things went on, the same way, a little longer. Poor Lena was not feeling any joy to have a baby. She was scared the way she had been when she was so sick on the water. She was scared now every time when anything would hurt her. She was scared and still and lifeless, and sure that every minute she would die. Lena had no power to be strong in this kind of trouble, she could only sit still and be scared, and dull, and lifeless, and sure that every minute she would die.

Before very long, Lena had her baby. He was a good, healthy little boy, the baby. Herman cared very much to have the baby. When Lena was a little stronger he took a house next door to the old couple, so he and his own family could eat and sleep and do the way they wanted.

This did not seem to make much change now for Lena. She was just the same as when she was waiting with her baby. She just dragged around and was careless with her clothes and all lifeless, and she acted always and lived on just as if she had no feeling. She always did everything regular with the work, the way she always had had to do it, but she never got back any spirit in her. Herman was always good and kind, and always helped her with her working. He did everything he knew to help her. He always did all the active new things in the house and for the baby. Lena did what she had to do the way she always had been taught it. She always just kept going now with her working, and she was always careless, and dirty, and a little dazed, and lifeless. Lena never got any better in herself of this way of being that she had had ever since she had been married.

Mrs. Haydon never saw any more of her niece, Lena. Mrs. Haydon had now so much trouble with her own house, and her daughters getting married, and her boy, who was growing up, and who always was getting so much worse to manage. She knew she had done right by Lena. Herman Kreder was a good man, she would be glad to get one so good, sometimes, for her own daughters, and now they had a home to live in together, separate from the old people, who had made their trouble for them. Mrs. Haydon felt she had done very well by her niece, Lena, and she never thought now she needed any more to go and see her. Lena would do very well now without her aunt to trouble herself any more about her.

The good german cook who had always scolded, still tried to do her duty like a mother to poor Lena. It was very hard now to do right by Lena. Lena never seemed to hear now what anyone was saying to her. Herman was always doing everything he could to help her. Herman always, when he was home, took good care of the baby. Herman loved to take care of his baby. Lena never thought to take him out or to do anything she didn't have to.

The good cook sometimes made Lena come to see her. Lena would come with her baby and sit there in the kitchen, and watch the good woman cooking, and listen to her sometimes a little, the way she used to, while the good german woman scolded her for going around looking so careless when now she had no trouble, and sitting there so dull, and always being just so thankless. Sometimes Lena would wake up a little and get back into her face her old, gentle, patient, and unsuffering sweetness, but mostly Lena did not seem to hear much when the good german woman scolded. Lena always liked it when Mrs. Aldrich her good mistress spoke to her kindly, and then Lena would seem to go back and feel herself to be like she was when she had been in service. But mostly Lena just lived along and was careless in her clothes, and dull, and lifeless.

By and by Lena had two more little babies. Lena was not so much scared now when she had the babies. She did not seem to notice very much when they hurt her, and she never seemed to feel very much now about anything that happened to her.

They were very nice babies, all these three that Lena had, and Herman took good care of them always. Herman never really cared much about his wife, Lena. The only things Herman ever really cared for were his babies. Herman always was very good to his children. He always had a gentle, tender way when he held them. He learned to be very handy with them. He spent all the time he was not working, with them. By and by he began to work all day in his own home so that he could have his children always in the same room with him.

Lena always was more and more lifeless and Herman now mostly never thought about her. He more and more took all the care of their three children. He saw to their eating right and their washing, and he dressed them every morning, and he taught them the right way to do things, and he put them to their sleeping, and he was now always every minute with them. Then there was to come to them, a fourth baby. Lena went to the hospital near by to have the baby. Lena seemed to be going to have much trouble with it. When the baby was come out at last, it was like its mother lifeless.

While it was coming, Lena had grown very pale and sicker. When it was all over Lena had died, too, and nobody knew just how it had happened to her.

The good german cook who had always scolded Lena, and had always to the last day tried to help her, was the only one who ever missed her. She remembered how nice Lena had looked all the time she was in service with her, and how her voice had been so gentle and sweet-sounding, and how she always was a good girl, and how she never had to have any trouble with her, the way she always had with all the other girls who had been taken into the house to help her. The good cook sometimes spoke so of Lena when she had time to have a talk with Mrs. Aldrich, and this was all the remembering there now ever was of Lena.

Herman Kreder now always lived very happy, very gentle, very quiet, very well content alone with his three children. He never had a woman any more to be all the time around him. He always did all his own work in his house, when he was through every day with the work he was always doing for his father. Herman always was alone, and he always worked alone, until his little ones were big enough to help him. Herman Kreder was very well content now and he always lived very regular and peaceful, and with every day just like the next one, always alone now with his three good, gentle children.

FINIS

1909

from **The Making of Americans**

Once an angry man dragged his father along the ground through his own orchard. "Stop!" cried the groaning old man at last, "Stop! I did not drag my father beyond this tree."

It is hard living down the tempers we are born with. We all begin well, for in our youth there is nothing we are more intolerant of than our own sins writ large in others and we fight them fiercely in ourselves; but we grow old and we see that these our sins are of all sins the really harmless ones to own, nay that they give a charm to any character, and so our struggle with them dies away.

It has always seemed to me a rare privilege, this, of being an American, a real American, one whose tradition it has taken scarcely sixty years to create. We need only realise our parents, remember our grandparents and know ourselves and our history is complete.

The old people in a new world, the new people made out of the old, that is the story that I mean to tell, for that is what really is and what I really know.

Some of the fathers we must realise so that we can tell our story really, were little boys then, and they came across the water with their parents, the grandparents we need only just remember. Some of these our fathers and our mothers, were not even made then, and the women, the young mothers, our grandmothers we perhaps just have seen once, carried these our fathers and our mothers into the new world inside them, those women of the old world strong to bear them. Some looked very weak and little women, but even these so weak and little, were strong always, to bear many children.

These certain men and women, our grandfathers and grandmothers, with their children born and unborn with them, some whose children were gone ahead to prepare a home to give them; all countries were full of women who brought with them many children; but only certain men and women and the children they had in them, to make many generations for them, will fill up this history for us of a family and its progress.

Many kinds of all these women were strong to bear many children.

One was very strong to bear them and then always she was very strong to lead them.

One was strong to bear them and then always she was strong to suffer with them.

One, a little gentle weary woman was strong to bear many children, and then always after she would sadly suffer for them, weeping for the sadness of all sinning, wearying for the rest she knew her death would bring them.

And then there was one sweet good woman, strong just to bear many children, and then she died away and left them, for that was all she knew then to do for them.

And these four women and the husbands they had with them and the children born and unborn in them will make up the history for us of a family and its progress.

Other kinds of men and women and the children they had with them, came at different times to know them; some, poor things, who never found how they could make a living, some who dreamed while others fought a way to help them, some whose children went to pieces with them, some who thought and thought and then their children rose to greatness through them, and some of all these kinds of men and women and the children they had in them will help to make the history for us of this family and its progress.

These first four women, the grandmothers we need only just remember, mostly never saw each other. It was their children and grandchildren who, later, wandering over the new land, where they were seeking first, just to make a living, and then later, either to grow rich or to gain wisdom, met with one another and were married, and so together they made a family whose progress we are now soon to be watching. . . .

Old ones come to be dead. There are old ones in family living in some family livings and these when they come to be old enough ones come to be dead. Any one coming to be an old enough one comes then to be a dead one.

Doing something is done by some in family living. Some family living is existing. Some are doing something in family living. Some one in a family living is doing something and family living is existing and family living is going on being existing and that one is doing something in family living.

That one has been doing something in family living, that one is doing something in family living, that one is going to be doing something in family living. That one has been doing something in family living and that one is doing that thing and any one in the family living is being one being in the family living and that one the one doing something in the family living is completely remembering that every one being in the family living is in the family living. That one is remembering something of this thing about every one being in the family living, is remembering something about each one being in the family living, is completely remembering something about each one being in the family living and any one in the family living can come to be remembering that that one the one completely remembering something about each one being in the family living is remembering something about each one in the family living being in the family living.

The one remembering completely remembering something about each one being in the family living has been completely remembering everything about any one being in the family living, is remembering completely remembering everything about some being in the family living, is completely remembering something about every one being in the family living, will be completely remembering everything about some being in the family living will completely remember something about every one being in the family living. Family living can be existing. Very many are remembering that family living can be existing.

Very many can go on living remembering that family living is existing. Very many are living and are remembering that family living can go on existing. Very many can go on living remembering that family living can go on existing. . . .

Family living can go on existing. Very many are remembering this thing are remembering that family living living can go on existing. Very many are quite certain that family living can go on existing. Very many are remembering that they are quite certain that family living can go on exiting.

Any family living going on existing is going on and every one can come to be a dead one and there are then not any more living in that family living and that family is not then existing if there are not then any more having come to be living. Any family living is existing if there are some more being living when very many have come to be dead ones. Family living can be existing if not every one in the family living has come to be a dead one. Family living can be existing if there have come to be some existing who have not come to be dead ones. Family living can be existing and there can be some who are not completely remembering any such thing. Family living can be existing and there can be some who have been completely remembering such a thing. Family living can be existing and there can be some remembering something of such a thing. Family living can be existing and some can come to be old ones and then dead ones and some can have been then quite expecting some such thing. Family living can be existing and some can come to be old ones and not yet dead ones and some can be remembering something of some such thing. Family living can be existing and some one can come to be an old one and some can come to be a pretty old one and some can come to be completely expecting such a thing and completely remembering expecting such a thing. Family living can be existing and every one can come to be a dead one and not any one then is remembering any such thing. Family living can be existing and every one can come to be a dead one and some are remembering some such thing. Family living can be existing and any one can come to be a dead one and every one is then a dead one and there are then not any more being living. Any old one can come to be a dead one. Every old one came come to be a dead one. Any family being existing is one having some being then not having come to be a dead one. Any family living can be existing when to every one has come to be a dead one. Every one in a family living have come to be dead ones some are remembering something of some such thing. Some being living not have come to be dead ones can be ones being in a family living. Some being living and having come to be old ones can come then to be dead ones. Some being living and being in a family living and coming then to be old ones can come then to be dead ones. Any one can be certain that some can remember such a thing. Any family living can be one being existing and some can remember something of some such thing.

1906–1911, 1925

Susie Asado

Sweet sweet sweet sweet sweet tea.
    Susie Asado.
Sweet sweet sweet sweet sweet tea.
    Susie Asado.
Susie Asado which is a told tray sure.
A lean on the shoe this means slips slips hers.
When the ancient light grey is clean it is yellow, it is a silver seller.
This is a please this is a please there are the saids to jelly. These are the wets these say the sets to leave a crown to Incy.
Incy is short for incubus.
A pot. A pot is a beginning of a rare bit of trees. Trees tremble, the old vats are in bobbles, bobbles which shade and shove and render clean, render clean must.
    Drink pups.
Drink pups drink pups lease a sash hold, see it shine and a bobolink his pins. It shows a nail.
What is a nail. A nail is unison.
Sweet sweet sweet sweet sweet tea.

1913, 1922

Preciosilla

Cousin to Clare washing.

In the win all the band beagles which have cousin lime sign and arrange a weeding match to presume a certain point to exstate to exstate a certain pass lint to exstate a lean sap prime lo and shut shut is life.

Bait, bait, tore, tore her clothes, toward it, toward a bit, toward a sit, sit down in, in vacant surely lots, a single mingle, bait and wet, wet a single establishment that has a lily lily grow. Come to the pen come in the stem, come in the grass grown water.

Lily wet lily wet while. This is so pink so pink in stammer, a long bean which shows bows is collected by a single curly shady, shady get, get set wet bet.

It is a snuff a snuff to be told and have can wither, can is it and sleep sleep knot, it is a lily scarf the pink and blue yellow, not blue not odour sun, nobles are bleeding bleeding two seats two seats on end. Why is grief. Grief is strange black. Sugar is melting. We will not swim.

Preciosilla

Please be please be get, please get wet, wet naturally, naturally in weather. Could it be fire more firier. Could it be so in ate struck. Could it be gold up, gold up stringing, in it while while which is hanging, hanging in dingling, dingling in pinning, not so. Not so dots large dressed dots, big sizes, less laced, less laced diamonds, diamonds white, diamonds bright, diamonds in the in the light, diamonds light diamonds door diamonds hanging to be four, two four, all before, this bean, lessly, all most, a best, willow, vest, a green guest, guest, go go go go go go, go. Go go. Not guessed. Go go.

Toasted susie is my ice-cream.

1913, 1926

Ladies' Voices

Curtain Raiser

Ladies' voices give pleasure.

The acting two is easily lead. Leading is not in winter. Here the winter is sunny.

Does that surprise you.

Ladies voices together and then she came in.

Very well good night.

Very well good night.

(Mrs. Cardillac.)

That's silver.

You mean the sound.

Yes the sound.

Act II

Honest to God Miss Williams I don't mean to say that I was older.
But you were.
Yes I was. I do not excuse myself. I feel that there is no reason for
passing an archduke.
You like the word.
You know very well that they all call it their house.
As Christ was to Lazarus so was the founder of the hill to Mahon.
You really mean it.
I do.

Act III

Yes Genevieve does not know it. What. That we are seeing Caesar.
Caesar kisses.
Kisses today.
Caesar kisses every day.
Genevieve does not know that it is only in this country that she
could speak as she does.
She does speak very well doesn't she. She told them that there was
not the slightest intention on the part of her countrymen to eat the fish
that was not caught in their country.
In this she was mistaken.

Act IV

What are ladies voices.
Do you mean to believe me.
Have you caught the sun.
Dear me have you caught the sun.

Scene II

Did you say they were different. I said it made no difference.
Where does it. Yes.
Mr. Richard Sutherland. This is a name I know.
Yes.
The Hotel Victoria.
Many words spoken to me have seemed English.
Yes we do hear one another and yet what are called voices the best
decision in telling of balls.
Masked balls.
Yes masked balls.
Poor Augustine.

1916, 1922

Miss Furr and Miss Skeene

Helen Furr had quite a pleasant home. Mrs. Furr was quite a pleasant woman. Mr. Furr was quite a pleasant man. Helen Furr had quite a pleasant voice a voice quite worth cultivating. She did not mind working. She worked to cultivate her voice. She did not find it gay living in the same place where she had always been living. She went to a place where some were cultivating something, voices and other things needing cultivating. She met Georgine Skeene there who was cultivating her voice which some thought was quite a pleasant one. Helen Furr and Georgine Skeene lived together then. Georgine Skeene liked travelling. Helen Furr did not care about travelling, she liked to stay in one place and be gay there. They were together then and traveled to another place and stayed there and were gay there.

They stayed there and were gay there, not very gay there, just gay there. They were both gay there, they were regularly working there both of them cultivating their voices there, they were both gay there. Georgine Skeene was gay there and she was regular, regular in being gay, regular in not being gay, regular in being a gay one who was one not being gay longer than was needed to be one being quite a gay one. They were both gay then there and both working there then.

They were in a way both gay there where there were many cultivating something. They were both regular in being gay there. Helen Furr was gay there, she was gayer and gayer there and really she was just gay there, she was gayer and gayer there, that is to say she found ways of being gay there that she was using in being gay there. She was gay There, not gayer and gayer, just gay there, that is to say she was not gayer by using the things she found there that were gay things, she was gay there, always she was gay there.

There were quite regularly gay there, Helen Furr and Georgine Skeene, they were regularly gay there where they were gay. They were very regularly gay.

To be regularly gay was to do every day the gay thing that they did every day. To be regularly gay was to end every day at the same time after they had been regularly gay. they were regularly gay. They were gay every day. They ended every day in the same way, at the same time, and they had been every day regularly gay.

The voice Helen Furr was cultivating was quite a pleasant one. The voice Georgine Skeene was cultivating was, some said, a better one. The voice Helen Furr was cultivating she cultivated and it was quite completely a pleasant enough one then, a cultivated enough one then. The voice Georgine Skeene was cultivating she did not cultivate too much. She cultivated it quite some. She cultivated and she would sometime go on cultivating it and it was not then an unpleasant one, it would not be then an unpleasant one, it would be a quite richly enough cultivated one, it would be quite richly enough to be a pleasant enough one.

They were gay where there were many cultivating something. The two were gay there, were regularly gay there. Georgine Skeene would have liked to do more travelling. They did some travelling, not very much travelling, Georgine Skeene would have liked to do more travelling. Helen Furr did not care about doing travelling, she liked to stay in a place and be gay there.

They stayed in a place and were gay there, both of them stayed there, they stayed together there, they were gay there, they were regularly gay there.

They went quite often, not very often, but they did go back to where Helen Furr had a pleasant enough home and then Georgine Skeene went to a place where her brother had quite some distinction. They both went, every few years, went visiting to where Helen Furr had quite a pleasant home. Certainly Helen Furr would not find it gay to stay, she did not find it gay, she said she would not stay, she said she did not find it gay, she said she would not stay where she did not find it gay, she said she found it gay where she did stay and she did stay there where very many were cultivating something. She did stay there. She always did find it gay there.

She went to see them where she had always been living and where she did not find it gay. She had a pleasant home there, Mrs. Furr was a pleasant enough woman, Mr. Furr was a pleasant enough man, Helen told them and they were not worrying, that she did not find it gay living where she had always been living.

Georgine Skeene and Helen Furr were living where they were both cultivating their voices and they were gay there. They visited where Helen Furr had come from and then they went to where they were living where they were then regularly living.

There were some dark and heavy men there then. There were some who were not so heavy and some who were not so dark. Helen Furr and Georgine Skeene sat regularly with them. They sat regularly with the ones who were dark and heavy. They sat regularly with the ones who were not so dark. They sat regularly with the ones that were not so heavy. They sat with them regularly, sat with some of them. They went with them regularly went with them. They were regular then, they were gay then, they were where they wanted to be then where it was gay to be then, they were regularly gay then. There were men there then who were dark and heavy and they sat with them with Helen Furr and Georgine Skeene and they went with them with Miss Furr and Miss Skeene, and they went with the heavy and dark men Miss Furr and Miss Skeene went with them, and they sat with them, Miss Furr and Miss Skeene sat with them, and there were other men, some were not heavy men and they sat with Miss Furr and Miss Skeene and Miss Furr and Miss Skeene sat with them, and there were other men who were not dark men and they sat with Miss Furr and Miss Skeene and Miss Furr and Miss Skeene sat with them. Miss Furr and Miss Skeene went with them and they went with Miss Furr and Miss Skeene, some who were not heavy men, some who were not dark men. Miss Furr and Miss Skeene sat regularly, they sat with some men. Miss Furr and Miss Skeene went and there were some men with them. There were men and Miss Furr and Miss Skeene went with them, went somewhere with them, went with some of them.

Helen Furr and Georgine Skeene were regularly living where very many were living and cultivating in themselves something. Helen Furr and Georgine Skeene were living very regularly then, being very regular then in being gay then. They did then learn many ways to be gay and they were then being gay being quite regular in being gay, being gay and they were learning little things, little things in ways of being gay, they were very regular then, they were learning very many little things in ways of being gay, they were being gay and using these little things they were learning to have to be gay with regularly gay with then, and they were gay the same amount they had been gay. They were quite gay, they were quite regular, they were learning little things, gay little things, they were gay inside them the same amount they had been gay, they were gay the same length of time they had been gay every day.

They were regular in being gay, they learned little things that are things in being gay, they learned many little things that are things in being gay, they were gay every day, they were regular, they were gay, they were gay the same length of time every day, they were gay, they were quite regularly gay.

Georgine Skeene went away to stay two months with her brother. Helen Furr did not go then to stay with her father and her mother. Helen Furr stayed there where they had been regularly living the two of them and she would then certainly not be lonesome, she would go on being gay. She did go on being gay. She was not any more gay but she was gay longer every day than they had been being gay when they were together being gay. She was gay then quite exactly the same way. She learned a few more little ways of being in being gay. She was quite gay and in the same way, the same way she had been gay and she was gay a little longer in the day, more of each day she was gay. She was gay longer every day than when the two of them had been being gay. She was gay quite in the way they had been gay, quite in the same way.

She was not lonesome then, she was not at all feeling any need of having Georgine Skeene. She was not astonished at this thing. She would have been a little astonished by this thing but she knew she was not astonished at anything and so she was not astonished at this thing not astonished at not feeling any need of having Georgine Skeene.

Helen Furr had quite a completely pleasant voice and it was quite well enough cultivated and she could use it and she did use it but then there was not any way of working at cultivating a completely pleasant voice when it has become a quite completely well enough cultivated one, and there was not much use in using it when one was not wanting it to be helping to make one a gay one. Helen Furr was not needing using her voice to be a gay one. She was gay then and sometimes she used her voice and she was not using it very often. It was quite completely enough cultivated and it was quite completely a pleasant one and she did not use it very often. She was then, she was quite exactly as gay as she had been, she was gay a little longer in the day than she had been.

She was gay exactly the same way. She was never tired of being gay that way. She had learned very many little ways to use in being gay. Very many were telling about using other ways in being gay. She was gay enough, she was always gay exactly the same way, she was always learning little things to use in being gay, she was telling about using other ways in being gay, she was telling about learning other ways in being gay, she was learning other ways in being gay, she would be using other ways in being gay, she would always be gay in the same way, when Georgine Skeene was there not so long each day as when Georgine Skeene was away.

She came to using many ways in being gay, she came to use every way in being gay. She went on living where many were cultivating something and she was gay, she had used every way to be gay.

They did not live together then Helen Furr and Georgine Skeene. Helen Furr lived there the longer where they had been living regularly together. Then neither of them were living there any longer. Helen Furr was living somewhere else then and telling some about being gay and she was gay then and she was living quite regularly then. She was regularly gay then. She was quite regular in being gay then. She remembered all the little ways of being gay. She used all the little ways of being gay. She was quite regularly gay. She told many then the way of being gay, she taught very many then little ways they could use in being gay. She was living very well, she was gay then, she went on living then, she was regular in being gay, she always was living very well and was gay very well and was telling about little ways one could be learning to use in being gay, and later was telling them quite often, telling them again and again.

1923

from **Composition as Explanation**

There is singularly nothing that makes a difference a difference in beginning and in the middle and in ending except that each generation has something different at which they are all looking. By this I mean so simply that anybody knows it that composition is the difference which makes each and all of them then different from other generations and this is what makes everything different otherwise they are all alike and everybody knows it because everybody says it.

It is very likely that nearly every one has been very nearly certain that something that is interesting is interesting them. Can they and do they. It is very interesting that nothing inside in them, that is when you consider the very long history of how every one ever acted or has felt, it is very interesting that nothing inside in them in all of them makes it connectedly different. By this I mean this. The only thing that is different from one time to another is what is seen and what is seen depends upon how everybody is doing everything. This makes the thing we are looking at very different and this makes what those who describe it make of it, it makes a composition, it confuses, it shows, it is, it looks, it likes it as it is, and this makes what is seen as it is seen. Nothing changes from generation to generation except the thing seen and that makes a composition. Lord Grey remarked that when the generals before the war talked about the war they talked about it as a nineteenth century war although to be fought with twentieth century weapons. That is because war is a thing that decides how it is to be when it is to be done. It is prepared and to that degree it is like all academies it is not a thing made by being made it is a thing prepared. Writing and painting and all that, is like that, for those who occupy themselves with it and don't make it as it is made. Now the few who make it as it is made, and it is to be remarked that the most decided of them usually are prepared just as the world around them is preparing, do it in this way and so I if you do not mind I will tell you how it happens. Naturally one does not know how it happened until it is well over beginning happening.

To come back to the part that the only thing that is different is what is seen when it seems to be being seen, in other words, composition and time-sense.

No one is ahead of his time, it is only that the particular variety of creating his time is the one that his contemporaries who also are creating their own time refuse to accept. And they refuse to accept it for a very simple reason and that is that they do not have to accept it for any reason. They themselves that is everybody in their entering the modern composition and they do enter it, if they do not enter it they are not so to speak in it they are out of it and so they do enter it; but in as you may say the non-competitive efforts where if you are not in it nothing is lost except nothing at all except what is not had, there are naturally all the refusals, and the things refused are only important if unexpectedly somebody happens to need them. In the case of the arts it is very definite. Those who are creating the modern composition authentically are naturally only of importance when they are dead because by that time the modern composition having become past is classified and the description of it is classical. That is the reason why the creator of the new composition in the arts is an outlaw until he is a classic, there is hardly a moment in between and it is really too bad very much too bad naturally for the creator but also very much too bad for the enjoyer, they all really would enjoy the created so much better just after it has been made than when it is already a classic, but it is perfectly simple that there is no reason why the contemporaries should see, because it would not make any difference as they lead their lives in the new composition anyway, and as everyone one is naturally indolent why naturally they don't see. For this reason as in quoting Lord Grey it is quite certain that nations not actively threatened are at least several generations behind themselves militarily so æsthetically they are more than several generations behind themselves and it is very much too bad, it is so very much more exciting and satisfactory for everybody if one can have contemporaries, if all one's contemporaries could be one's contemporaries.

There is almost not an interval.

For a very long time everybody refuses and then almost without a pause almost everybody accepts. In this history of the refused in the arts and literature the rapidity of the change is always startling. Now the only difficulty with the *volte-face* concerning the arts is this. When the acceptance comes, by that acceptance the thing created becomes a classic. It is a natural phenomena a rather extraordinary natural phenomena that a thing accepted becomes a classic. And what is the characteristic quality of a classic. The characteristic quality of a classic is that it is beautiful. Now of course it is perfectly true that a more or less first rate work of art is beautiful but the trouble is that when that first rate work of art becomes a classic because it is accepted the only thing that is important from then on to the majority of the acceptors the enormous majority, the most intelligent majority of the acceptors is that it is so wonderfully beautiful. Of course it is wonderfully beautiful, only when it is still a thing irritating annoying stimulating then all quality of beauty is denied to it....

1926

WILLIAM CARLOS WILLIAMS
1883–1963

Since his death in 1963, William Carlos Williams's centrality among the American modernist poets has been assured by a spate of critical studies elucidating his innovative poetics, his use of American language and scene, and his ties to revolutionary currents in the visual arts. In formal experiment and in modulation of poetic voice from the highly objective to the intimately autobiographical, Williams's influence on the writing of younger generations of poets has been extensive. Beyond this emphasis on craft, however, lies his essential humanity and what he called "contact" with the immediate world: from close attention to the flora and landscape of his native northern New Jersey to his concern with the struggle, pathos, and comic resilience of the working class. A writer of amazing shifts and changes, Williams's interest in process and discovery led him to reflect the fragmentation and disjunction of modern life.

Born in Rutherford, New Jersey, Williams spent most of his life there except for periods of education and travel. For him, remaining in the United States became an example to set against the expatriation of Ezra Pound and T. S. Eliot. Yet he was far from provincial. From 1897 to 1899, he studied with his younger brother at schools near Geneva and in Paris. Home again, he commuted to the Horace Mann School in New York until 1902. Finally deciding a career in medicine would offer the support his writing demanded, Williams attended the University of Pennsylvania Medical School, graduating in 1906. After an internship in New York City, he spent a year in Europe, visiting Pound in London and traveling on the continent. He was convinced, however, that the United States provided richer materials for the native writer attentive to the "local" and the vital language of his people.

Of mixed heritage, Williams thought himself a quintessential American. His mother had been born in Puerto Rico of Basque and French-Dutch-Jewish descent; his father, born in England and raised in the West Indies, retained British citizenship after settling with his new wife in the U.S. The family spoke Spanish at home when Williams was a boy. In his parents' experience—including his mother's three years of art study as a young woman in Paris and his father's business trips to Latin and South America—as well as in his own knowledge of the immigrant life of many of his patients, Williams found the basis for his celebration of cultural diversity.

In 1912, two years after he began medical practice, Williams married Florence Herman, daughter of a prosperous local family and later the Flossie of numerous poems. The next year they bought a house at 9 Ridge Road in Rutherford to serve as home and office; here they raised two sons and resided the rest of their lives. His practice among the poor and the middle class would become a source of characters, settings, and images throughout his work.

Influenced by early reading and imitation of Walt Whitman and John Keats, Williams was to find his way after publication of *Poems 1909* through Imagism and interest in modernist art to a new attitude toward poetic form and treatment of immediate reality. Although Ezra Pound, with whom he began a lifelong friendship at the University of Pennsylvania, could not fully convert him to Imagism's tenets, his ideas helped to free Williams from a more conventional Romanticism.

With publication of *Al Que Quiere!* in 1917, Williams first displayed the qualities of his mature work: the short enjambed lines characterizing his visual style contrasted with more colloquial verse shaped by what he called the "American idiom" (typified by "Danse Russe"); the brash, no-nonsense voice of the social man contrasted with a lyrical, romantic strain; precise, almost photographic recording of scene contrasted with evocation of intimate emotion. In large measure, Williams's break with traditional forms and with aesthetic attitudes toward mimesis and beauty was a response to contemporary movements in painting and photography. In the work of the Cubists, Dadaists, and Precisionists exhibited at Alfred Stieglitz's galleries and at Walter Arensberg's studio, as well as in the dense lyrics of Marianne Moore, Williams found support for a radically new approach to verse.

The early 1920s were for Williams a time of aggressive experimentation. Typical of the range of his writing during this period are the three poems "Spring and All," "The Rose," and "To Elsie." In each Williams begins with the importance of the particular, the near-at-hand, affirming his later insistence in *Paterson* on "no ideas but in things." The potential for quickening he perceives in the drear landscape and the possibility for renewal of outmoded conceptions communicated in the painting—these, Williams implies, await only our imaginative response.

With *Paterson*, Book I (1946), Williams undertook the long poem for which he had been preparing since the preliminary study, "Paterson" (1927). Composed eventually of five books, this modernist epic centers on the doctor-poet

Paterson's search for a redeeming language, exploring the estrangement of men and women from their environment and from each other. Using collage-like techniques, Williams juxtaposes material from newspapers, letters, documents, and interviews with passages in lyric, descriptive, and dramatic forms to create a portrait of his time as significant as those in the long poems of Eliot and Pound.

In his later work, Williams often employed what he referred to as the "variable foot," a triadic or step-down form he first discovered in writing "The Descent" in *Paterson*, Book II. Line length in "The Pink Locust," for example, is sometimes determined by grammatical units, sometimes by the emphasis Williams places on phrases or individual words. The speaker's voice is direct, personal. Like the pink locust, Williams persisted during the last fifteen years of his life, weathering a series of heart attacks and strokes and a nervous collapse, to write a number of psychologically complex and hauntingly beautiful poems. He is considered the most diverse and challenging poet of his generation.

Theodora Rapp Graham
Pennsylvania State University at Harrisburg

PRIMARY WORKS

Poetry: *Poems*, 1909; *The Tempers*, 1913; *Al Que Quiere!*, 1917; *Sour Grapes*, 1921; *Spring and All*, 1923; *Collected Poems 1906–1938*, 1938; *Paterson*, 1946, 1948, 1949, 1951, 1958, 1963 (revised edition, 1992); *The Desert Music*, 1954; *Journey to Love*, 1955; *Pictures from Breghel*, 1962; A. Walton Litz and Christopher MacGowan, eds., *Collected Poems of William Carlos Williams*, Vol. I, 1986, *Collected Poems*, Vol. II, 1988; Fiction: *The Great American Novel*, 1923; *A Voyage to Pagany*, 1928; A Trilogy: *White Mule*, 1937; *In the Money*, 1940; *The Build-Up*, 1952; *Collected Stories*, 1961 (1996); Non-Fiction: *Kora in Hell: Improvisations*, 1920; *In the American Grain*, 1925; *Autobiography*, 1951.

Danse Russe[1]

If when my wife is sleeping
and the baby and Kathleen[2]
are sleeping
and the sun is a flame-white disc
in silken mists   5
above shining trees,—
if I in my north room
dance naked, grotesquely
before my mirror
waving my shirt round my head   10
and singing softly to myself:
"I am lonely, lonely.
I was born to be lonely,
I am best so!"

[1] In 1916 Nijinsky and the Ballets Russes appeared in New York.

[2] "Kathleen" was nursemaid for the Williams children.

If I admire my arms, my face,   15
my shoulders, flanks, buttocks
against the yellow drawn shades,—

Who shall say I am not
the happy genius of my household?

                                                  1916

The Young Housewife

At ten A.M. the young housewife
moves about in negligee behind
the wooden walls of her husband's house.
I pass solitary in my car.

Then again she comes to the curb   5
to call the ice-man, fish-man, and stands
shy, uncorseted, tucking in
stray ends of hair, and I compare her
to a fallen leaf.

The noiseless wheels of my car   10
rush with a crackling sound over
dried leaves as I bow and pass smiling.

                                                  1917

Portrait of a Lady

Your thighs are appletrees
whose blossoms touch the sky.
Which sky? The sky
where Watteau hung a lady's
slipper. Your knees   5
are a southern breeze—or
a gust of snow. Agh! what
sort of man was Fragonard?[1]
—as if that answered
anything. Ah, yes—below   10
the knees, since the tune
drops that way, it is
one of those white summer days,

[1]Watteau and Fragonard were 18th-century French painters. The painting referred to is not by Watteau but Fragonard's "The Swing."

the tall grass of your ankles
flickers upon the shore—   15
Which shore?—
the sand clings to my lips—
Which shore?
Agh, petals maybe. How
should I know?   20
Which shore? Which shore?
I said petals from an appletree.

                                                                 1920

Spring and All

By the road to the contagious hospital
under the surge of the blue
mottled clouds driven from the
northeast—a cold wind. Beyond, the
waste of broad, muddy fields   5
brown with dried weeds, standing and fallen

patches of standing water
the scattering of tall trees

All along the road the reddish
purplish, forked, upstanding, twiggy   10
stuff of bushes and small trees
with dead, brown leaves under them
leafless vines—
Lifeless in appearance, sluggish
dazed spring approaches—   15

They enter the new world naked,
cold, uncertain of all
save that they enter. All about them
the cold, familiar wind—

Now the grass, tomorrow   20
the stiff curl of wildcarrot leaf

One by one objects are defined—
It quickens:[1] clarity, outline of leaf

---

[1]Medical term given to pregnant woman's
first feeling of movement of fetus.

But now the stark dignity of
entrance—Still, the profound change   25
has come upon them: rooted, they
grip down and begin to awaken

1923

The Red Wheelbarrow

so much depends
upon

a red wheel
barrow

glazed with rain   5
water

beside the white
chickens

1923

The Pot of Flowers[1]

Pink confused with white
flowers and flowers reversed
take and spill the shaded flame
darting it back
into the lamp's horn   5

petals aslant darkened with mauve

red where in whorls
petal lays its glow upon petal
round flamegreen throats

petals radiant with transpiercing light   10
contending
         above

[1]Free rendering into poetry of Charles
Demuth's "Tuberoses" (1922), which Williams owned.

the leaves
reaching up their modest green
from the pot's rim   15

and there, wholly dark, the pot
gay with rough moss.

                                                               1923

The Rose

The rose is obsolete
but each petal ends in
an edge, the double facet
cementing the grooved
columns of air—The edge   5
cuts without cutting
meets—nothing—renews
itself in metal or porcelain—

whither? It ends—
But if it ends   10
the start is begun
so that to engage roses
becomes a geometry—

Sharper, neater, more cutting
figured in majolica—   15
the broken plate
glazed with a rose

Somewhere the sense
makes copper roses
steel roses—   20

The rose carried weight of love
but love is at an end—of roses

It is at the edge of the
petal that love waits

Crisp, worked to defeat   25
laboredness—fragile
plucked, moist, half-raised
cold, precise, touching

What

The place between the petal's   30
edge and the

From the petal's edge a line starts
that being of steel
infinitely fine, infinitely
rigid penetrates   35
the Milky Way
without contact—lifting
from it—neither hanging
nor pushing—

The fragility of the flower   40
unbruised
penetrates space.

                                                                 1923

To Elsie[1]

The pure products of America
go crazy—
mountain folk from Kentucky

or the ribbed north end of
Jersey   5
with its isolate lakes and

valleys, its deaf-mutes, thieves
old names
and promiscuity between

devil-may-care men who have taken   10
to railroading
out of sheer lust of adventure—

and young slatterns, bathed
in filth
from Monday to Saturday   15

---

[1]Elsie was a mentally handicapped nursemaid from the state orphanage who worked for the Williams family after Kathleen departed (see "Danse Russe").

to be tricked out that night
with gauds
from imaginations which have no

peasant traditions to give them
character   20
but flutter and flaunt

sheer rags—succumbing without
emotion
save numbed terror

under some hedge of choke-cherry   25
or viburnum—
which they cannot express—

Unless it be that marriage
perhaps
with a dash of Indian blood   30
will throw up a girl so desolate
so hemmed round
with disease or murder

that she'll be rescued by an
agent—   35
reared by the state and

sent out at fifteen to work in
some hard-pressed
house in the suburbs—

some doctor's family, some Elsie—   40
voluptuous water
expressing with broken

brain the truth about us—
her great
ungainly hips and flopping breasts   45

addressed to cheap
jewelry
and rich young men with fine eyes

as if the earth under our feet
were   50
an excrement of some sky

and we degraded prisoners
destined
to hunger until we eat filth

while the imagination strains   55
after deer
going by fields of goldenrod in

the stifling heat of September
Somehow
it seems to destroy us   60

It is only in isolate flecks that
something
is given off

No one
to witness   65
and adjust, no one to drive the car

                                                                1923

Young Sycamore

I must tell you
this young tree
whose round and firm trunk
between the wet

pavement and the gutter   5
(where water
is trickling) rises
bodily

into the air with
one undulant   10
thrust half its height—
and then

dividing and waning
sending out
young branches on   15
all sides—

hung with cocoons
it thins
till nothing is left of it
but two   20

eccentric knotted
twigs
bending forward
hornlike at the top

                                                                1927

The Flower

A petal, colorless and without form
the oblong towers lie

beyond the low hill and northward the great
bridge stanchions,
small in the distance, have appeared,   5
pinkish and incomplete—

It is the city,
approaching over the river. Nothing

of it is mine, but visibly
for all that it is petal of a flower—my own.   10

It is a flower through which the wind
combs the whitened grass and a black dog

with yellow legs stands eating from a
garbage barrel. One petal goes eight blocks

past two churches and a brick school beyond   15
the edge of the park where under trees

leafless now, women having nothing else to do
sit in summer—to the small house

in which I happen to have been born. Or
a heap of dirt, if you care   20

to say it, frozen and sunstreaked in
the January sun, returning.

Then they hand you—they who wish to God
you'd keep your fingers out of

their business—science or philosophy or   25
anything else they can find to throw off

to distract you. But Madame Lenine[1]
is a benefactress when under her picture

in the papers she is quoted as saying:
Children should be especially protected   30

from religion. Another petal
reaches to San Diego, California where

a number of young men, New Yorkers most
of them, are kicking up the dust.

A flower, at its heart (the stamens, pistil,   35
etc.) is a naked woman, about 38, just

out of bed, worth looking at both for
her body and her mind and what she has seen

and done. She it was put me straight
about the city when I said, It   40

makes me ill to see them run up
a new bridge like that in a few months

and I can't find time even to get
a book written. They have the power,

that's all, she replied. That's what you all   45
want. If you can't get it, acknowledge

at least what it is. And they're not
going to give it to you. Quite right.

For years I've been tormented by
that miracle, the buildings all lit up—   50

[1]French spelling of the name of Lenin's
widow, an educational leader in Russia.

unable to say anything much to the point
though it is the major sight

of this region. But foolish to rhapsodize over
strings of lights, the blaze of a power

in which I have not the least part.   55
Another petal reaches

into the past, to Puerto Rico
when my mother was a child bathing in a small

river and splashing water up on
the yucca leaves to see them roll back pearls.   60

The snow is hard on the pavements. This
is no more a romance than an allegory.

I plan one thing—that I could press
buttons to do the curing of or caring for

the sick that I do laboriously now by hand   65
for cash, to have the time

when I am fresh, in the morning, when
my mind is clear and burning—to write.

                                                                       1930

The Poor

It's the anarchy of poverty
delights me, the old
yellow wooden house indented
among the new brick tenements

Or a cast-iron balcony   5
with panels showing oak branches
in full leaf. It fits
the dress of the children

reflecting every stage and
custom of necessity—   10
Chimneys, roofs, fences of
wood and metal in an unfenced

age and enclosing next to
nothing at all: the old man
in a sweater and soft black   15
hat who sweeps the sidewalk—

his own ten feet of it—
in a wind that fitfully
turning his corner has
overwhelmed the entire city   20

                                                               1938

Burning the Christmas Greens

Their time past, pulled down
cracked and flung to the fire
—go up in a roar
All recognition lost, burnt clean

clean in the flame, the green   5
dispersed, a living red,
flame red, red as blood wakes
on the ash—

and ebbs to a steady burning
the rekindled bed become   10
a landscape of flame

At the winter's midnight
we went to the trees, the coarse
holly, the balsam and
the hemlock for their green   15

At the thick of the dark
the moment of the cold's
deepest plunge we brought branches
cut from the green trees

to fill our need, and over   20
doorways, about paper Christmas
bells covered with tinfoil
and fastened by red ribbons

we stuck the green prongs
in the windows hung   25

woven wreaths and above pictures
the living green. On the

mantle we built a green forest
and among those hemlock
sprays put a herd of small   30
white deer as if they

were walking there. All this!
and it seemed gentle and good
to us. Their time past,
relief! The room bare. We   35

stuffed the dead grate
with them upon the half burnt out
log's smoldering eye, opening
red and closing under them

and we stood there looking down.   40
Green is a solace
a promise of peace, a fort
against the cold (though we

did not say so) a challenge
above the snow's   45
hard shell. Green (we might
have said) that, where

small birds hide and dodge
and lift their plaintive
rallying cries, blocks for them   50
and knocks down

the unseeing bullets of
the storm. Green spruce boughs
pulled down by a weight of
snow—Transformed!   55

Violence leaped and appeared.
Recreant! roared to life
as the flame rose through and
our eyes recoiled from it.

In the jagged flames green   60
to red, instant and alive. Green!

those sure abutments ... Gone!
lost to mind

and quick in the contracting
tunnel of the grate   65
appeared a world! Black
mountains, black and red—as

yet uncolored—and ash white,
an infant landscape of shimmering
ash and flame and we, in   70
that instant, lost,

breathless to be witnesses,
as if we stood
ourselves refreshed among
the shining fauna of that fire.   75

                                                          1944

The Descent

The descent beckons
            as the ascent beckoned.
                        Memory is a kind
of accomplishment,
            a sort of renewal   5
even
an initiation, since the spaces it opens are new places
            inhabited by hordes
                        heretofore unrealized,

of new kinds—   10
            since their movements
                        are toward new objectives
(even though formerly they were abandoned).

No defeat is made up entirely of defeat—since
the world it opens is always a place   15
            formerly
                        unsuspected. A
world lost,
            a world unsuspected,
                        beckons to new places   20
and no whiteness (lost) is so white as the memory
of whiteness.

With evening, love wakens
      though its shadows
            which are alive by reason   25
of the sun shining—
      grow sleepy now and drop away
          from desire.

Love without shadows stirs now
      beginning to awaken   30
    as night
advances.

The descent
      made up of despairs
          and without accomplishment   35
realizes a new awakening:
        which is a reversal
of despair.
      For what we cannot accomplish, what
is denied to love,   40
what we have lost in the anticipation—
a descent follows,
endless and indestructible

                   1954

The Pink Locust

I'm persistent as the pink locust,
      once admitted
          to the garden,
you will not easily get rid of it.
      Tear it from the ground,   5
        if one hair-thin rootlet
remain
    it will come again.
        It is
flattering to think of myself   10
    so. It is also
        laughable.
A modest flower,
      resembling a pink sweet-pea,
        you cannot help   15
but admire it
    until its habits
      become known.

Are we not most of us
           like that? It would be   20
                  too much
if the public
           pried among the minutiae
                  of our private affairs.
Not   25
           that we have anything to hide
                  but could *they*
stand it? Of course
           the world would be gratified
                  to find out   30
what fools we have made of ourselves.
           The question is,
                  would they
be generous with us—
           as we have been   35
                  with others? It is,
as I say,
           a flower
                  incredibly resilient
under attack!   40
           Neglect it
                  and it will grow into a tree.
I wish I could *so* think of myself
           and of what
                  is to become of me.   45
The poet himself,
           what does he think of himself
                  facing his world?
It will not do to say,
           as he is inclined to say: 50
                  Not much. The poem
would be in *that* betrayed.
           He might as well answer—
                  "a rose is a rose
is a rose"[1] and let it go at that.   55
           A rose *is* a rose
                  and the poem equals it
if it be well made.
           The poet
                  cannot slight himself   60
without slighting
           his poem—
                  which would be

[1]The phrase quoted is Gertrude Stein's.

ridiculous.
      Life offers   65
            no greater reward.
And so,
      like this flower,
            I persist—
for what there may be in it.   70
      I am not,
            I know,
in the galaxy of poets
      a rose
            but *who*, among the rest,   75
will deny me
      my place.

                                            1955

EUGENE O'NEILL
1888–1953

"The best play by an American we have seen," raved the *Brooklyn Eagle*; "an exceedingly juvenile performance," lamented the *New York Post*. The mixed reviews of *The Hairy Ape*'s first production in Greenwich Village in 1922 were not unusual for a new O'Neill play during that decade. Despite winning three Pulitzer Prizes for drama between 1920 and 1928, O'Neill repeatedly battled not only skeptical critics, but also hostile censors, who resisted the staging of plays depicting interracial marriage (*All God's Chillun Got Wings*, 1924), infanticide (*Desire Under the Elms*, 1924), and infidelity and abortion (*Strange Interlude*, 1928). The controversy continues today, though its focus now is literary. O'Neill simultaneously spiritualized and democratized the modern stage by discovering "the transfiguring nobility of tragedy" in "seemingly the most ignoble, debased lives"—such as that of Yank Smith—thereby forging a trail later followed by Arthur Miller and Tennessee Williams. O'Neill's keen ear for native dialects (like the Bronx accent of Yank) brought numerous varieties of spoken American English onto our stage in a serious way for the first time, an achievement comparable to that of Mark Twain in fiction.

If O'Neill's literary merit is the subject of debate, his work's autobiographical nature is not. His father was the famous actor James O'Neill, who became a wealthy man—and sacrificed much of his talent—by touring in the title role of the melodrama *The Count of Monte Cristo*, which he performed over 5,000 times. Perhaps the young O'Neill's taste for strong theatrical effects, so evident in *Ape*'s stage directions, can be traced to his early, repeated exposure to this source; certainly, the polar conflict between Yank and Mildred (typical of the extreme oppositions in O'Neill's plays) is the stuff of melodrama, though here it dramatizes psychological, social, and philosophical issues rather than moral ones. The central conflict also points toward the playwright's mother. Ella Quinlan O'Neill's long-lasting addiction to morphine caused a frequent personal remoteness that deeply wounded her youngest son—who was sent off to Roman Catholic boarding schools as a young boy, partially to prevent his knowledge of her condition. His traumatic discovery of it at fourteen was comparable in his mind to the biblical fall from grace (a recurrent motif in his work), and Yank's sense of not "belonging" anywhere after his encounter with the ghostly Mildred projects the spiritual anguish that subsequently tormented O'Neill throughout his life. He never fully forgave his mother, and the women in his work frequently embody cultural stereotypes that reveal O'Neill's deep fear and mistrust of women. He also grew to resent bitterly the Christian God who, he felt, permitted his mother's addiction and failed to answer his prayers to cure it. Later, this disillusion took the form of a restless quest for alternative faiths—not unlike Yank's agonized search—that led him to the works of Nietzsche, Schopenhauer, Jung, Freud, and Asian mystical religions, systems that inform his drama throughout the twenties.

O'Neill's discovery of writing as his vocation occurred only after a period of alcoholism, sea travel, and bohemianism culminated in 1912 in a failed suicide attempt and his contracting of tuberculosis. Recovering from the disease, he started reading ancient and modern drama—Sophocles, Aeschylus, Wedekind, Ibsen, Shaw, and (especially) Strindberg—and, with the help of George Pierce Baker's drama workshop at Harvard, began writing his own plays, many about the sea. One of them, *Bound East for Cardiff*, was produced on Cape Cod in 1916 by the Provincetown Players, one of numerous, idealistic "little theater" companies formed in America after 1900 to produce and promote artistic drama without regard for commercial considerations. As guided by George Cram Cook—Susan Glaspell's husband—the Players helped develop O'Neill's sense of theater's sacred mission; more important, they encouraged his experimentation and established his reputation when they began producing his plays in New York in the fall of 1916. Within four years, O'Neill had scored his first Broadway success with *Beyond the Horizon*, a realistic tragedy. Within two more years, the original Provincetown Players had disbanded, but not before producing two of O'Neill's most daring expressionistic works, *The Emperor Jones* (1921) and *The Hairy Ape*. Even after his plays moved permanently to Broadway, O'Neill continued to take artistic risks, though he now often turned to classical sources for inspiration. *The Great God Brown* (1926) used masks to explore psychological conflicts within and between the characters, *Strange Interlude* (1928) borrowed the Elizabethan soliloquy for prolonged "thought asides" that resembled the stream of consciousness technique in modernist novels, and *Mourning Becomes Electra* (1931) drew on Aeschylus' *Oresteia* for a tragic trilogy that explored the Freudian family romance in an aristocratic nineteenth-century New England clan. All were essentially religious dramas that focused on inner, spiritual conflicts, seeking to "interpret Life in terms of lives"; only with *Ah, Wilderness!* (1933), his mature comedy, did he relax.

In his final plays, written during a period of withdrawal from the stage between 1934 and 1946, O'Neill returned to the mode of realism. He worked assiduously on a cycle of eleven plays tracing the history of an American family, "A Tale of Possessors Self-dispossessed," but destroyed most before his death in 1953; only *A Touch of the Poet* (completed in 1942, produced in 1957) survived in finished form, though *More Stately Mansions* (1963) and *The Calms of Capricorn* (1982) have been completed and published with the help of O'Neill scholars. But O'Neill produced his most powerful work when he courageously faced his personal ghosts in *The Iceman Cometh* (1939), *Long Day's Journey into Night* (1941, published and produced 1955), *Hughie* (1942), and *A Moon for the Misbegotten* (1943). The latter two exorcise the demon of his older brother Jamie, an alcoholic "Broadway loafer" who had died in 1923; the former two, set in 1912, are even closer to home. Revisiting the Bowery bar where O'Neill had attempted suicide, *Iceman* dramatizes a self-deluding salesman's attempt to rob derelicts of their sustaining life-lies; revisiting the New London, Connecticut, home where O'Neill grew up, *Journey* depicts his mother's readdiction to morphine upon discovery of his tuberculosis. Appropriately, the climactic acts of both plays revolve around confessions, for here O'Neill confronted not only harrowing memories, but also (in *Journey*) the radical cause of his alienation and his tragic vision: his guilt over being born, the original sin that had first caused his mother to take morphine in 1888.

Within two years of completing *Journey*, O'Neill had to end his writing career due to Parkinson's disease; within another ten years, he was dead.

James A. Robinson
late of University of Maryland

PRIMARY WORKS

Comments on the Drama and the Theater: A Source Book, 1987; *Complete Plays* (three volumes), 1988; *Selected Letters*, 1988.

The Hairy Ape

A Comedy of Ancient and Modern Life in Eight Scenes

CHARACTERS

ROBERT SMITH, "YANK"
PADDY
LONG
MILDRED DOUGLAS
HER AUNT
SECOND ENGINEER
A GUARD
A SECRETARY OF AN ORGANIZATION
STOKERS, LADIES, GENTLEMEN, ETC.

SCENES

SCENE I: The firemen's forecastle of an ocean liner—an hour after sailing from New York.
SCENE II: Section of promenade deck, two days out—morning.
SCENE III: The stokehole. A few minutes later.
SCENE IV: Same as Scene One. Half an hour later.
SCENE V: Fifth Avenue, New York. Three weeks later.
SCENE VI: An island near the city. The next night.
SCENE VII: In the city. About a month later.
SCENE VIII: In the city. Twilight of the next day.

Scene One

The firemen's forecastle of a transatlantic liner an hour after sailing from New York for the voyage across. Tiers of narrow, steel bunks, three deep, on all sides. An entrance in rear. Benches on the floor before the bunks. The room is crowded with men, shouting, cursing, laughing, singing—a confused, inchoate uproar swelling into a sort of unity, a meaning—the bewildered, furious, baffled defiance of a beast in a cage. Nearly all the men are drunk. Many bottles are passed from hand to hand. All are dressed in dungaree pants, heavy ugly shoes. Some wear singlets, but the majority are stripped to the waist.

The treatment of this scene, or of any other scene in the play, should by no means be naturalistic. The effect sought after is a cramped space in the bowels of a ship, imprisoned by white steel. The lines of bunks, the uprights supporting them, cross each other like the steel framework of a cage. The ceiling crushes down upon the men's heads. They cannot stand upright. This accentuates the natural stooping posture which shoveling coal and the resultant over-development of back and shoulder muscles have given them. The men themselves should resemble those pictures in which the appearance of Neanderthal Man is guessed at. All are hairy-chested, with long arms of tremendous power, and low, receding brows above their small, fierce, resentful eyes. All the civilized white races are represented, but except for the slight differentiation in color of hair, skin, eyes, all these men are alike.

The curtain rises on a tumult of sound. YANK *is seated in the foreground. He seems broader, fiercer, more truculent, more powerful, more sure of himself than the rest. They respect his superior strength—the grudging respect of fear. Then, too, he represents to them a self-expression, the very last word in what they are, their most highly developed individual.*

VOICES: Gif me trink dere, you!
　　　'Ave a wet!
　　　Salute!
　　　Gesundheit!
　　　Skoal![1]

[1]Scandinavian drinking toast.

Drunk as a lord, God stiffen you!
Here's how!
Luck!
Pass back that bottle, damn you!
Pourin' it down his neck!
Ho, Froggy! Where the devil have you been?
La Touraine.[2]
I hit him smash in yaw, py Gott!
Jenkins—the First—he's a rotten swine—
And the coppers nabbed him—and I run—
I like peer better. It don't pig head gif you.
A slut, I'm saying'! She robbed me aslape—
To hell with 'em all!
You're a bloody liar!
Say dot again! (*Commotion. Two men about to fight are pulled apart.*)
No scrappin' now!
Tonight—
See who's the best man!
Bloody Dutchman!
Tonight on the for'ard square.
I'll bet on Dutchy.
He packa da wallop, I tella you!
Shut up, Wop!
No fightin', maties. We're all chums, ain't we?
(*A voice starts bawling a song.*)

> "*Beer, beer, glorious beer!*
> *Fill yourselves right up to here.*"

YANK. (*for the first time seeming to take notice of the uproar about him, turns around threateningly—in a tone of contemptuous authority*) Choke off dat noise! Where d'yuh get dat beer stuff? Beer, hell! Beer's for goils—and Dutchmen. Me for somep'n wit a kick to it! Gimme a drink, one of youse guys. (*Several bottles are eagerly offered. He takes a tremendous gulp at one of them; then, keeping the bottle in his hand, glares belligerently at the owner, who hastens to acquiesce in this robbery by saying*) All righto, Yank. Keep it and have another. (YANK *contemptuously turns his back on the crowd again. For a second there is an embarrassed silence. Then—*)

VOICES. We must be passing the Hook.[3]
    She's beginning to roll to it.
    Six days in hell—and then Southampton.[4]
    Py Yesus, I vish somepody take my first vatch for me!
    Gittin' seasick, Square-head?

---

[2]A French ocean liner.
[3]Sandy Hook, a narrow sandy New Jersey peninsula at the entrance to lower New York Bay.

[4]English port city.

Drink up and forget it!

What's in your bottle?

Gin.

Dot's nigger trink.

Absinthe? It's doped. You'll go off your chump, Froggy!

Cochon![5]

Whisky, that's the ticket!

Where's Paddy?

Going asleep.

Sing us that whisky song, Paddy. (*They all turn to an old, wizened Irishman who is dozing, very drunk, on the benches forward. His face is extremely monkey-like with all the sad, patient pathos of that animal in his small eyes.*)

Singa da song, Caruso[6] Pat!

He's gettin' old. The drink is too much for him.

He's too drunk.

PADDY. (*blinking about him, starts to his feet resentfully, swaying, holding on to the edge of a bunk*) I'm never too drunk to sing. 'Tis only when I'm dead to the world I'd be wishful to sing at all. (*With a sort of sad contempt*) "Whisky Johnny," ye want? A chanty, ye want? Now that's a queer wish from the ugly like of you, God help you. But no matther. (*He starts to sing in a thin, nasal, doleful tone:*)

> "Oh, whisky is the life of man!
>   Whisky! O Johnny! (They all join in on this.)
> Oh, whisky is the life of man!
>   Whisky for my Johnny! (Again chorus.)
>
> "Oh, whisky drove my old man mad!
>   Whisky! O Johnny!
> Oh, whisky drove my old man mad!
>   Whisky for my Johnny!"

YANK. (*again turning around scornfully*) Aw hell! Nix on dat old sailing ship stuff! All dat bull's dead, see? And you're dead, too, yuh damned old Harp,[7] on'y yuh don't know it. Take it easy, see. Give us a rest. Nix on de loud noise. (*With a cynical grin*) Can't youse see I'm tryin' to t'ink?

ALL. (*repeating the word after him as one with the same cynical amused mockery*) Think! (*The chorused word has a brazen metallic quality as if their throats were phonograph horns. It is followed by a general uproar of hard, barking laughter.*)

VOICES. Don't be cracking your head wit ut, Yank.

You gat headache, py yingo!

---

[5]"Pig!" (French).
[6]Enrico Caruso, Italian operatic tenor (1873–1921).

[7]Irishman (slang).

One thing about it—it rhymes with drink!

Ha, ha, ha!

Drink, don't think!

Drink, don't think!

Drink, don't think! *(A whole chorus of voices has taken up this refrain, stamping on the floor, pounding on the benches with fists.)*

YANK. *(taking a gulp from his bottle—good-naturedly)* Aw right. Can de noise. I got yuh de foist time. *(The uproar subsides. A very drunken sentimental tenor begins to sing):*

> *"Far away in Canada,*
> *Far across the sea,*
> *There's a lass who fondly waits*
> *Making a home for me—"*

YANK. *(fiercely contemptuous)* Shut up, yuh lousy boob! Where d'yuh get dat tripe? Home? Home, hell! I'll make a home for yuh! I'll knock yuh dead. Home! T'hell wit home! Where d'yuh get dat tripe? Dis is home, see? What d'yuh want wit home? *(Proudly)* I runned away from mine when I was a kid. On'y too glad to beat it, dat was me. Home was lickings for me, dat's all. But yuh can bet your shoit no one ain't never licked me since! Wanter try it, any of youse? Huh! I guess not. *(In a more placated but still contemptuous tone)* Goils waitin' for yuh, huh? Aw, hell! Dat's all tripe. Dey don't wait for no one. Dey'd double-cross yuh for a nickel. Dey're all tarts, get me? Treat 'em rough, dat's me. To hell wit 'em. Tarts, dat's what, de whole bunch of 'em.

LONG. *(very drunk, jumps on a bench exictedly, gesticulating with a bottle in his hand)* Listen 'ere, Comrades! Yank 'ere is right. 'E says this 'ere stinkin' ship is our 'ome. And 'e says as 'ome is 'ell. And 'e's right! This is 'ell. We lives in 'ell, Comrades—and right enough we'll die in it. *(Raging)* And who's ter blame, I arsks yer? We ain't. We wasn't born this rotten way. All men is born free and ekal. That's in the bleedin' Bible, maties. But what d'they care for the Bible—them lazy, bloated swine what travels first cabin? Them's the ones. They dragged us down 'til we're on'y wage slaves in the bowels of a bloody ship, sweatin', burnin' up, eatin' coal dust! Hit's them's ter blame—the damned Capitalist clarss! *(There had been a gradual murmur of contemptuous resentment rising among the men until now he is interrupted by a storm of catcalls, hisses, boos, hard laughter.)*

VOICES. Turn it off!

Shut up!

Sit down!

Closa da face!

Tamn fool! *(Etc.)*.

YANK. *(standing up and glaring at* LONG) Sit down before I knock yuh down! (LONG *makes haste to efface himself.* YANK *goes on contemptuously)* De Bible, huh? De Cap'tlist class, huh? Aw nix on dat Salvation Army-Socialist bull. Git a soapbox! Hire a hall! Come and be saved, huh? Jerk us to Jesus, huh?

Aw g'wan! I've listened to lots of guys like you, see. Yuh're all wrong. Wanter know what I t'ink? Yuh ain't no good for no one. Yuh're de bunk. Yuh ain't got no noive, get me? Yuh're yellow, dat's what. Yellow, dat's you. Say! What's dem slobs in de foist cabin got to do wit us? We're better men dan dey are, ain't we? Sure! One of us guys could clean up de whole mob wit one mitt. Put one of 'em down here for one watch in de stokehole, what'd happen? Dey'd carry him off on a stretcher. Dem boids don't amount to nothin'. Dey're just baggage. Who makes dis old tub run? Ain't it us guys? Well den, we belong, don't we? We belong and dey don't. Dat's all. (*A loud chorus of approval.* YANK *goes on*) As for dis bein' hell—aw, nuts! Yuh lost your noive, dat's what. Dis is a man's job, get me? It belongs. It runs dis tub. No stiffs[8] need apply. But yuh're a stiff, see? Yuh're yellow, dat's you.

VOICES. (*with a great hard pride in them*)

> Righto!
> A man's job!
> Talk is cheap, Long.
> He never could hold up his end.
> Divil take him!
> Yank's right. We make it go.
> Py Gott, Yank say right ting!
> We don't need no one cryin' over us.
> Makin' speeches.
> Throw him out!
> Yellow!
> Chuck him overboard!
> I'll break his jaw for him!
> (*They crowd around* LONG *threateningly.*)

YANK. (*half good-natured again—contemptuously*) Aw, take it easy. Leave him alone. He ain't woith a punch. Drink up. Here's how, whoever owns dis. (*He takes a long swallow from his bottle. All drink with him. In a flash all is hilarious amiability again, back-slapping, loud talk, etc.*)

PADDY. (*who has been sitting in a blinking, melancholy daze—suddenly cries out in a voice full of old sorrow*) We belong to this, you're saying? We make the ship to go, you're saying? Yerra[9] then, that Almighty God have pity on us! (*His voice runs into the wail of a keen,*[10] *he rocks back and forth on his bench. The men stare at him, startled and impressed in spite of themselves*) Oh, to be back in the fine days of my youth, ochone![11] Oh, there was fine beautiful ships them days—clippers wid tall masts touching the sky—fine strong men in them—men that was sons of the sea as if 'twas the mother that bore them. Oh, the clean skins of them, and the clear eyes, the straight backs and full chests of them! Brave men they was, and bold men surely! We'd be sailing out, bound down round the Horn[12] maybe. We'd

---

[8]Slang expression for an overformal, inhibited person, as well as a corpse.
[9]"Truly" (Irish).

[10]Irish lamentation for the dead.
[11]"Alas!" (Irish).
[12]Cape Horn, southern end of South America.

be making sail in the dawn, with a fair breeze, singing a chanty song wid no care to it. And astern the land would be sinking low and dying out, but we'd give it no heed but a laugh, and never a look behind. For the day that was, was enough, for we was free men—and I'm thinking 'tis only slaves do be giving heed to the day that's gone or the day to come—until they're old like me. *(With a sort of religious exaltation)* Oh, to be scudding south again wid the power of the Trade Wind driving her on steady through the nights and the days! Full sail on her! Nights and days! Nights when the foam of the wake would be flaming wid fire, when the sky'd be blazing and winking wid stars. Or the full of the moon maybe. Then you'd see her driving through the gray night, her sails stretching aloft all silver and white, not a sound on the deck, the lot of us dreaming dreams, till you'd believe 'twas no real ship at all you was on but a ghost ship like the *Flying Dutchman*[13] they say does be roaming the seas forevermore widout touching a port. And there was the days, too. A warm sun on the clean decks. Sun warming the blood of you, and wind over the miles of shiny green ocean like strong drink to your lungs. Work—aye, hard work—but who'd mind that at all? Sure, you worked under the sky and 'twas work wid skill and daring to it. And wid the day done, in the dog watch, smoking me pipe at ease, the lookout would be raising land maybe, and we'd see the mountains of South Americy wid the red fire of the setting sun painting their white tops and the clouds floating by them! *(His tone of exaltation ceases. He goes on mournfully)* Yerra, what's the use of talking? 'Tis a dead man's whisper. *(To* YANK *resentfully)* 'Twas them days men belonged to ships, not now. 'Twas them days a ship was part of the sea, and a man was part of a ship, and the sea joined all together and made it one. *(Scornfully)* Is it one wid this you'd be, Yank—black smoke from the funnels smudging the sea, smudging the decks—the bloody engines pounding and throbbing and shaking—wid divil a sight of sun or a breath of clean air—choking our lungs wid coal dust—breaking our backs and hearts in the hell of the stokehole—feeding the bloody furnace—feeding our lives along wid the coal, I'm thinking—caged in by steel from a sight of the sky like bloody apes in the Zoo! *(With a harsh laugh)* Ho-ho, divil mend you! Is it to belong to that you're wishing? Is it a flesh and blood wheel of the engines you'd be?

YANK. *(who has been listening with a contemptuous sneer, barks out the answer)* Sure ting! Dat's me. What about it?

PADDY. *(as if to himself—with great sorrow)* Me time is past due. That a great wave wid sun in the heart of it may sweep me over the side sometime I'd be dreaming of the days that's gone!

YANK. Aw, yuh crazy Mick![14] *(He springs to his feet and advances on* PADDY *threateningly—then stops, fighting some queer struggle within himself—lets*

---

[13]Legendary ship carrying a mariner condemned to sail the seas against the wind until Judgment Day.

[14]Irishman (slang).

his hands fall to his sides—contemptuously) Aw, take it easy. Yuh're aw right, at dat. Yuh're bugs, dat's all—nutty as a cuckoo. All dat tripe yuh been pullin'—Aw, dat's all right. On'y it's dead, get me? Yuh don't belong no more, see. Yuh don't get de stuff. Yuh're too old. *(Disgustedly)* But aw say, come up for air onct in a while, can't yuh? See what's happened since yuh croaked. *(He suddenly bursts forth vehemently, growing more and more excited)* Say! Sure! Sure I meant it! What de hell—Say, lemme talk! Hey! Hey, you old Harp! Hey, youse guys! Say, listen to me—wait a moment—I gotter talk, see. I belong and he don't. He's dead but I'm livin'. Listen to me! Sure I'm part of de engines! Why de hell not! Dey move, don't dey? Dey're speed, ain't dey? Dey smash trou, don't dey? Twenty-five knots a hour! Dat's goin' some! Dat's new stuff! Dat belongs! But him, he's too old. He gets dizzy. Say, listen. All dat crazy tripe about nights and days; all dat crazy tripe about stars and moons; all dat crazy tripe about suns and winds, fresh air and de rest of it—Aw hell, dat's all a dope dream! Hittin' de pipe of de past, dat's what he's doin'. He's old and don't belong no more. But me, I'm young! I'm in de pink! I move wit it. It, get me! I mean de ting dat's de guts of all dis. It ploughs trou all de tripe he's been sayin'. It blows dat up! It knocks dat dead! It slams dat offen de face of de oith! It, get me! De engines and de coal and de smoke and all de rest of it! He can't breathe and swallow coal dust, but I kin, see? Dat's fresh air for me! Dat's food for me! I'm new, get me? Hell in de stokehole? Sure! It takes a man to work in hell. Hell, sure, dat's my fav'rite climate. I eat it up! I git fat on it! It's me makes it hot! It's me makes it roar! It's me makes it move! Sure, on'y for me everyting stops. It all goes dead, get me? De noise and smoke and all de engines movin' de woild, dey stop. Dere ain't nothin' no more! Dat's what I'm sayin'. Everyting else dat makes de woild move, somep'n makes it move. It can't move witout somep'n else, see? Den yuh get down to me. I'm at de bottom, get me! Dere ain't nothin' foither. I'm de end! I'm de start! I start somep'n and de woild moves! It—dat's me!—de new dat's moiderin' de old! I'm de ting in coal dat makes it boin; I'm steam and oil for de engines; I'm de ting in noise dat makes yuh hear it; I'm smoke and express trains and steamers and factory whistles; I'm de ting in gold dat makes it money! And I'm what makes iron into steel! Steel, dat stands for de whole ting! And I'm steel—steel—steel! I'm de muscles in steel, de punch behind it! *(As he says this he pounds with his fist against the steel bunks. All the men, roused to a pitch of frenzied self-glorification by his speech, do likewise. There is a deafening metallic roar, through which* YANK'S *voice can be heard bellowing)* Slaves, hell! We run de whole woiks. All de rich guys dat tink dey're somep'n, dey ain't nothin'! Dey don't belong. But us guys, we're in de move, we're at de bottom, de whole ting is us! *(*PADDY *from the start of* YANK's *speech has been taking one gulp after another from his bottle, at first frightenedly, as if he were afraid to listen, then desperately, as if to drown his senses, but finally has achieved complete indifferent, even amused, drunkenness.* YANK *sees his lips moving. He quells the uproar with a shout)* Hey, youse guys, take it easy! Wait a moment! De nutty Harp is sayin' somep'n.

PADDY. *(is heard now—throws his head back with a mocking burst of laughter)* Ho-ho-ho-ho-ho—

YANK. *(drawing back his fist, with a snarl)* Aw! Look out who yuh're givin' the bark!

PADDY. *(begins to sing, the "Miller of Dee" with enormous good nature)*

> "I care for nobody, no, not I,
> And nobody cares for me."

YANK. *(good-natured himself in a flash, interrupts* PADDY *with a slap on the bare back like a report)* Dat's de stuff! Now yuh're gettin' wise to somep'n. Care for nobody, dat's de dope! To hell with 'em all! And nix on nobody else carin'. I kin care for myself, get me! *(Eight bells sound, muffled, vibrating through the steel walls as if some enormous brazen gong were imbedded in the heart of the ship. All the men jump up mechanically, file through the door silently close upon each other's heels in what is very like a prisoner's lockstep.* YANK *slaps* PADDY *on the back)* Our watch, yuh old Harp! *(Mockingly)* Come on down in hell. Eat up de coal dust. Drink in de heat. It's it, see! Act like yuh liked it, yuh better—or croak yuhself.

PADDY. *(with jovial defiance)* To the divil wid it! I'll not report this watch. Let thim log[15] me and be damned. I'm no slave the like of you. I'll be sittin' here at me ease, and drinking, and thinking, and dreaming dreams.

YANK. *(contemptuously)* Tinkin' and dreamin', what'll that get yuh? What's tinkin' got to do wit it? We move, don't we? Speed, ain't it? Fog, dat's all you stand for. But we drive trou dat, don't we? We split dat up and smash trou—twenty-five knots a hour! *(Turns his back on* PADDY *scornfully)* Aw, yuh make me sick! Yuh don't belong! *(He strides out the door in rear.* PADDY *hums to himself, blinking drowsily.)*

CURTAIN

Scene Two

Two days out. A section of the promenade deck. MILDRED DOUGLAS *and her aunt are discovered reclining in deck chairs. The former is a girl of twenty, slender, delicate, with a pale, pretty face marred by a self-conscious expression of disdainful superiority. She looks fretful, nervous and discontented, bored by her own anemia. Her aunt is a pompous and proud—and fat—old lady. She is a type even to the point of a double chin and lorgnettes.[16] She is dressed pretentiously, as if afraid her face alone would never indicate her position in life.* MILDRED *is dressed all in white.*

The impression to be conveyed by this scene is one of the beautiful, vivid life of the sea all about—sunshine on the deck in a great flood, the fresh sea wind blowing across it. In the midst of this, these two incongruous, artificial figures,

---

[15]Note his absence by entering his name in the ship's log, a record of daily activities and routines.

[16]Eyeglasses with a short handle, a fashion accessory of some upper-class women of the time.

inert and disharmonious, the elder like a gray lump of dough touched up with rouge, the younger looking as if the vitality of her stock had been sapped before she was conceived, so that she is the expression not of its life energy but merely of the artificialities that energy had won for itself in the spending.

MILDRED. *(looking up with affected dreaminess)* How the black smoke swirls back against the sky! Is it not beautiful?

AUNT. *(without looking up)* I dislike smoke of any kind.

MILDRED. My great-grandmother smoked a pipe—a clay pipe.

AUNT. *(ruffling)* Vulgar!

MILDRED. She was too distant a relative to be vulgar. Time mellows pipes.

AUNT. *(pretending boredom but irritated)* Did the sociology you took up at college teach you that—to play the ghoul on every possible occasion, excavating old bones? Why not let your great-grandmother rest in her grave?

MILDRED. *(dreamily)* With her pipe beside her—puffing in Paradise.

AUNT. *(with spite)* Yes, you are a natural born ghoul. You are even getting to look like one, my dear.

MILDRED. *(in a passionless tone)* I detest you, Aunt. *(Looking at her critically)* Do you know what you remind me of? Of a cold pork pudding against a background of linoleum tablecloth in the kitchen of a—but the possibilities are wearisome. *(She closes her eyes.)*

AUNT. *(with a bitter laugh)* Merci[17] for your candor. But since I am and must be your chaperon—in appearance, at least—let us patch up some sort of armed truce. For my part you are quite free to indulge any pose of eccentricity that beguiles you—as long as you observe the amenities—

MILDRED. *(drawling)* The inanities?

AUNT. *(going on as if she hadn't heard)* After exhausting the morbid thrills of social service work on New York's East Side[18]—how they must have hated you, by the way, the poor that you made so much poorer in their own eyes!—you are now bent on making your slumming international. Well, I hope Whitechapel[19] will provide the needed nerve tonic. Do not ask me to chaperon you there, however. I told your father I would not. I loathe deformity. We will hire an army of detectives and you may investigate everything—they allow you to see.

MILDRED. *(protesting with a trace of genuine earnestness)* Please do not mock my attempts to discover how the other half lives. Give me credit for some sort of groping sincerity in that at least. I would like to help them. I would like to be some use in the world. Is it my fault I don't know how? I would like to be sincere, to touch life somewhere. *(With weary bitterness)* But I'm afraid I have neither the vitality nor integrity. All that was burnt out in our stock before I was born. Grandfather's blast furnaces, flaming to the sky, melting steel, making millions—then father keeping those home fires burning, making more millions—and little me at the tail-end

---

[17]Thank you" (French).

[18]A Manhattan slum district, inhabited mainly by first generation immigrants.

[19]A London slum district.

of it all. I'm a waste product in the Bessemer process[20]—like the millions. Or rather, I inherit the acquired trait of the by-product, wealth, but none of the energy, none of the strength of the steel that made it. I am sired by gold and damned[21] by it, as they say at the race track—damned in more ways than one. *(She laughs mirthlessly.)*

AUNT. *(unimpressed—superciliously)* You seem to be going in for sincerity today. It isn't becoming to you, really—except as an obvious pose. Be as artificial as you are, I advise. There's a sort of sincerity in that, you know. And, after all, you must confess you like that better.

MILDRED. *(again affected and bored)* Yes, I suppose I do. Pardon me for my outburst. When a leopard complains of its spots, it must sound rather grotesque. *(In a mocking tone)* Purr, little leopard. Purr, scratch, tear, kill, gorge yourself and be happy—only stay in the jungle where your spots are camouflage. In a cage they make you conspicuous.

AUNT. I don't know what you are talking about.

MILDRED. It would be rude to talk about anything to you. Let's just talk. *(She looks at her wrist watch)* Well, thank goodness, it's about time for them to come for me. That ought to give me a new thrill, Aunt.

AUNT. *(affectedly troubled)* You don't mean to say you're really going? The dirt—the heat must be frightful—

MILDRED. Grandfather started as a puddler.[22] I should have inherited an immunity to heat that would make a salamander[23] shiver. It will be fun to put it to the test.

AUNT. But don't you have to have the captain's—or someone's—permission to visit the stokehole?

MILDRED. *(with a triumphant smile)* I have it—both his and the chief engineer's. Oh, they didn't want to at first, in spite of my social service credentials. They didn't seem a bit anxious that I should investigate how the other half lives and works on a ship. So I had to tell them that my father, the president of Nazareth Steel,[24] chairman of the board of directors of this line, had told me it would be all right.

AUNT. He didn't.

MILDRED. How naïve age makes one! But I said he did, Aunt. I even said he had given me a letter to them—which I had lost. And they were afraid to take the chance that I might be lying. *(Excitedly)* So it's ho! for the stokehole. The second engineer is to escort me. *(Looking at her watch again)* It's time. And here he comes, I think. *(The* SECOND ENGINEER *enters. He is a husky, fine-looking man of thirty-five or so. He stops before the two and tips his cap, visibly embarrassed and ill-at-ease.)*

SECOND ENGINEER. Miss Douglas?

MILDRED. Yes. *(Throwing off her rugs and getting to her feet)* Are we all ready to start?

---

[20]A method for making steel by burning out excess impurities.
[21]Pun on "dammed" (mothered).
[22]A steelworker.

[23]A mythical creature, resembling a lizard, once believed capable of living in fire.
[24]Allusion to Bethlehem Steel, a large American steel corporation.

SECOND ENGINEER. In just a second, ma'am. I'm waiting for the Fourth.[25] He's coming along.

MILDRED. *(with a scornful smile)* You don't care to shoulder this responsibility alone, is that it?

SECOND ENGINEER. *(forcing a smile)* Two are better than one. *(Disturbed by her eyes, glances out to sea—blurts out)* A fine day we're having.

MILDRED. Is it?

SECOND ENGINEER. A nice warm breeze—

MILDRED. It feels cold to me.

SECOND ENGINEER. But it's hot enough in the sun—

MILDRED. Not hot enough for me. I don't like Nature. I was never athletic.

SECOND ENGINEER. *(forcing a smile)* Well, you'll find it hot enough where you're going.

MILDRED. Do you mean hell?

SECOND ENGINEER. *(flabbergasted, decides to laugh)* Ho-ho! No, I mean the stoke-hole.

MILDRED. My grandfather was a puddler. He played with boiling steel.

SECOND ENGINEER. *(all at sea—uneasily)* Is that so? Hum, you'll excuse me, ma'am, but are you intending to wear that dress?

MILDRED. Why not?

SECOND ENGINEER. You'll likely rub against oil and dirt. It can't be helped.

MILDRED. It doesn't matter. I have lots of white dresses.

SECOND ENGINEER. I have an old coat you might throw over—

MILDRED. I have fifty dresses like this. I will throw this one into the sea when I come back. That ought to wash it clean, don't you think?

SECOND ENGINEER. *(doggedly)* There's ladders to climb down that are none too clean—and dark alleyways—

MILDRED. I will wear this very dress and none other.

SECOND ENGINEER. No offense meant. It's none of my business. I was only warning you—

MILDRED. Warning? That sounds thrilling.

SECOND ENGINEER. *(looking down the deck—with a sigh of relief)* There's the Fourth now. He's waiting for us. If you'll come—

MILDRED. Go on. I'll follow you. *(He goes.* MILDRED *turns a mocking smile on her aunt)* An oaf—but a handsome, virile oaf.

AUNT. *(scornfully)* Poser!

MILDRED. Take care. He said there were dark alleyways—

AUNT. *(in the same tone)* Poser!

MILDRED. *(biting her lips angrily)* You are right. But would that my millions were not so anemically chaste!

AUNT. Yes, for a fresh pose I have no doubt you would drag the name of Douglas in the gutter!

MILDRED. From which it sprang. Good-by, Aunt. Don't pray too hard that I may fall into the fiery furnace.

---

[25]Fourth Engineer.

AUNT. Poser!

MILDRED. *(viciously)* Old hag! *(She slaps her aunt insultingly across the face and walks off, laughing gaily.)*

AUNT. *(screams after her)* I said poser!

CURTAIN

Scene Three

The stokehole. In the rear, the dimly-outlined bulks of the furnaces and boilers. High overhead one hanging electric bulb sheds just enough light through the murky air laden with coal dust to pile up masses of shadows everywhere. A line of men, stripped to the waist, is before the furnace doors. They bend over, looking neither to right nor left, handling their shovels as if they were part of their bodies, with a strange, awkward, swinging rhythm. They use the shovels to throw open the furnace doors. Then from these fiery round holes in the black a flood of terrific light and heat pours full upon the men who are outlined in silhouette in the crouching, inhuman attitudes of chained gorillas. The men shovel with a rhythmic motion, swinging as on a pivot from the coal which lies in heaps on the floor behind to hurl it into the flaming mouths before them. There is a tumult of noise—the brazen clang of the furnace doors as they are flung open or slammed shut, the grating, teeth-gritting grind of steel against steel, of crunching coal. This clash of sounds stuns one's ears with its rending dissonance. But there is order in it, rhythm, a mechanical regulated recurrence, a tempo. And rising above all, making the air hum with the quiver of liberated energy, the roar of leaping flames in the furnaces, the monotonous throbbing beat of the engines.

As the curtain rises, the furnace doors are shut. The men are taking a breathing spell. One or two are arranging the coal behind them, pulling it into more accessible heaps. The others can be dimly made out leaning on their shovels in relaxed attitudes of exhaustion.

PADDY. *(from somewhere in the line—plaintively)* Yerra, will this divil's own watch nivir end? Me back is broke. I'm destroyed entirely.

YANK. *(from the center of the line—with exuberant scorn)* Aw, yuh make me sick! Lie down and croak, why don't yuh? Always beefin', dat's you! Say, dis is a cinch! Dis was made for me! It's my meat, get me! *(A whistle is blown—a thin, shrill note from somewhere overhead in the darkness.* YANK *curses without resentment)* Dere's de damn engineer crackin' de whip. He tinks we're loafin'.

PADDY. *(vindictively)* God stiffen him!

YANK. *(in an exultant tone of command)* Come on, youse guys! Git into de game! She's gittin' hungry! Pile some grub in her. Trow it into her belly! Come on now, all of youse! Open her up! *(At this last all the men, who have followed his movements of getting into position, throw open their furnace doors with a deafening clang. The fiery light floods over their shoulders as they bend round for the coal. Rivulets of sooty sweat have traced maps on their backs. The enlarged muscles form bunches of high light and shadow.)*

YANK. *(chanting a count as he shovels without seeming effort)* One—two—tree— *(His voice rising exultantly in the joy of battle)* Dat's de stuff! Let her have it! All togedder now! Sling it into her! Let her ride! Shoot de piece now! Call de toin on her! Drive her into it! Feel her move! Watch her smoke! Speed, dat's her middle name! Give her coal, youse guys! Coal, dat's her booze! Drink it up, baby! Let's see yuh sprint! Dig in and gain a lap! Dere she go-o-es. *(This last in the chanting formula of the gallery gods at the six-day bike race. He slams his furnace door shut. The others do likewise with as much unison as their wearied bodies will permit. The effect is of one fiery eye after another being blotted out with a series of accompanying bangs.)*

PADDY. *(groaning)* Me back is broke. I'm bate out—bate— *(There is a pause. Then the inexorable whistle sounds again from the dim regions above the electric light. There is a growl of cursing rage from all sides.)*

YANK. *(shaking his fist upward—contemptuously)* Take it easy dere, you! Who d'yuh tink's runnin' dis game, me or you? When I git ready, we move. Not before! When I git ready, get me!

VOICES. *(approvingly)* That's the stuff!

> *Yank tal him, py golly!*
> *Yank ain't affeerd.*
> *Goot poy, Yank!*
> *Give him hell!*
> *Tell 'im 'e's a bloody swine!*
> *Bloody slave-driver!*

YANK. *(contemptuously)* He ain't got no noive. He's yellow, get me? All de engineers is yellow. Dey got streaks a mile wide. Aw, to hell wit him! Let's move, youse guys. We had a rest. Come on, she needs it! Give her pep! It ain't for him. Him and his whistle, dey don't belong. But we belong, see! We gotter feed de baby! Come on! *(He turns and flings his furnace door open. They all follow his lead. At this instant the* SECOND *and* FOURTH ENGINEERS *enter from the darkness on the left with* MILDRED *between them. She starts, turns paler, her pose is crumbling, she shivers with fright in spite of the blazing heat, but forces herself to leave the* ENGINEERS *and take a few steps nearer the men. She is right behind* YANK. *All this happens quickly while the men have their backs turned.)*

YANK. Come on, youse guys! *(He is turning to get coal when the whistle sounds again in a peremptory, irritating note. This drives* YANK *into a sudden fury. While the other men have turned full around and stopped dumbfounded by the spectacle of* MILDRED *standing there in her white dress,* YANK *does not turn far enough to see her. Besides, his head is thrown back, he blinks upward through the murk trying to find the owner of the whistle, he brandishes his shovel murderously over his head in one hand, pounding on his chest, gorilla-like, with the other, shouting)* Toin off dat whistle! Come down outa dere, yuh yellow, brass-buttoned, Belfast bum, yuh! Come down and I'll knock yer brains out! Yuh lousy, stinkin', yellow mut of a Catholic-moiderin' bastard! Come down and I'll moider yuh! Pullin' dat whistle on me, huh? I'll show yuh! I'll crash yer skull in! I'll drive yer teet' down yer troat! I'll slam yer nose trou de back of yer head! I'll cut yer guts out for a nickel, yuh lousy boob, yuh dirty, crummy, muck-eatin' son of a—(*Suddenly he becomes conscious of all the other men staring at something directly behind his back. He whirls defensively with a snarling, murderous growl, crouching to spring, his lips drawn back over his teeth, his small eyes gleaming ferociously. He sees* MILDRED, *like a white apparition in the full light from the open furnace doors. He glares into her eyes, turned to stone. As for her, during his speech she has listened, paralyzed with horror, terror, her whole personality crushed, beaten in, collapsed, by the terrific impact of this unknown, abysmal brutality, naked and shameless. As she looks at his gorilla face, as his eyes bore into hers, she utters a low, choking cry and shrinks away from him, putting both hands up before her eyes to shut out the sight of his face, to protect her own. This startles* YANK *to a reaction. His mouth falls open, his eyes grow bewildered.*)

MILDRED. (*about to faint—to the* ENGINEERS, *who now have her one by each arm—whimperingly*) Take me away! Oh, the filthy beast! (*She faints. They carry her quickly back, disappearing in the darkness at the left, rear. An iron door clangs shut. Rage and bewildered fury rush back on* YANK. *He feels himself insulted in some unknown fashion in the very heart of his pride. He roars* "God Damn yuh!" *and hurls his shovel after them at the door which has just closed. It hits the steel bulkhead with a clang and falls clattering on the steel floor. From overhead the whistle sounds again in a long, angry, inconsistent command.*)

CURTAIN

Scene Four

The firemen's forecastle. YANK'S *watch has just come off duty and had dinner. Their faces and bodies shine from a soap-and-water scrubbing but around their eyes, where a hasty dousing does not touch, the coal dust sticks like black make-up, giving them a queer, sinister expression.* YANK *has not washed either face or body. He stands out in contrast to them, a blackened, brooding figure. He is seated forward on a bench in the exact attitude of Rodin's "The Thinker."*[26] *The others, most of them smoking pipes, are staring at* YANK *half-apprehensively, as if fearing an outburst; half-amusedly, as if they saw a joke somewhere that tickled them.*

VOICES. He ain't ate nothin'.
    Py golly, a fallar gat to gat grub in him.
    Divil a lie.
    Yank feeda da fire, no feeda da face.
    Ha-ha.

[26]Statue by French sculptor Auguste Rodin (1840–1917) of seated nude man with chin propped on fist.

He ain't even washed hisself.

He's forgot.

Hey, Yank, you forgot to wash.

YANK. *(sullenly)* Forgot nothin'! To hell wit washin'.

VOICES. It'll stick to you.

It'll get under your skin.

Give yer the bleedin' itch, that's wot.

It makes spots on you—like a leopard.

Like a piebald[27] nigger, you mean.

Better wash up, Yank.

You sleep better.

Wash up, Yank!

Wash up! Wash up!

YANK. *(resentfully)* Aw say, youse guys. Lemme alone. Can't youse see I'm tryin' to tink?

ALL. *(repeating the word after him as one with cynical mockery)* Think! *(The word has a brazen, metallic quality as if their throats were phonograph horns. It is followed by a chorus of hard, barking laughter.)*

YANK. *(springing to his feet and glaring at them belligerently)* Yes, tink! Tink, dat's what I said! What about it? *(They are silent, puzzled by his sudden resentment at what used to be one of his jokes.* YANK *sits down again in the same attitude of "The Thinker."*)

VOICES. Leave him alone.

He's got a grouch on.

Why wouldn't he?

PADDY. *(with a wink at the others)* Sure I know what's the matther. 'Tis aisy to see. He's fallen in love, I'm telling you.

ALL. *(repeating the word after him as one with cynical mockery)* Love! *(The word has a brazen, metallic quality as if their throats were phonograph horns. It is followed by a chorus of hard, barking laughter.)*

YANK. *(with a contemptuous snort)* Love, Hell! Hate, dat's what. I've fallen in hate, get me?

PADDY. *(philosophically)* 'Twould take a wise man to tell one from the other. *(With a bitter, ironical scorn, increasing as he goes on)* But I'm telling you it's love that's in it. Sure what else but love for us poor bastes in the stokehole would be bringing a fine lady, dressed like a white quane, down a mile of ladders and steps to be havin' a look at us? *(A growl of anger goes up from all sides.)*

LONG. *(jumping on a bench—hectically)* Hinsultin' us! Hinsultin' us, the bloody cow! And them bloody engineers! What right 'as they got to be exhibitin' us 's if we was bleedin' monkeys in a menagerie? Did we sign for hinsults to our dignity as 'onest workers? Is that in the ship's articles?[28] You kin bloody well bet it ain't! But I knows why they done it. I arsked a deck steward 'o she

---

[27]Spotted or patched, especially in black and white.   [28]Regulations concerning employment.

was and 'e told me. 'Er old man's a bleedin' millionaire, a bloody Capitalist! 'E's got enuf bloody gold to sink this bleedin' ship! 'E makes arf the bloody steel in the world! 'E owns this bloody boat! And you and me, Comrades, we're 'is slaves! And the skipper and mates and engineers, they're 'is slaves! And she's 'is bloody daughter and we're all 'er slaves, too! And she gives 'er orders as 'ow she wants to see the bloody animals below decks and down they takes 'er! *(There is a roar of rage from all sides.)*

YANK. *(blinking at him bewilderedly)* Say! Wait a moment! Is all dat straight goods?

LONG. Straight as string! The bleedin' steward as waits on 'em, 'e told me about 'er. And what're we goin' ter do, I arsks yer? 'Ave we got ter swaller 'er hinsults like dogs? It ain't in the ship's articles. I tell yer we got a case. We kin go to law—

YANK. *(with abysmal contempt)* Hell! Law!

ALL. *(repeating the word after him as one with cynical mockery)* Law! *(The word has a brazen metallic quality as if their throats were phonograph horns. It is followed by a chorus of hard, barking laughter.)*

LONG. *(feeling the ground slipping from under his feet—desperately)* As voters and citizens we kin force the bloody governments—

YANK. *(with abysmal contempt)* Hell! Governments!

ALL. *(repeating the word after him as one with cynical mockery)* Governments! *(The word has a brazen metallic quality as if their throats were phonograph horns. It is followed by a chorus of hard, barking laughter.)*

LONG. *(hysterically)* We're free and equal in the sight of God—

YANK. *(with abysmal contempt)* Hell! God!

ALL. *(repeating the word after him as one with cynical mockery)* God! *(The word has a brazen metallic quality as if their throats were phonograph horns. It is followed by a chorus of hard, barking laughter.)*

YANK. *(witheringly)* Aw, join de Salvation Army!

ALL. Sit down! Shut up! Damn fool! Sea-lawyer![29] (LONG *slinks back out of sight.)*

PADDY. *(continuing the trend of his thoughts as if he had never been interrupted—bitterly)* And there she was standing behind us, and the Second pointing at us like a man you'd hear in a circus would be saying: In this cage is a queerer kind of baboon than ever you'd find in darkest Africy. We roast them in their own sweat—and be damned if you won't hear some of thim saying they like it! *(He glances scornfully at* YANK.*)*

YANK. *(with a bewildered uncertain growl)* Aw!

PADDY. And there was Yank roarin' curses and turning round wid his shovel to brain her—and she looked at him, and him at her—

YANK. *(slowly)* She was all white. I tought she was a ghost. Sure.

PADDY. *(with heavy, biting sarcasm)* 'Twas love at first sight, divil a doubt of it! If you'd seen the endearin' look on her pale mug when she shriveled away with her hands over her eyes to shut out the sight of him! Sure, 'twas as if she'd seen a great hairy ape escaped from the Zoo!

---

[29]"Troublemaker" (slang).

YANK. (*stung—with a growl of rage*) Aw!

PADDY. And the loving way Yank heaved his shovel at the skull of her, only she was out the door! (*A grin breaking over his face*) 'Twas touching, I'm telling you! It put the touch of home, swate home in the stokehole. (*There is a roar of laughter from all.*)

YANK. (*glaring at* PADDY *menacingly*) Aw, choke dat off, see!

PADDY. (*not heeding him—to the others*) And her grabbin' at the Second's arm for protection. (*With a grotesque imitation of a woman's voice*) Kiss me, Engineer dear, for it's dark down here and me old man's in Wall Street making money! Hug me tight, darlin', for I'm afeerd in the dark and me mother's on deck makin' eyes at the skipper! (*Another roar of laughter.*)

YANK. (*threateningly*) Say! What yuh tryin' to do, kid me, yuh old Harp?

PADDY. Divil a bit! Ain't I wishin' myself you'd brained her?

YANK. (*fiercely*) I'll brain her! I'll brain her yet, wait 'n' see! (*Coming over to* PADDY—*slowly*) Say, is dat what she called me—a hairy ape?

PADDY. She looked it at you if she didn't say the word itself.

YANK. (*grinning horribly*) Hairy ape, huh? Sure! Dat's de way she looked at me, aw right. Hairy ape! So dat's me, huh? (*Bursting into rage—as if she were still in front of him*) Yuh skinny tart! Yuh white-faced bum, yuh! I'll show yuh who's a ape! (*Turning to the others, bewilderment seizing him again*) Say, youse guys. I was bawlin' him out for pullin' de whistle on us. You heard me. And den I seen youse lookin' at somep'n and I tought he'd sneaked down to come up in back of me, and I hopped round to knock him dead wit de shovel. And dere she was wit de light on her! Christ, yuh coulda pushed me over with a finger! I was scared, get me? Sure! I thought she was a ghost, see? She was all in white like dey wrap around stiffs. You seen her. Kin yuh blame me? She didn't belong, dat's what. And den when I come to and seen it was a real skoit and seen de way she was lookin' at me—like Paddy said—Christ, I was sore, get me? I don't stand for dat stuff from nobody. And I flung de shovel—on'y she'd beat it. (*Furiously*) I wished it'd banged her! I wished it'd knocked her block off!

LONG. And be 'anged for murder or 'lectrocuted? She ain't bleedin' well worth it.

YANK. I don't give a damn what! I'd be square wit her, wouldn't I? Tink I wanter let her put somep'n over on me? Tink I'm goin' to let her git away wit dat stuff? Yuh don't know me! No one ain't never put nothin' over on me and got away wit it, see!—not dat kind of stuff—no guy and no skoit neither! I'll fix her! Maybe she'll come down again—

VOICE. No chance, Yank. You scared her out of a year's growth.

YANK. I scared her? Why de hell should I scare her? Who de hell is she? Ain't she de same as me? Hairy ape, huh? (*With his old confident bravado*) I'll show her I'm better'n her, if she on'y knew it. I belong and she don't, see! I move and she's dead! Twenty-five knots a hour, dat's me! Dat carries her but I make dat. She's on'y baggage. Sure! (*Again bewilderedly*) But, Christ, she was funny lookin'! Did yuh pipe her hands? White and skinny.

Yuh could see de bones through 'em. And her mush, dat was dead white, too. And her eyes, dey was like dey'd seen a ghost. Me, dat was! Sure! Hairy ape! Ghost, huh? Look at dat arm! *(He extends his right arm, swelling out of the great muscles)* I coulda took her wit dat, wit just my little finger even, and broke her in two. *(Again bewilderedly)* Say, who is dat skoit, huh? What is she? What's she come from? Who made her? Who give her de noive to look at me like dat? Dis ting's got my goat right. I don't get her. She's new to me. What does a skoit like her mean, huh? She don't belong, get me! I can't see her. *(With growing anger)* But one ting I'm wise to, aw right, aw right! Youse all kin bet your shoits I'll git even wit her. I'll show her if she tinks she—She grinds de organ and I'm on de string, huh? I'll fix her! Let her come down again and I'll fling her in de furnace! She'll move den! She won't shiver at nothin', den! Speed, dat'll be her! She'll belong den! *(He grins horribly.)*

PADDY. She'll never come. She's had her belly-full, I'm telling you. She'll be in bed now, I'm thinking, wid ten doctors and nurses feedin' her salts[30] to clean the fear out of her.

YANK. *(enraged)* Yuh tink I made her sick, too, do yuh? Just lookin' at me, huh? Hairy ape, huh? *(In a frenzy of rage)* I'll fix her! I'll tell her where to git off! She'll git down on her knees and take it back or I'll bust de face offen her! *(Shaking one fist upward and beating on his chest with the other)* I'll find yuh! I'm comin', d'yuh hear? I'll fix yuh, God damn yuh! *(He makes a rush for the door.)*

VOICES. Stop him!
    He'll get shot!
    He'll murder her!
    Trip him up!
    Hold him!
    He's gone crazy!
    Gott, he's strong!
    Hold him down!
    Look out for a kick!
    Pin his arms!

(They have all piled on him and, after a fierce struggle, by sheer weight of numbers have borne him to the floor just inside the door.)

PADDY. *(who has remained detached)* Kape him down till he's cooled off. (Scornfully) Yerra, Yank, you're a great fool. Is it payin' attention at all you are to the like of that skinny sow widout one drop of rale blood in her?

YANK. *(frenziedly, from the bottom of the heap)* She done me doit! She done me doit, didn't she? I'll git square wit her! I'll get her some way! Git offen me, youse guys! Lemme up! I'll show her who's a ape!

CURTAIN

---

[30]Epsom salts, a laxative.

Scene Five

Three weeks later. A corner of Fifth Avenue in the Fifties on a fine Sunday morning. A general atmosphere of clean, well-tidied, wide street; a flood of mellow, tempered sunshine; gentle, genteel breezes. In the rear, the show windows of two shops, a jewelry establishment on the corner, a furrier's next to it. Here the adornments of extreme wealth are tantalizingly displayed. The jeweler's window is gaudy with glittering diamonds, emeralds, rubies, pearls, etc., fashioned in ornate tiaras, crowns, necklaces, collars, etc. From each piece hangs an enormous tag from which a dollar sign and numerals in intermittent electric lights wink out the incredible prices. The same in the furrier's. Rich furs of all varieties hang there bathed in a downpour of artificial light. The general effect is of a background of magnificence cheapened and made grotesque by commercialism, a background in tawdry disharmony with the clear light and sunshine on the street itself.

Up the side street YANK *and* LONG *come swaggering.* LONG *is dressed in shore clothes, wears a black Windsor tie, cloth cap.* YANK *is in his dirty dungarees. A fireman's cap with black peak is cocked defiantly on the side of his head. He has not shaved for days and around his fierce, resentful eyes—as around those of* LONG *to a lesser degree—the black smudge of coal dust still sticks like make-up. They hesitate and stand together at the corner, swaggering, looking about them with a forced, defiant contempt.*

LONG. (*indicating it all with an oratorical gesture*) Well, 'ere we are. Fif' Avenoo. This 'ere's their bleedin' private lane, as yer might say. (*Bitterly*) We're trespassers 'ere. Proletarians keep orf the grass!

YANK. (*dully*) I don't see no grass, yuh boob. (*Staring at the sidewalk*) Clean, ain't it? Yuh could eat a fried egg offen it. The white wings[31] got some job sweepin' dis up. (*Looking up and down the avenue—surlily*) Where's all de white-collar stiffs yuh said was here—and de skoits—her kind?

LONG. In church, blarst 'em! Arskin' Jesus to give 'em more money.

YANK. Choich, huh? I useter go to choich onct—sure—when I was a kid. Me old man and woman, dey made me. Dey never went demselves, dough. Always got too big a head on Sunday mornin', dat was dem. (*With a grin*) Dey was scrappers for fair, bot' of dem. On Satiday nights when dey bot' got a skinful dey could put up a bout oughter been staged at de Garden.[32] When dey got trough dere wasn't a chair or table wit a leg under it. Or else dey bot' jumped on me for somep'n. Dat was where I loined to take punishment. (*With a grin and a swagger*) I'm a chip offen de old block, get me?

LONG. Did yer old man follow the sea?

YANK. Naw. Worked along shore. I runned away when me old lady croaked wit de tremens.[33] I helped at truckin' and in de market. Den I shipped in

---

[31]Streetcleaners, dressed in white.
[32]New York City's Madison Square Garden, site of prize fights.

[33]Delirium tremens, a nervous affliction suffered by heavy drinkers.

de stokehole. Sure. Dat belongs. De rest was nothin'. *(Looking around him)* I ain't never seen dis before. De Brooklyn waterfront, dat was where I was dragged up. *(Taking a deep breath)* Dis ain't so bad at dat, huh?

LONG. Not bad? Well, we pays for it wiv our bloody sweat, if yer wants to know!

YANK. *(with sudden angry disgust)* Aw, hell! I don't see no one, see—like her. All dis gives me a pain. It don't belong. Say, ain't dere a back room around dis dump? Let's go shoot a ball.[34] All dis is too clean and quiet and dolled-up, get me! It gives me a pain.

LONG. Wait and yer'll bloody well see—

YANK. I don't wait for no one. I keep on de move. Say, what yuh drag me up here for, anyway? Tryin' to kid me, yuh simp, yuh?

LONG. Yer wants to get back at 'er, don't yer? That's what yer been sayin' every bloomin' hour since she hinsulted yer.

YANK. *(vehemently)* Sure ting I do! Didn't I try to get even wit her in South-ampton? Didn't I sneak on de dock and wait for her by de gangplank? I was goin' to spit in her pale mug, see! Sure, right in her pop-eyes! Dat woulda made me even, see? But no chanct. Dere was a whole army of plainclothes bulls around. Dey spotted me and gimme de bum's rush. I never seen her. But I'll git square wit her yet, you watch. *(Furiously)* De lousy tart! She tinks she kin get away wit moider—but not wit me! I'll fix her! I'll tink of a way!

LONG. *(as disgusted as he dares to be)* Ain't that why I brought yer up 'ere—to show yer? Yer been lookin' at this 'ere 'ole affair wrong. Yer been actin' an' talkin' 's if it was all a bleedin' personal matter between yer and that bloody cow. I wants to convince yer she was on'y a representative of 'er clarss. I wants to awaken yer bloody clarss consciousness. Then yer'll see it's 'er clarss yer've got to fight, not 'er alone. There's a 'ole mob of 'em like 'er, Gawd blind 'em!

YANK. *(spitting on his hands—belligerently)* De more de merrier when I gits started. Bring on de gang!

LONG. Yer'll see 'em in arf a mo', when that church lets out. *(He turns and sees the window display in the two stores for the first time)* Blimey![35] Look at that, will yer? *(They both walk back and stand looking in the jeweler's.* LONG *flies into a fury)* Just look at this 'ere bloomin' mess! Just look at it! Look at the bleedin' prices on 'em—more'n our 'ole bloody stokehole makes in ten voyages sweatin' in 'ell! And they—'er and 'er bloody clarss—buys 'em for toys to dangle on 'em! One of these 'ere would buy scoff[36] for a star-vin' family for a year!

YANK. Aw, cut de sob stuff! T' hell wit de starvin' family! Yuh'll be passin' de hat to me next. *(With naïve admiration)* Say, dem tings is pretty, huh? Bet yuh dey'd hock for a piece of change aw right. *(Then turning away, bored)* But, aw hell, what good are dey? Let her have 'em. Dey don't belong no

[34]Shoot pool.
[35]"God blind me" (British slang).
[36]"Food" (slang).

more'n she does. (With a gesture of sweeping the jewelers into oblivion) All dat don't count, get me?

LONG. (who has moved to the furrier's—indignantly) And I s'pose this 'ere don't count neither—skins of poor, 'armless animals slaughtered so as 'er and 'ers can keep their bleedin' noses warm!

YANK. (who has been staring at something inside—with queer excitement) Take a slant at dat! Give it de once-over! Monkey fur—two t'ousand bucks! (Bewilderedly) Is dat straight goods—monkey fur? What de hell—?

LONG. (bitterly) It's straight enuf. (With grim humor) They wouldn't bloody well pay that for a 'airy ape's skin—no, nor for the 'ole livin' ape with all 'is 'ead, and a body, and soul thrown in!

YANK. (clenching his fists, his face growing pale with rage as if the skin in the window were a personal insult) Trowin' it up in my face! Christ! I'll fix her!

LONG. (excitedly) Church is out. 'Ere they come, the bleedin' swine. (After a glance at YANK'S lowering face—uneasily) Easy goes, Comrade. Keep yer bloomin' temper. Remember force defeats itself. It ain't our weapon. We must impress our demands through peaceful means—the votes of the on-marching proletarians of the bloody world!

YANK. (with abysmal contempt) Votes, hell! Votes is a joke, see. Votes for women! Let dem do it!

LONG. (still more uneasily) Calm, now. Treat 'em wiv the proper contempt. Observe the bleedin' parasites but 'old yer 'orses.

YANK. (angrily) Git away from me! Yuh're yellow, dat's what. Force, dat's me! De punch, dat's me every time, see! (The crowd from church enter from the right, sauntering slowly and affectedly, their heads held stiffly up, looking nei-ther to right nor left, talking in toneless, simpering voices. The women are rouged, calcimined,[37] dyed, overdressed to the nth degree. The men are in Prince Alberts[38] high hats, spats, canes, etc. A procession of gaudy mario-nettes, yet with something of the relentless horror of Frankensteins[39] in their detached, mechanical unawareness.)

VOICES. Dear Doctor Caiphas![40] He is so sincere!

What was the sermon? I dozed off.

About the radicals, my dear—and the false doctrines that are being preached.

We must organize a hundred per cent American bazaar.

And let everyone contribute one one-hundredth per cent of their income tax.

What an original idea!

We can devote the proceeds to rehabilitating the veil of the temple.[41]

But that has been done so many times.

---

[37]Made up with calcimine, a white liquid used as a wash for walls and ceilings.

[38]Long-tailed suit coats, very formal wear.

[39]I.e., the Frankenstein monster.

[40]A possible allusion to Caiaphas, the Jewish high priest who presided over the council that condemned Jesus.

[41]A curtain hung before the sanctuary of a church.

YANK. (*glaring from one to the other of them—with an insulting snort of scorn*) Huh! Huh! (*Without seeming to see him, they make wide detours to avoid the spot where he stands in the middle of the sidewalk.*)

LONG. (*frightenedly*) Keep yer bloomin' mouth shut, I tells yer.

YANK. (*viciously*) G'wan! Tell it to Sweeney! (*He swaggers away and deliberately lurches into a top-hatted gentleman, then glares at him pugnaciously*) Say, who d'yuh tink yuh're bumpin'? Tink yuh own de oith?

GENTLEMAN. (*coldly and affectedly*) I beg your pardon. (*He has not looked at* YANK *and passes on without a glance, leaving him bewildered.*)

LONG. (*rushing up and grabbing* YANK'S *arm*) 'Ere! Come away! This wasn't what I meant. Yer'll 'ave the bloody coppers down on us.

YANK. (*savagely—giving him a push that sends him sprawling*) G'wan!

LONG. (*picks himself up—hysterically*) I'll pop orf then. This ain't what I meant. And whatever 'appens, yer can't blame me. (*He slinks off left.*)

YANK. T' hell wit youse! (*He approaches a lady—with a vicious grin and smirking wink*) Hello, Kiddo. How's every little ting? Got anything on for tonight? I know an old boiler down to de docks we kin crawl into. (*The lady stalks by without a look, without a change of pace.* YANK *turns to others—insultingly*) Holy smokes, what a mug! Go hide yuhself before de horses shy at yuh. Gee, pipe de heine on dat one! Say, youse, yuh look like de stoin of a ferryboat. Paint and powder! All dolled up to kill! Yuh look like stiffs laid out for de boneyard! Aw, g'wan, de lot of youse! Yuh give me de eyeache. Yuh don't belong, get me! Look at me, why don't youse dare? I belong, dat's me! (*Pointing to a skyscraper across the street which is in process of construction—with bravado*) See dat building goin' up dere? See de steel work? Steel, dat's me! Youse guys live on it and tink yuh're somep'n. But I'm *in* it, see! I'm de hoistin' engine dat makes it go up! I'm it—de inside and bottom of it! Sure! I'm steel and steam and smoke and de rest of it! It moves—speed—twenty-five stories up—and me at de top and bottom—movin'! Youse simps don't move. Yuh're on'y dolls I winds up to see 'm spin. Yuh're de garbage, get me—de leavin's—de ashes we dump over de side! Now, what 'a' yuh gotta say? (*But as they seem neither to see nor hear him, he flies into a fury*) Bums! Pigs! Tarts! Bitches! (*He turns in a rage on the men, bumping viciously into them but not jarring them the least bit. Rather it is he who recoils after each collision. He keeps growling*) Git off de oith! G'wan, yuh bum! Look where yuh're goin', can't yuh? Git outa here! Fight, why don't yuh? Put up yer mits! Don't be a dog! Fight or I'll knock yuh dead! (*But, without seeming to see him, they all answer with mechanical affected politeness* "I beg your pardon." *Then at a cry from one of the women, they all scurry to the furrier's window.*)

THE WOMAN. (*ecstatically, with a gasp of delight*) Monkey fur! (*The whole crowd of men and women chorus after her in the same tone of affected delight* "Monkey fur!")

YANK. (*with a jerk of his head back on his shoulders, as if he had received a punch full in the face—raging*) I see yuh, all in white! I see yuh, yuh white-faced tart, yuh! Hairy ape, huh? I'll hairy ape yuh! (*He bends down and grips at* *the street curbing as if to pluck it out and hurl it. Foiled in this, snarling with passion, he leaps to the lamp-post on the corner and tries to pull it up for a club. Just at that moment a bus is heard rumbling up. A fat, high-hatted, spatted gentleman runs out from the side street. He calls out plaintively "Bus! Bus! Stop there!" and runs full tilt into the bending, straining* YANK, *who is bowled off his balance.*)

YANK. (*seeing a fight—with a roar of joy as he springs to his feet*) At last! Bus, huh? I'll bust yuh! (*He lets drive a terrific swing, his fist landing full on the fat gentleman's face. But the gentleman stands unmoved as if nothing had happened.*)

GENTLEMAN. I beg your pardon. (*Then irritably*) You have made me lose my bus. (*He claps his hands and begins to scream*) Officer! Officer! (*Many police whistles shrill out on the instant and a whole platoon of policemen rush in on* YANK *from all sides. He tries to fight but is clubbed to the pavement and fallen upon. The crowd at the window have not moved or noticed this disturbance. The clanging gong of the patrol wagon approaches with a clamoring din.*)

CURTAIN

Scene Six

Night of the following day. A row of cells in the prison on Blackwells Island.[42] *The cells extend back diagonally from right front to left rear. They do not stop, but disappear in the dark background as if they ran on, numberless, into infinity. One electric bulb from the low ceiling of the narrow corridor sheds its light through the heavy steel bars of the cell at the extreme front and reveals part of the interior.* YANK *can be seen within, crouched on the edge of his cot in the attitude of Rodin's "The Thinker." His face is spotted with black and blue bruises. A blood-stained bandage is wrapped around his head.*

YANK. (*suddenly starting as if awakening from a dream, reaches out and shakes the bars—aloud to himself, wonderingly*) Steel. Dis is de Zoo, huh? (*A burst of hard, barking laughter comes from the unseen occupants of the cells, runs back down the tier, and abruptly ceases.*)

VOICES. (*mockingly*) The Zoo? That's a new name for this coop—a damn good name!
    Steel, eh? You said a mouthful. This is the old iron house.
    Who is that boob talkin'?
    He's the bloke they brung in out of his head. The bulls had beat him up fierce.

YANK. (*dully*) I musta been dreamin'. I tought I was in a cage at de Zoo—but de apes don't talk, do dey?

VOICES. (*with mocking laughter*) You're in a cage aw right.
    A coop!
    A pen!

[42]In New York City's East River; now Roosevelt Island.

A sty!

A kennel! *(Hard laughter—a pause.)*

Say, guy! Who are you? No, never mind lying. What are you?

Yes, tell us your sad story. What's your game?

What did they jug yuh for?

YANK. *(dully)* I was a fireman—stokin' on de liners. *(Then with sudden rage, rattling his cell bars)* I'm a hairy ape, get me? And I'll bust youse all in de jaw if yuh don't lay off kiddin' me.

VOICES. Huh! You're a hard boiled duck, ain't you!

When you spit, it bounces! *(Laughter.)*

Aw, can it. He's a regular guy. Ain't you?

What did he say he was—a ape?

YANK. *(defiantly)* Sure ting! Ain't dat what youse all are—apes? *(A silence. Then a furious rattling of bars from down the corridor.)*

A VOICE. *(thick with rage)* I'll show yuh who's a ape, yuh bum!

VOICES. Ssshh! Nix!

Can de noise!

Piano![43]

You'll have the guard down on us!

YANK. *(scornfully)* De guard? Yuh mean de keeper, don't yuh? *(Angry exclamations from all the cells.)*

VOICE. *(placatingly)* Aw, don't pay no attention to him. He's off his nut from the beatin'-up he got. Say, you guy! We're waitin' to hear what they landed you for—or ain't yuh tellin'?

YANK. Sure, I'll tell youse. Sure! Why de hell not? On'y—youse won't get me. Nobody gets me but me, see? I started to tell de Judge and all he says was: "'Toity days to tink it over."—Tink it over! Christ, dat's all I been doin' for weeks! *(After a pause)* I was tryin' to git even wit someone, see?—someone dat done me doit.

VOICES. *(cynically)* De old stuff, I beg. Your goil, huh?

Give yuh the double-cross, huh?

That's them every time!

Did yuh beat up de odder guy?

YANK. *(disgustedly)* Aw, yuh're all wrong! Sure dere was a skoit in it—but not what youse mean, not dat old tripe. Dis was a new kind of skoit. She was dolled up all in white—in de stokehole. I tought she was a ghost. Sure. *(A pause.)*

VOICES. *(whispering)* Gee, he's still nutty.

Let him rave. It's fun listenin'.

YANK. *(unheeding—groping in his thoughts)* Her hands—dey was skinny and white like dey wasn't real but painted on somep'n. Dere was a million miles from me to her—twenty-five knots a hour. She was like some dead ting de cat brung in. Sure, dat's what. She didn't belong. She belonged in de window of a toy store, or on de top of a garbage can, see! Sure! *(He*

---

[43]"Softly" (Italian).

breaks out angrily) But would yuh believe it, she had de noive to do me doit. She lamped[44] me like she was seein' somep'n broke loose from de menagerie. Christ, yuh'd oughter seen her eyes! (*He rattles the bars of his cell furiously*) But I'll get back at her yet, you watch! And if I can't find her I'll take it out on de gang she runs wit. I'm wise to where dey hangs out now. I'll show her who belongs! I'll show her who's in de move and who ain't. You watch my smoke!

VOICES. (*serious and joking*) Dat's de talkin'!

Take her for all she's got!

What was this dame, anyway? Who was she, eh?

YANK. I dunno. First cabin stiff. Her old man's a millionaire, dey says—name of Douglas.

VOICES. Douglas? That's the president of the Steel Trust, I bet.

Sure. I seen his mug in de papers.

He's filthy with dough.

VOICE. Hey, feller, take a tip from me. If you want to get back at that dame, you better join the Wobblies. You'll get some action then.

YANK. Wobblies? What de hell's dat?

VOICE. Ain't you ever heard of the I.W.W.?[45]

YANK. Naw. What is it?

VOICE. A gang of blokes—a tough gang. I been readin' about 'em today in the paper. The guard give me the *Sunday Times*. There's a long spiel about 'em. It's from a speech made in the Senate by a guy named Senator Queen. (*He is in the cell next to* YANK'S. *There is a rustling of paper*) Wait'll I see if I got light enough and I'll read you. Listen. (*He reads*) "There is a menace existing in this country today which threatens the vitals of our fair Republic—as foul a menace against the very life-blood of the American Eagle as was the foul conspiracy of Catiline[46] against the eagles of ancient Rome!"

VOICE. (*disgustedly*) Aw, hell! Tell him to salt de tail of dat eagle!

VOICE. (*reading*) "I refer to that devil's brew of rascals, jailbirds, murderers and cutthroats who libel all honest working men by calling themselves the Industrial Workers of the World; but in the light of their nefarious plots, I call them the Industrious *Wreckers* of the World!"

YANK. (*with vengeful satisfaction*) Wreckers, dat's de right dope! Dat belongs! Me for dem!

VOICE. Ssshh! (*Reading*) "This fiendish organization is a foul ulcer on the fair body of our Democracy—"

VOICE. Democracy, hell! Give him the boid, fellers—the raspberry! (*They do.*)

VOICE. Ssshh! (*Reading*) "Like Cato[47] I say to this Senate, the I.W.W. must be destroyed! For they represent an ever-present dagger pointed at the heart of the greatest nation the world has ever known, where all men are born

[44]"Looked at" (slang).
[45]Industrial Workers of the World, a radical socialist/anarchist group whose members were called "Wobblies."

[46]Roman revolutionary (108–62 B.C.).
[47]Roman senator (234–189 B.C.) who argued for the destruction of Rome's enemy, Carthage.

free and equal, with equal opportunities to all, where the Founding Fathers have guaranteed to each one happiness, where Truth, Honor, Liberty, Justice, and the Brotherhood of Man are a religion absorbed with one's mother's milk, taught at our father's knee, sealed, signed, and stamped upon in the glorious Constitution of these United States!" *(A perfect storm of hisses, catcalls, boos, and hard laughter.)*

VOICES. *(scornfully)* Hurrah for de Fort' of July!

> Pass de hat!
> Liberty!
> Justice!
> Honor!
> Opportunity!
> Brotherhood!

ALL. *(with abysmal scorn)* Aw, hell!

VOICE. Give that Queen Senator guy the bark! All togedder now—one—two—tree—*(A terrific chorus of barking and yapping.)*

GUARD. *(from a distance)* Quiet there, youse—or I'll git the hose. *(The noise subsides.)*

YANK. *(with growling rage)* I'd like to catch dat senator guy alone for a second. I'd loin him some trute!

VOICE. Ssshh! Here's where he gits down to cases on the Wobblies. *(Reads)* "They plot with fire in one hand and dynamite in the other. They stop not before murder to gain their ends, nor at the outraging of defenseless womanhood. They would tear down society, put the lowest scum in the seats of the mighty, turn Almighty God's revealed plan for the world topsy-turvy, and make of our sweet and lovely civilization a shambles, a desolation where man, God's masterpiece, would soon degenerate back to the ape!"

VOICE. *(to YANK)* Hey, you guy. There's your ape stuff again.

YANK. *(with a growl of fury)* I got him. So dey blow up tings, do dey? Dey turn tings round, do dey? Hey, lend me dat paper, will yuh?

VOICE. Sure. Give it to him. On'y keep it to yourself, see. We don't wanter listen to no more of that slop.

VOICE. Here you are. Hide it under your mattress.

YANK. *(reaching out)* Tanks. I can't read much but I kin manage. *(He sits, the paper in the hand at his side, in the attitude of Rodin's "The Thinker." A pause. Several snores from down the corridor. Suddenly YANK jumps to his feet with a furious groan as if some appalling thought had crashed on him—bewilderedly)* Sure—her old man—president of de Steel Trust—makes half de steel in de world—steel—where I tought I belonged—drivin' trou—movin'—in dat—to make *her*—and cage me in for her to spit on! Christ! *(He shakes the bars of his cell door till the whole tier trembles. Irritated, protesting exclamations from those awakened or trying to get to sleep)* He made dis—dis cage! Steel! *It* don't belong, dat's what! Cages, cells, locks, bolts, bars—dat's what it means!—holdin' me down wit him at de top! But I'll drive trou! Fire, dat melts it! I'll be fire—under de heap—fire dat never goes out—hot as hell—breakin' out in de night—(*While he has been saying this last he has shaken his cell door to a clanging accompaniment. As he comes to the "breakin' out" he seizes one bar with both hands and, putting his two feet up against the others so that his position is parallel to the floor like a monkey's, he gives a great wrench backwards. The bar bends like a licorice stick under his tremendous strength. Just at this moment the* PRISON GUARD *rushes in, dragging a hose behind him.*)

GUARD. (*angrily*) I'll loin youse bums to wake me up! (*Sees* YANK) Hello, it's you, huh? Got the D.T.'s[48] hey? Well, I'll cure 'em. I'll drown your snakes for yuh! (*Noticing the bar*) Hell, look at dat bar bended! On'y a bug is strong enough for dat!

YANK. (*glaring at him*) Or a hairy ape, yuh big yellow bum! Look out! Here I come! (*He grabs another bar.*)

GUARD. (*scared now—yelling off left*) Toin de hose on, Ben!—full pressure! And call de others—and a straitjacket! (*The curtain is falling. As it hides* YANK *from view, there is a splattering smash as the steam of water hits the steel of* YANK'S *cell.*)

CURTAIN

Scene Seven

Nearly a month later. An I.W.W. local near the waterfront, showing the interior of a front room on the ground floor, and the street outside. Moonlight on the narrow street, buildings massed in black shadow. The interior of the room, which is general assembly room, office, and reading room, resembles some dingy settlement boys' club. A desk and high stool are in one corner. A table with papers, stacks of pamphlets, chairs about it, is at center. The whole is decidedly cheap, banal, commonplace and unmysterious as a room could well be. The SECRETARY *is perched on the stool making entries in a large ledger. An eye shade casts his face into shadows. Eight or ten men, longshoremen, iron workers, and the like, are grouped about the table. Two are playing checkers. One is writing a letter. Most of them are smoking pipes. A big signboard is on the wall at the rear, "Industrial Workers of the World—Local No. 57."*

YANK comes down the street outside. He is dressed as in Scene Five. He moves cautiously, mysteriously. He comes to a point opposite the door; tiptoes softly up to it, listens, is impressed by the silence within, knocks carefully, as if he were guessing at the password to some secret rite. Listens. No answer. Knocks again a bit louder. No answer. Knocks impatiently, much louder.

SECRETARY. (*turning around on his stool*) What the hell is that—someone knocking? (*Shouts*) Come in, why don't you? (*All the men in the room look up.* YANK *opens the door slowly, gingerly, as if afraid of an ambush. He looks around for secret doors, mystery, is taken aback by the commonplaceness of the room and the men in it, thinks he may have gotten in the wrong place, then sees the signboard on the wall and is reassured.*)

---

[48]Delirium tremens.

YANK. (*blurts out*) Hello.

MAN. (*reservedly*) Hello.

YANK. (*more easily*) I thought I'd bumped into de wrong dump.

SECRETARY. (*scrutinizing him carefully*) Maybe you have. Are you a member?

YANK. Naw, not yet. Dat's what I come for—to join.

SECRETARY. That's easy. What's your job—longshore?

YANK. Naw. Fireman—stoker on de liners.

SECRETARY. (*with satisfaction*) Welcome to our city. Glad to know you people are waking up at last. We haven't got many members in your line.

YANK. Naw. Dey're all dead to de woild.

SECRETARY. Well, you can help to wake 'em. What's your name? I'll make out your card.

YANK. (*confused*) Name? Lemme tink.

SECRETARY. (*sharply*) Don't you know your own name?

YANK. Sure; but I been just Yank for so long—Bob, dat's it—Bob Smith.

SECRETARY. (*writing*) Robert Smith. (*Fills out the rest of the card*) Here you are. Cost you half a dollar.

YANK. Is dat all—four bits? Dat's easy. (*Gives the* SECRETARY *the money.*)

SECRETARY. (*throwing it in drawer*) Thanks. Well, make yourself at home. No introductions needed. There's literature on the table. Take some of those pamphlets with you to distribute aboard ship. They may bring results. Sow the seed, only go about it right. Don't get caught and fired. We got plenty out of work. What we need is men who can hold their jobs—and work for us at the same time.

YANK. Sure. (*But he still stands, embarrassed and uneasy.*)

SECRETARY. (*looking at him—curiously*) What did you knock for? Think we had a coon[49] in uniform to open doors?

YANK. Naw, I tought it was locked—and dat yuh'd wanter give me the once-over trou a peep-hole or somep'n to see if I was right.

SECRETARY. (*alert and suspicious but with an easy laugh*) Think we were running a crap game? That door is never locked. What put that in your nut?

YANK. (*with a knowing grin, convinced that this is all camouflage, a part of the secrecy*) Dis burg is full of bulls, ain't it?

SECRETARY. (*sharply*) What have the cops got to do with us? We're breaking no laws.

YANK. (*with a knowing wink*) Sure. Youse wouldn't for woilds. Sure. I'm wise to dat.

SECRETARY. You seem to be wise to a lot of stuff none of us knows about.

YANK. (*with another wink*) Aw, dat's aw right, see. (*Then made a bit resentful by the suspicious glances from all sides*) Aw, can it! Youse needn't put me trou de toid degree. Can't youse see I belong? Sure! I'm reg'lar. I'll stick, get me? I'll shoot de woiks for youse. Dat's why I wanted to join in.

---

[49]African (slang).

SECRETARY. *(breezily, feeling him out)* That's the right spirit. Only are you sure you understand what you've joined? It's all plain and above board; still, some guys get a wrong slant on us. *(Sharply)* What's your notion of the purpose of the I.W.W.?

YANK. Aw, I know all about it.

SECRETARY. *(sarcastically)* Well, give us some of your valuable information.

YANK. *(cunningly)* I know enough not to speak outa my toin. *(Then resentfully again)* Aw, say! I'm reg'lar. I'm wise to de game. I know yuh got to watch your step wit a stranger. For all youse know, I might be a plain-clothes dick, or somep'n, dat's what yuh're tinkin', huh? Aw, forget it! I belong, see? Ask any guy down to de docks if I don't.

SECRETARY. Who said you didn't?

YANK. After I'm 'nitiated, I'll show yuh.

SECRETARY. *(astounded)* Initiated? There's no initiation.

YANK. *(disappointed)* Ain't there no password—no grip nor nothin'?

SECRETARY. What'd you think this is—the Elks—or the Black Hand?[50]

YANK. De Elks, hell! De Black Hand, dey're a lot of yellow back stickin' Ginees.[51] Naw. Dis is a man's gang, ain't it?

SECRETARY. You said it! That's why we stand on our two feet in the open. We got no secrets.

YANK. *(surprised but admiringly)* Yuh mean to say yuh always run wide open— like dis?

SECRETARY. Exactly.

YANK. Den yuh sure got your noive wit youse!

SECRETARY. *(sharply)* Just what was it made you want to join us? Come out with that straight.

YANK. Yuh call me? Well, I got noive, too! Here's my hand. Yuh wanter blow tings up, don't yuh? Well, dat's me! I belong!

SECRETARY. *(with pretended carelessness)* You mean change the unequal conditions of society by legitimate direct action—or with dynamite?

YANK. Dynamite! Blow it offen de oith—steel—all de cages—all de factories, steamers, buildings, jails—de Steel Trust and all dat makes it go.

SECRETARY. So—that's your idea, eh? And did you have any special job in that line you wanted to propose to us? *(He makes a sign to the men, who get up cautiously one by one and group behind* YANK.*)*

YANK. *(boldly)* Sure, I'll come out wit it. I'll show youse I'm one of de gang. Dere's dat millionaire guy, Douglas—

SECRETARY. President of the Steel Trust, you mean? Do you want to assassinate him?

YANK. Naw, dat don't get yuh nothin'. I mean blow up de factory, de woiks, where he makes de steel. Dat's what I'm after—to blow up de steel, knock

---

[50] A secret Sicilian terrorist group active in the United States in the early years of the twentieth century.

[51] Italians (slang; literally "Guineas").

all de steel in de woild up to de moon. Dat'll fix tings! *(Eagerly, with a touch of bravado)* I'll do it by me lonesome! I'll show yuh! Tell me where his woiks is, how to git there, all de dope. Gimme de stuff, de old butter—and watch me do de rest! Watch de smoke and see it move! I don't give a damn if dey nab me—long as it's done! I'll soive life for it—And give 'em de laugh! *(Half to himself)* And I'll write her a letter and tell her de hairy ape done it. Dat'll square tings.

SECRETARY. *(stepping away from* YANK) Very interesting. *(He gives a signal. The men, huskies all, throw themselves on* YANK *and before he knows it they have his legs and arms pinioned. But he is too flabbergasted to make a struggle, anyway. They feel him over for weapons.)*

MAN. No gat, no knife. Shall we give him what's what and put the boots to him?

SECRETARY. No. He isn't worth the trouble we'd get into. He's too stupid. *(He comes closer and laughs mockingly in* YANK'S *face)* Ho-ho! By God, this is the biggest joke they've put up on us yet. Hey, you Joke! Who sent you—Burns or Pinkerton?[52] No, by God, you're such a bonehead I'll bet you're in the Secret Service! Well, you dirty spy, you rotten agent provocator, you can go back and tell whatever skunk is paying you blood-money for betraying your brothers that he's wasting his coin. You couldn't catch a cold. And tell him that all he'll ever get on us, or ever has got, is just his own sneaking plots that he's framed up to put us in jail. We are what our manifesto says we are, neither more nor less—and we'll give him a copy of that any time he calls. And as for you—(*He glares scornfully at* YANK, *who is sunk in an oblivious stupor)* Oh, hell, what's the use of talking? You're a brainless ape.

YANK. *(aroused by the word to fierce but futile struggles)* What's dat, you Sheeny[53] bum, yuh!

SECRETARY. Throw him out, boys. *(In spite of his struggles, this is done with gusto and éclat. Propelled by several parting kicks,* YANK *lands sprawling in the middle of the narrow cobbled street. With a growl he starts to get up and storm the closed door, but stops bewildered by the confusion in his brain, pathetically impotent. He sits there, brooding, in as near to the attitude of Rodin's "The Thinker" as he can get in his position.)*

YANK. *(bitterly)* So dem boids don't tink I belong, neider. Aw, to hell wit 'em! Dey're in de wrong pew—de same old bull—soap-boxes and Salvation Army—no guts! Cut out an hour offen de job a day and make me happy! Gimme a dollar more a day and make me happy! Tree square a day, and cauliflowers in de front yard—ekal rights—a woman and kids—a lousy vote—and I'm all fixed for Jesus, huh? Aw, hell! What does dat get yuh? Dis ting's in your inside, but it ain't your belly. Feedin' your face—sinkers and coffee—dat don't touch it. It's way down—at de bottom. Yuh can't

---

[52]Famous detective agencies of the time.   [53]Jewish (slang).

grab it, and yuh can't stop it. It moves, and everything moves. It stops and de whole woild stops. Dat's me now—I don't tick, see?—I'm a busted Ingersoll,[54] dat's what. Steel was me, and I owned de woild. Now I ain't steel, and de woild owns me. Aw, hell! I can't see—it's all dark, get me? It's all wrong! (*He turns a bitter mocking face up like an ape gibbering at the moon*) Say, youse up dere, Man in de Moon, yuh look so wise, gimme de answer, huh? Slip me de inside dope, de information right from de stable—where do I get off at, huh?

A POLICEMAN. (*who has come up the street in time to hear this last—with grim humor*) You'll get off at the station, you boob, if you don't get up out of that and keep movin'.

YANK. (*looking up at him—with a hard, bitter laugh*) Sure! Lock me up! Put me in a cage! Dat's de on'y answer yuh know. G'wan, lock me up!

POLICEMAN. What you been doin'?

YANK. Enuf to gimme life for! I was born, see? Sure, dat's de charge. Write it in de blotter. I was born, get me!

POLICEMAN. (*jocosely*) God pity your old woman! (*Then matter-of-factly*) But I've no time for kidding. You're soused. I'd run you in but it's too long a walk to the station. Come on now, get up, or I'll fan your ears with this club. Beat it now! (*He hauls* YANK *to his feet.*)

YANK. (*in a vague mocking tone*) Say, where do I go from here?

POLICEMAN. (*giving him a push—with a grin, indifferently*) Go to hell.

CURTAIN

Scene Eight

Twilight of the next day. The monkey house at the Zoo. One spot of clear gray light falls on the front of one cage so that the interior can be seen. The other cages are vague, shrouded in shadow from which chatterings pitched in a conversational tone can be heard. On the one cage a sign from which the word "gorilla" stands out. The gigantic animal himself is seen squatting on his haunches on a bench in much the same attitude as Rodin's "The Thinker." YANK *enters from the left. Immediately a chorus of angry chattering and screeching breaks out. The gorilla turns his eyes but makes no sound or move.*

YANK. (*with a hard, bitter laugh*) Welcome to your city, huh? Hail, hail, de gang's all here! (*At the sound of his voice the chattering dies away into an attentive silence.* YANK *walks up to the gorilla's cage and, leaning over the railing, stares in at its occupant, who stares back at him, silent and motionless. There is a pause of dead stillness. Then* YANK *begins to talk in a friendly confidential tone, half mockingly, but with a deep undercurrent of sympathy*) Say, yuh're some hard-lookin' guy, ain't yuh? I seen lots of tough nuts dat de gang called gorillas, but yuh're de foist real one I ever seen. Some chest yuh got, and shoulders, and dem arms and mits! I bet yuh got a punch in

---

[54]A popular watch brand of the time.

eider fist dat'd knock 'em all silly! (*This with genuine admiration. The gorilla, as if he understood, stands upright, swelling out his chest and pounding on it with fist.* YANK *grins sympathetically*) Sure, I get yuh. Yuh challenge de whole woild, huh? Yuh got what I was sayin' even if yuh muffed de woids. (*Then bitterness creeping in*) And why wouldn't yuh get me? Ain't we both members of de same club—de Hairy Apes? (*They stare at each other—a pause—then* YANK *goes on slowly and bitterly.*) So yuh're what she seen when she looked at me, de white-faced tart! I was you to her, get me? On'y outa de cage—broke out—free to moider her, see? Sure! Dat's what she tought. She wasn't wise dat I was in a cage, too—worser'n yours— sure—a damn sight—'cause you got some chanct to bust loose—but me—(*He grows confused*) Aw, hell! It's all wrong, ain't it? (*A pause*) I s'pose yuh wanter know what I'm doin' here, huh? I been warmin' a bench down to de Battery[55]—ever since last night. Sure. I seen de sun come up. Dat was pretty, too—all red and pink and green. I was lookin' at de skycrapers— steel—and all de ships comin' in, sailin' out, all over de oith— and dey was steel, too. De sun was warm, dey wasn't no clouds, and dere was a breeze blowin'. Sure, it was great stuff. I got it aw right—what Paddy said about dat bein' de right dope—on'y I couldn't get *in* it, see? I couldn't belong in dat. It was over my head. And I kept tinkin'—and den I beat it up here to see what youse was like. And I waited till dey was all gone to git yuh alone. Say, how d'yuh feel sittin' in dat pen all de time, havin' to stand for 'em comin' and starin' at yuh—de white-faced, skinny tarts and de boobs what marry 'em—makin' fun of yuh, laughin' at yuh, gittin' scared of yuh—damn 'em! (*He pounds on the rail with his fist. The gorilla rattles the bars of his cage and snarls. All the other monkeys set up an angry chattering in the darkness.* YANK *goes on excitedly*) Sure! Dat's de way it hits me, too. On'y yuh're lucky, see? Yuh don't belong wit 'em and yuh know it. But me, I belong wit 'em—but I don't, see? Dey don't belong wit me, dat's what. Get me? Tinkin' is hard—(*He passes one hand across his forehead with a painful gesture. The gorilla growls impatiently.* YANK *goes on gropingly*) It's dis way, what I'm drivin' at. Youse can sit and dope dream in de past, green woods, de jungle and de rest of it. Den yuh belong and dey don't. Den yuh kin laugh at 'em, see? Yuh're de champ of de world. But me—I ain't got no past to tink in, nor nothin' dat's comin', on'y what's now—and dat don't belong. Sure, you're de best off! You can't tink, can yuh? Yuh can't talk neider. But I kin make a bluff at talkin' and tinkin'—a'most git away wit it—a'most!—and dat's where de joker comes in. (*He laughs*) I ain't on oith and I ain't in heaven, get me? I'm in de middle tryin' to separate 'em, takin' all de woist punches from bot' of 'em. Maybe dat's what dey call hell, huh? But you, yuh're at de bottom. You belong! Sure! Yuh're de on'y one in de woild dat does, yuh lucky stiff! (*The

---

[55]A park on the southern end of Manhattan where artillery was mounted during colonial and revolutionary times.

gorilla growls proudly) And dat's why dey gotter put yuh in a cage, see? *(The gorilla roars angrily)* Sure! Yuh get me. It beats it when you try to tink it or talk it—it's way down—deep—behind—you 'n' me we feel it. Sure! Bot' members of dis club! *(He laughs—then in a savage tone)* What de hell! T' hell wit it! A little action, dat's our meat! Dat belongs! Knock 'em down and keep bustin' 'em till dey croaks yuh wit a gat—wit steel! Sure! Are yuh game? Dey've looked at youse, ain't dey—in a cage? Wanter git even? Wanter wind up like a sport 'stead of croakin' slow in dere? *(The gorilla roars an emphatic affirmative.* YANK *goes on with a sort of furious exaltation)* Sure! Yuh're reg'lar! Yuh'll stick to de finish! Me 'n' you, huh?—bot' members of dis club! We'll put up one last star bout dat'll knock 'em offen deir seats! Dey'll have to make de cages stronger after we're trou! *(The gorilla is straining at his bars, growling, hopping from one foot to the other.* YANK *takes a jimmy from under his coat and forces the lock on the cage door. He throws this open)* Pardon from de governor! Step out and shake hands. I'll take yuh for a walk down Fif' Avenoo. We'll knock 'em offen de oith and croak wit de band playin'. Come on, Brother. *(The gorilla scrambles gingerly out of his cage. Goes to* YANK *and stands looking at him.* YANK *keeps his mocking tone—holds out his hand)* Shake—de secret grip of our order. *(Something, the tone of mockery, perhaps, suddenly enrages the animal. With a spring he wraps his huge arms around* YANK *in a murderous hug. There is a crackling snap of crushed ribs—a gasping cry, still mocking, from* YANK*)* Hey, I didn't say kiss me! *(The gorilla lets the crushed body slip to the floor; stands over it uncertainly, considering; then picks it up, throws it in the cage, shuts the door, and shuffles off menacingly into the darkness at left. A great uproar of frightened chattering and whimpering comes from the other cages. Then* YANK *moves, groaning, opening his eyes, and there is silence. He mutters painfully)*

Say—dey oughter match him—with Zybszko.[56] He got me, aw right, I'm trou.Even him didn't tink I belonged. *(Then, with sudden passionate despair)* Christ, where do I get off at? Where do I fit in? *(Checking himself as suddenly)* Aw, what de hell! No squawkin', see! No quittin', get me! Croak wit your boots on! *(He grabs hold of the bars of the cage and hauls himself painfully to his feet—looks around him bewilderedly—forces a mocking laugh)* In de cage? huh? *(In the strident tones of a circus barker)* Ladies and gents, step forward and take a slant at de one and only— *(His voice weakening)* one and original—Hairy Ape from de wilds of— *(He slips in a heap on the floor and dies. The monkeys set up a chattering, whimpering wail. And, perhaps, the Hairy Ape at last belongs.)*

CURTAIN

1922

---

[56]Stanislaus Zbyszko, famous wrestler during the 1920s.

■   ELIZABETH MADOX ROBERTS   ■
                      1881–1941

Elizabeth Madox Roberts was one of eight children born to Mary Elizabeth Brent and Simpson Roberts, two strong-minded, passionate people, who, through stories and written memoirs, blended fact and imagination. This background helped shape Roberts's complex sensibility. Elizabeth loved to listen to the rich tales her father and maternal grandmother spun about ancestors dating back to the early eighteenth century, and to the stories recounted from Bulfinch's *The Age of Fable*. Much of this after-dinner lore was woven into her novels and short stories, especially her historical novel *The Great Meadow*.

Ardent southern sympathizers, her parents struggled meagerly through the Civil War and the Reconstruction period in Perryville, Kentucky. In 1884, the family moved to Springfield, a small, agrarian community, which bustled to life once a month on County Court Day to catch up with trading, haggling, and gossiping. Roberts, a keen observer, later depicted these Pigeon River country scenes with skill and flair. In spite of being situated in a particular time and place, and making use of "local color" devices, her novels take on archetypal dimensions and become universal in theme.

Elizabeth Madox Roberts was intelligent, sensitive, and artistic even as a child. She had a great love for music; in fact, the folksong, as well as the symphony, gave substance and shape to her art. Having excelled as a student in the small private schools of Springfield, she was sent by her parents to Covington to complete high school in a city school system. With little money and ill health, Roberts did not attend college full-time for another eighteen years. During these years she taught in various rural towns, boarding with residents and noting in detail the idiom of the people, their mores and customs. On June 8, 1917, she enrolled in the University of Chicago, her long-awaited dream come true. She graduated at the age of forty.

During her four years in Chicago, Roberts studied with Robert Morss Lovett and was active in a group of writers that included Glenway Wescott, Yvor Winters, and Harriet Monroe. Members read their own works, discussed the current literary scene (including Edgar Lee Masters, Carl Sandburg, Vachel Lindsay, and Sherwood Anderson), and shared an intense interest in literature and the arts. Roberts's writing career began with the publication of *Under the Tree* (1922), a volume of "child poems," "butterbeans" she called them, for which she won the Fiske Poetry Prize. She returned home frail and ill both physically and emotionally, but brought with her a Bachelor of Philosophy degree.

The Time of Man (1926) and *The Great Meadow* (1930) represent Roberts at her best, and with these novels she achieved the status of one of America's most popular and critically acclaimed novelists. In both novels Roberts uses a feminine central consciousness to shape her subject: "the total mind, not thinking or reason, but the instincts and emotions of all memories, imaginings, sensations of the whole being." In 1932 she published her first volume of stories, *The Haunted Mirror*. Her stories demonstrate her innovative craftsmanship, her use of "symbolism working through poetic realism" and regionalism, her belief in the intimate connection between the past and the present, and her penetrating dramatization of psychological crises. "Life is from within," she would say, "and thus the noise outside is a wind blowing in a mirror."

Roberts never married. She seldom made public appearances and, except for medical reasons, rarely traveled. During the last few years of her life, she spent the cold winter months in Orlando, Florida, where she died after years of suffering from a severe skin ailment and what was finally diagnosed as Hodgkin's disease. Although her writing career was comparatively short, she was surprisingly productive and original. With *The Time of Man*, her richest novel, she claimed her place as the first major novelist of the Southern Renascence. Her style markedly influenced later southern writers such as Jesse Stuart and William Faulkner, as well as Robert Penn Warren, who acknowledged this indebtedness when he said: "Elizabeth Madox Roberts was that rare thing, a true artist. . . . She was one of the indispensables."

Sheila Hurst Donnelly
Orange County Community College

PRIMARY WORKS

Under the Tree, 1922; *The Time of Man*, 1926; *My Heart and My Flesh*, 1927; *The Great Meadow*, 1930; *A Buried Treasure*, 1931; *The Haunted Mirror*, 1932; *He Sent Forth a Raven*, 1935; *Black Is My Truelove's Hair*, 1938; *Song in the Meadow*, 1940; *Not by Strange Gods*, 1941.

Death at Bearwallow

He had been to see his grandmother and the way home was growing dark, the ground at his feet imperfectly seen, moving nearer than his feet, as if his feet stepped into it and out again, as if they walked into an open substance which was like sponge. He had run out of the road to chase a rabbit, off into a cornfield, and now he was sorry for this. His father would flog him when he reached home, that he knew, for not being at hand to help with the night work. The moon was already in the sky, there when the sun set, prepared for the night, hastening the night. The thorn bushes at the roadside were familiar, known in all their contours and sensed in all their power, known too well. The hills beyond the running line of the fence and the field sank into the dark of the sky, cool and even, a terror, going to the night too easily, joining the dark. All the familiar things of the road and the day fitted into the dark, rising out of it. He was too far from his grandmother's house to return there; he had been on the road now since long before sundown.

He was more afraid as he came near to Terry Polin's house, fearful of it, for old Terry Polin threw stones at the children and he was bent as if he were squared to the earth he walked unevenly over. Coming near to the house he stopped in the road and would not dare to pass farther. There were strange ticking noises, irregularly placed, like some diminutive speech put into the bushes beyond the fence where scrub cedars grew out of a bramble, but he was not afraid of the sounds. It was the earth that arose to engulf him, to open his grave before his feet. The dusty stones in the road threatened, rising familiarly into the light, already accurately known. He blunted his fear of the house before his renewed sense of the earth and walked heedlessly past Polin's cabin where it stood close by the roadside as a threat standing clear in the moonlight. When he was well past it, he saw that the light on the window was not the light of the moon. A lamp burned inside, and out of the walls came the low outcry of voices.

He came then to the creek that ran past Polin's house, but the way downward toward the ford seemed short. Then the water was over the stepping stones, and he was unable to see the stones in the dark, running freshet that had come from the rain of the early afternoon in the hills. He tried to find one stone with a long stick, and he thought that if he could strike one of them he would be able to work out the others, but the water was high and the stones were lost. The dark of the earth lay under his feet, ready to yawn, his abysmal place, and he went back along the road and stopped in the open under the moon, above the creek bank, well away from the shade about the ford. The dark bushes at the side of the road, twiggy and rugged against the white of the moon, arose out of the black of the earth. Over in the field beyond the fence, out of sight in the shaded hummocks of the stubble, some hogs were working at the soil, rooting their food out of it, deeply breathing and grunting their content. He looked again at the dark of the ford, and he tried again and again to probe the water with a stick, but in the end he left the creek hurriedly and walked back along the way toward the moonlight. The dusty stones of the road were misty with their own defeat as they sank out of the light and carried understanding with them as they went, too vividly known, already familiar of old. He cried in his terror, the sobbing cry of a child, and he stood in the road shuddering. A sudden increase of fear arose suffusing the entire night that threatened to split asunder to let terror out, a threat like the threatened crack of doom. Crack-of-doom stood in his path and waited upon a thunder crash. He ran back along the road and, pushing open the door, he went into the house without knocking.

There was a dim light in the room, a light that seemed fogged beside the light of the moon. Two men whose names he knew, Sam Mulligan and Leo Scruggs, sat beside the table laying cards up on the dim board, scraping their feet on the floor when they rocked forward. Another man lay in the bed, lying very still.

"If here ain't Thompson Nally's boy," Scruggs said. "If here ain't that youngone, Dave Nally."

"What's he out so late for?" Mulligan asked.

There was a great laugh, the two of them joining to make it burst through the dim light and knock at the corners of the ceiling. The cards fell evenly from their hands, falling now one and now another to the table.

"God's sake, I bet that-there youngone was caught out. Afeared to go home by hisself."

"Come in to help old Terry Polin die."

"Doc says to me: 'Somebody's got to sit up tonight along with old Terry Polin. Somebody's got to.' Then I says: 'I don't mind if I do. As lief as not.'"

"I judge it's time now to be a-readen the prayer for the departen," Scruggs said. "I judge we best begin."

"Plenty time yet. Play on the cards. Quit your always a-blocken a game. It'll be a pretty while yet as I see."

He sat in the corner on the bare floor, near the door, between the light of the moon and the light of the lamp, touched by both. The man on the bed lay very still, but presently Sam Mulligan moved aside and the light fell toward the bed, and then by lifting his head and straining forward from the corner he could see the face that lay horizontal with the dull, yellowed pillow. The man on the bed was Terry Polin, the owner of the house. On the road old Terry threw stones at the children when they laughed and called out to him.

He knew that Terry Polin was on his bed to die and that the two men, Leo Scruggs and Sam Mulligan, were there to assist him. He himself was a small shape crouched in the corner, gathering himself to the smallest possible size, gathering inward his fear. He folded his hands into the warmth that was made where his arms touched his sides and bent his body toward the hollow where the two walls joined, drawing inward. He was glad that old Terry Polin was bound to die, that this would be the end of him, that he would not be throwing rocks on the road along with his curses when some child called him a name. His fears grew dim before sleep and he sank into a surrounding oblivion. The voices at the table went first, leaving the dim square of the room with its blocked shadows, but these trembled softly and broke into fragments, dissolved. He dreamed a story of hoofs thundering on the turf at the place where the grown boys raced their horses, the coming rush of feet throwing up the sod in little balls that were sprayed with dust.

"You threw back your slobbers inside the water bucket," a loud voice said. "You can just go to the spring and get more water now."

Voices had waked him with a great clamor. The men were up in the floor, shaking the floor with their steps. They were calling out roughly in anger.

"I'll not do it. I never threw back my slobbers. I didn't have no slobbers left. I drank it up to the bottom of the dipper."

"You threw back your slobbers, Leo Scruggs. I seen you. You lie to me if you say you didn't."

"You call me a lie and I'll smear your face up. I didn't throw back no slobbers."

"I'll throw this-here water out the door, the whole bucketful, and you can get more or go dry the balance of the night. You're a lie, Leo Scruggs. I see you throw back slobbers."

"You throw out this-here water and I'll knock hell outen you. You can take back your lie, too, Sam Mulligan. You don't call me a lie and pass it off like the time of day. You can take back your words."

"I never take back nothing. God Almighty, who you think I am?"

The boards of the house shook with their trampled feet as they scuffled, as they tried to grapple each the other's throat. The table was brushed aside, the lamp uncertainly poised in the movement, but it did not fall. Their great shadows lurched among the corners of the room, and Terry Polin twitched his hands at the quilt's edge. Then the fight ended suddenly and both men laughed. Scruggs had overturned the water bucket by some accident. The water slopped over the floor, and the bucket rolled along the boards near the chimney, spilling the dipper. A foot kicked the dipper away.

They settled to their places again, both of them breathing deeply after the fight. They both laughed again and told incidents of the struggle over and over. Then Sam Mulligan took up the cards from the floor and began to set them straight.

"I reckon it's about time now to read the prayer for the departen," Scruggs said when he had cooled a little from the fight. "We best read now."

"Aw, no. The night's young as I see it."

They set themselves to the cards again, but Dave was afraid to sleep. The untended lamp burned dully and smoked the chimney, and Leo Scruggs scraped the wick with a long splinter. One after the other, they would deal the cards, the dealer spraying one portion of the cards upon the other as if the pages of two books were mingled into one mass. Another sound came steadily beside the dropping of the cards on the table and the irregular outcries of the game, and presently he knew that the other sound was the long slow breathing of the man on the bed, each breath lying between long spaces of quiet. At the end of a round the men burst into comments, a loud scuffle of voices that broke into enforced sleep. "God, I had a club hand! Whoop law, and a lousy queen! I says to Hick: 'Where'd you-all get that-there haimstrung thoroughbred?'" The voice came starkly then out of his sleep:

"Her dress gaped open and I saw her meat, saw her naked meat a-showen."

"Saw Claudie Burk's meat. God, what was that to see?"

"I know it's time now to be a-readen the prayer for the departen."

Mulligan peered down across the dim light toward the bed, stretching his neck to see the progress there, waiting while he peered. "Naw, not yet. Deal again. I reckon I know. Deal on the cards."

Morning would come, he thought, sinking against the wall, fading into the hard lines of the wall, meeting the contours of the plaster. His back ached for sleep and his legs cramped as they were crumpled beneath him. After long intervals a deep breath shuddered through the dying man. The wall was merciful, inviting oblivion, and he sank toward it again and entered into it more nearly. A long interval of semi-knowing passed when the sounds found their accustomed rhythms and fell away entirely. Suddenly then a rough call splitting the density of forgetfulness.

Voice: I know it's time to be a-readen. I know it's getten time to be a-readen the prayer for the departen.

Voice: Aw, not yet. I know.

Voice: What's he a-tryen to say?

Voice: He's a-callen Kate. K-k-k-k-ka-kate. Used to be his old woman. Kate Polin, don't you recollect?

Voice: We better begin to read the prayer for the departen.

Voice: Pick up that-there deuce offen the floor. Play the cards. He ain't a-dyen easy, by gosh. Doc said afore morning. Come on now. It's four and four.

Voice: Doc says to me: "Somebody's got to sit up with old Terry Polin . . ."

Voice: I disgust bad cards, but these-here are plumb stinken.

The event on the bed stood between him and the morning which would never come. He fell again into semi-sleep. The water would be over the stones until daylight. A great hand tended the lamp again, lifting away the chimney and clearing the wick, the shapes of fingers shadowing the room, great palms obliterating the ceiling and the bed. It seemed a long while after the incident of the fingers that a quick outcry rent the substances of the wall into which he had sunk. The men were leaping to the floor, the voices blended.

"I told you it was time . . ."

"God Almighty, where's that-there prayer book?"

"Find the place inside. Hold that-there lamp. Hold it higher. Quit your fool doens now. That's not the prayer book. God Almighty, where's the prayer book? Get the right book, you damned-to-hell fool. Get the prayer book, Leo Scruggs. Hunt it up. Hold the lamp steady now. Find that-there prayer book. . . ."

He ran out the door of the house. One light bare step on the floor and another on the door sill and he was beyond the reach of the lamplight. He ran down to the dark ford and waited among the cold shadows.

Valeria was dead, Bob Newton's girl, and the banns had been ready to publish. Dave Nally drove his plow through the crumpled dolomite soil making ground ready for winter wheat, and as he walked he knew his height suddenly and knew what it was to stand high above the ground in the stature of a man. This knowledge had grown upon him with the years and had not been openly confessed to his sense. The bell ringing at St. Rose came faintly across many hills and was dispersed among the stony rises and bushy hollows, shallow and thin. Hearing the bell he remembered the mission that would begin at St. Rose in two weeks, and a vague excitement surged in his breast and in his throat, for the mission would be someplace to go every night. But Valeria was dead. Going to the mission would not be what it had formerly been to Bob Newton, to himself, to his sister Piety, to Clel Tobin; the mission was gutted of its rich core. The earth he cut with the plowshare was dark with hard sand and the plow scraped the stones. As he walked behind the plow, one foot limping deeply into the furrow, he arose momently above the soil and sank anew into it, fluctuating with each roughly placed step. He knew then what it was to stand above the ground in the shape of a man, having all of a man's parts.

Valeria lay in a bed somewhere in her father's house. From the field he could see the crumpled gable of the house as it stood, small, almost invisible, out of two hills.

Across the road from his plowing lay the marsh where tall rushes grew, and out of it some water birds were crying. Old men at the store, talking about the country and about the early days, often said that once the bears had come there to wallow, that the bears had carried away the mud on their backs and had made the great pond. He knew how the water stood above the clay or sank into it, and the great oaks had been there when the bears had lain in the mire. Bears had eaten the nuts from the tall hickory trees. The marsh seemed more curious, as one of the wonders of the earth, since he had heard of the bears, but on this morning as his gaze was fastened on the marsh while the plow rode across the rise of the field, he saw it in its relation to Valeria. His brother Dominic had walked across the field going to the still that was hidden down inside the bushy glen, had walked that way an hour earlier, and passing he had said:

"Valery, she's dead. Valery."

"Dead! How? Valery?"

"She died a right smart while ago this morning. She was taken bad last night at bedtime with a gripe in her heart and she died soon after daylight."

Valeria came acutely into his vision as he drove the team up the field, cutting the dirt apart for the winter seeds. At first a still pang lay within his breast, awe, disappointment, annoyance. Slowly the past tense gathered about her name and the present was sifted out of it. By the time he had plowed two rings about the field Valeria was dead, the matter settled and done, reported, closed. The beasts dragged at the heavy plow over the hill's rim, and the earth lay away, hill following hill, each interlocking with another. Coming across the brow, as the stubble rolled back to reveal its crumbled inner part, he saw swiftly into the earth, into the dark of the dirt. Year after year the plow but turned it over, wheeled it in procession. His eyes saw into it and saw the darkness under it.

As he went down the hill's farther side, slapping the plow rope on the mare's haunch, tears dimmed his eyes. Valeria had been Bob's girl, a warm creature with gray eyes, round arms and hips, soft to touch, warm to feel. Bob had known what it was to have her in his arms, and the banns were ready. He could hear clearly now the clatter of her laugh and feel her coming nearer, her swift step. Her hair was dark and her voice was kind for Bob and for Bob's friends, or impudently full of life. He had gone with Bob acutely in mind, knowing his way with her. Seeing them kiss, and seeing his sister Piety with Clel Tobin, he had turned to Pearl Janes and had kissed there, trying to want what he did, but she was forbidding even when she invited. There was a hardness in her, a dull woodenness. They had walked to the graveyard and had looked at the place where the first to come into the country were buried, trying to find dates on the eaten stones. He had known intently what Valeria and Bob held between them and he had read their joy and their sense of each other. He had stood between them minutely while they looked together, their eyes full of their greetings, and he had gone with them in their frank caress. Now the tears dried on his face, the tears of his first surprise at the news, and he moved unevenly after the plow iron, holding it into the earth, his eyes searching the ground where it rolled apart.

His sister Piety was coming across the field toward the plow. She seemed very small as she bent to struggle against the rough furrows and clods, very delicate and small, a child, as she worked her way through the crumbled clods to the inner island of unplowed stubble where she waited until he came near, her apron folded over her head to shield her from the sun.

"Valery's dead," she said. She seemed untouched by grief, being too near the event herself. He saw her then as a woman standing in the heart of the field, speaking out of the stubble. Her hands were warm and moist as she held the apron over her shoulder and her body swelled its woman's curves. She was a part of what lay on Valeria's bed, of what had gone with Valeria.

"Dominic told me. Where's Bob at now?"

"He came by our house a right smart while ago. He's gone back home now to his pappy's. He was here, but now he's gone."

He looked at her, comprehending. They looked toward each other and away.

"Did Bob take on?"

"He wouldn't talk. He just set in his chair. They want you to stay there tonight. To sit up. With the corpse."

The horses stood at ease, resting, the harness falling limp across their tired flanks. He stood with his feet buried in the crumbled loam, accepting the need where it reached toward him, making no sign. He was seeing Piety as Clel Tobin saw her, as Bob had seen Valeria, and this understanding over-spread his thought and made him slow in acquiescing. She stood a moment before him, the warmth of her life issuing from her body, from her face, from her hair, infinitely capable of sustaining itself, of continuing. Her breasts, lifted with her lifted arm, throbbed with it before him, denoting warm being, the same as that which had moved in the other girl. They were the same to him, both something distinguished by the two boys, his friends, Bob and Clel Tobin. It was unthinkable that any disaster could bring it any hurt. Warm life darted now about Piety's mouth as she spoke and sat quietly on her eyes, or sat again on her small full shoulders and her back, her hips and her legs, her ankles. He nodded his willingness to the request and gathered taut the plow lines.

"I best put a stitch in your shirt with the blue stripe," she said. "I best mend it a little by the collar."

He remembered the garment, and remembered that he would have to put on his other clothes. "I'll quit up work early, in time to get there against night sets in. They might want help."

He saw her go back across the plowed space, picking her way slowly and with trouble through the broken earth. He saw a small blue shape, Piety, rising and falling in a struggle with the gullies and stony rises.

Two candles burned at Valeria's feet and the room was very still. Her people had gone to the other room, or they had gone above to the loft chamber. One or two sat on the chairs of the room or knelt at the prayers. When they stood, the uneven boards creaked under the carpet Valeria herself had helped to weave at the loom. Her hands had gathered the winter bouquet, goldenrod and sassafras and thorn apples, gathered idly, not meant to keep; but now it would be saved on the shelf, standing on the mantel beyond the crucifix. At any moment of its gathering she was near to tossing it into the gully, caring then to keep only what Bob gave her.

He was staring at the light on the wall where the throb of the candle burst and spread unevenly. The other watcher was an old man, Ben Hester, and he had fallen asleep over his prayers where he knelt in a corner. The night moved slowly, and the weariness of the plow pulled at his limbs but he had no mind to sleep. He had read the prayers for the repose of the dead and he had been through the circle of the rosary, and now he stared at the beating light on the wall. Valeria was still, was waxen like an image at the altar. He turned his back to the room and sat facing the light that throbbed uneasily on the wall just beyond the crucifix and the dried bouquet of autumn. Bob's joy in Valeria arose as a spectre to question him, and the book had fallen from his hands to lie unheeded on the floor. The ground at his feet moved nearer, imperfectly seen, making a pool about his ankles, arising to engulf him. "It's time now to be a-readen the prayer for the departen," a flat voice said, far back in his memory, one with his breath, "the prayer for the departen." This which Bob had with Valeria stood set apart, warm within itself, but his only by the knowing of it, it being theirs to have privately. A cry beat at his throat and sank deeply into his mind. He was staring at the wall and his feet were sinking into the dark of the floor. Within his own breath, the speech lying back of his inner disorder, the words lay perpetually, "It's time now to be a-readen that-there prayer for the departen."

The man on the bed was himself, Dave Nally, his head on the pillow, his feet stretched out far and cold. As he lay, his eyes looked up at the ceiling which was a fixity holding length and depth in a four-square design. His throat struggled with the words of the rosary, the words pushed against his throat as against shut gates that held firmly, that rattled on lock and hinges, "Hail Mary, full of grace, blessed art thou among women." His entire self from first to the present moment lay back in his being, and he was one, breathing and living, the same he had always been. He could leap back to the beginning or forward to the end, the now, the last moment. It was night and he and Dominic were beside the fire, Dominic taking a piece of food from their mother's hands. He was holding his hands, the same hands he now had, to the warmth of the fire, saying over and over: "Six times seven is forty-two, six times seven. That's my word to remember." The hammering words of the prayer still beat at the hinges of his shut throat, and his fingers felt the hard little berries of the rosary, but when he lifted his hands under the quilt he found that they were cold and empty. There were no beads.

The two candles burned behind him at Valeria's feet and she was still, like wax. The light shook on the yellowed wall, leaping and falling slowly. His hands were at the quilt's edge, adjusting the world. He was cold and he ought to have gloves, his hands smarting, hard and stiff and raw with deep chapped places that bled. His mammy would knit him some gloves if she were still living. He would sit close to the fire and the heat would glide into his bones slowly, a little at a time. He would take his coat off to let the warmth in, and he would sit and hear the log crackle and settle itself into a quiet lapping flame, until he would float on the warmth and the cold would sink back and away. His own warmth, all for him, would sink inside his shirt, the same inside he had always had. Ten hail-maries and then one our-father, in his hands as marbles on a string. A sudden outcry: You threw back your slobbers. I see you do it. You lie to me if you say you didn't. I didn't do it. I never threw my slobbers back. I drank it all to the last drop. You did so throw back your slobbers. I never had no slobbers. You lie and I'll tear your guts out. You'll eat back your words. I never take nothing back. God Almighty who you think I am. It's time now to be a-readen the prayer for the departen. Naw, not yet, plenty time yet as I see. Play down your hand, quit a-blocken a game.

He was with a pack of boys, hunting across fields and into woods. A pack of boys, himself one, and a little girl hiding. She was running down a thicket, her skimp little dress, drab, showing now and then in the brush. Hoarse cries, unknown to themselves, were coming out of their throats. Four boys, himself one. She was gone, swallowed up by the ground or slipped away through some fence, Sallie Bent, lost to them, safe. Down into a deep hollow where the path ran cool, and she was lost to them, two of the boys off after a rabbit and one, Wes Hyte, lagging behind in the cool brush, lying on the moss, loving the moss.

Slowly he came back to the light of the lamp behind the smoky chimney and then to the hands that lifted regularly over the edge of the table and dropped the cards. "There's my high and the ace ain't out. A queen for high. Her dress gapped open and I see her naked meat a-showen. I see old man Hicks come down the pike a-driven a haimstrung critter. Where'd he get that-there haimstrung nag? Deal out again, egad, and give me something this-here time." The voice took tone:

"Is it time now to be a-readen the prayer for the departen?"

The lamp made pink streams across the space before the window, long colored lines running down into the light across the powdered dark of the room. The air was still except that something rattled slowly in long waves, a rattling lying across the continued stillness. A great head stood up above the turned shoulders, nose, mouth, eyes and hair. The eyes looked down across the quiet space, peering and staring at him out of their shadowed lids.

"Naw, not yet. Deal again. Plenty time. Reckon I know."

The cards fell slowly one on the other, making no sounds, but now and then a hand thumped the table impatiently. Fragments of the prayer for the departing appeared in mind, imperfectly remembered, the litany for the dying, never learned in life. "Lord have mercy on him. Christ have mercy on him. Lord have mercy ... Holy Mary pray for him ... All ye holy angels and arch-angels ..." The supplications were rising and falling away ... "All ye choirs of the just ... Have pity, Lord, on his sighs, have pity on his tears. Loosed from the bonds of flesh ..." Somebody would have to read the words from the book.

He was sitting in the pew with Piety and his mother, at late mass. A wasp was dipping up and down slowly over old Mrs. Hester's bonnet, touching the black of the crown. Piety was kneeling, saying prayers, her eyes half asleep, her feet set upright behind the hem of her dress, her lips whispering rapid, wordless motions. He was turning through the prayer book, watching the leaves fall over the brim of it, motions of leaves, the worn edges soft like rag. His eyes had read without seeing, The Litany of the Saints, The Ordinary of the Mass, Prayer for one Departing this Life. The words stood on the page like poetry in a book.

> St. Mary Magdalen,
> St. Lucy
> All ye holy virgins and widows.

He fingered the edge of the quilt to settle the edges of the world into order, to make all right, to straighten a crease. A great hand shadowed the lamp and the light fell through the gapped fingers and became a turmoil that threatened to wrench his hold from the side of the quilt. "I know you did throw your slobbers back. I did not so. You call me a lie and I'll tear your guts outen your belly ..." There was something he, Terry Polin, had always been wanting, needing, and he could not now gather the name of it or the meaning. It was something he was always wanting and getting and wanting again. He could not divine how it was called. It was gone now and the name of it gone. It was something that ran in his limbs, in his legs and arms and sides. It was kate; he had found the name for it. It seemed very far away now, forgotten in the way of its going, but the name was now assembled, kate in his arms and legs, in his breastbone.

Slowly this sense grew definite and firm, gathering a person about it, Kate, a warm moving body, a blood-containing flesh, hands lifted and rising before the puffed breasts as she sewed. Hurrying down to the chickenhouse with a pan of meal dough or going in at the door of the house, closing the door. Ask Kate. Tell Kate. These were incessant sayings, never refuted. Tell Kate about the low price of hogs, himself almost giving them away. She was the mother of his children, Tony and Mag and Terry B. Kate moved down a film of air, her hands moving, setting food out or cooking food, making a bed, combing her hair, drawing on her clothes that smelt warm and full, like her body and like the things she handled all day, food, chickens, feathers, ashes, earth, children. He would ask Kate, tell Kate, tell her now. A great cry formed in his body and rushed up into his throat, into his loose throat, and there it hung on folds of flesh entangled with breath and struggled forth in a dry hissing sound. "K-k-k-k-ka-Kate!" Two great heads stood up above a mass of shoulders and turned wide-opened eyes toward him. He brought his gaze down from the dispersed light of the room and centered it upon the two heads that turned toward him staring, they being the world. The rattle that shook through the quiet of the room was his breath, his own, climbing down long slow stairs with great steps. He was one, the same he had always been, as when he ran out at the door in a little blue dress, climbing up the hen ladder.

Voice: I know now it's time to be a-readen the prayer for the departen. . . .

Voice: Find me that-there prayer book. . . .

Voice: God Almighty, where's that-there book? Find it quick. Find the place. I never take nothing back. Who you think I am?

Voice: Lord have mercy on him
      Christ have mercy on him
      Lord have mercy
      Holy Mary pray for him
      All ye holy angels. . . .
      Holy Abel . . .
      Thy creature not made by strange gods but by thee. . . .
      Loosed from the bonds of flesh he may attain . . . may attain . . .
          may attain. . . .

He arose and went bending toward the house door, looking past the candles that burned at Valeria's feet. The night was cool outside, the crying of the night noises an infinity of sound sinking back and arising perpetually in the three-ply space of the night-quiet. The darkness was complete, no part of it distinguished from any other part.

1932

H.D. (HILDA DOOLITTLE)
1886–1961

H.D.'s life and work recapitulate the central themes of literary modernism: the emergence from Victorian norms and certainties, the entry into an age characterized by rapid technological change and the violence of two world wars, the disruptions of conventional gender roles with the rise of feminism, and the development of literary modes that reflected the disintegration of traditional symbolic systems and the myth-making quest for new meanings. Writing under the *nom de plume* H.D., she is known mainly as a poet, especially for her imagist poetry (as in *Sea Garden*) and her epics of the forties and fifties (*Trilogy* and *Helen in Egypt*). She was the first woman to receive the prestigious Award of Merit Medal for Poetry from the American Academy of Arts and Letters (1960). H.D. has also been highly praised for her Greek translations. Often compared to

Virginia Woolf and Gertrude Stein, H.D. is increasingly recognized for her experimental fiction (*HERmione, Bid Me to Live*, and *Asphodel*) and her personal essays (*Tribute to Freud*).

Like the modernist poetry of her friends, Ezra Pound, T. S. Eliot, and William Carlos Williams, H.D.'s early poetry originated in the avant-garde, *vers libre* movements of 1910–1920 (especially imagism), influenced by Sappho, Japanese haiku, Troubadour lyrics, Bergsonian philosophy, and post-impressionist art. H.D. was known as the "most perfect" of the imagist poets for her innovative musical rhythms, crystalline lines, and stark images. Like *The Cantos, The Waste Land*, and *Paterson*, H.D.'s later long sequence poems featured the poet as prophet wandering in the wilderness of the modern world, drawing on the fragments of many cultures to forge new myths that might give meaning to a world shattered by war, technology, and alienation. Like the modernist novels of Virginia Woolf, James Joyce, and William Faulkner that she admired, H.D.'s fiction fractured narrative perspective and chronology in order to capture the shifting subjectivities of consciousness. This prose centers on the experience of the creative woman who wants both love and vocation in a world perpetually split open by violence.

H.D.'s distinctive emphasis as a modernist grew out of her extensive involvement with classical Greece and ancient Egypt, cinema, psychoanalysis, esoteric religion, and occult mysticism. Her perspective as a woman further permeated her revisions of these traditions. Analyzed by Sigmund Freud (1933, 1934), for example, she transformed his androcentric theories of femininity into the basis of a redemptive female voice and vision. Like Woolf, H.D. was profoundly concerned with the issues of war and violence. To counter the forces of death, her work reconstitutes gender, language, and myth to serve her search for a vision of personal and cultural rebirth.

Loving the forests and sea coasts of the United States, H.D. grew up in Pennsylvania: first Bethlehem and then a Philadelphia suburb. Her mother was a Moravian artist and musician, and her father was a well-known professor of astronomy. Withdrawing from Bryn Mawr College in her sophomore year with poor grades, she later went to Europe in 1911 to join the circle of artists around Pound, Yeats, and Joyce. Although she remained intensely American throughout her residences in London and Switzerland, she visited the United States only four times. Bisexually oriented, H.D. almost married Ezra Pound, married fellow imagist Richard Aldington in 1913, separated from him in 1919, divorced him in 1938, and lived with Bryher (Winifred Ellerman) from 1919 through 1946.

Susan Stanford Friedman
University of Wisconsin at Madison

PRIMARY WORKS

Sea Garden, 1916; *Collected Poems*, 1925; *Palimpsest*, 1926; *Hedylus*, 1928; *By Avon River*, 1949; *Tribute to Freud*, 1956; *Bid Me to Live (A Madrigal)*, 1960; *Helen in Egypt*, 1961; *Hermetic Definition*, 1972; *Trilogy, 1944–1946*, 1973; *End to Torment: A Memoir of Ezra Pound*, 1979; *HERmione*, 1981; *Collected Poems, 1912–1944*, 1983; *Paint It Today*, 1992; *Asphodel*, 1992.

Sea Rose

Rose, harsh rose,
marred and with stint of petals,
meagre flower, thin,
sparse of leaf,

more precious   5
than a wet rose
single on a stem—
you are caught in the drift.

Stunted, with small leaf,
you are flung on the sand,   10
you are lifted
in the crisp sand
that drives in the wind.

Can the spice-rose
drip such acrid fragrance   15
hardened in a leaf?

                                                                 1916

The Helmsman[1]

O be swift—
we have always known you wanted us.
We fled inland with our flocks,
we pastured them in hollows,
cut off from the wind   5
and the salt track of the marsh.

We worshipped inland—
we stepped past wood-flowers,
we forgot your tang,
we brushed wood-grass.   10

We wandered from pine-hills
through oak and scrub-oak tangles,
we broke hyssop and bramble,
we caught flower and new bramble-fruit
in our hair: we laughed   15

---

[1]Possible allusion to Charon, the ferryman who carried the souls of the dead across the river Styx to the Underworld in Greek mythology.

as each branch whipped back,
we tore our feet in half buried rocks
and knotted roots and acorn-cups.

We forgot—we worshipped,
we parted green from green,   20
we sought further thickets,
we dipped our ankles
through leaf-mould and earth,
and wood and wood-bank enchanted us—

and the feel of the clefts in the bark,   25
and the slope between tree and tree—
and a slender path strung field to field
and wood to wood
and hill to hill
and the forest after it.   30

We forgot—for a moment
tree-resin, tree-bark,
sweat of a torn branch
were sweet to the taste.

We were enchanted with the fields,   35
the tufts of coarse grass
in the shorter grass—
we loved all this.

But now, our boat climbs—hesitates—drops—
climbs—hesitates—crawls back—   40
climbs—hesitates—
O be swift—
we have always known you wanted us.

                                                            1916

Oread[1]

Whirl up, sea—
whirl your pointed pines,
splash your great pines
on our rocks,
hurl your green over us,   5
cover us with your pools of fir.

                                                            1914

[1]Mountain nymph in Greek mythology.

Helen[1]

All Greece hates
the still eyes in the white face,
the lustre as of olives
where she stands,
and the white hands.   5

All Greece reviles
the wan face when she smiles,
hating it deeper still
when it grows wan and white,
remembering past enchantments   10
and past ills.

Greece sees unmoved,
God's daughter, born of love,
the beauty of cool feet
and slenderest knees,   15
could love indeed the maid,
only if she were laid,
white ash amid funereal cypresses.

1923

from **Trilogy**

from *The Walls Do Not Fall*
[43]

Still the walls do not fall,
I do not know why;

there is zrr-hiss,
lightning in a not-known,

unregistered dimension;   5
we are powerless,

dust and powder fill our lungs
our bodies blunder

[1]Beautiful daughter of Zeus and Leda, and wife of the Greek king Menelaus, Helen was abducted from Sparta and taken to Troy by Paris, the Trojan prince. Her kidnapping led to the Trojan War.

through doors twisted on hinges,
and the lintels slant   10

cross-wise;
we walk continually

on thin air
that thickens to a blind fog,

then step swiftly aside,   15
for even the air

is independable,
thick where it should be fine

and tenuous
where wings separate and open,   20

and the ether
is heavier than the floor,

and the floor sags
like a ship floundering;

we know no rule   25
of procedure,

we are voyagers, discoverers
of the not-known,

the unrecorded;
we have no map;   30

possibly we will reach haven,
heaven.

1944

from *Tribute to the Angels*

[8]

Now polish the crucible[1]
and in the bowl distill

[1]In alchemy, the vessel in which the alchemist
tried to purify matter into gold through fire.

a word most bitter, *marah*,[2]
a word bitterer still, *mar*,[3]

sea, brine, breaker, seducer,   5
giver of life, giver of tears;

now polish the crucible
and set the jet of flame

under, till *marah-mar*[4]
are melted, fuse and join   10

and change and alter,
mer, mere, mère, mater, Maia, Mary,

Star of the Sea,
Mother.[5]

[12]

Swiftly re-light the flame,   15
Aphrodite,[6] holy name,

Astarte,[7] hull and spar
of wrecked ships lost your star,

forgot the light at dusk,
forgot the prayer at dawn;   20

return, O holiest one,
Venus[8] whose name is kin

to venerate,
venerator.

[2]Hebrew word for bitter in feminine form; the place where the Hebrews first camped after crossing the Red Sea, and where Moses made the bitter waters sweet (Exodus 15:23); and the name Naomi took to signify her bitter fate after the death of her sons (Ruth 1:20).
[3]Hebrew adjective for bitter in masculine form; Hebrew title for Mr.; and Hebrew verb for ruin, mar, break.
[4]In the alchemical crucible, the alchemist fired together materials thought to be masculine and feminine.
[5]In French, *mer* means sea; *mère* means mother. In Latin, *mater* means mother. Maia is an early Greek goddess and mother of Hermes by Zeus. In Christian tradition, Mary is the mother of Jesus and is sometimes known by the name Stella Maris, Latin for Star of the Sea. This name indicates her protection of sailors as a beacon of light in the planet Venus, also associated with the Egyptian goddess Isis, the Babylonian goddess Ishtar, the Phoenecian goddess Astarte, the Greek goddess Aphrodite, and the Roman goddess Venus.
[6]Greek goddess of love.
[7]Phoenecian goddess of love.
[8]Roman goddess of love.

[19]

. . . . . .
we asked for no sign   25
but she[9] gave a sign unto us;

sealed with the seal of death,
we thought not to entreat her

but prepared us for burial;
then she set a charred tree before us,   30

burnt and stricken to the heart;
was it may-tree or apple?

[20]

Invisible, indivisible Spirit,
how is it you come so near,

how is it that we dare   35
approach the high-altar?

we crossed the charred portico,
passed through a frame—doorless—

entered a shrine; like a ghost,
we entered a house through a wall;   40

then still not knowing
whether (like the wall)

we were there or not-there,
we saw the tree flowering;

it was an ordinary tree   45
in an old garden-square.

[9]The goddess of the Near-eastern, Egyptian, Greek, and Roman mystery religions in all her many forms; also associated in *Trilogy* with the Virgin Mary and Mary Magdalene, the former prostitute who first saw the risen Christ according to Christian tradition.

[23]

. . . .
it was the Holy Ghost[10]—

a half-burnt-out-apple-tree
blossoming;

this the flowering of the rood,[11]   50
this is the flowering of the wood,

where Annael,[12] we pause to give
thanks that we rise again from death and live.

[43]

And the point in the spectrum
where all lights become one,   55

is white and white is not no-colour,
as we were told as children,

but all-colour;
where the flames mingle

and the wings meet, when we gain   60
the arc of perfection,

we are satisfied, we are happy,
we begin again;

I *John saw. I testify*
to rainbow feathers, to the span of heaven

and walls of colour,
and colonnades of jasper;
but when the jewel   15
melts in the crucible,

---

[10]Third member of the Trinity (Father, Son,
Holy Ghost) in Christianity, often associated
with the feminine.
[11]Cross or crucifix, symbolizing the death and
resurrection of Christ.
[12]Angel of peace in the Judeo-Christian tradition, associated with Venus. H.D. links

Annael and the six other angels in *Tribute to
the Angels* with the seven unnamed angels
around God's throne in the book of Revelation in the Bible.

we find not ashes, not ash-of-rose,
not a tall vase and a staff of lilies,

not *vas spirituale*,
not *rosa mystica* even,   20

but a cluster of garden-pinks
or a face like a Christmas-rose.

This is the flowering of the rod,
this is the flowering of the burnt-out wood,

where, Zadkiel, we pause to give   25
thanks that we rise again from death and live.

London, May 17–31, 1944

Political Poetry in the Modern Period

THE HISTORY OF AMERICAN POLITICAL POETRY IS CONTINUOUS WITH THE HISTORY of the nation itself; there is no period, for example, when poetry reflecting on and critical of the dominant values in American social life was not being written and read. But the history of the moments when oppositional political poetry became highly visible and influential—either within important subcultures or more broadly—is far more discontinuous. The high points of political poetry include the abolitionist poetry of the mid-nineteenth century and the poetry and song of the late-nineteenth- and early-twentieth-century labor movement. In the twentieth century, a proper definition of political poetry would certainly encompass much of the work of the New Negro Renaissance. For contemporary readers, the history of political poetry also includes the 1960s poetry of black liberation, the antiwar poetry written during the Vietnam War, and much contemporary Chicano, feminist, Asian American, and Native American poetry.

But in no decade was political poetry as pervasive as it was in the 1930s. As the Great Depression deepened in the early 1930s, large numbers of people, including many writers, were drawn to the political Left or to the Communist Party. They shared a widespread conviction that capitalism had failed, that the old order could not be restored, and that only the most thoroughgoing social and political change could bring about social and economic justice. As a result, the generalized sense of alienation common to modernism became much more focused; many poets felt specifically alienated from capitalism and its social institutions, rather than from modern life as a whole. They joined a number of active poets who had already been writing from that perspective in the 1920s, for the much heralded "roaring twenties" had not brought economic health to everyone.

What this actually meant began to become clear in 1926 and 1927 when protests against the planned execution of Sacco and Vanzetti in Massachusetts gathered force. A broad coalition, reaching far beyond writers with established progressive commitments, formed to oppose the verdict. When the execution occurred despite mass protests, many writers concluded that American institutions were too corrupt to be reformed. A few years later, when the depression took hold, some of these writers found themselves documenting the decay of American life and urging revolutionary change. It would take a full decade, until 1936 and 1937 and the advent of the Spanish Civil War, before a coalition as broad as that protesting Sacco's and Vanzetti's executions would form again, but in the meantime many writers were radicalized, and the poetry of the Great Depression reached a wide audience.

As even this brief selection of poems demonstrates, the political poetry of the Great Depression and subsequent decades was far more varied formally and stylistically than is conventionally assumed. At least on the political Left, modernist experimentation could sometimes coexist with forms as traditional as the ballad stanza. As poems like Rolfe's "First Love" and "Elegia" suggest, the language of political poetry was often lyrical, though lyricism and anger here often occur together. This intense period of social and political consciousness for many lasted beyond the decade. Those radical poets of the 1930s who maintained their Left commitments and who lived through the 1950s found themselves taking up, in turn, critiques of capitalism, racism, fascism, and McCarthyism. Thus a poet like Rolfe was writing protest poetry until his death in 1954. This poetry does, therefore, display common themes and political views, a pattern poets were aware of and sought to underline.

On the one hand, Kay Boyle's "A Communication to Nancy Cunard," based on the Scottsboro case in which nine young black men were unjustly accused and convicted of the rape of two white women that had not even taken place, and Genevieve Taggard's poem sequence "To the Negro People" represent the great number of poems that white authors produced to protest American racism and explore African American culture. Rolfe's "First Love" and "Elegia" and Taggard's "To the Veterans of the Abraham Lincoln Brigade," on the other hand, represent many poems written in support of the Spanish Republic and of the Americans who fought on its behalf after Francisco Franco and other army officers supported by Hitler and Mussolini led a revolt against it in 1936. The Spanish Civil War came to an end with Franco's victory in 1939, but American poets who came of age in the 1920s and 1930s continued to write poems about it through the 1950s.

Poems about the Great Depression and about American labor fill out this selection. They include Lola Ridge's protest against labor leader Tom Mooney's unjust imprisonment for a crime he did not commit, Tillie Olsen's exposé of the exploitation of Mexican American seamstresses in the Southwest, and Alfred Hayes's simultaneously anguished and sardonic narrative about an economically disenfranchised generation. Stylistically, they range from Joseph Kalar's almost expressionist portrait of an abandoned factory to Kenneth Fearing's satires about American business and politics, from Taggard's effort to mix blunt realism with metaphoric intensity in "Up State—Depression Summer," her narrative of a farm family's decline, to Rolfe's fusion of realism and surreal moments in "Season of Death," his poem about the unemployed.

Not every reader today will find the revolutionary sentiments here appealing, but many of the social issues these poets took up remain strikingly relevant. Economic hardship and exploitation in the city and on the farm have not changed enough to date these poems, nor have race relations in America so improved as to make the poems about race irrelevant. Taggard's poem about immigration, diversity, and national identity, "Ode in Time of Crisis," reads as if it might have been written yesterday. And it is uncanny, certainly, to realize that the damage asbestos could do to a worker was evident to some as early as 1933. These are among the points of entrance we may use in deciding whether the passions of this period have any bearing on our own.

Cary Nelson
University of Illinois

PRIMARY WORKS

Kenneth Fearing, *Social Poetry of the 1930s*, 1978; *Complete Poems*, 1994; Kay Boyle, *Collected Poems*, 1991; Langston Hughes, *Good Morning Revolution: Uncollected Writings of Social Protest*, 1992; *Collected Poems*, 1994; Edwin Rolfe, *Collected Poems*, 1993.

JOSEPH KALAR
1906–1972

Papermill

Not to be believed, this blunt savage wind
Blowing in chill empty rooms, this tornado
Surging and bellying across the oily floor
Pushing men out in streams before it;
Not to be believed, this dry fall   5
Of unseen fog drying the oil
And emptying the jiggling greasecups;
Not to be believed, this unseen hand
Weaving a filmy rust of spiderwebs
Over these turbines and grinding gears,   10
These snarling chippers and pounding jordans;[1]
These fingers placed to lips saying shshsh;
Keep silent, keep silent, keep silent;
Not to be believed hardly, this clammy silence
Where once feet stamped over the oily floor,   15
Dinnerpails clattered, voices rose and fell
In laughter, curses, and songs. Now the guts
Of this mill have ceased their rumbling, now
The fires are banked and red changes to black,
Steam is cold water, silence is rust, and quiet   20
Spells hunger. Look at these men, now,
Standing before the iron gates, mumbling,
"Who could believe it? Who could believe it?"

1931

---

[1]Machines employed at a paper mill.

KENNETH FEARING
1902–1961

1933

You heard the gentleman, with automatic precision, speak
    the truth.
    Cheers. Triumph.
    And then mechanically it followed the gentleman lied.
    Deafening applause. Flashlights, cameras, microphones.   5
    Floral tribute. Cheers.

Down Mrs. Hogan's alley, your hand with others reaching
    among the ashes, cinders, scrapiron, garbage, you
    found the rib of sirloin wrapped in papal docu-
    ments. Snatched it. Yours by right, the title clear.   10
    Looked up. Saw lips twitch in the smiling head thrust
    from the museum window. "A new deal."

And ran. Escaped. You returned the million dollars. You
    restored the lady's virginity.
    You were decorated 46 times in rapid succession by   15
    the King of Italy. Took a Nobel prize. Evicted
    again, you went downtown, slept at the movies,
    stood in the breadline, voted yourself a limousine.
    Rage seized the Jewish Veterans of Foreign Wars. In
    footnotes, capitals, Latin, italics, the poet of the   20
    Sunday supplements voiced steamheated grief. The
    RFC expressed surprise.
    And the news, at the Fuller Brush hour, leaked out.
    Shouts. Cheers. Stamping of feet. Blizzard of con-
    fetti. Thunderous applause.   25

But the stocks were stolen. The pearls of the actress, stolen
    again. The books embezzled.
    Inexorably, the thief pursued. Captured inexorably.
    Tried. Inexorably acquitted.

And again you heard the gentleman, with automatic   30
    precision, speak the truth.
    Saw, once more, the lady's virginity restored.

In the sewers of Berlin, the directors prepared, the room
    dark for the seance, she a simple Baroness, you a

lowly millionaire, came face to face with John D.   35
    Christ.
Shook hands, his knife at your back, your knife at his.
    Sat down.
Saw issue from his throat the ectoplasm of Pius VIII,
    and heard "A test of the people's faith." You said   40
    amen, voted to endorse but warned against default,
    you observed the astral form of Nicholas II, and
    heard "Sacred union of all." Saw little "Safe for
    democracy" Nell. Listened to Adolph "Safety of
    France and society" Thiers.   45
And beheld the faith, the union of rags, blackened
    hands, stacked carrion, breached barricades in flame,
no default, credit restored, Union Carbide $94^3/_8$, call
    money 10%, disarm, steel five points up, rails rise,
    Dupont up, disarm, disarm, and heard again,   50
ghost out of ghost out of ghost out of ghost,
the voice of the senator reverberate through all the
    morgues of all the world, echo again for liberty in
    the catacombs of Rome, again sound through the
    sweatshops, ghettoes, factories, mines, hunger again   55
    repealed, circle the London cenotaph once more
    annulling death, saw ten million dead returned to
    life, shot down again, again restored,

Heard once more the gentleman speak, with automatic
    precision, the final truth,   60
once more beheld the lady's virginity, the lady's de-
    cency, the lady's purity, the lady's innocence,
paid for, certified, and restored.

Crawled amorously into bed. Felt among the maggots for
    the mouldering lips. The crumbled arms. Found   65
    them.
Tumult of cheers. Music and prayer by the YMCA.
    Horns, rockets. Spotlight.
The child was nursed on government bonds. Cut its
    teeth on a hand grenade. Grew fat on shrapnel.   70
    Bullets. Barbed wire. Chlorine gas. Laughed at
    the bayonet through its heart.

These are the things you saw and heard, these are the
    things you did, this is your record,
you.   75

                                                         1934

▪ ALFRED HAYES ▪
1911–1985

In a Coffee Pot

Tonight, like every night, you see me here
Drinking my coffee slowly, absorbed, alone.
A quiet creature at a table in the rear
Familiar at this evening hour and quite unknown.
The coffee steams. The Greek who runs the joint   5
Leans on the counter, sucks a dead cigar.
His eyes are meditative, sad, lost in what it is
Greeks think about the kind of Greeks they are.

I brood upon myself. I rot
Night after night in this cheap coffee pot.   10
I am twenty-two I shave each day
I was educated at a public school
They taught me what to read and what to say
The nobility of man my country's pride
How Nathan Hale died   15
And Grant took Richmond.
Was it on a summer or a winter's day?
Was it Sherman burned the Southland to the sea?
The men the names the dates have worn away
The classes words the books commencement prize   20
Here bitter with myself I sit
Holding the ashes of their prompted lies.

The bright boys, where are they now?
Fernando, handsome wop who led us all
The orator in the assembly hall   25
Arista man the school's big brain.
He's bus boy in an eat-quick joint
At seven per week twelve hours a day.
His eyes are filled with my own pain
His life like mine is thrown away.   30
Big Jorgensen the honest, blond, six feet,
And Daniels, cunning, sly,—all, all—
You'll find them reading Sunday's want ad sheet.
Our old man didnt know someone

Our mother gave no social teas   35
You'll find us any morning now
Sitting in the agencies.

You'll find us there before the office opens
Crowding the vestibule before the day begins
The secretary yawns from last night's date   40
The elevator boy's black face looks out and grins.
We push we crack our bitter jokes we wait
These mornings always find us waiting there
Each one of us has shined his broken shoes
Has brushed his coat and combed his careful hair   45
Dance hall boys pool parlor kids wise guys
The earnest son the college grad all, all
Each hides the question twitching in his eyes
And smokes and spits and leans against the wall.

We meet each other sometimes on the street   50
Sixth Avenue's high L bursts overhead
Freak shows whore gypsies hotdog stands
Cajole our penniless eyes our bankrupt hands.
"Working yet?" "The job aint come
Got promised but a runaround."   55
The L shakes building store and ground
"What's become of Harry? and what's become
Of Charley? Martinelli? Brooklyn Jones?"
"He's married—got a kid—and broke."
And Charley's on Blackwell's, Martinelli's through—   60
Met him in Grand Central—he's on the bum—
We're all of us on the bum—"
A freak show midget's pounding on a drum
The high L thunders redflag auctioneers
Are selling out a bankrupt world—   65
The hammer falls—a bid! a bid!—and no one hears . . .

The afternoon will see us in the park
With pigeons and our feet in peanut shells.
We pick a bench apart. We brood.

                                                                      1934

■   TILLIE LERNER OLSEN   ■
                            1912–2007

I Want You Women up North to Know

(Based on a Letter by Felipe Ibarro in New Masses, *Jan. 9th, 1934.)*

i want you women up north to know
how those dainty children's dresses you buy
   at macy's, wanamakers, gimbels, marshall fields,
are dyed in blood, are stitched in wasting flesh,
down in San Antonio, "where sunshine spends the winter."   5

I want you women up north to see
the obsequious smile, the salesladies trill
   "exquisite work, madame, exquisite pleats"
vanish into a bloated face, ordering more dresses,
   gouging the wages down,   10
dissolve into maria, ambrosa, catalina,
   stitching these dresses from dawn to night,
   in blood, in wasting flesh.

Catalina Rodriguez, 24,
   body shrivelled to a child's at twelve,   15
catalina rodriguez, last stages of consumption,
   works for three dollars a week from dawn to midnight.
A fog of pain thickens over her skull, the parching heat
   breaks over her body.
and the bright red blood embroiders the floor of her room.   20
   White rain stitching the night, the bourgeois poet would say,
   white gulls of hands, darting, veering,
   white lightning, threading the clouds,
this is the exquisite dance of her hands over the cloth,
and her cough, gay, quick, staccato,   25
   like skeleton's bones clattering,
is appropriate accompaniment for the esthetic dance
   of her fingers,
and the tremolo, tremolo when the hands tremble with pain.
Three dollars a week,   30
two fifty-five,
seventy cents a week,
no wonder two thousands eight hundred ladies of joy
are spending the winter with the sun after he goes down—

for five cents (who said this was a rich man's world?) you can   35
    get all the lovin you want
"clap and syph aint much worse than sore fingers, blind eyes, and
    t.m."

Maria Vasquez, spinster,
    for fifteen cents a dozen stitches garments for children she has never   40
    had,
Catalina Torres, mother of four,
    to keep the starved body starving, embroiders from dawn to
    night.
Mother of four, what does she think of,   45
    as the needle pocked fingers shift over the silk—
    of the stubble-coarse rags that stretch on her own brood,
    and jut with the bony ridge that marks hunger's landscape
    of fat little prairie-roll bodies that will bulge in the
    silk she needles?   50
(Be not envious, Catalina Torres, look!
    on your own children's clothing, embroidery,
    more intricate than any a thousand hands could fashion,
    there where the cloth is ravelled, or darned,
    designs, multitudinous, complex and handmade by Poverty   55
    herself.)

Ambrosa Espinoza trusts in god,
    "Todos es de dios, everything is from god,"
    through the dwindling night, the waxing day, she bolsters herself up with
    it—   60
but the pennies to keep god incarnate, from ambrosa,
and the pennies to keep the priest in wine, from ambrosa,
ambrosa clothes god and priest with hand-made children's dresses.

Her brother lies on an iron cot, all day and watches,
on a mattress of rags he lies.   65
For twenty-five years he worked for the railroad, then they laid him off.
    (racked days, searching for work; rebuffs; suspicious eyes of policemen.)
    goodbye ambrosa, mebbe in dallas I find work; desperate swing for a
        freight,
    surprised hands, clutching air, and the wheel goes over a   70
    leg,
    the railroad cuts it off, as it cut off twenty-five years of his life.)
She says that he prays and dreams of another world, as he lies there, a
    heaven (which he does not know was brought to earth in 1917 in
    Russia, by workers like him).   75
Women up north, I want you to know
when you finger the exquisite hand made dresses
what it means, this working from dawn to midnight,

on what strange feet the feverish dawn must come
    to maria, catalina, ambrosa,   80
how the malignant fingers twitching over the pallid faces jerk them to work,
and the sun and the fever mounts with the day—
    long plodding hours, the eyes burn like coals, heat jellies the flying fingers,
down comes the night like blindness.
    long hours more with the dim eye of the lamp, the breaking back, 85
    weariness crawls in the flesh like worms, gigantic like earth's in winter.
And for Catalina Rodriguez comes the night sweat and the blood
    embroidering the darkness.
    for Catalina Torres the pinched faces of four huddled
    children,   90
    the naked bodies of four bony children,
    the chant of their chorale of hunger.
And for twenty eight hundred ladies of joy the grotesque act gone over—
    the wink—the grimace—the "feeling like it baby?"
And for Maria Vasquez, spinster, emptiness, emptiness.   95
    flaming with dresses for children she can never fondle.
And for Ambrosa Espinoza—the skeleton body of her brother on his mattress
of rags, boring twin holes in the dark with his eyes to the image of christ
remembering a leg, and twenty-five years cut off from his life by the railroad.

Women up north, I want you to know,   100
I tell you this can't last forever.

I swear it won't.

                                   1934

KAY BOYLE
1903–1993

A Communication to Nancy Cunard[1]

These are not words set down for the rejected
Nor for outcasts cast by the mind's pity

---

[1]The poem is based on the famous Scottsboro case in which nine young black men (Charlie Weems, Ozie Powell, Clarence Norris, Olen Montgomery, Willie Robertson, Haywood Patterson, Andy Wright, Roy Wright, Eugene Williams) were convicted of raping Ruby Bates and Victoria Price in 1931 in Alabama. The convictions, based on false testimony, produced death sentences and worldwide protest.

> Beyond the aid of lip or hand or from the speech
> Of fires lighted in the wilderness by lost men
> Reaching in fright and passion to each other.   5
> This is not for the abandoned to hear.

It begins in the dark on a box-car floor, the groaning timber
Stretched from bolt to bolt above the freight-train wheels
That grind and cry aloud like hounds upon the trail, the breathing
    weaving   10
Unseen within the dark from mouth to nostril, nostril to speaking mouth.
This is the theme of it, stated by one girl in a box-car saying:
"Christ, what they pay you don't keep body and soul together."
"Where was you working?" "Working in a mill-town."
The other girl in the corner saying: "Working the men when we could 15
    get them."
"Christ, what they pay you," wove the sound of breathing, "don't keep
    shoes on your feet.
Don't feed you. That's why we're shoving on."
(This is not for Virginia Price or Ruby Bates, the white girls dressed like 20
boys to go; not for Ozie Powell, six years in a cell playing the harp he
played tap-dancing on the box-car boards; not for Olen Montgomery,
the blind boy travelling towards Memphis that night, hopping a ride to
find a doctor who could cure his eyes; not for Eugene Williams or
Charlie Weems, not for Willie Robertson nor for Leroy and Andy 25
Wright, thirteen years old the time in March they took him off the train
in Paint Rock, Alabama; this is not for Clarence Norris or Haywood
Patterson, sentenced three times to die.)

This is for the sheriff with a gold lodge pin
    And for the jury venireman who said: "Now, mos' folk don't go on 30
    And think things out. The Bible never speaks
    Of sexual intercourses. It jus' says a man knows a woman.
    So after Cain killed Abel he went off and knew a woman
    In the land of Nod. But the Bible tells as how
    There couldn't be no human folk there then.   35
    Now, jus' put two and two together. Cain had off-spring
    In the land of Nod so he musta had him a female baboon
    Or chimpanzee or somethin' like it.
    And that's how the nigger race begun."

This is for the Sunday-school teacher with the tobacco-plug   40
Who addressed the jury, the juice splattering on the wall,
Pleading: "Whether in overalls or furs a woman is protected by the
    Alabama law
Against the vilest crime the human species knows. Now, even dogs
    choose their mates,   45

But these nine boys are lower than the birds of the air,
Lower than the fish in the sea, lower than the beasts of the fields.
There is a law reaching down from the mountain-tops to the swamps
    and caves—
It's the wisdom of the ages, there to protect the sacred parts of the   50
    female species
Without them having to buckle around their middles
Six-shooters or some other method of defense."

    This is set down for the others: people who go and come,
    Open a door and pass through it, walk in the streets   55
    With the shops lit, loitering, lingering, gazing.
    This is for two men riding, Deputy Sheriff Sandlin, Deputy Sheriff
        Blacock,
    With Ozie Powell, handcuffed. Twelve miles out of Cullman
    They shot him through the head.   60

The Testimony

Haywood Patterson:	*Victoria Price:*
"So here goes an I shell try	
Faithfully an I possibly can	"I
Reference to myself in particularly	cain't
And concerning the other boys personal pride	remember."
And life time upto now.	65
You must be patience with me and remember	"I
Most of my English is not of much interest	cain't
And that I am continually	remember."
Stopping and searching for the word."	

So here goes and I shall try faithfully as possible to tell you as I understand if not mistaken that Olen Montgomery, who was part blind then, kept saying because of the dark there was inside the box-car and outside it: "It sure don't seem to me we're getting anywheres. It sure don't seem like it to me." I and my three comrades whom were with me, namely Roy Wright and his brother Andy and Eugene Williams, and about my character I have always been a good natural sort of boy, but as far as I am personally concerned about those pictures of me in the papers, why they are more or less undoubtedly not having the full likeness of me for I am a sight better-looking than those pictures make me out. Why all my life I spent in and around working for Jews in their stores and so on and I have quite a few Jew friends whom can and always have gave me a good reputation as having regards for those whom have regards for me. The depression ran me away from home, I was off on my way to try my very best to find some work some elsewhere but misfortune befalled me without a moving cause. For it is events and misfortune which happens to people and how some must whom are less fortunate have their lives taken from them and how people die in chair for what they do not do.

The Spiritual for Nine Voices

I went last night to a turkey feast (Oh, God, don't fail your children now!)
My people were sitting there the way they'll sit in heaven
With their wings spread out and their hearts all singing
Their mouths full of food and the table set with glass
(Oh, God, don't fail your children now!)   90
There were poor men sitting with their fingers dripping honey
All the ugly sisters were fair. I saw my brother who never had a penny
With a silk shirt on and a pair of golden braces
And gems strewn through his hair.

(Were you looking, Father, when the sheriffs came in?   95
Was your face turned towards us when they had their say?)

    There was baked sweet potato and fried corn pone
    There was eating galore, there was plenty in the horn.

(Were you there when Victoria Price took the stand?
Did you see the state attorney with her drawers in his hand?   100
Did you hear him asking for me to burn?)
    There were oysters cooked in amplitude
    There was sauce in every mouth.
    There was ham done slow in spice and clove
    And chicken enough for the young and the old.   105

(Was it you stilled the waters on horse-swapping day
When the mob came to the jail? Was it you come out in a long
   tail coat
Come dancing high with the word in your mouth?)

    I saw my sister who never had a cent   110
    Come shaking and shuffling between the seats.
    Her hair was straight and her nails were pointed
    Her breasts were high and her legs double-jointed.

(Oh, God, don't fail your children now!)

The Sentence

Hear how it goes, the wheels of it travelling fast on the rails   115
  The box-cars, the gondolas running drunk through the night.
Hear the long high wail as it flashes through stations unlit
  Past signals ungiven running wild through a country
          A time when sleepers rouse in their beds and listen
              And cannot sleep again.   120
          Hear it passing in no direction, to no destination
          Carrying people caught in the box-cars, trapped on the coupled chert-
              cars
          (Hear the rattle of gravel as it rides whistling through the day and
              night.)   125
          Not the old or the young on it, nor people with any difference in their
              color or shape,
          Not girls or men, negroes or white, but people with this in common:
          People that no one had use for, had nothing to give to, no place to offer
          But the cars of a freight-train careening through Paint Rock, through   130
              Memphis,
          Through town after town without halting.
          The loose hands hang down, and swing with the swing of the train in
              the darkness,
          Holding nothing but poverty, syphilis white as a handful of dust, taking 135
              nothing as baggage
          But the sound of the harp Ozie Powell is playing or the voice of Mont-
              gomery
          Half-blind in oblivion saying: "It sure don't seem to me like we're
              getting anywheres.   140
          It don't seem to me like we're getting anywheres at all."

                                                                    1937

LANGSTON HUGHES
1902–1967

Goodbye Christ

Listen, Christ,
You did all right in your day, I reckon—
But that day's gone now.
They ghosted you up a swell story, too.

Called it the Bible—   5
But it's dead now.
The popes and the preachers 've
Made too much money from it.
They've sold you to too many
Kings, generals, robbers, and killers—   10
Even to the Tzar and the Cossacks,
Even to Rockefeller's Church,
Even to the Saturday Evening Post.
You ain't no good no more.
They've pawned you   15
Till you've done wore out.
Goodbye.
Christ Jesus Lord God Jehovah,
Beat it on away from here now.
Make way for a new guy with no religion at all—   20
A real guy named
Marx Communist Lenin Peasant Stalin Worker ME—
I said, ME!
Go ahead on now,
You're getting in the way of things, Lord,   25
And please take Saint Ghandi with you when you go,
And Saint Pope Pius,
And Saint Aimee McPherson,[1]
And big black Saint Becton
Of the Consecrated Dime.   30
And step on the gas, Christ!
Move!
Don't be so slow about movin'!
The world is mine from now on—
And nobody's gonna sell ME   35
To a king, or a general,
Or a millionaire.

Goodbye Christ, good morning Revolution!

                                                                          1932

---

[1]Aimee McPherson (1890–1944), American
evangelist.

FINE LIVING ... *a la carte* ?? *Come t*

Listen Hungry Ones!

Look! See what **Vanity Fair** says about the new
Waldorf Astoria:
"**All the luxuries of private home . . .** "
Now, won't that be charming when the last flop-
house has turned you down this winter? Furthermore:
"It is far beyond anything hitherto attempted in the
hotel world. . . ." It cost twenty-eight million
dollars. The famous Oscar Tschirky is in charge
of banqueting. Alexandre Gastaud is chef. It
will be a distinguished background for society.
So when you've got no place else to go, homeless and
hungry ones,
choose the Waldorf as a background for your
rags—
(Or do you still consider the subway after midnight
good enough?)

Roomers

Take a room at the new Waldorf, you down-and-
outers—sleepers in charity flop-houses where
God pulls a long face, and you have to pray to
get a bed.
They serve swell board at the Waldorf Astoria.
Look at this menu, will you:
GUMBO CREOLE
CRABMEAT IN CASSOLETTE
BOILED BRISKET OF BEEF
SMALL ONIONS IN CREAM
WATERCRESS SALAD
PEACH MELBA
Have luncheon there this afternoon, all you jobless.
Why not?
Dine with some of the men and women who got
rich off of your labor, who clip coupons with

Illustration by Walter Steinhilber

the Waldorf-Astoria!

clean white fingers because your hands dug coal,
drilled stone, sewed garments, poured steel—to
let other people draw dividends and live easy.
(Or haven't you had enough yet of the soup-lines
and the bitter bread of charity?)
Walk through Peacock Alley tonight before dinner,
and get warm, anyway. You've got nothing else
to do.

Evicted Families

All you families put out in the street: Apartments
in the Towers are only $10,000 a year. (Three
rooms and two baths.) Move in there until
times get good, and you can do better. $10,000
and $1.00 are about the same to you, aren't they?
Who cares about money with a wife and kids homeless, and nobody in the family working? Would-
n't a duplex high above the street be grand,
with a view of the richest city in the world at
your nose?
"A lease, if you prefer; or an arrangement terminable
at will."

Negroes

O, Lawd, I done forgot Harlem!
Say, you colored folks, hungry a long time in 135th
Street—they got swell music at the Waldorf-Astoria. It sure is a mighty nice place to shake hips
in, too. There's dancing after supper in a big
warm room. It's cold as hell on Lenox Avenue.
All you've had all day is a cup of coffee. Your
pawnshop overcoat's a ragged banner on your
hungry frame. . . . You know, down-town folks
are just crazy about Paul Robeson. Maybe they'd
like you, too, black mob from Harlem. Drop in
at the Waldorf this afternoon for tea. Stay to
dinner. Give Park Avenue a lot of darkie color
—free—for nothing! Ask the Junior Leaguers
to sing a spiritual for you. They probably know
'em better than you do—and their lips won't be
so chapped with cold after they step out of their
closed cars in the undercover driveways.
Hallelujah! under-cover driveways!
Ma soul's a witness for de Waldorf-
Astoria!
(A thousand nigger section-hands keep the road-
beds smooth, so investments in railroads pay

ladies with diamond necklaces staring at Cert
murals.)
Thank God A-Mighty!
(And a million niggers bend their backs on rubber
plantations, for rich behinds to ride on thick
tires to the Theatre Guild tonight.)
Ma soul's a witness!
(And here we stand, shivering in the cold, in Har-
lem.)
Glory be to God—
De Waldorf-Astoria's open!

Everybody

So get proud and rare back, everybody! The new
Waldorf-Astoria's open!
(Special siding for private cars from the railroad
yards.)
You ain't been there yet?
(A thousand miles of carpet and a million bath
rooms.)
What's the matter? You haven't seen the ads in the
papers? Didn't you get a card? Don't you know
they specialize in American cooking?
Ankle on down to 49th Street at Park Avenue. Get
up off that subway bench tonight with the evening POST for cover! Come on out o' that
flop-house! Stop shivering your guts out all
day on street corners under the L.
Jesus, ain't you tired yet?

Christmas Card

Hail Mary, Mother of God!
The new Christ child of the Revolution's about to
be born.
(Kick hard, red baby, in the bitter womb of the
mob.)
Somebody, put an ad in **Vanity Fair** quick!
Call Oscar of the Waldorf—for Christ's sake!
It's almost Christmas, and that little girl—turned
whore because her belly was too hungry to stand
it any more—wants a nice clean bed for the Im-
maculate Conception.
Listen, Mary, Mother of God, wrap your new born
babe in the red flag of Revolution:
The Waldorf-Astoria's the best manger we've got.
For reservations: Telephone
ELdorado 5-3000.

by Langston Hughes

Air Raid over Harlem

Scenario for a Little Black Movie

Who you gonna put in it?
Me.
Who the hell are you?
Harlem.
Alright, then.   5
               AIR RAID OVER HARLEM
You're not talkin' 'bout Harlem, are you?
That's where my home is,
My bed is, my woman is, my kids is!
Harlem, that's where I live!   10
Look at my streets
Full of black and brown and
Yellow and high-yellow
Jokers like me.
Lenox, Seventh, Edgecombe, 145th.   15
Listen,
Hear 'em talkin' and laughin'?
Bombs over Harlem'd kill
People like me—
Kill ME!   20

Sure, I know
The Ethiopian war broke out last night:[1]
BOMBS OVER HARLEM
Cops on every corner
Most of 'em white   25
COPS IN HARLEM
Guns and billy-clubs
Double duty in Harlem
Walking in pairs
Under every light   30
Their faces
WHITE
In Harlem
And mixed in with 'em
A black cop or two   35
for the sake of the vote in Harlem
GUGSA A TRAITOR TOO
No, sir,
I ain't talking' 'bout you,

---

[1] In 1935 Italian forces under Mussolini invaded the African nation of Ethiopia, an act that aroused protest among blacks throughout the United States.

Mister Policeman!   40
No, indeed!
I know we got to keep
ORDER OVER HARLEM
Where the black millions sleep
Shepherds over Harlem   45
Their armed watch keep
Lest Harlem stirs in its sleep
And maybe remembers
And remembering forgets
To be peaceful and quiet   50
And has sudden fits
Of raising a black fist
Out of the dark
And that black fist
Becomes a red spark   55
PLANES OVER HARLEM
Bombs over Harlem
You're just making up
A fake funny picture, ain't you?
Not real, not real?   60
Did you ever taste blood
From an iron heel
Planted in your mouth
In the slavery-time South
Where to whip a nigger's   65
Easy as hell—
And not even a *living* nigger
Has a tale to tell
Lest the kick of a boot
Bring more blood to his mouth   70
In the slavery-time South
And a long billy-club
Split his head wide
And a white hand draw
A gun from its side   75
And send bullets splaying
Through the streets of Harlem
Where the dead're laying
Lest you stir in your sleep
And remember something   80
You'd best better keep
In the dark, in the dark
Where the ugly things hide
Under the white lights
With guns by their side   85

In Harlem?
Say, what are yuh tryin' to do?
Start a riot?
You keep quiet!
You niggers keep quiet! 90
BLACK WORLD
Never wake up
Lest you knock over the cup
Of gold that the men who
Keep order guard so well 95
And then—well, then
There'd be hell
To pay
And bombs over Harlem

                AIR RAID OVER HARLEM 100
Bullets through Harlem
And someday
A sleeping giant waking
To snatch bombs from the sky
And push the sun up with a loud cry 105
Of to hell with the cops on the corners at night
Armed to the teeth under the light
Lest Harlem see red
And suddenly sit on the edge of its bed
And shake the whole world with a new dream 110
As the squad cars come and the sirens scream
And a big black giant snatches bombs from the sky
And picks up a cop and lets him fly
Into the dust of the Jimcrow past
And laughs and hollers 115
Kiss my
!x!&!

Hey!
Scenario For A Little Black Movie,
You say? 120
A RED MOVIE TO MR. HEARST
Black and white workers united as one
In a city where
There'll never be
Air raids over Harlem 125
FOR THE WORKERS ARE FREE
What workers are free?
THE BLACK AND WHITE WORKERS—

You and me!
Looky here, everybody!   130
Look at me!

I'M HARLEM!

Harlem, 1935

LOLA RIDGE
1873–1941

Stone Face

They have carved you into a stone face, Tom Mooney,[1]
You, there lifted high in California
Over the salt wash of the Pacific,
With your eyes . . . crying in many tongues,
Goading, innumerable eyes of the multitudes,   5
Holding in them all hopes, fears, persecutions,
Forever straining one way.

Even in the Sunday papers,
  and your face tight-bitten like a pierced fist,
The eyes have a transfixed gleam   10
  as they had glimpsed some vision and there hung
Impaled as on a bright lance.

Too much lip-foam has dripped on you, too many
And dislinete signatures are scrawled on your stone face
    that all   15
Have set some finger on, to say who made you for the
    years
To mouth as waves mouth rock . . . you, a rough man,
Rude-nurtured, casually shouldering
Through a May-day crowd in San Francisco,   20
To be cast up out of the dark mass—terribly gestating,
    swarming without feature,
And raised with torsion to identity.

---

[1]Tom Mooney (1892–1942), labor leader who was falsely convicted of planting a bomb that killed ten people at a 1916 parade in San Francisco. Despite revelations that the testimony against him was perjured, Mooney remained in prison for twenty-three years.

Now they—who wrote you plain, with Sacco and the fish-
    monger,   25
High on the scroll of the Republic—
Look up with a muddled irritation at your clenched face,
It set up in full sight under the long
Gaze of the generations—to be there
Haggard in the sunrise, when San Quentin   30
Prison shall be caved in and its steel ribs
Food for the ant-rust ... and Governor Rolph[2]
A fleck of dust among the archives.

                                            1935

EDWIN ROLFE
1909–1954

Asbestos[1]

Knowing (as John did) nothing of the way
men act when men are roused from lethargy,
and having nothing (as John had) to say
to those he saw were starving just as he

starved, John was like a workhorse. Day by day   5
he saw his sweat cement the granite tower
(the edifice his bone had built), to stay
listless as ever, older every hour.

John's deathbed is a curious affair:
the posts are made of bone, the spring of nerves,   10
the mattress bleeding flesh. Infinite air,
compressed from dizzy altitudes, now serves

his skullface as a pillow. Overhead
a vulture leers in solemn mockery,
knowing what John had never known: that dead   15
workers are dead before they cease to be.

                                              1928

[2]California governor who refused to pardon
Mooney.
[1]Titled "The 100 Percenter" when published
in 1928. Retitled "Asbestos" when reprinted
in 1933.

Season of Death

This is the sixth winter:
this is the season of death
when lungs contract and the breath of homeless men
freezes on restaurant window panes—men seeking
the sight of rare food   5
before the head is lowered into the upturned collar
and the shoulders hunched and the shuffling feet
move away slowly, slowly disappear
into a darkened street.

This is the season when rents go up: 10
men die, and their dying is casual.
I walk along a street, returning
at midnight from my unit. Meet a man
leaning against an illumined wall
and ask him for a light.   15
                              His open eyes
stay fixed on mine. And cold rain falling
trickles down his nose, his chin.
"Buddy," I begin . . . and look more closely—
and flee in horror from the corpse's grin.   20

The eyes pursue you even in sleep and
when you awake they stare at you from the ceiling;
you see the dead face peering from your shoes;
the eggs at Thompson's are the dead man's eyes.
Work dims them for eight hours, but then—   25
the machines silent—they appear again.

Along the docks, in the terminals, in the subway,
     on the street,
in restaurants—the eyes
are focused from the river   30
among the floating garbage
that other men fish for,
their hands around poles
almost in prayer—
wanting to live,   35
wanting to live! who also soon
will stand propped by death against a stone-cold wall.

                                                                                              1935

First Love[1]

Again I am summoned to the eternal field
green with the blood still fresh at the roots of flowers,
green through the dust-rimmed memory of faces
that moved among the trees there for the last time
before the final shock, the glazed eye, the hasty mound.   5

But why are my thoughts in another country?
Why do I always return to the sunken road through corroded hills,
with the Moorish castle's shadow casting ruins over my shoulder
and the black-smocked girl approaching, her hands laden with
          grapes?   10

I am eager to enter it, eager to end it.
Perhaps this one will be the last one.
And men afterward will study our arms in museums
and nod their heads, and frown, and name the inadequate dates
and stumble with infant tongues over the strange place-names.   15

But my heart is forever captive of that other war
that taught me first the meaning of peace and of comradeship
and always I think of my friend who amid the apparition of bombs
saw on the lyric lake the single perfect swan.

                                                                     1943

Elegia

Madrid   Madrid   Madrid   Madrid[1']
I call your name endlessly, savor it like a lover.
Ten irretrievable years have exploded like bombs
since last I saw you, since last I slept
in your arms of tenderness and wounded granite.   5
Ten years since I touched your face in the sun,
ten years since the homeless Guadarrama winds[2]
moaned like shivering orphans through your veins

[1]Written when the author was in training in the U.S. Army during World War II. He is reflecting on his volunteer service (1937–1938) in the Abraham Lincoln Battalion on the side of the Spanish Republic during the Spanish Civil War.

[1']The Spanish capital. Hoping to end the civil war he started with one decisive stroke, Franco ordered a major assault against the city in 1936. German troops assisted him with massive bombing against civilians. The city did not fall until the war's end (and Franco's victory) in 1939; its suffering and defense were symbolic of the war in its entirety.

[2]Madrid is encircled by the Guadarrama mountains to the north. The winds that sweep down off them are a distinctive part of the city's climate.

and I moaned with them.
                When I think of you, Madrid,   10
locked in the bordello of the Universal Pimp,[3]
the blood that rushes to my heart and head
blinds me, and I could strangle your blood-bespattered jailors,
choke them with these two hands which once embraced you.
When I think of your breathing body of vibrancy and sun,   15
silently I weep, in my own native land
which I love no less because I love you more.
Yet I know, in the heart of my heart, that until your liberation
rings through the world of free men near and far
I must wander like an alien everywhere.   20

Madrid, in these days of our planet's anguish,
forged by the men whose mock morality
begins and ends with the tape of the stock exchanges,
I too sometimes despair. I weep with your dead young poet.
Like him I curse our age and cite the endless wars,   25
the exiles, dangers, fears, our weariness
of blood, and blind survival, when so many
homes, wives, even memories, are lost.

Yes, I weep with Garcilaso.[4] I remember
your grave face and your subtle smile   30
and the heart-leaping beauty of your daughters
    and even
the tattered elegance of your poorest sons.
I remember the gaiety of your *milicianos*—[5]
my comrades-in-arms. What other city   35
in history ever raised a battalion of barbers
or reared its own young shirt-sleeved generals?
And I recall them all. If I ever forget you,
Madrid, Madrid, may my right hand lose its cunning.
I speak to you, Madrid, as lover, husband, son.   40
Accept this human trinity of passion.
I love you, therefore I am faithful to you
and because to forget you would be to forget
everything I love and value in the world.
Who is not true to you is false to every man   45
and he to whom your name means nothing never
    loved
and they who would use your flesh and blood again

[3]Francisco Franco.
[4]Garcilaso de la Vega (1501–1536) was a sol-
dier-poet, the undisputed classic poet of the
Golden Age of Spanish literature. The recurrent theme in his poetry is love, typically
viewed with melancholy and frustrated
idealism.
[5]Soldiers.

as a whore for their wars and their wise investments,
may they be doubly damned! the double murderers   50
of you and their professed but fictional honor,
of everything untarnished in our time.

Wandering, bitter, in this bitter age,
I dream of your broad avenues like brooks in summer
with your loveliest children alive in them like trout.   55
In my memory I walk the Calle de Velasquez[6]
to the green Retiro[7] and its green gardens.
Sometimes when I pace the streets of my own city
I am transported to the flowing Alcalá[8]
and my footsteps quicken, I hasten to the spot   60
where all your living streams meet the Gateway to the Sun.[9]
Sometimes I brood in the shadowed Plaza Mayor[10]
with the ghosts of old Kings and Inquisitors
agitating the balconies with their idiot stares
(which Goya[11] later knew) and under whose stone arches,   65
those somber rooms beneath the colonnades,
the old watchmaker dreams of tiny, intricate minutes,
the old woman sells pencils and gaudy amber combs,
dreaming of the days when her own body was young,
and the rheumatic peasant with fingers gnarled as grapevines   70
eagerly displays his muscat raisins;
and the intense boys of ten, with smouldering agèd eyes,
kneel, and gravely, quixotically,
polish the rawhide boots of the soldiers in for an hour
from the mined trenches of the Casa de Campo,[12]   75
from their posts, buzzing with death, within the skeleton
of University City.[13]

      And the girls stroll by,
the young ones, conscious of their womanhood,
and I hear in my undying heart called Madrid   80
the soldiers boldly calling to them: Oye, guapa, oye!
I remember your bookshops, the windows always crowded

[6]Street where the International Brigades building was located and where Rolfe edited its English language newspaper.
[7]Park in the middle of Madrid.
[8]A major highway that heads east from its origin in the Puerta del Sol.
[9]Puerta del Sol, the central plaza of Madrid.
[10]A seventeenth-century square, frequent site for public spectacles, from processions of flagellants to bullfights and the crowning of kings. The Inquisition held its *autos-da-fe* and executed its victims here.
[11]Francisco de Goya (1746–1828), one of Spain's great painters.
[12]A sprawling wooded park northwest of the city that was the scene of major fighting during the attacks on Madrid.
[13]The hillside campus of the University of Madrid that was the scene of dramatic fighting.

with new editions of the Gypsy Ballads,[14]
with *Poetas en la España Leal*
and *Romanceros de los Soldados en las Trincheras.*[15]   85
There was never enough food, but always poetry.
Ah the flood of song that gushed with your blood
into the world during your three years of glory!

And I think: it is a fine thing to be a man
only when man has dignity and manhood.   90
It is a fine thing to be proud and fearless
only when pride and courage have direction, meaning.
And in our world no prouder words were spoken
in those three agonized years than *I am from Madrid.*

Now ten years have passed with small explosions of hope,   95
yet you remain, Madrid, the conscience of our lives.
So long as you endure, in chains, in sorrow,
I am not free, no one of us is free.
Any man in the world who does not love Madrid
as he loves a woman, as he values his sex,   100
that man is less than a man and dangerous,
and so long as he directs the affairs of our world
I must be his undying enemy.

Madrid   Madrid   Madrid   Madrid
Waking and sleeping, your name sings in my heart   105
and your need fills all my thoughts and acts
(which are gentle but have also been intimate with rifles).
Forgive me, I cannot love you properly from afar—
no distant thing is ever truly loved—
but this, in the wrathful impotence of distance,   110
I promise: Madrid, if I ever forget you,
may my right hand lose its human cunning,
may my arms and legs wither in their sockets,
may my body be drained of its juices and my brain
go soft and senseless as an imbecile's.   115
And if I die before I can return to you,
or you, in fullest freedom, are restored to us,
my sons will love you as their father did
Madrid   Madrid   Madrid

                                                                           1948

---

[14]*Romancero Gitano*, 1928: A book of poems by Federico Garcia Lorca. Lorca was murdered by Nationalist partisans just after the outbreak of the Spanish Civil War.

[15]Two wartime poetry anthologies issued in Spain by Loyalist supporters.

▪ # GENEVIEVE TAGGARD
1894–1948
▪

Up State—Depression Summer

One of many patient farms under a cloud—
Clap-boarded house on up-land, Yankee as
   cider;
Mortgage the cloud, with another, second mortgage;
One old cloud with another one, drawn closer,   5
Size of a silver dollar, pouring trouble;
Bad luck everyway, short rations, and the old horse
   spavined.
Two cents a quart for milk and the feed sky-high.

June was sinister sweet. Can you eat wild flowers?   10
The world outside gilt-green, inside bone-bare.
No sugar, coffee . . . So the evil had them . . .
Evil, devil, pain in the belly hit them.
Taxes, words with the grocer, rage. . . .
                     The trouble veered   15
And found a body small, for spring infection,
White as the May, slim shoulders and naked ear
Open for poison.
            Behind June-morning eyes
The torpor spread.   20
            Suddenly the kid was sick.

Emma found her in the yellow spare-room
That opened north, asleep across her doll
Face on the floor in stupor with thick breath.
And in her bed she hardly ever groaned.   25
Shut her eyes, stretched arms up, and went down
Deeper in stupor.
            And days and weeks went by.
At first no telephone could get the doctor.
                       Emma sat   30
Rubbing Nan's chest with goose grease, whipping egg
To make her vomit phlegm. Tom stormed and peeped
   at the child.
Banging the kitchen pots with no relief.
                   "Why haven't we   35
Medicine here, Emma," ranted Tom,
Knocking the bottles off the window-sill.

"Thermometer. Damn. This is like you.
You let the time go by till the kid gets sick
Before you even think to look or get one.   40
Go get some sleep. We both don't need to watch.
Go on, I tell you."
                         Emma left the door
Open. Tom closed it. It was the closing door
That felt like death. Emma stared and stood.   45
And emerald lightning went on out of doors
Too vaguely flashed to rain and cut the web
Of woven heat that clustered in the trees.

And it was weeks along and still she lay.

The doctor came and went and wanted medicine   50
No one could buy. And weeks went on.
Hot spell came on; and rank weeds wilted. Haze.
Night's indifferent noise
Went slowly on. Day was the easier night-mare.

One day no one came out to feed the cows.   55
The house was like a rock stuck in the earth.
Tom's half-gone Ford
Stopped in the barn-yard middle. There the hens
Fluffed dust and slept beneath it. Desolation
Sat busy in the yard somewhere. The cows stamped on   60
Inside the barn with caking heavy udders.
The wind-mill pined and swung a point or two.
And Fanny, the cow, bore her calf and licked it clean.
No one molested. Nothing came
Out of the house till evening.   65
                         Then poor Tom
Blundered about the porch and milked a little
And pumped some water and went in, afraid.
And the kid died as slowly as she could.
Then Emma was sick and would lie and look at   70
     nothing,
Or look at the elms and maples in the sky.
Or she spent a useless day with silent toil,
While the heat broke slowly. Cooking with no sense;
War on all living dirt; anger and fret   75
At all inanimate things that balked her hands.
Because the fire smoked she cried in a rage.

Tom found his cows, his second haying, found
The solid substance that he walked upon.
The roughness of his tools, the excellent   80

Hard silence of his clumsy cultivator.
And milking had its comfort, morning and evening.
In the gloom he came into the kitchen, bumping in,
To warn her not to let herself go on
While he was there to eat.   85
                  Not possible now
To even roughly kiss her.
                They slept apart
Like grieving beasts that fall to sleep and lie
Their sour blood, their agony in them.   90

They sold the calf. That fall the bank took over.

                          1936

To the Negro People

I. Spirituals

My way's cloudy, I cry out,
Cloudy, Lord.
        Who found this way to speak?
Where is this poet's grave?
South is his burying ground. River Mississippi wide   5
Washes his dust along.
                The Gulf dances level
Sapphire blue near his elbow, where his bones
Sleep in the dust of song, where we lift up our voices
Crying with the dark man when we cry   10
My way's cloudy.

                          1939

II. City of the Blues

St. Louis, Mo.;
                river side, piles rotted with river,
Y'hoo, Y'hoo, river whistle tuned harsh.
Get me back to St. Louis.
Burdocks, castor oil plants; ground pecked over by chickens,   5
    smeared
With droppings and moulted feathers. Fence, coop, mash-
    pans, wire
And a tub of white-wash. Faded rag rug and flat bottle.
(This nook and nobody here but the half-grown hens.)   10
Tug going by, puffpuff, small wave tapered. St. Louis dock

Stacked high, six blocks away, belted with wharves,
Coal smoke, winches, shovels,—crash of freight,
Pillars of white puffed upward, stiff white from the trains.
Bank all slums and slime, frame houses. Dark, wet, cold.   15
(So sweet, so cold, so fair.)
Castor oil plants and acanthus.
                           (When they kill, they kill
Here, and dump the body here.) The river, pale clay
Deep down stream. Y'hoo, Y'hoo yell the trains,   20
And the boats yell, too.
                  But the silence, the silence
Blows clean through your bones.
In the chicken yard, listlessly, beside the piles, waiting for
    nothing   25
The Negro boy, head bent, beating out his tattoo
Nimble and complex, on the fence . . .
Get ready to blow, trumpets, trumpets, trumpets,
O Gabriel,[1] O Willie Smith[2]
               Take it away.   30

                        1939

III. Proud Day

(Marian Anderson on the steps of the Lincoln Memorial)[1']

Our sister sang on the Lincoln steps. Proud day.
We came to hear our sister sing. Proud day.
Voice out of depths, poise with memory,
What goodness, what splendor lay long under foot!
Our sister with a lasso of sorrow and triumph   5
Caught America, made it listen. Proud day.

The peaceful Lincoln sat so still. Proud day.
Waiting the Republic to be born again. Proud day.
Never, never forget how the dark people rewarded us
Giving out of their want and their little freedom   10
This blazing star. This blazing star.
Something spoke in my patriot heart. Proud day.

                        1939

[1]An angel named in both the Old and New Testaments. He is to blow the trumpet on Judgment Day.
[2]Willie Smith (1897–1973), legendary American jazz pianist.

[1']Marian Anderson (1902–1993), American singer renowned for her performance of spirituals. She also devoted herself to the struggle for civil rights.

IV. Chant for the Great Negro Poet of America Not Yet Born

He comes soon now, this spanning poet, the wide
Man, the dark, conscious of the apex, the place of his people.
He is sure to come,—up from the sorrowing side,
Born, awake, with the urgent rising of his people.

He will be our poet when he comes, he will wear   5
Scars. And a dazzling joy will give him the mark of his
    people.
We will hear his voice; in our nearness share
The struggle he joins, with the powerful mass of his people.

His ancestors are splendid; they are ours also; but he is heir.   10
The Hebrew poets, so long the fellows of his people.
Those who Englished them, anonymous, and also their
Kin—Blake, Whitman, and the honest preachers of his
    people.

He comes to us with the authority of those who cried   15
In darkness. He, to be the poet of all rising people.
A fervent kiss from all of us who have died
Going down, singing, for him, rising up in majesty, singing
                       with the universal
                       singing of his people.   20

                                     1941

Ode in Time of Crisis[1]

Now in the fright of change when bombed towns vanish
In fountains of debris
We say to the stranger coming across the sea
Not here, not here, go elsewhere!
Here we keep   5
Bars up. Wall out the danger, tightly seal
The ports, the intake from the alien world we fear.
It is a time of many errors now.
And this the error of children when they feel
But cannot say their terror. To shut off the stream   10
In which we moved and still move, if we move.
The alien is the nation, nothing more or less.

---

[1]Alludes to several crises of national identity during World War II, from America's refusal to accept refugees from Nazi Germany to our decision to imprison American citizens of Japanese descent for the duration of the war.

How set ourselves at variance to prove
The alien is not the nation. And so end the dream.
Forbid our deep resource from whence we came,   15
And the very seed of greatness.

                          This is to do
Something like suicide; to choose
Sterility—forget the secret of our past
Which like a magnet drew   20
A wealth of men and women hopeward. And now to lose
In ignorant blindness what we might hold fast.
The fright of change, not readiness. Instead
Inside our wall we will today pursue
The man we call the alien, take his print,   25
Give him a taste of the thing from which he fled,
Suspicion him. And again we fail.
How shall we release his virtue, his good-will
If by such pressure we hold his life in jail?
The alien is the nation. Nothing else.   30
And so we fail and so we jail ourselves.
Landlocked, the stagnant stream.
So ends the dream.

O country-men, are we working to undo
Our lusty strength, our once proud victory?   35
Yes, if by this fright we break our strength in two.
If we make of every man we jail the enemy.
If we make ourselves the jailer locked in jail.
Our laboring wills, our brave, too brave to fail
Remember this nation by millions believed to be   40
Great and of mighty forces born; and resolve to be free,
To continue and renew.

                                               1940

To the Veterans of the Abraham Lincoln Brigade[1]

Say of them
They knew no Spanish
At first, and nothing of the arts of war
At first,
      how to shoot, how to attack, how to retreat   5
How to kill, how to meet killing

[1]Written after these veterans of the Spanish
Civil War had their loyalty questioned by the
House Un-American Activities Committee.

At first.
Say they kept the air blue
Grousing and griping,
Arid words and harsh faces. Say   10
They were young;
The haggard in a trench, the dead on the olive slope
All young. And the thin, the ill and the shattered,
Sightless, in hospitals, all young.

Say of them they were young, there was much they did not   15
    know,
They were human. Say it all; it is true. Now say
When the eminent, the great, the easy, the old,
And the men on the make
Were busy bickering and selling,   20
Betraying, conniving, transacting, splitting hairs,
Writing bad articles, signing bad papers,
Passing bad bills,
Bribing, blackmailing,
Whimpering, meaching, garroting,—they   25
Knew and acted
          understood and died.

Or if they did not die came home to peace
That is not peace.
          Say of them   30
They are no longer young, they never learned
The arts, the stealth of peace, this peace, the tricks of fear;
And what they knew, they know.
And what they dared, they dare.

                                                1941

E. E. CUMMINGS
1894–1962

Edward Estlin Cummings, the son of Edward Cummings, a Unitarian minister, and Rebecca Haswell Clarke, a woman of distinguished literary and intellectual ancestry, grew up in Cambridge, Massachusetts, a community dominated by the learning of Harvard University and the literary spirit of Longfellow and Lowell. Although he was educated at the Cambridge Latin School and Harvard (A.B. in classics, 1915; A.M. in English, 1916), he soon became a rebel against the Cambridge atmosphere.

While at Harvard, Cummings became intensely interested in the new movements in the visual arts: impressionism, post-impressionism, cubism, and futurism, and he began painting in the modern manner. He read the new poets: Pound, H.D., Sandburg, and Amy Lowell, and he started to write free verse and follow the imagist principles. But seeking fresh and unusual effects, he began, by 1916, to create a style of his own, a form of literary cubism, breaking up his material and attempting to present it so that its appearance on the page directed the reader toward its meaning.

When the United States entered the European war in 1917, Cummings volunteered for service in the Norton-Harjes Ambulance Corps. While he was on duty in France, his pacifist leanings led to his being imprisoned in a French concentration camp under suspicion of espionage. This experience formed the basis of his autobiographical book *The Enormous Room*. Continuing to write verse, Cummings established, by 1919, a distinctive poetic style that had its own grammatical usages, its own punctuation, and its own rules for capitalization, in the freest kind of verse.

His work, published in *Tulips and Chimneys* and later volumes, met with much critical hostility, expressed in complaints about his "exploded fragments," "eccentric punctuation," and "jigsaw puzzle" arrangements. His harsh satirical verse as well as his erotic poems served also to identify him as a social iconoclast. But Cummings's trip to Russia in 1931 and two troublesome marriages brought about a change in his youthful and exuberant outlook. He became politically more conservative and more irascible in temper, as seen in such volumes as *Eimi*, an account of his experience in Russia, and *No Thanks*, a collection of his most experimental verse. At the same time, he continued to give voice to a basic affirmation of life, especially in whatever was simple, natural, individual, or unique, and he expressed powerful opposition to any social forces that would hinder uniqueness, forces such as conformity, groupiness, imitation, and artificiality. His poem "anyone lived in a pretty how town" gives mythic expression to these attitudes.

The horrors of World War II, the atomic bomb, and the cruel Russian suppression of the Hungarian revolution all made their impact upon Cummings's later work, but he was still able to express moods of serenity, particularly in response to the beauties of the natural world.

Like Joyce, Eliot, Faulkner, and other literary innovators, Cummings gradually taught his audience how to read his work, and with Pound and others he carried free verse into visually directive forms. The appearance on the page of much present-day poetry owes something to the flexibility Cummings introduced into American verse.

Richard S. Kennedy
Temple University

PRIMARY WORKS

The Enormous Room, 1922; *Tulips and Chimneys,* 1923 (complete edition, 1976); *Is 5,* 1926; *Him,* 1927; *ViVa,* 1931; *Eimi,* 1933; *No Thanks,* 1935; *50 Poems,* 1940; *1 × 1,* 1944; *Xiape,* 1950; *i: six non-lectures,* 1953; *Etcetera,* 1983; *Complete Poems,* 1904–1962, 1991.

[Buffalo Bill's]

Buffalo Bill 's
defunct
      who used to
      ride a watersmooth-silver
                     stallion   5
and break onetwothreefourfive pigeonsjustlikethat
                         Jesus

he was a handsome man
             and what i want to know is
how do you like your blueeyed boy   10
Mister Death

                     1920, 1923

[into the strenuous briefness]

into the strenuous briefness
Life:
handorgans and April
darkness,friends

i charge laughing.   5
Into the hair-thin tints
of yellow dawn,
into the women-coloured twilight

i smilingly
glide. I   10
into the big vermilion departure
swim,sayingly;

(Do you think?)the
i do, world
is probably made   15
of roses & hello:

(of solongs and,ashes)

                                                                        1923

[the Cambridge ladies who live in furnished souls]

the Cambridge ladies who live in furnished souls
are unbeautiful and have comfortable minds
(also, with the church's protestant blessings
daughters,unscented shapeless spirited)
they believe in Christ and Longfellow,both dead,   5
are invariably interested in so many things—
at the present writing one still finds
delighted fingers knitting for the is it Poles?
perhaps. While permanent faces coyly bandy
scandal of Mrs. N and Professor D   10
.... the Cambridge ladies do not care,above
Cambridge if sometimes in its box of
sky lavender and cornerless,the
moon rattles like a fragment of angry candy

                                                                        1923

[i like my body when it is with your]

i like my body when it is with your
body. It is so quite new a thing.
Muscles better and nerves more.
i like your body.   i like what it does,
i like its hows.   i like to feel the spine   5
of your body and its bones,and the trembling
-firm-smooth ness and which i will
again and again and again
kiss,   i like kissing this and that of you,
i like, slowly stroking the, shocking fuzz   10
of your electric fur, and what-is-it comes
over parting flesh.... And eyes big love-crumbs,

and possibly i like the thrill

of under me you so quite new

                                                                        1925

[my sweet old etcetera]

my sweet old etcetera
aunt lucy during the recent

war could and what
is more did tell you just
what everybody was fighting   5

for,
my sister

isabel created hundreds
(and
hundreds)of socks not to   10
mention shirts fleaproof earwarmers

etcetera wristers etcetera,my

mother hoped that

i would die etcetera
bravely of course my father used   15
to become hoarse talking about how it was
a privilege and if only he
could meanwhile my

self etcetera lay quietly
in the deep mud et   20

cetera
(dreaming,
et
   cetera,of
Your smile   25
eyes knees and of your Etcetera)

                                                               1926

[since feeling is first]

since feeling is first
who pays any attention
to the syntax of things
will never wholly kiss you;

wholly to be a fool   5
while Spring is in the world

my blood approves,
and kisses are a better fate
than wisdom
lady i swear by all flowers. Don't cry   10
—the best gesture of my brain is less than
your eyelids' flutter which says

we are for each other:then
laugh,leaning back in my arms
for life's not a paragraph   15

And death i think is no parenthesis

                                                                                      1926

[i sing of Olaf glad and big]

XXX

i sing of Olaf glad and big
whose warmest heart recoiled at war:
a conscientious object-or

his wellbelovéd colonel(trig
westpointer most succinctly bred)   5
took erring Olaf soon in hand;
but—though an host of overjoyed
noncoms(first knocking on the head
him)do through icy waters roll
that helplessness which others stroke   10
with brushes recently employed
anent this muddy toiletbowl,
while kindred intellects evoke
allegiance per blunt instruments—
Olaf(being to all intents   15
a corpse and wanting any rag
upon what God unto him gave)
responds, without getting annoyed
"I will not kiss your fucking flag"

straightway the silver bird looked grave   20
(departing hurriedly to shave)

but—though all kinds of officers
(a yearning nation's blueeyed pride)
their passive prey did kick and curse
until for wear their clarion   25
voices and boots were much the worse,
and egged the firstclassprivates on
his rectum wickedly to tease
by means of skilfully applied
bayonets roasted hot with heat—   30
Olaf(upon what were once knees)
does almost ceaselessly repeat
"there is some shit I will not eat"

our president,being of which
assertions duly notified   35
threw the yellowsonofabitch
into a dungeon,where he died

Christ(of His mercy infinite)
i pray to see;and Olaf, too

preponderatingly because   40
unless statistics lie he was
more brave than me:more blond than you.

                                                                       1931

[Picasso]

Picasso[1]
you give us Things
which
bulge:grunting lungs pumped full of sharp thick mind

you make us shrill   5
presents always
shut in the sumptuous screech of
simplicity

(out of the
black unbunged   10
Something gushes vaguely a squeak of planes
or

---

[1]Twentieth-century Spanish painter; the origi-
nator of the cubist technique.

between squeals of
Nothing grabbed with circular shrieking tightness
solid screams whisper.)   15
Lumberman of The Distinct

your brain's
axe only chops hugest inherent
Trees of Ego,from
whose living and biggest   20

bodies lopped
of every
prettiness

you hew form truly

                                                                     1925

[anyone lived in a pretty how town]

anyone lived in a pretty how town
(with up so floating many bells down)
spring summer autumn winter
he sang his didn't he danced his did.

Women and men(both little and small)   5
cared for anyone not at all
they sowed their isn't they reaped their same
sun moon stars rain

children guessed(but only a few
and down they forgot as up they grew   10
autumn winter spring summer)
that noone loved him more by more

when by now and tree by leaf
she laughed his joy she cried his grief
bird by snow and stir by still   15
anyone's any was all to her

someones married their everyones
laughed their cryings and did their dance
(sleep wake hope and then)they
said their nevers they slept their dream   20

stars rain sun moon
(and only the snow can begin to explain

how children are apt to forget to remember
with up so floating many bells down)

one day anyone died i guess   25
(and noone stooped to kiss his face)
busy folk buried them side by side
little by little and was by was

all by all and deep by deep
and more by more they dream their sleep   30
noone and anyone earth by april
wish by spirit and if by yes.

Women and men(both dong and ding)
summer autumn winter spring
reaped their sowing and went their came   35
sun moon stars rain

                                                              1940

[plato told]

plato told

him:he couldn't
believe it(jesus

told him;he
wouldn't believe   5
it)lao

tsze
certainly told
him,and general
(yes   10

mam)
sherman;[1]
and even
(believe it
or   15

not)you
told him:i told

[1]General in the American Civil War who said,
"War is hell."

him;we told him
(he didn't believe it,no

sir)it took   20
a nipponized bit of
the old sixth

avenue
el;[2]in the top of his head:to tell
him   25

                                                                                        1944

[what if a much of a which of a wind]

what if a much of a which of a wind
gives the truth to summer's lie;
bloodies with dizzying leaves the sun
and yanks immortal stars awry?
Blow king to beggar and queen to seem   5
(blow friend to fiend:blow space to time)
—when skies are hanged and oceans drowned,
the single secret will still be man

what if a keen of a lean wind flays
screaming hills with sleet and snow: 10
strangles valleys by ropes of thing
and stifles forests in white ago?
Blow hope to terror;blow seeing to blind
(blow pity to envy and soul to mind)
—whose hearts are mountains,roots are trees,   15
it's they shall cry hello to the spring

what if a dawn of a doom of a dream
bites this universe in two,
peels forever out of his grave
and sprinkles nowhere with me and you?   20
Blow soon to never and never to twice
(blow life to isn't:blow death to was)
—all nothing's only our hugest home;
the most who die,the more we live

                                                                                        1944

[2]Cummings supposes that when the Sixth Av-   the scrap iron was sold to the Japanese for
enue elevated train tracks were demolished,   reuse in munitions making.

[pity this busy monster, manunkind]

pity this busy monster,manunkind,

not. Progress is a comfortable disease:
your victim(death and life safely beyond)

plays with the bigness of his littleness
—electrons deify one razorblade   5
into a mountainrange;lenses extend

unwish through curving wherewhen till unwish
returns on its unself.
                 A world of made
is not a world of born—pity poor flesh   10

and trees,poor stars and stones,but never this
fine specimen of hypermagical

ultraomnipotence. We doctors know

a hopeless case if—listen:there's a hell
of a good universe next door;let's go   15

                   1944

■   # T. S. ELIOT   ■

1888–1965

Born in St. Louis, Missouri, Thomas Stearns Eliot was the son of Charlotte Stearns, a sometime amateur poet strictly committed to New England beliefs, and Henry Ware Eliot, a successful businessman. His grandfather, William Greenleaf Eliot, a Unitarian minister with a strong sense of civic and religious duty, had moved from Massachusetts in 1831, founding the local church, school, and the college that subsequently became Washington University. Thus, growing up a "South Westerner," Eliot was nonetheless always aware of his New England heritage, an awareness deepened by his mother's tutelage, by regular family summer vacations on Cape Ann, and by his education at Milton Academy (1905–1906) and Harvard (1906–1910, 1911–1914).

However strong these American influences, Eliot chose to live almost his entire adult life abroad. In 1910 he went to the Sorbonne for a year, and after three graduate years studying philosophy at Harvard, he went to Merton College at Oxford on a fellowship. In September 1914, he met Ezra Pound, to whom he read "The Love Song of J. Alfred Prufrock." Pound immediately recognized its merit and persuaded Harriet Monroe to publish it in *Poetry* in June 1915, the same month Eliot married Vivien Haigh-Wood. His family strongly disapproved of the sudden marriage and temporarily withdrew support. Faced with the necessity of making a living, Eliot taught in public schools for two years. By 1917 he had completed his doctoral dissertation on F. H. Bradley, but he did not return to Harvard to receive the degree and join the philosophy department, despite his outspoken dislike of grammar school teaching. Instead he became a bank clerk at Lloyd's, which he also found wearing. It was not until 1925 that, through the efforts of influential literary friends, Eliot obtained a congenial position as a director at the publishing firm of Faber and Gwyer, a post he retained for the rest of his life.

Ultimately, the strongest force in keeping him abroad was his growing reputation in literary London, a reputation enhanced by the publication of *Prufrock and Other Observations* (1917) and *Poems* (1920). He also had begun to establish himself as a critic, with the first collection of his essays, *The Sacred Wood*, appearing in 1920. With the publication of *The Waste Land* in 1922, he achieved the status he was to hold for the next two decades as the most influential poet and critic writing in English.

In his private life, however, and especially at the time he was writing *The Waste Land*, Eliot was at the point of despair. His sense of conflict with his parents, his dislike of his job, and, above all, the strain of his marriage brought him close to collapse. After years of tension and unhappiness, to which both undoubtedly contributed, Eliot arranged a formal separation from Vivien in 1932, as he made his first return home to give a series of lectures at Harvard. There is much evidence in "The Family Reunion" and elsewhere of the guilt he continued to feel over forcing the separation. As for Vivien Eliot, always high-strung, her intermittent instability eventually worsened into a nervous break-down, and she was institutionalized from 1939 until her death in 1947. Eliot did not remarry until 1958, his seventieth year, and he seems to have been supremely happy in these last years with Valerie Eliot.

As Eliot was being recognized as the premier poet of the 1920s, he was also noted for his essays on literature. Certain of his theories, abbreviated in catch phrases, are still part of the critical vocabulary—the "impersonality" of the poet; "dissociation of sensibility" into thought and feeling; the "objective correlative" by which an emotion is expressed. Essays on Donne, the Metaphysical Poets, Dryden, and, especially, early seventeenth-century dramatists, given what was by now Eliot's almost magisterial literary authority, were highly influential in contributing to a reconsideration of these figures. Eliot's role as a major critical voice was facilitated by his launching of *Criterion* in 1922, a journal that he edited until 1939, and he continued to publish a wide range of essays there and elsewhere throughout the 1920s.

In 1935 "Burnt Norton" was published, followed by "East Coker" (1940), "The Dry Salvages" (1941), and "Little Gidding" (1942). They were collected as *Four Quartets* in 1943, the major opus of the last part of Eliot's career. Both external and internal evidence indicates that he did not at the outset envisage *Four Quartets* as a unified poem, although read together, the *Quartets* provide a better sense of the total thrust, not only of the four pieces, but of Eliot's entire work. The differences between the early and late poetry are marked, but there is also an essential thematic continuity.

Many readers have regarded *Four Quartets* as Eliot's culminating achievement, appropriately recognized by the Nobel Prize in 1948. Others have entered demurrals. Several close readings have recently presented Eliot as a poet essentially torn between romantic yearning and intellectual detachment, unwilling or unable in this final major effort to maintain the temper of negative capability so movingly evident in his earlier poems. In this view, *Four Quartets* becomes an assertion in desperation, a falling off from the poetry of experience to the more prosaic, discursive mode of "a man reasoning with himself in solitude," with a consequent loss of intensity and even credibility. Whether or not one finds validity in such "corrections" to previous understandings of Eliot, they are valuable in underlining the importance of continued examination of his writing. In any reading, his work stands as one of the most distinctive contributions of the twentieth century to the literary tradition.

Sam S. Baskett
Michigan State University

PRIMARY WORKS

Selected Essays, 1932, 1960; *The Complete Poems and Plays of T. S. Eliot*, 1952, 1962; *The Complete Plays of T. S. Eliot*, 1967; *The Waste Land: A Facsimile and Transcript of the Original Drafts Including the Annotations of Ezra Pound*, 1971; *Inventions of the March Hare*, ed. Christopher Ricks, 1997; *Letters*, Vols. 1–2 (Revised Editions), ed. Hugh Haughton, Valerie Eliot, and John Haffenden, 2009–2011.

The Love Song of J. Alfred Prufrock

S'io credessi che mia risposta fosse
a persona che mai tornasse al mondo,
questa fiamma staria senza più scosse.
Ma per ciò che giammai di questo fondo
non tornò vivo alcun, s'i'odo il vero,
senza tema d'infamia ti rispondo.[1]

Let us go then, you and I,
When the evening is spread out against the sky
Like a patient etherised upon a table;
Let us go, through certain half-deserted streets,
The muttering retreats   5
Of restless nights in one-night cheap hotels
And sawdust restaurants with oyster-shells:

---

[1]"If I thought my answer were to one who could ever return to the world, this flame would move no more; but since no one has ever returned alive from this depth, if what I hear be true, without fear of infamy I answer you." (Dante, *Inferno* XXVII, 61–66.) Guido da Montefeltro, in Hell as punishment for giving false counsel without repenting, thus confesses to Dante since he believes he cannot return to earth and report Guido's shame.

Streets that follow like a tedious argument
Of insidious intent
To lead you to an overwhelming question . . .   10
Oh, do not ask, 'What is it?'
Let us go and make our visit.

In the room the women come and go
Talking of Michelangelo.

The yellow fog that rubs its back upon the window-panes,   15
The yellow smoke that rubs its muzzle on the window-panes,
Licked its tongue into the corners of the evening,
Lingered upon the pools that stand in drains,
Let fall upon its back the soot that falls from chimneys,
Slipped by the terrace, made a sudden leap,   20
And seeing that it was a soft October night,
Curled once about the house, and fell asleep.

And indeed there will be time
For the yellow smoke that slides along the street
Rubbing its back upon the window-panes;   25
There will be time, there will be time
To prepare a face to meet the faces that you meet;
There will be time to murder and create,
And time for all the works and days of hands
That lift and drop a question on your plate;   30
Time for you and time for me,
And time yet for a hundred indecisions,
And for a hundred visions and revisions,
Before the taking of a toast and tea.

In the room the women come and go   35
Talking of Michelangelo.

And indeed there will be time
To wonder, 'Do I dare?' and, 'Do I dare?'
Time to turn back and descend the stair,
With a bald spot in the middle of my hair—   40
(They will say: 'How his hair is growing thin!')
My morning coat, my collar mounting firmly to the chin,
My necktie rich and modest, but asserted by a simple pin—
(They will say: 'But how his arms and legs are thin!')
Do I dare   45
Disturb the universe?
In a minute there is time
For decisions and revisions which a minute will reverse.

For I have known them all already, known them all—
Have known the evenings, mornings, afternoons,   50
I have measured out my life with coffee spoons;
I know the voices dying with a dying fall
Beneath the music from a farther room.
    So how should I presume?

And I have known the eyes already, known them all—   55
The eyes that fix you in a formulated phrase,
And when I am formulated, sprawling on a pin,
When I am pinned and wriggling on the wall,
Then how should I begin
To spit out all the butt-ends of my days and ways?   60
    And how should I presume?

And I have known the arms already, known them all—
Arms that are braceleted and white and bare
(But in the lamplight, downed with light brown hair!)
Is it perfume from a dress   65
That makes me so digress?
Arms that lie along a table, or wrap about a shawl.
    And should I then presume?
    And how should I begin?

Shall I say, I have gone at dusk through narrow streets   70
And watched the smoke that rises from the pipes
Of lonely men in shirt-sleeves, leaning out of windows? . . .

I should have been a pair of ragged claws
Scuttling across the floors of silent seas.

And the afternoon, the evening, sleeps so peacefully!   75
Smoothed by long fingers,
Asleep . . . tired . . . or it malingers,
Stretched on the floor, here beside you and me.
Should I, after tea and cakes and ices,
Have the strength to force the moment to its crisis?   80
But though I have wept and fasted, wept and prayed,
Though I have seen my head (grown slightly bald) brought in
    upon a platter,[2]

---

[2]Mark 6:17–20 and Matthew 14:3–11 recount the story of John the Baptist, forerunner and baptiser of Christ. He was beheaded at the request of Salome, who then presented his head to Queen Herodias.

I am no prophet—and here's no great matter;
I have seen the moment of my greatness flicker,   85
And I have seen the eternal Footman hold my coat, and snicker,
And in short, I was afraid.

And would it have been worth it, after all,
After the cups, the marmalade, the tea,
Among the porcelain, among some talk of you and me,   90
Would it have been worth while,
To have bitten off the matter with a smile,
To have squeezed the universe into a ball[3]
To roll it towards some overwhelming question,
To say: 'I am Lazarus,[4] come from the dead,   95
Come back to tell you all, I shall tell you all'—
If one, settling a pillow by her head,
    Should say: 'That is not what I meant at all.
    That is not it, at all.'

And would it have been worth it, after all,   100
Would it have been worth while,
After the sunsets and the dooryards and the sprinkled streets,
After the novels, after the teacups, after the skirts that trail along
        the floor—
And this, and so much more?—   105
It is impossible to say just what I mean!
But as if a magic lantern threw the nerves in patterns on a screen:
Would it have been worth while
If one, settling a pillow or throwing off a shawl,
And turning toward the window, should say: 110
    'That is not it at all,
    That is not what I meant, at all.'

No! I am not Prince Hamlet, nor was meant to be;
Am an attendant lord, one that will do
To swell a progress, start a scene or two,   115
Advise the prince; no doubt, an easy tool,
Deferential, glad to be of use,
Politic, cautious, and meticulous;
Full of high sentence, but a bit obtuse;[5]
At times, indeed, almost ridiculous—   120
Almost, at times, the Fool.

[3]Here, as in line 23, an echo of the seductive *carpe diem* plea of Andrew Marvell's "To His Coy Mistress."
[4]Luke 16:19–31 and John 11:1–44 recount the resurrection of Lazarus.

[5]Qualities associated with Polonius in Shakespeare's *Hamlet*. Line 74 echoes Hamlet's mocking of Polonius, II. ii. 205–6: "you yourself, sir, should be as old as I am, if like a crab you could go backward."

I grow old ... I grow old ...
I shall wear the bottoms of my trousers rolled.

Shall I part my hair behind? Do I dare to eat a peach?
I shall wear white flannel trousers, and walk upon the beach.
I have heard the mermaids[6] singing, each to each.   125

I do not think that they will sing to me.

I have seen them riding seaward on the waves
Combing the white hair of the waves blown back
When the wind blows the water white and black.   130

We have lingered in the chambers of the sea
By sea-girls wreathed with seaweed red and brown
Till human voices wake us, and we drown.

                                                                       1915

Preludes

I

The winter evening settles down
With smell of steaks in passageways.
Six o'clock.
The burnt-out ends of smoky days.
And now a gusty shower wraps   5
The grimy scraps
Of withered leaves about your feet
And newspapers from vacant lots;
The showers beat
On broken blinds and chimney-pots,   10
And at the corner of the street
A lonely cab-horse steams and stamps.
And then the lighting of the lamps.

II

The morning comes to consciousness
Of faint stale smells of beer   15
From the sawdust-trampled street
With all its muddy feet that press
To early coffee-stands.
With the other masquerades

---

[6]The "mermaid passage" may be read in the context of the Siren Tradition—mermaids/ sirens considered as muses, "not wholly evil, but very far from entirely good."

That time resumes,   20
One thinks of all the hands
That are raising dingy shades
In a thousand furnished rooms.

III

You tossed a blanket from the bed,
You lay upon your back, and waited;   25
You dozed, and watched the night revealing
The thousand sordid images
Of which your soul was constituted;
They flickered against the ceiling.
And when all the world came back   30
And the light crept up between the shutters
And you heard the sparrows in the gutters,
You had such a vision of the street
As the street hardly understands;
Sitting along the bed's edge, where   35
You curled the papers from your hair,
Or clasped the yellow soles of feet
In the palms of both soiled hands.

IV

His soul stretched tight across the skies
That fade behind a city block,   40
Or trampled by insistent feet
At four and five and six o'clock;
And short square fingers stuffing pipes,
And evening newspapers, and eyes
Assured of certain certainties,   45
The conscience of a blackened street
Impatient to assume the world.

   I am moved by fancies that are curled
Around these images, and cling:
The notion of some infinitely gentle   50
Infinitely suffering thing.

   Wipe your hand across your mouth, and laugh;
The worlds revolve like ancient women
Gathering fuel in vacant lots.

                                                                 1917

Tradition and the Individual Talent[1]

In English writing we seldom speak of tradition, though we occasionally apply its name in deploring its absence. We cannot refer to "the tradition" or to "a tradition"; at most, we employ the adjective in saying that the poetry of So-and-so is "traditional" or even "too traditional." Seldom, perhaps, does the word appear except in a phrase of censure. If otherwise, it is vaguely approbative, with the implication, as to the work approved, of some pleasing archaeological reconstruction. You can hardly make the word agreeable to English ears without this comfortable reference to the reassuring science of archaeology.

Certainly the word is not likely to appear in our appreciations of living or dead writers. Every nation, every race, has not only its own creative, but its own critical turn of mind; and is even more oblivious of the shortcomings and limitations of its critical habits than of those of its creative genius. We know, or think we know, from the enormous mass of critical writing that has appeared in the French language the critical method or habit of the French; we only conclude (we are such unconscious people) that the French are "more critical" than we, and sometimes even plume ourselves a little with the fact, as if the French were the less spontaneous. Perhaps they are; but we might remind ourselves that criticism is as inevitable as breathing, and that we should be none the worse for articulating what passes in our minds when we read a book and feel an emotion about it, for criticizing our own minds in their work of criticism. One of the facts that might come to light in this process is our tendency to insist, when we praise a poet, upon those aspects of his work in which he least resembles any one else. In these aspects or parts of his work we pretend to find what is individual, what is the peculiar essence of the man. We dwell with satisfaction upon the poet's difference from his predecessors, especially his immediate predecessors; we endeavour to find something that can be isolated in order to be enjoyed. Whereas if we approach a poet without this prejudice we shall often find that not only the best, but the most individual parts of his work may be those in which the dead poets, his ancestors, assert their immortality most vigorously. And I do not mean the impressionable period of adolescence, but the period of full maturity.

Yet if the only form of tradition, of handing down, consisted in following the ways of the immediate generation before us in a blind or timid adherence to its successes, "tradition" should positively be discouraged. We have seen many such simple currents soon lost in the sand; and novelty is better than repetition. Tradition is a matter of much wider significance. It cannot be inherited, and if you want it you must obtain it by great labour. It involves, in the first place, the historical sense, which we may call nearly indispensable to any one who would continue to be a poet beyond his twenty-

---

[1]From *The Sacred Wood* (1920), first published in *The Egoist* (1919).

fifth year; and the historical sense involves a perception, not only of the pastness of the past, but of its presence; the historical sense compels a man to write not merely with his own generation in his bones, but with a feeling that the whole of the literature of Europe from Homer and within it the whole of the literature of his own country has a simultaneous existence and composes a simultaneous order. This historical sense, which is a sense of the timeless as well as of the temporal and of the timeless and of the temporal together, is what makes a writer traditional. And it is at the same time what makes a writer most acutely conscious of his place in time, of his own contemporaneity.

No poet, no artist of any art, has his complete meaning alone. His significance, his appreciation is the appreciation of his relation to the dead poets and artists. You cannot value him alone; you must set him, for contrast and comparison, among the dead. I mean this as a principle of aesthetic, not merely historical, criticism. The necessity that he shall conform, that he shall cohere, is not onesided; what happens when a new work of art is created is something that happens simultaneously to all the works of art which preceded it. The existing monuments form an ideal order among themselves, which is modified by the introduction of the new (the really new) work of art among them. The existing order is complete before the new work arrives; for order to persist after the supervention of novelty, the *whole* existing order must be, if ever so slightly, altered; and so the relations, proportions, values of each work of art toward the whole are readjusted; and this is conformity between the old and the new. Whoever has approved this idea of order, of the form of European, of English literature will not find it preposterous that the past should be altered by the present as much as the present is directed by the past. And the poet who is aware of this will be aware of great difficulties and responsibilities.

In a peculiar sense he will be aware also that he must inevitably be judged by the standards of the past. I say judged, not amputated, by them; not judged to be as good as, or worse or better than, the dead; and certainly not judged by the canons of dead critics. It is a judgment, a comparison, in which two things are measured by each other. To conform merely would be for the new work not really to conform at all; it would not be new, and would therefore not be a work of art. And we do not quite say that the new is more valuable because it fits in; but its fitting in is a test of its value—a test, it is true, which can only be slowly and cautiously applied, for we are none of us infallible judges of conformity. We say: it appears to conform, and is perhaps individual, or it appears individual, and may conform; but we are hardly likely to find that it is one and not the other.

To proceed to a more intelligible exposition of the relation of the poet to the past: he can neither take the past as a lump, an indiscriminate bolus, nor can he form himself wholly on one or two private admirations, nor can he form himself wholly upon one preferred period. The first course is inadmissible, the second is an important experience of youth, and the third is a pleasant and highly desirable supplement. The poet must be very conscious of the main current, which does not at all flow invariably through the most distinguished reputations. He must be quite aware of the obvious fact that art never improves, but that the material of art is never quite the same. He must be aware that the mind of Europe—the mind of his own country—a mind which he learns in time to be much more important than his own private mind—is a mind which changes, and that this change is a development which abandons nothing *en route*, which does not superannuate either Shakespeare, or Homer, or the rock drawing of the Magdalenian[2] draughtsmen. That this development, refinement perhaps, complication certainly, is not, from the point of view of the artist, any improvement. Perhaps not even an improvement from the point of view of the psychologist or not to the extent which we imagine; perhaps only in the end based upon a complication in economics and machinery. But the difference between the present and the past is that the conscious present is an awareness of the past in a way and to an extent which the past's awareness of itself cannot show.

Some one said: "The dead writers are remote from us because we *know* so much more than they did." Precisely, and they are that which we know.

I am alive to a usual objection to what is clearly part of my programme for the *métier* of poetry. The objection is that the doctrine requires a ridiculous amount of erudition (pedantry), a claim which can be rejected by appeal to the lives of poets in any pantheon. It will even be affirmed that much learning deadens or perverts poetic sensibility. While, however, we persist in believing that a poet ought to know as much as will not encroach upon his necessary receptivity and necessary laziness, it is not desirable to confine knowledge to whatever can be put into a useful shape for examinations, drawing-rooms, or the still more pretentious modes of publicity. Some can absorb knowledge, the more tardy must sweat for it. Shakespeare acquired more essential history from Plutarch[3] than most men could from the whole British Museum. What is to be insisted upon is that the poet must develop or procure the consciousness of the past and that he should continue to develop this consciousness throughout his career.

What happens is a continual surrender of himself as he is at the moment to something which is more valuable. The progress of an artist is a continual self-sacrifice, a continual extinction of personality.

There remains to define this process of depersonalization and its relation to the sense of tradition. It is in this depersonalization that art may be said to approach the condition of science. I, therefore, invite you to consider, as a suggestive analogy, the action which takes place when a bit of finely filiated platinum is introduced into a chamber containing oxygen and sulphur dioxide.

---

[2]Named for La Madeleine in France, where the drawings of this advanced stage of Paleolithic culture were discovered.

[3]First century (A.D.) Greek biographer from whom Shakespeare took the plots of his Roman plays.

II

Honest criticism and sensitive appreciation are directed not upon the poet but upon the poetry. If we attend to the confused cries of the newspaper critics and the *susurrus*[4] of popular repetition that follows, we shall hear the names of poets in great numbers; if we seek not Blue-book[5] knowledge but the enjoyment of poetry, and ask for a poem, we shall seldom find it. I have tried to point out the importance of the relation of the poem to other poems by other authors, and suggested the conception of poetry as a living whole of all the poetry that has ever been written. The other aspect of this Impersonal theory of poetry is the relation of the poem to its author. And I hinted, by an analogy, that the mind of the mature poet differs from that of the immature one not precisely in any valuation of "personality," not being necessarily more interesting, or having "more to say," but rather by being a more finely perfected medium in which special, or very varied, feelings are at liberty to enter into new combinations.

The analogy was that of the catalyst. When the two gases previously mentioned are mixed in the presence of a filament of platinum, they form sulphurous acid. This combination takes place only if the platinum is present; nevertheless the newly formed acid contains no trace of platinum, and the platinum itself is apparently unaffected; has remained inert, neutral, and unchanged. The mind of the poet is the shred of platinum. It may partly or exclusively operate upon the experience of the man himself; but, the more perfect the artist, the more completely separate in him will be the man who suffers and the mind which creates; the more perfectly will the mind digest and transmute the passions which are its material.

The experience, you will notice, the elements which enter the presence of the transforming catalyst, are of two kinds: emotions and feelings. The effect of a work of art upon the person who enjoys it is an experience different in kind from any experience not of art. It may be formed out of one emotion, or may be a combination of several; and various feelings, inhering for the writer in particular words or phrases or images, may be added to compose the final result. Or great poetry may be made without the direct use of any emotion whatever: composed out of feelings solely. Canto XV of the *Inferno* (Brunetto Latini)[6] is a working up of the emotion evident in the situation; but the effect, though single as that of any work of art, is obtained by considerable complexity of detail. The last quatrain gives an image, a feeling attaching to an image, which "came," which did not develop simply out of what precedes, but which was probably in suspension in the poet's mind until the proper combination arrived for it to add itself to. The poet's mind is in fact a receptacle for seizing and storing up numberless

[4]"Murmuring" in Latin.
[5]British official government publication.
[6]Late thirteenth-century philosopher; Dante's master. Dante describes the punishment he is eternally undergoing for his unnatural lusts, but greets him with compassion.

feelings, phrases, images, which remain there until all the particles which can unite to form a new compound are present together.

If you compare several representative passages of the greatest poetry you see how great is the variety of types of combination, and also how completely any semi-ethical criterion of "sublimity" misses the mark. For it is not the "greatness," the intensity, of the emotions, the components, but the intensity of the artistic process, the pressure, so to speak, under which the fusion takes place, that counts. The episode of Paolo and Francesca[7] employs a definite emotion, but the intensity of the poetry is something quite different from whatever intensity in the supposed experience it may give the impression of. It is no more intense, furthermore, than Canto XXVI, the voyage of Ulysses,[8] which has not the direct dependence upon an emotion. Great variety is possible in the process of transmutation of emotion: the murder of Agamemnon,[9] or the agony of Othello,[10] gives an artistic effect apparently closer to a possible original than the scenes from Dante. In the *Agamemnon*, the artistic emotion approximates to the emotion of an actual spectator; in *Othello* to the emotion of the protagonist himself. But the difference between art and the event is always absolute; the combination which is the murder of Agamemnon is probably as complex as that which is the voyage of Ulysses. In either case there has been a fusion of elements. The ode of Keats[11] contains a number of feelings which have nothing particular to do with the nightingale, but which the nightingale, partly, perhaps, because of its attractive name, and partly because of its reputation, served to bring together.

The point of view which I am struggling to attack is perhaps related to the metaphysical theory of the substantial unity of the soul: for my meaning is, that the poet has, not a "personality" to express, but a particular medium, which is only a medium and not a personality, in which impressions and experiences combine in peculiar and unexpected ways. Impressions and experiences which are important for the man may take no place in the poetry, and those which become important in the poetry may play quite a negligible part in the man, the personality.

I will quote a passage which is unfamiliar enough to be regarded with fresh attention in the light—or darkness—of these observations:

> *And now methinks I could e'en chide myself*
> *For doating on her beauty, though her death*
> *Shall be revenged after no common action.*
> *Does the silkworm expend her yellow labours*
> *For thee? For thee does she undo herself?*
> *Are lordships sold to maintain ladyships*
> *For the poor benefit of a bewildering minute?*

---

[7]Dante describes the punishment of these illicit lovers in *Inferno*, V.

[8]Ulysses, who is being punished for false counseling, tells Dante of his final voyage, actually Dante's addition to Homer.

[9]In Aeschylus' tragedy, Agamemnon is killed by his wife and her lover.

[10]In Shakespeare's tragedy, Othello agonizes over having killed his wife out of jealousy.

[11]"Ode to a Nightingale."

> *Why does yon fellow falsify highways,*
> *And put his life between the judge's lips,*
> *To refine such a thing—keeps horse and men*
> *To beat their valours for her? . . .*[12]

In this passage (as is evident if it is taken in its context) there is a combination of positive and negative emotions: an intensely strong attraction toward beauty and an equally intense fascination by the ugliness which is contrasted with it and which destroys it. This balance of contrasted emotion is in the dramatic situation to which the speech is pertinent, but that situation alone is inadequate to it. This is, so to speak, the structural emotion, provided by the drama. But the whole effect, the dominant tone, is due to the fact that a number of floating feelings, having an affinity to this emotion by no means superficially evident, have combined with it to give us a new art emotion.

It is not in his personal emotions, the emotions provoked by particular events in his life, that the poet is in any way remarkable or interesting. His particular emotions may be simple, or crude, or flat. The emotion in his poetry will be a very complex thing, but not with the complexity of the emotions of people who have very complex or unusual emotions in life. One error, in fact, of eccentricity in poetry is to seek for new human emotions to express; and in this search for novelty in the wrong place it discovers the perverse. The business of the poet is not to find new emotions, but to use the ordinary ones and, in working them up into poetry, to express feelings which are not in actual emotions at all. And emotions which he has never experienced will serve his turn as well as those familiar to him. Consequently, we must believe that "emotion recollected in tranquillity"[13] is an inexact formula. For it is neither emotion, nor recollection, nor, without distortion of meaning, tranquillity. It is a concentration, and a new thing resulting from the concentration, of a very great number of experiences which to the practical and active person would not seem to be experiences at all; it is a concentration which does not happen consciously or of deliberation. These experiences are not "recollected," and they finally unite in an atmosphere which is "tranquil" only in that it is a passive attending upon the event. Of course this is not quite the whole story. There is a great deal, in the writing of poetry, which must be conscious and deliberate. In fact, the bad poet is usually unconscious where he ought to be conscious, and conscious where he ought to be unconscious. Both errors tend to make him "personal." Poetry is not a turning loose of emotion, but an escape from emotion; it is not the expression of personality, but an escape from personality. But, of course, only those who have personality and emotions know what it means to want to escape from these things.

---

[12]From Cyril Tourneur's *The Revenger's Tragedy* (1607), III. v. 68–78.

[13]Wordsworth's "formula" for poetry expressed in his Preface to *Lyrical Ballads*.

III

ὁ δὲ νοῦς ἴοως Θειότερόν τι χαὶ ἀπαθές ἐοτιν.[14]

This essay proposes to halt at the frontier of metaphysics or mysticism, and confine itself to such practical conclusions as can be applied by the responsible person interested in poetry. To divert interest from the poet to the poetry is a laudable aim: for it would conduce to a juster estimation of actual poetry, good and bad. There are many people who appreciate the expression of sincere emotion in verse, and there is a smaller number of people who can appreciate technical excellence. But very few know when there is an expression of *significant* emotion, emotion which has its life in the poem and not in the history of the poet. The emotion of art is impersonal. And the poet cannot reach this impersonality without surrendering himself wholly to the work to be done. And he is not likely to know what is to be done unless he lives in what is not merely the present, but the present moment of the past, unless he is conscious, not of what is dead, but of what is already living.

1919

The Waste Land[1]

*"Nam Sibyllam quidem Cumis ego ipse oculis meis vidi in ampullapendere,
et cum illi pueri dicerent: Σιβυλλα τί θέλεις; respondebat illa
ἀποθανείν θέλω."*[2]

—FOR EZRA POUND
il miglior fabbro.[3]

I. The Burial of the Dead[4]

April is the cruellest month, breeding
Lilacs out of the dead land, mixing
Memory and desire, stirring
Dull roots with spring rain.
Winter kept us warm, covering   5

---

[14]Aristotle, *De Anima* ("On the Soul"), I. 4. "No doubt the mind is something divine and not subject to external impressions."

[1]In the first hard-cover edition of *The Waste Land*, Eliot included several pages of "Notes," acknowledging his indebtedness to Miss Jessie L. Weston's book on the Grail Legend, *From Ritual to Romance*, as suggesting "the title ... the plan and a good deal of the incidental symbolism of the poem." He also cited as a source the volumes of James G. Frazer's *The Golden Bough* which deal with "vegetation ceremonies." As deemed particularly helpful, Eliot's notes are summarized in these footnotes.

[2]Petronius's *Satyricon* (first century A.D.) recounts the story of the Sibyl of Cumae, given eternal life, but thus doomed to perpetual old age: "For once I myself saw with my own eyes, the Sibyl at Cumae hanging in a cage, and when the children said to her, 'Sibyl, what do you want?' she replied, 'I want to die.'"

[3]"The better maker," Eliot's recognition of Pound for his extensive, sensitive help in shaping the poem. The quotation, from Dante's *Purgatorio* XXVI, 117, was a tribute to the Provençal poet Arnaut Daniel.

[4]The phrase is from the burial service of the Anglican Church.

Earth in forgetful snow, feeding
A little life with dried tubers.
Summer surprised us, coming over the Starnbergersee[5]
With a shower of rain; we stopped in the colonnade,
And went on in sunlight, into the Hofgarten,[6]   10
And drank coffee, and talked for an hour.
Bin gar keine Russin, stamm' aus Litauen, echt deutsch.[7]
And when we were children, staying at the archduke's,
My cousin's, he took me out on a sled,
And I was frightened. He said, Marie,   15
Marie, hold on tight. And down we went.
In the mountains, there you feel free.
I read, much of the night, and go south in the winter.

What are the roots that clutch, what branches grow
Out of this stony rubbish? Son of man,[8]   20
You cannot say, or guess, for you know only
A heap of broken images, where the sun beats,
And the dead tree gives no shelter, the cricket no relief,[9]
And the dry stone no sound of water. Only
There is shadow under this red rock,[10]   25
(Come in under the shadow of this red rock),
And I will show you something different from either
Your shadow at morning striding behind you
Or your shadow at evening rising to meet you;
I will show you fear in a handful of dust.   30

> *Frisch weht der Wind*
> *Der Heimat zu*
> *Mein irisch Kind,*
> *Wo weilest du?*[11]

"You gave me hyacinths first a year ago;   35
"They called me the hyacinth girl."[12]
—Yet when we came back, late, from the Hyacinth garden,
Your arms full, and your hair wet, I could not
Speak, and my eyes failed, I was neither

---

[5]A lake near Munich. Lines 8–16 echo passages in Countess Marie Larisch's *My Past* (1913).

[6]A Munich public park with cafés, formerly the grounds of a palace.

[7]"I am no Russian, I come from Lithuania, a real German."

[8]Eliot's note: "Cf. Ezekiel II, i." God addresses Ezekiel as "Son of man," and calls upon him to "stand upon thy feet, and I will speak unto thee."

[9]Eliot's note: "Cf. Ecclesiastes XII," The Preacher points to old age when "the grasshopper shall be a burden and desire shall fail."

[10]Isaiah 32:1–2 prophesies that when the Messiah comes it "shall be . . . as rivers of water in a dry place, as the shadow of a great rock in a weary land."

[11]Eliot's note: "*Tristan und Isolde*, I, verses 5–8." In Wagner's opera, the lines are sung by a sailor aboard Tristan's ship, thinking of his beloved in Ireland: "Fresh blows the wind ward; my Irish child, where are you waiting?"

[12]In Ovid's *Metamorphoses*, X, Hyacinth is a young boy slain by a rival for Apollo's love.

Living nor dead, and I knew nothing,   40
Looking into the heart of light, the silence.
Oed' und leer das Meer.[13]

Madame Sosostris,[14] famous clairvoyante,
Had a bad cold, nevertheless
Is known to be the wisest woman in Europe,   45
With a wicked pack of cards.[15] Here, said she,
Is your card, the drowned Phoenician Sailor,[16]
(Those are pearls that were his eyes.[17] Look!)
Here is Belladonna, the Lady of the Rocks,[18]
The lady of situations.   50
Here is the man with three staves, and here the Wheel,[19]
And here is the one-eyed merchant,[20] and this card,
Which is blank, is something he carries on his back,
Which I am forbidden to see. I do not find
The Hanged Man. Fear death by water.   55
I see crowds of people, walking round in a ring.
Thank you. If you see dear Mrs. Equitone,
Tell her I bring the horoscope myself:
One must be so careful these days.

Unreal City,[21]   60
Under the brown fog of a winter dawn,

[13]"Wide and empty the sea," the message given the dying Tristan, waiting for the ship bringing Isolde.

[14]The name alludes to Sesostris, a 12th-dynasty Egyptian king, adapted by Aldous Huxley in *Chrome Yellow* (1921) to Sesostris, the Sorceress of Ectabana, a woman fortune-teller.

[15]The reference is to the Tarot deck once, but no longer, significant in Eastern magic. Its four suits, cup, dish, lance, and sword, are life symbols in the Grail Legend. Eliot's note: "I am not familiar with the exact constitution of the Tarot pack of cards, from which I have obviously departed to suit my own convenience. The Hanged Man, a member of the traditional pack, fits my purpose in two ways: because he is associated in my mind with the Hanged God of Frazer, and because I associate him with the hooded figure in the passage of the disciples to Emmaus in Part V. The Phoenician Sailor and the Merchant appear later; also the 'crowds of people,' and Death by Water is executed in Part IV. The Man with Three Staves (an authentic member of the Tarot pack) I associate, quite arbitrarily, with the Fisher King himself." Eliot's disclaimer should be attended, since the Phoenician Sailor, for example, is not a member of the pack.

[16]According to Eliot's note, the Smyrna merchant (1. 209) "melts into the Phoenician Sailor." The Phoenicians were seagoing merchants who spread Egyptian fertility cults throughout the Mediterranean. He is a type of the fertility god annually "drowned" as a symbol of the death of winter.

[17]From Ariel's song in Shakespeare's *The Tempest*, I. ii. 398. Ariel sings of the transformation from supposed death to "something rich and strange." See also "A Game of Chess," 1. 125.

[18]Suggestive of several "situations": literally, beautiful lady, the name ambiguously expands into the names of the poisonous nightshade, of a cosmetic and of the Madonna, or Virgin Mary, painted by Leonardo da Vinci as *Madonna of the Rocks*.

[19]The Wheel on one of the Tarot cards is the Wheel of Fortune.

[20]Cf. Mr. Eugenides, 1. 209; on the Tarot card he is shown in profile, thus "one-eyed."

[21]Eliot's note: "Cf. Baudelaire: 'Fourmillante cité, cité pleine de rêves,/ Où le spectre en plein jour raccroche le passant.'" In translation: "Swarming city, city full of dreams,/ Where the specter in full day accosts the passerby." *Les Fleurs du Mal (The Flowers of Evil)*.

A crowd flowed over London Bridge, so many,
I had not thought death had undone so many.[22]
Sighs, short and infrequent, were exhaled,[23]
And each man fixed his eyes before his feet.   65
Flowed up the hill and down King William Street,
To where Saint Mary Woolnoth kept the hours
With a dead sound on the final stroke of nine.[24]
There I saw one I knew, and stopped him, crying: "Stetson!
"You who were with me in the ships at Mylae![25]   70
"That corpse you planted last year in your garden,
"Has it begun to sprout? Will it bloom this year?
"Or has the sudden frost disturbed its bed?
"Oh keep the Dog far hence, that's friend to men,
"Or with his nails he'll dig it up again![26]   75
"You! hypocrite lecteur!—mon semblable,—mon frère!"[27]

II. A Game of Chess[28]

The Chair she sat in, like a burnished throne,
Glowed on the marble,[29] where the glass
Held up by standards wrought with fruited vines
From which a golden Cupidon peeped out   80
(Another hid his eyes behind his wing)
Doubled the flames of sevenbranched candelabra

[22]A rendering of *Inferno*, III, 55–57, quoted in Eliot's note. Canto III deals with those living without praise or blame.

[23]A rendering of *Inferno* IV, 25–27, quoted in Eliot's note. Canto IV deals with those in Limbo who had lived virtuously but died before Christ, and were thus excluded from Christian salvation.

[24]Eliot's note wryly comments, "A Phenomenon which I have often noticed." Indeed he had, for it was partly the route Eliot took for many years to his desk at Lloyd's. If he passed under the clock of the "Bankers Church" at nine, he would have been on time at the office, a few steps down the street. The church is also possibly an allusion to the Chapel Perilous in the Grail Legend. See also Lines 388–89.

[25]Rome won a naval battle at Mylae (260 B.C.) in a commercial war against Carthage.

[26]Lines 71–75 constitute a parody of the anticipation of the resurrection of the fertility god. Eliot's note refers to Webster's *The White Devil*. A Roman woman fears her murdered relatives will be disinterred: "But keep the wolf far thence, that's foe to men,/ For with his nails he'll dig them up again." In

welding his "theft,"—Eliot's term for such literary "borrowing"—into something "new" he made two significant changes: "foe" to "friend" and "wolf" to "Dog," thus alluding to the "Dog Star"—the bright star Sirius whose annual positioning coincided with the flooding of the Nile in consonance with the fertility ceremonies. The passage has occasioned a great deal of speculative comment with reference to naturalistic and humanistic suggestions that seem at odds with the rebirth of the god.

[27]Eliot's note refers to Baudelaire's *Fleurs du Mal*. The apposite lines in the introductory poem to the volume may be rendered, "Hypocrite reader!—my likeness—my brother!"

[28]The title alludes to Thomas Middleton's *A Game of Chess* (1627), about a marriage for political purposes, and *Women Beware Women* (1657), in which a chess game is used as a means of keeping a woman occupied while her daughter-in-law is being seduced, the seduction being described in terms of chess. See also 1. 137.

[29]Shakespeare's *Anthony and Cleopatra*, II. ii. 190–1: "The barge she sat in, like a burnished throne,/ Burn'd on the water."

Reflecting light upon the table as
The glitter of her jewels rose to meet it,
From satin cases poured in rich profusion;   85
In vials of ivory and coloured glass
Unstoppered, lurked her strange synthetic perfumes,
Unguent, powdered, or liquid—troubled, confused
And drowned the sense in odours; stirred by the air
That freshened from the window, these ascended   90
In fattening the prolonged candle-flames,
Flung their smoke into the laquearia,[30]
Stirring the pattern on the coffered ceiling.
Huge sea-wood fed with copper
Burned green and orange, framed by the coloured stone,   95
In which sad light a carvèd dolphin swam.
Above the antique mantel was displayed
As though a window gave upon the sylvan scene[31]
The change of Philomel, by the barbarous king
So rudely forced; yet there the nightingale   100
Filled all the desert with inviolable voice
And still she cried, and still the world pursues,
"Jug Jug"[32] to dirty ears.
And other withered stumps of time
Were told upon the walls; staring forms   105
Leaned out, leaning, hushing the room enclosed.
Footsteps shuffled on the stair.
Under the firelight, under the brush, her hair
Spread out in fiery points
Glowed into words, then would be savagely still.   110

"My nerves are bad to-night. Yes, bad. Stay with me.
"Speak to me. Why do you never speak. Speak.
　　"What are you thinking of? What thinking? What?
"I never know what you are thinking. Think."

---

[30]An echo of the "paneled ceiling" of the banquet hall in which Queen Dido of Carthage received Aeneas, *Aenid*, I, 726. She commits suicide after Aeneas leaves her to found Rome.

[31]Eliot's note for line 98 refers to *Paradise Lost*, IV, 140 for "sylvan scene," the phrase used in Satan's first visit to the Garden. The actual scene, however, is that of the "change of Philomel"; and Eliot for line 99 refers to "Ovid *Metamorphoses*, VI, Philomela." Thus the two failures of love are conjoined—and added to the two previous failures figured in the opulent furnishing of the lady's boudoir. Eve's temptation by Satan will lead to carnal debauchery and expulsion from the Garden. Ovid recounts the rape of Philomela by Tereus, her sister's husband. Eventually, to escape his wrath, she is transformed into a nightingale. The motif of the transformation of suffering into art continues through line 103 and, pointed to by Eliot's note, in lines 206–9.

[32]The stylized representation of the song of the nightingale in Elizabethan poetry.

I think we are in rats' alley   115
Where the dead men lost their bones.

    "What is that noise?"
                      The wind under the door.
"What is that noise now? What is the wind doing?"
                      Nothing again nothing.   120
                                        "Do
"You know nothing? Do you see nothing? Do you remember
"Nothing?"

    I remember
Those are pearls that were his eyes.   125
"Are you alive, or not? Is there nothing in your head?"
                      But

O O O O that Shakespeherian Rag—
It's so elegant
So intelligent   130
"What shall I do now? What shall I do?"
"I shall rush out as I am, and walk the street
"With my hair down, so. What shall we do to-morrow?
"What shall we ever do"
                      The hot water at ten.   135
And if it rains, a closed car at four.
And we shall play a game of chess,
Pressing lidless eyes and waiting for a knock upon the door.

When Lil's husband got demobbed,[33] I said—
I didn't mince my words, I said to her myself,   140
HURRY UP PLEASE ITS TIME[34]
Now Albert's coming back, make yourself a bit smart.
He'll want to know what you done with that money he gave you
To get yourself some teeth. He did, I was there.
You have them all out, Lil, and get a nice set,   145
He said, I swear, I can't bear to look at you.
And no more can't I, I said, and think of poor Albert,
He's been in the army four years, he wants a good time,
And if you don't give it him, there's others will, I said.
Oh is there, she said. Something o' that, I said.   150
Then I'll know who to thank, she said, and give me a straight
    look.

---

[33]Slang for "demobilized" from the army after
  World War I.

[34]Announcement by the "pub" bartender that
  it is closing time.

HURRY UP PLEASE ITS TIME
If you don't like it you can get on with it, I said.
Others can pick and choose if you can't.   155
But if Albert makes off, it won't be for lack of telling.
You ought to be ashamed, I said, to look so antique.
(And her only thirty-one.)
I can't help it, she said, pulling a long face,
It's them pills I took, to bring it off, she said.   160
(She's had five already, and nearly died of young George.)
The chemist[35] said it would be all right, but I've never been the
    same.
You are a proper fool, I said.
Well, if Albert won't leave you alone, there it is, I said,   165
What you get married for if you don't want children?
HURRY UP PLEASE ITS TIME
Well, that Sunday Albert was home, they had a hot gammon,[36]
And they asked me in to dinner, to get the beauty of it hot—
HURRY UP PLEASE ITS TIME   170
HURRY UP PLEASE ITS TIME
Goonight Bill. Goonight Lou. Goonight May. Goonight.
Ta ta. Goonight. Goonight.
Good night, ladies, good night, sweet ladies, good night, good
    night.[37]   175

III. The Fire Sermon[38]

The river's tent is broken: the last fingers of leaf
Clutch and sink into the wet bank. The wind
Crosses the brown land, unheard. The nymphs are departed.
Sweet Thames, run softly, till I end my song.[39]
The river bears no empty bottles, sandwich papers,   180
Silk handkerchiefs, cardboard boxes, cigarette ends
Or other testimony of summer nights. The nymphs are departed.
And their friends, the loitering heirs of city directors;

[35]Druggist.
[36]Ham or the lower end of a side of bacon; suggestively, thigh.
[37]Alludes to both Ophelia's words before drowning herself, *Hamlet*, IV. v. 72 and to a popular song "Good night ladies, we're going to leave you now."
[38]The title of this section is especially evocative. It serves as a kind of rubric for the various scenes of lust, past and present, which follow, and it anticipates the express references to Buddha's *Fire Sermon* and St. Augustine's *Confessions* in the concluding

lines and in Eliot's notes to those lines (310–12). Given the accurate London geography of the poem and the fact that *The Waste Land* began as, and to some extent remains, a poem about London in the Dryden vein, it is worth noting that overlooking the scenes mentioned, especially in lines 262–268, is the imposing Monument to the Great Fire of London of 1666.
[39]The refrain of Edmund Spenser's *Prothalamion*, a late sixteenth-century celebration of marriage in the then pastoral setting along the Thames River near London.

Departed, have left no addresses.
By the waters of Leman I sat down and wept . . .[40]   185
Sweet Thames, run softly till I end my song,
Sweet Thames, run softly, for I speak not loud or long.
But at my back in a cold blast I hear[41]
The rattle of the bones, and chuckle spread from ear to ear.
A rat crept softly through the vegetation   190
Dragging its slimy belly on the bank
While I was fishing in the dull canal
On a winter evening round behind the gashouse
Musing upon the king my brother's wreck[42]
And on the king my father's death before him.   195
White bodies naked on the low damp ground
And bones cast in a little low dry garret,
Rattled by the rat's foot only, year to year.
But at my back from time to time I hear
The sound of horns and motors, which shall bring   200
Sweeney to Mrs. Porter in the spring.[43]
O the moon shone bright on Mrs. Porter
And on her daughter
They wash their feet in soda water[44]
Et O ces voix d'enfants, chantant dans la coupole![45]   205

Twit twit twit
Jug jug jug jug jug jug
So rudely forc'd.
Tereu[46]
Unreal City   210
Under the brown fog of a winter noon
Mr. Eugenides, the Smyrna merchant
Unshaven, with a pocket full of currants

[40]In Psalms 137:1 the exiled Jews express their longing for home: "By the rivers of Babylon, there we sat down, yea, we wept, when we remembered Zion." Eliot largely finished the poem at Lake Leman, as Lake Geneva is also called, at a sanatorium where he had gone for care.

[41]Lines 188 and 199 allude to Andrew Marvell's "To His Coy Mistress," lines 21–24.

[42]An allusion, again, to *The Tempest*. Ferdinand, believing his father dead, is "Sitting on a bank,/ Weeping again the King my father's wreck," I., ii. 389–90.

[43]Eliot's note quotes the relevant lines from John Day's *Parliament of Bees*: "When of a sudden, listening, you shall hear, A noise of horns and hunting, which shall bring/ Actaeon to Diana in the spring/ Where all shall see her naked skin . . ." As a punishment for thus seeing the goddess of chastity naked, Actaeon was changed into a stag, hunted, and killed.

[44]Eliot here uses some sanitized lines from a bawdy song of World War I, which actually was a parody of the popular ballad, "Little Redwing."

[45]Eliot's note calls attention to Paul Verlaine's sonnet, "Parsifal," the last line of which goes, "And O those children singing in the choir." The feet of Parsifal, in Wagner's opera, are washed before he enters the sanctuary. The children are singing at the ceremony. In Verlaine's poem, there are sexual implications.

[46]See Notes 31, 32.

C.i.f.[47] London: documents at sight,
Asked me in demotic French   215
To luncheon at the Cannon Street Hotel
Followed by a weekend at the Metropole.[48]

At the violet hour, when the eyes and back
Turn upward from the desk, when the human engine waits
Like a taxi throbbing waiting,   220
I Tiresias,[49] though blind, throbbing between two lives.
Old man with wrinkled female breasts, can see
At the violet hour, the evening hour that strives
Homeward, and brings the sailor home from sea,
The typist home at teatime, clears her breakfast, lights   225
Her stove, and lays out food in tins.
Out of the window perilously spread
Her drying combinations touched by the sun's last rays,
On the divan are piled (at night her bed)
Stockings, slippers, camisoles, and stays.   230
I Tiresias, old man with wrinkled dugs
Perceived the scene, and foretold the rest—
I too awaited the expected guest.
He, the young man carbuncular, arrives,
A small house agent's clerk, with one bold stare,   235
One of the low on whom assurance sits
As a silk hat on a Bradford[50] millionaire.
The time is now propitious, as he guesses,
The meal is ended, she is bored and tired,
Endeavours to engage her in caresses   240
Which still are unreproved, if undesired.
Flushed and decided, he assaults at once;
Exploring hands encounter no defence;

---

[47]Eliot's explanation, "carriage and insurance free to London," has been corrected by Mrs. Valerie Eliot to "cost, insurance and freight."

[48]The Cannon Street Hotel is a commercial hotel in that area of the City, the Metropole, a hotel in Brighton popular for assignations.

[49]Eliot's note: "Tiresias, although a mere spectator and not indeed a 'character,' is yet the most important personage in the poem, uniting all the rest. Just as the one-eyed merchant, seller of currants, melts into the Phoenician Sailor, and the latter is not wholly distinct from Ferdinand Prince of Naples, so all the women are one woman, and the two sexes meet in Tiresias. What Tiresias *sees*, in fact is the substance of the poem. The whole passage from Ovid is of great anthropological interest." The Latin passage that is quoted may be summarized as follows: Tiresias saw two snakes copulating, separated them and became a woman; after seven years he saw the same sight, again separated them, became a man again. When Jove and Juno disputed whether more pleasure in love was enjoyed by male or female, they referred the question to Tiresias, who said women. Juno in her anger blinded him, but Jove, unable to undo her action, gave him the power of infallible divination.

[50]A manufacturing town in Yorkshire, England, noted for the rapid fortunes made during World War I.

His vanity requires no response,
And makes a welcome of indifference.   245
(And I Tiresias have foresuffered all
Enacted on this same divan or bed;
I who have sat by Thebes below the wall
And walked among the lowest of the dead.)[51]
Bestows one final patronizing kiss,   250
And gropes his way, finding the stairs unlit . . .

She turns and looks a moment in the glass,
Hardly aware of her departed lover;
Her brain allows one half-formed thought to pass:
"Well now that's done: and I'm glad it's over."   255
When lovely woman stoops to folly and
Paces about her room again, alone,
She smoothes her hair with automatic hand,
And puts a record on the gramophone.[52]
"This music crept by me upon the waters"[53]   260
And along the Strand, up Queen Victoria Street.
O City city, I can sometimes hear
Beside a public bar in Lower Thames Street,
The pleasant whining of a mandoline
And a clatter and a chatter from within   265
Where fishmen lounge at noon: where the walls
Of Magnus Martyr hold
Inexplicable splendour of Ionian white and gold.[54]

The river sweats[55]
Oil and tar   270
The barges drift
With the turning tide
Red sails
Wide
To leeward, swing on the heavy spar.   275
The barges wash
Drifting logs

---

[51]The site of Tiresias' prophecies and of his witnessing the fate of Oedipus and Creon.

[52]Eliot's note refers to the song in Goldsmith's *The Vicar of Wakefield*: "When lovely woman stoops to folly/ And finds too late that men betray/ What charm can sooth her melancholy,/ What art can wash her guilt away?/ The only art her guilt to cover,/ To hide her shame from every eye,/ To give repentance to her lover/ And wring his bosom—is to die."

[53]An exact quotation from Ariel's song of transformation in *The Tempest*, I. ii. 391.

[54]Eliot's note: "The interior of St Magnus Martyr is to my mind one of the finest among Wren's interiors." Nearby the Billingsgate Fishmarket and across the street from "The Cock," "where fishmen lounge at noon," it was known as the "Fishmen's Church."

[55]Eliot's note: "The Song of the (three) Thames-daughters begins here. From line 295 to 309 inclusive they speak in turn. V. *Götterdämmerung*, III, i: the Rhine-daughters."

Down Greenwich reach
Past the Isle of Dogs.
      Weialala leia   280
      Wallala leialala

Elizabeth and Leicester[56]
Beating oars
The stern was formed
A gilded shell   285
Red and gold
The brisk swell
Rippled both shores
Southwest wind
Carried down stream   290
The peal of bells
White towers
      Weialala leia
      Wallala leialala

      "Trams and dusty trees.   295
Highbury bore me. Richmond and Kew
Undid me. By Richmond I raised my knees
Supine on the floor of a narrow canoe."

      "My feet are at Moorgate,[57] and my heart
Under my feet. After the event   300
He wept. He promised 'a new start.'
I made no comment. What should I resent?"

      "On Margate Sands.[58]
I can connect
Nothing with nothing.   305
The broken fingernails of dirty hands.
My people humble people who expect
Nothing."
         la la

To Carthage then I came[59]   310

---

[56]A reference to the fruitless love affair of Queen Elizabeth and the Earl of Leicester, referred to in Eliot's note.

[57]Highbury, Richmond, Kew, and Moorgate are all areas in or around London.

[58]A resort on the sea where Eliot, suffering from stress, spent a short period before going to the sanatorium on Lake Geneva.

[59]The last five lines of "The Fire Sermon" Eliot virtually instructs the reader to consider together. Of line 310 he quotes St. Augustine's Confessions, "to Carthage then I came, where a cauldron of unholy love sang all about my ears." Of line 311, he points to "The complete text of the Buddha's Fire Sermon (which corresponds in importance to the Sermon on the Mount) from which these words are taken...." Of line 312, after citing *Confessions* again, "The collocation of these two representatives of eastern and western asceticism, as the culmination of this part of the poem, is not an accident."

Burning burning burning burning
O Lord Thou pluckest me out
O Lord Thou pluckest

burning

IV. Death by Water[60]

Phlebas the Phoenician, a fortnight dead,   315
Forgot the cry of gulls, and the deep sea swell
And the profit and loss.
                          A current under sea
Picked his bones in whispers. As he rose and fell
He passed the stages of his age and youth   320
Entering the whirlpool.
                          Gentile or Jew
O you who turn the wheel and look to windward,
Consider Phlebas, who was once handsome and tall as you.

V. What the Thunder Said[61]

After the torchlight red on sweaty faces   325
After the frosty silence in the gardens
After the agony in stony places
The shouting and the crying
Prison and palace and reverberation
Of thunder of spring over distant mountains   330
He who was living is now dead
We who were living are now dying
With a little patience[62]

Here is no water but only rock
Rock and no water and the sandy road   335
The road winding above among the mountains
Which are mountains of rock without water
If there were water we should stop and drink
Amongst the rock one cannot stop or think

[60]There is no consensus as to whether this short section, drastically cut by Ezra Pound, is in anticipation of rebirth or annihilation. Interestingly, it is translated from the concluding lines of Eliot's "Dans le Restaurant," written in French.

[61]Eliot's note: "In the first part of Part V three themes are employed: the journey to Emmaus, the approach to the Chapel Perilous (see Miss Weston's book) and the present decay of eastern Europe." See lines 363, 391, 372, respectively.

[62]Lines 325–333 allude to Christ's travail in the gardens of Gethsemane and Golgotha—but also to that of the other slain gods of anthropology through whom new life was invoked.

Sweat is dry and feet are in the sand 340
If there were only water amongst the rock
Dead mountain mouth of carious teeth that cannot spit
Here one can neither stand nor lie nor sit
There is not even silence in the mountains
But dry sterile thunder without rain 345
There is not even solitude in the mountains
But red sullen faces sneer and snarl
From doors of mudcracked houses
     If there were water
And no rock 350
If there were rock
And also water
And water
A spring
A pool among the rock 355
If there were the sound of water only
Not the cicada
And dry grass singing
But sound of water over a rock
Where the hermit-thrush sings in the pine trees 360
Drip drop drip drop drop drop drop
But there is no water
Who is the third who walks always beside you?
When I count, there are only you and I together
But when I look ahead up the white road 365
There is always another one walking beside you
Gliding wrapt in a brown mantle, hooded
I do not know whether a man or a woman
—But who is that on the other side of you?
What is that sound high in the air 370
Murmur of maternal lamentation
Who are those hooded hordes swarming
Over endless plains, stumbling in cracked earth
Ringed by the flat horizon only
What is the city over the mountains 375
Cracks and reforms and bursts in the violet air
Falling towers
Jerusalem Athens Alexandria
Vienna London
Unreal 380

A woman drew her long black hair out tight
And fiddled whisper music on those strings
And bats with baby faces in the violet light
Whistled, and beat their wings

And crawled head downward down a blackened wall   385
And upside down in air were towers
Tolling reminiscent bells, that kept the hours
And voices singing out of empty cisterns and exhausted wells.

In this decayed hole among the mountains
In the faint moonlight, the grass is singing   390
Over the tumbled graves, about the chapel
There is the empty chapel, only the wind's home.
It has no windows, and the door swings,
Dry bones can harm no one.
Only a cock stood on the rooftree   395
Co co rico co co rico[63]
In a flash of lightning. Then a damp gust
Bringing rain
Ganga[64] was sunken, and the limp leaves
Waited for rain, while the black clouds   400
Gathered far distant, over Himavant.[65]
The jungle crouched, humped in silence.
Then spoke the thunder
DA[66]
Datta: what have we given?   405
My friend, blood shaking my heart
The awful daring of a moment's surrender
Which an age of prudence can never retract
By this, and this only, we have existed
Which is not to be found in our obituaries   410
Or in memories draped by the beneficent spider[67]
Or under seals broken by the lean solicitor
In our empty rooms
DA
Dayadhvam: I have heard the key[68]   415
Turn in the door once and turn once only
We think of the key, each in his prison
Thinking of the key, each confirms a prison
Only at nightfall, aethereal rumours

[63]In folklore, the cock's crow was thought to indicate the departure of ghosts. In Matthew, as Christ has predicted, Peter denies him three times before the cock crows.
[64]The Ganges River in India is sacred to Hindus, a place of purification.
[65]A Himalayan mountain.
[66]Eliot's note: "'DaTa, dayadhvam, damyata' (Give, sympathise, control)." With this introduction of the onomatopoetic Sanskrit, the density of allusion, only partially accommodated in these footnotes for reasons of space and clarity of progression, seems to intensify.
[67]Eliot's note refers to Webster's *The White Devil:* "they'll remarry/ Ere the worm pierce your winding-sheet, ere the spider/ Make a thin curtain for your epitaphs."
[68]Eliot's note refers to Dante's Ugolino in *Inferno*, XXXIII, 46 starved to death in the locked tower and to F. H. Bradley's postulation that "my experience falls within my own circle.... the whole world for each is peculiar and private to that soul."

Revive for a moment a broken Coriolanus[69]   420
DA
Damyata: The boat responded
Gaily, to the hand expert with sail and oar
The sea was calm, your heart would have responded
Gaily, when invited, beating obedient   425
To controlling hands

                    I sat upon the shore
Fishing,[70] with the arid plain behind me
Shall I at least set my lands in order?
London Bridge is falling down falling down falling down   430
Poi s'ascose nel foco che gli affina[71]
Quando fiam uti chelidon[72]—O swallow swallow
Le Prince d'Aquitaine à la tour abolie[73]
These fragments I have shored against my ruins
Why then Ile fit you. Hieronymo's mad againe.[74]   435
Datta, Dayadhvam. Damyata.
    Shantih   shantih   shantih[75]

                                          1922

The Dry Salvages

(The Dry Salvages—presumably *les trois sauvages*—is a small group of rocks, with a beacon, off the N.E. coast of Cape Ann, Massachusetts. *Salvages* is pronounced to rhyme with *assuages*. *Groaner:* a whistling buoy.)

---

[69]Coriolanus, threatened with banishment from Rome, chose exile, and, although he tried to return, was eventually "broken." Shakespeare's *Coriolanus* deals with his tragedy.

[70]Eliot's note directs the reader to Weston's "chapter on the Fisher King." The king in the Grail legends typically lived on a river or seashore. Fish is a fertility or life symbol. This meaning was often forgotten, however, and the title of the Fisher King in medieval romances was accounted for by describing him as fishing.

[71]"Then he hid himself in the fire that refines them." Eliot's note refers to *Purgatorio,* XXVI, 145–48, where the poet Arnaut Daniel, remembering his lechery, speaks this line.

[72]"When shall I be like the swallow?" Eliot's note refers to the Latin poem, *Pervigilium Veneris,* with its echo of Philomela, recalling the idea of finding a voice through suffering. In this anonymous poem, the myth is imaged in the swallow. "O Swallow, Swallow" appears in one of the songs in Tennyson's "The Princess."

[73]"The Prince of Aquitaine in the ruined tower" is from Gérard de Nerval's sonnet *"El Desdichado"* ("The Disinherited One").

[74]When Hieronymo in Thomas Kyd's play, *The Spanish Tragedy, Hieronymo's Mad Againe* (1594), is asked to write a court play, he replies, "I'll fit [supply] you." Through the play, despite his madness, he is able to revenge himself on the murderers of his son in a pattern similar to that of *Hamlet.*

[75]Eliot's note: "Shantih. Repeated as here, a formal ending to an Upanishad [sacred Hindu text]. 'The Peace which passeth understanding' is our equivalent to this word."

I

I do not know much about gods; but I think that the river
Is a strong brown god—sullen, untamed and intractable,
Patient to some degree, at first recognised as a frontier;
Useful, untrustworthy, as a conveyor of commerce;
Then only a problem confronting the builder of bridges.   5
The problem once solved, the brown god is almost forgotten
By the dwellers in cities—ever, however, implacable,
Keeping his seasons and rages, destroyer, reminder
Of what men choose to forget. Unhonoured, unpropitiated
By worshippers of the machine, but waiting, watching and waiting.   10
His rhythm was present in the nursery bedroom,
In the rank ailanthus of the April dooryard,[1]
In the smell of grapes on the autumn table,
And the evening circle in the winter gaslight.

The river is within us, the sea is all about us;   15
The sea is the land's edge also, the granite
Into which it reaches, the beaches where it tosses
Its hints of earlier and other creation:
The starfish, the horseshoe crab, the whale's backbone;
The pools where it offers to our curiosity   20
The more delicate algae and the sea anemone.
It tosses up our losses, the torn seine,
The shattered lobsterpot, the broken oar
And the gear of foreign dead men. The sea has many voices,
Many gods and many voices.   25
                    The salt is on the briar rose,
The fog is in the fir trees.
                  The sea howl
And the sea yelp, are different voices
Often together heard: the whine in the rigging,   30
The menace and caress of wave that breaks on water,
The distant rote in the granite teeth,
And the wailing warning from the approaching headland
Are all sea voices, and the heaving groaner
Rounded homewards, and the seagull: 35
And under the oppression of the silent fog
The tolling bell
Measures time not our time, rung by the unhurried
Ground swell, a time

---

[1]Here and in lines 36 and 48, Eliot alludes to Whitman's "When Lilacs Last in the Dooryard Bloom'd." These echoes of the clanging bells and the April dooryard have been seen as effecting "a reconciliation with Whitman and America—a kind of homecoming," with Eliot discovering poetically "the home key at last, the right relation of the personal and the primitive, of the natural and the human orders."

Older than the time of chronometers, older   40
Than time counted by anxious worried women
Lying awake, calculating the future,
Trying to unweave, unwind, unravel
And piece together the past and the future,
Between midnight and dawn, when the past is all deception,   45
The future futureless, before the morning watch
When time stops and time is never ending;
And the ground swell, that is and was from the beginning,
Clangs
The bell.   50

II

Where is there an end of it, the soundless wailing,
The silent withering of autumn flowers
Dropping their petals and remaining motionless;
Where is there an end to the drifting wreckage,
The prayer of the bone on the beach, the unprayable   55
Prayer at the calamitous annunciation?

There is no end, but addition: the trailing
consequence of further days and hours,
While emotion takes to itself the emotionless
Years of living among the breakage   60
Of what was believed in as the most reliable—
And therefore the fittest for renunciation.

There is the final addition, the failing
Pride or resentment at failing powers,
The unattached devotion which might pass for devotionless,   65
In a drifting boat with a slow leakage,
The silent listening to the undeniable
Clamour of the bell of the last annunciation.

Where is the end of them, the fishermen sailing
Into the wind's tail, where the fog cowers?   70
We cannot think of a time that is oceanless
Or of an ocean not littered with wastage
Or of a future that is not liable
Like the past, to have no destination.

We have to think of them as forever bailing,   75
Setting and hauling, while the North East lowers
Over shallow banks unchanging and erosionless
Or drawing their money, drying sails at dockage;

Not as making a trip that will be unpayable
For a haul that will not bear examination.   80

There is no end of it, the voiceless wailing,
No end to the withering of withered flowers,
To the movement of pain that is painless and motionless,
To the drift of the sea and the drifting wreckage,
The bone's prayer to Death its God. Only the hardly, barely   85
    prayable
Prayer of the one Annunciation.

It seems, as one becomes older,
That the past has another pattern, and ceases to be a mere
    sequence—   90
Or even development: the latter a partial fallacy
Encouraged by superficial notions of evolution,
Which becomes, in the popular mind, a means of disowning the
    past.
The moments of happiness—not the sense of well-being,   95
Fruition, fulfilment, security or affection,
Or even a very good dinner, but the sudden illumination—
We had the experience but missed the meaning,
And approach to the meaning restores the experience
In a different form, beyond any meaning   100
We can assign to happiness. I have said before
That the past experience revived in the meaning
Is not the experience of one life only
But of many generations—not forgetting
Something that is probably quite ineffable: 105
The backward look behind the assurance
Of recorded history, the backward half-look
Over the shoulder, towards the primitive terror.
Now, we come to discover that the moments of agony
(Whether, or not, due to misunderstanding,   110
Having hoped for the wrong things or dreaded the wrong things,
Is not in question) are likewise permanent
With such permanence as time has. We appreciate this better
In the agony of others, nearly experienced,
Involving ourselves, than in our own.   115
For our own past is covered by the currents of action,
But the torment of others remains an experience
Unqualified, unworn by subsequent attrition.
People change, and smile: but the agony abides.
Time the destroyer is time the preserver,   120
Like the river with its cargo of dead negroes, cows and chicken
    coops,

The bitter apple and the bite in the apple.
And the ragged rock in the restless waters,
Waves wash over it, fogs conceal it;   125
On a halcyon day it is merely a monument,
In navigable weather it is always a seamark
To lay a course by: but in the sombre season
Or the sudden fury, is what it always was.

III

I sometimes wonder if that is what Krishna meant—   130
Among other things—or one way of putting the same thing:
That the future is a faded song, a Royal Rose or a lavender spray
Of wistful regret for those who are not yet here to regret,
Pressed between yellow leaves of a book that has never been
    opened.   135
And the way up is the way down, the way forward is the way
    back.
You cannot face it steadily, but this thing is sure,
That time is no healer: the patient is no longer here.
When the train starts, and the passengers are settled   140
To fruit, periodicals and business letters
(And those who saw them off have left the platform)
Their faces relax from grief into relief,
To the sleepy rhythm of a hundred hours.
Fare forward, travellers! not escaping from the past   145
Into different lives, or into any future;
You are not the same people who left that station
Or who will arrive at any terminus,
While the narrowing rails slide together behind you;
And on the deck of the drumming liner   150
Watching the furrow that widens behind you,
You shall not think 'the past is finished'
Or 'the future is before us'.
At nightfall, in the rigging and the aerial,
Is a voice descanting (though not to the ear,   155
The murmuring shell of time, and not in any language)
'Fare forward, you who think that you are voyaging;
You are not those who saw the harbour
Receding, or those who will disembark.
Here between the hither and the farther shore   160
While time is withdrawn, consider the future
And the past with an equal mind.
At the moment which is not of action or inaction
You can receive this: "on whatever sphere of being
The mind of a man may be intent   165

At the time of death"—that is the one action
(And the time of death is every moment)
Which shall fructify in the lives of others:
And do not think of the fruit of action.
Fare forward.   170
                    O voyagers, O seamen,
You who come to port, and you whose bodies
Will suffer the trial and judgement of the sea
Or whatever event, this is your real destination.'
So Krishna, as when he admonished Arjuna   175
On the field of battle.[2]
                    Not fare well,
But fare forward, voyagers.

IV

Lady, whose shrine stands on the promontory,
Pray for all those who are in ships, those   180
Whose business has to do with fish, and
Those concerned with every lawful traffic
And those who conduct them.

Repeat a prayer also on behalf of
Women who have seen their sons or husbands   185
Setting forth, and not returning:
Figlia del tuo figlio,[3]
Queen of Heaven.

Also pray for those who were in ships, and
Ended their voyage on the sand, in the sea's lips   190
Or in the dark throat which will not reject them
Or wherever cannot reach them the sound of the sea bell's
Perpetual angelus.

V

To communicate with Mars, converse with spirits,
To report the behaviour of the sea monster,   195
Describe the horoscope, haruspicate or scry,
Observe disease in signatures, evoke
Biography from the wrinkles of the palm
And tragedy from fingers; release omens
By sortilege, or tea leaves, riddle the inevitable   200

---

[2]Krishna, one of the principal Hindu gods,   [3]The daughter of Thy Son.
thus admonishes the hero of the *Bhagavad-
Gita* "on the field of battle."

With playing cards, fiddle with pentagrams
Or barbituric acids, or dissect
The recurrent image into pre-conscious terrors—
To explore the womb, or tomb, or dreams; all these are usual
Pastimes and drugs, and features of the press: 205
And always will be, some of them especially
When there is distress of nations and perplexity
Whether on the shores of Asia, or in the Edgware Road.
Men's curiosity searches past and future
And clings to that dimension. But to apprehend   210
The point of intersection of the timeless
With time, is an occupation for the saint—
No occupation either, but something given
And taken, in a lifetime's death in love,
Ardour and selflessness and self-surrender.   215
For most of us, there is only the unattended
Moment, the moment in and out of time,
The distraction fit, lost in a shaft of sunlight,
The wild thyme unseen, or the winter lightning
Or the waterfall, or music heard so deeply   220
That it is not heard at all, but you are the music
While the music lasts. These are only hints and guesses,
Hints followed by guesses; and the rest
Is prayer, observance, discipline, thought and action.
The hint half guessed, the gift half understood, is Incarnation.   225
Here the impossible union
Of spheres of existence is actual,
Here the past and future
Are conquered, and reconciled,
Where action were otherwise movement   230
Of that which is only moved
And has in it no source of movement—
Driven by dæmonic, chthonic
Powers. And right action is freedom
From past and future also.   235
For most of us, this is the aim
Never here to be realised;
Who are only undefeated
Because we have gone on trying;
We, content at the last   240
If our temporal reversion nourish
(Not too far from the yew-tree)
The life of significant soil.

                                                                          1941

F. SCOTT FITZGERALD
1896–1940

When F. Scott Fitzgerald was born in St. Paul, Minnesota, on September 24, 1896, he was named after Frances Scott Key, a relative on his father's side and the author of the National Anthem. Fitzgerald's parents had great pride in his father's ancestry, but their financial stability came from his mother's side of wealthy Irish merchants. "I am half...Irish and half old American stock with the usual exaggerated ancestral pretensions," Fitzgerald told John O'Hara in a 1933 letter. The "Irish half of the family had the money and looked down upon the Maryland side of the family who had, and really had, that certain series of reticences and obligations that go under the poor old shattered word 'breeding.'" Although well-bred, Fitzgerald's father suffered a series of business catastrophes that resulted in his financial dependence upon his wife's family. The most devastating of these failures was his father's losing his job at Proctor & Gamble in 1908.

Vowing to have a different fate than his father, Fitzgerald sought to make his mark with writing. He started at the Newman School, a preparatory school in New Jersey, where he published his first story. Pursuing his literary ambitions at Princeton University, he neglected his studies to write for the Triangle Club, the *Princeton Tiger*, and *Nassau Literary Magazine*. With little hopes of graduating, Fitzgerald joined the army in 1917, commissioning as a second lieutenant. As an army officer, he continued writing, completing a novel called "The Romantic Egoist."

In 1918, while stationed at Camp Sheridan, Fitzgerald met and fell in love with Zelda Sayre, the daughter of an Alabama Supreme Court judge. After the war ended and he was discharged, he took a job with the Barron Collier advertising agency in New York, but Zelda was not satisfied with his financial prospects and broke off their engagement. In an attempt to win her back, Fitzgerald quit his job and returned to St. Paul to revise "The Romantic Egoist." It became *This Side of Paradise*, which Scribners published in 1920. With the publication of *This Side of Paradise*, Fitzgerald's earnings jumped; in April of that same year, he and Zelda were married. They became instant celebrities with tumultuous, public lives.

Fitzgerald's literary career took off after the stunning debut of his first novel. In addition to his subsequent novels—*The Beautiful and Damned*, *The Great Gatsby*, *Tender Is the Night*, and *The Last Tycoon*—Fitzgerald wrote short stories for widely read periodicals like *The Saturday Evening Post* and *Esquire* to support his extravagant lifestyle. Collectively, these works depict how America was changing in the 1920s, characterizing the Jazz Age that Fitzgerald named and came to personify. Fitzgerald not only glamorized the era's excesses of consumer culture, he also critiqued them. "All the stories that came into my head had a touch of disaster in them," he insisted, "the lovely young creatures in my novels went to ruin, the diamond mountains of my short stories blew up, [and] my millionaires were as beautiful and damned as Thomas Hardy's peasants."

"Babylon Revisited" explores the quest for dignity in the face of disaster, a fitting subject during the Great Depression. Like Charlie Wales, Fitzgerald had to piece his life together after a series of personal and professional failures. Despite Fitzgerald's admission that "I had been only a mediocre caretaker of most of the things left in my hands, even of my talent," he succeeded in making his literary mark. Today Fitzgerald is among the most-read American authors, compelling generations of readers to consider, in the words of *The Great Gatsby*'s narrator, Nick Carraway, "the last and greatest of all human dreams."

Lauren Rule Maxwell
The Citadel

PRIMARY WORKS

This Side of Paradise, 1920; *Flappers and Philosophers*, 1921; *The Beautiful and Damned*, 1922; *Tales of the Jazz Age*, 1922; *The Vegetable or from President to Postman*, 1923; *The Great Gatsby*, 1925; *All the Sad Young Men*, 1926; *Tender Is the Night*, 1934; *Taps at Reveille*, 1935; *The Last Tycoon*, ed. by Edmund Wilson, 1941; *The Crack-Up*, ed. by Edmund Wilson, 1945; *Correspondence of F. Scott Fitzgerald*, ed. by Matthew J. Bruccoli and Margaret M. Duggan, 1980; *The Short Stories*, ed. Matthew J. Bruccoli, 1989; *A Life in Letters*, ed. Matthew J. Bruccoli, 1994; *Trimalchio: An Early Version of* The Great Gatsby, ed. James L. W. West III, 2000.

Babylon Revisited

"And where's Mr. Campbell?" Charlie asked.

"Gone to Switzerland. Mr. Campbell's a pretty sick man, Mr. Wales."

"I'm sorry to hear that. And George Hardt?" Charlie inquired.

"Back in America, gone to work."

"And where is the Snow Bird?"

"He was in here last week. Anyway, his friend, Mr. Schaeffer, is in Paris."

Two familiar names from the long list of a year and a half ago. Charlie scribbled an address in his notebook and tore out the page.

"If you see Mr. Schaeffer, give him this," he said. "It's my brother-in-law's address. I haven't settled in a hotel yet."

He was not really disappointed to find Paris so empty. But the stillness in the Ritz bar was strange and portentous. It was not an American bar any more—he felt polite in it, and not as if he owned it. It had gone back into France. He felt the stillness from the moment he got out of the taxi and saw the doorman, usually in a frenzy of activity at this hour, gossiping with a *chasseur*[1] by the servants' entrance.

Passing through the corridor, he heard only a single, bored voice in the once-clamorous women's room. When he turned into the bar he travelled the twenty feet of green carpet with his eyes fixed straight ahead by old habit; and then, with his foot firmly on the rail, he turned and surveyed the room, encountering only a single pair of eyes that fluttered up from a

[1]French: "porter."

newspaper in the corner. Charlie asked for the head barman, Paul, who in the latter days of the bull market had come to work in his own custom-built car—disembarking, however, with due nicety at the nearest corner. But Paul was at his country house today and Alix giving him information.

"No, no more," Charlie said, "I'm going slow these days."

Alix congratulated him: "You were going pretty strong a couple of years ago."

"I'll stick to it all right," Charlie assured him. "I've stuck to it for over a year and a half now."

"How do you find conditions in America?"

"I haven't been to America for months. I'm in business in Prague, representing a couple of concerns there. They don't know about me down there."

Alix smiled.

"Remember the night of George Hardt's bachelor dinner here?" said Charlie. "By the way, what's become of Claude Fessenden?"

Alix lowered his voice confidentially, "He's in Paris, but he doesn't come here any more. Paul doesn't allow it. He ran up a bill of thirty thousand francs, charging all his drinks and his lunches, and usually his dinner, for more than a year. And when Paul finally told him he had to pay, he gave him a bad check."

Alix shook his head sadly.

"I don't understand it, such a dandy fellow. Now he's all bloated up—" He made a plump apple of his hands.

Charlie watched a group of strident queens installing themselves in a corner.

"Nothing affects them," he thought. "Stocks rise and fall, people loaf or work, but they go on forever." The place oppressed him. He called for the dice and shook with Alix for the drink.

"Here for long, Mr. Wales?"

"I'm here for four or five days to see my little girl."

"Oh-h! You have a little girl?"

Outside, the fire-red, gas blue, ghost-green signs shone smokily through the tranquil rain. It was late afternoon and the streets were in movement; the *bistros* gleamed. At the corner of the Boulevard des Capucines he took a taxi. The Place de la Concorde moved by in pink majesty; they crossed the logical Seine, and Charlie felt the sudden provincial quality of the Left Bank.

Charlie directed his taxi to the Avenue de l'Opera, which was out of his way. But he wanted to see the blue hour spread over the magnificent façade, and imagine that the cab horns, playing endlessly the first few bars of *La Plus que Lente*, were the trumpets of the Second Empire. They were closing the iron grill in front of Brentano's Book-store, and people were already at dinner behind the trim little bourgeois hedge of Duval's. He had never eaten at a really cheap restaurant in Paris. Five-course dinner, four francs fifty, eighteen cents, wine included. For some odd reason he wished that he had.

As they rolled to the Left Bank and he felt its sudden provincialism, he thought, "I spoiled this city for myself. I didn't realize it, but the days came along one after another, and then two years were gone, and everything was gone, and I was gone."

He was thirty-five, and good to look at. The Irish mobility of his face was sobered by a deep wrinkle between his eyes. As he rang his brother-in-law's bell in the Rue Palatine, the wrinkle deepened till it pulled down his brows; he felt a cramping sensation in his belly. From behind the maid who opened the door darted a lovely little girl of nine who shrieked "Daddy!" and flew up, struggling like a fish, into his arms. She pulled his head around by one ear and set her cheek against his.

"My old pie," he said.

"Oh, daddy, daddy, daddy, daddy, dads, dads, dads!"

She drew him into the salon where the family waited, a boy and girl his daughter's age, his sister-in-law and her husband. He greeted Marion with his voice pitched carefully to avoid either feigned enthusiasm or dislike, but her response was more frankly tepid, though she minimized her expression of unalterable distrust by directing her regard toward his child. The two men clasped hands in a friendly way and Lincoln Peters rested his for a moment on Charlie's shoulder.

The room was warm and comfortably American. The three children moved intimately about, playing through the yellow oblongs that led to other rooms; the cheer of six o'clock spoke in the eager smacks of the fire and the sounds of French activity in the kitchen. But Charlie did not relax; his heart sat up rigidly in his body and he drew confidence from his daughter, who from time to time came close to him, holding in her arms the doll he had brought.

"Really extremely well," he declared in answer to Lincoln's question. "There's a lot of business there that isn't moving at all, but we're doing even better than ever. In fact, damn well. I'm bringing my sister over from America next month to keep house for me. My income last year was bigger than it was when I had money. You see, the Czechs—"

His boasting was for a specific purpose; but after a moment, seeing a faint restiveness in Lincoln's eye, he changed the subject:

"Those are fine children of yours, well brought up, good manners."

"We think Honoria's a great little girl too."

Marion Peters came back from the kitchen. She was a tall woman with worried eyes, who had once possessed a fresh American loveliness. Charlie had never been sensitive to it and was always surprised when people spoke of how pretty she had been. From the first there had been an instinctive antipathy between them.

"Well, how do you find Honoria?" she asked.

"Wonderful. I was astonished how much she's grown in ten months. All the children are looking well."

"We haven't had a doctor for a year. How do you like being back in Paris?"

"It seems very funny to see so few Americans around."

"I'm delighted," Marion said vehemently. "Now at least you can go into a store without their assuming you're a millionaire. We've suffered like everybody, but on the whole it's a good deal pleasanter."

"But it was nice while it lasted," Charlie said. "We were sort of royalty, almost infallible, with a sort of magic around us. In the bar this afternoon"—he stumbled, seeing his mistake—"there wasn't a man I knew."

She looked at him keenly. "I should think you'd had enough of bars."

"I only stayed a minute. I take one drink every afternoon, and no more."

"Don't you want a cocktail before dinner?" Lincoln asked.

"I take only one drink every afternoon, and I've had that."

Her dislike was evident in the coldness with which she spoke, but Charlie only smiled; he had larger plans. Her very aggressiveness gave him an advantage, and he knew well enough to wait. He wanted them to initiate the discussion of what they knew had brought him to Paris.

At dinner he couldn't decide whether Honoria was most like him or her mother. Fortunate if she didn't combine the traits of both that had brought them to disaster. A great wave of protectiveness went over him. He thought he knew what to do for her. He believed in character; he wanted to jump back a whole generation and trust in character again as the eternally valuable element. Everything wore out.

He left soon after dinner, but not to go home. He was curious to see Paris by night with clearer and more judicious eyes than those of other days. He bought a *strapontin*[2] for the Casino and watched Josephine Baker[3] go through her chocolate arabesques.

After an hour he left and strolled toward Montmartre, up the Rue Pigalle into the Place Blanche. The rain had stopped and there were a few people in evening clothes disembarking from taxis in front of cabarets, and *cocottes*[4] prowling singly or in pairs, and many Negroes. He passed a lighted door from which issued music, and stopped with the sense of familiarity; it was Bricktop's, where he had parted with so many hours and so much money. A few doors farther on he found another ancient rendezvous and incautiously put his head inside. Immediately an eager orchestra burst into sound, a pair of professional dancers leaped to their feet and a maître d'hôtel swooped toward him, crying, "Crowd just arriving, sir!" But he withdrew quickly.

"You have to be damn drunk," he thought.

Zelli's was closed, the bleak and sinister cheap hotels surrounding it were dark; up the Rue Blanche there was more light and a local, colloquial French crowd. The Poet's Cave had disappeared, but the two great mouths of the Café of Heaven and the Café of Hell still yawned—even devoured, as he watched, the meager contents of a tourist bus—a German, a Japanese, and an American couple who glanced at him with frightened eyes.

So much for the effort and ingenuity of Montmartre. All the catering to vice and waste was on an utterly childish scale, and he suddenly realized the meaning of the word "dissipate"—to dissipate into thin air; to make

---

[2]Folding chair.

[3]Black American entertainer who toured Paris in the 1920s and 1930s.

[4]Prostitutes.

nothing out of something. In the little hours of the night every move from place to place was an enormous human jump, an increase of paying for the privilege of slower and slower motion.

He remembered thousand-franc notes given to an orchestra for playing a single number, hundred-franc notes tossed to a doorman for calling a cab.

But it hadn't been given for nothing.

It had been given, even the most wildly squandered sum, as an offering to destiny that he might not remember the things most worth remembering, the things that now he would always remember—his child taken from his control, his wife escaped to a grave in Vermont.

In the glare of a *brasserie*[5] a woman spoke to him. He bought her some eggs and coffee, and then, eluding her encouraging stare, gave her a twenty-franc note and took a taxi to his hotel.

II

He woke upon a fine fall day—football weather. The depression of yesterday was gone and he liked the people on the streets. At noon he sat opposite Honoria at Le Grant Vatel, the only restaurant he could think of not reminiscent of champagne dinners and long luncheons that began at two and ended in a blurred vague twilight.

"Now, how about vegetables? Oughn't you to have some vegetables?"

"Well, yes."

"Here's *épinards* and *chou-fleur* and carrots and *haricots*."[6]

"I'd like *chou-fleur*."

"Wouldn't you like to have two vegetables?"

"I usually only have one at lunch."

The waiter was pretending to be inordinately fond of children. "*Qu'elle est mignonne la petite! Elle parle exactement comme une Française.*"[7]

How about dessert? Shall we wait and see?"

The waiter disappeared. Honoria looked at her father expectantly.

"What are we going to do?"

"First, we're going to that toy store in the Rue Saint-Honoré and buy you anything you like. And then we're going to the vaudeville at the Empire."

She hesitated. "I like it about the vaudeville, but not the toy store."

"Why not?"

"Well, you brought me this doll." She had it with her. "And I've got lots of things. And we're not rich any more, are we?"

"We never were. But today you are to have anything you want."

"All right," she agreed resignedly.

When there had been her mother and a French nurse he had been inclined to be strict; now he extended himself, reached out for a new

---

[5]Restaurant-bar.
[6]French: "spinach," "cauliflower," "beans."

[7]French: "What a darling little one. She speaks exactly like a French girl."

tolerance; he must be both parents to her and not shut any of her out of communication.

"I want to get to know you," he said gravely. "First let me introduce myself. My name is Charles J. Wales, of Prague."

"Oh daddy!" her voice cracked with laughter.

"And who are you, please?" he persisted, and she accepted a rôle immediately: "Honoria Wales, Rue Palatine, Paris."

"Married or single?"

"No, not married. Single."

He indicated the doll. "But I see you have a child, madame."

Unwilling to disinherit it, she took it to her heart and thought quickly: "Yes, I've been married, but I'm not married now. My husband is dead."

He went on quickly, "And the child's name?"

"Simone. That's after my best friend at school."

"I'm very pleased that you're doing so well at school."

"I'm third this month," she boasted. "Elsie"—that was her cousin—"is only about eighteenth, and Richard is about at the bottom."

"You like Richard and Elsie, don't you?"

"Oh, yes. I like Richard quite well and I like her all right."

Cautiously and casually he asked: "Aunt Marion and Uncle Lincoln—which do you like best?"

"Oh, Uncle Lincoln, I guess."

He was increasingly aware of her presence. As they came in, a murmur of "... adorable" followed them, and now the people at the next table bent all their silences upon her, staring as if she were something no more conscious than a flower.

"Why don't I live with you?" she asked suddenly. "Because mamma's dead?"

"You must stay here and learn more French. It would have been hard for daddy to take care of you so well."

"I don't really need much taking care of any more. I do everything for myself."

Going out of the restaurant, a man and a woman unexpectedly hailed him.

"Well, the old Wales!"

"Hello there, Lorraine.... Dunc."

Sudden ghosts out of the past: Duncan Schaeffer, a friend from college. Lorraine Quarrles, a lovely, pale blonde of thirty; one of a crowd who had helped them make months into days in the lavish times of three years ago.

"My husband couldn't come this year," she said, in answer to his question. "We're poor as hell. So he gave me two hundred a month and told me I could do my worst on that.... This your little girl?"

"What about coming back and sitting down?" Duncan asked.

"Can't do it" He was glad for an excuse. As always, he felt Lorraine's passionate, provocative attraction, but his own rhythm was different now.

"Well, how about dinner?" she asked.

"I'm not free. Give me your address and let me call you."

"Charlie, I believe you're sober," she said judicially. "I honestly believe he's sober, Dunc. Pinch him and see if he's sober."

Charlie indicated Honoria with his head. They both laughed.

"What's your address?" said Duncan skeptically.

He hesitated, unwilling to give the name of his hotel.

"I'm not settled yet. I'd better call you. We're going to see the vaudeville at the Empire."

"There! That's what I want to do," Lorraine said. "I want to see some clowns and acrobats and jugglers. That's just what we'll do, Dunc."

"We've got to do an errand first," said Charlie. "Perhaps we'll see you there."

"All right, you snob.... Good-by, beautiful little girl."

"Good-by."

Honoria bobbed politely.

Somehow, an unwelcomed encounter. They liked him because he was functioning, because he was serious; they wanted to see him, because he was stronger than they were now because they wanted to draw a certain sustenance from his strength.

At the Empire, Honoria proudly refused to sit upon her father's folded coat. She was already an individual with a code of her own, and Charlie was more and more absorbed by the desire of putting a little of himself into her before she crystallized utterly. It was hopeless to try to know her in so short a time.

Between the acts they came upon Duncan and Lorraine in the lobby where the band was playing.

"Have a drink?"

"All right, but not up at the bar. We'll take a table."

"The perfect father."

Listening abstractedly to Lorraine, Charlie watched Honoria's eyes leave their table, and he followed them wistfully about the room, wondering what they saw. He met her glance and she smiled.

"I liked that lemonade," she said.

What had she said? What had he expected? Going home in a taxi afterward, he pulled her over until her head rested against his chest.

"Darling, do you ever think about your mother?"

"Yes, sometimes," she answered vaguely.

"I don't want you to forget her. Have you got a picture of her?"

"Yes, I think so. Anyhow, Aunt Marion has. Why don't you want me to forget her?"

"She loved you very much."

"I loved her too."

They were silent for a moment.

"Daddy, I want to come and live with you," she said suddenly.

His heart leaped; he had wanted it to come like this.

"Aren't you perfectly happy?"

"Yes, but I love you better than anybody. And you love me better than anybody, don't you, now that mummy's dead?"

"Of course I do. But you won't always like me best, honey. You'll grow up and meet somebody your own age and go marry him and forget you ever had a daddy."

"Yes, that's true," she agreed tranquilly.

He didn't go in. He was coming back at nine o'clock and he wanted to keep himself fresh and new for the thing he must say then.

"When you're safe inside, just show yourself in that window."

"All right. Good-by, dads, dads, dads, dads."

He waited in the dark street until she appeared, all warm and glowing, in the window above and kissed her fingers out into the night,

III

They were waiting. Marion sat behind the coffee service in a dignified black dinner dress that just faintly suggested mourning. Lincoln was walking up and down with the animation of one who had already been talking. They were as anxious as he was to get into the question. He opened it almost immediately:

"I suppose you know what I want to see you about—why I really came to Paris."

Marion played with the black stars on her necklace and frowned.

"I'm awfully anxious to have a home," he continued. "And I'm awfully anxious to have Honoria in it. I appreciate your taking in Honoria for her mother's sake, but things have changed now"—he hesitated and then continued more forcibly—"changed radically with me, and I want to ask you to reconsider the matter. It would be silly for me to deny that about three years ago I was acting badly—"

Marion looked up at him with hard eyes.

"—But all that's over. As I told you, I haven't had more than a drink a day for over a year, and I take that drink deliberately, so that the idea of alcohol won't get too big in my imagination. You see the idea?"

"No," said Marion succinctly.

"It's a sort of stunt I set myself. It keeps the matter in proportion."

"I get you," said Lincoln. "You don't want to admit it's got any attraction for you."

"Something like that. Sometimes I forget and don't take it. But I try to take it. Anyhow, I couldn't afford to drink in my position. The people I represent are more than satisfied with what I've done, and I'm bringing my sister over from Burlington to keep house for me, and I want awfully to have Honoria too. You know that even when her mother and I weren't getting along well we never let anything that happened touch Honoria. I know she's fond of me and I know I'm able to take care of her and—well, there you are. How do you feel about it?"

He knew that now he would have to take a beating. It would last an hour or two hours, and it would be difficult but if he modulated his inevitable resentment to the chastened attitude of the reformed sinner, he might win his point in the end.

Keep your temper, he told himself. You don't want to be justified. You want Honoria.

Lincoln spoke first: "We've been talking it over ever since we got your letter last month. We're happy to have Honoria here. She's a dear little thing, and we're glad to be able to help her, but of course that isn't the question—"

Marion interrupted suddenly. "How long are you going to stay sober, Charlie?" she asked.

"Permanently, I hope."

"How can anybody count on that?"

"You know I never did drink heavily until I gave up business and came over here with nothing to do. Then Helen and I began to run around with—"

"Please leave Helen out of it. I can't bear to hear you talk about her like that."

He stared at her grimly; he had never been certain how fond of each other the sisters were in life.

"My drinking only lasted about a year and a half—from the time we came over until I—collapsed."

"It was time enough."

"It was time enough," he agreed.

"My duty is entirely to Helen," she said. "I try to think what she would have wanted me to do. Frankly, from the night you did that terrible thing you haven't really existed for me. I can't help that. She was my sister."

"Yes."

"When she was dying she asked me to look out for Honoria. If you hadn't been in a sanitarium then, it might have helped matters."

He had no answer.

"I'll never in my life be able to forget the morning when Helen knocked at my door, soaked to the skin and shivering, and said you'd locked her out."

Charlie gripped the sides of the chair. This was more difficult than he expected; he wanted to launch out into a long expostulation and explanation, but he only said: "The night I locked her out—" and she interrupted, "I don't feel up to going over that again."

After a moment's silence Lincoln said: "We're getting off the subject. You want Marion to set aside her legal guardianship and give you Honoria. I think the main point for her is whether she has confidence in you or not."

"I don't blame Marion," Charlie said slowly, "but I think she can have entire confidence in me. I had a good record up to three years ago. Of course, it's within human possibilities I might go wrong at any time. But if we wait much longer I'll lose Honoria's childhood and my chance for a home." He shook his head, "I'll simply lose her, don't you see?"

"Yes, I see," said Lincoln.

"Why didn't you think of all this before?" Marion asked.

"I suppose I did, from time to time, but Helen and I were getting along badly. When I consented to the guardianship, I was flat on my back in a sanitarium and the market had cleaned me out. I knew I'd acted badly, and I thought if it would bring any peace to Helen, I'd agree to anything. But now it's different. I'm functioning, I'm behaving damn well, so far as—"

"Please don't swear at me," Marion said.

He looked at her, startled. With each remark the force of her dislike became more and more apparent. She had built up all her fear of life into one wall and faced it toward him. This trivial reproof was possibly the result of some trouble with the cook several hours before. Charlie became increasingly alarmed at leaving Honoria in this atmosphere of hostility against himself; sooner or later it would come out, in a word here, a shake of the head there, and some of that distrust would be irrevocably implanted in Honoria. But he pulled his temper down out of his face and shut it up inside him; he had won a point, for Lincoln realized the absurdity of Marion's remark and asked her lightly since when she had objected to the word "damn."

"Another thing," Charlie said: "I'm able to give her certain advantages now. I'm going to take a French governess to Prague with me. I've got a lease on a new apartment—"

He stopped, realizing that he was blundering. They couldn't be expected to accept with equanimity the fact that his income was again twice as large as their own.

"I suppose you can give her more luxuries than we can," said Marion. "When you were throwing away money we were living along watching every ten francs. . . . I suppose you'll start doing it again."

"Oh, no," he said. "I've learned. I worked hard for ten years, you know—until I got lucky in the market, like so many people. Terribly lucky. It didn't seem any use working any more, so I quit. It won't happen again."

There was a long silence. All of them felt their nerves straining, and for the first time in a year Charlie wanted a drink. He was sure now that Lincoln Peters wanted him to have his child.

Marion shuddered suddenly; part of her saw that Charlie's feet were planted on the earth now, and her own maternal feeling recognized the naturalness of his desire; but she had lived for a long time with a prejudice—a prejudice founded on a curious disbelief in her sister's happiness, in which, in the shock of one terrible night, had turned to hatred for him. It had all happened at a point in her life where the discouragement of ill health and adverse circumstances made it necessary for her to believe in tangible villainy and a tangible villain.

"I can't help what I think!" she cried out suddenly. "How much you were responsible for Helen's death, I don't know. It's something you'll have to square with your own conscience."

An electric current of agony surged through him; for a moment he was almost on his feet, an unuttered sound echoing in his throat. He hung on to himself for a moment, another moment.

"Hold on there," said Lincoln uncomfortably. "I never thought you were responsible for that."

"Helen died of heart trouble," Charlie said dully.

"Yes, heart trouble." Marion spoke as if the phrase had another meaning for her.

Then, in the flatness that followed her outburst, she saw him plainly and she knew he had somehow arrived at control over the situation. Glancing at her husband, she found no help from him, and as abruptly as if it were a matter of no importance, she threw up the sponge.

"Do what you like!" she cried, springing up from her chair. "She's your child. I'm not the person to stand in your way. I think if it were my child I'd rather see her—" She managed to check herself. "You two decide it. I can't stand this. I'm sick. I'm going to bed."

She hurried from the room; after a moment Lincoln said:

"This has been a hard day for her. You know how strongly she feels—" His voice was almost apologetic: "When a woman gets an idea in her head."

"Of course."

"It's going to be all right. I think she sees now that you—can provide for the child, and so we can't very well stand in your way or Honoria's way."

"Thank you, Lincoln."

"I'd better go along and see how she is."

"I'm going."

He was still trembling when he reached the street but a walk down the Rue Bonaparte to the quais set him up, and as he crossed the Seine, fresh and new by the quai lamps, he felt exultant. But back in his room he couldn't sleep. The image of Helen haunted him. Helen whom he had loved so until they had senselessly begun to abuse each other's love, tear it into shreds. On that terrible February night that Marion remembered so vividly, a slow quarrel had gone on for hours. There was a scene at the Florida, and then he attempted to take her home, and then she kissed young Webb at a table; after that there was what she had hysterically said. When he arrived home alone he turned the key in the lock in wild anger. How could he know she would arrive an hour later alone, that there would be a snowstorm in which she wandered about in slippers, too confused to find a taxi? Then the aftermath, her escaping pneumonia by a miracle, and all the attendant horror. They were "reconciled," but that was the beginning of the end, and Marion, who had seen with her own eyes and who imagined it to be one of many scenes from her sister's martyrdom, never forgot.

Going over it again brought Helen nearer, and in the white, soft light that steals upon half sleep near morning he found himself talking to her again. She said that he was perfectly right about Honoria and that she wanted Honoria to be with him. She said she was glad he was being good and doing better. She said a lot of other things—very friendly things—but she was in a swing in a white dress, and swinging faster and faster all the time, so that at the end he could not hear clearly all that she said.

IV

He woke up feeling happy. The door of the world was open again. He made plans, vistas, futures for Honoria and himself, but suddenly he grew sad, remembering all the plans he and Helen had made. She had not planned to die. The present was one thing—work to do and someone to love. But not to love too much, for he knew the injury that a father can do to a daughter or a mother to a son by attaching them too closely: afterward, out in the world, the child would seek in the marriage partner the same blind tenderness and, failing probably to find it, turn against love and life.

It was another bright, crisp day. He called Lincoln Peters at the bank where he worked and asked if he could count on taking Honoria when he left for Prague. Lincoln agreed that there was no reason for delay. One thing—the legal guardianship. Marion wanted to retain that a while longer. She was upset by the whole matter, and it would oil things if she felt that the situation was still in her control for another year. Charlie agreed, wanting only the tangible, visible child.

Then the question of a governess. Charles sat in a gloomy agency and talked to a cross Bérnaise and to a boxom Breton peasant, neither of whom he could have endured. There were others whom he would see tomorrow.

He lunched with Lincoln Peters at Griffons, trying to keep down his exultation.

"There's nothing quite like your own child," Lincoln said. "But you understand how Marion feels too."

"She's forgotten how hard I worked for seven years there," Charlie said. "She just remembers one night."

"There's another thing." Lincoln hesitated. "While you and Helen were tearing around Europe throwing money away, we were just getting along. I didn't touch any of the prosperity because I never got ahead enough to carry anything but my insurance. I think Marion felt there was some kind of injustice in it—you not even working toward the end, and getting richer and richer."

"It went just as quick as it came," said Charlie.

"Yes, a lot of it stayed in the hands of *chasseurs* and saxophone players and maîtres d'hôtel—well, the big party's over now. I just said that to explain Marion's feeling about those crazy years. If you drop in about six o'clock tonight before Marion's too tired, we'll settle the details on the spot."

Back at his hotel, Charlie found a *pneumatique*[8] that had been redirected from the Ritz bar where Charlie had left his address for the purpose of finding a certain man.

> DEAR CHARLIE: *You were so strange when we saw you the other day that I wondered if I did something to offend you. If so, I'm not conscious of it. In fact, I have thought about you too much for the last year, and it's always*

---

[8]A written note; because telephones were unreliable, messages were transmitted throughout Paris via a network of pneumatic tubes.

*been in the back of my mind that I might see you if I came over here. We did
have such good times that crazy spring, like the night you and I stole the
butcher's tricycle, and the time we tried to call on the president and you had
the old derby rim and the wire cane. Everybody seems so old lately, but I
don't feel old a bit. Couldn't we get together some time today for old time's
sake? I've got a vile hang-over for the moment, but will be feeling better this
afternoon and will look for you about five in the sweet-shop at the Ritz.*

Always devotedly,
LORRAINE.

His first feeling was one of awe that he had actually, in his mature years,
stolen a tricycle and pedalled Lorraine all over the Étoile between the small
hours and dawn. In retrospect it was a nightmare. Locking out Helen didn't
fit in with any other act of his life, but the tricycle incident did—it was one
of many. How many weeks or months of dissipation to arrive at that condition of utter irresponsibility?

He tried to picture how Lorraine had appeared to him then—very
attractive; Helen was unhappy about it, though she said nothing. Yesterday,
in the restaurant, Lorraine had seemed trite, blurred, worn away. He
emphatically did not want to see her, and he was glad Alix had not given
away his hotel address. It was a relief to think, instead, of Honoria, to think
of Sundays spent with her and of saying good morning to her and of knowing she was there in his house at night, drawing her breath in the darkness.

At five he took a taxi and bought presents for all the Peters—a piquant
cloth doll, a box of Roman soldiers, flowers for Marion, big linen handkerchiefs for Lincoln.

He saw, when he arrived in the apartment, that Marion had accepted
the inevitable. She greeted him now as though he were a recalcitrant member of the family, rather than a menacing outsider. Honoria had been told
she was going; Charlie was glad to see that her tact made her conceal her excessive happiness. Only on his lap did she whisper her delight and the question "When?" before she slipped away with the other children.

He and Marion were alone for a minute in the room, and on an impulse
he spoke out boldly.

"Family quarrels are bitter things. They don't go according to any rules.
They're not like aches or wounds; they're more like splits in the skin that
won't heal because there's not enough material. I wish you and I could be on
better terms."

"Some things are hard to forget," she answered. "It's a question of confidence." There was no answer to this and presently she asked, "When do you
propose to take her?"

"As soon as I can get a governess. I hoped the day after tomorrow."

"That's impossible. I've got to get her things in shape. Not before Saturday."

He yielded. Coming back into the room, Lincoln offered him a drink.

"I'll take my daily whisky," he said.

It was warm here, it was a home, people together by a fire. The children felt very safe and important; the mother and father were serious, watchful. They had things to do for the children more important than his visit here. A spoonful of medicine was, after all, more important than the strained relations between Marion and himself. They were not dull people, but they were very much in the grip of life and circumstances. He wondered if he couldn't do something to get Lincoln out of his rut at the bank.

A long peal at the door-bell; the *bonne à tout faire*[9] passed through and went down the corridor. The door opened upon another long ring, and then voices, and the three in the salon looked up expectantly; Lincoln moved to bring the corridor within his range of vision, and Marion rose. Then the maid came back alone the corridor, closely followed by the voices, which developed under the light into Duncan Schaeffer and Lorraine Quarrles.

They were gay, they were hilarious, they were roaring with laughter. For a moment Charlie was astounded; unable to understand how they ferreted out the Peters' address.

"Ah-h-h!" Duncan wagged his finger roguishly at Charlie "A-h-h!"

They both slid down another cascade of laughter. Anxious and at a loss, Charlie shook hands with them quickly and presented them to Lincoln and Marion. Marion nodded, scarcely speaking. She had drawn back a step toward the fire; her little girl stood beside her, and Marion put an arm about her shoulder.

With growing annoyance at the intrusion, Charlie waited for them to explain themselves. After some concentration Duncan said:

"We came to invite you out to dinner. Lorraine and I insist that all this shishi, cagy business 'bout your address got to stop."

Charlie came closer to them, as if to force them backward down the corridor.

"Sorry, but I can't. Tell me where you'll be and I'll phone you in half an hour."

This made no impression. Lorraine sat down suddenly on the side of a chair, and focusing her eyes on Richard, cried, "Oh, what a nice little boy! Come here, little boy." Richard glanced at his mother, but did not move. With a perceptible shrug of her shoulders, Lorraine turned back to Charlie:

"Come and dine. Sure your cousins won' mine. See you so sel'om. Or solemn."

"I can't," said Charlie sharply. "You two have dinner and I'll phone you."

Her voice became suddenly unpleasant. "All right, we'll go. But I remember once when you hammered on my door at four A.M. I was enough of a good sport to give you a drink. Come on, Dunc."

Still in slow motion, with blurred, angry faces, with uncertain feet, they retired along the corridor.

"Good night," Charlie said.

"Good night!" responded Lorraine emphatically.

[9]French: "maid-of-all-work."

When he went back into the salon Marion had not moved, only now her son was standing in the circle of her other arm. Lincoln was still swinging Honoria back and forth like a pendulum from side to side.

"What an outrage!" Charlie broke out. "What an absolute outrage!"

Neither of them answered. Charlie dropped into an armchair, picked up his drink, set it down again and said:

"People I haven't seen for two years having the colossal nerve—"

He broke off. Marion had made the sound "Oh!" in one swift, furious breath, turned her body from him with a jerk and left the room.

Lincoln set down Honoria carefully.

"You children go in and start your soup," he said, and when they obeyed, he said to Charlie:

"Marion's not well and she can't stand shocks. That kind of people make her really physically sick."

"I didn't tell them to come here. They wormed your name out of somebody. They deliberately—"

"Well, it's too bad. It doesn't help matters. Excuse me a minute."

Left alone, Charlie sat tense in his chair. In the next room he could hear the children eating, talking in monosyllables, already oblivious to the scene between their elders. He heard a murmur of conversation from a farther room and then the ticking bell of a telephone receiver picked up, and in a panic he moved to the other side of the room and out of earshot.

In a minute Lincoln came back. "Look here, Charlie. I think we'd better call off dinner for tonight. Marion's in bad shape."

"Is she angry with me?"

"Sort of," he said, almost roughly. "She's not strong and—"

"You mean she's changed her mind about Honoria?"

"She's pretty bitter right now. I don't know. You phone me at the bank tomorrow."

"I wish you'd explain to her I never dreamed these people would come here. I'm just as sore as you are."

"I couldn't explain anything to her now."

Charlie got up. He took his coat and hat and started down the corridor. Then he opened the door of the dining room and said in a strange voice, "Good night, children."

Honoria rose and ran around the table to hug him.

"Good night, sweetheart," he said vaguely, and then trying to make his voice more tender, trying to conciliate something, "Good night, dear children."

V

Charlie went directly to the Ritz bar with the furious idea of finding Lorraine and Duncan, but they were not there, and he realized that in any case there was nothing he could do. He had not touched his drink at the Peters', and now he ordered a whisky-and-soda. Paul came over to say hello.

"It's a great change," he said sadly. "We do about half the business we did. So many fellows I hear about back in the States lost everything, maybe not in the first crash, but then in the second. Your friend George Hardt lost every cent, I hear. Are you back in the States?"

"No. I'm in business in Prague."

"I heard you lost a lot in the crash."

"I did," and he added grimly, "but I lost everything I wanted in the boom."

"Selling short."

"Something like that."

Again the memory of those days swept over him like a nightmare—the people they had met travelling; then people who couldn't add a row of figures or speak a coherent sentence. The little man Helen had consented to dance with at the ship's party, who had insulted her ten feet from the table; the women and girls carried screaming with drink or drugs out of public places—

—The men who locked their wives out in the snow, because the snow of twenty-nine wasn't real snow. If you didn't want it to be snow, you just paid some money.

He went to the phone and called the Peters' apartment; Lincoln answered.

"I called up because this thing is on my mind. Has Marion said anything definite?"

"Marion's sick," Lincoln answered shortly. "I know this thing isn't altogether your fault, but I can't have her go to pieces about it. I'm afraid we'll have to let it slide for six months; I can't take the chance of working her up to this stage again."

"I see."

"I'm sorry, Charlie."

He went back to his table. His whisky glass was empty, but he shook his head when Alix looked at it questioningly. There wasn't much he could do now except send Honoria some things; he would send her a lot of things tomorrow. He thought rather angrily that this was just money—he had given so many people money....

"No, no more," he said to another waiter. "What do I owe you?"

He would come back some day; they couldn't make him pay forever. But he wanted his child, and nothing was much good now, beside the fact. He wasn't young any more, with a lot of nice thoughts and dreams to have by himself. He was absolutely sure Helen wouldn't have wanted him to be so alone.

1935

KATHERINE ANNE PORTER
1890–1980

In 1936, Katherine Anne Porter explained the initial step in her process of writing fiction as the "exercise of memory." At a certain point, she explained, "thousands of memories converge, harmonize, arrange themselves around a central idea in a coherent form, and I write a story." By pointing out the artist's memory as an essential ingredient in the process, she acknowledged the autobiographical element in each of her works. She was speaking to the American Women's Club in Paris when she proffered her explanation of the way her fiction was made. By then, what she had to say on the subject of art was significant. She was established as an important writer—one of the modernists whose voices informed a literary age.

Katherine Anne Porter, christened Callie Russell Porter, was born May 15, 1890, in the frontier community of Indian Creek, Texas, the fourth child of Harrison Boone Porter and Mary Alice Jones Porter. After Mary Alice died in 1892, Callie went with her father, brother, and sisters to live with her widowed grandmother, Catherine Ann Skaggs Porter, in Hays County. When her grandmother died in 1901, Callie set forth with her father and siblings on several years of vagabondage. During that time, she sporadically attended convent schools, spent a full year at the Thomas School in San Antonio, informally changed her name to Katherine, and began her lifelong self-education. Her adolescence ended in 1906, when at sixteen she married John Henry Koontz, son of a prosperous Texas rancher.

Katherine endured her husband's physical abuse and infidelities while she continued to read widely and to write stories and poems. She finally fled from the marriage in 1914 and went to Chicago, where she worked briefly in the movies before returning to Texas and divorcing Koontz in 1915, asking in the decree that her name be formally changed to Katherine Porter. Soon she began giving her name as Katherine Anne Porter, signaling her identification with her paternal grandmother, whose strength and grace she hoped to match. For the next four years, her struggle was indeed "ungodly," as she later described that period of her life, marked by life-threatening tuberculosis and influenza, two more failed marriages, and apprenticeships in the newsrooms of Texas papers and the *Rocky Mountain News* in Denver. In 1919, when she went to New York, she was ready to become the artist she knew she could be.

She was in New York City barely a year before she went to Mexico, where a cultural revolution was in full swing, to live inexpensively and to find time for what she called her "artist-writing." She became acquainted with all the important revolutionaries, including the new president, Álvaro Obregón, as well as Mexican artists and intellectuals. Between 1920 and 1923, she was in Mexico three different times, assessing politics and art in Mexico and continuing to write both fiction and nonfiction. In 1922, she published her first story, "María Concepción." By 1930 she had published a total of nine stories (including "He" and "Flowering Judas"), and Harcourt, Brace published six of them in a limited edition entitled *Flowering Judas*. Extraordinarily high praise from reviewers fixed Porter's position in American letters. "No other writer has a talent quite like [Porter's]," Louise Bogan wrote in the *New Republic*, and other reviewers agreed. The collection revealed that Porter's time in Mexico had released her creative force and that, beginning with "He" in 1927, she had looked beyond Mexico to recollect her Texas experiences as another source for her art. Something of herself would appear in everything she wrote, and the controlling themes of her evolving fictional canon were betrayal (including self-betrayal) and the progress toward spiritual maturity through one's ongoing search for truth.

Porter had gone to Mexico again in the spring of 1930, and she stayed until the late summer of 1931, when she received a Guggenheim Fellowship and sailed with Eugene Pressly from Veracruz to Bremen, Germany, before settling in Paris for four years. By the time she gave up her exile in France and moved back the United States, she had married Pressly, formed important friendships in the expatriate community, and published three more small books, three more long stories, and the first three stories that featured her autobiographical character Miranda—"The Grave," "The Circus," and "The Old Order" (later retitled "The Journey").

Between 1936 and 1941, she further enhanced her already stellar reputation with publication of four more stories and *Pale Horse, Pale Rider: Three Short Novels*. She also had divorced Pressly and married Albert Russel Erskine, Jr. By that time, a novel she had conceived in the late 1920s had focused exclusively on one of its three parts and was developing into her only long novel, *Ship of Fools*. During the next twenty years, she divorced Erskine, worked as a scriptwriter in Hollywood, accepted speaking engagements and academic appointments at colleges and universities, undertook a Fulbright assignment in Belgium, and published segments of her novel-in-progress as well as two more stories. When *Ship of Fools* was published in 1962, reviews ranged from Mark Schorer's enthusiastic assessment in the *New York Times* to scathing attacks in *Commentary* and several German newspapers. Although the novel, a satire in the spirit of Swift and Erasmus, ran afoul of 1960s literary aesthetics, its popular success led to an award-winning film and brought Porter substantial wealth.

For the remaining eighteen years of her life, Porter lived in Washington, D.C., and Maryland, publishing only works that had been written earlier but reaping the rewards of her literary success. In 1966, she received both the Pulitzer Prize and the National Book Award for her *Collected Stories* (1965). She was awarded the Gold Medal for Fiction from the American Academy of Arts and Letters and continued to receive honorary degrees, which she had begun gathering in the 1940s. When she died on September 18, 1980, she left behind a body of work that many consider unexcelled in its crystalline prose, classical style, and deep insight into the human condition.

Darlene Unrue
University of Nevada, Las Vegas

PRIMARY WORKS

Flowering Judas, 1930; *Flowering Judas and Other Stories*, 1935; *The Leaning Tower and Other Stories*, 1944; *The Days Before*, 1952; *Ship of Fools*, 1962; *The Collected Stories of Katherine Anne Porter*, 1965; *The Collected Essays and Occasional Writings of*

Katherine Anne Porter, 1970; *The Never-Ending Wrong,* 1977; *Katherine Anne Porter: Conversations,* ed. Joan Givner, 1987; *Letters of Katherine Anne Porter,* ed. Isabel Bayley, 1990; *Uncollected Early Prose of Katherine Anne Porter,* ed. Ruth M. Alvarez and Thomas F. Walsh, 1993; *"This Strange, Old World" and Other Book Reviews of Katherine Anne Porter,* ed. Darlene Harbour Unrue, 1993; *Katherine Anne Porter's Poetry,* ed. Darlene Harbour Unrue, 1996.

He

Life was very hard for the Whipples. It was hard to feed all the hungry mouths, it was hard to keep the children in flannels during the winter, short as it was: "God knows what would become of us if we lived north," they would say: keeping them decently clean was hard. "It looks like our luck won't never let up on us," said Mr. Whipple, but Mrs. Whipple was all for taking what was sent and calling it good, anyhow when the neighbors were in earshot. "Don't ever let a soul hear us complain," she kept saying to her husband. She couldn't stand to be pitied. "No, not if it comes to it that we have to live in a wagon and pick cotton around the country," she said, "nobody's going to get a chance to look down on us."

Mrs. Whipple loved her second son, the simple-minded one, better than she loved the other two children put together. She was forever saying so, and when she talked with certain of her neighbors, she would even throw in her husband and her mother for good measure.

"You needn't keep on saying it around," said Mr. Whipple, "you'll make people think nobody else has any feelings about Him but you."

"It's natural for a mother," Mrs. Whipple would remind him. "You know yourself it's more natural for a mother to be that way. People don't expect so much of fathers, some way."

This didn't keep the neighbors from talking plainly among themselves. "A Lord's pure mercy if He should die," they said. "It's the sins of the fathers," they agreed among themselves.[1] "There's bad blood and bad doings somewhere, you can bet on that." This behind the Whipples' backs. To their faces everybody said, "He's not so bad off. He'll be all right yet. Look how He grows!"

Mrs. Whipple hated to talk about it, she tried to keep her mind off it, but every time anybody set foot in the house, the subject always came up, and she had to talk about Him first, before she could get on to anything else. It seemed to ease her mind. "I wouldn't have anything happen to Him for all the world, but it just looks like I can't keep Him out of mischief. He's so strong and active, He's always into everything; He was like that since He could walk. It's actually funny sometimes, the way He can do anything; it's laughable to see Him up to His tricks. Emly has more accidents; I'm forever tying up her bruises, and Adna can't fall a foot without cracking a bone. But

---

[1] See Exodus 20:5: "You shall not worship or serve them; for I, the Lord your God, am a jealous God, visiting the iniquity of the fathers on the children, on the third and fourth generations of those who hate me."

He can do anything and not get a scratch. The preacher said such a nice thing once when he was here. He said, and I'll remember it to my dying day, 'The innocent walk with God—that's why He don't get hurt.'" Whenever Mrs. Whipple repeated these words, she always felt a warm pool spread in her breast, and the tears would fill her eyes, and then she could talk about something else.

He did grow and He never got hurt. A plank blew off the chicken house and struck Him on the head and He never seemed to know it. He had learned a few words, and after this He forgot them. He didn't whine for food as the other children did, but waited until it was given Him; He ate squatting in the corner, smacking and mumbling. Rolls of fat covered Him like an overcoat, and He could carry twice as much wood and water as Adna. Emly had a cold in the head most of the time—"she takes that after me," said Mrs. Whipple—so in bad weather they gave her the extra blanket off His cot. He never seemed to mind the cold.

Just the same, Mrs. Whipple's life was a torment for fear something might happen to Him. He climbed the peach trees much better than Adna and went skittering along the branches like a monkey, just a regular monkey. "Oh, Mrs. Whipple, you hadn't ought to let Him do that. He'll lose His balance sometime. He can't rightly know what He's doing."

Mrs. Whipple almost screamed out at the neighbor. "He *does* know what He's doing! He's as able as any other child! Come down out of there, you!" When He finally reached the ground she could hardly keep her hands off Him for acting like that before people, a grin all over His face and her worried sick about Him all the time.

"It's the neighbors," said Mrs. Whipple to her husband. "Oh, I do mortally wish they would keep out of our business. I can't afford to let Him do anything for fear they'll come nosing around about it. Look at the bees, now. Adna can't handle them, they sting him up so; I haven't got time to do everything, and now I don't dare let Him. But if He gets a sting He don't really mind."

"It's just because He ain't got sense enough to be scared of anything," said Mr. Whipple.

"You ought to be ashamed of yourself," said Mrs. Whipple, "talking that way about your own child. Who's to take up for Him if we don't, I'd like to know? He sees a lot that goes on, He listens to things all the time. And anything I tell Him to do He does it. Don't never let anybody hear you say such things. They'd think you favored the other children over Him."

"Well, now I don't, and you know it, and what's the use of getting all worked up about it? You always think the worst of everything. Just let Him alone, He'll get along somehow. He gets plenty to eat and wear, don't He?" Mr. Whipple suddenly felt tired out. "Anyhow, it can't be helped now."

Mrs. Whipple felt tired too, she complained in a tired voice. "What's done can't never be undone, I know that good as anybody; but He's my child, and I'm not going to have people say anything. I get sick of people coming around saying things all the time."

In the early fall Mrs. Whipple got a letter from her brother saying he and his wife and two children were coming over for a little visit next Sunday week. "Put the big pot in the little one," he wrote at the end. Mrs. Whipple read this part out loud twice, she was so pleased. Her brother was a great one for saying funny things. "We'll just show him that's no joke," she said, "we'll just butcher one of the sucking pigs."

"It's a waste and I don't hold with waste the way we are now," said Mr. Whipple. "That pig'll be worth money by Christmas."

"It's a shame and a pity we can't have a decent meal's vittles once in a while when my own family comes to see us," said Mrs. Whipple. "I'd hate for his wife to go back and say there wasn't a thing in the house to eat. My God, it's better than buying up a great chance of meat in town. There's where you'd spend the money!"

"All right, do it yourself then," said Mr. Whipple. "Christamighty, no wonder we can't get ahead!"

The question was how to get the little pig away from his ma, a great fighter, worse than a Jersey cow.[2] Adna wouldn't try it: "That sow'd rip my insides out all over the pen." "All right, old fraidy," said Mrs. Whipple, "*He's* not scared. Watch *Him* do it." And she laughed as though it was all a good joke and gave Him a little push toward the pen. He sneaked up and snatched the pig right away from the teat and galloped back and was over the fence with the sow raging at His heels. The little black squirming thing was screeching like a baby in a tantrum, stiffening its back and stretching its mouth to the ears. Mrs. Whipple took the pig with her face stiff and sliced its throat with one stroke. When He saw the blood He gave a great jolting breath and ran away. "But He'll forget and eat plenty, just the same," thought Mrs. Whipple. Whenever she was thinking, her lips moved making words. "He'd eat it all if I didn't stop Him. He'd eat up every mouthful from the other two if I'd let Him."

She felt badly about it. He was ten years old now and a third again as large as Adna, who was going on fourteen. "It's a shame, a shame," she kept saying under her breath, "and Adna with so much brains!"

She kept on feeling badly about all sorts of things. In the first place it was the man's work to butcher; the sight of the pig scraped pink and naked made her sick. He was too fat and soft and pitiful-looking. It was simply a shame the way things had to happen. By the time she had finished it up, she almost wished her brother would stay at home.

Early Sunday morning Mrs. Whipple dropped everything to get Him all cleaned up. In an hour He was dirty again, with crawling under fences after a possum, and straddling along the rafters of the barn looking for eggs in the hayloft. "My Lord, look at you now after all my trying! And here's Adna and Emly staying so quiet. I get tired trying to keep you decent. Get off that shirt and put on another, people will say I don't half dress you!" And she boxed

[2]Jersey cows, small dairy cows, are known for especially rich milk, but Jersey bulls are notoriously fierce and aggressive.

Him on the ears, hard. He blinked and blinked and rubbed His head, and His face hurt Mrs. Whipple's feelings. Her knees began to tremble, she had to sit down while she buttoned His shirt. "I'm just all gone before the day starts."

The brother came with his plump healthy wife and two great roaring hungry boys. They had a grand dinner, with the pig roasted to a crackling in the middle of the table, full of dressing, a pickled peach in his mouth and plenty of gravy for the sweet potatoes.

"This looks like prosperity all right," said the brother; "you're going to have to roll me home like I was a barrel when I'm done."

Everybody laughed out loud; it was fine to hear them laughing all at once around the table. Mrs. Whipple felt warm and good about it. "Oh, we've got six more of these; I say it's as little as we can do when you come to see us so seldom."

He wouldn't come into the dining room, and Mrs. Whipple passed it off very well. "He's timider than my other two," she said, "He'll just have to get used to you. There isn't everybody He'll make up with, you know how it is with some children, even cousins." Nobody said anything out of the way.

"Just like my Alfy here," said the brother's wife. "I sometimes got to lick him to make him shake hands with his own grand-mammy."

So that was over, and Mrs. Whipple loaded up a big plate for Him first, before everybody. "I always say He ain't to be slighted, no matter who else goes without," she said, and carried it to Him herself.

"He can chin Himself on the top of the door," said Emly, helping along.

"That's fine, He's getting along fine," said the brother.

They went away after supper. Mrs. Whipple rounded up the dishes, and sent the children to bed and sat down and unlaced her shoes. "You see?" she said to Mr. Whipple. "That's the way my whole family is. Nice and considerate about everything. No out-of-the-way remarks—they *have* got refinement. I get awfully sick of people's remarks. Wasn't that pig good?"

Mr. Whipple said, "Yes, we're out three hundred pounds of pork, that's all. It's easy to be polite when you come to eat. Who knows what they had in their minds all along?"

"Yes, that's like you," said Mrs. Whipple. "I don't expect anything else from you. You'll be telling me next that my own brother will be saying around that we made Him eat in the kitchen! Oh, my God!" She rocked her head in her hands, a hard pain started in the very middle of her forehead. "Now it's all spoiled, and everything was so nice and easy. All right, you don't like them and you never did—all right, they'll not come here again soon, never you mind! But they *can't* say He wasn't dressed every lick as good as Adna—oh, honest, sometimes I wish I was dead!"

"I wish you'd let up," said Mr. Whipple. "It's bad enough as it is."

It was a hard winter. It seemed to Mrs. Whipple that they hadn't ever known anything but hard times, and now to cap it all a winter like this. The crops were about half of what they had a right to expect; after the cotton was in it didn't do much more than cover the grocery bill. They swapped off one of the plow horses, and got cheated, for the new one died of the heaves.[3] Mrs. Whipple kept thinking all the time it was terrible to have a man you couldn't depend on not to get cheated. They cut down on everything, but Mrs. Whipple kept saying there are things you can't cut down on, and they cost money. It took a lot of warm clothes for Adna and Emly, who walked four miles to school during the three-months session. "He sets around the fire a lot, He won't need so much," said Mr. Whipple. "That's so," said Mrs. Whipple, "and when He does the outdoor chores He can wear your tarpaullion coat. I can't do no better, that's all."

In February He was taken sick, and lay curled up under His blanket looking very blue in the face and acting as if He would choke. Mr. and Mrs. Whipple did everything they could for Him for two days, and then they were scared and sent for the doctor. The doctor told them they must keep Him warm and give Him plenty of milk and eggs. "He isn't as stout as He looks, I'm afraid," said the doctor. "You've got to watch them when they're like that. You must put more cover onto Him, too."

"I just took off His big blanket to wash," said Mrs. Whipple, ashamed. "I can't stand dirt."

"Well, you'd better put it back on the minute it's dry," said the doctor, "or He'll have pneumonia."

Mr. and Mrs. Whipple took a blanket off their own bed and put His cot in by the fire. "They can't say we didn't do everything for Him," she said, "even to sleeping cold ourselves on His account."

When the winter broke He seemed to be well again, but He walked as if His feet hurt Him. He was able to run a cotton planter during the season.

"I got it all fixed up with Jim Ferguson about breeding the cow next time," said Mr. Whipple. "I'll pasture the bull this summer and give Him some fodder in the fall. That's better than paying out money when you haven't got it."

"I hope you didn't say such a thing before Jim Ferguson," said Mrs. Whipple. "You oughtn't to let him know we're so down as all that."

"Godamighty, that ain't saying we're down. A man is got to look ahead sometimes. *He* can lead the bull over today. I need Adna on the place."

At first Mrs. Whipple felt easy in her mind about sending Him for the bull. Adna was too jumpy and couldn't be trusted. You've got to be steady around animals. After He was gone she started thinking, and after a while she could hardly bear it any longer. She stood in the lane and watched for Him. It was nearly three miles to go and a hot day, but He oughtn't to be so long about it. She shaded her eyes and stared until colored bubbles floated in her eyeballs. It was just like everything else in life, she must always worry and never know a moment's peace about anything. After a long time she saw Him turn into the side lane, limping. He came on very slowly, leading

---

[3]A chronic lung disorder of cattle and horses.

the big hulk of an animal by a ring in the nose, twirling a little stick in His hand, never looking back or sideways, but coming on like a sleepwalker with His eyes half shut.

Mrs. Whipple was scared sick of bulls; she had heard awful stories about how they followed on quietly enough, and then suddenly pitched on with a bellow and pawed and gored a body to pieces. Any second now that black monster would come down on Him, my God, He'd never have sense enough to run.

She mustn't make a sound nor a move; she mustn't get the bull started. The bull heaved his head aside and horned the air at a fly. Her voice burst out of her in a shriek, and she screamed at Him to come on, for God's sake. He didn't seem to hear her clamor, but kept on twirling His switch and limping on, and the bull lumbered along behind him as gently as a calf. Mrs. Whipple stopped calling and ran toward the house, praying under her breath: "Lord, don't let anything happen to Him. Lord, you *know* people will say we oughtn't to have sent Him. You *know* they'll say we didn't take care of Him. Oh, get Him home, safe home, safe home, and I'll look out for Him better! Amen."

She watched from the window while He led the beast in, and tied him up in the barn. It was no use trying to keep up, Mrs. Whipple couldn't bear another thing. She sat down and rocked and cried with her apron over her head.

From year to year the Whipples were growing poorer and poorer. The place just seemed to run down of itself, no matter how hard they worked. "We're losing our hold," said Mrs. Whipple. "Why can't we do like other people and watch for our best chances? They'll be calling us poor white trash next."

"When I get to be sixteen I'm going to leave," said Adna. "I'm going to get a job in Powell's grocery store. There's money in that. No more farm for me."

"I'm going to be a schoolteacher," said Emly. "But I've got to finish the eighth grade, anyhow. Then I can live in town. I don't see any chances here."

"Emly takes after my family," said Mrs. Whipple. "Ambitious every last one of them, and they don't take second place for anybody."

When fall came Emly got a chance to wait on table in the railroad eating-house in the town near by, and it seemed such a shame not to take it when the wages were good and she could get her food too, that Mrs. Whipple decided to let her take it, and not bother with school until the next session. "You've got plenty of time," she said. "You're young and smart as a whip."

With Adna gone too, Mr. Whipple tried to run the farm with just Him to help. He seemed to get along fine, doing His work and part of Adna's without noticing it. They did well enough until Christmas time, when one morning He slipped on the ice coming up from the barn. Instead of getting up He thrashed round and round, and when Mr. Whipple got to Him, He was having some sort of fit.

They brought Him inside and tried to make Him sit up, but He blubbered and rolled, so they put Him to bed and Mr. Whipple rode to town for the doctor. All the way there and back he worried about where the money was to come from: it sure did look like he had about all the troubles he could carry.

From then on He stayed in bed. His legs swelled up double their size, and the fits kept coming back. After four months, the doctor said, "It's no use, I think you'd better put Him in the County Home for treatment right away. I'll see about it for you. He'll have good care there and be off your hands."

"We don't begrudge Him any care, and I won't let Him out of my sight," said Mrs. Whipple. "I won't have it said I sent my sick child off among strangers."

"I know how you feel," said the doctor. "You can't tell me anything about that, Mrs. Whipple. I've got a boy of my own. But you'd better listen to me. I can't do anything more for Him, that's the truth."

Mr. and Mrs. Whipple talked it over a long time that night after they went to bed. "It's just charity," said Mrs. Whipple, "that's what we've come to, charity! I certainly never looked for this."

"We pay taxes to help support the place just like everybody else," said Mr. Whipple, "and I don't call that taking charity. I think it would be fine to have Him where He'd get the best of everything . . . and besides, I can't keep up with these doctor bills any longer."

"Maybe that's why the doctor wants us to send Him—he's scared he won't get his money," said Mrs. Whipple.

"Don't talk like that," said Mr. Whipple, feeling pretty sick, "or we won't be able to send Him."

"Oh, but we won't keep Him there long," said Mrs. Whipple. "Soon's He's better, we'll bring Him right back home."

"The doctor has told you and told you time and again He can't ever get better, and you might as well stop talking," said Mr. Whipple.

"Doctors don't know everything," said Mrs. Whipple, feeling almost happy. "But anyhow, in the summer Emly can come home for a vacation, and Adna can get down for Sundays: we'll all work together and get on our feet again, and the children will feel they've got a place to come to."

All at once she saw it full summer again, with the garden going fine, and new white roller shades up all over the house, and Adna and Emly home, so full of life, all of them happy together. Oh, it could happen, things would ease up on them.

They didn't talk before Him much, but they never knew just how much He understood. Finally the doctor set the day and a neighbor who owned a double-seated carry-all offered to drive them over.[4] The hospital would have sent an ambulance, but Mrs. Whipple couldn't stand to see Him going away looking so sick as all that. They wrapped Him in blankets, and the neighbor

---

[4]A carry-all is a horse-driven buggy with seats for four people.

and Mr. Whipple lifted Him into the back seat of the carry-all beside Mrs. Whipple, who had on her black shirtwaist. She couldn't stand to go looking like charity.

"You'll be all right, I guess I'll stay behind," said Mr. Whipple. "It don't look like everybody ought to leave the place at once."

"Besides, it ain't as if He was going to stay forever," said Mrs. Whipple to the neighbor. "This is only for a little while."

They started away, Mrs. Whipple holding to the edges of the blankets to keep Him from sagging sideways. He sat there blinking and blinking. He worked His hands out and began rubbing His nose with His knuckles, and then with the end of the blanket. Mrs. Whipple couldn't believe what she saw; He was scrubbing away big tears that rolled out of the corners of His eyes. He sniveled and made a gulping noise. Mrs. Whipple kept saying, "Oh, honey, you don't feel so bad, do you? You don't feel so bad, do you?" for He seemed to be accusing her of something. Maybe He remembered that time she boxed His ears, maybe He had been scared that day with the bull, maybe He had slept cold and couldn't tell her about it; maybe He knew they were sending Him away for good and all because they were too poor to keep Him. Whatever it was, Mrs. Whipple couldn't bear to think of it. She began to cry, frightfully, and wrapped her arms tight around Him. His head rolled on her shoulder: she had loved Him as much as she possibly could, there were Adna and Emly who had to be thought of too, there was nothing she could do to make up to Him for His life. Oh, what a moral pity He was ever born.

They came in sight of the hospital, with the neighbor driving very fast, not daring to look behind him.

1927

Flowering Judas[1]

Braggioni sits heaped upon the edge of a straight-backed chair much too small for him, and sings to Laura in a furry, mournful voice. Laura has begun to find reasons for avoiding her own house until the latest possible moment, for Braggioni is there almost every night. No matter how late she is, he will be sitting there with a surly, waiting expression, pulling at his kinky yellow hair, thumbing the strings of his guitar, snarling a tune under his breath. Lupe the Indian maid meets Laura at the door, and says with a flicker of a glance towards the upper room, "He waits."[2]

Laura wishes to lie down, she is tired of her hairpins and the feel of her long tight sleeves, but she says to him, "Have you a new song for me this evening?" If he says yes, she asks him to sing it. If he says no, she

[1]The title refers to Judas Iscariot, whose name, according to legend, was given to the species of redbud tree from which he hanged himself, and to T. S. Eliot's poem "Gerontian" (1920): "In the juvenescence of the year / Came Christ the tiger / In depraved May, dogwood and chestnut, flowering Judas, / To be eaten, to be divided, to be drunk / Among whispers."
[2]The Last Supper of Jesus and his disciples took place in an "upper room" (see Mark 14:12–15).

remembers his favorite one, and asks him to sing it again. Lupe brings her a cup of chocolate and a plate of rice, and Laura eats at the small table under the lamp, first inviting Braggioni, whose answer is always the same: "I have eaten, and besides, chocolate thickens the voice."

Laura says, "Sing, then," and Braggioni heaves himself into song. He scratches the guitar familiarly as though it were a pet animal, and sings passionately off key, taking the high notes in a prolonged painful squeal. Laura, who haunts the markets listening to the ballad singers, and stops every day to hear the blind boy playing his reed-flute in Sixteenth of September Street,[3] listens to Braggioni with pitiless courtesy, because she dares not smile at his miserable performance. Nobody dares to smile at him. Braggioni is cruel to everyone, with a kind of specialized insolence, but he is so vain of his talents, and so sensitive to slights, it would require a cruelty and vanity greater than his own to lay a finger on the vast cureless wound of his self-esteem. It would require courage, too, for it is dangerous to offend him, and nobody has this courage.

Braggioni loves himself with such tenderness and amplitude and eternal charity that his followers—for he is a leader of men, a skilled revolutionist, and his skin has been punctured in honorable warfare—warm themselves in the reflected glow, and say to each other: "He has a real nobility, a love of humanity raised above mere personal affections." The excess of this self-love has flowed out, inconveniently for her, over Laura, who, with so many others, owes her comfortable situation and her salary to him. When he is in a very good humor, he tells her, "I am tempted to forgive you for being a *gringa. Gringita!*"[4] and Laura, burning, imagines herself leaning forward suddenly, and with a sound back-handed slap wiping the suety smile from his face. If he notices her eyes at these moments he gives no sign.

She knows what Braggioni would offer her, and she must resist tenaciously without appearing to resist, and if she could avoid it she would not admit even to herself the slow drift of his intention. During these long evenings which have spoiled a long month for her, she sits in her deep chair with an open book on her knees, resting her eyes on the consoling rigidity of the printed page when the sight and sound of Braggioni singing threaten to identify themselves with all her remembered afflictions and to add their weight to her uneasy premonitions of the future. The gluttonous bulk of Braggioni has become a symbol of her many disillusions, for a revolutionist should be lean, animated by heroic faith, a vessel of abstract virtues. This is nonsense, she knows it now and is ashamed of it. Revolution must have leaders, and leadership is a career for energetic men. She is, her comrades tell her, full of romantic error, for what she defines as cynicism in them is merely "a developed sense of reality." She is almost too willing to say, "I am wrong, I suppose I don't really understand the principles," and afterward

[3]Street named to commemorate the beginning of the 1810 War of Mexican Independence from Spain.

[4]Foreign woman; little foreign woman.

she makes a secret truce with herself, determined not to surrender her will to such expedient logic. But she cannot help feeling that she has been betrayed irreparably by the disunion between her way of living and her feeling of what life should be, and at times she is almost contented to rest in this sense of grievance as a private store of consolation. Sometimes she wishes to run away, but she stays. Now she longs to fly out of this room, down the narrow stairs, and into the street where the houses lean together like conspirators under a single mottled lamp, and leave Braggioni singing to himself.

Instead she looks at Braggioni, frankly and clearly, like a good child who understands the rules of behavior. Her knees cling together under sound blue serge, and her round white collar is not purposely nun-like. She wears the uniform of an idea, and has renounced vanities. She was born Roman Catholic, and in spite of her fear of being seen by someone who might make a scandal of it, she slips now and again into some crumbling little church, kneels on the chilly stone, and says a Hail Mary on the gold rosary she bought in Tehuantepec.[5] It is no good and she ends by examining the altar with its tinsel flowers and ragged brocades, and feels tender about the battered doll-shape of some male saint whose white, lace-trimmed drawers hang limply around his ankles below the hieratic dignity of his velvet robe. She has encased herself in a set of principles derived from her early training, leaving no detail of gesture or of personal taste untouched, and for this reason she will not wear lace made on machines. This is her private heresy, for in her special group the machine is sacred, and will be the salvation of the workers. She loves fine lace, and there is a tiny edge of fluted cobweb on this collar, which is one of twenty precisely alike, folded in blue tissue paper in the upper drawer of her clothes chest.

Braggioni catches her glance solidly as if he had been waiting for it, leans forward, balancing his paunch between his spread knees, and sings with tremendous emphasis, weighing his words. He has, the song relates, no father and no mother, nor even a friend to console him; lonely as a wave of the sea he comes and goes, lonely as a wave.[6] His mouth opens round and yearns sideways, his balloon cheeks grow oily with the labor of song. He bulges marvelously in his expensive garments. Over his lavender collar, crushed upon a purple necktie, held by a diamond hoop: over his ammunition belt of tooled leather worked in silver, buckled cruelly around his gasping middle: over the tops of his glossy yellow shoes Braggioni swells with ominous ripeness, his mauve silk hose stretched taut, his ankles bound with the stout leather thongs of his shoes.

When he stretches his eyelids at Laura she notes again that his eyes are the true tawny yellow cat's eyes. He is rich, not in money, he tells her, but

[5]A town and surrounding area in the southeast section of the state of Oaxaca.
[6]The song is "A la Orilla de un Palmar": "I am alone by the palm-grove. I am a little orphan, alas. I have no father, and no mother, not even a friend who comes, alas, to console me. I pass my life by the shore of the palm-grove and all alone come and go like the waves of the sea."

in power, and this power brings with it the blameless ownership of things, and the right to indulge his love of small luxuries. "I have a taste for the elegant refinements," he said once, flourishing a yellow silk handkerchief before her nose. "Smell that? It is Jockey Club, imported from New York."[7] Nonetheless he is wounded by life. He will say so presently. "It is true everything turns to dust in the hand, to gall on the tongue." He sighs and his leather belt creaks like a saddle girth. "I am disappointed in everything as it comes. Everything." He shakes his head. "You, poor thing, you will be disappointed too. You are born for it. We are more alike than you realize in some things. Wait and see. Some day you will remember what I have told you, you will know that Braggioni was your friend."

Laura feels a slow chill, a purely physical sense of danger, a warning in her blood that violence, mutilation, a shocking death, wait for her with lessening patience. She has translated this fear into something homely, immediate, and sometimes hesitates before crossing the street. "My personal fate is nothing, except as the testimony of a mental attitude," she reminds herself, quoting from some forgotten philosophic primer, and is sensible enough to add, "Anyhow, I shall not be killed by an automobile if I can help it."

"It may be true I am as corrupt, in another way, as Braggioni," she thinks in spite of herself, "as callous, as incomplete," and if this is so, any kind of death seems preferable. Still she sits quietly, she does not run. Where could she go? Uninvited she has promised herself to this place; she can no longer imagine herself as living in another country, and there is no pleasure in remembering her life before she came here.

Precisely what is the nature of this devotion, its true motives, and what are its obligations? Laura cannot say. She spends part of her days in Xochimilco,[8] near by, teaching Indian children to say in English, "The cat is on the mat." When she appears in the classroom they crowd about her with smiles on their wise, innocent, clay-colored faces, crying, "Good morning, my titcher!" in immaculate voices, and they make of her desk a fresh garden of flowers every day.

During her leisure she goes to union meetings and listens to busy important voices quarreling over tactics, methods, internal politics. She visits the prisoners of her own political faith in their cells, where they entertain themselves with counting cockroaches, repenting of their indiscretions, composing their memoirs, writing out manifestoes and plans for their comrades who are still walking about free, hands in pockets, sniffing fresh air. Laura brings them food and cigarettes and a little money, and she brings messages disguised in equivocal phrases from the men outside who dare not set foot in the prison for fear of disappearing into the cells kept empty for them. If the prisoners confuse night and day, and complain, "Dear little Laura, time doesn't pass in this infernal hole, and I won't know when it is

---

[7]A line of men's fragrances produced by Caswell-Massey; refers also to the Jockey Club in Mexico City, a luxurious gathering place for socially prominent Mexicans.

[8]Idyllic Indian village south of Mexico City known for its canals and ancient traditions.

time to sleep unless I have a reminder," she brings them their favorite narcotics, and says in a tone that does not wound them with pity, "Tonight will really be night for you," and though her Spanish amuses them, they find her comforting, useful. If they lose patience and all faith, and curse the slowness of their friends in coming to their rescue with money and influence, they trust her not to repeat everything, and if she inquires, "Where do you think we can find money, or influence?" they are certain to answer, "Well, there is Braggioni, why doesn't he do something?"

She smuggles letters from headquarters to men hiding from firing squads in back streets in mildewed houses, where they sit in tumbled beds and talk bitterly as if all Mexico were at their heels, when Laura knows positively they might appear at the band concert in the Alameda on Sunday morning, and no one would notice them.[9] But Braggioni says, "Let them sweat a little. The next time they may be careful. It is very restful to have them out of the way for a while." She is not afraid to knock on any door in any street after midnight, and enter in the darkness, and say to one of these men who is really in danger: "They will be looking for you—seriously—tomorrow morning after six. Here is some money from Vicente. Go to Vera Cruz and wait."

She borrows money from the Roumanian agitator to give to his bitter enemy the Polish agitator. The favor of Braggioni is their disputed territory, and Braggioni holds the balance nicely, for he can use them both. The Polish agitator talks love to her over café tables, hoping to exploit what he believes is her secret sentimental preference for him, and he gives her misinformation which he begs her to repeat as the solemn truth to certain persons. The Roumanian is more adroit. He is generous with his money in all good causes, and lies to her with an air of ingenuous candor, as if he were her good friend and confidant. She never repeats anything they may say. Braggioni never asks questions. He has other ways to discover all that he wishes to know about them.

Nobody touches her, but all praise her gray eyes, and the soft, round under lip which promises gayety, yet is always grave, nearly always firmly closed: and they cannot understand why she is in Mexico. She walks back and forth on her errands, with puzzled eyebrows, carrying her little folder of drawings and music and school papers. No dancer dances more beautifully than Laura walks, and she inspires some amusing, unexpected ardors, which cause little gossip, because nothing comes of them. A young captain who had been a soldier in Zapata's army attempted, during a horseback ride near Cuernavaca, to express his desire for her with the noble simplicity befitting a rude folk-hero: but gently, because he was gentle.[10] This gentleness was his defeat, for when he alighted, and removed her foot from the

---

[9]The Alameda is a historic park in central Mexico City.

[10]The Liberation Army of the South, led by revolutionist Emiliano Zapata (1879–1919).

Cuernavaca is the capital city of the state of Morelo, about fifty miles from Mexico City.

stirrup, and essayed to draw her down into his arms, her horse, ordinarily a tame one, shied fiercely, reared and plunged away. The young hero's horse careered blindly after his stable-mate, and the hero did not return to the hotel until rather late that evening. At breakfast he came to her table in full charro dress, gray buckskin jacket and trousers with strings of silver buttons down the leg, and he was in a humorous, careless mood.[11] "May I sit with you?" and "You are a wonderful rider. I was terrified that you might be thrown and dragged. I should never have forgiven myself. But I cannot admire you enough for your riding!"

"I learned to ride in Arizona," said Laura.

"If you will ride with me again this morning, I promise you a horse that will not shy with you," he said. But Laura remembered that she must return to Mexico City at noon.

Next morning the children made a celebration and spent their playtime writing on the blackboard, "We lov ar ticher," and with tinted chalks they drew wreaths of flowers around the words. The young hero wrote her a letter: "I am a very foolish, wasteful, impulsive man. I should have first said I love you, and then you would not have run away. But you shall see me again." Laura thought, "I must send him a box of colored crayons," but you was trying to forgive herself for having spurred her horse at the wrong moment.

A brown, shock-haired youth came and stood in her patio one night and sang like a lost soul for two hours, but Laura could think of nothing to do about it. The moonlight spread a wash of gauzy silver over the clear spaces of the garden, and the shadows were cobalt blue. The scarlet blossoms of the Judas tree were dull purple, and the names of the colors repeated themselves automatically in her mind, while she watched not the boy, but his shadow, fallen like a dark garment across the fountain rim, trailing in the water.[12] Lupe came silently and whispered expert counsel in her ear: "If you will throw him one little flower, he will sing another song or two and go away." Laura threw the flower, and he sang a last song and went away with the flower tucked in the band of his hat. Lupe said, "He is one of the organizers of the Typographers Union, and before that he sold corridos in the Merced market, and before that, he came from Guanajuato, where I was born.[13] I would not trust any man, but I trust least those from Guanajuato."

She did not tell Laura that he would be back again the next night, and the next, nor that he would follow her at a certain fixed distance around the Merced market, through the Zócolo, up Francisco I. Madero Avenue, and so

---

[11]Charro is the traditional costume of a horseman or cowboy from the state of Jalisco.

[12]The blossoms mark the arrival of spring, when redtree blossoms include purple as well as red.

[13]Corridos are broadsides printed with words and music of ballads. Merced is Mexico City's largest market, selling wares from the smallest items to large pieces of furniture. Guanajuato is the capital city of state by the same name about 230 miles north of Mexico City.

along the Paseo de la Reforma to Chapultepec Park, and into the Philosopher's Footpath, still with that flower withering in his hat, and an indivisible attention in his eyes.[14]

Now Laura is accustomed to him, it means nothing except that he is
nineteen years old and is observing a convention with all propriety, as
though it were founded on a law of nature, which in the end it might well
prove to be. He is beginning to write poems which he prints on a wooden
press, and he leaves them stuck like handbills in her door. She is pleasantly
disturbed by the abstract, unhurried watchfulness of his black eyes which
will in time turn easily towards another object. She tells herself that throwing the flower was a mistake, for she is twenty-two years old and knows better; but she refuses to regret it, and persuades herself that her negation of
all external events as they occur is a sign that she is gradually perfecting
herself in the stoicism she strives to cultivate against that disaster she fears,
though she cannot name it.

She is not at home in the world. Every day she teaches children who
remain strangers to her, though she loves their tender round hands and
their charming opportunist savagery. She knocks at unfamiliar doors not
knowing whether a friend or a stranger shall answer, and even if a known
face emerges from the sour gloom of that unknown interior, still it is the
face of a stranger. No matter what this stranger says to her, nor what her
message to him, the very cells of her flesh reject knowledge and kinship in
one monotonous word. No. No. No. She draws her strength from this one
holy talismanic word which does not suffer her to be led into evil. Denying
everything, she may walk anywhere in safety, she looks at everything without amazement.

No, repeats this firm unchanging voice of her blood; and she looks at
Braggioni without amazement. He is a great man, he wishes to impress this
simple girl who covers her great round breasts with thick dark cloth, and
who hides long, invaluably beautiful legs under a heavy skirt. She is almost
thin except for the incomprehensible fullness of her breasts, like a nursing
mother's, and Braggioni, who considers himself a judge of women, speculates again on the puzzle of her notorious virginity, and takes the liberty of
speech which she permits without a sign of modesty, indeed, without any
sort of sign, which is disconcerting.

"You think you are so cold, *gringita*! Wait and see. You will surprise
yourself some day! May I be there to advise you!" He stretches his eyelids at
her, and his ill-humored cat's eyes waver in a separate glance for the two
points of light marking the opposite ends of a smoothly drawn path

[14]Zócolo is the correct spelling of a major town square in Mexico City also known as the Plaza de la Constitution. Madero Avenue is a Mexico City street commemorating the uprising against dictator Porfirio Díaz (1830–1915) led by Francisco Ignacio Madero (1873–1913). The paseo is a grand boulevard in Mexico City honoring the liberal reforms of President Benito Juárez (1806–1872). The Philosopher's Footpath is a 1,600-acre park on the outskirts of Mexico City and site of the Poet's Footpath and the castle that was once the home of Maximilian I of Mexico (1832–1867), and the Empress Carlota (1840–1927).

between the swollen curve of her breasts. He is not put off by that blue serge, nor by her resolutely fixed gaze. There is all the time in the world. His cheeks are bellying with the wind of song. "O girl with the dark eyes," he sings, and reconsiders. "But yours are not dark. I can change all that. O girl with the green eyes,[15] you have stolen my heart away!" then his mind wanders to the song, and Laura feels the weight of his attention being shifted elsewhere. Singing thus, he seems harmless, he is quite harmless, there is nothing to do but sit patiently and say "No," when the moment comes. She draws a full breath, and her mind wanders also, but not far. She dares not wander too far.

Not for nothing has Braggioni taken pains to be a good revolutionist and a professional lover of humanity. He will never die of it. He has the malice, the cleverness, the wickedness, the sharpness of wit, the hardness of heart, stipulated for loving the world profitably. *He will never die of it*. He will live to see himself kicked out from his feeding trough by other hungry world-saviors. Traditionally he must sing in spite of his life which drives him to bloodshed, he tells Laura, for his father was a Tuscany peasant who drifted to Yucatan and married a Maya woman: a woman of race, an aristocrat. They gave him the love and knowledge of music, thus: and under the rip of his thumbnail, the strings of the instrument complain like exposed nerves.

Once he was called Delgadito by all the girls and married women who ran after him; he was so scrawny all his bones showed under his thin cotton clothing, and he could squeeze his emptiness to the very backbone with his two hands.[16] He was a poet and the revolution was only a dream then; too many women loved him and sapped away his youth, and he could never find enough to eat anywhere, anywhere! Now he is a leader of men, crafty men who whisper in his ear, hungry men who wait for hours outside his office for a word with him, emaciated men with wild faces who waylay him at the street gate with a timid, "Comrade, let me tell you ..." and they blow the foul breath from their empty stomachs in his face.

He is always sympathetic. He gives them handfuls of small coins from his own pocket, he promises them work, there will be demonstrations, they must join the unions and attend the meetings, above all they must be on the watch for spies. They are closer to him than his own brothers, without them he can do nothing—until tomorrow, comrade!

Until tomorrow. "They are stupid, they are lazy, they are treacherous, they would cut my throat for nothing," he says to Laura. He has good food and abundant drink, he hires an automobile and drives in the Paseo on Sunday morning, and enjoys plenty of sleep in a soft bed beside a wife who dares not disturb him; and he sits pampering his bones in easy billows of fat, singing to Laura, who knows and thinks these things about him. When he was fifteen, he tried to drown himself because he loved a girl, his first

[15]"Aquellos Ojos Verdes," translated into English in 1929.

[16]Delgadito means little slim one.

love, and she laughed at him. "A thousand women have paid for that," and his tight little mouth turns down at the corners. Now he perfumes his hair with Jockey Club, and confides to Laura: "One woman is really as good as another for me, in the dark. I prefer them all."

His wife organizes unions among the girls in the cigarette factories, and walks in picket lines, and even speaks at meetings in the evening. But she cannot be brought to acknowledge the benefits of true liberty. "I tell her I must have my freedom, net.[17] She does not understand my point of view." Laura has heard this many times. Braggioni scratches the guitar and meditates. "She is an instinctively virtuous woman, pure gold, no doubt of that. If she were not, I should lock her up, and she knows it."

His wife, who works so hard for the good of the factory girls, employs part of her leisure lying on the floor weeping because there are so many women in the world, and only one husband for her, and she never knows where nor when to look for him. He told her: "Unless you can learn to cry when I am not here, I must go away for good." That day he went away and took a room at the Hotel Madrid.

It is this month of separation for the sake of higher principles that has been spoiled not only for Mrs. Braggioni, whose sense of reality is beyond criticism, but for Laura, who feels herself bogged in a nightmare. Tonight Laura envies Mrs. Braggioni, who is alone, and free to weep as much as she pleases about a concrete wrong. Laura has just come from a visit to the prison, and she is waiting for tomorrow with a bitter anxiety as if tomorrow may not come, but time may be caught immovably in this hour, with herself transfixed, Braggioni singing on forever, and Eugenio's body not yet discovered by the guard.

Braggioni says: "Are you going to sleep?" Almost before she can shake her head, he begins telling her about the May-day disturbances coming on in Morelia, for the Catholics hold a festival in honor of the Blessed Virgin, and the Socialists celebrate their martyrs on that day.[18] "There will be two independent processions, starting from either end of town, and they will march until they meet, and the rest depends ..." He asks her to oil and load his pistols. Standing up, he unbuckles his ammunition belt, and spreads it laden across her knees. Laura sits with the shells slipping through the cleaning cloth dipped in oil, and he says again he cannot understand why she works so hard for the revolutionary idea unless she loves some man who is in it. "Are you not in love with someone?" "No," says Laura. "And no one is in love with you?" "No." "Then it is your own fault. No woman need go begging. Why, what is the matter with you? The legless beggar woman in the Alameda has a perfectly faithful lover. Did you know that?"

Laura peers down the pistol barrel and says nothing, but a long, slow faintness rises and subsides in her? Braggioni curves his swollen fingers

[17]To cast his net wider.
[18]The reference is to the clash between Catholics and anticlerical factions in Morelia on May 8, 1921.

around the throat of the guitar and softly smothers the music out of it, and when she hears him again he seems to have forgotten her, and is speaking in the hypnotic voice he uses when talking in small rooms to a listening, close-gathered crowd. Some day this world, now seemingly so composed and eternal, to the edges of every sea shall be merely a tangle of gaping trenches, of crashing walls and broken bodies. Everything must be torn from its accustomed place where it has rotted for centuries, hurled skyward and distributed, cast down again clean as rain, without separate identity. Nothing shall survive that the stiffened hands of poverty have created for the rich and no one shall be left alive except the elect spirits destined to procreate a new world cleansed of cruelty and injustice, ruled by benevolent anarchy: "Pistols are good, I love them, cannon are even better, but in the end I pin my faith to good dynamite," he concludes, and strokes the pistol lying in her hands. "Once I dreamed of destroying this city, in case if offered resistance to General Ortíz, but it fell into his hands like an overripe pear."[19]

He is made restless by his own words, rises and stands waiting. Laura holds up the belt to him: "Put that on, and go kill somebody in Morelia, and you will be happier," she says softly. The presence of death in the room makes her bold. "Today, I found Eugenio going into a stupor. He refused to allow me to call the prison doctor. He had taken all the tablets I brought him yesterday. He said he took them because he was bored."

"He is a fool, and his death is his own business," says Braggioni, fastening his belt carefully.

"I told him if he had waited only a little while longer, you would have got him set free," says Laura. "He said he did not want to wait."

"He is a fool and we are well rid of him," says Braggioni, reaching for his hat.

He goes away. Laura knows his mood has changed, she will not see him any more for a while. He will send word when he needs her to go on errands into strange streets, to speak to the strange faces that will appear, like clay masks with the power of human speech, to mutter their thanks to Braggioni for his help. Now she is free, and she thinks, I must run while there is time. But she does not go.

Braggioni enters his own house where for a month his wife has spent many hours every night weeping and tangling her hair upon her pillow. She is weeping now, and she weeps more at the sight of him, the cause of all her sorrows. He looks about the room. Nothing is changed, the smells are good and familiar, he is well acquainted with the woman who comes toward him with no reproach except grief on her face. He says to her tenderly: "You are so good, please don't cry any more, you dear good creature." She says, "Are you tired, my angel? Sit here and I will wash your feet."[20] She brings a bowl of water, and kneeling, unlaces his shoes, and when from her knees she raises her sad eyes under her blackened lids, he is sorry for everything, and bursts

[19]Pascual Ortiz Rubio (1877–1963), president of Mexico, 1930–1932.

[20]See John 13:1–15, which describes Jesus washing his disciples' feet.

into tears. "Ah, yes, I am hungry, I am tired, let us eat something together," he says, between sobs. His wife leans her head on his arm and says, "Forgive me!" and this time he is refreshed by the solemn, endless rain of her tears.

Laura takes off her serge dress and puts on a white linen nightgown and goes to bed. She turns her head a little to one side, and lying still, reminds herself that it is time to sleep. Numbers tick in her brain like little clocks, soundless doors close of themselves around her. If you would sleep, you must not remember anything, the children will say tomorrow, good morning, my teacher, the poor prisoners who come every day bringing flowers to their jailor. 1-2-3-4-5—it is monstrous to confuse love with revolution, night with day, life with death—ah, Eugenio!

The tolling of the midnight bell is a signal, but what does it mean? Get up, Laura, and follow me[21]: come out of your sleep, out of your bed, out of this strange house. What are you doing in this house? Without a word, without fear she rose and reached for Eugenio's hand, but he eluded her with a sharp, sly smile and drifted away. This is not all, you shall see—Murderer, he said, follow me, I will show you a new country, but it is far away and we must hurry. No, said Laura, not unless you take my hand, no; and she clung first to the stair rail, and then to the topmost branch of the Judas tree that bent down slowly and set her upon the earth, and then to the rocky ledge of a cliff, and then to the jagged wave of a sea that was not water but a desert of crumbling stone. Where are you taking me, she asked in wonder but without fear. To death, and it is a long way off, and we must hurry, said Eugenio. No, said Laura, not unless you take my hand. Then eat these flowers, poor prisoner, said Eugenio in a voice of pity, take and eat: and from the Judas tree he stripped the warm bleeding flowers, and held them to her lips. She saw that his hand was fleshless, a cluster of small white petrified branches, and his eye sockets were without light, but she ate the flowers greedily for they satisfied both hunger and thirst. Murderer! said Eugenio, and Cannibal! This is my body and my blood.[22] Laura cried No! and at the sound of her own voice, she awoke trembling, and was afraid to sleep again.

1930

The Grave

The Grandfather, dead for more than thirty years, had been twice disturbed in his long repose by the constancy and possessiveness of his widow. She removed his bones first to Louisiana and then to Texas as if she had set out to find her own burial place, knowing well she would never return to the places she had left. In Texas she set up a small cemetery in a corner of her

[21] Jesus's words in many passages in the Bible; for example, Matthew 16:24: "If anyone desires to come after me, let him deny himself, and take up his cross, and follow me."

[22] Matthew 26:26–28: "And as they were eating, Jesus took bread, and blessed it, and broke it and gave it to the disciples, and said, 'Take, eat; this is my body.' And he took the cup, and gave thanks, and gave it to them, saying, 'Drink ye all of it, for this is my blood of the covenant, which is poured out for many for the forgiveness of sins.'"

first farm, and as the family connection grew, and oddments of relations came over from Kentucky to settle, it contained at last about twenty graves. After the Grandmother's death, part of her land was to be sold for the benefit of certain of her children, and the cemetery happened to lie in the part set aside for sale. It was necessary to take up the bodies and bury them again in the family plot in the big new public cemetery, where the Grandmother had been buried. At last her husband was to lie beside her for eternity, as she had planned.

The family cemetery had been a pleasant small neglected garden of tangled rose bushes and ragged cedar trees and cypress, the simple flat stones rising out of uncropped sweet-smelling wild grass.[1] The graves were lying open and empty one burning day when Miranda and her brother Paul, who often went together to hunt rabbits and doves, propped their twenty-two Winchester rifles carefully against the rail fence, climbed over and explored among the graves. She was nine years old and he was twelve.

They peered into the pits all shaped alike with such purposeful accuracy, and looking at each other with pleased adventurous eyes, they said in solemn tones: "These were graves!" trying by words to shape a special, suitable emotion in their minds, but they felt nothing except an agreeable thrill of wonder: they were seeing a new sight, doing something they had not done before. In them both there was also a small disappointment at the entire commonplaceness of the actual spectacle. Even if it had once contained a coffin for years upon years, when the coffin was gone a grave was just a hole in the ground. Miranda leaped into the pit that had held her grandfather's bones. Scratching around aimlessly and pleasurably as any young animal, she scooped up a lump of earth and weighed it in her palm. It had a pleasantly sweet, corrupt smell, being mixed with cedar needles and small leaves, and as the crumbs fell apart, she saw a silver dove no larger than a hazel nut, with spread wings and a neat fanshaped tail. The breast had a deep round hollow in it. Turning it up to the fierce sunlight, she saw that the inside of the hollow was cut in little whorls. She scrambled out, over the pile of loose earth that had fallen back into one end of the grave, calling to Paul that she had found something, he must guess what ... His head appeared smiling over the rim of another grave. He waved a closed hand at her. "I've got something too!" They ran to compare treasures, making a game of it, so many guesses each, all wrong, and a final showdown with opened palms. Paul had found a thin wide gold ring carved with intricate flowers and leaves. Miranda was smitten at sight of the ring and wished to have it. Paul seemed more impressed by the dove. They made a trade, with some little bickering. After he had got the dove in his hand, Paul said, "Don't you know what this is? This is a screw head for a *coffin*! ... I'll bet nobody else in the world has one like this!"

---

[1] An allusion to Part 6 of Whitman's *Song of Myself*, which includes, in a long catalog of answers to the child's question "What is the Grass," the line "And now it seems to me the beautiful uncut hair of graves."

Miranda glanced at it without covetousness. She had the gold ring on her thumb; it fitted perfectly. "Maybe we ought to go now," she said, "maybe one of the niggers'll see us and tell somebody." They knew the land had been sold, the cemetery was no longer theirs, and they felt like trespassers. They climbed back over the fence, slung their rifles loosely under their arms—they had been shooting at targets with various kinds of firearms since they were seven years old—and set out to look for the rabbits and doves or whatever small game might happen along. On these expeditions Miranda always followed at Paul's heels along the path, obeying instructions about handling her gun when going through fences; learning how to stand it up properly so it would not slip and fire unexpectedly; how to wait her time for a shot and not just bang away in the air without looking, spoiling shots for Paul, who really could hit things if given a chance. Now and then, in her excitement at seeing birds whizz up suddenly before her face, or a rabbit leap across her very toes, she lost her head, and almost without sighting she flung her rifle up and pulled the trigger. She hardly ever hit any sort of mark. She had no proper sense of hunting at all. Her brother would be often completely disgusted with her. "You don't care whether you get your bird or not," he said. "That's no way to hunt." Miranda could not understand his indignation. She had seen him smash his hat and yell with fury when he had missed his aim. "What I like about shooting," said Miranda, with exasperating inconsequence, "is pulling the trigger and hearing the noise."

"Then, by golly," said Paul, "whyn't you go back to the range and shoot at bulls-eyes?"

"I'd just as soon," said Miranda, "only like this, we walk around more."

"Well, you just stay behind and stop spoiling my shots," said Paul, who, when he made a kill, wanted to be certain he had made it. Miranda, who alone brought down a bird once in twenty rounds, always chimed as her own any game they got when they fired at the same moment. It was tiresome and unfair and her brother was sick of it.

"Now, the first dove we see, or the first rabbit, is mine," he told her. "And the next will be yours. Remember that and don't get smarty."

"What about snakes?" asked Miranda idly. "Can I have the first snake?"

Waving her thumb gently and watching her gold ring glitter, Miranda lost interest in shooting. She was wearing her summer roughing outfit: dark blue overalls, a light blue shirt, a hired-man's straw hat, and thick brown sandals. Her brother had the same outfit except his was a sober hickory-nut color. Ordinarily Miranda preferred her overalls to any other dress, though it was making rather a scandal in the countryside, for the year was 1903, and in the back country the law of female decorum had teeth in it. Her father had been criticized for letting his girls dress like boys and go careering around astride barebacked horses. Big sister Maria, the really independent and fearless one, in spite of her rather affected ways, rode at a dead run with only a rope knotted around her horse's nose. It was said the motherless family was running down, with the Grandmother no longer there to hold it together. It was known that she had discriminated against her son Harry in her will, and that he was in straits about money. Some of his old neighbors reflected with vicious satisfaction that now he would probably not be so stiff-necked, nor have any more high-stepping horses either. Miranda knew this, though she could not say how. She had met along the road old women of the kind who smoked corn-cob pipes, who had treated her grandmother with most sincere respect. They slanted their gummy old eyes side-ways at the granddaughter and said, "Ain't you ashamed of yo-self, Missy? It's against the Scriptures to dress like that. Whut yo Pappy thinkin about?" Miranda, with her powerful social sense, which was like a fine set of antennae radiating from every pore of her skin, would feel ashamed because she knew well it was rude and ill-bred to shock anybody, even bad-tempered old crones, though she had faith in her father's judgment and was perfectly comfortable in the clothes. Her father had said, "They're just what you need, and they'll save your dresses for school. . . ." This sounded quite simple and natural to her. She had been brought up in rigorous economy. Wastefulness was vulgar. It was also a sin. These were truths; she had heard them repeated many times and never once disputed.

Now the ring, shining with the serene purity of fine gold on her rather grubby thumb, turned her feelings against her overalls and sockless feet, toes sticking through the thick brown leather straps. She wanted to go back to the farmhouse, take a good cold bath, dust herself with plenty of Maria's violent talcum powder—provided Maria was not present to object, of course—put on the thinnest, most becoming dress she owned, with a big sash, and sit in a wicker chair under the trees. . . . These things were not all she wanted, of course; she had vague stirrings of desire for luxury and a grand way of living which could not take precise form in her imagination but were founded on family legend of past wealth and leisure. These immediate comforts were what she could have, and she wanted them at once. She lagged rather far behind Paul, and once she thought of just turning back without a word and going home. She stopped, thinking that Paul would never do that to her, and so she would have to tell him. When a rabbit leaped, she let Paul have it without dispute. He killed it with one shot.

When she came up with him, he was already kneeling, examining the wound, the rabbit trailing from his hands. "Right through the head," he said complacently, as if he had aimed for it. He took out his sharp, competent bowie knife and started to skin the body. He did it very cleanly and quickly. Uncle Jimbilly knew how to prepare the skins so that Miranda always had fur coats for her dolls, for though she never cared much for her dolls she liked seeing them in fur coats. The children knelt facing each other over the dead animal. Miranda watched admiringly while her brother stripped the skin away as if he were taking off a glove. The flayed flesh emerged dark scarlet, sleek, firm; Miranda with thumb and finger felt the long fine muscles with the silvery flat strips binding them to the joints. Brother lifted the oddly bloated belly. "Look," he said, in a low amazed voice. "It was going to have young ones."

Very carefully he slit the thin flesh from the center ribs to the flanks, and a scarlet bag appeared. He slit again and pulled the bag open, and there lay a bundle of tiny rabbits, each wrapped in a thin scarlet veil. The brother pulled these off and there they were, dark gray, their sleek wet down lying in minute even ripples, like a baby's head just washed, their unbelievably small delicate ears folded close, their little blind faces almost featureless.

Miranda said, "Oh, I want to *see*," under her breath. She looked and looked—excited but not frightened, for she was accustomed to the sight of animals killed in hunting—filled with pity and astonishment and a kind of shocked delight in the wonderful little creatures for their own sakes, they were so pretty. She touched one of them ever so carefully. "Ah, there's blood running over them," she said and began to tremble without knowing why. Yet she wanted most deeply to see and to know. Having seen, she felt at once as if she had known all along. The very memory of her former ignorance faded, she had always known just this. No one had ever told her anything outright, she had been rather unobservant of the animal life around her because she was so accustomed to animals. They seemed simply disorderly and unaccountably rude in their habits, but altogether natural and not very interesting. Her brother had spoken as if he had known about everything all along. He may have seen all this before. He had never said a word to her, but she knew now a part at least of what he knew. She understood a little of the secret, formless intuitions in her own mind and body, which had been clearing up, taking form, so gradually and so steadily she had not realized that she was learning what she had to know. Paul said cautiously, as if he were talking about something forbidden: "They were just about ready to be born." His voice dropped on the last word. "I know," said Miranda, "like kittens. I know, like babies." She was quietly and terribly agitated, standing again with her rifle under her arm, looking down at the bloody heap. "I don't want the skin," she said, "I won't have it." Paul buried the young rabbits again in their mother's body, wrapped the skin around her, carried her to a clump of sage brushes, and hid her away. He came out again at once and said to Miranda, with an eager friendliness, a confidential tone quite unusual in him, as if he were taking her into an important secret on equal terms: "Listen now. Now you listen to me, and don't ever forget. Don't you ever tell a living soul that you saw this. Don't tell a soul. Don't tell Dad because I'll get into trouble. He'll say I'm leading you into things you ought not to do. He's always saying that. So now don't you go and forget and blab out sometime the way you're always doing.... Now, that's a secret. Don't you tell."

Miranda never told, she did not even wish to tell anybody. She thought about the whole worrisome affair with confused unhappiness for a few days. Then it sank quietly into her mind and was heaped over by accumulated thousands of impressions, for nearly twenty years. One day she was picking her path among the puddles and crushed refuse of a market street in a strange city of a strange country, when without warning, plain and clear in its true colors as if she looked through a frame upon a scene that had not stirred nor changed since the moment it happened, the episode of that faroff day leaped from its burial place before her mind's eye. She was so reasonlessly horrified she halted suddenly staring, the scene before her eyes dimmed by the vision back of them. An Indian vendor had held up before her a tray of dyed sugar sweets, in the shapes of all kinds of small creatures: birds, baby chicks, baby rabbits, lambs, baby pigs. They were in gay colors and smelled of vanilla, maybe. . . . It was a very hot day and the smell in the market, with its piles of raw flesh and wilting flowers, was like the mingled sweetness and corruption she had smelled that other day in the empty cemetery at home: the day she had remembered always until now vaguely as the time she and her brother had found treasure in the opened graves. Instantly upon this thought the dreadful vision faded, and she saw clearly her brother, whose childhood face she had forgotten, standing again in the blazing sunshine, again twelve years old, a pleased sober smile in his eyes, turning the silver dove over and over in his hands.

1935

MARIANNE MOORE
1887–1972

Marianne Moore enjoyed a reputation among her fellow American poets as a distinctive and stylish innovator because of her fastidious diction and off-beat subject matter. In her later years, she was known to a wider public for her mild eccentricities and polished image, though her poems remained—at times at least—abstruse and difficult. Raised in Kirkwood, Missouri, and Carlisle, Pennsylvania, she attended Bryn Mawr College, from which she graduated in 1909. She taught at the U.S. Indian School in Carlisle and worked as a secretary and assistant librarian in New York City from 1911 to 1915, where her literary efforts began to receive notice. Her first professional publications in England and the United States in 1915 brought her considerable acclaim, perhaps most notably from Ezra Pound. She befriended both William Carlos Williams and Wallace Stevens and in 1925 was given *The Dial* magazine award for *Observations* (1924). Five consecutive issues of *The Dial* lauded her work; she soon became editor of the journal, which was perhaps the most prestigious American magazine of literature and art during the 1920s.

During her four years with *The Dial*, she published little of her own work, but in the 1930s, Moore accumulated awards as critics and other poets lauded her craftsmanship and precision of observation. Her greatest accolade came from T. S. Eliot, who, in the introduction to her *Selected Poems* (1935), said she was one of the few writers who had made a contribution to the language. Moore remained "a poet's poet" until 1952 when, following publication of *Collected Poems* (1951), she garnered outstanding praise, including the National Book Award, the Pulitzer Prize, and the Bollingen Prize.

Even after such acclaim, however, her work was seldom included in the school anthologies, which give most Americans their first acquaintance with the work of poets. Her portrait in a three-cornered hat and her idiosyncratic conversation created a public "character," however, and by the 1960s, she was a favorite of *Life* magazine and the *New York Times*. Being lionized as a celebrity, curiously at odds with her aesthetic, apparently did not disturb her impersonal and objective stances. Although she was an intelligent and serious poet, her public image reduced her to stereotypes of eccentric "genius" and benevolent grandmotherly dottiness.

Her reputation for difficulty arose from the habit in her early poems of breaking words at the ends of lines, even though the lines did not extend to the page margins. This effect is produced by syllabic verse—where the count of syllables measures the line—and was heightened by her stanzas, which often have an arbitrary but strict form. Thus the six-line stanzas in "Abundance" open with three lines of five or six syllables each; these are followed by two lines of ten or eleven and one of seven or eight. These metrics support the careful, precise statement of "observation" that a poem deals with. Another source for the opinion that Moore's work is difficult may have been the fact that she was determined to be as relatively objective as her male peers; much recent feminist criticism has examined the sexist patterns in the reception of her work and the gendered significance of her poetics.

Moore possessed a strict sense of moral values, and her good friend Elizabeth Bishop saw this as a close analogue to her concern with responsive social manners. She managed to find her values exemplified in a broad range of subjects, natural and cultural; these came from the wide reading, of material commonplace and erudite, that was one of her principal sources of experience. Her rigorous view considered abundance not as a plethora of luxuries but devotion to duty, fortitude as one of the primary necessities for survival, and good poetry as making room for the "genuine." She took much delight in things well-made, whether the product of human craftsmanship or creatures of nature such as the pangolin, a scaly anteater that she saw as "an armored animal." Her depicted animals became forms of subtle self-emblematizing, as they conveyed her thought and feeling with a combination of physical, aesthetic, and religious grace. On occasion known to be fussy in her endless revising and fondness for exact detail, her "gusto," a favorite term, frequently produced tones of delight mixed with a fastidious sense of right and wrong. Her fascination with the play of the mind gives her work the endurance she sought.

Bernard F. Engel
Michigan State University

Charles Molesworth
Queens College, City University of New York

PRIMARY WORKS

Poems, 1921; *Observations,* 1924; *Selected Poems,* 1935; *The Pangolin and Other Verse,* 1936; *What Are Years?,* 1941; *Nevertheless,* 1944; *Collected Poems,* 1951; *The Complete Prose of Marianne Moore,* 1989; *The Complete Poems of Marianne Moore,* 1994; *Selected Letters,* 1998; *The Poems of Marianne Moore,* ed. Grace Schulman, 2003; *The Poems of Marianne Moore,* 2005.

Poetry[1]

I, too, dislike it: there are things that are important beyond
    all this fiddle.
Reading it, however, with a perfect contempt for it, one
    discovers in
it after all, a place for the genuine.   5
    Hands that can grasp, eyes
        that can dilate, hair that can rise
           if it must, these things are important not because a

high-sounding interpretation can be put upon them but because
    they are   10
useful. When they become so derivative as to become
    unintelligible,
the same thing may be said for all of us, that we
        do not admire what
           we cannot understand: the bat   15
              holding on upside down or in quest of something to

eat, elephants pushing, a wild horse taking a roll, a tireless wolf
    under
a tree, the immovable critic twitching his skin like a horse that
    feels a flea, the base-   20
ball fan, the statistician—
    nor is it valid
        to discriminate against 'business documents and

school-books';[2] all these phenomena are important. One must
    make a distinction   25
however: when dragged into prominence by half poets, the
    result is not poetry,
nor till the poets among us can be
    'literalists of
    the imagination'[3]—above   30
        insolence and triviality and can present
for inspection, 'imaginary gardens with real toads in them', shall
    we have

---

[1]This is the well-known version of the poem. The *Collected Poems* (1981) prints only the first four words of lines 1–5. The notes, however, give the full version that appears here.

[2]*Diary of Tolstoy*, p. 84: "Poetry is verse: prose is not verse. Or the poetry is everything with the exception of business documents and school books" (from Moore's notes).

[3]W. B. Yeats, *Ideas of Good and Evil*, 1903, p. 182: "The limitation of his view was from the very intensity of his vision; he was a too literal realist of imagination, as others are of nature...." (from Moore's notes).

it. In the meantime, if you demand on the one hand,
the raw material of poetry in   35
   all its rawness and
   that which is on the other hand
      genuine, you are interested in poetry.

                  1921

England

with its baby rivers and little towns, each with its abbey or its
                       cathedral,
with voices—one voice perhaps, echoing through the transept—
                       the
criterion of suitability and convenience: and Italy   5
with its equal shores—contriving an epicureanism
from which the grossness has been extracted:

and Greece with its goat and its gourds,
the nest of modified illusions: and France,
the "chrysalis of the nocturnal butterfly,"[1]   10
in whose products mystery of construction
diverts one from what was originally one's object—
substance at the core: and the East with its snails, its emotional

shorthand and jade cockroaches, its rock crystal and its
                     imperturbability,   15
all of museum quality: and America where there
is the little old ramshackle victoria in the south,
where cigars are smoked on the street in the north;
where there are no proof-readers, no silkworms, no digressions;
the wild man's land; grassless, linksless, languageless country in   20
                   which letters are written
not in Spanish, not in Greek, not in Latin, not in shorthand,
but in plain American which cats and dogs can read!
The letter *a* in psalm and calm when
pronounced with the sound of *a* in candle, is very noticeable, but   25

why should continents of misapprehension
have to be accounted for by the fact?
Does it follow that because there are poisonous toadstools
which resemble mushrooms, both are dangerous?
Of mettlesomeness which may be mistaken for appetite,   30

[1]Moore's notes attribute the quotation to Erté (Romain de Tirtoff, 1892–1990), Russian-born graphics artist who became a celebrity designer for fashion houses and the theater in Paris, London, and New York.

of heat which may appear to be haste,
no conclusions may be drawn.

To have misapprehended the matter is to have confessed that
                                    one has not looked far enough.
The sublimated wisdom of China, Egyptian discernment,   35
the cataclysmic torrent of emotion
compressed in the verbs of the Hebrew language,
the books of the man who is able to say,
"I envy nobody but him, and him only,
who catches more fish than I do"—[2]   40
the flower and fruit of all that noted superiority—
if not stumbled upon in America,
must one imagine that it is not there?
It has never been confined to one locality.

                                                                    1921

To a Chameleon[1]

Hid by the august foliage and fruit of the grape-vine
    twine
        your anatomy
            round the pruned and polished stem,
                Chameleon.   5
                Fire laid upon
            an emerald as long as
        the Dark King's[2'] massy
    one,
could not snap the spectrum up for food as you have done.   10

                                                                    1921

An Egyptian Pulled Glass Bottle in the Shape of a Fish

Here we have thirst
and patience, from the first,
    and art, as in a wave held up for us to see
    in its essential perpendicularity;

---

[2]Moore took the quotation from Izaak Walton
(1593–1683), author of *The Compleat Angler*
(1653, rev. 1655), the best-known book on
fishing as a recreation.
[1]Chameleon: any of a number of lizards that
can change skin color. The shape of the poem

on the page seems meant to suggest the way
the lizard can "twine" around a stem.
[2']Dark King: alludes to Prester John, a perhaps legendary medieval king and priest,
said to have ruled in Ethiopia or western
Asia.

not brittle but   5
intense—the spectrum, that
    spectacular and nimble animal the fish,
    whose scales turn aside the sun's sword by their polish.

1924

The Pangolin

Another armored animal[1]—scale
    lapping scale with spruce-cone regularity until they
form the uninterrupted central
    tail-row! This near artichoke with head and legs and grit-
      equipped gizzard,   5

the night miniature artist engineer is,
    yes, Leonardo da Vinci's replica—[2]
      impressive animal and toiler of whom we seldom hear.
    Armor seems extra. But for him,
      the closing ear-ridge—[3]   10
        or bare ear lacking even this small
        eminence and similarly safe

contracting nose and eye apertures
    impenetrably closable, are not; a true ant-eater,
not cockroach-eater, who endures   15
    exhausting solitary trips through unfamiliar ground at night,
    returning before sunrise; stepping in the moonlight,
      on the moonlight peculiarly,[4] that the outside
      edges of his hands may bear the weight and save the
    claws   20
      for digging. Serpentined about
        the tree, he draws
          away from danger unpugnaciously,
          with no sound but a harmless hiss; keeping

the fragile grace of the Thomas-   25
    of-Leighton Buzzard Westminster Abbey wrought-iron vine,[5]
      or

[1]"Pangolin" is the name given to a number of scaly, ant-eating mammals of Asia and Africa. The word "another" suggests a bit of humor, since Moore wrote several poems on creatures having thick hides or other "armor."

[2]Leonardo da Vinci (1452–1519), Renaissance man of all talents, was both artist and engineer.

[3]Moore's notes say that "the closing ear-ridge" and certain other details are from Robert T. Hatt, "Pangolins," *Natural History* (December 1935).

[4]Moore's notes say that "stepping … peculiarly" is an idea taken from Richard Lydekker (1849–1915), English naturalist.

[5]Alludes to "a fragment of ironwork in Westminster Abbey" (from Moore's note).

rolls himself into a ball that has
    power to defy all effort to unroll it; strongly intailed, neat
head for core, on neck not breaking off, with curled-in feet.   30
        Nevertheless he has sting-proof scales; and nest
            of rocks closed with earth from inside, which he can thus
        darken.
        Sun and moon and day and night and man and beast
            each with a splendor   35
                which man in all his vileness cannot
                set aside; each with an excellence!

"Fearful yet to be feared,"[6] the armored
    ant-eater met by the driver-ant does not turn back, but
engulfs what he can, the flattened sword-   40
        edged leafpoints on the tail and artichoke set leg- and body-
        plates
    quivering violently when it retaliates
            and swarms on him. Compact like the furled fringed frill
                on the hat-brim of Gargallo's hollow iron head of a   45
            matador,[7] he will drop and will
                then walk away
                    unhurt, although if unintruded on,
                    he cautiously works down the tree, helped

by his tail. The giant-pangolin-   50
    tail, graceful tool, as prop or hand or broom or ax, tipped
    like
an elephant's trunk with special skin,
    is not lost on this ant- and stone-swallowing uninjurable
    artichoke which simpletons thought a living fable   55
        whom the stones had nourished, whereas ants had done
            so. Pangolins are not aggressive animals; between
        dusk and day they have the not unchain-like machine-like
                form and frictionless creep of a thing
                made graceful by adversities, con-   60

versities. To explain grace requires
    a curious hand. If that which is at all were not forever,
why would those who graced the spires
    with animals and gathered there to rest, on cold luxurious
    low stone seats—a monk and monk and monk—between the   65
    thus

---

[6]"Fearful yet to be feared": Moore gives no
source. She may have been quoting; or she
may have used quotation marks to highlight
the expression or to give it an air of factuality.

[7]Pablo Gargallo (1881–1934) was a Spanish
painter and sculptor.

ingenious roof-supports, have slaved to confuse
    grace with a kindly manner, time in which to pay a debt,
the cure for sins, a graceful use
    of what are yet   70
        approved stone mullions[8] branching out across
        the perpendiculars? A sailboat
was the first machine. Pangolins, made
    for moving quietly also, are models of exactness,
on four legs; on hind feet plantigrade,   75
  with certain postures of a man. Beneath sun and moon, man
    slaving
  to make his life more sweet, leaves half the flowers worth
    having,
        needing to choose wisely how to use his strength;   80
          a paper-maker like the wasp; a tractor of foodstuffs,
      like the ant; spidering a length
        of web from bluffs
           above a stream; in fighting, mechanicked
           like the pangolin; capsizing in   85
disheartenment. Bedizened or stark
    naked, man, the self, the being we call human, writing-
master to this world, griffons[9] a dark
    "Like does not like like that is obnoxious"; and writes error
    with four   90
  r's. Among animals, *one* has a sense of humor.
        Humor saves a few steps, it saves years. Unignorant,
        modest and unemotional, and all emotion,
    he has everlasting vigor,
        power to grow,   95
        though there are few creatures who can make one
        breathe faster and make one erecter.

Not afraid of anything is he,
    and then goes cowering forth, tread paced to meet an obstacle
at every step. Consistent with the   100
    formula—warm blood, no gills, two pairs of hands and a few
    hairs—that
is a mammal; there he sits in his own habitat,
      serge-clad, strong-shod. The prey of fear, he, always
        curtailed, extinguished, thwarted by the dusk, work partly 105
        done,

---

[8]Vertical dividing bars between panels or window panes.
[9]Probably alludes to the griffin, a mythical beast having an eagle's head and wings, and a lion's body. The word is used here as a verb.

says to the alternating blaze,
   "Again the sun!
      anew each day; and new and new and new,
      that comes into and steadies my soul."   110

                                                          1936

What Are Years?

   What is our innocence,
what is our guilt? All are
   naked, none is safe. And whence
is courage: the unanswered question,
the resolute doubt,—   5
dumbly calling, deafly listening—that
in misfortune, even death,
     encourages others
       and in its defeat, stirs
   the soul to be strong? He   10
sees deep and is glad, who
   accedes to mortality
and in his imprisonment rises
upon himself as
the sea in a chasm, struggling to be   15
free and unable to be,
     in its surrendering
     finds its continuing.

   So he who strongly feels,
behaves. The very bird,   20
   grown taller as he sings, steels
his form straight up. Though he is captive,
his mighty singing
says, satisfaction is a lowly
thing, how pure a thing is joy.   25
     This is mortality,
     this is eternity.

                                                            1941

Nevertheless

you've seen a strawberry
   that's had a struggle; yet
   was, where the fragments met,

a hedgehog or a star-
    fish for the multitude   5
    of seeds. What better food

than apple seeds—the fruit
    within the fruit—locked in
    like counter-curved twin

hazelnuts? Frost that kills   10
    the little rubber-plant-
    leaves of *kok-saghyz*[1]-stalks, can't

harm the roots; they still grow
    in frozen ground. Once where
    there was a prickly-pear-   15

leaf clinging to barbed wire,
    a root shot down to grow
    in earth two feet below;

as carrots form mandrakes[2]
    or ram's-horn root some-   20
    times. Victory won't come

to me unless I go
    to it; a grape tendril
    ties a knot in knots till

knotted thirty times—so   25
    the bound twig that's under-
    gone and over-gone, can't stir.

The weak overcomes its
    menace, the strong over-
    comes itself. What is there   30

like fortitude! What sap
    went through that little thread
    to make the cherry red!

1944

[1]Russian dandelion; its roots yield a form of rubber.

[2]Poisonous plants thought to look like the human body.

The Mind Is an Enchanting Thing[1]

is an enchanted thing
    like the glaze on a
katydid-wing
        subdivided by sun
        till the nettings are legion.   5
Like Gieseking playing Scarlatti;[2]

like the apteryx-awl
    as a beak, or the
kiwi's rain shawl
        of haired feathers, the mind   10
        feeling its way as though blind,
walks along with its eyes on the ground.

It has memory's ear
    that can hear without
having to hear.   15
        Like the gyroscope's fall,
        truly unequivocal
because trued by regnant certainty,

it is a power of
    strong enchantment. It   20
is like the dove-
        neck animated by
        sun; it is memory's eye;
it's conscientious inconsistency.

It tears off the veil; tears   25
    the temptation, the
mist the heart wears,
        from its eyes—if the heart
        has a face; it takes apart
dejection. It's fire in the dove-neck's   30

iridescence; in the
    inconsistencies

[1]This poem may be compared with the later "The Mind, Intractable Thing."
[2]Walter W. Gieseking (1895–1956), a German pianist, was well known for his playing of pieces by the Italian composer Domenico Scarlatti (1685–1757).

of Scarlatti.
       Unconfusion submits
           its confusion to proof; it's   35
not a Herod's oath that cannot change.

                                                                            1944

LOUISE BOGAN
1897–1970

Born in Livermore, Maine, Bogan attended private school in New Hampshire
and, after her family moved to Boston, the Girls' Latin School, graduating in
1915. Later, she remembered her five years at the school—renowned for its rigorous classical curriculum—as stimulating and happy. By age fifteen she considered herself a writer. However, having completed one year at Boston University,
she married an army officer and accompanied him to Panama, where they had a
daughter. After his death in 1920, Bogan lived in New York, supporting herself
with jobs in a bookstore and at the public library. During these difficult, but
exciting years, she frequented literary gatherings in Greenwich Village and met
writers associated with Alfred Kreymborg and his magazine, *Others*, among
them William Carlos Williams, Lola Ridge, and Conrad Aiken. She also developed
a lasting friendship with the writer-critic Edmund Wilson. By 1922, her verse
had appeared in such leading journals as *Poetry*, *Vanity Fair*, and *The New Republic*. Early recognition led in 1923 to her first book, *Body of This Death*.

From 1925 to 1937, Bogan was married to Raymond Holden, a poet and for
several years managing editor of *The New Yorker*. In 1931 she became poetry
reviewer for the magazine, a position she held for thirty-eight years. Her essays
and reviews are collected in two volumes of criticism. From 1933, when she was
awarded the first of two Guggenheim Fellowships for creative writing, she spent
periods of time in Europe.

The detachment typical of Bogan's verse is absent in "Women" (1922). In
an accusing tone, the speaker berates women for reducing their talent and imagination to attain a life-denying contentment, perpetuating their own meager
conditions. Although the speaker implies male standards against which to judge
women's actions, the point is, surely, that women *should* have "wilderness in
them," should journey with courage, and both think and imagine beyond narrowly defined limits. When the poem appeared, Bogan herself was not one of
the "provident," cautious women she describes.

Two poems from the 1930s reveal the influence of Yeats and Rilke as well
as the range of Bogan's poetic skill. In lines alive with alliteration, "Roman
Fountain" echoes the startling rise and fall of the fountain, shaped by the
bronze spout to achieve its zenith just a moment before falling. Like the fountain's maker, the poet crafts her materials in dramatic, intricate patterns to

capture the image. In contrast to this response to outer reality, "The Sleeping Fury" details the speaker's conflict with an inner self, both sister and avenger of "the kissed-out lie." Driven by this punishing force, she must finally acknowledge her mask and its false love. In place of the flame-enshrouded demon, she discovers upon relinquishing her passion a childlike figure of dreamless sleep that mirrors her hard-won peace. In long, fluid lines, Bogan conveys deep personal anguish without revealing its factual source.

A late poem, "The Dragonfly," exemplifies Bogan's rare experiment with short free verse lines, capturing through vivid imagery the insect's appearance and movement. Like Moore's animals, Bogan's dragonfly embodies certain human characteristics: the "Unending hunger/Grappling love" that cause the beautiful predator to "rocket into the day," only to lose "design and purpose" as the season runs its course. In its faultless diction and elegant simplicity, Bogan's finest verse possesses lyric power of a high order.

Theodora Rapp Graham
Pennsylvania State University at Harrisburg

PRIMARY WORKS

Poetry: *Body of This Death*, 1923; *Dark Summer*, 1929; *The Sleeping Fury*, 1937; *Poems and New Poems*, 1941; *Collected Poems, 1923–1953*, 1954; *The Blue Estuaries: Poems 1923–1968*, 1968, 1977; Criticism: *Achievement in American Poetry, 1900–1950*, 1951; *Selected Criticism: Poetry and Prose*, 1955; *A Poet's Alphabet: Reflections on the Literary Art and Vocation*, ed. Robert Phelps and Ruth Limmer, 1970; *What the Woman Lived: Selected Letters of Louise Bogan, 1920–1970*, ed. Ruth Limmer, 1973; *Journey Around My Room: The Autobiography of Louise Bogan: A Mosaic*, ed. Ruth Limmer, 1980.

Women

Women have no wilderness in them,
They are provident instead,
Content in the tight hot cell of their hearts
To eat dusty bread.

They do not see cattle cropping red winter grass,   5
They do not hear
Snow water going down under culverts
Shallow and clear.

They wait, when they should turn to journeys,
They stiffen, when they should bend.   10
They use against themselves that benevolence
To which no man is friend.

They cannot think of so many crops to a field
Or of clean wood cleft by an axe.

Their love is an eager meaninglessness   15
Too tense, or too lax.

They hear in every whisper that speaks to them
A shout and a cry.
As like as not, when they take life over their door-sills
They should let it go by.   20

1922

The Sleeping Fury

You are here now,
Who were so loud and feared, in a symbol before me,
Alone and asleep, and I at last look long upon you.

Your hair fallen on your cheek, no longer in the semblance of
    serpents,   5
Lifted in the gale; your mouth, that shrieked so, silent.
You, my scourge, my sister, lie asleep, like a child,
Who, after rage, for an hour quiet, sleeps out its tears.

The days close to winter
Rough with strong sound. We hear the sea and the forest,   10
And the flames of your torches fly, lit by others,
Ripped by the wind, in the night. The black sheep for sacrifice
Huddle together. The milk is cold in the jars.

All to no purpose, as before, the knife whetted and plunged,
The shout raised, to match the clamor you have given them.   15
You alone turn away, not appeased; unaltered, avenger.

Hands full of scourges, wreathed with your flames and adders,
You alone turned away, but did not move from my side,
Under the broken light, when the soft nights took the torches.

At thin morning you showed, thick and wrong in that calm,   20
The ignoble dream and the mask, sly, with slits at the eyes,
Pretence and half-sorrow, beneath which a coward's hope
    trembled.

You uncovered at night, in the locked stillness of houses,
False love due the child's heart, the kissed-out lie, the embraces,   25
Made by the two who for peace tenderly turned to each other.

You who know what we love, but drive us to know it;
You with your whips and shrieks, bearer of truth and of solitude;
You who give, unlike men, to expiation your mercy.

Dropping the scourge when at last the scourged advances to meet   30
    it,
You, when the hunted turns, no longer remain the hunter
But stand silent and wait, at last returning his gaze.

Beautiful now as a child whose hair, wet with rage and tears
Clings to its face. And now I may look upon you,   35
Having once met your eyes. You lie in sleep and forget me.
Alone and strong in my peace, I look upon you in yours.

                                                        1937

Roman Fountain

Up from the bronze, I saw
Water without a flaw
Rush to its rest in air,
Reach to its rest, and fall.
Bronze of the blackest shade,   5
An element man-made,
Shaping upright the bare
Clear gouts of water in air.

O, as with arm and hammer,
Still it is good to strive   10
To beat out the image whole,
To echo the shout and stammer
When full-gushed waters, alive,
Strike on the fountain's bowl
After the air of summer.   15

                                                        1937

After the Persian

I

I do not wish to know
The depths of your terrible jungle:
From what nest your leopard leaps
Or what sterile lianas are at once your serpents' disguise and
    home.   5

I am the dweller on the temperate threshold,
The strip of corn and vine,
Where all is translucence (the light!)
Liquidity, and the sound of water.

Here the days pass under shade   10
And the nights have the waxing and the waning moon.
Here the moths take flight at evening;
Here at morning the dove whistles and the pigeons coo.
Here, as night comes on, the fireflies wink and snap
Close to the cool ground,   15
Shining in a profusion
Celestial or marine.

Here it is never wholly dark but always wholly green,
And the day stains with what seems to be more than the sun
What may be more than my flesh.   20

II

I have wept with the spring storm;
Burned with the brutal summer.
Now, hearing the wind and the twanging bow-strings,
I know what winter brings.

The hunt sweeps out upon the plain   25
And the garden darkens.
They will bring the trophies home
To bleed and perish
Beside the trellis and the lattices,
Beside the fountain, still flinging diamond water,   30
Beside the pool
(Which is eight-sided, like my heart).

III

All has been translated into treasure:
Weightless as amber,
Translucent as the currant on the branch,   35
Dark as the rose's thorn.

Where is the shimmer of evil?
This is the shell's iridescence
And the wild bird's wing.

IV

Ignorant, I took up my burden in the wilderness.   40
Wise with great wisdom, I shall lay it down upon flowers.

V

Goodbye, goodbye!
There was so much to love, I could not love it all;
I could not love it enough.

Some things I overlooked, and some I could not find.   45
Let the crystal clasp them
When you drink your wine, in autumn.

1937

The Dragonfly

You are made of almost nothing
But of enough
To be great eyes
And diaphanous double vans;
To be ceaseless movement,   5
Unending hunger
Grappling love.

Link between water and air,
Earth repels you.
Light touches you only to shift into iridescence   10
Upon your body and wings.

Twice-born, predator,
You split into the heat.
Swift beyond calculation or capture
You dart into the shadow   15
Which consumes you.

You rocket into the day.
But at last, when the wind flattens the grasses,
For you, the design and purpose stop.

And you fall   20
With the other husks of summer.

1963

Night

The cold remote islands
And the blue estuaries
Where what breathes, breathes
The restless wind of the inlets,
And what drinks, drinks   5
The incoming tide;

Where shell and weed
Wait upon the salt wash of the sea,
And the clear nights of stars
Swing their lights westward   10
To set behind the land;

Where the pulse clinging to the rocks
Renews itself forever;
Where, again on cloudless nights,
The water reflects   15
The firmament's partial setting;

—O remember
In your narrowing dark hours
That more things move
Than blood in the heart.   20

1963

ERNEST HEMINGWAY
1899–1961

Ernest Miller Hemingway, like the matadors he admired, "lived life all the way up." He witnessed three wars, traveled extensively, enjoyed big game hunting and fishing, married four times, and ultimately became an icon of American masculinity and one of the most celebrated and significant American writers of the twentieth century.

Born the second of six children (and oldest son) to a physician father, Clarence, and an opera-singer-turned-music-teacher mother, Grace, the young Hemingway chafed against the middle-class provincialism of his upbringing in the conservative and affluent Chicago suburb of Oak Park. He preferred the adventure and freedom of the summers his family spent in Upper Michigan. Almost-

Edenic Michigan settings figure prominently in his fiction, particularly in stories related to his most autobiographical protagonist, Nick Adams. Although Hemingway was critical of both his parents—he found his mother domineering (he resented, among other things, her decision to "twin" him with his older sister, Marcelline, by dressing and coifing them alike as young children) and his father weak and unavailable (Clarence suffered from depression and eventually committed suicide in 1928)—both parents influenced him greatly. He adopted his mother's love of the arts and his father's passion for the outdoors, particularly hunting and fishing. He also struggled with the bourgeois morality he rebelled against in his parents throughout his life.

As soon as he graduated high school in 1917, Hemingway left Oak Park, settling into a job with *The Kansas City Star* after he was rejected from service in the army due to poor eyesight. Less than a year later, Hemingway signed on with American Red Cross ambulance corps. He arrived in Italy in June 1918; a month later, he was wounded in Fossalta di Piave while delivering chocolate and cigarettes to soldiers. His wounds were serious—he had over 200 pieces of shrapnel in his legs—and he arguably suffered from shell shock (today known as posttraumatic stress disorder). While recovering in Milan, he fell in love with Agnes von Kurowsky, an American nurse eight years his senior; she broke off their relationship. Hemingway later transformed these experiences into several short stories and one of his most successful novels, *A Farewell to Arms* (1929).

After enjoying a minor celebrity as the first American wounded on the Italian front upon returning to the United States, Hemingway again longed for adventure. In 1921 he married Hadley Richardson, and shortly after he arrived in Paris with a job as a foreign correspondent for the *Toronto Star*, armed with letters of introduction to influential artists and writers from well-known American author, Sherwood Anderson, whom he and Hadley had met in Chicago. As Gertrude Stein, one of Hemingway's mentors during this period, famously observed, "Paris was where the twentieth century was," and it was here, under the tutelage of Stein and Ezra Pound, that Hemingway forged his unique style. This taut, action-based style combines Stein's cadences and use of repetition with Pound's emphasis on concrete language, but it also is indebted to the direct writing and adventure- and romance-driven plotlines popular in pulp magazines of his youth and his training as a journalist. By the end of his six transformative years in Paris, Hemingway had become a well-known figure in the Parisian literary world, and, more importantly, he had published two significant books—the experimental *In Our Time* (1925) and the generation-defining *The Sun Also Rises* (1926). He also divorced his first wife, with whom he had a son, John, and married the stylish and wealthy Pauline Pfeiffer.

Hemingway lived with Pauline and their two sons, Patrick and Gregory, in Key West, Florida, for most of the 1930s. Curiously, after the resounding success of *Farewell* in1929, the established fiction author dedicated himself to nonfiction: *Green Hills of Africa* (1935) based on his African safari (1934–1935) and *Death in the Afternoon* (1932), an expert study of the Spanish bullfight. During this period, Hemingway's fame and public persona arguably began to dominate his literary reputation. In addition to the personality-driven nonfiction works, he published short pieces in popular magazines such as *Esquire*. Toward the end of the decade, he divorced Pauline and married a young writer and journalist,

Martha Gellhorn. The couple moved to the Finca Vigìa in San Francisco de Paula, Cuba, which remained Hemingway's home base until the Cuban Revolution in 1959.

The 1940s began with the tremendous success of *For Whom the Bell Tolls* (1940), based on Hemingway's experiences as a correspondent during the Spanish Civil War (1936–1939). He traveled to China with Martha, and the two worked as correspondents during World War II. Gellhorn's commitment to her career antagonized Hemingway, and he eventually left her for a less competitive journalist, Mary Welsh, who gave up her career to become his fourth and final wife. Although Hemingway's celebrity never waned, his literary reputation did. His World War II novel, *Across the River and into the Trees* (1950), is generally considered a failure. With the publication of *The Old Man and the Sea* in 1952, however, Hemingway reclaimed his position as a serious writer and won a Pulitzer. He also won the Nobel Prize for Literature in 1954.

In the last decade of his life, Hemingway began to revisit significant sites from his youth. He returned to Africa for a second safari in 1953 and 1954 and spent time in Spain in 1959. In his last years, Hemingway suffered from increasingly intense bouts of depression and erratic behavior. He was hospitalized and treated for depression, including primitive use of electroshock therapy. On July 2, 1961, he committed suicide at his home in Ketchum, Idaho.

Hemingway's fame, however, has lived on through his mythic status in American culture and through a series of posthumously published works, including *A Moveable Feast* (1964), *Islands in the Stream* (1970), *The Dangerous Summer* (1985), *The Garden of Eden* (1986), and *True at First Light* (1999; republished in a scholarly edition, *Under Kilimanjaro* [2005]). In particular, *The Garden of Eden*, which explores the gender and sexual experiments of a young couple on their honeymoon in the 1920s, prompted a critical re-evaluation of Hemingway's iconic hypermasculine persona and inspired a new wave of criticism informed by gender and sexuality studies, cultural studies, and ecological criticism (among others). From this work, a new Hemingway—complex, compassionate, and sensitive—has emerged, challenging and enriching previous understandings of the man and his work.

Suzanne del Gizzo
Chestnut Hill College

PRIMARY WORKS

In Our Time, 1925; *The Sun Also Rises*, 1926; *The Torrents of Spring*, 1926; *Men Without Women*, 1927; *A Farewell to Arms*, 1929; *Death in the Afternoon*, 1932; *Winner Take Nothing*, 1933; *Green Hills of Africa*, 1935; *To Have and Have Not*, 1937; *The Fifth Column and the First Forty-nine Stories*, 1938; *For Whom the Bell Tolls*, 1940; *Across the River and into the Trees*, 1950; *The Old Man and the Sea*, 1952; *A Moveable Feast*, 1964; *Islands in the Stream*, 1970; *The Nick Adams Stories*, ed. by Philip Young, 1972; *Selected Letters, 1917–1961*, ed. by Carlos Baker, 1981; *That Dangerous Summer*, 1985; *The Garden of Eden*, 1986; *The Complete Short Stories of Ernest Hemingway*, 1987; *True at First Light*, 1999; *Under Kilimanjaro*, 2005.

Hills Like White Elephants

The hills across the valley of the Ebro[1] were long and white. On this side there was no shade and no trees and the station was between two lines of rails in the sun. Close against the side of the station there was the warm shadow of the building and a curtain, made of strings of bamboo beads, hung across the open door into the bar, to keep out flies. The American and the girl with him sat at a table in the shade, outside the building. It was very hot and the express from Barcelona would come in forty minutes. It stopped at this junction for two minutes and went on to Madrid.

"What should we drink?" the girl asked. She had taken off her hat and put it on the table.

"It's pretty hot," the man said.

"Let's drink beer."

"Dos cervezas," the man said into the curtain.

"Big ones?" a woman asked from the doorway.

"Yes. Two big ones."

The woman brought two glasses of beer and two felt pads. She put the felt pads and the beer glasses on the table and looked at the man and the girl. The girl was looking off at the line of hills. They were white in the sun and the country was brown and dry.

"They look like white elephants," she said.

"I've never seen one," the man drank his beer.

"No, you wouldn't have."

"I might have," the man said. "Just because you say I wouldn't have doesn't prove anything."

The girl looked at the bead curtain. "They've painted something on it," she said. "What does it say?"

"Anis del Toro. It's a drink."

"Could we try it?"

The man called "Listen" through the curtain. The woman came out from the bar.

"Four reales."

"We want two Anis del Toro."

"With water?"

"Do you want it with water?"

"I don't know," the girl said. "Is it good with water?"

"It's all right."

"You want them with water?" asked the woman.

"Yes, with water."

"It tastes like licorice," the girl said and put the glass down.

"That's the way with everything."

[1]River in northeast Spain that empties into the Mediterranean between Barcelona and Valencia.

"Yes," said the girl. "Everything tastes of licorice. Especially all the things you've waited so long for, like absinthe."

"Oh, cut it out."

"You started it," the girl said. "I was being amused. I was having a fine time."

"Well, let's try and have a fine time."

"All right. I was trying. I said the mountains looked like white elephants. Wasn't that bright?"

"That was bright."

"I wanted to try this new drink. That's all we do, isn't it—look at things and try new drinks?"

"I guess so."

The girl looked across at the hills.

"They're lovely hills," she said. "They don't really look like white elephants. I just meant the coloring of their skin through the trees."

"Should we have another drink?"

"All right."

The warm wind blew the bead curtain against the table.

"The beer's nice and cool," the man said.

"It's lovely," the girl said.

"It's really an awfully simple operation, Jig," the man said. "It's not really an operation at all."

The girl looked at the ground the table legs rested on.

"I know you wouldn't mind it, Jig. It's really not anything. It's just to let the air in."

The girl did not say anything.

"I'll go with you and I'll stay with you all the time. They just let the air in and then it's all perfectly natural."

"Then what will we do afterward?"

"We'll be fine afterward. Just like we were before."

"What makes you think so?"

"That's the only thing that bothers us. It's the only thing that's made us unhappy."

The girl looked at the bead curtain, put her hand out and took hold of two of the strings of beads.

"And you think then we'll be all right and be happy."

"I know we will. You don't have to be afraid. I've known lots of people that have done it."

"So have I," said the girl. "And afterward they were all so happy."

"Well," the man said, "if you don't want to you don't have to. I wouldn't have you do it if you didn't want to. But I know it's perfectly simple."

"And you really want to?"

"I think it's the best thing to do. But I don't want you to do it if you don't really want to."

"And if I do it you'll be happy and things will be like they were and you'll love me?"

"I love you now. You know I love you."

"I know. But if I do it, then it will be nice again if I say things are like white elephants, and you'll like it?"

"I'll love it. I love it now but I just can't think about it. You know how I get when I worry."

"If I do it you won't ever worry?"

"I won't worry about that because it's perfectly simple."

"Then I'll do it. Because I don't care about me."

"What do you mean?"

"I don't care about me."

"Well, I care about you."

"Oh, yes. But I don't care about me. And I'll do it and then everything will be fine."

"I don't want you to do it if you feel that way."

The girl stood up and walked to the end of the station. Across, on the other side, were fields of grain and trees along the banks of the Ebro. Far away, beyond the river, were mountains. The shadow of a cloud moved across the field of grain and she saw the river through the trees.

"And we could have all this," she said. "And we could have everything and every day we make it more impossible."

"What did you say?"

"I said we could have everything."

"We can have everything."

"No, we can't."

"We can have the whole world."

"No, we can't."

"We can go everywhere."

"No, we can't. It isn't ours any more."

"It's ours."

"No, it isn't. And once they take it away, you never get it back."

"But they haven't taken it away."

"We'll wait and see."

"Come on back in the shade," he said. "You mustn't feel that way."

"I don't feel any way," the girl said. "I just know things."

"I don't want you to do anything that you don't want to do—"

"Nor that isn't good for me," she said. "I know. Could we have another beer?"

"All right. But you've got to realize—"

"I realize," the girl said. "Can't we maybe stop talking?"

They sat down at the table and the girl looked across at the hills on the dry side of the valley and the man looked at her and at the table.

"You've got to realize," he said, "that I don't want you to do it if you don't want to. I'm perfectly willing to go through with it if it means anything to you."

"Doesn't it mean anything to you? We could get along."

"Of course it does. But I don't want anybody but you. I don't want any one else. And I know it's perfectly simple."

"Yes, you know it's perfectly simple."

"It's all right for you to say that, but I do know it."

"Would you do something for me now?"

"I'd do anything for you."

"Would you please please please please please please please stop talking?"

He did not say anything but looked at the bags against the wall of the station. There were labels on them from all the hotels where they had spent nights.

"But I don't want you to," he said, "I don't care anything about it."

"I'll scream," the girl said.

The woman came out through the curtains with two glasses of beer and put them down on the damp felt pads. "The train comes in five minutes," she said.

"What did she say?" asked the girl.

"That the train is coming in five minutes."

The girl smiled brightly at the woman, to thank her.

"I'd better take the bags over to the other side of the station," the man said. She smiled at him.

"All right. Then come back and we'll finish the beer."

He picked up the two heavy bags and carried them around the station to the other tracks. He looked up the tracks but could not see the train. Coming back, he walked through the barroom, where people waiting for the train were drinking. He drank an Anis at the bar and looked at the people. They were all waiting reasonably for the train. He went out through the bead curtain. She was sitting at the table and smiled at him.

"Do you feel better?" he asked.

"I feel fine," she said. "There's nothing wrong with me. I feel fine."

1927

WALLACE STEVENS
1879–1955

Wallace Stevens, the poet of lush word patterns and evocative images, lived a circumspect daily life that contrasted dramatically with the profession of poet. In his position as vice president of the Hartford Accident and Indemnity Insurance Company, Stevens used his law degree for the betterment of his field and never mentioned to his associates that he was also a poet. Even when his

Collected Poems won the Pulitzer Prize and the National Book Award, he remained first an insurance executive.

The son of an attorney, Stevens was born and reared in Reading, Pennsylvania. He attended Harvard for three years as a special student, studying languages and publishing poems in the *Harvard Advocate*. George Santayana befriended him during that time. For a year he wrote for the New York *Herald Tribune*, but he did not enjoy journalism. He then entered the New York University Law School, and in 1904 was admitted to the New York Bar and began to practice law. A partnership failed; he worked in several firms and, in 1909, married Elsie Moll. His move to the insurance field occurred in 1916.

Although Stevens began to publish his mature poems in *Poetry* and elsewhere in 1914, it was 1923 before *Harmonium*, his first book, was published. Many of Stevens's best-known poems were included in that collection, but little notice of it was taken until 1931, when it was reissued. Then Stevens published three collections in quick succession, establishing himself as one of the most skilled and original of America's modernists. In 1946 he was chosen as a member of the National Institute of Arts and Letters; in 1950 he won the Bollingen Prize for Poetry, and in 1955 both the Pulitzer Prize for Poetry and the National Book Award.

A distinctively original poet, Stevens was not afraid to write about seemingly "philosophical" subjects, even in a period when the modernist writers concentrated on objects (and Williams said, "No ideas but in things"). Stevens's art was usually grounded in those things, however, and he called himself a poet of the earth. He met the sometimes rigid demands of the modernists and yet preserved his own inclination to re-create beauty—the sheer colors of a tropical landscape, the efflorescence of the ocean depths, the stark icy silhouette of a snow-covered tree. For all his interest in abstractions, Stevens was a highly visual poet. He was also the poet of language as sounded speech, and many of his best poems are most effective when read aloud. Stevens did not write from the point of view of a persona—either himself or a disguised person—but he did write with such a true sense of inflected speech that his line, his sound, were his own. "One must have a mind of winter," "The Snow Man" opens, and while the reader is not sure the speaking voice is that of Stevens, he or she is convinced that it is the voice of some observer or listener. Authenticity rather than personality marks Stevens's writing.

Most of Stevens's poems are far from somber, although their meditative pace and generally long lines suggest a seriousness that might turn dour. Instead, he sparks parts of single poems (which are often lengthy) as well as entire collections with comic touches. Like Roethke, Stevens sees with the childlike eyes of innocence. Like Cummings, he was not afraid to share his vision with a world that might have scoffed at its ingenuousness. All the joy and power of language used at its best, and for a myriad of its best effects, is evident in Stevens's work.

Linda Wagner-Martin
University of North Carolina at Chapel Hill

PRIMARY WORKS

Harmonium, 1923, 1931; *Ideas of Order*, 1935; *The Man with the Blue Guitar*, 1937; *Parts of a World*, 1942; *Transport to Summer*, 1947; *The Auroras of Autumn*, 1950; *The Necessary Angel*, 1951; *Collected Poems*, 1954; *Letters*, 1966; *Sur Plusiers Beaux Sujects: Wallace Stevens' Commonplace Book*, ed. Milton J. Bates, 1989; *Collected Poetry and Prose*, 1997.

Sunday Morning

I

Complacencies of the peignoir, and late
Coffee and oranges in a sunny chair,
And the green freedom of a cockatoo
Upon a rug mingle to dissipate
The holy hush of ancient sacrifice.   5
She dreams a little, and she feels the dark
Encroachment of that old catastrophe,
As a calm darkens among water-lights.
The pungent oranges and bright, green wings
Seem things in some procession of the dead,   10
Winding across wide water, without sound.
The day is like wide water, without sound,
Stilled for the passing of her dreaming feet
Over the seas, to silent Palestine,
Dominion of the blood and sepulchre.   15

II

Why should she give her bounty to the dead?
What is divinity if it can come
Only in silent shadows and in dreams?
Shall she not find in comforts of the sun,
In pungent fruit and bright, green wings, or else   20
In any balm or beauty of the earth,
Things to be cherished like the thought of heaven?
Divinity must live within herself:
Passions of rain, or moods in falling snow;
Grievings in loneliness, or unsubdued   25
Elations when the forest blooms; gusty
Emotions on wet roads on autumn nights;
All pleasures and all pains, remembering
The bough of summer and the winter branch.
These are the measures destined for her soul.   30

III

Jove[1] in the clouds had his inhuman birth.
No mother suckled him, no sweet land gave
Large-mannered motions to his mythy mind.
He moved among us, as a muttering king,
Magnificent, would move among his hinds,   35
Until our blood, commingling, virginal,
With heaven, brought such requital to desire
The very hinds discerned it, in a star.
Shall our blood fail? Or shall it come to be
The blood of paradise? And shall the earth,   40
Seem all of paradise that we shall know?
The sky will be much friendlier then than now,
A part of labor and a part of pain,
And next in glory to enduring love,
Not this dividing and indifferent blue.   45

IV

She says, "I am content when wakened birds,
Before they fly, test the reality
Of misty fields, by their sweet questionings;
But when the birds are gone, and their warm fields
Return no more, where, then, is paradise?"   50
There is not any haunt of prophecy,
Nor any old chimera[2] of the grave,
Neither the golden underground, nor isle
Melodious, where spirits gat them home,
Nor visionary south, nor cloudy palm   55
Remote on heaven's hill, that has endured
As April's green endures; or will endure
Like her remembrance of awakened birds,
Or her desire for June and evening, tipped
By the consummation of the swallow's wings.   60

V

She says, "But in contentment I still feel
The need of some imperishable bliss."
Death is the mother of beauty; hence from her,
Alone, shall come fulfilment to our dreams
And our desires. Although she strews the leaves   65

[1]Jupiter, the chief deity in Roman mythology.
[2]A fabulous fire-breathing monster in Greek
mythology.

Of sure obliteration on our paths,
The path sick sorrow took, the many paths
Where triumph rang its brassy phrase, or love
Whispered a little out of tenderness,
She makes the willow shiver in the sun   70
For maidens who were wont to sit and gaze
Upon the grass, relinquished to their feet.
She causes boys to pile new plums and pears
On disregarded plate. The maidens taste
And stray impassioned in the littering leaves.   75

VI

Is there no change of death in paradise?
Does ripe fruit never fall? Or do the boughs
Hang always heavy in that perfect sky,
Unchanging, yet so like our perishing earth,
With rivers like our own that seek for seas   80
They never find, the same receding shores
That never touch with inarticulate pang?
Why set the pear upon those river-banks
Or spice the shores with odors of the plum?
Alas, that they should wear our colors there,   85
The silken weavings of our afternoons,
And pick the strings of our insipid lutes!
Death is the mother of beauty, mystical,
Within whose burning bosom we devise
Our earthly mothers waiting, sleeplessly.   90

VII

Supple and turbulent, a ring of men
Shall chant in orgy on a summer morn
Their boisterous devotion to the sun,
Not as a god, but as a god might be,
Naked among them, like a savage source.   95
Their chant shall be a chant of paradise,
Out of their blood, returning to the sky;
And in their chant shall enter, voice by voice,
The windy lake wherein their lord delights,
The trees, like serafin, and echoing hills,   100
That choir among themselves long afterward.
They shall know well the heavenly fellowship
Of men that perish and of summer morn.
And whence they came and whither they shall go
The dew upon their feet shall manifest.   105

VIII

She hears, upon that water without sound,
A voice that cries, "The tomb in Palestine
Is not the porch of spirits lingering.
It is the grave of Jesus, where he lay."
We live in an old chaos of the sun,   110
Or old dependency of day and night,
Or island solitude, unsponsored, free,
Of that wide water, inescapable.
Deer walk upon our mountains, and the quail
Whistle about us their spontaneous cries;   115
Sweet berries ripen in the wilderness;
And, in the isolation of the sky,
At evening, casual flocks of pigeons make
Ambiguous undulations as they sink,
Downward to darkness, on extended wings.   120

                                                                 1923

The Snow Man

One must have a mind of winter
To regard the frost and the boughs
Of the pine-trees crusted with snow;

And have been cold a long time
To behold the junipers shagged with ice,   5
The spruces rough in the distant glitter

Of the January sun; and not to think
Of any misery in the sound of the wind,
In the sound of a few leaves,

Which is the sound of the land   10
Full of the same wind
That is blowing in the same bare place

For the listener, who listens in the snow,
And, nothing himself, beholds
Nothing that is not there and the nothing that is.   15

                                                                 1923

Peter Quince at the Clavier[1]

I

Just as my fingers on these keys
Make music, so the selfsame sounds
On my spirit make a music, too.

Music is feeling, then, not sound;
And thus it is that what I feel,   5
Here in this room, desiring you,

Thinking of your blue-shadowed silk,
Is music. It is like the strain
Waked in the elders by Susanna.[2]

Of a green evening, clear and warm,   10
She bathed in her still garden, while
The red-eyed elders watching, felt

The basses of their beings throb
In witching chords, and their thin blood
Pulse pizzicati of Hosanna.[3]   15

II

In the green water, clear and warm,
Susanna lay.
She searched
The touch of springs,
And found   20
Concealed imaginings.
She sighed,
For so much melody.
Upon the bank, she stood
In the cool   25
Of spent emotions.

[1]The keyboard of an organ, harpsichord, or piano.
[2]The story of Susanna and the elders is told in the thirteenth chapter of Daniel, in the Apocrypha. Susanna, a Jewish woman of the Babylonian diaspora famed for her beauty and virtue, is caught alone in her garden by two wicked elders who attempted to coerce sex with her. She cries out for assistance, but when her house servants arrive, the elders accuse her of committing adultery with a young man who has just eluded them, a crime for which she is condemned to death. Susanna is rescued and her accusers executed instead when Daniel exposes their false testimony.
[3]Pizzicati are notes made by plucking a stringed instrument; a Hosanna is an exclamation of praise to God.

She felt, among the leaves,
The dew
Of old devotions.

She walked upon the grass,   30
Still quavering.
The winds were like her maids,
On timid feet,
Fetching her woven scarves,
Yet wavering.   35

A breath upon her hand
Muted the night.
She turned—
A cymbal crashed,
And roaring horns.   40

III

Soon, with a noise like tambourines,
Came her attendant Byzantines.[4]

They wondered why Susanna cried
Against the elders by her side;

And as they whispered, the refrain   45
Was like a willow swept by rain.

Anon, their lamps' uplifted flame
Revealed Susanna and her shame.

And then, the simpering Byzantines
Fled, with a noise like tambourines.   50

IV

Beauty is momentary in the mind—
The fitful tracing of a portal;
But in the flesh it is immortal.
The body dies; the body's beauty lives.
So evenings die, in their green going,   55
A wave, interminably flowing.
So gardens die, their meek breath scenting
The cowl of winter, done repenting.

[4]Natives of Byzantium.

So maidens die, to the auroral
Celebration of a maiden's choral.   60

Susanna's music touched the bawdy strings
Of those white elders; but, escaping,
Left only Death's ironic scraping.
Now, in its immortality, it plays
On the clear viol of her memory,   65
And makes a constant sacrament of praise.

                                                     1923

Anecdote of the Jar

I placed a jar in Tennessee,
And round it was, upon a hill.
It made the slovenly wilderness
Surround that hill.

The wilderness rose up to it,   5
And sprawled around, no longer wild.
The jar was round upon the ground
And tall and of a port in air.

It took dominion everywhere.
The jar was gray and bare.   10
It did not give of bird or bush,
Like nothing else in Tennessee.

                                                     1923

A High-Toned Old Christian Woman

Poetry is the supreme fiction, madame.
Take the moral law and make a nave of it
And from the nave build haunted heaven. Thus,
The conscience is converted into palms,
Like windy citherns[1] hankering for hymns.   5
We agree in principle. That's clear. But take
The opposing law and make a peristyle,
And from the peristyle project a masque
Beyond the planets. Thus, our bawdiness,
Unpurged by epitaph, indulged at last,   10
Is equally converted into palms,

[1]A stringed instrument of the guitar family
popular in medieval times.

Squiggling like saxophones. And palm for palm,
Madame, we are where we began. Allow,
Therefore, that in the planetary scene
Your disaffected flagellants,[2] well-stuffed,   15
Smacking their muzzy bellies in parade,
Proud of such novelties of the sublime,
Such tink and tank and tunk-a-tunk-tunk,
May, merely may, madame, whip from themselves
A jovial hullabaloo among the spheres.   20
This will make widows wince. But fictive things
Wink as they will. Wink most when widows wince.

                                                                     1923

Of Modern Poetry

The poem of the mind in the act of finding
What will suffice. It has not always had
To find: the scene was set; it repeated what
Was in the script.
                    Then the theatre was changed   5
To something else. Its past was a souvenir.

It has to be living, to learn the speech of the place.
It has to face the men of the time and to meet
The women of the time. It has to think about war
And it has to find what will suffice. It has   10
To construct a new stage. It has to be on that stage
And, like an insatiable actor, slowly and
With meditation, speak words that in the ear,
In the delicatest ear of the mind, repeat,
Exactly, that which it wants to hear, at the sound   15
Of which, an invisible audience listens,
Not to the play, but to itself, expressed
In an emotion as of two people, as of two
Emotions becoming one. The actor is
A metaphysician in the dark, twanging   20
An instrument, twanging a wiry string that gives
Sounds passing through sudden rightnesses, wholly
Containing the mind, below which it cannot descend,
Beyond which it has no will to rise.
                    It must   25
Be the finding of a satisfaction, and may

[2]Persons who whip themselves as a religious
discipline.

Be a man of skating, a woman dancing, a woman
Combing. The poem of the act of the mind.

1942

The Course of a Particular

Today the leaves cry, hanging on branches swept by wind,
Yet the nothingness of winter becomes a little less.
It is still full of icy shades and shapen snow.

The leaves cry ... One holds off and merely hears the cry.
It is a busy cry, concerning someone else.   5
And though one says that one is part of everything,

There is a conflict, there is a resistance involved;
And being part is an exertion that declines:
One feels the life of that which gives life as it is.

The leaves cry. It is not a cry of divine attention,   10
Nor the smoke-drift of puffed-out heroes, nor human cry.
It is the cry of leaves that do not transcend themselves,

In the absence of fantasia, without meaning more
Than they are in the final finding of the ear, in the thing
Itself, until, at last, the cry concerns no one at all.   15

1950

Of Mere Being

The palm at the end of the mind,
Beyond the last thought, rises
In the bronze distance,

A gold-feathered bird
Sings in the palm, without human meaning,   5
Without human feeling, a foreign song.

You know then that it is not the reason
That makes us happy or unhappy.
The bird sings. Its feathers shine.

The palm stands on the edge of space.   10
The wind moves slowly in the branches.
The bird's fire-fangled feathers dangle down.

1955

▪   WILLIAM FAULKNER   ▪
                          1897–1962

The great-grandson and namesake of Colonel William C. Falkner, a Civil War hero who was also a popular writer, William Cuthbert Faulkner aspired to greatness, even as a small child, when he listened mesmerized to tales and legends from his distinguished family's past, a history that had paled by the time it reached his rather ordinary and sometimes hostile father, Murray Falkner. William was born in New Albany, Mississippi, but the family soon moved to nearby Oxford, where Faulkner would spend most of his life.

In June 1918, Faulkner joined the Royal Air Force of Canada; he trained as a cadet pilot in Toronto until November, when the Armistice sent him homeward again. Back in Oxford, after swaggering around the square in his uniform, telling spurious tales about his combat in France, he renewed his attempts to become both an artist and a poet. He had learned to draw from his artistically inclined grandmother and mother; enrolling as a special student at the University of Mississippi, he illustrated several campus publications, as well as some poetry sequences he wrote for various girlfriends. After dropping out of the university in 1921, Faulkner took a brief job in a New York bookstore; there he met the future wife of Sherwood Anderson, Elizabeth Prall. Returning to Oxford in December, he accepted a position as postmaster at the university, a job he held, despite a lackadaisical attitude, until late 1924. His first book of poetry, *The Marble Faun* (1924), continued his work in the decadent/neo-romantic vein.

Faulkner moved to New Orleans in 1925, where his friendship with Elizabeth Prall led to an apprenticeship with Sherwood Anderson, whom she had married. In Anderson's literary circle, Faulkner became acquainted with Freud's theories of sexuality, the mythic world of anthropologist Sir James Frazer's *Golden Bough*, and the sweeping implications of the literary innovations of T. S. Eliot and James Joyce. He also absorbed the ennui and despair of the postwar generation, and melded all these influences, first in a series of literary sketches published by the *New Orleans Times Picayune* and *The Double Dealer* (a literary magazine) and then in a first novel, *Soldier's Pay*. Faulkner meanwhile left for Europe, spending time in Italy and England but reacting most strongly to France, beginning a lifelong love affair with that country. Returning to Mississippi, Faulkner took a series of jobs while working on his second novel, *Mosquitoes* (1927).

For Faulkner, 1929 marked the beginning of what critics have come to call "the great years" (extending to 1942), when he wrote the seven novels (in a total of twenty) that have been judged masterworks. The impetus for this extraordinary outburst came in *Sartoris* (1929), when Faulkner, on the advice of Anderson, decided to concentrate on what he came to call his "little postage-stamp of soil," Yoknapatawpha County; all the great novels are set there, in or around Jefferson, the county seat. The town and county obviously depict Oxford and its surrounding Lafayette County. As a result of this focus, Faulkner was able to create a mythic "cosmos" of his own, with interconnected mythic structures and characters, populating his world with all the various folk he had encountered in life; he made a determined effort to render the experience of women, blacks, and American Indians as well and showed nostalgia for lost traditions and the vanishing wilderness while simultaneously decrying rampant materialist culture and racial injustice.

Faulkner's first masterwork, *The Sound and the Fury*, was published in 1929. Faulkner wrote this book thinking of a little girl with muddy drawers climbing a pear tree to look in on her grandmother's body lying in state in the parlor, thereby finding a metaphor for the narrative of the fall of a proud southern family. The story, told in three successive first-person narrations by three brothers and finally through the consciousness of their black nurse/housekeeper, keeps circling back to the same issues in different voices, adding new levels of understanding. Documenting, in a radical new prose style, both the loss of familial love and honor and the decline of a great culture, the book caused a sensation among critics but sold poorly, as did its successor, *As I Lay Dying* (1930), which detailed the efforts of a poor white family to bury their unembalmed mother.

Faulkner, desperate for money, embarked on the first of several unhappy stints in Hollywood as a scriptwriter (1932–1936; 1942–1945; parts of 1951 and 1954). He found intermittent happiness during his Hollywood years. He wrote much of his next novel, *Light in August* (1932), during a trip to New York. One of his two or three greatest works, it details the deceptively simple frame story of Lena Grove, a country woman wandering the South searching for the father of her unborn child. This narrative interconnects on many levels with the one it encloses, the much longer and tragic tale of Joe Christmas, an orphan like Lena, who may or may not have black blood. The novel probes deeply into race, religion, and sexuality and the role of memory and the past in the human consciousness.

Absalom, Absalom! (1936) is generally considered Faulkner's most monumental achievement. Four narrators, including Quentin Compson of *The Sound and the Fury* and his Harvard roommate, Shreve McCannon, attempt to decipher the mysteries surrounding the rise and fall of Thomas Sutpen, a self-made planter and God-like creator of Supten's Hundreds, a huge plantation. The novel plunges into the darker recesses of personal histories, exploring incest, interracial love, psychic perversion, and materialist obsession, while simultaneously rendering the sufferings of blacks and whites during the Civil War and Reconstruction and the South's attempts to come to terms with its tragic history.

Faulkner experimented with counterpoint in *The Wild Palms* (1939), alternating chapters of two discrete narratives, one concerning a convict's efforts to bring a woman and her baby safely out of a Mississippi flood, the other focusing on a tragic and adulterous love affair. He returned to form in his last two masterworks, *The Hamlet* (1940) and *Go Down, Moses* (1942). The former, Faulkner's finest comedy, begins a trilogy of novels about the rise of the Snopes family, which continues in *The Town* (1957) and *The Mansion* (1959). *Go Down, Moses*, generated by Faulkner's revision and union of existing stories, concerns the efforts of Ike McCaslin to repudiate the tragic racial history of his family, which includes his grandfather's siring of a child on his mulatto daughter. The narrative builds to a climax in what is perhaps Faulkner's most powerful and sustained piece of writing, "The Bear," which uses a hunt to explore the meaning of history, manhood, and responsibility to nature.

The course of his career was always uncertain, and all of his books except *Sanctuary* were out of print before Malcolm Cowley's publication of *The Portable Faulkner* in 1946, which began a reassessment of Faulkner's career. Faulkner's *Collected Stories* appeared in 1950, setting the stage for his acceptance of the Nobel Prize for literature in Stockholm, where his short but powerful acceptance speech caused a sensation; he predicted that man would not only endure; he would prevail.

Faulkner's last decade combined increasing bouts with illness, accident, and alcoholism with public appearances and pronouncements. He traveled widely for the State Department (most memorably to Japan in 1955) and eventually accepted a position at the University of Virginia in Charlottesville.

His dogged, often heroic commitment to a dissection of racism indicates an agreement with W.E.B. Du Bois's assertion that "the problem of the twentieth century is the problem of the color line." Faulkner's profound sense of history and tradition was in no way a curb on his appetite for modernist solutions—both stylistic and philosophical—to literary, social, and spiritual problems. He stated, a few years before his death, that "the writer's first job ..." is "always to search the soul ... To search his own soul, and to give a proper, moving picture of man in the human dilemma." At its best, Faulkner's complex work courageously meets this standard.

John Lowe
University of Georgia

PRIMARY WORKS

The Marble Faun, 1924; *Soldier's Pay,* 1926; *Mosquitoes,* 1927; *Sartoris,* 1929; *The Sound and the Fury,* 1929; *As I Lay Dying,* 1930; *Sanctuary,* 1931; *Light in August,* 1932; *Pylon,* 1935; *Absalom, Absalom!,* 1936; *The Unvanquished,* 1938; *The Wild Palms,* 1939; *The Hamlet,* 1940; *Go Down, Moses,* 1942; *Intruder in the Dust,* 1948; *Collected Stories of William Faulkner,* 1950; *Requiem for a Nun,* 1951; *A Fable,* 1954; *The Town,* 1957; *The Mansion,* 1959; *Early Prose and Poetry,* ed. Carvel Collins, 1962; *The Reivers,* 1962; *Essays, Speeches and Public Letters,* ed. James B. Meriwether, 1965; *Selected Letters of William Faulkner,* ed. Joseph L. Blotner, 1977; *Novels, 1926–1929,* 2006; *Novels, 1930–1935,* 1985; *Novels, 1936–1940,* 1990; *Novels, 1942–1954,* 1994; *Novels, 1957–1962,* 1999.

Delta Autumn

Soon now they would enter the Delta. The sensation was familiar to old Isaac McCaslin. It had been renewed like this each last week in November for more than fifty years—the last hill, at the foot of which the rich unbroken alluvial flatness began as the sea began at the base of its cliffs, dissolving away beneath the unhurried November rain as the sea itself would dissolve away.

At first they had come in wagons: the guns, the bedding, the dogs, the food, the whiskey, the keen heartlifting anticipation of hunting; the young men who could drive all night and all the following day in the cold rain and pitch a camp in the rain and sleep in the wet blankets and rise at daylight the next morning and hunt. There had been bear then. A man shot a doe or a fawn as quickly as he did a buck, and in the afternoons they shot wild turkey with pistols to test their stalking skill and marksmanship, feeding all but the breast to the dogs. But that time was gone now. Now they went in cars, driving faster and faster each year because the roads were better and they had farther and farther to drive, the territory in which game still existed drawing yearly inward as his life was drawing inward, until now he was the last of those who had once made the journey in wagons without feeling it and now those who accompanied him were the sons and even grandsons of the men who had ridden for twenty-four hours in the rain or sleet behind the steaming mules. They called him "Uncle Ike" now, and he no longer told anyone how near eighty he actually was because he knew as well as they did that he no longer had any business making such expeditions, even by car.

In fact, each time now, on that first night in camp, lying aching and sleepless in the harsh blankets, his blood only faintly warmed by the single thin whiskey-and-water which he allowed himself, he would tell himself that this would be his last. But he would stand that trip—he still shot almost as well as he ever had, still killed almost as much of the game he saw as he ever killed; he no longer even knew how many deer had fallen before his gun—and the fierce long heat of the next summer would renew him. Then November would come again, and again in the car with two of the sons of his old companions, whom he had taught not only how to distinguish between the prints left by a buck or a doe but between the sound they made in moving, he would look ahead past the jerking arc of the windshield wiper and see the land flatten suddenly and swoop, dissolving away beneath the rain as the sea itself would dissolve, and he would say, "Well, boys, there it is again."

This time though, he didn't have time to speak. The driver of the car stopped it, slamming it to a skidding halt on the greasy pavement without warning, actually flinging the two passengers forward until they caught themselves with their braced hands against the dash. "What the hell, Roth!" the man in the middle said. "Can't you whistle first when you do that? Hurt you, Uncle Ike?"

"No," the old man said. "What's the matter?" The driver didn't answer. Still leaning forward, the old man looked sharply past the face of the man between them, at the face of his kinsman. It was the youngest face of them all, aquiline, saturnine, a little ruthless, the face of his ancestor too, tempered a little, altered a little, staring sombrely through the streaming windshield across which the twin wipers flicked and flicked.

"I didn't intend to come back in here this time," he said suddenly and harshly.

"You said that back in Jefferson last week," the old man said. "Then you changed your mind. Have you changed it again? This ain't a very good time to——"

"Oh, Roth's coming," the man in the middle said. His name was Legate. He seemed to be speaking to no one, as he was looking at neither of them. "If it was just a buck he was coming all this distance for, now. But he's got a doe in here. Of course a old man like Uncle Ike can't be interested in no doe, not one that walks on two legs—when she's standing up, that is. Pretty light-colored, too. The one he was after them nights last fall when he said he was coon-hunting, Uncle Ike. The one I figured maybe he was still running when he was gone all that month last January. But of course a old man like Uncle Ike ain't got no interest in nothing like that." He chortled, still looking at no one, not completely jeering.

"What?" the old man said. "What's that?" But he had not even so much as glanced at Legate. He was still watching his kinsman's face. The eyes behind the spectacles were the blurred eyes of an old man, but they were quite sharp too; eyes which could still see a gun-barrel and what ran beyond it as well as any of them could. He was remembering himself now: how last year, during the final stage by motor boat in to where they camped, a box of food had been lost overboard and how on the next day his kinsman had gone back to the nearest town for supplies and had been gone overnight. And when he did return, something had happened to him. He would go into the woods with his rifle each dawn when the others went, but the old man, watching him, knew that he was not hunting. "All right," he said. "Take me and Will on to shelter where we can wait for the truck, and you can go on back."

"I'm going in," the other said harshly. "Don't worry. Because this will be the last of it."

"The last of deer hunting, or doe hunting?" Legate said. This time the old man paid no attention to him even by speech. He still watched the young man's savage and brooding face.

"Why?" he said.

"After Hitler gets through with it? Or Smith or Jones or Roosevelt or Willkie or whatever he will call himself in this country?"

"We'll stop him in this country," Legate said. "Even if he calls himself George Washington."

"How?" Edmonds said. "By singing 'God Bless America' in bars at midnight and wearing dime-store flags in our lapels?"

"So that's what's worrying you," the old man said. "I ain't noticed this country being short of defenders yet, when it needed them. You did some of it yourself twenty-odd years ago, before you were a grown man even. This country is a little mite stronger than any one man or group of men, outside of it or even inside of it either. I reckon, when the time comes and some of you have done got tired of hollering we are whipped if we don't go to war and some more are hollering we are whipped if we do, it will cope with one Austrian paper-hanger, no matter what he will be calling himself. My pappy and some other better men than any of them you named tried once to tear it in two with a war, and they failed."

"And what have you got left?" the other said. "Half the people without jobs and half the factories closed by strikes. Half the people on public dole that won't work and half that couldn't work even if they would. Too much cotton and corn and hogs, and not enough for people to eat and wear. The country full of people to tell a man how he can't raise his own cotton whether he will or won't, and Sally Rand with a sergeant's stripes and not even the fan couldn't fill the army rolls. Too much not-butter and not even the guns———"

"We got a deer camp—if we ever get to it," Legate said. "Not to mention does."

"It's a good time to mention does," the old man said. "Does and fawns both. The only fighting anywhere that ever had anything of God's blessing on it has been when man fought to protect does and fawns. If it's going to come to fighting, that's a good thing to mention and remember too."

"Haven't you discovered in—how many years more than seventy is it?—that women and children are one thing there's never any scarcity of?" Edmonds said.

"Maybe that's why all I am worrying about right now is that ten miles of river we still have got to run before we can make camp," the old man said. "So let's get on."

They went on. Soon they were going fast again, as Edmonds always drove, consulting neither of them about the speed just as he had given neither of them any warning when he slammed the car to stop. The old man relaxed again. He watched, as he did each recurrent November while more than sixty of them passed, the land which he had seen change. At first there had been only the old towns along the River and the old towns along the hills, from each of which the planters with their gangs of slaves and then of hired laborers had wrested from the impenetrable jungle of water-standing cane and cypress, gum and holly and oak and ash, cotton patches which, as the years passed, became fields and then plantations. The paths made by deer and bear became roads and then highways, with towns in turn springing up along them and along the rivers Tallahatchie and Sunflower which joined and became the Yazoo, the River of the Dead of the Choctaws—the thick, slow, black, unsunned streams almost without current, which once each year ceased to flow at all and then reversed, spreading, drowning the rich land and subsiding again, leaving it still richer.

Most of that was gone now. Now a man drove two hundred miles from Jefferson before he found wilderness to hunt in. Now the land lay open from the cradling hills on the east to the rampart of levee on the west, standing horseman-tall with cotton for the world's looms—the rich black land, imponderable and vast, fecund up to the very doorsteps of the Negroes who worked it and of the white men who owned it; which exhausted the hunting life of a dog in one year, the working life of a mule in five and of a man in twenty—the land in which neon flashed past them from the little countless towns, and countless shining this-year's automobiles sped past them on the broad plumb-ruled highways, yet in which the only permanent mark of man's occupation seemed to be the tremendous gins, constructed in sections of sheet iron and in a week's time though they were, since no man, millionaire though he be, would build more than a roof and walls to shelter the camping equipment he lived from, when he knew that once each ten years or so his house would be flooded to the second storey and all within it ruined;—the land across which there came now no scream of panther but instead the long hooting of locomotives: trains of incredible length and drawn by a single engine, since there was no gradient anywhere and no elevation save those raised by forgotten aboriginal hands as refuges from the yearly water and used by their Indian successors to sepulchre their fathers' bones, and all that remained of that old time were the Indian names on the little towns and usually pertaining to water—Aluschaskuna, Tillatoba, Homochitto, Yazoo.

By early afternoon, they were on water. At the last little Indian-named town at the end of pavement they waited until the other car and the two trucks—the one carrying the bedding and tents and food, the other the horses—overtook them. They left the concrete and, after another mile or so, the gravel too. In caravan they ground on through the ceaselessly dissolving afternoon, with skid-chains on the wheels now, lurching and splashing and sliding among the ruts, until presently it seemed to him that the retrograde of his remembering had gained an inverse velocity from their own slow progress, that the land had retreated not in minutes from the last spread of gravel but in years, decades, back toward what it had been when he first knew it: the road they now followed once more the ancient pathway of bear and deer, the diminishing fields they now passed once more scooped punily and terrifically by axe and saw and mule-drawn plow from the wilderness' flank, out of the brooding and immemorial tangle, in place of ruthless mile-wide parallelograms wrought by ditching the dyking machinery.

They reached the river landing and unloaded, the horses to go overland down stream to a point opposite the camp and swim the river, themselves and the bedding and food and dogs and guns in the motor launch. It was himself, though no horseman, no farmer, not even a countryman save by his distant birth and boyhood, who coaxed and soothed the two horses, drawing them by his own single frail hand until, backing, filling, trembling a little, they surged, halted, then sprang scrambling down from the truck, possessing no affinity for them as creatures, beasts, but being merely insulated by his years and time from the corruption of steel and oiled moving parts which tainted the others.

Then, his old hammer double gun which was only twelve years younger than he standing between his knees, he watched even the last puny marks of man—cabin, clearing, the small and irregular fields which a year ago were jungle and in which the skeleton stalks of this year's cotton stood almost as tall and rank as the old cane had stood, as if man had had to marry his planting to the wilderness in order to conquer it—fall away and vanish. The twin banks marched with wilderness as he remembered it—the tangle of brier and cane impenetrable even to sight twenty feet away, the tall tremendous soaring of oak and gum and ash and hickory which had rung to no axe save the hunter's, had echoed to no machinery save the beat of old-time steam boats traversing it or to the snarling of launches like their own of people going into it to dwell for a week or two weeks because it was still wilderness. There was some of it left, although now it was two hundred miles from Jefferson when once it had been thirty. He had watched it, not being conquered, destroyed, so much as retreating since its purpose was served now and its time an outmoded time, retreating southward through this inverted-apex, this ∇-shaped section of earth between hills and River until what was left of it seemed now to be gathered and for the time arrested in one tremendous density of brooding and inscrutable impenetrability at the ultimate funnelling tip.

They reached the site of their last-year's camp with still two hours left of light. "You go on over under that driest tree and set down," Legate told him. "—if you can find it. Me and these other young boys will do this." He did neither. He was not tired yet. That would come later. *Maybe it won't come at all this time*, he thought, as he had thought at this point each November for the last five or six of them. *Maybe I will go out on stand in the morning too;* knowing that he would not, not even if he took the advice and sat down under the driest shelter and did nothing until camp was made and supper cooked. Because it would not be the fatigue. It would be because he would not sleep tonight but would lie instead wakeful and peaceful on the cot amid the tent-filling snoring and the rain's whisper as he always did on the first night in camp; peaceful, without regret or fretting, telling himself that was all right too, who didn't have so many of them left as to waste one sleeping.

In his slicker he directed the unloading of the boat—the tents, the stove, the bedding, the food for themselves and the dogs until there should be meat in camp. He sent two of the Negroes to cut firewood; he had the cook-tent raised and the stove up and a fire going and supper cooking while the big tent was still being staked down. Then in the beginning of dusk he crossed in the boat to where the horses waited, backing and snorting at the water. He took the lead-ropes and with no more weight than that and his voice, he drew them down into the water and held them beside the boat with only their heads above the surface, as though they actually were suspended from his frail and strengthless old man's hands, while the boat recrossed and each horse in turn lay prone in the shallows, panting and trembling, its eyes rolling in the dusk, until the same weightless hand and unraised voice gathered it surging upward, splashing and thrashing up the bank.

Then the meal was ready. The last of light was gone now save the thin stain of it snared somewhere between the river's surface and the rain. He had the single glass of thin whiskey-and-water, then, standing in the churned mud beneath the stretched tarpaulin, he said grace over the fried slabs of pork, the hot soft shapeless bread, the canned beans and molasses and coffee in iron plates and cups,—the town food, brought along with them—then covered himself again, the others following. "Eat," he said. "Eat it all up. I don't want a piece of town meat in camp after breakfast tomorrow. Then you boys will hunt. You'll have to. When I first started hunting in this bottom sixty years ago with old General Compson and Major de Spain and Roth's grandfather and Will Legate's too, Major de Spain wouldn't allow but two pieces of foreign grub in his camp. That was one side of pork and one ham or beef. And not to eat for the first supper and breakfast neither. It was to save until along toward the end of camp when everybody was so sick of bear meat and coon and venison that we couldn't even look at it."

"I thought Uncle Ike was going to say the pork and beef was for the dogs," Legate said, chewing. "But that's right; I remember. You just shot the dogs a mess of wild turkey every evening when they got tired of deer guts."

"Times are different now," another said. "There was game here then."

"Yes," the old man said quietly. "There was game here then."

"Besides, they shot does then too," Legate said. "As it is now, we ain't got but one doe-hunter in——"

"And better men hunted it," Edmonds said. He stood at the end of the rough plank table, eating rapidly and steadily as the others ate. But again the old man looked sharply across at the sullen, handsome, brooding face which appeared now darker and more sullen still in the light of the smoky lantern. "Go on. Say it."

"I didn't say that," the old man said. "There are good men everywhere, at all times. Most men are. Some are just unlucky, because most men are a little better than their circumstances give them a chance to be. And I've known some that even the circumstances couldn't stop."

"Well, I wouldn't say—" Legate said.

"So you've lived almost eighty years," Edmonds said, "and that's what you finally learned about the other animals you lived among. I suppose the question to ask you is, where have you been all the time you were dead?"

There was a silence; for the instant even Legate's jaw stopped chewing while he gaped at Edmonds. "Well, by God, Roth—" the third speaker said. But it was the old man who spoke, his voice still peaceful and untroubled and merely grave:

"Maybe so," he said. "But if being what you call alive would have learned me any different, I reckon I'm satisfied, wherever it was I've been."

"Well, I wouldn't say that Roth—" Legate said.

The third speaker was still leaning forward a little over the table, looking at Edmonds. "Meaning that it's only because folks happen to be watching him that a man behaves at all," he said. "Is that it?"

"Yes," Edmonds said. "A man in a blue coat, with a badge on it watching him. Maybe just the badge."

"I deny that," the old man said. "I don't——"

The other two paid no attention to him. Even Legate was listening to them for the moment, his mouth still full of food and still open a little, his knife with another lump of something balanced on the tip of the blade arrested halfway to his mouth. "I'm glad I don't have your opinion of folks," the third speaker said. "I take it you include yourself."

"I see," Edmonds said. "You prefer Uncle Ike's opinion of circumstances. All right. Who makes the circumstances?"

"Luck," the third said. "Chance. Happen-so. I see what you are getting at. But that's just what Uncle Ike said: that now and then, maybe most of the time, man is a little better than the net result of his and his neighbors' doings, when he gets the chance to be."

This time Legate swallowed first. He was not to be stopped this time. "Well, I wouldn't say that Roth Edmonds can hunt one doe every day and night for two weeks and was a poor hunter or a unlucky one neither. A man that still have the same doe left to hunt on again next year——"

"Have some meat," the man next to him said.

"—ain't so unlucky— What?" Legate said.

"Have some meat." The other offered the dish.

"I got some," Legate said.

"Have some more," the third speaker said. "You and Roth Edmonds both. Have a heap of it. Clapping your jaws together that way with nothing to break the shock." Someone chortled. Then they all laughed, with relief, the tension broken. But the old man was speaking, even into the laughter, in that peaceful and still untroubled voice:

"I still believe. I see proof everywhere. I grant that man made a heap of his circumstances, him and his living neighbors between them. He even inherited some of them already made, already almost ruined even. A while ago Henry Wyatt there said how there used to be more game here. There was. So much that we even killed does. I seem to remember Will Legate mentioning that, too—" Someone laughed, a single guffaw, stillborn. It ceased and they all listened, gravely, looking down at their plates. Edmonds was drinking his coffee, sullen, brooding, inattentive.

"Some folks still kill does," Wyatt said. "There won't be just one buck hanging in this bottom tomorrow night without any head to fit it."

"I didn't say all men," the old man said. "I said most men. And not just because there is a man with a badge to watch us. We probably won't even see him unless maybe he will stop here about noon tomorrow and eat dinner with us and check our licenses——"

"We don't kill does because if we did kill does in a few years there wouldn't even be any bucks left to kill, Uncle Ike," Wyatt said.

"According to Roth yonder, that's one thing we won't never have to worry about," the old man said. "He said on the way here this morning that does and fawns—I believe he said women and children—are two things this world ain't ever lacked. But that ain't all of it," he said. "That's just the mind's reason a man has to give himself because the heart don't always have time to bother with thinking up words that fit together. God created man and He created the world for him to live in and I reckon He created the kind of world He would have wanted to live in if He had been a man—the ground to walk on, the big woods, the trees and the water, and the game to live in it. And maybe He didn't put the desire to hunt and kill game in man but I reckon He knew it was going to be there, that man was going to teach it to himself, since he wasn't quite God himself yet——"

"When will he be?" Wyatt said.

"I think that every man and woman, at the instant when it don't even matter whether they marry or not, I think that whether they marry then or afterward or don't never, at that instant the two of them together were God."

"Then there are some Gods in this world I wouldn't want to touch, and with a damn long stick," Edmonds said. He set his coffee cup down and looked at Wyatt. "And that includes myself, if that's what you want to know. I'm going to bed." He was gone. There was a general movement among the others. But it ceased and they stood again about the table, not looking at the old man, apparently held there yet by his quiet and peaceful voice as the heads of the swimming horses had been held above the water by his weightless hand. The three Negroes—the cook and his helper and old Isham—were sitting quietly in the entrance of the kitchen tent, listening too, the three faces dark and motionless and musing.

"He put them both here: man, and the game he would follow and kill, foreknowing it. I believe He said, 'So be it.' I reckon He even foreknew the end. But He said, 'I will give him his chance. I will give him warning and foreknowledge too, along with the desire to follow and the power to slay. The woods and fields he ravages and the game he devastates will be the consequence and signature of his crime and guilt, and his punishment.'— Bed time," he said. His voice and inflection did not change at all. "Breakfast at four o'clock, Isham. We want meat on the ground by sunup time."

There was a good fire in the sheet-iron heater; the tent was warm and was beginning to dry out, except for the mud underfoot. Edmonds was already rolled into his blankets, motionless, his face to the wall. Isham had made up his bed too—the strong, battered iron cot, the stained mattress which was not quite soft enough, the worn, often-washed blankets which as the years passed were less and less warm enough. But the tent was warm; presently, when the kitchen was cleaned up and readied for breakfast, the young Negro would come in to lie down before the heater, where he could be roused to put fresh wood into it from time to time. And then, he knew now he would not sleep tonight anyway; he no longer needed to tell himself that perhaps he would. But it was all right now. The day was ended now and night faced him, but alarmless, empty of fret. *Maybe I came for this*, he thought: *Not to hunt, but for this. I would come anyway, even if only to go back home tomorrow.* Wearing only his bagging woolen underwear, his spectacles folded away in the worn case beneath the pillow where he could reach them readily and his lean body fitted easily into the old worn groove of mattress and blankets, he lay on his back, his hands crossed on his breast and his eyes closed while the others undressed and went to bed and the last of the sporadic talking died into snoring. Then he opened his eyes and lay peaceful and quiet as a child, looking up at the motionless belly of rain-murmured canvas upon which the glow of the heater was dying slowly away and would fade still further until the young Negro, lying on two planks before it, would sit up and stoke it and lie back down again.

They had a house once. That was sixty years ago, when the Big Bottom was only thirty miles from Jefferson and old Major de Spain, who had been his father's cavalry commander in '61 and '2 and '3 and '4, and his cousin (his older brother; his father too) had taken him into the woods for the first time. Old Sam Fathers was alive then, born in slavery, son of a Negro slave and a Chickasaw chief, who had taught him how to shoot, not only when to shoot but when not to; such a November dawn as tomorrow would be and the old man led him straight to the great cypress and he had known the buck would pass exactly there because there was something running in Sam Fathers' veins which ran in the veins of the buck too, and they stood there against the tremendous trunk, the old man of seventy and the boy of twelve, and there was nothing save the dawn until suddenly the buck was there, smoke-colored out of nothing, magnificent with speed: and Sam Fathers said, 'Now. Shoot quick and shoot slow:' and the gun levelled rapidly without haste and crashed and he walked to the buck lying still intact and still in the shape of that magnificent speed and bled it with Sam's knife and Sam dipped his hands into the hot blood and marked his face forever while he stood trying not to tremble, humbly and with pride too though the boy of twelve had been unable to phrase it then: *I slew you; my bearing must not shame your quitting life. My conduct forever onward must become your death;* marking him for that and for more than that: that day and himself and McCaslin juxtaposed, not against the wilderness but against the tamed land, the old wrong and shame itself, in repudiation and denial at least of the land and the wrong and shame, even if he couldn't cure the wrong and erad- icate the shame, who at fourteen when he learned of it had believed he could do both when he became competent, and when at twenty-one he became competent he knew that he could do neither but at least he could repudiate the wrong and shame, at least in principle, and at least the land itself in fact, for his son at least: and did, thought he had: then (married then) in a rented cubicle in a back-street stock-traders' boarding-house, the first and last time he ever saw her naked body, himself and his wife juxta- posed in their turn against that same land, that same wrong and shame from whose regret and grief he would at least save and free his son and, sav- ing and freeing his son, lost him.

They had the house then. That roof, the two weeks of each November which they spent under it, had become his home. Although since that time they had lived during the two fall weeks in tents and not always in the same place two years in succession and now his companions were the sons and even the grandsons of them with whom he had lived in the house, and for almost fifty years now the house itself had not even existed, the conviction, the sense and feeling of home, had been merely transferred into the canvas. He owned a house in Jefferson, a good house though small, where he had had a wife and lived with her and lost her, ay, lost her even though he had lost her in the rented cubicle before he and his old clever dipsomaniac part- ner had finished the house for them to move into it: but lost her, because she loved him. But women hope for so much. They never live too long to still believe that anything within the scope of their passionate wanting is likewise within the range of their passionate hope: and it was still kept for him by his dead wife's widowed niece and her children, and he was comfortable in it, his wants and needs and even the small trying harmless crochets of an old man looked after by blood at least related to the blood which he had elected out of all the earth to cherish. But he spent the time within those walls waiting for November, because even this tent with its muddy floor and the bed which was not wide enough nor soft enough nor even warm enough, was his home and these men, some of whom he only saw during these two November weeks and not one of whom even bore any name he used to know—De Spain and Compson and Ewell and Hogganbeck—were more his kin than any. Because this was his land——

The shadow of the youngest Negro loomed. It soared, blotting the heater's dying glow from the ceiling, the wood billets thumping into the iron maw until the glow, the flame, leaped high and bright across the canvas. But the Negro's shadow still remained, by its length and breadth, standing, since it covered most of the ceiling, until after a moment he raised himself on one elbow to look. It was not the Negro, it was his kinsman; when he spoke the other turned sharp against the red firelight the sullen and ruthless profile.

"Nothing," Edmonds said. "Go on back to sleep."

"Since Will Legate mentioned it," McCaslin said, "I remember you had some trouble sleeping in here last fall too. Only you called it coon-hunting then. Or was it Will Legate called it that?" The other didn't answer. Then he turned and went back to his bed. McCaslin, still propped on his elbow, watched until the other's shadow sank down the wall and vanished, became one with the mass of sleeping shadows. "That's right," he said. "Try to get some sleep. We must have meat in camp tomorrow. You can do all the setting up you want to after that." He lay down again, his hands crossed again on his breast, watching the glow of the heater on the canvas ceiling. It was steady again now, the fresh wood accepted, being assimilated; soon it would begin to fade again, taking with it the last echo of that sudden upflare of a young man's passion and unrest. Let him lie awake for a little while, he thought; He will lie still some day for a long time without even dissatisfaction to disturb him. And lying awake here, in these surroundings, would soothe him if anything could, if anything could soothe a man just forty years old. Yes, he thought; Forty years old or thirty, or even the trembling and sleepless ardor of a boy; already the tent, the rain-murmured canvas globe, was once more filled with it. He lay on his back, his eyes closed, his breathing quiet and peaceful as a child's, listening to it—that silence which was never silence but was myriad. He could almost see it, tremendous, primeval, looming, musing downward upon this puny, evanescent clutter of human sojourn which after a single brief week would vanish and in another week would be completely healed, traceless in the unmarked solitude. Because it was his land, although he had never owned a foot of it. He had never wanted to, not even after he saw plain its ultimate doom, watching it retreat year by year before the onslaught of axe and saw and log-lines and then dynamite and tractor plows, because it belonged to no man. It belonged to all; they had only to use it well, humbly and with pride. Then suddenly he knew why he had never wanted to own any of it, arrest at least that much of what people called progress, measure his longevity at least against that much of its ultimate fate. It was because there was just exactly enough of it. He seemed to see the two of them—himself and the wilderness—as coevals, his own span as a hunter, a woodsman, not contemporary with his first breath but transmitted to him, assumed by him gladly, humbly, with joy and pride, from that old Major de Spain and that old Sam Fathers who had taught him to hunt, the two spans running out together, not toward oblivion, nothingness, but into a dimension free of both time and space, where once more the untreed land warped and wrung to mathematical squares of rank cotton for the frantic old-world people to turn into shells to shoot at one another, would find ample room for both—the names, the faces of the old men he had known and loved and for a little while outlived, moving again among the shades of tall unaxed trees and sightless brakes where the wild strong immortal game ran forever before the tireless belling immortal hounds, falling and rising phoenix-like to the soundless guns.

He had been asleep. The lantern was lighted now. Outside in the darkness the oldest Negro, Isham, was beating a spoon against the bottom of a tin pan and crying, "Raise up and get yo foa clock coffy. Raise up and get yo foa clock coffy," and the tent was full of low talk and of men dressing, and Legate's voice, repeating: "Get out of here now and let Uncle Ike sleep. If you wake him up, he'll go out with us. And he ain't got any business in the woods this morning."

So he didn't move. He lay with his eyes closed, his breathing gentle and peaceful, and heard them one by one leave the tent. He listened to the breakfast sounds from the table beneath the tarpaulin and heard them depart—the horses, the dogs, the last voice until it died away and there was only the sounds of the Negroes clearing breakfast away. After a while he might possibly even hear the first faint clear cry of the first hound ring through the wet woods from where the buck had bedded, then he would go back to sleep again— The tent-flap swung in and fell. Something jarred sharply against the end of the cot and a hand grasped his knee through the blanket before he could open his eyes. It was Edmonds, carrying a shotgun in place of his rifle. He spoke in a harsh, rapid voice:

"Sorry to wake you. There will be a———"

"I was awake," McCaslin said. "Are you going to shoot that shotgun today?"

"You just told me last night you want meat," Edmonds said. "There will be a———"

"Since when did you start having trouble getting meat with your rifle?"

"All right," the other said, with that harsh, restrained, furious impatience. Then McCaslin saw in his hand a thick oblong: an envelope. "There will be a message here some time this morning, looking for me. Maybe it won't come. If it does, give the messenger this and tell h— say I said No."

"A what?" McCaslin said. "Tell who?" He half rose onto his elbow as Edmonds jerked the envelope onto the blanket, already turning toward the entrance, the envelope striking solid and heavy and without noise and already sliding from the bed until McCaslin caught it, divining by feel through the paper as instantaneously and conclusively as if he had opened the envelope and looked, the thick sheaf of banknotes. "Wait," he said. "Wait:"—more than the blood kinsman, more even than the senior in years, so that the other paused, the canvas lifted, looking back, and McCaslin saw that outside it was already day. "Tell her No," he said. "Tell her." They stared at one another—the old face, wan, sleep-raddled above the tumbled bed, the dark and sullen younger one at once furious and cold. "Will Legate was right. This is what you called coon-hunting. And now this." He didn't raise the envelope. He made no motion, no gesture to indicate it. "What did you promise her that you haven't the courage to face her and retract?"

"Nothing!" the other said. "Nothing! This is all of it. Tell her I said No." He was gone. The tent flap lifted on an in-waft of faint light and the constant murmur of rain, and fell again, leaving the old man still half-raised onto one elbow, the envelope clutched in the other shaking hand. Afterward it seemed to him that he had begun to hear the approaching boat almost immediately, before the other could have got out of sight even. It seemed to him that there had been no interval whatever: the tent flap falling on the same out-waft of faint and rain-filled light like the suspiration and expiration of the same breath and then in the next second lifted again—the mounting snarl of the outboard engine, increasing, nearer and nearer and louder and louder then cut short off, ceasing with the absolute instantaneity of a blown-out candle, into the lap and plop of water under the bows as the skiff slid in to the bank, the youngest Negro, the youth, raising the tent flap beyond which for that instant he saw the boat—a small skiff with a Negro man sitting in the stern beside the upslanted motor—then the woman entering, in a man's hat and a man's slicker and rubber boots, carrying the blanket-swaddled bundle on one arm and holding the edge of the unbuttoned raincoat over it with the other hand: and bringing something else, something intangible, an effluvium which he knew he would recognize in a moment because Isham had already told him, warned him, by sending the young Negro to the tent to announce the visitor instead of coming himself, the flap falling at last on the young Negro and they were alone—the face indistinct and as yet only young and with dark eyes, queerly colorless but not ill and not that of a country woman despite the garments she wore, looking down at him where he sat upright on the cot now, clutching the envelope, the soiled undergarment bagging about him and the twisted blankets huddled about his hips.

"Is this his?" he cried. "Don't lie to me!"

"Yes," she said. "He's gone."

"Yes. He's gone. You won't jump him here. Not this time. I don't reckon even you expected that. He left you this. Here." He fumbled at the envelope.

It was not to pick it up, because it was still in his hand; he had never put it down. It was as if he had to fumble somehow to co-ordinate physically his heretofore obedient hand with what his brain was commanding of it, as if he had never performed such an action before, extending the envelope at last, saying again, "Here. Take it. Take it:" until he became aware of her eyes, or not the eyes so much as the look, the regard fixed now on his face with that immersed contemplation, that bottomless and intent candor, of a child. If she had ever seen either the envelope or his movement to extend it, she did not show it.

"You're Uncle Isaac," she said.

"Yes," he said. "But never mind that. Here. Take it. He said to tell you No." She looked at the envelope, then she took it. It was sealed and bore no superscription. Nevertheless, even after she glanced at the front of it he watched her hold it in the one free hand and tear the corner off with her teeth and manage to rip it open and tilt the neat sheaf of bound notes onto the blanket without even glancing at them and look into the empty envelope and take the edge between her teeth and tear it completely open before she crumpled and dropped it.

"That's just money," she said.

"What did you expect? What else did you expect? You have known him long enough or at least often enough to have got that child, and you don't know him any better than that?"

"Not very often. Not very long. Just that week here last fall, and in January he sent for me and we went west, to New Mexico. We were there six weeks, where I could at least sleep in the same apartment where I cooked for him and looked after his clothes———"

"But not marriage," he said. "Not marriage. He didn't promise you that. Don't lie to me. He didn't have to."

"No. He didn't have to. I didn't ask him to. I knew what I was doing. I knew that to begin with, long before honor, I imagine he called it, told him the time had come to tell me in so many words what his code, I suppose he would call it, would forbid him forever to do. And we agreed. Then we agreed again before he left New Mexico, to make sure. That that would be all of it. I believed him. No, I don't mean that; I mean I believed myself. I wasn't even listening to him any more by then because by that time it had been a long time since he had anything else to tell me for me to have to hear. By then I wasn't even listening enough to ask him to please stop talking. I was listening to myself. And I believed it. I must have believed it. I don't see how I could have helped but believe it, because he was gone then as we had agreed and he didn't write as we had agreed, just the money came to the bank in Vicksburg in my name but coming from nobody as we had agreed. So I must have believed it. I even wrote him last month to make sure again and the letter came back unopened and I was sure. So I left the hospital and rented myself a room to live in until the deer season opened so I could make sure myself and I was waiting beside the road yesterday when your car passed and he saw me and so I was sure."

"Then what do you want?" he said. "What do you want? What do you expect?"

"Yes," she said. And while he glared at her, his white hair awry from the pillow and his eyes, lacking the spectacles to focus them, blurred and irisless and apparently pupilless, he saw again that grave, intent, speculative and detached fixity like a child watching him. "His great great— Wait a minute—great great *great* grandfather was your grandfather. McCaslin. Only it got to be Edmonds. Only it got to be more than that. Your cousin McCaslin was there that day when your father and Uncle Buddy won Tennie from Mr. Beauchamp for the one that had no name but Terrel so you called him Tomey's Terrel, to marry. But after that it got to be Edmonds." She regarded him, almost peacefully, with that unwinking and heatless fixity—the dark, wide, bottomless eyes in the face's dead and toneless pallor which to the old man looked anything but dead, but young and incredibly and even ineradicably alive—as though she were not only not looking at anything, she was not even speaking to anyone but herself. "I would have made a man of him. He's not a man yet. You spoiled him. You, and Uncle Lucas and Aunt Mollie. But mostly you."

"Me?" he said. "Me?"

"Yes. When you gave to his grandfather that land which didn't belong to him, not even half of it, by will or even law."

"And never mind that too," he said. "Never mind that too. You," he said. "You sound like you have been to college even. You sound almost like a Northerner even, not like the draggle-tailed women of these Delta peckerwoods. Yet you meet a man on the street one afternoon just because a box of groceries happened to fall out of a boat. And a month later you go off with him and live with him until he got a child on you: and then, by your own statement, you sat there while he took his hat and said goodbye and walked out. Even a Delta peckerwood would look after even a draggle-tail better than that. Haven't you got any folks at all?"

"Yes," she said. "I was living with one of them. My aunt, in Vicksburg. I came to live with her two years ago when my father died; we lived in Indianapolis then. But I got a job, teaching school here in Aluschaskuna, because my aunt was a widow, with a big family, taking in washing to sup——"

"Took in what?" he said. "Took in washing?" He sprang, still seated even, flinging himself backward onto one arm, awry-haired, glaring. Now he understood what it was she had brought into the tent with her, what old Isham had already told him by sending the youth to bring her in to him— the pale lips, the skin pallid and dead-looking yet not ill, the dark and tragic and foreknowing eyes. *Maybe in a thousand or two thousand years in America,* he thought. *But not now! Not now!* He cried, not loud, in a voice of amazement, pity, and outrage: "You're a nigger!"

"Yes," she said. "James Beauchamp—you called him Tennie's Jim though he had a name—was my grandfather. I said you were Uncle Isaac."

"And he knows?"

"No," she said. "What good would that have done?"

"But you did," he cried. "But you did. Then what do you expect here?"

"Nothing."

"Then why did you come here? You said you were waiting in Aluschas-kuna yesterday and he saw you. Why did you come this morning?"

"I'm going back North. Back home. My cousin brought me up the day before yesterday in his boat. He's going to take me on to Leland to get the train."

"Then go," he said. Then he cried again in that thin not loud and griev-ing voice: "Get out of here! I can do nothing for you! Can't nobody do noth-ing for you!" She moved; she was not looking at him again, toward the entrance. "Wait," he said. She paused again, obediently still, turning. He took up the sheaf of banknotes and laid it on the blanket at the foot of the cot and drew his hand back beneath the blanket. "There," he said.

Now she looked at the money, for the first time, one brief blank glance, then away again. "I don't need it. He gave me money last winter. Besides the money he sent to Vicksburg. Provided. Honor and code too. That was all arranged."

"Take it," he said. His voice began to rise again, but he stopped it. "Take it out of my tent." She came back to the cot and took up the money; where-upon once more he said, "Wait:" although she had not turned, still stooping, and he put out his hand. But, sitting, he could not complete the reach until she moved her hand, the single hand which held the money, until he touched it. He didn't grasp it, he merely touched it—the gnarled, bloodless, bone-light, bone-dry old man's fingers touching for a second the smooth young flesh where the strong old blood ran after its long lost journey back to home. "Tennie's Jim," he said. "Tennie's Jim." He drew the hand back beneath the blanket again: he said harshly now: "It's a boy, I reckon. They usually are, except that one that was its own mother too."

"Yes," she said. "It's a boy." She stood for a moment longer, looking at him. Just for an instant her free hand moved as though she were about to lift the edge of the raincoat away from the child's face. But she did not. She turned again when once more he said Wait and moved beneath the blanket.

"Turn your back," he said. "I am going to get up. I ain't got my pants on." Then he could not get up. He sat in the huddled blanket, shaking, while again she turned and looked down at him in dark interrogation. "There," he said harshly, in the thin and shaking old man's voice. "On the nail there. The tent-pole."

"What?" she said.

"The horn!" he said harshly. "The horn." She went and got it, thrust the money into the slicker's side pocket as if it were a rag, a soiled handkerchief, and lifted down the horn, the one which General Compson had left him in his will, covered with the unbroken skin from a buck's shank and bound with silver.

"What?" she said.

"It's his. Take it."

"Oh," she said. "Yes. Thank you."

"Yes," he said, harshly, rapidly, but not so harsh now and soon not harsh at all but just rapid, urgent, until he knew that his voice was running away with him and he had neither intended it nor could stop it: "That's right. Go back North. Marry: a man in your own race. That's the only salvation for you—for a while yet, maybe a long while yet. We will have to wait. Marry a black man. You are young, handsome, almost white; you could find a black man who would see in you what it was you saw in him, who would ask nothing of you and expect less and get even still less than that, if it's revenge you want. Then you will forget all this, forget it ever happened, that he ever existed—" until he could stop it at last and did, sitting there in his huddle of blankets during the instant when, without moving at all, she blazed silently down at him. Then that was gone too. She stood in the gleaming and still dripping slicker, looking quietly down at him from under the sodden hat.

"Old man," she said, "have you lived so long and forgotten so much that you don't remember anything you ever knew or felt or even heard about love?"

Then she was gone too. The waft of light and the murmur of the constant rain flowed into the tent and then out again as the flap fell. Lying back once more, trembling, panting, the blanket huddled to his chin and his hands crossed on his breast, he listened to the pop and snarl, the mounting then fading whine of the motor until it died away and once again the tent held only silence and the sound of rain. And cold too: he lay shaking faintly and steadily in it, rigid save for the shaking. This Delta, he thought: This Delta. *This land which man has deswamped and denuded and derivered in two generations so that white men can own plantations and commute every night to Memphis and black men own plantations and ride in Jim Crow cars to Chicago to live in millionaires' mansions on Lake Shore Drive; where white men rent farms and live like niggers and niggers crop on shares and live like animals; where cotton is planted and grows man-tall in the very cracks of the sidewalks, and usury and mortgage and bankruptcy and measureless wealth, Chinese and African and Aryan and Jew, all breed and spawn together until no man has time to say which one is which nor cares.* . . . No wonder the ruined woods I used to know don't cry for retribution! he thought: The people who have destroyed it will accomplish its revenge.

The tent flap jerked rapidly in and fell. He did not move save to turn his head and open his eyes. It was Legate. He went quickly to Edmonds' bed and stooped, rummaging hurriedly among the still-tumbled blankets.

"What is it?" he said.

"Looking for Roth's knife," Legate said. "I come back to get a horse. We got a deer on the ground." He rose, the knife in his hand, and hurried toward the entrance.

"Who killed it?" McCaslin said. "Was it Roth?"

"Yes," Legate said, raising the flap.

"Wait," McCaslin said. He moved, suddenly, onto his elbow. "What was it?" Legate paused for an instant beneath the lifted flap. He did not look back.

"Just a deer, Uncle Ike," he said impatiently. "Nothing extra." He was gone; again the flap fell behind him, wafting out of the tent again the faint light and the constant and grieving rain. McCaslin lay back down, the blanket once more drawn to his chin, his crossed hands once more weightless on his breast in the empty tent.

"It was a doe," he said.

1940

Barn Burning

The store in which the Justice of the Peace's court was sitting smelled of cheese. The boy, crouched on his nail keg at the back of the crowded room, knew he smelled cheese, and more: from where he sat he could see the ranked shelves close-packed with the solid, squat, dynamic shapes of tin cans whose labels his stomach read, not from the lettering which meant nothing to his mind but from the scarlet devils and the silver curve of fish—this, the cheese which he knew he smelled and the hermetic meat which his intestines believed he smelled coming in intermittent gusts momentary and brief between the other constant one, the smell and sense just a little of fear because mostly of despair and grief, the old fierce pull of blood. He could not see the table where the Justice sat and before which his father and his father's enemy (*our enemy* he thought in that despair; *ourn! mine and hisn both! He's my father!*) stood, but he could hear them, the two of them that is, because his father had said no word yet:

"But what proof have you, Mr. Harris?"

"I told you. The hog got into my corn. I caught it up and sent it back to him. He had no fence that would hold it. I told him so, warned him. The next time I put the hog in my pen. When he came to get it I gave him enough wire to patch up his pen. The next time I put the hog up and kept it. I rode down to his house and saw the wire I gave him still rolled on to the spool in his yard. I told him he could have the hog when he paid me a dollar pound fee.[1] That evening a nigger came with the dollar and got the hog. He was a strange nigger. He said, 'He say to tell you wood and hay kin burn.' I said, 'What?' 'That whut he say to tell you,' the nigger said. 'Wood and hay kin burn.' That night my barn burned. I got the stock out but I lost the barn."

"Where is the nigger? Have you got him?"

"He was a strange nigger, I tell you. I don't know what became of him."

"But that's not proof. Don't you see that's not proof?"

"Get that boy up here. He knows." For a moment the boy thought too that the man meant his older brother until Harris said, "Not him. The little one. The boy," and, crouching, small for his age, small and wiry like his father, in patched and faded jeans even too small for him, with straight,

---

[1] In many rural cultures, property owners may "impound" domestic animals that stray onto their land. The animal's owner must pay a "fee" to redeem them.

uncombed, brown hair and eyes gray and wild as storm scud, he saw the men between himself and the table part and become a lane of grim faces, at the end of which he saw the Justice, a shabby, collarless, graying man in spectacles, beckoning him. He felt no floor under his bare feet; he seemed to walk beneath the palpable weight of the grim turning faces. His father, stiff in his black Sunday coat donned not for the trial but for the moving, did not even look at him. *He aims for me to lie,* he thought, again with that frantic grief and despair. *And I will have to do hit.*

"What's your name, boy?" the Justice said.

"Colonel Sartoris Snopes," the boy whispered.

"Hey?" the Justice said. "Talk louder. Colonel Sartoris? I reckon anybody named for Colonel Sartoris in this country can't help but tell the truth, can they?" The boy said nothing. *Enemy! Enemy!* he thought; for a moment he could not even see, could not see that the Justice's face was kindly nor discern that his voice was troubled when he spoke to the man named Harris: "Do you want me to question this boy?" But he could hear, and during those subsequent long seconds while there was absolutely no sound in the crowded little room save that of quiet and intent breathing it was as if he had swung outward at the end of a grape vine, over a ravine, and at the top of the swing had been caught in a prolonged instant of mesmerized gravity, weightless in time.

"No!" Harris said violently, explosively. "Damnation! Send him out of here!" Now time, the fluid world, rushed beneath him again, the voices coming to him again through the smell of cheese and sealed meat, the fear and despair and the old grief of blood:

"This case is closed. I can't find against you, Snopes, but I can give you advice. Leave this country and don't come back to it."

His father spoke for the first time, his voice cold and harsh, level, without emphasis: "I aim to. I don't figure to stay in a country among people who . . ." he said something unprintable and vile, addressed to no one.

"That'll do," the Justice said. "Take your wagon and get out of this country before dark. Case dismissed."

His father turned, and he followed the stiff black coat, the wiry figure walking a little stiffly from where a Confederate provost's man's musket ball had taken him in the heel on a stolen horse thirty years ago, followed the two backs now, since his older brother had appeared from somewhere in the crowd, no taller than the father but thicker, chewing tobacco steadily, between the two lines of grim-faced men and out of the store and across the worn gallery and down the sagging steps and among the dogs and half-grown boys in the mild May dust, where as he passed a voice hissed:

"Barn burner!"

Again he could not see, whirling; there was a face in a red haze, moon-like, bigger than the full moon, the owner of it half again his size, he leaping in the red haze toward the face, feeling no blow, feeling no shock when his head struck the earth, scrabbling up and leaping again, feeling no blow this time either and tasting no blood, scrabbling up to see the other boy in full flight and himself already leaping into pursuit as his father's hand jerked him back, the harsh, cold voice speaking above him: "Go get in the wagon."

It stood in a grove of locusts and mulberries across the road. His two hulking sisters in their Sunday dresses and his mother and her sister in calico and sunbonnets were already in it, sitting on and among the sorry residue of the dozen and more movings which even the boy could remember—the battered stove, the broken beds and chairs, the clock inlaid with mother-of-pearl, which would not run, stopped at some fourteen minutes past two o'clock of a dead and forgotten day and time, which had been his mother's dowry. She was crying, though when she saw him she drew her sleeve across her face and began to descend from the wagon. "Get back," the father said.

"He's hurt. I got to get some water and wash his ..."

"Get back in the wagon," his father said. He got in too, over the tailgate. His father mounted to the seat where the older brother already sat and struck the gaunt mules two savage blows with the peeled willow, but without heat. It was not even sadistic; it was exactly that same quality which in later years would cause his descendants to over-run the engine before putting a motor car into motion, striking and reining back in the same movement. The wagon went on, the store with its quiet crowd of grimly watching men dropped behind; a curve in the road hid it. *Forever* he thought. *Maybe he's done satisfied now, now that he has* ... stopping himself, not to say it aloud even to himself. His mother's hand touched his shoulder.

"Does hit hurt?" she said.

"Naw," he said. "Hit don't hurt. Lemme be."

"Can't you wipe some of the blood off before hit dries?"

"I'll wash to-night," he said. "Lemme be, I tell you."

The wagon went on. He did not know where they were going. None of them ever did or ever asked, because it was always somewhere, always a house of sorts waiting for them a day or two days or even three days away. Likely his father had already arranged to make a crop on another farm before he ... Again he had to stop himself. He (the father) always did. There was something about his wolflike independence and even courage when the advantage was at least neutral which impressed strangers, as if they got from his latent ravening ferocity not so much a sense of dependability as a feeling that his ferocious conviction in the rightness of his own actions would be of advantage to all whose interest lay with his.

That night they camped, in a grove of oaks and beeches where a spring ran. The nights were still cool and they had a fire against it, of a rail lifted from a nearby fence and cut into lengths—a small fire, neat, niggard almost, a shrewd fire; such fires were his father's habit and custom always, even in freezing weather. Older, the boy might have remarked this and wondered why not a big one; why should not a man who had not only seen the waste and extravagance of war, but who had in his blood an inherent voracious prodigality with material not his own, have burned everything in sight? Then he might have gone a step farther and thought that that was the reason: that niggard blaze was the living fruit of nights passed during those four years in the woods hiding from all men, blue or gray, with his strings of horses (captured horses, he called them). And older still, he might have divined the true reason: that the element of fire spoke to some deep mainspring of his father's being, as the element of steel or of powder spoke to other men, as the one weapon for the preservation of integrity, else breath were not worth the breathing, and hence to be regarded with respect and used with discretion.

But he did not think this now and he had seen those same niggard blazes all his life. He merely ate his supper beside it and was already half asleep over his iron plate when his father called him, and once more he followed the stiff back, the stiff and ruthless limp, up the slope and on to the starlit road where, turning, he could see his father against the stars but without face or depth—a shape black, flat, and bloodless as though cut from tin in the iron folds of the frockcoat which had not been made for him, the voice harsh like tin and without heat like tin:

"You were fixing to tell them. You would have told him." He didn't answer. His father struck him with the flat of his hand on the side of the head, hard but without heat, exactly as he had struck the two mules at the store, exactly as he would strike either of them with any stick in order to kill a horse fly, his voice still without heat or anger: "You're getting to be a man. You got to learn. You got to learn to stick to your own blood or you ain't going to have any blood to stick to you. Do you think either of them, any man there this morning, would? Don't you know all they wanted was a chance to get at me because they knew I had them beat? Eh?" Later, twenty years later, he was to tell himself, "If I had said they wanted only truth, justice, he would have hit me again." But now he said nothing. He was not crying. He just stood there. "Answer me," his father said.

"Yes," he whispered. His father turned.

"Get on to bed. We'll be there tomorrow."

To-morrow they were there. In the early afternoon the wagon stopped before a paintless two-room house identical almost with the dozen others it had stopped before even in the boy's ten years, and again, as on the other dozen occasions, his mother and aunt got down and began to unload the wagon, although his two sisters and his father and brother had not moved.

"Likely hit ain't fitten for hawgs," one of the sisters said.

"Nevertheless, fit it will and you'll hog it and like it," his father said. "Get out of them chairs and help your Ma unload."

The two sisters got down, big, bovine, in a flutter of cheap ribbons; one of them drew from the jumbled wagon bed a battered lantern, the other a worn broom. His father handed the reins to the older son and began to climb stiffly over the wheel. "When they get unloaded, take the team to the barn and feed them." Then he said, and at first the boy thought he was still speaking to his brother: "Come with me."

"Me?" he said.

"Yes," his father said. "You."

"Abner," his mother said. His father paused and looked back—the harsh level stare beneath the shaggy, graying, irascible brows.

"I reckon I'll have a word with the man that aims to begin to-morrow owning me body and soul for the next eight months."

They went back up the road. A week ago—or before last night, that is— he would have asked where they were going, but not now. His father had struck him before last night but never before had he paused afterward to explain why; it was as if the blow and the following calm, outrageous voice still rang, repercussed, divulging nothing to him save the terrible handicap of being young, the light weight of his few years, just heavy enough to prevent his soaring free of the world as it seemed to be ordered but not heavy enough to keep him footed solid in it, to resist it and try to change the course of its events.

Presently he could see the grove of oaks and cedars and the other flowering trees and shrubs where the house would be, though not the house yet. They walked beside a fence massed with honeysuckle and Cherokee roses and came to a gate swinging open between two brick pillars, and now, beyond a sweep of drive, he saw the house for the first time and at that instant he forgot his father and the terror and despair both, and even when he remembered his father again (who had not stopped) the terror and despair did not return. Because, for all the twelve movings, they had sojourned until now in a poor country, a land of small farms and fields and houses, and he had never seen a house like this before. *Hit's big as a courthouse* he thought quietly, with a surge of peace and joy whose reason he could not have thought into words, being too young for that: *They are safe from him. People whose lives are a part of this peace and dignity are beyond his touch, he no more to them than a buzzing wasp: capable of stinging for a little moment but that's all; the spell of this peace and dignity rendering even the barns and stable and cribs which belong to it impervious to the puny flames he might contrive ...* this, the peace and joy, ebbing for an instant as he looked again at the stiff black back, the stiff and implacable limp of the figure which was not dwarfed by the house, for the reason that it had never looked big anywhere and which now, against the serene columned backdrop, had more than ever that impervious quality of something cut ruthlessly from tin, depthless, as though, sidewise to the sun, it would cast no shadow. Watching him, the boy remarked the absolutely undeviating course which his father held and saw the stiff foot come squarely down in a pile of fresh droppings where a horse had stood in the drive and which his father could have avoided by a simple change of stride. But it ebbed only for a moment, though he could not have thought this into words either, walking on in the spell of the house, which he could ever want but without envy, without sorrow, certainly never with that ravening and jealous rage which unknown to him walked in the ironlike black coat before him: *Maybe he will feel it too. Maybe it will even change him now from what maybe he couldn't help but be.*

They crossed the portico. Now he could hear his father's stiff foot as it came down on the boards with clocklike finality, a sound out of all proportion to the displacement of the body it bore and which was not dwarfed either by the white door before it, as though it had attained to a sort of vicious and ravening minimum not to be dwarfed by anything—the flat, wide, black hat, the formal coat of broadcloth which had once been black but which had now that friction-glazed greenish cast of the bodies of old house flies, the lifted sleeve which was too large, the lifted hand like a curled claw. The door opened so promptly that the boy knew the Negro must have been watching them all the time, an old man with neat grizzled hair, in a linen jacket, who stood barring the door with his body, saying, "Wipe yo foots, white man, fo you come in here. Major ain't home nohow."

"Get out of my way, nigger," his father said, without heat too, flinging the door back and the Negro also and entering, his hat still on his head. And now the boy saw the prints of the stiff foot on the doorjamb and saw them appear on the pale rug behind the machinelike deliberation of the foot which seemed to bear (or transmit) twice the weight which the body compassed. The Negro was shouting "Miss Lula! Miss Lula!" somewhere behind them, then the boy, deluged as though by a warm wave by a suave turn of carpeted stair and a pendant glitter of chandeliers and a mute gleam of gold frames, heard the swift feet and saw her too, a lady—perhaps he had never seen her like before either—in a gray, smooth gown with lace at the throat and an apron tied at the waist and the sleeves turned back, wiping cake or biscuit dough from her hands with a towel as she came up the hall, looking not at his father at all but at the tracks on the blond rug with an expression of incredulous amazement.

"I tried," the Negro cried. "I tole him to . . ."

"Will you please go away?" she said in a shaking voice. "Major de Spain is not at home. Will you please go away?"

His father had not spoken again. He did not speak again. He did not even look at her. He just stood stiff in the center of the rug, in his hat, the shaggy iron-gray brows twitching slightly above the pebble-colored eyes as he appeared to examine the house with brief deliberation. Then with the same deliberation he turned; the boy watched him pivot on the good leg and saw the stiff foot drag round the arc of the turning, leaving a final long and fading smear. His father never looked at it, he never once looked down at the rug. The Negro held the door. It closed behind them, upon the hysteric and indistinguishable woman-wail. His father stopped at the top of the steps and scraped his boot clean on the edge of it. At the gate he stopped again. He stood for a moment, planted stiffly on the stiff foot, looking back at the house. "Pretty and white, ain't it?" he said. "That's sweat. Nigger sweat. Maybe it ain't white enough yet to suit him. Maybe he wants to mix some white sweat with it."

Two hours later the boy was chopping wood behind the house within which his mother and aunt and the two sisters (the mother and aunt, not the two girls, he knew that; even at this distance and muffled by walls the flat loud voices of the two girls emanated an incorrigible idle inertia) were setting up the stove to prepare a meal, when he heard the hooves and saw the linen-clad man on a fine sorrel mare, whom he recognized even before he saw the rolled rug in front of the Negro youth following on a fat bay carriage horse—a suffused, angry face vanishing, still at full gallop, beyond the corner of the house where his father and brother were sitting in the two tilted chairs; and a moment later, almost before he could have put the axe down, he heard the hooves again and watched the sorrel mare go back out of the yard, already galloping again. Then his father began to shout one of the sisters' names, who presently emerged backward from the kitchen door dragging the rolled rug along the ground by one end while the other sister walked behind it.

"If you ain't going to tote, go on and set up the wash pot," the first said.

"You, Sarty!" the second shouted. "Set up the wash pot!" His father appeared at the door, framed against that shabbiness, as he had been against that other bland perfection, impervious to either, the mother's anxious face at his shoulder.

"Go on," the father said. "Pick it up." The two sisters stooped, broad, lethargic; stooping, they presented an incredible expanse of pale cloth and a flutter of tawdry ribbons.

"If I thought enough of a rug to have to git hit all the way from France I wouldn't keep hit where folks coming in would have to tromp on hit," the first said. They raised the rug.

"Abner," the mother said. "Let me do it."

"You go back and git dinner," his father said. "I'll tend to this."

From the woodpile through the rest of the afternoon the boy watched them, the rug spread flat in the dust beside the bubbling wash-pot, the two sisters stooping over it with that profound and lethargic reluctance, while the father stood over them in turn, implacable and grim, driving them though never raising his voice again. He could smell the harsh homemade lye they were using; he saw his mother come to the door once and look toward them with an expression not anxious now but very like despair; he saw his father turn, and he fell to with the axe and saw from the corner of his eye his father raise from the ground a flattish fragment of field stone and examine it and return to the pot, and this time his mother actually spoke: "Abner. Abner. Please don't. Please, Abner."

Then he was done too. It was dusk; the whippoorwills had already begun. He could smell coffee from the room where they would presently eat the cold food remaining from the mid-afternoon meal, though when he entered the house he realized they were having coffee again probably because there was a fire on the hearth, before which the rug now lay spread over the backs of the two chairs. The tracks of his father's foot were gone. Where they had been were now long, water-cloudy scoriations resembling the sporadic course of a lilliputian[2] mowing machine.

---

[2]Extremely small, like the 6-inch inhabitants of the land of Lilliput in Jonathan Swift's *Gulliver's Travels* (1726).

It still hung there while they ate the cold food and then went to bed, scattered without order or claim up and down the two rooms, his mother in one bed, where his father would later lie, the older brother in the other, himself, the aunt, and the two sisters on pallets on the floor. But his father was not in bed yet. The last thing the boy remembered was the depthless, harsh silhouette of the hat and coat bending over the rug and it seemed to him that he had not even closed his eyes when the silhouette was standing over him, the fire almost dead behind it, the stiff foot prodding him awake. "Catch up the mule," his father said.

When he returned with the mule his father was standing in the black door, the rolled rug over his shoulder. "Ain't you going to ride?" he said.

"No. Give me your foot."

He bent his knee into his father's hand, the wiry, surprising power flowed smoothly, rising, he rising with it, on to the mule's bare back (they had owned a saddle once; the boy could remember it though not when or where) and with the same effortlessness his father swung the rug up in front of him. Now in the starlight they retraced the afternoon's path, up the dusty road rife with honeysuckle, through the gate and up the black tunnel of the drive to the lightless house, where he sat on the mule and felt the rough warp of the rug drag across his thighs and vanish.

"Don't you want me to help?" he whispered. His father did not answer and now he heard again that stiff foot striking the hollow portico with that wooden and clocklike deliberation, that outrageous overstatement of the weight it carried. The rug, hunched, not flung (the boy could tell that even in the darkness) from his father's shoulder struck the angle of wall and floor with a sound unbelievably loud, thunderous, then the foot again, unhurried and enormous; a light came on in the house and the boy sat, tense, breathing steadily and quietly and just a little fast, though the foot itself did not increase its beat at all, descending the steps now; now the boy could see him.

"Don't you want to ride now?" he whispered. "We kin both ride now," the light within the house altering now, flaring up and sinking. *He's coming down the stairs now*, he thought. He had already ridden the mule up beside the horse block; presently his father was up behind him and he doubled the reins over and slashed the mule across the neck, but before the animal could begin to trot the hard, thin arm came round him, the hard, knotted hand jerking the mule back to a walk.

In the first red rays of the sun they were in the lot, putting plow gear on the mules. This time the sorrel mare was in the lot before he heard it at all, the rider collarless and even bareheaded, trembling, speaking in a shaking voice as the woman in the house had done, his father merely looking up once before stooping again to the hame[3] he was buckling, so that the man on the mare spoke to his stooping back:

[3]One of two curved wooden or metal pieces of a harness.

"You must realize you have ruined that rug. Wasn't there anybody here, any of your women ..." he ceased, shaking, the boy watching him, the older brother leaning now in the stable door, chewing, blinking slowly and steadily at nothing apparently. "It cost a hundred dollars. But you never had a hundred dollars. You never will. So I'm going to charge you twenty bushels of corn against your crop. I'll add it in your contract and when you come to the commissary you can sign it. That won't keep Mrs. de Spain quiet but maybe it will teach you to wipe your feet off before you enter her house again."

Then he was gone. The boy looked at his father, who still had not spoken or even looked up again, who was now adjusting the logger-head[4] in the hame.

"Pap," he said. His father looked at him—the inscrutable face, the shaggy brows beneath which the gray eyes glinted coldly. Suddenly the boy went toward him, fast, stopping as suddenly. "You done the best you could!" he cried. "If he wanted hit done different why didn't he wait and tell you how? He won't git no twenty bushels! He won't git none! We'll gether hit and hide hit! I kin watch ..."

"Did you put the cutter back in that straight stock like I told you?"[5]

"No, sir," he said.

"Then go do it."

That was Wednesday. During the rest of that week he worked steadily, at what was within his scope and some which was beyond it, with an industry that did not need to be driven nor even commanded twice; he had this from his mother, with the difference that some at least of what he did he liked to do, such as splitting wood with the half-size axe which his mother and aunt had earned; or saved money somehow, to present him with at Christmas. In company with the two older women (and on one afternoon, even one of the sisters), he built pens for the shoat and the cow which were a part of his father's contract with the landlord, and one afternoon, his father being absent, gone somewhere on one of the mules, he went to the field.

They were running a middle buster now, his brother holding the plow straight while he handled the reins, and walking beside the straining mule, the rich black soil shearing cool and damp against his bare ankles, he thought *Maybe this is the end of it. Maybe even that twenty bushels that seems hard to have to pay for just a rug will be a cheap price for him to stop forever and always from being what he used to be*; thinking, dreaming now, so that his brother had to speak sharply to him to mind the mule: *Maybe he even won't collect the twenty bushels. Maybe it will all add up and balance and vanish—corn, rug, fire; the terror and grief, the being pulled two ways like between two teams of horses—gone, done with for ever and ever.*

Then it was Saturday; he looked up from beneath the mule he was harnessing and saw his father in the black coat and hat. "Not that," his father

[4]Plowhead; harness piece.
[5]Cutter ... straight stock: the blade and frame of a plow.

said. "The wagon gear." And then, two hours later, sitting in the wagon bed behind his father and brother on the seat, the wagon accomplished a final curve, and he saw the weathered paintless store with its tattered tobacco- and patent-medicine posters and the tethered wagons and saddle animals below the gallery. He mounted the gnawed steps behind his father and brother, and there again was the lane of quiet, watching faces for the three of them to walk through. He saw the man in spectacles sitting at the plank table and he did not need to be told this was a Justice of the Peace; he sent one glare of fierce, exultant, partisan defiance at the man in collar and cravat now, whom he had seen but twice before in his life, and that on a galloping horse, who now wore on his face an expression not of rage but of amazed unbelief which the boy could not have known was at the incredible circumstance of being sued by one of his own tenants, and came and stood against his father and cried at the Justice: "He ain't done it! He ain't burnt . . ."

"Go back to the wagon," his father said.

"Burnt?" the Justice said. "Do I understand this rug was burned too?"

"Does anybody here claim it was?" his father said. "Go back to the wagon." But he did not, he merely retreated to the rear of the room, crowded as that other had been, but not to sit down this time, instead, to stand pressing among the motionless bodies, listening to the voices:

"And you claim twenty bushels of corn is too high for the damage you did to the rug?"

"He brought the rug to me and said he wanted the tracks washed out of it. I washed the tracks out and took the rug back to him."

"But you didn't carry the rug back to him in the same condition it was in before you made the tracks on it."

His father did not answer, and now for perhaps half a minute there was no sound at all save that of breathing, the faint, steady suspiration of complete and intent listening.

"You decline to answer that, Mr. Snopes?" Again his father did not answer. "I'm going to find against you, Mr. Snopes. I'm going to find that you were responsible for the injury to Major de Spain's rug and hold you liable for it. But twenty bushels of corn seems a little high for a man in your circumstances to have to pay. Major de Spain claims it cost a hundred dollars. October corn will be worth about fifty cents. I figure that if Major de Spain can stand a ninety-five dollar loss on something he paid cash for, you can stand a five-dollar loss you haven't earned yet. I hold you in damages to Major de Spain to the amount of ten bushels of corn over and above your contract with him, to be paid to him out of your crop at gathering time. Court adjourned."

It had taken no time hardly, the morning was but half begun. He thought they would return home and perhaps back to the field, since they were late, far behind all other farmers. But instead his father passed on behind the wagon, merely indicating with his hand for the older brother to follow with it, and crossed the road toward the blacksmith shop opposite, pressing on after his father, overtaking him, speaking, whispering up at the harsh, calm face beneath the weathered hat: "He won't git no ten bushels neither. He won't git one. We'll ..." until his father glanced for an instant down at him, the face absolutely calm, the grizzled eyebrows tangled above the cold eyes, the voice almost pleasant, almost gentle:

"You think so? Well, we'll wait till October anyway."

The matter of the wagon—the setting of a spoke or two and the tightening of the tires—did not take long either, the business of the tires accomplished by driving the wagon into the spring branch behind the shop and letting it stand there, the mules nuzzling into the water from time to time, and the boy on the seat with the idle reins, looking up the slope and through the sooty tunnel of the shed where the slow hammer rang and where his father sat on an upended cypress bolt, easily, either talking or listening, still sitting there when the boy brought the dripping wagon up out of the branch and halted it before the door.

"Take them on to the shade and hitch," his father said. He did so and returned. His father and the smith and a third man squatting on his heels inside the door were talking, about crops and animals; the boy, squatting too in the ammoniac dust and hoof-parings and scales of rust, heard his father tell a long and unhurried story out of the time before the birth of the older brother even when he had been a professional horsetrader. And then his father came up beside him where he stood before a tattered last year's circus poster on the other side of the store, gazing rapt and quiet at the scarlet horses, the incredible poisings and convolutions of tulle and tights and the painted leers of comedians, and said, "It's time to eat."

But not at home. Squatting beside his brother against the front wall, he watched his father emerge from the store and produce from a paper sack a segment of cheese and divide it carefully and deliberately into three with his pocket knife and produce crackers from the same sack. They all three squatted on the gallery and ate, slowly, without talking; then in the store again, they drank from a tin dipper tepid water smelling of the cedar bucket and of living beech trees. And still they did not go home. It was a horse lot this time, a tall rail fence upon and along which men stood and sat and out of which one by one horses were led, to be walked and trotted and then cantered back and forth along the road while the slow swapping and buying went on and the sun began to slant westward, they—the three of them— watching and listening, the older brother with his muddy eyes and his steady, inevitable tobacco, the father commenting now and then on certain of the animals, to no one in particular.

It was after sundown when they reached home. They ate supper by lamplight, then, sitting on the doorstep, the boy watched the night fully accomplish, listening to the whippoorwills and the frogs, when he heard his mother's voice: "Abner! No! No! Oh, God. Oh, God. Abner!" and he rose, whirled, and saw the altered light through the door where a candle stub now burned in a bottle neck on the table and his father, still in the hat and coat, at once formal and burlesque as though dressed carefully for some shabby and ceremonial violence, emptying the reservoir of the lamp back into the five-gallon kerosene can from which it had been filled, while the mother tugged at his arm until he shifted the lamp to the other hand and flung her back, not savagely or viciously, just hard, into the wall, her hands flung out against the wall for balance, her mouth open and in her face the same quality of hopeless despair as had been in her voice. Then his father saw him standing in the door. "Go to the barn and get that can of oil we were oiling the wagon with," he said. The boy did not move. Then he could speak.

"What . . ." he cried. "What are you . . ."

"Go get that oil," his father said. "Go."

Then he was moving, running, outside the house, toward the stable: this the old habit, the old blood which he had not been permitted to choose for himself, which had been bequeathed him willy nilly and which had run for so long (and who knew where, battening on what of outrage and savagery and lust) before it came to him. *I could keep on*, he thought. *I could run on and on and never look back, never need to see his face again. Only I can't. I can't*, the rusted can in his hand now, the liquid sploshing in it as he ran back to the house and into it, into the sound of his mother's weeping in the next room, and handed the can to his father.

"Ain't you going to even send a nigger?" he cried. "At least you sent a nigger before!"

This time his father didn't strike him. The hand came even faster than the blow had, the same hand which had set the can on the table with almost excruciating care flashing from the can toward him too quick for him to follow it, gripping him by the back of his shirt and on to tiptoe before he had seen it quit the can, the face stooping at him in breathless and frozen ferocity, the cold, dead voice speaking over him to the older brother who leaned against the table, chewing with that steady, curious, sidewise motion of cows:

"Empty the can into the big one and go on. I'll catch up with you."

"Better tie him up to the bedpost," the brother said.

"Do like I told you," the father said. Then the boy was moving, his bunched shirt and the hard, bony hand between his shoulder-blades, his toes just touching the floor, across the room and into the other one, past the sisters sitting with spread heavy thighs in the two chairs over the cold hearth, and to where his mother and aunt sat side by side on the bed, the aunt's arms about his mother's shoulders.

"Hold him," the father said. The aunt made a startled movement. "Not you," the father said. "Lennie. Take hold of him. I want to see you do it." His mother took him by the wrist. "You'll hold him better than that. If he gets loose don't you know what he is going to do? He will go up yonder." He jerked his head toward the road. "Maybe I'd better tie him."

"I'll hold him," his mother whispered.

"See you do then." Then his father was gone, the stiff foot heavy and measured upon the boards, ceasing at last.

Then he began to struggle. His mother caught him in both arms, he jerking and wrenching at them. He would be stronger in the end, he knew that. But he had no time to wait for it. "Lemme go!" he cried. "I don't want to have to hit you!"

"Let him go!" the aunt said. "If he don't go, before God, I am going up there myself!"

"Don't you see I can't?" his mother cried. "Sarty! Sarty! No! No! Help me, Lizzie!"

Then he was free. His aunt grasped at him but it was too late. He whirled, running, his mother stumbled forward on to her knees behind him, crying to the nearer sister: "Catch him, Net! Catch him!" But that was too late too, the sister (the sisters were twins, born at the same time, yet either of them now gave the impression of being, encompassing as much living meat and volume and weight as any other two of the family) not yet having begun to rise from the chair, her head, face, alone merely turned, presenting to him in the flying instant an astonishing expanse of young female features untroubled by any surprise even, wearing only an expression of bovine interest. Then he was out of the room, out of the house, in the mild dust of the starlit road and the heavy rifeness of honeysuckle, the pale ribbon unspooling with terrific slowness under his running feet, reaching the gate at last and turning in, running, his heart and lungs drumming, on up the drive toward the lighted house, the lighted door. He did not knock, he burst in, sobbing for breath, incapable for the moment of speech; he saw the astonished face of the Negro in the linen jacket without knowing when the Negro had appeared.

"De Spain!" he cried, panted. "Where's ..." then he saw the white man too emerging from a white door down the hall. "Barn!" he cried. "Barn!"

"What?" the white man said. "Barn?"

"Yes!" the boy cried. "Barn!"

"Catch him!" the white man shouted.

But it was too late this time too. The Negro grasped his shirt, but the entire sleeve, rotten with washing, carried away, and he was out that door too and in the drive again, and had actually never ceased to run even while he was screaming into the white man's face.

Behind him the white man was shouting, "My horse! Fetch my horse!" and he thought for an instant of cutting across the park and climbing the fence into the road, but he did not know the park nor how high the vine-massed fence might be and he dared not risk it. So he ran on down the drive, blood and breath roaring; presently he was in the road again though he could not see it. He could not hear either: the galloping mare was almost upon him before he heard her, and even then he held his course, as if the very urgency of his wild grief and need must in a moment more find him wings, waiting until the ultimate instant to hurl himself aside and into the weed-choked roadside ditch as the horse thundered past and on, for an instant in furious silhouette against the stars, the tranquil early summer night sky which, even before the shape of the horse and rider vanished, stained abruptly and violently upward: a long, swirling roar incredible and soundless, blotting the stars, and he springing up and into the road again, running again, knowing it was too late yet still running even after he heard the shot and, an instant later, two shots, pausing now without knowing he had ceased to run, crying "Pap! Pap!," running again before he knew he had begun to run, stumbling, tripping over something and scrabbling up again without ceasing to run, looking backward over his shoulder at the glare as he got up, running on among the invisible trees, panting, sobbing, "Father! Father!"

At midnight he was sitting on the crest of a hill. He did not know it was midnight and he did not know how far he had come. But there was no glare behind him now and he sat now, his back toward what he had called home for four days anyhow, his face toward the dark woods which he would enter when breath was strong again, small, shaking steadily in the chill darkness, hugging himself into the remainder of his thin, rotten shirt, the grief and despair now no longer terror and fear but just grief and despair. *Father. My father*, he thought. "He was brave!" he cried suddenly, aloud but not loud, no more than a whisper: "He was! He was in the war! He was in Colonel Sartoris' cav'ry!" not knowing that his father had gone to that war a private in the fine old European sense, wearing no uniform, admitting the authority of and giving fidelity to no man or army or flag, going to war as Malbrouck[6] himself did: for booty—it meant nothing and less than nothing to him if it were enemy booty or his own.

The slow constellations wheeled on. It would be dawn and then sun-up after a while and he would be hungry. But that would be to-morrow and now he was only cold, and walking would cure that. His breathing was easier now and he decided to get up and go on, and then he found that he had been asleep because he knew it was almost dawn, the night almost over. He could tell that from the whippoorwills. They were everywhere now among the dark trees below him, constant and inflectioned and ceaseless, so that, as the instant for giving over to the day birds drew nearer and nearer, there was no interval at all between them. He got up. He was a little stiff, but walking would cure that too as it would the cold, and soon there would be the sun. He went on down the hill, toward the dark woods within which the liquid silver voices of the birds called unceasing—the rapid and urgent beating of the urgent and quiring heart of the late spring night. He did not look back.

1938

---

[6]Malbrouck, the hero of an eighteenth-century French nursery rhyme, *"Malbrouck s'en va-t-en guerre"* ("Malbrouck has gone to war").

HART CRANE
1899–1932

The only child of a successful candy manufacturer and a difficult, possessive mother, Hart Crane grew up in a household of domestic turmoil that did not end even with his parents' divorce in 1916. He had a sketchy formal education but a precocious self-education derived from reading the experimental writing published in the little magazines of the period. He published his first poem, "C-33," in one such magazine, *Bruno's Weekly*, when he was seventeen. During this period, he voraciously read not only nativist writers such as Edgar Lee Masters and Sherwood Anderson, but also Ezra Pound and T. S. Eliot and the French poets Rimbaud and Laforgue.

He left school and went to New York for a brief stay in 1916, returned to Ohio to work for his father from 1919 to 1923, and finally settled in New York. Nourished by the break with his family, Crane was nonetheless troubled by financial difficulties, which kept him unhappily dependent upon his relatives. Benefactors such as financier Otto Kahn, who provided support for part of the writing of the long poem *The Bridge*, also helped Crane through troubled times.

In 1922, he started work on a three-part poem "For the Marriage of Faustus and Helen," which was to express the union of science and beauty, of technology and art, in the modern world. The oddly disparate three parts of the poem open with the poet's meeting Helen of Troy, symbol of beauty, in a streetcar (Part I), then move to an evocation of the jazz age (Part II), and end with a vision of wholeness beyond the ravages of modern warfare (Part III). This poem is important as a precursor of *The Bridge* as well as an expression of Crane's visionary hope.

During this period of his life, Crane was alternately productive and dejected. His first volume of poetry, *White Buildings*, was published in 1926. He continued to work on *The Bridge* through 1927, but he did not complete it until 1929 when he was encouraged by a promise from Harry Crosby, the owner of the Black Sun Press, to publish the poem. Crane never revived the inspiration that inaugurated the long work, and the last poems that he wrote for it lacked the power and vitality of the beginning. However, because he published the poems not in the sequence in which they were written but in the sequence outlined very early in the composition (he wrote, for example, the last section first), *The Bridge* is a difficult poem to read as a whole. It moves through changes of mood, as it struggles to maintain the positive vision of America that Crane first imagined. The poem starts and ends with a paean to the Brooklyn Bridge, symbolized as "O harp and altar, of the fury fused."

In the middle sections of the long poem, Crane moves back and forth in American history: back to trace the voyage of Columbus, forward to track the modern subway traveler, back to the Indians, forward to the airplane age, in an effort to unite past and present, nature and technology, America and the spiritual possibilities of the new age. Some parts, written late in the process of composition, express Crane's flagging spirits even when, in the sequence of the long work, they are designed to move positively toward the affirmation of the ending. As a result, *The Bridge* has presented problems in interpretation. Assured of its power, readers have been less certain about its purpose.

Long before he completed *The Bridge*, Crane lost faith in his vision of America and in his own ability as a poet. After a period of creative inactivity and personal discontent, Crane was awarded a Guggenheim Fellowship and moved to Mexico. On his return from Mexico in April 1927, he committed suicide by jumping from the ship carrying him to New York. Among the poems that he had been working on in his final years, "The Broken Tower" indicates a new range of control and verbal mastery. It expresses a return to the subject of poetry and to his own role as a poet of "the visionary company of love." Crane's poetry is marked by visionary power, verbal difficulty, and jammed syntax.

Margaret Dickie
late of University of Georgia

PRIMARY WORKS

White Buildings, 1926; *The Bridge*, 1930; *The Collected Poems of Hart Crane*, 1933; *The Letters of Hart Crane, 1916–1932*, ed. Brom Weber, 1952, 1965; *Letters of Hart Crane and His Family*, ed. Thomas S.W. Lewis, 1974; *Hart Crane and Yvor Winters: Their Literary Correspondence*, ed. Thomas F. Parkinson, 1978; *Complete Poems and Selected Letters*, 2006.

Black Tambourine

The interests of a black man in a cellar
Mark tardy judgment on the world's closed door.
Gnats toss in the shadow of a bottle,
And a roach spans a crevice in the floor.

Æsop,[1] driven to pondering, found   5
Heaven with the tortoise and the hare;
Fox brush and sow ear top his grave
And mingling incantations on the air.

The black man, forlorn in the cellar,
Wanders in some mid-kingdom, dark, that lies,   10
Between his tambourine, stuck on the wall,
And, in Africa, a carcass quick with flies.

1926

---

[1] A Greek slave to whom many beast fables are attributed.

Chaplinesque[1]

We make our meek adjustments,
Contented with such random consolations
As the wind deposits
In slithered and too ample pockets.

For we can still love the world, who find   5
A famished kitten on the step, and know
Recesses for it from the fury of the street,
Or warm torn elbow coverts.

We will sidestep, and to the final smirk
Dally the doom of that inevitable thumb[2]   10
That slowly chafes its puckered index toward us,
Facing the dull squint with what innocence
And what surprise!

And yet these fine collapses are not lies
More than the pirouettes of any pliant cane;   15
Our obsequies are, in a way, no enterprise.
We can evade you, and all else but the heart:
What blame to us if the heart live on.[3]

The game enforces smirks; but we have seen
The moon in lonely alleys make   20
A grail of laughter of an empty ash can,
And through all sound of gaiety and quest
Have heard a kitten in the wilderness.

1926

At Melville's Tomb[1']

Often beneath the wave, wide from this ledge
The dice of drowned men's bones he saw bequeath
An embassy. Their numbers as he watched,
Beat on the dusty shore and were obscured.

And wrecks passed without sound of bells,   5
The calyx of death's bounty giving back

---

[1] In the style of Charlie Chaplin, the silent movie star whom Crane had seen in *The Kid* in 1921.
[2] Of the policeman.
[3] Crane claimed to use this term as a deliberate pun on his first name.

[1'] Herman Melville (1819–1891) is buried at Woodlawn Cemetery in New York City. Crane refers to the sea as Melville's tomb.

A scattered chapter, livid hieroglyph,
The portent wound in corridors of shells.

Then in the circuit calm of one vast coil,
Its lashings charmed and malice reconciled,   10
Frosted eyes there were that lifted altars;
And silent answers crept across the stars.

Compass, quadrant and sextant contrive
No farther tides ... High in the azure steeps
Monody shall not wake the mariner.   15
This fabulous shadow only the sea keeps.

                                                          1926

from **The Bridge**

To Brooklyn Bridge

How many dawns, chill from his rippling rest
The seagull's wings shall dip and pivot him,
Shedding white rings of tumult, building high
Over the chained bay waters Liberty—

Then, with inviolate curve, forsake our eyes   5
As apparitional as sails that cross
Some page of figures to be filed away;
—Till elevators drop us from our day ...

I think of cinemas, panoramic sleights
With multitudes bent toward some flashing scene   10
Never disclosed, but hastened to again,
Foretold to other eyes on the same screen;

And Thee, across the harbor, silver-paced
As though the sun took step of thee, yet left
Some motion ever unspent in thy stride,—   15
Implicity thy freedom staying thee!

Out of some subway scuttle, cell or loft
A bedlamite[1] speeds to thy parapets,
Tilting there momently, shrill shirt ballooning,
A jest falls from the speechless caravan.   20

---

[1] A madman, inhabitant of Bedlam, the earliest established insane asylum in England.

Down Wall,[2] from girder into street noon leaks,
A rip-tooth of the sky's acetylene;
All afternoon the cloud-flown derricks turn . . .
Thy cables breathe the North Atlantic still.

And obscure as that heaven of the Jews,   25
Thy guerdon[3] . . . Accolade thou dost bestow
Of anonymity time cannot raise:
Vibrant reprieve and pardon thou dost show.

O harp and altar, of the fury fused,
(How could mere toil align thy choiring strings!)   30
Terrific threshold of the prophet's pledge,
Prayer of pariah, and the lover's cry,—

Again the traffic lights that skim thy swift
Unfractioned idiom, immaculate sigh of stars,
Beading thy path—condense eternity: 35
And we have seen night lifted in thine arms.

Under thy shadow by the piers I waited;
Only in darkness is thy shadow clear.
The City's fiery parcels all undone,
Already snow submerges an iron year . . .   40

O Sleepless as the river under thee,
Vaulting the sea, the prairies' dreaming sod,
Unto us lowliest sometime sweep, descend
And of the curveship lend a myth to God.

                                                              1930

The River[1]

Stick your patent name on a signboard
brother—all over—going west—young man   . . . *and past*
Tintex—Japalac—Certain-teed Overalls ads[2']   *the din and*
and lands sakes! under the new playbill ripped   *slogans of the*
in the guaranteed corner—see Bert Williams[3'] what? *year—*   5

Minstrels when you steal a chicken just
save me the wing for if it isn't

---

[2]Wall Street in Manhattan, the financial center.
[3]A reward.
[1]The Mississippi River.

[2']A take-off on advertisements of the day.
[3']One of the most talented Negro comedians of the twentieth century, who flourished from about 1895 until his death in 1922.

Erie it ain't for miles around a
Mazda—and the telegraphic night coming on Thomas

a Ediford—and whistling down the tracks   10
a headlight rushing with the sound—can you
imagine—while an EXpress makes time like
SCIENCE—COMMERCE AND THE HOLYGHOST
RADIO ROARS IN EVERY HOME WE HAVE THE NORTHPOLE
WALLSTREET AND VIRGINBIRTH WITHOUT STONES OR   15
WIRES OR EVEN RUNning brooks[4] connecting ears
and no more sermons windows flashing roar
breathtaking—as you like it ... eh?
                    So the 20th Century—so
whizzed the Limited[5]—roared by and left   20
three men, still hungry on the tracks, ploddingly
watching the tail lights wizen and converge, slipping gimleted and neatly out of sight.

The last bear, shot drinking in the Dakotas
Loped under wires that span the mountain stream.   25
Keen instruments, strung to a vast precision
Bind town to town and dream to ticking dream.   *to those*
But some men take their liquor slow—and count   *whose addresses*
—Though they'll confess no rosary nor clue—   *are never near*
The river's minute by the far brook's year.   30
Under a world of whistles, wires and steam
Caboose-like they go ruminating through
Ohio, Indiana—blind baggage—
To Cheyenne tagging ... Maybe Kalamazoo.

Time's rendings, time's blendings they construe   35
As final reckonings of fire and snow;
Strange bird-wit, like the elemental gist
Of unwalled winds they offer, singing low
My Old Kentucky Home and *Casey Jones,*
Some Sunny Day. I heard a road-gang chanting so.   40
And afterwards, who had a colt's eyes—one said,
"Jesus! Oh I remember watermelon days!" And sped
High in a cloud of merriment, recalled
"—And when my Aunt Sally Simpson smiled," he
        drawled—   45

---

[4]"books in the running brooks, / Sermons in   [5]Twentieth-Century Limited was a fast train.
stones," William Shakespeare, *As You Like It,*
Act II, Scene 1, ll. 16–17.

"It was almost Louisiana, long ago."
"There's no place like Booneville though, Buddy,"
One said, excising a last burr from his vest,
"—For early trouting." Then peering in the can,
"—But I kept on the tracks." Possessed, resigned,   50
He trod the fire down pensively and grinned,
Spreading dry shingles of a beard . . .

Behind

My father's cannery works I used to see
Rail-squatters ranged in nomad raillery,   55
The ancient men—wifeless or runaway
Hobo-trekkers that forever search
An empire wilderness of freight and rails.
Each seemed a child, like me, on a loose perch,
Holding to childhood like some termless play.   60
John, Jake or Charley, hopping the slow freight
—Memphis to Tallahassee—riding the rods,
Blind fists of nothing, humpty-dumpty clods.

Yet they touch something like a key perhaps.
From pole to pole across the hills, the states   65
—They know a body under the wide rain;   *but who have*
Youngsters with eyes like fjords, old reprobates   *touched her,*
With racetrack jargon,—dotting immensity   *knowing her*
They lurk across her, knowing her yonder breast   *without name*
Snow-silvered, sumac-stained or smoky blue—   70
Is past the valley-sleepers, south or west.
—As I have trod the rumorous midnights, too,

And past the circuit of the lamp's thin flame
(O Nights that brought me to her body bare!)[6]
Have dreamed beyond the print that bound her name.   75
Trains sounding the long blizzards out—I heard
Wail into distances I knew were hers.
Papooses crying on the wind's long mane
Screamed redskin dynasties that fled the brain,
—Dead echoes! But I knew her body there,   80
Time like a serpent down her shoulder, dark,
And space, an eaglet's wing, laid on her hair.[7]
Under the Ozarks, domed by Iron Mountain,   *nor the*
The old gods of the rain lie wrapped in pools   *myths of her*
Where eyeless fish curvet a sunken fountain   *fathers . . .*   85
and re-descend with corn from querulous crows.

---

[6]Crane identifies the body of the American continent with the Indian princess Pocahontas.

[7]The union of serpent and eagle symbolizes the union of time and space, land and air.

Such pilferings make up their timeless eatage,
Propitiate them for their timber torn
By iron, iron—always the iron dealt cleavage!
They doze now, below axe and powder horn.   90

And Pullman breakfasters glide glistening steel
From tunnel into field—iron strides the dew—
Straddles the hill, a dance of wheel on wheel.
You have a half-hour's wait at Siskiyou,
Or stay the night and take the next train through.   95
Southward, near Cairo[8] passing, you can see
The Ohio merging,—borne down Tennessee;
And if it's summer and the sun's in dusk
Maybe the breeze will lift the River's musk
—As though the waters breathed that you might know   100
Memphis Johnny, Steamboat Bill, Missouri Joe.[9]
Oh, lean from the window, if the train slows down,
As though you touched hands with some ancient
        clown,
—A little while gaze absently below   105
And hum *Deep River* with them while they go.

Yes, turn again and sniff once more—look see,
O Sheriff, Brakeman and Authority—
Hitch up your pants and crunch another quid,
For you, too, feed the River timelessly.   110
And few evade full measure of their fate;
Always they smile out eerily what they seem.
I could believe he joked at heaven's gate—
Dan Midland[10]—jolted from the cold brake-beam.

Down, down—born pioneers in time's despite,   115
Grimed tributaries to an ancient flow—
They win no frontier by their wayward plight,
But drift in stillness, as from Jordan's brow.[11]

You will not hear it as the sea; even stone
Is not more hushed by gravity ... But slow,   120
As loth to take more tribute—sliding prone
Like one whose eyes were buried long ago

---

[8]In southern Illinois where the Ohio River
merges with the Mississippi.
[9]Old Mississippi folk songs. "Deep River" is
also a Mississippi River song.

[10]A storied hobo who fell from the brake
beam while "riding the rods."
[11]The shore of the river Jordan in Palestine.

The River, spreading, flows—and spends your dream.
What are you, lost within this tideless spell?
You are your father's father, and the stream—   125
A liquid theme that floating niggers swell.

Damp tonnage and alluvial march of days—
Nights turbid, vascular with silted shale
And roots surrendered down of moraine clays:
The Mississippi drinks the farthest dale.   130

O quarrying passion, undertowed sunlight!
The basalt surface drags a jungle grace
Ochreous and lynx-barred in lengthening might;
Patience! and you shall reach the biding place!
Over De Soto's[12] bones the freighted floors   135
Throb past the City storied of three thrones.
Down two more turns the Mississippi pours
(Anon tall ironsides up from salt lagoons)

And flows within itself, heaps itself free.
All fades but one thin skyline 'round . . . Ahead   140
No embrace opens but the stinging sea;
The River lifts itself from its long bed,

Poised wholly on its dream, a mustard glow
Tortured with history, its one will—flow!
—The Passion[13] spreads in wide tongues, choked and slow,   145
Meeting the Gulf, hosannas silently below.

                                                                  1930

The Broken Tower

The bell-rope that gathers God at dawn[1]
Dispatches me as though I dropped down the knell
Of a spent day—to wander the cathedral lawn
From pit to crucifix, feet chill on steps from hell.

Have you not heard, have you not seen that corps   5
Of shadows in the tower, whose shoulders sway

---

[12]To prevent hostile Indians from discovering the death of Hernando DeSoto, who discovered the Mississippi in 1541, his men buried him in the river, near New Orleans, whose history involved the three thrones of Spain, France, and England.

[13]The river is associated with the Passion (suffering on the Cross) of Christ. The Gulf (of Mexico) becomes an emblem of eternity.
[1]The angelus commemorates the Incarnation of Christ.

Antiphonal carillons launched before
The stars are caught and hived in the sun's ray?

The bells, I say, the bells break down their tower;
And swing I know not where. Their tongues engrave   10
Membrane through marrow, my long-scattered score
Of broken intervals ... And I, their sexton slave!

Oval encyclicals in canyons heaping
The impasse high with choir. Banked voices slain!
Pagodas, campaniles with reveilles outleaping—   15
O terraced echoes prostrate on the plain! ...
And so it was I entered the broken world
To trace the visionary company of love, its voice
An instant in the wind (I know not whither hurled)
but not for long to hold each desperate choice.   20

My word I poured. But was it cognate, scored
Of that tribunal monarch of the air[2]
Whose thigh embronzes earth, strikes crystal Word[3]
In wounds pledged once to hope—cleft to despair?

The steep encroachments of my blood left me   25
No answer (could blood hold such a lofty tower
As flings the question true?)—or is it she
Whose sweet mortality stirs latent power?—

And through whose pulse I hear, counting the strokes
My veins recall and add, revived and sure   30
The angelus of wars my chest evokes;
What I hold healed, original now, and pure ...

And builds, within, a tower that is not stone
(Not stone can jacket heaven)—but slip
Of pebbles,—visible wings of silence sown   35
In azure circles, widening as they dip

The matrix of the heart, lift down the eye
That shrines the quiet lake and swells a tower ...
The commodious, tall decorum of that sky
Unseals her earth, and lifts love in its shower.   40

                                                1932

---

[2]Christ as judge and king.   [3]Divine revelation and the poet's words.

America in the World/The World in America—Expatriation, Immigration, and the Rise of the Celebrity-Publicity Culture

THIS IN FOCUS CHARACTERIZES THE ANXIETIES AND MOOD OF AMERICA FROM THE 1910s to the 1930s, emphasizing the conflicting intellectual undercurrents and political positions debating the direction America was taking. Walter Lippmann's *Drift and Mastery* reveals the degree to which commentators feared modernity had cost America its moral moorings—although, unlike many contemporaries, Lippmann refused to resort to a facile nostalgia for the past, insisting instead that the future required a commitment to forging new ideals. The excerpt from Harold E. Stearns's *Civilization and American Culture* reveals the strain of intellectual disdain for democracy inherent in these debates, with Stearns openly insisting that it flattens all thinking into a provincialism that is indicative of the "feminization" of American culture. While *Civilization and American Culture* is often cited as the Bible of American expatriates, Harry Crosby's short list of reasons for living abroad documents the dissatisfactions that drove many artists to relocate to London, Paris, Berlin, and other sites in the 1920s. Two speeches debating the Immigration Act of 1924 (the Johnson-Reed Act), meanwhile, illustrate the anxieties over American ethnic identity that drove the sixty-eighth U.S. Congress to impose severe, xenophobic limits on immigration to control the influx of "undesirable" populations that would remain in effect for the next forty years. Finally, the Marcus Garvey editorial from the Negro Improvement Association documents the African nationalist movement's response to the uncertainties of the age.

Kirk Curnutt,
Troy University–Montgomery, Alabama

WALTER LIPPMANN
1889–1974

from Drift and Mastery: An Attempt to Diagnose the Current Unrest[1]

The issues that we face are very different from those of the last century and a half. The difference, I think, might be summed up roughly this way: those who went before inherited a conservatism and overthrew it; we inherit freedom, and have to use it. The sanctity of property, the patriarchal family, hereditary caste, the dogma of sin, obedience to authority,—the rock of ages, in brief, has been blasted for us. Those who are young to-day are born into a world in which the foundations of the older order survive only as habits or by default. So Americans can carry through their purposes when they have them. If the standpatter is still powerful amongst us it is because we have not learned to use our power, and direct it to fruitful ends. The American conservative, it seems to me, fills the vacuum where democratic purpose should be.... The battle for us, in short, does not lie against crusted prejudice, but against the chaos of a new freedom....

Tradition will not work in the complexity of modern life. For if you ask Americans to remain true to the traditions of all their Fathers, there would be a pretty confusion if they followed your advice. There is great confusion, as it is, due in large measure to the persistency with which men follow tradition in a world unsuited to it. They modify a bit, however, they apply "the rule of reason" to their old loyalties, and so a little adjustment is possible. But there can be no real cohesion for America in following scrupulously the inherited ideals of our people. Between the Sons of the Revolution, the Ancient Order of Hibernians, the Orangemen, the plantation life of the South, the refugees from Russia, the Balkan Slavs, there is in their traditions a conflict of prejudice and custom that would make all America as clamorous as the Stock Exchange on a busy day.[2] Nor is there going to be lasting inspiration for Bulgarian immigrants in the legend of the Mayflower.

The only possible cohesion now is a loyalty that looks forward. America is preeminently the country where there is practical substance in Nietzsche's advice that we should not live for our fatherland but for our children's land.

To do this men have to substitute purpose for tradition: and that is, I believe, the profoundest change that has ever taken place in human history. We can no longer treat life as something that has trickled down to us. We

[1]Walter Lippmann, *Drift and Mastery: An Attempt to Diagnose the Current Unrest* (1914), 16–17, 146–47.
[2]The Sons of the Revolution is an American fraternal organization of descendants of military patriots in the Revolutionary War. The Ancient Order of Hibernians is an Irish Catholic fraternal organization, whereas "Orangemen" is the popular name for members of the Orange Institution, a Protestant fraternal organization founded in Ireland in 1795.

have to deal with it deliberately, devise its social organization, alter its tools, formulate its method, educate and control it. In endless ways we put intention where custom has reigned. We break up routines, make decisions, choose our ends, select means.

1914

■   ## HAROLD STEARNS   ■
1891–1943

from **The Intellectual Life**[1]

When Professor Einstein aroused the ire of the women's clubs by stating that "women dominate the entire life of America," and that "there are cities with a million population, but cities suffering from terrible poverty—the poverty of intellectual things," he was but repeating a criticism of our life now old enough to almost be a cliché.[2] Hardly any intelligent foreigner has failed to observe and comment upon the extraordinary feminization of American social life, and oftenest he has coupled this observation with a few biting remarks concerning the intellectual anemia or torpor that seems to accompany it. Naturally the attitude is resented, and the indiscreet visitor is told that he has been rendered astigmatic by too limited observation. He is further informed that he should travel in our country more extensively, see more people, and live among us longer. The inference is that this chastening process will in due time acquaint him with a beauty and a thrilling intellectual vitality coyly hidden from the superficial impressionist.

Now the thesis of this paper is that the spontaneous judgment of the perceptive foreigner is to a remarkable degree correct. But it is a judgment which has to be modified in certain respects rather sharply. Moreover, even long residence in the United States is not likely to give a visitor as vivid a sense of the historical background that has so largely contributed to the present situation as is aroused in the native American, who in his own family hears the folklore of the two generations preceding him and to whom the pioneer tradition is a reality more imaginatively plausible than, say, the emancipations of glory from English fields or the aura of ancient pomp enwrapping an Italian castle. The foreigner is too likely to forget that in a young country, precisely because it is young, traditions have a social sanction unknown in an older country where the memory of the past goes so far

[1]Harold E. Stearns, "The Intellectual Life," *Civilization and American Culture* (New York: Harcourt, Brace, 1920), 135–37, 141–43.

[2]The reference is to Albert Einstein (1879–1955).

back as to become shadowy and unreal. It is a paradox of history that from ancient cultures usually come those who "were born too soon," whereas from young and groping civilization spring the panoplied defenders of conventions. It is usually when a tradition is fresh that it is respected most; it is only when it has been followed for years sufficient to make it meaningless that it can create its repudiators. America is a very young country—and in no respect younger than that of all Western nations it has the oldest form of established government; our naïve respect for the fathers is surest proof that we are still in the cultural awkward age. We have not sufficiently grown up but that we must still cling to our father and mother. In a word, we still *think* in pioneer terms, whatever the material and economic facts of a day that has already outgrown their applicability.

And it is the pioneer point of view, once thoroughly understood, which will most satisfactorily explain the peculiar development of the intellectual life in the United States. For the life of the mind is no fine flower of impoverishment, and if the beginnings of human reflection were the wayward reveries of seamen in the long watches of the night or of a shepherd lying on his back idly watching the summer clouds float past, as surely have the considered intellectual achievements of modern men been due to the commercial and industrial organization which, whether or not conducive to the general happiness, has at least made leisure possible for the few. But for the pioneer community leisure cannot exist, even for the few; the struggle is too merciless, the stake—life itself, possibly—too high. The pioneer must almost of necessity hate the thinker, even when he does not despise thought in itself, because the thinker is a liability to a community that can afford only assets; he is non-productive in himself and a dangerous subversive example to others. Of course, the pioneer will tolerate the minister, exactly as primitive tribes tolerated the medicine men—and largely for the same reasons. The minister if he cannot bring rain or ward off pestilence as the medicine man at least pretended he could, can soften the hardness of the human lot and can show the road to a future kingdom that will amply compensate for the drudgery of the world. He has, in brief, considerable utilitarian value. The thinker *per se*, however, has none; not only that, he is a reproach and a challenge to the man who must labour by the seat of his brow—it is as if he said, "For what end, all this turmoil and effort, merely to live? But do you know if life is worth while on such terms?" Questions like these the pioneer must cast far from him, and for the very good reason that if they were tolerated, new communities might never become settled. S[k]epticism is an expensive luxury possible only to men in cities living off the fruit of others' toil. Certainly America, up to the end of the reconstruction period following the Civil War, had little practical opportunity and less native impulse for the cultivation of this tolerant attitude towards ultimate values, an atmosphere which is a talisman that a true intellectual life is flourishing.

... To an extent almost incomprehensible to the peoples of other cultures, the things of the mind and spirit have been given over, in America, into the almost exclusive custody of women. This has certainly been true of art, certainly of music, certainly of education. The spinster school-marm has settled in the impressionable, adolescent minds of boys the conviction that the cultural interests are largely an affair of the other sex; the intellectual life can have no connection with native gaiety, with sexual curiosity, with play, with creative dreaming, or with adventure. These more genuine impulses, he is made to feel, are not merely distinguishable from the intellectual life, but actually at war with it. In my own day at Harvard the Westerner in my class looked with considerable suspicion upon those who specialized in literature, the classics, or philosophy—a man's education should be science, economics, engineering. Only "sissies," I was informed, took courses in poetry out in that virile West. And to this day for a boy to be taught to play the piano, for example, is regarded as "queer," whereas for a girl to be so taught is entirely in the nature of things. That is, natural aptitude has nothing do with it; some interests are proper for women, others for men. Of course there are exceptions enough to make even the boldest hesitate at generalizations, yet assuredly the contempt, as measured in the only terms we thoroughly understand, money, with which male teachers, male professors (secretly), male ministers, and male artists are universally held should convince the most prejudiced that, speaking broadly, this generalization is in substance correct.

In fact, when we try to survey the currents of our entire national life, to assess these vagrant winds of doctrine free from the ingenuousness that our own academic experience or training may give us, the more shall we perceive that the dichotomy between the cultural and intellectual life of men and women in this country has been carried farther than anywhere else in the world. We need only recall the older women's clubs of the comic papers—in truth, the actual women's clubs of to-day as revealed by small-town newspaper reports of their meetings—the now deliquescent Browning Clubs, the Chautauquas, the church festivals, the rural normal schools for teachers, the women's magazines, the countless national organizations for improving, elevating, uplifting this, that, or the other.[3] One shudders slightly and turns to the impeccable style, the slightly tired and sensuous irony of Anatole France (not yet censored, if we read him in French) for relief.[4] Or if we are so fortunate as to be "regular" Americans instead of unhappy intellectuals educated beyond our environment, we go gratefully back to our work at the office. Beside the stilted artificiality of this world of higher ethical values the business world, where men haggle, cheat, and steal with whole-hearted devotion is at least real. And it is this world, the world of making money, in which alone the American man can feel thoroughly at home. If the French

[3]Browning Clubs were poetry appreciation groups devoted to studying the works of Robert Browning (1812–1889). Chautauqua assemblies were early twentieth-century civic groups that sponsored lecture series and musical performances for edification.

[4]Anatole France was a French author (1844–1924) considered scandalous in mainstream America but old hat among intellectuals.

romanticists of the 18th century invented the phrase *la femme mécomprise*, a modern Gallic visitor would be tempted to observe that in this 20th century the United States was the land of *l'homme mécompris*.[5]

These, then, are the cruder historical forces that have led directly to the present remarkable situation.... The surface of the contemporary social structure shows us suffrage, the new insights into the world of industry which the war gave so many women for the first time, the widening of professional opportunity, co-education, and, in the life which perhaps those of us who have contributed to this volume know best, a genuine intellectual camaraderie. Nevertheless, I believe the underlying thesis cannot be successfully challenged. Where men and women in America to-day share their intellectual life on terms of equality and perfect understanding, closer examination reveals that the phenomenon is not a sharing but a capitulation. The men have been feminized.

1920

HARRY CROSBY
1898–1924

Harry Crosby's Reasons for Expatriating[1]

I prefer to live outside America

1. because in America the *stars* were all suffocated inside
2. because I do not wish to devote myself to perpetual hypocrisy
3. because outside America there is nothing to remind me of my childhood
4. because I prefer perihelion to aphelion
5. because I love flagons of wine
6. because I am an enemy of society and here I can hunt with other enemies of society
7. because I want to be in at the death (of Europe)
8. because I like tumults and chances better than security
9. because I prefer transitional orgasms to atlantic monthlies
10. because I am not coprophagous
11. because I would rather be an eagle gathering sun than a spider gathering poison

[5]The disillusioned man (French).
[1]"Harry Crosby's Reasons for Expatriating," *Transition* (1928), reprinted in *Altogether* *Elsewhere: Writers on Exile*, ed. Marc Robinson (Boston: Faber and Faber), 208.

12. because by living outside of America New York can still remain for me the City of a Thousand and One Nights
13. because the Rivers of Suicide are more inviting than the Prairies of Prosperity
14. because I prefer explosions to whimperings.

1928

■ # U.S. CONGRESS ■

A Congressman and a Senator Debate the Immigration Act of 1924 (the Johnson-Reed Act)

Robert H. Clancy, D-Michigan (1882–1962)[1]

Since the foundations of the American commonwealth were laid in colonial times over 300 years ago, vigorous complaint and more or less bitter persecution have been aimed at newcomers to our shores. Also the congressional reports of about 1840 are full of abuse of English, Scotch, Welsh immigrants as paupers, criminals, and so forth.

Old citizens in Detroit of Irish and German descent have told me of the fierce tirades and propaganda directed against the great waves of Irish and Germans who came over from 1840 on for a few decades to escape civil, racial, and religious persecution in their native lands.

The "Know-Nothings," lineal ancestors of the Ku-Klux Klan, bitterly denounced the Irish and Germans as mongrels, scum, foreigners, and a menace to our institutions, much as other great branches of the Caucasian race of glorious history and antecedents are berated to-day. All are riff-raff, unassimilables, "foreign devils," swine not fit to associate with the great chosen people—a form of national pride and hallucination as old as the division of races and nations.

But to-day it is the Italians, Spanish, Poles, Jews, Greeks, Russians, Balkanians, and so forth, who are the racial lepers. And it is eminently fitting and proper that so many Members of this House with names as Irish as Paddy's pig, are taking the floor these days to attack once more as their kind has attacked for seven bloody centuries the fearful fallacy of chosen peoples and inferior peoples. The fearful fallacy is that one is made to rule and the other to be abominated. . . .

---

[1]Speech by Robert H. Clancy, April 8, 1924, *Congressional Record*, 68th Congress, 1st Session (Washington, D.C.: Government Printing Office, 1924), vol. 65, 5929–32.

In this bill we find racial discrimination at its worst—a deliberate attempt to go back 84 years in our census taken every 10 years so that a blow may be aimed at peoples of eastern and southern Europe, particularly at our recent allies in the Great War—Poland and Italy.

Jews in Detroit are Good Citizens

Of course the Jews too are aimed at, not directly, because they have no country in Europe they can call their own, but they are set down among the inferior peoples. Much of the animus against Poland and Russia, old and new, with the countries that have arisen from the ruins of the dead Czar's European dominions, is directed against the Jew.

We have many American citizens of Jewish descent in Detroit, tens of thousands of them—active in every profession and every walk of life. They are particularly active in charities and merchandising. One of our greatest judges, if not the greatest, is a Jew. Surely no fair-minded person with a knowledge of the facts can say the Jews or Detroit are a menace to the city's or the country's well-being. . . .

Forty or fifty thousand Italian-Americans live in my district in Detroit. They are found in all walks and classes of life—common hard labor, the trades, business, law, medicine, dentistry, art, literature, banking, and so forth.

They rapidly become Americanized, build homes, and make themselves into good citizens. They brought hardihood, physique, hope, and good humor with them from their outdoor life in Sunny Italy, and they bear up under the terrific strain of life and work in busy Detroit.

One finds them by thousands digging streets, sewers, and building foundations, and in the automobile and iron and steel fabric factories of various sorts. They do the hard work that the native-born American dislikes. Rapidly they rise in life and join the so-called middle and upper classes. . . .

The Italian-Americans of Detroit played a glorious part in the Great War. They showed themselves as patriotic as the native born in offering the supreme sacrifice.

In all, I am informed, over 300,000 Italian-speaking soldiers enlisted in the American Army, almost 10 percent of our total fighting force. Italians formed about 4 percent of the population of the United States and they formed 10 percent of the American military force. Their casualties were 12 percent. . . .

Detroit Satisfied with the Poles

I wish to take the liberty of informing the House that from my personal knowledge and observation of tens of thousands of Polish-Americans living in my district in Detroit that their Americanism and patriotism are unassailable from any fair or just standpoint.

The Polish-Americans are as industrious and as frugal and as loyal to our institutions as any class of people who have come to the shores of this country in the past 300 years. They are essentially home builders, and they have come to this country to stay. They learn the English language as quickly as possible, and take pride in the rapidity with which they become assimilated and adopt our institutions.

Figures available to all show that in Detroit in the World War the proportion of American volunteers of Polish blood was greater than the proportion of Americans of any other racial descent....

Polish-Americans do not merit slander nor defamation. If not granted charitable or sympathetic judgment, they are at least entitled to justice and to the high place they have won in American and European history and citizenship.

The force behind the Johnson bill and some of its champions in Congress charge that opposition to the racial discrimination feature of the 1800 quota basis arises from "foreign blocs." They would give the impression that 100 percent Americans are for it and that the sympathies of its opponents are of the "foreign-bloc" variety, and bear stigma of being "hyphenates." I meet that challenge willingly. I feel my Americanism will stand any test.

Every American Has Foreign Ancestors

The foreign born of my district writhe under the charge of being called "hyphenates." The people of my own family were all hyphenates—English-Americans, German-Americans, Irish-Americans. They began to come in the first ship or so after the *Mayflower*. But they did not come too early to miss the charge of anti-Americanism. Roger Williams was driven out of the Puritan colony of Salem to die in the wilderness because he objected "violently" to blue laws and the burning or hanging of rheumatic old women on witchcraft charges. He would not "assimilate" and was "a grave menace to American Institutions and democratic government."

My family put 11 men and boys into the Revolutionary War, and I am sure they and their women and children did not suffer so bitterly and sacrifice until it hurt to establish the autocracy of bigotry and intolerance which exists in many quarters to-day in this country. Some of these men and boys shed their blood and left their bodies to rot on American battle fields. To me real Americanism and the American flag are the product of the blood of men and of the tears of women and children of a different type than the rampant "Americanizers" of to-day.

My mother's father fought in the Civil War, leaving his six small children in Detroit when he marched away to the southern battle fields to fight against racial distinctions and protect his country. My mother's little brother, about 14 years old, and the eldest child, fired by the traditions of his family, plodded off to the battle fields to do his bit. He aspired to be a drummer boy and inspire the men in battle, but he was found too small to carry a drum and was put at the ignominious task of driving army mules, hauling cannons and wagons.

I learned more of the spirit of American history at my mother's knee than I ever learned in my four years of high school study of American history and in my five and a half years of study at the great University of Michigan.

All that study convinces me that the racial discriminations of this bill are un-American...

It must never be forgotten also that the Johnson bill, although it claims to favor the northern and western European peoples only, does so on a basis of comparison with the southern and western European peoples. The Johnson bill cuts down materially the number of immigrants allowed to come from northern and western Europe, the so-called Nordic peoples....

Then I would be true to the principles for which my forefathers fought and true to the real spirit of the magnificent United States of to-day. I can not stultify myself by voting for the present bill and overwhelm my country with racial hatreds and racial lines and antagonisms drawn even tighter than they are to-day. [Applause.]

Ellison DuRant Smith, D-South Carolina (1909–1944)[2]

It seems to me the point as to this measure—and I have been so impressed for several years—is that the time has arrived when we should shut the door. We have been called the melting pot of the world. We had an experience just a few years ago, during the great World War, when it looked as though we had allowed influences to enter our borders that were about to melt the pot in place of us being the melting pot.

I think that we have sufficient stock in America now for us to shut the door, Americanize what we have, and save the resources of America for the natural increase of our population. We all know that one of the most prolific causes of war is the desire for increased land ownership for the overflow of a congested population. We are increasing at such a rate that in the natural course of things in a comparatively few years the landed resources, the natural resources of the country, shall be taken up by the natural increase of our population. It seems to me the part of wisdom now that we have throughout the length and breadth of continental America a population which is beginning to encroach upon the reserve and virgin resources of the country to keep it in trust for the multiplying population of the country.

I do not believe that political reasons should enter into the discussion of this very vital question. It is of greater concern to us to maintain the institutions of America, to maintain the principles upon which this Government is founded, than to develop and exploit the underdeveloped resources of the country. There are some things that are dearer to us, fraught with more benefit to us, than the immediate development of the undeveloped resources of the country. I believe that our particular ideas, social, moral, religious, and political, have demonstrated, by virtue of the progress we have made and the character of people that we are, that we have the highest ideals of any member of the human family or any nation. We have demonstrated the

[2]Speech by Ellison DuRant Smith, April 9, 1924, *Congressional Record*, 68th Congress, 1st Session (Washington, D.C.: Government Printing Office, 1924), vol. 65, 5961–2.

fact that the human family, certainty the predominant breed in America, can govern themselves by a direct government of the people. If this Government shall fail, it shall fail by virtue of the terrible law of inherited tendency. Those who come from the nations which from time immemorial have been under the dictation of a master fall more easily by the law of inheritance and the inertia of habit into a condition of political servitude than the descendants of those who cleared the forests, conquered the savage, stood at arms and won their liberty from their mother country, England.

I think we now have sufficient population in our country for us to shut the door and to breed up a pure, unadulterated American citizenship. I recognize that there is a dangerous lack of distinction between people of a certain nationality and the breed of the dog. Who is an American? Is he an immigrant from Italy? Is he an immigrant from Germany? If you were to go abroad and some one were to meet you and say, "I met a typical American," what would flash into your mind as a typical American, the typical representative of that new Nation? Would it be the son of an Italian immigrant, the son of a German immigrant, the son of any of the breeds from the Orient, the son of the denizens of Africa? We must not get our ethnological distinctions mixed up with out anthropological distinctions. It is the breed of the dog in which I am interested. I would like for the Members of the Senate to read that book just recently published by Madison Grant, *The Passing of a Great Race*. Thank God we have in America perhaps the largest percentage of any country in the world of the pure, unadulterated Anglo-Saxon stock; certainly the greatest of any nation in the Nordic breed. It is for the preservation of that splendid stock that has characterized us that I would make this not an asylum for the oppressed of all countries, but a country to assimilate and perfect that splendid type of manhood that has made America the foremost Nation in her progress and in her power, and yet the youngest of all the nations. I myself believe that the preservation of her institutions depends upon us now taking counsel with our condition and our experience during the last World War.

Without offense, but with regard to the salvation of our own, let us shut the door and assimilate what we have, and let us breed pure American citizens and develop our own American resources. I am more in favor of that than I am of our quota proposition. Of course, it may not meet the approbation of the Senate that we shall shut the door—which I unqualifiedly and unreservedly believe to be our duty—and develop what we have, assimilate and digest what we have into pure Americans, with American aspirations, and thoroughly familiar with the love of American institutions, rather than the importation of any number of men from other countries. If we may not have that, then I am in favor of putting the quota down to the lowest possible point, with every selective element in it that may be.

The great desideratum of modern times has been education not alone book knowledge, but that education which enables men to think right, to think logically, to think truthfully, men equipped with power to appreciate the rapidly developing conditions that are all about us, that have converted the world in the last 50 years into a brand new world and made us masters of forces that are revolutionizing production. We want men not like dumb, driven cattle from those nations where the progressive thought of the times has scarcely made a beginning and where they see men as mere machines; we want men who have an appreciation of the responsibility brought about by the manifestation of the power of that individual. We have not that in this country to-day. We have men here to-day who are selfishly utilizing the enormous forces discovered by genius, and if we are not careful as statesmen, if we are not careful in our legislation, these very masters of the tremendous forces that have been made available to us will bring us under their domination and control by virtue of the power they have in multiplying their wealth.

We are struggling to-day against the organized forces of man's brain multiplied a million times by materialized thought in the form of steam and electricity as applied in the everyday affairs of man. We have enough in this country to engage the brain of every lover of his country in solving the problems of a democratic government in the midst of the imperial power that genius is discovering and placing in the hands of man. We have population enough to-day without throwing wide our doors and jeopardizing the interests of this country by pouring into it men who willingly become the slaves of those who employ them in manipulating these forces of nature, and they few reap the enormous benefits that accrue therefrom.

We ought to Americanize not only our population but our forces. We ought to Americanize our factories and our vast material resources, so that we can make each contribute to the other and have an abundance for us under the form of the government laid down by our fathers.

The Senator from Georgia [William J. Harris] has introduced an amendment to shut the door. It is not a question of politics. It is a question of maintaining that which has made you and me the beneficiaries of the greatest hope that ever burned in the human breast for the most splendid future that ever stood before mankind, where the boy in the gutter can look with confidence to the seat of the Presidency of the United States; where the boy in the gutter can look forward to the time when, paying the price of a proper citizen, he may fill a seat in this hall; where the boy to-day poverty-stricken, standing in the midst of all the splendid opportunities of America, should have and, please God, if we do our duty, will have an opportunity to enjoy the marvelous wealth that the genius and brain of our country is making possible for us all.

We do not want to tangle the skein of America's progress by those who imperfectly understand the genius of our Government and the opportunities that lie about us. Let up keep what we have, protect what we have, make what we have the realization of the dream of those who wrote the Constitution.

I am more concerned about that than I am about whether a new railroad shall be built or whether there shall be diversified farming next year or whether a certain coal mine shall be mined. I would rather see American citizenship refined to the last degree in all that makes America what we hope it will be than to develop the resources of America at the expense of the citizenship of our country. The time has come when we should shut the door and keep what we have for what we hope our own people to be.

MARCUS GARVEY
1887–1940

from **Editorial: Universal Negro Improvement Association**[1]

[New York City, September 2, 1924]

Fellow Men of the Negro Race, Greeting:

Our Fourth International Convention of the Negro Peoples of the World has risen and the delegates and deputies are now on their way back to their respective homes and habitats, to further promulgate and carry on the work of the Universal Negro Improvement Association, the cause for which they were assembled.[2] Great has been the result of this [A]ugust convention. We, as a people, ought to feel glad that there is in existence such a movement like the Universal Negro Improvement Association, to afford us the opportunity of legislating for our own common good rather than allowing us to depend upon the good will of others to do for us. There is no doubt about it, that the convention was a splendid success. As usual, we stirred the curiosity and attention of the whole world, and now that we have risen, the convention has left its program to be discussed by the entire civilized world. Among the many things that we did during the month of August, was to lay a foundation for the new education of our race, educating them to the policy of self appreciation and it is hoped that the four hundred million members of our race the world over will follow the advice given.

The Enemies at Work

During the whole of the convention and a little prior thereto, the enemies of our cause tried to provoke and confuse our deliberation by the many

---

[1]Marcus Garvey, Universal Negro Improvement Association Editorial (1924): African nationalism, www.international.ucla.edu/africa/mgpp/sample06.asp.

[2]Jamaica-born Garvey founded the UNIA in 1914 to promote "black humanity." Despite its efforts to improve minority business and education opportunities, the UNIA became known for advocating the separatist establishment of an African American "homeland" in Liberia.

unpleasant things they systematically published against the Universal Negro Improvement Association. Our enemies in America, especially the Negro Republican politicians of New York, used the general time fuse to explode on our tranquility and thereby destroy the purpose for which we were met, but as is customary, the Universal Negro Improvement Association is always ready for the enemy. They had arranged among themselves to get certain individuals of the Liberian government along with Ernest Lyons, the Liberian Consul-General, in Baltimore, himself a reactionary Negro politician of the old school, to circulate through the Negro press and other agencies such unpleasant news purported to be from Liberia as to create consternation in our ranks and bring about the demoralization that they hoped and calculated for, but as usual, the idiots counted without their hosts. The Universal Negro Improvement Association cannot be destroyed that way, in that it is not only an organization, but is the expression of the spiritual desires of the four hundred million black peoples of the world.

Our Colonization Program

As everybody knows, we were preparing to carry out our Liberian colonization program during this and succeeding months. Every arrangement was practically made toward this end. Men were shipped to Liberia as well as materials to the cost of over $50,000.00. Two consignments of materials were shipped from New York, one on the 25th of June, 1924, and the next on the *S.S. West Irmo*, on the 25th of July, 1924, consigned to the Association, in care of Chief Justice J. J. Dossen, of Cape Palmas, Liberia, in keeping with the understanding and arrangements entered into with the Universal Negro Improvement Association and the representatives of the Liberian government, and a local committee of Liberians, appointed in said government by the direction of President Charles King, all of which culminated in a higher industrial and commercial development of Liberia as a permanent home for the black race, in keeping with the constitution of that great little black republic. Unfortunately, after all arrangements had been made in this direction, our steamship secured to carry the colonists and all plans laid, these enemies of progress worked in every way to block the carrying out of the plan. For the purpose of deceiving the public and carrying out their obstruction, they tried to make out by the protest that was filed by Ernest Lyons of Baltimore, with the government at Washington, that our Association was of an incendiary character and that it was the intention of the organization to disturb the good relationship that existed between Liberia and other friendly powers. A greater nonsense could not have been advanced by any idiot. What could an organization like the Universal Negro Improvement Association do to destroy the peace of countries that are already established and recognized? It is supposed that England and France are the countries referred to when, in fact, the authors of that statement know that England and France are only waiting an opportunity to seize more land in Liberia and to keep Liberia in a state of stagnation, so as to justify their argument that the blacks are not competent of self government in Africa as well as elsewhere. If Edwin Barclay[3] had any sense, he would know that the Universal Negro Improvement Association is more friendly to Liberia, because it is made up of Negroes, than England and France could be in a thousand years. Lyons' protest was camouflage.

Negroes Double-Crossing

Everybody knows that the hitch in the colonization plan of the Universal Negro Improvement Association in Liberia came about because of double-crossing. The Firestone Rubber and Tire Company, of Ohio, has been spending large sums of money among certain people. The offer, no doubt, was so attractive as to cause certain persons to found the argument to destroy the Universal Negro Improvement Association, so as to favor the Firestone Rubber and Tire Company who, subsequently, got one million acres of Liberian land for actually nothing, to be exploited for rubber and minerals, and in the face of the fact that Liberia is one of the richest rubber countries in the world, an asset that should have been retained for the Liberian people and members of the black race, but now wantonly given over to a white company to be exploited in the interest of white capital, and to create another international complication, as evidenced in the subsequent subjugation of Haiti and the Haitians, after the New York City Bank established itself in Haiti in a similar way as the Firestone Rubber and Tire Company will establish itself in Liberia. Why, every Negro who is doing a little thinking, knows that after the Firestone Rubber and Tire Company gets into Liberia to exploit the one million acres of land, it is only a question of time when the government will be taken out of the hands of the Negroes who rule it, and Liberia will become a white man's country in violation of the constitution of that government as guaranteeing its soil as a home for all Negroes of all climes and nationalities who desire to return to their native land. The thing is so disgraceful that we, ourselves, are ashamed to give full publicity to it, but we do hope that the people of Liberia, who control the government of Liberia, will be speedily informed so that they, through the Senate and House of Representatives, will repudiate the concessions granted to the Firestone Rubber and Tire Company, so as to save their country from eternal spoilation. If the Firestone Rubber and Tire Company should get the concessions in Liberia of one million acres of land, which should have been granted to the Universal Negro Improvement Association for development by Negroes for the good of Negroes, it simply means that in another short while thousands of white men will be sent away from America by the Firestone Rubber and Tire Company to exploit their concessions. These white

[3]Edwin James Barclay (1882–1955) was the secretary of state of Liberia from 1920 to 1930 and subsequently served as its president from 1930 to 1944.

men going out to colonize, as they generally regard tropical countries, will carry with them the spirit of all other white colonists, superiority over and subjugation of native peoples; hence it will only be a question of time when these gentlemen will change the black population of Liberia into a mongrel race, as they have done in America, [the] West Indies and other tropical countries, and there create another race problem such as is confusing us now in these United States of America. These white gentlemen are not going to allow black men to rule and govern them, so, like China and other places, there will be such complications as to ultimately lead to the abrogation of all native control and government and the setting up of new authority in a country that once belonged to the natives.

Marcus Garvey, President-General
Universal Negro Improvement Association

1924

H. T. TSIANG
1899–1971

Born on May 3, 1899, into a world that he perceived as fundamentally unfair, H. T. Tsiang from a young age sought its revolution. Eventually, he chose writing as his contribution to the cause. "With our paper bullets," one of his characters declares, "we shall change the direction of the wind." By the end of his life, Tsiang's paper bullets found published form in one volume of poetry, three novels, and one play.

Tsiang grew up poor in Qi'an, a village in the district of Nantong, Jiangsu Province in China. His father, a grain store worker, died when he was nine, and his mother, a maid, died four years later. In addition to these tragic circumstances, Tsiang came of age during a tumultuous period in Chinese history, just as the Qing Dynasty fell, and different factions fought for control of the country. Two events, however, gave Tsiang hope: the 1911 Chinese Revolution led by Sun Yatsen and the 1917 Bolshevik Revolution led by Vladimir Lenin. Tsiang learned to read English-language newspapers in order to keep up with world events, and he earned scholarships to the Tongzhou Teachers' School in Jiangsu and Southeastern University in Nanjing, where he received a B.A. in political economy in 1925. For a short time, Tsiang served as Sun Yat-sen's secretary, but when Sun died in March of 1925, Chiang Kai-shek took over the reins of the Kuomintang (Nationalist Party). Vocally critical of Chiang's conservative politics, which he deemed a betrayal of Sun's more communist ideals, Tsiang drew the ire of his former party and had to flee to America in 1926. While the Chinese Exclusion Act of 1882 prevented "Chinese laborers" from entering the country, Tsiang took advantage of the exemption for students. Nominally, Tsiang studied at Stanford University, but he spent much of his time and energy rallying Americans, including Chinese Americans, against Chiang's policies. To this end, he helped to found a bilingual newspaper, *Chinese Guide to America*, and led protests against visiting dignitaries from Chiang's government. In 1928 he was arrested, and the *Los Angeles Times* branded him "the leader of the radicals."

Searching for a community more welcoming of his leftist politics, Tsiang moved to New York and enrolled at Columbia University. Encouraged by his professors, he published poems in the *New Masses* and the *Daily Worker*. Tsiang self-published a collection, *Poems of the Chinese Revolution*, in 1929. Two of these poems, "Chinaman, Laundryman" and "Sacco, Vanzetti," were set to music by Ruth Crawford Seeger and performed in Carnegie Hall in 1933. Interested in experimentation and genre, Tsiang turned next to writing novels. In 1931 he self-published an epistolary novel entitled *China Red*, which tells the story of lovers separated by distance (one at home in China, the other studying abroad in America) and by politics (one more conservative, the other an awakening leftist). In 1935 Tsiang experimented with combining poetic, dramatic, and novelistic conventions in *The Hanging on Union Square*, which he subtitled, "An American Epic." In 1937 he secured a conventional publisher for his novel *And China Has Hands*, which tells the story of Wong Wan-Lee, an immigrant Chinese laundry-worker, and Pearl Chang, a half-black, half-Chinese aspiring actress from the South. Both pursue their versions of the American Dream until they find that economic and social systems, namely capitalism and racism, stymie their efforts. Eventually, they find themselves allied, if not romantically, at least politically, protesting in a remarkable march that includes: "The white, the yellow, and the black, / The ones between yellow and black, / The ones between yellow and white, / And the ones between white and black."

To promote his books and incite revolution in other ways, Tsiang also performed his works. Of course, he acted in his own 1938 play, *China Marches On*, which adapted the Fa Mulan legend to tell the story of contemporary Chinese resistance to Japanese imperialism, but he also adapted *The Hanging on Union Square* for the stage. In these efforts, he was aided by the playwright, director, and dramatic theorist Edwin Piscator, with whom he worked at the New School for Social Research. After World War II began, political and literary tastes changed, and Tsiang turned to making his living as a film actor, often playing stereotypical roles, such as Japanese generals and Chinese houseboys. He never stopped writing and performing his more radical work, however. Even while detained at Ellis Island for possible deportation, he wrote poetry on toilet paper, and when no one came to his one-man version of *Hamlet*, which critiqued not the rotten state of Denmark but the contemporary state of the world, he would pay a taxi driver to sit in the audience. Radical, experimental, and quirky to the end, Tsiang died in Los Angeles on July 16, 1971.

Floyd Cheung
Smith College

PRIMARY WORKS

Poems of the Chinese Revolution, 1929; *China Red*, 1931; *The Hanging on Union Square: An American Epic*, 1935; *And China Has Hands*, 1937; *China Marches On*, 1938.

"Chinaman, Laundryman"

"Chinaman"!
"Laundryman"!
Don't call me "man"!
I am worse than a slave.

Wash! wash!
Why can I wash away
The dirt of others' clothes
But not the hatred of my heart?
My skin is yellow,
Does my yellow skin color the clothes?
Why do you pay me less
For the same work?
Clever boss!
You know

How to scatter the seeds of hatred
Among your ignorant slaves.

Iron! iron!
Why can I smooth away
The wrinkles of others' dresses
But not the miseries of my heart?
Why should I come to America
To wash clothes?
Do you think "Chinamen" in China
Wear no dresses?
I came to America
Three days after my marriage.
When can I see her again?
Only the almighty "Dollar" knows!

Dry! dry!
Why do clothes dry,
But not' my tears?
I work
Twelve hours a day,
He pays
Fifteen dollars a week.
My boss says,
"Chinaman,
Go back to China
If you don't feel satisfied!
There,
Unlimited hours of toil:
Two silver dollars a week,
If
You can find a job."
"Think you, Boss!
For you remind me.
I know
Bosses are robbers
Everywhere!"

Chinese boss says;
"You Chinaman,
Me Chinaman,
Come work for me—
Work for your fellow countryman!
By the way,
You 'Wong', me 'Wong'—

Do we not belong; to same family?
Ha! ha!
We are cousins!
O yes!
You 'Hai Shan', me 'Hai Shan',[1]
Do we not come from same district?
O, come work for me;
I will treat you better!"
"GET away from here,
What is the difference,
When you come to exploit me?"

"Chinaman"!
"Laundryman"!
Don't call me "Chinaman"!
Yes, I am a "Laundryman"!
The workingman!
Don't call me "Chinaman",
I am the Worldman,
"The International Soviet
Shall be his human race"!

"Chinaman".
"Laundryman !"
All, the workingman!
Here is the brush
Made of Marxism.
Here is the soap
Made of Leninism.
Let us all
Wash with the blood!
Let us all
Press with the iron!
Wash!
Brush!
Dry!
Iron!
Then we shall have
A clean world.

1928

---

[1]Huashan District is located in Anhui Province, just west of where Tsiang grew up in
Jiangsu Province, China.

from **The Hanging on Union Square**

XII. Before the Arrival of an Ambulance

> *"Heaven is above*
> *Hell below,*
> *Nothing in pocket,*
> *Where to go?"*

It was Mr. Nut poetizing.

One o'clock.

At the corner of Fourteenth Street and First Avenue, Mr. Nut saw a gar-bage-can standing in front of another cafeteria.

He stopped.

He looked in.

He put his right hand in.

To see if there was anything inside.

An old man came running towards him. He yelled:

"Get away from here! This is my station. I've got a sick wife to feed. You're a young fellow: why don't you go to the Relief Building?[1] You have the strength. They have to feed you! They are afraid that you will make trouble."

The old man covered the garbage-can with his whole body to keep it from Mr. Nut. Picking! Eating! And murmuring!

Nut moved to the other side of the can.

"Don't touch this can!" continued the old man. "This is my station!"

"What do you mean," asked Nut, "your station?"

"You heard me! Can't you understand English? I have been living by this can for three months now."

Nut moved back a few steps. Still looking on.

The snow whitened the pavement.

And the melting snow washed away all the dirt from the old man's bony hands. They were as pale and bloodless as wax.

While the old man kept on digging, a tin box of Drainpipe Solvent appeared, alongside of a piece of rotten apple-pie. The old man picked up the pie with joy, and was ready to swallow it.

Nut dashed forward and grabbed the old man's hand. He dropped the pie on the ground.

"You bastard! You take the food from an old man's mouth! You damned hero!"

"Now look here. This pie, with that white powder on, is poison! It can put your stomach and lungs out of commission. It will kill you!"

"Is that so?" said the disappointed old man. "Now you, young fellow, you have spoiled my opportunity. I'm sick. I'm tired. I'm a coward and can't

---

[1]Located on 507 West Street in New York City, this establishment sponsored by the American Seamen's Friends Society offered food and shelter to destitute sailors.

kill myself. I've prayed that some day I will die just in the way you tell me, and so get rid of my misery. Now you have delayed my voyage to Heaven."

Nut was hungry.

Nut had to move.

He went back to Third Avenue and from Fourteenth Street he followed the Third Avenue Elevated towards downtown.

He reached Thirteenth Street.

A half-drunk and half-awake bum approached him and asked for a cigarette.

"'Who the hell wants to work?" the fellow began talking. "I ain't no sap. It's snowing so I'll have good business tomorrow. I'll make lots of nickels and pennies! Who wants to work? The big shots do nothing but enjoy everything. They drink champagne, I drink wood alcohol! Poison. They are yachting! Me? Around Third Avenue! Tell me, ain't that justice? For heaven's sake, give me a cigarette!"

Nut had no cigarette to give.

He walked from Twelfth Street to Eleventh.

A middle-aged fellow with a Southern accent approached Nut and asked him if he could spare a penny so that he would have thirty-five cents with which to go to a cheap hotel on the Bowery.[2] He was a farmer. He had come from the South to this city and tried to find a job here. And he hadn't slept for two nights. He already had thirty-four cents.

Nut had no penny to spare.

Nut walked on from Eleventh Street to Tenth Street.

Another fellow came to him and asked him if he had a match.

Mr. Nut stopped. Searched.

In addition to a match, which Nut gave to the fellow, he felt something small, round and solid in the corner of his vest-pocket.

Before using his eyes to see it, Nut prayed: "Let it not be a button. I have lots of buttons. Let it be a dime."

If it were a dime, Nut would be able to have a bowl of soup together with a piece of butter, and two Big, Big Rolls!

For Heaven's sake! It was a penny.

Nut went back a block.

He found the Southern fellow standing there, shivering.

"I've just found a penny in my pocket. Take it and go to sleep."

"Thanks a lot," the fellow smiled gratefully.

"Don't mention it. One penny will do me no good anyhow."

---

[2]The Bowery is the section of Lower Manhattan in New York City that served as the center of the city's theatre life in the 1860s and 1870s, but by the 1880s had become an economically depressed area.

"God bless J. P. Morgan," said the Southern follow, "last year he made a speech on the radio. This is real Block Aid!"[3]

Snow was falling, heavier and heavier.
Snow was falling, faster and faster.
Nut followed the Third Avenue El again, walking back in the downtown direction.
He saw a woman about fifty who walked as if one of her legs were long and one short.
She called out to him:
"Say, whaddaya say?"
Nut had nothing to say.

At the corner of Ninth Street, he turned west to Fourth Avenue.
On his way he saw many people crowded in a hallway. At the place where the street was darker, he saw many people lying on the stone floors of a hallway. They were covered with newspapers and were sleeping.
Nut walked and walked.
He reached Washington Square and Fifth Avenue.
He saw a fellow rather well-dressed, lying on the sidewalk.
His body was stiff, the two legs straight, the two feet parted. The two hands coming from his overcoat sleeves had their palms upward. His face was half-covered with his hat. His mouth was open. The man wasn't breathing. His body was very stiff.

"Complete, dignified funeral for $150, with ornamented casket.
"As inexpensive as required and as impressive as desired."

Nut would like to know, Who, how, and why? A policeman stood nearby and smiled at him and said icily, "Starvation! Take a walk, it's none of your business! Or I'll hang you!"

1935

from **And China Has Hands**

Fifteen

From a waiter of a Chinese restaurant to the owner of a Chinese laundry, and from the owner of a Chinese laundry, Wong Wan-Lee now became a busboy in a Chinese cafeteria.
He worked in the same cafeteria where Pearl Chang worked.

[3]A system in which block chairmen would solicit donations of 10 cents to $1 a week for twenty weeks from residents of their block or blocks to assist unemployed people and their families in New York. By April 1932, 7,597 blocks were officially organized in the Bronx, Manhattan, Brooklyn, and Queens. ("Block Aid Covers Whole City," *New York Times*, 1 April 1932.)

Twelve hours a day.

Ten dollars a week.

He might get more than what he had made in his own laundry, but what went on in his mind was changed.

There was no more vanity, and he had to put on a uniform, and he was exactly a servant.

There was no more hope and his wages were all he could get; no tips were available.[1]

Poor Wong Wan-Lee, who had made no ten thousand fortunes, was a failure; but his cousin Wong Lung had made a million and had become the hero of *The Good Earth*—Horatio Alger![2]

Poor Pearl C.[3], who had become no star, was a failure; but her cousin Pearl B. had married her boss, a publisher.

The thing that made him feel better was that though he had lost his laundry, the two Chinese laundry associations[4] had stopped their quarrel and merged into one. Through this new organization, the other Chinese laundrymen from now on would be protected by it and would not be mistreated by the corrupt politicians and greedy loan sharks, as he had been.

The thing that made him feel better was that, according to what he read in the Chinese paper, the Chinese Communists and Nationalists were reconciled, and China and Russia again became friends to fight the Japanese, and America made a loan to China and sold her many, many airplanes.

Mo No![5]

The thing that made him feel better was that he was now working together with Pearl Chang and he could see her every day.

In this cafeteria there were two white busgirls besides Pearl Chang, since there were not enough Chinese girls. To have white girls, the boss thought, would be good for business in a way.

---

[1]Early in the novel, we learn that Wong Wan-Lee's name means "'ten thousand fortunes' ... and ten thousand fortunes was all he intended to make in America." He had planned to make his fortune as the owner-operator of a laundry but was forced out of business.

[2]Wong Lung, *The Good Earth*, Horatio Alger, and Pearl B.: Wang Lung is the protagonist of Pearl Buck's bestselling novel, *The Good Earth* (1931), published by her husband, John Day. In this narrative, Wang Lung is represented as having what Tsiang perceives as Algeresque values. Horatio Alger's enor-

mously popular books, like *Ragged Dick* (1868), feature poor, patient, and virtuous heroes who, by dint of hard work and good luck, rise to middle-class respectability.

[3]Pearl Chang is half-black and half-Chinese from the U.S. South. She had aspired to movie stardom.

[4]The Chinese Hand Laundry Alliance, whose slogan was "To Save China, To Save Ourselves," formed in 1933 to protect and promote their business and to organize against Japanese imperialism in China.

[5]Cantonese slang meaning "no brains" or stupid.

There were two white busboys besides Wong Wan-Lee. When white men worked in the place, the boss thought, the white customers would behave better.

When the boss talked to the Chinese workers, he would say the whites were no good. The whites were jealous of the Chinese—a yellow race. When the boss talked to the white workers, he would say that "Chinks" were no good—easygoing, weeping too much. He was an internationalist and was doing his best to create jobs for poor men.

He advertised in a radical paper that he was a radical, and he advertised in Hearst papers that he was a true American and a friend of Hitler.

He sold an established Chinese cafeteria to an American, and he bought a bankrupt American cafeteria from an American and opened a new Chinese one.

The boss was a very rich man: He had two gambling houses, two wet-wash companies, one poolroom, and one noodle factory, besides his new enterprise—Chinese cafeterias.

The boss was a charitable man: He gave free meals to the Chinese who came to the gambling houses—you did not have to gamble—and he gave free excursions to the Chinese who came to the boat in the summer—you did not have to gamble.

The boss was a cautious man: He wore, even when there was no Tong War,[6] a steel vest.

The boss was a ruthless man: He could smile at you and talk to you one minute and fix you up another minute.

But he had never killed anybody himself, for he was always good-hearted enough to let some other fellow have a chance to make eight hundred dollars a head.

Because of the capital he had and the shrewdness of his business management, his pocketbook grew fatter and fatter.

When Chinatown raised money to send back to defend China against the Japanese, he contributed nothing.

Oh, what a charitable, what a patriotic man he was!

The workers who worked in this cafeteria grew thinner and thinner.

And there was a strike.

One day Wong Wan-Lee, "the descendant of the great Huang Ti, the great-great-grandson of the Han Dynasty, the great-grandson of the Tang Dynasty, the grandson of the Sung Dynasty, and the son of the Ming Dynasty," and Pearl Chang, "the future movie star," and many other workers quit their jobs and paraded in front of the Chinese cafeteria in which they worked.

Wong Wan-Lee was not afraid of the boss, of the cafeteria as a boss. But he was afraid that he was a Tong man. However, he joined.

---

[6]Tongs in the true sense are mutual aid societies that meet in a "tong" or "hall," but the term came to designate Chinese gangs, which sometimes fought over criminal interests.

All the workers in this cafeteria paraded.
The workers in the other cafeterias joined:
The white, the yellow, and the black,
The ones between yellow and black,
The ones between yellow and white,
And the ones between white and black.
They were marching on, singing their song:
The song of the white,
The song of the yellow,
The song of the black,
The song of the ones who were neither yellow nor white,
The song of the ones who were neither yellow nor black,
The song of the ones who were neither black nor white,
And the song that knows nothing of white, yellow, or black.

They wanted better wages.
They wanted shorter hours.

The author of *Poems of the Chinese Revolution, China Red*, and *The Hanging on Union Square*[7] also participated, for he thought that since he had written so much about revolution, he had better do something about it. And picketing is a revolution in a small way.

He had been warned, watched, and finally bounced out by the owner of this cafeteria while he had been trying to peddle his books inside. What a joy it would be for him to see this cafeteria have trouble and eventually be unionized! Furthermore, since the few fakers of letters were trying to fix him up, it would be well for him to vindicate himself—not in leafleting, but in action.

As the party line had been changed, and Earl Browder[8] was smoking a cigar instead of a tobacco pipe, our author, as a sympathizer and follower, had just had a fresh haircut.

By now, our author had secured a publisher for his fourth book,[9] and the publisher was taking a deep interest in observing the moves of his writer—hoping the author would get his head clubbed so his picture would appear in the papers and, by-productingly, his books be mentioned.

Wong Wan-Lee and Pearl Chang marched together. They had to, for the cops were yelling, "Two by two! Keep moving!"

---

[7]A reference to Tsiang himself, who self-published most of his books. Without conventional book distribution, he had to "peddle" them on street corners and in cafeterias.

[8]Earl Browder, the leader of the Communist Party of the United States (CPUSA), shifted the party's rhetoric from one of Marxist revolution to one of progressive reform after 1936. With a more clean-cut image and new party line, called the Popular Front, the CPUSA attracted much broader public support.

[9]*And China Has Hands* was published by the Robert Speller Publishing Corporation.

When the mass demonstration was over, the strikers paraded in shifts of two.

Wong Wan-Lee and Pearl Chang were in the same shift.

Everything was quiet. Suddenly there came a shot! Another and then another.

Pearl Chang thought they were either firecrackers or tires bursting, but she saw a Chinese running away.

Wong Wan-Lee screamed and then dropped unconscious on the sidewalk.

Pearl Chang saw blood flowing from Wong Wan-Lee's breast: It colored all his clothes.

She took her white skirt and sopped some blood with it. Then, kneeling, she lifted his head into her lap.

It reddened her dress.

1937

THE NEW NEGRO RENAISSANCE

On the evening of March 21, 1924, one hundred ten Harlem luminaries converged on Manhattan's Civic Club in order to celebrate the publication of Jessie Harris Fauset's *There Is Confusion*. But the event was soon transformed into a sort of brokerage affair that would ease access between a select few of black America's "talented tenth" and certain well-heeled patrons of public opinion. The project of literary history/renovation would be tremendously simplified if we could sweep away the complexities and designate this glittering social event (or any other one like it) as the "beginning" of that period of dense cultural legacy called the "New Negro (or "Harlem") Renaissance." Enough of the younger generation of African American writers were invited to Charles S. Johnson's bash to flatter one's fantasies of uncomplicated and veritable origins: Eric Walrond, Gwendolyn Bennett, Countee Cullen, Langston Hughes, Georgia Douglass Johnson, Walter White, and Alain Locke (among others) were present, as the names, from the distance of almost eight decades, sound the roll of black cultural heroes who inscribed African American literary personality upon the twentieth century. That this formidable project was launched under the auspices of food and drink and in the midst, too, of important "midwives" such as Horace Liveright, whose house had published Jean Toomer's *Cane* the year before, enriches our notions of sociopolitical engagement. Absent from the Johnson fête, Toomer was not particularly eager to proffer his name and reputation to the movement stirring around him, but at least Arna Bontemps believed that *Cane* (1923)—despite the author's own wishes—really started it all.

Though the Great Depression is considered to have ended the New Negro Renaissance, its beginning remains elusive and open to debate. Though Nathan Huggins's important study of the period does not specify a precise commencement, his opening chapter focuses on the year of war, 1914, when James Weldon Johnson moved to Harlem and New York for the second time. David Levering Lewis begins his stunning narrative on the period with the return of New York National Guard's Fifteenth Regiment and a triumphal march along Fifth Avenue on a "clear, sharp" February morning, 1919. In her study of gender politics of the era, Gloria Hull offers a later date that forces us to reinterpret events both before and after that point: "The year is 1927," Hull notes, and Alice Dunbar-Nelson "is writing lively, informative columns" for Washington, D.C.'s *Eagle*. These scholars and critics offer a longer perspective than the customary shorter view of the Renaissance years that confines its investigation to the poetry, fiction, and nonfiction by African American writers published between 1923 and 1929.

Offering a radically different conceptual formulation of the inquiry, Houston Baker's 1987 study of the period tracks the New Negro Renaissance as the fruition of a discursive mastery wielded by Booker T. Washington in his address before the Atlantic Exposition on September 18, 1895. That scholars and students of the phenomenon might arguably adopt the long or short view and account for "deep" and "immediate" forces at work that converge on the period would suggest that these years—years rich with the promise and project of political and economic liberation—specify an especially dramatic moment in the long and perilous journey of cultural apprenticeship of African Americans within the context of the African Diaspora.

We can say, then, with some certainty that the New Negro Renaissance, the literary and artistic arm of a massive social movement with roots in the broken promises of post-Reconstruction America, offers at least a decade of *communal* and nationalist assertion, focused in the work of African American artists. The Renaissance becomes, in fact, the most vividly named outcome of a *second* African Diaspora, when large numbers of black people living in the southern United States fled the high tide of a "reign of terror," staged in the terrorist maneuvers of the Ku Klux Klan. From this angle, 1918 speaks volumes in its record number of lynchings. Seeking the more advantageous labor opportunities spawned by the war effort and pursuing a freer space in which to live their lives, southern black people in unprecedented number followed the tracks northward. From the midsouth and urban areas like Memphis and Little Rock, the migratory patterns ran straight to the major cities of the Midwest—Chicago, primarily. Even Cairo, Illinois, for the southern person, reared on the farm, represented that place of greater freedom. Likely an apocryphal story, train conductors in "the old days" were said to have declared, once outside Memphis, on the way to "yonder in Cairo," "black and white together!"

From the coastal regions of the South—Georgia, Virginia, and the Carolinas—"Mecca" was thought to have resided in cities like New York, Philadelphia, Hartford, and Boston. It is probably not at all accidental that Chicago in recent times is sometimes playfully referred to as an overgrown Mississippi town, or that the grandparents and parents of one's contemporaries in various East Coast cities are often indigenous to Charleston, South Carolina, or Greensboro or Rocky Mount, North Carolina, say. Even though Alain Locke might not have had the "masses" in mind, though he purportedly spoke for them in *The New Negro* (1925), the historical ground of the Renaissance is embedded in far less glamorous circumstances than the *haut monde* of the literary salon, or the charming dinner antics of what Zora Neale Hurston mockingly termed "niggerati."

An exceedingly complex historical movement that gained force at the close of World War I and that was largely checked by the economic collapse of the 1930s, the New Negro Renaissance was marked by a number of important developments. Among the most crucial was the extent to which African Americans gained access, even if limited, to certain engines of public opinion and evaluation. The Niagara Movement (1909–1910) had created the National Association for the Advancement of Colored People (NAACP), which founded, in turn, *Crisis Magazine*, which became, under the general editorship of W.E.B. Du Bois and the literary editorship of Jessie Fauset, one of the major sources for the dissemination of writings by African Americans. Langston Hughes's "The Negro Speaks of Rivers," published in *Crisis* before the poet attained wide celebrity, may be thought of as the poem that helped promote him to a place of acclaim. Published under the auspices of the National Urban League and originally intended to serve as a journal of sociology and a forum for the discussion of "race" issues, Charles S. Johnson's *Opportunity* easily slipped, by cunning design, into a nerve center that monitored the literary productions of black writers. Marcus Garvey's United Negro Improvement Association and its newspapers must also be taken into account as a crucial political force of the age.

Though not the first time, by any means, that black Americans realized and practiced the efficacies of collective effort, the period is noteworthy as a time of pointed critical consciousness. In addition to the journals of the NAACP and the National Urban League, Locke's anthology and James Weldon Johnson's 1922 *The Book of American Negro Poetry* not only signaled a new spirit abroad on the urban scene, but also underscored its merits as a collective enterprise that encompassed male and female artists and African American artists indigenous to the United States as well as to certain Caribbean communities, particularly Jamaica—the homeland of Marcus and Amy Jacques Garvey and Claude McKay. The apparent democracy of artistic expressiveness that embraced a literary agenda as divergent as Claude McKay's sonnets, Georgia Douglass Johnson's and Countee Cullen's lyrics, and Langston Hughes's experimentation with 12-bar blues mode in verse sustained, in fact, an international dimension that has not been fully appreciated. In her study of the Francophone-focused Negritude movement, critic Lilyan Lagneau-Kesteloot outlines contact between Renaissance figures, such as Alain Locke, and West African expatriate intellectuals living in Paris, including Leopold Senghor, future president of Senegal, and the author and future statesman Aimé Césaire.

Although students of the period usually focus on its literary production, the music generated in Harlem clubs of the time participated fully in a crucial synthesis of idioms that we would come to recognize as "modern jazz." Langston Hughes's "Jazzonia," for instance, which limns "six long-headed jazzers" "in a Harlem cabaret," "in a whirling cabaret," seems to lay hold of the romance of night-clubbing and the simple kaleidoscopic flicker of ceiling lights through a colored filter. Much of the poetry and fiction of Hughes, in their articulation of urban idioms of speech, might be thought of as the thematic intersection of the "folks" and new modes of being.

In the lyrics of Countee Cullen and Claude McKay, the traditional sonnet form is appropriated to alternative modes of address as both poets instigate an Afrocentric poetic *persona* at the center of their inquiry. In "Yet Do I Marvel," Cullen invokes the mythic dilemmas of Tantalus and Sisyphus in explaining the speaker's self-reflexive marveling—"To make a poet black, and bid him sing!" Ultimately, the poetry of the Renaissance reflects two major currents: (1) experimentation with verse form that takes its inspiration from African American musical idiom—for example, the work song and the blues in the poetic canon of Langston Hughes and Sterling Brown, and (2) the exploration of traditional verse forms, including free verse technique that rewrites aspects of European courtly love tradition in projecting a romanticized and aestheticized figure of the "black woman" (Cullen's "A Song of Praise" offers a case in point) and generally adapts romantic and heroic lyricisms to speak a range of emotion through black personality. (Anne Spencer's "At the Carnival," Gwendolyn Bennett's "To a Dark Girl," Claude McKay's "Harlem Dancer" and "Harlem Shadows," and Arna Bontemps's "A Black Man Talks of Reaping" all belong to this category.)

But perhaps the boldest artistic project of the period is embodied in *Cane*, a text that explodes generic boundaries in a stunningly innovative fashion. Not altogether poetry, prose, or drama, Jean Toomer's work encompasses all three. Synthesizing the symbolic valences of male/female, light/dark, North/South, black/white, urban/countryside, narrative closure/fragmentation, this brooding text refuses easy resolution and can be said to anticipate late twentieth-century developments in creative writing and critical discourse.

Though New Negro Renaissance poetry is more widely known than its fiction, it was in the latter arena that two significant women writers of the period made their appearance—Nella Larsen and Zora Neale Hurston. Marked by the publication of two important novels—*Quicksand* in 1928 and *Passing* in 1929— the truncated career of Nella Larsen represents yet another case of how the voices of women writers can fall strangely silent. Perhaps her own fiction provides a clue to the apparent creative impasse that Larsen encountered. Published in 1937, Hurston's *Their Eyes Were Watching God* was prepared for in the shorter fiction that she produced during the Renaissance years and has become one of the best-known and most influential novels written by an African American woman.

It seems entirely plausible to claim the New Negro Renaissance years as not only a burst of social and artistic activity of a freed American people, but also the "genesis" of African American personality as "modern man/woman." Even though Phillis Wheatley wrote her neoclassical verse almost a full two centuries before Gwendolyn Bennett and Countee Cullen set pen to paper, it is with the opening of the twentieth century and specifically the Renaissance period that the community can name a literature for itself. The proliferation of texts from those years offers an early model for what we know now as the new national pluralism. One of the United States' "modernisms," alongside Gertrude Stein's "lost generation," the New Negro Renaissance pursued a fairly amazing idea— an art directly tied to the fortunes of a political agenda.

Hortense Spillers
Cornell University

■ ALAIN LOCKE ■
1885–1954

That young Alain Leroy Locke grew up to be an educator is no surprise. By the time of his birth on September 13, 1885, education had become something of a family business. But that he would also be known as an influential philosopher and cultural critic is indeed surprising. Less than twenty years before Locke entered Harvard University to study philosophy, W.E.B. Du Bois had been cautioned against that discipline by William James, who feared that a Negro philosopher, even one with a degree from Harvard, would be hard put to make a living. Du Bois chose history instead; Locke sought to prove James wrong, even while taking up elements of Jamesian pragmatism in his own work. Locke's use of criti-cal philosophy, which questioned traditional Western faith in ultimate truths and absolute meanings, became an important element in his more widely known cultural work. He was a prolific reviewer of literature and drama; a critic, histo-rian, and collector of fine art, including African sculpture; an early student and advocate of African American music; and, of course, the prime mover behind the primarily artistic New Negro Renaissance, officially initiated in 1925 with the an-thology edited by Locke, titled simply *The New Negro: An Interpretation.*

Throughout his criticism, Locke moves between a deep appreciation of the Western high art forms he had come to know as a child in his late-Victorian, middle-class household, and an impassioned regard for African and African American folk art forms. Locke's view of culture was influenced by the Victorian Matthew Arnold, but early on, Locke began to depict the individual as an active producer rather than a passive consumer of culture. This view of cultural pro-duction became important for the political aspects of the New Negro Renais-sance. Unlike many of his white contemporaries in academia, Locke was always committed to social action and an awareness of what Du Bois called the "prob-lem of the color-line."

Locke graduated with honors from Central High School in Philadelphia in 1902, then furthered his studies at the Philadelphia School of Pedagogy. Matriculated at Harvard in 1904, he began his studies in philosophy and litera-ture at an advanced level. Upon graduating magna cum laude and Phi Beta Kappa in 1907, Locke accepted the first Rhodes scholarship ever awarded to an African American.

Race awareness was thrust upon Locke before he even arrived in England: five Oxford colleges denied him admission, in spite of his prestigious award. Finally settling in at one of the smaller and newer colleges, Hertford, the dark-skinned Locke had difficulty finding a comfortable social footing among his white classmates. He did, however, find company and intellectual stimulation with many African scholars at Oxford, friendships he pursued in later years as his interest in Pan-Africanism and international politics grew. Following his three years as a Rhodes scholar, Locke moved on for a year of study at the Uni-versity of Berlin, as Du Bois had done just before the century's turn. Locke returned to Harvard in 1916 to complete his dissertation, "The Problem of Clas-sification in the Theory of Value," under the direction of Ralph Barton Perry. Locke was now on his way to becoming one of the African American intellectual elite, those whom Du Bois exhorted to become "co-workers in the kingdom of culture."

Locke constantly challenged what it meant to be an intellectual. Many of the artists whom he actively supported charged him with elitism and Eurocen-trism, and often bristled at his (sometimes heavy-handed) editorial recommen-dations. Some, like Claude McKay, were embarrassed by Locke's perfect evocation of the "Aframerican roccoco." Though he certainly courted beauty in all its forms, and sometimes questioned the "blind practicality of the common man," Locke was never satisfied with the role of the decadent aesthete or the sedentary academic. Accepting the professorship at Howard University in 1912 that he would hold (with some interruption) until his retirement in 1953, Locke immediately became active in campus politics and student life; he supported both the Howard literary journal and the theater department and lobbied for parity among black and white faculty members. This latter effort resulted in his dismissal in 1925, but student and faculty protests made it clear that Locke was a highly valued member of the Howard community and that the community would no longer stand for the unjust practices of the white university president. In 1928 Howard's first African American president, Mordecai W. Johnson, reappointed Locke.

Locke did not officially take up residence in that district of upper Manhattan called Harlem until his retirement. But with the publication of the special Harlem issue of the journal *Survey Graphic* in 1925 (which resulted in the anthology published in the same year), Locke knew Harlem well enough to assert that "it is—or promises at least to be—a race capital." Indeed, the "pulse of the Negro world [had] begun to beat in Harlem." Though Locke acknowledged important urban movements elsewhere in the North and central Midwest, it was Harlem that could offer the New Negro Movement the "cosmopolitan scale" necessary to rise above racial provincialism.

In the 1930s and 1940s, Locke spent less time supporting the arts, due in part to World War II. Throughout the late 1940s, Locke continued teaching, often as a visiting professor. After his retirement in 1953, he finally moved to Manhattan, his spiritual hometown, and began work on the ambitious project *The Negro in American Culture*. On June 9, 1954, Alain Locke died of heart failure at New York's Mount Sinai Hospital.

Beth Helen Stickney
City University of New York

PRIMARY WORKS

The New Negro: An Interpretation, 1925; *The Negro and His Music,* 1936; *When Peoples Meet: A Study in Race and Culture Contacts,* 1942; *The Negro in Art,* 1971; *The Negro in American Culture,* 1972; *The Critical Temper of Alain Locke: A Selection of his Essays on Art and Culture,* 1983; *The Philosophy of Alain Locke: Harlem Renaissance and Beyond,* 1989; *Race Contacts and Interracial Relations: Lectures on the Theory and Practice of Race,* ed. Jeffrey C. Stewart, 1992.

The New Negro

In the last decade something beyond the watch and guard of statistics has happened in the life of the American Negro and the three norns who have traditionally presided over the Negro problem have a changeling in their laps. The Sociologist, the Philanthropist, the Race-leader are not unaware of the New Negro, but they are at a loss to account for him. He simply cannot be swathed in their formulae. For the younger generation is vibrant with a new psychology; the new spirit is awake in the masses, and under the very eyes of the professional observers is transforming what has been a perennial problem into the progressive phases of contemporary Negro life.

Could such a metamorphosis have taken place as suddenly as it has appeared to? The answer is no; not because the New Negro is not here, but because the Old Negro had long become more of a myth than a man. The

Old Negro, we must remember, was a creature of moral debate and historical controversy. His has been a stock figure perpetuated as an historical fiction partly in innocent sentimentalism, partly in deliberate reactionism. The Negro himself has contributed his share to this through a sort of protective social mimicry forced upon him by the adverse circumstances of dependence. So for generations in the mind of America, the Negro has been more of a formula than a human being—a something to be argued about, condemned or defended, to be "kept down," or "in his place," or "helped up," to be worried with or worried over, harassed or patronized, a social bogey or a social burden. The thinking Negro even has been induced to share this same general attitude, to focus his attention on controversial issues, to see himself in the distorted perspective of a social problem. His shadow, so to speak, has been more real to him than his personality. Through having had to appeal from the unjust stereotypes of his oppressors and traducers to those of his liberators, friends and benefactors he has had to subscribe to the traditional positions from which his case has been viewed. Little true social or self-understanding has or could come from such a situation.

But while the minds of most of us, black and white, have thus burrowed in the trenches of the Civil War and Reconstruction, the actual march of development has simply flanked these positions, necessitating a sudden reorientation of view. We have not been watching in the right direction; set North and South on a sectional axis, we have not noticed the East till the sun has us blinking.

Recall how suddenly the Negro spirituals revealed themselves; suppressed for generations under the stereotypes of Wesleyan hymn harmony, secretive, half-ashamed, until the courage of being natural brought them out—and behold, there was folk-music. Similarly the mind of the Negro seems suddenly to have slipped from under the tyranny of social intimidation and to be shaking off the psychology of imitation and implied inferiority. By shedding the old chrysalis of the Negro problem we are achieving something like a spiritual emancipation. Until recently, lacking self-understanding, we have been almost as much of a problem to ourselves as we still are to others. But the decade that found us with a problem has left us with only a task. The multitude perhaps feels as yet only a strange relief and a new vague urge, but the thinking few know that in the reaction the vital inner grip of prejudice has been broken.

With this renewed self-respect and self-dependence, the life of the Negro community is bound to enter a new dynamic phase, the buoyancy from within compensating for whatever pressure there may be of conditions from without. The migrant masses, shifting from countryside to city, hurdle several generations of experience at a leap, but more important, the same thing happens spiritually in the life-attitudes and self-expression of the Young Negro, in his poetry, his art, his education and his new outlook, with the additional advantage, of course, of the poise and greater certainty of knowing what it is all about. From this comes the promise and warrant of a new leadership. As one of them has discerningly put it:

We have tomorrow
Bright before us
Like a flame.

Yesterday, a night-gone thing
A sun-down name.

And dawn today
Broad arch above the road we came.
We march!

This is what, even more than any "most creditable record of fifty years of freedom," requires that the Negro of to-day be seen through other than the dusty spectacles of past controversy. The day of "aunties," "uncles" and "mammies" is equally gone. Uncle Tom and Sambo have passed on, and even the "Colonel" and "George" play barnstorm rôles from which they escape with relief when the public spotlight is off. The popular melodrama has about played itself out, and it is time to scrap the fictions, garret the bogeys and settle down to a realistic facing of facts.

First we must observe some of the changes which since the traditional lines of opinion were drawn have rendered these quite obsolete. A main change has been, of course, that shifting of the Negro population which has made the Negro problem no longer exclusively or even predominantly Southern. Why should our minds remain sectionalized, when the problem itself no longer is? Then the trend of migration has not only been toward the North and the Central Midwest, but cityward and to the great centers of industry—the problems of adjustment are new, practical, local and not peculiarly racial. Rather they are an integral part of the large industrial and social problems of our present-day democracy. And finally, with the Negro rapidly in process of class differentiation, if it ever was warrantable to regard and treat the Negro *en masse* it is becoming with every day less possible, more unjust and more ridiculous.

In the very process of being transplanted, the Negro is becoming transformed.

The tide of Negro migration, northward and city-ward, is not to be fully explained as a blind flood started by the demands of war industry coupled with the shutting off of foreign migration, or by the pressure of poor crops coupled with increased social terrorism in certain sections of the South and Southwest. Neither labor demand, the bollweevil nor the Ku Klux Klan is a basic factor, however contributory any or all of them may have been. The wash and rush of this human tide on the beach line of the northern city centers is to be explained primarily in terms of a new vision of opportunity, of social and economic freedom, of a spirit to seize, even in the face of an extortionate and heavy toll, a chance for the improvement of conditions. With each successive wave of it, the movement of the Negro becomes more and more a mass movement toward the larger and the more democratic chance—in the Negro's case a deliberate flight not only from countryside to city, but from medieval America to modern.

Take Harlem as an instance of this. Here in Manhattan is not merely the largest Negro community in the world, but the first concentration in history of so many diverse elements of Negro life. It has attracted the African, the West Indian, the Negro American; has brought together the Negro of the North and the Negro of the South; the man from the city and the man from the town and village; the peasant, the student, the business man, the professional man, artist, poet, musician, adventurer and worker, preacher and criminal, exploiter and social outcast. Each group has come with its own separate motives and for its own special ends, but their greatest experience has been the finding of one another. Proscription and prejudice have thrown these dissimilar elements into a common area of contact and interaction. Within this area, race sympathy and unity have determined a further fusing of sentiment and experience. So what began in terms of segregation becomes more and more, as its elements mix and react, the laboratory of a great race-welding. Hitherto, it must be admitted that American Negroes have been a race more in name than in fact, or to be exact, more in sentiment than in experience. The chief bond between them has been that of a common condition rather than a common consciousness; a problem in common rather than a life in common. In Harlem, Negro life is seizing upon its first chances for group expression and self-determination. It is—or promises at least to be—a race capital. That is why our comparison is taken with those nascent centers of folk-expression and self-determination which are playing a creative part in the world to-day. Without pretense to their political significance, Harlem has the same rôle to play for the New Negro as Dublin has had for the New Ireland or Prague for the New Czechoslovakia.

Harlem, I grant you, isn't typical—but it is significant, it is prophetic. No sane observer, however sympathetic to the new trend, would contend that the great masses are articulate as yet, but they stir, they move, they are more than physically restless. The challenge of the new intellectuals among them is clear enough—the "race radicals" and realists who have broken with the old epoch of philanthropic guidance, sentimental appeal and protest. But are we after all only reading into the stirrings of a sleeping giant the dreams of an agitator? The answer is in the migrating peasant. It is the "man farthest down" who is most active in getting up. One of the most characteristic symptoms of this is the professional man, himself migrating to recapture his constituency after a vain effort to maintain in some Southern corner what for years back seemed an established living and clientele. The clergyman following his errant flock, the physician or lawyer trailing his clients, supply the true clues. In a real sense it is the rank and file who are leading, and the leaders who are following. A transformed and transforming psychology permeates the masses.

When the racial leaders of twenty years ago spoke of developing race-pride and stimulating race-consciousness, and of the desirability of race solidarity, they could not in any accurate degree have anticipated the abrupt feeling that has surged up and now pervades the awakened centers. Some of the recognized Negro leaders and a powerful section of white opinion identified with "race work" of the older order have indeed attempted to discount this feeling as a "passing phase," an attack of "race nerves" so to speak, an "aftermath of the war," and the like. It has not abated, however, if we are to gauge by the present tone and temper of the Negro press, or by the shift in popular support from the officially recognized and orthodox spokesmen to those of the independent, popular, and often radical type who are unmistakable symptoms of a new order. It is a social disservice to blunt the fact that the Negro of the Northern centers has reached a stage where tutelage, even of the most interested and well-intentioned sort, must give place to new relationships, where positive self-direction must be reckoned with in ever increasing measure. The American mind must reckon with a fundamentally changed Negro.

The Negro too, for his part, has idols of the tribe to smash. If on the one hand the white man has erred in making the Negro appear to be that which would excuse or extenuate his treatment of him, the Negro, in turn, has too often unnecessarily excused himself because of the way he has been treated. The intelligent Negro of to-day is resolved not to make discrimination an extenuation for his shortcomings in performance, individual or collective; he is trying to hold himself at par, neither inflated by sentimental allowances nor depreciated by current social discounts. For this he must know himself and be known for precisely what he is, and for that reason he welcomes the new scientific rather than the old sentimental interest. Sentimental interest in the Negro has ebbed. We used to lament this as the falling off of our friends; now we rejoice and pray to be delivered both from self-pity and condescension. The mind of each racial group has had a bitter weaning, apathy or hatred on one side matching disillusionment or resentment on the other; but they face each other to-day with the possibility at least of entirely new mutual attitudes.

It does not follow that if the Negro were better known, he would be better liked or better treated. But mutual understanding is basic for any subsequent coöperation and adjustment. The effort toward this will at least have the effect of remedying in large part what has been the most unsatisfactory feature of our present stage of race relationships in America, namely the fact that the more intelligent and representative elements of the two race groups have at so many points got quite out of vital touch with one another.

The fiction is that the life of the races is separate, and increasingly so. The fact is that they have touched too closely at the unfavorable and too lightly at the favorable levels.

While inter-racial councils have sprung up in the South, drawing on forward elements of both races, in the Northern cities manual laborers may brush elbows in their everyday work, but the community and business leaders have experienced no such interplay or far too little of it. These segments must achieve contact or the race situation in America becomes desperate.

Fortunately this is happening. There is a growing realization that in social effort the co-operative basis must supplant long-distance philanthropy, and that the only safeguard for mass relations in the future must be provided in the carefully maintained contacts of the enlightened minorities of both race groups. In the intellectual realm a renewed and keen curiosity is replacing the recent apathy; the Negro is being carefully studied, not just talked about and discussed. In art and letters, instead of being wholly caricatured, he is being seriously portrayed and painted.

To all of this the New Negro is keenly responsive as an augury of a new democracy in American culture. He is contributing his share to the new social understanding. But the desire to be understood would never in itself have been sufficient to have opened so completely the protectively closed portals of the thinking Negro's mind. There is still too much possibility of being snubbed or patronized for that. It was rather the necessity for fuller, truer self-expression, the realization of the unwisdom of allowing social discrimination to segregate him mentally, and a counterattitude to cramp and fetter his own living—and so the "spite-wall" that the intellectuals built over the "color-line" has happily been taken down. Much of this reopening of intellectual contacts has centered in New York and has been richly fruitful not merely in the enlarging of personal experience, but in the definite enrichment of American art and letters and in the clarifying of our common vision of the social tasks ahead.

The particular significance in the re-establishment of contact between the more advanced and representative classes is that it promises to offset some of the unfavorable reactions of the past, or at least to re-surface race contacts somewhat for the future. Subtly the conditions that are molding a New Negro are molding a new American attitude.

However, this new phase of things is delicate; it will call for less charity but more justice; less help, but infinitely closer understanding. This is indeed a critical stage of race relationships because of the likelihood, if the new temper is not understood, of engendering sharp group antagonism and a second crop of more calculated prejudice. In some quarters, it has already done so. Having weaned the Negro, public opinion cannot continue to paternalize. The Negro to-day is inevitably moving forward under the control largely of his own objectives. What are these objectives? Those of his outer life are happily already well and finally formulated, for they are none other than the ideals of American institutions and democracy. Those of his inner life are yet in process of formation, for the new psychology at present is more of a consensus of feeling than of opinion, of attitude rather than of program. Still some points seem to have crystallized.

Up to the present one may adequately describe the Negro's "inner objectives" as an attempt to repair a damaged group psychology and reshape a warped social perspective. Their realization has required a new mentality for the American Negro. And as it matures we begin to see its effects; at first, negative, iconoclastic, and then positive and constructive. In this new group psychology we note the lapse of sentimental appeal, then the development of a more positive self-respect and self-reliance; the repudiation of social dependence, and then the gradual recovery from hyper-sensitiveness and "touchy" nerves, the repudiation of the double standard of judgment with its special philanthropic allowances and then the sturdier desire for objective and scientific appraisal; and finally the rise from social disillusionment to race pride, from the sense of social debt to the responsibilities of social contribution, and offsetting the necessary working and commonsense acceptance of restricted conditions, the belief in ultimate esteem and recognition. Therefore the Negro to-day wishes to be known for what he is, even in his faults and shortcomings, and scorns a craven and precarious survival at the price of seeming to be what he is not. He resents being spoken of as a social ward or minor, even by his own, and to being regarded a chronic patient for the sociological clinic, the sick man of American Democracy. For the same reasons, he himself is through with those social nostrums and panaceas, the so-called "solutions" of his "problem," with which he and the country have been so liberally dosed in the past. Religion, freedom, education, money—in turn, he has ardently hoped for and peculiarly trusted these things; he still believes in them, but not in blind trust that they alone will solve his life-problem.

Each generation, however, will have its creed, and that of the present is the belief in the efficacy of collective effort, in race co-operation. This deep feeling of race is at present the mainspring of Negro life. It seems to be the outcome of the reaction to proscription and prejudice; an attempt, fairly successful on the whole, to convert a defensive into an offensive position, a handicap into an incentive. It is radical in tone, but not in purpose and only the most stupid forms of opposition, misunderstanding or persecution could make it otherwise. Of course, the thinking Negro has shifted a little toward the left with the world-trend, and there is an increasing group who affiliate with radical and liberal movements. But fundamentally for the present the Negro is radical on race matters, conservative on others, in other words, a "forced radical," a social protestant rather than a genuine radical. Yet under further pressure and injustice iconoclastic thought and motives will inevitably increase. Harlem's quixotic radicalisms call for their ounce of democracy to-day lest to-morrow they be beyond cure.

The Negro mind reaches out as yet to nothing but American wants, American ideas. But this forced attempt to build his Americanism on race values is a unique social experiment, and its ultimate success is impossible except through the fullest sharing of American culture and institutions. There should be no delusion about this. American nerves in sections unstrung with race hysteria are often fed the opiate that the trend of Negro advance is wholly separatist, and that the effect of its operation will be to encyst the Negro as a benign foreign body in the body politic. This cannot be—even if it were desirable. The racialism of the Negro is no limitation or reservation with respect to American life; it is only a constructive effort to build the obstructions in the stream of his progress into an efficient dam of social energy and power. Democracy itself is obstructed and stagnated to the extent that any of its channels are closed. Indeed they cannot be selectively closed. So the choice is not between one way for the Negro and another way for the rest, but between American institutions frustrated on the one hand and American ideals progressively fulfilled and realized on the other.

There is, of course, a warrantably comfortable feeling in being on the right side of the country's professed ideals. We realize that we cannot be undone without America's undoing. It is within the gamut of this attitude that the thinking Negro faces America, but with variations of mood that are if anything more significant than the attitude itself. Sometimes we have it taken with the defiant ironic challenge of McKay:

> Mine is the future grinding down to-day
> Like a great landslip moving to the sea,
> Bearing its freight of débris far away
> Where the green hungry waters restlessly
> Heave mammoth pyramids, and break and roar
> Their eerie challenge to the crumbling shore.

Sometimes, perhaps more frequently as yet, it is taken in the fervent and almost filial appeal and counsel of Weldon Johnson's:

> O Southland, dear Southland!
> Then why do you still cling
> To an idle age and a musty page,
> To a dead and useless thing?

But between defiance and appeal, midway almost between cynicism and hope, the prevailing mind stands in the mood of the same author's *To America*, an attitude of sober query and stoical challenge:

> How would you have us, as we are?
>   Or sinking 'neath the load we bear,
> Our eyes fixed forward on a star,
>   Or gazing empty at despair?
>
> Rising or falling? Men or things?
>   With dragging pace or footsteps fleet?
> Strong, willing sinews in your wings,
>   Or tightening chains about your feet?

More and more, however, an intelligent realization of the great discrepancy between the American social creed and the American social practice forces upon the Negro the taking of the moral advantage that is his. Only the steadying and sobering effect of a truly characteristic gentleness of spirit prevents the rapid rise of a definite cynicism and counter-hate and a defiant superiority feeling. Human as this reaction would be, the majority still deprecate its advent, and would gladly see it forestalled by the speedy amelioration of its causes. We wish our race pride to be a healthier, more positive achievement than a feeling based upon a realization of the shortcomings of others. But all paths toward the attainment of a sound social attitude have been difficult; only a relatively few enlightened minds have been able as the phrase puts it "to rise above" prejudice. The ordinary man has had until recently only a hard choice between the alternatives of supine and humiliating submission and stimulating but hurtful counter-prejudice. Fortunately from some inner, desperate resourcefulness has recently sprung up the simple expedient of fighting prejudice by mental passive resistance, in other words by trying to ignore it. For the few, this manna may perhaps be effective, but the masses cannot thrive upon it.

Fortunately there are constructive channels opening out into which the balked social feelings of the American Negro can flow freely.

Without them there would be much more pressure and danger than there is. These compensating interests are racial but in a new and enlarged way. One is the consciousness of acting as the advance-guard of the African peoples in their contact with Twentieth Century civilization; the other, the sense of a mission of rehabilitating the race in world esteem from that loss of prestige for which the fate and conditions of slavery have so largely been responsible. Harlem, as we shall see, is the center of both these movements; she is the home of the Negro's "Zionism." The pulse of the Negro world has begun to beat in Harlem. A Negro newspaper carrying news material in English, French and Spanish, gathered from all quarters of America, the West Indies and Africa has maintained itself in Harlem for over five years. Two important magazines, both edited from New York, maintain their news and circulation consistently on a cosmopolitan scale. Under American auspices and backing, three pan-African congresses have been held abroad for the discussion of common interests, colonial questions and future co-operative development of Africa. In terms of the race question as a world problem, the Negro mind has leapt, so to speak, upon the parapets of prejudice and extended its cramped horizons. In so doing it has linked up with the growing group consciousness of the dark-peoples and is gradually learning their common interests. As one of our writers has recently put it: "It is imperative that we understand the white world in its relations to the non-white world." As with the Jew, persecution is making the Negro international.

As a world phenomenon this wider race consciousness is a different thing from the much asserted rising tide of color. Its inevitable causes are not of our making. The consequences are not necessarily damaging to the best interests of civilization. Whether it actually brings into being new Armadas of conflict or argosies of cultural exchange and enlightenment can only be decided by the attitude of the dominant races in an era of critical change. With the American Negro, his new internationalism is primarily an effort to recapture contact with the scattered peoples of African derivation. Garveyism may be a transient, if spectacular, phenomenon, but the possible rôle of the American Negro in the future development of Africa is one of the most constructive and universally helpful missions that any modern people can lay claim to.

Constructive participation in such causes cannot help giving the Negro valuable group incentives, as well as increased prestige at home and abroad. Our greatest rehabilitation may possibly come through such channels, but for the present, more immediate hope rests in the revaluation by white and black alike of the Negro in terms of his artistic endowments and cultural contributions, past and prospective. It must be increasingly recognized that the Negro has already made very substantial contributions, not only in his folk-art, music especially, which has always found appreciation, but in larger, though humbler and less acknowledged ways. For generations the Negro has been the peasant matrix of that section of America which has most under-valued him, and here he has contributed not only materially in labor and in social patience, but spiritually as well. The South has unconsciously absorbed the gift of his folk-temperament. In less than half a generation it will be eas-ier to recognize this, but the fact remains that a leaven of humor, senti-ment, imagination and tropic nonchalance has gone into the making of the South from a humble, unacknowledged source. A second crop of the Negro's gifts promises still more largely. He now becomes a conscious contributor and lays aside the status of a beneficiary and ward for that of a collaborator and participant in American civilization. The great social gain in this is the releasing of our talented group from the arid fields of controversy and debate to the productive fields of creative expression. The especially cultural recognition they win should in turn prove the key to that revaluation of the Negro which must precede or accompany any considerable further better-ment of race relationships. But whatever the general effect, the present gen-eration will have added the motives of self-expression and spiritual development to the old and still unfinished task of making material head-way and progress. No one who understandingly faces the situation with its substantial accomplishment or views the new scene with its still more abun-dant promise can be entirely without hope. And certainly, if in our lifetime the Negro should not be able to celebrate his full initiation into American democracy, he can at least, on the warrant of these things, celebrate the attainment of a significant and satisfying new phase of group development, and with it a spiritual Coming of Age.

1925

JEAN TOOMER
1894–1967

Born and raised in Washington, D.C., Nathan Eugene Toomer was the only child of Nina Pinchback, and her husband, Nathan Toomer. Soon after his son's birth, however, Nathan, Sr., disappeared, and Nina was forced, through economic need, to return to live with her father, Pinckney Benton Stewart Pinchback, who had been a controversial figure in Louisiana Reconstruction politics. She remarried in 1906 and took her son with her to New Rochelle, New York. Following her untimely death in 1909, Toomer returned to Washington and remained there until he left for college in 1914. Thereafter, intermittently, he lived for varying periods of time with his grandparents, until their deaths in the 1920s.

As a young man, Jean Toomer took a long time choosing a profession. He attended six separate institutions of higher education, but never graduated. However, even as a child, he enjoyed literature, and as early as when he lived in New York, he attempted to write. In 1919 he made up his mind to pursue a literary career.

Cane, his most important work, was published in 1923. This book grew out of a trip to the South in September 1921, at a time when he was frustrated with the slow progress of his writing. Toomer's encounter with rural African American folk culture inspired him, and the visit served as the catalyst for ideas that connected his identity, positively, to his creative impulses. *Cane* was highly praised upon publication. Toomer's friends and associates were mostly white avant-garde writers, but black writers of the early New Negro Renaissance claimed him as their own. As the first book to emerge from that period, *Cane* was called the herald of a new day in African American letters, and Toomer the most promising of the upcoming new writers. In its artistic achievement, his work had surpassed all prior literary descriptions of the African American experience. His future seemed assured.

Although composed of three separate parts, *Cane* unifies the northern and southern African American experiences through its circular movement. In the first section, six vignettes of southern women and twelve poems, in lyrical, vivid, mystical, and sensuous language, highlight the duality of black southern life in their portrayal of conflicts, pressures, and racial and economic oppression. The second section is a kaleidoscope of impressions of the death of black spirituality in a wasteland of urban materialism and technology. In the final section, a drama, a black northerner searches for and discovers his identity in the South of his ancestors. The most enduring aspect of *Cane* is its revelation of an intrinsic strength and beauty in black American culture even in the face of white oppression.

Toomer's other works of note include several plays written between 1922 and 1929 in which he experimented with expressionist techniques, then new to America. Among American playwrights, only Eugene O'Neill surpassed him in this respect. But by the beginning of 1924, angered by the negative impact of racial identity in American society and in search of a philosophy that would permit him a sense of internal unity, Toomer turned away from literature and became a follower of mystic George Gurdjieff. From 1924 to 1932, he worked as a teacher of Gurdjieff's philosophy, one which promised him the unity he sought. He continued to write, but never again about the black experience, or with the qualities of his masterpiece, *Cane*. Publishers refused the new work on its nonliterary merits. His final publication, a long Whitmanesque poem entitled "The Blue Meridian" (1936), pays tribute to Americans of all races, creeds, and colors.

Toomer was a gifted artist who turned his back on what might have been a brilliant writing career for a principle regarding the meaning of race in America.

For this reason, his life and work remain especially interesting to scholars. His grandfather claimed a black identity, although he was sufficiently light-skinned to pass for white. As the equally fair-skinned Toomer grew up and learned about racial politics, he declared himself a member of the American race rather than belonging to a particular ethnic group. This caused him many difficulties, especially as others accused him of denying his African American heritage, a charge he stoutly refuted. He stood firm, maintaining that he was the conscious representative of a people with a heritage of multiple bloodlines, and that others would understand this in time. By privileging no one of his bloodlines, Toomer perceived himself as having taken an important step toward solving America's racial problems.

Nellie Y. McKay
University of Wisconsin–Madison

PRIMARY WORKS

Cane, 1923; *Essentials*, 1931; *The Wayward and the Seeking: A Collection of Writings by Jean Toomer*, ed. Darwin Turner, 1980; *The Collected Poems of Jean Toomer*, ed. Robert B. Jones and Margery Toomer Latimer, 1988.

from **Cane**

Karintha

Her skin is like dusk on the eastern horizon,
O cant you see it, O cant you see it,
Her skin is like dusk on the eastern horizon
... When the sun goes down.

Men had always wanted her, this Karintha, even as a child, Karintha carrying beauty, perfect as dusk when the sun goes down. Old men rode her hobby-horse upon their knees. Young men danced with her at frolics when they should have been dancing with their grown-up girls. God grant us youth, secretly prayed the old men. The young fellows counted the time to pass before she would be old enough to mate with them. This interest of the male, who wishes to ripen a growing thing too soon, could mean no good to her.

Karintha, at twelve, was a wild flash that told the other folks just what it was to live. At sunset, when there was no wind, and the pine-smoke from over by the sawmill hugged the earth, and you couldnt see more than a few feet in front, her sudden darting past you was a bit of vivid color, like a black bird that flashes in light. With the other children one could hear, some distance off, their feet flopping in the two-inch dust. Karintha's running was a whir. It had the sound of the red dust that sometimes makes a spiral in the road. At dusk, during the hush just after the sawmill had closed down, and before any of the women had started their supper getting-ready songs, her voice, high-pitched, shrill, would put one's ears to itching. But no one ever thought to make her stop because of it. She stoned the cows, and beat her dog, and fought the other children ... Even the preacher, who caught her at mischief, told himself that she was as innocently lovely as a November cotton flower. Already, rumors were out about her. Homes in Georgia are most often built on the two-room plan. In one, you cook and eat, in the other you sleep, and there love goes on. Karintha had seen or heard, perhaps she had felt her parents loving. One could but imitate one's parents, for to follow them was the way of God. She played "home" with a small boy who was not afraid to do her bidding. That started the whole thing. Old men could no longer ride her hobby-horse upon their knees. But young men counted faster.

> Her skin is like dusk,
> O cant you see it,
> Her skin is like dusk,
> When the sun goes down.

Karintha is a woman. She who carries beauty, perfect as dusk when the sun goes down. She has been married many times. Old men remind her that a few years back they rode her hobby-horse upon their knees. Karintha smiles, and indulges them when she is in the mood for it. She has contempt for them. Karintha is a woman. Young men run stills to make her money. Young men go to the big cities and run on the road. Young men go away to college. They all want to bring her money. These are the young men who thought that all they had to do was to count time. But Karintha is a woman, and she has had a child. A child fell out of her womb onto a bed of pine-needles in the forest. Pine-needles are smooth and sweet. They are elastic to the feet of rabbits ... A sawmill was nearby. Its pyramidal sawdust pile smouldered. It is a year before one completely burns. Meanwhile, the smoke curls up and hangs in odd wraiths about the trees, curls up, and spreads itself out over the valley ... Weeks after Karintha returned home the smoke was so heavy you tasted it in water. Some one made a song:

> Smoke is on the hills. Rise up.
> Smoke is on the hills, O rise
> And take my soul to Jesus.

Karintha is a woman. Men do not know that the soul of her was a growing thing ripened too soon. They will bring their money; they will die not having found it out ... Karintha at twenty, carrying beauty, perfect as dusk when the sun goes down. Karintha ...

> Her skin is like dusk on the eastern horizon,
> O cant you see it, O cant you see it,
> Her skin is like dusk on the eastern horizon
> ... When the sun goes down.

> Goes down ...

1923

Song of the Son

Pour O pour that parting soul in song,
O pour it in the sawdust glow of night,
Into the velvet pine-smoke air to-night,
And let the valley carry it along.
And let the valley carry it along.   5

O land and soil, red soil and sweet-gum tree,
So scant of grass, so profligate of pines,
Now just before an epoch's sun declines
Thy son, in time, I have returned to thee,
Thy son, I have in time returned to thee.   10

In time, for though the sun is setting on
A song-lit race of slaves, it has not set;
Though late, O soil, it is not too late yet
To catch thy plaintive soul, leaving, soon gone,
Leaving, to catch thy plaintive soul soon gone.   15

O Negro slaves, dark purple ripened plums,
Squeezed, and bursting in the pine-wood air,
Passing, before they stripped the old tree bare
One plum was saved for me, one seed becomes

An everlasting song, a singing tree,   20
Caroling softly souls of slavery,
What they were, and what they are to me,
Caroling softly souls of slavery.

                                                                    1923

Blood-Burning Moon

1

Up from the skeleton stone walls, up from the rotting floor boards and the solid hand-hewn beams of oak of the pre-war cotton factory, dusk came. Up from the dusk the full moon came. Glowing like a fired pine-knot, it illumined the great door and soft showered the Negro shanties aligned along the single street of factory town. The full moon in the great door was an omen. Negro women improvised songs against its spell.

Louisa sang as she came over the crest of the hill from the white folks' kitchen. Her skin was the color of oak leaves on young trees in fall. Her breasts, firm and up-pointed like ripe acorns. And her singing had the low murmur of winds in fig trees. Bob Stone, younger son of the people she worked for, loved her. By the way the world reckons things, he had won her.

By measure of that warm glow which came into her mind at thought of him, he had won her. Tom Burwell, whom the whole town called Big Boy, also loved her. But working in the fields all day, and far away from her, gave him no chance to show it. Though often enough of evenings he had tried to. Somehow, he never got along. Strong as he was with hands upon the ax or plow, he found it difficult to hold her. Or so he thought. But the fact was that he held her to factory town more firmly than he thought for. His black balanced, and pulled against, the white of Stone, when she thought of them. And her mind was vaguely upon them as she came over the crest of the hill, coming from the white folks' kitchen. As she sang softly at the evil face of the full moon.

A strange stir was in her. Indolently, she tried to fix upon Bob or Tom as the cause of it. To meet Bob in the canebrake, as she was going to do an hour or so later, was nothing new. And Tom's proposal which she felt on its way to her could be indefinitely put off. Separately, there was no unusual significance to either one. But for some reason, they jumbled when her eyes gazed vacantly at the rising moon. And from the jumble came the stir that was strangely within her. Her lips trembled. The slow rhythm of her song grew agitant and restless. Rusty black and tan spotted hounds, lying in the dark corners of porches or prowling around back yards, put their noses in the air and caught its tremor. They began plaintively to yelp and howl. Chickens woke up and cackled. Intermittently, all over the countryside dogs barked and roosters crowed as if heralding a weird dawn or some ungodly awakening. The women sang lustily. Their songs were cotton-wads to stop their ears. Louisa came down into factory town and sank wearily upon the step before her home. The moon was rising towards a thick cloud-bank which soon would hide it.

> Red nigger moon. Sinner!
> Blood-burning moon. Sinner!
> Come out that fact'ry door.

2

Up from the deep dusk of a cleared spot on the edge of the forest a mellow glow arose and spread fan-wise into the low-hanging heavens. And all around the air was heavy with the scent of boiling cane. A large pile of cane-stalks lay like ribboned shadows upon the ground. A mule, harnessed to a pole, trudged lazily round and round the pivot of the grinder. Beneath a swaying oil lamp, a Negro alternately whipped out at the mule, and fed cane-stalks to the grinder. A fat boy waddled pails of fresh ground juice between the grinder and the boiling stove. Steam came from the copper boiling pan. The scent of cane came from the copper pan and drenched the forest and the hill that sloped to factory town, beneath its fragrance. It drenched the men in circle seated around the stove. Some of them chewed at the white pulp of stalks, but there was no need for them to, if all they wanted was to taste the cane. One tasted it in factory town. And from factory town one could see the soft haze thrown by the glowing stove upon the low-hanging heavens.

Old David Georgia stirred the thickening syrup with a long ladle, and ever so often drew it off. Old David Georgia tended his stove and told tales about the white folks, about moonshining and cotton picking, and about sweet nigger gals, to the men who sat there about his stove to listen to him. Tom Burwell chewed cane-stalk and laughed with the others till some one mentioned Louisa. Till some one said something about Louisa and Bob Stone, about the silk stockings she must have gotten from him. Blood ran up Tom's neck hotter than the glow that flooded from the stove. He sprang up. Glared at the men and said, "She's my gal." Will Manning laughed. Tom strode over to him. Yanked him up and knocked him to the ground. Several of Manning's friends got up to fight for him. Tom whipped out a long knife and would have cut them to shreds if they hadnt ducked into the woods. Tom had had enough. He nodded to Old David Georgia and swung down the path to factory town. Just then, the dogs started barking and the roosters began to crow. Tom felt funny. Away from the fight, away from the stove, chill got to him. He shivered. He shuddered when he saw the full moon rising towards the cloud-bank. He who didnt give a godam for the fears of old women. He forced his mind to fasten on Louisa. Bob Stone. Better not be. He turned into the street and saw Louisa sitting before her home. He went towards her, ambling, touched the brim of a marvelously shaped, spotted, felt hat, said he wanted to say something to her, and then found that he didnt know what he had to say, or if he did, that he couldnt say it. He shoved his big fists in his overalls, grinned, and started to move off.

"Youall want me, Tom?"

"Thats what us wants, sho, Louisa."

"Well, here I am—"

"An here I is, but that aint ahelpin none, all th same."

"You wanted to say something? . ."

"I did that, sho. But words is like th spots on dice: no matter how y fumbles em, there's times when they jes wont come. I dunno why. Seems like th love I feels fo yo done stole m tongue. I got it now. Whee! Louisa, honey, I oughtnt tell y, I feel I oughtnt cause yo is young an goes t church an I has had other gals, but Louisa I sho do love y. Lil gal, Ise watched y from them first days when youall sat right here befo yo door befo th well an sang sometimes in a way that like t broke m heart. Ise carried y with me into th fields, day after day, an after that, an I sho can plow when yo is there, an I can pick cotton. Yassur! Come near beatin Barlo yesterday. I sho did. Yassur! An next year if ole Stone'll trust me, I'll have a farm. My own. My bales will buy yo what y gets from white folks now. Silk stockings an purple dresses—course I dont believe what some folks been whisperin as t how y gets them things now. White folks always did do for niggers what they likes. An they jes cant help alikin yo, Louisa. Bob Stone likes y. Course he does. But not the way folks is awhisperin. Does he, hon?"

"I dont know what you mean, Tom."

"Course y dont. Ise already cut two niggers. Had t hon, t tell em so. Niggers always tryin t make somethin out a nothin. An then besides, white folks aint up t them tricks so much nowadays. Godam better not be. Leastawise not with yo. Cause I wouldnt stand f it. Nassur."

"What would you do, Tom?"

"Cut him jes like I cut a nigger."

"No, Tom—"

"I said I would an there aint no mo to it. But that aint th talk f now. Sing, honey Louisa, an while I'm listenin t y I'll be makin love."

Tom took her hand in his. Against the tough thickness of his own, hers felt soft and small. His huge body slipped down to the step beside her. The full moon sank upward into the deep purple of the cloud-bank. An old woman brought a lighted lamp and hung it on the common well whose bulky shadow squatted in the middle of the road, opposite Tom and Louisa. The old woman lifted the well-lid, took hold the chain, and began drawing up the heavy bucket. As she did so, she sang. Figures shifted, restlesslike, between lamp and window in the front rooms of the shanties. Shadows of the figures fought each other on the gray dust of the road. Figures raised the windows and joined the old woman in song. Louisa and Tom, the whole street, singing:

> *Red nigger moon. Sinner!*
> *Blood-burning moon. Sinner!*
> *Come out that fact'ry door.*

3

Bob Stone sauntered from his veranda out into the gloom of fir trees and magnolias. The clear white of his skin paled, and the flush of his cheeks turned purple. As if to balance this outer change, his mind became consciously a white man's. He passed the house with its huge open hearth which, in the days of slavery, was the plantation cookery. He saw Louisa bent over that hearth. He went in as a master should and took her. Direct, honest, bold. None of this sneaking that he had to go through now. The contrast was repulsive to him. His family had lost ground. Hell no, his family still owned the niggers, practically. Damned if they did, or he wouldnt have to duck around so. What would they think if they knew? His mother? His sister? He shouldnt mention them, shouldnt think of them in this connection. There in the dusk he blushed at doing so. Fellows about town were all right, but how about his friends up North? He could see them incredible, repulsed. They didnt know. The thought first made him laugh. Then, with their eyes still upon him, he began to feel embarrassed. He felt the need of explaining things to them. Explain hell. They wouldnt understand, and moreover, who ever heard of a Southerner getting on his knees to any Yankee, or anyone. No sir. He was going to see Louisa to-night, and love her. She was lovely—in her way. Nigger way. What way was that? Damned if he knew. Must know. He'd known her long enough to know. Was there something about niggers that you couldnt know? Listening to them at church didnt tell you anything. Looking at them didnt tell you anything. Talking to them didnt tell you anything—unless it was gossip, unless they wanted to talk. Of course, about farming, and licker, and craps—but those werent nigger. Nigger was something more. How much more? Something to be afraid of, more? Hell no. Who ever heard of being afraid of a nigger? Tom Burwell. Cartwell had told him that Tom went with Louisa after she reached home. No sir. No nigger had ever been with his girl. He'd like to see one try. Some position for him to be in. Him, Bob Stone, of the old Stone family, in a scrap with a nigger over a nigger girl. In the good old days ... Ha! Those were the days. His family had lost ground. Not so much, though. Enough for him to have to cut through old Lemon's canefield by way of the woods, that he might meet her. She was worth it. Beautiful nigger gal. Why nigger? Why not, just gal? No, it was because she was nigger that he went to her. Sweet ... The scent of boiling cane came to him. Then he saw the rich glow of the stove. He heard the voices of the men circled around it. He was about to skirt the clearing when he heard his own name mentioned. He stopped. Quivering. Leaning against a tree, he listened.

"Bad nigger. Yassur, he sho is one bad nigger when he gets started."

"Tom Burwell's been on th gang three times fo cuttin men."

"What y think he's agwine t do t Bob Stone?"

"Dunno yet. He aint found out. When he does—Baby!"

"Aint no tellin."

"Young Stone aint no quitter an I ken tell y that. Blood of th old uns in his veins."

"That's right. He'll scrap, sho."

"Be gettin too hot f niggers round this away."

"Shut up, nigger. Y dont know what y talkin bout."

Bob Stone's ears burned as though he had been holding them over the stove. Sizzling heat welled up within him. His feet felt as if they rested on red-hot coals. They stung him to quick movement. He circled the fringe of the glowing. Not a twig cracked beneath his feet. He reached the path that led to factory town. Plunged furiously down it. Halfway along, a blindness within him veered him aside. He crashed into the bordering canebrake. Cane leaves cut his face and lips. He tasted blood. He threw himself down and dug his fingers in the ground. The earth was cool. Cane-roots took the fever from his hands. After a long while, or so it seemed to him, the thought came to him that it must be time to see Louisa. He got to his feet and walked calmly to their meeting place. No Louisa. Tom Burwell had her. Veins in his forehead bulged and distended. Saliva moistened the dried blood on his lips. He bit down on his lips. He tasted blood. Not his own blood; Tom Burwell's blood. Bob drove through the cane and out again upon the road. A hound swung down the path before him towards factory town. Bob couldnt see it. The dog loped aside to let him pass. Bob's blind rushing made him stumble over it. He fell with a thud that dazed him. The hound yelped. Answering yelps came from all over the countryside. Chickens cackled. Roosters crowed, heralding the bloodshot eyes of southern awakening. Singers in the town were silenced. They shut their windows down. Palpitant between the rooster crows, a chill hush settled upon the huddled forms of Tom and Louisa. A figure rushed from the shadow and stood before them. Tom popped to his feet.

"Whats y want?"

"I'm Bob Stone."

"Yassur—an I'm Tom Burwell. Whats y want?"

Bob lunged at him. Tom side-stepped, caught him by the shoulder, and flung him to the ground. Straddled him.

"Let me up."

"Yassur—but watch yo doins, Bob Stone."

A few dark figures, drawn by the sound of scuffle, stood about them. Bob sprang to his feet.

"Fight like a man, Tom Burwell, and I'll lick y."

Again he lunged. Tom side-stepped and flung him to the ground. Straddled him.

"Get off me, you godam nigger you."

"Yo sho has started somethin now. Get up."

Tom yanked him up and began hammering at him. Each blow sounded as if it smashed into a precious, irreplaceable soft something. Beneath them, Bob staggered back. He reached in his pocket and whipped out a knife.

"Thats my game, sho."

Blue flash, a steel blade slashed across Bob Stone's throat. He had a sweetish sick feeling. Blood began to flow. Then he felt a sharp twitch of pain. He let his knife drop. He slapped one hand against his neck. He pressed the other on top of his head as if to hold it down. He groaned. He turned, and staggered towards the crest of the hill in the direction of white town. Negroes who had seen the fight slunk into their homes and blew the lamps out. Louisa, dazed, hysterical, refused to go indoors. She slipped, crumbled, her body loosely propped against the woodwork of the well. Tom Burwell leaned against it. He seemed rooted there.

Bob reached Broad Street. White men rushed up to him. He collapsed in their arms.

"Tom Burwell. . . ."

White men like ants upon a forage rushed about. Except for the taut hum of their moving, all was silent. Shotguns, revolvers, rope, kerosene, torches. Two high-powered cars with glaring search-lights. They came together. The taut hum rose to a low roar. Then nothing could be heard but the flop of their feet in the thick dust of the road. The moving body of their silence preceded them over the crest of the hill into factory town. It flattened the Negroes beneath it. It rolled to the wall of the factory, where it stopped. Tom knew that they were coming. He couldnt move. And then he saw the search-lights of the two cars glaring down on him. A quick shock went through him. He stiffened. He started to run. A yell went up from the mob. Tom wheeled about and faced them. They poured down on him. They swarmed. A large man with dead-white face and flabby cheeks came to him and almost jabbed a gun-barrel through his guts.

"Hands behind y, nigger."

Tom's wrists were bound. The big man shoved him to the well. Burn him over it, and when the woodwork caved in, his body would drop to the bottom. Two deaths for a godam nigger. Louisa was driven back. The mob pushed in. Its pressure, its momentum was too great. Drag him to the factory. Wood and stakes already there. Tom moved in the direction indicated. But they had to drag him. They reached the great door. Too many to get in there. The mob divided and flowed around the walls to either side. The big man shoved him through the door. The mob pressed in from the sides. Taut humming. No words. A stake was sunk into the ground. Rotting floor boards piled around it. Kerosene poured on the rotting floor boards. Tom bound to the stake. His breast was bare. Nails' scratches let little lines of blood trickle down and mat into the hair. His face, his eyes were set and stony. Except for irregular breathing, one would have thought him already dead. Torches were flung onto the pile. A great flare muffled in black smoke shot upward. The mob yelled. The mob was silent. Now Tom could be seen within the flames. Only his head, erect, lean, like a blackened stone. Stench of burning flesh soaked the air. Tom's eyes popped. His head settled downward. The mob yelled. Its yell echoed against the skeleton stone walls and sounded like a hundred yells. Like a hundred mobs yelling. Its yell thudded against the thick front wall and fell back. Ghost of a yell slipped through the flames and out the great door of the factory. It fluttered like a dying thing down the single street of factory town. Louisa, upon the step before her home, did not hear it, but her eyes opened slowly. They saw the full moon glowing in the great door. The full moon, an evil thing, an omen, soft showering the homes of folks she knew. Where were they, these people? She'd sing, and perhaps they'd come out and join her. Perhaps Tom Burwell would come. At any rate, the full moon in the great door was an omen which she must sing to:

> *Red nigger moon. Sinner!*
> *Blood-burning moon. Sinner!*
> *Come out that fact'ry door.*

1923

Seventh Street

> *Money burns the pocket, pocket hurts,*
> *Bootleggers in silken shirts,*
> *Ballooned, zooming Cadillacs,*
> *Whizzing, whizzing down the street-car tracks.*

Seventh Street is a bastard of Prohibition and the War. A crude-boned, soft-skinned wedge of nigger life breathing its loafer air, jazz songs and love, thrusting unconscious rhythms, black reddish blood into the white and whitewashed wood of Washington. Stale soggy wood of Washington. Wedges rust in soggy wood ... Split it! In two! Again! Shred it! .. the sun. Wedges are brilliant in the sun; ribbons of wet wood dry and blow away. Black reddish blood. Pouring for crude-boned soft-skinned life, who set you flowing? Blood suckers of the War would spin in a frenzy of dizziness if they drank your blood. Prohibition would put a stop to it. Who set you flowing? White and whitewash disappear in blood. Who set you flowing? Flowing down the smooth asphalt of Seventh Street, in shanties, brick office buildings, theaters, drug stores, restaurants, and cabarets? Eddying on the corners? Swirling like a blood-red smoke up where the buzzards fly in heaven? God would not dare to suck black red blood. A Nigger God! He would duck his head in shame and call for the Judgment Day. Who set you flowing?

> *Money burns the pocket, pocket hurts,*
> *Bootleggers in silken shirts,*
> *Ballooned, zooming Cadillacs,*
> *Whizzing, whizzing down the street-car tracks.*

1923

Box Seat

1

Houses are shy girls whose eyes shine reticently upon the dusk body of the street. Upon the gleaming limbs and asphalt torso of a dreaming nigger. Shake your curled wool-blossoms, nigger. Open your liver lips to the lean, white spring. Stir the root-life of a withered people. Call them from their houses, and teach them to dream.

Dark swaying forms of Negroes are street songs that woo virginal houses.

Dan Moore walks southward on Thirteenth Street. The low limbs of budding chestnut trees recede above his head. Chestnut buds and blossoms are wool he walks upon. The eyes of houses faintly touch him as he passes them. Soft girl-eyes, they set him singing. Girl-eyes within him widen upward to promised faces. Floating away, they dally wistfully over the dusk body of the street. Come on, Dan Moore, come on. Dan sings. His voice is a little hoarse. It cracks. He strains to produce tones in keeping with the houses' loveliness. Cant be done. He whistles. His notes are shrill. They hurt him. Negroes open gates, and go indoors, perfectly. Dan thinks of the house he's going to. Of the girl. Lips, flesh-notes of a forgotten song, plead with him ...

Dan turns into a side-street, opens an iron gate, bangs it to. Mounts the steps, and searches for the bell. Funny, he cant find it. He fumbles around. The thought comes to him that some one passing by might see him, and not understand. Might think that he is trying to sneak, to break in.

Dan: Break in. Get an ax and smash in. Smash in their faces. I'll show em. Break into an engine-house, steal a thousand horse-power fire truck. Smash in with the truck. I'll show em. Grab an ax and brain em. Cut em up.

Jack the Ripper. Baboon from the zoo. And then the cops come. "No, I aint a baboon. I aint Jack the Ripper. I'm a poor man out of work. Take your hands off me, you bull-necked bears. Look into my eyes. I am Dan Moore. I was born in a canefield. The hands of Jesus touched me. I am come to a sick world to heal it. Only the other day, a dope fiend brushed against me—Dont laugh, you mighty, juicy, meat-hook men. Give me your fingers and I will peel them as if they were ripe bananas.

Some one might think he is trying to break in. He'd better knock. His knuckles are raw bone against the thick glass door. He waits. No one comes. Perhaps they havent heard him. He raps again. This time, harder. He waits. No one comes. Some one is surely in. He fancies that he sees their shadows on the glass. Shadows of gorillas. Perhaps they saw him coming and dont want to let him in. He knocks. The tension of his arms makes the glass rattle. Hurried steps come towards him. The door opens.

"Please, you might break the glass—the bell—oh, Mr. Moore! I thought it must be some stranger. How do you do? Come in, wont you? Muriel? Yes. I'll call her. Take your things off, wont you? And have a seat in the parlor. Muriel will be right down. Muriel! Oh Muriel! Mr. Moore to see you. She'll be right down. You'll pardon me, wont you? So glad to see you."

Her eyes are weak. They are bluish and watery from reading newspapers. The blue is steel. It gimlets Dan while her mouth flaps amiably to him.

Dan: Nothing for you to see, old mussel-head. Dare I show you? If I did, delirium would furnish you headlines for a month. Now look here. Thats enough. Go long, woman. Say some nasty thing and I'll kill you. Huh. Better damned sight not. Ta-ta, Mrs. Pribby.

Mrs. Pribby retreats to the rear of the house. She takes up a newspaper. There is a sharp click as she fits into her chair and draws it to the table. The click is metallic like the sound of a bolt being shot into place. Dan's eyes sting. Sinking into a soft couch, he closes them. The house contracts about him. It is a sharp-edged, massed, metallic house. Bolted. About Mrs. Pribby. Bolted to the endless rows of metal houses. Mrs. Pribby's house. The rows of houses belong to other Mrs. Pribbys. No wonder he couldn't sing to them.

Dan: What's Muriel doing here? God, what a place for her. Whats she doing? Putting her stockings on? In the bathroom. Come out of there, Dan Moore. People must have their privacy. Peeping-toms. I'll never peep. I'll listen. I like to listen.

Dan goes to the wall and places his ear against it. A passing street car and something vibrant from the earth sends a rumble to him. That rumble comes from the earth's deep core. It is the mutter of powerful underground races. Dan has a picture of all the people rushing to put their ears against walls, to listen to it. The next world-savior is coming up that way. Coming up. A continent sinks down. The new-world Christ will need consummate skill to walk upon the waters where huge bubbles burst . . . Thuds of Muriel coming down. Dan turns to the piano and glances through a stack of jazz music sheets. Ji-ji-bo, JI-JI-BO! . .

"Hello, Dan, stranger, what brought you here?"

Muriel comes in, shakes hands, and then clicks into a high-armed seat under the orange glow of a floor-lamp. Her face is fleshy. It would tend to coarseness but for the fresh fragrant something which is the life of it. Her hair like an Indian's. But more curly and bushed and vagrant. Her nostrils flare. The flushed ginger of her cheeks is touched orange by the shower of color from the lamp.

"Well, you havent told me, you havent answered my question, stranger. What brought you here?"

Dan feels the pressure of the house, of the rear room, of the rows of houses, shift to Muriel. He is light. He loves her. He is doubly heavy.

"Dont know, Muriel—wanted to see you—wanted to talk to you—to see you and tell you that I know what you've been through—what pain the last few months must have been—"

"Lets dont mention that."

"But why not, Muriel? I—"

"Please."

"But Muriel, life is full of things like that. One grows strong and beautiful in facing them. What else is life?"

"I dont know, Dan. And I dont believe I care. Whats the use? Lets talk about something else. I hear there's a good show at the Lincoln this week."

"Yes, so Harry was telling me. Going?"

"To-night."

Dan starts to rise.

"I didnt know. I dont want to keep you."

"Its all right. You dont have to go till Bernice comes. And she wont be here till eight. I'm all dressed. I'll let you know."

"Thanks."

Silence. The rustle of a newspaper being turned comes from the rear room.

Muriel: Shame about Dan. Something awfully good and fine about him. But he dont fit in. In where? Me? Dan, I could love you if I tried. I dont have to try. I do. O Dan, dont you know I do? Timid lover, brave talker that you are. Whats the good of all you know if you dont know that? I wont let myself. I? Mrs. Pribby who reads newspapers all night wont. What has she got to do with me? She *is* me, somehow. No she's not. Yes she is. She is the town, and the town wont let me love you, Dan. Dont you know? You could make it let me if you would. Why wont you? Youre selfish. I'm not strong enough to buck it. Youre too selfish to buck it, for me. I wish you'd go. You irritate me. Dan, please go.

"What are you doing now, Dan?"

"Same old thing, Muriel. Nothing, as the world would have it. Living, as I look at things. Living as much as I can without—"

"But you cant live without money, Dan. Why dont you get a good job and settle down?"

Dan: Same old line. Shoot it at me, sister. Hell of a note, this loving business. For ten minutes of it youve got to stand the torture of an intolerable heaviness and a hundred platitudes. Well, damit, shoot on.

"To what? my dear. Rustling newspapers?"

"You mustnt say that, Dan. It isnt right. Mrs. Pribby has been awfully good to me."

"Dare say she has. Whats that got to do with it?"

"Oh, Dan, youre so unconsiderate and selfish. All you think of is yourself."

"I think of you."

"Too much—I mean, you ought to work more and think less. Thats the best way to get along."

"Mussel-heads get along, Muriel. There is more to you than that—"

"Sometimes I think there is, Dan. But I dont know. I've tried. I've tried to do something with myself. Something real and beautiful, I mean. But whats the good of trying? I've tried to make people, every one I come in contact with, happy—"

Dan looks at her, directly. Her animalism, still unconquered by zoo-restrictions and keeper-taboos, stirs him. Passion tilts upward, bringing with it the elements of an old desire. Muriel's lips become the flesh-notes of a futile, plaintive longing. Dan's impulse to direct her is its fresh life.

"Happy, Muriel? No, not happy. Your aim is wrong. There is no such thing as happiness. Life bends joy and pain, beauty and ugliness, in such a way that no one may isolate them. No one should want to. Perfect joy, or perfect pain, with no contrasting element to define them, would mean a monotony of consciousness, would mean death. Not happy, Muriel. Say that you have tried to make them create. Say that you have used your own capacity for life to cradle them. To start them upward-flowing. Or if you cant say that you have, then say that you will. My talking to you will make you aware of your power to do so. Say that you will love, that you will give yourself in love—"

"To you, Dan?"

Dan's consciousness crudely swerves into his passions. They flare up in his eyes. They set up quivers in his abdomen. He is suddenly over-tense and nervous.

"Muriel—"

The newspaper rustles in the rear room.

"Muriel—"

Dan rises. His arms stretch towards her. His fingers and his palms, pink in the lamplight, are glowing irons. Muriel's chair is close and stiff about her. The house, the rows of houses locked about her chair. Dan's fingers and arms are fire to melt and bars to wrench and force and pry. Her arms hang loose. Her hands are hot and moist. Dan takes them. He slips to his knees before her.

"Dan, you mustnt."

"Muriel—"

"Dan, really you mustnt. No, Dan. No."

"Oh, come, Muriel. Must I—"

"Shhh. Dan, please get up. Please. Mrs. Pribby is right in the next room. She'll hear you. She may come in. Dont, Dan. She'll see you—"

"Well then, lets go out."

"I cant. Let go, Dan. Oh, wont you please let go."

Muriel tries to pull her hands away. Dan tightens his grip. He feels the strength of his fingers. His muscles are tight and strong. He stands up. Thrusts out his chest. Muriel shrinks from him. Dan becomes aware of his crude absurdity. His lips curl. His passion chills. He has an obstinate desire to possess her.

"Muriel I love you. I want you, whatever the world of Pribby says. Damn your Pribby. Who is she to dictate my love? I've stood enough of her. Enough of you. Come here."

Muriel's mouth works in and out. Her eyes flash and waggle. She wrenches her hands loose and forces them against his breast to keep him off. Dan grabs her wrists. Wedges in between her arms. Her face is close to him. It is hot and blue and moist. Ugly.

"Come here now."

"Dont, Dan. Oh, dont. What are you killing?"

"Whats weak in both of us and a whole litter of Pribbys. For once in your life youre going to face whats real, by God—"

A sharp rap on the newspaper in the rear room cuts between them. The rap is like cool thick glass between them. Dan is hot on one side. Muriel, hot on the other. They straighten. Gaze fearfully at one another. Neither moves. A clock in the rear room, in the rear room, the rear room, strikes eight. Eight slow, cool sounds. Bernice. Muriel fastens on her image. She smooths her dress. She adjusts her skirt. She becomes prim and cool. Rising, she skirts Dan as if to keep the glass between them. Dan, gyrating nervously above the easy swing of his limbs, follows her to the parlor door. Muriel retreats before him till she reaches the landing of the steps that lead upstairs. She smiles at him. Dan sees his face in the hall mirror. He runs his fingers through his hair. Reaches for his hat and coat and puts them on. He moves towards Muriel. Muriel steps backward up one step. Dan's jaw shoots out. Muriel jerks her arm in warning of Mrs. Pribby. She gasps and turns and starts to run. Noise of a chair scraping as Mrs. Pribby rises from it, ratchets down the hall. Dan stops. He makes a wry face, wheels round, goes out, and slams the door.

2

People come in slowly ... mutter, laughs, flutter, whishadwash, "I've changed my work-clothes—" ... and fill vacant seats of Lincoln Theater. Muriel, leading Bernice who is a cross between a washerwoman and a blue-blood lady, a washer-blue, a washer-lady, wanders down the right aisle to the lower front box. Muriel has on an orange dress. Its color would clash with the crimson box draperies, its color would contradict the sweet rose smile her face is bathed in, should she take her coat off. She'll keep it on. Pale purple shadows rest on the planes of her cheeks. Deep purple comes from her thick-shocked hair. Orange of the dress goes well with these. Muriel presses her coat down from around her shoulders. Teachers are not supposed to have bobbed hair. She'll keep her hat on. She takes the first chair, and indicates that Bernice is to take the one directly behind her. Seated thus, her eyes are level with, and near to, the face of an imaginary man upon the stage. To speak to Berny she must turn. When she does, the audience is square upon her.

People come in slowly ... "—for my Sunday-go-to-meeting dress. O glory God! O shout Amen!" ... and fill vacant seats of Lincoln Theater. Each one is a bolt that shoots into a slot, and is locked there. Suppose the Lord should ask, where was Moses when the light went out? Suppose Gabriel should blow his trumpet! The seats are slots. The seats are bolted houses. The mass grows denser. Its weight at first is impalpable upon the box. Then Muriel begins to feel it. She props her arm against the brass box-rail, to ward it off. Silly. These people are friends of hers: a parent of a child she teaches, an old school friend. She smiles at them. They return her courtesy, and she is free to chat with Berny. Berny's tongue, started, runs on, and on. O washer-blue! O washer-lady!

Muriel: Never see Dan again. He makes me feel queer. Starts things he doesnt finish. Upsets me. I am not upset. I am perfectly calm. I am going to enjoy the show. Good show. I've had some show! This damn tame thing. O Dan. Wont see Dan again. Not alone. Have Mrs. Pribby come in. She *was* in. Keep Dan out. If I love him, can I keep him out? Well then, I dont love him. Now he's out. Who is that coming in? Blind as a bat. Ding-bat. Looks like Dan. He mustnt see me. Silly. He cant reach me. He wont dare come in here. He'd put his head down like a goring bull and charge me. He'd trample them. He'd gore. He'd rape! Berny! He wont dare come in here.

"Berny, who was that who just came in? I havent my glasses."

"A friend of yours, a *good* friend so I hear. Mr. Daniel Moore, Lord."

"Oh. He's no friend of mine."

"No? I hear he is."

"Well, he isnt."

Dan is ushered down the aisle. He has to squeeze past the knees of seated people to reach his own seat. He treads on a man's corns. The man grumbles, and shoves him off. He shrivels close beside a portly Negress whose huge rolls of flesh meet about the bones of seat-arms. A soil-soaked fragrance comes from her. Through the cement floor her strong roots sink down. They spread under the asphalt streets. Dreaming, the streets roll over on their bellies, and suck their glossy health from them. Her strong roots sink down and spread under the river and disappear in blood-lines that waver south. Her roots shoot down. Dan's hands follow them. Roots throb. Dan's heart beats violently. He places his palms upon the earth to cool them. Earth throbs. Dan's heart beats violently. He sees all the people in the house rush to the walls to listen to the rumble. A new-world Christ is coming up. Dan comes up. He is startled. The eyes of the woman dont belong to her. They look at him unpleasantly. From either aisle, bolted masses press in. He doesnt fit. The mass grows agitant. For an instant, Dan's and Muriel's eyes meet. His weight there slides the weight on her. She braces an arm against the brass rail, and turns her head away.

Muriel: Damn fool; dear Dan, what did you want to follow me here for? Oh cant you ever do anything right? Must you always pain me, and make me hate you? I do hate you. I wish some one would come in with a horse-whip and lash you out. I wish some one would drag you up a back alley and brain you with the whip-butt.

Muriel glances at her wrist-watch.

"Quarter of nine. Berny, what time have you?"

"Eight-forty. Time to begin. Oh, look Muriel, that woman with the plume; doesnt she look good! They say she's going with, oh, whats his name. You know. Too much powder. I can see it from here. Here's the orchestra now. O fine! Jim Clem at the piano!"

The men fill the pit. Instruments run the scale and tune. The saxophone moans and throws a fit. Jim Clem, poised over the piano, is ready to begin. His head nods forward. Opening crash. The house snaps dark. The curtain recedes upward from the blush of the footlights. Jazz overture is over. The first act is on.

Dan: Old stuff. Muriel—bored. Must be. But she'll smile and she'll clap. Do what youre bid, you she-slave. Look at her. Sweet, tame woman in a brass box seat. Clap, smile, fawn, clap. Do what youre bid. Drag me in with you. Dirty me. Prop me in your brass box seat. I'm there, am I not? because of you. He-slave. Slave of a woman who is a slave. I'm a damned sight worse than you are. I sing your praises, Beauty! I exalt thee, O Muriel! A slave, thou art greater than all Freedom because I love thee.

Dan fidgets, and disturbs his neighbors. His neighbors glare at him. He glares back without seeing them. The man whose corns have been trod upon speaks to him.

"Keep quiet, cant you, mister. Other people have paid their money besides yourself to see the show."

The man's face is a blur about two sullen liquid things that are his eyes. The eyes dissolve in the surrounding vagueness. Dan suddenly feels that the man is an enemy whom he has long been looking for.

Dan bristles. Glares furiously at the man.

"All right. All right then. Look at the show. I'm not stopping you."

"Shhh," from some one in the rear.

Dan turns around.

"Its that man there who started everything. I didnt say a thing to him until he tried to start something. What have I got to do with whether he has paid his money or not? Thats the manager's business. Do I look like the manager?"

"Shhhh. Youre right. Shhhh."

"Dont tell me to shhh. Tell him. That man there. He started everything. If what he wanted was to start a fight, why didnt he say so?"

The man leans forward.

"Better be quiet, sonny. I aint said a thing about fight, yet."

"Its a good thing you havent."

"Shhhh."

Dan grips himself. Another act is on. Dwarfs, dressed like prize-fighters, foreheads bulging like boxing gloves, are led upon the stage. They are going to fight for the heavyweight championship. Gruesome. Dan glances at Muriel. He imagines that she shudders. His mind curves back into himself, and picks up tail-ends of experiences. His eyes are open, mechanically. The dwarfs pound and bruise and bleed each other, on his eyeballs.

Dan: Ah, but she was some baby! And not vulgar either. Funny how some women can do those things. Muriel dancing like that! Hell. She rolled and wabbled. Her buttocks rocked. She pulled up her dress and showed her pink drawers. Baby! And then she caught my eyes. Dont know what my eyes had in them. Yes I do. God, dont I though! Sometimes I think, Dan Moore, that your eyes could burn clean ... burn clean ... BURN CLEAN! ..

The gong rings. The dwarfs set to. They spar grotesquely, playfully, until one lands a stiff blow. This makes the other sore. He commences slugging. A real scrap is on. Time! The dwarfs go to their corners and are sponged and fanned off. Gloves bulge from their wrists. Their wrists are necks for the tight-faced gloves. The fellow to the right lets his eyes roam over the audience. He sights Muriel. He grins.

Dan: Those silly women arguing feminism. Here's what I should have said to them. "It should be clear to you women, that the proposition must be stated thus:

> Me, horizontally above her.
> Action: perfect strokes downward oblique.
> Hence, man dominates because of limitation.
> Or, so it shall be until women learn their stuff.

So framed, the proposition is a mental-filler, Dentist, I want gold teeth. It should become cherished of the technical intellect. I hereby offer it to posterity as one of the important machine-age designs. P.S. It should be noted, that because it *is* an achievement of this age, its growth and hence its causes, up to the point of maturity, antedate machinery. Ery ..."

The gong rings. No fooling this time. The dwarfs set to. They clinch. The referee parts them. One swings a cruel upper-cut and knocks the other down. A huge head hits the floor. Pop! The house roars. The fighter, groggy, scrambles up. The referee whispers to the contenders not to fight so hard. They ignore him. They charge. Their heads jab like boxing-gloves. They kick and spit and bite. They pound each other furiously. Muriel pounds. The house pounds. Cut lips. Bloody noses. The referee asks for the gong. Time! The house roars. The dwarfs bow, are made to bow. The house wants more. The dwarfs are led from the stage.

Dan: Strange I never really noticed him before. Been sitting there for years. Born a slave. Slavery not so long ago. He'll die in his chair. Swing low, sweet chariot. Jesus will come and roll him down the river Jordan. Oh, come along, Moses, you'll get lost; stretch out your rod and come across. LET MY PEOPLE GO! Old man. Knows everyone who passes the corners. Saw the first horse-cars. The first Oldsmobile. And he was born in slavery. I did see his eyes. Never miss eyes. But they were bloodshot and watery. It hurt to look at them. It hurts to look in most people's eyes. He saw Grant and Lincoln. He saw Walt—old man, did you see Walt Whitman? Did you see Walt Whitman! Strange force that drew me to him. And I went up to see. The woman thought I was crazy. I told him to look into the heavens. He did, and smiled. I asked him if he knew what that rumbling is that comes up from the ground. Christ, what a stroke that was. And the jabbering idiots crowding around. And the crossing-cop leaving his job to come over and wheel him away . . .

The house applauds. The house wants more. The dwarfs are led back. But no encore. Must give the house something. The attendant comes out and announces that Mr. Barry, the champion, will sing one of his own songs, "for your approval." Mr. Barry grins at Muriel as he wabbles from the wing. He holds a fresh white rose, and a small mirror. He wipes blood from his nose. He signals Jim Clem. The orchestra starts. A sentimental love song. Mr. Barry sings, first to one girl, and then another in the audience. He holds the mirror in such a way that it flashes in the face of each one he sings to. The light swings around.

Dan: I am going to reach up and grab the girders of this building and pull them down. The crash will be a signal. Hid by the smoke and dust Dan Moore will arise. In his right hand will be a dynamo. In his left, a god's face that will flash white light from ebony. I'll grab a girder and swing it like a walking-stick. Lightning will flash. I'll grab its black knob and swing it like a crippled cane. Lightning . . . Some one's flashing . . . some one's flashing . . . Who in hell is flashing that mirror? Take it off me, godam you.

Dan's eyes are half blinded. He moves his head. The light follows. He hears the audience laugh. He hears the orchestra. A man with a high-pitched, sentimental voice is singing. Dan sees the dwarf. Along the mirror flash the song comes. Dan ducks his head. The audience roars. The light swings around to Muriel. Dan looks. Muriel is too close. Mr. Barry covers his mirror. He sings to her. She shrinks away. Nausea. She clutches the brass box-rail. She moves to face away. The audience is square upon her. Its eyes smile. Its hands itch to clap. Muriel turns to the dwarf and forces a smile at him. With a showy blare of orchestration, the song comes to its close. Mr. Barry bows. He offers Muriel the rose, first having kissed it. Blood of his battered lips is a vivid stain upon its petals. Mr. Barry offers Muriel the rose. The house applauds. Muriel flinches back. The dwarf steps forward, diffident; threatening. Hate pops from his eyes and crackles like a brittle heat about the box. The thick hide of his face is drawn in tortured wrinkles. Above his eyes, the bulging, tight-skinned brow. Dan looks at it. It grows calm and massive. It grows profound. It is a thing of wisdom and tenderness, of suffering and beauty. Dan looks down. The eyes are calm and luminous. Words come from them . . . Arms of the audience reach out, grab Muriel, and hold her there. Claps are steel fingers that manacle her wrists and move them forward to acceptance. Berny leans forward and whispers:

"Its all right. Go on—take it."

Words form in the eyes of the dwarf:

> *Do not shrink. Do not be afraid of me.*
> Jesus
> *See how my eyes look at you.*
> the Son of God
> *I too was made in His image.*
> was once—
> *I give you the rose.*

Muriel, tight in her revulsion, sees black, and daintily reaches for the offering. As her hand touches it, Dan springs up in his seat and shouts: "JESUS WAS ONCE A LEPER!"

Dan steps down.

He is as cool as a green stem that has just shed its flower.

Rows of gaping faces strain towards him. They are distant, beneath him, impalpable. Squeezing out, Dan again treads upon the corn-foot man. The man shoves him.

"Watch where youre going, mister. Crazy or no, you aint going to walk over me. Watch where youre going there."

Dan turns, and serenely tweaks the fellow's nose. The man jumps up. Dan is jammed against a seat-back. A slight swift anger flicks him. His fist hooks the other's jaw.

"Now you have started something. Aint no man living can hit me and get away with it. Come on on the outside."

The house, tumultuously stirring, grabs its wraps and follows the men.

The man leads Dan up a black alley. The alley-air is thick and moist with smells of garbage and wet trash. In the morning, singing niggers will drive by and ring their gongs ... Heavy with the scent of rancid flowers and with the scent of fight. The crowd, pressing forward, is a hollow roar. Eyes of houses, soft girl-eyes, glow reticently upon the hubbub and blink out. The man stops. Takes off his hat and coat. Dan, having forgotten him, keeps going on.

1923

LANGSTON HUGHES
1902–1967

Langston Hughes was one of the most original and versatile of twentieth-century black writers. Born in Joplin, Missouri, to James Nathaniel and Carrie Mercer Langston Hughes, he was reared for a time by his grandmother in

Lawrence, Kansas, after his parents' divorce. Influenced by the poetry of Paul Laurence Dunbar and Carl Sandburg, he began writing creatively while still a boy. After his graduation from high school in Cleveland, he spent fifteen months in Mexico with his father; upon his return to the United States in 1921, Hughes attended Columbia University for a year. Disillusioned with formal education, in 1923 he joined the crew of the *SS Malone* bound for Africa, where the ship visited thirty-odd ports. Before returning to New York, Hughes lived in Paris, Venice, and Genoa.

Despite the celebrated story of Hughes's being "discovered" by the white poet Vachel Lindsay while working as a hotel busboy in 1925, by that point Hughes had already established himself as a bright young star of the New Negro Renaissance. One of his most famous and innovative poems, "The Negro Speaks of Rivers" (dedicated to W.E.B. Du Bois), appeared in the *Crisis* in 1921; the poem was conceived as a proud rejoinder to his absentee father's bitter rejection of American possibilities for African American life. In 1923, the New York's *Amsterdam News* carried his "The Weary Blues." Two years later, his first collection, also entitled *The Weary Blues*, was published.

The most important stage in Langston Hughes's development as a writer was his discovery of New York, of Harlem, of the cultural life and literary circle of the "New Negro" writers: Countee Cullen, Arna Bontemps, Wallace Thurman, Zora Neale Hurston, Eric Walrond, and others. The black revue *Shuffle Along* was on Broadway, and Harlem was the center of a thriving theater and the new music—jazz. Hughes steeped himself in the language, music, and feeling of the common people of Harlem. Proud of his folk heritage, Hughes made the spirituals, blues, and jazz the bases of his poetic expression. Hughes wrote, he contended, "to explain and illuminate the Negro condition in America." As his friends said of him, "No one enjoyed being a Negro as much as Langston Hughes." He portrayed the humor, wit, endurance, and faith of his people with extraordinary skill. Subjected to discrimination and segregation, he remained steadfast in his devotion to human rights. His well-known defense of black writers was typical: "We younger Negro artists who create now intend to express our individual dark skinned selves without fear or shame...."

The versatility of Langston Hughes is evident in his capacity to create in every literary genre—poetry, fiction, drama, essay, and history. He was also the most prolific of black writers; more than twelve volumes of his poetry appeared in his lifetime. Hughes won several prizes, awards, and fellowships and was in constant demand for readings and lectures throughout the world. His fiction is equally distinguished. In addition to his fine coming-of-age novel, *Not Without Laughter* (1930), Langston Hughes created the character of Jesse B. Simple, a lively embodiment of urban black life, whose folk wit and wisdom allowed Hughes to undermine the bourgeois pretensions of our society while pointing out the hypocritical nature of American racism. Like Whitman, Hughes enhances our love of humanity, our vision of the just society with a spiritual transcendence and ever-widening horizons of joy and hope. In its spontaneity and race pride, his poetry found a response among poets of Africa and the Caribbean; and in his own country Hughes served as both an inspiration and a mentor for the younger black writers who came of age in the 1960s. With his rich poetic voice, nurturing generosity, warm humor, and abiding love of black people,

Langston Hughes was one of the dominant voices in American literature of the twentieth century and the single most influential black poet.

Charles H. Nichols
Brown University

PRIMARY WORKS

Poetry: *The Weary Blues,* 1926; *Fine Clothes to the Jew,* 1927; *Shakespeare in Harlem,* 1942; *Montage of a Dream Deferred,* 1951; Fiction: *Not Without Laughter,* 1930; *The Ways of White Folks,* 1934; *The Best of Simple,* 1961; *Something in Common and Other Stories,* 1963; Autobiography: *The Big Sea,* 1940; *I Wonder as I Wander,* 1956; Anthologies edited by Hughes: *The Poetry of the Negro* (with Arna Bontemps), 1949; *The Book of Negro Folklore* (with Arna Bontemps), 1958; *New Negro Poets: U.S.A.,* 1964; *The Best Short Stories by Negro Writers,* 1967; Histories: *A Pictorial History of the Negro in America* (with Milton Meltzer), 1956; *Famous Negro Heroes of America,* 1958; *Fight for Freedom: The Story of the NAACP,* 1962; *Collected Poems,* ed. Arnold Rampersad and David E. Roessel, 1994.

The Negro Speaks of Rivers

I've known rivers:
I've known rivers ancient as the world and older than the flow of
      human blood in human veins.

My soul has grown deep like the rivers.

I bathed in the Euphrates when dawns were young.   5
I built my hut near the Congo and it lulled me to sleep.
I looked upon the Nile and raised the pyramids above it.
I heard the singing of the Mississippi when Abe Lincoln
      went down to New Orleans, and I've seen its muddy
      bosom turn all golden in the sunset.   10

I've known rivers:
Ancient, dusky rivers.

My soul has grown deep like the rivers.

                                             1921

Drum

Bear in mind
That death is a drum
Beating forever
Till the last worms come
To answer its call,   5

Till the last stars fall,
Until the last atom
Is no atom at all,
Until time is lost
And there is no air   10
And space itself
Is nothing nowhere,
Death is a drum,
A signal drum,
Calling life   15
To come!
Come!
Come!

                                                                       1931

The Same

It is the same everywhere for me:
On the docks at Sierra Leone,
In the cotton fields of Alabama,
In the diamond mines of Kimberley,

On the coffee hills of Haiti,   5
The banana lands of Central America,
The streets of Harlem,
And the cities of Morocco and Tripoli.

Black:
Exploited, beaten, and robbed,   10
Shot and killed.
Blood running into

          DOLLARS
          POUNDS
          FRANCS   15
          PESETAS
          LIRE

For the wealth of the exploiters—
Blood that never comes back to me again.
Better that my blood   20
Runs into the deep channels of Revolution,
Runs into the strong hands of Revolution,
Stains all flags red,
Drives me away from

SIERRA LEONE 25
KIMBERLEY
ALABAMA
HAITI
CENTRAL AMERICA
HARLEM 30
MOROCCO
TRIPOLI

And all the black lands everywhere.
The force that kills,
The power that robs, 35
And the greed that does not care.
Better that my blood makes one with the blood
Of all the struggling workers in the world—
Till every land is free of

DOLLAR ROBBERS 40
POUND ROBBERS
FRANC ROBBERS
PESETA ROBBERS
LIRE ROBBERS
LIFE ROBBERS— 45

Until the Red Armies of the International Proletariat
Their faces, black, white, olive, yellow, brown,
Unite to raise the blood-red flag that
Never will come down!

1932

Negro

I am a Negro:
  Black as the night is black,
  Black like the depths of my Africa.

I've been a slave:
  Caesar told me to keep his door-steps clean. 5
  I brushed the boots of Washington.

I've been a worker:
  Under my hand the pyramids arose.
  I made mortar for the Woolworth Building.

I've been a singer: 10
    All the way from Africa to Georgia
    I carried my sorrow songs.
    I made ragtime.

I've been a victim:
    The Belgians cut off my hands in the Congo.   15
    They lynch me still in Mississippi.

I am a Negro:
    Black as the night is black,
    Black like the depths of my Africa.

                        1922

Bad Luck Card

Cause you don't love me
Is awful, awful hard.
Gypsy done showed me
My bad luck card.

There ain't no good left   5
In this world for me.
Gypsy done tole me—
Unlucky as can be.

I don't know what
Po' weary me can do.   10
Gypsy says I'd kill my self
If I was you.

                        1927

I, Too

I, too, sing America.

I am the darker brother.
They send me to eat in the kitchen
When company comes,
But I laugh,   5
And eat well,
And grow strong.

Tomorrow,
I'll be at the table
When company comes.   10
Nobody'll dare
Say to me,
"Eat in the kitchen,"
Then.

Besides,   15
They'll see how beautiful I am
And be ashamed—

I, too, am America.

1925

Dream Variations

To fling my arms wide
In some place of the sun,
To whirl and to dance
Till the white day is done.
Then rest at cool evening   5
Beneath a tall tree
While night comes on gently,
        Dark like me—
That is my dream!

To fling my arms wide   10
In the face of the sun,
Dance! Whirl! Whirl!
Till the quick day is done.
Rest at pale evening . . .
A tall, slim tree . . .   15
Night coming tenderly
        Black like me.

1924

Harlem

What happens to a dream deferred?

    Does it dry up
    like a raisin in the sun?
    Or fester like a sore—

And then run?   5
Does it stink like rotten meat?
Or crust and sugar over—
like a syrupy sweet?

Maybe it just sags
like a heavy load.   10

Or does it explode?

                                                     1951

Freedom Train

I read in the papers about the
    Freedom Train.
I heard on the radio about the
    Freedom Train.
I seen folks talkin' about the   5
    Freedom Train.
Lord, I been a-waitin' for the
    Freedom Train!
Down South in Dixie only train I see's
Got a Jim Crow car set aside for me.   10
I hope there ain't no Jim Crow on the Freedom Train,
No back door entrance to the Freedom Train,
No signs FOR COLORED on the Freedom Train,
No WHITE FOLKS ONLY on the Freedom Train.

        I'm gonna check up on this   15
            Freedom Train.

Who's the engineer on the Freedom Train?
Can a coal black man drive the Freedom Train?
Or am I still a porter on the Freedom Train?
Is there ballot boxes on the Freedom Train?   20
When it stops in Mississippi will it be made plain
Everybody's got a right to board the Freedom Train?

        Somebody tell me about this
            Freedom Train!

The Birmingham station's marked COLORED and WHITE.   25
The white folks go left, the colored go right—
They even got a segregated lane.
Is that the way to get aboard the Freedom Train?

I got to know about this
Freedom Train!   30

If my children ask me, *Daddy, please explain*
Why there's Jim Crow stations for the Freedom Train?
What shall I tell my children? . . . *You* tell me—
'Cause freedom ain't freedom when a man ain't free.

But maybe they explains it on the   35
Freedom Train.

When my grandmother in Atlanta, 83 and black,
Gets in line to see the Freedom,
Will some white man yell, *Get back!*
A Negro's got no business on the Freedom Track!   40

Mister, I thought it were the
Freedom Train!

Her grandson's name was Jimmy. He died at Anzio.
He died for real. It warn't no show.
The freedom that they carryin' on this Freedom Train,   45
Is it for real—or just a show again?

Jimmy wants to know about the
Freedom Train.

Will *his* Freedom Train come zoomin' down the track
Gleamin' in the sunlight for white and black?   50
Not stoppin' at no stations marked COLORED nor WHITE,
Just stoppin' in the fields in the broad daylight,
Stoppin' in the country in the wide-open air
Where there never was no Jim Crow signs nowhere,
No Welcomin' Committees, nor Politicians of note,   55
No Mayors and such for which colored can't vote,
And nary a sign of a color line—
For the Freedom Train will be yours and mine!

Then maybe from their graves in Anzio
The G.I.'s who fought will say, *We wanted it so!*   60
Black men and white will say, *Ain't it fine?*
At home they got a train that's yours and mine!

Then I'll shout, *Glory for the*
Freedom Train!

I'll holler, *Blow your whistle,*
   Freedom Train!
Thank God-A-Mighty! Here's the
   Freedom Train!
Get on board our Freedom Train!

65

1947

Big Meeting

The early stars had begun to twinkle in the August night as Bud and I neared the woods. A great many Negroes, old and young, were plodding down the dirt road on foot on their way to the Big Meeting. Long before we came near the lantern-lighted tent, we could hear early arrivals singing, clapping their hands lustily, and throwing out each word distinct like a drumbeat. Songs like "When the Saints Go Marching Home" and "That Old-Time Religion" filled the air.

In the road that ran past the woods, a number of automobiles and buggies belonging to white people had stopped near the tent so that their occupants might listen to the singing. The whites stared curiously through the hickory trees at the rocking figures in the tent. The canvas, except behind the pulpit, was rolled up on account of the heat, and the meeting could easily be seen from the road, so there beneath a tree Bud and I stopped, too. In our teens, we were young and wild and didn't believe much in revivals, so we stayed outside in the road where we could smoke and laugh like the white folks. But both Bud's mother and mine were under the tent singing, actively a part of the services. Had they known we were near, they would certainly have come out and dragged us in.

From frequent attendance since childhood at these Big Meetings held each summer in the South, we knew the services were divided into three parts. The testimonials and the song-service came first. This began as soon as two or three people were gathered together, continuing until the minister himself arrived. Then the sermon followed, with its accompanying songs and shouts from the audience. Then the climax came with the calling of the lost souls to the mourners' bench, and the prayers for sinners and backsliders. This was where Bud and I would leave. We were having too good a time being sinners, and we didn't want to be saved—not yet, anyway.

When we arrived, old Aunt Ibey Davis was just starting a familiar song:

> *"Where shall I be when that first trumpet sound?*
> *Lawdy, where shall I be when it sound so loud?"*

The rapidly increasing number of worshipers took up the tune in full volume, sending a great flood of melody billowing beneath the canvas roof. With heads back, feet and hands patting time, they repeated the chorus again and again. And each party of new arrivals swung into rhythm as they walked up the aisle by the light of the dim oil lanterns hanging from the tent poles.

Standing there at the edge of the road beneath a big tree, Bud and I watched the people as they came—keeping our eyes open for the girls. Scores of Negroes from the town and nearby villages and farms came, drawn by the music and the preaching. Some were old and gray-headed; some in the prime of life; some mere boys and girls; and many little barefooted children. It was the twelfth night of the Big Meeting. They came from miles around to bathe their souls in a sea of song, to shout and cry and moan before the flow of Reverend Braswell's eloquence, and to pray for all the sinners in the county who had not yet seen the light. Although it was a colored folks' meeting, whites liked to come and sit outside in the road in their cars and listen. Sometimes there would be as many as ten or twelve parties of whites parked there in the dark, smoking and listening, and enjoying themselves, like Bud and I, in a not very serious way.

Even while old Aunt Ibey Davis was singing, a big red Buick drove up and parked right behind Bud and me beneath the tree. It was full of white people, and we recognized the driver as Mr. Parkes, the man who owned the drugstore in town where colored people couldn't buy a glass of soda at the fountain.

> "It will sound so loud it will wake up the dead!
> Lawdy, where shall I be when it sound?"

"You'll hear some good singing out here," Mr. Parkes said to a woman in the car with him.

"I always did love to hear darkies singing," she answered from the back seat.

Bud nudged me in the ribs at the word "darkie."

"I hear 'em," I said, sitting down on one of the gnarled roots of the tree and pulling out a cigarette.

The song ended as an old black woman inside the tent got up to speak. "I rise to testify dis evenin' fo' Jesus!" she said. "Ma Saviour an' ma Redeemer an' de chamber wherein I resusticates ma soul. Pray fo' me, brothers and sisters. Let yo' mercies bless me in all I do an' yo' prayers go with me on each travelin' voyage through dis land."

"Amen! Hallelujah!" cried my mother.

Just in front of us, near the side of the tent, a woman's clear soprano voice began to sing:

> "I am a po' pilgrim of sorrow
> Out in this wide world alone ..."

Soon others joined with her and the whole tent was singing:

> "Sometimes I am tossed and driven,
> Sometimes I don't know where to go ..."

"Real pretty, ain't it?" said the white woman in the car behind us.

> "But I've heard of a city called heaven
> And I've started to make it my home."

When the woman finished her song, she rose and told how her husband left her with six children, her mother died in a poorhouse, and the world had always been against her—but still she was going on!

"My, she's had a hard time," giggled the woman in the car.

"Sure has," laughed Mr. Parkes, "to hear her tell it."

And the way they talked made gooseflesh come out on my skin.

"Trials and tribulations surround me—but I'm goin' on," the woman in the tent cried. Shouts and exclamations of approval broke out all over the congregation.

"Praise God!"

"Bless His Holy Name!"

"That's right, sister!"

"Devils beset me—but I'm goin' on!" said the woman. "I ain't got no friends—but I'm goin' on!"

"Jesus yo' friend, sister! Jesus yo' friend!" came the answer.

"God bless Jesus! I'm goin' on!"

"Dat's right!" cried Sister Mabry, Bud's mother, bouncing in her seat and flinging her arms outward. "Take all this world, but gimme Jesus!"

"Look at Mama," Bud said half amused, sitting there beside me smoking. "She's getting happy."

"Whoo-ooo-o-o! Great Gawd A'mighty!" yelled old man Walls near the pulpit. "I can't hold it dis evenin'! Dis mawnin', dis evenin', dis mawnin', Lawd!"

"Pray for me—cause I'm goin' on!" said the woman. In the midst of the demonstration she had created, she sat down exhausted, her armpits wet with sweat and her face covered with tears.

"Did you hear her, Jehover?" someone asked.

"Yes! He heard her! Halleloo!" came the answer.

"Dis mawnin', dis evenin', dis mawnin', Lawd!"

Brother Nace Eubanks began to line a song:

> *"Must Jesus bear his cross alone*
> *An' all de world go free?"*

Slowly they sang it line by line. Then the old man rose and told of a vision that had come to him long ago on that day when he had been changed from a sinner to a just man.

"I was layin' in ma bed," he said, "at de midnight hour twenty-two years past at Seven hundred fourteen Pine Street in dis here city when a snow-white sheep come in ma room an' stood behind de washbowl. Dis here sheep, hit spoke to me wid tongues o' fiah an' hit said, 'Nace, git up! Git up, an' come wid me!' Yes, suh! He had a light round 'bout his head like a moon, an' wings like a dove, an' he walked on hoofs o' gold an' dis sheep hit said, 'I once were lost, but now I'm saved, an' you kin be like me!' Yes, suh! An' ever since dat night, brothers an' sisters, I's been a chile o' de Lamb! Pray fo' me!"

"Help him, Jesus!" Sister Mabry shouted.

"Amen!" chanted Deacon Laws. "Amen! Amen!"

> *"Glory! Hallelujah!*
> *Let de halleluian roll*
>
> *I'll sing ma Saviour's praises far an' wide!"*

It was my mother's favorite song, and she sang it like a paean of triumph, rising from her seat.

"Look at Ma," I said to Bud, knowing that she was about to start her nightly shouting.

"Yah," Bud said. "I hope she don't see me while she's standing up there, or she'll come out here and make us go up to the mourners' bench."

"We'll leave before that," I said.

> *"I've opened up to heaven*
> *All de windows of ma soul,*
>
> *An' I'm livin' on de halleluian side!"*

Rocking proudly to and fro as the second chorus boomed and swelled beneath the canvas, Mama began to clap her hands, her lips silent now in this sea of song she had started, her head thrown back in joy—for my mother was a great shouter. Stepping gracefully to the beat of the music, she moved out toward the center aisle into a cleared space. Then she began to spring on her toes with little short rhythmical hops. All the way up the long aisle to the pulpit gently she leaped to the clap-clap of hands, the pat of feet, and the steady booming song of her fellow worshipers. Then Mama began to revolve in a dignified circle, slowly, as a great happiness swept her gleaming black features, and her lips curved into a smile.

> *"I've opened up to heaven*
> *All de windows of my soul . . ."*

Mama was dancing before the Lord with her eyes closed, her mouth smiling, and her head held high.

> *"I'm livin' on de halleluian side!"*

As she danced, she threw her hands upward away from her breasts, as though casting off all the cares of the world.

Just then the white woman in Mr. Parkes's car behind us laughed. "My Lord, John, it's better than a show!"

Something about the way she laughed made my blood boil. That was *my mother* dancing and shouting. Maybe it was better than a show, but nobody had any business laughing at her, least of all white people.

I looked at Bud, but he didn't say anything. Maybe he was thinking how often we, too, made fun of the shouters, laughing at our parents as though they were crazy—but deep down inside us we understood why they came to Big Meeting. Working all day all their lives for white folks, they *had* to believe there was a "halleluian side."

I looked at Mama standing there singing, and I thought about how many years she had prayed and shouted and praised the Lord at church meetings and revivals, then came home for a few hours' sleep before getting up at dawn to go cook and scrub and clean for others. And I didn't want any white folks, especially whites who wouldn't let a Negro drink a glass of soda in their drugstore or give one a job, sitting in a car laughing at Mama.

"Gimme a cigarette, Bud. If these dopes behind us say any more, I'm gonna get up and tell 'em something they won't like."

"To hell with 'em," Bud answered.

I leaned back against the gnarled roots of the tree by the road and inhaled deeply. The white people were silent again in their car, listening to the singing. In the dark I couldn't see their faces to tell if they were still amused or not. But that was mostly what they wanted out of Negroes—work and fun—without paying for it, I thought, work and fun.

To a great hand-clapping body-rocking foot-patting rhythm, Mama was repeating the chorus over and over. Sisters leaped and shouted and perspiring brothers walked the aisles, bowing left and right, beating time, shaking hands, laughing aloud for joy, and singing steadily when, at the back of the tent, the Reverend Duke Braswell arrived.

A tall, powerful jet-black man, he moved with long steps through the center of the tent, his iron-gray hair uncovered, his green-black coat jim-swinging to his knees, his fierce eyes looking straight toward the altar. Under his arm he carried a Bible.

Once on the platform, he stood silently wiping his brow with a large white handkerchief while the singing swirled around him. Then he sang, too, his voice roaring like a cyclone, his white teeth shining. Finally he held up his palms for silence and the song gradually lowered to a hum, hum, hum, hands and feet patting, bodies still moving. At last, above the broken cries of the shouters and the undertones of song, the minister was able to make himself heard.

"Brother Garner, offer up a prayer."

Reverend Braswell sank on his knees and every back bowed. Brother Garner, with his head in his hands, lifted his voice against a background of moans:

"Oh, Lawd, we comes befo' you dis evenin' wid fear an' tremblin'—unworthy as we is to enter yo' house an' speak yo' name. We comes befo' you, Lawd, 'cause we knows you is mighty an' powerful in all de lands, an' great above de stars, an' bright above de moon. Oh, Lawd, you is bigger den de world. You holds de sun in yo' right hand an' de mornin' star in you' left, an' we po' sinners ain't nothin', not even so much as a grain o' sand beneath yo' feet. Yet we calls on you dis evenin' to hear us, Lawd, to send down yo' sweet Son Jesus to walk wid us in our sorrows to comfort us on our weary road 'cause sometimes we don't know which-a-way to turn! We pray you dis evenin', Lawd, to look down at our wanderin' chilluns what's gone from home. Look down in St. Louis, Lawd, an' look in Memphis, an' look down in Chicago if they's usin' Thy name in vain dis evenin', if they's gamblin' tonight, Lawd, if they's doin' any ways wrong—reach down an' pull 'em up,

Lawd, an' say, 'Come wid me, cause I am de Vine an' de Husbandman an' de gate dat leads to Glory!'"

Remembering sons in faraway cities, "Help him, Jesus!" mothers cried.

"Whilst you's lookin' down on us dis evenin', keep a mighty eye on de sick an' de 'flicted. Ease Sister Hightower, Lawd, layin' in her bed at de pint o' death. An' bless Bro' Carpenter what's come out to meetin' here dis evenin' in spite o' his broken arm from fallin' off de roof. An' Lawd, aid de pastor dis evenin' to fill dis tent wid yo' Spirit, an' to make de sinners tremble an' backsliders shout, an' dem dat is without de church to come to de moaners' bench an' find rest in Jesus! We ask Thee all dese favors dis evenin'. Also to guide us an' bless us wid Thy bread an' give us Thy wine to drink fo' Christ de Holy Saviour's sake, our Shelter an' our Rock. Amen!"

"There's not a friend like de lowly Jesus ..."

Some sister began, high and clear after the passion of the prayer,

"No, not one! ... No, not one!"

Then the preacher took his text from the open Bible. "Ye now therefore have sorrow: but I will see you again, and your hearts shall rejoice, and your joy no man taketh from you."

He slammed shut the Holy Book and walked to the edge of the platform. "That's what Jesus said befo' he went to the cross, children—'I will see you again, and yo' hearts shall rejoice!'"

"Yes sir!" said the brothers and sisters. "'Deed he did!"

Then the minister began to tell the familiar story of the death of Christ. Standing in the dim light of the smoking oil lanterns, he sketched the life of the man who had had power over multitudes.

"Power," the minister said. "Power! Without money and without titles, without position, he had power! And that power went out to the poor and afflicted. For Jesus said, 'The first shall be last, and the last shall be first.'"

"He sho did!" cried Bud's mother.

"Hallelujah!" Mama agreed loudly. "Glory be to God!"

"Then the big people of the land heard about Jesus," the preacher went on, "the chief priests and the scribes, the politicians, the bootleggers, and the bankers—and they begun to conspire against Jesus because *He had power!* This Jesus with His twelve disciples preachin' in Galilee. Then came that eve of the Passover, when he set down with His friends to eat and drink of the vine and the settin' sun fell behind the hills of Jerusalem. And Jesus knew that ere the cock crew, Judas would betray Him, and Peter would say, 'I know Him not,' and all alone by Hisself He would go to His death. Yes, sir, He knew! So He got up from the table and went into the garden to pray. In this hour of trouble, Jesus went to pray!"

Away at the back of the tent some old sister began to sing:

"Oh, watch with me one hour
While I go yonder and pray ..."

And the crowd took up the song, swelled it, made its melody fill the hot tent while the minister stopped talking to wipe his face with his white handkerchief.

Then, to the humming undertone of the song, he continued, "They called it Gethsemane—that garden where Jesus fell down on His face in the grass and cried to the Father, 'Let this bitter hour pass from me! Oh, God, let this hour pass.' Because He was still a young man who did not want to die, He rose up and went back into the house—but His friends was all asleep. While Jesus prayed, His friends done gone to sleep! But, 'Sleep on,' he said, 'for the hour is at hand.' Jesus said, 'Sleep on.'"

"Sleep on, sleep on," chanted the crowd, repeating the words of the minister.

"He was not angry with them. But as Jesus looked out of the house, He saw that garden alive with men carryin' lanterns and swords and staves, and the mob was everywhere. So He went to the door. Then Judas come out from among the crowd, the traitor Judas, and kissed Him on the cheek— oh, bitter friendship! And the soldiers with handcuffs fell upon the Lord and took Him prisoner.

"The disciples was awake by now, oh yes! But they fled away because they was afraid. And the mob carried Jesus off.

"Peter followed Him from afar, followed Jesus in chains till they come to the palace of the high priest. There Peter went in, timid and afraid, to see the trial. He set in the back of the hall. Peter listened to the lies they told about Christ—and didn't dispute 'em. He watched the high priest spit in Christ's face—and made no move. He saw 'em smite Him with the palms of they hands—and Peter uttered not a word for his poor mistreated Jesus."

"Not a word! . . . Not a word! . . . Not a word!"

"And when the servants of the high priest asked Peter, 'Does you know this man?' he said, 'I do not!'

"And when they asked him a second time, he said, 'No!'

"And yet a third time, 'Do you know Jesus?'

"And Peter answered with an oath, 'I told you, no!'

"Then the cock crew."

"De cock crew!" cried Aunt Ibey Davis. "De cock crew! Oh, ma Lawd! De cock crew!"

"The next day the chief priests taken counsel against Jesus to put Him to death. They brought Him before Pilate, and Pilate said, 'What evil hath he done?'

"But the people cried, 'Crucify Him!' because they didn't care. So Pilate called for water and washed his hands.

"The soldiers made sport of Jesus where He stood in the Council Hall. They stripped Him naked, and put a crown of thorns on His head, a red robe about His body, and a reed from the river in His hands.

"They said, 'Ha! Ha! So you're the King! Ha! Ha!' And they bowed down in mockery before Him, makin' fun of Jesus.

"Some of the guards threw wine in His face. Some of the guards was drunk and called Him out o' His name—and nobody said, 'Stop! That's Jesus!'"

The Reverend Duke Braswell's face darkened with horror as he pictured the death of Christ. "Oh yes! Peter denied Him because he was afraid. Judas betrayed Him for thirty pieces of silver. Pilate said, 'I wash my hands—take Him and kill Him.'

"And His friends fled away! ... Have mercy on Jesus! ... His friends done fled away!"

"His friends!"

"His friends done fled away!"

The preacher chanted, half moaning his sentences, not speaking them. His breath came in quick, short gasps, with an indrawn "umn!" between each rapid phrase. Perspiration poured down his face as he strode across the platform, wrapped in this drama that he saw in the very air before his eyes. Peering over the heads of his audience out into the darkness, he began the ascent to Golgotha, describing the taunting crowd at Christ's heels and the heavy cross on His shoulders.

"Then a black man named Simon, blacker than me, come and took the cross and bore it for Him. Umn!

"Then Jesus were standin' alone on a high hill, in the broilin' sun, while they put the crosses in the ground. No water to cool His throat! No tree to shade His achin' head! Nobody to say a friendly word to Jesus! Umn!

"Alone, in that crowd on the hill of Golgotha, with two thieves bound and dyin', and the murmur of the mob all around. Umn!

"They laid they hands on Him, and they tore the clothes from His body—and then, and then"—loud as a thunderclap, the minister's voice broke through the little tent—"they raised Him to the cross!"

A great wail went up from the crowd. Bud and I sat entranced in spite of ourselves, forgetting to smoke. Aunt Ibey Davis wept. Sister Mabry moaned. In their car behind us the white people were silent as the minister went on:

> "They brought four long iron nails
> And put one in the palm of His left hand.
> The hammer said ... Bam!
> They put one in the palm of His right hand.
> The hammer said ... Bam!
> They put one through His left foot ... Bam!
> And one through His right foot ... Bam!"

"Don't drive it!" a woman screamed. "Don't drive them nails! For Christ's sake! Oh! Don't drive 'em!"

> "And they left my Jesus on the cross!
> Nails in His hands! Nails in His feet!
> Sword in His side! Thorns circlin' His head!
> Mob cussin' and hootin' my Jesus! Umn!
> The spit of the mob in His face! Umn!

His body hangin' on the cross! Umn!
Gimme piece of His garment for a souvenir! Umn!
Castin' lots for His garments! Umn!
Blood from His wounded side! Umn!
Streamin' down His naked legs! Umn!
Droppin' in the dust—umn—
That's what they did to my Jesus!
They stoned Him first, they stoned Him!
Called Him everything but a child of God.
Then they lynched Him on the cross."

In song I heard my mother's voice cry:

"Were you there when they crucified my Lord?
Were you there when they nailed Him to the tree?"

The Reverend Duke Braswell stretched wide his arms against the white canvas of the tent. In the yellow light his body made a cross-like shadow on the canvas.

"Oh, it makes me to tremble, tremble!
Were you there when they crucified my Lord?"

"Let's go," said the white woman in the car behind us. "This is too much for me!" They started the motor and drove noisily away in a swirl of dust.

"Don't go," I cried from where I was sitting at the root of the tree. "Don't go," I shouted, jumping up. "They're about to call for sinners to come to the mourners' bench. Don't go!" But their car was already out of earshot.

I didn't realize I was crying until I tasted my tears in my mouth.

1935

The Negro Artist and the Racial Mountain[1]

One of the most promising of the young Negro poets said to me once, "I want to be a poet—not a Negro poet," meaning, I believe, "I want to write like a white poet"; meaning subconsciously, "I would like to be a white poet"; meaning behind that, "I would like to be white." And I was sorry the young man said that, for no great poet has ever been afraid of being himself. And I doubted then that, with his desire to run away spiritually from his race, this boy would ever be a great poet. But this is the mountain standing in the way of any true Negro art in America—this urge within the race toward whiteness, the desire to pour racial individuality into the mold of American standardization, and to be as little Negro and as much American as possible.

But let us look at the immediate background of this young poet. His family is of what I suppose one would call the Negro middle class: people

---

[1]This essay can fruitfully be read as a response to George Schuyler's "The Negro-Art Hokum" (p. 1631), which had appeared in *The Nation* the week before Hughes's "The Negro Artist."

who are by no means rich yet never uncomfortable nor hungry—smug, contented, respectable folk, members of the Baptist church. The father goes to work every morning. He is a chief steward at a large white club. The mother sometimes does fancy sewing or supervises parties for the rich families of the town. The children go to a mixed school. In the home they read white papers and magazines. And the mother often says "Don't be like niggers" when the children are bad. A frequent phrase from the father is, "Look how well a white man does things." And so the word white comes to be unconsciously a symbol of all the virtues. It holds for the children beauty, morality, and money. The whisper of "I want to be white" runs silently through their minds. This young poet's home is, I believe, a fairly typical home of the colored middle class. One sees immediately how difficult it would be for an artist born in such a home to interest himself in interpreting the beauty of his own people. He is never taught to see that beauty. He is taught rather not to see it, or if he does, to be ashamed of it when it is not according to Caucasian patterns.

For racial culture the home of a self-styled "high-class" Negro has nothing better to offer. Instead there will perhaps be more aping of things white than in a less cultured or less wealthy home. The father is perhaps a doctor, lawyer, landowner, or politician. The mother may be a social worker, or a teacher, or she may do nothing and have a maid. Father is often dark but he has usually married the lightest woman he could find. The family attend a fashionable church where few really colored faces are to be found. And they themselves draw a color line. In the North they go to white theatres and white movies. And in the South they have at least two cars and a house "like white folks." Nordic manners, Nordic faces, Nordic hair, Nordic art (if any), and an Episcopal heaven. A very high mountain indeed for the would-be racial artist to climb in order to discover himself and his people.

But then there are the low-down folks, the so-called common element, and they are the majority—may the Lord be praised! The people who have their nip of gin on Saturday nights and are not too important to themselves or the community, or too well fed, or too learned to watch the lazy world go round. They live on Seventh Street in Washington or State Street in Chicago and they do not particularly care whether they are like white folks or anybody else. Their joy runs, bang! into ecstasy. Their religion soars to a shout. Work maybe a little today, rest a little tomorrow. Play awhile. Sing awhile. O, let's dance! These common people are not afraid of spirituals, as for a long time their more intellectual brethren were, and jazz is their child. They furnish a wealth of colorful, distinctive material for any artist because they still hold their own individuality in the face of American standardizations. And perhaps these common people will give to the world its truly great Negro artist, the one who is not afraid to be himself. Whereas the better-class Negro would tell the artist what to do, the people at least let him alone when he does appear. And they are not ashamed of him—if they know he exists at all. And they accept what beauty is their own without question.

Certainly there is, for the American Negro artist who can escape the restrictions the more advanced among his own group would put upon him, a great field of unused material ready for his art. Without going outside his race, and even among the better classes with their "white" culture and conscious American manners, but still Negro enough to be different, there is sufficient matter to furnish a black artist with a lifetime of creative work. And when he chooses to touch on the relations between Negroes and whites in this country with their innumerable overtones and undertones surely, and especially for literature and the drama, there is an inexhaustible supply of themes at hand. To these the Negro artist can give his racial individuality, his heritage of rhythm and warmth, and his incongruous humor that so often, as in the Blues, becomes ironic laughter mixed with tears. But let us look again at the mountain.

A prominent Negro clubwoman in Philadelphia paid eleven dollars to hear Raquel Meller sing Andalusian popular songs. But she told me a few weeks before she would not think of going to hear "that woman," Clara Smith, a great black artist, sing Negro folksongs. And many an upper-class Negro church, even now, would not dream of employing a spiritual in its services. The drab melodies in white folks' hymnbooks are much to be preferred. "We want to worship the Lord correctly and quietly. We don't believe in 'shouting.' Let's be dull like the Nordics," they say, in effect.

The road for the serious black artist, then, who would produce a racial art is most certainly rocky and the mountain is high. Until recently he received almost no encouragement for his work from either white or colored people. The fine novels of Chesnutt go out of print with neither race noticing their passing. The quaint charm and humor of Dunbar's dialect verse brought to him, in his day, largely the same kind of encouragement one would give a sideshow freak (A colored man writing poetry! How odd!) or a clown (How amusing!).

The present vogue in things Negro, although it may do as much harm as good for the budding colored artist, has at least done this: it has brought him forcibly to the attention of his own people among whom for so long, unless the other race had noticed him beforehand, he was a prophet with little honor. I understand that Charles Gilpin acted for years in Negro theatres without any special acclaim from his own, but when Broadway gave him eight curtain calls, Negroes, too, began to beat a tin pan in his honor. I know a young colored writer, a manual worker by day, who had been writing well for the colored magazines for some years, but it was not until he recently broke into the white publications and his first book was accepted by a prominent New York publisher that the "best" Negroes in his city took the trouble to discover that he lived there. Then almost immediately they decided to give a grand dinner for him. But the society ladies were careful to whisper to his mother that perhaps she'd better not come. They were not sure she would have an evening gown.

The Negro artist works against an undertow of sharp criticism and misunderstanding from his own group and unintentional bribes from the whites. "Oh, be respectable, write about nice people, show how good we are," say the Negroes. "Be stereotyped, don't go too far, don't shatter our illusions about you, don't amuse us too seriously. We will pay you," say the whites. Both would have told Jean Toomer not to write *Cane*. The colored people did not praise it. The white people did not buy it. Most of the colored people who did read *Cane* hate it. They are afraid of it. Although the critics gave it good reviews the public remained indifferent. Yet (excepting the work of Du Bois) *Cane* contains the finest prose written by a Negro in America. And like the singing of Robeson, it is truly racial.

But in spite of the Nordicized Negro intelligentsia and the desires of some white editors we have an honest America Negro literature already with us. Now I await the rise of the Negro theatre. Our folk music, having achieved world-wide fame, offers itself to the genius of the great individual American composer who is to come. And within the next decade I expect to see the work of a growing school of colored artists who paint and model the beauty of dark faces and create with new technique the expressions of their own soul-world. And the Negro dancers who will dance like flame and the singers who will continue to carry our songs to all who listen—they will be with us in even greater numbers tomorrow.

Most of my own poems are racial in theme and treatment, derived from the life I know. In many of them I try to grasp and hold some of the meanings and rhythms of jazz. I am as sincere as I know how to be in these poems and yet after every reading I answer questions like these from my own people: Do you think Negroes should always write about Negroes? I wish you wouldn't read some of your poems to white folks. How do you find anything interesting in a place like a cabaret? Why do you write about black people? You aren't black. What makes you do so many jazz poems?

But jazz to me is one of the inherent expressions of Negro life in America; the eternal tom-tom beating in the Negro soul—the tom-tom of revolt against weariness in a white world, a world of subway trains, and work, work, work; the tom-tom of joy and laughter, and pain swallowed in a smile. Yet the Philadelphia clubwoman is ashamed to say that her race created it and she does not like me to write about it. The old subconscious "white is best" runs through her mind. Years of study under white teachers, a lifetime of white books, pictures, and papers, and white manners, morals, and Puritan standards made her dislike the spirituals. And now she turns up her nose at jazz and all its manifestations—likewise almost everything else distinctly racial. She doesn't care for the Winold Reiss portraits of Negroes because they are "too Negro." She does not want a true picture of herself from anybody. She wants the artist to flatter her, to make the white world believe that all Negroes are as smug and as near white in soul as she wants to be. But, to my mind, it is the duty of the younger Negro artist, if he accepts any duties at all from outsiders, to change through the force of his art that old whispering "I want to be white," hidden in the aspirations of his people, to "Why should I want to be white? I am a Negro— and beautiful!"

So I am ashamed for the black poet who says, "I want to be a poet, not a Negro poet," as though his own racial world were not as interesting as any other world. I am ashamed, too, for the colored artist who runs from the painting of Negro faces to the painting of sunsets after the manner of the academicians because he fears the strange un-whiteness of his own features. An artist must be free to choose what he does, certainly, but he must also never be afraid to do what he might choose.

Let the blare of Negro jazz bands and the bellowing voice of Bessie Smith singing Blues penetrate the closed ears of the colored near-intellectuals until they listen and perhaps understand. Let Paul Robeson singing "Water Boy," and Rudolph Fisher writing about the streets of Harlem, and Jean Toomer holding the heart of Georgia in his hands, and Aaron Douglas drawing strange black fantasies cause the smug Negro middle class to turn from their white, respectable, ordinary books and papers to catch a glimmer of their own beauty. We younger Negro artists who create now intend to express our individual dark-skinned selves without fear or shame. If white people are pleased we are glad. If they are not, it doesn't matter. We know we are beautiful. And ugly too. The tom-tom cries and the tom-tom laughs. If colored people are pleased we are glad. If they are not, their displeasure doesn't matter either. We build our temples for tomorrow, strong as we know how, and we stand on top of the mountain, free within ourselves.

1926

When the Negro Was in Vogue

The 1920s were the years of Manhattan's black Renaissance. It began with *Shuffle Along, Running Wild,* and the Charleston. Perhaps some people would say even with *The Emperor Jones,* Charles Gilpin, and the tom-toms at the Provincetown. But certainly it was the musical revue, *Shuffle Along,* that gave a scintillating send-off to that Negro vogue in Manhattan, which reached its peak just before the crash of 1929, the crash that sent Negroes, white folks, and all rolling down the hill toward the Works Progress Administration.

Shuffle Along was a honey of a show. Swift, bright, funny, rollicking, and gay, with a dozen danceable, singable tunes. Besides, look who were in it: The now famous choir director, Hall Johnson, and the composer, William Grant Still, were a part of the orchestra. Eubie Blake and Noble Sissle wrote the music and played and acted in the show. Miller and Lyles were the comics. Florence Mills skyrocketed to fame in the second act. Trixie Smith sang "He May Be Your Man But He Comes to See Me Sometimes." And Caterina Jarboro, now a European prima donna, and the internationally celebrated Josephine Baker were merely in the chorus. Everybody was in the audience—including me. People came back to see it innumerable times. It was always packed.

To see *Shuffle Along* was the main reason I wanted to go to Columbia. When I saw it, I was thrilled and delighted. From then on I was in the gallery of the Cort Theatre every time I got a chance. That year, too, I saw Katharine Cornell in *A Bill of Divorcement*, Margaret Wycherly in *The Verge*, Maugham's *The Circle* with Mrs. Leslie Carter, and the Theatre Guild production of Kaiser's *From Morn Till Midnight*. But I remember *Shuffle Along* best of all. It gave just the proper push—a pre-Charleston kick—to that Negro vogue of the 20's, that spread to books, African sculpture, music, and dancing.

Put down the 1920's for the rise of Roland Hayes, who packed Carnegie Hall, the rise of Paul Robeson in New York and London, of Florence Mills over two continents, of Rose McClendon in Broadway parts that never measured up to her, the booming voice of Bessie Smith and the low moan of Clara on thousands of records, and the rise of that grand comedienne of song, Ethel Waters, singing: "Charlie's elected now! He's in right for sure!" Put down the 1920's for Louis Armstrong and Gladys Bentley and Josephine Baker.

White people began to come to Harlem in droves. For several years they packed the expensive Cotton Club on Lenox Avenue. But I was never there, because the Cotton Club was a Jim Crow club for gangsters and monied whites. They were not cordial to Negro patronage, unless you were a celebrity like Bojangles. So Harlem Negroes did not like the Cotton Club and never appreciated its Jim Crow policy in the very heart of their dark community. Nor did ordinary Negroes like the growing influx of whites toward Harlem after sundown, flooding the little cabarets and bars where formerly only colored people laughed and sang, and where now the strangers were given the best ringside tables to sit and stare at the Negro customers—like amusing animals in a zoo.

The Negroes said: "We can't go downtown and sit and stare at you in your clubs. You won't even let us in your clubs." But they didn't say it out loud—for Negroes are practically never rude to white people. So thousands of whites came to Harlem night after night, thinking the Negroes loved to have them there, and firmly believing that all Harlemites left their houses at sundown to sing and dance in cabarets, because most of the whites saw nothing but the cabarets, not the houses.

Some of the owners of Harlem clubs, delighted at the flood of white patronage, made the grievous error of barring their own race, after the manner of the famous Cotton Club. But most of these quickly lost business and folded up, because they failed to realize that a large part of the Harlem attraction for downtown New Yorkers lay in simply watching the colored customers amuse themselves. And the smaller clubs, of course, had no big floor shows or a name band like the Cotton Club, where Duke Ellington usually held forth, so, without black patronage, they were not amusing at all.

Some of the small clubs, however, had people like Gladys Bentley, who was something worth discovering in those days, before she got famous, acquired an accompanist, specially written material, and conscious vulgarity. But for two or three amazing years, Miss Bentley sat, and played a big piano all night long, literally all night, without stopping—singing songs like "The

St. James Infirmary," from ten in the evening until dawn, with scarcely a break between the notes, sliding from one song to another, with a powerful and continuous underbeat of jungle rhythm. Miss Bentley was an amazing exhibition of musical energy—a large, dark, masculine lady, whose feet pounded the floor while her fingers pounded the keyboard—a perfect piece of African sculpture, animated by her own rhythm.

But when the place where she played became too well known, she began to sing with an accompanist, became a star, moved to a larger place, then downtown, and is now in Hollywood. The old magic of the woman and the piano and the night and the rhythm being one is gone. But everything goes, one way or another. The '20's are gone and lots of fine things in Harlem night life have disappeared like snow in the sun—since it became utterly commercial, planned for the downtown tourist trade, and therefore dull.

The lindy-hoppers at the Savoy even began to practise acrobatic routines, and to do absurd things for the entertainment of the whites, that probably never would have entered their heads to attempt merely for their own effortless amusement. Some of the lindy-hoppers had cards printed with their names on them and became dance professors teaching the tourists. Then Harlem nights became show nights for the Nordics.

Some critics say that that is what happened to certain Negro writers, too—that they ceased to write to amuse themselves and began to write to amuse and entertain white people, and in so doing distorted and over-colored their material, and left out a great many things they thought would offend their American brothers of a lighter complexion. Maybe—since Negroes have writer-racketeers, as has any other race. But I have known almost all of them, and most of the good ones have tried to be honest, write honestly, and express their world as they saw it.

All of us know that the gay and sparkling life of the so-called Negro Renaissance of the '20's was not so gay and sparkling beneath the surface as it looked. Carl Van Vechten, in the character of Byron in *Nigger Heaven*, captured some of the bitterness and frustration of literary Harlem that Wallace Thurman later so effectively poured into his *Infants of the Spring*—the only novel by a Negro about that fantastic period when Harlem was in vogue.

It was a period when, at almost every Harlem upper-crust dance or party, one would be introduced to various distinguished white celebrities there as guests. It was a period when almost any Harlem Negro of any social importance at all would be likely to say casually: "As I was remarking the other day to Heywood—," meaning Heywood Broun. Or: "As I said to George—," referring to George Gershwin. It was a period when local and visiting royalty were not at all uncommon in Harlem. And when the parties of A'Lelia Walker, the Negro heiress, were filled with guests whose names would turn any Nordic social climber green with envy. It was a period when Harold Jackman, a handsome young Harlem school teacher of modest means, calmly announced one day that he was sailing for the Riviera for a fortnight, to attend Princess Murat's yachting party. It was a period when Charleston preachers opened up shouting churches as sideshows for white tourists. It was a period when at least one charming colored chorus girl, amber enough to pass for a Latin American, was living in a pent house, with all her bills paid by a gentleman whose name was banker's magic on Wall Street. It was a period when every season there was at least one hit play on Broadway acted by a Negro cast. And when books by Negro authors were being published with much greater frequency and much more publicity than ever before or since in history. It was a period when white writers wrote about Negroes more successfully (commercially speaking) than Negroes did about themselves. It was the period (God help us!) when Ethel Barrymore appeared in blackface in *Scarlet Sister Mary!* It was the period when the Negro was in vogue.

I was there. I had a swell time while it lasted. But I thought it wouldn't last long. (I remember the vogue for things Russian, the season the Chauve-Souris first came to town.) For how could a large and enthusiastic number of people be crazy about Negroes forever? But some Harlemites thought the millennium had come. They thought the race problem had at last been solved through Art plus Gladys Bentley. They were sure the New Negro would lead a new life from then on in green pastures of tolerance created by Countee Cullen, Ethel Waters, Claude McKay, Duke Ellington, Bojangles, and Alain Locke.

I don't know what made any Negroes think that—except that they were mostly intellectuals doing the thinking. The ordinary Negroes hadn't heard of the Negro Renaissance. And if they had, it hadn't raised their wages any. As for all those white folks in the speakeasies and night clubs of Harlem— well, maybe a colored man could find *some* place to have a drink that the tourists hadn't yet discovered.

Then it was that house-rent parties began to flourish—and not always to raise the rent either. But, as often as not, to have a get-together of one's own, where you could do the black-bottom with no stranger behind you trying to do it, too. Non-theatrical, non-intellectual Harlem was an unwilling victim of its own vogue. It didn't like to be stared at by white folks. But perhaps the downtowners never knew this—for the cabaret owners, the entertainers, and the speakeasy proprietors treated them fine—as long as they paid.

The Saturday night rent parties that I attended were often more amusing than any night club, in small apartments where God knows who lived— because the guests seldom did—but where the piano would often be augmented by a guitar, or an odd cornet, or somebody with a pair of drums walking in off the street. And where awful bootleg whiskey and good fried fish or steaming chitterling were sold at very low prices. And the dancing and singing and impromptu entertaining went on until dawn came in at the windows.

These parties, often termed whist parties or dances, were usually announced by brightly colored cards stuck in the grille of apartment house elevators. Some of the cards were highly entertaining in themselves:

We got yellow girls, we've got black and tan
Will you have a good time? - YEAH MAN !

A Social Whist Party

—GIVEN BY—

MARY WINSTON

147 West 145th Street   Apt. 5

SATURDAY EVE., MARCH 19th, 1932

GOOD MUSIC   REFRESHMENTS

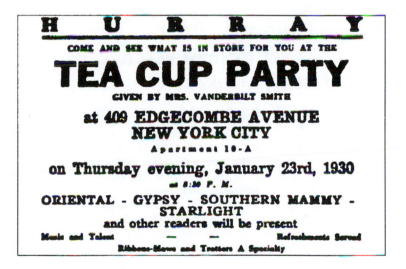

H U R R A Y

COME AND SEE WHAT IS IN STORE FOR YOU AT THE

TEA CUP PARTY

GIVEN BY MRS. VANDERBILT SMITH

at 409 EDGECOMBE AVENUE
NEW YORK CITY

Apartment 10-A

on Thursday evening, January 23rd, 1930

at 8:30 P. M.

ORIENTAL - GYPSY - SOUTHERN MAMMY - STARLIGHT
and other readers will be present

Music and Talent   —   —   Refreshments Served

Ribbons-Bows and Trotters A Specialty

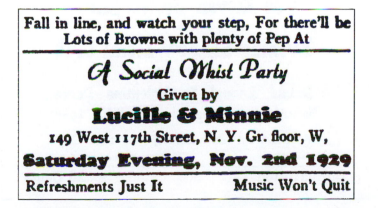

Fall in line, and watch your step, For there'll be
Lots of Browns with plenty of Pep At

A Social Whist Party

Given by

Lucille & Minnie

149 West 117th Street, N. Y. Gr. floor, W,

Saturday Evening, Nov. 2nd 1929

Refreshments Just It   Music Won't Quit

If Sweet Mamma is running wild, and you are looking
for a Do-right child, just come around and
linger awhile at a

SOCIAL WHIST PARTY

GIVEN BY

PINKNEY & EPPS

260 West 129th Street   Apartment 10

SATURDAY EVENING, JUNE 9, 1928

GOOD MUSIC   REFRESHMENTS

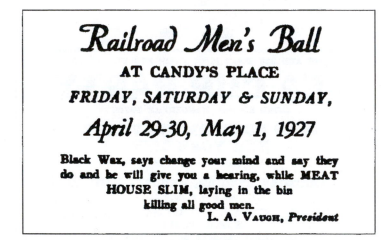

Railroad Men's Ball

AT CANDY'S PLACE

FRIDAY, SATURDAY & SUNDAY,

April 29-30, May 1, 1927

Black Wax, says change your mind and say they
do and he will give you a hearing, while MEAT
HOUSE SLIM, laying in the bin
killing all good men.

L. A. VAUGH, *President*

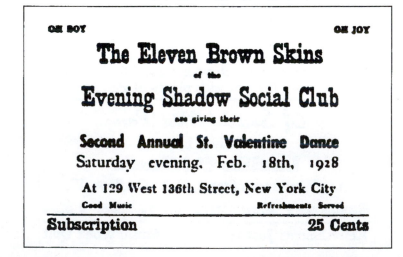

OH BOY   OH JOY

The Eleven Brown Skins

of the

Evening Shadow Social Club

are giving their

Second Annual St. Valentine Dance

Saturday evening. Feb. 18th, 1928

At 129 West 136th Street, New York City

Good Music   Refreshments Served

Subscription   **25 Cents**

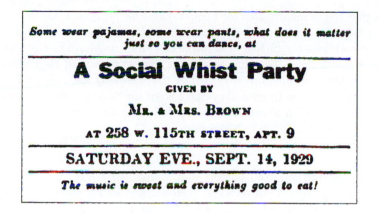

Some wear pajamas, some wear pants, what does it matter just so you can dance, at

A Social Whist Party

GIVEN BY

Mr. & Mrs. Brown

AT 258 W. 115TH STREET, APT. 9

SATURDAY EVE., SEPT. 14, 1929

The music is sweet and everything good to eat!

Almost every Saturday night when I was in Harlem I went to a house-rent party. I wrote lots of poems about house-rent parties, and ate thereat many a fried fish and pig's foot—with liquid refreshments on the side. I met ladies' maids and truck drivers, laundry workers and shoe shine boys, seamstresses and porters. I can still hear their laughter in my ears, hear the soft slow music, and feel the floor shaking as the dancers danced.

1940

Radioactive Red Caps

"How wonderful," I said, "that Negroes today are being rapidly integrated into every phase of American life from the Army and Navy to schools to industries—advancing, advancing!"

"I have not advanced one step," said Simple. "Still the same old job, same old salary, same old kitchenette, same old Harlem and the same old color."

"You are just one individual," I said. "I am speaking of our race in general. Look how many colleges have opened up to Negroes in the last ten years. Look at the change in restrictive covenants. You can live anywhere."

"You mean *try* to live anywhere."

"Look at the way you can ride unsegregated in interstate travel."

"And get throwed off the bus."

"Look at the ever greater number of Negroes in high places."

"Name me one making an atom bomb."

"That would be top-secret information," I said, "even if I knew. Anyway, you are arguing from supposition, not knowledge. How do you know what our top Negro scientists are doing?"

"I don't," said Simple. "But I bet if one was making an atom bomb, they would have his picture on the cover of *Jet* every other week like Eartha Kitt, just to make Negroes think the atom bomb is an integrated bomb. Then, next thing you know, some old Southern senator would up and move to have that Negro investigated for being subversive, because he would be mad that a Negro ever got anywhere near an atom bomb. Then that Negro would be removed from his job like Miss Annie Lee Moss, and have to hire a lawyer to get halfway back. Then they would put that whitewashed Negro to making plain little old-time ordinary bombs that can only kill a few folks at a time. You know and I know, they don't want no Negroes nowhere near no bomb that can kill a whole state full of folks like an atom bomb can. Just think what would happen to Mississippi. Wow!"

"Your thinking borders on the subversive," I warned. "Do you want to fight the Civil War over again?"

"Not without an atom bomb," said Simple. "If I was in Mississippi, I would be Jim Crowed out of bomb shelters, so I would need some kind of protection. By the time I got the N.A.A.C.P. to take my case to the Supreme Court, the war would be over, else I would be atomized."

"Absurd!" I said. "Bomb shelters will be for everybody."

"Not in Mississippi," said Simple. "Down there they will have some kind of voting test, else loyalty test, in which they will find some way of flunking Negroes out. You can't tell me them Dixiecrats are going to give Negroes free rein of bomb shelters. On the other hand, come to think of it, they might *have* to let us in to save their own skins, because I hear tell in the next war everything that ain't sheltered will be so charged with atoms a human can't touch it. Even the garbage is going to get radioactive when the bombs start falling. I read last week in the *News* that, in case of a bombing, it will be a problem as to where to put our garbage, because it will be radioactive up to a million years. So you sure can't keep garbage around. If you dump it in the sea, it will make the fish radioactive, too, like them Japanese tunas nobody could eat. I am wondering what the alley cats will eat— because if all the garbage is full of atomic rays, and the cats eat the garbage, and my wife pets a strange cat, Joyce will be radioactive, too. Then if I pet my wife, what will happen to me?"

"You are stretching the long arm of coincidence mighty far," I said. "What is more likely to happen is, if the bombs fall, you will be radioactive long before the garbage will."

"That will worry white folks," said Simple. "Just suppose all the Negroes down South got atomized, charged up like hot garbage, who would serve the white folks' tables, nurse their children, Red Cap their bags, and make up their Pullman berths? Just think! Suppose all the colored Red Caps carrying bags on the Southern Railroad was atom-charged! Suitcases would get atomized, too, and all that is packed in them. Every time a white man took out his toothbrush to wash his teeth on the train, his teeth would get atom-charged. How could he kiss his wife when he got home?"

"I believe you are charged now," I said.

"No," said Simple, "I am only thinking how awful this atom bomb can be! If one fell up North in Harlem and charged me, then I went downtown and punched that time clock where I work, the clock would be charged. Then a white fellow would come along behind me and punch the time clock, and he would be charged. Then both of us would be so full of atoms for the next million years, that at any time we would be liable to explode like firecrackers on the Fourth of July. And from us, everybody else in the plant would get charged. Atoms, they tell me, is catching. What I read in the *News* said that if you even look at an atom bomb going off, the rays are so strong your eyes will water the rest of your life, your blood will turn white, your hair turn gray, and your children will be born backwards. Your breakfast eggs will no longer be sunny-side up, but scrambled, giving off sparks—and people will give off sparks, too. If you walk down the street, every doorbell you pass will ring without your touching it. If you pick up a phone, whoever answers it will be atomized. So if you know somebody you don't like, for example, just phone them—and you can really fix them up! That's what they call a chain reaction. I am getting my chain ready now—the first person I am going to telephone is my former landlady! When she picks up the phone, I hope to atomize her like a Japanese tuna! She will drive a Geiger counter crazy after I say, 'Hello!'"

"My dear boy," I said, "what makes you think you, of all people, would be able to go around transferring atomic radiation to others? You would probably be annihilated yourself by the very first bomb blast."

"Me? Oh, no," said Simple. "Negroes are very hard to annihilate. I am a Negro—so I figure I would live to radiate and, believe me, once charged, I will take charge."

"In other words, come what may, you expect to survive the atom bomb?"

"If Negroes can survive white folks in Mississippi," said Simple, "we can survive anything."

1961

Thank You, M'am

She was a large woman with a large purse that had everything in it but a hammer and nails. It had a long strap, and she carried it slung across her shoulder. It was about eleven o'clock at night, dark, and she was walking alone, when a boy ran up behind her and tried to snatch her purse. The strap broke with the sudden single tug the boy gave it from behind. But the boy's weight and the weight of the purse combined caused him to lose his balance. Instead of taking off full blast as he had hoped, the boy fell on his back on the sidewalk and his legs flew up. The large woman simply turned around and kicked him right square in his blue-jeaned sitter. Then she reached down, picked the boy up by his shirt front, and shook him until his teeth rattled.

After that the woman said, "Pick up my pocketbook, boy, and give it here."

She still held him tightly. But she bent down enough to permit him to stoop and pick up her purse. Then she said, "Now ain't you ashamed of yourself?"

Firmly gripped by his shirt front, the boy said, "Yes'm."

The woman said, "What did you want to do it for?"

The boy said, "I didn't aim to."

She said, "You a lie!"

By that time two or three people passed, stopped, turned to look, and some stood watching.

"If I turn you loose, will you run?" asked the woman.

"Yes'm," said the boy.

"Then I won't turn you loose," said the woman. She did not release him.

"Lady, I'm sorry," whispered the boy.

"Um-hum! Your face is dirty. I got a great mind to wash your face for you. Ain't you got nobody home to tell you to wash your face?"

"No'm," said the boy.

"Then it will get washed this evening," said the large woman, starting up the street, dragging the frightened boy behind her.

He looked as if he were fourteen or fifteen, frail and willow-wild, in tennis shoes and blue jeans.

The woman said, "You ought to be my son. I would teach you right from wrong. Least I can do right now is to wash your face. Are you hungry?"

"No'm," said the being-dragged boy. "I just want you to turn me loose."

"Was I bothering *you* when I turned that corner?" asked the woman.

"No'm."

"But you put yourself in contact with *me*," said the woman. "If you think that that contact is not going to last awhile, you got another thought coming. When I get through with you, sir, you are going to remember Mrs. Luella Bates Washington Jones."

Sweat popped out on the boy's face and he began to struggle. Mrs. Jones stopped, jerked him around in front of her, put a half nelson about his neck, and continued to drag him up the street. When she got to her door, she dragged the boy inside, down a hall, and into a large kitchenette-furnished room at the rear of the house. She switched on the light and left the door open. The boy could hear other roomers laughing and talking in the large house. Some of their doors were open, too, so he knew he and the woman were not alone. The woman still had him by the neck in the middle of her room.

She said, "What is your name?"

"Roger," answered the boy.

"Then, Roger, you go to that sink and wash your face," said the woman, whereupon she turned him loose—at last. Roger looked at the door—looked at the woman—looked at the door—*and went to the sink.*

"Let the water run until it gets warm," she said. "Here's a clean towel."

"You gonna take me to jail?" asked the boy, bending over the sink.

"Not with that face, I would not take you nowhere," said the woman. "Here I am trying to get home to cook me a bite to eat, and you snatch my pocketbook! Maybe you ain't been to your supper either, late as it be. Have you?"

"There's nobody home at my house," said the boy.

"Then we'll eat," said the woman. "I believe you're hungry—or been hungry—to try to snatch my pocketbook!"

"I want a pair of blue suede shoes," said the boy.

"Well, you didn't have to snatch *my* pocketbook to get some suede shoes," said Mrs. Luella Bates Washington Jones. "You could of asked me."

"M'am?"

The water dripping from his face, the boy looked at her. There was a long pause. A very long pause. After he had dried his face and not knowing what else to do, dried it again, the boy turned around, wondering what next. The door was open. He could make a dash for it down the hall. He could run, run, run, *run!*

The woman was sitting on the day bed. After a while she said, "I were young once and I wanted things I could not get."

There was another long pause. The boy's mouth opened. Then he frowned, not knowing he frowned.

The woman said, "Um-hum! You thought I was going to say *but,* didn't you? You thought I was going to say, *but I didn't snatch people's pocketbooks.* Well, I wasn't going to say that." Pause. Silence. "I have done things, too, which I would not tell you, son—neither tell God, if He didn't already know. Everybody's got something in common. So you set down while I fix us something to eat. You might run that comb through your hair so you will look presentable."

In another corner of the room behind a screen was a gas plate and an icebox. Mrs. Jones got up and went behind the screen. The woman did not watch the boy to see if he was going to run now, nor did she watch her purse, which she left behind her on the day bed. But the boy took care to sit on the far side of the room, away from the purse, where he thought she could easily see him out of the corner of her eye if she wanted to. He did not trust the woman *not* to trust him. And he did not want to be mistrusted now.

"Do you need somebody to go to the store," asked the boy, "maybe to get some milk or something?"

"Don't believe I do," said the woman, "unless you just want sweet milk yourself. I was going to make cocoa out of this canned milk I got here."

"That will be fine," said the boy.

She heated some lima beans and ham she had in the icebox, made the cocoa, and set the table. The woman did not ask the boy anything about where he lived, or his folks, or anything else that would embarrass him. Instead, as they ate, she told him about her job in a hotel beauty shop that stayed open late, what the work was like, and how all kinds of women came in and out, blondes, redheads, and Spanish. Then she cut him a half of her ten-cent cake.

"Eat some more, son," she said.

When they were finished eating, she got up and said, "Now here, take this ten dollars and buy yourself some blue suede shoes. And next time, do not make the mistake of latching onto *my* pocketbook *nor nobody else's*—because shoes got by devilish ways will burn your feet. I got to get my rest now. But from here on in, son, I hope you will behave yourself."

She led him down the hall to the front door and opened it. "Good night! Behave yourself, boy!" she said, looking out into the street as he went down the steps.

The boy wanted to say something other than, "Thank you, m'am," to Mrs. Luella Bates Washington Jones, but although his lips moved, he couldn't even say that as he turned at the foot of the barren stoop and looked up at the large woman in the door. Then she shut the door.

1959

▪ # COUNTEE CULLEN ▪
1903–1946

The exact date of birth and birthplace of Countee Cullen remain a mystery. The best guess is that he was born in 1903 in Louisville, Kentucky. What is known is that he went to live with the Reverend Frederick Asbury Cullen and his wife, Carolyn in 1917 or 1918 after the death of the woman who appears to have been his grandmother. Frederick Cullen founded the Salem United Methodist Church in Harlem as an uptown mission of the St. Marks Methodist Episcopal Church in 1903 and built it up from a storefront to one of the most important black churches in New York. Though it seems that Frederick and Carolyn Cullen never formally adopted Countee Cullen, he assumed their last name. An outstanding student, Cullen attended De Witt Clinton High School and New York University, where he was elected to Phi Beta Kappa.

Cullen was generally recognized as the leading poet of the Harlem or New Negro Renaissance during most of the 1920s and the early 1930s—though Cullen's critical standing has fallen since then as those of Langston Hughes, Sterling Brown, and Claude McKay have risen. His acclaim as a poet began when he was a high school student and continued through college and beyond. He won major prizes and fellowships, including the Witt Bynner Prize, the John Reed Prize of *Poetry* magazine, and the Amy Spingarn Award of the NAACP's journal *The Crisis*, all while was in his twenties. He was only the second African American to win a Guggenheim Fellowship. He published more collections of poetry with mainstream presses than any other black writer of the period, and he edited the influential anthology of African American poetry, *Caroling Dusk*. In addition to poetry, he also wrote fiction, drama, and critical essays. Despite his reputation as relatively staid and middle-class in manner, Cullen was a political radical for much of his adult life, publicly endorsing the Communist Party Presidential and Vice-Presidential candidates in 1932 and supporting Sacco and Vanzetti in the 1920s and the Scottsboro defendants in the 1930s. For most of his working life, he taught English and French in the New York City public school system.

Cullen was and to some extent still is unfairly typed as being too imitative of Romantic and Victorian British poetry, of being insufficiently grounded in the modern and incapable of developing a distinctly African American voice. However fond he may have been of Keats and Tennyson, his work was most akin to those moderns, particularly women poets such as Edna St. Vincent-Millay, who used such forms as the sonnet and the ballad to explore interpersonal politics as they were inflected by gender, race, and sexuality. Cullen was gay, but also a serious Christian. In this contradiction between faith and sexuality, Cullen resembles the Christian gay poet W. H. Auden, who, too, saw this conflict as an irresolvable fact of his life. Given the legal, social, professional repercussions (especially for a school teacher) of publicly coming out as gay in the 1920s and 1930s (though Cullen's sexuality was widely known in Harlem at the time), Cullen tended to displace his sense of a transgressive sexuality into a vocabulary of race and opposed terms of "pagan" and "civilized." This is not to say that Cullen did not take racial identity and racism seriously, only that race in his poetry is rarely simply about race.

James Smethurst
University of Massachusetts Amherst

PRIMARY WORKS

Color, 1925; *The Ballad of the Brown Girl*, 1927; *Caroling Dusk: An Anthology of Verse by Negro Poets*, 1927; *Copper Sun*, 1927; *The Black Christ and Other Poems*, 1929; *One Way to Heaven*, 1932; *The Medea and Other Poems*, 1935; *The Lost World*, 1940; *On These I Stand*, 1947; *My Soul's High Song: The Collected Writings of Countee Cullen, Voice of the Harlem Renaissance*, ed. Gerald Lynn Early, 1991.

Incident

Once riding in old Baltimore,
    Heart-filled, head-filled with glee,
I saw a Baltimorean
    Keep looking straight at me.

Now I was eight and very small,   5
    And he was no whit bigger,
And so I smiled, but he poked out
    His tongue, and called me, "Nigger."

I saw the whole of Baltimore
    From May until December;   10
Of all the things that happened there
    That's all that I remember.

1924

From the Dark Tower

We shall not always plant while others reap
The olden increment of bursting fruit,
Not always countenance, abject and mute,
That lesser men should hold their brothers cheap;
Not everlastingly while others sleep   5
Shall we beguile their limbs with mellow flute,
Not always bend to some more subtle brute;
We were not made eternally to weep.

The night whose sable breast relieves the stark,
White stars is no less lovely being dark,   10
And there are buds that cannot bloom at all
In light, but crumple, piteous, and fall;
So in the dark we hide the heart that bleeds,
And wait, and tend our agonizing seeds.

                                                            1924

Simon the Cyrenian Speaks

He never spoke a word to me,
    And yet He called my name;
He never gave a sign to me,
    And yet I knew and came.

At first I said, "I will not bear   5
    His cross upon my back;
He only seeks to place it there
    Because my skin is black."

But He was dying for a dream,
    And He was very meek,   10
And in His eyes there shone a gleam
    Men journey far to seek.

It was Himself my pity bought;
    I did for Christ alone
What all of Rome could not have wrought   15
    With bruise of lash or stone.

                                                            1924

Yet Do I Marvel

I doubt not God is good, well-meaning, kind,
And did He stoop to quibble could tell why
The little buried mole continues blind,
Why flesh that mirrors Him must some day die,
Make plain the reason tortured Tantalus   5
Is baited by the fickle fruit, declare
If merely brute caprice dooms Sisyphus
To struggle up a never-ending stair.
Inscrutable His ways are, and immune
To catechism by a mind too strewn   10
With petty cares to slightly understand
What awful brain compels his awful hand.
Yet do I marvel at this curious thing:
To make a poet black, and bid him sing!

                                                        1925

Pagan Prayer

Not for myself I make this prayer,
    But for this race of mine
That stretches forth from shadowed places
    Dark hands for bread and wine.

For me, my heart is pagan mad,   5
    My feet are never still,
But give them hearths to keep them warm
    In homes high on a hill.

For me, my faith lies fallowing,
    I bow not till I see,   10
But these are humble and believe;
    Bless their credulity.

For me, I pay my debts in kind,
    And see no better way,
Bless these who turn the other cheek   15
    For love of you, and pray.

Our Father, God, our Brother, Christ—
    So are we taught to pray;
Their kinship seems a little thing
    Who sorrow all the day.   20

Our Father, God; our Brother, Christ,
    Or are we bastard kind,
That to our plaints your ears are closed,
    Your doors barred from within?

Our Father, God; our Brother, Christ,   25
    Retrieve my race again;
So shall you compass this black sheep,
    That flushes this wild fruit?

                1925

Heritage

For Harold Jackman

What is Africa to me:
Copper sun or scarlet sea,
Jungle star or jungle track,
Strong bronzed men, or regal black
Women from whose loins I sprang   5
When the birds of Eden sang?
One three centuries removed
From the scenes his fathers loved,
Spicy grove, cinnamon tree,
What is Africa to me?   10

So I lie, who all day long
Want no sound except the song
Sung by wild barbaric birds
Goading massive jungle herds,
Juggernauts of flesh that pass   15
Trampling tall defiant grass
Where young forest lovers lie,
Plighting troth beneath the sky.
So I lie, who always hear,
Though I cram against my ear   20
Both my thumbs, and keep them there,
Great drums throbbing through the air.
So I lie, whose fount of pride,
Dear distress, and joy allied.
Is my somber flesh and skin,   25
With the dark blood dammed within
Like great pulsing tides of wine
That, I fear, must burst the fine
Channels of the chafing net
Where they surge and foam and fret.   30

Africa? A book one thumbs
Listlessly, till slumber comes.
Unremembered are her bats
Circling through the night, her cats
Crouching in the river reeds,   35
Stalking gentle flesh that feeds
By the river brink; no more
Does the bugle-throated roar
Cry that monarch claws have leapt
From the scabbards where they slept.   40
Silver snakes that once a year
Doff the lovely coats you wear,
Seek no covert in your fear
Lest a mortal eye should see;
What's your nakedness to me?   45
Here no leprous flowers rear
Fierce corollas in the air;
Here no bodies sleek and wet,
Dripping mingled rain and sweat,
Tread the savage measures of   50
Jungle boys and girls in love.
What is last year's snow to me,
Last year's anything? The tree
Budding yearly must forget
How its past arose or set—   55
Bough and blossom, flower, fruit,
Even what shy bird with mute
Wonder at her travail there,
Meekly labored in its hair.
One three centuries removed   60
From the scenes his fathers loved,
Spicy grove, cinnamon tree,
What is Africa to me?

So I lie, who find no peace
Night or day, no slight release   65
From the unremittant beat
Made by cruel padded feet
Walking through my body's street.
Up and down they go, and back,
Treading out a jungle track.   70
So I lie, who never quite
Safely sleep from rain at night—
I can never rest at all
When the rain begins to fall;
Like a soul gone mad with pain   75

I must match its weird refrain;
Ever must I twist and squirm,
Writhing like a baited worm,
While its primal measures drip
Through my body, crying, "Strip!   80
Doff this new exuberance.
Come and dance the Lover's Dance!"
In an old remembered way
Rain works on me night and day.

Quaint, outlandish heathen gods   85
Black men fashion out of rods,
Clay, and brittle bits of stone,
In a likeness like their own,
My conversion came high-priced;
I belong to Jesus Christ,   90
Preacher of humility,
Heathen gods are naught to me.
Father, Son, and Holy Ghost,
So I make an idle boast;
Jesus of the twice-turned cheek,   95
Lamb of God, although I speak
With my mouth thus, in my heart
Do I play a double part.
Ever at Thy glowing altar
Must my heart grow sick and falter,   100
Wishing He I served were black,
Thinking then it would not lack
Precedent of pain to guide it,
Let who would or might deride it;
Surely then this flesh would know   105
Yours had borne a kindred woe.
Lord, I fashion dark gods, too,
Daring even to give You
Dark despairing features where,
Crowned with dark rebellious hair,   110
Patience wavers just so much as
Mortal grief compels, while touches
Quick and hot, of anger, rise
To smitten cheek and weary eyes.
Lord, forgive me if my need   115
Sometimes shapes a human creed.
All day long and all night through,
One thing only must I do:
Quench my pride and cool my blood,
Lest I perish in the flood,   120

Lest a hidden ember set
Timber that I thought was wet
Burning like the dryest flax,
Melting like the merest wax,
Lest the grave restore its dead.   125
Not yet has my heart or head
In the least way realized
They and I are civilized.

1925

Scottsboro, Too, Is Worth Its Song

(A poem to American poets)

I said:
Now will the poets sing,—
Their cries go thundering
Like blood and tears
Into the nation's ears,   5
Like lightning dart
Into the nation's heart.
Against disease and death and all things fell,
And war,
Their strophes rise and swell   10
To jar
The foe smug in his citadel.
Remembering their sharp and pretty
Tunes for Sacco and Vanzetti,
I said: 15
Here too's a cause divinely spun
For those whose eyes are on the sun,
Here in epitome
Is all disgrace
And epic wrong,   20
Like wine to brace
The minstrel heart, and blare it into song.

Surely, I said,
Now will the poets sing.
But they have raised no cry.   25
I wonder why.

1934

GWENDOLYN B. BENNETT
1902–1981

Gwendolyn Bennett was born in Giddings, Texas, on July 8, 1902, to Joshua Robin and Mayme F. Abernathy Bennett. While African Americans were riding the first wave of the Great Migration, traveling from the South to the North and from rural to urban communities, Bennett's parents moved in a slightly different direction. Shortly after Gwendolyn's birth, Joshua and Mayme moved their family to Nevada, where they served as teachers at a school on a Native American reservation. Five years later, the couple moved to Washington, D.C., and subsequently divorced. Although Mayme got custody of young Gwendolyn, Joshua disagreed with the decision, kidnapped his daughter, and moved her to Harrisburg, Pennsylvania. Bennett would not see her mother again until her father remarried and moved his new family to Brooklyn, New York.

Bennett excelled academically and artistically at Brooklyn's Girls High school, where she graduated in 1921. She was the first black student to be elected to the school's literary and drama societies, and it was here that she pursued her interests in the fine arts. After graduation, Bennett studied art at Columbia University and Pratt Institute, where she earned a bachelor's degree in 1924. During that time, she also joined Harlem's flourishing movement of artistic expression and enjoyed the publication of her artwork, poetry, and short stories in all of the major journals and collections of the period, including *The New Negro*, *The Crisis*, *Opportunity*, the short-lived *Fire!!*, *The Book of American Negro Poetry*, *Caroling Dusk*, *Anthology of Magazine Verse*, and *Yearbook of American Poetry*. The same year she graduated from college, she moved back to Washington, D.C., to teach at Howard University. The following year, she traveled to Paris on a $1,000 scholarship from Delta Sigma Theta Sorority to study watercolor, oil, woodcuts, pen and ink, and batik. When she returned from Paris, Charles S. Johnson, editor of *Opportunity Magazine*, hired Bennett as assistant editor to write a literary and fine arts column, which she called "The Ebony Flute" and described as a forum for "literary and social chit-chat."

In 1927, Bennett married Alfred Jackson and moved south to Tennessee and Florida, where Jackson set up his medical practice. Forced to discontinue her column, Bennett found herself increasingly unhappy with her marriage and her life in the segregated South away from her literary circle. In the early 1930s, the couple returned to New York, but the deepening Great Depression had affected the Harlem arts movement. Jackson passed away in 1932, and Bennett turned her attention to community-based projects and employment with the Works Progress Administration. Bennett, who moved to Kutztown, Pennsylvania, with her second husband, Richard Crosscup, spent her later years as an antiques dealer. She died of congestive heart failure on May 30, 1981.

Crystal J. Lucky
Villanova University

Heritage

I want to see the slim palm trees,
Pulling at the clouds
With little pointed fingers ...

I want to see lithe Negro girls,
Etched dark against the sky   5
While sunset lingers.

I want to hear the silent sands
Singing to the moon
Before the spinx-still face ...
I want to hear the chinting   10
Around a heathen fire
Of a strange black race.

I want to breathe the lotus flower,
Sighing to the stars
With tendrils drinking at the Nile ...   15

I want to feel the surging
Of my sad people's soul
Hidden by a minstrel smile.

1923

To Usward

Let us be still
As ginger jars are still
Upon a Chinese shelf
And let us be contained
By entities of self....   5
Not still with lethargy and sloth
But quiet with the Pushing of our growth
Not self-contained with smug identity
But conscious of the strength of entity.

If any have a song to sing   10
That's different from the rest,
Oh let them sing
Before the urgency of youth's behest!
For some of us have songs to sing
Of jungle heat and fires,   15

And some of us are solemn grown
With pitiful desires,
And there are those who feel the pull
Of seas beneath the skies,
And some there be who want to croon   20
Of Negro lullabies
We claim no part with racial dearth,
We want to sing the songs of birth!

And so we stand like ginger jars
Like ginger jars bound round   25
With dust and age;
Like jars of ginger we are sealed
By nature's heritage.

But let us break the seal of years
With pungent thrusts of song   30
For there is joy in long-dried tears
For whetted passions of a throng.

                                                                      1924

Advice

You were a sophist,
Pale and quite remote,
As you bade me
Write poems—
Brown poems   5
of dark words
And prehistoric rhythms ...
Your pallor stifled my posey.
But I remembered a tapestry
that I would someday weave   10
Of dim purples and fine reds
And blues
Like night and death—
The keen precision of your words
Wove a silver thread   15
Through the dusk softness
Of my dream-stuff....

                                                                      1927

Lines Written at the Grave of Alexandre Dumas

Cemeteries are places for departed souls
And bones interred,
Or hearts with shattered loves.
A woman with lips made warm for laughter
Would find grey stones and roving spirits   5
Too chill for living, moving pulses . . .
And thou, great spirit, wouldst shiver in thy granite shroud
Should idle mirth or empty talk
Disturb thy tranquil sleeping.

A cemetery is a place for shattered loves   10
And broken hearts. . . .
Bowed before the crystal chalice of thy soul,
I find the multi-colored fragrance of thy mind
Has lost itself in Death's transparency.

Oh, stir the lucid waters of thy sleep   15
And coin for me a tale
Of happy loves and gems and joyous limbs
And hearts where love is sweet!

A cemetery is a place for broken hearts
And silent thought . . .   20
And silence never moves,
Nor speaks nor sings.

1927

■   STERLING A. BROWN   ■
1901–1989

After graduating with a Harvard M.A. in 1923, Sterling A. Brown went south, as he said, to learn something of his people. There a whole new world of black experience opened up to his acute and sensitive artistic vision, causing in him not just a geographical realignment from north to south but the profound shaping of a folk-based aesthetic. At Virginia Seminary and College in Lynchburg (1923–1926), where the precocious twenty-three-year-old instructor played "red-ink" man in English classes, the teacher by day became student at night as seminarians introduced him to Calvin "Big Boy" Davis, itinerate guitar player, and Mrs. Bibby, "illiterate, and somehow very wise"—two of the many individuals whose lives, language, and lore Brown would celebrate in memorable literary portraits.

The genteel circumstances of Brown's birth would seemingly have mitigated against so complete an absorption of black folk life. He was born into the rather "high-brow" gentility of Washington, D.C.'s, black middle class, to Adelaide Allen and Sterling Nelson Brown, a famous pastor, theologian, and social activist who numbered John Mercer Langston and Blanche K. Bruce among his friends. Graduating valedictorian from the prestigious Dunbar High School in 1918 earned Brown a scholarship to Williams College, where an essay in 1922, "The Comic Spirit in Shakespeare and Molière," and election to Phi Beta Kappa won him a Clark Fellowship to Harvard for graduate work (1922–1923). By the time Brown began a second period of study at Harvard (1931–1932), a marvelous synthesis of formal and folk training had coalesced into an early maturing scholarship and a deeply sensitive creative writing.

An unpublished course thesis entitled "Plays of the Irish Character: A Study in Reinterpretation" (1932), for example, anticipated the critical approach of some of his most important scholarship of the 1930s: "Negro Character as Seen by White Authors" (1933), *Negro Poetry and Drama* (1938), and *The Negro in American Fiction* (1938). It is in this vein that, as editor on Negro Affairs for the Federal Writers' Project (1938–1940) and as researcher for the Carnegie-Myrdal Study (1939–1940), Brown was a custodian guarding against the proliferation of stereotypes of blacks in the American Guidebooks series as well as in Gunnar Myrdal's *An American Dilemma* (1944). Against the tiresome argument that blacks had contributed little to American cultural history, Brown set forth *The Negro Caravan* (1941), an anthology of black writing coedited with Arthur P. Davis and Ulysses Lee. By making "comprehensiveness" an editorial aim, the *Caravan* effectively expanded the canons of black and Euro-American literatures by historicizing nineteenth-century black formal and folk literatures, bringing previously unacknowledged writers into prominence, and advocating a single standard of literary criticism. A 1942 Rosenwald Foundation grant supported his work on "A Negro Looks at the South," a proposed book-length travelogue.

The context established by Brown's scholarship and teaching is a window through which to view his poetry. After his early experiments with conventional Victorian verse forms, two seemingly unrelated traditions coalesced in Brown's poetry: the democratic impulse of the New American Poetry and the richly textured aesthetic forms and experiences of black folk life. Carl Sandburg, Robert Frost, Edwin Arlington Robinson, Edgar Lee Masters, and Vachel Lindsay resonate throughout Brown's writing. In their startling experiments with free verse, bold use of idiom and regional vernaculars, and mining of "ordinary" life for its extraordinary meaning, these poets established an American poetry that diverged both from artificial nineteenth-century conventions and from the concern for myth, symbol, and image voiced by Pound, Eliot, and others of the "high modernist" mode.

The other tradition animating Brown's poetry, the untapped world of black folk experience, suffered from *a priori* assumptions of blacks as contented slaves, exotic primitives, and other literary stereotypes. By situating his sensibility in the American literary trend called "critical realism," Brown the scholar refuted such representations. But his poetry became an affirmation of black life while insisting upon a recognition of black humanity. Under his influence, the blues,

Negro spirituals, humor, folktales, aphorisms, and work songs became more than cultural artifacts; they became crucibles of experience that when transformed became the stuff of good art.

The blues presented more than a music of pain, suffering, and lost love. Its culturally specific verse form and its highly metaphoric language were raw materials awaiting the craftsman's hand. In the Negro spirituals, Brown detected a tonic shrewdness, or what a critic later described as a "distilled metaphysic." Lines such as "Ben down so long, / Down don't bother me" and "I don't know why my mother wants to stay here for / This world ain't been no friend to her" reveal his desire to get at certain qualities in the language of black people, "a flavor, a color, a pungency of speech." Later, he continues, "I came to something more important—I wanted to get an understanding of people, to acquire an accuracy in the portrayal of their lives."

Expanding black language into a philosophical vehicle conveying the character of a people—a way of life, in effect—revises the conventional idea that black language is inherently limited and racially demeaning. In much the same way, Brown's adaptation of black folk humor revises the shopworn notion of blacks "laughing to keep from crying," by exploiting the familiar purposes of satire to instruct and delight and to instruct through delighting. And black life, largely misunderstood and poorly represented, enjoys one of its most articulate and enthusiastic celebrants.

John Edgar Tidwell
University of Kansas

PRIMARY WORKS

Southern Road, 1932; "A Son's Return: 'Oh, Didn't He Ramble,'" in *Chant of Saints,* eds. Michael S. Harper and Robert B. Stepto, 1979; *The Collected Poems of Sterling A. Brown,* 1980; *A Son's Return,* ed. Mark A. Sanders, 1996.

When de Saints Go Ma'ching Home

(To Big Boy Davis, Friend.
In Memories of Days Before He Was
Chased Out of Town for Vagrancy.)[1]

I

He'd play, after the bawdy songs and blues,
After the weary plaints
Of "Trouble, Trouble deep down in muh soul,"
Always one song in which he'd lose the rôle
Of entertainer to the boys. He'd say,   5
"My mother's favorite." And we knew
That what was coming was his chant of saints,

---

[1]As a faculty member at Virginia Seminary and College in Lynchburg (1923–1926), Brown befriended Calvin "Big Boy" Davis, a former coal miner turned itinerate blues guitarist.

"When de saints go ma'chin' home...."[2]
And that would end his concert for the day.

Carefully as an old maid over needlework,   10
Oh, as some black deacon, over his Bible, lovingly,
He'd tune up specially for this. There'd be
No chatter now, no patting of the feet.
After a few slow chords, knelling and sweet—
Oh when de saints go ma'chin' home,   15
Oh when de sayaints goa ma'chin' home....
He would forget
The quieted bunch, his dimming cigarette
Stuck into a splintered edge of the guitar;
Sorrow deep hidden in his voice, a far   20
And soft light in his strange brown eyes;
Alone with his masterchords, his memories....
    Lawd I wanna be one in nummer
    When de saints go ma'chin' home.
Deep the bass would rumble while the treble scattered high,   25
For all the world like heavy feet a-trompin' toward the sky,
With shrill-voiced women getting 'happy'
All to celestial tunes.
The chap's few speeches helped me understand
The reason why he gazed so fixedly   30
Upon the burnished strings.
For he would see
A gorgeous procession to 'de Beulah Land,'—
Of saints—his friends—"a-climbin' fo' deir wings."
Oh when de saints go ma'chin' home....   35
Lawd I wanna be one o' dat nummer
When de saints goa ma'chin' home....

II

There'd be—so ran his dream:
    "Ole Deacon Zachary
    With de asthmy in his chest,   40
    A-puffin' an' a-wheezin'
    Up de golden stair;
    Wid de badges of his lodges
    Strung acrost his heavin' breast
    An' de hoggrease jes' shinin'   45
    In his coal black hair....

[2]Adaptation of the Negro spiritual "When de
Saints Go Ma'chin' In."

"An' ole Sis Joe
In huh big straw hat,
An' huh wrapper flappin',
Flappin' in de heavenly win',   50
An' huh thin-soled easy walkers
Goin' pitty pitty pat,—
Lawd she'd have to ease her corns
When she got in!"

Oh when de saints go ma'chin' home.   55
        "Ole Elder Peter Johnson
Wid his corncob jes' a-puffin',
An' de smoke a-rollin'
Lak stormclouds out behin';
Crossin' de cloud mountains   60
Widout slowin' up fo' nuffin,
Steamin' up de grade
Lak Wes' bound No. 9.

        "An' de little brown-skinned chillen
Wid deir skinny legs a-dancin',   65
Jes' a-kickin' up ridic'lous
To de heavenly band;
Lookin' at de Great Drum Major
On a white hoss jes' a-prancin',
Wid a gold and silver drumstick   70
A-waggin' in his han'."
Oh when de sun refuse to shine
Oh when de mo-on goes down
        In Blood
        "Ole Maumee Annie   75
Wid huh washin' done,
An' huh las' piece o' laundry
In de renchin' tub,
A wavin' sof' pink han's
To de much obligin' sun,   80
An' her feet a-moverin' now
To a swif' rub-a-dub;

        "An' old Grampa Eli
Wid his wrinkled old haid,
A-puzzlin' over summut   85
He ain' understood,
Intendin' to ask Peter
Pervidin' he ain't skyaid,
'Jes' what mought be de meanin'
Of de moon in blood?' ..."   90
When de saints go ma'chin' home....

III

"Whuffolks,"[3] he dreams, "will have to stay outside
Being so onery." But what is he to do
With that red brakeman who once let him ride
An empty going home? Or with that kind-faced man   95
Who paid his songs with board and drink and bed?
Or with the Yankee Cap'n who left a leg
At Vicksburg? *Mought be a place, he said,*
Mought be another mansion fo' white saints,
A smaller one than his'n ... not so gran'.   100
As fo' the rest ... oh let 'em howl and beg.
Hell would be good enough—if big enough—
Widout no shade trees, lawd, widout no rain.
Whuffolks sho' to bring nigger out behin',
Excep'—"when de saints go ma'chin' home."   105

IV

Sportin' Legs would not be there—nor lucky Sam,
Nor Smitty, nor Hambone, nor Hardrock Gene,
An' not too many guzzlin', cuttin' shines,
Not bootleggers to keep his pockets clean.
An' Sophie wid de sof' smile on her face,   110
Her foolin' voice, her strappin' body, brown
Lak coffee doused wid milk—she had been good
To him, wid lovin', money and wid food.—
But saints and heaven didn't seem to fit
Jes' right wid Sophy's Beauty—nary bit—   115
She mought stir trouble, somehow, in dat peaceful place
Mought be some dressed-up dudes in dat fair town.

V

Ise got a dear ole mudder,
She is in hebben I know—
He sees: 120
      Mammy,
      Li'l mammy—wrinkled face,
      Her brown eyes, quick to tears—to joy—
      With such happy pride in her
      Guitar-plunkin' boy.   125
      Oh kain't I be one in nummer?

---

[3]Black vernacular pronunciation of white folks.

Mammy
With deep religion defeating the grief
Life piled so closely about her,
Ise so glad trouble doan last alway,   130
And her dogged belief
That some fine day
She'd go a-ma'chin'
When de saints go ma'chin' home.

He sees her ma'chin' home, ma'chin' along,   135
Her perky joy shining in her furrowed face,
Her weak and quavering voice singing her song—
The best chair set apart for her worn out body
In that restful place....
   I pray to de Lawd I'll meet her   140
   When de saints go ma'chin' home.

VI

He'd shuffle off from us, always, at that,—
His face a brown study beneath his torn brimmed hat,
His broad shoulders slouching, his old box strung
Around his neck;—he'd go where we
Never could follow him—to Sophie probably,
Or to his dances in old Tinbridge flat.

1927

Strong Men

   The young men keep coming on
   The strong men keep coming on.

—*Sandburg*

They dragged you from homeland,
They chained you in coffles,[1]
They huddled you spoon-fashion[2] in filthy hatches,
They sold you to give a few gentlemen ease.

They broke you in like oxen,   5
They scourged you,

[1] A line or file of slaves chained together in transit.
[2] A method of chaining and stowing slaves below
ship deck in the hold, resembling the arrangement of spoons in a silverware chest.

They branded you,
They made your women breeders,
They swelled your numbers with bastards....
They taught you the religion they disgraced.   10

You sang:
     Keep a-inchin' along
     Lak a po' inch worm....

You sang:
     Bye and bye   15
     I'm gonna lay down dis heaby load....

You sang:
     Walk togedder, chillen,
     Dontcha git weary....[3]
         The strong men keep a-comin' on   20
         The strong men git stronger.

They point with pride to the roads you built for them,
They ride in comfort over the rails you laid for them.
They put hammers in your hands
And said—Drive so much before sundown.[4]   25

You sang:
     Ain't no hammah
     In dis lan',
     Strikes lak mine, bebby,
     Strikes lak mine.   30

They cooped you in their kitchens,
They penned you in their factories,
They gave you the jobs that they were too good for,
They tried to guarantee happiness to themselves
By shunting dirt and misery to you.   35

You sang:
     Me an' muh baby gonna shine, shine
     Me an' muh baby gonna shine.[5]
         The strong men keep a-comin' on
         The strong men git stronger....   40

[3]Lines from old Negro spirituals.   [5]Lines from Negro secular folksongs.
[4]Injunction to lay railroad track.

They bought off some of your leaders
You stumbled, as blind men will . . .
They coaxed you, unwontedly soft-voiced. . . .
You followed a way.
Then laughed as usual.   45

They heard the laugh and wondered;
Uncomfortable,
Unadmitting a deeper terror. . . .
   The strong men keep a-comin' on
   Gittin' stronger. . . .   50

What, from the slums
Where they have hemmed you,
What, from the tiny huts
They could not keep from you—
What reaches them   55
Making them ill at ease, fearful?
Today they shout prohibition at you
"Thou shalt not this"
"Thou shalt not that"
"Reserved for whites only"   60
You laugh,

One thing they cannot prohibit—
   The strong men . . . coming on
   The strong men gittin' stronger.
   Strong men. . . .   65
   Stronger. . . .

                  1931

Ma Rainey[1]

I

When Ma Rainey
Comes to town,
Folks from anyplace
Miles aroun',
From Cape Girardeau,   5
Poplar Bluff,

[1]Gertrude Malissa Nix Pridgett "Ma" Rainey (1886–1939), a former vaudeville entertainer who sang minstrel and popular songs with the Rabbit Foot Minstrels, was taken with "strange" and "weird" music, which she eventually helped propel into national prominence as the classic blues.

Flocks in to hear
Ma do her stuff;
Comes flivverin' in,[2]
Or ridin' mules,   10
Or packed in trains,
Picknickin' fools....
That's what it's like,
Fo' miles on down,
To New Orleans delta   15
An' Mobile town,
When Ma hits
Anywheres aroun'.

II

Dey comes to hear Ma Rainey from de little river settlements,
From blackbottom cornrows and from lumber camps;   20
Dey stumble in de hall, jes a-laughin' an' a-cacklin',
Cheerin' lak roarin' water, lak wind in river swamps.

An' some jokers keeps deir laughs a-goin' in de crowded aisles,
An' some folks sits dere waitin' wid deir aches an' miseries,
Till Ma comes out before dem, a-smilin' gold-toofed smiles   25
An' Long Boy ripples minors on de black an' yellow keys.

III

O Ma Rainey,
Sing yo' song;
Now you's back
Whah you belong,   30
Git way inside us,
Keep us strong....
O Ma Rainey,
Li'l an' low;
Sing us 'bout de hard luck   35
Roun' our do';
Sing us 'bout de lonesome road
We mus' go....

[2]Brown makes a verb of *flivver*, a slang term
of unknown origin for an old or cheap car.

IV

I talked to a fellow, an' the fellow say,
"She jes' catch hold of us, somekindaway.   40
She sang Backwater Blues one day:

    'It rained fo' days an' de skies was dark as night,
    Trouble taken place in de lowlands at night.

    'Thundered an' lightened an' the storm begin to roll
    Thousan's of people ain't got no place to go.   45

    'Den I went an' stood upon some high ol' lonesome hill,
    An' looked down on the place where I used to live.'

An' den de folks, dey natchally bowed dey heads an' cried,
Bowed dey heavy heads, shet dey moufs up tight an' cried,
An' Ma lef' de stage, an' followed some de folks outside."   50

Dere wasn't much more de fellow say:
She jes' gits hold of us dataway.

                             1932

Slim in Hell[1]

I

Slim Greer went to heaven;
   St. Peter said, "Slim,
You been a right good boy."
   An' he winked at him.

  "You been a travelin' rascal   5
     In yo' day.
   You kin roam once mo';
     Den you comes to stay.

  "Put dese wings on yo' shoulders,
     An' save yo' feet."   10
Slim grin, and he speak up
     "Thankye, Pete."

[1]In addition to the tall-tale tradition made famous by Mark Twain, the poem draws from two other vernacular traditions: "the colored man in heaven" folktale and the myth of Orpheus and Eurydice.

Den Peter say, "Go
  To Hell an' see,
All dat is doing, and   15
  Report to me.

"Be sure to remember
  How everything go."
Slim say, "I be seein' yuh
  On de late watch, bo."   20

  Slim got to cavortin',
    Swell as you choose,
  Like Lindy in de "Spirit
    Of St. Louis Blues!"

He flew an' he flew,   25
  Till at last he hit
A hangar wid de sign readin'
  DIS IS IT.

  Den he parked his wings,
    An' strolled aroun'   30
  Gettin' used to his feet
    On de solid ground.

II

Big bloodhound came aroarin'
  Like Niagry Falls,
Sicked on by white devils   35
  In overhalls.

Now Slim warn't scared,
  Cross my heart, it's a fac',
An' de dog went on a bayin'
  Some po' devil's track.   40

  Dem Slim saw a mansion
    An' walked right in;
  De Devil looked up
    Wid a sickly grin.

"Suttinly didn't look   45
  Fo' you, Mr. Greer,
How it happen you comes
  To visit here?"

Slim say—"Oh, jes' thought
   I'd drap by a spell."
"Feel at home, seh, an' here's   50
   De keys to Hell."

Den he took Slim around
   An' showed him people
Raisin' hell as high as   55
   De First Church Steeple.

   Lots of folks fightin'
      At de roulette wheel,
   Like old Rampart Street,
      Or leastwise Beale.[2]   60

Showed him bawdy houses
   An' cabarets,
Slim thought of New Orleans
   An' Memphis days.

   Each devil was busy   65
      Wid a devilish broad,
   An' Slim cried, "Lawdy,
      Lawd, Lawd, Lawd."

Took him in a room
   Where Slim see   70
De preacher wid a brownskin
   On each knee.

   Showed him giant stills,
      Going everywhere
   Wid a passel of devils,   75
      Stretched dead drunk there.

Den he took him to de furnace
   Dat some devils was firing,
Hot as hell, an' Slim start
   A mean presspirin';   80

   White devils wid pitchforks
      Threw black devils on,
   Slim thought he'd better
      Be gittin' along.

[2]Sites of booze and bordellos, Rampart Street in New Orleans and Beale Street in Memphis were birthplaces of blues and jazz during the first quarter of the twentieth century.

An' he say—"Dis makes   85
  Me think of home—
Vicksburg, Little Rock, Jackson,
  Waco, and Rome."

  Den de devil gave Slim
    De big Ha-Ha;   90
  An' turned into a cracker,
    Wid a sheriff's star.

Slim ran fo' his wings,
  Lit out from de groun'
Hauled it back to St. Peter,   95
  Safety boun'.

III

  St. Peter said, "Well,
    You got back quick.
  How's de devil? An' what's
    His latest trick?"   100

An' Slim say, "Peter,
  I really cain't tell,
De place was Dixie
  Dat I took for Hell."

Then Peter say, "You must   105
  Be crazy, I vow,
Where'n hell dja think Hell *was*,
  Anyhow?

"Git on back to de yearth,
  Cause I got de fear,   110
You'se a leetle too dumb,
  Fo' to stay up here ..."

1932

Remembering Nat Turner[1]

(For R.C.L.)

We saw a bloody sunset over Courtland, once Jerusalem,
As we followed the trail that old Nat took

[1]Nat Turner (1800–1831) led one of the few black slave uprisings in which white people were killed. According to various accounts, seventy-five slaves slew fifty-five whites in this August 21, 1831, revolt. After eluding capture for several weeks, Turner was caught, convicted, and eventually hanged on November 11, 1831.

When he came out of Cross Keys down upon Jerusalem,[2]
In his angry stab for freedom a hundred years ago.
The land was quiet, and the mist was rising,   5
Out of the woods and the Nottaway swamp,
Over Southampton the still night fell,
As we rode down to Cross Keys where the march began.

When we got to Cross Keys, they could tell us little of him,
The Negroes had only the faintest recollections: 10
    "I ain't been here so long, I come from up roun' Newsome;
    Yassah, a town a few miles up de road,
    The old folks who coulda told you is all dead an' gone.
    I heard something, sometime; I doan jis remember what.
    'Pears lak I heard that name somewheres or other.   15
    So he fought to be free. Well, you doan say."

An old white woman recalled exactly
How Nat crept down the steps, axe in his hand,
After murdering a woman and child in bed,
"Right in this here house at the head of these stairs"   20
(In a house built long after Nat was dead).
She pointed to a brick store where Nat was captured,
(Nat was taken in the swamp, three miles away)
With his men around him, shooting from the windows
(She was thinking of Harpers Ferry and old John Brown).[3]   25
She cackled as she told how they riddled Nat with bullets
(Nat was tried and hanged at Courtland, ten miles away).
She wanted to know why folks would come miles
Just to ask about an old nigger fool.
    "Ain't no slavery no more, things is going all right,   30
    Pervided thar's a good goober market this year.
    We had a sign post here with printing on it,
    But it rotted in the hole, and thar it lays,
    And the nigger tenants split the marker for kindling.
    Things is all right, now, ain't no trouble with the niggers   35
    Why they make this big to-do over Nat?"

As we drove from Cross Keys back to Courtland,
Along the way that Nat came down upon Jerusalem,
A watery moon was high in the cloud-filled heavens,
The same moon he dreaded a hundred years ago.   40
The tree they hanged Nat on is long gone to ashes,
The trees he dodged behind have rotted in the swamps.

[2]Then county seat of Southampton County, Virginia.
[3]A white abolitionist leader (1800–1859) who attacked Harpers Ferry, Virginia, October 16, 1859, site of a federal armory; his militance earned for him the status of martyr from Union soldiers, who took up the song "John Brown's Body" as a battle hymn.

The bus for Miami and the trucks boomed by,
And touring cars, their heavy tires snarling on the pavement.
Frogs piped in the marshes, and a hound bayed long,   45
And yellow lights glowed from the cabin windows.

As we came back the way that Nat led his army,
Down from Cross Keys, down to Jerusalem,
We wondered if his troubled spirit still roamed the Nottaway,
Or if it fled with the cock-crow at daylight,   50
Or lay at peace with the bones in Jerusalem,
Its restlessness stifled by Southampton clay.

We remembered the poster rotted through and falling,
The marker split for kindling a kitchen fire.

1939

Song of Triumph

Let the band play Dixie.
And let the Rebel Yell resound.
Let daughters of the Confederacy
Be proud that once more virginal loveliness
Even in dingy courtrooms   5
Receives the homage of the poets.

Let us rush to Stone Mountain[1]
Uncover our heads, stand speechless before
Granite embodiments of our knighthood
Unfinished but everlasting,   10
"And truth and honor established here, forever."
Lo! Stonewall, preux chevalier,[2]
And Lee, majestic Arthur,[3] facing East.

Behind them, to the West
Scottsboro, Decatur.   15
Eight cowering Negroes in a jail[4]
Waiting for the justice

[1]Site near Atlanta infamous for the Ku Klux Klan rallies in the 1920s.
[2]Confederate general Thomas "Stonewall" Jack-son (1824–1863) is described literally as "pure knight," or gallant and valiant warrior.
[3]The metaphor of knighthood is continued in this reference to Robert E. Lee, another general fighting for the Confederacy, with this comparison to King Arthur, whose medieval knights of the Round Table became synonymous with chivalry.
[4]The infamous Scottsboro Boys case, in which nine black youths were accused of raping two white prostitutes hoboing on a train near this small Alabama town, was a *cause célèbre* beginning in 1931.

Chivalry as ever extends to them,
Still receiving the benefactions
Of Noblesse Oblige.[5]   20

Oh, let us be proud.
Oh, let us, undefeated, raise again
The Rebel Yell.

1980

ZORA NEALE HURSTON
1891–1960

An author who died in poverty in 1960, Zora Neale Hurston now holds a posthumous reputation that she herself might not have imagined. Her best-known
novel, *Their Eyes Were Watching God* (1937), has sold over 200,000 copies since
the mid-1980s, and more of her work is in print now than at any period during
her lifetime. A writer who never earned appreciable royalties on any of her
books, Hurston understood the vagaries of literary fortune: "I have been in sorrow's kitchen and licked out all the pots. Then I have stood on the peaky mountain wrapped in rainbows, with a harp and a sword in my hands."

Why should this particular woman have such an impact? For two reasons.
Her life illustrates the folk wisdom of Hurston's mother, who told her daughter
to "jump at de sun. You might not land on the sun, but at least you'll get off
the ground." At the same time, her work celebrates black culture and leads us to
an appreciation of the courage and humor, art and intellect, life and society,
of black people living in the rural South in the early decades of the twentieth
century—men and women who didn't jump at the sun so much as labor under
its rays from "can" in the morning till "can't" at night.

Born in the all-black town of Eatonville, Florida, Zora Neale Hurston
attended Howard University, and in 1928 graduated from Barnard College, where
she studied with anthropologists Franz Boas and Gladys Reichard. While living in
New York in the twenties, an exuberant participant with Langston Hughes,
Countee Cullen, and others in the artist's uprising they labeled "The Harlem Renaissance," she grew fascinated with the scholarly study of her home town's natural ways, which the anthropologists on Morningside Heights called "folklore."

Hurston spent the late 1920s and early 1930s collecting the folklore she
knew best, the stories, songs, tales, proverbs, and crafts of black southern people. With a pistol in her pocketbook and a cheap dress in her suitcase, she
roamed the backroads of Florida, Mississippi, and Louisiana, swapping tales at

[5]French for "nobility obligates." Persons of
high rank or nobility are expected to adopt a
benevolent and honorable air toward those
less fortunate than they are.

turpentine camps, holding "lying sessions" at jook joints, and learning hoodoo rituals from conjure doctors. If questioned too closely about being a single woman in the sole possession of a Chevrolet coupe, she usually explained that she was a bootlegger's woman on the lam.

In the mid-1930s she began publishing folklore collections (*Mules and Men*, 1935), novels (*Jonah's Gourd Vine*, 1934; *Moses: Man of the Mountain*, 1939), and Caribbean travel books (*Tell My Horse*, 1938). Well received by reviewers and critics, these books earned her a modest reputation, which reached its peak in 1942, when her autobiography, *Dust Tracks on a Road*, won a national race relations award and *The Saturday Review* featured her portrait on its cover.

The last twenty years of her life saw this reputation steadily decline for a variety of reasons, including her own withdrawal following a false morals charge in 1948 and increasing financial difficulties. In 1952 she was discovered working as a maid the same week that the *Saturday Evening Post* published one of her stories.

At Hurston's death in Fort Pierce, Florida, friends collected small change from school children to help pay for her burial. Until Alice Walker, the Pulitzer Prize–winning author of *The Color Purple*, made a pilgrimage to Fort Pierce to erect a memorial, however, she lay buried in an unmarked grave in a segregated cemetery.

As fascinating as her life is, however, Hurston's influence arises from her art. As Walker says, "We love Zora Neale Hurston for her work, first." At a time when the Ku Klux Klan was still a major force in national politics, in an era when "negro coeds" were expected to limit their horizons to school teaching, Hurston single-handedly, against great odds, became the best black woman writer in America.

"Sweat" and "The Gilded Six-Bits" are early short stories, written before Hurston reached her peak in the mid-thirties, but they illustrate the strengths of her writing. Focusing on the lives of common folks—black people usually represented as only sociological statistics—she demonstrates both the complexity of their lives and the richness of their folk culture. In these stories, particularly, she also explores the tangle of sexual power and personal oppression that can characterize relationships between men and women.

Robert E. Hemenway
University of Kansas

PRIMARY WORKS

Jonah's Gourd Vine, 1934; *Mules and Men*, 1935; *Their Eyes Were Watching God*, 1937; *Tell My Horse*, 1938; *Moses: Man of the Mountain*, 1939; *Dust Tracks on a Road*, 1942; *Seraph on the Swanee*, 1948; *Folklore, Memoirs, and Other Writings*, 1995; *Novels and Stories*, 1995; *Every Tongue Got to Confess: Negro Folk-Tales from the Gulf States*, ed. Carla Kaplan, 2001; *A Life in Letters*, ed. Carla Kaplan, 2002.

Sweat

It was eleven o'clock of a Spring night in Florida. It was Sunday. Any other night, Delia Jones would have been in bed for two hours by this time. But she was a washwoman, and Monday morning meant a great deal to her.

So she collected the soiled clothes on Saturday when she returned the clean things. Sunday night after church, she sorted them and put the white things to soak. It saved her almost a half day's start. A great hamper in the bedroom held the clothes that she brought home. It was so much neater than a number of bundles lying around.

She squatted in the kitchen floor beside the great pile of clothes, sorting them into small heaps according to color, and humming a song in a mournful key, but wondering through it all where Sykes, her husband, had gone with her horse and buckboard.

Just then something long, round, limp and black fell upon her shoulders and slithered to the floor beside her. A great terror took hold of her. It softened her knees and dried her mouth so that it was a full minute before she could cry out or move. Then she saw that it was the big bull whip her husband liked to carry when he drove.

She lifted her eyes to the door and saw him standing there bent over with laughter at her fright. She screamed at him.

"Sykes, what you throw dat whip on me like dat? You know it would skeer me—looks just like a snake, an' you knows how skeered Ah is of snakes."

"Course Ah knowed it! That's how come Ah done it." He slapped his leg with his hand and almost rolled on the ground in his mirth. "If you such a big fool dat you got to have a fit over a earth worm or a string, Ah don't keer how bad Ah skeer you."

"You aint got no business doing it. Gawd knows it's a sin. Some day Ah'm gointuh drop dead from some of yo' foolishness. 'Nother thing, where you been wid mah rig? Ah feeds dat pony. He aint fuh you to be drivin' wid no bull whip."

"You sho is one aggravatin' nigger woman!" he declared and stepped into the room. She resumed her work and did not answer him at once. "Ah done tole you time and again to keep them white folks' clothes outa dis house."

He picked up the whip and glared down at her. Delia went on with her work. She went out into the yard and returned with a galvanized tub and set it on the washbench. She saw that Sykes had kicked all of the clothes together again, and now stood in her way truculently, his whole manner hoping, *praying*, for an argument. But she walked calmly around him and commenced to re-sort the things.

"Next time, Ah'm gointer kick 'em outdoors," he threatened as he struck a match along the leg of his corduroy breeches.

Delia never looked up from her work, and her thin, stooped shoulders sagged further.

"Ah aint for no fuss t'night Sykes. Ah just come from taking sacrament at the church house."

He snorted scornfully. "Yeah, you just come from de church house on a Sunday night, but heah you is gone to work on them clothes. You ain't nothing but a hypocrite. One of them amen-corner Christians—sing, whoop, and shout, then come home and wash white folks clothes on the Sabbath."

He stepped roughly upon the whitest pile of things, kicking them helter-skelter as he crossed the room. His wife gave a little scream of dismay, and quickly gathered them together again.

"Sykes, you quit grindin' dirt into these clothes! How can Ah git through by Sat'day if Ah don't start on Sunday?"

"Ah don't keer if you never git through. Anyhow, Ah done promised Gawd and a couple of other men, Ah aint gointer have it in mah house. Don't gimme no lip neither, else Ah'll throw 'em out and put mah fist up side yo' head to boot."

Delia's habitual meekness seemed to slip from her shoulders like a blown scarf. She was on her feet; her poor little body, her bare knuckly hands bravely defying the strapping hulk before her.

"Looka heah, Sykes, you done gone too fur. Ah been married to you fur fifteen years, and Ah been takin' in washin' for fifteen years. Sweat, sweat, sweat! Work and sweat, cry and sweat, pray and sweat!"

"What's that got to do with me?" he asked brutally.

"What's it got to do with you, Sykes? Mah tub of suds is filled yo' belly with vittles more times than yo' hands is filled it. Mah sweat is done paid for this house and Ah reckon Ah kin keep on sweatin' in it."

She seized the iron skillet from the stove and struck a defensive pose, which act surprised him greatly, coming from her. It cowed him and he did not strike her as he usually did.

"Naw you won't," she panted, "that ole snaggle-toothed black woman you runnin' with aint comin' heah to pile up on *mah* sweat and blood. You aint paid for nothin' on this place, and Ah'm gointer stay right heah till Ah'm toted out foot foremost."

"Well, you better quit gittin' me riled up, else they'll be totin' you out sooner than you expect. Ah'm so tired of you Ah don't know whut to do. Gawd! how Ah hates skinny wimmen!"

A little awed by this new Delia, he sidled out of the door and slammed the back gate after him. He did not say where he had gone, but she knew too well. She knew very well that he would not return until nearly daybreak also. Her work over, she went on to bed but not to sleep at once. Things had come to a pretty pass!

She lay awake, gazing upon the debris that cluttered their matrimonial trail. Not an image left standing along the way. Anything like flowers had long ago been drowned in the salty stream that had been pressed from her heart. Her tears, her sweat, her blood. She had brought love to the union and he had brought a longing after the flesh. Two months after the wedding, he had given her the first brutal beating. She had the memory of his numerous trips to Orlando with all of his wages when he had returned to her penniless, even before the first year had passed. She was young and soft then, but now she thought of her knotty, muscled limbs, her harsh knuckly hands, and drew herself up into an unhappy little ball in the middle of the big feather bed. Too late now to hope for love, even if it were not Bertha it would be someone else. This case differed from the others only in that she was bolder than the others. Too late for everything except her little home. She had built it for her old days, and planted one by one the trees and flowers there. It was lovely to her, lovely.

Somehow, before sleep came, she found herself saying aloud: "Oh well, whatever goes over the Devil's back, is got to come under his belly. Sometime or ruther, Sykes, like everybody else, is gointer reap his sowing." After that she was able to build a spiritual earthworks against her husband. His shells could no longer reach her. *Amen.* She went to sleep and slept until he announced his presence in bed by kicking her feet and rudely snatching the covers away.

"Gimme some kivah heah, an' git yo' damn foots over on yo' own side! Ah oughter mash you in yo' mouf fuh drawing dat skillet on me."

Delia went clear to the rail without answering him. A triumphant indifference to all that he was or did.

The week was as full of work for Delia as all other weeks, and Saturday found her behind her little pony, collecting and delivering clothes.

It was a hot, hot day near the end of July. The village men on Joe Clarke's porch even chewed cane listlessly. They did not hurl the cane-knots as usual. They let them dribble over the edge of the porch. Even conversation had collapsed under the heat.

"Heah come Delia Jones," Jim Merchant said, as the shaggy pony came 'round the bend of the road toward them. The rusty buckboard was heaped with baskets of crisp, clean laundry.

"Yep," Joe Lindsay agreed. "Hot or col', rain or shine, jes ez reg'lar ez de weeks roll roun' Delia carries 'em an' fetches 'em on Sat'day."

"She better if she wanter eat," said Moss. "Syke Jones aint wuth de shot an' powder hit would tek tuh kill 'em. Not to *huh* he aint."

"He sho' aint," Walter Thomas chimed in. "It's too bad, too, cause she wuz a right pritty lil trick when he got huh. Ah'd uh mah'ied huh mahseff if he hadnter beat me to it."

Delia nodded briefly at the men as she drove past.

"Too much knockin' will ruin *any* 'oman. He done beat huh 'nough tuh kill three women, let 'lone change they looks," said Elijah Moseley. "How Syke kin stommuck dat big black greasy Mogul he's layin' roun wid, gits me. Ah swear dat eight-rock couldn't kiss a sardine can Ah done throwed out de back do' 'way las' yeah."

"Aw, she's fat, thass how come. He's allus been crazy 'bout fat women," put in Merchant. "He'd a' been tied up wid one long time ago if he could a' found one tuh have him. Did Ah tell yuh 'bout him come sidlin' roun' *mah* wife—bringin' her a basket uh pecans outa his yard fuh a present? Yessir, mah wife! She tol' him tuh take 'em right straight back home, cause Delia works so hard ovah dat washtub she reckon everything on de place taste lak sweat an' soapsuds. Ah jus' wisht Ah'd a' caught 'im 'roun' dere! Ah'd a' made his hips ketch on fiah down dat shell road."

"Ah know he done it, too. Ah sees 'im grinnin' at every 'oman dat passes," Walter Thomas said. "But even so, he useter eat some mighty big hunks uh humble pie tuh git dat lil' 'oman he got. She wuz ez pritty ez a speckled pup! Dat wuz fifteen yeahs ago. He useter be so skeered uh losin' huh, she could make him do some parts of a husband's duty. Dey never wuz de same in de mind."

"There oughter be a law about him," said Lindsay. "He aint fit tuh carry guts tuh a bear."

Clarke spoke for the first time. "Taint no law on earth dat kin make a man be decent if it aint in 'im. There's plenty men dat takes a wife lak dey do a joint uh sugar-cane. It's round, juicy an' sweet when dey gits it. But dey squeeze an' grind, squeeze an' grind an' wring tell dey wring every drop uh pleasure dat's in 'em out. When dey's satisfied dat dey is wrung dry, dey treats 'em jes lak dey do a cane-chew. Dey throws 'em away. Dey knows whut dey is doin' while dey is at it, an' hates theirselves fuh it but they keeps on hangin' after huh tell she's empty. Den dey hates huh fuh bein' a cane-chew an' in de way."

"We oughter take Syke an' dat stray 'oman uh his'n down in Lake Howell swamp an' lay on de rawhide till they cain't say Lawd a' mussy. He allus wuz uh ovahbearin' niggah, but since dat white 'oman from up north done teached 'im how to run a automobile, he done got too biggety to live—an' we oughter kill 'im," Old Man Anderson advised.

A grunt of approval went around the porch. But the heat was melting their civic virtue, and Elijah Moseley began to bait Joe Clarke.

"Come on, Joe, git a melon outa dere an' slice it up for yo' customers. We'se all sufferin' wid de heat. De bear's done got *me!*"

"Thass right, Joe, a watermelon is jes' whut Ah needs tuh cure de eppizudicks," Walter Thomas joined forces with Moseley. "Come on dere, Joe. We all is steady customers an' you aint set us up in a long time. Ah chooses dat long, bowlegged Floridy favorite."

"A god, an' be dough. You all gimme twenty cents and slice way," Clarke retorted. "Ah needs a col' slice m'self. Heah, everybody chip in. Ah'll lend y'll mah meat knife."

The money was quickly subscribed and the huge melon brought forth. At that moment, Sykes and Bertha arrived. A determined silence fell on the porch and the melon was put away again.

Merchant snapped down the blade of his jackknife and moved toward the store door.

"Come on in, Joe, an' gimme a slab uh sow belly an' uh pound uh coffee—almost fuhgot 'twas Sat'day. Got to git on home." Most of the men left also.

Just then Delia drove past on her way home, as Sykes was ordering magnificently for Bertha. It pleased him for Delia to see.

"Git whutsoever yo' heart desires, Honey. Wait a minute, Joe. Give huh two botles uh strawberry soda-water, uh quart uh parched ground-peas, an' a block uh chewin' gum."

With all this they left the store, with Sykes reminding Bertha that this was his town and she could have it if she wanted it.

The men returned soon after they left, and held their watermelon feast.

"Where did Syke Jones git da 'oman from nohow?" Lindsay asked.

"Ovah Apopka. Guess dey musta been cleanin' out de town when she lef'. She don't look lak a thing but a hunk uh liver wid hair on it."

"Well, she sho' kin squall," Dave Carter contributed. "When she gits ready tuh laff, she jes' opens huh mouf an' latches it back tuh de las' notch. No ole grandpa alligator down in Lake Bell ain't got nothin' on huh."

Bertha had been in town three months now. Sykes was still paying her room rent at Della Lewis'—the only house in town that would have taken her in. Sykes took her frequently to Winter Park to "stomps." He still assured her that he was the swellest man in the state.

"Sho' you kin have dat lil' ole house soon's Ah kin git dat 'oman outa dere. Everything b'longs tuh me an' you sho' kin have it. Ah sho' 'bominates uh skinny 'oman. Lawdy, you sho' is got one portly shape on you! You kin git *anything* you wants. Dis is *mah* town an' you sho' kin have it."

Delia's work-worn knees crawled over the earth in Gethsemane and up the rocks of Calvary many, many times during these months. She avoided the villagers and meeting places in her efforts to be blind and deaf. But Bertha nullified this to a degree, by coming to Delia's house to call Sykes out to her at the gate.

Delia and Sykes fought all the time now with no peaceful interludes. They slept and ate in silence. Two or three times Delia had attempted a timid friendliness, but she was repulsed each time. It was plain that the breaches must remain agape.

The sun had burned July to August. The heat streamed down like a million hot arrows, smiting all things living upon the earth. Grass withered, leaves browned, snakes went blind in shedding and men and dogs went mad. Dog days!

Delia came home one day and found Sykes there before her. She wondered, but started to go on into the house without speaking, even though he was standing in the kitchen door and she must either stoop under his arm or ask him to move. He made no room for her. She noticed a soap box beside the steps, but paid no particular attention to it, knowing that he must have brought it there. As she was stooping to pass under his outstretched arm, he suddenly pushed her backward, laughingly.

"Look in de box dere Delia, Ah done brung yuh somethin'!"

She nearly fell upon the box in her stumbling, and when she saw what it held, she all but fainted outright.

"Syke! Syke, mah Gawd! You take dat rattlesnake 'way from heah! You *gottuh*. Oh, Jesus, have mussy!"

"Ah aint gut tuh do nuthin' uh de kin'—fact is Ah aint got tuh do nothin' but die. Taint no use uh you puttin' on airs makin' out lak you skeered uh dat snake—he's gointer stay right heah tell he die. He wouldn't bite me cause Ah knows how tuh handle 'im. Nohow he wouldn't risk breakin' out his fangs 'gin yo' skinny laigs."

"Naw, now Syke, don't keep dat thing 'roun' heah tuh skeer me tuh death. You knows Ah'm even feared uh earth worms. Thass de biggest snake Ah evah did see. Kill 'im Syke, please."

"Doan ast me tuh do nothin' fuh yuh. Goin' roun' trying' tuh be so damn asterperious. Naw, Ah aint gonna kill it. Ah think uh damn sight mo' uh him dan you! Dat's a nice snake an' anybody doan lak 'im kin jes' hit de grit."

The village soon heard that Sykes had the snake, and came to see and ask questions.

"How de hen-fire did you ketch dat six-foot rattler, Syke?" Thomas asked.

"He's full uh frogs so he caint hardly move, thass how. Ah eased up on 'm. But Ah'm a snake charmer an' knows how tuh handle 'em. Shux, dat aint nothin'. Ah could ketch one eve'y day if Ah so wanted tuh."

"Whut he needs is a heavy hick'ry club leaned real heavy on his head. Dat's de bes 'way tuh charm a rattlesnake."

"Naw, Walt, y'll jes' don't understand dese diamon' backs lak Ah do," said Sykes in a superior tone of voice.

The village agreed with Walter, but the snake stayed on. His box remained by the kitchen door with its screen wire covering. Two or three days later it had digested its meal of frogs and literally came to life. It rattled at every movement in the kitchen or the yard. One day as Delia came down the kitchen steps she saw his chalky-white fangs curved like scimitars hung in the wire meshes. This time she did not run away with averted eyes as usual. She stood for a long time in the doorway in a red fury that grew bloodier for every second that she regarded the creature that was her torment.

That night she broached the subject as soon as Sykes sat down to the table.

"Syke, Ah wants you tuh take dat snake 'way fum heah. You done starved me an' Ah put up widcher, you done beat me an Ah took dat, but you done kilt all mah insides bringin' dat varmint heah."

Sykes poured out a saucer full of coffee and drank it deliberately before he answered her.

"A whole lot Ah keer 'bout how you feels inside uh out. Dat snake aint goin' no damn wheah till Ah gits ready fuh 'im tuh go. So fur as beatin' is concerned, yuh aint took near all dat you gointer take ef yuh stay 'roun' me."

Delia pushed back her plate and got up from the table. "Ah hates you, Sykes," she said calmly. "Ah hates you tuh de same degree dat Ah useter love yuh. Ah done took an' took till mah belly is full up tuh mah neck. Dat's de reason Ah got mah letter fum de church an' moved mah membership tuh Woodbridge—so Ah don't haftuh take no sacrament wid yuh. Ah don't wantuh see yuh 'roun' me atall. Lay 'roun' wid dat 'oman all yuh wants tuh, but gwan 'way fum me an' mah house. Ah hates yuh lak uh suck-egg dog."

Sykes almost let the huge wad of corn bread and collard greens he was chewing fall out of his mouth in amazement. He had a hard time whipping himself up to the proper fury to try to answer Delia.

"Well, Ah'm glad you does hate me. Ah'm sho' tiahed uh you hangin' ontuh me. Ah don't want yuh. Look at yuh stringey ole neck! Yo' rawbony laigs an' arms is enough tuh cut uh man tuh death. You looks jes' lak de dev-vul's doll-baby tuh *me*. You cain't hate me no worse dan Ah hates you. Ah been hatin' *you* fuh years."

"Yo' ole black hide don't look lak nothin' tuh me, but uh passle uh wrin-kled up rubber, wid yo' big ole yeahs flappin' on each side lak uh paih uh buzzard wings. Don't think Ah'm gointuh be run 'way fum mah house nei-ther. Ah'm goin' tuh de white folks bout *you*, mah young man, de very nex' time you lay yo' han's on me. Mah cup is done run ovah." Delia said this with no signs of fear and Sykes departed from the house, threatening her, but made not the slightest move to carry out any of them.

That night he did not return at all, and the next day being Sunday, Delia was glad she did not have to quarrel before she hitched up her pony and drove the four miles to Woodbridge.

She stayed to the night service—"love feast"—which was very warm and full of spirit. In the emotional winds her domestic trials were borne far and wide so that she sang as she drove homeward.

> *"Jurden water, black an' col'*
> *Chills de body, not de soul*
> *An' Ah wantah cross Jurden in uh calm time."*

She came from the barn to the kitchen door and stopped.

"Whut's de mattah, ol' satan, you aint kickin' up yo' racket?" She addressed the snake's box. Complete silence. She went on into the house with a new hope in its birth struggles. Perhaps her threat to go to the white folks had frightened Sykes! Perhaps he was sorry! Fifteen years of misery and suppression had brought Delia to the place where she would hope *any-thing* that looked towards a way over or through her wall of inhibitions.

She felt in the march safe behind the stove at once for a match. There was only one there.

"Dat niggah wouldn't fetch nothin' heah tuh save his rotten neck, but he kin run thew whut Ah brings quick enough. Now he done toted off nigh on tuh haff uh box uh matches. He done had dat 'oman heah in mah house, too."

Nobody but a woman could tell how she knew this even before she struck the match. But she did and it put her into a new fury.

Presently she brought in the tubs to put the white things to soak. This time she decided she need not bring the hamper out of the bedroom; she would go in there and do the sorting. She picked up the pot-bellied lamp and went in. The room was small and the hamper stood hard by the foot of the white iron bed. She could sit and reach through the bedposts—resting as she worked.

"Ah wantah cross Jurden in uh calm time," She was singing again. The mood of the "love feast" had returned. She threw back the lid of the basket almost gaily. Then, moved by both horror and terror, she sprang back to-ward the door. *There lay the snake in the basket!* He moved sluggishly at first, but even as she turned round and round, jumped up and down in an insanity of fear, he began to stir vigorously. She saw him pouring his awful beauty from the basket upon the bed, then she seized the lamp and ran as fast as she could to the kitchen. The wind from the open door blew out the light and the darkness added to her terror. She sped to the darkness of the yard, slamming the door after her before she thought to set down the lamp. She did not feel safe even on the ground, so she climbed up in the hay barn.

There for an hour or more she lay sprawled upon the hay a gibbering wreck.

Finally, she grew quiet, and after that, coherent thought. With this, stalked through her a cold, bloody rage. Hours of this. A period of introspection, a space of retrospection, then a mixture of both. Out of this an awful calm.

"Well, Ah done de bes' Ah could. If things aint right, Gawd knows taint mah fault."

She went to sleep—a twitch sleep—and woke up to a faint gray sky. There was a loud hollow sound below. She peered out. Sykes was at the wood-pile, demolishing a wire-covered box.

He hurried to the kitchen door, but hung outside there some minutes before he entered, and stood some minutes more inside before he closed it after him.

The gray in the sky was spreading. Delia descended without fear now, and crouched beneath the low bedroom window. The drawn shade shut out the dawn, shut in the night. But the thin walls held back no sound.

"Dat ol' scratch is woke up now!" She mused at the tremendous whirr inside, which every woodsman knows, is one of the sound illusions. The rattler is a ventriloquist. His whirr sounds to the right, to the left, straight ahead, behind, close –under foot—everywhere but where it is. Woe to him who guesses wrong unless he is prepared to hold up his end of the argument! Sometimes he strikes without rattling at all.

Inside, Sykes heard nothing until he knocked a pot lid off the stove while trying to reach the match safe in the dark. He had emptied his pockets at Bertha's.

The snake seemed to wake up under the stove and Sykes made a quick leap into the bedroom. In spite of the gin he had had, his head was clearing now.

"Mah Gawd!" he chattered, "ef Ah could on'y strack uh light!"

The rattling ceased for a moment as he stood paralyzed. He waited. It seemed that the snake waited also.

"Oh, fuh de light! Ah thought he'd be too sick"—Sykes was muttering to himself when the whirr began again, closer, right underfoot this time. Long before this, Sykes' ability to think had been flattened down to primitive instinct and he leaped—onto the bed.

Outside Delia heard a cry that might have come from a maddened chimpanzee, a stricken gorilla. All the terror, all the horror, all the rage that man possibly could express, without a recognizable human sound.

A tremendous stir inside there, another series of animal screams, the intermittent whirr of the reptile. The shade torn violently down from the window, letting in the red dawn, a huge brown hand seizing the window stick, great dull blows upon the wooden floor punctuating the gibberish of sound long after the rattle of the snake had abruptly subsided. All this Delia could see and hear from her place beneath the window, and it made her ill. She crept over to the four-o'clocks and stretched herself on the cool earth to recover.

She lay there. "Delia. Delia!" She could hear Sykes calling in a most despairing tone as one who expected no answer. The sun crept on up, and he called. Delia could not move—her legs were gone flabby. She never moved, he called, and the sun kept rising.

"Mah Gawd!" She heard him moan, "Mah Gawd fum Heben!" She heard him stumbling about and got up from her flower-bed. The sun was growing warm. As she approached the door she heard him call out hopefully, "Delia, is dat you Ah heah?"

She saw him on his hands and knees as soon as she reached the door. He crept an inch or two toward her—all that he was able, and she saw his horribly swollen neck and his one open eye shining with hope. A surge of pity too strong to support bore her away from that eye that must, could not, fail to see the tubs. He would see the lamp. Orlando with its doctors was too far. She could scarcely reach the Chi-naberry tree, where she waited in the growing heat while inside she knew the cold river was creeping up and up to extinguish that eye which must know by now that she knew.

1926

The Gilded Six-Bits

It was a Negro yard around a Negro house in a Negro settlement that looked to the payroll of the G. and G. Fertilizer works for its support.

But there was something happy about the place. The front yard was parted in the middle by a sidewalk from gate to doorstep, a sidewalk edged on either side by quart bottles driven neck down into the ground on a slant. A mess of homey flowers planted without a plan but blooming cheerily from their helter-skelter places. The fence and house were whitewashed. The porch and steps scrubbed white.

The front door stood open to the sunshine so that the floor of the front room could finish drying after its weekly scouring. It was Saturday. Everything clean from the front gate to the privy house. Yard raked so that the strokes of the rake would make a pattern. Fresh newspaper cut in fancy edge on the kitchen shelves.

Missie May was bathing herself in the galvanized washtub in the bedroom. Her dark-brown skin glistened under the soapsuds that skittered down from her washrag. Her stiff young breasts thrust forward aggressively, like broad-based cones with the tips lacquered in black.

She heard men's voices in the distance and glanced at the dollar clock on the dresser.

"Humph! Ah'm way behind time t'day! Joe gointer be heah 'fore Ah git mah clothes on if Ah don't make haste."

She grabbed the clean mealsack at hand and dried herself hurriedly and began to dress. But before she could tie her slippers, there came the ring of singing metal on wood. Nine times.

Missie May grinned with delight. She had not seen the big tall man come stealing in the gate and creep up the walk grinning happily at the joyful mischief he was about to commit. But she knew that it was her husband throwing silver dollars in the door for her to pick up and pile beside her plate at dinner. It was this way every Saturday afternoon. The nine dollars hurled into the open door, he scurried to a hiding place behind the Cape jasmine bush and waited.

Missie May promptly appeared at the door in mock alarm.

"Who dat chunkin' money in mah do'way?" she demanded. No answer from the yard. She leaped off the porch and began to search the shrubbery. She peeped under the porch and hung over the gate to look up and down the road. While she did this, the man behind the jasmine darted to the chinaberry tree. She spied him and gave chase.

"Nobody ain't gointer be chunkin' money at me and Ah not do 'em nothin'," she shouted in mock anger. He ran around the house with Missie May at his heels. She overtook him at the kitchen door. He ran inside but could not close it after him before she crowded in and locked with him in a rough-and-tumble. For several minutes the two were a furious mass of male and female energy. Shouting, laughing, twisting, turning, tussling, tickling each other in the ribs; Missie May clutching onto Joe and Joe trying, but not too hard, to get away.

"Missie May, take yo' hand out mah pocket!" Joe shouted out between laughs.

"Ah ain't, Joe, not lessen you gwine gimme whateve' it is good you got in yo' pocket. Turn it go, Joe, do Ah'll tear yo' clothes."

"Go on tear 'em. You de one dat pushes de needles round heah. Move yo' hand, Missie May."

"Lemme git dat paper sak out yo' pocket. Ah bet it's candy kisses."

"Tain't. Move yo' hand. Woman ain't got no business in a man's clothes nohow. Go way."

Missie May gouged way down and gave an upward jerk and triumphed.

"Unhhunh! Ah got it! It 'tis so candy kisses. Ah knowed you had somethin' for me in yo' clothes. Now Ah got to see whut's in every pocket you got."

Joe smiled indulgently and let his wife go through all of his pockets and take out the things that he had hidden for her to find. She bore off the chewing gum, the cake of sweet soap, the pocket handkerchief as if she had wrested them from him, as if they had not been bought for the sake of this friendly battle.

"Whew! dat play-fight done got me all warmed up!" Joe exclaimed. "Got me some water in de kittle?"

"Yo' water is on de fire and yo' clean things is cross de bed. Hurry up and wash yo'self and git changed so we kin eat. Ah'm hongry." As Missie said this, she bore the steaming kettle into the bedroom.

"You ain't hongry, sugar," Joe contradicted her. "Youse jes' a little empty. Ah'm de one whut's hongry. Ah could eat up camp meetin', back off 'ssociation, and drink Jurdan dry. Have it on de table when Ah git out de tub."

"Don't you mess wid mah business, man. You git in yo' clothes. Ah'm a real wife, not no dress and breath. Ah might not look lak one, but if you burn me, you won't git a thing but wife ashes."

Joe splashed in the bedroom and Missie May fanned around in the kitchen. A fresh red-and-white checked cloth on the table. Big pitcher of buttermilk beaded with pale drops of butter from the churn. Hot fried mullet, crackling bread, ham hock atop a mound of string beans and new potatoes, and perched on the windowsill a pone of spicy potato pudding.

Very little talk during the meal but that little consisted of banter that pretended to deny affection but in reality flaunted it. Like when Missie May reached for a second helping of the tater pone. Joe snatched it out of her reach.

After Missie May had made two or three unsuccessful grabs at the pan, she begged, "Aw, Joe, gimme some mo' dat tater pone."

"Nope, sweetenin' is for us menfolks. Y'all pritty lil frail eels don't need nothin' lak dis. You too sweet already."

"Please, Joe."

"Naw, naw. Ah don't want you to git no sweeter than whut you is already. We goin' down de road a lil piece t'night so you go put on yo' Sunday-go-to-meetin' things."

Missie May looked at her husband to see if he was playing some prank. "Sho nuff, Joe?"

"Yeah. We goin' to de ice cream parlor."

"Where de ice cream parlor at, Joe?"

"A new man done come heah from Chicago and he done got a place and took and opened it up for a ice cream parlor, and bein' as it's real swell, Ah wants you to be one de first ladies to walk in dere and have some set down."

"Do Jesus, Ah ain't knowed nothin' bout it. Who de man done it?"

"Mister Otis D. Slemmons, of spots and places—Memphis, Chicago, Jacksonville, Philadelphia and so on."

"Dat heavyset man wid his mouth full of gold teeths?"

"Yeah. Where did you see 'im at?"

"Ah went down to de sto' tuh git a box of lye and Ah seen 'im standin' on de corner talkin' to some of de mens, and Ah come on back and went to scrubbin' de floor, and he passed and tipped his hat whilst Ah was scourin' de steps. Ah thought Ah never seen *him* befo'."

Joe smiled pleasantly. "Yeah, he's up-to-date. He got de finest clothes Ah ever seen on a colored man's back."

"Aw, he don't look no better in his clothes than you do in yourn. He got a puzzlegut on 'im and he so chuckleheaded he got a pone behind his neck."

Joe looked down at his own abdomen and said wistfully: "Wisht Ah had a build on me lak he got. He ain't puzzlegutted, honey. He jes' got a corperation. Dat make 'm look lak a rich white man. All rich mens is got some belly on 'em."

"Ah seen de pitchers of Henry Ford and he's a spare-built man and Rockefeller look lak he ain't got but one gut. But Ford and Rockefeller and dis Slemmons and all de rest kin be as many-gutted as dey please, Ah's satisfied wid you jes' lak you is, baby. God took pattern after a pine tree and built you noble. Youse a pritty man, and if Ah knowed any way to make you mo' pritty still Ah'd take and do it."

Joe reached over gently and toyed with Missie May's ear. "You jes' say dat cause you love me, but Ah know Ah can't hold no light to Otis D. Slemmons. Ah ain't never been nowhere and Ah ain't got nothin' but you."

Missie May got on his lap and kissed him and he kissed back in kind. Then he went on. "All de womens is crazy 'bout 'im everywhere he go."

"How you know dat, Joe?"

"He tole us so hisself."

"Dat don't make it so. His mouf is cut crossways, ain't it? Well, he kin lie jes' lak anybody else."

"Good Lawd, Missie! You womens sho is hard to sense into things. He's got a five-dollar gold piece for a stickpin and he got a ten-dollar gold piece on his watch chain and his mouf is jes' crammed full of gold teeths. Sho wisht it wuz mine. And whut make it so cool, he got money 'cumulated. And womens give it all to 'im."

"Ah don't see whut de womens see on 'im. Ah wouldn't give 'im a wink if de sheriff wuz after 'im."

"Well, he tole us how de white womens in Chicago give 'im all dat gold money. So he don't 'low nobody to touch it at all. Not even put day finger on it. Dey told 'im not to. You kin make 'miration at it, but don't tetch it."

"Whyn't he stay up dere where dey so crazy 'bout 'im?"

"Ah reckon dey done made 'im vast-rich and he wants to travel some. He says dey wouldn't leave 'im hit a lick of work. He got mo' lady people crazy 'bout him than he kin shake a stick at."

"Joe, Ah hates to see you so dumb. Dat stray nigger jes' tell y'all anything and y'all b'lieve it."

"Go 'head on now, honey, and put on yo' clothes. He talkin' 'bout his pritty womens—Ah want 'im to see *mine*."

Missie May went off to dress and Joe spent the time trying to make his stomach punch out like Slemmons's middle. He tried the rolling swagger of the stranger, but found that his tall bone-and-muscle stride fitted ill with it. He just had time to drop back into his seat before Missie May came in dressed to go.

On the way home that night Joe was exultant. "Didn't Ah say ole Otis was swell? Can't he talk Chicago talk? Wuzn't dat funny whut he said when great big fat ole Ida Armstrong come in? He asted me, 'Who is dat broad wid de forte shake?' Dat's a new word. Us always thought forty was a set of figgers but he showed us where it means a whole heap of things. Sometimes he don't say forty, he jes' say thirty-eight and two and dat mean de same thing. Know whut he told me when Ah wuz payin' for our ice cream? He say, Ah have to hand it to you, Joe. Dat wife of yours is jes' thirty-eight and two. Yessuh, she's forte!' Ain't he killin'?"

"He'll do in case of a rush. But he sho is got uh heap uh gold on 'im. Dat's de first time Ah ever seed gold money. It lookted good on him sho nuff, but it'd look a whole heap better on you."

"Who, me? Missie May, youse crazy! Where would a po' man lak me git gold money from?"

Missie May was silent for a minute, then she said, "Us might find some goin' long de road some time. Us could."

"Who would be losin' gold money round heah? We ain't even seen none dese white folks wearin' no gold money on dey watch chain. You must be figgerin' Mister Packard or Mister Cadillac goin' pass through heah."

"You don't know whut been lost 'round heah. Maybe somebody way back in memorial times lost they gold money and went on off and it ain't never been found. And then if we wuz to find it, you could wear some 'thout havin' no gang of womens lak dat Slemmons say he got."

Joe laughed and hugged her. "Don't be so wishful 'bout me. Ah'm satisfied de way Ah is. So long as Ah be yo' husband. Ah don't keer 'bout nothin' else. Ah'd ruther all de other womens in de world to be dead than for you to have de toothache. Less we go to bed and git our night rest."

It was Saturday night once more before Joe could parade his wife in Slemmons's ice cream parlor again. He worked the night shift and Saturday was his only night off. Every other evening around six o'clock he left home, and dying dawn saw him hustling home around the lake, where the challenging sun flung a flaming sword from east to west across the trembling water.

That was the best part of life—going home to Missie May. Their whitewashed house, the mock battle on Saturday, the dinner and ice cream parlor afterwards, church on Sunday nights when Missie outdressed any woman in town—all, everything, was right.

One night around eleven the acid ran out at the G. and G. The foreman knocked off the crew and let the steam die down. As Joe rounded the lake on his way home, a lean moon rode the lake in a silver boat. If anybody had asked Joe about the moon on the lake, he would have said he hadn't paid it any attention. But he saw it with his feelings. It made him yearn painfully for Missie. Creation obsessed him. He thought about children. They had been married more than a year now. They had money put away. They ought to be making little feet for shoes. A little boy child would be about right.

He saw a dim light in the bedroom and decided to come in through the kitchen door. He could wash the fertilizer dust off himself before presenting himself to Missie May. It would be nice for her not to know that he was there until he slipped into his place in bed and hugged her back. She always liked that.

He eased the kitchen door open slowly and silently, but when he went to set his dinner bucket on the table he bumped it into a pile of dishes, and something crashed to the floor. He heard his wife gasp in fright and hurried to reassure her.

"Iss me, honey. Don't git skeered."

There was a quick, large movement in the bedroom. A rustle, a thud, and a stealthy silence. The light went out.

What? Robbers? Murderers? Some varmint attacking his helpless wife, perhaps. He struck a match, threw himself on guard and stepped over the doorsill into the bedroom.

The great belt on the wheel of Time slipped and eternity stood still. By the match light he could see the man's legs fighting with his breeches in his frantic desire to get them on. He had both chance and time to kill the intruder in his helpless condition—half in and half out of his pants—but he was too weak to take action. The shapeless enemies of humanity that live in the hours of Time had waylaid Joe. He was assaulted in his weakness. Like Samson awakening after his haircut. So he just opened his mouth and laughed.

The match went out and he struck another and lit the lamp. A howling wind raced across his heart, but underneath its fury he heard his wife sobbing and Slemmons pleading for his life. Offering to buy it with all that he had. "Please, suh, don't kill me. Sixty-two dollars at de sto'. Gold money."

Joe just stood. Slemmons looked at the window, but it was screened. Joe stood out like a rough-backed mountain between him and the door. Barring him from escape, from sunrise, from life.

He considered a surprise attack upon the big clown that stood there laughing like a chessy cat. But before his fist could travel an inch, Joe's own rushed out to crush him like a battering ram. Then Joe stood over him.

"Git into yo' damn rags, Slemmons, and dat quick."

Slemmons scrambled to his feet and into his vest and coat. As he grabbed his hat, Joe's fury overrode his intentions and he grabbed at Slemmons with his left hand and struck at him with his right. The right landed. The left grazed the front of his vest. Slemmons was knocked a somersault into the kitchen and fled through the open door. Joe found himself alone with Missie May, with the golden watch charm clutched in his left fist. A short bit of broken chain dangled between his fingers.

Missie May was sobbing. Wails of weeping without words. Joe stood, and after a while he found out that he had something in his hand. And then he stood and felt without thinking and without seeing with his natural eyes. Missie May kept on crying and Joe kept on feeling so much, and not knowing what to do with all his feelings, he put Slemmons's watch charm in his pants pocket and took a good laugh and went to bed.

"Missie May, whut you cryin' for?"

"Cause Ah love you so hard and Ah know you don't love *me* no mo'."

Joe sank his face into the pillow for a spell, then he said huskily, "You don't know de feelings of dat yet, Missie May."

"Oh Joe, honey, he said he wuz gointer give me dat gold money and he jes' kept on after me—"

Joe was very still and silent for a long time. Then he said, "Well, don't cry no mo', Missie May. Ah got yo' gold piece for you."

The hours went past on their rusty ankles. Joe still and quiet on one bed rail and Missie May wrung dry of sobs on the other. Finally the sun's tide crept upon the shore of night and drowned all its hours. Missie May with her face stiff and streaked towards the window saw the dawn come into her yard. It was day. Nothing more. Joe wouldn't be coming home as usual. No need to fling open the front door and sweep off the porch, making it nice for Joe. Never no more breakfast to cook; no more washing and starching of Joe's jumper-jackets and pants. No more nothing. So why get up?

With this strange man in her bed, she felt embarrassed to get up and dress. She decided to wait till he had dressed and gone. Then she would get up, dress quickly and be gone forever beyond reach of Joe's looks and laughs. But he never moved. Red light turned to yellow, then white.

From beyond the no-man's land between them came a voice. A strange voice that yesterday had been Joe's.

"Missie May, ain't you gonna fix me no breakfus'?"

She sprang out of bed. "Yeah, Joe. Ah didn't reckon you wuz hongry."

No need to die today. Joe needed her for a few more minutes anyhow.

Soon there was a roaring fire in the cookstove. Water bucket full and two chickens killed. Joe loved fried chicken and rice. She didn't deserve a thing and good Joe was letting her cook him some breakfast. She rushed hot biscuits to the table as Joe took his seat.

He ate with his eyes in his plate. No laughter, no banter.

"Missie May, you ain't eatin' yo' breakfus'."

"Ah don't choose none, Ah thank yuh."

His coffee cup was empty. She sprang to refill it. When she turned from the stove and bent to set the cup beside Joe's plate, she saw the yellow coin on the table between them.

She slumped into her seat and wept into her arms.

Presently Joe said calmly, "Missie May, you cry too much. Don't look back lak Lot's wife and turn to salt."

The sun, the hero of every day, the impersonal old man that beams as brightly on death as on birth, came up every morning and raced across the blue dome and dipped into the sea of fire every morning. Water ran downhill and birds nested.

Missie knew why she didn't leave Joe. She couldn't. She loved him too much, but she could not understand why Joe didn't leave her. He was polite, even kind at times, but aloof.

There were no more Saturday romps. No ringing silver dollars to stack beside her plate. No pockets to rifle. In fact, the yellow coin in his trousers was like a monster hiding in the cave of his pockets to destroy her.

She often wondered if he still had it, but nothing could have induced her to ask nor yet to explore his pockets to see for herself. Its shadow was in the house whether or no.

One night Joe came home around midnight and complained of pains in the back. He asked Missie to rub him down with liniment. It had been three months since Missie had touched his body and it all seemed strange. But she rubbed him. Grateful for the chance. Before morning youth triumphed and Missie exulted. But the next day, as she joyfully made up their bed, beneath her pillow she found the piece of money with the bit of chain attached.

Alone to herself, she looked at the thing with loathing, but look she must. She took it into her hands with trembling and saw first thing that it was no gold piece. It was a gilded half dollar. Then she knew why Slemmons had forbidden anyone to touch his gold. He trusted village eyes at a distance not to recognize his stickpin as a gilded quarter, and his watch charm as a four-bit piece.

She was glad at first that Joe had left it there. Perhaps he was through with her punishment. They were man and wife again. Then another thought came clawing at her. He had come home to buy from her as if she were any woman in the longhouse. Fifty cents for her love. As if to say that he could pay as well as Slemmons. She slid the coin into his Sunday pants pocket and dressed herself and left his house.

Halfway between her house and the quarters she met her husband's mother, and after a short talk she turned and went back home. Never would she admit defeat to that woman who prayed for it nightly. If she had not the substance of marriage she had the outside show. Joe must leave *her*. She let him see she didn't want his old gold four-bits, too.

She saw no more of the coin for some time though she knew that Joe could not help finding it in his pocket. But his health kept poor, and he came home at least every ten days to be rubbed.

The sun swept around the horizon, trailing its robes of weeks and days. One morning as Joe came in from work, he found Missie May chopping wood. Without a word he took the ax and chopped a huge pile before he stopped.

"You ain't got no business choppin' wood, and you know it."

"How come? Ah been choppin' it for de last longest."

"Ah ain't blind. You makin' feet for shoes."

"Won't you be glad to have a lil baby chile, Joe?"

"You know dat 'thout astin' me."

"Iss gointer be a boy chile and de very spit of you."

"You reckon, Missie May?"

"Who else could it look lak?"

Joe said nothing, but he thrust his hand deep into his pocket and fingered something there.

It was almost six months later Missie May took to bed and Joe went and got his mother to come wait on the house.

Missie May was delivered of a fine boy. Her travail was over when Joe come in from work one morning. His mother and the old woman were drinking great bowls of coffee around the fire in the kitchen.

The minute Joe came into the room his mother called him aside.

"How did Missie May make out?" he asked quickly.

"Who, dat gal? She strong as a ox. She gointer have plenty mo'. We done fixed her wid de sugar and lard to sweeten her for de nex' one."

Joe stood silent awhile.

"You ain't ask 'bout de baby, Joe. You oughter be mighty proud cause he sho is de spittin' image of yuh, son. Dat's yourn all right, if you never git another one, dat un is yourn. And you know Ah'm mighty proud too, son, cause Ah never thought well of you marryin' Missie May cause her ma used tuh fan her foot round right smart and Ah been mighty skeered dat Missie May wuz gointer git misput on her road."

Joe said nothing. He fooled around the house till late in the day, then, just before he went to work, he went and stood at the foot of the bed and asked his wife how she felt. He did this every day during the week.

On Saturday he went to Orlando to make his market. It had been a long time since he had done that.

Meat and lard, meal and flour, soap and starch. Cans of corn and toma-toes. All the staples. He fooled around town for a while and bought bananas and apples. Way after while he went around to the candy store.

"Hello, Joe," the clerk greeted him. "Ain't seen you in a long time."

"Nope, Ah ain't been heah. Been round in spots and places."

"Want some of them molasses kisses you always buy?"

"Yessuh." He threw the gilded half dollar on the counter. "Will dat spend?"

"What is it, Joe? Well, I'll be doggone! A gold-plated four-bit piece. Where'd you git it, Joe?"

"Offen a stray nigger dat come through Eatonville. He had it on his watch chain for a charm—goin' round making out iss gold money. Ha ha! He had a quarter on his tiepin and it wuz all golded up too. Tryin' to fool people. Makin' out he so rich and everything. Ha! Ha! Tryin' to tole off folk-ses wives from home."

"How did you git it, Joe? Did he fool you, too?"

"Who, me? Naw suh! He ain't fooled me none. Know whut Ah done? He come round me wid his smart talk. Ah hauled off and knocked 'im down and took his old four-bits away from 'im. Gointer buy my wife some good ole lasses kisses wid it. Gimme fifty cents worth of dem candy kisses."

"Fifty cents buys a mighty lot of candy kisses, Joe. Why don't you split it up and take some chocolate bars, too? They eat good, too."

"Yessuh, dey do, but Ah wants all dat in kisses. Ah got a lil boy chile home now. Tain't a week old yet, but he kin suck a sugar tit and maybe eat one them kisses hisself."

Joe got his candy and left the store. The clerk turned to the next cus-tomer. "Wisht I could be like these darkies. Laughin' all the time. Nothin' worries 'em."

Back in Eatonville, Joe reached his own front door. There was the ring of singing metal on wood. Fifteen times. Missie May couldn't run to the door, but she crept there as quickly as she could.

"Joe Banks, Ah hear you chunkin' money in mah do'way. You wait till Ah got mah strength back and Ah'm gointer fix you for dat."

1933

CLAUDE MCKAY
1889–1948

Of the many gifted writers who contributed to the rich literary legacy of the Harlem Renaissance, Claude McKay, a Jamaican immigrant, was clearly the most militant. McKay's most famous poem, "If We Must Die," an eloquent and provocative sonnet, was inspired by the violent race riots that erupted in Chicago and other cities in 1919. In other deeply moving, carefully crafted poems, McKay voices his outrage at the treatment of blacks in a racist society. The poem "The Lynching," for example, is a chilling indictment against the hatred and vigilantism that cost many black Americans their lives in the 1920s and 1930s. However, the social protest verse upon which McKay's reputation as a poet ultimately rests represents only a small portion of his approximately two hundred published poems.

Born in the Clarendon Hills of Jamaica, McKay began writing poetry in childhood. He published two books of dialect verse in 1912. In recognition of this achievement, the Jamaican Institute of Arts and Sciences awarded McKay a medal and a stipend that allowed him to study agriculture briefly at Tuskegee Institute and later at Kansas State University (1912–1914). McKay left Kansas State in 1914 to pursue a writing career in New York City, where he became involved with the socialist movement and wrote for radical journals like Max Eastman's *Liberator*, for which he served as an editor. As the Harlem Renaissance began to flower, McKay published *Harlem Shadows* (1922), a landmark collection of poems. McKay also published three novels, including the popular and controversial *Home to Harlem* (1928), as well as other books and essays. The majority of McKay's fiction was written between 1923 and 1934, when he was an expatriate, living variously in France, Great Britain, and North Africa, and his work reflects the broad range of black experience in what is now termed the Diaspora. He died in Chicago in 1948. His *Selected Poems* appeared posthumously in 1953.

Like his friend and fellow Renaissance poet Countee Cullen, McKay preferred the traditional verse forms of the British masters, particularly the sonnet and short lyric. Thematically, McKay's poetry includes nostalgic lyrics about rural Jamaica, and poems celebrating nature, love, and Christian faith, in addition to the powerful protest verses. McKay's best poetry sparkles with sharp, fresh images and resonates with an indomitable passion for life.

Elvin Holt
Texas State University–San Marcos

PRIMARY WORKS

Songs of Jamaica, 1912; *Spring in New Hampshire,* 1920; *Harlem Shadows,* 1922; *Home to Harlem,* 1928; *Banjo,* 1929; *Gingertown,* 1932; *Banana Bottom,* 1933; *A Long Way from Home,* 1937; *Harlem: Negro Metropolis,* 1940; *Selected Poems,* 1953; *The Passion of Claude McKay: Selected Poetry and Prose, 1912–948,* ed. Wayne F. Cooper, 1973.

The Harlem Dancer

Applauding youths laughed with young prostitutes
And watched her perfect, half-clothed body sway;
Her voice was like the sound of blended flutes
Blown by black players upon a picnic day.
She sang and danced on gracefully and calm,   5
The light gauze hanging loose about her form;
To me she seemed a proudly-swaying palm
Grown lovelier for passing through a storm.
Upon her swarthy neck black shiny curls
Luxuriant fell; and tossing coins in praise,   10
The wine-flushed, bold-eyed boys, and even the girls,
Devoured her shape with eager, passionate gaze;
But looking at her falsely-smiling face,
I knew her self was not in that strange place.

1917

If We Must Die

If we must die, let it not be like hogs
Hunted and penned in an inglorious spot,
While round us bark the mad and hungry dogs,
Making their mock at our accursed lot.
If we must die, O let us nobly die,   5
So that our precious blood may not be shed
In vain; then even the monsters we defy
Shall be constrained to honor us though dead!
O kinsmen! we must meet the common foe!
Though far outnumbered let us show us brave,   10
And for their thousand blows deal one deathblow!
What though before us lies the open grave?
Like men we'll face the murderous, cowardly pack,
Pressed to the wall, dying, but fighting back!

1919

The Lynching

His Spirit in smoke ascended to high heaven.
His father, by the cruelest way of pain,
Had bidden him to his bosom once again;
The awful sin remained still unforgiven.
All night a bright and solitary star   5
(Perchance the one that ever guided him,
Yet gave him up at last to Fate's wild whim)
Hung pitifully o'er the swinging char.
Day dawned, and soon the mixed crowds came to view
The ghastly body swaying in the sun.   10
The women thronged to look, but never a one
Showed sorrow in her eyes of steely blue.

And little lads, lynchers that were to be,
Danced round the dreadful thing in fiendish glee.

                                                          1920

Harlem Shadows

I hear the halting footsteps of a lass
    In Negro Harlem when the night lets fall
Its veil. I see the shapes of girls who pass
    To bend and barter at desire's call.
Ah, little dark girls who in slippered feet   5
Go prowling through the night from street to street!

Through the long night until the silver break
    Of day the little gray feet know no rest;
Through the lone night until the last snow-flake
    Has dropped from heaven upon the earth's white breast,   10
The dusky, half-clad girls of tired feet
Are trudging, thinly shod, from street to street.

Ah, stern harsh world, that in the wretched way
    Of poverty, dishonor and disgrace,
Has pushed the timid little feet of clay,   15
    The sacred brown feet of my fallen race!
Ah, heart of me, the weary, weary feet
In Harlem wandering from street to street.

                                                          1920

I Shall Return

I shall return again. I shall return
To laugh and love and watch with wonder-eyes
At golden noon the forest fires burn,
Wafting their blue-black smoke to sapphire skies.
I shall return to loiter by the streams   5
That bathe the brown blades of the bending grasses,
And realize once more my thousand dreams
Of waters rushing down the mountain passes.
I shall return to hear the fiddle and fife
Of village dances, dear delicious tunes   10
That stir the hidden depths of native life,
Stray melodies of dim-remembered runes.
I shall return. I shall return again
To ease my mind of long, long years of pain.

                                                                      1920

America

Although she feeds me bread of bitterness,
And sinks into my throat her tiger's tooth,
Stealing my breath of life, I will confess
I love this cultured hell that tests my youth!
Her vigor flows like tides into my blood,   5
Giving me strength erect against her hate.
Her bigness sweeps my being like a flood.
Yet as a rebel fronts a king in state,
I stand within her walls with not a shred
Of terror, malice, not a word of jeer.   10
Darkly I gaze into the days ahead,
And see her might and granite wonders there,
Beneath the touch of Time's unerring hand,
Like priceless treasures sinking in the sand.

                                                                      1921

In Bondage

I would be wandering in distant fields
Where man, and bird, and beast, lives leisurely,
And the old earth is kind, and ever yields
Her goodly gifts to all her children free;
Where life is fairer, lighter, less demanding,   5
And boys and girls have time and space for play

Before they come to years of understanding—
Somewhere I would be singing, far away.
For life is greater than the thousand wars
Men wage for it in their insatiate lust,   10
And will remain like the eternal stars,
When all that shines today is drift and dust
But I am bound with you in your mean graves,
O black men, simple slaves of ruthless slaves.

                                                                        1920

Flame-Heart

So much I have forgotten in ten years,
So much in ten brief years! I have forgot
What time the purple apples come to juice,
And what month brings the shy forget-me-not.
I have forgot the special, startling season   5
Of the pimento's flowering and fruiting;
What time of year the ground doves brown the fields
And fill the noonday with their curious fluting.
I have forgotten much, but still remember
The poinsettia's red, blood-red, in warm December.   10

I still recall the honey-fever grass,
But cannot recollect the high days when
We rooted them out of the ping-wing path
To stop the mad bees in the rabbit pen.
I often try to think in what sweet month   15
The languid painted ladies used to dapple
The yellow by-road mazing from the main,
Sweet with the golden threads of the rose-apple.
I have forgotten—strange—but quite remember
The poinsettia's red, blood-red, in warm December.   20
What weeks, what months, what time of the mild year
We cheated school to have our fling at tops?
What days our wine-thrilled bodies pulsed with joy
Feasting upon blackberries in the copse?
Oh some I know! I have embalmed the days,   25
Even the sacred moments when we played,
All innocent of passion, uncorrupt,
At noon and evening in the flame-heart's shade.
We were so happy, happy, I remember,
Beneath the poinsettia's red in warm December.   30

                                                                        1922

Flower of Love

The perfume of your body dulls my sense.
    I want nor wine nor weed; your breath alone
Suffices. In this moment rare and tense
    I worship at your breast. The flower is blown,
The saffron petals tempt my amorous mouth,   5
    The yellow heart is radiant now with dew
Soft-scented, redolent of my loved South;
    O flower of love! I give myself to you.
Uncovered on your couch of figured green,
    Here let us linger indivisible.   10
The portals of your sanctuary unseen
    Receive my offering, yielding unto me.
Oh, with our love the night is warm and deep!
    The air is sweet, my flower, and sweet the flute
Whose music lulls our burning brain to sleep,   15
    While we lie loving, passionate and mute.

          1953

A Red Flower

Your lips are like a southern lily red,
    Wet with soft rain-kisses of the night,
In which the brown bee buries deep its head,
    When still the dawn's a silver sea of light.

Your lips betray the secret of your soul,   5
    The dark delicious essence that is you,
A mystery of life, the flaming goal
    I seek through mazy pathways strange and new.

Your lips are the red symbol of a dream.
    What visions of warm lilies they impart,   10
That line the green bank of a fair blue stream,
    With butterflies and bees close to each heart!

Brown bees that murmur sounds of music rare,
    That softly fall upon the languorous breeze,
Wafting them gently on the quiet air   15
    Among untended avenues of trees.

O were I hovering, a bee, to probe
    Deep down within your scented heart, fair flower,
Enfolded by your soft vermilion robe,
    Amorous of sweets, for but one perfect hour!   20

          1953

■   ANNE SPENCER   ■
                      1882–1975

Born Annie Bethel Scales in Bramwell, West Virginia, Anne Spencer was educated at the Virginia Seminary in Lynchburg. Selected to deliver the major student address at the commencement on May 8, 1899, Annie, for her uplifting
oration, merited widespread acclaim and respect. Accompanying a gift—a four-
volume set of Emerson—that Dr. Richard H. Bolling, head of the Negro Baptist
Publishing Board of Nashville, had given Annie was a maxim: "Take what you
have and make what you want." This advice she treasured, and it evolved
through the years as her personal philosophy. Two years later, Annie married
Edward Spencer, a former classmate, and they settled in Lynchburg.

Annie was intensely interested in the world about her, yet remained apart
from active society, except when cultivating literary friends and visitors such as
W.E.B. Du Bois, James Weldon Johnson, Walter White, and others. She also corresponded with Carl Van Vechten and H. L. Mencken. Yet, under certain conditions, Spencer was an initiator, organizer, and a fighter for human rights. She
helped mobilize black citizens to oppose political and civil injustices in the
Lynchburg community. An independent thinker and doer, she assumed the pen
name Anne Spencer by which her poetry is identified. Having read Emerson's
works closely throughout her life, she asserted, "Do your 'own thing' is right out
of Emerson ... it is not new." During her midlife, she became the librarian at
the Dunbar High School to supplement her family's income when her children
reached college age.

She began writing poetry before the Harlem Renaissance, but her poetry
first appeared during this period, notably in Countee Cullen's *Caroling Dusk*
(1927). Spencer's verse is somewhat conventional and, like much of the poetry
of William Stanley Braithwaite and Cullen, is nonracial in theme. She admitted
that she possessed "no civilized articulation for the things she hated." Spencer
develops vibrant images to communicate a uniquely private experience that
becomes profound, reflecting her sensibility to a moral code that man evidences,
her fidelity to exoticism as a romantic component, her innate love of nature,
her search for the ideal while acknowledging reality, and her dual treatment of
the imagination involving both character and reader.

Spencer never had a volume of her own poems published. She was content
to probe and pursue her private musings, often, however, interacting or collaborating with other writers who sought her views and valued her editorial comments. Through several decades her creativity has been respected and admired,
for her poems have appeared in nearly every anthology of African American literature; moreover, she created new poems and revised previous compositions
until her final year: her poem titled "1975" was composed in 1974. Spencer's poetry of affirmation will endure, appealing to all who seek insights concerning
humankind's relationship to the past, present, and future.

Evelyn H. Roberts
late of St. Louis Community College–Meramec

Lines to a Nasturtium

(A Lover Muses)[1]

Flame-flower, Day-torch, Mauna Loa,
I saw a daring bee, today, pause, and soar,
   Into your flaming heart;
Then did I hear crisp, crinkled laughter
As the furies after tore him apart?   5
   A bird, next, small and humming,
Looked into your startled depths and fled....
Surely, some dread sight, and dafter
   Than human eyes as mine can see,
Set the stricken air waves drumming   10
   In his flight.

Day-torch, Flame-flower, cool-hot Beauty,
I cannot see, I cannot hear your flutey
Voice lure your loving swain,
But I know one other to whom you are in beauty   15
Born in vain:
Hair like the setting sun,
Her eyes a rising star,
Motions gracious as reeds by Babylon, bar
All your competing;   20
Hands like, how like, brown lilies sweet,
Cloth of gold were fair enough to touch her feet ...
Ah, how the sense reels at my repeating,
As once in her fire-lit heart I felt the furies
Beating, beating.   25

                                      1926

Substitution[1']

Is Life itself but many ways of thought,
How real the tropic storm or lambent breeze
Within the slightest convolution wrought
Our mantled world and men-freighted seas?

---

[1]Slightly revised from the version as first published in *Palms*, IV (October 1926),
[1']Revised in 1973 from the version as first published in Countee Cullen, ed., *Caroling*
Dusk: An Anthology of Verse by Negro Poets, 1927, 48.

God thinks ... and being comes to ardent things: 5
The splendor of the day-spent sun, love's birth,—
Or dreams a little, while creation swings
The circle of His mind and Time's full girth ...
As here within this noisy peopled room
My thought leans forward ... quick! you're lifted clear   10
Of brick and frame to moonlit garden bloom,—
Absurdly easy, now, our walking, dear,
Talking, my leaning close to touch your face ...
His All-Mind bids us keep this sacred place!

1927

For Jim, Easter Eve[1]

If ever a garden was a Gethsemane,
with old tombs set high against
the crumpled olive tree—and lichen,
this, my garden has been to me.
For such as I none other is no sweet: 5
Lacking old tombs, here stands my grief,
and certainly its ancient tree.

Peace is here and in every season
a quiet beauty.
The sky falling about me   10
evenly to the compass ...
What is sorrow but tenderness now
in this earth-close frame of land and sky
falling constantly into horizons
of east and west, north and south;   15
what is pain but happiness here
amid these green and wordless patterns,—
indefinite texture of blade and leaf:

Beauty of an old, old tree,
last comfort in Gethsemane.   20

1949

[1]Written in 1948 and first published in Langston Hughes and Arna Bontemps, eds., *The Poetry of the Negro, 1746–1949*, 1949, 65.

NELLA LARSEN
1891–1964

Until the early 1970s when previously "lost" work by women writers began to be recovered and reprinted, Nella Larsen was one of several women writers of the New Negro Renaissance relegated to the back pages of that movement's literary history, a curious fate since her career had such an auspicious beginning. Touted as a promising writer by blacks and whites alike, Larsen was encouraged by some of the most influential names on the 1920s arts scene. Walter White, onetime director of the NAACP, read drafts of *Quicksand* and urged Larsen along to its completion. Carl Van Vechten, popularly credited with promoting many Harlem Renaissance writers, introduced the novel to his publisher, Knopf. These efforts paid off. Larsen won second prize in literature in 1928 for *Quicksand* from the Harmon Foundation, which celebrated outstanding achievement by Negroes.

Quicksand was also well received by the critics. In his review of the novel, W.E.B. Du Bois praised it as the "best piece of fiction that Negro America has produced since the heyday of Chesnutt." *Passing* was similarly lauded. One reviewer gave the novel high marks for capturing, as did no other novel of the genre, the psychology of racial passing with "consummate art." Due largely to the success of these first two novels, Larsen won a Guggenheim fellowship in 1930—the first black female creative writer to be so honored—to do research on a third novel in Spain and France. That novel was never published.

After the release of *Passing*, Larsen published her last piece, a story entitled "Sanctuary." The subject of much controversy, many speculate that the scandal it created helped to send Larsen into obscurity. Following the appearance of the story in 1930, Larsen was accused of plagiarism. One reader wrote to the editor of the magazine about the striking resemblance of Larsen's story to one by Sheila Kaye-Smith entitled "Mrs. Adis," published in the January 1922 issue of *Century* magazine. The editor of *The Forum* conducted an investigation and was finally convinced that the resemblance between the stories was an extraordinary coincidence. In compliance with the editor's request, Larsen wrote a detailed explanation of the way in which she came by the germ for her story, trying to vindicate herself. Despite her editor's support, Larsen never recovered from the shock of the charge and disappeared from the literary scene altogether.

Why a career with such auspicious beginnings had such an inauspicious ending has continued to perplex students of the New Negro Renaissance. Many search for answers in the scattered fragments of Larsen's biography, which reveal a delicate and unstable person. Though there is very little information about Larsen, some pieces of her life's puzzle are fairly widely known. Born in Chicago in 1891 (though no birth certificate has been found), she was the daughter of a Danish mother and a black West Indian father who died when Larsen was a young girl. Larsen's mother remarried, this time a white man who treated his step-daughter with some disfavor. Never feeling connected to this newly configured family, Larsen searched vainly for the sense of belonging it could not provide. Fickle and unsettled, Larsen roamed from place to place, searching for some undefined and undefinable "something." She studied at Fisk University in Nashville, Tennessee; audited classes at the University of Copenhagen; and studied nursing at Lincoln Hospital Training School for Nurses in New York, graduating in 1915.

For a brief time after her nurses' training, she was superintendent of nurses at Tuskegee Institute in Alabama. Unable to tolerate its stifling atmosphere, she left after only a year and returned to New York. There she worked as a nurse between 1916 and 1918 at the hospital where she was trained and between 1918 and 1921 for New York City's Department of Health. Dissatisfied with this career, she began work in 1921 at the children's division of the New York Public Library, enrolling in its training program. During her employment as a librarian, she published her only two novels. She died in Brooklyn in 1964, practically in obscurity, having toiled as a nurse for her last two decades.

Both *Quicksand* and *Passing* illuminate the peculiar pressures on Nella Larsen as a woman writer during the male-dominated New Negro Renaissance. They show her grappling with the conflicting demands of her racial and sexual identities and the contradictions of a black and feminine aesthetic. While these novels often appear to be concessions to the dominant ideology of romance—marriage and motherhood—viewed from a feminist perspective, they can be seen as radical and original efforts to acknowledge a female sexual experience, repressed, more often than not, in both literary and social realms.

Deborah E. McDowell
University of Virginia

PRIMARY WORKS

Quicksand, 1928; *Passing*, 1929; *An Intimation of Things Distant: The Collected Fiction of Nella Larsen*, ed. Charles R. Larson, 1992; *Complete Fiction*, ed. Charles R. Larson and Marita Golden, 1992, 2001.

Passing

Part One. Encounter

One

It was the last letter in Irene Redfield's little pile of morning mail. After her other ordinary and clearly directed letters the long envelope of thin Italian paper with its almost illegible scrawl seemed out of place and alien. And there was, too, something mysterious and slightly furtive about it. A thin sly thing which bore no return address to betray the sender. Not that she hadn't immediately known who its sender was. Some two years ago she had one very like it in outward appearance. Furtive, but yet in some peculiar, determined way a little flaunting. Purple ink. Foreign paper of extraordinary size.

It had been, Irene noted, postmarked in New York the day before. Her brows came together in a tiny frown. The frown, however, was more from perplexity than from annoyance; though there was in her thoughts an element of both. She was wholly unable to comprehend such an attitude towards danger as she was sure the letter's contents would reveal; and she disliked the idea of opening and reading it.

This, she reflected, was of a piece with all that she knew of Clare Kendry. Stepping always on the edge of danger. Always aware, but not drawing back or turning aside. Certainly not because of any alarms or feeling of outrage on the part of others.

And for a swift moment Irene Redfield seemed to see a pale small girl sitting on a ragged blue sofa, sewing pieces of bright red cloth together, while her drunken father, a tall, powerfully built man, raged threateningly up and down the shabby room, bellowing curses and making spasmodic lunges at her which were not the less frightening because they were, for the most part, ineffectual. Sometimes he did manage to reach her. But only the fact that the child had edged herself and her poor sewing over to the farthermost corner of the sofa suggested that she was in any way perturbed by this menace to herself and her work.

Clare had known well enough that it was unsafe to take a portion of the dollar that was her weekly wage for the doing of many errands for the dressmaker who lived on the top floor of the building of which Bob Kendry was janitor. But that knowledge had not deterred her. She wanted to go to her Sunday school's picnic, and she had made up her mind to wear a new dress. So, in spite of certain unpleasantness and possible danger, she had taken the money to buy the material for that pathetic little red frock.

There had been, even in those days, nothing sacrificial in Clare Kendry's idea of life, no allegiance beyond her own immediate desire. She was selfish, and cold, and hard. And yet she had, too, a strange capacity of transforming warmth and passion, verging sometimes almost on theatrical heroics.

Irene, who was a year or more older than Clare, remembered the day that Bob Kendry had been brought home dead, killed in a silly saloon-fight. Clare, who was at that time a scant fifteen years old, had just stood there with her lips pressed together, her thin arms folded across her narrow chest, staring down at the familiar pasty-white face of her parent with a sort of disdain in her slanting black eyes. For a very long time she had stood like that, silent and staring. Then, quite suddenly, she had given way to a torrent of weeping, swaying her thin body, tearing at her bright hair, and stamping her small feet. The outburst had ceased as suddenly as it had begun. She glanced quickly about the bare room, taking everyone in, even the two policemen, in a sharp look of flashing scorn. And, in the next instant, she had turned and vanished through the door.

Seen across the long stretch of years, the thing had more the appearance of an outpouring of pent-up fury than of an overflow of grief for her dead father; though she had been, Irene admitted, fond enough of him in her own rather catlike way.

Catlike. Certainly that was the word which best described Clare Kendry, if any single word could describe her. Sometimes she was hard and apparently without feeling at all; sometimes she was affectionate and rashly impulsive. And there was about her an amazing soft malice, hidden well away until provoked. Then she was capable of scratching, and very effectively too. Or, driven to anger, she would fight with a ferocity and impetuousness that disregarded or forgot any danger; superior strength, numbers, or other unfavourable circumstances. How savagely she had clawed those boys the day they had hooted her parent and sung a derisive rhyme, of their own composing, which pointed out certain eccentricities in his careening gait! And how deliberately she had—

Irene brought her thoughts back to the present, to the letter from Clare Kendry that she still held unopened in her hand. With a little feeling of apprehension, she very slowly cut the envelope, drew out the folded sheets, spread them, and began to read.

It was, she saw at once, what she had expected since learning from the postmark that Clare was in the city. An extravagantly phrased wish to see her again. Well, she needn't and wouldn't, Irene told herself, accede to that. Nor would she assist Clare to realize her foolish desire to return for a moment to that life which long ago, and of her own choice, she had left behind her.

She ran through the letter, puzzling out, as best she could, the carelessly formed words or making instinctive guesses at them.

"... For I am lonely, so lonely ... cannot help longing to be with you again, as I have never longed for anything before; and I have wanted many things in my life.... You can't know how in this pale life of mine I am all the time seeing the bright pictures of that other that I once thought I was glad to be free of.... It's like an ache, a pain that never ceases...." Sheets upon thin sheets of it. And ending finally with, "and it's your fault, 'Rene dear. At least partly. For I wouldn't now, perhaps, have this terrible, this wild desire if I hadn't seen you that time in Chicago...."

Brilliant red patches flamed in Irene Redfield's warm olive cheeks.

"That time in Chicago." The words stood out from among the many paragraphs of other words, bringing with them a clear, sharp remembrance, in which even now, after two years, humiliation, resentment, and rage were mingled.

Two

This is what Irene Redfield remembered.

Chicago. August. A brilliant day, hot, with a brutal staring sun pouring down rays that were like molten rain. A day on which the very outlines of the buildings shuddered as if in protest at the heat. Quivering lines sprang up from baked pavements and wriggled along the shining car-tracks.[1] The automobiles parked at the kerbs were a dancing blaze, and the glass of the

---

[1]Rails through city streets for the operation of street-cars or trolleys; the Chicago Surface   Lines then comprised the largest street-car system in existence.

shop-windows threw out a blinding radiance. Sharp particles of dust rose from the burning sidewalks, stinging the seared or dripping skins of wilting pedestrians. What small breeze there was seemed like the breath of a flame fanned by slow bellows.

It was on that day of all others that Irene set out to shop for the things which she had promised to take home from Chicago to her two small sons, Brian junior and Theodore. Characteristically, she had put it off until only a few crowded days remained of her long visit. And only this sweltering one was free of engagements till the evening.

Without too much trouble she had got the mechanical aeroplane for Junior. But the drawing-book, for which Ted had so gravely and insistently given her precise directions, had sent her in and out of five shops without success.

It was while she was on her way to a sixth place that right before her smarting eyes a man toppled over and became an inert crumpled heap on the scorching cement. About the lifeless figure a little crowd gathered. Was the man dead, or only faint? someone asked her. But Irene didn't know and didn't try to discover. She edged her way out of the increasing crowd, feeling disagreeably damp and sticky and soiled from contact with so many sweating bodies.

For a moment she stood fanning herself and dabbing at her moist face with an inadequate scrap of handkerchief. Suddenly she was aware that the whole street had a wobbly look, and realized that she was about to faint. With a quick perception of the need for immediate safety, she lifted a wavering hand in the direction of a cab parked directly in front of her. The perspiring driver jumped out and guided her to his car. He helped, almost lifted her in. She sank down on the hot leather seat.

For a minute her thoughts were nebulous. They cleared.

"I guess," she told her Samaritan, "it's tea I need. On a roof somewhere."

"The Drayton,[2] ma'am?" he suggested. "They do say as how it's always a breeze up there."

"Thank you. I think the Drayton'll do nicely," she told him.

There was that little grating sound of the clutch being slipped in as the man put the car in gear and slid deftly out into the boiling traffic. Reviving under the warm breeze stirred up by the moving cab, Irene made some small attempts to repair the damage that the heat and crowds had done to her appearance.

All too soon the rattling vehicle shot towards the sidewalk and stood still. The driver sprang out and opened the door before the hotel's decorated attendant could reach it. She got out, and thanking him smilingly as well as in a more substantial manner for his kind helpfulness and understanding, went in through the Drayton's wide doors.

Stepping out of the elevator that had brought her to the roof, she was led to a table just in front of a long window whose gently moving curtains suggested a cool breeze. It was, she thought, like being wafted upward on a

[2]Fictional hotel, modeled on two fashionable Chicago hotels: the Drake (located on the Gold Coast end of Michigan Avenue and Walton Place at Lakeshore Drive) and the Morrison (located in the Loop at Madison and Clark streets in the 1920s and known for its Terrace Garden Restaurant).

magic carpet to another world, pleasant, quiet, and strangely remote from the sizzling one that she had left below.

The tea, when it came, was all that she had desired and expected. In fact, so much was it what she had desired and expected that after the first deep cooling drink she was able to forget it, only now and then sipping, a little absently, from the tall green glass, while she surveyed the room about her or looked out over some lower buildings at the bright unstirred blue of the lake reaching away to an undetected horizon.

She had been gazing down for some time at the specks of cars and people creeping about in streets, and thinking how silly they looked, when on taking up her glass she was surprised to find it empty at last. She asked for more tea and while she waited, began to recall the happenings of the day and to wonder what she was to do about Ted and his book. Why was it that almost invariably he wanted something that was difficult or impossible to get? Like his father. For ever wanting something that he couldn't have.

Presently there were voices, a man's booming one and a woman's slightly husky. A waiter passed her, followed by a sweetly scented woman in a fluttering dress of green chiffon whose mingled pattern of narcissuses, jonquils, and hyacinths was a reminder of pleasantly chill spring days. Behind her there was a man, very red in the face, who was mopping his neck and forehead with a big crumpled handkerchief.

"Oh dear!" Irene groaned, rasped by annoyance, for after a little discussion and commotion they had stopped at the very next table. She had been alone there at the window and it had been so satisfyingly quiet. Now, of course, they would chatter.

But no. Only the woman sat down. The man remained standing, abstractedly pinching the knot of his bright blue tie. Across the small space that separated the two tables his voice carried clearly.

"See you later, then," he declared, looking down at the woman. There was pleasure in his tones and a smile on his face.

His companion's lips parted in some answer, but her words were blurred by the little intervening distance and the medley of noises floating up from the streets below. They didn't reach Irene. But she noted the peculiar caressing smile that accompanied them.

The man said: "Well, I suppose I'd better," and smiled again, and said good-bye, and left.

An attractive-looking woman, was Irene's opinion, with those dark, almost black, eyes and that wide mouth like a scarlet flower against the ivory of her skin. Nice clothes too, just right for the weather, thin and cool without being mussy, as summer things were so apt to be.

A waiter was taking her order. Irene saw her smile up at him as she murmured something—thanks, maybe. It was an odd sort of smile. Irene couldn't quite define it, but she was sure that she would have classed it, coming from another woman, as being just a shade too provocative for a waiter. About this one, however, there was something that made her hesitate to name it that. A certain impression of assurance, perhaps.

The waiter came back with the order. Irene watched her spread out her napkin, saw the silver spoon in the white hand slit the dull gold of the melon. Then, conscious that she had been staring, she looked quickly away.

Her mind returned to her own affairs. She had settled, definitely, the problem of the proper one of two frocks for the bridge party that night, in rooms whose atmosphere would be so thick and hot that every breath would be like breathing soup. The dress decided, her thoughts had gone back to the snag of Ted's book, her unseeing eyes far away on the lake, when by some sixth sense she was acutely aware that someone was watching her.

Very slowly she looked around, and into the dark eyes of the woman in the green frock at the next table. But she evidently failed to realize that such intense interest as she was showing might be embarrassing, and continued to stare. Her demeanour was that of one who with utmost singleness of mind and purpose was determined to impress firmly and accurately each detail of Irene's features upon her memory for all time, nor showed the slightest trace of disconcertment at having been detected in her steady scrutiny.

Instead, it was Irene who was put out. Feeling her colour heighten under the continued inspection, she slid her eyes down. What, she wondered, could be the reason for such persistent attention? Had she, in her haste in the taxi, put her hat on backwards? Guardedly she felt at it. No. Perhaps there was a streak of powder somewhere on her face. She made a quick pass over it with her handkerchief. Something wrong with her dress? She shot a glance over it. Perfectly all right. *What* was it?

Again she looked up, and for a moment her brown eyes politely returned the stare of the other's black ones, which never for an instant fell or wavered. Irene made a little mental shrug. Oh well, let her look! She tried to treat the woman and her watching with indifference, but she couldn't. All her efforts to ignore her, it, were futile. She stole another glance. Still looking. What strange languorous eyes she had!

And gradually there rose in Irene a small inner disturbance, odious and hatefully familiar. She laughed softly, but her eyes flashed.

Did that woman, could that woman, somehow know that here before her very eyes on the roof of the Drayton sat a Negro?

Absurd! Impossible! White people were so stupid about such things for all that they usually asserted that they were able to tell; and by the most ridiculous means, finger-nails, palms of hands, shapes of ears, teeth, and other equally silly rot. They always took her for an Italian, a Spaniard, a Mexican, or a gipsy. Never, when she was alone, had they even remotely seemed to suspect that she was a Negro. No, the woman sitting there staring at her couldn't possibly know.

Nevertheless, Irene felt, in turn, anger, scorn, and fear slide over her. It wasn't that she was ashamed of being a Negro, or even of having it declared. It was the idea of being ejected from any place, even in the polite and tactful way in which the Drayton would probably do it, that disturbed her.

But she looked, boldly this time, back into the eyes still frankly intent upon her. They did not seem to her hostile or resentful. Rather, Irene had the feeling that they were ready to smile if she would. Nonsense, of course. The feeling passed, and she turned away with the firm intention of keeping her gaze on the lake, the roofs of the buildings across the way, the sky, anywhere but on that annoying woman. Almost immediately, however, her eyes were back again. In the midst of her fog of uneasiness she had been seized by a desire to outstare the rude observer. Suppose the woman did know or suspect her race. She couldn't prove it.

Suddenly her small fright increased. Her neighbour had risen and was coming towards her. What was going to happen now?

"Pardon me," the woman said pleasantly, "but I think I know you." Her slightly husky voice held a dubious note.

Looking up at her, Irene's suspicions and fears vanished. There was no mistaking the friendliness of that smile or resisting its charm. Instantly she surrendered to it and smiled too, as she said: "I'm afraid you're mistaken."

"Why, of course, I know you!" the other exclaimed. "Don't tell me you're not Irene Westover. Or do they still call you 'Rene?"

In the brief second before her answer, Irene tried vainly to recall where and when this woman could have known her. There, in Chicago. And before her marriage. That much was plain. High school? College? Y. W. C. A. committees? High school, most likely. What white girls had she known well enough to have been familiarly addressed as 'Rene by them? The woman before her didn't fit her memory of any of them. Who was she?

"Yes, I'm Irene Westover. And though nobody calls me 'Rene any more, it's good to hear the name again. And you—" She hesitated, ashamed that she could not remember, and hoping that the sentence would be finished for her.

"Don't you know me? Not really, 'Rene?"

"I'm sorry, but just at the minute I can't seem to place you."

Irene studied the lovely creature standing beside her for some clue to her identity. Who could she be? Where and when had they met? And through her perplexity there came the thought that the trick which her memory had played her was for some reason more gratifying than disappointing to her old acquaintance, that she didn't mind not being recognized.

And, too, Irene felt that she was just about to remember her. For about the woman was some quality, an intangible something, too vague to define, too remote to seize, but which was, to Irene Redfield, very familiar. And that voice. Surely she'd heard those husky tones somewhere before. Perhaps before time, contact, or something had been at them, making them into a voice remotely suggesting England. Ah! Could it have been in Europe that they had met? 'Rene. No.

"Perhaps," Irene began, "you—"

The woman laughed, a lovely laugh, a small sequence of notes that was like a trill and also like the ringing of a delicate bell fashioned of a precious metal, a tinkling.

Irene drew a quick sharp breath. "Clare!" she exclaimed, "not really Clare Kendry?"

So great was her astonishment that she had started to rise.

"No, no, don't get up," Clare Kendry commanded, and sat down herself. "You've simply got to stay and talk. We'll have something more. Tea? Fancy meeting you here! It's simply too, too lucky!"

"It's awfully surprising," Irene told her, and, seeing the change in Clare's smile, knew that she had revealed a corner of her own thoughts. But she only said: "I'd never in this world have known you if you hadn't laughed. You are changed, you know. And yet, in a way, you're just the same."

"Perhaps," Clare replied. "Oh, just a second."

She gave her attention to the waiter at her side. "M-mm, let's see. Two teas. And bring some cigarettes. Y-es, they'll be all right. Thanks." Again that odd upward smile. Now, Irene was sure that it was too provocative for a waiter.

While Clare had been giving the order, Irene made a rapid mental calculation. It must be, she figured, all of twelve years since she, or anybody that she knew, had laid eyes on Clare Kendry.

After her father's death she'd gone to live with some relatives, aunts or cousins two or three times removed, over on the west side: relatives that nobody had known the Kendrys' possessed until they had turned up at the funeral and taken Clare away with them.

For about a year or more afterwards she would appear occasionally among her old friends and acquaintances on the south side for short little visits that were, they understood, always stolen from the endless domestic tasks in her new home. With each succeeding one she was taller, shabbier, and more belligerently sensitive. And each time the look on her face was more resentful and brooding. "I'm worried about Clare, she seems so unhappy," Irene remembered her mother saying. The visits dwindled, becoming shorter, fewer, and further apart until at last they ceased.

Irene's father, who had been fond of Bob Kendry, made a special trip over to the west side about two months after the last time Clare had been to see them and returned with the bare information that he had seen the relatives and that Clare had disappeared. What else he had confided to her mother, in the privacy of their own room, Irene didn't know.

But she had had something more than a vague suspicion of its nature. For there had been rumours. Rumours that were, to girls of eighteen and nineteen years, interesting and exciting.

There was the one about Clare Kendry's having been seen at the dinner hour in a fashionable hotel in company with another woman and two men, all of them white. And *dressed!* And there was another which told of her driving in Lincoln Park[3] with a man, unmistakably white, and evidently rich. Packard limousine,[4] chauffeur in livery, and all that. There had been others

---

[3]North Side Chicago park area, bounded by North Avenue and Fullerton Avenue, Clark Street and Lakeshore Drive; home of the Lincoln Park Zoo, the Chicago Historical Society, and the Chicago Academy of Science.

[4]Luxury, chauffeur-driven automobile perfected by J. W. Packard and W. D. Packard and produced from 1899 to 1958.

whose context Irene could no longer recollect, but all pointing in the same glamorous direction.

And she could remember quite vividly how, when they used to repeat and discuss these tantalizing stories about Clare, the girls would always look knowingly at one another and then, with little excited giggles, drag away their eager shining eyes and say with lurking undertones of regret or disbelief some such thing as: "Oh, well, maybe she's got a job or something," or "After all, it mayn't have been Clare," or "You can't believe all you hear."

And always some girl, more matter-of-fact or more frankly malicious than the rest, would declare: "Of course it was Clare! Ruth said it was and so did Frank, and they certainly know her when they see her as well as we do." And someone else would say: "Yes, you can bet it was Clare all right." And then they would all join in asserting that there could be no mistake about it's having been Clare, and that such circumstances could mean only one thing. Working indeed! People didn't take their servants to the Shelby[5] for dinner. Certainly not all dressed up like that. There would follow insincere regrets, and somebody would say: "Poor girl, I suppose it's true enough, but what can you expect. Look at her father. And her mother, they say, would have run away if she hadn't died. Besides, Clare always had a—a—having way with her."

Precisely that! The words came to Irene as she sat there on the Drayton roof, facing Clare Kendry. "A having way." Well, Irene acknowledged, judging from her appearance and manner, Clare seemed certainly to have succeeded in having a few of the things that she wanted.

It was, Irene repeated, after the interval of the waiter, a great surprise and a very pleasant one to see Clare again after all those years, twelve at least.

"Why, Clare, you're the last person in the world I'd have expected to run into. I guess that's why I didn't know you."

Clare answered gravely: "Yes. It is twelve years. But I'm not surprised to see you, 'Rene. That is, not so very. In fact, ever since I've been here, I've more or less hoped that I should, or someone. Preferably you, though. Still, I imagine that's because I've thought of you often and often, while you—I'll wager you've never given me a thought."

It was true, of course. After the first speculations and indictments, Clare had gone completely from Irene's thoughts. And from the thoughts of others too—if their conversation was any indication of their thoughts.

Besides, Clare had never been exactly one of the group, just as she'd never been merely the janitor's daughter, but the daughter of Mr. Bob Kendry, who, it was true, was a janitor, but who also, it seemed, had been in college with some of their fathers. Just how or why he happened to be a janitor, and a very inefficient one at that, they none of them quite knew.

[5]Fictional hotel, modeled on the Sherman, a Chicago hotel and restaurant located at Clark and Randolph streets in the Loop.

One of Irene's brothers, who had put the question to their father, had been told: "That's something that doesn't concern you," and given him the advice to be careful not to end in the same manner as "poor Bob."

No, Irene hadn't thought of Clare Kendry. Her own life had been too crowded. So, she supposed, had the lives of other people. She defended her—their—forgetfulness. "You know how it is. Everybody's so busy. People leave, drop out, maybe for a little while there's talk about them, or questions; then, gradually they're forgotten."

"Yes, that's natural," Clare agreed. And what, she inquired, had they said of her for that little while at the beginning before they'd forgotten her altogether?

Irene looked away. She felt the telltale colour rising in her cheeks. "You can't," she evaded, "expect me to remember trifles like that over twelve years of marriages, births, deaths, and the war."

There followed that trill of notes that was Clare Kendry's laugh, small and clear and the very essence of mockery.

"Oh, 'Rene!" she cried, "of course you remember! But I won't make you tell me, because I know just as well as if I'd been there and heard every unkind word. Oh, I know, I know. Frank Danton saw me in the Shelby one night. Don't tell me he didn't broadcast that, and with embroidery. Others may have seen me at other times. I don't know. But once I met Margaret Hammer in Marshall Field's.[6] I'd have spoken, was on the very point of doing it, but she cut me dead. My dear 'Rene, I assure you that from the way she looked through me, even I was uncertain whether I was actually there in the flesh or not. I remember it clearly, too clearly. It was that very thing which, in a way, finally decided me not to go out and see you one last time before I went away to stay. Somehow, good as all of you, the whole family, had always been to the poor forlorn child that was me, I felt I shouldn't be able to bear that. I mean if any of you, your mother or the boys or—Oh, well, I just felt I'd rather not know it if you did. And so I stayed away. Silly, I suppose. Sometimes I've been sorry I didn't go."

Irene wondered if it was tears that made Clare's eyes so luminous.

"And now 'Rene, I want to hear all about you and everybody and everything. You're married, I s'pose?"

Irene nodded.

"Yes," Clare said knowingly, "you would be. Tell me about it."

And so for an hour or more they had sat there smoking and drinking tea and filling in the gap of twelve years with talk. That is, Irene did. She told Clare about her marriage and removal to New York, about her husband, and about her two sons, who were having their first experience of being separated from their parents at a summer camp, about her mother's death,

[6]Chicago's premiere department store, founded in 1881 and located at Randolph, Wabash, Washington, and State streets. A pioneer in modern retail merchandising, and in the 1920s the world's largest retail store, Marshall Field and Company was world-famous for both customer service and for architectural features: Tiffany Dome, Great Clock (a Chicago landmark), and atrium fountain.

about the marriages of her two brothers. She told of the marriages, births and deaths in other families that Clare had known, opening up, for her, new vistas on the lives of old friends and acquaintances.

Clare drank it all in, these things which for so long she had wanted to know and hadn't been able to learn. She sat motionless, her bright lips slightly parted, her whole face lit by the radiance of her happy eyes. Now and then she put a question, but for the most part she was silent.

Somewhere outside, a clock struck. Brought back to the present, Irene looked down at her watch and exclaimed: "Oh, I must go, Clare!"

A moment passed during which she was the prey of uneasiness. It had suddenly occurred to her that she hadn't asked Clare anything about her own life and that she had a very definite unwillingness to do so. And she was quite well aware of the reason for that reluctance. But, she asked herself, wouldn't it, all things considered, be the kindest thing not to ask? If things with Clare were as she—as they all—had suspected, wouldn't it be more tactful to seem to forget to inquire how she had spent those twelve years?

If? It was that "if" which bothered her. It might be, it might just be, in spite of all gossip and even appearances to the contrary, that there was nothing, had been nothing, that couldn't be simply and innocently explained. Appearances, she knew now, had a way sometimes of not fitting facts, and if Clare hadn't—Well, if they had all been wrong, then certainly she ought to express some interest in what had happened to her. It would seem queer and rude if she didn't. But how was she to know? There was, she at last decided, no way; so she merely said again: "I must go, Clare."

"Please, not so soon, 'Rene," Clare begged, not moving.

Irene thought: "She's really almost too good-looking. It's hardly any wonder that she—"

"And now, 'Rene dear, that I've found you, I mean to see lots and lots of you. We're here for a month at least. Jack, that's my husband, is here on business. Poor dear! in this heat. Isn't it beastly? Come to dinner with us tonight, won't you?" And she gave Irene a curious little sidelong glance and a sly, ironical smile peeped out on her full red lips, as if she had been in the secret of the other's thoughts and was mocking her.

Irene was conscious of a sharp intake of breath, but whether it was relief or chagrin that she felt, she herself could not have told. She said hastily: "I'm afraid I can't, Clare. I'm filled up. Dinner and bridge. I'm so sorry."

"Come tomorrow instead, to tea," Clare insisted. "Then you'll see Margery—she's just ten—and Jack too, maybe, if he hasn't got an appointment or something."

From Irene came an uneasy little laugh. She had an engagement for tomorrow also and she was afraid that Clare would not believe it. Suddenly, now, that possibility disturbed her. Therefore it was with a half-vexed feeling at the sense of undeserved guilt that had come upon her that she explained that it wouldn't be possible because she wouldn't be free for tea, or for luncheon or dinner either. "And the next day's Friday when I'll be going away for the week-end, Idlewild,[7] you know. It's quite the thing now." And then she had an inspiration.

"Clare!" she exclaimed, "why don't you come up with me? Our place is probably full up—Jim's wife has a way of collecting mobs of the most impossible people—but we can always manage to find room for one more. And you'll see absolutely everybody."

In the very moment of giving the invitation she regretted it. What a foolish, what an idiotic impulse to have given way to! She groaned inwardly as she thought of the endless explanations in which it would involve her, of the curiosity, and the talk, and the lifted eyebrows. It wasn't she assured herself, that she was a snob, that she cared greatly for the petty restrictions and distinctions with which what called itself Negro society chose to hedge itself about; but that she had a natural and deeply rooted aversion to the kind of front-page notoriety that Clare Kendry's presence in Idlewild, as her guest, would expose her to. And here she was, perversely and against all reason, inviting her.

But Clare shook her head. "Really, I'd love to, 'Rene," she said, a little mournfully. "There's nothing I'd like better. But I couldn't. I mustn't, you see. It wouldn't do at all. I'm sure you understand. I'm simply crazy to go, but I can't." The dark eyes glistened and there was a suspicion of a quaver in the husky voice. "And believe me, 'Rene, I do thank you for asking me. Don't think I've entirely forgotten just what it would mean for you if I went. That is, if you still care about such things."

All indication of tears had gone from her eyes and voice, and Irene Redfield, searching her face, had an offended feeling that behind what was now only an ivory mask lurked a scornful amusement. She looked away, at the wall far beyond Clare. Well, she deserved it, for, as she acknowledged to herself, she *was* relieved. And for the very reason at which Clare had hinted. The fact that Clare had guessed her perturbation did not, however, in any degree lessen that relief. She was annoyed at having been detected in what might seem to be an insincerity; but that was all.

The waiter came with Clare's change. Irene reminded herself that she ought immediately to go. But she didn't move.

The truth was, she was curious. There were things that she wanted to ask Clare Kendry. She wished to find out about this hazardous business of "passing," this breaking away from all that was familiar and friendly to take one's chance in another environment, not entirely strange, perhaps, but certainly not entirely friendly. What, for example, one did about background, how one accounted for oneself. And how one felt when one came into contact with other Negroes. But she couldn't. She was unable to think of a

---

[7]Black resort in Lake County, Michigan, seventy-nine miles north of Grand Rapids. Founded in 1912 and developed over the next decade, Idlewild was marketed nationally to middle-class urbanites as a first-class vacation retreat with beaches, crystal lake waters, fish and game, wild flowers, hotel accommodations, and myriad opportunities for outside sports. By the late 1920s, Idlewild was the premiere black resort in the United States.

single question that in its context or its phrasing was not too frankly curious, if not actually impertinent.

As if aware of her desire and her hesitation, Clare remarked, thoughtfully: "You know, 'Rene, I've often wondered why more coloured girls, girls like you and Margaret Hammer and Esther Dawson and—oh, lots of others—never 'passed' over. It's such a frightfully easy thing to do. If one's the type, all that's needed is a little nerve."

"What about background? Family, I mean. Surely you can't just drop down on people from nowhere and expect them to receive you with open arms, can you?"

"Almost," Clare asserted. "You'd be surprised, 'Rene, how much easier that is with white people than with us. Maybe because there are so many more of them, or maybe because they are secure and so don't have to bother. I've never quite decided."

Irene was inclined to be incredulous. "You mean that you didn't have to explain where you came from? It seems impossible."

Clare cast a glance of repressed amusement across the table at her. "As a matter of fact, I didn't. Though I suppose under any other circumstances I might have had to provide some plausible tale to account for myself. I've a good imagination, so I'm sure I could have done it quite creditably, and credibly. But it wasn't necessary. There were my aunts, you see, respectable and authentic enough for anything or anybody."

"I see. They were 'passing' too."

"No. They weren't. They were white."

"Oh!" And in the next instant it came back to Irene that she had heard this mentioned before; by her father, or, more likely, her mother. They were Bob Kendry's aunts. He had been a son of their brother's, on the left hand.[8] A wild oat.

"They were nice old ladies," Clare explained, "very religious and as poor as church mice. That adored brother of theirs, my grandfather, got through every penny they had after he'd finished his own little bit."

Clare paused in her narrative to light another cigarette. Her smile, her expression, Irene noticed, was faintly resentful.

"Being good Christians," she continued, "when dad came to his tipsy end, they did their duty and gave me a home of sorts. I was, it was true, expected to earn my keep by doing all the housework and most of the washing. But do you realize, 'Rene, that if it hadn't been for them, I shouldn't have had a home in the world?"

Irene's nod and little murmur were comprehensive, understanding.

Clare made a small mischievous grimace and proceeded. "Besides, to their notion, hard labour was good for me. I had Negro blood and they belonged to the generation that had written and read long articles headed:

[8]The offspring of a morganatic marriage or similar legal marriage between partners of unequal rank or status, in which the partner of lower status and the couple's offspring are excluded from sharing in the estate. Clare's father, Bob Kendry, is thus the son of a black mother and a white father, whose racial status he cannot inherit.

'Will the Blacks Work?' Too, they weren't quite sure that the good God hadn't intended the sons and daughters of Ham[9] to sweat because he had poked fun at old man Noah once when he had taken a drop too much. I remember the aunts telling me that that old drunkard had cursed Ham and his sons for all time."

Irene laughed. But Clare remained quite serious.

"It was more than a joke, I assure you, 'Rene. It was a hard life for a girl of sixteen. Still, I had a roof over my head, and food, and clothes—such as they were. And there were the Scriptures, and talks on morals and thrift and industry and the loving-kindness of the good Lord."

"Have you ever stopped to think, Clare," Irene demanded, "how much unhappiness and downright cruelty are laid to the loving-kindness of the Lord? And always by His most ardent followers, it seems."

"Have I?" Clare exclaimed. "It, they, made me what I am today. For, of course, I was determined to get away, to be a person and not a charity or a problem, or even a daughter of the indiscreet Ham. Then, too, I wanted things. I knew I wasn't bad-looking and that I could 'pass.' You can't know, 'Rene, how, when I used to go over to the south side, I used almost to hate all of you. You had all the things I wanted and never had had. It made me all the more determined to get them, and others. Do you, can you understand what I felt?"

She looked up with a pointed and appealing effect, and, evidently finding the sympathetic expression on Irene's face sufficient answer, went on. "The aunts were queer. For all their Bibles and praying and ranting about honesty, they didn't want anyone to know that their darling brother had seduced—ruined, they called it—a Negro girl. They could excuse the ruin, but they couldn't forgive the tar-brush.[10] They forbade me to mention Negroes to the neighbours, or even to mention the south side. You may be sure that I didn't. I'll bet they were good and sorry afterwards."

She laughed and the ringing bells in her laugh had a hard metallic sound.

"When the chance to get away came, that omission was of great value to me. When Jack, a schoolboy acquaintance of some people in the neighbourhood, turned up from South America with untold gold, there was no one to tell him that I was coloured, and many to tell him about the severity and the religiousness of Aunt Grace and Aunt Edna. You can guess the rest. After he came, I stopped slipping off to the south side and slipped off to meet him instead. I couldn't manage both. In the end I had no great difficulty in convincing him that it was useless to talk marriage to the aunts.

---

[9]Literally, the Canaanites, the descendants of Ham, one of the three sons of Noah, saved from God's destruction of a wicked world by flooding (Genesis 9:20–27). Ham was punished for mocking his father's drunkenness and nakedness. Ham's punishment for disrespecting his father fell upon his children who were cursed to become the slaves of his brothers' children; slave holders in the United States applied this Biblical account to Africans and used it as a justification for slavery.

[10]A reference to African ancestry; derived from the descriptive saying, "Black as tar."

So on the day that I was eighteen, we went off and were married. So that's that. Nothing could have been easier."

"Yes, I do see that for you it was easy enough. By the way! I wonder why they didn't tell father that you were married. He went over to find out about you when you stopped coming over to see us. I'm sure they didn't tell him. Not that you were married."

Clare Kendry's eyes were bright with tears that didn't fall. "Oh, how lovely! To have cared enough about me to do that. The dear sweet man! Well, they couldn't tell him because they didn't know it. I took care of that, for I couldn't be sure that those consciences of theirs wouldn't begin to work on them afterwards and make them let the cat out of the bag. The old things probably thought I was living in sin, wherever I was. And it would be about what they expected."

An amused smile lit the lovely face for the smallest fraction of a second. After a little silence she said soberly: "But I'm sorry if they told your father so. That was something I hadn't counted on."

"I'm not sure that they did," Irene told her. "He didn't say so, anyway."

"He wouldn't, 'Rene dear. Not your father."

"Thanks. I'm sure he wouldn't."

"But you've never answered my question. Tell me, honestly, haven't you ever thought of 'passing'?"

Irene answered promptly: "No. Why should I?" And so disdainful was her voice and manner that Clare's face flushed and her eyes glinted. Irene hastened to add: "You see, Clare, I've everything I want. Except, perhaps, a little more money."

At that Clare laughed, her spark of anger vanished as quickly as it had appeared. "Of course," she declared, "that's what everybody wants, just a little more money, even the people who have it. And I must say I don't blame them. Money's awfully nice to have. In fact, all things considered, I think, 'Rene, that it's even worth the price."

Irene could only shrug her shoulders. Her reason partly agreed, her instinct wholly rebelled. And she could not say why. And though conscious that if she didn't hurry away, she was going to be late to dinner, she still lingered. It was as if the woman sitting on the other side of the table, a girl that she had known, who had done this rather dangerous and, to Irene Redfield, abhorrent thing successfully and had announced herself well satisfied, had for her a fascination, strange and compelling.

Clare Kendry was still leaning back in the tall chair, her sloping shoulders against the carved top. She sat with an air of indifferent assurance, as if arranged for, desired. About her clung that dim suggestion of polite insolence with which a few women are born and which some acquire with the coming of riches or importance.

Clare, it gave Irene a little prick of satisfaction to recall, hadn't got that by passing herself off as white. She herself had always had it.

Just as she'd always had that pale gold hair, which, unsheared still, was drawn loosely back from a broad brow, partly hidden by the small close hat.

Her lips, painted a brilliant geranium-red, were sweet and sensitive and a little obstinate. A tempting mouth. The face across the forehead and cheeks was a trifle too wide, but the ivory skin had a peculiar soft lustre. And the eyes were magnificent! dark, sometimes absolutely black, always luminous, and set in long, black lashes. Arresting eyes, slow and mesmeric, and with, for all their warmth, something withdrawn and secret about them.

Ah! Surely! They were Negro eyes! mysterious and concealing. And set in that ivory face under that bright hair, there was about them something exotic.

Yes, Clare Kendry's loveliness was absolute, beyond challenge, thanks to those eyes which her grandmother and later her mother and father had given her.

Into those eyes there came a smile and over Irene the sense of being petted and caressed. She smiled back.

"Maybe," Clare suggested, "you can come Monday, if you're back. Or, if you're not, then Tuesday."

With a small regretful sigh, Irene informed Clare that she was afraid she wouldn't be back by Monday and that she was sure she had dozens of things for Tuesday, and that she was leaving Wednesday. It might be, however, that she could get out of something Tuesday.

"Oh, do try. Do put somebody else off. The others can see you any time, while I—Why, I may never see you again! Think of that, 'Rene! You'll have to come. You'll simply have to! I'll never forgive you if you don't."

At that moment it seemed a dreadful thing to think of never seeing Clare Kendry again. Standing there under the appeal, the caress, of her eyes, Irene had the desire, the hope, that this parting wouldn't be the last.

"I'll try, Clare," she promised gently. "I'll call you—or will you call me?"

"I think, perhaps, I'd better call you. Your father's in the book, I know, and the address is the same. Sixty-four eighteen. Some memory, what? Now remember, I'm going to expect you. You've got to be able to come."

Again that peculiar mellowing smile.

"I'll do my best, Clare."

Irene gathered up her gloves and bag. They stood up. She put out her hand. Clare took and held it.

"It has been nice seeing you again, Clare. How pleased and glad father'll be to hear about you!"

"Until Tuesday, then," Clare Kendry replied. "I'll spend every minute of the time from now on looking forward to seeing you again. Good-bye, 'Rene dear. My love to your father, and this kiss for him."

The sun had gone from overhead, but the streets were still like fiery furnaces. The languid breeze was still hot. And the scurrying people looked even more wilted than before Irene had fled from their contact.

Crossing the avenue in the heat, far from the coolness of the Drayton's roof, away from the seduction of Clare Kendry's smile, she was aware of a sense of irritation with herself because she had been pleased and a little flattered at the other's obvious gladness at their meeting.

With her perspiring progress homeward this irritation grew, and she began to wonder just what had possessed her to make her promise to find time, in the crowded days that remained of her visit, to spend another afternoon with a woman whose life had so definitely and deliberately diverged from hers; and whom, as had been pointed out, she might never see again.

Why in the world had she made such a promise?

As she went up the steps to her father's house, thinking with what interest and amazement he would listen to her story of the afternoon's encounter, it came to her that Clare had omitted to mention her marriage name. She had referred to her husband as Jack. That was all. Had that, Irene asked herself, been intentional?

Clare had only to pick up the telephone to communicate with her, or to drop her a card, or to jump into a taxi. But she couldn't reach Clare in any way. Nor could anyone else to whom she might speak of their meeting.

"As if I should!"

Her key turned in the lock. She went in. Her father, it seemed, hadn't come in yet.

Irene decided that she wouldn't, after all, say anything to him about Clare Kendry. She had, she told herself, no inclination to speak of a person who held so low an opinion of her loyalty, or her discretion. And certainly she had no desire or intention of making the slightest effort about Tuesday. Nor any other day for that matter.

She was through with Clare Kendry.

Three

On Tuesday morning a dome of grey sky rose over the parched city, but the stifling air was not relieved by the silvery mist that seemed to hold a promise of rain, which did not fall.

To Irene Redfield this soft foreboding fog was another reason for doing nothing about seeing Clare Kendry that afternoon.

But she did see her.

The telephone. For hours it had rung like something possessed. Since nine o'clock she had been hearing its insistent jangle. Awhile she was resolute, saying firmly each time: "Not in, Liza, take the message." And each time the servant returned with the information: "It's the same lady, ma'am; she says she'll call again."

But at noon, her nerves frayed and her conscience smiting her at the reproachful look on Liza's ebony face as she withdrew for another denial, Irene weakened.

"Oh, never mind. I'll answer this time, Liza."

"It's her again."

"Hello.... Yes."

"It's Clare, 'Rene.... Where *have* you been? ... Can you be here around four? ... What? ... But, 'Rene, you promised! Just for a little while.... You can if you want to.... I am *so* disappointed. I had counted so on seeing you.... Please be nice and come. Only for a minute. I'm sure you can manage it if you try.... I won't beg you to stay.... Yes.... I'm going to expect you ... It's the Morgan ...[11] Oh, yes! The name's Bellew, Mrs. John Bellew.... About four, then.... I'll be so happy to see you! ... Goodbye."

"Damn!"

Irene hung up the receiver with an emphatic bang, her thoughts immediately filled with self-reproach. She'd done it again. Allowed Clare Kendry to persuade her into promising to do something for which she had neither time nor any special desire. What was it about Clare's voice that was so appealing, so very seductive?

Clare met her in the hall with a kiss. She said: "You're good to come, 'Rene. But, then, you always were nice to me." And under her potent smile a part of Irene's annoyance with herself fled. She was even a little glad that she had come.

Clare led the way, stepping lightly, towards a room whose door was standing partly open, saying: "There's a surprise. It's a real party. See."

Entering, Irene found herself in a sitting-room, large and high, at whose windows hung startling blue draperies which triumphantly dragged attention from the gloomy chocolate-coloured furniture. And Clare was wearing a thin floating dress of the same shade of blue, which suited her and the rather difficult room to perfection.

For a minute Irene thought the room was empty, but turning her head, she discovered, sunk deep in the cushions of a huge sofa, a woman staring up at her with such intense concentration that her eyelids were drawn as though the strain of that upward glance had paralysed them. At first Irene took her to be a stranger, but in the next instant she said in an unsympathetic, almost harsh voice: "And how are you, Gertrude?"

The woman nodded and forced a smile to her pouting lips. "I'm all right," she replied. "And you're just the same, Irene. Not changed a bit."

"Thank you." Irene responded, as she chose a seat. She was thinking: "Great goodness! Two of them."

For Gertrude too had married a white man, though it couldn't be truthfully said that she was "passing." Her husband—what was his name?—had been in school with her and had been quite well aware, as had his family and most of his friends, that she was a Negro. It hadn't, Irene knew, seemed to matter to him then. Did it now, she wondered? Had Fred—Fred Martin, that was it—had he ever regretted his marriage because of Gertrude's race? Had Gertrude?

Turning to Gertrude, Irene asked: "And Fred, how is he? It's unmentionable years since I've seen him."

"Oh, he's all right," Gertrude answered briefly.

For a full minute no one spoke. Finally out of the oppressive little silence Clare's voice came pleasantly, conversationally: "We'll have tea right away. I know that you can't stay long, 'Rene. And I'm so sorry you won't see

[11]Fictional hotel modeled on the Morrison.
See note 2, Part One, Chapter Two.

Margery. We went up the lake over the week end to see some of Jack's people, just out of Milwaukee. Margery wanted to stay with the children. It seemed a shame not to let her, especially since it's so hot in town. But I'm expecting Jack any second."

Irene said briefly: "That's nice."

Gertrude remained silent. She was, it was plain, a little ill at ease. And her presence there annoyed Irene, roused in her a defensive and resentful feeling for which she had at the moment no explanation. But it did seem to her odd that the woman that Clare was now should have invited the woman that Gertrude was. Still, of course, Clare couldn't have known. Twelve years since they had met.

Later, when she examined her feeling of annoyance, Irene admitted, a shade reluctantly, that it arose from a feeling of being outnumbered, a sense of aloneness, in her adherence to her own class and kind; not merely in the great thing of marriage, but in the whole pattern of her life as well.

Clare spoke again, this time at length. Her talk was of the change that Chicago presented to her after her long absence in European cities. Yes, she said in reply to some question from Gertrude, she'd been back to America a time or two, but only as far as New York and Philadelphia, and once she had spent a few days in Washington. John Bellew, who, it appeared, was some sort of international banking agent, hadn't particularly wanted her to come with him on this trip, but as soon as she had learned that it would probably take him as far as Chicago, she made up her mind to come anyway.

"I simply had to. And after I once got here, I was determined to see someone I knew and find out what had happened to everybody. I didn't quite see how I was going to manage it, but I meant to. Somehow. I'd just about decided to take a chance and go out to your house, 'Rene, or call up and arrange a meeting, when I ran into you. What luck!"

Irene agreed that it was luck. "It's the first time I've been home for five years, and now I'm about to leave. A week later and I'd have been gone. And how in the world did you find Gertrude?"

"In the book. I remembered about Fred. His father still has the meat market."

"Oh, yes," said Irene, who had only remembered it as Clare had spoken, "on Cottage Grove[12] near—"

Gertrude broke in. "No. It's moved. We're on Maryland Avenue—used to be Jackson—now. Near Sixty-third Street.[13] And the market's Fred's. His name's the same as his father's."

---

[12]A major north-south street on the South Side of Chicago.

[13]Nella Larsen's personal joke; her parents owned a small South Side Chicago apartment house on Maryland Avenue, whose name had been changed from Jackson at the time of the 1893 World's Columbian Exposition when the area was marketed as McChesney's World's Fair Subdivision; Sixty-third Street was the business and commercial district in this area, known as Woodland and adjacent to the site of the Columbian Exposition, and where the Chicago Surface Lines had a terminal station and the Illinois Central Railway operated the Woodland Park Station.

Gertrude, Irene thought, looked as if her husband might be a butcher. There was left of her youthful prettiness, which had been so much admired in their high-school days, no trace. She had grown broad, fat almost, and though there were no lines on her large white face, its very smoothness was somehow prematurely ageing. Her black hair was clipt, and by some unfortunate means all the live curliness had gone from it. Her over-trimmed Georgette *crêpe* dress was too short and showed an appalling amount of leg, stout legs in sleazy stockings of a vivid rose-beige shade. Her plump hands were newly and not too competently manicured—for the occasion, probably. And she wasn't smoking.

Clare said—and Irene fancied that her husky voice held a slight edge—"Before you came, Irene, Gertrude was telling me about her two boys. Twins. Think of it! Isn't it too marvellous for words?"

Irene felt a warmness creeping into her cheeks. Uncanny, the way Clare could divine what one was thinking. She was a little put out, but her manner was entirely easy as she said: "That is nice. I've two boys myself, Gertrude. Not twins, though. It seems that Clare's rather behind, doesn't it?"

Gertrude, however, wasn't sure that Clare hadn't the best of it. "She's got a girl. I wanted a girl. So did Fred."

"Isn't that a bit unusual?" Irene asked. "Most men want sons. Egotism, I suppose."

"Well, Fred didn't."

The tea-things had been placed on a low table at Clare's side. She gave them her attention now, pouring the rich amber fluid from the tall glass pitcher into stately slim glasses, which she handed to her guests, and then offered them lemon or cream and tiny sandwiches or cakes.

After taking up her own glass she informed them: "No, I have no boys and I don't think I'll ever have any. I'm afraid. I nearly died of terror the whole nine months before Margery was born for fear that she might be dark. Thank goodness, she turned out all right. But I'll never risk it again. Never! The strain is simply too—too hellish."

Gertrude Martin nodded in complete comprehension.

This time it was Irene who said nothing.

"You don't have to tell me!" Gertrude said fervently. "I know what it is all right. Maybe you don't think I wasn't scared to death too. Fred said I was silly, and so did his mother. But, of course, they thought it was just a notion I'd gotten into my head and they blamed it on my condition. They don't know like we do, how it might go way back, and turn out dark no matter what colour the father and mother are."

Perspiration stood out on her forehead. Her narrow eyes rolled first in Clare's, then in Irene's direction. As she talked she waved her heavy hands about.

"No," she went on, "no more for me either. Not even a girl. It's awful the way it skips generations and then pops out. Why, he actually said he didn't care what colour it turned out, if I would only stop worrying about it. But, of course, nobody wants a dark child." Her voice was earnest and she took for granted that her audience was in entire agreement with her.

Irene, whose head had gone up with a quick little jerk, now said in a voice of whose even tones she was proud: "One of my boys is dark."

Gertrude jumped as if she had been shot at. Her eyes goggled. Her mouth flew open. She tried to speak, but could not immediately get the words out. Finally she managed to stammer: "Oh! And your husband, is he—is he—er—dark, too?"

Irene, who was struggling with a flood of feelings, resentment, anger, and contempt, was, however, still able to answer as coolly as if she had not that sense of not belonging to and of despising the company in which she found herself drinking iced tea from tall amber glasses on that hot August afternoon. Her husband, she informed them quietly, couldn't exactly "pass."

At that reply Clare turned on Irene her seductive caressing smile and remarked a little scoffingly: "I do think that coloured people—we—are too silly about some things. After all, the thing's not important to Irene or hundreds of others. Not awfully, even to you, Gertrude. It's only deserters like me who have to be afraid of freaks of the nature. As my inestimable dad used to say, 'Everything must be paid for.' Now, please one of you tell me what ever happened to Claude Jones. You know, the tall, lanky specimen who used to wear that comical little moustache that the girls used to laugh at so. Like a thin streak of soot. The moustache, I mean."

At that Gertrude shrieked with laughter. "Claude Jones!" and launched into the story of how he was no longer a Negro or a Christian but had become a Jew.

"A Jew!" Clare exclaimed.

"Yes, a Jew. A black Jew, he calls himself. He won't eat ham and goes to the synagogue on Saturday. He's got a beard now as well as a moustache. You'd die laughing if you saw him. He's really too funny for words. Fred says he's crazy and I guess he is. Oh, he's a scream all right, a regular scream!" And she shrieked again.

Clare's laugh tinkled out. "It certainly sounds funny enough. Still, it's his own business. If he gets along better by turning—"

At that, Irene, who was still hugging her unhappy don't-care feeling of rightness, broke in, saying bitingly: "It evidently doesn't occur to either you or Gertrude that he might possibly be sincere in changing his religion. Surely everyone doesn't do everything for gain."

Clare Kendry had no need to search for the full meaning of that utterance. She reddened slightly and retorted seriously: "Yes, I admit that might be possible—his being sincere, I mean. It just didn't happen to occur to me, that's all. I'm surprised," and the seriousness changed to mockery, "that you should have expected it to. Or did you really?"

"You don't, I'm sure, imagine that that is a question that I can answer," Irene told her. "Not here and now."

Gertrude's face expressed complete bewilderment. However, seeing that little smiles had come out on the faces of the two other women and not recognizing them for the smiles of mutual reservations which they were, she smiled too.

Clare began to talk, steering carefully away from anything that might lead towards race or other thorny subjects. It was the most brilliant exhibition of conversational weightlifting that Irene had ever seen. Her words swept over them in charming well-modulated streams. Her laughs tinkled and pealed. Her little stories sparkled.

Irene contributed a bare "Yes" or "No" here and there. Gertrude, a "You don't say!" less frequently.

For a while the illusion of general conversation was nearly perfect. Irene felt her resentment changing gradually to a silent, somewhat grudging admiration.

Clare talked on, her voice, her gestures colouring all she said of wartime in France, of after-the-wartime in Germany, of the excitement at the time of the general strike in England, of dressmaker's openings in Paris, of the new gaiety of Budapest.[14]

But it couldn't last, this verbal feat. Gertrude shifted in her seat and fell to fidgeting with her fingers. Irene, bored at last by all this repetition of the selfsame things that she had read all too often in papers, magazines, and books, set down her glass and collected her bag and handkerchief. She was smoothing out the tan fingers of her gloves preparatory to putting them on when she heard the sound of the outer door being opened and saw Clare spring up with an expression of relief saying: "How lovely! Here's Jack at exactly the right minute. You can't go now, 'Rene dear."

John Bellew came into the room. The first thing that Irene noticed about him was that he was not the man that she had seen with Clare Kendry on the Drayton roof. This man, Clare's husband, was a tallish person, broadly made. His age she guessed to be somewhere between thirty-five and forty. His hair was dark brown and waving, and he had a soft mouth, somewhat womanish, set in an unhealthy-looking dough-coloured face. His steel-grey opaque eyes were very much alive, moving ceaselessly between thick bluish lids. But there was, Irene decided, nothing unusual about him, unless it was an impression of latent physical power.

"Hello, Nig," was his greeting to Clare.

Gertrude who had started slightly, settled back and looked covertly towards Irene, who had caught her lip between her teeth and sat gazing at husband and wife. It was hard to believe that even Clare Kendry would permit this ridiculing of her race by an outsider, though he chanced to be her husband. So he knew, then, that Clare was a Negro? From her talk the other day Irene had understood that he didn't. But how rude, how positively insulting, for him to address her in that way in the presence of guests!

---

[14]Clare's account of her sojourn in France, Germany, England, and Austria-Hungary during World War I (1914–1918) and its aftermath (1919–1926), when Europe underwent enormous changes and upheavals in its political, social, and economic life, including workers' strikes in the postwar period (such as the week-long May 1926 General Strike in England by the major transport, railway, and mining unions mentioned in the text), and the emergence of Paris in the 1920s as the capital of the fashion industry.

In Clare's eyes, as she presented her husband, was a queer gleam, a jeer, it might be. Irene couldn't define it.

The mechanical professions that attend an introduction over, she inquired: "Did you hear what Jack called me?"

"Yes," Gertrude answered, laughing with a dutiful eagerness.

Irene didn't speak. Her gaze remained level on Clare's smiling face.

The black eyes fluttered down. "Tell them, dear, why you call me that."

The man chuckled, crinkling up his eyes, not, Irene was compelled to acknowledge, unpleasantly. He explained: "Well, you see, it's like this. When we were first married, she was as white as—as—well as white as a lily. But I declare she's gettin' darker and darker. I tell her if she don't look out, she'll wake up one of these days and find she's turned into a nigger."

He roared with laughter. Clare's ringing bell-like laugh joined his. Gertrude after another uneasy shift in her seat added her shrill one. Irene, who had been sitting with lips tightly compressed, cried out: "That's good!" and gave way to gales of laughter. She laughed and laughed and laughed. Tears ran down her cheeks. Her sides ached. Her throat hurt. She laughed on and on and on, long after the others had subsided. Until, catching sight of Clare's face, the need for a more quiet enjoyment of this priceless joke, and for caution, struck her. At once she stopped.

Clare handed her husband his tea and laid her hand on his arm with an affectionate little gesture. Speaking with confidence as well as with amusement, she said: "My goodness, Jack! What difference would it make if, after all these years, you were to find out that I was one or two per cent coloured?"

Bellew put out his hand in a repudiating fling, definite and final. "Oh, no, Nig," he declared, "nothing like that with me. I know you're no nigger, so it's all right. You can get as black as you please as far as I'm concerned, since I know you're no nigger. I draw the line at that. No niggers in my family. Never have been and never will be."

Irene's lips trembled almost uncontrollably, but she made a desperate effort to fight back her disastrous desire to laugh again, and succeeded. Carefully selecting a cigarette from the lacquered box on the tea-table before her, she turned an oblique look on Clare and encountered her peculiar eyes fixed on her with an expression so dark and deep and unfathomable that she had for a short moment the sensation of gazing into the eyes of some creature utterly strange and apart. A faint sense of danger brushed her, like the breath of a cold fog. Absurd, her reason told her, as she accepted Bellew's proffered light for her cigarette. Another glance at Clare showed her smiling. So, as one always ready to oblige, was Gertrude.

An on-looker, Irene reflected, would have thought it a most congenial tea-party, all smiles and jokes and hilarious laughter. She said humorously: "So you dislike Negroes, Mr. Bellew?" But her amusement was at her thought, rather than her words.

John Bellew gave a short denying laugh. "You got me wrong there, Mrs. Redfield. Nothing like that at all. I don't dislike them, I hate them. And so does Nig, for all she's trying to turn into one. She wouldn't have a nigger maid around her for love nor money. Not that I'd want her to. They give me the creeps. The black scrimy devils."

This wasn't funny. Had Bellew, Irene inquired, ever known any Negroes? The defensive tone of her voice brought another start from the uncomfortable Gertrude, and, for all her appearance of serenity, a quick apprehensive look from Clare.

Bellew answered: "Thank the Lord, no! And never expect to! But I know people who've known them, better than they know their black selves. And I read in the papers about them. Always robbing and killing people. And," he added darkly, "worse."

From Gertrude's direction came a queer little suppressed sound, a snort or a giggle. Irene couldn't tell which. There was a brief silence, during which she feared that her self control was about to prove too frail a bridge to support her mounting anger and indignation. She had a leaping desire to shout at the man beside her: "And you're sitting here surrounded by three black devils, drinking tea."

The impulse passed, obligated by her consciousness of the danger in which such rashness would involve Clare, who remarked with a gentle reprovingness: "Jack dear, I'm sure 'Rene doesn't care to hear all about your pet aversions. Nor Gertrude either. Maybe they read the papers too, you know." She smiled on him, and her smile seemed to transform him, to soften and mellow him, as the rays of the sun does a fruit.

"All right, Nig, old girl. I'm sorry," he apologized. Reaching over, he playfully touched his wife's pale hands, then turned back to Irene. "Didn't mean to bore you, Mrs. Redfield. Hope you'll excuse me," he said sheepishly. "Clare tells me you're living in New York. Great city, New York. The city of the future."

In Irene, rage had not retreated, but was held by some dam of caution and allegiance to Clare. So, in the best casual voice she could muster, she agreed with Bellew. Though, she reminded him, it was exactly what Chicagoans were apt to say of their city. And all the while she was speaking, she was thinking how amazing it was that her voice did not tremble, that outwardly she was calm. Only her hands shook slightly. She drew them inward from their rest in her lap and pressed the tips of her fingers together to still them.

"Husband's a doctor, I understand. Manhattan, or one of the other boroughs?"

Manhattan, Irene informed him, and explained the need for Brian to be within easy reach of certain hospitals and clinics.

"Interesting life, a doctor's."

"Ye-es. Hard, though. And, in a way, monotonous. Nerve-racking too."

"Hard on the wife's nerves at least, eh? So many lady patients." He laughed, enjoying, with a boyish heartiness, the hoary joke.

Irene managed a momentary smile, but her voice was sober as she said: "Brian doesn't care for ladies, especially sick ones. I sometimes wish he did. It's South America that attracts him."

"Coming place, South America, if they ever get the niggers out of it. It's run over—"

"Really, Jack!" Clare's voice was on the edge of temper.

"Honestly, Nig, I forgot." To the others he said: "You see how henpecked I am." And to Gertrude: "You're still in Chicago, Mrs.—er—Mrs. Martin?"

He was, it was plain, doing his best to be agreeable to these old friends of Clare's. Irene had to concede that under other conditions she might have liked him. A fairly good-looking man of amiable disposition, evidently, and in easy circumstances. Plain and with no nonsense about him.

Gertrude replied that Chicago was good enough for her. She'd never been out of it and didn't think she ever should. Her husband's business was there.

"Of course, of course. Can't jump up and leave a business."

There followed a smooth surface of talk about Chicago, New York, their differences and their recent spectacular changes.

It was, Irene, thought, unbelievable and astonishing that four people could sit so unruffled, so ostensibly friendly, while they were in reality seething with anger, mortification, shame. But no, on second thought she was forced to amend her opinion. John Bellew, most certainly, was as undisturbed within as without. So, perhaps, was Gertrude Martin. At least she hadn't the mortification and shame that Clare Kendry must be feeling, or, in such full measure, the rage and rebellion that she, Irene, was repressing.

"More tea, 'Rene," Clare offered.

"Thanks, no. And I must be going. I'm leaving tomorrow, you know, and I've still got packing to do."

She stood up. So did Gertrude, and Clare, and John Bellew.

"How do you like the Drayton, Mrs. Redfield?" the latter asked.

"The Drayton? Oh, very much. Very much indeed," Irene answered, her scornful eyes on Clare's unrevealing face.

"Nice place, all right. Stayed there a time or two myself," the man informed her.

"Yes, it is nice," Irene agreed. "Almost as good as our best New York places." She had withdrawn her look from Clare and was searching in her bag for some non-existent something. Her understanding was rapidly increasing, as was her pity and her contempt. Clare was so daring, so lovely, and so "having."

They gave their hands to Clare with appropriate murmurs. "So good to have seen you." . . . "I do hope I'll see you again soon."

"Good-bye," Clare returned. "It was good of you to come, 'Rene dear. And you too, Gertrude."

"Good-bye, Mr. Bellew." . . . "So glad to have met you." It was Gertrude who had said that. Irene couldn't, she absolutely couldn't bring herself to utter the polite fiction or anything approaching it.

He accompanied them out into the hall, summoned the elevator.

"Good-bye," they said again, stepping in.

Plunging downward they were silent.

They made their way through the lobby without speaking.

But as soon as they had reached the street Gertrude, in the manner of one unable to keep bottled up for another minute that which for the last hour she had had to retain, burst out: "My God! What an awful chance! She must be plumb crazy."

"Yes, it certainly seems risky," Irene admitted.

"Risky! I should say it was. Risky! My God! What a word! And the mess she's liable to get herself into!"

"Still, I imagine she's pretty safe. They don't live here, you know. And there's a child. That's a certain security."

"It's an awful chance, just the same," Gertrude insisted. "I'd never in the world have married Fred without him knowing. You can't tell what will turn up."

"Yes, I do agree that it's safer to tell. But then Bellew wouldn't have married her. And, after all, that's what she wanted."

Gertrude shook her head. "I wouldn't be in her shoes for all the money she's getting out of it, when he finds out. Not with him feeling the way he does. Gee! Wasn't it awful? For a minute I was so mad I could have slapped him."

It had been, Irene acknowledged, a distinctly trying experience, as well as a very unpleasant one. "I was more than a little angry myself."

"And imagine her not telling us about him feeling that way! Anything might have happened. We might have said something."

That, Irene pointed out, was exactly like Clare Kendry. Taking a chance, and not at all considering anyone else's feelings.

Gertrude said: "Maybe she thought we'd think it a good joke. And I guess you did. The way you laughed. My land! I was scared to death he might catch on."

"Well, it was rather a joke," Irene told her, "on him and us and maybe on her."

"All the same, it's an awful chance. I'd hate to be her."

"She seems satisfied enough. She's got what she wanted, and the other day she told me it was worth it."

But about that Gertrude was sceptical. "She'll find out different," was her verdict. "She'll find out different all right."

Rain had begun to fall, a few scattered large drops.

The end-of-the-day crowds were scurrying in the directions of street-cars and elevated roads.

Irene said: "You're going south? I'm sorry. I've got an errand. If you don't mind, I'll just say good-bye here. It has been nice seeing you, Gertrude. Say hello to Fred for me, and to your mother if she remembers me. Good-bye."

She had wanted to be free of the other woman, to be alone; for she was still sore and angry.

What right, she kept demanding of herself, had Clare Kendry to expose her, or even Gertrude Martin, to such humiliation, such downright insult?

And all the while, on the rushing ride out to her father's house, Irene Redfield was trying to understand the look on Clare's face as she had said good-bye. Partly mocking, it had seemed, and partly menacing. And something else for which she could find no name. For an instant a recrudescence of that sensation of fear which she had had while looking into Clare's eyes that afternoon touched her. A slight shiver ran over her.

"It's nothing," she told herself. "Just somebody walking over my grave, as the children say." She tried a tiny laugh and was annoyed to find that it was close to tears.

What a state she had allowed that horrible Bellew to get her into!

And late that night, even, long after the last guest had gone and the old house was quiet, she stood at her window frowning out into the dark rain and puzzling again over that look on Clare's incredibly beautiful face. She couldn't, however, come to any conclusion about its meaning, try as she might. It was unfathomable, utterly beyond any experience or comprehension of hers.

She turned away from the window, at last, with a still deeper frown. Why, after all, worry about Clare Kendry? She was well able to take care of herself, had always been able. And there were, for Irene, other things, more personal and more important to worry about.

Besides, her reason told her, she had only herself to blame for her disagreeable afternoon and its attendant fears and questions. She ought never to have gone.

Four

The next morning, the day of her departure for New York, had brought a letter, which, at first glance, she had instinctively known came from Clare Kendry, though she couldn't remember ever having had a letter from her before. Ripping it open and looking at the signature, she saw that she had been right in her guess. She wouldn't, she told herself, read it. She hadn't the time. And, besides, she had no wish to be reminded of the afternoon before. As it was, she felt none too fresh for her journey; she had had a wretched night. And all because of Clare's innate lack of consideration for the feelings of others.

But she did read it. After father and friends had waved good-bye, and she was being hurled eastward, she became possessed of an uncontrollable curiosity to see what Clare had said about yesterday. For what, she asked, as she took it out of her bag and opened it, could she, what could anyone, say about a thing like that?

Clare Kendry had said:

'Rene dear:

However am I to thank you for your visit? I know you are feeling that under the circumstances I ought not to have asked you to come, or, rather, insisted. But if you could know how glad, how excitingly happy, I was to meet you and how I ached to see more of you (to see everybody and couldn't), you would understand my wanting to see you again, and maybe forgive me a little.

My love to you always and always and to your dear father, and all my poor thanks.

Clare.

And there was a postscript which said:

It may be, 'Rene dear, it may just be, that, after all, your way may be the wiser and infinitely happier one. I'm not sure just now. At least not so sure as I have been.

C.

But the letter hadn't conciliated Irene. Her indignation was not lessened by Clare's flattering reference to her wiseness. As if, she thought wrathfully, anything could take away the humiliation, or any part of it, of what she had gone through yesterday afternoon for Clare Kendry.

With an unusual methodicalness she tore the offending letter into tiny ragged squares that fluttered down and made a small heap in her black *crêpe de Chine* lap. The destruction completed, she gathered them up, rose, and moved to the train's end. Standing there, she dropped them over the railing and watched them scatter, on tracks, on cinders, on forlorn grass, in rills of dirty water.

And that, she told herself, was that. The chances were one in a million that she would ever again lay eyes on Clare Kendry. If, however, that millionth chance should turn up, she had only to turn away her eyes, to refuse her recognition.

She dropped Clare out of her mind and turned her thoughts to her own affairs. To home, to the boys, to Brian. Brian, who in the morning would be waiting for her in the great clamourous station. She hoped that he had been comfortable and not too lonely without her and the boys. Not so lonely that that old, queer, unhappy restlessness had begun again within him, that craving for some place strange and different, which at the beginning of her marriage she had had to make such strenuous efforts to repress, and which yet faintly alarmed her, though it now sprang up at gradually lessening intervals.

Part Two. Re-Encounter

One

Such were Irene Redfield's memories as she sat there in her room, a flood of October sunlight streaming in upon her, holding that second letter of Clare Kendry's.

Laying it aside, she regarded with an astonishment that had in it a mild degree of amusement the violence of the feelings which it stirred in her.

It wasn't the great measure of anger that surprised and slightly amused her. That, she was certain, was justified and reasonable, as was the fact that it could hold, still strong and unabated, across the stretch of two years' time entirely removed from any sight or sound of John Bellew, or of Clare. That even at this remote date the memory of the man's words and manner had power to set her hands to trembling and to send the blood pounding against her temples did not seem to her extraordinary. But that she should retain that dim sense of fear, of panic, was surprising, silly.

That Clare should have written, should even all things considered, have expressed a desire to see her again, did not so much amaze her. To count as nothing the annoyances, the bitterness, or the suffering of others, that was Clare.

Well—Irene's shoulders went up—one thing was sure: that she needn't, and didn't intend to, lay herself open to any repetition of a humiliation as galling and outrageous as that which, for Clare Kendry's sake, she had borne "that time in Chicago." Once was enough.

If, at the time of choosing, Clare hadn't precisely reckoned the cost, she had, nevertheless, no right to expect others to help make up the reckoning. The trouble with Clare was, not only that she wanted to have her cake and eat it too, but that she wanted to nibble at the cakes of other folk as well.

Irene Redfield found it hard to sympathize with this new tenderness, this avowed yearning of Clare's for "my own people."

The letter which she just put out of her hand was, to her taste, a bit too lavish in its wordiness, a shade too unreserved in the manner of its expression. It roused again that old suspicion that Clare was acting, not consciously, perhaps—that is, not too consciously—but, none the less, acting. Nor was Irene inclined to excuse what she termed Clare's downright selfishness.

And mingled with her disbelief and resentment was another feeling, a question. Why hadn't she spoken that day? Why, in the face of Bellew's ignorant hate and aversion, had she concealed her own origin? Why had she allowed him to make his assertions and express his misconceptions undisputed? Why, simply because of Clare Kendry, who had exposed her to such torment, had she failed to take up the defence of the race to which she belonged?

Irene asked these questions, felt them. They were, however, merely rhetorical, as she herself was well aware. She knew their answers, every one, and it was the same for them all. The sardony of it![15] She couldn't betray Clare, couldn't even run the risk of appearing to defend a people that were being maligned, for fear that that defence might in some infinitesimal degree lead the way to final discovery of her secret. She had to Clare Kendry a duty. She was bound to her by those very ties of race, which, for all her repudiation of them, Clare had been unable to completely sever.

And it wasn't, as Irene knew, that Clare cared at all about the race or what was to become of it. She didn't. Or that she had for any of its members great, or even real, affection, though she professed undying gratitude for the small kindnesses which the Westover family had shown her when she was a child. Irene doubted the genuineness of it, seeing herself only as a

[15]Mocking bitterness; scornful, cynical humor; Larsen creates a noun form of the adjective "sardonic."

means to an end where Clare was concerned. Nor could it be said that she had even the slight artistic or sociological interest in the race that some members of other races displayed. She hadn't. No, Clare Kendry cared nothing for the race. She only belonged to it.

"Not another damned thing!" Irene declared aloud as she drew a fragile stocking over a pale beige-coloured foot.

"Aha! Swearing again, are you, madam? Caught you in the act that time."

Brian Redfield had come into the room in that noiseless way which, in spite, of the years of their life together, still had the power to disconcert her. He stood looking down on her with that amused smile of his, which was just the faintest bit supercilious and yet was somehow very becoming to him.

Hastily Irene pulled on the other stocking and slipped her feet into the slippers beside her chair.

"And what brought on this particular outburst of profanity? That is, if an indulgent but perturbed husband may inquire. The mother of sons too! The times, alas, the times!"

"I've had this letter," Irene told him. "And I'm sure that anybody'll admit it's enough to make a saint swear. The nerve of her!"

She passed the letter to him, and in the act made a little mental frown. For, with a nicety of perception, she saw that she was doing it instead of answering his question with words, so that he might be occupied while she hurried through her dressing. For she was late again, and Brian, she well knew, detested that. Why, oh why, couldn't she ever manage to be on time? Brian had been up for ages, had made some calls for all she knew, besides having taken the boys downtown to school. And she wasn't dressed yet; had only begun. Damn Clare! This morning it was her fault.

Brian sat down and bent his head over the letter, puckering his brows slightly in his effort to make out Clare's scrawl.

Irene, who had risen and was standing before the mirror, ran a comb through her black hair, then tossed her head with a light characteristic gesture, in order to disarrange a little the set locks. She touched a powder-puff to her warm olive skin, and then put on her frock with a motion so hasty that it was with some difficulty properly adjusted. At last she was ready, though she didn't immediately say so, but stood, instead, looking with a sort of curious detachment at her husband across the room.

Brian, she was thinking, was extremely good-looking. Not, of course, pretty or effeminate; the slight irregularity of his nose saved him from the prettiness, and the rather marked heaviness of his chin saved him from the effeminacy. But he was, in a pleasant masculine way, rather handsome. And yet, wouldn't he, perhaps, have been merely ordinarily good-looking but for the richness, the beauty of his skin, which was of an exquisitely fine texture and deep copper colour.

He looked up and said: "Clare? That must be the girl you told me about meeting the last time you were out home. The one you went to tea with?"

Irene's answer to that was an inclination of the head.

"I'm ready," she said.

They were going downstairs, Brian deftly, unnecessarily, piloting her round the two short curved steps, just before the centre landing.

"You're not," he asked, "going to see her?"

His words, however, were in reality not a question, but, as Irene was aware, an admonition.

Her front teeth just touched. She spoke through them, and her tones held a thin sarcasm. "Brian, darling, I'm really not such an idiot that I don't realize that if a man calls me a nigger, it's his fault the first time, but mine if he has the opportunity to do it again."

They went into the dining-room. He drew back her chair and she sat down behind the fat-bellied German coffee-pot, which sent out its morning fragrance, mingled with the smell of crisp toast and savoury bacon, in the distance. With his long, nervous fingers he picked up the morning paper from his own chair and sat down.

Zulena, a small mahogany-coloured creature, brought in the grapefruit.

They took up their spoons.

Out of the silence Brian spoke. Blandly. "My dear, you misunderstand me entirely. I simply meant that I hope you're not going to let her pester you. She will, you know, if you give her half a chance and she's anything at all like your description of her. Anyway, they always do. Besides," he corrected, "the man, her husband, didn't call you a nigger. There's a difference, you know."

"No, certainly he didn't. Not actually. He couldn't, not very well, since he didn't know. But he would have. It amounts to the same thing. And I'm sure it was just as unpleasant."

"U-mm, I don't know. But it seems to me," he pointed out, "that you, my dear, had all the advantage. You knew what his opinion of you was, while he—Well 'twas ever thus. We know, always have. They don't. Not quite. It has, you will admit, its humorous side, and, sometimes, its conveniences."

She poured the coffee.

"I can't see it. I'm going to write Clare. Today, if I can find a minute. It's a thing we might as well settle definitely, and immediately. Curious, isn't it, that knowing, as she does, his unqualified attitude, she still—"

Brian interrupted: "It's always that way. Never known it to fail. Remember Albert Hammond, how he used to be for ever haunting Seventh Avenue, and Lenox Avenue, and the dancing-places, until some 'shine' took a shot at him for casting an eye towards his 'sheba?'[16] They always come back. I've seen it happen time and time again."

"But why?" Irene wanted to know. "Why?"

"If I knew that, I'd know what race is."

"But wouldn't you think that having got the thing, or things, they were after, and at such risk, they'd be satisfied? Or afraid?"

[16]Primary streets identified with the heart of 1920s Harlem for their subway stops, theatres, cabarets, restaurants, strolling, and parades; "shine" is slang for a black man, derived from the negative notion of shiny black skin, and "sheba" is slang for a black woman, derived from the Biblical Queen of Sheba (I Kings: 10), an Arabian ruler who brought gold, spices, and precious stones to King Solomon.

"Yes," Brian agreed, "you certainly would think so. But, the fact remains, they aren't. Not satisfied, I mean. I think they're scared enough most of the time, when they give way to the urge and slip back. Not scared enough to stop them, though. Why, the good God only knows."

Irene leaned forward, speaking, she was aware, with a vehemence absolutely unnecessary, but which she could not control.

"Well, Clare can just count me out. I've no intention of being the link between her and her poorer darker brethren. After that scene in Chicago too! To calmly expect me—" She stopped short, suddenly too wrathful for words.

"Quite right. The only sensible thing to do. Let her miss you. It's an unhealthy business, the whole affair. Always is."

Irene nodded. "More coffee," she offered.

"Thanks, no." He took up his paper again, spreading it open with a little rattling noise.

Zulena came in bringing more toast. Brian took a slice and bit into it with that audible crunching sound that Irene disliked so intensely, and turned back to his paper.

She said: "It's funny about 'passing.' We disapprove of it and at the same time condone it. It excites our contempt and yet we rather admire it. We shy away from it with an odd kind of revulsion, but we protect it."

"Instinct of the race to survive and expand."

"Rot! Everything can't be explained by some general biological phrase."

"Absolutely everything can. Look at the so-called whites, who've left bastards all over the known earth. Same thing in them. Instinct of the race to survive and expand."

With that Irene didn't at all agree, but many arguments in the past had taught her the futility of attempting to combat Brian on ground where he was more nearly at home than she. Ignoring his unqualified assertion, she slid away from the subject entirely.

"I wonder," she asked, "if you'll have time to run me down to the printing office. It's on a Hundred and Sixteenth Street. I've got to see about some handbills and some more tickets for the dance."

"Yes, of course. How's it going? Everything all set?"

"Ye-es. I guess so. The boxes are all sold and nearly all the first batch of tickets. And we expect to take in almost as much again at the door. Then, there's all that cake to sell. It's a terrible lot of work, though."

"I'll bet it is. Uplifting the brother's no easy job.[17] I'm as busy as a cat with fleas, myself." And over his face there came a shadow. "Lord! how I

[17]Uplift, an ethic of service and racial self-help fueled by self-interests and focused on the black masses, permeated black middle-class ideology from emancipation through the first decades of the twentieth century, when social advancement was considered the distinguishing feature of racial progress. The work of racial uplift for middle-class blacks in the helping professions, such as medicine, teaching, and social work, became more difficult after World War I when mass black migration from the rural South to northern urban areas, in particular New York City and Chicago, threatened to overwhelm the resources for improving the living conditions of poor blacks.

hate sick people, and their stupid, meddling families, and smelly, dirty rooms, and climbing filthy steps in dark hallways."

"Surely," Irene began, fighting back the fear and irritation that she felt, "surely—"

Her husband silenced her, saying sharply: "Let's not talk about it, please." And immediately, in his usual, slightly mocking tone he asked: "Are you ready to go now? I haven't a great deal of time to wait."

He got up. She followed him out into the hall without replying. He picked up his soft brown hat from the small table and stood a moment whirling it round on his long tea-coloured fingers.

Irene, watching him, was thinking: "It isn't fair, it isn't fair." After all these years to still blame her like this. Hadn't his success proved that she'd been right in insisting that he stick to his profession right there in New York? Couldn't he see, even now, that it *had* been best? Not for her, oh no, not for her—she had never really considered herself—but for him and the boys. Was she never to be free of it, that fear which crouched, always, deep down within her, stealing away the sense of security, the feeling of permanence, from the life which she had so admirably arranged for them all, and desired so ardently to have remain as it was? That strange, and to her fantastic, notion of Brian's of going off to Brazil, which, though unmentioned, yet lived within him; how it frightened her, and—yes, angered her!

"Well?" he asked lightly.

"I'll just get my things. One minute," she promised and turned upstairs.

Her voice had been even and her step was firm, but in her there was no slackening of the agitation, of the alarms, which Brian's expression of discontent had raised. He had never spoken of his desire since that long-ago time of storm and strain, of hateful and nearly disastrous quarrelling, when she had so firmly opposed him, so sensibly pointed out its utter impossibility and its probable consequences to her and the boys, and had even hinted at a dissolution of their marriage in the event of his persistence in his idea. No, there had been, in all the years that they had lived together since then, no other talk of it, no more than there had been any other quarrelling or any other threats. But because, so she insisted, the bond of flesh and spirit between them was so strong, she knew, had always known, that his dissatisfaction had continued, as had his dislike and disgust for his profession and his country.

A feeling of uneasiness stole upon her at the inconceivable suspicion that she might have been wrong in her estimate of her husband's character. But she squirmed away from it. Impossible! She couldn't have been wrong. Everything proved that she had been right. More than right, if such a thing could be. And all, she assured herself, because she understood him so well, because she had, actually, a special talent for understanding him. It was, as she saw it, the one thing that had been the basis of the success which she had made of a marriage that had threatened to fail. She knew him as well as he knew himself, or better.

Then why worry? The thing, this discontent which had exploded into words, would surely die, flicker out, at last. True, she had in the past often been tempted to believe that it had died, only to become conscious, in some instinctive, subtle way, that she had been merely deceiving herself for a while and that it still lived. But it *would* die. Of that she was certain. She had only to direct and guide her man, to keep him going in the right direction.

She put on her coat and adjusted her hat.

Yes, it would die, as long ago she had made up her mind that it should. But in the meantime, while it was still living and still had the power to flare up and alarm her, it would have to be banked, smothered, and something offered in its stead. She would have to make some plan, some decision, at once. She frowned, for it annoyed her intensely. For, though temporary, it would be important and perhaps disturbing. Irene didn't like changes, particularly changes that affected the smooth routine of her household. Well, it couldn't be helped. Something would have to be done. And immediately.

She took up her purse and drawing on her gloves, ran down the steps and out through the door which Brian held open for her and stepped into the waiting car.

"You know," she said, settling herself into the seat beside him, "I'm awfuly glad to get this minute alone with you. It does seem that we're always so busy—I do hate that—but what can we do? I've had something on my mind for ever so long, something that needs talking over and really serious consideration."

The car's engine rumbled as it moved out from the kerb and into the scant traffic of the street under Brian's expert guidance.

She studied his profile.

They turned into Seventh Avenue. Then he said: "Well, let's have it. No time like the present for the settling of weighty matters."

"It's about Junior. I wonder if he isn't going too fast in school? We do forget that he's not eleven yet. Surely it can't be good for him to—well, if he is, I mean. Going too fast, you know. Of course, you know more about these things than I do. You're better able to judge. That is, if you've noticed or thought about it at all."

"I do wish, Irene, you wouldn't be for ever fretting about those kids. They're all right. Perfectly all right. Good, strong, healthy boys, especially Junior. Most especially Junior."

"We-ll, I s'pose you're right. You're expected to know about things like that, and I'm sure you wouldn't make a mistake about your own boy." (Now, why had she said that?) "But that isn't all. I'm terribly afraid he's picked up some queer ideas about things—some things—from the older boys, you know."

Her manner was consciously light. Apparently she was intent of the maze of traffic, but she was still watching Brian's face closely. On it was a peculiar expression. Was it, could it possibly be, a mixture of scorn and distaste?

"Queer ideas?" he repeated. "D'you mean ideas about sex, Irene?"

"Ye-es. Not quite nice ones. Dreadful jokes, and things like that."

"Oh, I see," he threw at her. For a while there was silence between them. After a moment he demanded bluntly: "Well, what of it? If sex isn't a joke, what is it? And what is a joke?"

"As you please, Brian. He's your son, you know." Her voice was clear, level, disapproving.

"Exactly! And you're trying to make a molly-coddle out of him. Well, just let me tell you, I won't have it. And you needn't think I'm going to let you change him to some nicer kindergarten kind of a school because he's getting a little necessary education. I won't! He'll stay right where he is. The sooner and the more he learns about sex, the better for him. And most certainly if he learns that it's a grand joke, the greatest in the world. It'll keep him from lots of disappointments later on."

Irene didn't answer.

They reached the printing-shop. She got out, emphatically slamming the car's door behind her. There was a piercing agony of misery in her heart. She hadn't intended to behave like this, but her extreme resentment at his attitude, the sense of having been wilfully misunderstood and reproved, drove her to fury.

Inside the shop, she stilled the trembling of her lips and drove back her rising anger. Her business transacted, she came back to the car in a chastened mood. But against the armour of Brian's stubborn silence she heard herself saying in a calm, metallic voice: "I don't believe I'll go back just now. I've remembered that I've got to do something about getting something decent to wear. I haven't a rag that's fit to be seen. I'll take the bus downtown."

Brian merely doffed his hat in that maddening polite way which so successfully curbed and yet revealed his temper.

"Good-bye," she said bitingly. "Thanks for the lift," and turned towards the avenue.

What, she wondered contritely, was she to do next? She was vexed with herself for having chosen, as it had turned out, so clumsy an opening for what she had intended to suggest: some European school for Junior next year, and Brian to take him over. If she had been able to present her plan, and he had accepted it, as she was sure that he would have done, with other more favourable opening methods, he would have had that to look forward to as a break in the easy monotony that seemed, for some reason she was wholly unable to grasp, so hateful to him.

She was even more vexed at her own explosion of anger. What could have got into her to give way to it in such a moment?

Gradually her mood passed. She drew back from the failure of her first attempt at substitution, not so much discouraged as disappointed and ashamed. It might be, she reflected, that, in addition to her ill-timed loss of temper, she had been too hasty in her eagerness to distract him, had rushed too closely on the heels of his outburst, and had thus aroused his suspicions and his obstinacy. She had but to wait. Another more appropriate time would come, tomorrow, next week, next month. It wasn't now, as it had been once, that she was afraid that he would throw everything aside and rush off to that remote place of his heart's desire. He wouldn't, she knew. He was fond of her, loved her, in his slightly undemonstrative way. And there were the boys.

It was only that she wanted him to be happy, resenting, however, his inability to be so with things as they were, and never acknowledging that though she did want him to be happy, it was only in her own way and by some plan of hers for him that she truly desired him to be so. Nor did she admit that all other plans, all other ways, she regarded as menaces, more or less indirect, to that security of place and substance which she insisted upon for her sons and in a lesser degree for herself.

Two

Five days had gone by since Clare Kendry's appealing letter. Irene Redfield had not replied to it. Nor had she had any other word from Clare.

She had not carried out her first intention of writing at once because on going back to the letter for Clare's address, she had come upon something which, in the rigour of her determination to maintain unbroken between them the wall that Clare herself had raised, she had forgotten, or not fully noted. It was the fact that Clare had requested her to direct her answer to the post office's general delivery.

That had angered Irene, and increased her disdain and contempt for the other.

Tearing the letter across, she had flung it into the scrap-basket. It wasn't so much Clare's carefulness and her desire for secrecy in their relations—Irene understood the need for that—as that Clare should have doubted her discretion, implied that she might not be cautious in the wording of her reply and the choice of a posting-box. Having always had complete confidence in her own good judgment and tact, Irene couldn't bear to have anyone seem to question them. Certainly not Clare Kendry.

In another, calmer moment she decided that it was, after all, better to answer nothing, to explain nothing, to refuse nothing; to dispose of the matter simply by not writing at all. Clare, of whom it couldn't be said that she was stupid, would not mistake the implication of that silence. She might—and Irene was sure that she would—choose to ignore it and write again, but that didn't matter. The whole thing would be very easy. The basket for all letters, silence for their answers.

Most likely she and Clare would never meet again. Well, she, for one, could endure that. Since childhood their lives had never really touched. Actually they were strangers. Strangers in their ways and means of living. Strangers in their desires and ambitions. Strangers even in their racial consciousness. Between them the barrier was just as high, just as broad, and just as firm as if in Clare did not run that strain of black blood. In truth, it was higher, broader, and firmer; because for her there were perils, not known, or imagined, by those others who had no such secrets to alarm or endanger them.

The day was getting on toward evening. It was past the middle of October. There had been a week of cold rain, drenching the rotting leaves which had fallen from the poor trees that lined the street on which the Redfields' house was located, and sending a damp air of penetrating chill into the house, with a hint of cold days to come. In Irene's room a low fire was burning. Outside, only a dull grey light was left of the day. Inside, lamps had already been lighted.

From the floor above there was the sound of young voices. Sometimes Junior's serious and positive; again, Ted's deceptively gracious one. Often there was laughter, or the noise of commotion, tussling, or toys being slammed down.

Junior, tall for his age, was almost incredibly like his father in feature and colouring; but his temperament was hers, practical and determined, rather than Brian's. Ted, speculative and withdrawn, was, apparently, less positive in his ideas and desires. About him there was a deceiving air of candour that was, Irene knew, like his father's show of reasonable acquiescence. If, for the time being, and with a charming appearance of artlessness, he submitted to the force of superior strength, or some other immovable condition or circumstance, it was because of his intense dislike of scenes and unpleasant argument. Brian over again.

Gradually Irene's thought slipped away from Junior and Ted, to become wholly absorbed in their father.

The old fear, with strength increased, the fear for the future, had again laid its hand on her. And, try as she might, she could not shake it off. It was as if she had admitted to herself that against that easy surface of her husband's concordance with her wishes, which had, since the war had given him back to her physically unimpaired, covered an increasing inclination to tear himself and his possessions loose from their proper setting, she was helpless.

The chagrin which she had felt at her first failure to subvert this latest manifestation of his discontent had receded, leaving in its wake an uneasy depression. Were all her efforts, all her labours, to make up to him that one loss, all her silent striving to prove to him that her way had been best, all her ministrations to him, all her outward sinking of self, to count for nothing in some unperceived sudden moment? And if so, what, then, would be the consequences to the boys? To her? To Brian himself? Endless searching had brought no answer to these questions. There was only an intense weariness from their shuttle-like procession in her brain.

The noise and commotion from above grew increasingly louder. Irene was about to go to the stairway and request the boys to be quieter in their play when she heard the doorbell ringing.

Now, who was that likely to be? She listened to Zulena's heels, faintly tapping on their way to the door, then to the shifting sound of her feet on the steps, then to her light knock on the bedroom door.

"Yes. Come in," Irene told her.

Zulena stood in the doorway. She said: "Someone to see you, Mrs. Redfield." Her tone was discreetly regretful, as if to convey that she was reluctant to disturb her mistress at that hour, and for a stranger. "A Mrs. Bellew."

Clare!

"Oh dear! Tell her, Zulena," Irene began, "that I can't—No. I'll see her. Please bring her up here."

She heard Zulena pass down the hall, down the stairs, then stood up, smoothing out the tumbled green and ivory draperies of her dress with light stroking pats. At the mirror she dusted a little powder on her nose and brushed out her hair.

She meant to tell Clare Kendry at once, and definitely, that it was of no use, her coming, that she couldn't be responsible, that she'd talked it over with Brian, who had agreed with her that it was wiser, for Clare's own sake, to refrain—

But that was as far as she got in her rehearsal. For Clare had come softly into the room without knocking, and before Irene could greet her, had dropped a kiss on her dark curls.

Looking at the woman before her, Irene Redfield had a sudden inexplicable onrush of affectionate feeling. Reaching out, she grasped Clare's two hands in her own and cried with something like awe in her voice: "Dear God! But aren't you lovely, Clare!"

Clare tossed that aside. Like the furs and small blue hat which she threw on the bed before seating herself slantwise in Irene's favourite chair, with one foot curled under her.

"Didn't you mean to answer my letter, 'Rene?" she asked gravely.

Irene looked away. She had that uncomfortable feeling that one has when one has not been wholly kind or wholly true.

Clare went on: "Every day I went to that nasty little post-office place. I'm sure they were all beginning to think that I'd been carrying on an illicit love-affair and that the man had thrown me over. Every morning the same answer: 'Nothing for you.' I got into an awful fright, thinking that something might have happened to your letter, or to mine. And half the nights I would lie awake looking out at the watery stars—hopeless things, the stars—worrying and wondering. But at last it soaked in, that you hadn't written and didn't intend to. And then—well, as soon as ever I'd seen Jack off for Florida, I came straight here. And now, 'Rene, please tell me quite frankly why you didn't answer my letter."

"Because, you see—" Irene broke off and kept Clare waiting while she lit a cigarette, blew out the match, and dropped it into a tray. She was trying to collect her arguments, for some sixth sense warned her that it was going to be harder than she thought to convince Clare Kendry of the folly of Harlem for her. Finally she proceeded: "I can't help thinking that you ought not to come up here, ought not to run the risk of knowing Negroes."

"You mean you don't want me, 'Rene?"

Irene hadn't supposed that anyone could look so hurt. She said, quite gently, "No, Clare, it's not that. But even you must see that it's terribly foolish, and not just the right thing."

The tinkle of Clare's laugh rang out, while she passed her hands over the bright sweep of her hair. "Oh, 'Rene!" she cried, "you're priceless! And you haven't changed a bit. The right thing!" Leaning forward, she looked curiously into Irene's disapproving brown eyes. "You don't, you really can't mean exactly that! Nobody could. It's simply unbelievable."

Irene was on her feet before she realized that she had risen. "What I really mean," she retorted, "is that it's dangerous and that you ought not to run such silly risks. No one ought to. You least of all."

Her voice was brittle. For into her mind had come a thought, strange and irrelevant, a suspicion, that had surprised and shocked her and driven her to her feet. It was that in spite of her determined selfishness the woman before her was yet capable of heights and depths of feeling that she, Irene Redfield, had never known. Indeed, never cared to know. The thought, the suspicion, was gone as quickly as it had come.

Clare said: "Oh, me!"

Irene touched her arm caressingly, as if in contrition for that flashing thought. "Yes, Clare, you. It's not safe. Not safe at all."

"Safe!"

It seemed to Irene that Clare had snapped her teeth down on the word and then flung it from her. And for another flying second she had that suspicion of Clare's ability for a quality of feeling that was to her strange, and even repugnant. She was aware, too, of a dim premonition of some impending disaster. It was as if Clare Kendry had said to her, for whom safety, security, were all-important: "Safe! Damn being safe!" and meant it.

With a gesture of impatience she sat down. In a voice of cool formality, she said: "Brian and I have talked the whole thing over carefully and decided that it isn't wise. He says it's always a dangerous business, this coming back. He's seen more than one come to grief because of it. And, Clare, considering everything—Mr. Bellew's attitude and all that—don't you think you ought to be as careful as you can?"

Clare's deep voice broke the small silence that had followed Irene's speech. She said, speaking almost plaintively: "I ought to have known. It's Jack. I don't blame you for being angry, though I must say you behaved beautifully that day. But I did think you'd understand, 'Rene. It was that, partly, that has made me want to see other people. It just swooped down and changed everything. If it hadn't been for that, I'd have gone on to the end, never seeing any of you. But that did something to me, and I've been so lonely since! You can't know. Not close to a single soul. Never anyone to really talk to."

Irene pressed out her cigarette. While doing so, she saw again the vision of Clare Kendry staring disdainfully down at the face of her father, and thought that it would be like that that she would look at her husband if he lay dead before her.

Her own resentment was swept aside and her voice held an accent of pity as she exclaimed: "Why, Clare! I didn't know. Forgive me. I feel like seven beasts. It was stupid of me not to realize."

"No. Not at all. You couldn't. Nobody, none of you, could," Clare moaned. The black eyes filled with tears that ran down her cheeks and spilled into her lap, ruining the priceless velvet of her dress. Her long hands were a little uplifted and clasped tightly together. Her effort to speak moderately was obvious, but not successful. "How could you know? How could you? You're free. You're happy. And," with faint derision, "safe."

Irene passed over that touch of derision, for the poignant rebellion of the other's words had brought the tears to her own eyes, though she didn't allow them to fall. The truth was that she knew weeping did not become her. Few women, she imagined, wept as attractively as Clare. "I'm beginning to believe," she murmured, "that no one is ever completely happy, or free, or safe."

"Well, then, what does it matter? One risk more or less, if we're not safe anyway, if even you're not, it can't make all the difference in the world. It can't to me. Besides, I'm used to risks. And this isn't such a big one as you're trying to make it."

"Oh, but it is. And it can make all the difference in the world. There's your little girl, Clare. Think of the consequences to her."

Clare's face took on a startled look, as though she were totally unprepared for this new weapon with which Irene had assailed her. Seconds passed, during which she sat with stricken eyes and compressed lips. "I think," she said at last, "that being a mother is the cruellest thing in the world." Her clasped hands swayed forward and back again, and her scarlet mouth trembled irrepressibly.

"Yes," Irene softly agreed. For a moment she was unable to say more, so accurately had Clare put into words that which, not so definitely defined, was so often in her own heart of late. At the same time she was conscious that here, to her hand, was a reason which could not be lightly brushed aside. "Yes," she repeated, "and the most responsible, Clare. We mothers are all responsible for the security and happiness of our children. Think what it would mean to your Margery if Mr. Bellew should find out. You'd probably lose her. And even if you didn't, nothing that concerned her would ever be the same again. He'd never forget that she had Negro blood. And if she should learn—Well, I believe that after twelve it is too late to learn a thing like that. She'd never forgive you. You may be used to risks, but this is one you mustn't take, Clare. It's a selfish whim, an unnecessary and—"

"Yes, Zulena, what is it?" she inquired, a trifle tartly, of the servant who had silently materialized in the doorway.

"The telephone's for you, Mrs. Redfield. It's Mr. Wentworth."[18]

"All right. Thank you. I'll take it here." And, with a muttered apology to Clare, she took up the instrument.

[18]Hugh and Bianca Wentworth are characters modeled on novelist Carl Van Vechten and his actress wife, Fania Marinoff, who ignored the social separation of the races in New York by inviting blacks to their home and by frequenting both the public gatherings and the private homes of blacks in the 1920s.

"Hello.... Yes, Hugh.... Oh, quite.... And you? ... I'm sorry, every single thing's gone.... Oh, too bad.... Ye-es, I s'pose you could. Not very pleasant, though.... Yes, of course, in a pinch everything goes.... Wait! I've got it! I'll change mine with whoever's next to you, and you can have that.... No.... I mean it.... I'll be so busy I shan't know whether I'm sitting or standing.... As long as Brian has a place to drop down now and then.... Not a single soul.... No, don't.... That's nice.... My love to Bianca.... I'll see to it right away and call you back.... Good-bye."

She hung up and turned back to Clare, a little frown on her softly chiselled features. "It's the N. W. L. dance," she explained, "the Negro Welfare League,[19] you know. I'm on the ticket committee, or, rather, I *am* the committee. Thank heaven it comes off tomorrow night and doesn't happen again for a year. I'm about crazy, and now I've got to persuade somebody to change boxes with me."

"That wasn't," Clare asked, "Hugh Wentworth? Not *the* Hugh Wentworth?"

Irene inclined her head. On her face was a tiny triumphant smile. "Yes, *the* Hugh Wentworth. D'you know him?"

"No. How should I? But I do know about him. And I've read a book or two of his."

"Awfully good, aren't they?"

"U-umm, I s'pose so. Sort of contemptuous, I thought. As if he more or less despised everything and everybody."

"I shouldn't be a bit surprised if he did. Still, he's about earned the right to. Lived on the edges of nowhere in at least three continents. Been through every danger in all kinds of savage places. It's no wonder he thinks the rest of us are a lazy self-pampering lot. Hugh's a dear, though, generous as one of the twelve disciples; give you the shirt off his back. Bianca—that's his wife—is nice too."

"And he's coming up here to your dance?"

Irene asked why not.

"It seems rather curious, a man like that, going to a Negro dance."

This, Irene told her, was the year 1927 in the city of New York, and hundreds of white people of Hugh Wentworth's type came to affairs in Harlem, more all the time. So many that Brian had said: "Pretty soon the coloured people won't be allowed in at all, or will have to sit in Jim Crowed sections."

"What do they come for?"

"Same reason you're here, to see Negroes."

"But why?"

[19]Fictitious organization based on the National Urban League, established in New York City in 1911 to assist blacks who migrated from rural areas to urban centers in obtaining jobs, housing, education, and services. The National Urban League's official magazine, *Opportunity*, founded in 1923 and edited by sociologist Charles S. Johnson, became one of the major publishing outlets for writers during the Harlem Renaissance.

"Various motives," Irene explained. "A few purely and frankly to enjoy themselves. Others to get material to turn into shekels.[20] More, to gaze on these great and near great while they gaze on the Negroes."

Clare clapped her hands. "'Rene, suppose I come too! It sounds terribly interesting and amusing. And I don't see why I shouldn't."

Irene, who was regarding her through narrowed eyelids, had the same thought that she had had two years ago on the roof of the Drayton, that Clare Kendry was just a shade too good-looking. Her tone was on the edge of irony as she said: "You mean because so many other white people go?"

A pale rose-colour came into Clare's ivory cheeks. She lifted a hand in protest. "Don't be silly! Certainly not! I mean that in a crowd of that kind I shouldn't be noticed."

On the contrary, was Irene's opinion. It might be even doubly dangerous. Some friend or acquaintance of John Bellew or herself might see and recognize her.

At that, Clare laughed for a long time, little musical trills following one another in sequence after sequence. It was as if the thought of any friend of John Bellew's going to a Negro dance was to her the most amusing thing in the world.

"I don't think," she said, when she had done laughing, "we need worry about that."

Irene, however, wasn't so sure. But all her efforts to dissuade Clare were useless. To her, "You never can tell whom you're likely to meet there," Clare's rejoinder was: "I'll take my chance on getting by."

"Besides, you won't know a soul and I shall be too busy to look after you. You'll be bored stiff."

"I won't, I won't. If nobody asks me to dance, not even Dr. Redfield, I'll just sit and gaze on the great and the near great, too. Do, 'Rene, be polite and invite me."

Irene turned away from the caress of Clare's smile, saying promptly and positively: "I will not."

"I mean to go anyway," Clare retorted, and her voice was no less positive than Irene's.

"Oh, no. You couldn't possibly go there alone. It's a public thing. All sorts of people go, anybody who can pay a dollar, even ladies of easy virtue looking for trade. If you were to go there alone, you might be mistaken for one of them, and that wouldn't be too pleasant."

Clare laughed again. "Thanks. I never have been. It might be amusing. I'm warning you, 'Rene, that if you're not going to be nice and take me, I'll still be among those present. I suppose, my dollar's as good as anyone's."

[20]The opportunistic practice of whites from downtown capitalizing on the 1920s' vogue for "things Negro" by spending time uptown in Harlem to collect materials on black culture and race matters—music, dance, styles, beliefs, practices, and trends—to use in their art for profit. Larsen's friend, Carl Van Vechten, was accused of this practice when his 1926 novel, *Nigger Heaven*, appeared to exploit his black acquaintances and the access to Harlem life they had provided him.

"Oh, the dollar! Don't be a fool, Clare. I don't care where you go, or what you do. All I'm concerned with is the unpleasantness and possible danger which your going might incur, because of your situation. To put it frankly, I shouldn't like to be mixed up in any row of the kind." She had risen again as she spoke and was standing at the window lifting and spreading the small yellow chrysanthemums in the grey stone jar on the sill. Her hands shook slightly, for she was in a near rage of impatience and exasperation.

Clare's face looked strange, as if she wanted to cry again. One of her satin-covered feet swung restlessly back and forth. She said vehemently, violently almost: "Damn Jack! He keeps me out of everything. Everything I want. I could kill him! I expect I shall, some day."

"I wouldn't," Irene advised her, "you see, there's still capital punishment, in this state at least. And really, Clare, after everything's said, I can't see that you've a right to put all the blame on him. You've got to admit that there's his side to the thing. You didn't tell him you were coloured, so he's got no way of knowing about this hankering of yours after Negroes, or that it galls you to fury to hear them called niggers and black devils. As far as I can see, you'll just have to endure some things and give up others. As we've said before, everything must be paid for. Do, please, be reasonable."

But Clare, it was plain, had shut away reason as well as caution. She shook her head. "I can't, I can't," she said. "I would if I could, but I can't. You don't know, you can't realize how I want to see Negroes, to be with them again, to talk with them, to hear them laugh."

And in the look she gave Irene, there was something groping, and hopeless, and yet so absolutely determined that it was like an image of the futile searching and the firm resolution in Irene's own soul, and increased the feeling of doubt and compunction that had been growing within her about Clare Kendry.

She gave in.

"Oh, come if you want to. I s'pose you're right. Once can't do such a terrible lot of harm."

Pushing aside Clare's extravagant thanks, for immediately she was sorry that she had consented, she said briskly: "Should you like to come up and see my boys?"

"I'd love to."

They went up, Irene thinking that Brian would consider that she'd behaved like a spineless fool. And he would be right. She certainly had.

Clare was smiling. She stood in the doorway of the boys' playroom, her shadowy eyes looking down on Junior and Ted, who had sprung apart from their tusselling. Junior's face had a funny little look of resentment. Ted's was blank.

Clare said: "Please don't be cross. Of course, I know I've gone and spoiled everything. But maybe, if I promise not to get too much in the way, you'll let me come in, just the same."

"Sure, come in if you want to," Ted told her. "We can't stop you, you know." He smiled and made her a little bow and then turned away to a shelf that held his favourite books. Taking one down, he settled himself in a chair and began to read.

Junior said nothing, did nothing, merely stood there waiting.

"Get up, Ted! That's rude. This is Theodore, Mrs. Bellew. Please excuse his bad manners. He does know better. And this is Brian junior. Mrs. Bellew is an old friend of mother's. We used to play together when we were little girls."

Clare had gone and Brian had telephoned that he'd been detained and would have his dinner downtown. Irene was a little glad for that. She was going out later herself, and that meant she wouldn't, probably, see Brian until morning and so could put off for a few more hours speaking of Clare and the N. W. L. dance.

She was angry with herself and with Clare. But more with herself, for having permitted Clare to tease her into doing something that Brian had, all but expressly, asked her not to do. She didn't want him ruffled, not just then, not while he was possessed of that unreasonable restless feeling.

She was annoyed, too, because she was aware that she had consented to something which, if it went beyond the dance, would involve her in numerous petty inconveniences and evasions. And not only at home with Brian, but outside with friends and acquaintances. The disagreeable possibilities in connection with Clare Kendry's coming among them loomed before her in endless irritating array.

Clare, it seemed, still retained her ability to secure the thing that she wanted in the face of any opposition, and in utter disregard of the convenience and desire of others. About her there was some quality, hard and persistent, with the strength and endurance of rock, that would not be beaten or ignored. She couldn't, Irene thought, have had an entirely serene life. Not with that dark secret for ever crouching in the background of her consciousness. And yet she hadn't the air of a woman whose life had been touched by uncertainty or suffering. Pain, fear, and grief were things that left their mark on people. Even love, that exquisite torturing emotion, left its subtle traces on the countenance.

But Clare—she had remained almost what she had always been, an attractive, somewhat lonely child—selfish, wilful, and disturbing.

Three

The things which Irene Redfield remembered afterward about the Negro Welfare League dance seemed, to her, unimportant and unrelated.

She remembered the not quite derisive smile with which Brian had cloaked his vexation when she informed him—oh, so apologetically—that she had promised to take Clare, and related the conversation of her visit.

She remembered her own little choked exclamation of admiration, when, on coming downstairs a few minutes later than she had intended, she had rushed into the living-room where Brian was waiting and had found Clare there too. Clare, exquisite, golden, fragrant, flaunting, in a stately gown of shining black taffeta, whose long, full skirt lay in graceful folds about her slim golden feet; her glistening hair drawn smoothly back into a small twist at the nape of her neck; her eyes sparkling like dark jewels. Irene, with her new rose-coloured chiffon frock ending at the knees, and her cropped curls, felt dowdy and commonplace. She regretted that she hadn't counselled Clare to wear something ordinary and inconspicuous. What on earth would Brian think of deliberate courting of attention? But if Clare Kendry's appearance had in it anything that was, to Brian Redfield, annoying or displeasing, the fact was not discernible to his wife as, with an uneasy feeling of guilt, she stood there looking into his face while Clare explained that she and he had made their own introductions, accompanying her words with a little deferential smile for Brian, and receiving in return one of his amused, slightly mocking smiles.

She remembered Clare's saying, as they sped northward: "You know, I feel exactly as I used to on the Sunday we went to the Christmas-tree celebration. I knew there was to be a surprise for me and couldn't quite guess what it was to be. I am *so* excited. You can't possibly imagine! It's marvellous to be really on the way! I can hardly believe it!"

At her words and tone a chilly wave of scorn had crept through Irene. All those superlatives! She said, taking care to speak indifferently: "Well, maybe in some ways you will be surprised, more, probably, than you anticipate."

Brian, at the wheel, had thrown back: "And then again, she won't be so very surprised after all, for it'll no doubt be about what she expects. Like the Christmas-tree."

She remembered rushing around here and there, consulting with this person and that one, and now and then snatching a part of a dance with some man whose dancing she particularly liked.

She remembered catching glimpses of Clare in the whirling crowd, dancing, sometimes with a white man, more often with a Negro, frequently with Brian. Irene was glad that he was being nice to Clare, and glad that Clare was having the opportunity to discover that some coloured men were superior to some white men.

She remembered a conversation she had with Hugh Wentworth in a free half-hour when she had dropped into a chair in an emptied box and let her gaze wander over the bright crowd below.

Young men, old men, white men, black men; youthful women, older women, pink women, golden women; fat men, thin men, tall men, short men; stout women, slim women, stately women, small women moved by. An old nursery rhyme popped into her head. She turned to Wentworth, who had just taken a seat beside her, and recited it:

> "Rich man, poor man,
> Beggar man, thief,
> Doctor, lawyer,
> Indian chief."

"Yes," Wentworth said, "that's it. Everybody seems to be here and a few more. But what I'm trying to find out is the name, status, and race of the blonde beauty out of the fairy-tale. She's dancing with Ralph Hazelton at the moment. Nice study in contrasts, that."

It was. Clare fair and golden, like a sunlit day. Hazelton dark, with gleaming eyes, like a moonlit night.

"She's a girl I used to know a long time ago in Chicago. And she wanted especially to meet you."

"'S awfully good of her, I'm sure. And now, alas! the usual thing's happened. All these others, these—er—'gentlemen of colour' have driven a mere Nordic from her mind."

"Stuff!"

"'S a fact, and what happens to all the ladies of my superior race who're lured up here. Look at Bianca. Have I laid eyes on her tonight except in spots, here and there, being twirled about by some Ethiopian? I have not."

"But, Hugh, you've got to admit that the average coloured man is a better dancer than the average white man—that is, if the celebrities and 'butter and egg' men[21] who find their way up here are fair specimens of white Terpsichorean art."

"Not having tripped the light fantastic[22] with any of the males, I'm not in a position to argue the point. But I don't think it's merely that. 'S something else, some other attraction. They're always raving about the good looks of some Negro, preferably an unusually dark one. Take Hazelton there, for example. Dozens of women have declared him to be fascinatingly handsome. How about you, Irene? Do you think he's—er—ravishingly beautiful?"

"I do not! And I don't think the others do either. Not honestly, I mean. I think that what they feel is—well, a kind of emotional excitement. You know, the sort of thing you feel in the presence of something strange, and even, perhaps, a bit repugnant to you; something so different that it's really at the opposite end of the pole from all your accustomed notions of beauty."

"Damned if I don't think you're halfway right!"

"I'm sure I am. Completely. (Except, of course, when it's just patronizing kindness on their part.) And I know coloured girls who've experienced the same thing—the other way round, naturally."

"And the men? You don't subscribe to the general opinion about their reason for coming up here. Purely predatory. Or, do you?"

"N-no. More curious, I should say."

Wentworth, whose eyes were a clouded amber colour, had given her a long, searching look that was really a stare. He said: "All this is awfully interestin', Irene. We've got to have a long talk about it some time soon. There's your friend from Chicago, first time up here and all that. A case in point."

---

[21]Expression for wealthy men or big spenders.   [22]Slang for dancing.

Irene's smile had only just lifted the corners of her painted lips. A match blazed in Wentworth's broad hands as he lighted her cigarette and his own, and flickered out before he asked: "Or isn't she?"

Her smile changed to a laugh. "Oh, Hugh! You're so clever. You usually know everything. Even how to tell the sheep from the goats. What do you think? Is she?"

He blew a long contemplative wreath of smoke. "Damned if I know! I'll be as sure as anything that I've learned the trick. And then in the next minute I'll find I couldn't pick some of 'em if my life depended on it."

"Well, don't let that worry you. Nobody can. Not by looking."

"Not by looking, eh? Meaning?"

"I'm afraid I can't explain. Not clearly. There are ways. But they're not definite or tangible."

"Feeling of kinship, or something like that?"

"Good heavens, no! Nobody has that, except for their in-laws."

"Right again! But go on about the sheep and the goats."

"Well, take my own experience with Dorothy Thompkins.[23] I'd met her four or five times, in groups and crowds of people, before I knew she wasn't a Negro. One day I went to an awful tea, terribly dicty.[24] Dorothy was there. We got talking. In less than five minutes, I knew she was 'fay.'[25] Not from anything she did or said or anything in her appearance. Just—just something. A thing that couldn't be registered."

"Yes, I understand what you mean. Yet lots of people 'pass' all the time."

"Not on our side, Hugh. It's easy for a Negro to 'pass' for white. But I don't think it would be so simple for a white person to 'pass' for coloured."

"Never thought of that."

"No, you wouldn't. Why should you?"

He regarded her critically through mists of smoke. "Slippin' me, Irene?"[26]

She said soberly: "Not you, Hugh. I'm too fond of you. And you're too sincere."

And she remembered that towards the end of the dance Brian had come to her and said: "I'll drop you first and then run Clare down." And that he had been doubtful of her discretion when she had explained to him that he wouldn't have to bother because she had asked Bianca Wentworth to take her down with them. Did she, he had asked, think it had been wise to tell them about Clare?

---

[23]Fictitious character, probably based on Dorothy Fields (1905–1974), a white song writer who began her career in the 1920s by writing material for black shows at the Cotton Club and who achieved her first major success by writing songs for the hit show *Blackbirds of 1928*.

[24]High-toned; person assuming airs and mannerisms of the upper class.

[25]Short form of "ofay," slang for white people.

[26]Slang for tricking or hoodwinking, putting something over on someone.

"I told them nothing," she said sharply, for she was unbearably tired, "except that she was at the Walsingham. It's on their way. And, really, I haven't thought anything about the wisdom of it, but now that I do, I'd say it's much better for them to take her than you."

"As you please. She's your friend, you know," he had answered, with a disclaiming shrug of his shoulders.

Except for these few unconnected things the dance faded to a blurred memory, its outlines mingling with those of other dances of its kind that she had attended in the past and would attend in the future.

Four

But undistinctive as the dance had seemed, it was, nevertheless, important. For it marked the beginning of a new factor in Irene Redfield's life, something that left its trace on all the future years of her existence. It was the beginning of a new friendship with Clare Kendry.

She came to them frequently after that. Always with a touching gladness that welled up and overflowed on all the Redfield household. Yet Irene could never be sure whether her comings were a joy or a vexation.

Certainly she was no trouble. She had not to be entertained, or even noticed—if anyone could ever avoid noticing Clare. If Irene happened to be out or occupied, Clare could very happily amuse herself with Ted and Junior, who had conceived for her an admiration that verged on adoration, especially Ted. Or, lacking the boys, she would descend to the kitchen and, with—to Irene—an exasperating childlike lack of perception, spend her visit in talk and merriment with Zulena and Sadie.

Irene, while secretly resenting these visits to the playroom and kitchen, for some obscure reason which she shied away from putting into words, never requested that Clare make an end of them, or hinted that she wouldn't have spoiled her own Margery so outrageously, nor been so friendly with white servants.

Brian looked on these things with the same tolerant amusement that marked his entire attitude toward Clare. Never since his faintly derisive surprise at Irene's information that she was to go with them the night of the dance, had he shown any disapproval of Clare's presence. On the other hand, it couldn't be said that her presence seemed to please him. It didn't annoy or disturb him, so far as Irene could judge. That was all.

Didn't he, she once asked him, think Clare was extraordinarily beautiful?

"No," he had answered. "That is, not particularly."

"Brian, you're fooling!"

"No, honestly. Maybe I'm fussy. I s'pose she'd be an unusually good-looking white woman. I like my ladies darker. Beside an A-number-one sheba, she simply hasn't got 'em."

Clare went, sometimes with Irene and Brian, to parties and dances, and on a few occasions when Irene hadn't been able or inclined to go out, she had gone alone with Brian to some bridge party or benefit dance.

Once in a while she came formally to dine with them. She wasn't, how-ever, in spite of her poise and air of worldliness, the ideal dinner-party guest. Beyond the æsthetic pleasure one got from watching her, she contrib-uted little, sitting for the most part silent, an odd dreaming look in her hyp-notic eyes. Though she could for some purpose of her own—the desire to be included in some party being made up to go cabareting, or an invitation to a dance or a tea—talk fluently and entertainingly.

She was generally liked. She was so friendly and responsive, and so ready to press the sweet food of flattery on all. Nor did she object to appear-ing a bit pathetic and ill-used, so that people could feel sorry for her. And, no matter how often she came among them, she still remained someone apart, a little mysterious and strange, someone to wonder about and to admire and to pity.

Her visits were undecided and uncertain, being, as they were, dependent on the presence or absence of John Bellew in the city. But she did, once in a while, manage to steal uptown for an afternoon even when he was not away. As time went on without any apparent danger of discovery, even Irene ceased to be perturbed about the possibility of Clare's husband's stumbling on her racial identity.

The daughter, Margery, had been left in Switzerland in school, for Clare and Bellew would be going back in the early spring. In March, Clare thought. "And how I do hate to think of it!" she would say, always with a suggestion of leashed rebellion; "but I can't see how I'm going to get out of it. Jack won't hear of my staying behind. If I could have just a couple of months more in New York, alone I mean, I'd be the happiest thing in the world."

"I imagine you'll be happy enough, once you get away," Irene told her one day when she was bewailing her approaching departure. "Remember, there's Margery. Think how glad you'll be to see her after all this time."

"Children aren't everything," was Clare Kendry's answer to that. "There are other things in the world, though I admit some people don't seem to suspect it." And she laughed, more, it seemed, at some secret joke of her own than at her words.

Irene replied: "You know you don't mean that, Clare. You're only trying to tease me. I know very well that I take being a mother rather seriously. I *am* wrapped up in my boys and the running of my house. I can't help it. And, really, I don't think it's anything to laugh at." And though she was aware of the slight primness in her words and attitude, she had neither power nor wish to efface it.

Clare, suddenly very sober and sweet, said: "You're right. It's no laughing matter. It's shameful of me to tease you, 'Rene. You are so good." And she reached out and gave Irene's hand an affectionate little squeeze. "Don't think," she added, "whatever happens, that I'll ever forget how good you've been to me."

"Nonsense!"

"Oh, but you have, you have. It's just that I haven't any proper morals or sense of duty, as you have, that makes me act as I do."

"Now you are talking nonsense."

"But it's true, 'Rene. Can't you realize that I'm not like you a bit? Why, to get the things I want badly enough, I'd do anything, hurt anybody, throw anything away. Really, 'Rene, I'm not safe." Her voice as well as the look on her face had a beseeching earnestness that made Irene vaguely uncomfortable.

She said: "I don't believe it. In the first place what you're saying is so utterly, so wickedly wrong. And as for your giving up things—" She stopped, at a loss for an acceptable term to express her opinion of Clare's "having" nature.

But Clare Kendry had begun to cry, audibly, with no effort at restraint, and for no reason that Irene could discover.

Part Three. FINALE

One

The year was getting on towards its end. October, November had gone. December had come and brought with it a little snow and then a freeze and after that a thaw and some soft pleasant days that had in them a feeling of spring.

It wasn't, this mild weather, a bit Christmasy, Irene Redfield was thinking, as she turned out of Seventh Avenue into her own street. She didn't like it to be warm and springy when it should have been cold and crisp, or grey and cloudy as if snow was about to fall. The weather, like people, ought to enter into the spirit of the season. Here the holidays were almost upon them, and the streets through which she had come were streaked with rills of muddy water and the sun shone so warmly that children had taken off their hats and scarfs. It was all as soft, as like April, as possible. The kind of weather for Easter. Certainly not for Christmas.

Though, she admitted, reluctantly, she herself didn't feel the proper Christmas spirit this year, either. But that couldn't be helped, it seemed, any more than the weather. She was weary and depressed. And for all her trying, she couldn't be free of that dull, indefinite misery which with increasing tenaciousness had laid hold of her. The morning's aimless wandering through the teeming Harlem streets, long after she had ordered the flowers which had been her excuse for setting out, was but another effort to tear herself loose from it.

She went up the cream stone steps, into the house, and down to the kitchen. There were to be people in to tea. But that, she found, after a few words with Sadie and Zulena, need give her no concern. She was thankful. She didn't want to be bothered. She went upstairs and took off her things and got into bed.

She thought: "Bother those people coming to tea!"

She thought: "If I could only be sure that at bottom it's just Brazil."

She thought: "Whatever it is, if I only knew what it was, I could manage it."

Brian again. Unhappy, restless, withdrawn. And she, who had prided herself on knowing his moods, their causes and their remedies, had found it first unthinkable, and then intolerable, that this, so like and yet so unlike those other spasmodic restlessnesses of his, should be to her incomprehensible and elusive.

He was restless and he was not restless. He was discontented, yet there were times when she felt he was possessed of some intense secret satisfaction, like a cat who had stolen the cream. He was irritable with the boys, especially Junior, for Ted, who seemed to have an uncanny knowledge of his father's periods of off moods, kept out of his way when possible. They got on his nerves, drove him to violent outbursts of temper, very different from his usual gently sarcastic remarks that constituted his idea of discipline for them. On the other hand, with her he was more than customarily considerate and abstemious. And it had been weeks since she had felt the keen edge of his irony.

He was like a man marking time, waiting. But what was he waiting for? It was extraordinary that, after all these years of accurate perception, she now lacked the talent to discover what that appearance of waiting meant. It was the knowledge that, for all her watching, all her patient study, the reason for his humour still eluded her which filled her with foreboding dread. That guarded reserve of his seemed to her unjust, inconsiderate, and alarming. It was as if he had stepped out beyond her reach into some section, strange and walled, where she could not get at him.

She closed her eyes, thinking what a blessing it would be if she could get a little sleep before the boys came in from school. She couldn't, of course, though she was so tired, having had, of late, so many sleepless nights. Nights filled with questionings and premonitions.

But she did sleep—several hours.

She wakened to find Brian standing at her bedside looking down at her, an unfathomable expression in his eyes.

She said: "I must have dropped off to sleep," and watched a slender ghost of his old amused smile pass over his face.

"It's getting on to four," he told her, meaning, she knew, that she was going to be late again.

She fought back the quick answer that rose to her lips and said instead: "I'm getting right up. It was good of you to think to call me." She sat up.

He bowed. "Always the attentive husband, you see."

"Yes indeed. Thank goodness, everything's ready."

"Except you. Oh, and Clare's downstairs."

"Clare! What a nuisance! I didn't ask her. Purposely."

"I see. Might a mere man ask why? Or is the reason so subtly feminine that it wouldn't be understood by him?"

A little of his smile had come back. Irene, who was beginning to shake off some of her depression under his familiar banter, said, almost gaily: "Not at all. It just happens that this party happens to be for Hugh, and that Hugh happens not to care a great deal for Clare; therefore I, who happen to be giving the party, didn't happen to ask her. Nothing could be simpler. Could it?"

"Nothing. It's so simple that I can easily see beyond your simple explanation and surmise that Clare, probably, just never happened to pay Hugh the admiring attention that he happens to consider no more than his just due. Simplest thing in the world."

Irene exclaimed in amazement: "Why, I thought you liked Hugh! You don't, you can't, believe anything so idiotic!"

"Well, Hugh does think he's God, you know."

"That," Irene declared, getting out of bed, "is absolutely not true. He thinks ever so much better of himself than that, as you, who know and have read him, ought to be able to guess. If you remember what a low opinion he has of God, you won't make such a silly mistake."

She went into the closet for her things and, coming back, hung her frock over the back of a chair and placed her shoes on the floor beside it. Then she sat down before her dressing-table.

Brian didn't speak. He continued to stand beside the bed, seeming to look at nothing in particular. Certainly not at her. True, his gaze was on her, but in it there was some quality that made her feel that at that moment she was no more to him than a pane of glass through which he stared. At what? She didn't know, couldn't guess. And this made her uncomfortable. Piqued her.

She said: "It just happens that Hugh prefers intelligent women."

Plainly he was startled. "D'you mean that you think Clare is stupid?" he asked, regarding her with lifted eyebrows, which emphasized the disbelief of his voice.

She wiped the cold cream from her face, before she said: "No, I don't. She isn't stupid. She's intelligent enough in a purely feminine way. Eighteenth-century France would have been a marvellous setting for her, or the old South[27] if she hadn't made the mistake of being born a Negro."

"I see. Intelligent enough to wear a tight bodice and keep bowing swains whispering compliments and retrieving dropped fans. Rather a pretty picture. I take it, though, as slightly feline in its implication."

"Well, then, all I can say is that you take it wrongly. Nobody admires Clare more than I do, for the kind of intelligence she has, as well as for her decorative qualities. But she's not—She isn't—She hasn't—Oh, I can't explain it. Take Bianca, for example, or, to keep to the race, Felise Freeland. Looks *and* brains. Real brains that can hold their own with anybody. Clare has got brains of a sort, the kind that are useful too. Acquisitive, you know. But she'd bore a man like Hugh to suicide. Still, I never thought that even Clare would come to a private party to which she hadn't been asked. But, it's like her."

For a minute there was silence. She completed the bright red arch of her full lips. Brian moved towards the door. His hand was on the knob. He said: "I'm sorry, Irene. It's my fault entirely. She seemed so hurt at being left out that I told her I was sure you'd forgotten and to just come along."

Irene cried out: "But, Brian, I—" and stopped, amazed at the fierce anger that had blazed up in her.

Brian's head came round with a jerk. His brows lifted in an odd surprise.

Her voice, she realized, *had* gone queer. But she had an instinctive feeling that it hadn't been the whole cause of his attitude. And that little straightening motion of the shoulders. Hadn't it been like that of a man drawing himself up to receive a blow? Her fright was like a scarlet spear of terror leaping at her heart.

---

[27]Places and times placing a high premium on female beauty, in which women might get by being what Larsen terms "intelligent in a purely feminine way."

Clare Kendry! So that was it! Impossible. It couldn't be.

In the mirror before her she saw that he was still regarding her with that air of slight amazement. She dropped her eyes to the jars and bottles on the table and began to fumble among them with hands whose fingers shook slightly.

"Of course," she said carefully, "I'm glad you did. And in spite of my recent remarks, Clare does add to any party. She's so easy on the eyes."

When she looked again, the surprise had gone from his face and the expectancy from his bearing.

"Yes," he agreed. "Well, I guess I'll run along. One of us ought to be down, I s'pose."

"You're right. One of us ought to." She was surprised that it was in her normal tones she spoke, caught as she was by the heart since that dull indefinite fear had grown suddenly into sharp panic. "I'll be down before you know it," she promised.

"All right." But he still lingered. "You're quite certain. You don't mind my asking her? Not awfully, I mean? I see now that I ought to have spoken to you. Trust women to have their reasons for everything."

She made a little pretence at looking at him, managed a tiny smile, and turned away. Clare! How sickening!

"Yes, don't they?" she said, striving to keep her voice casual. Within her she felt a hardness from feeling, not absent, but repressed. And that hardness was rising, swelling. Why didn't he go? Why didn't he?

He had opened the door at last. "You won't be long?" he asked, admonished.

She shook her head, unable to speak, for there was a choking in her throat, and the confusion in her mind was like the beating of wings. Behind her she heard the gentle impact of the door as it closed behind him, and knew that he had gone. Down to Clare.

For a long minute she sat in strained stiffness. The face in the mirror vanished from her sight, blotted out by this thing which had so suddenly flashed across her groping mind. Impossible for her to put it immediately into words or give it outline, for, prompted by some impulse of self-protection, she recoiled from exact expression.

She closed her unseeing eyes and clenched her fists. She tried not to cry. But her lips tightened and no effort could check the hot tears of rage and shame that sprang into her eyes and flowed down her cheeks; so she laid her face in her arms and wept silently.

When she was sure that she had done crying, she wiped away the warm remaining tears and got up. After bathing her swollen face in cold, refreshing water and carefully applying a stinging splash of toilet water, she went back to the mirror and regarded herself gravely. Satisfied that there lingered no betraying evidence of weeping, she dusted a little powder on her dark-white face and again examined it carefully, and with a kind of ridiculing contempt.

"I do think," she confided to it, "that you've been something—oh, very much—of a damned fool."

Downstairs the ritual of tea gave her some busy moments, and that, she decided, was a blessing. She wanted no empty spaces of time in which her mind would immediately return to that horror which she had not yet gathered sufficient courage to face. Pouring tea properly and nicely was an occupation that required a kind of well-balanced attention.

In the room beyond, a clock chimed. A single sound. Fifteen minutes past five o'clock. That was all! And yet in the short space of half an hour all of life had changed, lost its colour, its vividness, its whole meaning. No, she reflected, it wasn't that that had happened. Life about her, apparently, went on exactly as before.

"Oh, Mrs. Runyon.... So nice to see you.... Two? ... Really? ... How exciting! ... Yes, I think Tuesday's all right...."

Yes, life went on precisely as before. It was only she that had changed. Knowing, stumbling on this thing, had changed her. It was as if in a house long dim, a match had been struck, showing ghastly shapes where had been only blurred shadows.

Chatter, chatter, chatter. Someone asked her a question. She glanced up with what she felt was a rigid smile.

"Yes ... Brian picked it up last winter in Haiti.[28] Terribly weird, isn't it? ... It *is* rather marvellous in its own hideous way.... Practically nothing, I believe. A few cents...."

Hideous. A great weariness came over her. Even the small exertion of pouring golden tea into thin old cups seemed almost too much for her. She went on pouring. Made repetitions of her smile. Answered questions. Manufactured conversation. She thought: "I feel like the oldest person in the world with the longest stretch of life before me."

"Josephine Baker? ...[29] No. I've never seen her.... Well, she might have been in *Shuffle Along*[30] when I saw it, but if she was, I don't remember her.... Oh, but you're wrong! ... I do think Ethel Waters[31] is awfully good. ..."

There were the familiar little tinkling sounds of spoons striking against frail cups, the soft running sounds of inconsequential talk, punctuated now

[28]Work of art produced in Haiti; Haitian art, in particular painting and sculpture, became popular during the cultural awakening of the Harlem Renaissance for its expressive relation to traditional African forms and to colorful, symbolic representations of black folk life.

[29]Josephine Baker (1906–1975) was a singer, dancer, and entertainer, initially made her mark as "the comedy chorus girl" in *Chocolate Dandies* (1924), after using her comic talents in a Boston production of *Shuffle Along*. In 1925 she was selected for *Revue Negre*, a show headed for Paris; there Baker immediately became a star and a headliner at the Follies Bergère and French nightclubs. By the end of the 1920s, she was the toast of France and the most famous American entertainer in Europe.

[30]1921 musical comedy written by the vaudeville team of Aubrey Lyles (1882–1932) and Flournoy Miller (1889–1971), with music by

Noble Sissle (1889–1975) and Eubie Blake (1883–1983), and hailed as the first popular all-black show of the decade and sometimes credited as the opening act of the Harlem Renaissance.

[31]Ethel Waters (1896–1977) was a singer, recording artist, and stage and film actress and was one of the busiest and most popular performers during the 1920s. While still a teenager, she toured in vaudeville and tent shows as "Sweet Mama Stringbean," but she graduated to appearances in New York and recordings for Black Swan records in 1921. She enjoyed success in musical reviews at New York's Lafayette Theatre (*Tan Town Topics*, 1925; *Too Bad*, 1925; and *Black Bottom Revue*, 1926), and on Broadway (*Africana*, 1927). Her stardom continued to rise in Europe and New York during the 1930s, when she also began working as a dramatic actress.

and then with laughter. In irregular small groups, disintegrating, coalescing, striking just the right note of disharmony, disorder in the big room, which Irene had furnished with a sparingness that was almost chaste, moved the guests with that slight familiarity that makes a party a success. On the floor and the walls the sinking sun threw long, fantastic shadows.

So like many other tea-parties she had had. So unlike any of those others. But she musn't think yet. Time enough for that after. All the time in the world. She had a second's flashing knowledge of what those words might portend. Time with Brian. Time without him. It was gone, leaving in its place an almost uncontrollable impulse to laugh, to scream, to hurl things about. She wanted, suddenly, to shock people, to hurt them, to make them notice her, to be aware of her suffering.

"Hello, Dave.... Felise.... Really your clothes are the despair of half the women in Harlem.... How do you do it? ... Lovely, is it Worth or Lanvin? ... Oh, a mere Babani...."

"Merely that," Felise Freeland acknowledged. "Come out of it, Irene, whatever it is. You look like the second grave-digger."

"Thanks, for the hint, Felise. I'm not feeling quite up to par. The weather, I guess."

"Buy yourself an expensive new frock, child. It always helps. Any time this child gets the blues, it means money out of Dave's pocket. How're those boys of yours?"

The boys! For once she'd forgotten them.

They were, she told Felise, very well. Felise mumbled something about that being awfully nice, and said she'd have to fly, because for a wonder she saw Mrs. Bellew sitting by herself, "and I've been trying to get her alone all afternoon. I want her for a party. Isn't she stunning today?"

Clare was. Irene couldn't remember ever having seen her look better. She was wearing a superlatively simple cinnamon-brown frock which brought out all her vivid beauty, and a little golden bowl of a hat. Around her neck hung a string of amber beads that would easily have made six or eight like one Irene owned. Yes, she was stunning.

The ripple of talk flowed on. The fire roared. The shadows stretched longer.

Across the room was Hugh. He wasn't, Irene hoped, being too bored. He seemed as he always did, a bit aloof, a little amused, and somewhat weary. And as usual he was hovering before the book-shelves. But he was not, she noticed, looking at the book he had taken down. Instead, his dull amber eyes were held by something across the room. They were a little scornful. Well, Hugh had never cared for Clare Kendry. For a minute Irene hesitated, then turned her head, though she knew what it was that held Hugh's gaze. Clare, who had suddenly clouded all her days. Brian, the father of Ted and Junior.

Clare's ivory face was what it always was, beautiful and caressing. Or maybe today a little masked. Unrevealing. Unaltered and undisturbed by any emotion within or without. Brian's seemed to Irene to be pitiably bare. Or was it too as it always was? That half-effaced seeking look, did he always have that? Queer, that now she didn't know, couldn't recall. Then she saw him smile, and the smile made his face all eager and shining. Impelled by some inner urge of loyalty to herself, she glanced away. But only for a moment. And when she turned towards them again, she thought that the look on his face was the most melancholy and yet the most scoffing that she had ever seen upon it.

In the next quarter of an hour she promised herself to Bianca Wentworth in Sixty-second Street, Jane Tenant at Seventh Avenue and a Hundred and Fiftieth Street, and the Dashields in Brooklyn for dinner all on the same evening and at almost the same hour.

Oh well, what did it matter? She had no thoughts at all now, and all she felt was a great fatigue. Before her tired eyes Clare Kendry was talking to Dave Freeland.[32] Scraps of their conversation, in Clare's husky voice, floated over to her: "... always admired you ... so much about you long ago ... everybody says so ... no one but you...." And more of the same. The man hung rapt on her words, though he was the husband of Felise Freeland, and the author of novels that revealed a man of perception and a devastating irony. And he fell for such pish-posh! And all because Clare had a trick of sliding down ivory lids over astonishing black eyes and then lifting them suddenly and turning on a caressing smile. Men like Dave Freeland fell for it. And Brian.

Her mental and physical languor receded. Brian. What did it mean? How would it affect her and the boys? The boys! She had a surge of relief. It ebbed, vanished. A feeling of absolute unimportance followed. Actually, she didn't count. She was, to him, only the mother of his sons. That was all. Alone she was nothing. Worse. An obstacle.

Rage boiled up in her.

There was a slight crash. On the floor at her feet lay the shattered cup. Dark stains dotted the bright rug. Spread. The chatter stopped. Went on. Before her, Zulena gathered up the white fragments.

As from a distance Hugh Wentworth's clipt voice came to her, though he was, she was aware, somehow miraculously at her side. "Sorry," he apologized. "Must have pushed you. Clumsy of me. Don't tell me it's priceless and irreplaceable."

It hurt. Dear God! How the thing hurt! But she couldn't think of that now. Not with Hugh sitting there mumbling apologies and lies. The significance of his words, the power of his discernment, stirred in her a sense of caution. Her pride revolted. Damn Hugh! Something would have to be done about him. Now. She couldn't, it seemed, help his knowing. It was too late

---

[32]Character based on the novelist and short story writer Rudolph Fisher (1897–1934), who was known for his sharp wit and sparkling conversation. A medical doctor specializing in roentgenology, Fisher divided his time between his practice in X-ray technology and his literary career. His satiric first novel, *The Walls of Jericho*, appeared in 1928 (the same year as Larsen's *Quicksand*), and contained Fisher's "Introduction to Contemporary Harlemese: Expurgated and Abridged," a dictionary of black slang and popular terms used in the 1920s.

for that. But she could and would keep him from knowing that she knew. She could, she would bear it. She'd have to. There were the boys. Her whole body went taut. In that second she saw that she could bear anything, but only if no one knew that she had anything to bear. It hurt. It frightened her, but she could bear it.

She turned to Hugh. Shook her head. Raised innocent dark eyes to his concerned pale ones. "Oh, no," she protested, "you didn't push me. Cross your heart, hope to die, and I'll tell you how it happened."

"Done!"

"Did you notice that cup? Well, you're lucky. It was the ugliest thing that your ancestors, the charming Confederates ever owned. I've forgotten how many thousands of years ago it was that Brian's great-great-grand-uncle owned it. But it has, or had, a good old hoary history. It was brought North by way of the subway. Oh, all right! Be English if you want to and call it the underground. What I'm coming to is the fact that I've never figured out a way of getting rid of it until about five minutes ago. I had an inspiration. I had only to break it, and I was rid of it for ever. So simple! And I'd never thought of it before."

Hugh nodded and his frosty smile spread over his features. Had she convinced him?

"Still," she went on with a little laugh that didn't, she was sure, sound the least bit forced, "I'm perfectly willing for you to take the blame and admit that you pushed me at the wrong moment. What are friends for, if not to help bear our sins? Brian will certainly be told that it was your fault.

"More tea, Clare? . . . I haven't had a minute with you. . . . Yes, it is a nice party. . . . You'll stay to dinner, I hope. . . . Oh, too bad! . . . I'll be alone with the boys. . . . They'll be sorry. Brian's got a medical meeting, or something. . . . Nice frock you're wearing. . . . Thanks. . . . Well, good-bye; see you soon, I hope."

The clock chimed. One. Two. Three. Four. Five. Six. Was it, could it be, only a little over an hour since she had come down to tea? One little hour.

"Must you go? . . . Good-bye. . . . Thank you so much. . . . So nice to see you. . . . Yes, Wednesday. . . . My love to Madge. . . . Sorry, but I'm filled up for Tuesday. . . . Oh, really? . . . Yes. . . . Good-bye. . . . Good-bye. . . ."

It hurt. It hurt like hell. But it didn't matter, if no one knew. If everything could go on as before. If the boys were safe.

It did hurt.

But it didn't matter.

Two

But it did matter. It mattered more than anything had ever mattered before.

What bitterness! That the one fear, the one uncertainty, that she had felt, Brian's ache to go somewhere else, should have dwindled to a childish triviality! And with it the quality of the courage and resolution with which she had met it. From the visions and dangers which she now perceived she shrank away. For them she had no remedy or courage. Desperately she tried to shut out the knowledge from which had risen this turmoil, which she had no power to moderate or still, within her. And half succeeded.

For, she reasoned, what was there, what had there been, to show that she was even half correct in her tormenting notion? Nothing. She had seen nothing, heard nothing. She had no facts or proofs. She was only making herself unutterably wretched by an unfounded suspicion. It had been a case of looking for trouble and finding it in good measure. Merely that.

With this self-assurance that she had no real knowledge, she redoubled her efforts to drive out of her mind the distressing thought of faiths broken and trusts betrayed which every mental vision of Clare, of Brian, brought with them. She could not, she would not, go again through the tearing agony that lay just behind her.

She must, she told herself, be fair. In all their married life she had had no slightest cause to suspect her husband of any infidelity, of any serious flirtation even. If—and she doubted it—he had had his hours of outside erratic conduct, they were unknown to her. Why begin now to assume them? And on nothing more concrete than an idea that had leapt into her mind because he had told her that he had invited a friend, a friend of hers, to a party in his own house. And at a time when she had been, it was likely, more asleep than awake. How could she without anything done or said, or left undone or unsaid, so easily believe him guilty? How be so ready to renounce all confidence in the worth of their life together?

And if, perchance, there were some small something—well, what could it mean? Nothing. There were the boys. There was John Bellew. The thought of these three gave her some slight relief. But she did not look the future in the face. She wanted to feel nothing, to think nothing; simply to believe that it was all silly invention on her part. Yet she could not. Not quite.

Christmas, with its unreality, its hectic rush, its false gaiety, came and went. Irene was thankful for the confused unrest of the season. Its irksomeness, its crowds, its inane and insincere repetitions of genialities, pushed between her and the contemplation of her growing unhappiness.

She was thankful, too, for the continued absence of Clare, who, John Bellew having returned from a long stay in Canada, had withdrawn to that other life of hers, remote and inaccessible. But beating against the walled prison of Irene's thoughts was the shunned fancy that, though absent, Clare Kendry was still present, that she was close.

Brian, too, had withdrawn. The house contained his outward self and his belongings. He came and went with his usual noiseless irregularity. He sat across from her at the table. He slept in his room next to hers at night. But he was remote and inaccessible. No use pretending that he was happy, that things were the same as they had always been. He wasn't and they weren't. However, she assured herself, it needn't necessarily be because of anything that involved Clare. It was, it must be, another manifestation of the old longing.

But she did wish it were spring, March, so that Clare would be sailing, out of her life and Brian's. Though she had come almost to believe that there was nothing but generous friendship between those two, she was very tired of Clare Kendry. She wanted to be free of her, and of her furtive comings and goings. If something would only happen, something that would make John Bellew decide on an earlier departure, or that would remove Clare. Anything. She didn't care what. Not even if it were that Clare's Margery were ill, or dying. Not even if Bellew should discover—

She drew a quick, sharp breath. And for a long time sat staring down at the hands in her lap. Strange, she had not before realized how easily she could put Clare out of her life! She had only to tell John Bellew that his wife—No. Not that! But if he should somehow learn of these Harlem visits—Why should she hesitate? Why spare Clare?

But she shrank away from the idea of telling that man, Clare Kendry's white husband, anything that would lead him to suspect that his wife was a Negro. Nor could she write it, or telephone it, or tell it to someone else who would tell him.

She was caught between two allegiances, different, yet the same. Herself. Her race. Race! The thing that bound and suffocated her. Whatever steps she took, or if she took none at all, something would be crushed. A person or the race. Clare, herself, or the race. Or, it might be, all three. Nothing, she imagined, was ever more completely sardonic.

Sitting alone in the quiet living-room in the pleasant firelight, Irene Redfield wished, for the first time in her life, that she had not been born a Negro. For the first time she suffered and rebelled because she was unable to disregard the burden of race. It was, she cried silently, enough to suffer as a woman, an individual, on one's own account, without having to suffer for the race as well. It was a brutality, and undeserved. Surely, no other people so cursed as Ham's dark children.[33]

Nevertheless, her weakness, her shrinking, her own inability to compass the thing, did not prevent her from wishing fervently that, in some way with which she had no concern, John Bellew would discover, not that his wife had a touch of the tar-brush—Irene didn't want that—but that she was spending all the time that he was out of the city in black Harlem. Only that. It would be enough to rid her forever of Clare Kendry.

Three

As if in answer to her wish, the very next day Irene came face to face with Bellew.

She had gone downtown with Felise Freeland to shop. The day was an exceptionally cold one, with a strong wind that had whipped a dusky red

---

[33]In the Biblical Table of Nations (Genesis 10: 6–20), the descendants of Noah's son Ham are the Semitic-speaking people of Canaan, then belonging to Egypt, and the Hamitic-speaking people of Northern Africa, including Egypt, Ethiopia, and Nubia.

into Felise's smooth golden cheeks and driven moisture into Irene's soft brown eyes.

Clinging to each other, with heads bent against the wind, they turned out of the Avenue[34] into Fifty-seventh Street. A sudden bluster flung them around the corner with unexpected quickness and they collided with a man.

"Pardon," Irene begged laughingly, and looked up into the face of Clare Kendry's husband.

"Mrs. Redfield!"

His hat came off. He held out his hand, smiling genially.

But the smile faded at once. Surprise, incredulity, and—was it understanding?—passed over his features.

He had, Irene knew, become conscious of Felise, golden, with curly black Negro hair, whose arm was still linked in her own. She was sure, now, of the understanding in his face, as he looked at her again and then back at Felise. And displeasure.

He didn't, however, withdraw his outstretched hand. Not at once.

But Irene didn't take it. Instinctively, in the first glance of recognition, her face had become a mask. Now she turned on him a totally uncomprehending look, a bit questioning. Seeing that he still stood with hand outstretched, she gave him the cool appraising stare which she reserved for mashers,[35] and drew Felise on.

Felise drawled: "Aha! Been 'passing,' have you? Well, I've queered that."[36]

"Yes, I'm afraid you have."

"Why, Irene Redfield! You sound as if you cared terribly. I'm sorry."

"I do, but not for the reason you think. I don't believe I've ever gone native[37] in my life except for the sake of convenience, restaurants, theatre tickets, and things like that. Never socially I mean, except once. You've just passed the only person that I've ever met disguised as a white woman."

"Awfully sorry. Be sure your sin will find you out and all that. Tell me about it."

"I'd like to. It would amuse you. But I can't."

Felise's laughter was as languidly nonchalant as her cool voice. "Can it be possible that the honest Irene has—Oh, do look at that coat! There. The red one. Isn't it a dream?"

Irene was thinking: "I had my chance and didn't take it. I had only to speak and to introduce him to Felise with the casual remark that he was Clare's husband. Only that. Fool. Fool." That instinctive loyalty to a race. Why couldn't she get free of it? Why should it include Clare? Clare, who'd shown little enough consideration for her, and hers. What she felt was not so much resentment as a dull despair because she could not change herself in this respect, could not separate individuals from the race, herself from Clare Kendry.

[34]Fifth Avenue, the area of New York City known for fine shopping and exclusive stores.
[35]Men making unwelcome sexual advances or passes.
[36]Slang for thwart, spoil, reverse, or ruin.
[37]Term for passing.

"Let's go home, Felise. I'm so tired I could drop."

"Why, we haven't done half the things we planned."

"I know, but it's too cold to be running all over town. But you stay down if you want to."

"I think I'll do that, if you don't mind."

And now another problem confronted Irene. She must tell Clare of this meeting. Warn her. But how? She hadn't seen her for days. Writing and telephoning were equally unsafe. And even if it was possible to get in touch with her, what good would it do? If Bellew hadn't concluded that he'd made a mistake, if he was certain of her identity—and he was nobody's fool—telling Clare wouldn't avert the results of the encounter. Besides, it was too late. Whatever was in store for Clare Kendry had already overtaken her.

Irene was conscious of a feeling of relieved thankfulness at the thought that she was probably rid of Clare, and without having lifted a finger or uttered one word.

But she did mean to tell Brian about meeting John Bellew.

But that, it seemed, was impossible. Strange. Something held her back. Each time she was on the very of saying: "I ran into Clare's husband on the street downtown today. I'm sure he recognized me, and Felise was with me," she failed to speak. It sounded too much like the warning she wanted it to be. Not even in the presence of the boys at dinner could she make the bare statement.

The evening dragged. At last she said good-night and went upstairs, the words unsaid.

She thought: "Why didn't I tell him? Why didn't I? If trouble comes from this, I'll never forgive myself. I'll tell him when he comes up."

She took up a book, but she could not read, so oppressed was she by a nameless foreboding.

What if Bellew should divorce Clare? Could he? There was the Rhinelander case.[38] But in France, in Paris, such things were very easy. If he

[38]A highly publicized 1920s trial involving race, sex, marriage, and passing. Leonard Kip Rhinelander, a member of one of New York's wealthiest and oldest families, married a mulatto chamber maid, Alice B. Jones, on 14 October 1924, one week after he had received a share of his family's stocks, real estate, jewels, and cash. After a month of marriage and under pressure from his family, Rhinelander sought an annulment on the grounds that Alice had fraudulently concealed her race. The sensational trial was front-page news in the New York newspapers for over one year, during which time Alice Jones Rhinelander was required to disrobe on the witness stand for an examination of her skin, frank courtship letters were read into evidence, and Leonard Rhinelander contradicted himself about his knowledge of Alice's race. The New York State Supreme Court jury found on April 5, 1925 that Alice had not been fraudulent about her racial identity and no annulment was granted. Leonard Rhinelander appealed the decision and fought it through the legal system for another year, but lost his appeals. In 1927, Alice Jones Rhinelander filed a suit for separation from her husband, whom she charged with abandonment, and in 1929, she sued his father, Philip Rhinelander, for ruining her marriage. When the case finally ended in 1929, Alice Jones received $31,500, plus $3,600 payable quarterly for the rest of her life; the divorce decree provided that she could no longer use the Rhinelander name. Kip Rhinelander died four years later of pneumonia.

divorced her—If Clare were free—But of all the things that could happen, that was the one she did not want. She must get her mind away from that possibility. She must.

Then came a thought which she tried to drive away. If Clare should die! Then—Oh, it was vile! To think, yes, to wish that! She felt faint and sick. But the thought stayed with her. She could not get rid of it.

She heard the outer door open. Close. Brian had gone out. She turned her face into her pillow to cry. But no tears came.

She lay there awake, thinking of things past. Of her courtship and marriage and Junior's birth. Of the time they had bought the house in which they had lived so long and so happily. Of the time Ted had passed his pneumonia crisis and they knew he would live. And of other sweet painful memories that would never come again.

Above everything else she had wanted, had striven, to keep undisturbed the pleasant routine of her life. And now Clare Kendry had come into it, and with her the menace of impermanence.

"Dear God," she prayed, "make March come quickly."

By and by she slept.

Four

The next morning brought with it a snowstorm that lasted throughout the day.

After a breakfast, which had been eaten almost in silence and which she was relieved to have done with, Irene Redfield lingered for a little while in the downstairs hall, looking out at the soft flakes fluttering down. She was watching them immediately fill some ugly irregular gaps left by the feet of hurrying pedestrians when Zulena came to her, saying: "The telephone, Mrs. Redfield. It's Mrs. Bellew."

"Take the message, Zulena, please."

Though she continued to stare out of the window, Irene saw nothing now, stabbed as she was by fear—and hope. Had anything happened between Clare and Bellew? And if so, what? And was she to be freed at last from the aching anxiety of the past weeks? Or was there to be more, and worse? She had a wrestling moment, in which it seemed that she must rush after Zulena and hear for herself what it was that Clare had to say. But she waited.

Zulena, when she came back, said: "She says, ma'am, that she'll be able to go to Mrs. Freeland's tonight. She'll be here some time between eight and nine."

"Thank you, Zulena."

The day dragged on to its end.

At dinner Brian spoke bitterly of a lynching that he had been reading about in the evening paper.

"Dad, why is it that they only lynch coloured people?" Ted asked.

"Because they hate 'em, son."

"Brian!" Irene's voice was a plea and a rebuke.

Ted said: "Oh! And why do they hate 'em?"

"Because they are afraid of them."

"But what makes them afraid of 'em?"

"Because—"

"Brian!"

"It seems, son, that is a subject we can't go into at the moment without distressing the ladies of our family," he told the boy with mock seriousness, "but we'll take it up some time when we're alone together."

Ted nodded in his engaging grave way. "I see. Maybe we can talk about it tomorrow on the way to school."

"That'll be fine."

"Brian!"

"Mother," Junior remarked, "that's the third time you've said 'Brian' like that."

"But not the last, Junior, never you fear," his father told him.

After the boys had gone up to their own floor, Irene said suavely: "I do wish, Brian, that you wouldn't talk about lynching before Ted and Junior. It was really inexcusable for you to bring up a thing like that at dinner. There'll be time enough for them to learn about such horrible things when they're older."

"You're absolutely wrong! If, as you're so determined, they've got to live in this damned country, they'd better find out what sort of thing they're up against as soon as possible. The earlier they learn it, the better prepared they'll be."

"I don't agree. I want their childhood to be happy and as free from the knowledge of such things as it possibly can be."

"Very laudable," was Brian's sarcastic answer. "Very laudable indeed, all things considered. But can it?"

"Certainly it can. If you'll only do your part."

"Stuff! You know as well as I do, Irene, that it can't. What was the use of our trying to keep them from learning the word 'nigger' and its connotation? They found out, didn't they? And how? Because somebody called Junior a dirty nigger."

"Just the same you're not to talk to them about the race problem. I won't have it."

They glared at each other.

"I tell you, Irene, they've got to know these things, and it might as well be now as later."

"They do not!" she insisted, forcing back the tears of anger that were threatening to fall.

Brian growled: "I can't understand how anybody as intelligent as you like to think you are can show evidences of such stupidity." He looked at her in a puzzled harassed way.

"Stupid!" she cried. "Is it stupid to want my children to be happy?" Her lips were quivering.

"At the expense of proper preparation for life and their future happiness, yes. And I'd feel I hadn't done my duty by them if I didn't give them some inkling of what's before them. It's the least I can do. I wanted to get them out of this hellish place years ago. You wouldn't let me. I gave up the idea, because you objected. Don't expect me to give up everything."

Under the lash of his words she was silent. Before any answer came to her, he had turned and gone from the room.

Sitting there alone in the forsaken dining-room, unconsciously pressing the hands lying in her lap, tightly together, she was seized by a convulsion of shivering. For, to her, there had been something ominous in the scene that she had just had with her husband. Over and over in her mind his last words: "Don't expect me to give up everything," repeated themselves. What had they meant? What could they mean? Clare Kendry?

Surely, she was going mad with fear and suspicion. She must not work herself up. She must not! Where were all the self-control, the common sense, that she was so proud of? Now, if ever, was the time for it.

Clare would soon be there. She must hurry or she would be late again, and those two would wait for her downstairs together, as they had done so often since that first time, which now seemed so long ago. Had it been really only last October? Why, she felt years, not months, older.

Drearily she rose from her chair and went upstairs to set about the business of dressing to go out when she would far rather have remained at home. During the process she wondered, for the hundredth time, why she hadn't told Brian about herself and Felise running into Bellew the day before, and for the hundredth time she turned away from acknowledging to herself the real reason for keeping back the information.

When Clare arrived, radiant in a shining red gown, Irene had not finished dressing. But her smile scarcely hesitated as she greeted her, saying: "I always seem to keep C. P. time,[39] don't I? We hardly expected you to be able to come. Felise will be pleased. How nice you look."

Clare kissed a bare shoulder, seeming not to notice a slight shrinking.

"I hadn't an idea in the world, myself, that I'd be able to make it; but Jack had to run down to Philadelphia unexpectedly. So here I am."

Irene looked up, a flood of speech on her lips. "Philadelphia. That's not very far, is it? Clare, I—?"

She stopped, one of her hands clutching the side of her stool, the other lying clenched on the dressing-table. Why didn't she go on and tell Clare about meeting Bellew? Why couldn't she?

But Clare didn't notice the unfinished sentence. She laughed and said lightly: "It's far enough for me. Anywhere, away from me, is far enough. I'm not particular."

Irene passed a hand over her eyes to shut out the accusing face in the glass before her. With one corner of her mind she wondered how long she

[39]Colored People's time, euphemism for being late.

had looked like that, drawn and haggard and—yes, frightened. Or was it only imagination?

"Clare," she asked, "have you ever seriously thought what it would mean if he should find you out?"

"Yes."

"Oh! You have! And what you'd do in that case?"

"Yes." And having said it, Clare Kendry smiled quickly, a smile that came and went like a flash, leaving untouched the gravity of her face.

That smile and the quiet resolution of that one word, "yes," filled Irene with a primitive paralysing dread. Her hands were numb, her feet like ice, her heart like a stone weight. Even her tongue was like a heavy dying thing. There were long spaces between the words as she asked: "And what should you do?"

Clare, who was sunk in a deep chair, her eyes far away, seemed wrapped in some pleasant impenetrable reflection. To Irene, sitting expectantly upright, it was an interminable time before she dragged herself back to the present to say calmly: "I'd do what I want to do more than anything else right now. I'd come up here to live. Harlem, I mean. Then I'd be able to do as I please, when I please."

Irene leaned forward, cold and tense. "And what about Margery?" Her voice was a strained whisper.

"Margery?" Clare repeated, letting her eyes flutter over Irene's concerned face. "Just this, 'Rene. If it wasn't for her, I'd do it anyway. She's all that holds me back. But if Jack finds out, if our marriage is broken, that lets me out. Doesn't it?"

Her gentle resigned tone, her air of innocent candour, appeared, to her listener, spurious. A conviction that the words were intended as a warning took possession of Irene. She remembered that Clare Kendry had always seemed to know what other people were thinking. Her compressed lips grew firm and obdurate. Well, she wouldn't know this time.

She said: "Do go downstairs and talk to Brian. He's got a mad on."

Though she had determined that Clare should not get at her thoughts and fears, the words had sprung, unthought of, to her lips. It was as if they had come from some outer layer of callousness that had no relation to her tortured heart. And they had been, she realized, precisely the right words for her purpose.

For as Clare got up and went out, she saw that that arrangement was as good as her first plan of keeping her waiting up there while she dressed—or better. She would only have hindered and rasped her. And what matter if those two spent one hour, more or less, alone together, one or many, now that everything had happened between them?

Ah! The first time that she had allowed herself to admit to herself that everything had happened, had not forced herself to believe, to hope, that nothing irrevocable had been consummated! Well, it had happened. She knew it, and knew that she knew it.

She was surprised that, having thought the thought, conceded the fact, she was no more hurt, cared no more, than during her previous frenzied endeavours to escape it. And this absence of acute, unbearable pain seemed to her unjust, as if she had been denied some exquisite solace of suffering which the full acknowledgment should have given her.

Was it, perhaps, that she had endured all that a woman could endure of tormenting humiliation and fear? Or was it that she lacked the capacity for the acme of suffering? "No, no!" she denied fiercely. "I'm human like everybody else. It's just that I'm so tired, so worn out, I can't feel any more." But she did not really believe that.

Security. Was it just a word? If not, then was it only by the sacrifice of other things, happiness, love, or some wild ecstasy that she had never known, that it could be obtained? And did too much striving, too much faith in safety and permanence, unfit one for these other things?

Irene didn't know, couldn't decide, though for a long time she sat questioning and trying to understand. Yet all the while, in spite of her searchings and feeling of frustration, she was aware that, to her, security was the most important and desired thing in life. Not for any of the others, or for all of them, would she exchange it. She wanted only to be tranquil. Only, unmolested, to be allowed to direct for their own best good the lives of her sons and her husband.

Now that she had relieved herself of what was almost like a guilty knowledge, admitted that which by some sixth sense she had long known, she could again reach out for plans. Could think again of ways to keep Brian by her side, and in New York. For she would not go to Brazil. She belonged in this land of rising towers. She was an American. She grew from this soil, and she would not be uprooted. Not even because of Clare Kendry, or a hundred Clare Kendrys.

Brian, too, belonged here. His duty was to her and to his boys.

Strange, that she couldn't now be sure that she had ever truly known love. Not even for Brian. He was her husband and the father of her sons. But was he anything more? Had she ever wanted or tried for more? In that hour she thought not.

Nevertheless, she meant to keep him. Her freshly painted lips narrowed to a thin straight line. True, she had left off trying to believe that he and Clare loved and yet did not love, but she still intended to hold fast to the outer shell of her marriage, to keep her life fixed, certain. Brought to the edge of distasteful reality, her fastidious nature did not recoil. Better, far better, to share him than to lose him completely. Oh, she could close her eyes, if need be. She could bear it. She could bear anything. And there was March ahead. March and the departure of Clare.

Horribly clear, she could now see the reason for her instinct to withhold—omit, rather—her news of the encounter with Bellew. If Clare was freed, anything might happen.

She paused in her dressing, seeing with perfect clearness that dark truth which she had from that first October afternoon felt about Clare Kendry and of which Clare herself had once warned her—that she got the things she wanted because she met the great condition of conquest, sacrifice. If she wanted Brian, Clare wouldn't revolt from the lack of money or place. It was as she had said, only Margery kept her from throwing all that away. And if things were taken out of her hands—Even if she was only alarmed, only suspected that such a thing was about to occur, anything might happen. Anything.

No! At all costs, Clare was not to know of that meeting with Bellew. Nor was Brian. It would only weaken her own power to keep him.

They would never know from her that he was on his way to suspecting the truth about his wife. And she would do anything, risk anything, to prevent him from finding out the truth. How fortunate that she had obeyed her instinct and omitted to recognize Bellew!

"Ever go up to the sixth floor, Clare?" Brian asked as he stopped the car and got out to open the door for them.

"Why, of course! We're on the seventeenth."

"I mean, did you ever go up by nigger-power?"[40]

"That's good!" Clare laughed. "Ask 'Rene. My father was a janitor, you know, in the good old days before every ramshackle flat had its elevator. But you can't mean we've got to walk up? Not here!"

"Yes, here. And Felise lives at the very top," Irene told her.

"What on earth for?"

"I believe she claims it discourages the casual visitor."

"And she's probably right. Hard on herself, though."

Brian said: "Yes, a bit. But she says she'd rather be dead than bored."

"Oh, a garden! And how lovely with that undisturbed snow!"

"Yes, isn't it? But keep to the walk with those foolish thin shoes. You too, Irene."

Irene walked beside them on the cleared cement path that split the whiteness of the courtyard garden. She felt a something in the air, something that had been between those two and would be again. It was like a live thing pressing against her. In a quick furtive glance she saw Clare clinging to Brian's other arm. She was looking at him with that provocative upward glance of hers, and his eyes were fastened on her face with what seemed to Irene an expression of wistful eagerness.

"It's this entrance, I believe," she informed them in quite her ordinary voice.

"Mind," Brian told Clare, "you don't fall by the wayside before the fourth floor. They absolutely refuse to carry anyone up more than the last two flights."

"Don't be silly!" Irene snapped.

[40]Reference to having to expend physical effort, sweat, and hard work in order to achieve something.

The party began gaily.

Dave Freeland was at his best, brilliant, crystal clear, and sparkling. Felise, too, was amusing, and not so sarcastic as usual, because she liked the dozen or so guests that dotted the long, untidy living-room. Brian was witty, though, Irene noted, his remarks were somewhat more barbed than was customary even with him. And there was Ralph Hazelton, throwing non-sensical shining things into the pool of talk, which the others, even Clare, picked up and flung back with fresh adornment.

Only Irene wasn't merry. She sat almost silent, smiling now and then, that she might appear amused.

"What's the matter, Irene?" someone asked. "Taken a vow never to laugh, or something? You're as sober as a judge."

"No. It's simply that the rest of you are so clever that I'm speechless, absolutely stunned."

"No wonder," Dave Freeland remarked, "that you're on the verge of tears. You haven't a drink. What'll you take?"

"Thanks. If I must take something, make it a glass of gingerale and three drops of Scotch. The Scotch first, please. Then the ice, then the ginger ale."

"Heavens! Don't attempt to mix that yourself, Dave darling. Have the butler in," Felise mocked.

"Yes, do. And the footman." Irene laughed a little, then said: "It seems dreadfully warm in here. Mind if I open this window?" With that she pushed open one of the long casement-windows of which the Freelands were so proud.

It had stopped snowing some two or three hours back. The moon was just rising, and far behind the tall buildings a few stars were creeping out. Irene finished her cigarette and threw it out, watching the tiny spark drop slowly down to the white ground below.

Someone in the room had turned on the phonograph. Or was it the radio? She didn't know which she disliked more. And nobody was listening to its blare. The talking, the laughter never for a minute ceased. Why must they have more noise?

Dave came with her drink. "You ought not," he told her, "to stand there like that. You'll take cold. Come along and talk to me, or listen to me gabble." Taking her arm, he led her across the room. They had just found seats when the door-bell rang and Felise called over to him to go and answer it.

In the next moment Irene heard his voice in the hall, carelessly polite: "Your wife? Sorry. I'm afraid you're wrong. Perhaps next—"

Then the roar of John Bellew's voice above all the other noises of the room: "I'm *not* wrong! I've been to the Redfields and I know she's with them. You'd better stand out of my way and save yourself trouble in the end."

"What is it, Dave?" Felise ran out to the door.

And so did Brian. Irene heard him saying: "I'm Redfield. What the devil's the matter with you?"

But Bellew didn't heed him. He pushed past them all into the room and strode towards Clare. They all looked at her as she got up from her chair, backing a little from his approach.

"So you're a nigger, a damned dirty nigger!" His voice was a snarl and a moan, an expression of rage and of pain.

Everything was in confusion. The men had sprung forward. Felise had leapt between them and Bellew. She said quickly: "Careful. You're the only white man here." And the silver chill of her voice, as well as her words, was a warning.

Clare stood at the window, as composed as if everyone were not staring at her in curiosity and wonder, as if the whole structure of her life were not lying in fragments before her. She seemed unaware of any danger or uncaring. There was even a faint smile on her full, red lips, and in her shining eyes.

It was the smile that maddened Irene. She ran across the room, her terror tinged with ferocity, and laid a hand on Clare's bare arm. One thought possessed her. She couldn't have Clare Kendry cast aside by Bellew. She couldn't have her free.

Before them stood John Bellew, speechless now in his hurt and anger. Beyond them the little huddle of other people, and Brian stepping out from among them.

What happened next, Irene Redfield never afterwards allowed herself to remember. Never clearly.

One moment Clare had been there, a vital glowing thing, like a flame of red and gold. The next she was gone.

There was a gasp of horror, and above it a sound not quite human, like a beast in agony. "Nig! My God! Nig!"

A frenzied rush of feet down long flights of stairs. The slamming of distant doors. Voices.

Irene stayed behind. She sat down and remained quite still, staring at a ridiculous Japanese print on the wall across the room.

Gone! The soft white face, the bright hair, the disturbing scarlet mouth, the dreaming eyes, the caressing smile, the whole torturing loveliness that had been Clare Kendry. That beauty that had torn at Irene's placid life. Gone! The mocking daring, the gallantry of her pose, the ringing bells of her laughter.

Irene wasn't sorry. She was amazed, incredulous almost.

What would the others think? That Clare had fallen? That she had deliberately leaned backward? Certainly one or the other. Not—

But she mustn't, she warned herself, think of that. She was too tired, and too shocked. And, indeed, both were true. She was utterly weary, and she was violently staggered. But her thoughts reeled on. If only she could be as free of mental as she was of bodily vigour; could only put from her memory the vision of her hand on Clare's arm!

"It was an accident, a terrible accident," she muttered fiercely. "It *was*."

People were coming up the stairs. Through the still open door their steps and talk sounded nearer, nearer.

Quickly she stood up and went noiselessly into the bedroom and closed the door softly behind her.

Her thoughts raced. Ought she to have stayed? Should she go back out there to them? But there would be questions. She hadn't thought of them, of afterwards, of this. She had thought of nothing in that sudden moment of action.

It was cold. Icy chills ran up her spine and over her bare neck and shoulders.

In the room outside there were voices. Dave Freeland's and others that she did not recognize.

Should she put on her coat? Felise had rushed down without any wrap. So had all the others. So had Brian. Brian! He mustn't take cold. She took up his coat and left her own. At the door she paused for a moment, listening fearfully. She heard nothing. No voices. No footsteps. Very slowly she opened the door. The room was empty. She went out.

In the hall below she heard dimly the sound of feet going down the steps, of a door being opened and closed, and of voices far away.

Down, down, down, she went, Brian's great coat clutched in her shivering arms and trailing a little on each step behind her.

What was she to say to them when at last she had finished going down those endless stairs? She should have rushed out when they did. What reason could she give for her dallying behind? Even she didn't know why she had done that. And what else would she be asked? There had been her hand reaching out towards Clare. What about that?

In the midst of her wonderings and questionings came a thought so terrifying, so horrible, that she had had to grasp hold of the banister to save herself from pitching downwards. A cold perspiration drenched her shaking body. Her breath came short in sharp painful gasps.

What if Clare was not dead?

She felt nauseated, as much at the idea of the glorious body mutilated as from fear.

How she managed to make the rest of the journey without fainting she never knew. But at last she was down. Just at the bottom she came on the others, surrounded by a little circle of strangers. They were all speaking in whispers, or in the awed, discreetly lowered tones adapted to the presence of disaster. In the first instant she wanted to turn and rush back up the way she had come. Then a calm desperation came over her. She braced herself, physically and mentally.

"Here's Irene now," Dave Freeland announced, and told her that, having only just missed her, they had concluded that she had fainted or something like that, and were on the way to find out about her. Felise, she saw, was holding on to his arm, all the insolent nonchalance gone out of her, and the golden brown of her handsome face changed to a queer mauve colour.

Irene made no indication that she had heard Freeland, but went straight to Brian. His face looked aged and altered, and his lips were purple and trembling. She had a great longing to comfort him, to charm away his suffering and horror. But she was helpless, having so completely lost control of his mind and heart.

She stammered: "Is she—is she—?"

It was Felise who answered. "Instantly, we think."

Irene struggled against the sob of thankfulness that rose in her throat. Choked down, it turned to a whimper, like a hurt child's. Someone laid a hand on her shoulder in a soothing gesture. Brian wrapped his coat about her. She began to cry rackingly, her entire body heaving with convulsive sobs. He made a slight perfunctory attempt to comfort her.

"There, there, Irene. You mustn't. You'll make yourself sick. She's—" His voice broke suddenly.

As from a long distance she heard Ralph Hazelton's voice saying: "I was looking right at her. She just tumbled over and was gone before you could say 'Jack Robinson.' Fainted, I guess. Lord! It was quick. Quickest thing I ever saw in all my life."

"It's impossible, I tell you! Absolutely impossible!"

It was Brian who spoke in that frenzied hoarse voice, which Irene had never heard before. Her knees quaked under her.

Dave Freeland said: "Just a minute, Brian. Irene was there beside her. Let's hear what she has to say."

She had a moment of stark craven fear. "Oh God," she thought, prayed, "help me."

A strange man, official and authoritative, addressed her. "You're sure she fell? Her husband didn't give her a shove or anything like that, as Dr. Redfield seems to think?"

For the first time she was aware that Bellew was not in the little group shivering in the small hallway. What did that mean? As she began to work it out in her numbed mind, she was shaken with another hideous trembling. Not that! Oh, not that!

"No, no!" she protested. "I'm quite certain that he didn't. I was there, too. As close as he was. She just fell, before anybody could stop her. I—"

Her quaking knees gave way under her. She moaned and sank down, moaned again. Through the great heaviness that submerged and drowned her she was dimly conscious of strong arms lifting her up. Then everything was dark.

Centuries after, she heard the strange man saying: "Death by misadventure, I'm inclined to believe. Let's go up and have another look at that window."

1929

GEORGE SAMUEL SCHUYLER
1895–1977

Born in Providence, Rhode Island, Schuyler received a public school education in Syracuse, New York, before enlisting in the army at age 17. During World War I, he produced satirical sketches for *The Service*, a military publication. When he mustered out as a first lieutenant in 1919, he began his long career as a professional journalist and wrote satirical columns for a series of black newspapers, including *The Messenger* (New York City) and the *Pittsburgh Courier*, the publication with which he was longest associated. At the same time he published essays, sketches, and satirical pieces in influential magazines such as *The Nation*, *The American Mercury*, and *Reader's Digest*. Schuyler also traveled overseas, especially to West Africa and Latin America, as a foreign correspondent. In his later years he moved away from his earlier socialistic bent to become a conservative anti-Communist, joining the John Birch Society and writing for William Loeb's *Manchester* (New Hampshire) *Union Leader*.

Best known for the stinging satires he published in the 1920s and 1930s, he ridiculed the "colorphobia" of both black and white Americans in articles such as "The Negro-Art Hokum" (1926), "Blessed Are the Sons of Ham" (1927), and "Our White Folks" (1927). *Black No More*, the first full-length satiric novel by a black American, hypothesizes an America in which a black doctor discovers a formula that makes blacks white. Chaos results as whites try to become as black as possible to distinguish themselves from their (formerly) black brethren. Schuyler's next novel, *Slaves Today*, savagely attacked the slave trade in Liberia in the 1920s. His autobiographical *Black and Conservative*, besides containing a wealth of information on just about every political, social, literary, and journalistic black personality of the first half of the century, is a shrill anti-Communist tract.

Because he maintained there was essentially no difference between black and white Americans except in color ("the Aframerican is merely a lampblacked Anglo-Saxon," he once wrote), and because he ridiculed black leaders from W.E.B. Du Bois to Martin Luther King, Schuyler was labeled in the heat of the 1960s as an "assimilationist" or "Uncle Tom" who thought "white" and sold out to the establishment. It was an unfair assessment; during his long career Schuyler demonstrated pride in his black heritage—a fact his critics too often ignored, mistaking his iconoclastic stance as race hatred.

Of course Schuyler was perversely proud of his reputation as a shatterer of idols. Such an attitude placed him in the company of several journalistic satirists of this century—Ambrose Bierce, for example, and H. L. Mencken, who befriended him and published some of his articles in the *American Mercury*. The NAACP's newspaper, *The Crisis*—in which he had once been praised by its founder, W.E.B. Du Bois—lamented in 1965 that Schuyler had become "a veteran dissenter and incurable iconoclast" who "dips his pen in his ever-handy bottle of acid." "The Negro Art-Hokum" appeared in the *Nation* in 1926 and is noteworthy because it constitutes yet another of Schuyler's sarcastic assaults on claims that there exist fundamental differences between blacks and whites. The essay also elicted from Langston Hughes one of the most important critical statements on black art of the time—"The Negro Artist and the Racial Mountain."

"Our Greatest Gift to America" was first published in *Ebony and Topaz* in 1927 and reprinted in V. F. Calverton's *Anthology of American Negro Literature* (1929). As a period piece, Schuyler's essay presents a dismal view of the racial situation in the 1920s. Its ironic, even savage, tone makes it uncomfortable reading. Slashing Juvenalian satire usually is. Yet underlying the attack is a more optimistic appeal to reason. In this as in his other works, Schuyler seems to say, "If Americans would only realize how absurd their colorphobia is, then perhaps they would put it aside and behave like human beings." It is a message as relevant today as it was in 1927.

During the 1930s, Schuyler published a number of nonsatirical pieces, some of them pseudonymously. These included eight African novellas, which were serialized in the *Pittsburgh Courier*. Two of them were innovative pieces of science fiction, "The Black Internationale" and "Black Empire," and were published together in 1991 as *Black Empire*. Two more novellas, a murder mystery ("The Ethiopian Murder Mystery") and an international adventure story ("Revolt in Ethiopia"), were collected under the title *Ethiopian Stories* in 1994.

Michael W. Peplow
Late of Western International University

PRIMARY WORKS

Black No More, 1931; *Slaves Today*, 1931; *Fifty Years of Progress in Negro Journalism*, 1950; *Black and Conservative*, 1966; *Black Empire*, ed., Robert A. Hill and R. Kent Rasmussen, 1991; *Ethiopian Stories*, ed. with an introduction by Robert A. Hill, 1994.

Our Greatest Gift to America

On divers occasions some eloquent Ethiop[1] arises to tell this enlightened nation about the marvelous contributions of his people to our incomparable civilization. With glib tongue or trenchant pen, he starts from the arrival of the nineteen unfortunate dinges at Jamestown in 1619,[2] or perhaps with the coming of the celebrated Columbus to these sacred shores with his Negro mate in 1492,[3] and traces the multiple gifts of the black brethren to the present day. He will tell us of the vast amount of cotton picked by the Negro, of the hundreds of roads and levees the black laborers have constructed, of the miles of floors Negro women have scrubbed, and the acres of clothes they have washed, of the numerous wars in which, for some unknown reason, the Sambo participated, of the dances and cookery he invented, or of the spirituals and work songs composed by the sons of Ham and given to a none too grateful nation. The more erudite of these self-appointed spokesmen of the race will even go back to the Garden of Eden, the walls of Babylon, the pyramids of Egypt and the palaces of Ethiopia by way of introduction and during their prefatory remarks, they will not fail, often, to claim for the Negro race every person of importance that has ever resided on the face of the earth. Ending with a forceful and fervent plea for

[1]Schuyler employs a number of racial epithets in vogue in the 1920s: for blacks, Ethiop, dinges, Sambo (see the children's story, "Little Black Sambo"), sons of Ham, shines, blackamoors, smokes, spades, coons, darkies, zigaboos; for whites, crackers, peckerwoods, the buckra majority, rednecks, ofays, etc.
[2]*The Chronological History of the Negro in America* (hereafter CHNA) quotes John

Rolfe's journal entry for August 20: "there came in a Dutch man-of-warre that sold us 20 negars." These were indentured servants.
[3]The CHNA cites the legend that one Pedro Alonzo Nino, a black man, was part of Columbus's crew.

justice, equality, righteousness, humanitarianism and other such things conspicuous in the world by their absence, they close amid a storm of applause from their sable auditors—and watch the collection plate.

This sort of thing has been going on regularly for the last century. No Negro meeting is a success without one or more such encouraging addresses, and no Negro publication that fails to carry one such article in almost every issue is considered worthy of purchase. So general has the practice become that even white audiences and magazines are no longer immune. It has become not unusual in the past few years for the Tired Society Woman's Club of Keokuk, Iowa, or the Delicatessen Proprietors' Chamber of Commerce or the Hot Dog Venders' Social Club to have literary afternoons devoted exclusively to the subject of the lowly smoke. On such occasions there will be some notable Aframerican speakers as Prof. Hambone of Moronia Institute[4] or Dr. Lampblack[5] of the Federal Society for the Exploitation of Lynching, who will eloquently hold forth for the better part of an hour on the blackamoor's gifts to the Great Republic and why, therefore, he should not be kept down. Following him there will usually be a soulful rendition by the Charcoal Singers of their selected repertoire of genuine spirituals and then, mayhap, one of the younger Negro poets will recite one of his inspiring verses anent[6] a ragged black prostitute gnawing out her soul in the dismal shadows of Hog Maw Alley.[7]

It was not so many years ago that Negro writers used to chew their fingernails and tear as much of their hair as they could get hold of because the adamantine editors of white magazines and journals invariably returned unread their impassioned manuscripts in which they sought to tell how valuable the Aframerican had always been to his country and what a dirty shame it was to incinerate a spade without benefit of jury. Not so today, my friends. The swarms of Negro hacks and their more learned associates have at last come into their own. They have ridden into popular demand on the waves of jazz music, the Charleston, Mammy Songs and the ubiquitous, if intricate, Black Bottom. Pick up almost any of the better class periodicals of national note nowadays and you are almost sure to find a lengthy paper by some sable literatus on the Negro's gifts to America, on his amazing progress in becoming just like other Americans in habit and thought, or on the horrible injustice of Jim Crow[8] cars. The cracker editors are paying generously for the stuff (which is more than the Negro editors did in the old

---

[4]Moronia Institute is Schuyler's jab at Tuskegee Institute, founded by Booker T. Washington and headed in the 1920s by Robert Russa Moton.

[5]Probably a reference to Dr. W.E.B. Du Bois, a founding member of the NAACP and editor of its periodical, *The Crisis*. The NAACP organized antilynching conferences and published annual surveys of lynchings in the United States. Du Bois not only published numerous racial uplift articles in *The Crisis*,

but also wrote *The Gift of Black Folk: Negroes in the Making of America* (1924).

[6]About.

[7]A probable reference to the poet Claude McKay's sentimental poem, "Young Prostitute."

[8]Any of a series of laws enforcing segregated public facilities. See Schuyler's "Traveling Jim Crow," which was published in *The American Mercury* (August 1930) and condensed in *Reader's Digest* (August 1930).

days) and, as a result, the black scribblers, along with the race orators, are now wallowing in the luxury of four-room apartments, expensive radios, Chickering pianos, Bond Street habiliments, canvas-back duck, pre-war Scotch and high yellow mistresses.

All of which is very well and good. It is only natural that the pecker-woods, having become bored to death with their uninteresting lives, should turn to the crows for inspiration and entertainment. It is probably part of their widespread rationalization of the urge they possess to mix with the virile blacks. One marvels, however, that the principal contribution of our zigaboos to the nation has been entirely overlooked by our dusky literati and peripatetic platform prancers. None of them, apparently, has ever thought of it. While they have been ransacking their brains and the shelves of the public libraries for new Negro gifts of which to inform their eager listeners at so much per word or per engagement, they have ignored the principal gift sprawling everywhere about them. They had but to lift their eyes from the pages of their musty tome and glance around. But they didn't.

"And what," I can hear these propagandists feverishly inquiring with poised fountain pens and notebooks, "is this unchronicled contribution to the worth of our nation?" Well, I am not unwilling to divulge this "secret" that has been all too apparent to the observing. And though the brownish intelligentsia are now able to pay for the information—and probably willing to do so—I modestly ask nothing save perhaps a quart of decent rye or possibly one of the numerous medals shoveled out every year to deserving coons. Hence, like all of the others, I now arise, flick a speck off my dinner jacket, adjust my horn-rimmed nose glasses and, striking an attitude, declaim the magic word: Flattery!

Yes, folks, the greatest gift we have made to America is flattery. Flattery, if you please, of the buckra majority; inflation of the racial ego of the dominant group by our mere proximity, by our actions and by our aspirations. "How come?" I am belligerently and skeptically quizzed, and very indulgently I elucidate. Imitation, someone has said, is the sincerest flattery. It is quite human to be pleased and feel very important when we are aped and imitated. Consider how we Negroes shove out our chests when an article appears in an enterprising darky newspaper from the pen of some prominent African chief saying that his dingy colleagues on the Dark Continent look to their American brethren, with their amazing progress, for inspiration. How sweet is flattery, the mother of pride. And pride, we have been told, is absolutely essential to progress and achievement. If all of this be true of the dark American, how much truer must it be of the pink American? By constant exposure to his energetic propagandists in press, on platform and in pulpit, the colored brother has forged ahead—to borrow an expression from the *Uplift*—until he can now eat with Rogers silver off Haviland china, sprawl on overstuffed couches and read spicy literature under the glow of ornate floor lamps, while the strains of "Beer Bucket Blues" are wafted over the radio. This is generally known as progress. Now, if the downtrodden Negro under the influence of his flattering propagandists has been able to attain such heights of material well-being, is it any wonder that the noble rednecks have leaped so much farther up the scale of living when surrounded by millions of black flatterers, both mute and vocal? Most certainly not.

Look, for example, at Isadore Shankersoff. By hook or by crook (probably the latter) he grabbed off enough coin of his native land to pay his passage to America. In Russia he was a nobody—hoofed by everybody—the mudsill of society. Quite naturally his inferiority complex was Brobdingnagian. Arriving under the shadow of the Statue of Liberty, he is still Isadore Shankersoff, the prey of sharpers and cheap grafters, but now he has moved considerably higher in the social scale. Though remaining mentally adolescent, he is no longer at the bottom; he is a white man! Over night he has become a member of the superior race. Ellis Island marked his metamorphosis. For the first time in his life he is better than somebody. Without the presence of the blackamoor in these wonderfully United States, he would still know himself for the thick-pated underling that he is; but how can he go on believing that when America is screaming to him on every hand that he is a white man and, as such, entitled to certain rights and privileges forbidden to Negro scientists, artists, clergymen, journalists and merchants. One can understand why Isadore walks with firmer tread.

Or glance at Cyrus Leviticus Dumbell. He is of Anglo-Saxon stock that is so old that it has very largely gone to seed. In the fastnesses of the Blue Ridge Mountains his racial strain has been safely preserved from pollution by black and red men, for over two hundred years. Thus he is a stalwart fellow untouched by thrift or education. Cy finally tires of the bushes and descends to one of the nearby towns. There he finds employment in a mill on a twelve-hour shift. The company paternalistically furnishes him everything he needs and thoughtfully deducts the cost regularly from his slender pay envelope, leaving him about two dollars for corn liquor and moving pictures. Cy has never had cause to think himself of any particular importance in the scheme of things, but his fellow workers tell him differently. He is a white man, they say, and therefore divinely appointed to "keep the nigger down." He must, they insist, protect white womanhood and preserve white supremacy. This country, he learns, is a white man's country and, although he owns none of it, the information strikes him not unpleasantly. Shortly he scrapes together ten dollars, buys Klan[9] regalia, and is soon engaged in attending midnight meetings, burning crosses, repeating ritual from the Kloran, flogging erring white womanhood for the greater purity of Anglo-Saxondom, and keeping vigilantly on the lookout for uppish and offensive zigaboos to lynch. Like the ancient Greeks and Romans, he now believes himself superior to everybody different from him. Nor does the presence of Jim Crow institutions on every hand contribute anything toward lessening

[9]The Ku Klux Klan was quite active during the 1920s (see the CHNA and Schuyler's own "Scripture for Lynchers" in *The Crisis* [January 1935] and his savage—and hilarious—novel, *Black No More* [1931]). The Kloran was the Klan's "bible."

that belief. Whatever his troubles may be, he has learned from his colleagues and the politicians to blame it all on the dark folks, who are, he is now positive, without exception his inferiors.

Think, also, of demure little Dorothy Dunce. For twelve years she attended the palatial public school. Now, at eighteen, having graduated, she is about to apply her Latin, Greek, English literature, ancient history, geometry and botany to her everyday work as packer in a spaghetti factory. When she was very young, before she entered the kindergarten, her indulgent parents used to scare her by issuing a solemn warning that a big, black nigger would kidnap her if she wasn't a good little girl. Now that she has had American popular education turned loose upon her, she naturally believes differently: i.e., that every big, burly, black nigger she meets on a dark street is ready to relieve her by force of what remains of her virtue. A value is placed upon her that she would not have in Roumania, Scotland, Denmark, or Montenegro. She is now a member of that exalted aggregation known as pure, white womanhood. She is also confident of her general superiority because education has taught her that Negroes are inferior, immoral, diseased, lazy, unprogressive, ugly, odoriferous, and should be firmly kept in their place at the bottom of the social and industrial scale. Quite naturally she swells with race pride for, no matter how low she falls, she will always be a white woman.

But enough of such examples. It is fairly well established, I think, that our presence in the Great Republic has been of incalculable psychological value to the masses of white citizens. Descendants of convicts, serfs and half-wits with the rest have been buoyed up and greatly exalted by being constantly assured of their superiority to all other races and their equality with each other. On the stages of a thousand music halls, they have had their vanity tickled by blackface performers parading the idiocies of mythical black roustabouts and rustics. Between belly-cracking guffaws they have secretly congratulated themselves on the fact that they are not like these buffoons. Their books and magazines have told them, or insinuated, that morality, beauty, refinement and culture are restricted to Caucasians. On every hand they have seen smokes endeavoring to change from black to white and from kinky hair to straight by means of deleterious chemicals; and constantly they hear the Negroes urging each other to do this and that "like white folks." Nor do the crackers fail to observe, either, that pink epidermis is as highly treasured among blacks as in Nordic America and that the most devastating charge that one Negro can make against another is that "he acts just like a nigger." Anything excellent they hear labeled by the race conscious Negroes as "like white folks," nor is it unusual for them, while loitering in the Negro ghetto, to hear black women compared to Fords, mulatto women to Cadillacs and white women to Packards. With so much flattery it is no wonder that the Caucasians have a very high opinion of themselves and attempt to live up to the lofty niche in which the Negroes have placed them. We should not marvel that every white elevator operator, school teacher and bricklayer identifies himself with Shakespeare, Julius Caesar, Napoleon,

Newton, Edison, Wagner, Tennyson, and Rembrandt as creators of this great civilization. As a result we have our American society, where everybody who sports a pink color believes himself to be the equal of all other whites by virtue of his lack of skin pigmentation and his classic Caucasian features.

It is not surprising, then, that democracy has worked better in this country than elsewhere. This belief in the equality of all white folks—making skin color the gauge of worth and the measure of citizenship rights—has caused the lowest to strive to become among the highest. Because of this great ferment, America has become the Utopia of the material world, the land of hope and opportunity. Without the transplanted African in their midst to bolster up the illusion, America would have unquestionably been a very different place; but instead the shine has served as a mudsill upon which all white people alike can stand and reach toward the stars. I submit that here is the gift par excellence of the Negro to America. To spur ten times our number on to great heights of achievement; to spare the nation the enervating presence of a destructive social caste system, such as exists elsewhere, by substituting a color caste system that rouses the hope and pride of teeming millions of ofays—this indeed is a gift of which we can well be proud.

1927

The Negro-Art Hokum

Negro art "made in America" is as non-existent as the widely advertised profundity of Cal Coolidge, the "seven years of progress" of Mayor Hylan, or the reported sophistication of New Yorkers. Negro art there has been, is, and will be among the numerous black nations of Africa; but to suggest the possibility of any such development among the ten million colored people in this republic is self-evident foolishness. Eager apostles from Greenwich Village, Harlem, and environs proclaimed a great renaissance of Negro art just around the corner waiting to be ushered on the scene by those whose hobby is taking races, nations, peoples, and movements under their wing. New art forms expressing the "peculiar" psychology of the Negro were about to flood the market. In short, the art of Homo Africanus was about to electrify the waiting world. Skeptics patiently waited. They still wait.

True, from dark-skinned sources have come those slave songs based on Protestant hymns and Biblical texts known as the spirituals, work songs and secular songs of sorrow and tough luck known as the blues, that outgrowth of ragtime known as jazz (in the development of which whites have assisted), and the Charleston, an eccentric dance invented by the gamins around the public market-place in Charleston, S.C. No one can or does deny this. But these are contributions of a caste in a certain section of the country. They are foreign to Northern Negroes, West Indian Negroes, and African Negroes. They are no more expressive or characteristic of the Negro race than the music and dancing of the Appalachian highlanders or the

Dalmatian peasantry are expressive or characteristic of the Caucasian race. If one wishes to speak of the musical contributions of the peasantry of the South, very well. Any group under similar circumstances would have produced something similar. It is merely a coincidence that this peasant class happens to be of a darker hue than the other inhabitants of the land. One recalls the remarkable likeness of the minor strains of the Russian mujiks to those of the Southern Negro.

As for the literature, painting, and sculpture of Aframericans—such as there is—it is identical in kind with the literature, painting, and sculpture of white Americans: that is, it shows more or less evidence of European influence. In the field of drama little if any merit has been written by and about Negroes that could not have been written by whites. The dean of the Aframerican literati is W.E.B. Du Bois, a product of Harvard and German universities; the foremost Aframerican sculptor is Meta Warwick Fuller, a graduate of leading American art schools and former student of Rodin; while the most noted Aframerican painter, Henry Ossawa Tanner, is dean of American painters in Paris and has been decorated by the French Government. Now the work of these artists is no more "expressive of the Negro soul"—as the gushers put it—than are the scribblings of Octavus Cohen or Hugh Wiley.

This, of course, is easily understood if one stops to realize that the Aframerican is merely a lampblacked Anglo-Saxon. If the European immigrant after two or three generations of exposure to our schools, politics, advertising, moral crusades, and restaurants becomes indistinguishable from the mass of Americans of the older stock (despite the influence of the foreign-language press), how much truer must it be of the sons of Ham who have been subjected to what the uplifters call Americanism for the last three hundred years. Aside from his color, which ranges from very dark brown to pink, your American Negro is just plain American. Negroes and whites from the same localities in this country talk, think, and act about the same. Because a few writers with a paucity of themes have seized upon imbecilities of the Negro rustics and clowns and palmed them off as authentic and characteristic Aframerican behavior, the common notion that the black American is so "different" from his white neighbor has gained wide currency. The mere mention of the word "Negro" conjures up in the average white American's mind a composite stereotype of Bert Williams, Aunt Jemima, Uncle Tom, Jack Johnson, Florian Slappey, and the various monstrosities scrawled by the cartoonists. Your average Aframerican no more resembles this stereotype than the average American resembles a composite of Andy Gump, Jim Jeffries, and a cartoon by Rube Goldberg.

Again, the Aframerican is subject to the same economic and social forces that mold the actions and thoughts of the white Americans. He is not living in a different world as some whites and a few Negroes would have us believe. When the jangling of his Connecticut alarm clock gets him out of his Grand Rapids bed to a breakfast similar to that eaten by his white brother across the street; when he toils at the same or similar work in mills, mines, factories, and commerce alongside the descendants of Spartacus, Robin Hood, and Erik the Red; when he wears similar clothing and speaks the same language with the same degree of perfection; when he reads the same Bible and belongs to the Baptist, Methodist, Episcopal, or Catholic church; when his fraternal affiliations also include the Elks, Masons, and Knights of Pythias; when he gets the same or similar schooling, lives in the same kind of houses, owns the same makes of cars (or rides in them), and nightly sees the same Hollywood version of life on the screen; when he smokes the same brands of tobacco and avidly peruses the same puerile periodicals; in short, when he responds to the same political, social, moral, and economic stimuli in precisely the same manner as his white neighbor, it is sheer nonsense to talk about "racial differences" as between the American black man and the American white man. Glance over a Negro newspaper (it is printed in good Americanese) and you will find the usual quota of crime news, scandal, personals, and uplift to be found in the average white newspaper—which, by the way, is more widely read by the Negroes than is the Negro press. In order to satisfy the cravings of an inferiority complex engendered by the colorphobia of the mob, the readers of the Negro newspapers are given a slight dash of racialistic seasoning. In the homes of the black and white Americans of the same cultural and economic level one finds similar furniture, literature, and conversation. How, then, can the black American be expected to produce art and literature dissimilar to that of the white American?

Consider Coleridge-Taylor, Edward Wilmot Blyden, and Claude McKay, the Englishmen; Pushkin, the Russian; Bridgewater, the Pole; Antar, the Arabian; Latino, the Spaniard; Dumas, *père* and *fils*, the Frenchmen; and Paul Laurence Dunbar, Charles W. Chesnutt, and James Weldon Johnson, the Americans. All Negroes; yet their work shows the impress of nationality rather than race. They all reveal the psychology and culture of their environment—their color is incidental. Why should Negro artists of America vary from the national artistic norm when Negro artists in other countries have not done so? If we can foresee what kind of white citizens will inhabit this neck of the woods in the next generation by studying the sort of education and environment the children are exposed to now, it should not be difficult to reason that the adults of today are what they are because of the education and environment they were exposed to a generation ago. And that education and environment were about the same for blacks and whites. One contemplates the popularity of the Negro-art hokum and murmurs, "How come?"

This nonsense is probably the last stand of the old myth palmed off by Negrophobists for all these many years, and recently rehashed by the sainted Harding, that there are "fundamental, eternal, and inescapable differences" between white and black Americans. That there are Negroes who will lend this myth a helping hand need occasion no surprise. It has been broadcast all over the world by the vociferous scions of slaveholders, "scientists" like Madison Grant and Lothrop Stoddard, and the patriots who flood the treasury of the Ku Klux Klan; and is believed, even today, by the majority of free, white citizens. On this baseless premise, so flattering to the white mob, that the blackamoor is inferior and fundamentally different, is erected the postulate that he must needs be peculiar; and when he attempts to portray life through the medium of art, it must of necessity be a peculiar art. While such reasoning may seem conclusive to the majority of Americans, it must be rejected with a loud guffaw by intelligent people.

1926

■ WALLACE THURMAN ■
1902–1934

Born in Salt Lake City, Utah, in 1902—the same year as Langston Hughes and Arna Bontemps—Wallace Henry Thurman took a few courses at both the University of Utah and the University of Southern California, but did not graduate with a degree from either. In Los Angeles, he tried unsuccessfully in the early 1920s to organize a literary community and also worked for some time as a postal clerk. Arriving in Harlem on Labor Day, 1925, he formed a circle of friends very quickly, moving almost seamlessly through many jobs and professional roles. Between 1925 and 1929, in addition to writing for the black press, he also published articles and book reviews in major white periodicals. Serving successively between 1925 and 1927 on the staff of *The Looking Glass*, *The Messenger*, and *The World Tomorrow*, he landed in 1928 an editorial job at the McFadden, publishers of over 20 magazines including the widely circulated *True Story*. In September 1932, he joined the Macaulay Company and served for some time as their editor-in-chief, the only black person during the period to have had such a job.

Acclaimed by both his Harlem Renaissance peers and some later historians as the most brilliant and radical among the younger writers of the period, Thurman was known until 2003 largely through a few magazine pieces and two of his novels. However, he wrote with savvy and success in almost all genres throughout his short life, often with a fury ignited possibly by a premonition of early death. He was a delightful raconteur and an energetic correspondent who wrote regularly to close friends, collaborators, and many others. A dynamic personality, Thurman had read everything because, as Hughes reports in *The Big Sea*, he could read "eleven lines at a time." Hughes acknowledges with admiration Thurman's amazing critical mind and notes his intermittent despondency about his chances of realizing his ambition of becoming "a *very* great writer, like Gorki or Thomas Mann."

The critical role Thurman played in the Harlem Renaissance has still not received full acknowledgment or critical evaluation. Throughout its peak years, Thurman lived a self-described "erotic, bohemian" lifestyle and engaged energetically in debates about black artistic expression through his literary essays and reviews such as "Nephews of Uncle Remus." Thurman was a provocateur par excellence, inspiring an assertive artistic independence among the young Negro artists that found its clearest expression in Hughes' 1926 essay, "The Negro Artist and the Racial Mountain." In an active leadership role, Thurman conspired with peers such as Hughes, Zora Neale Hurston, Gwendolyn Bennett, John D. Davis, Helene Johnson, Richard Bruce Nugent, Eric Walrond, and Aaron Douglas to organize a response through short-lived but ambitious small magazines, such as *Fire!!* and *Harlem*, to the prescriptive, overbearing demands on their art from both whites and blacks, including powerful players like W.E.B. Du Bois and Alain Locke. Thurman's successive quarters in Harlem—one of which was made famous as the "Niggeratti Manor" in his second novel, *Infants of the Spring* (1932)—were centers of activity and debate for most black young artists and for their friends of diverse backgrounds and sexual orientations. In August 1928, Thurman surprised his friends by marrying a woman friend, Louise Thompson, in what most of his friends saw as a marriage of convenience. In 1929 he published his first novel, *The Blacker the Berry*, and his play, *Harlem*, coauthored with William Jourdan Rapp, had a successful run on Broadway. In early 1934, he moved to Hollywood and wrote two screenplays for Bryan Foy's films *High School Girl* and *Tomorrow's Children*. These two films deal with unusual and tabooed subjects and highlight class conflicts in U.S. society by focusing exclusively on white characters. In 1932, Thurman had already published his third, coauthored novel, *The Interne*, a fictional exposé of the appalling conditions in the City Hospital on Welfare Island, where ironically, having been diagnosed with incurable tuberculosis, Thurman spent the last six months of his life before his death on December 22, 1934.

Most scholars have viewed Thurman not as the critically engaged thinker he was, but as an embodiment of the Harlem Renaissance whose death signals the end of an era, or as a "strangely brilliant black boy" who remained perpetually misunderstood and unappreciated. Even today, his deep inner conflicts as an individual are often viewed as centered in his unusually dark skin. However, his short story "Grist in the Mill" and the "salon" scene from *Infants of the Spring* expose Thurman's complex view of racial and skin-tone constructions in the United States as he learned to modulate his personal pain in response to the occasional slings and arrows of racial prejudice. His ability to collaborate with white individuals in warm collegial relationships is well demonstrated in his collaborations with Rapp and Abraham L. Furman, as well as his friendship with a rich white woman, Elisabeth Marbury, who assisted Thurman financially to help him finish *Infants of the Spring*, the only contemporaneous satire on the Harlem Renaissance. In *Infants of the Spring*—as in his social, biographical, and literary essays—Thurman displays not only his ability to laugh at himself and others, but also his prescient insights into the central challenges of race-inflected literary expression in the United States by both white and black writers and intellectuals.

Amritjit Singh
Ohio University

PRIMARY WORKS

The Blacker the Berry, 1929; *Infants of the Spring*, 1932, rpt. 1992; *The Interne*, 1932; *Collected Writings of Wallace Thurman*, 2003.

Nephews of Uncle Remus

It is too bad that Negro literature and literary material have had to be exploited by fad finders and sentimentalists. Too bad that the ballyhoo brigade which fostered the so-called Negro art "renaissance" has chosen to cheer and encourage indiscriminately anything which claims a Negroid ancestry or kinship. For as the overfed child gags when forced to swallow an extra spoonful of half sour milk, so will the gullible American public gag when too much of this fervid fetish known as Negro art is shoveled into its gaping minds and mouths, and the Afro-American artist will find himself as unchampioned and as unimpressive as he was before Carl Van Vechten commenced caroling of his charms in *Vanity Fair* and the *Survey Graphic* discovered the "New Negro" in 1924. Less so; for even in the prerenaissance days any Negro who achieved something in literature was regarded with wonderment even by the emancipated white intellectuals. But now so many Negroes have written a book or a story or a poem that the pale-faced public is no longer astonished by such phenomena.

There has, of course, been some compensation. Negroes have become more articulate and more coherent in their cries for social justice, and they have also begun to appreciate the advantages of racial solidarity and individual achievement. But speaking purely of the arts, the results of the renaissance have been sad rather than satisfactory, in that critical standards have been ignored, and the measure of achievement had been racial rather than literary. This is supposed to be valuable in a social way, for it is now current that the works produced by Negro artists will form the clauses in a second emancipation proclamation, and that because of the Negro artists and their works, the Afro-American will reap new fruits of freedom. But this will be true only inasmuch as the Negro artist produces dignified and worth-while work. Quick, tricky, atmospheric bits will be as ephemeral as they are sensational, and sentimental propaganda, unless presented in a style both vigorous and new, will have the effect of bird shot rather than that of shrapnel. Which is to say that the Negro will not be benefited by mediocre and ephemeral works, even if they are hailed by well-meaning, but for the moment, simple-minded, white critics as works of genius.

There is a constant controversy being waged as to whether or not there can be in America something specifically known as Negro literature. One school says yes, pointing out the fact that there are inherent differences between whites and blacks which will cause the artistic works of the two groups to be distinctly different. The other school contends that there can be no such thing in America as an individual Negro literature; that the

Afro-American is different from the white American in only one respect, namely, skin color, and that when he writes he will observe the same stylistic conventions and literary traditions.

This latter school seems to have the better of the argument. It is true that anthropologically the American Negro is really no Negro at all. He retains such an ethnological classification only because there seems to be nothing else to call him. There are probably no pure-blooded Negroes in America. The present-day American colored man is, as the Anthropological Department of Columbia University has advanced, neither Negro, Caucasian, nor Indian, but a combination of all three with the Negroid characteristics tending to dominate. Furthermore, the American Negro has absorbed all of the American white man's culture and cultural appurtenances. He uses the same language, attends the same schools, reads the same newspapers and books, lives in the same kind of houses, wears the same kind of clothes, and is no more keenly attuned to the African jungle or any of its aesthetic traditions than the average American white man.

It is hard to see, then, that the Negro in America can produce an individual literature. What he produces in the field of letters must be listed as American literature, just as the works of the Scotchman Burns or the Irishman Synge are listed as English literature. The Negro author can, by writing of certain race characteristics and institutions, introduce a Negro note into American literature, just as Yeats, Colum, A. E., Lady Gregory and others introduced a Celtic note in English literature, but in America this can be done by a white writer as well as by a black one, and there is a possibility of its being done much better by the former, in that he may approach his material with a greater degree of objectivity. For example, no Negro has written about his own people as beautifully or as sympathetically as has DuBose Heyward, the author of *Porgy*, purely because the Negro writer, for the most part, has seen fit to view his own people as sociological problems rather than as human beings, and has written of little else save the constant racial struggle between whites and blacks. Consequentially, he has limited himself and left a great deal of fresh vital material untouched.

It was to be hoped that the renaissance would make the Negro writer more aware of the value of the literary material provided by his own people. During this time, DuBose Heyward wrote *Porgy*, Julia Peterkin wrote *Green Thursday* and *Black April*, but as yet no Negro novelist has taken a hint from these white writers, let alone tried to surpass them.

The question arises: Must the Negro author write entirely of his own people? So many of the young Negro writers have asked this and then wailed that they did not wish to be known as *Negro* artists, but as *artists*. They seemed to think that by writing of white people they could produce better work and have a less restricted field of endeavor. In trying to escape from a condition their own mental attitude makes more harrowing, they forget that every facet of life can be found among Negroes, who being human beings, have all the natural emotional and psychological reactions of other human beings. They live, die, hate, love, and procreate. They dance and sing, play and fight. And if art is the universal expressed in terms of the particular, there is, if he has the talent, just as much chance for the Negro author to produce great literature by writing of his own people as if he were to write of Chinese or Laplanders. He will be labeled a *Negro* artist, with the emphasis on the Negro rather than on the artist, only as he fails to rise above the province of petty propaganda, or fails to find a means of escape from both himself and his environment.

The pioneer work done by Jean Toomer in freeing himself from restrictive racial bonds and letting the artist in him take flight where it will, and the determination with which Langston Hughes went about depicting his people, their rhythms and institutions, make these two appear to be the most important literary figures the renaissance has produced. They, of all the young Negro writers, have seemed to be the most objective and the most aware of the aesthetic value of literary material in their race. Their work is distinctive because it contains vestiges of that Negro note which will characterize the literature produced by truly talented, sincere Negro writers. Neither of them is worried by an inferiority complex which makes him wish to escape his race by not writing of it and at the same time binds him more tightly to the whipping post he would escape. The trouble with Mr. Toomer is that he has written too little. The trouble with Mr. Hughes is that he has written too much, in that he seems to lack, where his own work is concerned, that discriminating sense of selection which makes the complete artist as critical as he is creative. Urged on by a faddistic interest in the unusual, Mr. Hughes has been excessively prolific, and has exercised little restraint. The result is that his work is uneven to an alarming degree, and makes one fear that soon he will expend all of his spiritual energy in bubbling over in his adolescence rather than conserving himself until he matures. He needs to learn the use of the blue pencil and the waste-paper basket.

Eric Walrond can be classed with Mr. Toomer in that when writing of his own people he treats them objectively and as human beings. His *Tropic Death* was marred only by the writer's inability to master completely his style. He was attempting to forge a new method of expression, to escape, as Jean Toomer escaped, from the staid conventionality of stereotyped prose; and he succeeded to a degree that almost made one overlook those passages which were incoherent or tiresome. Nevertheless, it must be admitted that had his style been less esoteric or more controlled, the subject matter would have been more effective, a large order when one remembers such stories as "The Vampire Bat" and "The Black Pin."

Rudolph Fisher has written one very good short story of Negro life in Harlem, and a few more which, while vivid with local color, are weak in other respects. "The City of Refuge," which appeared in *The Atlantic Monthly* almost three years ago, and was later incorporated in *The New Negro*, that handbook of the renaissance edited by Alain Locke, was one of the first short stories written by a Negro about Negroes which did not follow the conventional formula. It told the story of a Southern Negro's coming to Harlem, the city of refuge, and of his struggles to adapt himself to a strange and complex environment. Here was drama of a new order, drama and color and life, a story as good as it was unusual. One waits expectantly for Mr. Fisher's first novel.

There are many more Negro writers who could be discussed in detail if the space allowed. Zora Neale Hurston is a good story-teller, but an indifferent craftsman. Walter White and Jessie Fauset have produced nothing out of the ordinary, or very good. James Weldon Johnson belongs to the elder generation of Negro writers, as his *Autobiography of an Ex-Colored Man*, recently reissued by Knopf, will prove. Despite Carl Van Vechten's enthusiastic introduction, there seems to be no real reason for reprinting this volume in the Blue Jade Library. It is well written, yes, and the author predicts the popularity of ragtime, but its content seems uninspired and stereotyped. Fifteen years ago it might have been a little more than just a well-written book; today it merely makes one wonder why the author didn't call it the autobiography of a colored man rather than that of an ex-colored man. Mr. Johnson's *God's Trombones* is of a different species. The majesty and eloquence of the sermon poems included therein, especially "Go Down Death" are searing and unforgettable. In these poems Mr. Johnson has been the artist rather than the propagandist, and *God's Trombones* will be remembered long after the *Autobiography* has been forgotten, even by sentimental white folk and Jeremiah-like Negroes.

Countee Cullen has published three volumes, *Color, Copper Sun*, and *The Ballad of the Brown Girl*, all of which tend to convince the critical investigator that although Mr. Cullen can say things beautifully and impressively, he really has nothing new to say, nor no new way in which to say it. He follows the tradition of a literary poet. His lyrics of love and death are reminiscent of Keats, Housman, and Edna Millay, and one gets the impression that Mr. Cullen writes not from his own experience, but from vicarious literary experiences which are not intense enough to be real and vital. His poetry is not an escape from life in the big sense, but from the narrow world in which he has been caged, and from which he seems to have made no great effort to escape.

Undoubtedly Mr. Cullen has more talent than any of his colored contemporaries. What he lacks is originality of theme and treatment, and the contact with life necessary to have had actual, rather than vicarious, emotional experiences. He is still young, and perhaps when some of the fanfare aroused when it was discovered that a *Negro* could write beautiful conventional verse has died down, he will be able to work out his own destiny. He has far to go if only he is given the chance and stimulation.

In a recent issue of *Opportunity, Journal of Negro Life*, there are reviews of two recent books. Both of the reviewers were white poets, both books were by Negro poets. The first was of Countee Cullen's *Copper Sun*, and in

dithyrambic prose the reviewer went to every possible verbal excess in praising the volume. According to him Countee Cullen is *the* thing in American
poetry—he equals Housman and surpasses Edna Millay. There is more such
lyric nonsense, all done in good faith, no doubt, but of no value whatsoever
either to Mr. Cullen or to the race to which he belongs. The second review,
while less turgid and more restrained, was excessive in its praise of *God's
Trombones*, and in neither piece was there any constructive criticism or intelligent evaluation.

These two reviews are typical of the attitude of a certain class of white
critics toward Negro writers. Urged on by their desire to do what in their
opinion is a "service," they dispense with all intelligence and let their sentimentality run riot. Fortunately, most of the younger Negro writers realize
this, and as most Negroes have always done, are laughing up their sleeves at
the antics of their Nordic patronizers. It is almost a certainty that Countee
Cullen and Langston Hughes know full well that there are perhaps a half
dozen young white poets in these United States doing just as good if not
better work than they, and who are not being acclaimed by the public or
pursued by publishers purely because dash of color is the style in literary
circles today.

If the Negro writer is to make any appreciable contribution to American
literature it is necessary that he be considered as a sincere artist trying to
do dignified work rather than a highly trained dog doing trick dances in a
public square. He is, after all, motivated and controlled by the same forces
which motivate and control a white writer, and like him he will be mediocre
or good, succeed or fail as his ability deserves. A man's complexion has little
to do with his talent. He either has it or has it not, and despite the dictates
of spiritually starved white sophisticates genius does not automatically
descend upon one cause one's grandmother happened to be sold down the
river "befo' de wah."

1927

Grist in the Mill

This is indeed an accidental cosmos, so much so, that even the most divine
mechanism takes an occasional opportunity to slip a cog and intensify the
reigning chaos. And to make matters more intriguing, more terrifying, there
seems to be a universal accompaniment of mocking laughter, coming from
the ethereal regions as well as from the more mundane spheres, to each mishap whether that mishap be experienced by a dislodged meteor, a moon-
bound planet, a sun-shrunken comet, or a determined man. All of which
serves to make this universe of ours a sometimes comic spectacle, serves to
push all unexpected cosmic experience just over the deviating border line
that divides the comic from the tragic, for there is always something delightfully humorous in an accident even if that accident be as earthly, as

insignificant (cosmically speaking) and as fatal as was the accident of Colonel Charles Summers, the second, of Louisiana.

Colonel Charles Summers, the second, was a relic; an anachronistic relic from pre-civil war days, being one of those rare sons of a dyed-in-the-wool southern father who had retained all the traditionary characteristics of his patrician papa. Even his aristocratic blood had escaped being diluted by poor white corpuscles making him indeed a phenomenal person among the decadent first families of the decadent south. Colonel Charles Summers, the second, was your true reborn Confederate, your true transplanted devotee of the doctrines of Jeff Davis, your true contemporary Colonel Charles Summers, the first, even to the petty affectation of an unearned military title, and a chronic case of pernicious anemia.

It was on one of those placid days when a wary human is always expecting the gods to play a scurvy trick upon him, one of those days when smiling nature might be expected to smirk at any moment, one of those days when all seems to be too well with the world that the first act of Colonel Summers' accident occurred. He should have sensed that all was not to be well with him on that day, for long, lonely isolated years of living with and nursing a dead ideal, had made him peculiarly attune to the ever variant vibrations of his environment. He had little companionship, for there were few kindred souls in the near vicinity. His wife, to him, was practically non-existent, being considered a once useful commodity now useless. He had no children, had not wanted any, for fear that they would become too seared with the customs and mannerisms of the moment to complacently follow in his footsteps. He could not abide the poor white or mongrel aristocrats who were his neighbors. He shrank from contact with the modern world, and preserved his feudal kingdom religiously, passionately, safeguarding it from the unsympathetic outside. Hence he communed with himself and with nature, and became intensely aware of his own mental and physical reactions and premonitions, so aware, in fact, that he privately boasted that no accident could befall him without his first receiving a sensory warning, but of course, he forgot to be aware at the proper time, even though the day was rampant with danger signals.

Mrs. Summers was an unemotional ninny, being one of those backwoods belles whom the fates failed to attend properly at birth. Her only basis of recognition in this world at all was that she was a direct descendant of an old southern family. She was one of those irritating persons who never think about a thing nor yet feel about it. Rather she met all phenomena dispassionately, practically, and seemed to be more mechanical than most other humans. When an interne from the hospital brought her the news that only a blood transfusion would save her husband's life, she accepted that without the slightest suggestion of having received a shock; and she had accepted the news of his sunstroke, induced by walking beneath a torrid, noonday Louisiana sun, and which had resulted in an acute aggravation of his chronic illness in the same "well, that's no news" manner.

"Blood transfusion," she stated rather than queried, "well, why not?"

"We thought, madame," the interne was polite, "that you might have been able to suggest—"

She gave a little shrug, the nearest approach to the expression of an emotion that she ever allowed herself. "I am no physician," and the door was closed deliberately, yet normally.

The hospital staff was thus placed in an embarrassing dilemma, for there was no professional blood donor available, and no volunteers forthcoming either from the village center or the outlying plantations. One must suffer from not having friends as well as suffer from having them—so the Colonel's life line continued to fray, his wife made perfunctory visits, and continued to appear disinterested, while the hospital staff pondered and felt criminal, not too criminal, you know, for they remembered that the Colonel had most insultingly refrained from ever donating to their building or upkeep fund, yet they could not let him die while there was a possible chance of saving him, so being both human and humanitarian they played a joke on the doughty old Colonel and at the same time saved his life.

Zacharia Davis had a suppressed desire, and the suppression of that desire was necessarily more potent than the desire itself, for Zacharia wished to make a happy hegira to the northland, and being in the south decided that it was best to keep this desire under cover until such time came that he would have what he called the "necessary mazuma."

Zacharia had been born and schooled in Illinois, and had been perfectly willing to remain there until a certain war-time conscription measure had made Mexico seem more desirable. Once in Mexico he had remained until the ink of the Armistice signatures had been dry five years, and then he had recrossed the border into the cattle lands of western Texas. There he had parked, and attempted to amass sufficient coin to enable him to return to and dazzle Chicago's south side black belt, but an untimely discovery of a pair of loaded dice on his person during an exciting crap game had made it necessary for him to journey by night and by freight to the cane-brake country of Southern Louisiana.

Here he had occupied himself by doing odd jobs about the various plantations and village shops, and by gambling down by the river bottom at night with the rice field and cane-brake laborers. He avoided trouble either with his fellow black men who were somewhat suspicious of this smooth talking "furriner," and with that white portion of his environment that demanded his quiescent respect. Consciously he adopted a protective cloak of meekness, and at first glance could not be distinguished from the native southern blacks; in fact, only a keen analyst could have discerned that Zacharia was continually laughing at all those about him, both white and black, and that he, unlike the southern native Negro suffered little, even unconsciously, and laughed much. Then, too, Zacharia washed the hospital windows every Saturday morning, and was thus drawn into the little comedy in which Colonel Summers was to play the star role.

Meanwhile there were other factors working to deter Zacharia from ever realizing the fruitation of his desire. The sheriff of the parish had finally decided to clamp down on the river bottom gambling activities where there had lately been a siege of serious cuttings and fatal shootings. Of course, normally it did not matter if all the "coons" insisted upon killing one another, but it did matter when northern migration was at its highest peak, and labor was both scarce and valuable to the plantation owners and it was at the instigation of these persons that the sheriff was moved to act. He planned his raid secretly and carefully, seeking the aid of the local K.K.K., and the more adventurous villagers. They had no intention of using firearms or of jailing any of the game participants. Neither did they have any intention of stopping the games completely. They merely hoped to lessen the attendance, and to inspire caution in those who would attend about the advisability of carrying firearms and knives.

Of course, it was in line with Zacharia's general luck that he should be in the midst of a winning streak on the night when the eager vigilantes swooped down upon the river bottom rendezvous like revengeful phantoms in the moonlight, and proceeded to do their chosen duty. And, of course, it was in line with Zacharia's general procedure to forgo immediate flight in order to gather up forsaken cash piles.

There was so much confusion there in the damp darkness. The fiery, white demons reveled in the raucous riot they had created, while the scuttling blacks cursed and cried out against the lash sting and the club beat. The rendezvous was surrounded, there was only one means of escape, the river, and the cornered ones shrank back from its cold, slimy, swift currents. Hysteria descended upon the more terrified. Knives were drawn, and temporarily reflected the gleaming moonlight as they were hurled recklessly into the mad white-black crowd. Periodic pistol shots punctuated the hoarse shouts of the conquerors and the pained moans of the vanquished. Torchlight flares carried by the invaders gave the scene the color and passion of a Walpurgis night. Marsh grass was trampled, its dew turned red by dripping blood. And the river—the muddy river—became riotous with struggling men, and chuckled to itself as an occasional body was unable to withstand the current, or unable to reach the other shore.

There was much more confusion there in the damp darkness. Bleeding heads emitted free blood streams, more groans, more blood, and then grew still, grew horribly inanimate. Wounded bodies squirmed and moaned. The flares were all extinguished. The river was once more quietly rippling undisturbed by super-imposed freight. The round-up had commenced, the injured whites were being carefully carried into the village hospital, while the wounded blacks were being dragged to jail. Thus the night wore on, and seemed a little weary of having witnessed such a carnal spectacle, such elemental chaos.

Among those hapless blacks who regained consciousness in the crowded jail was Zacharia who was nonchalantly nursing a cracked head, and a sock full of coin. Being in jail was no novelty, nor was having a cracked head an entirely new experience, but the sock of money, the sock that contained his pecuniary emancipation, the sock that contained the "necessary mazuma," ah, that was new, saliently new, and comforting.

The town was in an uproar. A deputy sheriff had died from a knife wound inflicted by some infuriated black during the conflict. No one had expected any of the invaders to come back wounded. No one had considered that the cornered colored man might stand at bay like a wild, jungle animal, and fight back. Everyone had considered the whole episode as an unusual chance to sock a few niggers upon the head, and to flay a few black hides with a long unused lash, but instead most of the blacks had fought their way to freedom, only a mere handful of the more seriously wounded were in custody, and they were being claimed by their plantation employers. Moreover, the hospital was overcrowded with wounded whites, and now, this death, this death of a white man at the hands of a nigger. Of course, some one had to pay. The plantation owners were not willing to part with any of their hired help, considering the cultivation of the rice and sugar cane crop of more importance now than the punishment of some unknown assailant. Oh, yes, catch some one and punish him, but don't take this nigger of mine, who is one of my best workmen, seemed to be the general attitude.

No one came to claim Zacharia, and he remained in his cell, awaiting to be released, and amusing himself meanwhile by trying to compute in his mind just how much money his beloved sock, so carefully hidden away, contained. No one came to claim him and finally he was accused of having murdered the deputy sheriff.

The trial was conducted rather leisurely. There was no hurry to cash in on the mob's vengeance. Their call for blood had been satiated by that river bottom battle. It was enough that they had a victim in custody whom they could torture at will, and whom they could put to death legally. Thus Zacharia found himself a participant in a mock trial, found himself being legally railroaded to the gallows, found himself being kept away from freedom— from Chicago—when he had the cash, the long desired cash. He was too amazed at first to realize just how completely he had been enveloped by a decidedly hostile environment. Realization came slowly, and noticeably. His bronze colored face grew wan and sickly. His beady eyes became more and more screwed up until it seemed as if they would completely retreat into the protective folds of their wrinkled sockets. Even the firm lower lip, his one sign of forceful character, drooped, and mutely asked for pity.

He was found guilty, and made ready to take his journey to the state penitentiary where he would be held until the date set for his hanging. The date of his departure drew near, and Zacharia became pitifully panic stricken. The four walls of his lousy cell seemed to be gyrating mirrors sordidly reflecting his certain doom. The bars running diagonally across the cell door and standing upright in the cell window all seemed to assume the personality of ballet dancers attired in hemp, and forming twirling circular figures, lunging at him with menacing loops. Everything choked him, his food—the air—even thought. Incipient nausea tortured him. And then one thought flashed across is mind, lingered there, shimmering with the glorified heat of potential hope. A spasm of grotesque smiles distorted the uneven, thick features, and the quivering lips called to the guards, and begged them to send for Colonel Summers.

Had Zacharia asked for anyone else besides Colonel Summers his request would have been either roughly refused or rudely ignored, but to have a condemned "nigger" ask for old stuck up Colonel Summers, well, well, well, what a chance for some fun at the Colonel's expense. The question was would the Colonel come. In all probability he wouldn't. Since he had recovered from that last illness of his, he had drawn more and more into himself. His wife had imported a sister for company, but the Colonel continued to tramp about his plantation, continued to commune with himself.

It was sheer accident that Colonel Summers happened to be in town on the same day that Zacharia had asked to see him. His wife's sister had had an attack of indigestion. In fact, it seemed to Colonel Summers that she was always having an attack of something. And she was always having prescriptions filled, always dispatching a servant to the drug store. Damned frump, the Colonel called her. Worrisum bitch, was what the black servants called her. However, on this day she had sent for medicine twice, and each time the little black boys had come back with the wrong brand, so impatient at both his sister-in-law, the stupid black boys, and the crafty druggist, the Colonel went into town himself.

Of course, once there the Colonel did the usual thing, *id est* wandered aimlessly about the streets and enjoyed himself by cursing the activities of these ambitious, pettily so, of course, poor trash. And in his wanderings he walked past the jail, was hailed, stopped to see what the insolent fellow wanted, gaped slightly when he heard, and without a word, or without an idea why he did so except that his pride would not let him appear to be placed at a disadvantage, strode into jail, and asked to see Zacharia.

Fifteen minutes later the amused eavesdropping guards and jail loiterers rushed into the cell passageway to see the Colonel striking through the bars with his cane, perspiring dreadfully, his face inordinately infused with blood, and to find Zacharia cowed against the further wall, his face a study in perplexity and pleading, his lips whimpering, "I didn't lie, I didn't lie, it was me, it was me," on and on in ceaseless reiteration.

The surprised and amused men plied the old Colonel with questions in a vain effort to find out what was wrong, but the old southern gentleman was incoherent with rage, and sick, both in body and in mind. He seemed on the verge of collapse and the more solicitous men in the group attempted to lead him into the warden's quarters where he could lie down. Someone even suggested a doctor, but all were overruled by Colonel Summers, who had meanwhile regained some of his strength and cried out, "The hospital, the hospital," and to the hospital the men carried him, not knowing that he did not wish to go there for treatment, or that he was seeking for verification—verification of what the doomed Zacharia had told him.

Twenty-four hours later he was taken home, babbling, unconscious, and pitiful. The hospital authorities had verified Zacharia's statement, and Colonel Summers now knew that it was the black man's blood that saved his life.

It commenced to rain about twilight time. Colonel Summers suddenly sat up in his bed, the most ambitious move that he had made in a week. He was alone in the room, alone with himself, and his fear, alone in the defeated twilight.

The rain drops increased in volume and velocity. Colonel Summers threw the covers back, struggled out of the bed, and staggered laboriously to the panel mirror set in his closet door. Eagerly, insanely he peered into it, and what he saw there evidently pleased him, for the drawn features relaxed a trifle, and only the eyes, the weak, pitiful eyes, remained intensely animate as they peered and peered into the mirror. Then his strength gave out, and he sank with a groan to the floor.

The rain drops began to come down in torrents, urged on by a rising wind. Colonel Summers once more drew himself up with the aid of the door knob, and once more peered and peered into the mirror. By this time he had ripped his night shirt from him, and stood there naked, his wasted body perspiring from the effort. Soon his strength gave out again, and as he sank to the floor there was a peaceful half smile striving for expression on his pained and fear-racked face.

"Still white, still white," he muttered, and then more loudly, "still white, still white, still white," the voice became hoarse again, "still white, thank God, A'hm still white."

Night came, greeted by the whistle of the frolicsome wind and the ceaseless chorus of the scampering rain drops. The bedroom became dark, and once more gaining consciousness the naked Colonel crawled across the carpeted floor to the nearest window. The darkness frightened him, he was seeking for light, and since the interior offered none, he sought for it or a reflection of it through the window panes. But on the outside was also the black night plus the cachinnating rain drops, and the playful wind. He shrank back in abject terror only to be confronted with the same terrifying darkness behind him.

He looked out of the window once more. A flash of lightning provided the wanted light, but it brought no release, brought only additional terror, for the tree tops, glistening wet and swaying with the wind, assumed the shapes of savage men, rhythmically moving to the tune of a tom-tom, rhythmically tossing to the intermittent thud of the reverberating thunder.

"Darkies," he murmured, and tried to draw from the window, "My God—darkies." Then the scene changed. His insane eyes set in a bearded skull conjured up strange figures when the lightning flashed. Each tree assumed a definite personality. That broken limb dangling from the tree just beyond the fence was Zacharia, and as it gyrated wildly in the mad night, it seemed to whisper to the wind. "He is my brother, my brother, my brother," while the wind broadcasted the whisper through the night. And then that tallest tree so close to the house was himself, a black reproduction of himself with savage sap surging through its veins. It too reveled in the wildness of the night; it too exulted in being pelted by the wind-driven rain drops and in responding to the rough rhythm of the thunder-god's tom-tom.

Someone lit a light in the hall, and laid their hand on the door knob preparatory to opening the door to the Colonel's room. Then someone else across the hall called, and the first person released their grip on the knob and treaded softly away.

The Colonel fell prostrate to the floor, and attempted to burrow his head deep into the thick protective nap of the carpet. He felt an inky blackness enveloping him, his whole form seemed to be seared with some indigo stain that burned and burned like an avid acid. Then his body began to revolt against this dusky intruder, began to writhe and wriggle upon the floor, began to twitch and turn, trying to rub itself clean, trying to shed this superimposed cloak, but the blackness could not be shed—it was sprouting from the inside, and being fertilized by the night.

Time passed. Voices were heard whispering in the hall. A door closed. More whispering. Outdoors all was jubilantly mad. In the bedroom the Colonel still lay upon the floor, panting, perspiring, exhausted from his insane efforts. His reason was now completely gone. His last ounce of life was being slowly nibbled away. The blackness became more intense, and then a black crow, stranded, befuddled by the storm, sought refuge upon the window ledge, and finding none there cawed out in distress, and to the dying maniac on the floor, it seemed to caw, "nigaw, nigaw, nigaw—"

Someone opened the door, turned on the light, and screamed.

1926

from **Infants of the Spring**

Thursday night came and so did the young hopefuls. The first to arrive was Sweetie May Carr. Sweetie May was a short story writer, more noted for her ribald wit and personal effervescence than for any actual literary work. She was a great favorite among those whites who went in for Negro prodigies.[1] Mainly because she lived up to their conception of what a typical Negro should be. It seldom occurred to any of her patrons that she did this with tongue in cheek. Given a paleface audience, Sweetie May would launch forth into a saga of the little all-colored Mississippi town where she claimed to have been born. Her repertoire of tales was earthy, vulgar and funny. Her darkies always smiled through their tears, sang spirituals on the slightest provocation, and performed buck dances when they should have been working. Sweetie May was a master of Southern dialect, and an able raconteur,

[1]Sweetie May Carr is Thurman's satiric portrait of Zora Neale Hurston. The scene takes place at "Niggerati Manor," Thurman's boarding house at 267 West 136th Street in Harlem.

but she was too indifferent to literary creation to transfer to paper that which she told so well. The intricacies of writing bored her, and her written work was for the most part turgid and unpolished. But Sweetie May knew her white folks.

"It's like this," she had told Raymond.[2] "I have to eat. I also wish to finish my education. Being a Negro writer these days is a racket and I'm going to make the most of it while it lasts. Sure I cut the fool. But I enjoy it, too. I don't know a tinker's damn about art. I care less about it. My ultimate ambition, as you know, is to become a gynecologist. And the only way I can live easily until I have the requisite training is to pose as a writer of potential ability. *Voila!* I get my tuition paid at Columbia. I rent an apartment and have all the furniture contributed by kind-hearted o'fays.[3] I receive bundles of groceries from various sources several times a week ... all accomplished by dropping a discreet hint during an evening's festivities. I find queer places for whites to go in Harlem ... out of the way primitive churches, side-street speakeasies. They fall for it. About twice a year I manage to sell a story. It is acclaimed. I am a genius in the making. Thank God for this Negro literary renaissance! Long may it flourish!"

Sweetie May was accompanied by two young girls, recently emigrated from Boston. They were the latest to be hailed as incipient immortals. Their names were Doris Westmore and Hazel Jamison.[4] Doris wrote short stories. Hazel wrote poetry. Both had become known through a literary contest fostered by one of the leading Negro magazines. Raymond liked them more than he did most of the younger recruits to the movement. For one thing, they were characterized by a freshness and naïveté which he and his cronies had lost. And, surprisingly enough for Negro prodigies, they actually gave promise of possessing literary talent. He was most pleased to see them. He was also amused by their interest and excitement. A salon! A literary gathering! It was one of the civilized institutions they had dreamed of finding in New York, one of the things they had longed and hoped for.

As time passed, others came in. Tony Crews, smiling and self-effacing, a mischievous boy, grateful for the chance to slip away from the backwoods college he attended.[5] Raymond had never been able to analyze this young poet. His work was interesting and unusual. It was also spotty. Spasmodically he gave promise of developing into a first rate poet. Already he had published two volumes, prematurely, Raymond thought. Both had been excessively praised by whites and universally damned by Negroes. Considering the nature of his work this was to be expected. The only unknown quantity was the poet himself. Would he or would he not fulfill the promise

[2]Thurman's protagonist, Raymond Taylor, is based on himself.

[3]An "o'fay" is period African American slang for a Caucasian. Sometimes said to derive from the Pig Latin derivation of *foe*, though most slang histories dispute the claim.

[4]Doris Westmore is Dorothy West (1907–1998), author of *The Living is Easy* (1948). West's 1970 memoir of Thurman, "Elephant's Memory," published in *Black World*, paved the way for Wallace's rediscovery. Hazel Jamison is poet Helene Johnson (1906–1995).

[5]Crews is Thurman's portrait of Langston Hughes. Crews also appears in Thurman's first novel, *The Blacker the Berry* (1929).

exemplified in some of his work? Raymond had no way of knowing and even an intimate friendship with Tony himself had failed to enlighten him. For Tony was the most close-mouthed and cagey individual Raymond had ever known when it came to personal matters. He fended off every attempt to probe into his inner self and did this with such an unconscious and naïve air that the prober soon came to one of two conclusions: Either Tony had no depth whatsoever, or else he was too deep for plumbing by ordinary mortals.

DeWitt Clinton, the Negro poet laureate, was there, too, accompanied, as usual, by his *fideles achates*, David Holloway.[6] David had been acclaimed the most handsome Negro in Harlem by a certain group of whites. He was in great demand by artists who wished to paint him. He had become a much touted romantic figure. In reality he was a fairly intelligent school teacher, quite circumspect in his habits, a rather timid beau, who imagined himself to be bored with life.

Dr. Parkes finally arrived, accompanied by Carl Denny, the artist, and Carl's wife, Annette.[7] Next to arrive was Cedric Williams, a West Indian, whose first book, a collection of short stories with a Caribbean background, in Raymond's opinion, marked him as one of the three Negroes writing who actually had something to say, and also some concrete idea of style. Cedric was followed by Austin Brown, a portrait painter whom Raymond personally despised, a Dr. Manfred Trout, who practiced medicine and also wrote exceptionally good short stories, Glenn Madison, who was a Communist, and a long, lean professorial person, Allen Fenderson, who taught school and had ambitions to become a crusader modeled after W.E.B. Du Bois.[8]

The roster was now complete. There was an hour of small talk and drinking of mild cocktails in order to induce ease and allow the various guests to become acquainted and voluble. Finally, Dr. Parkes ensconced himself in Raymond's favorite chair, where he could get a good view of all in the room, and clucked for order.

Raymond observed the professor closely. Paul's description never seemed more apt.[9] He was a mother hen clucking at her chicks. Small, dapper, with sensitive features, graying hair, a dominating head, and restless hands and feet, he smiled benevolently at his brood. Then, in his best continental manner, which he had acquired during four years at European Universities, he began to speak.

---

[6]Clinton is Countee Cullen; Holloway Cullen's rumored lover Harold Jackman (1901–1961), who also appears as a character in Carl Van Vechten's Harlem Renaissance novel, *Nigger Heaven* (1926).

[7]Dr. Parkes is Alain Locke; Carl Denny painter Aaron Douglas (1899–1979); Cedric Williams Eric D. Walrond (1898–1966), author of the story collection *Tropic Death* (1926) Thurman references here.

[8]Dr. Trout is Rudolph Fisher (1897–1934), author of *The Walls of Jericho* (1928) and *The*

Conjure-Man Dies (1932), often cited as the first African American detective novel.

[9]Paul Arbian is Richard Bruce Nugent (1906–1987), painter and author. Nugent's 1926 story "Smoke, Lilies, and Jade" is considered the first African American text to address openly gay issues. Nugent also resided at 267 West 136th Street and treats much of the same material as *Infants* in his unpublished novel *Gentleman Jigger*.

"You are," he perorated, "the outstanding personalities in a new generation. On you depends the future of your race. You are not, as were your
predecessors, concerned with donning armor, and clashing swords with the
enemy in the public square. You are finding both an escape and a weapon in
beauty, which beauty when created by you will cause the American white
man to reestimate the Negro's value to his civilization, cause him to realize
that the American black man is too valuable, too potential of utilitarian
accomplishment, to be kept downtrodden and segregated.

"Because of your concerted storming up Parnassus, new vistas will be
spread open to the entire race. The Negro in the south will no more know
peonage, Jim Crowism, or loss of the ballot, and the Negro everywhere in
America will know complete freedom and equality.

"But," and here his voice took on a more serious tone, "to accomplish
this, your pursuit of beauty must be vital and lasting. I am somewhat fearful
of the decadent strain which seems to have filtered into most of your work.
Oh, yes, I know you are children of the age and all that, but you must not,
like your paleface contemporaries, wallow in the mire of post-Victorian
license. You have too much at stake. You must have ideals. You should
become . . . well, let me suggest your going back to your racial roots, and cultivating a healthy paganism based on African traditions.

"For the moment that is all I wish to say. I now want you all to give expression to your own ideas. Perhaps we can reach a happy mean for guidance."

He cleared his throat and leaned contentedly back in his chair. No one
said a word. Raymond was full of contradictions, which threatened to ooze
forth despite his efforts to remain silent. But he knew that once the ooze
began there would be no stopping the flood, and he was anxious to hear
what some of the others might have to say.

However, a glance at the rest of the people in the room assured him that
most of them had not the slightest understanding of what had been said,
nor any ideas on the subject, whatsoever. Once more Dr. Parkes clucked for
discussion. No one ventured a word. Raymond could see that Cedric, like
himself, was full of argument, and also like him, did not wish to appear contentious at such an early stage in the discussion. Tony winked at Raymond
when he caught his eye, but the expression on his face was as inscrutable as
ever. Sweetie May giggled behind her handkerchief. Paul amused himself by
sketching the various people in the room. The rest were blank.

"Come, come, now," Dr. Parkes urged somewhat impatiently, "I'm not to
do all the talking. What have you to say, DeWitt?"

All eyes sought out the so-called Negro poet laureate. For a moment he
stirred uncomfortably in his chair, then in a high pitched, nasal voice proceeded to speak.

"I think, Dr. Parkes, that you have said all there is to say. I agree with
you. The young Negro artist must go back to his pagan heritage for inspiration and to the old masters for form."

Raymond could not suppress a snort. For DeWitt's few words had given
him a vivid mental picture of the poet's creative hours—eyes on a page of

Keats, fingers on typewriter, mind frantically conjuring African scenes. And there would of course be a bible nearby.

Paul had ceased being intent on his drawing long enough to hear "pagan heritage," and when DeWitt finished he inquired inelegantly:

"What old black pagan heritage?"

DeWitt gasped, surprised and incredulous.

"Why, from your ancestors."

"Which ones?" Paul pursued dumbly.

"Your African ones, of course." DeWitt's voice was full of disdain.

"What about the rest?"

"What rest?" He was irritated now.

"My German, English, and Indian ancestors," Paul answered willingly. "How can I go back to African ancestors when their blood is so diluted and their country and times so far away? I have no conscious affinity for them at all."

Dr. Parkes intervened: "I think you've missed the point, Paul."

"And I," Raymond was surprised at the suddenness with which he joined in the argument, "think he has hit the nail right on the head. Is there really any reason why *all* Negro artists should consciously and deliberately dig into African soil for inspiration and material unless they actually wish to do so?"

"I don't mean that. I mean you should develop your inherited spirit."

DeWitt beamed. The doctor had expressed his own hazy theory. Raymond was about to speak again, when Paul once more took the bit between his own teeth.

"I ain't got no African spirit."

Sweetie May giggled openly at this, as did Carl Denny's wife, Annette. The rest looked appropriately sober, save for Tony, whose eyes continued to telegraph mischievously to Raymond. Dr. Parkes tried to squelch Paul with a frown. He should have known better.

"I'm not an African," the culprit continued. "I'm an American and a perfect product of the melting pot."

"That's nothing to brag about," Cedric spoke for the first time.

"And I think you're all on the wrong track." All eyes were turned toward this new speaker, Allen Fenderson. "Dr. Du Bois has shown us the way. We must be militant fighters. We must not hide away in ivory towers and prate of beauty. We must fashion cudgels and bludgeons rather than sensitive plants. We must excoriate the white man, and make him grant us justice. We must fight for complete social and political and economic equality."

"What we ought to do," Glenn Madison growled intensely, "is to join hands with the workers of the world and overthrow the present capitalistic regime. We are of the proletariat and must fight our battles allied with them, rather than singly and selfishly."

"All of us?" Raymond inquired quietly.

"All of us who have a trace of manhood and are more interested in the rights of human beings than in gin parties and neurotic capitalists."

"I hope you're squelched," Paul stage whispered to Raymond.

"And how!" Raymond laughed. Several joined in. Dr. Parkes spoke quickly to Fenderson, ignoring the remarks of the Communist.

"But, Fenderson ... this is a new generation and must make use of new weapons. Some of us will continue to fight in the old way, but there are other things to be considered, too. Remember, a beautiful sonnet can be as effectual, nay more effectual, than a rigorous hymn of hate."

"The man who would understand and be moved by a hymn of hate would not bother to read your sonnet, and, even if he did, he would not know what it was all about."

"I don't agree. Your progress must be a boring in from the top, not a battle from the bottom. Convert the higher beings and the lower orders will automatically follow."

"Spoken like a true capitalistic minion," Glenn Madison muttered angrily.

Fenderson prepared to continue his argument, but he was forestalled by Cedric.

"What does it matter," he inquired diffidently, "what any of you do so long as you remain true to yourselves? There is no necessity for this movement becoming standardized. There is ample room for everyone to follow his own individual track. Dr. Parkes wants us all to go back to Africa and resurrect our pagan heritage, become atavistic. In this he is supported by Mr. Clinton. Fenderson here wants us all to be propagandists and yell at the top of our lungs at every conceivable injustice. Madison wants us all to take a cue from Leninism and fight the capitalistic bogey. Well ... why not let each young hopeful choose his own path? Only in that way will anything at all be achieved."

"Which is just what I say," Raymond smiled gratefully at Cedric. "One cannot make movements nor can one plot their course. When the work of a given number of individuals during a given period is looked at in retrospect, then one can identify a movement and evaluate its distinguishing characteristics. Individuality is what we should strive for. Let each seek his own salvation. To me, a wholesale flight back to Africa or a wholesale allegiance to Communism or a wholesale adherence to an antiquated and for the most part ridiculous propagandistic program are all equally futile and unintelligent."

Dr. Parkes gasped and sought for an answer. Cedric forestalled him.

"To talk of an African heritage among American Negroes *is* unintelligent. It is only in the West Indies that you can find direct descendents from African ancestors. Your primitive instincts among all but extreme proletariat have been ironed out. You're standardized Americans."

"Oh, no," Carl Denny interrupted suddenly. "You're wrong. It's in our blood. It's ..." he fumbled for a word, "fixed. Why ..." he stammered again, "remember Cullen's poem, 'Heritage':

> So I lie who find no peace
> Night or day, no slight release
> From the unremittent beat
> Made by cruel padded feet

Walking through my body's street.
Up and down they go, and back,
Treading out a jungle track.

"We're all like that. Negroes are the only people in America not standardized. The feel of the African jungle is in their blood. Its rhythms surge through their bodies. Look how Negroes laugh and dance and sing, all spontaneous and individual."

"Exactly." Dr. Parkes and DeWitt nodded assent.

"I have yet to see an intelligent or middle class American Negro laugh and sing and dance spontaneously. That's an illusion, a pretty sentimental fiction. Moreover your songs and dances are not individual. Your spirituals are mediocre folk songs, ignorantly culled from Methodist hymn books. There are white men who can sing them just as well as Negroes, if not better, should they happen to be untrained vocalists like Robeson, rather than highly trained technicians like Hayes.[10] And as for dancing spontaneously and feeling the rhythms of the jungle ... humph!"

Sweetie May jumped into the breach.

"I can do the Charleston better than any white person."[11]

"I particularly stressed ... intelligent people. The lower orders of any race have more vim and vitality than the illuminated tenth."

Sweetie May leaped to her feet.

"Why, you West Indian ..."

"Sweetie, Sweetie," Dr. Parkes was shocked by her polysyllabic expletive.

Pandemonium reigned. The master of ceremonies could not cope with the situation. Cedric called Sweetie an illiterate southern hussy. She called' him all types of profane West Indian monkey chasers. DeWitt and David were shocked and showed it. The literary doctor, the Communist and Fenderson moved uneasily around the room. Annette and Paul giggled. The two child prodigies from Boston looked on wide-eyed, utterly bewildered and dismayed. Raymond leaned back in his chair, puffing on a cigarette, detached and amused. Austin, the portrait painter, audibly repeated over and over to himself: "Just like niggers ... just like niggers." Carl Denny interposed himself between Cedric and Sweetie May. Dr. Parkes clucked for civilized behavior, which came only when Cedric stalked angrily out of the room.

After the alien had been routed and peace restored, Raymond passed a soothing cocktail. Meanwhile, Austin and Carl had begun arguing about painting. Carl did not possess a facile tongue. He always had difficulty

---

[10]Paul Robeson (1898–1976), the foremost African American concert singer; Roland Hayes (1877–1977), though less known today than Robeson, was equally an revered concert vocalist at the time. Robeson sang bass, Hayes tenor.

[11]The foremost dance of the 1920s, associated mostly with flappers, though it originated from a song ("The Charleston") in the African American Broadway hit *Runnin' Wild* (1923–1924).

formulating in words the multitude of ideas which seethed in his mind. Austin, to quote Raymond, was an illiterate cad. Having examined one of Carl's pictures on Raymond's wall, he had disparaged it. Raymond listened attentively to their argument. He despised Austin mainly because he spent most of his time imploring noted white people to give him a break by posing for a portrait. Having the gift of making himself pitiable, and having a glib tongue when it came to expatiating on the trials and tribulations of being a Negro, *he* found many sitters, all of whom thought they were encouraging a handicapped Negro genius. After one glimpse at the completed portrait, they inevitably changed their minds.

"I tell you," he shouted, "your pictures are distorted and grotesque. Art is art, I say. And art holds a mirror up to nature. No mirror would reflect a man composed of angles. God did not make man that way. Look at Sargent's portraits. He was an artist."

"But he wasn't," Carl expostulated. "We ... we of this age ... we must look at Matisse, Gauguin, Picasso and Renoir for guidance. They get the feel of the age ... They ..."

"Are all crazy and so are you," Austin countered before Carl could proceed.

Paul rushed to Carl's rescue. He quoted Wilde in rebuttal: Nature imitates art, then went on to blaspheme Sargent. Carl, having found some words to express a new idea fermenting in his brain, forgot the argument at hand, went off on a tangent and began telling the dazed Dr. Parkes about the Negroid quality in his drawings. DeWitt yawned and consulted his watch. Raymond mused that he probably resented having missed the prayer meeting which he attended every Thursday night. In another corner of the room the Communist and Fenderson had locked horns over the ultimate solution of the Negro problem. In loud voices each contended for his own particular solution. Karl Marx and Lenin were pitted against Du Bois and his disciples. The writing doctor, bored to death, slipped quietly from the room without announcing his departure or even saying good night. Being more intelligent than most of the others, he had wisely kept silent. Tony and Sweetie May had taken adjoining chairs, and were soon engaged in comparing their versions of original verses to the St. James infirmary, which Tony contended was soon to become as epical as the St. Louis Blues. Annette and Howard began gossiping about various outside personalities. The child prodigies looked from one to the other, silent, perplexed, uncomfortable, not knowing what to do or say. Dr. Parkes visibly recoiled from Carl's incoherent expository barrage, and wilted in his chair, willing but unable to effect a courteous exit. Raymond sauntered around the room, dispensing cocktails, chuckling to himself.

Such was the first and last salon.

1932

Blues Lyrics

ALTHOUGH THE WORD "BLUES," REFERRING TO ANXIETY OR SADNESS, DATES FROM around the sixteenth century, the music called the blues is more recent. The blues initially emerged in the 1890s, when the first generation of African Americans born after emancipation came into their majority subjected to the post-Reconstruction brand of freedom. While slaves were brutalized within a system in which they often had well-defined roles that sought to prevent much dignity or responsibility, the post-Reconstruction African American was brutalized by a more ambiguous and uncertain, but still inferior, status. The theoretical freedom created the illusion of the possibility of social and economic success, but the lack of education and economic independence, and continuing racial discrimination, was a prescription not only for failure, but also for haunting self-doubt. Lacking an older generation with this same experience to consult for advice, the new generation responded by expressing their reactions in a variety of new forms, including the blues, that were recognizably rooted in the African American tradition. Although critics may disagree on the particulars of the African influence on the blues, most agree that there are certain African elements in the blues as well as the work songs and field hollers from which the blues seem to have developed. The creations of people often unable to read and write, the texts of this tradition were not written down but passed on orally. From the common hopes, fears, and language of the people, the blues singers created songs that were, in turn, passed back to the audience in a form that was both traditional and individually creative.

The folk blues songs heard around the turn of the century, by people like Howard W. Odum and W. C. Handy, mirrored the variety of stanzas as employed in the blues tradition. The text of a blues stanza might consist of one "line" (sometimes rendered as two lines on the page, divided where a singer might pause in performance) repeated exactly or approximately twice (AA) or more; one line repeated twice or three times combined with a rhyming line to complete the thought expressed in the first line (AAB or AAAB); one line sung once followed by a rhyming line sung twice (ABB); two different lines followed by a refrain (AB refrain); or a variety of other patterns. The musical performances, executed with a fluid rather than a rigid sense of measures, tended toward eight-, twelve-, or sixteen-bar stanzas most often, and the songsters or musicians who performed these blues provided the tradition from which the first generation of recorded blues singers in the 1920s drew. Inevitably, phonograph recordings influenced the nature of the blues, helping establish the AAB stanza as the predominant form, changing the often traditional, nonthematic or associative texts into more original, thematic texts, and removing the song from its original performance context in the community. The first blues recordings by African Americans were the so-called vaudeville blues of the "Jazz Age" written by people like Handy who drew on both their knowledge of the oral tradition and on professional musical training that created a more sophisticated hybrid, sometimes straining for sexual innuendo, or creating the role of the rebellious "hot mama," but reaching their pinnacle in folk blues-based performances by such greats as Bessie Smith and Ma Rainey.

There is also disagreement about the nature of the blues performer and what the blues represent. While some see the blues as autobiographical laments, others have seen them as a recounting of "species experience." In reality they can be either or both. The singers may be describing what has or might have happened to someone like them, or may be conforming the lyrics to the idea of a mythological singer created over the years. Although the blues have been rejected by many middle-class blacks as old-fashioned and self-pitying, or as signs of resignation and defeat, others have seen in them a spirit of hope, a creativity, an unwillingness to capitulate to white middle-class values, and even a defiance and revolutionary resistance.

Blues performances are intended for entertainment and deal primarily with love relationships between men and women. The blues have been seen as a central expression of African American spirit, providing structures, rhythms, images, themes, and characters for literary artists like Langston Hughes, Sterling A. Brown, Zora Neale Hurston, Allen Ginsberg, John Berryman, Ralph Ellison, Albert Murray, Alice Walker, Etheridge Knight, and Gayl Jones. And the blues are still being created and performed today.

Steven C. Tracy
University of Massachusetts Amherst

PRIMARY WORKS

Paul Oliver, ed., *Early Blues Songbook*; Eric Sackheim, ed., *The Blues Line,* 1975; Jeff Titon, ed., *Downhome Blues Lyrics,* 1981; Michael Taft, *Blues Lyric Poetry: An Anthology,* 1983; Michael Taft, *Blues Lyric Poetry: A Concordance,* 1984; W.C. Handy, *Blues: An Anthology,* 1985; R. R. MacLeod, ed., *Yazoo 1–20* and *Yazoo 21–83,* 1988; *Document Blues–1,* 1993; *Document Blues–2* and *Document Blues–3,* 1995.

LANGSTON HUGHES
1902–1967

The Weary Blues

Droning a drowsy syncopated tune,
Rocking back and forth to a mellow croon,
    I heard a Negro play.
Down on Lenox Avenue the other night
By the pale dull pallor of an old gas light   5
    He did a lazy sway . . .
    He did a lazy sway . . .
To the tune o' those Weary Blues.
With his ebony hands on each ivory key
He made that poor piano moan with melody.   10
    O Blues!
Swaying to and fro on his rickety stool
He played that sad raggy tune like a musical fool.
    Sweet Blues!
Coming from a black man's soul.   15
    O Blues!
In a deep song voice with a melancholy tone
I heard that Negro sing, that old piano moan—
    "Ain't got nobody in all this world,
    Ain't got nobody but ma self.   20
    I's gwine to quit ma frownin'
    And put ma troubles on the shelf."
Thump, thump, thump, went his foot on the floor.
He played a few chords then he sang some more—
    "I got the Weary Blues   25
    And I can't be satisfied.
    Got the Weary Blues
    And can't be satisfied—
    I ain't happy no mo'
    And I wish that I had died."   30
And far into the night he crooned that tune.
    The stars went out and so did the moon.
    The singer stopped playing and went to bed
    While the Weary Blues echoed through his head.
    He slept like a rock or a man that's dead.   35

                                      1925

Blues Lyrics

Well, the blues come to Texas loping like a mule. (twice)
You take a high brown woman—man, she's hard to fool.

You can't ever tell what a woman's got on her mind.
Yes, you can't tell what a woman's got on her mind.
You might think she's crazy about you, she's leaving you all the
        time.

She ain't so good looking and her teeth don't shine like pearls,
She ain't so good looking, teeth don't shine like pearls,
But that nice disposition carry that woman all through the world.

I'm going to the river, gonna take my rocker chair.
Well, I'm going to the river, carry my rocker chair.
Gonna ask that transfer boat, "Have the worried blues reached
        here?"

I think I heard my good gal calling my name.
Hey, hey, good gal calling my name.
She don't call so loud, but she call so nice and plain.

I was raised in Texas, schooled in Tennessee. (twice)
Now, sugar, you can't make no fatmouth out of me.

Can't a woman act funny, quit you for another man. (twice)
She ain't gonna look at you straight, but she's always raising sand.

—Blind Lemon Jefferson

John Henry said to his captain, "A man ain't nothing but a man.
And before I let your steam drill beat me down
Die with a hammer in my hand." (twice)

When John Henry was a little boy he sit down on his father's
        knee,
He pointed his hand at a piece of steel,
Said, "That gonna be the death of me, Lord, Lord, Lord!
That gonna be the death of me."

John Henry hammered in the mountain 'til the head of his
        hammer catched afire.
Cryin' "Pick 'em up boys and let 'em down again,
One cool drink of water 'fore I die, die,
One cool drink of water 'fore I die."

—Traditional

Now she's the meanest woman that I've ever seen,
And when I asked for water give me gasoline.
Now, asked her for water, give me gasoline.
Lord, asked for water, give me gasoline.

—Ishmon Bracey

I did more for you than you understand.
You can tell by the bullet holes, mama, now, here in my hand.
Baby, now, you got to reap, baby,
Just what, what you sow.

—Peetie Wheatstraw

I need plenty grease in my frying pan 'cause I don't want my meat
    to burn.
You know I asked you first to get me some lard,
But it seems that you cannot learn.
You know I use plenty grease everyday,
But I ain't did no frying while you was away.
I need plenty grease in my frying pan 'cause I don't want my meat
    to burn.

—Margaret Carter

I've got a disposition and a way of my own.
When my man starts kicking I let him find another home.
I get full of good liquor, walk the streets all night,
Go home and put my man out if he don't act right.
Wild women don't worry,
Wild women don't have the blues.

—Ida Cox

I got all cut to pieces, aah aah, about a man I love. (twice)
I'm gonna get that a-woman just as sure as the sky's above.

Now, when my man left me I was half dead lying in my door.
When my man left me, aah, half dead lying in my door.
I was a-suffering and groaning, "Oh daddy, please don't go."

—Bessie Tucker

When I picked you up, baby, you was beat just like a slave.
    (twice)
You had one foot on a banana peeling, ooh well well, and the
    other foot in the grave.

—Peetie Wheatstraw

Mama get your hatchet, kill the fly on your baby's head. (twice)
Mama get your hatchet and run here to my bed.

—Furry Lewis

Crying, sun gonna shine in my back door some day.
(Now don't you hear me talking pretty mama?) Lord,
Sun gonna shine in my back door some day.
And the wind gonna change, gonna blow my blues away.

—*Tommy Johnson*

I've got to keep moving, I've got to keep moving.
Blues falling down like hail, Blues falling down like hail,
Blues falling down like hail, Blues falling down like hail.
And the day keeps on 'minding me there's a hellhound on my
    trail.
Hellhound on my trail, Hellhound on my trail.

—*Robert Johnson*

Black cat on my doorstep, black cat on my window sill. (twice)
If some black cat don't cross me, some other black cat will.

—*Ma Rainey*

I left my babe in Mississippi picking cotton down on her knees.
    (twice)
She says, "If you get to Chicago all right, please write me a letter
    if you please."

—*Tommy McClennan*

Poor people is like prisoners, but they just ain't got on a ball and
    chain. (twice)
But the way they are faring I swear it's all the same.

—*Walter Davis*

Early one morning when I was on my way home. (twice)
A policeman walked up and caught me by my arm.

I told him my name, and he wrote it down. (twice)
He said, "Come with me, this is your last night running
    'round."

I took him at his word and didn't have nothing to
    say. (twice)
I thought they would have my trial the very next day.

But they put me in jail, wouldn't give me no bond.
They put me in jail, wouldn't give me no bond.
It made me think about my peoples that's dead and gone.

On that third morning just about half past three. (twice)
They beat me and kicked me and put me through the third
    degree.

They put me in the cellar, got my clothes and shoes. (twice)
That's why I'm screaming, I got the third degree blues.

—*Blind Blake*

Got the backwoods blues but I don't want to go back home.
Got the blues so bad for the place that I come from.
Gonna see my folks but it's way too far,
You ride in a dusty old Jim Crow car,
Got the backwoods blues but I don't want to go back home . . .

Gonna stay right here right where I'm at,
Where there ain't no grinnin and snatchin off my hat,
Got the backwoods blues but I don't want to go back home . . .

Yes I'm from down there and I'm proud to say,
And from down there I'm gonna stay,
Got the backwoods blues but I don't want to go back home.

—*Rosa Henderson*

I walked down the track and the stars refused to shine,
Looked like every minute I was goin to lose my mind.
Now my knees was weak, my footsteps was all I heard,
Looked like every minute I was steppin in another world.

—*Charlie McCoy*

I don't mind workin, captain, from sun to sun,
I don't mind workin, captain, from sun to sun,
But I want my money, captain, when pay day comes.

—*Tom Dickson*

Comin a time B.D. womens ain't gonna need no men.
Comin a time B.D. womens ain't going to need no men.
Oh the way they treat us is a lowdown and dirty sin.

B.D. women, you sure can't understand,
B.D. women, you sure can't understand,
They got a head like a switch engine and they walk just like a natural
    man.

B.D. women, they all done learned their trade.
B.D. women, they all done learned their trade.
They can lay their jive just like a natural man.

–*Lucille Bogan*

E Pluribus Unum: Ideology, Patriotism, and Politesse

THIS IN FOCUS ILLUSTRATES THE EXTREMES OF CONSENSUS BUILDING NECESSARY TO speak of *an* American people. Both the actual language of the Sedition Act and Mitchell Palmer's defense of it reveal the controls necessary to stifle dissent to create the appearance of a democratic majority. Excerpts from the rampant racist discourse of the day—whether from the Ku Klux Klan or social scientist Lothrop Stoddard—likewise suggest the role spurious theories of racial superiority played in this effort by demonstrating how racism adapted the rhetoric of nationalism. Eugene V. Debs "Sound Socialist Tactics," meanwhile, reveals the aims by which the socialist movement of the period sought to redress the stifling of dissent by defining acceptable tactics of resistance.

With specific ethnic groups themselves, debates about appropriate degrees of assimilation were likewise front and center. The *Tejana* Jovita Idar provides here the more moderate view, manifesting no sense of contradiction in her argument that while *Tejano* children must learn English in order to function as full citizens of the United States, they must also continue to learn Spanish to cultivate their feelings of Mexican patriotism and love for the culture of their ancestors. In a much more radical vein, Soledad Flores de Peña responds to increasing violence against Mexicans in the United States by asserting a militaristic view of women's role in fighting Anglo-American incursions. Drawing directly from conceptions of "Spartan Motherhood" and envisioning Mexican communities in the United States as part of Mexico, Peña asserts that women must happily sacrifice their sons in defense of the fatherland and remain fiercely defiant in the face of "foreign invasion."

Peña's militaristic feminism provides an appropriate if unexpected segue to Margaret Sanger, perhaps the most divisive figure in debates over the role of women and the cultural regulation of femininity. Sanger's support of birth control encourages freedom from biological determinism but also makes irrefutable economic sense.

Finally, Franklin Delano Roosevelt's "The Four Freedoms" demonstrates how the national instabilities introduced by the first world war could be resolved and unified by finding common purpose in fighting the second. We end this section with the text of Roosevelt's Executive Order 9006 and the military orders implementing the forced relocation of Japanese Americans to internment camps to illustrate how essential suppression was to constructing that "common purpose."

Kirk Curnutt
Troy University–Montgomery

Yolanda Padilla
University of Pennsylvania

U.S. CONGRESS

from **Sedition Act (1918–1921)**

Section 3

Whoever, when the United States is at war, shall willfully make or convey false reports or false statements with intent to interfere with the operation or success of the military or naval forces of the United States, or to promote the success of its enemies, or shall willfully make or convey false reports or false statements, or say or do anything except by way of bona fide and not disloyal advice to an investor or investors, with intent to obstruct the sale by the United States of bonds or other securities of the United States or the making of loans by or to the United States, and whoever when the United States is at war, shall willfully cause or attempt to cause, or incite or attempt to incite, insubordination, disloyalty, mutiny, or refusal of duty, in the military or naval forces of the United States, or shall willfully obstruct or attempt to obstruct the recruiting or enlistment services of the United States, and whoever, when the United States is at war, shall willfully utter, print, write or publish any disloyal, profane, scurrilous, or abusive language about the form of government of the United States or the Constitution of the United States, or the military or naval forces of the United States, or the flag of the United States, or the uniform of the Army or Navy of the United States into contempt, scorn, contumely, or disrepute, or shall willfully utter, print, write, or publish any language intended to incite, provoke, or encourage resistance to the United States, or to promote the cause of its enemies, or shall willfully display the flag of any foreign enemy, or shall willfully by utterance, writing, printing, publication, or language spoken, urge, incite, or advocate any curtailment of production in this country of any thing or things, product or products, necessary or essential to the prosecution of the war in which the United States may be engaged, with intent by such curtailment to cripple or hinder the United States in the prosecution of war, and whoever shall willfully advocate, teach, defend, or suggest the doing of any of the acts or things in this section enumerated, and whoever shall by word or act support or favor the cause of any country with which the United States is at war or by word or act oppose the cause of the United States therein, shall be punished by a fine of not more than $10,000 or the imprisonment for not more than twenty years, or both: Provided, That any employee or official of the United States Government who commits any disloyal act or utters any unpatriotic or disloyal language, or who, in an abusive and violent manner criticizes the Army or Navy or the flag of the United States shall be at once dismissed from the service ...

Section 4

When the United States is at war, the Postmaster General may, upon evidence satisfactory to him that any person or concern is using the mails in violation of any of the provisions of this Act, instruct the postmaster at any post office at which mail is received addressed to such person or concern to return to the postmaster at the office at which they were originally mailed all letters or other matter so addressed, with the words "Mail to this address undeliverable under Espionage Act" plainly written or stamped upon the outside thereof, and all such letters or other matter so returned to such postmasters shall be by them returned to the senders thereof under such regulations as the Postmaster General may prescribe.

1918–1921

■   A. MITCHELL PALMER   ■
1872–1936

from **The Case against the "Reds"**[1]

In this brief review of the work which the Department of Justice has undertaken, to tear out the radical seeds that have entangled American ideas in their poisonous theories, I desire not merely to explain what the real menace of communism is, but also to tell how we have been compelled to clean up the country almost unaided by any virile legislation. Though I have not been embarrassed by political opposition, I have been materially delayed because the present sweeping processes of arrests and deportation of seditious aliens should have been vigorously pushed by Congress last spring. The failure of this is a matter of record in the Congressional files.

The anxiety of that period in our responsibility when Congress, ignoring the seriousness of these vast organizations that were plotting to overthrow the Government, failed to act, has passed. The time came when it was obviously hopeless to expect the hearty cooperation of Congress in the only way to stamp out these seditious societies in their open defiance of law by various forms of propaganda.

Like a prairie-fire, the blaze of revolution was sweeping over every American institution of law and order a year ago. It was eating its way into the homes of the American workmen, its sharp tongues of revolutionary heat

---

[1]A. Mitchell Palmer, "The Case against the 'Reds,'" *Forum* 63 (1920): 173–85.

were licking the altars of the churches, leaping into the belfry of the school bell, crawling into the sacred corners of American homes, seeking to replace marriage vows with libertine laws, burning up the foundations of society.

Robbery, not war, is the ideal of communism. This has been demonstrated in Russia, Germany, and in America. As a foe, the anarchist is fearless of his own life, for his creed is a fanaticism that admits no respect of any other creed. Obviously it is the creed of any criminal mind, which reasons always from motives impossible to clean thought. Crime is the degenerate factor in society.

Upon these two basic certainties, first that the "Reds" were criminal aliens and secondly that the American Government must prevent crime, it was decided that there could be no nice distinctions drawn between the theoretical ideals of the radicals and their actual violations of our national laws. An assassin may have brilliant intellectuality, he may be able to excuse his murder or robbery with fine oratory, but any theory which excuses crime is not wanted in America. This is no place for the criminal to flourish, nor will he do so so long as the rights of common citizenship can be exerted to prevent him.

Our Government in Jeopardy

It has always been plain to me that when American citizens unite upon any national issue they are generally right, but it is sometimes difficult to make the issue clear to them. If the Department of Justice could succeed in attracting the attention of our optimistic citizens to the issue of internal revolution in this country, we felt sure there would be no revolution. The Government was in jeopardy; our private information of what was being done by the organization known as the Communist Party of America, with headquarters in Chicago, of what was being done by the Communist Internationale under their manifesto planned at Moscow last March by Trotzky, Lenin and others addressed "To the Proletariats of All Countries," of what strides the Communist Labor Party was making, removed all doubt.[2] In this conclusion we did not ignore the definite standards of personal liberty, of free speech, which is the very temperament and heart of the people. The evidence was examined with the utmost care, with a personal leaning toward freedom of thought and word on all questions.

The whole mass of evidence, accumulated from all parts of the country, was scrupulously scanned, not merely for the written or spoken differences of viewpoint as to the Government of the United States, but, in spite of these things, to see if the hostile declarations might not be sincere in their

[2]Leon Trotsky was a Ukrainian-born Marxist (1879– 1940) who was a chief lieutenant in the Bolshevik Revolution that brought Lenin to power in 1917. Trotsky went into exile in 1929 after disagreeing with the Stalinists who controlled the Union of Soviet Socialist Republics after Lenin's death in 1923. He was assassinated by a Soviet agent in Mexico.

announced motive to improve our social order. There was no hope of such a thing.

By stealing, murder and lies, Bolshevism has looted Russia not only of its material strength but of its moral force. A small clique of outcasts from the East Side of New York has attempted this, with what success we all know. Because a disreputable alien (Leon Bronstein, the man who now calls himself Trotzky) can inaugurate a reign of terror from his throne room in the Kremlin, because this lowest of all types known to New York can sleep in the Czar's bed, while hundreds of thousands in Russia are without food or shelter, should Americans be swayed by such doctrines?

Such a question, it would seem, should receive but one answer from America.

My information showed that communism in this country was an organization of thousands of aliens who were direct allies of Trotzky. Aliens of the same misshapen caste of mind and indecencies of character, and it showed that they were making the same glittering promises of lawlessness, of criminal autocracy to Americans, that they had made to the Russian peasants. How the Department of Justice discovered upwards of 60,000 of these organized agitators of the Trotzky doctrine in the United States is the confidential information upon which the Government is now sweeping the nation clean of such alien filth. . . .

Will Deportation Check Bolshevism?

Behind, and underneath, my own determination to drive from our midst the agents of Bolshevism with increasing vigor and with greater speed, until there are no more of them left among us, so long as I have the responsible duty of that task, I have discovered the hysterical methods of these revolutionary humans with increasing amazement and suspicion. In the confused information that sometimes reaches the people they are compelled to ask questions which involve the reasons for my acts against the "Reds." I have been asked, for instance, to what extent deportation will check radicalism in this country. Why not ask what will become of the United States Government if these alien radicals are permitted to carry out the principles of the Communist Party as embodied in its so-called laws, aims and regulations?

There wouldn't be any such thing left. In place of the United States Government we should have the horror and terrorism of Bolsheviki tyranny such as is destroying Russia now. Every scrap of radical literature demands the overthrow of our existing government. All of it demands obedience to the instincts of criminal minds, that is, to the lower appetites, material and moral. The whole purpose of communism appears to be a mass formation of the criminals of the world to overthrow the decencies of private life, to usurp property that they have not earned, to disrupt the present order of life regardless of health, sex or religious rights. By a literature that promises the wildest dreams of such low aspirations, that can occur to only the criminal minds, communism distorts our social law. . . .

It has been inferred by the "Reds" that the United States Government, by arresting and deporting them, is returning to the autocracy of Czardom, adopting the system that created the severity of Siberian banishment. My reply to such charges is that in our determination to maintain our government we are treating our alien enemies with extreme consideration. To deny them the privilege of remaining in a country which they have openly deplored as an unenlightened community, unfit for those who prefer the privileges of Bolshevism, should be no hardship. It strikes me as an odd form of reasoning that these Russian Bolsheviks who extol the Bolshevik rule should be so unwilling to return to Russia. The nationality of most of the alien "Reds" is Russian and German. There is almost no other nationality represented among them.

It has been impossible in so short a space to review the entire menace of the internal revolution in this country as I know it, but this may serve to arouse the American citizen to its reality, its danger, and the great need of united effort to stamp it out, under our feet, if needs be. It is being done. The Department of Justice will pursue the attack of these "Reds" upon the Government of the United States with vigilance, and no alien, advocating the overthrow of existing law and order in this country, shall escape arrest and prompt deportation.

It is my belief that while they have stirred discontent in our midst, while they have caused irritating strikes, and while they have infected our social ideas with the disease of their own minds and their unclean morals we can get rid of them! and not until we have done so shall we have removed the menace of Bolshevism for good.

1920

H. H. BOWER

UNKNOWN DATES

Why I Am a Klansman

1. Because this is my Country, my **Native** Country, and **It's** flag is **my** Flag , unto **death.**
2. Because this is **America,** and **I** am an **American.**
3. Because **Protestant Anglo-Saxon blood** is the **Heart** and **Soul** of the **Foundation** of this **Republic.**
4. Because our Fore-Fathers were baptised in their own blood for the Constitutional Rights and privileges we now enjoy.
5. Because they **Nationalized,** and **Immortalized America.**
6. Because the Separation of Church and State, and free Public Schools, is a part of the Constitution of the United States.

7. Because the Roman Catholic Church is now, and has been, Insidously working (in various ways, and especially through our **Public Schools**) to make **America Catholic.**

8. Because the **Ku Klax Kian** is now using, and will continue to use Its mighty influence to forestall any and every such move by or for the **Catholic Church,** or any **Person** or **Power** from whatever source, alien or otherwise, who seek to 1interfere with, or encroach upon our **Inalienable, Constitutional Rights** and **privileges, subvert** or **Destroy our Government.**

9. Because the **Ku Klax Klan** is **100 per cent** for **White Supremacy, Restricted Immigration, Protestantism,** and **Americanism.**

10. Because the **Ku Klax Klan** stands **flat footed for Good Citizenship, Obedience to Law,** and **Law Enforcement.**

11. Because the **Ku Klax Klan** teaches **Physical, Social, Moral, Vocational, Patriotic, Domestic,** and **Imperial Klanishness.**

12. Because the **Ku Klax Klan** is the **Guardian** of our **Public Schools,** and **America's** best **Friend.**

13. Because the **Ku Klax Klan** has offered and is now teaching the only just and practical Solution of the Race question. It puts **Race Pride** and **Race Distinction First,** where it **belongs.**

14. Because our **Illustrious Imperial Emperor** and **Imperial Wizzard** are the men of the hour, **in and for America.**

And finally. Because of my unerring **belief in,** and my **Duty** and **Fidelity for,** the things here-in stated, is why

I AM A KLANSMAN

1923

LOTHROP STODDARD
1883–1950

from The Rising Tide of Colored against White World-Supremacy[1]

The man who, on a quiet spring evening of the year 1914, opened his atlas to a political map of the world and pored over its many-tinted patterns probably got one fundamental impression: the overwhelming preponderance of the white race in the ordering world's affairs. Judged by accepted canons of statecraft, the white man towered the indisputable master of the planet. Forth from Europe's teeming mother-hive the imperious Sons of Japhet had swarmed for centuries to plant their laws, their customs, and their

---

[1]Lothrop Stoddard, *The Rising Tide of Colored against White World-Conspiracy* (New York: Scribners, 1920): 3.

battle-flags at the uttermost ends of the earth.[2] Two whole continents, North America and Australia, had been made virtually as white in blood as the European motherland; two other continents, South America and Africa, had been extensively colonized by white stocks; while even huge Asia had seen its empty northern march, Siberia, pre-empted for the white man's abode. Even where white populations had not locked themselves to the soil few regions of the earth had escaped the white man's imperial sway, and vast areas inhabited by uncounted myriads of dusky folk obeyed the white man's will.

Beside the enormous area of white settlement or control, the regions under non-white governance bulked small indeed. In eastern Asia, China, Japan, and Siam; in western Asia, Turkey, Afghanistan, and Persia; in Africa, Abyssinia, and Liberia; and in America the minute state of Haiti; such was the brief list of lands under non-white rule. In other words, of the 53,000,000 square miles which (excluding the polar regions) constitute the land area of the globe, only 6,000,000 square miles had non-white governments, and nearly two-thirds of this relatively modest remainder was represented by China and its dependencies.

Since 1914 the world has been convulsed by the most terrible war in recorded history. This war was primarily a struggle between the white peoples, who have borne the brunt of the conflict and have suffered most of the losses. Nevertheless, one of the war's results has been a further whittling down of the areas standing outside white political control. Turkey is to-day practically an Anglo-French condominium, Persia is virtually a protectorate of the British Empire, while the United States has thrown over the endemic anarchy of Haiti the aegis of the *Pax Americana*. Study of the political map might thus apparently lead one to conclude that white world-predominance is immutable, since the war's ordeal has still further broadened the territorial basis of its authority....

[Yet] instead of a world politically nine-tenths white, we see a world of which only four-tenths at the most can be considered predominantly white in blood, the rest of the world being inhabited mainly by the other primary races of mankind—yellows, brown, blacks, and reds. Speaking by continents, Europe, North America to the Rio Grande, the southern portion of South America, the Siberian part of Asia, and Australasia constitute the real white world; while the bulk of Asia, virtually the whole of Africa, and most of Central and South America form the world of color. The respective areas of these two racially contrasted worlds are 22,000,000 square miles for the whites and 31,000,000 square miles for the colored races. Furthermore it must be remembered that fully one-third of the white area (notably Australasia and Siberia) is very thinly inhabited and is thus held by a very slender racial tenure—the only tenure which counts in the long run....

There can be no doubt that at present the colored races are increasing very much faster than the white. Treating the primary race-stocks as units,

[2]The youngest son of Noah, Japhet was said to have descendants in many Central European countries.

it would appear that whites tend to double in eighty years, yellow and browns in sixty years, blacks in forty years. The whites are thus the slowest breeders, and they will undoubtedly become slower still, since section after section of the white race is revealing that lowered birthrate which in Frances has reached the extreme of a stationary population.....

Now what must be the inevitable result of all this? It can mean only one thing: a tremendous and steadily augmenting outward thrust of surplus colored men from overcrowded colored homelands. Remember that these homelands are already populated up to the available limits of subsistence. Of course present limits in many cases can be pushed back by better living conditions, improved agriculture, and the ruse of modern machine industry such as is already under way in Japan. Nevertheless, in view of the tremendous population increases which must occur, these can only be palliatives. Where, then, should the congested color world tend to pour its accumulating human surplus, inexorably condemned to emigrate or starve? The answer is: into those emptier regions of the earth under white political control. But many of these relatively empty lands have been definitely set aside by the white man as his own special heritage. The upshot is that the rising flood of color finds itself walled in by white dikes debarring it from many a promised land which it would fain deluge with its dusky waves.

Thus the colored world, long restive under white political domination, is being welded by the most fundamental of instincts, the instinct of self-preservation, into a common solidarity of feeling against the dominant white man, and in the fire of a common purpose internecine differences tend, for the time at least, to be burned away. Before the supreme fact of white political world-domination, antipathies within the colored world must inevitably recede into the background ... [superseded by] the imperious urge of the colored world toward racial expansion.

1920

EUGENE V. DEBS
1855–1926

from **Sound Socialist Tactics**[1]

Socialists are practically all agreed as to the fundamental principles of their movement. But as to tactics there is wide variance among them. The matter of sound tactics, equally with the matter of sound principles, is of supreme

[1]Eugene V. Debs, "Sound Socialist Tactics" (1912), from Jean Y. Tussey, ed., *Eugene V. Debs Speaks* (New York: Pathfinder Press, 1970).

importance. The disagreements and dissensions among Socialists relate almost wholly to tactics. The party splits which have occurred in the past have been due to same cause, and if the party should ever divide again, which it is to be hoped it will not, it will be on the rock of tactics....

There has recently been some rather spirited discussion about a paragraph which appears in the pamphlet on "Industrial Socialism," by William D. Haywood and Frank Bohn. The paragraph follows:

When the worker, either through experience or study of Socialism, comes to know the truth, he acts accordingly. He retains absolutely no respect for the property "rights" of the property-takers. He will use any weapon which will win his fight. *He knows that the present laws of property are made by and for capitalists.* Therefore he does not hesitate to break them.

The sentences which I have italicized provoked the controversy.

We have a matter of tactics upon which a number of comrades of ability and prominence have sharply disagreed. For my own part I believe the paragraph to be entirely sound.

Certainly all Socialists, knowing how and to what end capitalist property "rights" are established, must hold such "rights" in contempt. In The *Manifesto* Marx says: "The Communist (Socialist) revolution is the most radical rupture with traditional property relations; no wonder that its development involves the most radical rupture with traditional ideas."

As a revolutionist I can have no respect for capitalist property laws, nor the least scruple about violating them. I hold all such laws to have been enacted through chicanery, fraud and corruption, with the sole end in view of dispossessing, robbing and enslaving the working class. But this does not imply that I propose making an individual lawbreaker of myself and butting my head against the stone wall of existing property laws. That might be called force, but it would not be that. It would be mere weakness and folly.

If I had the force to overthrow these despotic laws I would use it without an instant's hesitation or delay, but I haven't got it, and so I am law-abiding under protest—not from scruple—and bide my time.

Here let me say that for the same reason I am opposed to sabotage and to "direct action." I have not a bit of use for the "propaganda of the deed." These are the tactics of anarchist individuals and not of socialist collectivists. They were developed by and belong exclusively to our anarchist friends and accord perfectly with their philosophy. These and similar measures are reactionary, not revolutionary, and they invariably have a demoralizing effect upon those who practice them. If I believed in the doctrine of violence and destruction as party policy; if I regarded the class struggle as guerrilla warfare, I would join the anarchists and practice as well as preach such tactics.

It is not because these tactics involve the use of force that I am opposed to them, but because they do not. The physical forcist is the victim of his own boomerang. The blow he strikes reacts upon himself and his followers. The force that implies power is utterly lacking, and it can never be developed by such tactics.

The foolish and misguided, zealots and fanatics, are quick to applaud and employ such tactics, and the result is usually hurtful to themselves and to the cause they seek to advance. . . .

Sound tactics are constructive, not destructive. The collective reason of the workers repels the idea of individual violence where they are free to assert themselves by lawful and peaceable means.

The American workers are law-abiding and no amount of sneering or derision will alter that fact. Direct action will never appeal to any considerable number of them while they have the ballot and the right of industrial and political organization.

1912

JOVITA IDAR
(1885–1942)

For Our Race: Preservation of Nationalism[1]

In our previous article we stated that "most regrettably, we have seen Mexican teachers teaching students of their race English without taking into consideration, at all, their mother tongue." With that we did not intend to imply—not in the least—that the language of the land they inhabit should not be taught, as it is the medium available for direct contact with their neighbors, and that which will allow them to ensure that their rights are respected. What we wanted to suggest, simply, is that the national language should not be ignored, because it is the stamp that characterizes races and nations. Nations disappear and races sink when they forget their national language. For that reason, nations, like the Aztecs, no longer exist. Rome, through her language, profoundly influenced the people she had conquered. If the Jews today do not comprise a nation, it is because each one speaks the language of the land they inhabit.

We are not saying that English should not be taught to Mexican Texan children, but, whether appropriate or not, we are saying you should not forget to teach them Spanish. In the same way that arithmetic and grammar are useful to them, English is useful to those people who live among English speakers.

We are all creatures of our environment: we love things that we have seen since our infancy, and we believe in that which has permeated our souls since the first years of our lives. Therefore, if in the American school our children attend they teach Washington's biography and not Hidalgo's,

[1]Translated by Tonya E. Wolford.

and instead of the glorious accomplishments of Juárez they refer to the exploits of Lincoln, no matter how noble and fair these men were, that child will not know the glories of his homeland. He will not love his homeland, and will even view his parents' compatriots with indifference.

There was not one Mexican Texan who, with the best intentions in the world, did not adorn his jacket with a picture of the heroic Juarez on September 16, 1910. This uplifts any person who loves his race. Good and honorable Mexicans, who are so patriotic and worthy, why do you ignore the noble actions of those who have sacrificed their lives to give us freedom?

It is true that we are in the country of business, and that time is money, but while history and geography are not indispensable for earning a living, they are good for the preservation of patriotism.

Mexican-Texan youngsters need instruction to gain the esteem and sympathy of those around them; they need it to obtain a livelihood with greater ease and to be more influential.

We Should Work[1]

The modern woman, cognizant of and recognizing the need to contribute her quota to aid in the development of erudition among the masses, prepares herself valiantly and invades every field of industry, at all levels, without fear and without laziness. She abandons idleness and inactivity, since in the present age, so full of life opportunities and replete with energy and hope, there is no room for the socially indolent.

Inactivity and laziness are seen as contemptible today and, as such, are undone by all of those things that are considered factors in the development and progress of the people.

The modern woman does not spend her days lounging in a comfortable chair. This, not even the rich woman does, since those flattered by fortune also dedicate themselves to the practice of generosity or other philanthropic work, or to the organization of charitable or recreational clubs. What is desirable is to do something useful for yourself or for your fellow man.

The working-class woman, recognizing her rights, raises her head with pride and confronts the struggle; her period of degradation has passed. She is no longer the slave sold for a few coins, no longer the servant. She is an equal to man, his companion; he is her natural protector and not her master and lord.

Much has dealt with and been written about the feminist movement, but despite the opposition, already in California women can cast their vote as jury and occupy public office.

Those fastidious, superficial and unworthy souls make many mistakes in criticizing this type of woman who, brushing aside social convention, dedicates her energies to work for something beneficial and charitable; these critics do not realize the moral influence that this exerts, because a person dedicated to certain jobs or tasks does not have time to be bothered with

[1]Translated by Tonya E. Wolford.

futile and prejudicial things. She does more, the steadfast working woman, behind a counter and seated in front of her sewing machine or already an office worker, than the young lady with time to spare who occupies herself with making daily social calls or in going through, one by one, every store, which is a life filled with gossip and vulgar stories.

The single woman, decent and hardworking, does not demand a living at the expense of the head of her family, whether or not it be a father, brother or relative. No. A healthy woman, valiant and strong, dedicates her energy and her intelligence to helping her family, or at least, to providing for her own sustenance.

Just as decent and hardworking men regard unemployed and vagrant men with disdain, so too do working women disparage good-for-nothing and unemployed women.

1911

SOLEDAD PEÑA
DATES UNKNOWN

Speech[1]

Mr. President and Representatives
Respectable/esteemed/dear public:

Following my heart's desires, I have taken the opportunity to occupy this podium in order to share my humble opinion with respect to the work that this organization has proposed to carry out and to share a warm, sincere farewell to such dignified delegates as the active efforts of the Mexicanist Congress comes to a close.

The time has come to return to our homes. You leave us. Our ears hear the clattering of the train that shall be conducting, its whistle announcing that you are abandoning/leaving us; yet we will not remain alone. The seed you have planted has not fallen on sterile ground, the idea you have cultivated in our minds is redemptive and so we no longer fear that we will be abused or ridiculed now that we have brothers that fight for us.

Your efforts have arduous, but fruitful because you, humble gladiators of the Texas-Mexican's rights, have conquered the sympathies of an entire people. You leave, but you will no longer be alone in the battle. Thousands of hearts remain here that will support you. And for this, it is necessary to understand well each other's rights and to work according to those rights. Like you, I believe

[1]Given by the author, Mrs. Soledad Flores de Peña, at the First Mexicanist Congress. Translated by Omar Figueredo.

that the best way to achieve this is through the education of the woman, instructing her, giving her courage, spirit, and strength while respecting her.

However, we women in exchange must promise to do something, although it hardly represents our love for our heroines, our ancestral defenders and for the tireless fighters of today, that struggle for the well-being of a people living in a foreign land. We must help them, but how to do it? Listen! We women must promise to be strong, to order as the female Spartans our sons in case of a foreign invasion; giving them the sword and the flag and telling them, return, my son, with it or wrapped in it. For before surrendering herself to ridicule and as the mother of the conquerors, your mother will flee to the mountains to serve as pasture for the beasts.

But no, dear homeland! Your sons, instructed to save you and their intellects illuminated by high ideals, shall be your safeguards. Sleep peacefully and majestically at the foot of your mountains, let them crown your brown virginal forehead, like the Shulamite of the "Song of Songs," with garlands of roses from your own gardens and let your slender palm trees offer you their delicate fruit. Sleep, beloved homeland! Sleep to the majestic murmur of your seas and to the bright kiss of your constellations, that your sons shall know to die for you bloodied and epic. The fecund blood of the young heroes of Chapultepec will still give strength to your young, whom we, their mothers, will educate so that they never feel ashamed to say they are Mexican.

And now, Representatives, distinguished champions of a just cause, with our brotherly greeting receive the most sincere homage of our gratitude, and let science's always fruitful sun light the way for you to find the most efficient methods to redeem our race.

1911

■ MARGARET SANGER ■
1879–1966

from **Debate on Birth Control**[1]

Mr. Chairman, and ladies and gentlemen:

Mr. Russell and I seem to agree on some of the points of this argument, at least, but as usual, with most opponents of birth control, they have absolutely no intelligent argument.[2] (Laughter.) They always barricade themselves behind

[1]Margaret Sanger, *Debate on Birth Control* (1920), 9–14.
[2]Winter Russell was the "assistant corruption counsel" of New York and a leading opponent of the contraception movement.

the Bible or the terrible vengeance of an offended Nature. That is exactly what Mr. Russell is doing now.

Now, friends, I want to say, let us get down to fundamental principles. Let us get together and look at life the way it is now, now as it might have been had Nature acted thus so, not as it might be had God done thus and so, but as we find ourselves today. We have a few principles of life by which we must live, and I claim that every one of us has a right to health, to liberty and to the pursuit of happiness. I say furthermore that birth control is an absolutely essential factor in our living, and having those three principles of happiness. (Applause).

By birth control, I mean a voluntary, conscious control of the birth rate by means that prevent conception—scientific means that prevent conception. I don't mean birth control by abstinence or by continence or anything except the thing that agrees with most of us, and as we will develop later on, most of us are glad that there are means of science at the present time that are not injurious, not harmful, and all conception can be avoided.

Now let us look upon life as it really is, and we see society today is divided distinctly into two groups: those who use the means of birth control and those who do not.

On the one side we find those who do use means in controlling birth. What have they? They are the people who bring to birth few children. They are the people who have all the happiness, who have wealth and the leisure for culture and mental and spiritual development. They are people who rear their children to manhood and womanhood and who fill the universities and the colleges with their progeny. Nature has seemed to be very kind to that group of people. (Laughter.)

On the other hand we have the group who have large families and have for generations perpetuated large families, and I know from my work among them that the great percentage of these people that are brought into the world in poverty and misery have been unwanted. I know that most of these women are just as desirous to have means to control birth as the women of wealth. I know she tries desperately to obtain the information, not for selfish purposes, but for her own benefit and for that of her children. In this group, what do we have? We have poverty, misery, disease, overcrowding, congestion, child labor, infant mortality, maternal mortality, all the evils which today are grouped in the crowd where there are large families of unwanted and undesired children.

Take the first one and let us see how these mothers feel. I claim that a woman, whether she is rich or poor, has a right to be a mother or not when she feels herself fit to be so. She has just as much right not to be a mother as she has to be a mother. It is just as right and as moral for people to talk of small families and to demand them as to want large families. It is just as moral.

If we let, as we are supposed to do, Nature take her course, we know that any woman, from the age of puberty until the age of the period of menopause could have anywhere from 15 to 20 children in her lifetime, and it will only take one relationship between man and woman to give her one a year, to give her that large family. Let us not forget that.

Are we today, as women, who wish to develop, who wish to advance in life, are we willing to spend all of our time through those years of development in bringing forth children that the world does not appreciate? Certainly, anyone who looks into that will find that there is very little place in the world for children. And besides, if a woman does spend all her time in child bearing, do you know that, even with healthy women, one out of ten who have children as often as Nature sends them, dies from child bearing? One out of every ten women who lets Nature take her course and has from 12 to 16 children dies from child bearing. Furthermore, there are many cases where it is absolutely indispensable for a woman's health, for her life, in fact, to have means to control birth. There are cases . . . of syphilis, cases of tuberculosis; do you realize that out of every seven women who have tuberculosis today four of them die, not from tuberculosis, my friends, but from pregnancy. They die because they have not that knowledge of birth control because physicians and all the others who should be disseminating information and safeguarding those women's lives are not giving them the fundamental things to cure their disease, but allowing them to become pregnant. They keep them in ignorance of this particular knowledge that should assist them in recovering their health. Not only with tuberculosis, but there are other diseases that are inimical to woman's health and happiness. Heart disease is another thing that pregnancy absolutely stimulates and it means a woman's death. Not long ago a young girl came to me who had kidney disease. She was a telegraph operator. Her husband was a young working man, but he was not able to support a family. She had on two different occasions tried to have children, but she had kidney disease and they found her in convulsions; she had frothed at the mouth and was taken to a hospital in a serious and critical condition. The only thing they could do to her was to resort to abortion, and yet they send her back to her home, to her husband and family again in just the same way, with no information as to how to protect herself against another condition such as she had just gone through. That is what happens to our women today, even those who are suffering from disease where they should be protected with means and knowledge of birth control.

The only weapon that women have, and the most uncivilized weapon that they must use, if they will not submit to having children every year and a half, is abortion. We know how detrimental abortion is to the physical side as well as to the psychic side of woman's life. Yet there are in this nation, because of these generalities and opinions that are here before us, and that are stopping the tide of progress, more than one million women who have abortions performed on them each year.

What does this mean? It is a very bad sign when women indulge in it, and it means they are absolutely determined that they cannot continue bringing children into the world that they cannot clothe, feed and shelter. It is a woman's instinct, and she knows herself when she should and should not give birth to children, and it is much more natural to trust this instinct and to let her be the judge than it is to let her judge herself by some unknown God. I claim it is a woman's duty and right to have for herself the power to say when she shall and shall not have children.

1920

FRANKLIN DELANO ROOSEVELT
1882–1945

from **The Four Freedoms**[1]

In the future days, which we seek to make secure, we look forward to a world founded upon four essential human freedoms.

The first is freedom of speech and expression—everywhere in the world.

The second is freedom of every person to worship God in his own way—everywhere in the world.

The third is freedom from want—which, translated into world terms, means economic understandings which will secure to every nation a healthy peacetime life for its inhabitants—everywhere in the world.

The fourth is freedom from fear—which, translated into world terms, means a world-wide reduction of armaments to such a point and in such a thorough fashion that no nation will be in a position to commit an act of physical aggression against any neighbor—anywhere in the world.

That is no vision of a distant millennium. It is a definite basis for a kind of world attainable in our own time and generation. That kind of world is the very antithesis of the so-called new order of tyranny which the dictators seek to create with the crash of a bomb.

To that new order we oppose the greater conception—the moral order. A good society is able to face schemes of world domination and foreign revolutions alike without fear.

Since the beginning of our American history, we have been engaged in change—in a perpetual peaceful revolution—a revolution which goes on steadily, quietly adjusting itself to changing conditions—without the concentration camp or the quick-lime in the ditch. The world order which we seek is the cooperation of free countries, working together in a friendly, civilized society.

[1] *The Public Papers and Addresses of Franklin D. Roosevelt, 1940: War and Aid to Democracies,* Franklin Delano Roosevelt Presidential Library and Museum, http://www.fdrlibrary.marist.edu/4free.html.

This nation has placed its destiny in the hands and heads and hearts of its millions of free men and women; and its faith in freedom under the guidance of God. Freedom means the supremacy of human rights everywhere. Our support goes to those who struggle to gain those rights or keep them. Our strength is our unity of purpose.

To that high concept there can be no end save victory.

1941

Executive Order No. 9066

Executive Order Authorizing the Secretary of War to Prescribe Military Areas

Whereas the successful prosecution of the war requires every possible protection against espionage and against sabotage to national-defense material, national-defense premises, and national-defense utilities as defined in Section 4, Act of April 20, 1918, 40 Stat. 533, as amended by the Act of November 30, 1940, 54 Stat. 1220, and the Act of August 21, 1941, 55 Stat. 655 (U.S.C., Title 50, Sec. 104);

Now, therefore, by virtue of the authority vested in me as President of the United States, and Commander in Chief of the Army and Navy, I hereby authorize and direct the Secretary of War, and the Military Commanders whom he may from time to time designate, whenever he or any designated Commander deems such action necessary or desirable, to prescribe military areas in such places and of such extent as he or the appropriate Military Commander may determine, from which any or all persons may be excluded, and with respect to which, the right of any person to enter, remain in, or leave shall be subject to whatever restrictions the Secretary of War or the appropriate Military Commander may impose in his discretion. The Secretary of War is hereby authorized to provide for residents of any such area who are excluded there from, such transportation, food, shelter, and other accommodations as may be necessary, in the judgment of the Secretary of War or the said Military Commander, and until other arrangements are made, to accomplish the purpose of this order. The designation of military areas in any region or locality shall supersede designations of prohibited and restricted areas by the Attorney General under the Proclamations of December 7 and 8, 1941, and shall supersede the responsibility and authority of the Attorney General under the said Proclamations in respect of such prohibited and restricted areas.

I hereby further authorize and direct the Secretary of War and the said Military Commanders to take such other steps as he or the appropriate Military Commander may deem advisable to enforce compliance with the restrictions applicable to each Military area herein above authorized to be designated, including the use of Federal troops and other Federal Agencies, with authority to accept assistance of state and local agencies.

I hereby further authorize and direct all Executive Departments, independent establishments and other Federal Agencies, to assist the Secretary of War or the said Military Commanders in carrying out this Executive Order, including the furnishing of medical aid, hospitalization, food, clothing, transportation, use of land, shelter, and other supplies, equipment, utilities, facilities, and services.

This order shall not be construed as modifying or limiting in any way the authority heretofore granted under Executive Order No. 8972, dated December 12, 1941, nor shall it be construed as limiting or modifying the duty and responsibility of the Federal Bureau of Investigation, with respect to the investigation of alleged acts of sabotage or the duty and responsibility of the Attorney General and the Department of Justice under the Proclamations of December 7 and 8, 1941, prescribing regulations for the conduct and control of alien enemies, except as such duty and responsibility is superseded by the designation of military areas hereunder.

Franklin D. Roosevelt
The White House,
February 19, 1942.

WESTERN DEFENSE COMMAND AND FOURTH ARMY WARTIME CIVIL CONTROL ADMINISTRATION

Instructions to All Persons of Japanese Ancestry

Instructions to all persons of Japanese ancestry living in the following area: All that portion of the City and County of San Francisco, lying generally west of the north-south line established by Junipero Serra Boulevard, Worchester Avenue, and Nineteenth Avenue, and lying generally north of the east-west line established by California Street, to the intersection of Market Street, and thence on Market Street to San Francisco Bay.

All Japanese persons, both alien and non-alien, will be evacuated from the above designated area by 12:00 o'clock noon Tuesday, April 7, 1942.

No Japanese person will be permitted to enter or leave the above described area after 8:00 a.m., Thursday, April 2, 1942, without obtaining special permission from the Provost Marshal at the Civil Control Station located at:

1701 Van Ness Avenue
San Francisco, California

The Civil Control Station is equipped to assist the Japanese population affected by this evacuation in the following ways:

1. Give advise and instructions on the evacuation.
2. Provide services with respect to the management, leasing, sale, storage or other disposition of most kinds of property including real estate, business and professional equipment, household goods, boats, automobiles, live-stock, etc.
3. Provide temporary residence elsewhere for all Japanese in family groups.
4. Transport persons and a limited amount of clothing and equipment to their new residence as specified below.

The Following Instructions Must Be Observed:

1. A responsible member of each family, preferably the head of the family, or the person in whose name most of the property is held, and each individual living alone must report to the Civil Control Station to receive further instructions. This must be done between 8:00 a.m. and 5:00 p.m., Thursday, April 2, 1942, or between 8:00 a.m. and 5 p.m., Friday, April 3, 1942.

2. Evacuees must carry with them on departure for the Reception Center, the following property:
    a. Bedding and linens (no mattress) for each member of the family.
    b. Toilet articles for each member of the family.
    c. Extra clothing for each member of the family.
    d. Sufficient knives, forks, spoons, plates, bowls and cups for each member of the family.
    e. Essential personal effects for each member of the family.

All items carried will be securely packaged, tied and plainly marked with the name of the owner and numbered in accordance with instructions received at the Civil Control Station.

The size and number of packages is limited to that which can be carried by the individual or family group.

No contraband items as described in paragraph 6, Public Proclamation No. 3, Headquarters Western Defense Command and Fourth Army, dated March 24, 1942, will be carried.

3. The United States Government through its agencies will provide for the storage at the sole risk of the owner of the more substantial household items, such as iceboxes, washing machines, pianos and other heavy furniture. Cooking utensils and other small items will be accepted if crated, packed and plainly marked with the name and address of the owner. Only one name and address will be used by a given family.

4. Each family, and individual living alone, will be furnished transportation to the Reception Center. Private means of transportation will not be utilized. All instructions pertaining to the movement will be obtained at the Civil Control Station.

Go to the Civil Control Station at 1701 Van Ness Avenue, San Francisco, California, between 8:00 a.m. and 5:00 p.m., Thursday, April 2, 1942, or between 8:00 a.m. and 5:00 p.m., Friday, April 3, 1942, to receive further instructions.

J. L. DeWITT Lieutenant General,
U. S. Army Commanding
April 1, 1942

ISSUES AND VISIONS IN MODERN AMERICA

When the Puritans came to America they had a vision of a city on a hill, a sacred republic that would show the continuing force of God's promise to them and replace the security that was lost by the Fall from the Garden of Eden. Social problems, however, were not automatically answered by this vision. Yet it continued to give hope to those who felt such problems could be addressed. More complexly, the vision often determined what could be perceived as the problem, let alone its possible solutions. This same set of complexities faced Americans in the modern period as well. But the nature of the problem was generally conceded to be on a much larger scale, and there were inescapably numerous solutions that were being put forth with great feeling and skill.

The problem in modern society was perceived in many terms. For some it was a problem of scale: simply put, the difficulties in administering and governing a social collective that numbers in the tens or hundreds of millions had never been faced in previous centuries, and hardly even imagined. For others, the problem was one of legitimacy, that is, how could those who rule others lay claim to their power, especially if they could no longer claim that power by right of birth or "natural" endowment? For yet others, the problem was an old problem, but it had taken on new urgency in an industrialized society: how should we distribute the wealth?

Many of the writers in this section held to visions that would have supplied solutions, so they believed, even though no writer here ever claimed it would be easy. Mike Gold felt that the claims of distributive justice—the question of who should own what and how might they justly dispose of it—were paramount. Other writers preferred to concentrate on the problem rather than the solution. Thus, LeSueur devoted her artistic energy to depicting the outrages people had to suffer when the economic system of capitalism failed to provide even a minimally just distribution of society's goods.

The 1930s in America saw many writers turn to solutions based on collectivism, whether in the form of a general commitment to socialism or of a more specific identification with the communism of the Soviet Union. These solutions were in turn harshly attacked as being against the spirit of American individualism, even identified as the work of "foreign" agents. The New Deal of President Roosevelt, set forth in the Depression years, was a form of government intervention in the market system, and so was recognized as a form of social democracy, though others insisted on attacking it as an insidiously advanced form of collectivism. These issues were debated fiercely by American citizens and American writers, too.

Generally speaking, these issues can be seen under the heading of this country's perennial struggle between the principles of unity and plurality. America's famous motto—*e pluribus unum*—suggests that unity will arise out of plurality almost automatically. But unity and plurality are both subject to various rhetorical twists and turns, most obviously when the topic turns to immigration. In a sense all Americans, except the Native Americans, are immigrants. In another sense we "naturally" honor our various populations—but if so, what then can we claim as our principle of unity? Beyond the question of immigration there is the problem of integration: not only of one race with another, but of individual with community, and region with nation. Writers in this section as various as Randolph Bourne and Mary McCarthy have faced the insoluble aspects of integrating nation and self, unity and plurality.

One way of dealing with the apparently insoluble aspects of the problem is to celebrate diversity. This approach often works well, but it also arouses the suspicion of those who distrust any attempt to blur individual identity, the tactile grit of specific individuals faced with their separate and unabstractable lives. Writers like Warren and Ransom faced this dilemma, and they generally insisted on the specific, as they contributed to the vast wealth of regional literature in America. Both, however, were very sophisticated and conversant with abstract thought. In a sense, they dealt with one of the problems of modernism that affected writers during the New Negro Renaissance: can the use of folk or mythic material in literature successfully avoid creating a limited reception for the work of art? And how can a mass audience best be addressed without limiting the writer's vision and range of reference?

Immigrant writers had similar problems, for they had to be aware of the choice between speaking only to other immigrants (many of whom were unable to read very widely in the language of the "new" country), or to people who were part of the established and conventional population. If the vision of the immigrant such as Yezierska were to insist on its authentic specificity, it might very well consign itself to oblivion. But to do anything less would be to lose the self that had undergone the experience. Of course, there was the additional problem of the specific experiences of each immigrant group. Russians might see the new land quite differently from Chinese, say, and even inside any one national group there could be sharp class distinctions that would form separate frames of reference and perception.

This section is clearly a miscellany, including as it does not only regional writers and immigrant authors (popular writers and intellectuals), but also two Native American storytellers. In its inclusiveness, this unit celebrates diversity. However, it rests on two shared assumptions: that the self is distinctive, and that constant and nimble exploration is required in order to reveal the particular character of the self.

Charles Molesworth
Queens College, City University of New York

RANDOLPH BOURNE
1886–1918

Randolph Bourne was one of the most intellectual voices of his generation, a social critic of considerable acuity and an analyst of American national life and culture without peer in the first two decades of the twentieth century. He was born in Bloomfield, New Jersey, a small town of the sort he was to describe with X-ray accuracy in "The Social Order in an American Town" (1913). Though his spine and face were deformed at birth, Bourne went on to find a place for himself among the leading literary and intellectual figures of the day. Like Thorstein Veblen and other left-leaning critics of American society, Bourne constantly circled around the disjunction of our ideals and our practices. He often cultivated an ironic view of life, but never succumbed to the corrosive pessimism endemic to social criticism. At Columbia College in the early 1910s, he met Charles Beard and John Dewey and began to publish essays in journals like the *Atlantic Monthly* and the *Dial*. It was with the *New Republic*, founded in 1914, and its editors and writers such as Herbert Croly and Walter Lippmann, and later with the cultural magazine, *The Seven Arts*, that he came closest to finding a network of supportive friends. In fact he often lived in a sort of emotional isolation, however, admired by many but frequently troubled by his inability to find a permanent position for himself without compromising his ideals. He died in 1918, a victim of the influenza epidemic that spread throughout the country after the close of the war.

Perhaps the most important chapter in Bourne's intellectual odyssey came when he broke with his mentor, John Dewey, over America's entrance into the First World War. Bourne's polemical skills stood out in sharp relief during this episode, as essays like "Twilight of Idols" (1917) exposed the weak logic of those who had to change their principles in order to justify joining the national call to arms. During this time he also wrote his most important work, an unfinished theoretical piece called "The State" (1919); this bold set of formulations served later to increase speculation about his ultimate intellectual and political influence had he lived to write more along such lines.

"Trans-National America" (1916) must be read in the context of Bourne's rejection of the war fever that was beginning to overtake various ethnic groups in America in 1915, when the cry of "preparedness" was often a code for heightening the will to fight on an international scale. But the essay is also an extremely prescient work, the most challenging rethinking of the "melting pot" metaphor produced by any twentieth-century writer. Indeed it is fair to say that even today the thinking on multiculturalism and its political and social forms has rarely gone beyond Bourne's formulations, even though he acknowledged his own "vagueness."

Bourne used the image of the cultural center to organize his article, but he urged his readers not to accept the central "melting pot" metaphor to produce a culture that would be "washed out into a tasteless, colorless fluid of uniformity." Intellectuals at this time were just beginning to see the social ramifications of assimilation, and not all who analyzed the situation were favorably disposed to the cultural values of those increasingly referred to as "hyphenated" Americans. Far from thrilled by what he called the "flotsam and jetsam of American life," with its "leering cheapness and falseness of taste and spiritual outlook," Bourne saw further into the problem than most when he claimed that "if freedom means a democratic cooperation in determining the ideals and purposes and industrial and social institutions of a country, then the immigrant has not been free."

Bourne envisioned a nation of immigrants who could "retain that distinctiveness of their native cultures" and hence be "more valuable and interesting to each other for being different." This visionary state he called by various terms, such as a "Beloved Community," marked by a cosmopolitanism that embraced various cultural points of view. He saw, like Du Bois, the necessary double consciousness of modern life, though, unlike Du Bois, he considered this a possibility rather than a burden. Like Alain Locke, he recognized that cultural struggle and enrichment could provide a way beyond the narrow bitterness of political divisiveness and economic exploitation. Education, especially one provided by the modern college and university that contained the "seeds of [an] international intellectual world of the future" would prepare immigrants for the "Beloved Community." As with many visionaries, Bourne's formulations remain both a rebuke and a challenge.

Charles Molesworth
Queens College, City University of New York

PRIMARY WORKS

Youth and Life, 1913; *History of a Literary Radical and Other Essays*, ed. Van Wyck Brooks, 1920; *Letters*, 1981; *The Radical Will: Selected Writings 1911–1918*, ed. Olaf Hansen, 1992.

Trans-National America

No reverberatory effect of the great war has caused American public opinion more solicitude than the failure of the "melting-pot." The discovery of diverse nationalistic feelings among our great alien population has come to most people as an intense shock. It has brought out the unpleasant inconsistencies of our traditional beliefs. We have had to watch hard-hearted old Brahmins virtuously indignant at the spectacle of the immigrant refusing to be melted, while they jeer at patriots like Mary Antin who write about "our forefathers." We have had to listen to publicists who express themselves as stunned by the evidence of vigorous nationalistic and cultural movements in this country among Germans, Scandinavians, Bohemians, and Poles, while in the same breath they insist that the alien shall be forcibly assimilated to that Anglo-Saxon tradition which they unquestioningly label "American."

As the unpleasant truth has come upon us that assimilation in this country was proceeding on lines very different from those we had marked out for it, we found ourselves inclined to blame those who were thwarting our prophecies. The truth became culpable. We blamed the war, we blamed the Germans. And then we discovered with a moral shock that these movements had been making great headway before the war even began. We found that the tendency, reprehensible and paradoxical as it might be, has been for the national clusters of immigrants, as they became more and more firmly established and more and more prosperous, to cultivate more and more assiduously the literatures and cultural traditions of their homelands. Assimilation, in other words, instead of washing out the memories of Europe, made them more and more intensely real. Just as these clusters became more and more objectively American, did they become more and more German or Scandinavian or Bohemian or Polish.

To face the fact that our aliens are already strong enough to take a share in the direction of their own destiny, and that the strong cultural movements represented by the foreign press, schools, and colonies are a challenge to our facile attempts, is not, however, to admit the failure of Americanization. It is not to fear the failure of democracy. It is rather to urge us to an investigation of what Americanism may rightly mean. It is to ask ourselves whether our ideal has been broad or narrow—whether perhaps the time has not come to assert a higher ideal than the "melting-pot." Surely we cannot be certain of our spiritual democracy when, claiming to melt the nations within us to a comprehension of our free and democratic institutions, we fly into panic at the first sign of their own will and tendency. We act as if we wanted Americanization to take place only on our own terms, and not by the consent of the governed. All our elaborate machinery of settlement and school and union, of social and political naturalization, however, will move with friction just in so far as it neglects to take into account this strong and virile insistence that America shall be what the immigrant will have a hand in making it, and not what a ruling class, descendant of those British stocks which were the first permanent immigrants, decide that America shall be made. This is the condition which confronts us, and which demands a clear and general readjustment of our attitude and our ideal.

I

Mary Antin is right when she looks upon our foreign-born as the people who missed the Mayflower and came over on the first boat they could find. But she forgets that when they did come it was not upon other Mayflowers, but upon a "Maiblume," a "Fleur de Mai," a "Fior di Maggio," a "Majblomst." These people were not mere arrivals from the same family, to be welcomed as understood and long-loved, but strangers to the neighborhood, with whom a long process of settling down had to take place. For they brought with them their national and racial characters, and each new national quota had to wear slowly away the contempt with which its mere alienness got itself greeted. Each had to make its way slowly from the lowest strata of unskilled labor up to a level where it satisfied the accredited norms of social success.

We are all foreign-born or the descendants of foreign-born, and if distinctions are to be made between us they should rightly be on some other ground than indigenousness. The early colonists came over with motives no less colonial than the later. They did not come to be assimilated in an American melting-pot. They did not come to adopt the culture of the American Indian. They had not the smallest intention of "giving themselves without reservation" to the new country. They came to get freedom to live as they wanted to. They came to escape from the stifling air and chaos of the old world; they came to make their fortune in a new land. They invented no new social framework. Rather they brought over bodily the old ways to which they had been accustomed. Tightly concentrated on a hostile frontier, they were conservative beyond belief. Their pioneer daring was reserved for the objective conquest of material resources. In their folkways, in their social and political institutions, they were, like every colonial people, slavishly imitative of the mother country. So that, in spite of the "Revolution," our whole legal and political system remained more English than the English, petrified and unchanging, while in England law developed to meet the needs of the changing times.

It is just this English-American conservatism that has been our chief obstacle to social advance. We have needed the new peoples—the order of the German and Scandinavian, the turbulence of the Slav and Hun—to save us from our own stagnation. I do not mean that the illiterate Slav is now the equal of the New Englander of pure descent. He is raw material to be educated, not into a New Englander, but into a socialized American along such lines as those thirty nationalities are being educated in the amazing schools of Gary. I do not believe that this process is to be one of decades of evolution. The spectacle of Japan's sudden jump from mediaevalism to postmodernism should have destroyed that superstition. We are not dealing with individuals who are to "evolve." We are dealing with their children, who, with that education we are about to have, will start level with all of us. Let us cease to think of ideals like democracy as magical qualities inherent in certain peoples. Let us speak, not of inferior races, but of inferior civilizations. We are all to educate and to be educated. These peoples in America are in a common enterprise. It is not what we are now that concerns us, but what this plastic next generation may become in the light of a new cosmopolitan ideal.

We are not dealing with static factors, but with fluid and dynamic generations. To contrast the older and the newer immigrants and see the one class as democratically motivated by love of liberty, and the other by mere money-getting, is not to illuminate the future. To think of earlier nationalities as culturally assimilated to America, while we picture the later as a sodden and resistive mass, makes only for bitterness and misunderstanding. There may be a difference between these earlier and these later stocks, but it lies neither in motive for coming nor in strength of cultural allegiance to the homeland. The truth is that no more tenacious cultural allegiance to the mother country has been shown by any alien nation than by the ruling class of Anglo-Saxon descendants in these American States. English snobberies, English religion, English literary styles, English literary reverences and canons, English ethics, English superiorities, have been the cultural food that we have drunk in from our mothers' breasts. The distinctively American spirit—pioneer, as distinguished from the reminiscently English—that appears in Whitman and Emerson and James, has had to exist on sufferance alongside of this other cult, unconsciously belittled by our cultural makers of opinion. No country has perhaps had so great indigenous genius which had so little influence on the country's traditions and expressions. The unpopular and dreaded German-American of the present day is a beginning amateur in comparison with those foolish Anglophiles of Boston and New York and Philadelphia whose reversion to cultural type sees uncritically in England's cause the cause of Civilization, and, under the guise of ethical independence of thought, carries along European traditions which are no more "American" than the German categories themselves.

It speaks well for German-American innocence of heart or else for its lack of imagination that it has not turned the hyphen stigma into a "Tu quoque"! If there were to be any hyphens scattered about, clearly they should be affixed to those English descendants who had had centuries of time to be made American where the German had had only half a century. Most significantly has the war brought out of them this alien virus, showing them still loving English things, owing allegiance to the English Kultur, moved by English shibboleths and prejudice. It is only because it has been the ruling class in this country that bestowed the epithets that we have not heard copiously and scornfully of "hyphenated English-Americans." But even our quarrels with England have had the bad temper, the extravagance, of family quarrels. The Englishman of today nags us and dislikes us in that personal, peculiarly intimate way in which he dislikes the Australian, or as we may dislike our younger brothers. He still thinks of us incorrigibly as "colonials." America—official, controlling, literary, political America—is still, as a writer recently expressed it, "culturally speaking, a self-governing dominion of the British Empire."

The non-English American can scarcely be blamed if he sometimes thinks of the Anglo-Saxon predominance in America as little more than a predominance of priority. The Anglo-Saxon was merely the first immigrant, the first to found a colony. He has never really ceased to be the descendant of immigrants, nor has he ever succeeded in transforming that colony into a real nation, with a tenacious, richly woven fabric of native culture. Colonials from the other nations have come and settled down beside him. They found no definite native culture which should startle them out of their colonialism, and consequently they looked back to their mother country, as the earlier Anglo-Saxon immigrant was looking back to his. What has been offered the newcomer has been the chance to learn English, to become a citizen, to salute the flag. And those elements of our ruling classes who are responsible for the public schools, the settlements, all the organizations for amelioration in the cities, have every reason to be proud of the care and labor which they have devoted to absorbing the immigrant. His opportunities the immigrant has taken to gladly, with almost a pathetic eagerness to make his way in the new land without friction or disturbance. The common language has made not only for the necessary communication, but for all the amenities of life.

If freedom means the right to do pretty much as one pleases, so long as one does not interfere with others, the immigrant has found freedom, and the ruling element has been singularly liberal in its treatment of the invading hordes. But if freedom means a democratic cooperation in determining the ideals and purposes and industrial and social institutions of a country, then the immigrant has not been free, and the Anglo-Saxon element is guilty of just what every dominant race is guilty of in every European country: the imposition of its own culture upon the minority peoples. The fact that this imposition has been so mild and, indeed, semi-conscious does not alter its quality. And the war has brought out just the degree to which that purpose of "Americanizing," that is, "Anglo-Saxonizing," the immigrant has failed.

For the Anglo-Saxon now in his bitterness to turn upon the other peoples, talk about their "arrogance," scold them for not being melted in a pot which never existed, is to betray the unconscious purpose which lay at the bottom of his heart. It betrays too the possession of a racial jealousy similar to that of which he is now accusing the so-called "hyphenates." Let the Anglo-Saxon be proud enough of the heroic toil and heroic sacrifices which moulded the nation. But let him ask himself, if he had had to depend on the English descendants, where he would have been living today. To those of us who see in the exploitation of unskilled labor the strident red *leit-motif* of our civilization, the settling of the country presents a great social drama as the waves of immigration broke over it.

Let the Anglo-Saxon ask himself where he would have been if these races had not come? Let those who feel the inferiority of the non-Anglo-Saxon immigrant contemplate that region of the States which has remained the most distinctively "American," the South. Let him ask himself whether he would really like to see the foreign hordes Americanized into such an Americanization. Let him ask himself how superior this native civilization is to the great "alien" states of Wisconsin and Minnesota, where Scandinavians, Poles, and Germans have self-consciously labored to preserve their traditional culture, while being outwardly and satisfactorily American. Let him ask himself how much more wisdom, intelligence, industry and social leadership has come out of these alien states than out of all the truly American ones. The South, in fact, while this vast Northern development has gone on, still remains an English colony, stagnant and complacent, having progressed culturally scarcely beyond the early Victorian era. It is culturally sterile because it has had no advantage of cross-fertilization like the Northern states. What has happened in states such as Wisconsin and Minnesota is that strong foreign cultures have struck root in a new and fertile soil. America has meant liberation, and German and Scandinavian political ideas and social energies have expanded to a new potency. The process has not been at all the fancied "assimilation" of the Scandinavian or Teuton. Rather it has been a process of their assimilation of us—I speak as an Anglo-Saxon.

The foreign cultures have not been melted down or run together, made into some homogeneous Americanism, but have remained distinct but cooperating to the greater glory and benefit, not only of themselves but of all the native "Americanism" around them.

What we emphatically do not want is that these distinctive qualities should be washed out into a tasteless, colorless fluid of uniformity. Already we have far too much of this insipidity—masses of people who are cultural half-breeds, neither assimilated Anglo-Saxons nor nationals of another culture. Each national colony in this country seems to retain in its foreign press, its vernacular literature, its schools, its intellectual and patriotic leaders, a central cultural nucleus. From this nucleus the colony extends out by imperceptible gradations to a fringe where national characteristics are all but lost. Our cities are filled with these half-breeds who retain their foreign names but have lost the foreign savor. This does not mean that they have actually been changed into New Englanders or Middle Westerners. It does not mean that they have been really Americanized. It means that, letting slip from them whatever native culture they had, they have substituted for it only the most rudimentary American—the American culture of the cheap newspaper, the "movies," the popular song, the ubiquitous automobile. The unthinking who survey this class call them assimilated, Americanized. The great American public school has done its work. With these people our institutions are safe. We may thrill with dread at the aggressive hyphenate, but this tame flabbiness is accepted as Americanization. The same moulders of opinion whose ideal is to melt the different races into Anglo-Saxon gold hail this poor product as the satisfying result of their alchemy.

Yet a truer cultural sense would have told us that it is not the self-conscious cultural nuclei that sap at our American life, but these fringes. It is not the Jew who sticks proudly to the faith of his fathers and boasts of that venerable culture of his who is dangerous to America, but the Jew who has lost the Jewish fire and become a mere elementary, grasping animal. It is not the Bohemian who supports the Bohemian schools in Chicago whose influence is sinister, but the Bohemian who has made money and has got into ward politics. Just so surely as we tend to disintegrate these nuclei of nationalistic culture do we tend to create hordes of men and women without a spiritual country, cultural outlaws, without taste, without standards but those of the mob. We sentence them to live on the most rudimentary planes of American life. The influences at the centre of the nuclei are centripetal. They make for the intelligence and the social values which mean an enhancement of life. And just because the foreign-born retains this expressiveness he is likely to be a better citizen of the American community. The influences at the fringe, however, are centrifugal, anarchical. They make for detached fragments of peoples. Those who came to find liberty achieve only license. They become the flotsam and jetsam of American life, the downward undertow of our civilization with its leering cheapness and falseness of taste and spiritual outlook, the absence of mind and sincere feeling which we see in our slovenly towns, our vapid moving pictures, our popular novels, and in the vacuous faces of the crowds on the city street. This is the cultural wreckage of our time, and it is from the fringes of the Anglo-Saxon as well as the other stocks that it falls. America has as yet no impelling integrating force. It makes too easily for this detritus of cultures. In our loose, free country, no constraining national purpose, no tenacious folk-tradition and folk-style hold the people to a line.

The war has shown us that not in any magical formula will this purpose be found. No intense nationalism of the European plan can be ours. But do we not begin to see a new and more adventurous ideal? Do we not see how the national colonies in America, deriving power from the deep cultural heart of Europe and yet living here in mutual toleration, freed from the age-long tangles of races, creeds, and dynasties, may work out a federated ideal? America is transplanted Europe, but a Europe that has not been disintegrated and scattered in the transplanting as in some Dispersion. Its colonies live here inextricably mingled, yet not homogeneous. They merge but they do not fuse.

America is a unique sociological fabric, and it bespeaks poverty of imagination not to be thrilled at the incalculable potentialities of so novel a union of men. To seek no other goal than the weary old nationalism—belligerent, exclusive, inbreeding, the poison of which we are witnessing now in Europe—is to make patriotism a hollow sham, and to declare that, in spite of our boastings, America must ever be a follower and not a leader of nations.

II

If we come to find this point of view plausible, we shall have to give up the search for our native "American" culture. With the exception of the South and that New England which, like the Red Indian, seems to be passing into solemn oblivion, there is no distinctively American culture. It is apparently our lot rather to be a federation of cultures. This we have been for half a century, and the war has made it ever more evident that this is what we are destined to remain. This will not mean, however, that there are not expressions of indigenous genius that could not have sprung from any other soil. Music, poetry, philosophy, have been singularly fertile and new. Strangely enough, American genius has flared forth just in those directions which are least understanded [sic] of the people. If the American note is bigness, action, the objective as contrasted with the reflective life, where is the epic expression of this spirit? Our drama and our fiction, the peculiar fields for the expression of action and objectivity, are somehow exactly the fields of the spirit which remain poor and mediocre. American materialism is in some way inhibited from getting into impressive artistic form its own energy with which it bursts. Nor is it any better in architecture, the least romantic and subjective of all the arts. We are inarticulate of the very values which we profess to idealize. But in the finer forms—music, verse, the essay, philosophy— the American genius puts forth work equal to any of its contemporaries. Just in so far as our American genius has expressed the pioneer spirit, the adventurous, forward-looking drive of a colonial empire, is it representative of that whole America of the many races and peoples, and not of any partial or traditional enthusiasm. And only as that pioneer note is sounded can we really speak of the American culture. As long as we thought of Americanism in terms of the "melting-pot," our American cultural tradition lay in the past. It was something to which the new Americans were to be moulded. In the light of our changing ideal of Americanism, we must perpetrate the paradox that our American cultural tradition lies in the future. It will be what we all together make out of this incomparable opportunity of attacking the future with a new key.

Whatever American nationalism turns out to be, it is certain to become something utterly different from the nationalisms of twentieth-century Europe. This wave of reactionary enthusiasm to play the orthodox nationalistic game which is passing over the country is scarcely vital enough to last. We cannot swagger and thrill to the same national self-feeling. We must give new edges to our pride. We must be content to avoid the unnumbered woes that national patriotism has brought in Europe, and that fiercely heightened pride and self-consciousness. Alluring as this is, we must allow our imaginations to transcend this scarcely veiled belligerency. We can be serenely too proud to fight if our pride embraces the creative forces of civilization which armed contest nullifies. We can be too proud to fight if our code of honor transcends that of the schoolboy on the playground surrounded by his jeering mates. Our honor must be positive and creative, and not the mere jealous and negative protectiveness against metaphysical violations of our technical rights. When the doctrine is put forth that in one American flows the mystic blood of all our country's sacred honor, freedom, and prosperity, so that an injury to him is to be the signal for turning our whole nation into that clan-feud of horror and reprisal which would be war, then we find ourselves back among the musty schoolmen of the Middle Ages, and not in any pragmatic and realistic America of the twentieth century.

We should hold our gaze to what America has done, not what mediaeval codes of dueling she has failed to observe. We have transplanted European modernity to our soil, without the spirit that inflames it and turns all its energy into mutual destruction. Out of these foreign peoples there has somehow been squeezed the poison. An America, "hyphenated" to bitterness, is somehow non-explosive. For, even if we all hark back in sympathy to a European nation, even if the war has set every one vibrating to some emotional string twanged on the other side of the Atlantic, the effect has been one of almost dramatic harmlessness.

What we have really been witnessing, however unappreciatively, in this country has been a thrilling and bloodless battle of Kulturs. In that arena of friction which has been the most dramatic—between the hyphenated German-American and the hyphenated English-American—there have emerged rivalries of philosophies which show up deep traditional attitudes, points of view which accurately reflect the gigantic issues of the war. America has mirrored the spiritual issues. The vicarious struggle has been played out peacefully here in the mind. We have seen the stout resistiveness of the old moral interpretation of history on which Victorian England thrived and made itself great in its own esteem. The clean and immensely satisfying vision of the war as a contest between right and wrong; the enthusiastic support of the Allies as the incarnation of virtue-on-a-rampage; the fierce envisaging of their selfish national purposes as the ideals of justice, freedom, and democracy—all this has been thrown with intensest force against the German realistic inter- pretations in terms of the struggle for power and the virility of the integrated State. America has been the intellectual battleground of the nations.

III

The failure of the melting-pot, far from closing the great American demo- cratic experiment, means that it has only just begun. Whatever American nationalism turns out to be, we see already that it will have a color richer and more exciting than our ideal has hitherto encompassed. In a world which has dreamed of internationalism, we find that we have all unawares been building up the first international nation. The voices which have cried for a tight and jealous nationalism of the European pattern are failing. From the ideal, however valiantly and disinterestedly it has been set for us, time and tendency have moved us further and further away. What we have achieved has been rather a cosmopolitan federation of national colonies, of foreign cultures, from whom the sting of devastating competition has been removed. America is already the world-federation in miniature, the continent where for the first time in history has been achieved that miracle of hope, the peaceful living side by side, with character substantially pre- served, of the most heterogenous peoples under the sun. Nowhere else has such contiguity been anything but the breeder of misery. Here, notwith- standing our tragic failures of adjustment, the outlines are already too clear not to give us a new vision and a new orientation of the American mind in the world.

It is for the American of the younger generation to accept this cosmo- politanism, and carry it along with self-conscious and fruitful purpose. In his colleges, he is already getting, with the study of modern history and poli- tics, the modern literatures, economic geography, the privilege of a cosmo- politan outlook such as the people of no other nation of today in Europe can possibly secure. If he is still a colonial, he is no longer the colonial of one partial culture, but of many. He is a colonial of the world. Colonialism has grown into cosmopolitanism, and his motherland is no one nation, but all who have anything life-enhancing to offer to the spirit. That vague sym- pathy which the France of ten years ago was feeling for the world—a sym- pathy which was drowned in the terrible reality of war—may be the modern American's, and that in a positive and aggressive sense. If the American is parochial, it is in sheer wantonness or cowardice. His provincialism is the measure of his fear of bogies or the defect of his imagination.

Indeed, it is not uncommon for the eager Anglo-Saxon who goes to a vivid American university today to find his true friends not among his own race but among the acclimatized German or Austrian, the acclimatized Jew, the acclimatized Scandinavian or Italian. In them he finds the cosmopolitan note. In these youths, foreign-born or the children of foreign-born parents, he is likely to find many of his old inbred morbid problems washed away. These friends are oblivious to the repressions of that tight little society in which he so provincially grew up. He has a pleasurable sense of liberation from the stale and familiar attitudes of those whose ingrowing culture has scarcely created anything vital for his America of today. He breathes a larger air. In his new enthusiasms for continental literature, for unplumbed Russian depths, for French clarity of thought, for Teuton philosophies of power, he feels himself citizen of a larger world. He may be absurdly superficial, his outward-reaching wonder may ignore all the stiller and homelier virtues of his Anglo-Saxon home, but he has at least found the clue to that international mind which will be essential to all men and women of good-will if they are ever to save this Western world of ours from suicide. His new friends have gone through a similar evolution. America has burned most of the baser metal also from them. Meeting now with this common American background, all of them may yet retain that distinctiveness of their native cultures and their national spiritual slants. They are more valuable and interesting to each other for being different, yet that difference could not be creative were it not for this new cosmopolitan outlook which America has given them and which they all equally possess.

A college where such a spirit is possible even to the smallest degree, has within itself already the seeds of this international intellectual world of the future. It suggests that the contribution of America will be an intellectual internationalism which goes far beyond the mere exchange of scientific ideas and discoveries and the cold recording of facts. It will be an intellectual sympathy which is not satisfied until it has got at the heart of the different cultural expressions, and felt as they feel. It may have immense preferences, but it will make understanding and not indignation its end. Such a sympathy will unite and not divide.

Against the thinly disguised panic which calls itself "patriotism" and the thinly disguised militarism which calls itself "preparedness" the cosmopolitan ideal is set. This does not mean that those who hold it are for a policy of drift. They, too, long passionately for an integrated and disciplined America. But they do not want one which is integrated only for domestic economic exploitation of the workers or for predatory economic imperialism among the weaker peoples. They do not want one that is integrated by coercion or militarism, or for the truculent assertion of a mediaeval code of honor and of doubtful rights. They believe that the most effective integration will be one which coordinates the diverse elements and turns them consciously toward working out together the place of America in the world-situation. They demand for integration a genuine integrity, a wholeness and soundness of enthusiasm and purpose which can only come when no national colony within our America feels that it is being discriminated against or that its cultural case is being prejudged. This strength of cooperation, this feeling that all who are here may have a hand in the destiny of America, will make for a finer spirit of integration than any narrow "Americanism" or forced chauvinism.

In this effort we may have to accept some form of that dual citizenship which meets with so much articulate horror among us. Dual citizenship we may have to recognize as the rudimentary form of that international citizenship to which, if our words mean anything, we aspire. We have assumed unquestioningly that mere participation in the political life of the United States must cut the new citizen off from all sympathy with his old allegiance. Anything but a bodily transfer of devotion from one sovereignty to another has been viewed as a sort of moral treason against the Republic. We have insisted that the immigrant whom we welcomed escaping from the very exclusive nationalism of his European home shall forthwith adopt a nationalism just as exclusive, just as narrow, and even less legitimate because it is founded on no warm traditions of his own. Yet a nation like France is said to permit a formal and legal dual citizenship even at the present time. Though a citizen of hers may pretend to cast off his allegiance in favor of some other sovereignty, he is still subject to her laws when he returns. Once a citizen, always a citizen, no matter how many new citizenships he may embrace. And such a dual citizenship seems to us sound and right. For it recognizes that, although the Frenchman may accept the formal institutional framework of his new country and indeed become intensely loyal to it, yet his Frenchness he will never lose. What makes up the fabric of his soul will always be of this Frenchness, so that unless he becomes utterly degenerate he will always to some degree dwell still in his native environment.

Indeed, does not the cultivated American who goes to Europe practice a dual citizenship, which, if not formal, is no less real? The American who lives abroad may be the least expatriate of men. If he falls in love with French ways and French thinking and French democracy and seeks to saturate himself with the new spirit, he is guilty of at least a dual spiritual citizenship. He may be still American, yet he feels himself through sympathy also a Frenchman. And he finds that this expansion involves no shameful conflict within him, no surrender of his native attitude. He has rather for the first time caught a glimpse of the cosmopolitan spirit. And after wandering about through many races and civilizations he may return to America to find them all here living vividly and crudely, seeking the same adjustment that he made. He sees the new peoples here with a new vision. They are no longer masses of aliens, waiting to be "assimilated," waiting to be melted down into the indistinguishable dough of Anglo-Saxonism. They are rather threads of living and potent cultures, blindly striving to weave themselves into a novel international nation, the first the world has seen. In an Austria-Hungary or a Prussia the stronger of these cultures would be moving almost instinctively to subjugate the weaker. But in America those wills-to-power are turned in a different direction into learning how to live together.

Along with dual citizenship we shall have to accept, I think, that free and mobile passage of the immigrant between America and his native land again which now arouses so much prejudice among us. We shall have to accept the immigrant's return for the same reason that we consider justified our own flitting about the earth. To stigmatize the alien who works in America for a few years and returns to his own land, only perhaps to seek American fortune again, is to think in narrow nationalistic terms. It is to ignore the cosmopolitan significance of this migration. It is to ignore the fact that the returning immigrant is often a missionary to an inferior civilization.

This migratory habit has been especially common with the unskilled laborers who have been pouring into the United States in the last dozen years from every country in southeastern Europe. Many of them return to spend their earnings in their own country or to serve their country in war. But they return with an entirely new critical outlook, and a sense of the superiority of American organization to the primitive living around them. This continued passage to and fro has already raised the material standard of living in many regions of these backward countries. For these regions are thus endowed with exactly what they need, the capital for the exploitation of their natural resources, and the spirit of enterprise. America is thus educating these laggard peoples from the very bottom of society up, awakening vast masses to a new-born hope for the future. In the migratory Greek, therefore, we have not the parasitic alien, the doubtful American asset, but a symbol of that cosmopolitan interchange which is coming, in spite of all war and national exclusiveness.

Only America, by reason of the unique liberty of opportunity and traditional isolation for which she seems to stand, can lead in this cosmopolitan enterprise. Only the American—and in this category I include the migratory alien who has lived with us and caught the pioneer spirit and a sense of new social vistas—has the chance to become that citizen of the world. America is coming to be, not a nationality but a trans-nationality, a weaving back and forth, with the other lands, of many threads of all sizes and colors. Any movement which attempts to thwart this weaving, or to dye the fabric any one color, or disentangle the threads of the strands, is false to this cosmopolitan vision. I do not mean that we shall necessarily glut ourselves with the raw product of humanity. It would be folly to absorb the nations faster than we could weave them. We have no duty either to admit or reject. It is purely a question of expediency. What concerns us is the fact that the strands are here. We must have a policy and an ideal for an actual situation. Our question is, What shall we do with our America? How are we likely to get the more creative America—by confining our imaginations to the ideal of the melting-pot, or broadening them to some such cosmopolitan conception as I have been vaguely sketching?

The war has shown America to be unable, though isolated geographically and politically from a European world-situation, to remain aloof and irresponsible. She is a wandering star in a sky dominated by two colossal constellations of states. Can she not work out some position of her own, some life of being in, yet not quite of, this seething and embroiled European world? This is her only hope and promise. A trans-nationality of all the nations, it is spiritually impossible for her to pass into the orbit of any one. It will be folly to hurry herself into a premature and sentimental nationalism, or to emulate Europe and play fast and loose with the forces that drag into war. No Americanization will fulfill this vision which does not recognize the uniqueness of this trans-nationalism of ours. The Anglo-Saxon attempt to fuse will only create enmity and distrust. The crusade against "hyphenates" will only inflame the partial patriotism of trans-nationals, and cause them to assert their European traditions in strident and unwholesome ways. But the attempt to weave a wholly novel international nation out of our chaotic America will liberate and harmonize the creative power of all these peoples and give them the new spiritual citizenship, as so many individuals have already been given, of a world.

Is it a wild hope that the undertow of opposition to metaphysics in international relations, opposition to militarism, is less a cowardly provincialism than a groping for this higher cosmopolitan ideal? One can understand the irritated restlessness with which our proud pro-British colonists contemplate a heroic conflict across the seas in which they have no part. It was inevitable that our necessary inaction should evolve in their minds into the bogey of national shame and dishonor. But let us be careful about accepting their sensitiveness as final arbiter. Let us look at our reluctance rather as the first crude beginnings of assertion on the part of certain strands in our nationality that they have a right to a voice in the construction of the American ideal. Let us face realistically the America we have around us. Let us work with the forces that are at work. Let us make something of this trans-national spirit instead of outlawing it. Already we are living this cosmopolitan America. What we need is everywhere a vivid consciousness of the new ideal. Deliberate headway must be made against the survivals of the melting-pot ideal for the promise of American life.

We cannot Americanize America worthily by sentimentalizing and moralizing history. When the best schools are expressly renouncing the questionable duty of teaching patriotism by means of history, it is not the time to force shibboleth upon the immigrant. This form of Americanization has been heard because it appealed to the vestiges of our old sentimentalized and moralized patriotism. This has so far held the field as the expression of the new American's new devotion. The inflections of other voices have been drowned. They must be heard. We must see if the lesson of the war has not been for hundreds of these later Americans a vivid realization of their transnationality, a new consciousness of what America meant to them as a citizenship in the world. It is the vague historic idealisms which have provided the fuel for the European flame. Our American ideal can make no progress until we do away with this romantic gilding of the past.

All our idealisms must be those of future social goals in which all can participate, the good life of personality lived in the environment of the Beloved Community. No mere doubtful triumphs of the past, which redound to the glory of only one of our trans-nationalities, can satisfy us. It must be a future America, on which all can unite, which pulls us irresistibly toward it, as we understand each other more warmly.

To make real this striving amid dangers and apathies is work for a younger *intelligentsia* of America. Here is an enterprise of integration into which we can all pour ourselves, of a spiritual welding which should make us, if the final menace ever came, not weaker, but infinitely strong.

1916

Anzia Yezierska
1881(?)–1970

Anzia Yezierska, one of ten children, emigrated with her family from Russian Poland to New York's Lower East Side when she was about fifteen. She worked in sweatshops, laundries, and as a maid, studying English in night school. A settlement worker helped her get a scholarship to Columbia College's domestic science teacher training program; Yezierska invented a high school diploma to enter. These early experiences formed her fictional voice of the feisty immigrant waif who pulls herself up from poverty through wit and hard work.

While attending Rand School classes in social theory, she met radical feminist Henrietta Rodman, who encouraged her writing. She started using her European name of Anzia Yezierska, rather than Hattie Mayer, the name that she had received at Ellis Island. In 1910 Yezierska's brief marriage to lawyer Jacob Gordon was annulled. A year later, she married teacher Arnold Levitas, giving birth to their daughter Louise in 1912. When Yezierska and Levitas separated, she focused on her writing and visited Louise once a week. Her first published story, "The Free Vacation House" (1915), describes an overworked immigrant mother's frustration with both domestic life and organized charity's attempts to relieve her. Through the voice of the ghetto mother, Yezierska expressed the Yiddish-English dialect better than any previous writer had.

In 1917, Yezierska barged into the Columbia University office of philosopher and educator John Dewey to enlist his help in obtaining a permanent teaching certificate. From 1917 to 1918, she audited his seminars. Their brief and probably unconsummated romance ended after the summer of 1918. For Dewey, Yezierska was a window onto New York's Jewish ghetto and inspiration for over twenty love poems. For Yezierska, Dewey represented mainstream America and the paternal approval she did not receive from her own highly religious father, who believed women should be wives and not writers. Dewey, however, encouraged Yezierska and introduced her to editors.

Yezierska's most anthologized short story, "The Fat of the Land," was originally chosen the best of *Best Short Stories of 1919*; in 1920 Houghton Mifflin Company published *Hungry Hearts*, a collection of Yezierska's short stories. After newspapers publicized the book, Goldwyn movie studios hired her to write screenplays. The short stories of *Hungry Hearts*, and her first novel, *Salome of the Tenements*, became two movies, the prints and negatives of which have since disintegrated. Yezierska felt her creativity dry up in Hollywood (where she promoted herself as the "sweatshop Cinderella") and returned to New York. There she was somewhat reclusive, but occasionally met with the Algonquin group of writers.

Yezierska wrote more short stories (collected in *Children of Loneliness*) and three more novels (*Bread Givers*, her most polished; *Arrogant Beggar*; and *All I Could Never Be*, about her relationship with Dewey). This last work was written while Yezierska held a Zona Gale Fellowship for writers-in-residence at the University of Wisconsin (1928–1931). Back in New York, around 1935 or 1936, Yezierska joined the WPA Writer's Project, staying perhaps until 1938.

Her fictionalized autobiography, *Red Ribbon on a White Horse*, published in 1950 after an eighteen-year silence, renewed public interest in her writing, thanks in part to a glowing preface by the poet W. H. Auden. Most of the volume describes her Hollywood and WPA experiences. Throughout the Fifties, she wrote *New York Times* book reviews and sometimes lectured. Her fictional voice of the old woman, speaker for the disenfranchised, aged poor, developed at this time. Until 1966, Yezierska lived alone in New York, but then moved near her daughter, who hired transcribers for the writing Yezierska continued even when nearly blind. Yezierska died in a nursing home near Claremont, California, at close to ninety.

Critics have called Yezierska's fiction extremely autobiographical, but examination reveals it to be emotionally, rather than factually, true to her life. All of her writing, whether about young immigrant working-class Jewish women, or the elderly, isolated urban poor, expresses the feelings of characters considered by others to be marginal to the American mainstream. Her work has been recently rediscovered by those interested in women's, ethnic, immigrant, Jewish, urban, or working-class literature.

Sally Ann Drucker
Nassau Community College

PRIMARY WORKS

Hungry Hearts, 1920; *Salome of the Tenements*, 1922; *Children of Loneliness*, 1923; *Bread Givers*, 1925; *Arrogant Beggar*, 1927; *All I Could Never Be*, 1932; *Red Ribbon on a White Horse*, 1950. Paperback reprints: *Bread Givers*, 1975; *Hungry Hearts and Other Stories*, 1985; *Red Ribbon on a White Horse*, 1988; *The Open Cage* (a collection), 1979, 1993; *How I Found America: Collected Stories of Anzia Yezierska*, ed. Vivian Gornick, 1991.

America and I

As one of the dumb, voiceless ones I speak. One of the millions of immigrants beating, beating out their hearts at your gates for a breath of understanding.

Ach! America! From the other end of the earth from where I came, America was a land of living hope, woven of dreams, aflame with longing and desire.

Choked for ages in the airless oppression of Russia, the Promised Land rose up—wings for my stifled spirit—sunlight burning through my darkness—freedom singing to me in my prison—deathless songs tuning prison-bars into strings of a beautiful violin.

I arrived in America. My young, strong body, my heart and soul pregnant with the unlived lives of generations clamoring for expression.

What my mother and father and their mother and father never had a chance to give out in Russia, I would give out in America. The hidden sap of centuries would find release; colors that never saw light—songs that died unvoiced—romance that never had a chance to blossom in the black life of the Old World.

In the golden land of flowing opportunity I was to find my work that was denied me in the sterile village of my forefathers. Here I was to be free from the dead drudgery for bread that held me down in Russia. For the first time in America, I'd cease to be a slave of the belly. I'd be a creator, a giver, a human being! My work would be the living job of fullest self-expression.

But from my high visions, my golden hopes, I had to put my feet down on earth. I had to have food and shelter. I had to have the money to pay for it.

I was in America, among the Americans, but not of them. No speech, no common language, no way to win a smile of understanding from them, only my young, strong body and my untried faith. Only my eager, empty hands, and my full heart shining from my eyes!

God from the world! Here I was with so much richness in me, but my mind was not wanted without the language. And my body, unskilled, untrained, was not even wanted in the factory. Only one of two chances was left open to me: the kitchen, or minding babies.

My first job was as a servant in an Americanized family. Once, long ago, they came from the same village from where I came. But they were so well-dressed, so well-fed, so successful in America, that they were ashamed to remember their mother tongue.

"What were to be my wages?" I ventured timidly, as I looked up to the well-fed, well-dressed "American" man and woman.

They looked at me with a sudden coldness. What have I said to draw away from me their warmth? Was it so low from me to talk of wages? I shrank back into myself like a low-down bargainer. Maybe they're so high up in well-being they can't any more understand my low thoughts for money.

From his rich height the man preached down to me that I must not be so grabbing for wages. Only just landed from the ship and already thinking about money when I should be thankful to associate with "Americans."

The woman, out of her smooth, smiling fatness assured me that this was my chance for a summer vacation in the country with her two lovely children. My great chance to learn to be a civilized being, to become an American by living with them.

So, made to feel that I was in the hands of American friends, invited to share with them their home, their plenty, their happiness, I pushed out from my head the worry for wages. Here was my first chance to begin my life in the sunshine, after my long darkness. My laugh was all over my face as I said to them: "I'll trust myself to you. What I'm worth you'll give me." And I entered their house like a child by the hand.

The best of me I gave them. Their house cares were my house cares. I got up early. I worked till late. All that my soul hungered to give I put into the passion with which I scrubbed floors, scoured pots, and washed clothes. I was so grateful to mingle with the American people, to hear the music of the American language, that I never knew tiredness.

There was such a freshness in my brains and such a willingness in my heart that I could go on and on—not only with the work of the house, but work with my head—learning new words from the children, the grocer, the butcher, the iceman. I was not even afraid to ask for words from the police-man on the street. And every new word made me see new American things with American eyes. I felt like a Columbus, finding new worlds through every new word.

But words alone were only for the inside of me. The outside of me still branded me for a steerage immigrant. I had to have clothes to forget myself that I'm a stranger yet. And so I had to have money to buy these clothes.

The month was up. I was so happy! Now I'd have money. *My own, earned* money. Money to buy a new shirt on my back—shoes on my feet. Maybe yet an American dress and hat!

Ach! How high rose my dreams! How plainly I saw all that I would do with my visionary wages shining like a light over my head!

In my imagination I already walked in my new American clothes. How beautiful I looked as I saw myself like a picture before my eyes! I saw how I would throw away my immigrant rags tied up in my immigrant shawl. With money to buy—free money in my hands—I'd show them that I could look like an American in a day.

Like a prisoner in his last night in prison, counting the seconds that will free him from his chains, I trembled breathlessly for the minute I'd get the wages in my hand.

Before dawn I rose.

I shined up the house like a jewel-box.

I prepared breakfast and waited with my heart in my mouth for my lady and gentleman to rise. At last I heard them stirring. My eyes were jumping out of my head to them when I saw them coming in and seating themselves by the table.

Like a hungry cat rubbing up to its boss for meat, so I edged and simpered around them as I passed them the food. Without my will, like a beggar, my hand reached out to them.

The breakfast was over. And no word yet from my wages.

"*Gottuniu!*" I thought to myself. "Maybe they're so busy with their own things they forgot it's the day for my wages. Could they who have everything know what I was to do with my first American dollars? How could they, soak-ing in plenty, how could they feel the longing and the fierce hunger in me, pressing up through each visionary dollar? How could they know the gnawing ache of my avid fingers for the feel of my own, earned dollars? *My* dollars that I could spend like a free person. *My* dollars that would make me feel with everybody alike!"

Lunch came. Lunch past.

Oi-i weh! Not a word yet about my money.

It was near dinner. And not a word yet about my wages.

I began to set the table. But my head—it swam away from me. I broke a glass. The silver dropped from my nervous fingers. I couldn't stand it any longer. I dropped everything and rushed over to my American lady and gentleman.

"*Oi weh!* The money—my money—my wages!" I cried breathlessly.

Four cold eyes turned on me.

"Wages? Money?" The four eyes turned into hard stone as they looked me up and down. "Haven't you a comfortable bed to sleep, and three good meals a day? You're only a month here. Just came to America. And you already think about money. Wait till you're worth any money. What use are you without knowing English? You should be glad we keep you here. It's like a vacation for you. Other girls pay money yet to be in the country."

It went black for my eyes. I was so choked no words came to my lips. Even the tears went dry in my throat.

I left. Not a dollar for all my work.

For a long, long time my heart ached and ached like a sore wound. If murderers would have robbed me and killed me it wouldn't have hurt me so much. I couldn't think through my pain. The minute I'd see before me how they looked at me, the words they said to me—then everything began to bleed in me. And I was helpless.

For a long, long time the thought of ever working in an "American" family made me tremble with fear, like the fear of wild wolves. No—never again would I trust myself to an "American" family, no matter how fine their language and how sweet their smile.

It was blotted out in me all trust in friendship from "Americans." But the life in me still burned to live. The hope in me still craved to hope. In darkness, in dirt, in hunger and want, but only to live on!

There had been no end to my day—working for the "American" family.

Now rejecting false friendships from higher-ups in America, I turned back to the Ghetto. I worked on a hard bench with my own kind on either side of me. I knew before I began what my wages were to be. I knew what my hours were to be. And I knew the feeling of the end of the day.

From the outside my second job seemed worse than the first. It was in a sweatshop of a Delancey Street basement, kept up by an old, wrinkled woman that looked like a black witch of greed. My work was sewing on buttons. While the morning was still dark I walked into a dark basement. And darkness met me when I turned out of the basement.

Day after day, week after week, all the contact I got with America was handling dead buttons. The money I earned was hardly enough to pay for bread and rent. I didn't have a room to myself. I didn't even have a bed. I slept on a mattress on the floor in a rat-hole of a room occupied by a dozen other immigrants. I was always hungry—oh, so hungry! The scant meals I could afford only sharpened my appetite for real food. But I felt myself better off than working in the "American" family, where I had three good meals a day and a bed to myself. With all the hunger and darkness of the sweat-shop, I had at least the evening to myself. And all night was mine. When all were asleep, I used to creep up on the roof of the tenement and talk out my heart in silence to the stars in the sky.

"Who am I? What am I? What do I want with my life? Where is America? Is there an America? What is this wilderness in which I'm lost?"

I'd hurl my questions and then think and think. And I could not tear it out of me, the feeling that America must be somewhere, somehow—only I couldn't find it—*my America*, where I would work for love and not for a living. I was like a thing following blindly after something far off in the dark!

"*Oi weh!*" I'd stretch out my hand up in the air. "My head is so lost in America! What's the use of all my working if I'm not in it? Dead buttons is not me."

Then the busy season started in the shop. The mounds of buttons grew and grew. The long day stretched out longer. I had to begin with the buttons earlier and stay with them till later in the night. The old witch turned into a huge greedy maw for wanting more and more buttons.

For a glass of tea, for a slice of herring over black bread, she would buy us up to stay another and another hour, till there seemed no end to her demands.

One day, the light of self-assertion broke into my cellar darkness.

"I don't want the tea. I don't want your herring," I said with terrible boldness. "I only want to go home. I only want the evening to myself!"

"You fresh mouth, you!" cried the old witch. "You learned already too much in America. I want no clock-watchers in my shop. Out you go!"

I was driven out to cold and hunger. I could no longer pay for my mattress on the floor. I no longer could buy the bite in my mouth. I walked the streets. I knew what it is to be alone in a strange city, among strangers.

But I laughed through my tears. So I learned too much already in America because I wanted the whole evening to myself? Well America has yet to teach me still more: how to get not only the whole evening to myself, but a whole day a week like the American workers.

That sweat-shop was a bitter memory but a good school. It fitted me for a regular factory. I could walk in boldly and say I could work at something, even if it was only sewing on buttons.

Gradually, I became a trained worker. I worked in a light, airy factory, only eight hours a day. My boss was no longer a sweater and a blood-squeezer. The first freshness of the morning was mine. And the whole evening was mine. All day Sunday was mine.

Now I had better food to eat. I slept on a better bed. Now, I even looked dressed up like the American-born. But inside of me I knew that I was not yet an American. I choked with longing when I met an American-born, and I could say nothing.

Something cried dumb in me. I couldn't help it. I didn't know what it was I wanted. I only knew I wanted. I wanted. Like the hunger in the heart that never gets food.

An English class for foreigners started in our factory. The teacher had such a good, friendly face, her eyes looked so understanding, as if she could see right into my heart. So I went to her one day for an advice:

"I don't know what is with me the matter," I began. "I have no rest in me. I never yet done what I want."

"What is it you want to do, child?" she asked me.

"I want to do something with my head, my feelings. All day long, only with my hands I work."

"First you must learn English." She patted me as if I was not yet grown up. "Put your mind on that, and then we'll see."

So for a time I learned the language. I could almost begin to think with English words in my head. But in my heart the emptiness still hurt. I burned to give, to give something, to do something, to be something. The dead work with my hands was killing me. My work left only hard stones on my heart.

Again I went to our factory teacher and cried out to her: "I know already to read and write the English language, but I can't put it into words what I want. What is it in me so different that can't come out?"

She smiled at me down from her calmness as if I were a little bit out of my head. "What *do you want* to do?"

"I feel. I see. I hear. And I want to think it out. But I'm like dumb in me. I only feel I'm different—different from everybody."

She looked at me close and said nothing for a minute. "You ought to join one of the social clubs of the Women's Association," she advised.

"What's the Women's Association?" I implored greedily.

"A group of American women who are trying to help the working-girl find herself. They have a special department for immigrant girls like you."

I joined the Women's Association. On my first evening there they announced a lecture: "The Happy Worker and His Work," by the Welfare director of the United Mills Corporation.

"Is there such a thing as a happy worker at his work?" I wondered. Happiness is only by working at what you love. And what poor girl can ever find it to work at what she loves? My old dreams about my America rushed through my mind. Once I thought that in America everybody works for love. Nobody has to worry for a living. Maybe this welfare man came to show me the *real* America that till now I sought in vain.

With a lot of polite words the head lady of the Women's Association introduced a higher-up that looked like the king of kings of business. Never before in my life did I ever see a man with such a sureness in his step, such power in his face, such friendly positiveness in his eye as when he smiled upon us.

"Efficiency is the new religion of business," he began. "In big business houses, even in up-to-date factories, they no longer take the first comer and give him any job that happens to stand empty. Efficiency begins at the employment office. Experts are hired for the one purpose, to find out how best to fit the worker to his work. It's economy for the boss to make the worker happy." And then he talked a lot more on efficiency in educated language that was over my head.

I didn't know exactly what it meant—efficiency—but if it was to make the worker happy at his work, then that's what I had been looking for since I came to America. I only felt from watching him that he was happy by his job. And as I looked on this clean, well-dressed, successful one, who wasn't ashamed to say he rose from an office-boy, it made me feel that I, too, could lift myself up for a person.

He finished his lecture, telling us about the Vocational-Guidance Center that the Women's Association started.

The very next evening I was at the Vocational-Guidance Center. There I found a young, college-looking woman. Smartness and health shining from her eyes! She, too, looked as if she knew her way in America. I could tell at the first glance: here is a person that is happy by what she does.

"I feel you'll understand me," I said right away.

She leaned over with pleasure in her face: "I hope I can."

"I want to work by what's in me. Only, I don't know what's in me. I only feel I'm different."

She gave me a quick, puzzled look from the corner of her eyes. "What are you doing now?"

"I'm the quickest shirtwaist hand on the floor. But my heart wastes away by such work. I think and think, and my thoughts can't come out."

"Why don't you think out your thoughts in shirtwaists? You could learn to be a designer. Earn more money."

"I don't want to look on waists. If my hands are sick from waists, how could my head learn to put beauty into them?"

"But you must earn your living at what you know, and rise slowly from job to job."

I looked at her office sign: "Vocational Guidance." "What's your vocational guidance?" I asked. "How to rise from job to job—how to earn more money?"

The smile went out from her eyes. But she tried to be kind yet. "What *do* you want?" she asked, with a sigh of last patience.

"I want America to want me."

She fell back in her chair, thunderstruck with my boldness. But yet, in a low voice of educated self-control, she tried to reason with me:

"You have to *show* that you have something special for America before America has need of you."

"But I never had a chance to find out what's in me, because I always had to work for a living. Only, I feel it's efficiency for America to find out what's in me so different, so I could give it out by my work."

Her eyes half closed as they bored through me. Her mouth opened to speak, but no words came from her lips. So I flamed up with all that was choking in me like a house on fire:

"America gives free bread and rent to criminals in prison. They got grand houses with sunshine, fresh air, doctors and teachers, even for the crazy ones. Why don't they have free boarding-schools for immigrants— strong people—willing people? Here you see us burning up with something different, and America turns her head away from us."

Her brows lifted and dropped down. She shrugged her shoulders away from me with the look of pity we give to cripples and hopeless lunatics.

"America is no Utopia. First you must become efficient in earning a living before you can indulge in your poetic dreams."

I went away from the vocational-guidance office with all the air out of my lungs. All the light out of my eyes. My feet dragged after me like dead wood.

Till now there had always lingered a rosy veil of hope over my emptiness, a hope that a miracle would happen. I would open up my eyes some day and suddenly find the America of my dreams. As a young girl hungry for love sees always before her eyes the picture of lover's arms around her, so I saw always in my heart the vision of Utopian America.

But now I felt that the America of my dreams never was and never could be. Reality had hit me on the head as with a club. I felt that the America that I sought was nothing but a shadow—an echo—a chimera of lunatics and crazy immigrants.

Stripped of all illusion, I looked about me. The long desert of wasting days of drudgery stared me in the face. The drudgery that I had lived through, and the endless drudgery still ahead of me rose over me like a withering wilderness of sand. In vain were all my cryings, in vain were all frantic efforts of my spirit to find the living waters of understanding for my perishing lips. Sand, sand was everywhere. With every seeking, every reaching out I only lost myself deeper and deeper in a vast sea of sand.

I knew now the American language. And I knew now, if I talked to the Americans from morning till night, they could not understand what the Russian soul of me wanted. They could not understand *me* any more than if I talked to them in Chinese. Between my soul and the American soul were worlds of difference that no words could bridge over. What was that difference? What made the Americans so far apart from me?

I began to read the American history. I found from the first pages that America started with a band of Courageous Pilgrims. They had left their native country as I had left mine. They had crossed an unknown ocean and landed in an unknown country, as I.

But the great difference between the first Pilgrims and me was that they expected to make America, build America, create their own world of liberty. I wanted to find it ready made.

I read on. I delved deeper down into the American history. I saw how the Pilgrim Fathers came to a rocky desert country, surrounded by Indian savages on all sides. But undaunted, they pressed on—through danger—through famine, pestilence, and want—they pressed on. They did not ask the Indians for sympathy, for understanding. They made no demands on anybody, but on their own indomitable spirit of persistence.

And I—I was forever begging a crumb of sympathy, a gleam of understanding from strangers who could not understand.

I, when I encountered a few savage Indian scalpers, like the old witch of the sweat-shop, like my "Americanized" countryman, who cheated me of my wages—I, when I found myself on the lonely, untrodden path through which all seekers of the new world must pass, I lost heart and said: "There is no America!"

Then came a light—a great revelation! I saw America—a big idea—a deathless hope—a world still in the making. I saw that it was the glory of America that it was not yet finished. And I, the last comer, had her share to give, small or great, to the making of America, like those Pilgrims who came in the *Mayflower*.

Fired up by this revealing light, I began to build a bridge of understanding between the American-born and myself. Since their life was shut out from such as me, I began to open up my life and the lives of my people to them. And life draws life. In only writing about the Ghetto I found America.

Great chances have come to me. But in my heart is always a deep sadness. I feel like a man who is sitting down to a secret table of plenty, while his near ones and dear ones are perishing before his eyes. My very joy in doing the work I love hurts me like secret guilt, because all about me I see so many with my longings, my burning eagerness, to do and to be, wasting their days in drudgery they hate, merely to buy bread and pay rent. And America is losing all that richness of the soul.

The Americans of tomorrow, the America that is every day nearer coming to be, will be too wise, too open-hearted, too friendly-handed, to let the least lastcomer at their gates knock in vain with his gifts unwanted.

1923

■ # MICHAEL GOLD
1893–1967 ■

Michael Gold was the eldest of three sons born to the Graniches, Jewish immigrants living on New York's Lower East Side. During the Palmer Raids of 1919–1920 he took the name Michael Gold after a Jewish Civil War veteran he admired for having fought to "free the slaves." When his father's health and business failed, the son had to go to work at age twelve to help support the family. His anger at capitalism was initially more personal than political, more subjective than ideological: unlike the mass of impoverished ghetto dwellers, he had been reared to expect better.

He was twenty-one and his life was going nowhere when, having "no politics . . . except hunger," Granich happened to wander into Union Square one April day in 1914 during a demonstration, was knocked down by a policeman, and had the epiphany he describes at the end of *Jews Without Money*. The Jewish Messiah that the young boy of *Jews Without Money* prays for will not come in Gold's lifetime; but the Marxist Messiah, who will punish the guilty—*i.e.*, the capitalists, the exploiters—and reward the innocent—*i.e.*, the workers, the exploited—will.

The first time he read *The Masses*, the important revolutionary magazine edited by Max Eastman and Floyd Dell, Granich was amazed that poetry and fiction about being poor was publishable—he had been writing poems and stories that he assumed he could never publish. Four months after his Union Square epiphany in August 1914, *The Masses* published Granich's first piece, a poem about three anarchists who had died in a bomb explosion, and his fifty-year career as a writer was launched.

He left the Jewish, working-class Lower East Side and moved to Greenwich Village, where he started to move in the American and Bohemian leftist and literary circles then swirling around John Reed and Eugene O'Neill. Discovering he could support himself working for the leftist press, Granich ceased working as a manual laborer. In 1921 he became an editor of the *Liberator*, which had succeeded the suppressed *Masses* and became the cultural journal of the Communist Party. When the *Liberator* became wholly political in the mid-1920s, he helped found the *New Masses*, devoted to publishing literary works *by* workers rather than by literary leftists with working-class sympathies. He became editor-in-chief in 1928.

Jews Without Money, which Gold had been working on throughout the 1920s, was published in February 1930. Had it been published a year or two earlier when the Jazz Age still seemed to be booming, it might well have gone unnoticed; had it been published a year or two later in the midst of the Great Depression, it might have seemed old hat. The collapse of the economy had ruined the plans and destroyed the dreams of a whole generation, as the collapse of Papa Granich's business and health twenty years earlier had ruined the plans and destroyed the dreams of Yitzhak-already-Isaac-already-Irwin Granich. Although *Jews Without Money* was not *about* the 1930s and did not emerge from a 1930s sensibility, having been composed in the 1920s, it seemed to many the preeminent 1930s novel. By October it had gone into its eleventh printing.

The book's success was not based on its subject matter alone. It was Gold's description of a degrading ghetto existence—the diseases, the early deaths, the degenerates, crime, prostitution, filth—and his arraignment of capitalism as its progenitor and cause that made *Jews Without Money* seem so contemporary, so urgent, in 1930. The heroic center of *Jews Without Money* is Katie Gold, whose selflessness, whose love for fellow men and women, Jew and Gentile, and whose energy and indomitability are all channeled into an almost cosmic sense of responsibility to and for everyone she comes into contact with. Katie's persistent struggle to survive with dignity and generosity of spirit stands as a paradigm for the Workers' Revolution.

Gold became a national figure, cultural commissar of the Communist Party, arbiter of artistic value according to the artist's political allegiances. As the Twenties had buoyed up F. Scott Fitzgerald, the Thirties buoyed up Michael Gold—it was the decade for which he was born. In 1933 he became daily columnist for the *Daily Worker*, the mass circulation Communist Party newspaper. In 1935, in the introduction for a new edition of *Jews Without Money*, Gold noted that it had been translated into French, Swedish, Bohemian, Bulgarian, Romanian, Jugo-Slavian [sic], Italian, Japanese, Chinese, Ukrainian, Russian, Yiddish, Dutch, and Tatar and was particularly proud that "German radicals had translated it and were spreading it widely as a form of propaganda against the Nazi anti-Semitic lies."

Unlike many of the Marxists of his generation, Michael Gold never shifted gears, never changed with the times. Through the Forties, Fifties, and Sixties he remained remarkably—some would say foolishly, naively, stupidly even, given the revelation of the Stalinist purges—faithful to that twenty-one-year-old's epiphany: "O workers' Revolution! ... You are the true Messiah!" Gold's chance of surviving as a writer has come to depend much more on the religion and ethnicity that he abandoned than on his politics and ideology, much more on the Jewish identity he implicitly rejected at the end of *Jews Without Money* and that shaped the first twenty-one years of his life than on the Marxist identity he explicitly donned at the end of *Jews Without Money*.

Barry Gross
Michigan State University

PRIMARY WORKS

Jews Without Money, 1930; *The Hollow Men*, 1941; *Mike Gold: A Literary Anthology*, ed. by Michael Folsom, 1972.

from **Jews Without Money**

The Soul of a Landlord

1

On the East Side people buy their groceries a pinch at a time; three cents' worth of sugar, five cents' worth of butter, everything in penny fractions. The good Jewish black bread that smells of harvest time, is sliced into a dozen parts and sold for pennies. But that winter even pennies were scarce.

There was a panic on Wall Street. Multitudes were without work; there were strikes, suicides, and food riots. The prostitutes roamed our street like wolves; never was there so much competition among them.

Life froze. The sun vanished from the deathly gray sky. The streets reeked with snow and slush. There were hundreds of evictions. I walked down a street between dripping tenement walls. The rotten slush ate through my shoes. The wind beat on my face. I saw a stack of furniture before a tenement: tables, chairs, a washtub packed with crockery and bedclothes, a broom, a dresser, a lamp.

The snow covered them. The snow fell, too, on a little Jew and his wife and three children. They huddled in a mournful group by their possessions. They had placed a saucer on one of the tables. An old woman with a market bag mumbled a prayer in passing. She dropped a penny in the saucer. Other people did the same. Each time the evicted family lowered its eyes in shame. They were not beggars, but "respectable" people. But if enough pennies fell in the saucer, they might have rent for a new home. This was the one hope left them.

Winter. Building a snow fort one morning, we boys dug out a litter of frozen kittens and their mother. The little ones were still blind. They had been born into it, but had never seen our world.

Other dogs and cats were frozen. Men and women, too, were found dead in hallways and on docks. Mary Sugar Bum met her end in an alley. She was found half-naked, clutching a whiskey bottle in her blue claw. This was her last "love" affair.

Horses slipped on the icy pavement, and quivered there for hours with broken legs, until a policeman arrived to shoot them.

The boys built a snow man. His eyes were two coals; his nose a potato. He wore a derby hat and smoked a corncob pipe. His arms were flung wide; in one of them he held a broom, in the other a newspaper. This Golem[1] with his amazed eyes and idiotic grin amused us all for an afternoon.

The next morning we found him strangely altered. His eyes and nose had been torn out; his grin smashed, like a war victim's. Who had played this joke? The winter wind.

2

Mrs. Rosenbaum owned a grocery store on our street. She was a widow with four children, and lived in two rooms back of the store. She slaved from dawn until midnight; a big, clumsy woman with a chapped face and masses of untidy hair; always grumbling, groaning, gossiping about her ailments. Sometimes she was nervous and screamed at her children, and beat them. But she was a kind-hearted woman, and that winter suffered a great deal. Every one was very poor, and she was too good not to give them groceries on credit.

"I'm crazy to do it!" she grumbled in her icy store. "I'm a fool! But when a child comes for a loaf of bread, and I have the bread, and I know her family is starving, how can I refuse her? Yet I have my own children to think of! I am being ruined! The store is being emptied! I can't meet my bills!"

She was kind. Kindness is a form of suicide in a world based on the law of competition.

---

[1]According to Jewish folklore, the golem was an artificial figure in human form that Rabbi Low of Prague created in the sixteenth century to frighten the enemies of the Jews.

One day we watched the rewards of kindness. The sheriff's men arrived to seize Mrs. Rosenbaum's grocery. They tore down the shelves and fixtures, they carted off tubs of butter, drums of kerosene, sacks of rice, flour and potatoes.

Mrs. Rosenbaum stood by watching her own funeral. Her fat kind face was swollen with crying as with toothache. Her eyes blinked in bewilderment. Her children clung to her skirts and cried. Snow fell from the sky, a crowd muttered its sympathy, a policeman twirled his club.

What happened to her after that, I don't know. Maybe the Organized Charities helped her; or maybe she died. O golden dyspeptic God of America, you were in a bad mood that winter. We were poor, and you punished us harshly for this worst of sins.

3

My father lay in bed. His shattered feet ached in each bone. His painter's sickness came back on him; he suffered with lung and kidney pains.

He was always depressed. His only distraction was to read the Yiddish newspapers, and to make gloomy conversation at night over the suicides, the hungry families, the robberies, murders and catastrophes that newspapers record.

"It will come to an end!" said my father. "People are turning into wolves! They will soon eat each other! They will tear down the cities, and destroy the world in flames and blood!"

"Drink your tea," said my mother cheerfully, "God is still in the world. You will get better and work and laugh again. Let us not lose courage."

My father was fretful and nervous with an invalid's fears.

"But what if we are evicted, Katie?"

"We won't be evicted, not while I have my two hands and can work," said my mother.

"But I don't want you to work!" my father cried. "It breaks up our home!"

"It doesn't!" said my mother. "I have time and strength for everything."

4

At first my mother had feared going out to work in a cafeteria among Christians. But after a few days she settled easily into the life of the polyglot kitchen, and learned to fight, scold, and mother the Poles, Germans, Italians, Irish and Negroes who worked there. They liked her, and soon called her "Momma," which made her vain.

"You should hear how a big black dishwasher named Joe, how he comes to me to-day, and says, 'Momma, I'm going to quit. Every one is against me here because I am black,' he says. 'The whole world is against us black people.'"

"So I said to him, 'Joe, I am not against you. Don't be foolish, don't go out to be a bum again. The trouble with you here is you are lazy. If you would work harder the others would like you, too.' So he said, 'Momma, all right I'll stay,' So that's how it is in the restaurant. They call me Momma, even the black ones."

It was a large, high-priced cafeteria for businessmen on lower Broadway. My mother was a chef's helper, and peeled and scoured tons of vegetables for cooking. Her wages were seven dollars a week.

She woke at five, cooked our breakfast at home, then had to walk a mile to her job. She came home at five-thirty, and made supper, cleaned the house, was busy on her feet until bedtime. It hurt my father's masculine pride to see his wife working for wages. But my mother liked it all; she was proud of earning money, and she liked her fights in the restaurant.

My dear, tireless, little dark-faced mother! Why did she always have to fight? Why did she have to give my father a new variety of headache with accounts of her battles for "justice" in the cafeteria? The manager there was a fat blond Swede with a *Kaiserliche* mustache,[2] and the manners of a Mussolini.[3] All the workers feared this bull-necked tyrant, except my mother. She told him "what was what." When the meat was rotten, when the drains were clogged and smelly, or the dishwashers overworked, she told him so. She scolded him as if he were her child, and he listened meekly. The other workers fell into the habit of telling their complaints to my mother, and she would relay them to the Swedish manager.

"It's because he needs me," said my mother proudly. "That's why he lets me scold him. I am one of his best workers; he can depend on me in the rush. And he knows I am not like the other kitchen help; they work a day or two; then quit, but I stay on. So he's afraid to fire me, and I tell him what is what."

It was one of those super-cafeterias, with flowers on the tables, a string orchestra during the lunch hour, and other trimmings. But my mother had no respect for it. She would never eat the lunch served there to the employees, but took along two cheese sandwiches from home.

"Your food is *Dreck*,[4] it is fit only for pigs," she told the manager bluntly. And once she begged me to promise never to eat hamburger steak in a restaurant when I grew up.

"Swear it to me, Mikey!" she said. "Never, never eat hamburger!"

"I swear it, momma."

"Poison!" she went on passionately. "They don't care if they poison the people, so long as there's money in it. I've seen with my own eyes. If I could write English, I'd write a letter to all the newspapers."

"Mind your own business!" my father growled. "Such things are for Americans. It is their country and their hamburger steak."

---

[2]Kaiser Wilhelm II, Emperor of Germany and King of Prussia (1888–1918), had a very prominent and imposing mustache.

[3]Benito Mussolini founded the Italian Fascist Party in 1919 and was Prime Minister of Italy (1922–1943).

[4]Yiddish for feces.

5

Our tenement was nothing but a junk-heap of rotten lumber and brick. It was an old ship on its last voyage; in the battering winter storms, all its seams opened, and wind and snow came through.

The plaster was always falling down, the stairs were broken and dirty. Five times that winter the water pipes froze, and floods spurted from the plumbing, and dripped from the ceilings.

There was no drinking water in the tenement for days. The women had to put on their shawls and hunt in the street for water. Up and down the stairs they groaned, lugging pails of water. In December, when Mr. Zunzer the landlord called for rent, some of the neighbors told him he ought to fix the plumbing.

"Next week," he murmured into his scaly beard.

"Next week!" my mother sneered, after he had gone. "A dozen times he has told us that, the yellow-faced murderer! May the lice eat him next week! May his false teeth choke him to death next week!"

Some tenants set out hunting for other flats, but could find none. The cheap ones were always occupied, the better flats were too dear. Besides, it wasn't easy to move; it cost money, and it meant leaving one's old neighbors.

"The tenements are the same everywhere, the landlords the same," said a woman. "I have seen places to-day an Irisher[5] wouldn't live in, and the rents are higher than here."

Toward the end of January, during a cataclysmic spell of snow, ice, and iron frost, the pipes burst again, and for weeks every one suffered for lack of water; the babies, old people, the sick ones. The neighbors were indignant. They gathered in the halls and held wild conversations. Mrs. Cracauer suggested that some one send in a complaint to the Board of Health. Mrs. Schuman said this was useless, the Board of Health belonged to Tammany Hall,[6] and the landlord had a pull there.

Mrs. Tannenbaum exploded like a bomb of Jewish emotion. She was a worse agitator than my mother, a roly-poly hysterical hippopotamus with a piercing voice.

"Let's all move out together!" she shrieked. "Let's get axes and hack out the walls and smash the windows and then move out!"

"No," said my mother, "I know something better."

Then and now, on the East Side, there have been rent strikes of tenants against their landlords. East Side tenants, I am sure, have always been the most obstreperous that ever gave a landlord sleepless nights and indigestion. My mother suggested a rent strike. The neighbors agreed with

---

[5]Slang for someone from Ireland.
[6]Tammany Hall was the headquarters of the Tammany Society, a political organization that controlled New York City politics and plundered it of millions of dollars in the nineteenth century. In the twentieth century Tammany Hall was synonymous with political patronage in New York as dispensed by the Democratic party.

enthusiasm. They chattered about it in the weeks that followed. One told the other how she would curse the landlord when he came, and refuse to pay the rent.

"I'll spit in his face," said Mrs. Tannenbaum, "and tell him to kiss my *tochess*[7] for his rent. Then I'll slam the door on him. That's what I'll do."

There spread through our tenement that feeling of exhilarating tension which precedes a battle. One counted the days until the first of February, when the landlord called for rent. What would he do? What would he say?

The hour came. Mrs. Tannenbaum, the fat, wildeyed hippopotamus agitator, was the first tenant upon whose door the landlord knocked. She opened it meekly, paid the rent, and never spoke a word. Her husband had forbade her to make a fuss. He didn't want the bother of moving.

The next tenant, Mrs. Schuman across the hall, was so amazed at this treachery to the cause, that she paid her rent, too. Every one else paid, except my mother. She faced the landlord boldly, and said in a clear voice, for every one to hear:

"Fix first the plumbing, Mr. Zunzer, then I'll pay the rent."

Mr. Zunzer glared at her with his goggly eyes. For a minute he could not speak for rage. Then he yanked his red scrubby beard, and said:

"I'll throw you out! Mischief-maker, I know who you are! You're the one who has been starting the rent strike here!"

"Yes," said my mother coolly. "And you've scared the others into paying you, but you can't scare me."

"I can't?" sputtered the landlord. "I will show you. To-morrow I'll call the sheriff and throw your furniture on the street!"

"No!" said my mother. "First you will have to take me to court! I know what my rights are!"

"*Pfoo*[8] on your rights!" said the landlord. "I can do anything I want in this district. I have a pull with Tammany Hall!"

My mother put her hands on her hips, and asked him quietly: "But with God have you a pull, Mr. Zunzer?"

Mr. Zunzer was startled by this sally. He tried to meet it with haughtiness.

"Don't talk to me of God," he said. "I am more often in the synagogue than you and your husband together. I give a dozen times more money there."

"Every one knows you have money," said my mother quietly, "even the Angel of Death. Some day he will come for *all* your money, Mr. Zunzer."

The landlord's face paled; he trembled. He tried to speak, but the words choked him. He looked queer, as if he were about to faint. Then he pulled himself together, and walked away. My mother slammed the door after him, and laughed heartily. She rushed to the window, and called across the airshaft[9] to Mrs. Ashkenazi and other neighbors. They had been sitting at their windows, listening greedily to the quarrel.

[7]Yiddish for ass.
[8]Slang for "I spit on."
[9]In tenement buildings a narrow court enclosed within four walls but open at the top as a source of air supply for internal windows.

"Did you hear what hell I gave to that landlord? Didn't I give it to him good?"

"Madwoman!" my father called from the bedroom. "Where will we go when he puts us out to-morrow?"

"He won't put us out," said my mother confidently. "The landlord is scared of me, I could see it in his eyes."

My father sneered at her. Who ever heard of a landlord being scared of his tenant? But it was true this time; the landlord did not bother us again. He actually fixed the plumbing. He sent an agent to collect the rent. He was scared; my mother had made a lucky hit when she taunted him with the Angel of Death.

Mr. Zunzer was superstitious. His deepest fear was that burglars would break in some night and kill him and take his money. Dr. Solow told us the story one night:

6

"When Mr. Zunzer first came to America," Dr. Solow related, "he peddled neckties, shoelaces and collarbuttons from a tray. He was very poor. He slept on a mattress in a cobbler's damp cellar, and lived on herrings and dry bread. He starved and suffered for five years. That's how he got the yellow face you see on him.

"Every penny he could grab he saved like a miser. He tied the nickels and dimes in a bag which he hid in a crack under his mattress. He worried. Big rats ran across his face while he slept. They did not bother him a tenth as much as did thoughts of his money.

"Oh, how sacred was that money to him. It was money to bring his wife and children from Europe. He was hungry for them. He would cry at night thinking about them. The money was not money; it was his family, his peace, his happiness, his life and death.

"One night some one stole this money from under the mattress. It was the savings of three years. Mr. Zunzer almost went crazy. He was sick in a hospital for months. He refused to eat. He wanted to die. But he took heart and commenced saving again. In two years he was able to send for his wife and children.

"Happiness did not come with them. Mr. Zunzer had formed the habit of saving money. He was a miser. He grudged his wife and children every cent they needed. He gave them little to eat. His wife fell sick; he grudged her a doctor. She died. At the funeral he fought with the undertaker over the burial price. He was always thinking of money.

"His children grew up hating him for his miserly ways. One by one they left him. The eldest boy became a thief. The second boy joined the U.S. Army. The girl disappeared.

"Mr. Zunzer was left alone. He is rich now, he owns a pawnshop and several tenement houses. But he still lives on herring and dry bread, and saves pennies like a miser. It is a disease.

"He has fits," said Dr. Solow. "Every few months I am called to him. He is rolling on the floor, he knocks his head against furniture, he cuts his face on falling dishes. He screams robbers are killing him, and stealing his money. I talk to him quietly. I give him a medicine. I light the gas, to show him there are no burglars. All night I talk to him as to a child.

"About ten years ago a junkman he knew was murdered by thieves and robbed. Since then Mr. Zunzer has the fear the same thing will happen to him.

"'Listen,' I tell him, 'you must stop worrying about money. It is making you crazy, Mr. Zunzer.'

"He wrings his hands, he weeps, and says to me: 'Yes, Dr. Solow, it is making me crazy. But what can I do? It is in my blood, in my heart. Can I cut it out of me with a knife?'

"'No,' I answer him, 'there are other ways, Mr. Zunzer.'

"'What other ways?' he weeps. 'Shall I throw my money in the river? Shall I give it to the synagogue? What good would it do? How can one live without money? And if other men fight for money, must one not fight, too? The whole world is sick with this disease, Dr. Solow, I am not the only one.'

"So what can I answer? He will die in one of his fits. His money will disappear down the sewer. Sometimes I am sorry for him; it's not altogether his fault. It *is* a world sickness. Even we who are not misers suffer from it. How happy the world would be without money! Yet what's to be done?"

My mother wagged her head mournfully through this tale of Mr. Zunzer's sickness. She said:

"The poor man! Maybe he needs another wife."

Ach, my mother! She could be sorry for any one, even a landlord.

7

Yet she fought the landlord again that winter. The rent was due, and by a coincidence my brother, my sister, my mother and I all needed shoes. We had worn the old ones until they were in shreds. It was impossible to patch them any longer. My mother decided to pawn the family's diamond ring— the one my father had bought in a prosperous period.

I went with my mother to Mr. Zunzer's pawnshop. In summer it had swinging wicker doors like a saloon. Now we entered through heavy curtained doors that shut out the daylight.

It was a grim, crowded little store smelling of camphor. There were some gloomy East Side people standing around. The walls were covered with strange objects: guitars, shovels, blankets, clocks; with lace curtains, underwear and crutches; all these miserable trophies of the defeat of the poor.

Everything worth more than a quarter was taken in pawn by Mr. Zunzer, from an old man's false teeth to a baby's diapers. People were sure to redeem these little necessities. If he made ten cents on a transaction he was satisfied, for there were hundreds of them. At the end of a week there was a big total.

It was said in the neighborhood he also bought stolen things from the young thieves and pickpockets.

We waited for our turn. An old Irish worker in overalls, with merry blue eyes and a rosy face, was trying to pawn some tools. He was drunk, and pleaded that he be given a dollar. Mr. Zunzer gave him only half a dollar, and said, "Get the hell out." The white-haired Irishman jigged and sang as he left for the saloon.

A dingy little woman pawned a baby carriage. An old Jewish graybeard pawned his prayer book and praying shawl. A fat Polish woman with a blowsy, weepy face pawned an accordion. A young girl pawned some quilts; then our turn came.

The landlord wore a black alpaca coat[10] in the pawnshop, and a skull cap.[11] He crouched on a stool behind the counter. One saw only his scaly yellow face and bulging eyes; he was like an anxious spider. He picked up the ring my mother presented him, screwed a jeweler's glass into his eye, and studied it in the gaslight.

"Ten dollars," he said abruptly.

"I must have fifteen," said my mother.

"Ten dollars," said the landlord.

"No, fifteen," said my mother.

He looked up irritably and stared at her with his near-sighted eyes. He recognized her in the pawnshop gloom.

"You're my tenant, aren't you?" he asked, "the one that made all the trouble for me?"

"Yes," said my mother, "what of it?"

The landlord smiled bitterly.

"Nothing," he said, "but you are sure to come to a bad end."

"No worse end than yours," said my mother, "may the bananas grow in your throat!"

"Don't curse me in my own shop!" said the landlord. "I'll have you arrested. What do you want here?"

"I told you," said my mother, "I want fifteen dollars on this ring."

"It is worth only ten," said the landlord.

"To me you must give fifteen," said my mother boldly.

The landlord paled. He looked at my mother fearfully. She knew his secret. My mother mystified and alarmed him with her boldness. He was accustomed to people who cowered.

He wrote out a ticket for the ring, gave my mother fifteen dollars. She crowed over her victory as we walked home. Next day she bought shoes for my brother, my sister Esther, and myself. Her own shoes she forgot to buy. That's the way she generally arranged things.

1930

---

[10]A fine lightweight cloth made from the woolly hair of an alpaca, an animal similar to a llama.

[11]A close-fitting, brimless cloth cap worn by Orthodox Jewish males.

H. L. MENCKEN
1880–1956

Called by journalist Walter Lippmann in the 1920s "the most powerful personal influence on this whole generation of educated people," H. L. Mencken reigned as national literary arbiter during that decade as well as the most famous social and cultural commentator of his day. From the early days of the twentieth century he led the attack on the genteel tradition in American letters—the Anglo-American tradition that was associated in most readers' eyes with Henry James, William Dean Howells, and "polite letters." Mencken championed early literary naturalists and realists, particularly Theodore Dreiser and Sinclair Lewis, and in the pages of the *Smart Set* and the *American Mercury*, highly influential magazines that he edited for two decades, he attacked provincialism, puritanism, and censorship. A bitter critic of the American alliance with Great Britain in World War I—and, in fact, a critic of all things British—he fought for an expansion of the literary franchise to Americans of non-British descent. He had in mind German Americans (such as Dreiser) and eastern Europeans, but—as editor of *American Mercury*—he also published more African American writers than any other editor of his time.

Mencken came by his "prejudices" (as he termed them) honestly. The son of German American parents whose families had settled in Baltimore in the mid-nineteenth century, he grew up in a mid-Atlantic city dominated by Americans of British (and, often, southern) descent. Scorning a university education (although, he was quick to point out, the Menckens had been a learned family in Germany), he took to journalism in his teens and rose quickly on a series of Baltimore newspapers—all the while reading voraciously, trying his hand at poetry and fiction, and publishing books on Nietzsche and George Bernard Shaw in his twenties. In his late twenties he became literary editor of the stylish *Smart Set*, and by his mid-thirties he was editing the magazine. Silenced during World War I for his unpopular pro-German views, he broke out in 1919 with both fury and delight as he heaped abuse on nearly every aspect of American life: its small-town provincialism, its religious fundamentalism, its tawdry politics, its intellectual sterility. He was particularly rough on the American hinterlands, the South and the Midwest. Holding up a European—and an urban—ideal, and feeling the American East at least approached that ideal, he delighted in attacking those regions that he felt had become the home of American puritanism (by which he meant a sort of raw Calvinism in combination with Victorian propriety) and the hotbed of prohibitionist sentiment. He lambasted the provinces in his Baltimore *Sun* column, in nationally syndicated newspaper pieces, in the pages of the *Mercury*, and in a series of books—appropriately entitled *Prejudices*—that appeared throughout the 1920s.

Among his most famous essays are those he wrote during the Scopes evolution trial in Dayton, Tennessee, in 1925 (and, just after the trial, his vicious obituary essay on the life and career of the fundamentalist William Jennings Bryan) and his diatribe against southern culture, "The Sahara of the Bozart."

That essay and others earned Mencken the reputation of the most hated man in the South since Sherman—although his anti-South essays also stirred a number of young, iconoclastic southern writers (including Thomas Wolfe, Frances Newman, W. J. Cash, Paul Green, and Allen Tate—although Tate later repented of his Menckenism) and played some part in the southern literary renaissance of the 1920s and 1930s. His truth-telling about the South also influenced the young African American writer Richard Wright—who happened upon criticism of Mencken in a Memphis newspaper, turned to Mencken's own essays, and marveled at this writer who, as Wright later stated, denounced "everything American," laughed at the national circus, and used "words as a weapon . . . as one would use a club."

Mencken produced other books in the 1920s and 1930s—reflections on religion, politics, and the national life—but his period of greatest influence declined with the end of the 1920s. Although he regained readers and reputation in the 1940s with a series of autobiographical volumes as well as his multivolume work *The American Language* (he vastly preferred American English to British English), he never recaptured the boisterous spirit of the 1920s. During the Great Depression and World War II, Mencken's brand of satire no longer appeared so funny. His pro-German sympathies kept him from attacking Hitler (whom he characterized as a European version of a benighted southern demagogue), and certain of his writings led to charges of anti-Semitism.

It is with the 1920s, then, that the essential Mencken is to be identified. As an American social critic and humorist he is *sui generis*—the boldest, most outrageous critic of his time, writing in a language that seemed to sing and dance. Scholars have found for him European equivalents—Voltaire and Samuel Johnson are most often cited—but no American precedents. Mencken's own favorite American writer, Mark Twain, perhaps comes closest—with his own bold satire, his truth-telling, his love of the American language, his delight in exposing frauds and hypocrites of all kinds. At its best, Mencken's joyous nay-saying provides ample evidence for Walter Lippmann's shrewd assessment: Mencken "calls you a swine, and an imbecile, and . . . increases your will to live."

Fred Hobson
University of North Carolina at Chapel Hill

PRIMARY WORKS

Prejudices (6 vols.), 1919–27; *The American Language: An Inquiry into the Development of English in the United States*, 1936; *Happy Days*, 1940; *Newspaper Days*, 1941; *Heathen Days*, 1943; *The Diary of H. L. Mencken*, ed. Charles A. Fecher, 1989.

The Sahara of the Bozart

*Alas, for the South! Her books have grown fewer—She never was much
given to literature.*

In the lamented J. Gordon Coogler, author of these elegiac lines, there was the insight of a true poet. He was the last bard of Dixie, at least in the legitimate line. Down there a poet is now almost as rare as an oboe-player, a dry-point etcher or a meta-physician. It is, indeed, amazing to contemplate so vast a vacuity. One thinks of the interstellar spaces, of the colossal reaches of the now mythical ether. Nearly the whole of Europe could be lost in that stupendous region of fat farms, shoddy cities and paralyzed cerebrums: one could throw in France, Germany and Italy, and still have room for the British Isles. And yet, for all its size and all its wealth and all the "progress" it babbles of, it is almost as sterile, artistically, intellectually, culturally, as the Sahara Desert. There are single acres in Europe that house more first-rate men than all the states south of the Potomac; there are probably single square miles in America. If the whole of the late Confederacy were to be engulfed by a tidal wave tomorrow, the effect upon the civilized minority of men in the world would be but little greater than that of a flood on the Yang-tse-kiang. It would be impossible in all history to match so complete a drying-up of civilization.

I say a civilization because that is what, in the old days, the South had, despite the Baptist and Methodist barbarism that reigns down there now. More, it was a civilization of manifold excellences—perhaps the best that the Western Hemisphere has ever seen—undoubtedly the best that These States have ever seen. Down to the middle of the last century, and even beyond, the main hatchery of ideas on this side of the water was across the Potomac bridges. The New England shopkeepers and theologians never really developed a civilization; all they ever developed was a government. They were, at their best, tawdry and tacky fellows, oafish in manner and devoid of imagination; one searches the books in vain for mention of a salient Yankee gentleman; as well look for a Welsh gentleman. But in the south there were men of delicate fancy, urbane instinct and aristocratic manner—in brief, superior men—in brief, gentry. To politics, their chief diversion, they brought active and original minds. It was there that nearly all the political theories we still cherish and suffer under came to birth. It was there that the crude dogmatism of New England was refined and humanized. It was there, above all, that some attention was given to the art of living—that life got beyond and above the state of a mere infliction and became an exhilarating experience. A certain noble spaciousness was in the ancient southern scheme of things. The *Ur*-Confederate had leisure. He liked to toy with ideas. He was hospitable and tolerant. He had the vague thing that we call culture.

But consider the condition of his late empire today. The picture gives one the creeps. It is as if the Civil War stamped out every last bearer of the torch, and left only a mob of peasants on the field. One thinks of Asia Minor, resigned to Armenians, Greeks and wild swine, of Poland abandoned to the Poles. In all that gargantuan paradise of the fourth-rate there is not a single picture gallery worth going into, or a single orchestra capable of playing the nine symphonies of Beethoven, or a single opera-house, or a single theater devoted to decent plays, or a single public monument (built since the war) that is worth looking at, or a single workshop devoted to the making of beautiful things. Once you have counted Robert Loveman (an Ohioan by birth) and John McClure (an Oklahoman) you will not find a single southern poet above the rank of a neighborhood rhymester. Once you have counted James Branch Cabell (a lingering survivor of the *ancien régime:* a scarlet dragonfly imbedded in opaque amber) you will not find a single southern prose writer who can actually write. And once you have—but when you come to critics, musical composers, painters, sculptors, architects and the like, you will have to give it up, for there is not even a bad one between the Potomac mud-flats and the Gulf. Nor an historian. Nor a sociologist. Nor a philosopher. Nor a theologian. Nor a scientist. In all these fields the south is an awe-inspiring blank—a brother to Portugal, Serbia and Esthonia.

Consider, for example, the present estate and dignity of Virginia—in the great days indubitably the premier American state, the mother of Presidents and statesmen, the home of the first American university worthy of the name, the *arbiter elegantiarum* of the western world. Well, observe Virginia to-day. It is years since a first-rate man, save only Cabell, has come out of it; it is years since an idea has come out of it. The old aristocracy went down the red gullet of war; the poor white trash are now in the saddle. Politics in Virginia are cheap, ignorant, parochial, idiotic; there is scarcely a man in office above the rank of a professional job-seeker; the political doctrine that prevails is made up of hand-me-downs from the bumpkinry of the Middle West—Bryanism, Prohibition, vice crusading, all that sort of filthy claptrap; the administration of the law is turned over to professors of Puritanism and espionage; a Washington or a Jefferson, dumped there by some act of God, would be denounced as a scoundrel and jailed overnight. Elegance, *esprit,* culture? Virginia has no art, no literature, no philosophy, no mind or aspiration of her own. Her education has sunk to the Baptist seminary level; not a single contribution to human knowledge has come out of her colleges in twenty-five years; she spends less than half upon her common schools, *per capita,* than any northern state spends. In brief, an intellectual Gobi or Lapland. Urbanity, *politesse,* chivalry? Go to! It was in Virginia that they invented the device of searching for contraband whisky in women's underwear.... There remains, at the top, a ghost of the old aristocracy, a bit wistful and infinitely charming. But it has lost all its old leadership to fabulous monsters from the lower depths; it is submerged in an industrial plutocracy that is ignorant and ignominious. The mind of the state, as it is revealed to the nation, is pathetically naïve and inconsequential. It no longer reacts with energy and elasticity to great problems. It has fallen to the bombastic trivialities of the camp-meeting and the chautauqua. Its foremost exponent—if so flabby a thing may be said to have an exponent—is a stateman whose name is synonymous with empty words, broken pledges and false pretenses. One could no more imagine a Lee or a Washington in the Virginia of to-day than one could imagine a Huxley in Nicaragua.

I choose the Old Dominion, not because I disdain it, but precisely because I esteem it. It is, by long odds, the most civilized of the southern states, now as always. It has sent a host of creditable sons northward; the stream kept running into our own time. Virginians, even the worst of them, show the effects of a great tradition. They hold themselves above other southerners, and with sound pretension. If one turns to such a commonwealth as Georgia the picture becomes far darker. There the liberated lower orders of whites have borrowed the worst commercial bounderism of the Yankee and superimposed it upon a culture that, at bottom, is but little removed from savagery. Georgia is at once the home of the cotton-mill sweater and of the most noisy and vapid sort of chamber of commerce, of the Methodist parson turned Savonarola and of the lynching bee. A self-respecting European, going there to live, would not only find intellectual stimulation utterly lacking; he would actually feel a certain insecurity, as if the scene were the Balkans or the China Coast. The Leo Frank affair was no isolated phenomenon. It fitted into its frame very snugly. It was a natural expression of Georgian notions of truth and justice. There is a state with more than half the area of Italy and more population than either Denmark or Norway, and yet in thirty years it has not produced a single idea. Once upon a time a Georgian printed a couple of books that attracted notice, but immediately it turned out that he was little more than an amanuensis for the local blacks—that his works were really the products, not of white Georgia, but of black Georgia. Writing afterward *as* a white man, he swiftly subsided into the fifth rank. And he is not only the glory of the literature of Georgia; he is, almost literally, the whole of the literature of Georgia—nay, of the entire art of Georgia.

Virginia is the best of the south to-day, and Georgia is perhaps the worst. The one is simply senile; the other is crass, gross, vulgar and obnoxious. Between lies a vast plain of mediocrity, stupidity, lethargy, almost of dead silence. In the north, of course, there is also grossness, crassness, vulgarity. The north, in its way, is also stupid and obnoxious. But nowhere in the north is there such complete sterility, so depressing a lack of all civilized gesture and aspiration. One would find it difficult to unearth a second-rate city between the Ohio and the Pacific that isn't struggling to establish an orchestra, or setting up a little theater, or going in for an art gallery, or making some other effort to get into touch with civilization. These efforts often fail, and sometimes they succeed rather absurdly, but under them there is at least an impulse that deserves respect, and that is the impulse to seek beauty and to experiment with ideas, and so to give the life of every day a certain dignity and purpose. You will find no such impulse in the south. There are no committees down there cadging subscriptions for orchestras; if a string quartet is ever heard there, the news of it has never come out; an opera troupe, when it roves the land, is a nine days' wonder. The little theater movement has swept the whole country, enormously augmenting the public interest in sound plays, giving new dramatists their chance, forcing reforms upon the commercial theater. Everywhere else the wave rolls high—but along the line of the Potomac it breaks upon a rock-bound shore. There is no little theater beyond. There is no gallery of pictures. No artist ever gives exhibitions. No one talks of such things. No one seems to be interested in such things.

As for the cause of this unanimous torpor and doltishness, this curious and almost pathological estrangement from everything that makes for a civilized culture, I have hinted at it already, and now state it again. The south has simply been drained of all its best blood. The vast blood-letting of the Civil War half exterminated and wholly paralyzed the old aristocracy, and so left the land to the harsh mercies of the poor white trash, now its masters. The war, of course, was not a complete massacre. It spared a decent number of first-rate southerners—perhaps even some of the very best. Moreover, other countries, notably France and Germany, have survived far more staggering butcheries, and even showed marked progress thereafter. But the war not only cost a great many valuable lives; it also brought bankruptcy, demoralization and despair in its train—and so the majority of the first-rate southerners that were left, broken in spirit and unable to live under the new dispensation, cleared out. A few went to South America, to Egypt, to the Far East. Most came north. They were fecund; their progeny is widely dispersed, to the great benefit of the north. A southerner of good blood almost always does well in the north. He finds, even in the big cities, surroundings fit for a man of condition. His peculiar qualities have a high social value, and are esteemed. He is welcomed by the codfish aristocracy as one palpably superior. But in the south he throws up his hands. It is impossible for him to stoop to the common level. He cannot brawl in politics with the grandsons of his grandfather's tenants. He is unable to share their fierce jealousy of the emerging black—the cornerstone of all their public thinking. He is anæsthetic to their theological and political enthusiasms. He finds himself an alien at their feasts of soul. And so he withdraws into his tower, and is heard of no more. Cabell is almost a perfect example. His eyes, for years, were turned toward the past; he became a professor of the grotesque genealogizing that decaying aristocracies affect; it was only by a sort of accident that he discovered himself to be an artist. The south is unaware of the fact to this day; it regards Woodrow Wilson and Col. John Temple Graves as much finer stylists, and Frank L. Stanton as an infinitely greater poet. If it has heard, which I doubt, that Cabell has been hoofed by the Comstocks, it unquestionably views that assault as a deserved rebuke to a fellow who indulges a lewd passion for fancy writing, and is a covert enemy to the Only True Christianity.

What is needed down there, before the vexatious public problems of the region may be intelligently approached, is a survey of the population by competent ethnologists and anthropologists. The immigrants of the north have been studied at great length, and any one who is interested may now apply to the Bureau of Ethnology for elaborate data as to their racial strains, their stature and cranial indices, their relative capacity for education, and the changes that they undergo under American *Kultur*. But the older stocks of the south, and particularly the emancipated and dominant poor white trash, have never been investigated scientifically, and most of the current generalizations about them are probably wrong. For example, the generalization that they are purely Anglo-Saxon in blood. This I doubt very seriously.

The chief strain down there, I believe, is Celtic rather than Saxon, particularly in the hill country. French blood, too, shows itself here and there, and so does Spanish, and so does German. The last-named entered from the northward, by way of the limestone belt just east of the Alleghenies. Again, it is very likely that in some parts of the south a good many of the plebeian whites have more than a trace of negro blood. Interbreeding under concubinage produced some very light half-breeds at an early day, and no doubt appreciable numbers of them went over into the white race by the simple process of changing their abode. Not long ago I read a curious article by an intelligent negro, in which he stated that it is easy for a very light negro to pass as white in the south on account of the fact that large numbers of southerners accepted as white have distinctly negroid features. Thus it becomes a delicate and dangerous matter for a train conductor or a hotel-keeper to challenge a suspect. But the Celtic strain is far more obvious than any of these others. It not only makes itself visible in physical stigmata— *e.g.*, leanness and dark coloring—but also in mental traits. For example, the religious thought of the south is almost precisely identical with the religious thought of Wales. There is the same naïve belief in an anthropomorphic Creator but little removed, in manner and desire, from an evangelical bishop; there is the same submission to an ignorant and impudent sacerdotal tyranny, and there is the same sharp contrast between doctrinal orthodoxy and private ethics. Read Caradoc Evans' ironical picture of the Welsh Wesleyans in his preface to "My Neighbors," and you will be instantly reminded of the Georgia and Carolina Methodists. The most booming sort of piety, in the south, is not incompatible with the theory that lynching is a benign institution. Two generations ago it was not incompatible with an ardent belief in slavery.

It is highly probable that some of the worst blood of western Europe flows in the veins of the southern poor whites, now poor no longer. The original strains, according to every honest historian, were extremely corrupt. Philip Alexander Bruce (a Virginian of the old gentry) says in his "Industrial History of Virginia in the Seventeenth Century" that the first native-born generation was largely illegitimate. "One of the most common offenses against morality committed in the lower ranks of life in Virginia during the seventeenth century," he says, "was bastardy." The mothers of these bastards, he continues, were chiefly indentured servants, and "had belonged to the lowest class in their native country." Fanny Kemble Butler, writing of the Georgia poor whites of a century later, described them as "the most degraded race of human beings claiming an Anglo-Saxon origin that can be found on the face of the earth—filthy, lazy, ignorant, brutal, proud, penniless savages." The Sunday-school and the chautauqua, of course, have appreciably mellowed the descendants of these "savages," and their economic progress and rise to political power have done perhaps even more, but the marks of their origin are still unpleasantly plentiful. Every now and then they produce a political leader who puts their secret notions of the true, the good and the beautiful into plain words, to the amazement and scandal of the rest of the country. That amazement is turned into downright incredulity when news comes that his platform has got him high office, and that he is trying to execute it.

In the great days of the south the line between the gentry and the poor whites was very sharply drawn. There was absolutely no intermarriage. So far as I know there is not a single instance in history of a southerner of the upper class marrying one of the bondwomen described by Mr. Bruce. In other societies characterized by class distinctions of that sort it is common for the lower class to be improved by extra-legal crosses. That is to say, the men of the upper class take women of the lower class as mistresses, and out of such unions spring the extraordinary plebeians who rise sharply from the common level, and so propagate the delusion that all other plebeians would do the same thing if they had the chance—in brief, the delusion that class distinctions are merely economic and conventional, and not congenital and genuine. But in the south the men of the upper classes sought their mistresses among the blacks, and after a few generations there was so much white blood in the black women that they were considerably more attractive than the unhealthy and bedraggled women of the poor whites. This preference continued into our own time. A southerner of good family once told me in all seriousness that he had reached his majority before it ever occurred to him that a white woman might make quite as agreeable a mistress as the octaroons of his jejune fancy. If the thing has changed of late, it is not the fault of the southern white man, but of the southern mulatto women. The more slightly yellow girls of the region, with improving economic opportunities, have gained self-respect, and so they are no longer as willing to enter into concubinage as their grand-dams were.

As a result of this preference of the southern gentry for mulatto mistresses there was created a series of mixed strains containing the best white blood of the south, and perhaps of the whole country. As another result the poor whites went unfertilized from above, and so missed the improvement that so constantly shows itself in the peasant stocks of other countries. It is a commonplace that nearly all negroes who rise above the general are of mixed blood, usually with the white predominating. I know a great many negroes, and it would be hard for me to think of an exception. What is too often forgotten is that this white blood is not the blood of the poor whites but that of the old gentry. The mulatto girls of the early days despised the poor whites as creatures distinctly inferior to negroes, and it was thus almost unheard of for such a girl to enter into relations with a man of that submerged class. This aversion was based upon a sound instinct. The southern mulatto of to-day is a proof of it. Like all other half-breeds he is an unhappy man, with disquieting tendencies toward anti-social habits of thought, but he is intrinsically a better animal than the pure-blooded descendant of the old poor whites, and he not infrequently demonstrates it. It is not by accident that the negroes of the south are making faster progress, economically and culturally, than the masses of the whites. It is not by accident that the only visible æsthetic activity in the south is wholly in their hands. No southern composer has ever written music so good as that of half a dozen white-black composers who might be named. Even in politics, the negro reveals a curious superiority. Despite the fact that the race question has been the main political concern of the southern whites for two generations, to the practical exclusion of everything else, they have contributed nothing to the discussion that has impressed the rest of the world so deeply and so favorably as three or four books by southern negroes.

Entering upon such themes, of course, one must resign one's self to a vast misunderstanding and abuse. The south has not only lost its old capacity for producing ideas; it has also taken on the worst intolerance of ignorance and stupidity. Its prevailing mental attitude for several decades past has been that of its own hedge ecclesiastics. All who dissent from its orthodox doctrines are scoundrels. All who presume to discuss its ways realistically are damned. I have had, in my day, several experiences in point. Once, after I had published an article on some phase of the eternal race question, a leading southern newspaper replied by printing a column of denunciation of my father, then dead nearly twenty years—a philippic placarding him as an ignorant foreigner of dubious origin, inhabiting "the Baltimore ghetto" and speaking a dialect recalling that of Weber & Fields—two thousand words of incandescent nonsense, utterly false and beside the point, but exactly meeting the latter-day southern notion of effective controversy. Another time, I published a short discourse on lynching, arguing that the sport was popular in the south because the backward culture of the region denied the populace more seemly recreations. Among such recreations I mentioned those afforded by brass bands, symphony orchestras, boxing matches, amateur athletic contests, shoot-the-chutes, roof gardens, horse races, and so on. In reply another great southern journal denounced me as a man "of wineshop temperament, brass-jewelry tastes and pornographic predilections." In other words, brass bands, in the south, are classed with brass jewelry, and both are snares of the devil! To advocate setting up symphony orchestras is pornography! ... Alas, when the touchy southerner attempts a greater urbanity, the result is often even worse. Some time ago a colleague of mine printed an article deploring the arrested cultural development of Georgia. In reply he received a number of protests from patriotic Georgians, and all of them solemnly listed the glories of the state. I indulge in a few specimens:

> Who has not heard of Asa G. Candler, whose name is synonymous with Coca-Cola, a Georgia product?
> The first Sunday-school in the world was opened in Savannah.
> Who does not recall with pleasure the writings of ... Frank L. Stanton, Georgia's brilliant poet?
> Georgia was the first state to organize a Boys' Corn Club in the South— Newton county, 1904.
> The first to suggest a common United Daughters of the Confederacy badge was Mrs. Raynes, of Georgia.

The first to suggest a state historian of the United Daughters of the Confederacy was Mrs. C. Helen Plane (Macon convention, 1896).

The first to suggest putting to music Heber's "From Greenland's Icy Mountains" was Mrs. F. R. Goulding, of Savannah.

And so on, and so on. These proud boasts came, remember, not from obscure private persons, but from "Leading Georgians"—in one case, the state historian. Curious sidelights upon the ex-Confederate mind! Another comes from a stray copy of a negro paper. It describes an ordinance lately passed by the city council of Douglas, Ga., forbidding any trousers presser, on penalty of forfeiting a $500 bond, to engage in "pressing for both white and colored." This in a town, says the negro paper, where practically all of the white inhabitants have "their food prepared by colored hands," "their babies cared for by colored hands," and "the clothes which they wear right next to their skins washed in houses where negroes live"—houses in which the said clothes "remain for as long as a week at a time." But if you marvel at the absurdity, keep it dark! A casual word, and the united press of the south will be upon your trail, denouncing you bitterly as a scoundrelly Yankee, a Bolshevik Jew, an agent of the Wilhelmstrasse....

Obviously, it is impossible for intelligence to flourish in such an atmosphere. Free inquiry is blocked by the idiotic certainties of ignorant men. The arts, save in the lower reaches of the gospel hymn, the phonograph and the chautauqua harangue, are all held in suspicion. The tone of public opinion is set by an upstart class but lately emerged from industrial slavery into commercial enterprise—the class of "hustling" business men, of "live wires," of commercial club luminaries, of "drive" managers, of forward-lookers and right-thinkers—in brief, of third-rate southerners inoculated with all the worst traits of the Yankee sharper. One observes the curious effects of an old tradition of truculence upon a population now merely pushful and impudent, of an old tradition of chivalry upon a population now quite without imagination. The old repose is gone. The old romanticism is gone. The philistinism of the new type of town-boomer southerner is not only indifferent to the ideals of the old south; it is positively antagonistic to them. That philistinism regards human life, not as an agreeable adventure, but as a mere trial of rectitude and efficiency. It is overwhelmingly utilitarian and moral. It is inconceivably hollow and obnoxious. What remains of the ancient tradition is simply a certain charming civility in private intercourse—often broken down, alas, by the hot rages of Puritanism, but still generally visible. The southerner, at his worst, is never quite the surly cad that the Yankee is. His sensitiveness may betray him into occasional bad manners, but in the main he is a pleasant fellow—hospitable, polite, good-humored, even jovial.... But a bit absurd.... A bit pathetic.

1917

JOHN DOS PASSOS
1896–1970

Born the illegitimate son of a famous Wall Street lawyer, John Dos Passos attended Choate, toured Europe, and went on to Harvard to become first an aesthete and then, gradually, something of a political rebel. In 1917, like many young men of his background, he went to France as a volunteer ambulance driver. Horrified by the war's brutality, by the official lies, by the meaninglessness of the suffering he witnessed, he grew increasingly radical and further alienated from the world his father represented. In *Three Soldiers*, an attack on the army, he sought, through formal means, to break out of the narrow perspective of his own social class: this early novel is narrated in turn from the points of view of three different soldiers, one an artist and Harvard man, but the other two very much "average" soldiers.

Dos Passos's desire to broaden further the social perspective in his writing, along with his intense interest in postwar developments in the arts, led to the experimental novel *Manhattan Transfer*, published in 1925. Here the point of view shifts rapidly, providing over a hundred fragments of the lives of dozens of characters, so that no one individual, but rather Manhattan itself—dazzling, but lonely and alienating—emerges as the novel's protagonist.

Over the next ten years, Dos Passos became involved with a variety of left-wing causes, among them the *New Masses*, a political journal; the radical New Playwrights Theatre; the defense of Sacco and Vanzetti, two Italian American anarchists hastily accused of murder and finally executed in 1927; and the 1931 miners' strike in Harlan County, Kentucky. The fiction he wrote during this period, the trilogy *U.S.A.*, reflects Dos Passos's deepening radicalism as well as his increasing ambition as a writer, for the subject of *U.S.A.* is the history of American life in the first three decades of this century. His best work, the trilogy represents a culmination of Dos Passos's experimentation with literary form. In *U.S.A.*, Dos Passos found the technical means to delineate the connections between the kinds of alienation he dramatized in *Manhattan Transfer* and the social structures that produced it.

Most of this lengthy trilogy consists of twelve interwoven fictional narratives, each told from the point of view of its central character. These twelve narratives are interrupted not only by each other but by three kinds of formal devices: (1) sixty-eight "Newsreel" sections, carefully constructed collages of actual newspaper headlines, news story fragments, and snatches of song lyrics, political speeches, and advertisements that together trace mass culture and popular consciousness over the years; (2) twenty-seven biographies (like the two included here) of key public figures, people who shaped or represented or resisted the major social forces of the era; and (3) fifty-one "Camera Eye" sections, stream-of-consciousness fragments that depict the developing awareness of a sensitive and artistic individual (not unlike Dos Passos). These four components—narratives, Newsreels, biographies, and Camera Eye sections—work together to dramatize the impact of public events on private lives, to illustrate the very social nature of individual experience, and to indict capitalist America.

Dos Passos's writing after *U.S.A.* never approached the power of the trilogy. His experimenting had been very much tied up with his radical ideas, and he began rejecting those ideas in the late 1930s (becoming, in later life, extremely conservative). He returned to more traditional forms in a second trilogy, *District of Columbia* (1952), and in later novels; he began writing history, including a biography of Thomas Jefferson, and he continued the political journalism and travel writing he had been producing all his life. In 1961 he published *Midcentury*, which copies the form of his first trilogy but has none of its power; *Midcentury*'s attack on unions, psychoanalysis, teenagers, and other targets seems narrow and petulant next to the passionate critique of an entire social system that is Dos Passos's greatest achievement, *U.S.A.*

Robert C. Rosen
William Paterson University

PRIMARY WORKS

Three Soldiers, 1920; *Manhattan Transfer*, 1925; *U.S.A.*, 1938 (*The 42nd Parallel*, 1930; *Nineteen Nineteen*, 1932; *The Big Money*, 1936); *District of Columbia*, 1952; *Midcentury*, 1961; *The Best Times: An Informal Memoir*, 1966; *Novels, 1920–1925*, 2003.

from **U.S.A.**

The Body of an American

Whereasthe Congressoftheunitedstates byaconcurrentresolutionadoptedon the4thdayofmarch lastauthorizedthe Secretaryofwar to cause to be brought to theunitedstatesthe body of an Americanwhowasamemberoftheamerica-nexpeditionaryforcesineurope wholosthislifeduringtheworldwarandwhoseidentityhas notbeenestablished for burial inthememorialamphitheatreofthenationalcemeteryat arlingtonvirginia

In the tarpaper morgue at Chalons-sur-Marne in the reek of chloride of lime and the dead, they picked out the pine box that held all that was left of

enie menie minie moe plenty other pine boxes stacked up there containing what they'd scraped up of Richard Roe

and other person or persons unknown. Only one can go. How did they pick John Doe?

Make sure he aint a dinge, boys,

make sure he aint a guinea or a kike,[1]

how can you tell a guy's a hundredpercent when all you've got's a gunnysack full of bones, bronze buttons stamped with the screaming eagle and a pair of roll puttees?

... and the gagging chloride and the puky dirtstench of the yearold dead ...

*   *   *

---

[1]Derogatory terms for black, Italian, and Jew.

The day withal was too meaningful and tragic for applause. Silence, tears, songs and prayer, muffled drums and soft music were the instrumentalities today of national approbation.

John Doe was born (thudding din of blood in love into the shuddering soar of a man and a woman alone indeed together lurching into

and ninemonths sick drowse waking into scared agony and the pain and blood and mess of birth). John Doe was born

and raised in Brooklyn, in Memphis, near the lakefront in Cleveland, Ohio, in the stench of the stockyards in Chi, on Beacon Hill, in an old brick house in Alexandria Virginia, on Telegraph Hill, in a halftimbered Tudor cottage in Portland the city of roses,

in the Lying-In Hospital old Morgan[2] endowed on Stuyvesant Square,

across the railroad tracks, out near the country club, in a shack cabin tenement apartmenthouse exclusive residential suburb;

scion of one of the best families in the social register, won first prize in the baby parade at Coronado Beach, was marbles champion of the Little Rock grammarschools, crack basketballplayer at the Booneville High, quarterback at the State Reformatory, having saved the sheriff's kid from drowning in the Little Missouri River was invited to Washington to be photographed shaking hands with the President on the White House steps;—

though this was a time of mourning, such an assemblage necessarily has about it a touch of color. In the boxes are seen the court uniforms of foreign diplomats, the gold braid of our own and foreign fleets and armies, the black of the conventional morning dress of American statesmen, the varicolored furs and outdoor wrapping garments of mothers and sisters come to mourn, the drab and blue of soldiers and sailors, the glitter of musical instruments and the white and black of a vested choir

—busyboy harveststiff hogcaller boyscout champeen cornshucker of Western Kansas bellhop at the United States Hotel at Saratoga Springs office boy callboy fruiter telephone lineman longshoreman lumberjack plumber's helper,

worked for an exterminating company in Union City, filled pipes in an opium joint in Trenton, N.J.

Y.M.C.A. secretary, express agent, truckdriver, fordmechanic, sold books in Denver Colorado: Madam would you be willing to help a young man work his way through college?

President Harding, with a reverence seemingly more significant because of his high temporal station, concluded his speech:

We are met today to pay the impersonal tribute;
the name of him whose body lies before us took flight with his imperishable soul . . .

[2]J. Pierpont Morgan (1837–1913), powerful U.S. financier.

as a typical soldier of this representative democracy he fought and died
believing in the indisputable justice of his country's cause . . .

by raising his right hand and asking the thousands within the sound of
his voice to join in the prayer:

Our Father which art in heaven hallowed be thy name . . .

Naked he went into the army;
    they weighed you, measured you, looked for flat feet, squeezed your
penis to see if you had clap, looked up your anus to see if you had piles,
counted your teeth, made you cough, listened to your heart and lungs, made
you read the letters on the card, charted your urine and your intelligence,
    gave you a service record for a future (imperishable soul)
    and an identification tag stamped with your serial number to hang
around your neck, issued O D[3] regulation equipment, a condiment can and
a copy of the articles of war:
    Atten'SHUN suck in your gut you c——r wipe that smile off your face
eyes right wattja tink dis is a choirch-social? For-war-D'ARCH.

John Doe
and Richard Roe and other person or persons unknown
    drilled hiked, manual of arms, ate slum,[4] learned to salute, to soldier, to
loaf in the latrines, forbidden to smoke on deck, overseas guard duty, forty
men and eight horses,[5] shortarm inspection[6] and the ping of shrapnel and
the shrill bullets combing the air and the sorehead woodpeckers the machi-
neguns mud cooties gasmasks and the itch.
    Say feller tell me how I can get back to my outfit.
    John Doe had a head
for twentyodd years intensely the nerves of the eyes the ears the palate
the tongue the fingers the toes the armpits, the nerves warmfeeling under
the skin charged the coiled brain with hurt sweet warm cold mine must dont
sayings print headlines:
    Thou shalt not the multiplication table long division, Now is the time
for all good men knocks but once at a young man's door, It's a great life if
Ish gebibbel,[7] The first five years'll be the Safety First, Suppose a hun tried
to rape your my country right or wrong, Catch 'em young, What he dont
know wont treat 'em rough, Tell 'em nothin, He got what was coming to
him he got his, This is a white man's country, Kick the bucket, Gone west, If
you dont like it you can croaked him
    Say buddy cant you tell me how I can get back to my outfit?

            *   *   *

---

[3] Olive drab, military color.
[4] Slumgullion, or watery stew.
[5] Troop train capacity.

[6] Inspection for venereal disease.
[7] It doesn't matter to me (pseudo-Yiddish).

Cant help jumpin when them things go off, give me the trots[8] them things do. I lost my identification tag swimmin in the Marne, roughhousin with a guy while we was waitin to be deloused, in bed with a girl named Jeanne (Love moving picture wet French postcard dream began with saltpeter[9] in the coffee and ended at the propho[10] station);—

Say soldier for chrissake cant you tell me how I can get back to my outfit?
John Doe's
heart pumped blood:
alive thudding silence of blood in your ears
down in the clearing in the Oregon forest[11] where the punkins were punkincolor pouring into the blood through the yes and the fallcolored trees and the bronze hoopers were hopping through the dry grass, where tiny striped snails hung on the underside of the blades and the flies hummed, wasps droned, bumble-bees buzzed, and the woods smelt of wine and mushrooms and apples, homey smell of fall pouring into the blood,

and I dropped the tin hat and the sweaty pack and lay flat with the dogday sun licking my throat and adamsapple and the tight skin over the breastbone.

The shell had his number on it.

The blood ran into the ground.

The service record dropped out of the filing cabinet when the quartermaster sergeant got blotto that time they had to pack up and leave the billets in a hurry.
The identification tag was in the bottom of the Marne.

The blood ran into the ground, the brains oozed out of the cracked skull and were licked up by the trenchrats, the belly swelled and raised a generation of bluebottle flies,
and the incorruptible skeleton,
and the scraps of dried viscera and skin bundled in khaki
they took to Chalons-sur-Marne
and laid it out neat in a pine coffin
and took it home to God's Country on a battleship
and buried it in a sarcophagus in the Memorial Amphitheatre in the Arlington National Cemetery
and draped the Old Glory over it
and the bugler played taps
and Mr. Harding prayed to God and the diplomats and the generals and the admirals and the brasshats and the politicians and the handsomely

[8]Diarrhea.
[9]Chemical given to soldiers in an effort to reduce their sexual desire.
[10]Prophylactic.
[11]Argonne Forest, in northeastern France; scene of major World War I battle.

dressed ladies out of the society column of the *Washington Post* stood up solemn

and thought how beautiful sad Old Glory God's Country it was to have the bugler play taps and the three volleys made their ears ring.

Where his chest ought to have been they pinned

the Congressional Medal, the D.S.C.,[12] the Medaille Militaire, the Belgian Croix de Guerre, the Italian gold medal, the Vitutea Militara sent by Queen Marie of Rumania, the Czechoslovak war cross, the Virtuti Militari of the Poles, a wreath sent by Hamilton Fish, Jr.,[13] of New York, and a little wampum presented by a deputation of Arizona redskins in warpaint and feathers. All the Washingtonians brought flowers.

Woodrow Wilson brought a bouquet of poppies.

1932

The Bitter Drink

Veblen,

a greyfaced shambling man lolling resentful at his desk with his cheek on his hand, in a low sarcastic mumble of intricate phrases subtly paying out the logical inescapable rope of matteroffact for a society to hang itself by,

dissecting out the century with a scalpel so keen, so comical, so exact that the professors and students ninetenths of the time didn't know it was there, and the magnates and the respected windbags and the applauded loudspeakers never knew it was there.

Veblen

asked too many questions, suffered from a constitutional inability to say yes.

Socrates asked questions, drank down the bitter drink one night when the first cock crowed,

but Veblen

drank it in little sips through a long life in the stuffiness of classrooms, the dust of libraries, the staleness of cheap flats such as a poor instructor can afford. He fought the bogy all right, pedantry, routine, timeservers at office desks, trustees, collegepresidents, the plump flunkies of the ruling businessmen, all the good jobs kept for yesmen, never enough money, every broadening hope thwarted. Veblen drank the bitter drink all right.

The Veblens were a family of freeholding farmers.

The freeholders of the narrow Norwegian valleys were a stubborn hardworking people, farmers, dairymen, fishermen, rooted in their fathers'

---

[12]Distinguished Service Cross.

[13]Member of U.S. Congress; promoted Unknown Soldier memorial.

stony fields, in their old timbered farmsteads with carved gables they took their names from, in the upland pastures where they grazed the stock in summer.

During the early nineteenth century the towns grew; Norway filled up with landless men, storekeepers, sheriffs, moneylenders, bailiffs, notaries in black with stiff-collars and briefcases full of foreclosures under their arms. Industries were coming in. The townsmen were beginning to get profits out of the country and to finagle the farmers out of the freedom of their narrow farms.

The meanspirited submitted as tenants, daylaborers; but the strong men went out of the country

as their fathers had gone out of the country centuries before when Harald the Fairhaired[1] and St. Olaf[2] hacked to pieces the liberties of the northern men, who had been each man lord of his own creek, to make Christians and serfs of them,

only in the old days it was Iceland, Greenland, Vineland[3] the northmen had sailed west to; now it was America.

Both Thorstein Veblen's father's people and his mother's people had lost their farmsteads and with them the names that denoted them free men.

Thomas Anderson for a while tried to make his living as a traveling carpenter and cabinetmaker, but in 1847 he and his wife, Kari Thorsteinsdatter, crossed in a whalingship from Bremen and went out to join friends in the Scandihoovian[4] colonies round Milwaukee.

Next year his brother Haldor joined him.

They were hard workers; in another year they had saved up money to preempt a claim on 160 acres of uncleared land in Sheboygan County, Wisconsin; when they'd gotten that land part cleared they sold it and moved to an all-Norway colony in Manitowoc County, near Cato and a place named Valders after the valley they had all come from in the old country;

there in the house Thomas Anderson built with his own tools, the sixth of twelve children, Thorstein Veblen was born.

When Thorstein was eight years old, Thomas Anderson moved west again into the blacksoil prairies of Minnesota that the Sioux and the buffalo had only been driven off from a few years before. In the deed to the new farm Thomas Anderson took back the old farmstead name of Veblen.

He was a solid farmer, builder, a clever carpenter, the first man to import merino sheep and a mechanical reaper and binder; he was a man of standing in the group of Norway people farming the edge of the prairies, who kept their dialects, the manner of life of their narrow Norway valleys, their Lutheran pastors, their homemade clothes and cheese and bread, their suspicion and stubborn dislike of townsmen's ways.

---

[1] Harald I, King of Norway (c. 872–933).
[2] Patron saint of Norway and King (1016–1029).
[3] Area of northeastern North America visited by Norse explorers around A.D. 1000.
[4] Scandinavian (derogatory term).

The townspeople were Yankees mostly, smart to make two dollars grow where a dollar grew before, storekeepers, middlemen, speculators, money-lenders, with long heads for politics and mortgages; they despised the Scandihoovian dirtfarmers they lived off, whose daughters did their wives' kitchenwork.

The Norway people believed as their fathers had believed that there were only two callings for an honest man, farming or preaching.

Thorstein grew up a hulking lad with a reputation for laziness and wit. He hated the irk of everrepeated backbreaking chores round the farm. Reading he was happy. Carpentering he liked or running farmmachinery. The Lutheran pastors who came to the house noticed that his supple mind slid easily round the corners of their theology. It was hard to get farmwork out of him, he had a stinging tongue and was famous for the funny names he called people; his father decided to make a preacher out of him.

When he was seventeen he was sent for out of the field where he was working. His bag was already packed. The horses were hitched up. He was being sent to Carleton Academy in Northfield, to prepare for Carleton College.

As there were several young Veblens to be educated their father built them a house on a lot near the campus. Their food and clothes were sent to them from the farm. Cash money was something they never saw.

Thorstein spoke English with an accent. He had a constitutional inability to say yes. His mind was formed on the Norse sagas and on the matteroffact sense of his father's farming and the exact needs of carpenterwork and threshingmachines.

He could never take much interest in the theology, sociology, economics of Carleton College where they were busy trimming down the jagged dogmas of the old New England bibletaught traders to make stencils to hang on the walls of commissionmerchants' offices.

Veblen's collegeyears were the years when Darwin's assertions of growth and becoming were breaking the set molds of the Noah's Ark world,

when Ibsen's women were tearing down the portieres of the Victorian parlors,

and Marx's mighty machine was rigging the countinghouse's own logic to destroy the countinghouse.

When Veblen went home to the farm he talked about these things with his father, following him up and down at his plowing, starting an argument while they were waiting for a new load for the wheatthresher. Thomas Anderson had seen Norway and America; he had the squarebuilt mind of a carpenter and builder, and an understanding of tools and the treasured elaborated builtupseasonbyseason knowledge of a careful farmer,

a tough whetstone for the sharpening steel of young Thorstein's wits.

At Carleton College young Veblen was considered a brilliant unsound eccentric; nobody could understand why a boy of such attainments wouldn't settle down to the business of the day, which was to buttress property and profits with anything usable in the debris of Christian ethics and eighteenth-century economics that cluttered the minds of collegeprofessors, and to reinforce the sacred, already shaky edifice with the new strong girderwork of science Herbert Spencer[5] was throwing up for the benefit of the bosses.

People complained they never knew whether Veblen was joking or serious.

In 1880 Thorstein Veblen started to try to make his living by teaching. A year in an academy at Madison, Wisconsin, wasn't much of a success. Next year he and his brother Andrew started graduate work at Johns Hopkins. Johns Hopkins didn't suit, but boarding in an old Baltimore house with some ruined gentlewomen gave him a disdaining glimpse of an etiquette motheaten now but handed down through the lavish leisure of the slave-owning planters' mansions straight from the merry England of the landlord cavaliers.

(The valleyfarmers had always been scornful of outlanders' ways.)

He was more at home at Yale where in Noah Porter[6] he found a New England roundhead granite against which his Norway granite rang in clear dissent. He took his Ph.D. there. But there was still some question as to what department of the academic world he could best make a living in.

He read Kant and wrote prize essays. But he couldn't get a job. Try as he could he couldn't get his mouth round the essential yes.

He went back to Minnesota with a certain intolerant knowledge of the amenities of the higher learning. To his slight Norwegian accent he'd added the broad a.

At home he loafed about the farm and tinkered with inventions of new machinery and read and talked theology and philosophy with his father. In the Scandihoovian colonies the price of wheat and the belief in God and St. Olaf were going down together. The farmers of the Northwest were starting their long losing fight against the parasite businessmen who were sucking them dry. There was a mortgage on the farm, interest on debts to pay, always fertilizer, new machines to buy to speed production to pump in a halfcentury the wealth out of the soil laid down in a million years of buffalo-grass. His brothers kept grumbling about this sardonic loafer who wouldn't earn his keep.

Back home he met again his college sweetheart, Ellen Rolfe, the niece of the president of Carleton College, a girl who had railroad magnates and money in the family. People in Northfield were shocked when it came out that she was going to marry the drawling pernickety bookish badlydressed young Norwegian ne'er-do-well.

[5]English philosopher (1820–1903); argued that laissez-faire economics made for survival of the fittest and social progress.

[6]Conservative theologian and educator (1811–1892).

Her family hatched a plan to get him a job as economist for the Santa Fe Railroad but at the wrong moment Ellen Rolfe's uncle lost control of the line. The young couple went to live at Stacyville where they did everything but earn a living. They read Latin and Greek and botanized in the woods and along the fences and in the roadside scrub. They boated on the river and Veblen started his translation of the *Laxdaelasaga*.[7] They read *Looking Backward*[8] and articles by Henry George.[9] They looked at their world from the outside.

In '91 Veblen got together some money to go to Cornell to do postgraduate work. He turned up there in the office of the head of the economics department wearing a coonskin cap and grey corduroy trousers and said in his low sarcastic drawl, "I am Thorstein Veblen,"

but it was not until several years later, after he was established at the new University of Chicago that had grown up next to the World's Fair, and had published *The Theory of the Leisure Class*, put on the map by Howells'[10] famous review, that the world of the higher learning[11] knew who Thorstein Veblen was.

Even in Chicago as the brilliant young economist he lived pioneerfashion. (The valleyfarmers had always been scornful of outlanders' ways.) He kept his books in packingcases laid on their sides along the walls. His only extravagances were the Russian cigarettes he smoked and the red sash he sometimes sported. He was a man without smalltalk. When he lectured he put his cheek on his hand and mumbled out his long spiral sentences, reiterative like the eddas. His language was a mixture of mechanics' terms, scientific latinity, slang and Roget's Thesaurus. The other profs couldn't imagine why the girls fell for him so.

The girls fell for him so that Ellen Rolfe kept leaving him. He'd take summer trips abroad without his wife. There was a scandal about a girl on an ocean liner.

Tongues wagged so (Veblen was a man who never explained, who never could get his tongue around the essential yes; the valleyfarmers had always been scornful of the outlanders' ways, and their opinions) that his wife left him and went off to live alone on a timberclaim in Idaho and the president asked for his resignation.

Veblen went out to Idaho to get Ellen Rolfe to go with him to California when he succeeded in getting a job at a better salary at Leland Stanford, but in Palo Alto it was the same story as in Chicago. He suffered from woman trouble and the constitutional inability to say yes and an unnatural tendency to feel with the workingclass instead of with the profittakers. There

---

[7] Thirteenth-century Icelandic saga.
[8] Utopian novel (1888) by Edward Bellamy.
[9] U.S. economist (1839–1897) who advocated social reform through a "single tax" on land.
[10] William Dean Howells (1837–1920), American novelist.

[11] Allusion to Veblen's scathing attack on universities, *The Higher Learning in America* (1918).

were the same complaints that his courses were not constructive or attractive to big money bequests and didn't help his students to butter their bread, make Phi Beta Kappa, pick plums off the hierarchies of the academic grove. His wife left him for good. He wrote to a friend: "The president doesn't approve of my domestic arrangements; nor do I."

Talking about it he once said, "What is one to do if the woman moves in on you?"

He went back up to the shack in the Idaho woods.

Friends tried to get him an appointment to make studies in Crete, a chair at the University of Pekin, but always the bogy, routine, businessmen's flunkeys in all the university offices ... for the questioner the bitter drink.

His friend Davenport got him an appointment at the University of Missouri. At Columbia he lived like a hermit in the basement of the Davenports' house, helped with the work round the place, carpentered himself a table and chairs. He was already a bitter elderly man with a grey face covered with a net of fine wrinkles, a vandyke beard and yellow teeth. Few students could follow his courses. The college authorities were often surprised and somewhat chagrined that when visitors came from Europe it was always Veblen they wanted to meet.

These were the years he did most of his writing, trying out his ideas on his students, writing slowly at night in violet ink with a pen of his own designing. Whenever he published a book he had to put up a guarantee with the publishers. In *The Theory of Business Enterprise, The Instinct of Workmanship, The Vested Interests and the Common Man,*

he established a new diagram of a society dominated by monopoly capital, etched in irony

the sabotage of production by business,

the sabotage of life by blind need for money profits,

pointed out the alternatives: a warlike society strangled by the bureaucracies of the monopolies forced by the law of diminishing returns to grind down more and more the common man for profits,

or a new matteroffact commonsense society dominated by the needs of the men and women who did the work and the incredibly vast possibilities for peace and plenty offered by the progress of technology.

These were the years of Debs's[12] speeches, growing laborunions, the I.W.W.[13] talk about industrial democracy: these years Veblen still held to the hope that the workingclass would take over the machine of production before monopoly had pushed the western nations down into the dark again.

War cut across all that: under the cover of the bunting of Woodrow Wilson's phrases the monopolies cracked down. American democracy was crushed.

---

[12]Eugene V. Debs (1855–1926), labor leader and Socialist Party presidential candidate.

[13]Industrial Workers of the World, militant labor union founded in Chicago in 1905; its members were called "Wobblies."

The war at least offered Veblen an opportunity to break out of the airless greenhouse of academic life. He was offered a job with the Food Administration, he sent the Navy Department a device for catching submarines by trailing lengths of stout bindingwire. (Meanwhile the government found his books somewhat confusing. The postoffice was forbidding the mails to *Imperial Germany and the Industrial Revolution* while propaganda agencies were sending it out to make people hate the Huns. Educators were denouncing *The Nature of Peace* while Washington experts were clipping phrases out of it to add to the Wilsonian smokescreen.)

For the Food Administration Thorstein Veblen wrote two reports: in one he advocated granting the demands of the I.W.W. as a wartime measure and conciliating the workingclass instead of beating up and jailing all the honest leaders; in the other he pointed out that the Food Administration was a businessman's racket and was not aiming for the most efficient organization of the country as a producing machine. He suggested that, in the interests of the efficient prosecution of the war, the government step into the place of the middleman and furnish necessities to the farmers direct in return for raw materials;

but cutting out business was not at all the Administration's idea of making the world safe for democracy,

so Veblen had to resign from the Food Administration.

He signed the protests against the trial of the hundred and one wobblies in Chicago.[14]

After the armistice he went to New York. In spite of all the oppression of the war years, the air was freshening. In Russia the great storm of revolt had broken, seemed to be sweeping west, in the strong gusts from the new world in the east the warsodden multitudes began to see again. At Versailles[15] allies and enemies, magnates, generals, flunkey politicians were slamming the shutters against the storm, against the new, against hope. It was suddenly clear for a second in the thundering glare what war was about, what peace was about.

In America, in Europe, the old men won. The bankers in their offices took a deep breath, the bediamonded old ladies of the leisure class went back to clipping their coupons in the refined quiet of their safe deposit vaults,

the last puffs of the ozone of revolt went stale

in the whisper of speakeasy arguments.

Veblen wrote for the *Dial*,[16]

lectured at the New School for Social Research.

He still had a hope that the engineers, the technicians, the nonprofiteers whose hands were on the switchboard might take up the fight where the

[14]Mass trial in 1918; charges were numerous and indiscriminate, sentencing harsh.
[15]Site of major treaty (1919) officially ending World War I.
[16]Influential political and literary magazine.

workingclass had failed. He helped form the Technical Alliance.[17] His last hope was the British general strike.[18]

Was there no group of men bold enough to take charge of the magnificent machine before the pigeyed speculators and the yesmen at office desks irrevocably ruined it

and with it the hopes of four hundred years?

No one went to Veblen's lectures at the New School. With every article he wrote in the *Dial* the circulation dropped.

Harding's normalcy,[19] the new era was beginning;

even Veblen made a small killing on the stockmarket.

He was an old man and lonely.

His second wife had gone to a sanitarium suffering from delusions of persecution.

There seemed no place for a masterless man.

Veblen went back out to Palo Alto

to live in his shack in the tawny hills and observe from outside the last grabbing urges of the profit system taking on, as he put it, the systematized delusions of dementia praecox.

There he finished his translation of the *Laxdaelasaga*.

He was an old man. He was much alone. He let the woodrats take what they wanted from his larder. A skunk that hung round the shack was so tame he'd rub up against Veblen's leg like a cat.

He told a friend he'd sometimes hear in the stillness about him the voices of his boyhood talking Norwegian as clear as on the farm in Minnesota where he was raised. His friends found him harder than ever to talk to, harder than ever to interest in anything. He was running down. The last sips of the bitter drink.

He died on August 3, 1929.

Among his papers a penciled note was found:

It is also my wish, in case of death, to be cremated if it can conveniently be done, as expeditiously and inexpensively as may be, without ritual or ceremony of any kind; that my ashes be thrown loose into the sea or into some sizable stream running into the sea; that no tombstone, slab, epitaph, effigy, tablet, inscription or monument of any name or nature, be set up to my memory or name in any place or at any time; that no obituary, memorial, portrait or biography of me, nor any letters written to or by me be printed or published, or in any way reproduced, copied or circulated;

but his memorial remains

riveted into the language:

the sharp clear prism of his mind.

1936

---

[17]Organization of radical-left engineers.
[18]In 1926, in support of miners; it lasted nine days.

[19]Warren G. Harding, U.S. President (1921–1923), promised a return to "normalcy," away from internationalism and progressivist reform.

■   ALBERT MALTZ   ■
                            1908–1985

Albert Maltz was born in Brooklyn, New York, the son of immigrants; his father, beginning as a grocer's boy, had become a contractor and builder. Maltz attended public schools and Columbia University, where he majored in philosophy and graduated in 1930. He then enrolled in the Yale Drama School to study with George Pierce Baker, whose students had included Eugene O'Neill, Sidney Howard, S.N. Behrman, and Thomas Wolfe. Another important influence was that of fellow student George Sklar, whose radical politics ignited Maltz's own incipient leftist leanings. At first in collaboration with Sklar and then alone, Maltz wrote and saw several plays produced, among them an antiwar drama called *Peace on Earth*, and *Black Pit*, a study of conditions endured by coal miners in West Virginia.

Maltz soon turned to writing fiction, and it is on his stories and novels that his reputation rests. "Man on a Road," published in the *New Masses* in 1935, sparked a Congressional investigation of the dangers of silicosis to miners; this story was later widely reprinted. Maltz's excellent novella "Season of Celebration," which focuses on a dying man in a Bowery flophouse, and "The Happiest Man on Earth" both won recognition when they appeared in 1938. These and other stories were collected and published under the title *The Way Things Are*.

Both the principal strength and the central weakness of Maltz's work arise from his desire to fulfill an ideal of proletarian art and yet not betray "the great humanistic tradition of culture" by serving "an individual political purpose." The tension between these aims caused him some personal trouble as well as artistic ambivalence. In a 1946 essay entitled "What Shall We Ask of Writers?" he criticized the shallow aesthetic tenets of the left, questioning whether art was to be used as a weapon in the class war. For this he was bitterly denounced, and after two months of verbal siege, Maltz backed down; the *New Masses* published his retraction, in which he declared his earlier piece a "one-sided nondialectical treatment of complex issues."

Maltz is at his best when his political sympathies animate but do not overwhelm his narrative gift. In stories like "Man on a Road" and "The Happiest Man on Earth," a muted undercurrent of anger at injustice and suffering renders the protest extremely effective. But when he becomes openly didactic, Maltz's indignation subverts character, plot, and even feeling, as in his first novel, *The Underground Stream*, which focuses on the struggle between auto industry workers seeking to organize unions and the fascistic management who resist them. Here the characters act simply as one-dimensional mouthpieces, delivering various political viewpoints, rather than developing believably.

Maltz confronted his aesthetic dilemma with varying degrees of success in his next four novels; *The Cross and the Arrow* is his best. In part this novel was written as an answer to the theories of Robert Vansittart, a British diplomat who contended that the German people as a race were addicted to war, and that if this innate bellicosity could not be corrected by cultural reconditioning, it would be necessary to exterminate them. Maltz's narrative explores the life of a factory worker named Willi Wegler, who, though decorated with a German service cross, suddenly and heroically turns against his country's cause.

By this time Maltz was working in Hollywood as a screenwriter, but this career was to be interrupted in 1947 when the House Un-American Activities Committee reinstituted its investigation into Communist infiltration in the motion picture industry. Maltz, along with nine other writers and producers, a group thereafter known as "the Hollywood Ten," challenged the constitutional legitimacy of that committee on First Amendment grounds. Refusing to answer the committee's questions as to whether he was a member of the Communist Party and the Screenwriters' Guild, Maltz was fined and sentenced to a year's imprisonment in 1950. Blacklisted in Hollywood and so unable to work there for many years, he moved to Mexico after his release from prison and remained there until 1962.

During the time of the HUAC investigations, *The Journey of Simon McKeever* was published; squarely in the tradition of the novel of the road, this compact work recounts the adventures of a 73-year-old escapee from an old-age home, a representative American who comes at last to a reaffirmation of the communal ideal. *A Long Day in a Short Life* was written in Mexico and based on his nine-months' experience in a federal prison; a flatly realistic portrayal of the lives of prisoners in a Washington, D.C., jail, it voices Maltz's plea for human commitment and solidarity as the basis of true democracy. *A Tale of One January* was published in England and has never been printed in the United States; chronicling the escape of two women from Auschwitz, its narrative centers on one woman's rediscovery of her sense of self, her womanhood, and her relationship to the larger world.

Albert Maltz died in Los Angeles in 1985. His constant literary concern for an idealized vision of democracy links his work to the American tradition of Emerson and Whitman. His fiction regularly focuses on the individual's struggle for self-realization under confinement in some prison-like situation; always Maltz's faith in human decency, in the viability of the human struggle for a better life, and in the need for spiritual liberation triumph over the forces of repression. Among the most talented of the social protest writers shaped by the Depression years, Maltz projects an idealistic intensity in his best work that makes it worthy of wider recognition and publication.

Gabriel Miller
Rutgers University–Newark

PRIMARY WORKS

Peace on Earth, 1934; *Black Pit*, 1935; *The Way Things Are*, 1938; *The Underground Stream*, 1940; *The Cross and the Arrow*, 1944; *The Journey of Simon McKeever*, 1949; *The Citizen Writer*, 1950; *A Long Day in a Short Life*, 1957; *A Tale of One January*, 1966; *Afternoon in the Jungle*, 1971.

The Happiest Man on Earth

Jesse felt ready to weep. He had been sitting in the shanty waiting for Tom to appear, grateful for the chance to rest his injured foot, quietly, joyously anticipating the moment when Tom would say, "Why, of course, Jesse, you can start whenever you're ready!"

For two weeks he had been pushing himself, from Kansas City, Missouri, to Tulsa, Oklahoma, through nights of rain and a week of scorching sun, without sleep or a decent meal, sustained by the vision of that one moment. And then Tom had come into the office. He had come in quickly, holding a sheaf of papers in his hand; he had glanced at Jesse only casually, it was true—but long enough. He had not known him. He had turned away ... And Tom Brackett was his brother-in-law.

Was it his clothes? Jesse knew he looked terrible. He had tried to spruce up at a drinking fountain in the park, but even that had gone badly; in his excitement he had cut himself shaving, an ugly gash down the side of his cheek. And nothing could get the red gumbo dust out of his suit even though he had slapped himself till both arms were worn out ... Or was it just that he had changed so much?

True, they hadn't seen each other for five years; but Tom looked five years older, that was all. He was still Tom. God! Was he so different?

Brackett finished his telephone call. He leaned back in his swivel chair and glanced over at Jesse with small, clear, blue eyes that were suspicious and unfriendly. He was a heavy, paunchy man of forty-five, auburn-haired, rather dour-looking; his face was meaty, his features pronounced and forceful, his nose somewhat bulbous and reddish-hued at the tip. He looked like a solid, decent, capable businessman who was commander of his local branch of the American Legion—which he was. He surveyed Jesse with cold indifference, manifestly unwilling to spend time on him. Even the way he chewed his toothpick seemed contemptuous to Jesse.

"Yes?" Brackett said suddenly. "What to you want?"

His voice was decent enough, Jesse admitted. He had expected it to be worse. He moved up to the wooden counter that partitioned the shanty. He thrust a hand nervously through his tangled hair.

"I guess you don't recognize me, Tom," he said falteringly. "I'm Jesse Fulton."

"Huh?" Brackett said. That was all.

"Yes, I am, and Ella sends you her love."

Brackett rose and walked over to the counter until they were face to face. He surveyed Fulton incredulously, trying to measure the resemblance to his brother-in-law as he remembered him. This man was tall, about thirty. That fitted! He had straight good features and a lank erect body. That was right too. But the face was too gaunt, the body too spiny under the baggy clothes for him to be sure. His brother-in-law had been a solid, strong, young man with muscle and beef to him. It was like looking at a faded, badly taken photograph and trying to recognize the subject: The resemblance was there but the difference was tremendous. He searched the eyes. They at least seemed definitely familiar, gray, with a curiously shy but decent look in them. He had liked that about Fulton.

Jesse stood quiet. Inside he was seething. Brackett was like a man examining a piece of broken-down horseflesh; there was a look of pure pity in his eyes. It made Jesse furious. He knew he wasn't as far gone as all that.

"Yes, I believe you are," Brackett said finally, "but you sure have changed."

"By God, it's five years, ain't it?" Jesse said resentfully. "You only saw me a couple of times anyway." Then, to himself, with his lips locked together, in mingled vehemence and shame, "What if I have changed? Don't everybody? I ain't no corpse."

"You was solid looking," Brackett continued softly, in the same tone of incredulous wonder. "You lost weight, I guess?"

Jesse kept silent. He needed Brackett too much to risk antagonizing him. But it was only by deliberate effort that he could keep from boiling over. The pause lengthened, became painful. Brackett flushed. "Jiminy Christmas, excuse me," he burst out in apology. He jerked the counter up. "Come in. Take a seat. Good God, boy"—he grasped Jesse's hand and shook it—"I am glad to see you; don't think anything else! You just looked so peaked."

"It's all right," Jesse murmured. He sat down, thrusting his hand through his curly, tangled hair.

"Why are you limping?"

"I stepped on a stone; it jagged a hole through my shoe." Jesse pulled his feet back under the chair. He was ashamed of his shoes. They had come from the relief originally, and two weeks on the road had about finished them. All morning, with a kind of delicious, foolish solemnity, he had been vowing to himself that before anything else, before even a suit of clothes, he was going to buy himself a brand-new strong pair of shoes.

Brackett kept his eyes off Jesse's feet. He knew what was bothering the boy and it filled his heart with pity. The whole thing was appalling. He had never seen anyone who looked more down-and-out. His sister had been writing to him every week, but she hadn't told him they were as badly-off as this.

"Well now, listen," Brackett began, "tell me things. How's Ella?"

"Oh, she's pretty good," Jesse replied absently. He had a soft, pleasing shy voice that went with his soft gray eyes. He was worrying over how to get started.

"And the kids?"

"Oh, they're fine ... Well, you know," Jesse added, becoming more attentive, "the young one has to wear a brace. He can't run around, you know. But he's smart. He draws pictures and he does things, you know."

"Yes," Brackett said. "That's good." He hesitated. There was a moment's silence. Jesse fidgeted in his chair. Now that the time had arrived, he felt awkward. Brackett leaned forward and put his hand on Jesse's knee. "Ella didn't tell me things were so bad for you, Jesse. I might have helped."

"Well, goodness," Jesse returned softly, "you been having your own troubles, ain't you?"

"Yes." Brackett leaned back. His ruddy face became mournful and darkly bitter. "You know I lost my hardware shop?"

"Well sure, of course," Jesse answered, surprised. "You wrote us. That's what I mean."

"I forgot," Brackett said. "I keep on being surprised over it myself. Not that it was worth much," he added bitterly. "It was running downhill for three years. I guess I just wanted it because it was mine." He laughed pointlessly, without mirth. "Well, tell me about yourself," he added. "What happened to the job you had?"

Jesse burst out abruptly, with agitation, "Let it wait, Tom, I got something on my mind."

"It ain't you and Ella?" Brackett interrupted anxiously.

"Why no!" Jesse sat back. "Why, however did you come to think that? Why Ella and me . . ." He stopped, laughing. "Why, Tom, I'm just crazy about Ella. Why she's just wonderful. She's just my whole life, Tom."

"Excuse me. Forget it." Brackett chuckled uncomfortably, turned away. The naked intensity of the youth's burst of love had upset him. It made him wish savagely that he could do something for them. They were too decent to have had it so hard. Ella was like this boy too, shy and a little soft.

"Tom, listen," Jesse said, "I come here on purpose." He thrust his hand through his hair. "I want you to help me."

"Damn it, boy," Brackett groaned. He had been expecting this. "I can't much. I only get thirty-five a week and I'm damn grateful for it."

"Sure, I know," Jesse emphasized excitedly. He was feeling once again the wild, delicious agitation that had possessed him in the early hours of the morning. "I know you can't help us with money! But we met a man who works for you! He was in our city! He said you could give me a job!"

"Who said?"

"Oh, why didn't you tell me?" Jesse burst out reproachfully. "Why, as soon as I heard of it I started out. For two weeks now I been pushing ahead like crazy."

Brackett groaned aloud. "You come walking from Kansas City in two weeks so I could give you a job?"

"Sure, Tom, of course. What else could I do?"

"God Almighty, there ain't no jobs, Jesse! It's a slack season. And you don't know this oil business. It's special. I got my Legion friends here, but they couldn't do nothing now. Don't you think I'd ask for you as soon as there was a chance?"

Jesse felt stunned. The hope of the last two weeks seemed rolling up into a ball of agony in his stomach. Then, frantically, he cried, "But listen, this man said *you* could hire! He told me! He drives trucks for you! He said you always need men!"

"Oh! . . . You mean my department?" Brackett said in a low voice.

"Yes, Tom. That's it!"

"Oh, no, you don't want to work in my department," Brackett told him in the same low voice. "You don't know what it is."

"Yes, I do," Jesse insisted. "He told me all about it, Tom. You're a dispatcher, ain't you? You send the dynamite trucks out?"

"Who was the man, Jesse?"

"Everett, Everett, I think."

"Egbert? Man about my size?" Brackett asked slowly.

"Yes, Egbert. He wasn't a phony, was he?"

Brackett laughed. For the second time his laughter was curiously without mirth. "No, he wasn't a phony." Then, in a changed voice: "Jiminy, boy, you should have asked me before you trekked all the way down here."

"Oh, I didn't want to," Jesse explained with naive cunning. "I knew you'd say no. He told me it was risky work, Tom. But I don't care."

Brackett locked his fingers together. His solid, meaty face became very hard. "I'm going to say no anyway, Jesse."

Jesse cried out. It had not occurred to him that Brackett would not agree. It had seemed as though reaching Tulsa were the only problem he had to face. "Oh no," he begged, "you can't. Ain't there any jobs, Tom?"

"Sure there's jobs. There's even Egbert's job if you want it."

"He's quit?"

"He's dead!"

"Oh!"

"On the job, Jesse. Last night if you want to know."

"Oh!" ... Then, "I don't care!"

"Now you listen to me," Brackett said. "I'll tell you a few things that you should have asked before you started out. It ain't dynamite you drive. They don't use anything as safe as dynamite in drilling oil wells. They wish they could, but they can't. It's nitroglycerin! Soup!"

"But I know," Jesse told him reassuringly. "He advised me, Tom. You don't have to think I don't know."

"Shut up a minute," Brackett ordered angrily. "Listen! You just have to look at this soup, see? You just cough loud and it blows! You know how they transport it? In a can that's shaped like this, see, like a fan? That's to give room for compartments, because each compartment has to be lined with rubber. That's the only way you can even think of handling it."

"Listen, Tom ... "

"Now wait a minute, Jesse. For God's sake just put your mind to this. I know you had your heart set on a job, but you've got to understand. This stuff goes only in special trucks! At night! They got to follow a special route! They can't go through any city! If they lay over, it's got to be in a special garage! Don't you see what that means? Don't that tell you how dangerous it is?"

"I'll drive careful," Jesse said. "I know how to handle a truck. I'll drive slow."

Brackett groaned. "Do you think Egbert didn't drive careful or know how to handle a truck?"

"Tom," Jesse said earnestly, "you can't scare me. I got my mind fixed on only one thing: Egbert said he was getting a dollar a mile. He was making five to six hundred dollars a month for half a month's work, he said. Can I get the same?"

"Sure you can get the same," Brackett told him savagely. "A dollar a mile. It's easy. But why do you think the company has to pay so much? It's easy—until you run over a stone that your headlights didn't pick out, like Egbert did. Or get a blowout! Or get something in your eye so the wheel twists and you jar the truck! Or any other God damn thing that nobody ever knows! We can't ask Egbert what happened to him. There's no truck to give any evidence. There's no corpse. There's nothing! Maybe tomorrow some-body'll find a piece of twisted steel way off in a cornfield. But we never find the driver. Not even a fingernail. All we know is that he don't come in on schedule. Then we wait for the police to call us. You know what happened last night? Something went wrong on a bridge. Maybe Egbert was nervous. Maybe he brushed the side with his fender. Only there's no bridge anymore. No truck. No Egbert. Do you understand now? That's what you get for your God damn dollar a mile!"

There was a moment of silence. Jesse sat twisting his long thin hands. His mouth was sagging open, his face was agonized. Then he shut his eyes and spoke softly. "I don't care about that, Tom. You told me. Now you got to be good to me and give me that job."

Brackett slapped the palm of his hand down on his desk. "No!"

"Listen, Tom," Jesse said softly, "you just don't understand." He opened his eyes. They were filled with tears. They made Brackett turn away. "Just look at me, Tom. Don't that tell you enough? What did you think of me when you first saw me? You thought: 'Why don't that bum go away and stop panhandling?' Didn't you, Tom? Tom, I just can't live like this any more. I got to be able to walk down the street with my head up."

"You're crazy," Brackett muttered. "Every year there's one out of five drivers gets killed. That's the average. What's worth that?"

"Is my life worth anything now? We're just starvin' at home, Tom. They ain't put us back on relief yet."

"Then you should have told me," Brackett exclaimed harshly. "It's your own damn fault. A man has no right to have false pride when his family ain't eating. I'll borrow some money and we'll telegraph it to Ella. Then you go home and get back on relief."

"And then what?"

"And then wait, Got damn it! You're no old man. You got no right to throw your life away. Sometime you'll get a job."

"No!" Jesse jumped up. "No. I believed that too. But I don't now," he cried passionately. "I ain't getting a job no more than you're getting your hardware store back. I lost my skill, Tom. Linotyping is skilled work. I'm rusty now. I've been six years on relief. The only work I've had is pick and shovel. When I got that job this spring, I was supposed to be an A-1 man. But I wasn't. And they got new machines now. As soon as the slack started, they let me out."

"So what?" Brackett said harshly. "Ain't there other jobs?"

"How do I know?" Jesse replied. "There ain't been one for six years. I'd even be afraid to take one now. It's been too hard waiting so many weeks to get back on relief."

"Well, you got to have some courage," Brackett shouted. "You've got to keep up hope."

"I got all the courage you want," Jesse retorted vehemently, "but no, I ain't got no hope. The hope has dried up in me in six years waiting. You're the only hope I got."

"You're crazy," Brackett muttered. "I won't do it. For God's sake think of Ella for a minute."

"Don't you know I'm thinking about her?" Jesse asked softly. He plucked at Brackett's sleeve. "That's what decided me, Tom." His voice became muted into a hushed, pained, whisper. "The night Egbert was at our house I looked at Ella like I'd seen her for the first time. She ain't pretty anymore, Tom!" Brackett jerked his head and moved away. Jesse followed him, taking a deep, sobbing breath. "Don't that tell you, Tom? Ella was like a little doll or something, you remember. I couldn't walk down the street without somebody turning to look at her. She ain't twenty-nine yet, Tom, and she ain't pretty no more."

Brackett sat down with his shoulders hunched up wearily. He gripped his hands together and sat leaning forward, staring at the floor.

Jesse stood over him, his gaunt face flushed with emotion, almost unpleasant in its look of pleading and bitter humility. "I ain't done right for Ella, Tom. Ella deserved better. This is the only chance I see in my whole life to do something for her. I've just been a failure."

"Don't talk nonsense," Brackett commented without rancor. "You ain't a failure. No more than me. There's millions of men in the identical situation. It's just the depression, or the recession, or the God damn New Deal, or ... !" He swore and lapsed into silence.

"Oh no," Jesse corrected him in a knowing, sorrowful tone, "those things maybe excuse other men. But not me. It was up to me to do better. This is my own fault!"

"Oh, beans!" Brackett said. "It's more sun spots than it's you!"

Jesse's face turned an unhealthy mottled red. It looked swollen. "Well I don't care," he cried wildly. "I don't care! You got to give me this! I got to lift my head up. I went through one stretch of hell, but I can't go through another. You want me to keep looking at my little boy's legs and tell myself if I had a job he wouldn't be like that? Every time he walks he says to me, 'I got soft bones from the rickets and you give it to me because you didn't feed me right.' Jesus Christ, Tom, you think I'm going to sit there and watch him like that another six years?"

Brackett leaped to his feet. "So what if you do?" he shouted. "You say you're thinking about Ella. How's she going to like it when you get killed?"

"Maybe I won't," Jesse pleaded. "I've got to have some luck sometime."

"That's what they all think," Brackett replied scornfully. "When you take this job, your luck is a question mark. The only thing certain is that sooner or later you get killed."

"Okay then," Jesse shouted back. "Then I do! But meanwhile I got something, don't I? I can buy a pair of shoes. Look at me! I can buy a suit that don't say 'Relief' by the way it fits. I can smoke cigarettes. I can buy some candy for the kids. I can eat some myself. Yes, by God, I want to eat some candy. I want a glass of beer once a day. I want Ella dressed up. I want her to eat meat three times a week, four times maybe. I want to take my family to the movies."

Brackett sat down. "Oh, shut up," he said wearily.

"No," Jesse told him softly, passionately, "you can't get rid of me. Listen, Tom," he pleaded, "I got it all figured out. On six hundred a month look how much I can save! If I last only three months, look how much it is ... a thousand dollars ... more! And maybe I'll last longer. Maybe a couple years. I can fix Ella up for life!"

"You said it," Brackett interposed. "I suppose you think she'll enjoy living when you're on a job like that?"

"I got it all figured out," Jesse answered excitedly. "She don't know, see? I tell her I make only forty. You put the rest in a bank account for her, Tom."

"Oh, shut up," Brackett said. "You think you'll be happy? Every minute, waking and sleeping, you'll be wondering if tomorrow you'll be dead. And the worst days will be your days off, when you're not driving. They have to give you every other day free to get your nerve back. And you lay around the house eating your heart out. That's how happy you'll be."

Jesse laughed. "I'll be happy! Don't you worry, I'll be so happy, I'll be singing. Lord God, Tom, I'm going to feel proud of myself for the first time in seven years!"

"Oh, shut up, shut up," Brackett said.

The little shanty became silent. After a moment Jesse whispered: "You got to, Tom. You got to. You got to."

Again there was silence. Brackett raised both hands to his head, pressing the palms against his temples.

"Tom, Tom ... " Jesse said.

Brackett sighed. "Oh, God damn it," he said finally, "all right, I'll take you on, God help me." His voice was low, hoarse, infinitely weary. "If you're ready to drive tonight, you can drive tonight."

Jesse didn't answer. He couldn't. Brackett looked up. The tears were running down Jesse's face. He was swallowing and trying to speak, but only making an absurd, gasping noise.

"I'll send a wire to Ella," Brackett said in the same hoarse, weary voice. "I'll tell her you got a job, and you'll send her fare in a couple of days. You'll have some money then—that is, if you last the week out, you jackass!"

Jesse only nodded. His heart felt so close to bursting that he pressed both hands against it, as though to hold it locked within his breast.

"Come back here at six o'clock," Brackett said. "Here's some money. Eat a good meal."

"Thanks," Jesse whispered.

"Wait a minute," Brackett said. "Here's my address." He wrote it on a piece of paper, "Take any car going that way. Ask the conductor where to get off. Take a bath and get some sleep."

"Thanks," Jesse said. "Thanks, Tom."

"Oh, get out of here," Brackett said.

"Tom."

"What?"

"I just ..." Jesse stopped. Brackett saw his face. The eyes were still glistening with tears, but the gaunt face was shining now with a kind of fierce radiance.

Brackett turned away. "I'm busy," he said.

Jesse went out. The wet film blinded him, but the whole world seemed to have turned golden. He limped slowly, with the blood pounding his temples and a wild, incommunicable joy in his heart. "I'm the happiest man in the world," he whispered to himself. "I'm the happiest man on the whole earth."

Brackett sat watching till finally Jesse turned the corner of the alley and disappeared. Then he hunched himself over with his head in his hands. His heart was beating painfully like something old and clogged. He listened to it as it beat. He sat in desperate tranquillity, gripping his head in his hands.

1938

LILLIAN HELLMAN
1905–1984

Lillian Hellman's craftsmanship, powerful characterizations, and vigorous, persuasive themes assure her an important place in the history of the American stage. Born in 1905 and spending her childhood between New Orleans and New York, Hellman launched her dramatic career in 1934 with the production of *The Children's Hour*. She went on to write eight plays, including *Days to Come* (1936), *The Little Foxes* (1939), *Watch on the Rhine* (1941), *The Searching Wind* (1944), *Another Part of the Forest* (1946), *The Autumn Garden* (1951), and *Toys in the Attic* (1960), as well as four theatrical adaptations and numerous screenplays for Hollywood. Seven of the plays were chosen among the ten "Best Plays" of their seasons, and she received the New York Drama Critics' Circle Award for the best American drama of the season for both *Watch on the Rhine* and *Toys in the Attic*, as well as the Gold Medal for drama from the National Institute of Arts and Letters. In her Introduction to *Four Plays*, Hellman wrote, "I am a moral writer," and she saw her plays as an opportunity to exercise moral judgment. Although intended for the comfortable middle class that frequents Broadway, the plays, with their rigorous sense of justice and insistence on individual responsibility, compel audiences to confront themselves and their beliefs in light of Hellman's moral vigor. As Robert Brustein wrote of Hellman after her death, "she never wavered in her conviction that theater could be a force for change in what she considered an unethical, unjust, essentially venal world" and Hellman's work especially emphasized the dangers of American innocence to evil and injustice.

When publicly receiving an honorary Doctor of Letters at Smith College in 1974, Hellman was told "no stronger voice than yours has ever been raised against Fascism, the black comedy of the McCarthy period, or the frightening horror of Watergate and after." An example of the way Hellman followed the ethical ideals set out in her plays came during the McCarthy Era with its challenge to American civil liberties and freedom of inquiry. Hellman was called before the House Un-American Activities Committee (HUAC) in 1952, as were many people in the arts and entertainment industry. Risking the possibility of arrest, not to mention loss of property and livelihood, Hellman courageously told the Committee that while she was willing to speak about her own political activities, she refused, unlike so many called up before them, to "name names," to testify about the activities of friends and acquaintances. In her famous letter to HUAC, she insisted, "I cannot and will not cut my conscience to fit this year's fashions."

Hellman survived the Hollywood blacklisting that was in effect for years after her appearance before HUAC to launch a new career as a writer of the autobiographical memoirs that would become as well known as her plays. *An Unfinished Woman* appeared in 1969 and won the National Book Award; *Pentimento* came out in 1976, and one of its portraits was made into the 1977 film *Julia*. The last of these memoirs was *Maybe: A Story*, published in 1980. Hellman said that by far the hardest of her memoirs to write was *Scoundrel Time*, published in 1976. It had taken twenty-five years for her to bring herself to describe her experience before the House Un-American Committee during what is often referred as the McCarthy witchhunts, based on the dominant role played by Senator Joseph McCarthy and his Committee on Government Operations. With *Scoundrel Time*, Hellman said she wasn't out to write history, just to describe what happened to her. But in doing so, in pungent language with a definite point of view, she brings to life the repression of civil liberties in the name of Anti-Communism during the Cold War era of the 1950s. The selection here, culled from three places in the memoir, represents the underlying argument of the book. When *Scoundrel Time* was published, Hellman received high praise both for her portrayal of this period and for her actions during it. However, the memoir, as did much of Hellman's life, also engendered controversy and strong criticism, sometimes from the very intellectuals and writers Hellman's book indicted. And while Hellman did not think another McCarthy era could happen, she did tell interviewer Marilyn Berger that she thought contemporary Americans could be deprived of their civil liberties, that "something worse could happen based on a seeming sense and seeming rationality and seeming need ... in a much more quiet and simple way since very few of us any longer pay any attention to the small laws that are passed, or even the larger ones. We can be deprived of a great deal without knowing it; without realizing it; waking up to it."

Vivian Patraka
Bowling Green State University

PRIMARY WORKS

Lillian Hellman: The Collected Plays, 1971; *Six Plays*, 1979; *Three: An Unfinished Woman, Pentimento, Scoundrel Time*, 1979; *Maybe*, 1980.

from **Scoundrel Time**

I have tried twice before to write about what has come to be known as the McCarthy period but I didn't much like what I wrote. My reasons for not being able to write about my part in this sad, comic, miserable time of our history were simple to me, although some people thought I had avoided it for mysterious reasons. There was no mystery. I had strange hangups and they are always hard to explain. Now I tell myself that if I face them, maybe I can manage.

The prevailing eccentricity was and is my inability to feel much against the leading figures of the period, the men who punished me. Senators McCarthy and McCarran, Representatives Nixon, Walter and Wood, all of them, were what they were: men who invented when necessary, maligned even when it wasn't necessary. I do not think they believed much, if anything, of what they said: the time was ripe for a new wave in America, and they seized their political chance to lead it along each day's opportunity, spit-balling whatever and with whoever came into view.

But the new wave was not so new. It began with the Russian Revolution of 1917. The victory of the revolution, and thus its menace, had haunted us through the years that followed then twisted the tail of history when Russia was our ally in the Second World War and, just because that had been such an unnatural connection, the fears came back in fuller force after the war when it looked to many people as if Russia would overrun western Europe. Then the revolution in China caused an enormous convulsion in capitalist societies and somewhere along the line gave us the conviction that we could have prevented it if only. If only was never explained with any sense, but the times had very little need of sense.

The fear of Communism did not begin that year, but the new China, allied in those days with Russia, had a more substantial base and there were many honest men and women who were, understandably, frightened that their pleasant way of life could end in a day.

It was not the first time in history that the confusions of honest people were picked up in space by cheap baddies who, hearing a few bars of popular notes, made them into an opera of public disorder, staged and sung, as much of the congressional testimony shows, in the wards of an insane asylum.

A theme is always necessary, a plain, simple, unadorned theme to confuse the ignorant. The anti-Red theme was easily chosen from the grab bag, not alone because we were frightened of socialism, but chiefly, I think, to destroy the remains of Roosevelt and his sometimes advanced work. The McCarthy group—a loose term for all the boys, lobbyists, Congressmen, State Department bureaucrats, CIA operators—chose the anti-Red scare with perhaps more cynicism than Hitler picked anti-Semitism. He, history can no longer deny, deeply believed in the impurity of the Jew. But it is impossible to remember the drunken face of McCarthy, merry often with a kind of worldly malice, as if he were mocking those who took him seriously, and believe that he himself could take seriously anything but his boozed-up nightmares. And if all the rumors were true the nightmares could have concerned more than the fear of a Red tank on Pennsylvania Avenue, although it is possible that in his case a tank could have turned him on. Mr. Nixon's beliefs, if indeed they ever existed, are best left to jolly quarter-historians like Theodore White. But one has a right to believe that if Whittaker Chambers[1] was capable of thinking up a pumpkin, and he was, Mr. Nixon seized upon this strange hiding place with the eagerness of a man who already felt deep contempt for public intelligence. And he was right.

But none of them, even on the bad morning of my hearing before the House Un-American Activities Committee, interested me or disturbed me at a serious level. They didn't and they don't. They are what they are, or were, and are no relation to me by blood or background. (My own family held more interesting villains of another, wittier nature.)

I have written before that my shock and my anger came against what I thought had been the people of my world, although in many cases, of course, I did not know the men and women of that world except by name. I had, up to the late 1940's, believed that the educated, the intellectual, lived by what they claimed to believe: freedom of thought and speech, the right of each man to his own convictions, a more than implied promise, therefore, of aid to those who might be persecuted. But only a very few raised a finger when McCarthy and the boys appeared. Almost all, either by what they did or did not do, contributed to McCarthyism, running after a bandwagon which hadn't bothered to stop to pick them up.

Simply, then and now, I feel betrayed by the nonsense I had believed. I had no right to think that American intellectuals were people who would fight for anything if doing so would injure them; they have very little history that would lead to that conclusion. Many of them found in the sins of Stalin Communism—and there were plenty of sins and plenty that for a

---

[1]In August 1948 Whittaker Chambers appeared before the House Un-American Activities Committee. Chambers, a senior editor of *Time* magazine, told the Committee that he had once been a Communist and an underground courier. He named ten men as his former associates, the best known being Alger Hiss, formerly a high official of the State Department. Chambers accused Hiss of giving him secret government material, which Chambers preserved by placing it in a pumpkin at his farm in Maryland. Hiss was indicted, tried twice, and sent to jail for almost four years. In 1975 the secret pumpkin papers were found to contain nothing secret, nothing confidential. They were, in fact, non-classified, which is Washington's way of saying anybody who says "please" can have them.

long time I mistakenly denied—the excuse to join those who should have been their hereditary enemies.

To many intellectuals the radicals had become the chief, perhaps the only, enemy. (There had been a history of this that preceded my generation: Eugene Debs had been hounded into jail by Woodrow Wilson, and there had been the vicious trials of the men of the International Workers of the World.) Not alone because the radical's intellectual reasons were suspect, but because his convictions would lead to a world that deprived the rest of us what we had. Very few people are capable of admitting anything so simple: the radical had to be made into an immoral man who justified murder, prison camps, torture, any means to an end. And, in fact, he sometimes was just that. But the anti-radical camp contained the same divisions: often they were honest and thoughtful men, often they were men who turned down a dark road for dark reasons.

But radicalism or anti-radicalism should have had nothing to do with the sly, miserable methods of McCarthy, Nixon and colleagues, as they flailed at Communists, near-Communists, and nowhere-near-Communists. Lives were being ruined and few hands were raised in help. Since when do you have to agree with people to defend them from injustice? Certainly nobody in their right mind could have believed that the China experts, charged and fired by the State Department, did any more than recognize that Chiang Kai-shek was losing. Truth made you a traitor as it often does in a time of scoundrels. But there were very few who stood up to say so and there are almost none even now to remind us that one of the reasons we know so little and guess so badly about China is that we lost the only men who knew what they were talking about. Certainly the good magazines, the ones that published the most serious writers, should have come to the aid of those who were persecuted. *Partisan Review*, although through the years it has published many pieces protesting the punishment of dissidents in Eastern Europe, made no protest when people in this country were jailed or ruined. In fact, it never took an editorial position against McCarthy himself, although it did publish the results of anti-McCarthy symposiums and at least one distinguished piece by Irving Howe. *Commentary* didn't do anything. No editor or contributor ever protested against McCarthy. Indeed, Irving Kristol in that magazine wrote about McCarthy's critics, Henry Steele Commager among others, as if they were naughty children who needed Kristol to correct their innocence.

There were many thoughtful and distinguished men and women on both magazines. None of them, as far as I know, has yet found it a part of conscience to admit that their Cold War anti-Communism was perverted, possibly against their wishes, into the Vietnam War and then into the reign of Nixon, their unwanted but inevitable leader.

*   *   *

There were many broken lives along the path the boys [McCarthy, Cohn, and Schine] had bulldozed, but not so many that people needed to feel guilty if they turned their backs fast enough and told each other, as we were to do again after Watergate, that Americans justice will always prevail no matter how careless it seems to critical outsiders.

It is not true that when the bell tolls it tolls for thee: if it were true we could not have elected, so few years later, Richard Nixon, a man who had been closely allied with McCarthy. It was no accident that Mr. Nixon brought with him a group of high-powered operators who made Cohn and Schine look like cute little rascals from grammar school. The names and faces had been changed; the stakes were higher, because the prize was the White House. And one year after a presidential scandal of a magnitude still unknown, we have almost forgotten them, too. We are a people who do not want to keep much of the past in our heads. It is considered unhealthy in America to remember mistakes, neurotic to think about them, psychotic to dwell upon them.

1976

MARY McCARTHY
1912–1989

Mary McCarthy was an important intellectual writer whose work addressed many of the critical political issues of the twentieth century. Her novels and memoirs as well as her numerous collections of essays demonstrate that she was deeply concerned with social responsibility—a topic that inevitably involves an analysis of the traditional definitions of race, class, and gender. McCarthy's early theatre columns for *Partisan Review*, her autobiographical narratives, her fiction, especially her controversial novel *The Group*, and her penetrating essays in such collections as *On the Contrary* make it clear that she did not shrink from confrontation. Her keen analytical skills and caustic commentary were focused on national and international issues such as the Watergate scandal, the Vietnam War, and the invasion of Cambodia, as well as domestic concerns such as divorce, female sexuality, and birth control. Her refusal to resort to platitudes in her analyses of subjects as diverse as corruption in national government and dysfunctional family dynamics earned her a reputation as being "cold, steely, merciless." She became known as the "lady with a switchblade."

McCarthy's personal life was as complex as her writing. Born in Seattle in 1912, she was orphaned at the age of six when her parents died in the influenza epidemic that swept the United States in 1918. With her three younger brothers, Kevin, Preston, and Sheridan, she was sent to live with her great aunt and uncle. She recorded her bitter recollections of that time in *Memories of a Catholic*

Girlhood, How I Grew, and *Intellectual Memoirs*. Especially distressing was the cruel treatment she received from Uncle Myers, whose vicious criticisms and physical cruelty she never forgot. He is the prototype of the bombastic and self-indulgent men who appear in her fiction from "The Man in the Brooks Brothers Suit" to her descriptions of H. R. Haldeman and John Ehrlichman in *The Mask of State: Watergate Portraits*.

As an undergraduate at Vassar from 1929 to 1933, McCarthy was a voracious reader and an excellent student. After marrying and divorcing in the first three years after graduation, she embarked on an adventurous life in Greenwich Village during the Great Depression. During this time, McCarthy wrote theatre reviews for *Partisan Review* and lived with Philip Rahv, one of the editors of the journal. In 1938 she left Rahv to marry Edmund Wilson, a brilliant literary critic and essayist. Crediting Wilson with her career as a fiction writer, McCarthy reported that early in their marriage he insisted that she remain in her study until she had written a short story. She and Wilson had a son, Reuel, in 1939, and they divorced six years later. McCarthy married twice more and lived in Paris for many years with her fourth husband, James West.

During the 1930s, McCarthy was involved in political debates between the Stalinists and the supporters of Trotsky, whom she favored. She brilliantly evokes the political and social ferment of this period in the short stories "The Genial Host" and "Portrait of an Intellectual as a Yale Man," which were included in *The Company She Keeps*. The *New Yorker* responded with enthusiasm to this collection and invited McCarthy to join its staff of writers.

Following the Second World War, McCarthy and Hannah Arendt formed a friendship that lasted 30 years. McCarthy observed in *How I Grew* that "not love or marriage so much as friendship has promoted growth." McCarthy and Arendt became internationally acclaimed during the years of their friendship. When Arendt died in 1975, McCarthy devoted two years to editing Arendt's *The Life of the Mind*, which was published in two volumes in 1978.

Throughout her life, McCarthy disavowed any association with feminism, as did many women of her generation; nevertheless, a feminist sensibility underlies her work. One of the primary themes of her work is the battle of the sexes and the damaging consequences of the norms of masculine aggression and feminine passivity. Another of her concerns is the importance of psychological and financial autonomy for women. Economic and emotional dependence on men results in extraordinary paralysis in the lives of McCarthy's women protagonists, who are frequently caught in a web of feminine self-abnegation disguised as romantic love.

McCarthy dissected the perils of female passivity in the novel *The Group*, an immediate best-seller when published in 1963. The novel begins with the first inauguration of Franklin Roosevelt and ends with the inauguration of Truman. McCarthy observed that the novel is "about the idea of progress really, seen in the female sphere; the study of technology in the home, in the playpen, in the bed." Weaving interconnecting narratives about eight Vassar graduates from the class of 1933, this novel makes clear that, in spite of optimism about the possibilities of modern life, these women are as dependent on men for economic and social survival as their mothers were.

The writer Alison Lurie observed that Mary McCarthy invented "herself as a totally new type of woman who stood for both sense and sensibility; who was both coolly and professionally intellectual and frankly passionate." In spite of her sardonic and satiric view of sexual politics, McCarthy believed that it is necessary "to choose the self you want." Her boldly unconventional and accomplished life is a testament to the modernist credo that the individual is the locus of authority.

Wendy Martin
Claremont Graduate School

PRIMARY WORKS

Fiction: *The Oasis*, 1949; *The Groves of Academe*, 1952; *A Charmed Life*, 1955; *The Group*, 1963; *Birds of America*, 1965; *The Company She Keeps*, 1970; *Cannibals and Missionaries*, 1979; *The Hounds of Summer and Other Stories*, 1981. Nonfiction: *Cast a Cold Eye*, 1950; *Sights and Spectacles, 1937–1956*, 1956; *Venice Observed*, 1956; *The Stones of Florence*, 1959; *On the Contrary*, 1961; *Mary McCarthy's Theater Chronicles*, 1963; *Vietnam*, 1967; *Hanoi*, 1968; *The Writing on the Wall and Other Literary Essays*, 1970; *Medina*, 1972; *The Mask of State: Watergate Portraits*, 1974; *Memories of a Catholic Girlhood*, 1974; *The Seventeenth Degree*, 1974; *Ideas and the Novel*, 1980; *How I Grew*, 1985; *Occasional Prose*, 1985; *Intellectual Memoirs: New York 1936–1938*, 1992.

from Memories of a Catholic Girlhood

Names

Anna Lyons, Mary Louise Lyons, Mary von Phul, Emilie von Phul, Eugenia McLellan, Marjorie McPhail, Marie-Louise L'Abbé, Mary Danz, Julia Dodge, Mary Fordyce Blake, Janet Preston—these were the names (I can still tell them over like a rosary) of some of the older girls in the convent: the Virtues and Graces. The virtuous ones wore wide blue or green moire good-conduct ribbons, bandoleer-style, across their blue serge uniforms; the beautiful ones wore rouge and powder or at least were reputed to do so. Our class, the eighth grade, wore pink ribbons (I never got one myself) and had names like Patricia ("Pat") Sullivan, Eileen Donohoe, and Joan Kane. We were inelegant even in this respect; the best name we could show, among us, was Phyllis ("Phil") Chatham, who boasted that her father's name, Ralph, was pronounced "Rafe" as in England.

Names had a great importance for us in the convent, and foreign names, French, German, or plain English (which, to us, were foreign, because of their Protestant sound), bloomed like prize roses among a collection of spuds. Irish names were too common in the school to have any prestige either as surnames (Gallagher, Sheehan, Finn, Sullivan, McCarthy) or as Christian names (Kathleen, Eileen). Anything exotic had value: an "olive" complexion, for example. The pet girl of the convent was a fragile Jewish girl named Susie Lowenstein, who had pale red-gold hair and an exquisite retroussé nose, which, if we had had it, might have been called "pug." We liked her name too and the name of a child in the primary grades: Abbie Stuart Baillargeon. My favorite name, on the whole, though, was Emilie von Phul (pronounced "Pool"); her oldest sister, recently graduated, was called Celeste. Another name that appealed to me was Genevieve Albers, Saint Genevieve being the patron saint of Paris who turned back Attila from the gates of the city.

All these names reflected the still-pioneer character of the Pacific Northwest. I had never heard their like in the parochial school in Minneapolis, where "foreign" extraction, in any case, was something to be ashamed of, the whole drive being toward Americanization of first name and surname alike. The exceptions to this were the Irish, who could vaunt such names as Catherine O'Dea and the name of my second cousin, Mary Catherine Anne Rose Violet McCarthy, while an unfortunate German boy named Manfred was made to suffer for his. But that was Minneapolis. In Seattle, and especially in the convent of the Ladies of the Sacred Heart, foreign names suggested not immigration but emigration—distinguished exile. Minneapolis was a granary; Seattle was a port, which had attracted a veritable Foreign Legion of adventurers—soldiers of fortune, younger sons, gamblers, traders, drawn by the fortunes to be made in virgin timber and shipping and by the Alaska Gold Rush. Wars and revolutions had sent the defeated out to Puget Sound, to start a new life; the latest had been the Russian Revolution, which had shipped us, via Harbin, a Russian colony, complete with restaurant, on Queen Anne Hill. The English names in the convent, when they did not testify to direct English origin, as in the case of "Rafe" Chatham, had come to us from the South and represented a kind of internal exile; such girls as Mary Fordyce Blake and Mary McQueen Street (a class ahead of me; her sister was named Francesca) bore their double-barreled first names like titles of aristocracy from the ante-bellum South. Not all our girls, by any means, were Catholic; some of the very prettiest ones—Julia Dodge and Janet Preston, if I remember rightly—were Protestants. The nuns had taught us to behave with special courtesy to these strangers in our midst, and the whole effect was of some superior hostel for refugees of all the lost causes of the past hundred years. Money could not count for much in such an atmosphere; the fathers and grandfathers of many of our "best" girls were ruined men.

Names, often, were freakish in the Pacific Northwest, particularly girls' names. In the Episcopal boarding school I went to later, in Tacoma, there was a girl called De Vere Utter, and there was a girl called Rocena and another called Hermoine. Was Rocena a mistake for Rowena and Hermoine for Hermione? And was Vere, as we called her, Lady Clara Vere de Vere? Probably. You do not hear names like those often, in any case, east of the Cascade Mountains; they belong to the frontier, where books and libraries were few and memory seems to have been oral, as in the time of Homer.

Names have more significance for Catholics than they do for other people; Christian names are chosen for the spiritual qualities of the saints they are taken from; Protestants used to name their children out of the Old Testament and now they name them out of novels and plays, whose heroes and heroines are perhaps the new patron saints of a secular age. But with Catholics it is different. The saint a child is named for is supposed to serve, literally, as a model or pattern to imitate; your name is your fortune and it tells you what you are or must be. Catholic children ponder their names for a mystic meaning, like birthstones; my own, I learned, besides belonging to the Virgin and Saint Mary of Egypt, originally meant "bitter" or "star of the sea." My second name, Therese, could dedicate me either to Saint Theresa or to the saint called the Little Flower, Soeur Thérèse of Lisieux, on whom God was supposed to have descended in the form of a shower of roses. At Confirmation, I had added a third name (for Catholics then rename themselves, as most nuns do, yet another time, when they take orders); on the advice of a nun, I had taken "Clementina," after Saint Clement, an early pope—a step I soon regretted on account of "My Darling Clementine" and her number nine shoes. By the time I was in the convent, I would no longer tell anyone what my Confirmation name was. The name I had nearly picked was "Agnes," after a little Roman virgin martyr, always shown with a lamb, because of her purity. But Agnes would have been just as bad, I recognized in Forest Ridge Convent—not only because of the possibility of "Aggie," but because it was subtly, indefinably *wrong*, in itself. Agnes would have made me look like an ass.

The fear of appearing ridiculous first entered my life, as a governing motive, during my second year in the convent. Up to then, a desire for prominence had decided many of my actions and, in fact, still persisted. But in the eighth grade, I became aware of mockery and perceived that I could not seek prominence without attracting laughter. Other people could, but I couldn't. This laughter was proceeding, not from my classmates, but from the girls of the class just above me, in particular from two boon companions, Elinor Heffernan and Mary Harty, a clownish pair—oddly assorted in size and shape, as teams of clowns generally are, one short, plump, and baby-faced, the other tall, lean, and owlish—who entertained the high-school department by calling attention to the oddities of the younger girls. Nearly every school has such a pair of satirists, whose marks are generally low and who are tolerated just because of their laziness and non-conformity; one of them (in this case, Mary Harty, the plump one) usually appears to be half asleep. Because of their low standing, their indifference to appearances, the sad state of their uniforms, their clowning is taken to be harmless, which, on the whole, it is, their object being not to wound but to divert; such girls are bored in school. We in the eighth grade sat directly in front of the two wits in study hall, so that they had us under close observation; yet at first I was not afraid of them, wanting, if anything, to identify myself with their laughter, to be initiated into the joke. One of their specialties was giving people nicknames, and it was considered an honor to be the first in the eighth grade to be let in by Elinor and Mary on their latest invention. This often happened to me; they would tell me, on the playground, and I would tell the others. As their intermediary, I felt myself almost their friend and it did not occur to me that I might be next on their list.

I had achieved prominence not long before by publicly losing my faith and regaining it at the end of a retreat. I believe Elinor and Mary questioned me about this on the playground, during recess, and listened with serious, respectful faces while I told them about my conversations with the Jesuits. Those serious faces ought to have been an omen, but if the two girls used what I had revealed to make fun of me, it must have been behind my back. I never heard any more of it, and yet just at this time I began to feel something, like a cold breath on the nape of my neck, that made me wonder whether the new position I had won for myself in the convent was as secure as I imagined. I would turn around in study hall and find the two girls looking at me with speculation in their eyes.

It was just at this time, too, that I found myself in a perfectly absurd situation, a very private one, which made me live, from month to month, in horror of discovery. I had waked up one morning, in my convent room, to find a few small spots of blood on my sheet; I had somehow scratched a trifling cut on one of my legs and opened it during the night. I wondered what to do about this, for the nuns were fussy about bedmaking, as they were about our white collars and cuffs, and if we had an inspection those spots might count against me. It was best, I decided, to ask the nun on dormitory duty, tall, stout Mother Slattery, for a clean bottom sheet, even though she might scold me for having scratched my leg in my sleep and order me to cut my toenails. You never know what you might be blamed for. But Mother Slattery, when she bustled in to look at the sheet, did not scold me at all; indeed, she hardly seemed to be listening as I explained to her about the cut. She told me to sit down: she would be back in a minute. "You can be excused from athletics today," she added, closing the door. As I waited, I considered this remark, which seemed to me strangely munificent, in view of the unimportance of the cut. In a moment, she returned, but without the sheet. Instead, she produced out of her big pocket a sort of cloth girdle and a peculiar flannel object which I first took to be a bandage, and I began to protest that I did not need or want a bandage; all I needed was a bottom sheet. "The sheet can wait," said Mother Slattery, succinctly, handing me two large safety pins. It was the pins that abruptly enlightened me; I saw Mother Slattery's mistake, even as she was instructing me as to how this flannel article, which I now understood to be a sanitary napkin, was to be put on.

"Oh, no, Mother," I said, feeling somewhat embarrassed. "You don't understand. It's just a little cut, on my leg." But Mother, again, was not listening; she appeared to have grown deaf, as the nuns had a habit of doing when what you were saying did not fit in with their ideas. And now that I knew what was in her mind, I was conscious of a funny constraint; I did not feel it proper to name a natural process, in so many words, to a nun. It was like trying not to think of their going to the bathroom or trying not to see the straggling iron-grey hair coming out of their coifs (the common notion that they shaved their heads was false). On the whole, it seemed better just to show her my cut. But when I offered to do so and unfastened my black stocking, she only glanced at my leg, cursorily. "That's only a scratch, dear," she said. "Now hurry up and put this on or you'll be late for chapel. Have you any pain?" "No, no, Mother!" I cried. "You don't understand!" "Yes, yes, I understand," she replied soothingly, "and you will too, a little later. Mother Superior will tell you about it some time during the morning. There's nothing to be afraid of. You have become a woman."

"I know all about that," I persisted. "Mother, please listen. I just cut my leg. On the athletic field. Yesterday afternoon." But the more excited I grew, the more soothing, and yet firm, Mother Slattery became. There seemed to be nothing for it but to give up and do as I was bid. I was in the grip of a higher authority, which almost had the power to persuade me that it was right and I was wrong. But of course I was not wrong; that would have been too good to be true. While Mother Slattery waited, just outside my door, I miserably donned the equipment she had given me, for there was no place to hide it, on account of drawer inspection. She led me down the hall to where there was a chute and explained how I was to dispose of the flannel thing, by dropping it down the chute into the laundry. (The convent arrangements were very old-fashioned, dating back, no doubt, to the days of Louis Philippe.)

The Mother Superior, Madame MacIllvra, was a sensible woman, and all through my early morning classes, I was on pins and needles, chafing for the promised interview with her which I trusted would clear things up. "*Ma Mère*," I would begin, "Mother Slattery thinks ..." Then I would tell her about the cut and the athletic field. But precisely the same impasse confronted me when I was summoned to her office at recess-time. *I* talked about my cut, and *she* talked about becoming a woman. It was rather like a round, in which she was singing "Scotland's burning, Scotland's burning," and I was singing "Pour on water, pour on water." Neither of us could hear the other, or, rather, I could hear her, but she could not hear me. Owing to our different positions in the convent, she was free to interrupt me, whereas I was expected to remain silent until she had finished speaking. When I kept breaking in, she hushed me, gently, and took me on her lap. Exactly like Mother Slattery, she attributed all my references to the cut to a blind fear of this new, unexpected reality that had supposedly entered my life. Many young girls, she reassured me, were frightened if they had not been prepared. "And you, Mary, have lost your dear mother, who could have made this easier for you." Rocked on Madame MacIllvra's lap, I felt paralysis overtake me and I lay, mutely listening, against her bosom, my face being tickled by her white, starched, fluted wimple, while she explained to me how babies were born, all of which I had heard before.

There was no use fighting the convent. I had to pretend to have become a woman, just as, not long before, I had had to pretend to get my faith back—for the sake of peace. This pretense was decidedly awkward. For fear of being found out by the lay sisters downstairs in the laundry (no doubt an imaginary contingency, but the convent was so very thorough), I reopened the cut on my leg, so as to draw a little blood to stain the napkins, which were issued me regularly, not only on this occasion, but every twenty-eight days thereafter. Eventually, I abandoned this bloodletting, for fear of lock-jaw, and trusted to fate. Yet I was in awful dread of detection; my only hope, as I saw it, was either to be released from the convent or to become a woman in reality, which might take a year, at least, since I was only twelve. Getting out of athletics once a month was not sufficient compensation for the farce I was going through. It was not my fault; they had forced me into it; nevertheless, it was I who would look silly—worse than silly; half mad— if the truth ever came to light.

I was burdened with this guilt and shame when the nickname finally found me out. "Found me out," in a general sense, for no one ever did learn the particular secret I bore about with me, pinned to the linen band. "We've got a name for you," Elinor and Mary called out to me, one day on the play-ground. "What is it?" I asked, half hoping, half fearing, since not all their sobriquets were unfavorable. "Cye," they answered, looking at each other and laughing. "'Si'?" I repeated, supposing that it was based on Simple Simon. Did they regard me as a hick? "C.Y.E.," they elucidated, spelling it out in chorus. "The letters stand for something. Can you guess?" I could not and I cannot now. The closest I could come to it in the convent was "Clean Your Ears." Perhaps that was it, though in later life I have wondered whether it did not stand, simply, for "Clever Young Egg" or "Champion Young Eccentric." But in the convent I was certain that it stood for some-thing horrible, something even worse than dirty ears (as far as I knew, my ears were clean), something I could never guess because it represented some aspect of myself that the world could see and I couldn't, like a sign pinned on my back. Everyone in the convent must have known what the letters stood for, but no one would tell me. Elinor and Mary had made them prom-ise. It was like halitosis; not even my best friend, my deskmate, Louise, would tell me, no matter how much I pleaded. Yet everyone assured me that it was "very good," that is, very apt. And it made everyone laugh.

This name reduced all my pretensions and solidified my sense of *wrong-ness*. Just as I felt I was beginning to belong to the convent, it turned me into an outsider, since I was the only pupil who was not in the know. I liked the convent, but it did not like me, as people say of certain foods that dis-agree with them. By this, I do not mean that I was actively unpopular, either with the pupils or with the nuns. The Mother Superior cried when I left and predicted that I would be a novelist, which surprised me. And I had finally made friends; even Emilie von Phul smiled upon me softly out of her bright blue eyes from the far end of the study hall. It was just that I did not fit into the convent pattern; the simplest thing I did, like asking for a clean sheet, entrapped me in consequences that I never could have predicted. I was not bad; I did not consciously break the rules; and yet I could never, not even for a week, get a pink ribbon, and this was something I could not under-stand, because I was trying as hard as I could. It was the same case as with the hated name; the nuns, evidently, saw something about me that was in-visible to me.

The oddest part was all that pretending. There I was, a walking mass of lies, pretending to be a Catholic and going to confession while really I had lost my faith, and pretending to have monthly periods by cutting myself with nail scissors; yet all this had come about without my volition and even contrary to it. But the basest pretense I was driven to was the acceptance of the nickname. Yet what else could I do? In the convent, I could not live it down. To all those girls, I had become "Cye McCarthy." That was who I was. That was how I had to identify myself when telephoning my friends during vacations to ask them to the movies: "Hello, this is Cye." I loathed myself when I said it, and yet I succumbed to the name totally, making myself over into a sort of hearty to go with it—the kind of girl I hated. "Cye" was my new patron saint. This false personality stuck to me, like the name, when I entered public high school, the next fall, as a freshman, having finally persuaded my grandparents to take me out of the convent, although they could never get to the bottom of my reasons, since, as I admitted, the nuns were kind, and I had made many nice new friends. What I wanted was a fresh start, a chance to begin life over again, but the first thing I heard in the corridors of the public high school was that name called out to me, like the warmest of welcomes: "Hi, there, Si!" That was the way they thought it was spelled. But this time I was resolute. After the first weeks, I dropped the hearties who called me "Si" and I never heard it again. I got my own name back and sloughed off Clementina and even Therese—the names that did not seem to me any more to be mine but to have been imposed on me by others. And I preferred to think that Mary meant "bitter" rather than "star of the sea."

1957

CLIFFORD ODETS
1906–1963

Born into a middle-class family in Philadelphia, Odets grew up in predominantly Jewish neighborhoods in the Bronx. Like many successful American authors, he never attended college. After eleventh grade he found acting jobs on the radio and then drifted into work in small local theatre companies.

Odets's acting career was making little progress when in 1930 he became involved with the Group Theatre, a new and dynamic organization that was just beginning its influential decade in New York. After a number of minor acting roles with that company, he decided to try writing a contemporary family drama for them; his script was the genesis of *Awake and Sing* (1935), his first full-length play. The early draft of *Awake and Sing*, however, was rejected by the managers of the Group, and Odets put his script through extensive revisions before the play was eventually performed. In the meantime his rapidly written short play, *Waiting for Lefty* (1935), made him an instant theatrical celebrity.

A certain amount of theatrical mythology has grown up around the composition of *Waiting for Lefty*. It was, in fact, first produced in a small union hall; it was probably not, on the other hand, written in three nights or written as an entry in a contest with a $50 prize. It was quite clearly written in response to the urging of Odets's Communist friends (Odets had joined the party for his brief dalliance in the fall of 1934). More important about the play is the emotional heat which the young playwright was able to convey as well as the theatricality of the presentation. In part because it is a blatant "message" play that can be presented without the benefit of an elaborate stage or scenery, within a few months "Lefty" was being produced all over the country. The reception was predictably enthusiastic in almost every city where it was presented. Even when the play was condemned as mere propaganda, it managed to create enough of a stir to enhance the young playwright's reputation.

Thus the Great Depression and the Group Theatre were the two formative factors in Odets's career as dramatist. It is hard to imagine Odets's successes coming at any time other than during the depression. To the left-oriented, often militant American writers like Odets, "The theatre is a weapon" was a rallying cry. Yet the author of *Waiting for Lefty* went on to write for films, to marry a glamorous Hollywood movie queen, to live comfortably in Beverly Hills, to enjoy the night life of Las Vegas, and to speak openly about Communist infiltration of the arts when he testified in 1952 before the notorious House Un-American Activities Committee. These are only a few of the contradictions apparent in Odets's life.

His subsequent plays, the most popular of which are *Golden Boy* (1937) and *The Country Girl* (1950), demonstrate a mature craftsmanship. Some, like *The Flowering Peach*, even show a calm mood unexpected from the firebrand who wrote *Waiting for Lefty*. Yet Odets's reputation will probably rest heavily with the rich colloquial family drama, *Awake and Sing*, and the angry, experimental *Waiting for Lefty*, his first two produced dramas.

If Odets did not reach the full measure of fulfillment that any artist seeks, he did earn his niche in the history of American drama. His direct influence on playwrights like William Gibson and Arthur Miller is evident. Always the idealist rather than the doctrinaire leftist, Odets is best characterized not by the "Stormbirds of the Working Class" speech at the conclusion of *Waiting for Lefty*, but by the line he directed to the younger generation in *Awake and Sing*: "Go out and fight so life shouldn't be printed on dollar bills."

Michael J. Mendelsohn
University of Tampa

PRIMARY WORKS

Six Plays of Clifford Odets, 1935; *The Country Girl*, 1951.

Waiting for Lefty

As the curtain goes up we see a bare stage. On it are sitting six or seven men in a semi-circle. Lolling against the proscenium[1] down left is a young man chewing a toothpick: a gunman. A fat man of porcine appearance is talking directly to the audience. In other words he is the head of a union and the men ranged behind him are a committee of workers. They are now seated in interesting different attitudes and present a wide diversity of type, as we shall soon see. The fat man is hot and heavy under the collar, near the end of a long talk, but not too hot: he is well fed and confident. His name is HARRY FATT.

FATT: You're so wrong I ain't laughing. Any guy with eyes to read knows it. Look at the textile strike—out like lions and in like lambs. Take the San Francisco tie-up—starvation and broken heads. The steel boys wanted to walk out too, but they changed their minds. It's the trend of the times, that's what it is. All we workers got a good man behind us now.[2] He's top man of the country—looking out for our interests—the man in the White House is the one I'm referrin' to. That's why the times ain't ripe for a strike. He's working day and night—

VOICE *(from the audience)*: For who? *(The* GUNMAN *stirs himself.)*

FATT: For you! The records prove it. If this was the Hoover[3] régime, would I say don't go out, boys? Not on your tintype![4] But things is different now. You read the papers as well as me. You know it. And that's why I'm against the strike. Because we gotta stand behind the man who's standin' behind us! The whole country—

ANOTHER VOICE: Is on the blink! *(The* GUNMAN *looks grave.)*

FATT: Stand up and show yourself, you damn red![5] Be a man, let's see what you look like! *(Waits in vain.)* Yellow from the word go! Red and yellow makes a dirty color, boys. I got my eyes on four or five of them in the union here. What the hell'll they do for you? Pull you out and run away when trouble starts. Give those birds a chance and they'll have your sisters and wives in the whore houses, like they done in Russia. They'll tear Christ off his bleeding cross. They'll wreck your homes and throw your babies in the river. You think that's bunk? Read the papers! Now listen, we can't stay here all night. I gave you the facts in the case. You boys got hot suppers to go to and—

ANOTHER VOICE: Says you!

GUNMAN: Sit down, Punk!

ANOTHER VOICE: Where's Lefty? *(Now this question is taken up by the others in unison.* FATT *pounds with gavel.)*

---

[1]The archway, or frame, that forms the front of a traditional theatrical stage.
[2]Franklin Roosevelt, elected president in 1932.
[3]Roosevelt's predecessor, president from 1929–1933.
[4]Not a chance (slang).
[5]Fatt is calling the unseen heckler a communist agitator.

FATT: That's what I wanna know. Where's your pal, Lefty? You elected him chairman—where the hell did he disappear?

VOICES: We want Lefty! Lefty! Lefty!

FATT (*pounding*): What the hell is this—a circus? You got the committee here. This bunch of cowboys you elected. (*Pointing to man on extreme right end.*)

MAN: Benjamin.

FATT: Yeah, Doc Benjamin. (*Pointing to other men in circle in seated order*): Benjamin, Miller, Stein, Mitchell, Phillips, Keller. It ain't my fault Lefty took a run-out powder. If you guys—

A GOOD VOICE: What's the committee say?

OTHERS: The committee! Let's hear from the committee! (FATT *tries to quiet the crowd, but one of the seated men suddenly comes to the front. The* GUNMAN *moves over to center stage, but* FATT *says:*)

FATT: Sure, let him talk. Let's hear what the red boys gotta say! (*Various shouts are coming from the audience.* FATT *insolently goes back to his seat in the middle of the circle. He sits on his raised platform and relights his cigar. The* GUNMAN *goes back to his post.* JOE, *the new speaker, raises his hand for quiet. Gets it quickly. He is sore.*)

JOE: You boys know me. I ain't a red boy one bit! Here I'm carryin' a shrapnel that big I picked up in the war. And maybe I don't know it when it rains! Don't tell me red! You know what we are? The black and blue boys! We been kicked around so long we're black and blue from head to toes. But I guess anyone who says straight out he don't like it, he's a red boy to the leaders of the union. What's this crap about goin' home to hot suppers? I'm asking to your faces how many's got hot suppers to go home to? Anyone who's sure of his next meal, raise your hand! A certain gent sitting behind me can raise them both. But not in front here! And that's why we're talking strike—to get a living wage!

VOICE: Where's Lefty?

JOE: I honest to God don't know, but he didn't take no run-out powder. That Wop's got more guts than a slaughter house. Maybe a traffic jam got him, but he'll be here. But don't let this red stuff scare you. Unless fighting for a living scares you. We gotta make up our minds. My wife made up my mind last week, if you want the truth. It's plain as the nose on Sol Feinberg's face we need a strike. There's us comin' home every night—eight, ten hours on the cab. "God," the wife says, "eighty cents ain't money—don't buy beans almost. You're workin' for the company," she says to me, "Joe! you ain't workin' for me or the family no more!" She says to me, "If you don't start . . ."

I. Joe and Edna

The lights fade out and a white spot picks out the playing space within the space of seated men. The seated men are very dimly visible in the outer dark, but more prominent is FATT *smoking his cigar and often blowing the smoke in the lighted circle.*

A tired but attractive woman of thirty comes into the room, drying her hands on an apron. She stands there sullenly as JOE *comes in from the other side, home from work. For a moment they stand and look at each other in silence.*

JOE: Where's all the furniture, honey?

EDNA: They took it away. No installments paid.

JOE: When?

EDNA: Three o'clock.

JOE: They can't do that.

EDNA: Can't? They did it.

JOE: Why, the palookas,[6] we paid three-quarters.

EDNA: The man said read the contract.

JOE: We must have signed a phoney....

EDNA: It's a regular contract and you signed it.

JOE: Don't be so sour, Edna.... *(Tries to embrace her.)*

EDNA: Do it in the movies, Joe—they pay Clark Gable big money for it.

JOE: This is a helluva house to come home to. Take my word!

EDNA: Take MY word! Whose fault is it?

JOE: Must you start that stuff again?

EDNA: Maybe you'd like to talk about books?

JOE: I'd like to slap you in the mouth!

EDNA: No you won't.

JOE *(sheepishly)*: Jeez, Edna, you get me sore some time....

EDNA: But just look at me—I'm laughing all over!

JOE: Don't insult me. Can I help it if times are bad? What the hell do you want me to do, jump off a bridge or something?

EDNA: Don't yell. I just put the kids to bed so they won't know they missed a meal. If I don't have Emmy's shoes soled tomorrow, she can't go to school. In the meantime let her sleep.

JOE: Honey, I rode the wheels off the chariot today. I cruised around five hours without a call. It's conditions.

EDNA: Tell it to the A & P!

JOE: I booked two-twenty on the clock. A lady with a dog was lit ... she gave me a quarter tip by mistake. If you'd only listen to me—we're rolling in wealth.

EDNA: Yeah? How much?

JOE: I had "coffee and—" in a beanery. *(Hands her silver coins.)* A buck four.

EDNA: The second month's rent is due tomorrow.

JOE: Don't look at me that way, Edna.

EDNA: I'm looking through you, not at you.... Everything was gonna be so ducky! A cottage by the waterfall, roses in Picardy. You're a four-star-bust! If you think I'm standing for it much longer, you're crazy as a bedbug.

JOE: I'd get another job if I could. There's no work—you know it.

EDNA: I only know we're at the bottom of the ocean.

---

[6]A dumb, muscular type (slang).

JOE: What can I do?

EDNA: Who's the man in the family, you or me?

JOE: That's no answer. Get down to brass tacks. Christ, gimme a break, too! A coffee and java all day. I'm hungry, too, Babe. I'd work my fingers to the bone if—

EDNA: I'll open a can of salmon.

JOE: Not now. Tell me what to do!

EDNA: I'm not God!

JOE: Jeez, I wish I was a kid again and didn't have to think about the next minute.

EDNA: But you're not a kid and you do have to think about the next minute. You got two blondie kids sleeping in the next room. They need food and clothes. I'm not mentioning anything else—But we're stalled like a flivver[7] in the snow. For five years I laid awake at night listening to my heart pound. For God's sake, do something, Joe, get wise. Maybe get your buddies together, maybe go on strike for better money. Poppa did it during the war and they won out. I'm turning into a sour old nag.

JOE: (*defending himself*): Strikes don't work!

EDNA: Who told you?

JOE: Besides that means not a nickel a week while we're out. Then when it's over they don't take you back.

EDNA: Suppose they don't. What's to lose?

JOE: Well, we're averaging six-seven dollars a week now.

EDNA: That just pays for the rent.

JOE: That is something, Edna.

EDNA: It isn't. They'll push you down to three and four a week before you know it. Then you'll say, "That's somethin'," too!

JOE: There's too many cabs on the street, that's the whole damn trouble.

EDNA: Let the company worry about that, you big fool! If their cabs didn't make a profit, they'd take them off the streets. Or maybe you think they're in business just to pay Joe Mitchell's rent!

JOE: You don't know a-b-c, Edna.

EDNA: I know this—your boss is making suckers outa you boys every minute. Yes, and suckers out of all the wives and the poor innocent kids who'll grow up with crooked spines and sick bones. Sure, I see it in the papers, how good orange juice is for kids. But damnit our kids get colds one on top of the other. They look like little ghosts. Betty never saw a grapefruit. I took her to the store last week and she pointed to a stack of grapefruits. "What's that!" she said. My God, Joe—the world is supposed to be for all of us.

JOE: You'll wake them up.

EDNA: I don't care, as long as I can maybe wake you up.

JOE: Don't insult me. One man can't make a strike.

EDNA: Who says one? You got hundreds in your rotten union!

JOE: The union ain't rotten.

[7]A beat-up automobile (slang).

EDNA: No? Then what are they doing? Collecting dues and patting your back?

JOE: They're making plans.

EDNA: What kind?

JOE: They don't tell us.

EDNA: It's too damn bad about you. They don't tell little Joey what's happening in his bitsie witsie union. What do you think it is—a ping pong game?

JOE: You know they're racketeers. The guys at the top would shoot you for a nickel.

EDNA: Why do you stand for that stuff?

JOE: Don't you wanna see me alive?

EDNA (*after a deep pause*): No ... I don't think I do, Joe. Not if you can lift a finger to do something about it, and don't. No, I don't care.

JOE: Honey, you don't understand what—

EDNA: And any other hackie[8] that won't fight ... let them all be ground to hamburger!

JOE: It's one thing to—

EDNA: Take your hand away! Only they don't grind me to little pieces! I got different plans. (*Starts to take off her apron.*)

JOE: Where are you going?

EDNA: None of your business.

JOE: What's up your sleeve?

EDNA: My arm'd be up my sleeve, darling, if I had a sleeve to wear. (*Puts neatly folded apron on back of chair.*)

JOE: Tell me!

EDNA: Tell you what?

JOE: Where are you going?

EDNA: Don't you remember my old boy friend?

JOE: Who?

EDNA: Bud Haas. He still has my picture in his watch. He earns a living.

JOE: What the hell are you talking about?

EDNA: I heard worse than I'm talking about.

JOE: Have you seen Bud since we got married?

EDNA: Maybe.

JOE: If I thought ... (*He stands looking at her.*)

EDNA: See much? Listen, boy friend, if you think I won't do this it just means you can't see straight.

JOE: Stop talking bull.

EDNA: This isn't five years ago, Joe.

JOE: You mean you'd leave me and the kids?

EDNA: I'd leave *you* like a shot!

JOE: No....

EDNA: Yes! (JOE *turns away, sitting in a chair with his back to her. Outside the lighted circle of the playing stage we hear the other seated members of the strike committee. "She will ... she will ... it happens that way," etc. This*

---

[8]Taxi driver.

group should be used throughout for various comments, political, emotional and as general chorus. Whispering. . . . The fat boss now blows a heavy cloud of smoke into the scene.)

JOE *(finally)*: Well, I guess I ain't got a leg to stand on.

EDNA: No?

JOE *(suddenly mad)*: No, you lousy tart, no! Get the hell out of here. Go pick up that bull-thrower on the corner and stop at some cushy hotel downtown. He's probably been coming here every morning and laying you while I hacked my guts out!

EDNA: You're crawling like a worm!

JOE: You'll be crawling in a minute.

EDNA: You don't scare me that much! *(Indicates a half inch on her finger.)*

JOE: This is what I slaved for!

EDNA: Tell it to your boss.

JOE: He don't give a damn for you or me!

EDNA: That's what I say.

JOE: Don't change the subject!

EDNA: This is the subject, the *exact subject*! Your boss makes this subject. I never saw him in my life, but he's putting ideas in my head a mile a minute. He's giving your kids that fancy disease called the rickets. He's making a jelly-fish outa you and putting wrinkles in my face. This is the subject every inch of the way! He's throwing me into Bud Haas' lap. When in hell will you get wise—

JOE: I'm not so dumb as you think! But you are talking like a red.

EDNA: I don't know what that means. But when a man knocks you down you get up and kiss his fist! You gutless piece of boloney.

JOE: One man can't—

EDNA *(with great joy)*: I don't say one man! I say a hundred, a thousand, a whole million, I say. But start in your own union. Get those hack boys together! Sweep out those racketeers like a pile of dirt! Stand up like men and fight for the crying kids and wives. Goddamnit! I'm tired of slavery and sleepless nights.

JOE *(with her)*: Sure, sure! . . .

EDNA: Yes. Get brass toes on your shoes and know where to kick!

JOE *(suddenly jumping up and kissing his wife full on the mouth)*: Listen, Edna, I'm goin' down to 174th Street to look up Lefty Costello. Lefty was saying the other day . . . *(He suddenly stops.)* How about this Haas guy?

EDNA: Get out of here!

JOE: I'll be back! *(Runs out. For a moment* EDNA *stands triumphant. There is a blackout and when the regular lights come up,* JOE MITCHELL *is concluding what he has been saying):*

JOE: You guys know this stuff better than me. We gotta walk out! *(Abruptly he turns and goes back to his seat.)*

Blackout

II. Lab Assistant Episode

Discovered: MILLER, *a lab assistant, looking around; and* FAYETTE, *an industrialist.*

FAY: Like it?

MILLER: Very much. I've never seen an office like this outside the movies.

FAY: Yes, I often wonder if interior decorators and bathroom fixture people don't get all their ideas from Hollywood. Our country's extraordinary that way. Soap, cosmetics, electric refrigerators—just let Mrs. Consumer know they're used by the Crawfords and Garbos[9]—more volume of sale than one plant can handle!

MILL: I'm afraid it isn't that easy, Mr. Fayette.

FAY: No, you're right—gross exaggeration on my part. Competition is cutthroat today. Market's up flush against a stone wall. The astronomers had better hurry—open Mars to trade expansion.

MILL: Or it will be just too bad!

FAY: Cigar?

MILL: Thank you, don't smoke.

FAY: Drink?

MILL: Ditto, Mr. Fayette.

FAY: I like sobriety in my workers ... the trained ones, I mean. The pollacks and niggers, they're better drunk—keeps them out of mischief. Wondering why I had you come over?

MILL: If you don't mind my saying—very much.

FAY (*patting him on the knee*): I like your work.

MILL: Thanks.

FAY: No reason why a talented young man like yourself shouldn't string along with us—a growing concern. Loyalty is well repaid in our organization. Did you see Siegfried this morning?

MILL: He hasn't been in the laboratory all day.

FAY: I told him yesterday to raise you twenty dollars a month. Starts this week.

MILL: You don't know how happy my wife'll be.

FAY: Oh, I can appreciate it. (*He laughs.*)

MILL: Was that all, Mr. Fayette?

FAY: Yes, except that we're switching you to laboratory A tomorrow. Siegfried knows about it. That's why I had you in. The new work is very important. Siegfried recommended you very highly as a man to trust. You'll work directly under Dr. Brenner. Make you happy?

MILL: Very. He's an important chemist!

FAY (*leaning over seriously*): We think so, Miller. We think so to the extent of asking you to stay within the building throughout the time you work with him.

MILL: You mean sleep and eat in?

---

[9]Reference to two glamorous movie stars, Joan Crawford and Greta Garbo.

FAY: Yes. . . .

MILL: It can be arranged.

FAY: Fine. You'll go far, Miller.

MILL: May I ask the nature of the new work?

FAY (*looking around first*): Poison gas. . . .

MILL: Poison!

FAY: Orders from above. I don't have to tell you from where. New type poison gas for modern warfare.

MILL: I see.

FAY: You didn't know a new war was that close, did you?

MILL: I guess I didn't.

FAY: I don't have to stress the importance of absolute secrecy.

MILL: I understand!

FAY: The world is an armed camp today. One match sets the whole world blazing in forty-eight hours. Uncle Sam won't be caught napping!

MILL (*addressing his pencil*): They say 12 million men were killed in that last one and 20 million more wounded or missing.

FAY: That's not our worry. If big business went sentimental over human life there wouldn't be big business of any sort!

MILL: My brother and two cousins went in the last one.

FAY: They died in a good cause.

MILL: My mother says "no!"

FAY: She won't worry about you this time. You're too valuable behind the front.

MILL: That's right.

FAY: All right, Miller. See Siegfried for further orders.

MILL: You should have seen my brother—he could ride a bike without hands. . . .

FAY: You'd better move some clothes and shaving tools in tomorrow. Remember what I said—you're with a growing organization.

MILL: He could run the hundred yards in 9:8 flat. . . .

FAY: Who?

MILL: My brother. He's in the Meuse-Argonne Cemetery. Mama went there in 1926. . . .

FAY: Yes, those things stick. How's your handwriting, Miller, fairly legible?

MILL: Fairly so.

FAY: Once a week I'd like a little report from you.

MILL: What sort of report?

FAY: Just a few hundred words once a week on Dr. Brenner's progress.

MILL: Don't you think it might be better coming from the Doctor?

FAY: I didn't ask you that.

MILL: Sorry.

FAY: I want to know what progress he's making, the reports to be purely confidential—between you and me.

MILL: You mean I'm to watch him?

FAY: Yes!

MILL: I guess I can't do that. . . .

FAY: Thirty a month raise . . .

MILL: You said twenty. . . .

FAY: Thirty!

MILL: Guess I'm not built that way.

FAY: Forty. . . .

MILL: Spying's not in my line, Mr. Fayette!

FAY: You use ugly words, Mr. Miller!

MILL: For ugly activity? Yes!

FAY: Think about it, Miller. Your chances are excellent. . . .

MILL: No.

FAY: You're doing something for your country. Assuring the United States that when those goddamn Japs start a ruckus we'll have offensive weapons to back us up! Don't you read your newspapers, Miller?

MILL: Nothing but Andy Gump.[10]

FAY: If you were on the inside you'd know I'm talking cold sober truth! Now, I'm not asking you to make up your mind on the spot. Think about it over your lunch period.

MILL: No.

FAY: Made up your mind already?

MILL: Afraid so.

FAY: You understand the consequences?

MILL: I lose my raise—

Simultaneously: {
MILL: And my job!
FAY: And your job!
MILL: You misunderstand—
}

MILL: Rather dig ditches first!

FAY: That's a big job for foreigners.

MILL: But sneaking—and making poison gas—that's for Americans?

FAY: It's up to you.

MILL: My mind's made up.

FAY: No hard feelings?

MILL: Sure hard feelings! I'm not the civilized type, Mr. Fayette. Nothing suave or sophisticated about me. Plenty of hard feelings! Enough to want to bust you and all your kind square in the mouth! (*Does exactly that.*)

Blackout

III. The Young Hack and His Girl

Opens with girl and brother. FLORENCE *waiting for* SID *to take her to a dance.*

FLOR: I gotta right to have something out of life. I don't smoke, I don't drink. So if Sid wants to take me to a dance, I'll go. Maybe if you was in love you wouldn't talk so hard.

IRV: I'm saying it for your good.

---

[10]A comic strip character.

FLOR: Don't be so good to me.

IRV: Mom's sick in bed and you'll be worryin' her to the grave. She don't want that boy hanging around the house and she don't want you meeting him in Crotona Park.

FLOR: I'll meet him anytime I like!

IRV: If you do, yours truly'll take care of it in his own way. With just one hand, too!

FLOR: Why are you all so set against him?

IRV: Mom told you ten times—it ain't him. It's that he ain't got nothing. Sure, we know he's serious, that he's stuck on you. But that don't cut no ice.

FLOR: Taxi drivers used to make good money.

IRV: Today they're makin' five and six dollars a week. Maybe you wanta raise a family on that. Then you'll be back here living with us again and I'll be supporting two families in one. Well . . . over my dead body.

FLOR: Irv, I don't care—I love him!

IRV: You're a little kid with half-baked ideas!

FLOR: I stand there behind the counter the whole day. I think about him—

IRV: If you thought more about Mom it would be better.

FLOR: Don't I take care of her every night when I come home? Don't I cook supper and iron your shirts and . . . you give me a pain in the neck, too. Don't try to shut me up! I bring a few dollars in the house, too. Don't you see I want something else out of life. Sure, I want romance, love, babies. I want everything in life I can get.

IRV: You take care of Mom and watch your step!

FLOR: And if I don't?

IRV: Yours truly'll watch it for you!

FLOR: You can talk that way to a girl. . . .

IRV: I'll talk that way to your boy friend, too, and it won't be with words! Florrie, if you had a pair of eyes you'd see it's for your own good we're talking. This ain't no time to get married. Maybe later—

FLOR: "Maybe Later" never comes for me, though. Why don't we send Mom to a hospital? She can die in peace there instead of looking at the clock on the mantelpiece all day.

IRV: That needs money. Which we don't have!

FLOR: Money, Money, Money!

IRV: Don't change the subject.

FLOR: This is the subject!

IRV: You gonna stop seeing him? *(She turns away)*. Jesus, kiddie, I remember when you were a baby with curls down your back. Now I gotta stand here yellin' at you like this.

FLOR: I'll talk to him, Irv.

IRV: When?

FLOR: I asked him to come here tonight. We'll talk it over.

IRV: Don't get soft with him. Nowadays is no time to be soft. You gotta be hard as a rock or go under.

FLOR: I found that out. There's the bell. Take the egg off the stove I boiled for Mom. Leave us alone Irv. (SID *comes in—the two men look at each other for a second.* IRV *exits.*)

SID *(enters):* Hello, Florrie.

FLOR: Hello, Honey. You're looking tired.

SID: Naw, I just need a shave.

FLOR: Well, draw your chair up to the fire and I'll ring for brandy and soda ... like in the movies.

SID: If this was the movies I'd bring a big bunch of roses.

FLOR: How big?

SID: Fifty or sixty dozen—the kind with long, long stems—big as that. . . .

FLOR: You dope. . . .

SID: Your Paris gown is beautiful.

FLOR *(acting grandly):* Yes, Percy, velvet panels are coming back again. Madame La Farge told me today that Queen Marie herself designed it.

SID: Gee ... !

FLOR: Every princess in the Balkans is wearing one like this. *(Poses grandly.)*

SID: Hold it. *(Does a nose camera—thumbing nose and imitating grinding of camera with other hand. Suddenly she falls out of the posture and swiftly goes to him, to embrace him, to kiss him with love. Finally):*

SID: You look tired, Florrie.

FLOR: Naw, I just need a shave. *(She laughs tremulously.)*

SID: You worried about your mother?

FLOR: No.

SID: What's on your mind?

FLOR: The French and Indian War.

SID: What's on your mind?

FLOR: I got us on my mind, Sid. Night and day, Sid!

SID: I smacked a beer truck today. Did I get hell! I was driving along thinking of US, too. You don't have to say it—I know what's on your mind. I'm rat poison around here.

FLOR: Not to me. . . .

SID: I know to who ... and I know why. I don't blame them. We're engaged now for three years. . . .

FLOR: That's a long time. . . .

SID: My brother Sam joined the navy this morning—get a break that way. They'll send him down to Cuba with the hootchy-kootchy girls. He don't know from nothing, that dumb basket ball player!

FLOR: Don't you do that.

SID: Don't you worry, I'm not the kind who runs away. But I'm so tired of being a dog, Baby, I could choke. I don't even have to ask what's going on in your mind. I know from the word go, 'cause I'm thinking the same things, too.

FLOR: It's yes or no—nothing in between.

SID: The answer is no—a big electric sign looking down on Broadway!

FLOR: We wanted to have kids. . . .

SID: But that sort of life ain't for the dogs which is us. Christ, Baby! I get like thunder in my chest when we're together. If we went off together I could maybe look the world straight in the face, spit in its eye like a man should do. God-damnit, it's trying to be a man on the earth. Two in life together.

FLOR: But something wants us to be lonely like that—crawling alone in the dark. Or they want us trapped.

SID: Sure, the big shot money men want us like that.

FLOR: Highly insulting us—

SID: Keeping us in the dark about what is wrong with us in the money sense. They got the power and mean to be damn sure they keep it. They know if they give in just an inch, all the dogs like us will be down on them together—an ocean knocking them to hell and back and each singing cuckoo with stars coming from their nose and ears. I'm not raving, Florrie—

FLOR: I know you're not, I know.

SID: I don't have the words to tell you what I feel. I never finished school....

FLOR: I know....

SID: But it's relative, like the professors say. We worked like hell to send him to college—my kid brother Sam, I mean—and look what he done—joined the navy! The damn fool don't see the cards is stacked for all of us. The money man dealing himself a hot royal flush. Then giving you and me a phony hand like a pair of tens or something. Then keeping on losing the pots 'cause the cards is stacked against you. Then he says, what's the matter you can't win—no stuff on the ball, he says to you. And kids like my brother believe it 'cause they don't know better. For all their education, they don't know from nothing. But wait a minute! Don't he come around and say to you—this millionaire with a jazz band—listen Sam or Sid or what's-your-name, you're no good, but here's a chance. The whole world'll know who you are. Yes sir, he says, get up on that ship and fight those bastards who's making the world a lousy place to live in. The Japs, the Turks, the Greeks. Take this gun—kill the slobs like a real hero, he says, a real American. Be a hero! And the guy you're poking at? A real louse, just like you, 'cause they don't let him catch more than a pair of tens, too. On that foreign soil he's a guy like me and Sam, a guy who wants his baby like you and hot sun on his face! They'll teach Sam to point the guns the wrong way, that dumb basket ball player!

FLOR: I got a lump in my throat, Honey.

SID: You and me—we never even had a room to sit in somewhere.

FLOR: The park was nice ...

SID: In winter? The hallways ... I'm glad we never got together. This way we don't know what we missed.

FLOR (*in a burst*): Sid, I'll go with you—we'll get a room somewhere.

SID: Naw ... they're right. If we can't climb higher than this together—we better stay apart.

FLOR: I swear to God I wouldn't care.

SID: You would, you would—in a year, two years, you'd curse the day. I seen it happen.

FLOR: Oh, Sid....

SID: Sure, I know. We got the blues, Babe—the 1935 blues. I'm talkin' this way 'cause I love you. If I didn't, I wouldn't care. . . .

FLOR: We'll work together, we'll—

SID: How about the backwash? Your family needs your nine bucks. My family—

FLOR: I don't care for them!

SID: You're making it up, Florrie. Little Florrie Canary in a cage.

FLOR: Don't make fun of me.

SID: I'm not, Baby.

FLOR: Yes, you're laughing at me.

SID: I'm not. *(They stand looking at each other, unable to speak. Finally, he turns to a small portable phonograph and plays a cheap, sad, dance tune. He makes a motion with his hand; she comes to him. They begin to dance slowly. They hold each other tightly, almost as though they would merge into each other. The music stops, but the scratching record continues to the end of the scene. They stop dancing. He finally looses her clutch and seats her on the couch, where she sits, tense and expectant.)*

SID: Hello, Babe.

FLOR: Hello. *(For a brief time they stand as though in a dream.)*

SID *(finally)*: Good-bye, Babe. *(He waits for an answer, but she is silent. They look at each other.)*

SID: Did you ever see my Pat Rooney[11] imitation? *(He whistles Rosy O'Grady and soft-shoes to it. Stops. He asks:)*

SID: Don't you like it?

FLOR *(finally)*: No. *(Buries her face in her hands. Suddenly he falls on his knees and buries his face in her lap.)*

Blackout

IV. Labor Spy Episode

FATT: You don't know how we work for you. Shooting off your mouth won't help. Hell, don't you guys ever look at the records like me? Look in your own industry. See what happened when the hacks walked out in Philly three months ago! Where's Philly? A thousand miles away? An hour's ride on the train.

VOICE: Two hours!!

FATT: Two hours . . . what the hell's the difference. Let's hear from someone who's got the practical experience to back him up. Fellers, there's a man here who's seen the whole parade in Philly, walked out with his pals, got knocked down like the rest—and blacklisted after they went back. That's why he's here. He's got a mighty interestin' word to say. *(Announces): Tom Clayton! (As* CLAYTON *starts up from the audience,* FATT *gives him a hand which is sparsely followed in the audience.* CLAYTON *comes forward.)*

Fellers, this is a man with practical strike experience—Tom Clayton from little ole Philly.

---

[11]A vaudeville entertainer.

CLAYTON *a thin, modest individual*: Fellers, I don't mind your booing. If I thought it would help us hacks get better living conditions, I'd let you walk all over me, cut me up to little pieces. I'm one of you myself. But what I wanna say is that Harry Fatt's right. I only been working here in the big town five weeks, but I know conditions just like the rest of you. You know how it is—don't take long to feel the sore spots, no matter where you park.

CLEAR VOICE *(from the audience)*: Sit down!

CLAYTON: But Fatt's right. Our officers is right. The time ain't ripe. Like a fruit don't fall off the tree until it's ripe.

CLEAR VOICE: Sit down, you fruit!

FATT *(on his feet)*: Take care of him, boys.

VOICE *(in audience, struggling)*: No one takes care of me. *(Struggle in house and finally the owner of the voice runs up on stage, says to speaker)*:

SAME VOICE: Where the hell did you pick up that name! Clayton! This rat's name is Clancy, from the old Clancys, way back! Fruit! I almost wet myself listening to that one!

FATT *(gunman with him)*: This ain't a barn! What the hell do you think you're doing here!

SAME VOICE: Exposing a rat!

FATT: You can't get away with this. Throw him the hell outa here.

VOICE *(preparing to stand his ground)*: Try it yourself.... When this bozo throws that slop around. You know who he is? That's a company spy.

FATT: Who the hell are you to make—

VOICE: I paid dues in this union for four years, that's who's me! I gotta right and this pussy-footed rat ain't coming in here with ideas like that. You know his record. Lemme say it out—

FATT: You'll prove all this or I'll bust you in every hack outfit in town!

VOICE: I gotta right. I gotta right. Looka *him*, he don't say boo!

CLAYTON: You're a liar and I never seen you before in my life!

VOICE: Boys, he spent two years in the coal fields breaking up any organization he touched. Fifty guys he put in jail. He's ranged up and down the east coast—shipping, textiles, steel—he's been in everything you can name. Right now—

CLAYTON: That's a lie!

VOICE: Right now he's working for that Bergman outfit on Columbus Circle who furnishes rats for any outfit in the country, before, during, and after strikes. *(The man who is the hero of the next episode goes down to his side with other committee men.)*

CLAYTON: He's trying to break up the meeting, fellers!

VOICE: We won't search you for credentials....

CLAYTON: I got nothing to hide. Your own secretary knows I'm straight.

VOICE: Sure. Boys, you know who this sonovabitch is?

CLAYTON: I never seen you before in my life!

VOICE: Boys, I slept with him in the same bed sixteen years. HE'S MY OWN LOUSY BROTHER!!

FATT *(after pause)*: Is this true? *(No answer from* CLAYTON.*)*

VOICE (*to* CLAYTON): Scram, before I break your neck! (CLAYTON *scrams down center aisle.* VOICE *says, watching him:* Remember his map—he can't change that—Clancy! (*Standing in his place says*): Too bad you didn't know about this, Fatt! (*After a pause.*) The Clancy family tree is bearing nuts! (*Standing isolated clear on the stage is the hero of the next episode.*)

Blackout

V. Interne Episode

Dr. Barnes, an elderly distinguished man, is speaking on the telephone. He wears a white coat.

DR. BARNES: No, I gave you my opinion twice. You outvoted me. You did this to Dr. Benjamin yourself. That is why you can tell him yourself. (*Hangs up phone, angrily. As he is about to pour himself a drink from a bottle on the table, a knock is heard.*)

BARNES: Who is it?

BENJAMIN (*without*): Can I see you a minute, please?

BARNES (*hiding the bottle*): Come in, Dr. Benjamin, come in.

BENJ: It's important—excuse me—they've got Leeds up there in my place—He's operating on Mrs. Lewis—the historectomy—it's my job. I washed up, prepared ... they told me at the last minute. I don't mind being replaced, Doctor, but Leeds is a damn fool! He shouldn't be permitted—

BARNES (*dryly*): Leeds is the nephew of Senator Leeds.

BENJ: He's incompetent as hell.

BARNES (*obviously changing subject, picks up lab. jar*): They're doing splendid work in brain surgery these days. This is a very fine specimen. . . .

BENJ: I'm sorry, I thought you might be interested.

BARNES (*still examining jar*): Well, I am, young man, I am! Only remember it's a charity case!

BENJ: Of course. They wouldn't allow it for a second, otherwise.

BARNES: Her life is in danger?

BENJ: Of course! You know how serious the case is!

BARNES: Turn your gimlet eyes elsewhere, Doctor. Jigging around like a cricket on a hot grill won't help. Doctors don't run these hospitals. He's the Senator's nephew and there he stays.

BENJ: It's too bad.

BARNES: I'm not calling you down either. (*Plopping down jar suddenly.*) Goddamnit, do you think it's my fault?

BENJ (*about to leave*): I know ... I'm sorry.

BARNES: Just a minute. Sit down.

BENJ: Sorry, I can't sit.

BARNES: Stand then!

BENJ (*sits*): Understand, Dr. Barnes, I don't mind being replaced at the last minute this way, but ... well, this flagrant bit of class distinction—because she's poor—

BARNES: Be careful of words like that—"class distinction." Don't belong here. Lots of energy, you brilliant young men, but idiots. Discretion! Ever hear that word?

BENJ: Too radical?

BARNES: Precisely. And some day like in Germany, it might cost you your head.

BENJ: Not to mention my job.

BARNES: So they told you?

BENJ: Told me what?

BARNES: They're closing Ward C next month. I don't have to tell you the hospital isn't self-supporting. Until last year that board of trustees met deficits.... You can guess the rest. At a board meeting Tuesday, our fine feathered friends discovered they couldn't meet the last quarter's deficit—a neat little sum well over $100,000. If the hospital is to continue at all, its damn—

BENJ: Necessary to close another charity ward!

BARNES: So they say.... *(A wait.)*

BENJ: But that's not all?

BARNES *(ashamed)*: Have to cut down on staff too....

BENJ: That's too bad. Does it touch me?

BARNES: Afraid it does.

BENJ: But after all I'm top man here. I don't mean I'm better than others, but I've worked harder.

BARNES: And shown more promise....

BENJ: I always supposed they'd cut from the bottom first.

BARNES: Usually.

BENJ: But in this case?

BARNES: Complications.

BENJ: For instance? *(BARNES hesitant.)*

BARNES: I like you, Benjamin. It's one ripping shame.

BENJ: I'm no sensitive plant—what's the answer?

BARNES: An old disease, malignant, tumescent. We need an antitoxin for it.

BENJ: I see.

BARNES: What?

BENJ: I met that disease before—at Harvard first.

BARNES: You have seniority here, Benjamin.

BENJ: But I'm a Jew! *(BARNES nods his head in agreement. BENJ stands there a moment and blows his nose.)*

BARNES *(blows his nose)*: Microbes!

BENJ: Pressure from above?

BARNES: Don't think Kennedy and I didn't fight for you!

BENJ: Such discrimination, with all those wealthy brother Jews on the board?

BARNES: I've remarked before—doesn't seem to be much difference between wealthy Jews and rich Gentiles. Cut from the same piece!

BENJ: For myself I don't feel sorry. My parents gave up an awful lot to get me this far. They ran a little dry goods shop in the Bronx until their pitiful savings went in the crash last year. Poppa's peddling neckties. . . . Saul Ezra Benjamin—a man who's read Spinoza all his life.

BARNES: Doctors don't run medicine in this country. The men who know their jobs don't run anything here, except the motormen on trolley cars. I've seen medicine change—plenty—anesthesia, sterilization—but not because of rich men—in *spite* of them! In a rich man's country your true self's buried deep. Microbes! Less. . . . Vermin! See this ankle, this delicate sensitive hand? Four hundred years to breed that. Out of a revolutionary background! Spirit of '76! Ancestors froze at Valley Forge! What's it all mean! Slops! The honest workers were sold out then, in '76. The Constitution's for rich men then and now. Slops! *(The phone rings.)*

BARNES *(angrily)*: Dr. Barnes. *(Listens a moment, looks at* BENJAMIN.) I see. *(Hangs up, turns slowly to the younger Doctor.)* They lost your patient. *(*BENJ *stands solid with the shock of the news but finally hurls his operation gloves to the floor.)*

BARNES: That's right . . . that's right. Young, hot, go and do it! I'm very ancient, fossil, but life's ahead of you, Dr. Benjamin, and when you fire the first shot say, "This one's for old Doc Barnes!" Too much dignity— bullets. Don't shoot vermin! Step on them! If I didn't have an invalid daughter—*(*BARNES *goes back to his seat, blows his nose in silence):*
I have said my piece, Benjamin.

BENJ: Lots of things I wasn't certain of. Many things these radicals say . . . you don't believe theories until they happen to you.

BARNES: You lost a lot today, but you won a great point.

BENJ: Yes, to know I'm right? To really begin believing in something? Not to say, "What a world!", but to say, "Change the world!" I wanted to go to Russia. Last week I was thinking about it—the wonderful opportunity to do good work in their socialized medicine—

BARNES: Beautiful, beautiful!

BENJ: To be able to work—

BARNES: Why don't you go? I might be able—

BENJ: Nothing's nearer what I'd like to do!

BARNES: Do it!

BENJ: No! Our work's here—America! I'm scared. . . . What future's ahead, I don't know. Get some job to keep alive—maybe drive a cab—and study and work and learn my place—

BARNES: And step down hard!

BENJ: Fight! Maybe get killed, but goddamn! We'll go ahead! *(*BENJAMIN *stands with clenched fist raised high.)*

Blackout

AGATE: *Ladies and Gentlemen*, and don't let anyone tell you we ain't got some ladies in this sea of upturned faces! Only they're wearin' pants. Well, maybe I don't know a thing; maybe I fell outa the cradle when I was a kid and ain't been right since—you can't tell!

VOICE: Sit down, cockeye!

AGATE: Who's paying you for those remarks, Buddy?—Moscow Gold? Maybe I got a *glass eye*, but it come from working in a factory at the age of eleven. They hooked it out because they didn't have a shield on the works. But I wear it like a medal 'cause it tells the world where I belong—deep down in the working class! We had delegates in the union there—all kinds of secretaries and treasurers ... walkin' delegates, but not with blisters on their feet! Oh no! On their fat little ass from sitting on cushions and raking in mazuma.[12] (SECRETARY *and* GUNMAN *remonstrate in words and actions here.*) Sit down, boys. I'm just sayin' that about unions in general. I know it ain't true here! Why no, our officers is all aces. Why, I seen our own secretary Fatt walk outa his way not to step on a cockroach. No boys, don't think—

FATT (*breaking in*): You're out of order!

AGATE (*to audience*): Am I outa order?

ALL: No, no. Speak. Go on, etc.

AGATE: Yes, our officers is all aces. But I'm a member here—and no experience in Philly either! Today I couldn't wear my union button. The damnest thing happened. When I take the old coat off the wall, I see she's smoking. I'm a sonovagun if the old union button isn't on fire! Yep, the old celluloid was makin' the most god-awful stink: the landlady come up and give me hell! You know what happened? That old union button just blushed itself to death! Ashamed! Can you beat it?

FATT: Sit down, Keller! Nobody's interested!

AGATE: Yes they are!

GUNMAN: Sit down like he tells you!

AGATE (*continuing to audience*): And when I finish—(*His speech is broken by* FATT *and* GUNMAN *who physically handle him. He breaks away and gets to other side of stage. The two are about to make for him when some of the committee men come forward and get in between the struggling parties.* AGATE'S *shirt has been torn.*)

AGATE (*to audience*): What's the answer, boys? The answer is, if we're reds because we wanna strike, then we take over their salute too! Know how they do it? (*Makes Communist salute.*) What is it? An uppercut! The good old uppercut to the chin! Hell, some of us boys ain't even got a shirt to our backs. What's the boss class tryin' to do—make a nudist colony outa us? (*The audience laughs and suddenly* AGATE *comes to the middle of the stage so that the other cabmen back him up in a strong clump.*)

AGATE: Don't laugh! Nothing's funny! This is your life and mine! It's skull and bones every incha the road! Christ, we're dyin' by inches! For what? For the debutantees to have their sweet comin' out parties in the Ritz! Poppa's got a daughter she's gotta get her picture in the papers. Christ, they make 'em with our blood. Joe said it. Slow death or fight. It's war! (*Throughout this whole speech* AGATE *is backed up by the other six workers, so that from their activity it is plain that the whole group of them are saying these things. Several of them may take alternate lines out of this long last speech.*)

---

[12]Making a lot of money (slang).

You Edna, God love your mouth! Sid and Florrie, the other boys, old Doc
Barnes—fight with us for right! It's war! Working class, unite and fight! Tear
down the slaughter house of our old lives! Let freedom really ring.

These slick slobs stand here telling us about bogeymen. That's a new
one for the kids—the reds is bogeymen! But the man who got me food in
1932, he called me Comrade! The one who picked me up where I bled—
he called me Comrade too! What are we waiting for.... Don't wait for
Lefty! He might never come. Every minute— *(This is broken into by a man
who has dashed up on the center aisle from the back of the house. He runs up
on stage, says):*

MAN: Boys, they just found Lefty!

OTHERS: What? What? What?

SOME: Shhh.... Shhh....

MAN: They found Lefty....

AGATE: Where?

MAN: Behind the car barns with a bullet in his head!

AGATE *(crying):* Hear it, boys, hear it? Hell, listen to me! Coast to coast! HELLO
AMERICA! HELLO. WE'RE STORMBIRDS OF THE WORKING-CLASS.
WORKERS OF THE WORLD.... OUR BONES AND BLOOD! And when we
die they'll know what we did to make a new world! Christ, cut us up to
little pieces. We'll die for what is right! put fruit trees where our ashes are!
(To audience): Well, what's the answer?

ALL: STRIKE!

AGATE: LOUDER!

ALL: STRIKE!

AGATE and OTHERS on Stage: AGAIN!

ALL: STRIKE, STRIKE, STRIKE!!!

Curtain

1935

■   MERIDEL LESUEUR   ■
1900–1996

Often classified as a radical or working-class writer, Meridel LeSueur produced a
body of work that defies rigid categorization. Born in Murray, Iowa, in 1900,
LeSueur enjoyed a long and adventurous life, chronicling many aspects of it in
her fiction, nonfiction, poetry, essays, and journalism. Her childhood was
shaped by experiences living with her mother and grandmother (her parents
divorced early on), both of whom were known for embracing radical ideas. Her
mother would eventually marry Arthur LeSueur, a lawyer who worked on behalf

of the International Workers of the World (IWW) and the Non-Partisan League and later became the first Socialist mayor of Minot, North Dakota. Together, the family embraced a variety of social causes and entertained a number of radical visitors in their home.

During her young adulthood, LeSueur traveled to New York and California, pursuing a career on the stage and in film. However, after joining the Communist Party in the mid-1920s, she became increasingly involved in radical causes, and her acting career became a thing of the past. A protégé of Wisconsin writer Zona Gale, by the late 1920s, LeSueur was writing and publishing short stories to great critical acclaim. Many of her early stories were published in prominent little magazines and literary publications, including *The Dial*, *The American Mercury*, *Pagany*, *Story*, and *Scribner's Magazine*. She was also making a name for herself as a radical journalist, with essays and articles well known in early twentieth century radical circles, such as *New Masses*, *The Anvil*, *Partisan Review*, and *Masses and Mainstream*. The often radical nature of her writing would begin causing her political problems by the late 1940s, resulting in the diminishment of her publishing career, and she would be blacklisted during the height of the Cold War. Fortunately, a resurgence of interest in her work occurred in the late 1960s and into the 1970s which resulted in the publication or republication of a number of her novels and stories.

LeSueur's writing indeed has radical elements and inclinations, but to focus solely on those aspects is to ignore the larger impression of humanity she sought to capture in her work. In LeSueur's stories and journalism, there is an emphasis on individuals as they face conflict or struggle in their lives. In addition to fighting for a vision of the world as it should be, LeSueur captured the nuances of womanhood, the power of nature, and the beauty and depth of place and region in her writing. In many instances, her writing weaves these elements together in a unique way not captured by many other writers of the time. One notable example of this merging of ideas can be found in "Proletarian Literature and the Middle West," LeSueur's speech to the American Writer's Congress in 1935. In her platform as one of the few women to address the audience, she made an impassioned appeal for the merger of radicalism and place, citing the Midwest's long history as a perfect foundation for the building of a more equitable world.

The contrast of womanhood and nature can be found in LeSueur's short story "Annunciation" (1935). Focused on the thoughts of a pregnant young woman who is struggling to survive and protect her child while she and her husband are out of work, LeSueur parallels the development of the unborn child with the rich possibilities and fertility found in nature. While the young woman spends many of her days dodging the landlady because they are behind on their rent or walking the streets to stave off hunger when they have no money for food, her imagination transforms the world around her into a place pregnant with potential, the same potential she desires for her child. LeSueur balances the hope and optimism in her story with both the struggle of the couple's day to day existence and also the continued suggestion on the part of the woman that their lives would be easier if she just terminated the pregnancy. Ultimately, while the story does not suggest any happy ending, the recurring nature imagery, particularly in the symbolism of the pear tree, continue to suggest hope and potential in an otherwise dire world.

LeSueur's novel *The Girl*, written in 1939 but not published until 1978, continues to merge and develop many of her recurring themes. As with "Annunciation," once again LeSueur fails to name the narrator or central character of the story. The nameless "girl" functions as a representative everywoman, contributing further to the idea that LeSueur's characters have specific stories and characteristics but also symbolize womanhood or humanity in a larger way. *The Girl* conveys a stronger, more radical message regarding women and their rights than some of LeSueur's other stories. The narrator arrives rather naively from the country and takes a job as a waitress, slowly learning the realities of the larger world through her interactions with customers and conversations with her fellow women workers. LeSueur stated in an afterword to the novel that she based many of the characters and events in *The Girl* off of firsthand accounts she heard while working with a women's writing group in the 1930s. The authenticity of those experiences comes through clearly in her novel, particularly near the end when the girl is pregnant and facing the concerns of not having enough nourishment to sustain her developing child and not having any job or way to support the child once it is born. She is sustained throughout her struggles by the community of women around her. Ultimately that community of women assists in her childbirth and ushers in her baby girl, the newest member. LeSueur's depiction of the strength these women show while facing even the direst of struggles contributes valuable perspective to the development of American women's literature in the twentieth century.

LeSueur's work is valuable in helping readers understand many of the important cultural developments of the twentieth century and also speaks to the evolution of humanity into the twenty first century and beyond. Her strong invocations of the natural world, her commitment to portraying the strength and complexity of women, her emphatic desire to try and revolutionize the world into a better place, and her detailed observations of place and people make LeSueur an important American author.

Sara Kosiba
Troy University

PRIMARY WORKS

Annunciation, 1935; *Salute to Spring*, 1940; *North Star Country*, 1945; *Crusaders*, 1955; *Corn Village*, 1970; *Rites of Ancient Ripening*, 1975; *The Girl*, 1978; *Ripening: Selected Work, 1927–1980*, ed. Elaine Hedges, 1982. *I Hear Men Talking and Other Stories*, 1983; *The Dread Road*, 1991.

Annunciation

For Rachel

Ever since I have known I was going to have a child I have kept writing things down on these little scraps of paper. There is something I want to say, something I want to make clear for myself and others. One lives all one's life in a sort of way, one is alive and that is about all that there is to say about it. Then something happens.

There is the pear tree I can see in the afternoons as I sit on this porch writing these notes. It stands for something. It has had something to do with what has happened to me. I sit here all afternoon in the autumn sun and then I begin to write something on this yellow paper; something seems to be going on like a buzzing, a flying and circling within me, and then I want to write it down in some way. I have never felt this way before, except when I was a girl and was first in love and wanted then to set things down on paper so that they would not be lost. It is something perhaps like a farmer who hears the swarming of a host of bees and goes out to catch them so that he will have honey. If he does not go out right away, they will go, and he will hear the buzzing growing more distant in the afternoon.

My sweater pocket is full of scraps of paper on which I have written. I sit here many afternoons while Karl is out looking for work, writing on pieces of paper, unfolding, reading what I have already written.

We have been here two weeks at Mrs. Mason's boarding house. The leaves are falling and there is a golden haze over everything. This is the fourth month for me and it is fall. A rich powerful haze comes down from the mountains over the city. In the afternoon I go out for a walk. There is a park just two blocks from here. Old men and tramps lie on the grass all day. It is hard to get work. Many people besides Karl are out of work. People are hungry just as I am hungry. People are ready to flower and they cannot. In the evening we go there with a sack of old fruit we can get at the stand across the way quite cheap, bunches of grapes and old pears. At noon there is a hush in the air and at evening there are stirrings of wind coming from the sky, blowing in the fallen leaves, or perhaps there is a light rain, falling quickly on the walk. Early in the mornings the sun comes up hot in the sky and shines all day through the mist. It is strange, I notice all these things, the sun, the rain falling, the blowing of the wind. It is as if they had a meaning for me as the pear tree has come to have.

In front of Mrs. Mason's house there is a large magnolia tree with its blossoms yellow, hanging over the steps almost within reach. Its giant leaves are motionless and shining in the heat, occasionally as I am going down the steps toward the park one falls heavily on the walk.

This house is an old wooden one, that once was quite a mansion I imagine. There are glass chandeliers in the hall and fancy tile in the bathrooms. It was owned by the rich once and now the dispossessed live in it with the rats. We have a room three flights up. You go into the dark hallway and up the stairs. Broken settees and couches sit in the halls. About one o'clock the girls come down stairs to get their mail and sit on the front porch. The blinds go up in the old wooden house across the street. It is always quite hot at noon.

Next to our room lies a sick woman in what is really a kind of closet with no windows. As you pass you see her face on the pillow and a nauseating odor of sickness comes out the door. I haven't asked her what is the matter with her but everyone knows she is waiting for death. Somehow it is not easy to speak to her. No one comes to see her. She has been a housemaid all her life tending other people's children; now no one comes to see her. She gets up sometimes and drinks a little from the bottle of milk that is always sitting by her bed covered with flies.

Mrs. Mason, the landlady, is letting us stay although we have only paid a week's rent and have been here over a week without paying. But it is a bad season and we may be able to pay later. It is better perhaps for her than having an empty room. But I hate to go out and have to pass her door and I am always fearful of meeting her on the stairs. I go down as quietly as I can but it isn't easy, for the stairs creak frightfully.

The room we have on the top floor is a back room, opening out onto an old porch which seems to be actually tied to the wall of the house with bits of wire and rope. The floor of it slants downward to a rickety railing. There is a box perched on the railing that has geraniums in it. They are large, tough California geraniums. I guess nothing can kill them. I water them since I have been here and a terribly red flower has come. It is on this porch I am sitting. Just over the banisters stand the top branches of a pear tree.

Many afternoons I sit here. It has become a kind of alive place to me. The room is dark behind me, with only the huge walnut tree scraping against the one window over the kitchenette. If I go to the railing and look down I can see far below the back yard which has been made into a garden with two fruit trees and I can see where a path has gone in the summer between a small bed of flowers, now only dead stalks. The ground is bare under the walnut tree where little sun penetrates. There is a dog kennel by the round trunk but there doesn't ever seem to be a dog. An old wicker chair sits outdoors in rain or shine. A woman in an old wrapper comes out and sits there almost every afternoon. I don't know who she is, for I don't know anybody in this house, having to sneak downstairs as I do.

Karl says I am foolish to be afraid of the landlady. He comes home drunk and makes a lot of noise. He says she's lucky in these times to have anybody in her house, but I notice in the mornings he goes down the stairs quietly and often goes out the back way.

I'm alone all day so I sit on this rickety porch. Straight out from the rail so that I can almost touch it is the radiating frail top of the pear tree that has opened a door for me. If the pears were still hanging on it each would be alone and separate with a kind of bloom upon it. Such a bloom is upon me at this moment. Is it possible that everyone, Mrs. Mason who runs this boarding house, the woman next door, the girls downstairs, all in this dead wooden house have hung at one time, each separate in a mist and bloom upon some invisible tree? I wonder if it is so.

I am in luck to have this high porch to sit on and this tree swaying before me through the long afternoons and the long nights. Before we came here, after the show broke up in S.F. we were in an old hotel, a foul-smelling place with a dirty chambermaid and an old cat in the halls, and night and day we could hear the radio going in the office. We had a room with a window looking across a narrow way into another room where a lean man stood in the mornings looking across, shaving his evil face. By leaning out and looking up I could see straight up the sides of the tall building and above the smoky sky.

Most of the time I was sick from the bad food we ate. Karl and I walked the streets looking for work. Sometimes I was too sick to go. Karl would come in and there would be no money at all. He would go out again to perhaps borrow something. I know many times he begged although we never spoke of it, but I could tell by the way he looked when he came back with a begged quarter. He went in with a man selling Mexican beans but he didn't make much. I lay on the bed bad days feeling sick and hungry, sick too with the stale odor of the foul walls. I would lie there a long time listening to the clang of the city outside. I would feel thick with this child. For some reason I remember that I would sing to myself and often became happy as if mesmerized there in the foul room. It must have been because of this child. Karl would come back perhaps with a little money and we would go out to a dairy lunch and there have food I could not relish. The first alleyway I must give it up with the people all looking at me.

Karl would be angry. He would walk on down the street so people wouldn't think he was with me. Once we walked until evening down by the docks. "Why don't you take something?" he kept saying. "Then you wouldn't throw up your food like that. Get rid of it. That's what everybody does nowadays. This isn't the time to have a child. Everything is rotten. We must change it." He kept on saying, "Get rid of it. Take something why don't you?" And he got angry when I didn't say anything but just walked along beside him. He shouted so loud at me that some stevedores loading a boat for L.A. laughed at us and began kidding us, thinking perhaps we were lovers having a quarrel.

Some time later, I don't know how long it was, for I hadn't any time except the nine months I was counting off, but one evening Karl sold enough Mexican jumping beans at a carnival to pay our fare, so we got on a river boat and went up the river to a delta town. There might be a better chance of a job. On this boat you can sit up all night if you have no money to buy a berth. We walked all evening along the deck and then when it got cold we went into the saloon because we had pawned our coats. Already at that time I had got the habit of carrying slips of paper around with me and writing on them, as I am doing now. I had a feeling then that something was happening to me of some kind of loveliness I would want to preserve in some way. Perhaps that was it. At any rate I was writing things down. Perhaps it had something to do with Karl wanting me all the time to take something. "Everybody does it," he kept telling me. "It's nothing, then it's all over." I stopped talking to him much. Everything I said only made him angry. So writing was a kind of conversation I carried on with myself and with the child.

Well, on the river boat that night after we had gone into the saloon to get out of the cold, Karl went to sleep right away in a chair. But I couldn't sleep. I sat watching him. The only sound was the churning of the paddle wheel and the lap of the water. I had on then this sweater and the notes

I wrote are still in the breast pocket. I would look up from writing and see Karl sleeping like a young boy.

"Tonight, the world into which you are coming"—then I was speaking to the invisible child—"is very strange and beautiful. That is, the natural world is beautiful. I don't know what you will think of man, but the dark glisten of vegetation and the blowing of the fertile land wind and the delicate strong step of the sea wind, these things are familiar to me and will be familiar to you. I hope you will be like these things. I hope you will glisten with the glisten of ancient life, the same beauty that is in a leaf or a wild rabbit, wild sweet beauty of limb and eye. I am going on a boat between dark shores, and the river and the sky are so quiet that I can hear the scurryings of tiny animals on the shores and their little breathings seem to be all around. I think of them, wild, carrying their young now, crouched in the dark underbrush with the fruit-scented land wind in their delicate nostrils, and they are looking out at the moon and the fast clouds. Silent, alive, they sit in the dark shadow of the greedy world. There is something wild about us too something tender and wild about my having you as a child about your crouching so secretly here. There is something very tender and wild about it. We, too, are at the mercy of many hunters. On this boat I act like the other human beings, for I do not show that I have you, but really I know we are as helpless, as wild, as at bay as some tender wild animals who might be on the ship.

"I put my hand where you lie so silently. I hope you will come glistening with life power, with it shining upon you as upon the feathers of birds. I hope you will be a warrior and fierce for change, so all can live."

Karl woke at dawn and was angry with me for sitting there looking at him. Just to look at me makes him angry now. He took me out and made me walk along the deck although it was hardly light yet. I gave him the "willies" he said, looking at him like that. We walked round and round the decks and he kept talking to me in a low voice, trying to persuade me. It was hard for me to listen. My teeth were chattering with cold, but anyway I found it hard to listen to anyone talking, especially Karl. I remember I kept thinking to myself that a child should be made by machinery now, then there would be no fuss. I kept thinking of all the places I had been with this new child, traveling with the show from Tia Juana to S.F. In trains, over mountains, through deserts, in hotels and rooming houses, and myself in a trance of wonder. There wasn't a person I could have told it to, that I was going to have a child. I didn't want to be pitied. Night after night we played in the tent and the faces were all dust to me, but traveling, through the window the many vistas of the earth meant something—the bony skeleton of the mountains, like the skeleton of the world jutting through its flowery flesh. My child too would be made of bone. There were the fields of summer, the orchards fruiting, the berry fields and the pickers stooping, the oranges and the grapes. Then the city again in September and the many streets I walk looking for work, stopping secretly in doorways to feel beneath my coat.

It is better in this small town with the windy fall days and the sudden rain falling out of a sunny sky. I can't look for work any more. Karl gets a little work washing dishes at a wienie place. I sit here on the porch as if in a deep sleep waiting for this unknown child. I keep hearing this far flight of strange birds going on in the mysterious air about me. This time has come without warning. How can it be explained? Everything is dead and closed, the world a stone, and then suddenly everything comes alive as it has for me, like an anemone on a rock, opening itself, disclosing itself, and the very stones themselves break open like bread. It has all got something to do with the pear tree too. It has come about some way as I have sat here with this child so many afternoons, with the pear tree murmuring in the air.

The pears are all gone from the tree but I imagine them hanging there, ripe curves within the many scimitar leaves, and within them many pears of the coming season. I feel like a pear. I hang secret within the curling leaves, just as the pear would be hanging on its tree. It seems possible to me that perhaps all people at some time feel this, round and full. You can tell by looking at most people that the world remains a stone to them and a closed door. I'm afraid it will become like that to me again. Perhaps after this child is born, then everything will harden and become small and mean again as it was before. Perhaps I would even have a hard time remembering this time at all and it wouldn't seem wonderful. That is why I would like to write it down.

How can it be explained? Suddenly many movements are going on within me, many things are happening, there is an almost unbearable sense of sprouting, of bursting encasements, of moving kernels, expanding flesh. Perhaps it is such an activity that makes a field come alive with millions of sprouting shoots of corn or wheat. Perhaps it is something like that that makes a new world.

I have been sitting here and it seems as if the wooden houses around me had become husks that suddenly as I watched began to swarm with livening seed. The house across becomes a fermenting seed alive with its own movements. Everything seems to be moving along a curve of creation. The alley below and all the houses are to me like an orchard abloom, shaking and trembling, moving outward with shouting. The people coming and going seem to hang on the tree of life, each blossoming from himself. I am standing here looking at the blind windows of the house next door and suddenly the walls fall away, the doors open, and within I see a young girl making a bed from which she had just risen having dreamed of a young man who became her lover ... she stands before her looking-glass in love with herself.

I see in another room a young man sleeping, his bare arm thrown over his head. I see a woman lying on a bed after her husband has left her. There is a child looking at me. An old woman sits rocking. A boy leans over a table reading a book. A woman who has been nursing a child comes out and hangs clothes on the line, her dress in front wet with milk. A young woman comes to an open door looking up and down the street waiting for her young husband. I get up early to see this young woman come to the door in a pink wrapper and wave to her husband. They have only been married a short time, she stands waving until he is out of sight and even then she stands smiling to herself, her hand upraised.

Why should I be excited? Why should I feel this excitement, seeing a woman waving to her young husband, or a woman who has been nursing a child, or a young man sleeping? Yet I am excited. The many houses have become like an orchard blooming soundlessly. The many people have become like fruits to me, the young girl in the room alone before her mirror, the young man sleeping, the mother, all are shaking with their inward blossoming, shaken by the windy blooming, moving along a future curve.

I do not want it all to go away from me. Now many doors are opening and shutting, light is falling upon darkness, closed places are opening, still things are now moving. But there will come a time when the doors will close again, the shouting will be gone, the sprouting and the movement and the wondrous opening out of everything will be gone. I will be only myself. I will come to look like the women in this house. I try to write it down on little slips of paper, trying to preserve this time for myself so that afterwards when everything is the same again I can remember what all must have.

This is the spring there should be in the world, so I say to myself, "Lie in the sun with the child in your flesh shining like a jewel. Dream and sing, pagan, wise in your vitals. Stand still like a fat budding tree, like a stalk of corn athrob and aglisten in the heat. Lie like a mare panting with the dancing feet of colts against her sides. Sleep at night as the spring earth. Walk heavily as a wheat stalk at its full time bending toward the earth waiting for the reaper. Let your life swell downward so you become like a vase, a vessel. Let the unknown child knock and knock against you and rise like a dolphin within."

I look at myself in the mirror. My legs and head hardly make a difference, just a stem my legs. My hips are full and tight in back as if bracing themselves. I look like a pale and shining pomegranate, hard and tight, and my skin shines like crystal with the veins showing beneath blue and distended. Children are playing outside and girls are walking with young men along the walk. All that seems over for me. I am a pomegranate hanging from an invisible tree with the juice and movement of seed within my hard skin. I dress slowly. I hate the smell of clothes. I want to leave them off and just hang in the sun ripening . . . ripening.

It is hard to write it down so that it will mean anything. I've never heard anything about how a women feels who is going to have a child, or about how a pear tree feels bearing its fruit. I would like to read these things many years from now, when I am barren and no longer trembling like this, when I get like the women in this house, or like the woman in the closed room, I can hear her breathing through the afternoon.

When Karl has no money he does not come back at night. I go out on the street walking to forget how hungry I am. This is an old town and along the streets are many old strong trees. Night leaves hang from them ready to fall, dark and swollen with their coming death. Trees, dark, separate, heavy with their down-hanging leaves, cool surfaces hanging on the dark. I put my hand among the leaf sheaves. They strike with a cool surface, their glossy surfaces surprising me in the dark. I feel like a tree swirling upwards too, muscular sap alive, with rich surfaces hanging from me, flaring outward rocket-like and falling to my roots, a rich strong power in me to break through into a new life. And dark in me as I walk the streets of this decayed town are the buds of my child. I walk alone under the dark flaring trees. There are many houses with the lights shining out but you and I walk on the skirts of the lawns amidst the down-pouring darkness. Houses are not for us. For us many kinds of hunger, for us a deep rebellion.

Trees come from a far seed walking the wind, my child too from a far seed blowing from last year's rich and revolutionary dead. My child budding secretly from far-walking seed, budding secretly and dangerously in the night.

The woman has come out and sits in the rocker, reading, her fat legs crossed. She scratches herself, cleans her nails, picks her teeth. Across the alley lying flat on the ground is a garage. People are driving in and out. But up here it is very quiet and the movement of the pear tree is the only movement and I seem to hear its delicate sound of living as it moves upon itself silently, and outward and upward.

The leaves twirl and twirl all over the tree, the delicately curving tinkling leaves. They twirl and twirl on the tree and the tree moves far inward upon its stem, moves in an invisible wind, gently swaying. Far below straight down the vertical stem like a stream, black and strong into the ground, runs the trunk; and invisible, spiraling downward and outward in powerful radiation, lie the roots. I can see it spiraling upward from below, its stem straight, and from it, spiraling the branches season by season, and from the spiraling branches moving out in quick motion, the forked stems, and from the stems twirling fragilely the tinier stems holding out ward until they fall, the half-curled pear leaves.

Far below lies the yard, lying flat and black beneath the body of the upshooting tree, for the pear tree from above looks as if it had been shot instantaneously from the ground, shot upward like a rocket to break in showers of leaves and fruits twirling and falling. Its movement looks quick sudden and rocketing. My child when grown can be looked at in this way as if it suddenly existed ... but I know the slow time of making. The pear tree knows.

Far inside the vertical stem there must be a movement, a river of sap rising from below and radiating outward in many directions clear to the tips of the leaves. The leaves are the lips of the tree speaking in the wind or they move like many tongues. The fruit of the tree you can see has been a round speech, speaking in full tongue on the tree, hanging in ripe body, the fat curves hung within the small curves of the leaves. I imagine them there. The tree has shot up like a rocket, then stops in midair and its leaves flow out gently and its fruit curves roundly and gently in a long slow curve. All is gentle on the pear tree after its strong upward shooting movement.

I sit here all the afternoon as if in its branches, amidst the gentle and curving body of the tree. I have looked at it until it has become more familiar to me than Karl. It seems a strange thing that a tree might come to mean more to one than one's husband. It seems a shameful thing even. I am ashamed to think of it but it is so. I have sat here in the pale sun and the tree has spoken to me with its many tongued leaves, speaking through the afternoon of how to round a fruit. And I listen through the slow hours. I listen to the whispering of the pear tree, speaking to me, speaking to me. How can I describe what is said by a pear tree? Karl did not speak to me so. No one spoke to me in any good speech.

There is a woman coming up the stairs, slowly. I can hear her breathing. I can hear her behind me at the screen door.

She came out and spoke to me. I know why she was looking at me so closely. "I hear you're going to have a child," she said. "It's too bad." She is the same color as the dead leaves in the park. Was she once alive too?

I am writing on a piece of wrapping paper now. It is about ten o'clock. Karl didn't come home and I had no supper. I walked through the streets with their heavy, heavy trees bending over the walks and the lights shining from the houses and over the river the mist rising.

Before I came into this room I went out and saw the pear tree standing motionless, its leaves curled in the dark, its radiating body falling darkly, like a stream far below into the earth.

1935

from **The Girl**

Chapter 38

I'll never forget that summer as long as I live. That big old warehouse where we all lived, five floors, mostly women and it was cool too, with thick brick walls and high windows where sometimes the sun came through like in a temple. There was no heat and no light, and some women who had lived there in the winter had built fires on the wood floors and they had burnt through and made holes, so you could look down or holler down to the floor below. A guy had run electric wires from the outside to the floor we lived on, the second, so we could have lights and an electric plate when nobody was looking. Sometimes cops came, seeing a light, but we had a system of jiggers, it was called, jiggers the cops are coming. It would start at the bottom and go right up through the building.

It was said that it was owned by a widow of the lumber maggots, we called them, and that before the depression when it was rented she went to Europe every summer, but it had been empty now and had been taken over by girls and women who had no place to live.

On the second floor some women had made partitions, a few feet high, and some had hung blankets making a little privacy. Clara had an old mattress there without any springs. Belle in one corner had brought her stuff from above the German Village long after Hoinck was buried. I had a pallette on the floor. Amelia had her single cot. She had moved it in after the Workers Alliance offices had been raided and they barely got out with the mimeograph machine, which now sat in the middle of the floor and could be covered with an old oil cloth and boards to put over to make it look like a table. A Jesus lover named Sara, who had lived in the office, came too. Sitting in a rocking chair rocking with her coat and hat on no matter what the weather was Butch's crazy mother. She spooked me out because day and night she talked about Butch and sometimes I thought she knew this was Butch's baby.

She'd kind of grab me and hold me and say, They are playing out in the sand box, honey, Butch and Bill. Maybe you should keep an eye on them. I always had corn fritters for breakfast, she'd say, I make the best corn fritters. I'll make them for supper. Buckwheat cakes and Indian butter makes you fat and a little bit fatter, Butch always says. I keep my own hens. They been laying right good.

She made me turn cold.

It was goofy. Sometimes from all corners would come this singing and these goings on. Belle was trying on black veils to mourn for Hoinck and she would be saying, Yes sir, when Hoinck pawned his tools that was end of us all. What tools is to a man. He pawned his tools, he pawned more than his tools. He pawned his skill, being able to do something that gives a man pride. What can a man do without tools? He has to lick the boots of crazies like Ganz.

Clara before the shock treatments would be fixing her face, and singing and crying—I'd like to belong to a prominent family. I had my fortune told and there is something good around the corner. I'm going to miss the best pictures. Has Love in the Tropics gone away yet? Is it summer yet?

And Sara the Jesus lover would be singing—Jesus lover of my soul, let me to thy bosom fly.

Belle would howl, lord god jesus and the virgin mary if we all had a bosom to fly to.

Jesus will be waiting for you, Sara would say, Jesus loves you.

Jesus loves you this I know, cause the bible tells me so, Belle would sing.

Sara would bring her bible to read to us all—In his house are many mansions, if it were not so I would have told you.

Clara would say, I don't think I would need more than fourteen rooms, seven upstairs and seven down and I could have a room of my own.

It was a still hot bright afternoon when they brought Clara back from Hastings Mental hospital where she had the electric shock treatment and I never seen anything like she looked. It wasn't that she was white, she was always very white, it was that look in her eyes and her stillness. She was very very still as if she had gone out of herself, as if the shock like an explosion had sent the doves of her spirit flying away never to come back.

They were kind of walking her and the social worker who had refused her milk came in behind her and helped her to lie down.

She is going to be just fine, she said to all of us, you'll see. These treatments take away anxiety.

Did you bring the special food she was supposed to get, Amelia asked, going over to stroke Clara's head where it seemed like you could see bruises.

These things take time, the social worker said.

But death don't wait, Amelia said.

Sara began to sing, Shall we gather at the river, the beautiful the beautiful river.

She ought to be living in a better place but this will do till winter, the social worker said, and I hope you will be careful not to have any men up here. You can't get any help if there are goings on with men. You have to be mighty careful.

I waited for Clara to say something awful to her but her eyes seemed to be half closed and her little mouth hung open.

Belle said, O shit.

Amelia said, What about the cod liver oil?

That's the trouble with you people. You are alarmists. Hysterical. I have to fill out this paper. Do you own a trunk?

Belle hooted, We ain't got a pot to piss in or a window to throw it out.

Vulgarities will get you nowhere, she said.

Nothing will get us nowhere fast, Belle spat after her as she turned to go and had to walk around the hole burnt in the floor, through which I could see the frightened women gathered down below.

When left I started to read out loud the paper I had taken while at the relief office, the report on me. I got to the part where it said, the girl is maladjusted, emotionally unstable and a difficult problem to get to talk. A change of environment would be helpful....

Belle hooted, Miami or Pasadena...or the Bahamas...

Continuous casework should follow up the birth of the child. Educational interests should be encouraged to get her away from her friend Clara, a prostitute she lives with.

Shhh, Amelia said but Clara didn't hear. I knew already she was far away and it was too late.

I went on—In our opinion there should be a referral to a psychiatrist, if she shows symptoms of further emotional and mental disturbance.

Honey, Belle cries, it appears you are upset by something.

I went on reading, She should be tested for sterilization at the birth of her baby. In our opinion sterilization would be advisable.

Amelia was trying to give Clara a drink—It's because they don't need any more children from workers. They don't need us to reproduce our kind.

Belle threw the empty bottle against the wall. It's rotten, stinking, covered with slime! Men after you, the welfare workers after you, people living off each other like rats. I told you I would have no kids to bring into it. Thirteen abortions I had, got'em out of me.

Butch's mother said, It's wicked wicked, be careful for the children, that's the future. Where are my children? she suddenly howled like a wolf, my children. I thought they were outside playing in the sand box. It has gotten dark and Butch is gone.

I put my arms around her and rocked the chair and shhhed her.

Sara cried out, Woe! woe! to the Pharisees, Herod is waiting for the little one. Be careful.

Tears were just coming out of Clara's eyes and she looked so tiny. She was't saying anything or making a face, just tears came out of her eyes and Amelia wiped them away.

It's in the Bible, every man under his own tree. Every worker worthy of his hire to be paid by sundown. Now we see face to face, sisters, Sara said.

Amelia said, we all got to be together. Protect each other. Not lay down or give in. We got to fight for each other.

O maybe it's bad to have a child now, I cried, feeling it leap inside me like a fish in clear water. I put my arms around Clara—Don't cry Clara, we suffer together. We are women. Nothing can hold us apart. I hurt where you hurt. What did they do to your head? Your mouth is bleeding and torn.

Clara's eyes opened in an awful horror. Her little mouth formed a round O but nothing came out. I saw in her eyes a terrible thing.

I gave out a cry. It seemed like the women below gave out a cry and the women above, and Belle screamed.

Clara clung to me and I just rocked her. She was so tiny and smelled like scorch or burn. And the terrible deeps seemed to open up.

Chapter 39

It was a hot night. Even when Belle threw a whiskey bottle and broke out the tall warehouse windows that you couldn't open. And Amelia said—what about the winter?

The winter, Belle screamed, who's going to be here in the winter?

And I thought for the first time about the winter with a baby, and how mama lost her first baby with the croup the first winter. Where would we be? I thought of going home to mama, and then I thought of Amelia and the Workers Alliance, and I looked at the mimeograph machine sitting in the middle of the floor as if it was some kind of shrouded altar, like they covered the statues in the church, Friday before Easter rising.

I looked at Clara who had not moved in the night, and Butch's mother asleep in the rocking chair, who never took off her hat, waiting to go find Butch.

Amelia got up very early and took up her black hat and her bag of leaf-lets and went out, tiptoeing so as not to wake anyone. The demonstration for the fresh milk was at noon. I wasn't going to tell her about the little pains I had had all night, still about an hour apart. It was surely time now. Butch, I said into the hot still air, You always said, it's the timing. That was about robbing a bank, making a homer, ringing the bell, bring home the bacon. But women know the most about that. When you're going to have a baby there is some kind of strange timing. You can't wait for appropriations, or the social worker to sign the ambulance paper!

I began to think anyway how I would call the ambulance, if no one had a nickel or a dime. I didn't even have a watch to time the pains. I could count seconds, count one was a second, sixty made a minute. Belle must have some cash stashed away somewhere. Belle was sleeping amongst empty bottles with the newspaper clipping on Hoinck's death clutched in her hand. Her purse was under her pillow. In a little sewing box on the floor I found two pennies. I decided to wait till she woke.

The woman from downstairs stood at the big open door. It was so high it made people look small. It was not for people. I did not know her name. I knew she walked miles with Amelia, passing out leaflets.

I came for the leaflets, she said, and she lifted up her top skirt and inside she had like aprons with pockets. My husband is a hard shell, she said so I got these little pockets. I put the leaflets in here.

I wanted to ask her if she had a baby and how it was. Why hadn't I asked mama. O, if she was only here.

I got to jump a wink ahead of my husband, she said, putting the leaflets in all the pockets. Amelia called up through hole. Ho there, we got to get along. Pass these out downtown before the milk demonstration.

Coming! coming! the woman said, I thought joyfully I wished I was going too. I saw Clara was groaning kind of, and moving her hand up as if trying to wipe something away from her head. I ran over to her and took her hand which was real cold and clammy. I began to rub her and she pulled away like she was frightened.

It's me, It's me, I said, and she opened her bloodshot eyes. Her eyes were terrible, the whites bloody, and the pupils as if leaping right out of the sockets to tell you something. I remember the lovely eyes of Clara so full of summer flowers. Someone had taken her far away and I wanted to bring her back let her tell me about the fourteen room house and the sunken baths and a room of her own.

Clara! Clara! I cried—remember me, remember how you took me on your wanderings, how you showed me everything.

She didn't even smile. Those pupils leapt out though, as if to tell me something terrible. They told me. I saw it all, what they had done to her.

Clara! remember the German Village and those Saturday nights with the Booya and Bill, I cried, Bill and Butch, those pretty fellows, those wonderful foxes you used to call them, those slick cats you said. . . . Remember?

Was there a flicker, a kind of wink? One eye kind of closed and then opened. I felt I mustn't let her forget. They can't do that to her, I lifted up her cold thin body and her head rolled and it looked like her hair was greasy and bruises on the temples. What had they done?

I held her, I shook her, I caressed her, I shouted at her. Butch's mother woke and watched us. Sara sat up and wound her hair. Even Belle stirred.

Memory is all we got, I cried, we got to remember. We got to remember everything. It is the glory, Amelia said, the glory. We got to remember to be able to fight. Got to write down the names. Make a list. Nobody can be forgotten. They know if we don't remember we can't point them out. They got their guilt wiped out. The last thing they take is memory. Remember, Amelia says, the breasts of your mothers. O mama help us now. Clara remember your mama like you told me, going from city to city, to lousy jobs and getting children and taking them on her back, and locking them in rooms while she waited on tables, did laundry, Clara you got to remember your mama, I'll help you.

Then she smiled and the pupils changed kindly and she said—Baby. I grabbed my belly, Yes Clara, remember how you stood on the cold street to get enough money to help me. Yes, Clara, a baby. Remember, you want to see it. A pang went through me like a quake. I wasn't counting now. You're gonna hold it, I said. Yes you will see it, you remember the baby, see they can't wipe it out. Nothing can wipe it out. Remember that, Clara, we'll remember for you. We'll help you bit by bit, all of it, all our great lousy beautiful and terrible life, you'll see, we'll remember it all, all. I remember every insult those rich johns give you that night, Clara, and you shining like a light, that's what you are a light, Clara, a prairie city light. Don't forget it!

Sara came over and took hold of my shoulders and laid Clara down but her face was not so pale now, and her eyes followed me, and she said clearly but slowly, Clara, Clara, name the baby, she said, means Clear Light, the baby. Clara!

Yes, yes, I cried, Claro clara cleara light yes . . .

Sara walked me slowly away saying, What shall we do, our little sister has no breasts. . . .

O, a breast for all, I cried, and milk for all. . . .

Yes! yes! Sara said, she felt so tall and kind with an odor of strange love coming from her widow's weeds, her straight body like something defending, protecting you . . . Butch's mother rose, with a strange knowing as if she recognized me at last and she bowed and touched me and helped me into her rocking chair.

Butch is working just outside there on the street, she said, I can see him through the window. He'll come in for lunch. Butch, she cried softly, your girl is going to have corn fritters with us for lunch.

I bent over with a sudden pain and Belle cried, Is it starting? Holy Moses, I bet this is going to be some kid. I feel funny, I'm wet as a drowned cat, remember Susybelly? Say, did you get the signed paper for the ambulance. Say, you got to call them. Anybody got a nickel? Here in my sewing basket. . .

I took the two cents already, I said, but pennies aren't any good. You got to have the nickel for Ma Bell.

Somebody must have a nickel. Is it possible nobody has a nickel? Yes, it is possible. It is certainly possible. Cash scarce as hens' teeth. Hoinck's old suit, maybe some cash. I put money in old shoes too. I was going to buy some diapers.

I began to count the seconds, putting a finger up for each sixty making a minute. The next one came at eight minutes.

I felt good.

I thought of all my life with Butch. It makes you shake to come from your own loneliness and death. It makes you shake all over, but you've got to do it, you've got to take the chance to do it. It takes guts to speak out of the lonely room, after looking at yourself in a mirror, after smelling out yourself alone, after hearing emptiness sound off. It makes the sweat stand on you, and your blood starts up, for what is one voice alone, or what good is it to cry in a room with the door shut?

The pains got worse so I couldn't walk. Belle was making coffee and I sat down and looked at the clock. Now it was six minutes apart. It was exciting. I wanted to see it right away. Maybe it would look like Butch, with a lean black head and a sharp face. I could feel my blood like a river inside me, and my breast deep and thigh and womb ready for a new child, and strong labor for it and I liked it. I remember Amelia said once, I tell you when I like it, when there is something to it, when there's something doing, when you can see it, put your face in it, and double up your fist for it. That's when I like it, she said.

I had my teeth in it now for the first time. I could feel it bear down, bear heavy.

I'll go out on the street, Belle said, I'll phone. You got everything ready, kid?

I'm ready, I said.

Ain't you gonna take anything? Belle said.

I got nothing to take, I said, this tie of Butch's. The two cents. She can start to college on that.

Say kid, be careful, what about your income tax? I'll bring you a Doctor Pepper.

I'll need a doctor, I said and she hooted with laughter, and I could hear her with her wonderful heavy step going downstairs.

It was then I heard Clara, I cried, Clara don't go.

I got her little mirror from her purse, where she always looked at herself, I held it up to her mouth which was now in an awful O shape as if her last breath hurt.

The mirror was empty.

Chapter 40

I was glad to close her eyes over the horror they had given her and shut her silent screaming mouth. Butch's mother held the bucket while we washed her and brushed her golden hair. She was like a bird is when the life goes out of them, they seem so tiny, just bones and feathers. Amelia would say it was how a body got without proper food and being cold all winter and somebody after her.

Sara took from her things a white dress like a bride's with lace. We would make it cling and it had a high neck that covered the bruises, and

Sara was saying something from the bible, like—Set me as a seal upon thy heart, for love is stronger than death…many waters cannot quench love, neither can the floods drown it. We have a little sister and she has no breasts. What shall we do for our sister in the day when she shall be spoken for? If she be a wall we will build upon her a palace of silver and if she be a door we will enclose her with cedar. She made some sign upon her and her voice was low. Make haste, she said above her, be thou like a roe or a young deer upon the mountains of spices.

Butch's mother put a cloth rose between her hands.

I didn't need to count the pains now. I didn't worry about them, or the ambulance. And it wasn't long before it seemed all the people from the demonstration came, kind of anxious and hurrying, into the big room now full of noon sun—all the street girls and the sewing women from the project, and Amelia her face flushed and her hat gone, and when she knelt beside Clara the other women knelt too and each one was singing or saying whatever song or prayer she knew and some sobbed and cried out.

Belle came to me. How is it, kid? I called the ambulance but they seemed like they never heard of you, didn't get the requisition or whatever the hell it is. Kid you should have seen the demonstration, hundreds outside the courthouse and the cops threw tear gas out the windows and some of those ball players caught the bombs and threw them right back and kid, you should have seen those bureaucrats, like rats, pouring out of the building, and the street littered with those leaflets saying Milk and Iron Pills for Clara.

There was a big line going out into the hot noon sun and the cops were lined up across the street, but not one dared to come in. Pretty soon around Clara were gifts, like lip stick, old paper flowers, chains and medallions of the Virgin Mary, ribbons, belts, little pictures of saints. It looked like whatever a person had, they put there for Clara. Some combed her hair, patted her pretty dress, said a prayer and, and some sang little songs for her.

I couldn't get over it, that they should all care, as Amelia says a breast for all—the men kind of hung back but the women gathered and I tell you with the sun pouring down as if free for all, I never in my life saw anything like it. I felt I would stand there and just drop my child into their hands, the great Mothers, that's what I saw and will always see as long as I draw breath. I got no words but it will be like I had told Clara, inside us forever. Remembering always and appearing in everything, great mirrors like we held the picture of all, the suffering of all. I saw mama there, the same bend of back, the sagging belly, the look of sorrow, and of something else, something fierce, and the reason you have a child maybe.

Amelia held up her hands—Listen. Attention please, she said.

Sara said, We must have a mass for Clara.

Amelia said—Yes a Memorial for Clara, a mass meeting, let our voice be heard in the whole city—a trial, a judgment against the city fathers, a trial yes an accusation. We accuse. Yes, we point a finger. We hold them responsible.

There was a kind of roar that went down the stairs and out into the street as it was passed down from one person to another.

When? Tomorrow? The next day. Everyone seemed to agree on everything. Yes. Take it down, Sara. We have a good stencil left. Take all suggestions down, Amelia said, everything. All accusations. People called out. Clara is dead. Who killed Clara? Why didn't she have milk and iron pills? Who didn't care if she died? Who doesn't care that we are hungry? Some would begin to tell what had happened to them in the relief office but it would go on, everyone crying out something. I helped take down the ideas.

Was she a criminal? Was she a danger? Clara never got any wealth. She died a pauper. She never stole timber or wheat or made poor flour. She never stole anyone's land or took it for high interest on the mortgage. She never got rich on the labor of others. She never fattened off a war. She never made ammunition or guns. She never hurt no one. Who killed Clara? *Who will kill us?*

O it was something to hear and see their anger. And their power. Amelia looked like the mother of them all, nodding, smiling.

Did you get that? Put that down.

Sara said Amen.

Amelia said, Go, Sara and get that on the stencil. You can use the typewriter at the Labor Temple. They'll let you. Come back here as soon as you can. O yes, get some paper from them. Tell them about Clara and the girl. They'll give it.

They kept coming and coming, a steady line. Belle made me lie down on her bed. Amelia said she had delivered a hundred babies and would deliver a hundred more.

They made a little cave in the corner. Amelia rubbed me. Belle was crying and holding my hand. Then I saw Butch's mother and I touched her and she knew everything. And I thought of Butch and how he thought it was all a ball game. It ain't a ball game honey, I was laughing.

It is funny, Amelia said, and Butch's mother giggled in a high strange cry.

O it's shit to have to lie on the floor, Belle said.

Now breathe, Amelia said, bear down—Breathe—bear down—breathe—

O Butch, I laughed you didn't know what your mama knew, that little woman, door to you all. How did you do it I asked her? As she giggled, a high whinny, I saw her eye was like Butch's eye. I reached for her, put my arms around her, and she lay against me like a little wren, crying in that high voice.

It's the realest dream. I saw Amelia leaning between my legs looking at me saying breathe—push—wait—breathe. It was like being run over by a trunk when the pains came. But the women were pressing around now, I could look into their faces. They were pressing around now, I could look into their faces. They seem to breathe with me, a kind of great wind through their bodies like wind in a woods. Amelia said she delivered many babies and would many more. She kept talking. I didn't hear her and it was funny it was like when I left Butch on the prairie covering him with a blanket and his breath gone.

Breathe, Amelia kept saying, wait—push—stop—breathe—

He asked me before he died, Do we belong to the human race? Some people think we don't, I told him, but we do. Yes we do. This is your face, Butch, coming back down the great river, the great dark. I was bucking like a goat, lifting like a mountain. I heard the mimeograph start. A kind of beat.

It's crowning, Amelia cried, I never had heard that. The crown of its head. It's all right, just turn the head. Now, easy and strong girl, O girl it's coming, easy now. I felt all the river broke in me and poured and gave and opened. Was it my cry, the cry of the women, the cry of a child? The last breath of Butch the first of a child. Covered with a kind of slime and dark she lay the child on me. A girl, she cried, a girl, and she rubbed the slime and the child let a little gasp and breathed and before my eyes turned and glowed the dark memory, flushing. She turned golden as Clara, even her wet hair.

Belle was shouting, It's a girl, and the women murmured happily, It's a girl!

A woman, Amelia cried, still wiping the body with her hands.

Belle was shouting, and for a moment the mimeograph stopped then began again.

It's a woman, Belle was shouting, a sister a daughter. No dingle dangle, no rod of satan, no sword no third arm, a girl a woman a mother.

Amelia cried, Ho ho, a new woman.

Light, I said, Claro Clara.

Her name is Clara, the women said, a kind of woman's humming was all around me. I saw mama in them all, the bearing the suffering in us all, their seized bodies, bent bellies hanging, and the ferocity of their guarding. I felt fierce and she seemed to burrow to the nipple as I saw Amelia take the knife she had soaking in alcohol in a beer bottle and cut the cord.

Then Butch's mother said quite clearly, You keep the cord and then when the child is lost and wandering they come back to the grandmothers to find their road, the cord will tell them the road. The road.

I saw the women pressing in to see and I held her up for all to see and heard a kind of sound like AHHHHHHHH of wonder and delight.

Amelia said, Give me a newspaper to put the afterbirth in. And Butch's mother became very excited, Give it to me, she said, give it to me. Amelia wrapped it and gave it to her. They say, she said, it has more protein in it than any living thing.

Now I could cup her tiny bright head. I cried out. She had the tiny face of my mother. Like in a mirror.

O girl, I said down to her, giving her my full breast of milk.

1978

■ ## MURIEL RUKEYSER ■
1913–1980

From the outset, Muriel Rukeyser was at once a political poet and a visionary. At times, those qualities were intensified, and in those moments she was simultaneously a revolutionary and a mystic. However, to grasp the forces that drive her work—throughout the nearly 600 packed pages of her *Collected Poems*—we have to come to terms with a visionary impulse rooted in time, embedded in a struggle with lived history. Consider as case in point the rhapsodic images she crafts to voice the mother's anguish at the death of her sons in "Absalom," a poem from the beginning of a career that spanned five decades of American history. But that is not all. To understand her work, we must also embrace the larger, wiser notion of politics that underlies all her poetry. For she understood early on what so many of us could not: that politics encompasses all the ways that social life is hierarchically structured and made meaningful. Politics is not only the large-scale public life of nations. It is also the advantages, inequities, and illusions that make daily life very different for different groups among us. Thus Rukeyser understood that race and gender are integral parts of our social and political life. Never officially a feminist, she nonetheless devoted herself to voicing women's distinctive experience throughout her career.

Although Rukeyser was quite capable of writing short, tightly controlled poems—"The Minotaur" is a good example—it may well be that her most rich and suggestive accomplishments are her poem sequences. "Absalom" is from "The Book of the Dead," one of the major poem sequences of American modernism. Based on Rukeyser's own research in West Virginia, it combines historical background, congressional testimony, and the voices of a number of victims in telling the story of a 1930s industrial scandal: a company building a tunnel for a dam decided to double its profit by rapidly mining silica at the same time (without any of the necessary precautions). A great many workers died of lung disease as a result. "The Book of the Dead" is thus also one of Rukeyser's many poems that reflect and contribute to her political activism. "To Be a Jew in the Twentieth Century," published amid the Holocaust, served as a rallying cry for redeeming Jewish identity amid the carnage of the concentration camps. Rukeyser later expressed astonishment when the poem was reprinted in the prayer books of both Judaic reform and reconstruction movements.

During the 1930s Rukeyser regularly wrote for Communist Party publications like *New Masses*. She was in Spain to cover the antifascist Olympics in Barcelona when the Spanish Civil War broke out. She described that experience in the long poem "Mediterranean" and returned to the subject throughout her life. Years later, in 1975, she went to South Korea to protest the poet Kim Chi-Ha's imprisonment and anticipated execution; the poem sequence "The Gates" grew out of that trip. Rukeyser meditates on her poetics in *The Life of Poetry* (1949). She also published a novel, *The Orgy* (1966), as well as two biographies, *Willard Gibbs* (1942) and *The Traces of Thomas Harriot* (1971).

Cary Nelson
University of Illinois

PRIMARY WORKS

Willard Gibbs, 1942; *One Life*, 1957; *Body of Waking*, 1958; *Waterlily Fire*, 1962; *The Orgy*, 1965; *Bubbles*, 1967; *The Speed of Darkness*, 1968; *Mazes*, 1970; *The Traces of Thomas Hariot*, 1971; *Theory of Flight*, 1971; *The Life of Poetry*, 1974; *The Gates*, 1976; *The Collected Poems*, 1979, *Out of Silence: Selected Poems*, 1992; *Selected Poems*, 2004.

from **The Book of the Dead**

Absalom

I first discovered what was killing these men.
I had three sons who worked with their father in the tunnel:
Cecil, aged 23, Owen, aged 21, Shirley, aged 17.
They used to work in a coal mine, not steady work
for the mines were not going much of the time.   5
A power Co. foreman learned that we made home brew,
he formed a habit of dropping in evenings to drink,
persuading the boys and my husband—
give up their jobs and take this other work.
It would pay them better.   10
Shirley was my youngest son; the boy.
He went into the tunnel.

　　My heart   my mother   my heart   my mother
　　My heart   my coming into being.

My husband is not able to work.   15
He has it, according to the doctor.
We have been having a very hard time making a living since
　　this trouble came to us.
I saw the dust in the bottom of the tub.
The boy worked there about eighteen months,   20
came home one evening with a shortness of breath.
He said, "Mother, I cannot get my breath."
Shirley was sick about three months.
I would carry him from his bed to the table,
from his bed to the porch, in my arms.   25

　　My heart is mine in the place of hearts,
　　They gave me back my heart, it lies in me.

When they took sick, right at the start, I saw a doctor.
I tried to get Dr. Harless to X-ray the boys.
He was the only man I had any confidence in,   30
the company doctor in the Kopper's mine,
but he would not see Shirley.
He did not know where his money was coming from.
I promised him half if he'd work to get compensation,

but even then he would not do anything. 35
I went on the road and begged the X-ray money,
the Charleston hospital made the lung pictures,
he took the case after the pictures were made.
And two or three doctors said the same thing.
The youngest boy did not get to go down there with me, 40
he lay and said, "Mother, when I die,
"I want you to have them open me up and
"see if that dust killed me.
"Try to get compensation,
"you will not have any way of making your living 45
"when we are gone,
"and the rest are going too."

> I have gained mastery over my heart
> I have gained mastery over my two hands
> I have gained mastery over the waters 50
> I have gained mastery over the river.

The case of my son was the first of the line of lawsuits.
They sent the lawyers down and the doctors down;
they closed the electric sockets in the camps.
There was Shirley, and Cecil, Jeffrey and Oren, 55
Raymond Johnson, Clev and Oscar Anders,
Frank Lynch, Henry Palf, Mr. Pitch, a foreman;
a slim fellow who carried steel with my boys,
his name was Darnell, I believe. There were many others,
the towns of Glen Ferris, Alloy, where the white rock lies, 60
six miles away; Vanetta, Gauley Bridge,
Gamoca, Lockwood, the gullies,
the whole valley is witness.
I hitchhike eighteen miles, they make checks out.
They asked me how I keep the cow on $2. 65
I said one week, feed for the cow, one week, the children's
      flour.
The oldest son was twenty-three.
The next son was twenty-one.
The youngest son was eighteen. 70
They called it pneumonia at first.
They would pronounce it fever.
Shirley asked that we try to find out.
That's how they learned what the trouble was.

> I open out a way, they have covered my sky with crystal 75
> I come forth by day, I am born a second time,
> I force a way through, and I know the gate
> I shall journey over the earth among the living.

He shall not be diminished, never;
I shall give a mouth to my son.   80

                                                                                    1938

The Minotaur

Trapped, blinded, led; and in the end betrayed
Daily by new betrayals as he stays
Deep in his labyrinth, shaking and going mad.
Betrayed. Betrayed. Raving, the beaten head
Heavy with madness, he stands, half-dead and proud.   5
No one again will ever see his pride.
No one will find him by walking to him straight
But must be led circuitously about,
Calling to him and close and, losing the subtle thread,
Lose him again; while he waits, brutalized   10
By loneliness.   Later, afraid
Of his own suffering.   At last, savage and made
Ravenous, ready to prey upon the race
If it so much as learn the clews of blood
Into his pride his fear his glistening heart.   15
Now is the patient deserted in his fright
And love carrying salvage round the world
Lost in a crooked city; roundabout,
By the sea, the precipice, all the fantastic ways
Betrayal weaves its trap; loneliness knows the thread,   20
And the heart is lost, lost, trapped, blinded and led,
Deserted at the middle of the maze.

                                                                                    1944

from **Letter to the Front**

7. [To Be a Jew in The Twentieth Century]

To be a Jew in the twentieth century
Is to be offered a gift. If you refuse,
Wishing to be invisible, you choose
Death of the spirit, the stone insanity.
Accepting, take full life. Full agonies: 5
Your evening deep in labyrinthine blood
Of those who resist, fail, and resist; and God
Reduced to a hostage among hostages.

The gift is torment. Not alone the still
Torture, isolation; or torture of the flesh.   10
That may come also. But the accepting wish,
The whole and fertile spirit as guarantee
For every human freedom, suffering to be free,
Daring to live for the impossible.

1944

Folk Music Lyrics of the 1920s and 1930s

FOLK MUSIC EXISTED LONG BEFORE THE TERM ITSELF BECAME A RECOGNIZED category for describing a specific style or genre of popular song. With its roots in the oral tradition of poetry, folk may be said to descend from a range of sources as diverse as troubadour love ballads, lullabies, and narratives—about everything from history to murder to the supernatural—that were set to music and circulated for centuries in Anglo Europe.

Between 1882 and 1889, the Boston-born scholar Francis J. Child (1825–1896) collected about three hundred ephemeral story songs in his ten-volume *English and Scottish Ballads* and in doing so effectively established a canon that is informally known as "Child Ballads." The melodies and lyrics of these story songs were adapted by subsequent performers, who updated them to address their own conditions. The distances that these songs traveled as a result of immigration demonstrated their portability. In 1916, British musicologist Cecil J. Sharp (1859–1924) was stunned to discover that many ballads of English origin were in the repertoire of singers in Tennessee and Virginia who had never traveled outside the American southeast.

The settings in which these and other story songs were performed were as multifarious as their content. Just about every conceivable communal moment—work sites, family get-togethers, union meetings, rural barn dances, urban bars and pubs, churches, weddings and funerals—provided an opportunity for musical celebration.

In the early twentieth century, a music industry began to be built on the buying and selling of phonographic recordings and sheet-music transcriptions of songs, and a market for traditional music emerged. One of the earliest performers to make his mark in this field was Harry McClintock (1882–1957), also known as "Haywire Mac," who in 1928 released "Big Rock Candy Mountain," a paean to American plenitude likely based on the British ballad "An Invitation to Lubberland," which dates to 1685. McClintock was a long-term member of the International Workers of the World, a labor organization founded in 1905 by (among others) Eugene V. Debs. As with most "Wobblies" (as IWW members were known), McClintock believed in the power of music to create solidarity among the worker class, and his performances were integral to his efforts to help organize west Texas oil workers in the early 1920s. Yet McClintock also harbored aspirations of fame, and when a demand for "cowboy" songs emerged in the post–World War I era ("hillbilly music" being the forerunner of country and western), he was quick to accept an offer to record his compositions for commercial release on the Victor record label.

Thus began a tension that runs throughout the modern history of folk between music as a catalyst of community and social change and music as an entertainment commodity. It is further indicative of this tension that even as McClintock advocated the IWW agenda, he fought vigorously in the late 1920s to establish his copyright on songs like "Candy Mountain" and "Hallelujah, I'm a Bum." McClintock had been performing both works since he was a teenage busker in the late nineteenth century, but the degree to which he could appropriately claim "authorship" of a melody and lyrics whose variations were as well traveled as the singer himself remains hotly contested.

The onset of the depression in 1929 intensified the political potency of folk music, and songs about strikes and union loyalty became key tools for creating a collective community investment in fighting the capitalist exploitation of the working class. The core selections in this In Focus section thus functioned as rallying cries. They were designed to be participatory, with verses that told of individual struggle alternating with "sing-along" choruses to which an audience would be encouraged to add their voices.

To expedite this goal, songwriters often adapted familiar melodies. Thus, Joe Hill's "The Preacher and the Slave" (which McClintock also released commercially in its better-known version as "Pie in the Sky") is based on the familiar melody of "Sweet Bye and Bye." But whereas the original lyrics of that hymn preached the heavenly rewards promised in the Christian afterlife, "Pie" sarcastically mocks that passivity ("Work and pray, live on hay / You'll get pie when you die"). Hill's composition is also representative in its depiction of a stock adversary of folk, the status quo–supporting preacher who violates Christianity's "true" mission by sermonizing against labor unrest. Bosses and police were also common targets of ridicule because they enforced the institutions that sought to deprive individuals of their right to a livelihood.

One of the clever traits of this era's folk music—and its proletarian literature, in general—is that songwriters advocated class consciousness by appealing to workers' sense of oppressed individuality. That is, the socialist and Communist cause, grounded in the need for workers to relinquish the selfishness of self in the name of a greater class good, sought to gain adherents by insisting that capitalism had robbed the common man of the ability to advance his economic self-interest.

While McClintock's fame has faded to the point that more people are familiar with "The Big Rock Candy Mountain" than his career, at least one "star" would emerge from proletarian folk music to exert an enduring cultural influence. The son of an aspiring Oklahoma land speculator and a mother who died in an asylum in 1929 (of undiagnosed Huntington's disease), Woodrow "Woody" Guthrie (1912–1967) began playing guitar and harmonica as a teenager. He joined the mass migration of dust bowl refugees who headed west in the 1930s, developed a love for traveling on the open road, and built a repertoire of traditional music. Toward the end of the depression, he cohosted a Los Angeles radio show with Maxine "Lefty Lou" Crissman; that was when he began to compose a series of protest songs about the migration of fellow Oklahomans (or "Okies") to California. Released in 1940, *Dust Bowl Ballads* was a groundbreaking, two-set collection of proletarian narratives that were inspired by John Steinbeck's novel *The Grapes of Wrath* (1939). Guthrie admired Steinbeck's literary achievement and appreciated his recognition of the succor that music gave the downtrodden. Especially in Chapter 23 (excerpted here), Steinbeck depicted how a harmonica, guitar, and fiddle created a sense of community and provided relief from the brutal conditions of the migratory camps in which Oakies sought shelter. *Dust Bowl Ballads* overtly expresses Guthrie's appreciation of *The Grapes of Wrath*:

"The Ballad of Tom Joad" is a veritable outline of the book, ending with the pro-tagonist's famous pledge to his mother: "Wherever men are fightin' for their rights / That's where I'm gonna be, Ma." Steinbeck was delighted by the tribute and paid it back when he famously said, "Harsh voiced and nasal, his guitar hanging like a tire iron on a rusty rim, there is nothing sweet about Woody, and there is nothing sweet about the songs he sings. But there is something more important for those who will listen. There is the will of the people to endure and fight against oppression. I think we call this the American spirit."

Guthrie went on to write a celebrated fictional memoir, *Bound for Glory* (1943), along with hundreds of classic songs, most famously, "This Land Is Your Land" (1940). Despite a slew of practitioners—most notably, the indefatigable Pete Seeger (b. 1917)—Guthrie-style folk music was overshadowed by patriotic songs during World War II. Folk's fires would not rekindle until the late 1950s and early 1960s, when a folk renaissance launched the career of Guthrie devotee Bob Dylan (b. 1941). By then, Guthrie himself was disabled by Huntington's disease. He died in 1967, the same year that many of the songs reprinted here were compiled in Alan Lomax's *Hard Hitting Songs for Hard-Hit People*. Characteristically, Guthrie's notes on the songs are full of wry sarcasm and earnest devotion to the medium. "If you're too highbrow for [folk music]," he writes, "you can take your pants and go home right now, but please leave the book—some people might want to look through it."

Kirk Curnutt
Troy University–Montgomery, Alabama

PRIMARY SOURCES

Woody Guthrie, *Bound for Glory*, 1943; Alan Lomax, *Hard Hitting Songs for Hard-Hit People*, 1967; Terry E. Miller, *Folk Music in America: A Reference Guide*, 1986; Benjamin Filene, *Romancing the Folk: Public Memory and American Roots Music*, 2000; Ruth Crawford Seeger, *"The Music of American Folk Song" and Other Writings on American Folk Music*, 2001.

■ # JOHN STEINBECK
1902–1968 ■

from **The Grapes of Wrath**

from Chapter 23

A harmonica is easy to carry. Take it out of your hip pocket, knock it against your palm to shake out the dirt and pocket fuzz and bits of tobacco. Now it's ready. You can do anything with a harmonica: thin reedy single tone, or chords, or melody with rhythm chords. You can mold the music with curved hands, making it wail and cry like bagpipes, making it full and round like an organ, making it as sharp and bitter as the reed pipes of the hills. And you can play and put it back in your pocket. It is always with you, always in your pocket. And as you play, you learn new tricks, new ways to mold the tone with your hands, to pinch the tone with your lips, and no one teaches you. You feel around—sometimes alone in the shade at noon, sometimes in the tent door after supper when the women are washing up. Your foot taps gently on the ground. Your eyebrows rise and fall in rhythm. And if you lose it or break it, why, it's no great loss. You can buy another for a quarter.

A guitar is more precious. Must learn this thing. Fingers of the left hand must have callus caps. Thumb of the right hand a horn of callus. Stretch the left-hand fingers, stretch them like a spider's legs to get the hard pads on the frets.

This was my father's box. Wasn't no bigger'n a bug first time he give me C chord. An' when I learned as good as him, he hardly never played no more. Used to set in the door, an' listen an' tap his foot. I'm tryin' for a break, an' he'd scowl mean till I get her, an' then he'd settle back easy, an' he'd nod. "Play," he'd say. "Play nice." It's a good box. See how the head is wore. They's many a million songs wore down that wood an' scooped her out. Some day she'll cave in like a egg. But you can't patch her nor worry her no way or she'll lose tone. Play her in the evening, an' they's a harmonica player in the nex' tent. Makes it pretty nice together.

The fiddle is rare, hard to learn. No frets, no teacher.

Jes' listen to a ol' man an' try to pick it up. Won't tell how to double. Says it's a secret. But I watched. Here's how he done it.

Shrill as a wind, the fiddle, quick and nervous and shrill.

She ain't much of a fiddle. Give two dollars for her. Fella says they's fiddles four hundred years old, and they get mellow like whisky. Says they'll cost fifty-sixty thousan' dollars. I don't know. Soun's like a lie. Harsh ol' bastard, ain't she? Wanta dance? I'll rub up the bow with plenty rosin. Man! Then she'll squawk. Hear her a mile.

These three in the evening, harmonica and fiddle and guitar. Playing a reel and tapping out the tune, and the big deep strings of the guitar beating like a heart, and the harmonica's sharp chords and the skirl and squeal of the fiddle. People have to move close. They can't help it. "Chicken Reel" now, and the feet tap and a young lean buck takes three quick steps, and his arms hang limp. The square closes up and the dancing starts, feet on the bare ground, beating dull, strike with your heels. Hands 'round and swing. Hair falls down, and panting breaths. Lean to the side now.

Look at that Texas boy, long legs loose, taps four times for ever' damn step. Never seen a boy swing aroun' like that. Look at him swing that Chero-kee girl, red in her cheeks an' her toe points out. Look at her pant, look at her heave. Think she's tired? Think she's winded? Well, she ain't. Texas boy got his hair in his eyes, mouth's wide open, can't get air, but he pats four times for ever' darn step, an' he'll keep-a-goin' with the Cherokee girl.

The fiddle squeaks and the guitar bongs. Mouth-organ man is red in the face. Texas boy and the Cherokee girl, pantin' like dogs an' a-beatin' the groun'. Ol' folks stan' a-pattin' their han's. Smilin' a little, tappin' their feet.

Back home—in the schoolhouse, it was. The big moon sailed off to the westward. An' we walked, him an' me—a little ways. Didn' talk 'cause our throats was choked up. Didn' talk none at all. An' purty soon they was a haycock. Went right to it and laid down there. Seein' the Texas boy an' that girl a-steppin' away into the dark—think nobody seen 'em go. Oh, God! I wisht I was a-goin' with that Texas boy. Moon'll be up 'fore long. I seen that girl's ol' man move out to stop 'em, an' then he didn'. He knowed. Might as well stop the fall from comin', and might as well stop the sap from movin' in the trees. An' the moon'll be up 'fore long.

Play more—play the story songs—"As I Walked through the Streets of Laredo."

The fire's gone down. Be a shame to build her up. Little ol' moon'll be up 'fore long.

1939

HARRY McCLINTOCK
1882–1952

Big Rock Candy Mountain

One evening as the sun went down and the jungle fire was burning
Down the track came a hobo hiking and he said, "Boys, I'm not turning.
I'm headed for a land that's far away beside the crystal fountains
So come with me we'll go and see the Big Rock Candy Mountains."

In the Big Rock Candy Mountains there's a land that's fair and bright   5
Where the handouts grow on bushes and you sleep out every night
Where the boxcars all are empty and the sun shines every day
On the birds and the bees and the cigarette trees
The lemonade springs where the bluebird sings
In the Big Rock Candy Mountains   10

In the Big Rock Candy Mountains all the cops have wooden legs
And the bulldogs all have rubber teeth and the hens lay soft boiled eggs

The farmer's trees are full of fruit and the barns are full of hay
Oh, I'm bound to go where there ain't no snow
Where the rain don't fall the wind don't blow   15
In the Big Rock Candy Mountains

In the Big Rock Candy Mountains you never change your socks
And the little streams of alcohol come a-trickling down the rocks
The brakemen have to tip their hats and the railroad bulls are
    blind
There's a lake of stew and of whiskey too   20
You can paddle all around 'em in a big canoe
In the Big Rock Candy Mountains

In the Big Rock Candy Mountains the jails are made of tin
And you can walk right out again as soon as you are in
There ain't no short handled shovels, no axes saws or picks   25
I'm a goin to stay where you sleep all day
Where they hung the turk that invented work
In the Big Rock Candy Mountains

I'll see you all this coming fall in the Big Rock Candy Mountains.

1928

■   JOE HILL   ■
                          1879–1915

The Preacher and the Slave

Lyrics: Joe Hill
Music: "Sweet Bye and Bye"

Long-haired preachers come out every night
And they tell you what's wrong and what's right,
But when you ask them for something to eat,
They will answer in voices so sweet:

Chorus (repeat after each verse):   5
You will eat, bye and bye,

In that glorious land above the sky.
Work and pray, live on hay,
You'll get pie in the sky when you die.

Oh, the starvation army they play   10
And they sing and they clap and they pray,
Til they get all your coin on the drum
Then they'll tell you when you're on the bum.

Holy Rollers and Jumpers come out
And they holler, they jump and they shout: 15
"Give your money to Jesus," they say,
"He will cure all diseases today."

If you fight hard for children and wife
Try to get something good in this life,
You're a sinner and a bad man, they tell,   20
When you die you will sure go to Hell.

Workingmen of all countries, unite
Side by side we for freedom will fight,
When the world and its wealth we have gained
To the grafter we will sing this refrain: 25

Last chorus:
You will eat bye and bye
When you've learned how to cook and to fry
Chop some wood, 'twill do you good,
And you'll eat in the sweet bye and bye.   30

                                                                    1911

■   ANONYMOUS   ■

Winnsboro Cotton Mill Blues

Old man Sargent sitting at the desk,
The damned old fool won't give us no rest.
He'd take the nickels off a dead man's eyes,
To buy a Coco-cola and a Pomo Pie.

Chorus (reverse after each verse):   5
I've got the blues,
I've got the blues,
I've got the Winnsboro Cotton Mill blues.
Lordy, lordy, spoolin's hard.
You know and I know, I don't have to tell: 10
Work for Tom Watson, got to work like hell.
I've got the blues, I've got the blues,
I've got the Winnsboro Cotton Mill blues.

When I die, don't bury me at all,
Just hang me up on the spoolroom wall.   15
Place a knotter in my hand,
So I can spool in the Promised Land.

When I die, don't bury me deep,
Bury me down on 600 Street.
Place a bobbin in each hand,   20
So I can dolph in the Promised Land.

mid-1930s

ANONYMOUS

Working on the Project

I was workin' on the project, beggin' the relief for shoes,
I was workin' on the project, beggin' the relief for shoes,
Because the rock and concrete, oo boys, is giving my feet the blues.

Workin' on the project, with holes all in my clothes,
Workin' on the project, with holes all in my clothes,   5
Trying to make me a thin dime, oo boys, to keep the rent man from
    the do'.

I'm workin' on the project tryin' to make both ends meet,
I'm workin' on the project tryin' to make both ends meet,
But the payday is so long, till the grocery man won't let me eat.

Workin' on the project, my gal's spendin' all my dough,   10
Workin' on the project, my gal's spendin' all my dough,
Now I have waked up on her, well, well, and I won't be that weak
    no mo'.

Workin' on the project with payday three or four weeks away,
Workin' on the project, with payday three or four weeks away,
Now how can you live, well, well, well, when you can't get no pay.   15

mid-1930s

WOODY GUTHRIE
1912–1967

Union Maid

There once was a union maid who never was afraid
Of goons and ginks and company finks
And the deputy sheriffs who made the raids;
She went to the union hall when a meeting it was called,
And when the company boys came 'round   5
She always stood her ground.
Chorus (repeat after every verse):
Oh, you can't scare me, I'm sticking to the union.
I'm sticking to the union, I'm sticking to the union.
Oh, you can't scare me, I'm sticking to the union.   10
I'm sticking to the union till the day I die.

This union maid was wise to the tricks of company spies;
She never got fooled by a company stool, she'd always organize the guys;
She always got her way when she struck for higher pay;
She'd show her card to the company guard and this is what she'd say: 15

You gals who want to be free, just take a little tip from me:
Get you a man who's a union man and join the Ladies' Auxiliary;
Married life ain't hard when you've got a union card.
A union man has a happy life when he's got a union wife.

1940

Jesus Christ Was a Man

Jesus Christ was a man who traveled through the land,
A hard-working man and brave.
He said to the rich, "Give your goods to the poor,"
But they laid Jesus Christ in His grave.

Chorus   5
Jesus was a man, a carpenter by hand,
His followers true and brave.
One dirty little coward called Judas Iscariot
Has laid Jesus Christ in His grave.

He went to the preacher, He went to the sheriff,   10
He told them all the same,
"Sell all of your jewelry and give it to the poor,"
And they laid Jesus Christ in His grave.

When Jesus came to the town, the working folks around
Believed what He did say,   15
But the bankers and the preachers they nailed Him on a cross,
And they laid Jesus Christ in the grave. *(Chorus)*

And the people held their breath when they heard about His death,
Everybody wondered why,
It was the big landlord and the soldiers that they hired   20
To nail Jesus Christ in the sky.

This song it was wrote in New York City,
Of rich man, preacher and slave.
If Jesus was to preach what He preached in Galilee,
They would lay poor Jesus in His grave. *(Chorus)*   25

                                                                                1940

The Ballad of Tom Joad

Tom Joad got out of the old McAlester Pen.
There he got his parole
After four long years on a man killing charge.
Tom Joad come a walking down the road, poor boy.
Tom Joad come a walking down the road.   5

Tom Joad he met a truck driving man.
There he caught him a ride.
He said: "I just got loose from McAlester Pen
On a charge called Homicide,
A charge called Homicide."   10

That truck rolled away in a cloud of dust.
Tommy turned his face toward home.
He met Preacher Casey and they had a little drink,
But they found that his family they was gone.
He found that his family they was gone.   15

He found his mother's old fashioned shoe,
Found his daddy's hat,
And he found little Muley and Muley said:
"They've been tractored out by the cats.
They've been tractored out by the cats."   20

Tom Joad walked down to the neighbors farm,
Found his family.
They took Preacher Casey and loaded in a car.
And his mother said, "We've got to git away."
His mother said, "We've got to get away."   25

Now the twelve of the Joads made a mighty heavy load,
But Grandpa Joad did cry.
He picked up a handful of land in his hand,
Said: "I'm stayin' with the farm till I die.
Yes, I'm stayin' with my farm till I die."   30

They fed him short ribs and coffee and soothing syrup,
And Grandpa Joad did die.
They buried Grandpa Joad by the side of the road,
Grandma on the California side.
They buried Grandma on the California side.   35

They stood on a mountain and they looked to the West,
And it looked like the promised land,
That bright green valley with a river running through.
There was work for every single hand.
They thought, "There was work for every single hand."   40

The Joads road away to jungle camp,
There they cooked a stew.
And the hungry little kids of the jungle camp said:
"We'd like to have some too."
Said: "We'd like to have some too."   45

Now a Deputy Sheriff fired loose at a man,
Shot a woman in the back.
Before he could take his aim again,
Preacher Casey dropped him in his track.
Preacher Casey dropped him in his track.   50

They handcuffed Casey, and they took him to jail,
And then he got away.
And he met Tom Joad on the old river bridge,
And these few words he did say, poor boy.
These few words he did say: 55

"I preached for the Lord a mighty long time,
Preached about the rich and the poor.
Us workin' folks is all get together
Cause we ain't got a chance anymore.
We ain't got a chance anymore."   60

Now the Deputies come, and Tom and Casey run
To the bridge where the water run down.
But the vigilante thugs hit Casey with a club,
They laid Preacher Casey on the ground, poor Casey.
They laid Preacher Casey on the ground.   65

Tom Joad he grabbed that Deputy's club,
Hit him over the head.
Tom Joad took flight in the dark rainy night,
And a Deputy and a Preacher lying dead, two men,
A Deputy and a Preacher lying dead.   70

Tom run back where his mother was asleep,
He woke her up out of bed.
Then he kissed goodbye to the mother that he loved,
Said what Preacher Casey said. Tom Joad,
He said what Preacher Casey said: 75

"Ev'rybody might be just one big soul,
Well, it looks that a way to me.
Everywhere that you look in the day or night,

That's where I'm gonna be, Ma.
That's where I'm gonna be.   80

"Wherever little children are hungry and cry,
Wherever people ain't free,
Wherever men are fightin' for their rights,
That's where I'm gonna be, Ma.
That's where I'm a gonna be."   85

                                                                     1940

■ ## MOURNING DOVE (OKANOGAN) ■
1888–1936

Mourning Dove was born Christal Quintasket near Bonner's Ferry, Idaho. Besides her English name, she was given the name Hum-ishu-ma, or Mourning Dove. On her mother's side she was descended from an ancient line of warrior chieftains, and her paternal grandfather was an Irishman who worked for the Hudson's Bay Company. She received some education at Sacred Heart Convent at Ward, Washington, but left school to help care for four younger sisters and brothers. In her later teenage years, Mourning Dove lived with her maternal grandmother and through her developed an intense interest in the oral tradition of her people, the Okanogans, who today live in the western part of the Colville Reservation, near the Columbia and Okanogan Rivers and the Canadian border.

Cogewea, published in 1927, was considered the first novel written by an American Indian woman until the discovery of S. Alice Callahan's *Wynema: A Child of the Forest*, first published in 1891. Mourning Dove wrote in cooperation with Lucullus McWhorter, whom she met in 1914, by which time she had already drafted a version of the novel. McWhorter, who became her friend and mentor for twenty years, was a serious scholar of Indian traditions and had been adopted into the Yakima tribe. In contrast, Mourning Dove had little more than a third-grade education and some training in a business school. Thus she agreed to let McWhorter "fix up" the story by adding poetic epigraphs and elaborate notes on Okanogan traditions. His stylistic influence is also apparent in the often stilted language, including a self-conscious use of slang, which contrasts with the simple style of Mourning Dove's later drafts of some coyote stories. However, McWhorter knew what a white readership expected, and he was able, after a delay of many years, to find a publisher. While the novel is uneven, it gives an excellent picture of some Okanogan traditions, and the western romance plot made it acceptable in its time.

Meanwhile, in 1919 Mourning Dove had married Fred Galler, a Wenatchee. She had no children, and with Galler she became a migrant worker, camping out, working in the hop fields and apple orchards and lugging her typewriter along to work at her writing. McWhorter failed to mention this part of her life in his preface to *Cogewea;* instead, he gave a more idyllic picture of the deprivations of her life.

Coyote Stories, also published with the help of McWhorter, was much more Mourning Dove's own work. She agreed to Heister Dean Guie's receiving credit on the title page for illustrating and editing. Guie insisted on standardized spellings and verification of Okanogan beliefs. Mc-Whorter mediated between him and Mourning Dove. Unfortunately, neither Guie nor McWhorter regarded Mourning Dove as an authority on Okanogan folklore. A foreword by Chief Standing Bear probably helped sell the book because Standing Bear had published two popular autobiographies during the previous years, and his *Land of the Spotted Eagle*, focusing on Sioux beliefs and customs, appeared in the same year as *Coyote Stories*.

The stories give an impression of Mourning Dove's personality and tradition as well as of the folk material she gathered. Her introduction gives authenticity to her collection by describing her family heritage and the tribal setting in which these stories were passed on for education, entertainment, and social bonding.

The story "The Spirit Chief Names the Animal People" exemplifies all of these purposes, but also expresses the spiritual aspect of the coyote tradition by describing the concept of power *(squastenk')* and the origin of the sweat-house ritual. Both are central to Okanogan beliefs and indicate an aboriginal insight into the subtle connections between physical and psychological vitality and their grounding in cosmological mystery. Coyote himself is part of this mystery by being laughably human and divinely powerful at the same time.

Mourning Dove's later years were spent in relative obscurity. Occasionally she traveled to lecture in the East, but she was uncomfortable before strange audiences and could hardly afford the travel expenses. The single honor bestowed on her was her election as an honorary member of the Eastern Washington State Historical Society. Having for years been plagued with various illnesses, Mourning Dove died in a state hospital at Medical Lake, Washington, at the age of forty-eight.

Kristin Herzog
Independent Scholar

PRIMARY WORKS

Cogewea, the Half-Blood: A Depiction of the Great Montana Cattle Range, 1927, rpt. 1981; *Coyote Stories*, 1933, 1990; *Mourning Dove: A Salishan Autobiography*, ed. by Jay Miller, 1990; *Mourning Dove's Stories*, ed. Clifford E. Trafzer and Richard D. Scheuerman, 1991.

from **Coyote Stories**

Preface

The Animal People were here first—before there were any real people.

Coyote was the most important because, after he was put to work by the Spirit Chief, he did more than any of the others to make the world a good place to live. There were times, however, when Coyote was not busy for the Spirit Chief. Then he amused himself by getting into mischief and stirring up trouble. Frequently he got into trouble himself, and then everybody had a good laugh—everybody but Mole. She was Coyote's wife.

My people called Coyote *Sin-ka-lip'*, which means Imitator. He delighted in mocking and imitating others, or in trying to, and, as he was a great one to play tricks, sometimes he is spoken of as "Trick Person."

Our name for the Animal People is *Chip-chap-tiqulk* (the "k" barely is sounded), and we use the same word for the stories that are told about the Animal People and legendary times. To the younger generations, *chip-chap-tiqulk* are improbable stories; that is a result of the white man's schools. But to the old Indians, *chip-chap-tiqulk* are not at all improbable; they are accounts of what really happened when the world was very young.

My people are the Okanogan and the *Swhee-al-puh* (Colville), closely related Salishan tribes, and I also have relatives in the *En-koh-tu-me-whoh*, or Nicola, band of the Thompson River Indians in British Columbia. My father's mother was a Nicola, and his father was a Hudson's Bay Company man, a hardy, adventurous Celt. My father, Joseph *Quintasket* (Dark Cloud), was born in the Upper Okanogan community at Penticton, B.C., but he has lived, since a boy, with the

Lower Okanogan and the Colville, south of the international boundary. It is with the Lower, or River, Okanogan and the *Swhee-al-puh* on the Colville Reservation in north eastern Washington that I am identified.

The *Swhee-al-puh*—also called *Schu-ayl-pk*, *Schwelpi* and *Shoyelpee*—became known as the Colville following the establishment of Fort Colville by the Hudson's Bay Company in 1825–26. The fort, named after Andrew Colville, a London governor of the Company, was built near Kettle Falls in the Columbia River, in the heart of the *Swhee-al-puh* country.

My mother's name was Lucy *Stukin*. She was a *Swhee-al-puh* full blood. Her Grandfather was *See-whelh-ken*, who was head chief of the tribe for many years. His nephew, *Kin-kan-nawh*, whom the white people called Pierre Jerome, was chief when the American government made the tribe give up its home in the Colville Valley in 1872 and move to poorer land on the other side of the Columbia. My mother was born at Kettle Falls—the "Big Falls" of these legends—and she and father were married in a log church at that location. The church was built by Indians who had accepted the teachings of the missionaries.

I was born in a canoe on the Kootenai River, near Bonner's Ferry, Idaho, in the Moon of the Leaves (April), 1888. My parents were traveling with a packtrain, which my uncle, Louie *Stukin*, operated between Walla Walla, Washington and Fort Steele, B.C. during the mining rush that year. My mother and grandmother were being ferried across the river when I arrived. The Indian who was paddling their canoe stripped off his shirt and handed it to grandmother, who wrapped me up in it.

It used to be the custom for story-tellers to go from village to village and relate *chip-chap-tiqulk* to the children. How gladly were those tribal historians welcomed by busy mothers, and how glad were the boys and girls when one came to visit!

Vividly I recall old *S'whist-kane* (Lost-Head), also known as Old Narciss, and how, in the course of a narrative, he would jump up and mimic his characters, speaking or singing in a strong or weak voice, just as the Animal Persons were supposed to have done. And he would dance around the fire in the tule-mat covered lodge until the pines rang with the gleeful shouts of the smallest listeners. We thought of this as all fun and play, hardly aware that the tale-telling and impersonations were a part of our primitive education.

Another favorite was Broken Nose Abraham. He was old and crippled. He came to our village usually on a white horse, riding double with his blind wife, who held the reins and guided the horse at his direction. It always thrilled us to see Broken Nose ride into camp, he had a stock of such fascinating stories. Broken Nose could not dance for us. He could not even walk without the support of his two canes. But he sang exciting war songs, and we liked to sing with him.

Some of the women were noted story-tellers, but they never made it a business to go from village to village to tell them. We children would go to them. I particularly remember *Ka-at-qhu* (Big Lip), Old Jennie, *Tee-qualt*, or Long Thresa, and my maternal grandmother, *Soma-how-atqhu* (She-got-her-power-from-the-water). I loved these simple, kindly people, and I think of them often. And in my memory I treasure a picture of my dear mother, who, when I was a very little girl, made the bedtime hours happy for me with legends she told. She would tell them to me until I fell asleep. Two that are in this collection, "Why Marten's Face Is Wrinkled" and "Why Mosquitoes Bite People," she told over and over again, and I never grew tired of hearing them.

My father always enjoyed telling the old stories, and he does still. He and *Ste-heet-qhu* (Soup), **Toma Martin** and *Kleen-ment-itqu* are among the few men and women left who can tell chip-*chap-tiqulk*. I thank them for helping me. And I must acknowledge my debt to a blue-eyed "Indian," Lucullus Virgil McWhorter, whom the Yakimas adopted many snows ago and named *He-me⁻ne Ka⁻'wan* (Old Wolf). His heart is warm toward the red people. In him the Indians of the Pacific Northwest have a true friend. But for his insistence and encouragement, these legends would not have been set down by me for the children of another race to read.

MOURNING DOVE.

I. The Spirit Chief Names the Animal People

Hah-ah' eel-me'-whem, the great Spirit Chief,[1] called the Animal People together. They came from all parts of the world. Then the Spirit Chief told them there was to be a change, that a new kind of people was coming to live on the earth.

"All of you *Chip-chap-tiqulk*—Animal People—must have names," the Spirit Chief said. "Some of you have names now, some of you haven't. But tomorrow all will have names that shall be kept by you and your descendants forever. In the morning, as the first light of day shows in the sky, come to my lodge and choose your names. The first to come may choose any name that he or she wants. The next person may take any other name. That is the way it will go until all the names are taken. And to each person I will give work to do."

That talk made the Animal People very excited. Each wanted a proud name and the power to rule some tribe or some part of the world, and everyone determined to get up early and hurry to the Spirit Chief's lodge.

Sin-ka-lip'—Coyote—boasted that no one would be ahead of him. He walked among the people and told them that, that he would be the first. Coyote did not like his name; he wanted another. Nobody respected his name, Imitator, but it fitted him. He was called *Sin-ka-lip'* because he liked to imitate people. He thought that he could do anything that other persons did, and he pretended to know everything. He would ask a question, and when the answer was given he would say:

"I knew that before. I did not have to be told."

Such smart talk did not make friends for Coyote. Nor did he make friends by the foolish things he did and the rude tricks he played on people.

"I shall have my choice of the three biggest names," he boasted. "Those names are: *Kee-lau-naw*, the Mountain Person—Grizzly Bear, who will rule

---

[1]*Hah-ah',* or *Hwa-hwa'*—Spirit. *Eel-me'-whem*—Chief. While the Okanogan, Colville, and other Salishan stock tribes of the interior paid homage to a great variety of minor "powers" or deities (as many members of the tribes still do), they firmly believed in a Spirit Chief, or Chief Spirit, an all-powerful Man Above. This belief was theirs before they ever heard of Christianity, notwithstanding statements that have been made to the contrary.

the four-footed people; *Milka-noups*—Eagle,[2] who will rule the birds, and *En-tee-tee-ueh*, the Good Swimmer—Salmon. Salmon will be the chief of all the fish that the New People use for food."

Coyote's twin brother, Fox, who at the next sun took the name *Why-ay'-looh*—Soft Fur, laughed. "Do not be so sure, *Sin-ka-lip'*," said Fox. "Maybe you will have to keep the name you have. People despise that name. No one wants it."

"I am tired of that name," Coyote said in an angry voice. "Let someone else carry it. Let some old person take it—someone who cannot win in war. I am going to be a great warrior. My smart brother, I will make you beg of me when I am called Grizzly Bear, Eagle, or Salmon."

"Your strong words mean nothing," scoffed Fox, "Better go to your *sewhool-luh* (tepee) and get some sleep, or you will not wake up in time to choose any name."

Coyote stalked off to his tepee. He told himself that he would not sleep any that night; he would stay awake. He entered the lodge, and his three sons called as if with one voice:

"*Le-ee'-oo!*" ("Father")[3]

They were hungry, but Coyote had brought them nothing to eat. Their mother, who after the naming was known as *Pul'-laqu-whu*—Mole, the Mound Digger—sat on her foot at one side of the doorway. Mole was a good woman, always loyal to her husband in spite of his mean ways, his mischief-making, and his foolishness. She never was jealous, never talked back, never replied to his words of abuse. She looked up and said:

"Have you no food for the children? They are starving. I can find no roots to dig."

"*Eh-ha!*" Coyote grunted. "I am no common person to be addressed in that manner. I am going to be a great chief tomorrow. Did you know that? I will have a new name? I will be Grizzly Bear. Then I can devour my enemies with ease. And I shall need you no longer. You are growing too old and homely to be the wife of a great warrior and chief."

Mole said nothing. She turned to her corner of the lodge and collected a few old bones, which she put into a *klek'-chin* (cooking-basket). With two sticks she lifted hot stones from the fire and dropped them into the basket. Soon the water boiled, and there was weak soup for the hungry children.

"Gather plenty of wood for the fire," Coyote ordered. "I am going to sit up all night."

Mole obeyed. Then she and the children went to bed.

Coyote sat watching the fire. Half of the night passed. He got sleepy. His eyes grew heavy. So he picked up two little sticks and braced his eyelids

---

[2]*Milka-noups*—the "War Eagle," or "Man Eagle" (golden eagle), whose white plumes with black or brown tips are prized for decorative and ceremonial purposes, particularly for war bonnets and other headgear, dance bustles, coup sticks, and shields. The tail feathers of the bald eagle, *Pak-la-kin* (White-headed-bird) are not valued so highly. In the old days the use of eagle feathers was restricted to the men. Except in rare instances, women were not privileged to wear them.

[3]*Le-ee'-oo*. This form of address is employed only by males. A daughter calls her father *Mes-tem*, and her mother *Toom*. A son calls his mother *Se-go-ee*.

apart. "Now I can stay awake," he thought, but before long he was fast asleep, although his eyes were wide open.

The sun was high in the sky when Coyote awoke. But for Mole he would not have awakened then. Mole called him. She called him after she returned with her name from the Spirit Chief's lodge. Mole loved her husband. She did not want him to have a big name and be a powerful chief. For then, she feared, he would leave her. That was why she did not arouse him at daybreak. Of this she said nothing.

Only half-awake and thinking it was early morning, Coyote jumped at the sound of Mole's voice and ran to the lodge of the Spirit Chief. None of the other *Chip-chap-tiqulk* were there. Coyote laughed. Blinking his sleepy eyes, he walked into the lodge. "I am going to be *Kee-lau-naw*," he announced in a strong voice. "That shall be my name."

"The name Grizzly Bear was taken at dawn," the Spirit Chief answered.

"Then I shall be *Milka-noups*," said Coyote, and his voice was not so loud.

"Eagle flew away at sunup," the other replied.

"Well, I shall be called *En-tee-tee-ueh*," Coyote said in a voice that was not loud at all.

"The name Salmon also has been taken," explained the Spirit Chief. "All the names except your own have been taken. No one wished to steal your name."

Poor Coyote's knees grew weak. He sank down beside the fire that blazed in the great tepee, and the heart of *Hah-ah' Eel-mé-whem* was touched.

"*Sin-ka-lip'*," said that Person, "you must keep your name. It is a good name for you. You slept long because I wanted you to be the last one here. I have important work for you, much for you to do before the New People come. You are to be chief of all the tribes.

"Many bad creatures inhabit the earth. They bother and kill people, and the tribes cannot increase as I wish. These *En-alt-na Skil-ten*—People-Devouring Monsters—cannot keep on like that. They must be stopped. It is for you to conquer them. For doing that, for all the good things you do, you will be honored and praised by the people that are here now and that come afterward. But, for the foolish and mean things you do, you will be laughed at and despised. That you cannot help. It is your way.

"To make your work easier, I give you *squas-tenk'*. It is your own special magic power. No one else ever shall have it. When you are in danger, whenever you need help, call to your power. It will do much for you, and with it you can change yourself into any form, into anything you wish.

"To your twin brother, *Why-ay' -looh*, and to others I have given *shoo'-mesh*.[4] It is strong power. With that power Fox can restore your life should you be killed. Your bones may be scattered but, if there is one hair of your body left,

---

[4]*Shoo'-mesh*. With the exception of Coyote's "power," all "medicine" is spoken of as *shoo'-mesh*, which is regarded as definite aid communicated by the Spirit Chief through various mediums, inanimate objects as well as living creatures. Not infrequently an Indian will seek to test the potency of his medicine over that of another. Some present-day medicine-men and medicine-women are reputed to possess magic power strong enough to cause the sickness or even the death of enemies, of anyone incurring their displeasure.

Fox can make you live again. Others of the people can do the same with their *shoo'-mesh*. Now, go, *Sin-ka-lip'*! Do well the work laid for your trail!"

Well, Coyote was a chief after all, and he felt good again. After that day his eyes were different. They grew slant from being propped open that night while he sat by his fire. The New People, the Indians, got their slightly slant eyes from Coyote.

After Coyote had gone, the Spirit Chief thought it would be nice for the Animal People and the coming New People to have the benefit of the spiritual sweat-house. But all of the Animal People had names, and there was no one to take the name of Sweat-house—*Quil'-sten*, the Warmer.[5] So the wife of the Spirit Chief took the name. She wanted the people to have the sweat-house, for she pitied them. She wanted them to have a place to go to purify themselves, a place where they could pray for strength and good luck and strong medicine-power, and where they could fight sickness and get relief from their troubles.

[5]*Quil'-sten*—Sweat-house. A mystic shrine for both temporal and spiritual cleansing, the sweat-house is one of the most venerated institutions. Its use is governed by strict rules, said to have originated with Coyote, the great "law-giver." To break any of the rules is to invite misfortune, if not disaster.

Sweat-houses, or lodges, are mound-shaped, round, or oval at the base, three to four or five feet high at the center, and four to six feet in diameter, accommodating three to four persons. In some sweat-houses there is room but for one bather.

Pliant branches—usually willow or fir, depending upon the locality and growth available—are planted like interlocking croquet wickets to make the frame. Where these "ribs" cross, they are tied together with strips of bark. There are never less than eight ribs. The frame is covered with swamp tule mats, blankets, or canvas. In primitive times sheets of cottonwood bark, top-dressed with earth, frequently formed the covering. Where a permanent residence is established, the framework is covered with tule mats, top-dressed with three or more inches of soil that is well packed and smoothed. The floor is carpeted with matting, grass, ferns, or fir boughs. The last are regarded as "strong medicine," and always are used if obtainable. They give the bather strength, and they are liked, besides, for their aromatic odor. The Indians rub their bodies with the soft tips of the fir boughs, both for the purpose of deriving power and for the scent imparted.

Just within and at one side of the lodge entrance, a small hole serves as a receptacle for the stones that are heated in a brisk fire a few steps from the structure. The stones, the size of a man's fist, are smooth, unchipped,

"dry land" stones—never river-bed rocks. The latter crack and explode too easily when subjected to a combination of intense heat and cold water. By means of stout sticks, the heated stones are rolled from the fire into the sweat-house. Then the entrance is curtained tightly with mat or blanket, and the bather sprinkles cold water on the little pile of stones, creating a dense steam.

To the novice, five minutes spent in the sweltering, midnight blackness of the cramping structure seem an eternity and almost unendurable.

Several "sweats," each followed by a dip in a nearby stream or pool, properly constitute one sweat-bath. The customary period for a single sweat is ten to twenty minutes, although votaries from rival bands or tribes often crouch together in the steam for twice or thrice that time. Thus they display to one another their virility and hardihood. To further show their strength and their contempt for the discomfort of such protracted sweating, they will blow on their arms and chests. The forcing of the breath against the superheated skin produces a painful, burning sensation. Hours, even days, may be spent in "sweat-housing."

The stones used are saved and piled outside the sweat-lodge, where they remain undisturbed. For services rendered they are held in a regard bordering on reverence. An Indian would not think of spitting or stepping on these stones or of "desecrating" them in any way.

Old-time warriors and hunters always "sweat-housed" before starting on their expeditions, and many of the modern, school-educated Indian men and women often resort to the sweat-house to pray for good fortune and health.

The ribs, the frame poles, of the sweat-house represent the wife of *Hah-ah' Eel-me'-whem*. As she is a spirit, she cannot be seen, but she always is near. Songs to her are sung by the present generation. She hears them. She hears what her people say, and in her heart there is love and pity.

1933

JOHN JOSEPH MATHEWS (OSAGE)
1894–1979

John Joseph Mathews appears on the tribal roll as one-eighth Osage. He was acutely aware of his mixed-blood status as well as the changes that were over-taking reservation life in Indian Territory, later Oklahoma. After a varied youth during which he received degrees in natural sciences from the University of Oklahoma and Oxford and served as a flight instructor in aviation's infancy during World War I, he returned to Pawhuska, Oklahoma, and turned his intellect and talent to a life of public service and writing. His first book, *Wah'kon-tah: The Osage and The White Man's Road* (1929), became a Book-of-the-Month Club bestseller.

The title of his only novel, *Sundown* (1934), reflects Mathews's judgment that the traditional tribal life was passing away forever in Oklahoma. The novel is about young Challenge "Chal" Windzer, born to a progressive-minded father who hopes his son will be strong enough to make a very uncertain future full of change. The novel's plot is roughly autobiographical. Unlike Mathews, however, Chal returns from the University of Oklahoma and flight training in World War I and is unable to fit into his community, or find a meaningful vocation, or resist the blandishments of alcohol and other Anglo corruptions. The black oil derricks that ebb and flow ominously across Osage land symbolize the fatal consequences of the instant wealth brought by the exploitation of Indian resources. In the first of the passages that follows, Mathews draws a keenly insightful picture of the kinds of changes that were coming to the reservation. In the second, Chal has returned home to find his community expiring in the last trickle of money and alcohol from the oil boom. Though he is inspired by Roan Horse's example, his mother's sad but more knowledgeable evaluation of his character suggests that there is little hope for her son to fulfill his dream.

Andrew O. Wiget
New Mexico State University

PRIMARY WORK

Sundown, 1934.

from **Sundown**

I

The black derricks crept farther west. Sometimes near the town they "shot" a well with nitroglycerine, so that the strata might be loosened and allow a freer flow of the oil. At such times the citizens of the town would drive out and watch the spray of oil as it shot high into the air, and hear the gravels rattle on the woodwork of the derrick, like shot.

Everyone was happy and almost playful. On one occasion a mixedblood rushed into the spraying oil and had his new suit and a "damned good hat—a twenty-five-dollar hat" covered with oil. He said, "Whoopee!" He didn't give a damn.

They would troop back to town, feeling in their hearts that the indefinite glory was not far off now. The mixedbloods would stand in groups at the corners and discuss the well, some of them rattling the silver dollars in their pockets as they talked. They would shout jovially at anyone crossing the street; some pleasantry in Osage or in English.

DuBois joined one such group, expanding facetiously, "Say," he said, "by gawd, if I had a nose like that, I'd charge people to see it." The others laughed, and the one accused felt embarrassed, and attempted not to show in his face that his vanity had been wounded just a little. He shifted his tobacco, then said, "Well, I guess it's big all right, but they's one thing, it ain't in everybody's business." The laughter was then directed toward DuBois, who went to the curbing of the new sidewalk and spat onto the pavement, then came back. "Say," he said, desiring to change the subject, "was yu out to the well they shot this mornin'—looks like it's a-comin', don't it?" The others shook their heads in a way that would indicate that; "Sure looks that-away." DuBois continued.

"I's talkin' with a geologist the other day, and he said he thought they's oil all under the Osage—said if they found that Carsonville sand west o' here, that he knew it was all under the Osage."

The sun warmed the corner with a beneficence that seemed only for that particular corner of the world as they talked about the future; about that future which was sure to be glorious, though its particular glory was vague.

They moved over toward the sandstone building which had been the office building. Some of them sat on the broad window sill which had been worn smooth by generations of sitters. There was nothing to do except talk. Their incomes were so large now that they didn't think of working at anything; in fact, they had never worked except by spurts when some enthusiasm came over them. Some enthusiasm like starting a chicken farm and raising chickens for a market that didn't exist, or breeding white-faced cattle and pure-bred hogs.

But now, how could anyone keep his mind on anything except oil, when that tingling thrill was constantly with one; that thrill that expressed itself in expansive camaraderie and boisterousness? Besides, these people were only being true to the blood in their veins. Many of them were descendants of French gentleman adventurers who were buried in the Osage camps on the Missouri river, or lost forever in the wild forests of the new land. And many of them were descendants of laughing *coureurs du bois*, and of men who defeated Braddock from behind trees, and had come back with their allies, the great Osages, and married Osage women. The mixedblood descendants of these adventurers were usually handsome, careless and promiscuous. They had no tendency to acquisitiveness, and their lives were made sparkling by a series of enthusiasms. They lived merrily, whether they were definitely sure of the next meal or not.

From the earliest days of the Agency, they had sat in front of the traders' stores during the summer, hunted during the autumn, and sat around the big-bellied stoves and spat into the sawdust during the winter. As the Agency became a town they still sat and talked, and as the town grew they continued to talk and laugh, standing or sitting and watching the traffic.

Many of the older traders had come to the Agency out of the spirit of adventure and profit. They were in many cases men of some culture and family, and they developed a great respect and sometimes actual love for the Indian. Which was rather unique in that their large profit-taking was not always within the bounds of ethics, if the ethics of their religious training had anything to do with business practice. They did not compete with each other and perhaps ethics was not necessary.

They took much credit for allowing their Indian clients to have provisions on account, and even sacrificed comfort to haul provisions to far away camps during severe winters. During the great epidemic of smallpox they had even endangered themselves to supply the Indians with necessities, driving with their provisions to a designated rock or tree near an infected camp and leaving them there. To compensate for their sacrifices, they often added extra percentages to the bill. The interest from the tribal trust fund was definite and sure, but these early traders always felt a certain magnanimity in allowing the Indians to have whatever provisions and clothing they needed between the quarterly payments. Especially during the epidemic, when the desire for the continuance of the trade overbalanced their fears, they felt particularly self-righteous. They came back from these trips with the fear of the disease in their hearts, but they felt better after they had seen that all the saucers had been refilled with carbolic acid and set in the windows of their stores. And they kept these saucers filled in the windows at their homes, though they had sent their families out of the reservation during the period of the epidemic. They took no chances of germs wandering aimlessly into their homes through the windows.

Now, they too watched the black derricks spread from the east with an enthusiasm that was somehow dampened by the fact that such development would bring more competition. They worried when they thought of those riches under them and all around them going to others. The old reservation had been theirs and they still felt that the new county was theirs as well, and they felt vindictive toward all the people who were coming in to share the trade with them. The Agency was their home and the town became their home. They talked the language of their friends, the Osages, and felt sincerely protective toward them. But things were moving too fast, and they had difficulty adjusting themselves to the new tempo of Progress, having spent their youth in the hard tranquillity of an Indian nation, where a man's word was as good as his signature.

The new people who came in after the allotment were of all types, representing many professions or no profession in particular. Drifting artisans and laborers, lawyers, doctors, shopkeepers, bootleggers, shrewd and unscrupulous men who did business on the new curbs, and men and women with criminal tendencies who lacked the courage. There were representatives of oil companies, geologists and lease men, and oil field employees from the ends of the earth.

They came slowly at first as the black derricks moved toward the west, then they came in hundreds. After the war, however, when people all over the country spoke of "normalcy" and said that prosperity had come to the Federation of States, they came into the little town in swarms, and the mixedbloods stood on the corner and proudly guessed that there must be fifteen or twenty thousand people in town.

There were no factories, no mills, no industry except the cattle business which had flourished for years. There weren't even any oil refineries. These had been established in neighboring towns because the owners felt that it was too expensive to satisfy all the business men who seemed to have influence over the destinies of the town. A big railroad missed Kihekah by six miles for reasons which remained obscure.

The black derricks that sprang up among the blackjacks over night gave to the Osages and all the mixedbloods on the roll one-sixth of every forty-two-gallon barrel of oil. As more oil came out of the ground the quarterly payments became larger and larger, and as the payments became larger and larger, men's heads became filled with dreams and their lives became frenzied activity. So intoxicated did they become that they forgot to stop in their frantic grasping to point the finger of accusation at a neighbor. Still there was no keen competition. One had only to sit and think up schemes for bringing to himself more of the wealth which surrounded him.

One afternoon black clouds came up in the northwest and tumbled over each other in their attempts to be in the van; tumbling as though with deliberate design, as though directed by angry gods to destroy the town in the valley among the blackjacks. Lightning played against the black mass and there was distant thunder. The outer edges of the clouds were whipped by crazy little winds, and a deep silence settled over the valley. The rest of the sky was pale green.

In the town the people began thinking of the cellars. John walked to the front porch of his house, looked at the sky for some time, then went back in and sat down, picked up the *Trumpet* and began reading. Down the street DuBois had just come home from Goldie's, where he had spent the afternoon with one of the new girls. He went to the door and looked at the sky, and as he looked the first heavy drops spattered on the roof of his house. He went to the bedroom where his wife was lying, expecting a new baby. He made the sign of the cross over her bed as she slept, and did the same at each window of the room, then called the children. He led them into the cellar and made the sign of the cross again as he closed the door.

Jep Newberg, the leading merchant and general business man among the newcomers, telephoned to his wife and told her to go to the cellar. He stood at the large plate glass window of his store, and shifted his chewed, unlit cigar first to one side of his mouth and then to the other. He didn't like that sky. A raindrop spattered on the plate glass. He thought of his secretary sitting back in the office, and he went back and stood over her. She was bent over the books, adding the usual twenty per cent to the purchases of Indians made that day.

"Let that go," he said. "Leave that off." He laid his stubby finger on the page of the book. She looked up at him with a question. He said:

"Say, looks purty bad outside. Maybe you'd better go over to the Blue Front basement—might be blowy." He didn't give her time to adjust her hat properly, and she had just managed to get into one sleeve of her raincoat before he pushed her out the front door and told her to run. She wondered if he were really growing cold; becoming tired. "Maybe the old cat has been after him again," she thought as she went to the Blue Front drug store. The druggist was motioning to her from the top of the basement steps.

Jep saw that the sidewalk was profusely covered with dark splashes. He went back to the vault, stepped inside, and left the door half open. He shifted his cigar nervously as he stood there.

Chal was on the prairie on the other side of the creek from the village. When he noticed the clouds were so menacing he put his pony into a trot, but already the big drops had begun to fall, and suddenly the tall cottonwood along the little creek began to bend with the under sides of its leaves showing gray. He could hear the wind moaning in the blackjacks along the ridge to the west; it was like a protest.

He knew he couldn't make the village so he rode toward a hill where the small blackjack saplings were growing, He heard hoof beats behind him, and looked around. Three Osages on ponies came up to him; an old man whom he had seen many times but couldn't recall his name, young White Elk, and Sun-on-His-Wings. He was surprised and he had to keep looking forward to keep them from seeing the surprise on his face. Their faces were painted in a manner he hadn't seen for years, and he guessed that their bodies were naked. They were covered with their blankets which were pulled up around their heads. They greeted each other and rode on as though they had been together all day.

A terrific gust of wind hit them just as they neared the saplings. Chal looked up and saw the clouds boiling above them, and the old man looked as well, and as he did so he stopped his pony and slid off saying, "How." Chal and the others slid off of their ponies and all ran to the young blackjacks, each one lying down on his belly and each grasping tightly the thin, flexible stem of a sapling.

Everything was blurred. The wind howled and the rain came before it horizontally across the prairie. Objects flew past and the little trees bent and swished, but you heard only the roar of the wind, above which the thunder cracked and the earth seemed to shiver.

The wind died and the rain, still falling, began to slacken, and the skies began to clear. They stood up and looked around. They could hear the roaring of the water in the little creek. The ponies were gone. Chal looked at the faces of the three and that which had puzzled him became clear.

They had seen the storm coming and had prepared themselves for the ancient ritual of defiance and sacrifice. Though he had heard about it, he had never seen it, and thought that the people had discontinued the ceremony. But he could see it all now. They had seen the storm coming and had ridden out to the hill so that they might be visible to Wah 'Kon-Tah, and manifest their bravery by defying the storm, but ready to die by a bolt of lightning if it pleased the Great Mysteries. There was some reason why they had ridden out. Perhaps it was because Wah 'Kon-Tah had manifested his displeasure in some way, and they had wanted to show him that they were still Osages and were not afraid to die; that they would sacrifice themselves if he wished it for the benefit of the tribe. Chal didn't know why they had not carried their guns with them to shoot into the storm—they used to do that, he remembered. He guessed that they didn't want to attract the attention of white people who might chance to be near.

They had probably come down when they saw that cyclone coming— Wah 'Kon-Tah would not want them to face a cyclone, with death a certainty. They would have no chance that way. Lightning was fickle, or rather, it was directed by the Great Mysteries to a certain spot.

Chal's clothes were wet and he felt shivery as he walked with his companions toward the village. The little creek was bank full, and they unhesitatingly walked into the muddy, swirling water and swam across, climbing out several yards downstream. The water of the creek felt warm to Chal's chilled body.

When they had gone some distance from the roaring creek, they stopped and listened to a greater roar; a roar that shook the earth under their feet. The old man was visibly disturbed as he looked at the sky in all directions. The roar became louder and Chal thought that the old man looked bewildered, but no one said anything.

When they reached the village, all four of the ponies were there quietly grazing among the débris of wagons and lodge-coverings. The people were walking here and there, searching for their belongings, but most of them were standing in a group talking. Chal didn't even stop to think whether any of them had been hurt. He knew that they had all gone out and clung to the saplings and sumac bushes at the edge of the village.

When his little party came up to the group, the old man asked in Osage. "That roar, what is that thing which makes ground afraid?" Charging Bull pointed toward the town, "I told my son to go see about that thing. He is back now. He says it is gas well. He says lightning struck gas well."

"Ho-hoooo," said the old man and Chal was sure that he saw relief in his face.

Sun-on-His-Wings, shivering in his wet blanket, turned to Chal and said in English, "Let's go over there to my father's lodge—maybe there's a fire there." He pointed to one of the few lodges left standing.

When they were both naked and warming themselves and Chal was drying his clothes, Sun-on-His-Wings said, "That old man is Black Elk. He will say that lightning struck that gas well 'cause the Great Spirit don't want the white people to come here any more. He will say in council some time that Osages ought to see that, and run all the white people out of their land, I bet." They were silent for some time, then Sun-on-His-Wings raised his voice again above the roar, "He's an old man, though, and he don't know about these things. His body is here but his mind is back in a place where we lived many years ago."

Chal wanted to ask his friend why he had gone with old Black Elk to the hill, since Sun-on-His-Wings was now a Peyote worshipper, but he only smiled about the old man and said nothing.

Chal rode back to town with the constant roar of the fire in his ears, and as he drew near it became deafening. As he approached he could see the flame above the pipe. The derrick had burned and the flame didn't begin at the pipe but several feet above it, like a great jet.

People were standing in groups some distance from the flame; standing on the hillside and sitting on stone walls, and some had climbed to the roofs of barns and houses. Just watching. Several men were nearer than the others and Chal could see that they had rifles. He could see them point the guns at the flame, then white puffs of smoke, but the report was drowned. They were attempting to separate the thin column of roaring gas from the flame above, but they failed.

He stood there for some time and watched; the crowd amused him. White people seemed so helpless when they couldn't talk, and it was funny to see them so inefficient, standing there. He could see some of them move toward each other, not able to restrain themselves any longer, and attempt to talk above the terrific roar. For a moment as he sat there on his pony, he wondered if they were as great as he had always thought them to be. These doubts gave rise to confusion and he dismissed them after a moment.

His attention was attracted to some people standing around a man high up on the hill. The man standing on a stone wall and gesticulating. Here was something strange; some strange thing the white people were doing there upon the hill. He was intrigued.

He rode up to where the people were gathering and stopped outside the circle, but he could see over the heads of the others from his position. The thin man who was standing on the retaining wall was shouting and raising his hands to the sky. Chal thought he was one of those people who sell medicine at first, but he was not selling anything, that was plain. His face was distorted and his eyes had a wild light in them. The roar was not so loud here and Chal could hear some of the things he said:

"Come to Jesus, come to Jesus, come you sinners and repent! Jesus loves you—arms—I shall come—far—Jesus is good, Jesus is —square—"

The words would come indistinctly, and be lost as the little breeze that had sprung up carried the roar back over the hill. But Chal was fascinated by this man. He was fascinated by the veins that stood out on his neck and the way he moaned and shouted when he couldn't think of any more words. But eventually he would break into words again. Chal looked at the people around the speaker and he saw that they stood with their mouths open. On the outside of the circle some high school boys giggled and an older man turned and frowned at them.

The man would get down on his knees on the wall and lift his hands into the air, saying that that flaming gas well was a sign, and that everybody ought to make peace with their God. Then he would get up and pound the palm of his hand with the fist of the other, and point to the people in the front of the circle with a finger that shook.

Chal was surprised to see a man go forward and fall on his knees at the foot of the wall. Then a young girl and two women rushed forward and fell on their knees, weeping and groaning. He was startled by a cry close by him; like the cry of a rabbit caught by an owl, and a woman, scratching and clawing her way through the crowd, made his pony snort. Her hat was on the side of her head and her iron gray hair had fallen about her shoulders. She rushed forward to the wall and fell on her face shrieking.

Chal felt that a knot had come into his stomach, and the blood in his veins seemed to have turned to water, the water carrying some sort of poison. He turned his pony and rode away, shaking slightly.

He was glad to see that his father's house had not been disturbed by the cyclone; and he noticed that outside of a few trees and several houses some distance from the business district, very little damage had been done. He smiled to himself when he thought of what interpretation old Black Elk might put upon the fact that the village had been in the direct path of the storm, and that the town had been left intact.

After dinner he went back to the burning well with his father. People were still standing there, fascinated. He and his father stopped by a group of mixedbloods. They seemed to have doubts about the ability of the men running around below to put out the flame. DuBois shouted that they were "crazier 'n hell if they thought they was gonna put it out with rifles."

As they stood the flames lighted up the whole countryside, and the light could be seen for many miles that night. The terrific, ground-shivering roar and the light that spread over the whole valley; the light that made the blackjacks on the hills look like ghost trees, appeared to the mixedbloods standing there as a symbol of that indefinite glory that was coming. That light that you could see as far away as the old Cherokee country, and that roar that drowned all other sounds, gave them a feeling of vague greatness and importance in the universe. Here was the manifestation of a power that made the white man stand and wonder; a power that came out of their own hills, and that light, in which you could "pick up a pin a mile away," was certainly the light of glory.

Turning away from the spectacle, with a facetious remark in Osage, DuBois went home. He found one of the new doctors there. He had had a misunderstanding with the old government doctor, because he had forgotten to pay for former services rendered. He walked into the room where his wife lay, full of the emotion which had suffused him as he watched the fire. The doctor held the baby up to him and he saw that it was a boy.

"Well, Doc, he's already got a name," he said proudly, "Osage Oil DuBois."

II

The black derricks had crept from the blackjacks of the east, slowly over the hills; spreading to the south and north and on past the little town in the valley. They touched here and there, but climbed steadily west out of the valleys onto the high prairie; across the treeless hills, and on across Salt Creek that lay like a silver ribbon across the prairie, fringed by elms. Then they crept to the very edge of the old reservation and lapped over into the Kaw country. There they stopped. At the tip of the westward movement, half a dozen little towns grew up; not out of the earth like mushrooms, as they were not of this part of the earth; they had no harmony with the Osage. Later they were like driftwood carried in from strange lands on a high tide and left stranded when the tide went out.

Riding on the wave of oil the little town of Kihekah grew out of its narrow valley and climbed exuberantly up its surrounding hills, then grew along the lines of least resistance; along its elongated creek valley. The blackjacks moved back, stepping with dignity to protect their toes; standing around the town and throwing their shadows across gardens and the green lawns that crept up to their feet.

Then one day something happened. It didn't all happen in one day, but it seemed that way. The all-powerful life that had come with the creeping black derricks began to recede to the east. The population of the little towns at the tip of the movement seemed to melt into the air, and the brick buildings stood empty and fantastic on the prairie; singing sad songs in the prairie winds. The roar of activity faded into the lazy coughing of pumps, and the fever brightness of the Great Frenzy began to dim.

The derricks stood black against the prairie horizon in rows, and became the husks of a life force that had retreated back along its own trail. The houses in the town of the little valley stopped their encroachments on the blackjacks, then they gradually became husks too; like the shells of the cicadas clinging to the hillsides. The old trading store which had grown from primitive palisades into a domineering brick building closed its doors, and Ed Fancher took up a stand on the sunny corner of his old store, too old to believe what the more youthful were saying, that the oil would come back. The great store's empty windows stared out onto the streets like wondering eyes. Its owner expressing its surprised wonder when he said to a jovial, bankrupt mixedblood one day in the winter sun on the corner, that he "didn't see how 'Ye Shoppe' outfit across the street could keep goin." As he and the mixedblood talked about the past they backed up against the empty, staring windows. Above them was an extravagant advertisement announcing the arrival of a circus which had folded its canvas and left Kihekah the summer before.

Mixedblood families came back to the old Agency from their large homes in the mountains, in California, and elsewhere. They dropped their golf clubs and lost their homes and came back to wander aimlessly along the familiar streets. They asked with the other citizens of the town, "S'pose it'll come back?" All agreed that it would, but they wondered just the same.

One morning Jep Newberg was found with a bullet hole in his temple. Those who knew said that he sure was powder burned. He, with the sardonic humor of the hard-headed business man, had elected to float out sentimentally on the receding tide.

Doc Lawes, however, used a shotgun, and they said that he did a good job, all right.

When the population had shrunk to a few thousand and the citizens were still saying that times would be better, like a boy whistling in the dark, Federal investigators made an astonishing discovery. As a result, there was great interest in the fact that a group of citizens in the Big Hill country had been killing Big Hills for several years with the object of accumulating several headrights into the hands of one Indian woman who was married to one of the group. They were preparing to put her out of the way when they were caught. Running Elk had been the first relative to become a victim, but his death had aroused little interest, and the other victims were also disposed of in various ways during the roar of the Great Frenzy, and naturally little attention had been paid to the murders.

But now it was different. Here was an interest coming up just when a lively interest was needed, and good citizens rose early to be at the courtroom to hear the trial. Housewives left their breakfast dishes in order to get seats so that they might stare intently at the faces of the accused.

The little cloud that had hung over the town in the valley finally developed into a cumulus and spread over the sky. But there were no lightning-thrusts of an angry Jove. The senatorial committee came quietly and held their meetings in the courtroom. The members sat at a table, and successive witnesses took a chair and answered questions.

It was a dull day. A monotonous questioning of witnesses, and the only relief was the evident embarrassment of several guardians, and Roan Horse's speech. Chal sat in the back of the room, and when Roan Horse was called, he felt a deep, vicarious shame. Roan Horse was an insurgent and he believed that everything was wrong. He was the leader of the east moon faction of the Peyote church, and believed that Me-Ompah-Wee-Lee, the founder, was a deity, much to the disgust of the conservatives.

When he was called, he walked with quick dignity to the table, but refused to take the witness chair, and Chal's heart sank. He walked proudly to the dais of the judge's bench and stood there like one who is preparing to make an oration. His long hair fell over his black coat in two braids which were interbraided with red cheesecloth. Some tribal instinct caused his hand to move to his right breast, as though he were holding the edge of a blanket under his right arm, then with his right hand he made a gesture and said, "Gentleman of the senatorial investigating committee," then paused. The senator from the northwest Indian country sighed, and made a motion to the others that there was nothing to be done, then settled himself into a comfortable position. The others reared back in their chairs and pretended to be waiting.

Chal could see the anger in Roan Horse's face, and he looked down the bench where he was sitting as though he would escape if possible. Then again he heard Roan Horse's voice, "Gentlemen of the senatorial investigating committee: I am Roan Horse. I say this to you. You have come here twenty-five years too late." With a quick movement he descended to the table and shook hands with each of the members. When he came to the senator from the northwest Indian country, he stood at the senator's shoulder with his extended hand unnoticed. The senator was absorbed in some papers before him and apparently believed that Roan Horse was still speaking. He turned, surprised, and took the long bronze hand.

People laughed about Roan Horse's speech, and said it was good, and Chal felt quite proud of him. His speech came at a time in the investigation when the citizens were beginning to believe that the affair was going to be tame, after all. They had hoped that the committee might stir up something which would be of benefit to them, but had experienced that childish injury which intensely acquisitive people feel when they have been thwarted. Thus they felt, in some vague way, that Roan Horse had been their champion.

Chal felt the atmosphere which was charged with depression, and he felt almost disillusioned at times. The representatives of civilization changed from jovial backslapping, efficient people, around whom he had placed an aura of glory, to dour, reticent people who seemed afraid. The many ways which they had found to share in the wealth of the Osages, became less practical as the methods formerly used, now loomed in the quiescence, which before had been drowned in the frenzy. There was an attitude of waiting for something, and they told each other repeatedly that the Osage payments would become larger again.

The glamour was dimmed and Chal found that even corn whisky and home brew parties were of little aid in lifting his spirit from the effect of that strange atmosphere which had settled over the little town in the valley. He was annoyed with his mother because she didn't seem to understand that something had happened to the world. Fire Cloud would come with his wife, and the three of them would sit out in the shade under the postoak and talk as they had always talked. He thought they were like that postoak in a way. It had been standing there as long as he could remember; standing there in the shrill excitement of the frenzy, and standing there now with the same indifference under the pall of the dimmed glory. Chal was annoyed with them because they didn't seem to be aware that something important had happened to the little world of their blackjacks and prairie.

One hot June morning Chal drove home. He put the car in the garage, making as little noise as possible. Of course his mother never said anything about his absences, but he didn't want her to know that he had been drunk for the last two weeks.

This morning he had come from the hangout of Pug Wilson and his gang, and he couldn't remember how he had got there. As he drove in he was wondering how long he had been there and what he had done. He had received his June payment, which was certainly not much, but he didn't have a cent left this morning. As he rubbed his hand over his chin his straggly beard seemed to be inches long. He could remember only snatches of the conversations at Pug's hangout, and he could remember vaguely that there had been girls there. He remembered Pug and the way he could take his false teeth out and draw his cheeks in and pucker his mouth so that he didn't look like the same man. Pug had boasted to him that he always did that before he went into a bank. He said he always put his false teeth in his pocket and screwed his face up when he stuck the iron in their guts, so they couldn't recognize him later. He told Chal they'd play hell catchin' him by the description of him with his teeth out.

Chal walked slowly to the shade of the old postoak and sat down. He tried to recall some of the other things that had happened at Pug's hangout, but he couldn't remember. He was sure of one thing, and that was that he had not left the house; he was sure that he couldn't have accompanied them on one of their "jobs." This assurance gave him a pleasant feeling.

As he sat by the table this hot summer morning in the shade of the old oak, he felt lazily indifferent to everything. He slid back in his chair and watched a robin feeding her young; their quivering, jerky little heads reaching above the nest with wide mouths. The mother robin shook herself and flew away. A sparrow came hopping along the limb, chirruped, and looked about, then hopped to the edge of the nest. He cocked his head at the nestlings. They, hearing the sound at the edge of the nest, reached for the expected food. The sparrow looked quizzically at the little ones for a while, with his head cocked. He looked around several times, then reached in and lifted one of the nestlings out. He hopped along the limb for a short distance, then looking down at the ground, he let the little bird fall. Chal heard it spatter as it hit the earth. The sparrow looked down at it for a moment, then hopped back to the nest.

Chal was about to rise to scare him away when the mother robin appeared, and with much scolding, chased the sparrow away. When she came back she had a worm dangling from her bill and began to feed the remaining nestlings. She failed to realize that anything had happened to the fourth.

The door slammed, and Chal's mother came out with some coffee, and sat down in the other chair by the table. For some time they sat silently, and as he sipped his coffee Chal felt annoyed with her. He had felt antagonistic toward her for some time, and he wasn't sure why. He noticed that she had changed quite a bit. Her black hair was parted in the center and brushed back and done into a neat knot. Her long, copper-colored fingers played along the arm of the chair nervously. Her shoes looked neat on her very small feet, and she was dressed in a very attractive blue dress. About her, as usual, as long as he could remember, was the odor of soap; a simple, clean odor without the hint of perfume. He noticed that her hair was still damp from the strokes of a wet brush.

The coffee in the pot grew cold. Another sparrow came to the oak tree and looked about cautiously for the mother robin. Chal watched him for a moment, then said, "The sparrows are still purty bad." His mother looked at the ground in front of her, "Yes, seems like they're worse this year—I don' know why."

His antagonism left as a memory came back to him. He turned to his mother.

"'Member, I used to kill them with the arrows Uncle Fire Cloud made for me?"

"My son was a great hunter—he killed many sparrows." A smile came over her face, then left quickly, and there was another long silence. She looked straight ahead, then spoke softly, "Many white men are flying across the sea now."

It was only an observation, but Chal saw behind it into the Indian soul of his mother. He became very angry and almost hated her for a moment. An intense urge flooded him; an urge to vindicate himself before this woman. This woman sitting there was more than his mother—she was an Indian woman and she was questioning a man's courage. Suddenly he realized why he had almost hated her recently. She had been looking into his heart, as she had always looked into his heart.

As he sat there he was attempting to think of something to say which would vindicate him, but he was growing angrier in his futility. Then suddenly he was warmed by a thought. There was a primordial thing which thrilled him and made his stomach tingle, and he felt kindly toward his mother—toward this Indian woman who could see into a warrior's heart. Under the influence of this thought he got up from his chair and stood before her, instinctively straightening his body.

"Ah," he said, "there isn't anything to flyin'. Flyin' across the sea doesn't mean anything any more these days. It's not hard. We didn't have these parachutes and things. It was really dangerous when I was flyin'." He hesitated, then a definite, glorious feeling came over him as he stood there. "I'm goin' to Harvard law school, and take law—I'm gonna be a great orator." The thought that had so recently occurred to him for the first time, occurred to him the moment before, suffused him with glory, and he experienced an assurance and a courage that he hadn't felt for years, and he ended up with, "There isn't anything to flyin any more."

As his mother looked at him standing there, she didn't see a swaggering young man. She saw a little boy in breech clout and moccasins, holding up a cock sparrow for her approval. She could see again the marks of his fingers on his dirty face, and the little line of dirt in the crease of his neck. As he held the bird up to her he had frowned like a little warrior.

She thought that her heart might come into her face, so she looked at the ground and said, "Huhn-n-n-n." She got up quickly and went into the house.

Chal sat down in the chair and slid down on his back. He was filled with a calm pleasure. There was nothing definite except that hum of glory in his heart, subdued by the heat and the lazy tempo of life in the heated yard.

His heavy head lolled back and he fell asleep. The leaf-shadows made bizarre designs on his silk shirt, and moved slowly to the center of the table, then to the edge, and finally abandoned the table to the hot sun. The nestlings in the nest above settled down to digest their food. A flame-winged grasshopper rose in front of Chal's still form, and suspended there, made cracking sounds like electric sparks, then dropped to the grass and became silent. The flapping and splashing of the mother robin, as she bathed in the pan under the hydrant, was the only sound of activity.

1934

■ THOMAS S. WHITECLOUD (CHIPPEWA) ■
1914–1972

Thomas St. Germain Whitecloud was born in New York City, October 8, 1914. His mother was white and his father, Thomas S. Whitecloud, was Chippewa. The elder Whitecloud was a graduate of the Yale Law School but after his education chose not to cast his lot with white America. Thus the Whiteclouds divorced, and he returned to the Lac Du Flambeau Reservation in Wisconsin, where he remarried and reared a family. The young Whitecloud remained with his mother, but his childhood experiences included life on the reservation as well as in mainstream America.

The younger Whitecloud encountered difficult times growing up. He was in and out of public schools as well as federal Indian schools in Albuquerque, Chilocco, and Santa Fe. He made an unsuccessful attempt at college studies at the University of New Mexico but finally settled down to serious study at the University of Redlands, where he also met and married Barbara Ibanez. Meanwhile, during his youth, he had been a farm worker, truck driver, mechanic, handyman, and boxer, among others.

By the time Whitecloud entered Redlands, he had settled on medicine as a career. After graduation, in 1939 he entered the Tulane School of Medicine from which he earned his M.D. degree before entering military service in World War II. He served for over two years as a battalion surgeon with U.S. paratroops in Europe. As a practicing physician, he worked as an Indian Service doctor in Montana and Minnesota before entering private practice in Texas, where for over seven years he not only ran a county hospital but also served as county coroner and deputy sheriff. Because of ill health, he moved to Mississippi, settling finally at Picayune, where he had a limited practice, engaged in many civic activities, and served as a consultant to the Department of Health, Education, and Welfare. During his later years, he also wrote and lectured extensively.

While a student at Redlands, Whitecloud had contemplated careers other than medicine. He liked to write and apparently considered taking up literature. He wrote essays and Indian tales, some of which he sent to the aged Hamlin Garland, presumably for criticism. His only significant published literary work, "Blue Winds Dancing," appeared in his senior year. It has been a popular essay among readers of Indian literature because of its powerful theme and the quality of its style, which becomes almost lyrical at times. At his death, Whitecloud left a number of works in manuscript, including essays, tales, and poetry.

Daniel F. Littlefield, Jr.
University of Arkansas at Little Rock

PRIMARY WORK

Blue Winds Dancing, 1938.

Blue Winds Dancing[1]

There is a moon out tonight. Moon and stars and clouds tipped with moonlight. And there is a fall wind blowing in my heart. Ever since this evening, when against a fading sky I saw geese wedge southward. They were going home.... Now I try to study, but against the pages I see them again, driving southward. Going home.

Across the valley there are heavy mountains holding up the night sky, and beyond the mountains there is home. Home, and peace, and the beat of drums, and blue winds dancing over snow fields. The Indian lodge will fill with my people, and our gods will come and sit among them. I should be there then. I should be at home.

But home is beyond the mountains, and I am here. Here where fall hides in the valleys, and winter never comes down from the mountains. Here where all the trees grow in rows; the palms stand stiffly by the roadsides, and in the groves the orange trees line in military rows, and endlessly bear fruit. Beautiful, yes; there is always beauty in order, in rows of growing things! But it is the beauty of captivity. A pine fighting for existence on a windy knoll is much more beautiful.

[1]From *Scribner's Monthly*, 103 (February 1938), 59–61.

In my Wisconsin, the leaves change before the snows come. In the air there is the smell of wild rice and venison cooking; and when the winds come whispering through the forests, they carry the smell of rotting leaves. In the evenings, the loon calls, lonely; and birds sing their last songs before leaving. Bears dig roots and eat late fall berries, fattening for their long winter sleep. Later, when the first snows fall, one awakens in the morning to find the world white and beautiful and clean. Then one can look back over his trail and see the tracks following. In the woods there are tracks of deer and snowshoe rabbits, and long streaks where partridges slide to alight. Chipmunks make tiny footprints on the limbs; and one can hear squirrels busy in hollow trees, sorting acorns. Soft lake waves wash the shores, and sunsets burst each evening over the lakes, and make them look as if they were afire.

That land which is my home! Beautiful, calm—where there is no hurry to get anywhere, no driving to keep up in a race that knows no ending and no goal. No classes where men talk and talk, and then stop now and then to hear their own words come back to them from the students. No constant peering into the maelstrom of one's mind; no worries about grades and honors; no hysterical preparing for life until that life is half over; no anxiety about one's place in the thing they call Society.

I hear again the ring of axes in deep woods, the crunch of snow beneath my feet. I feel again the smooth velvet of ghost-birch bark. I hear the rhythm of the drums.... I am tired. I am weary of trying to keep up this bluff of being civilized. Being civilized means trying to do everything you don't want to, never doing anything you want to. It means dancing to the strings of custom and tradition; it means living in houses and never knowing or caring who is next door. These civilized white men want us to be like them—always dissatisfied, getting a hill and wanting a mountain.

Then again, maybe I am not tired. Maybe I'm licked. Maybe I am just not smart enough to grasp these things that go to make up civilization. Maybe I am just too lazy to think hard enough to keep up.

Still, I know my people have many things that civilization has taken from the whites. They know how to give; how to tear one's piece of meat in two and share it with one's brother. They know how to sing—how to make each man his own songs and sing them; for their music they do not have to listen to other men singing over a radio. They know how to make things with their hands, how to shape beads into design and make a thing of beauty from a piece of birch bark.

But we are inferior. It is terrible to have to feel inferior; to have to read reports of intelligence tests, and learn that one's race is behind. It is terrible to sit in classes and hear men tell you that your people worship sticks of wood—that your gods are all false, that the Manitou forgot your people and did not write them a book.

I am tired. I want to walk again among the ghost-birches. I want to see the leaves turn in autumn, the smoke rise from the lodgehouses, and to feel the blue winds. I want to hear the drums; I want to hear the drums and feel the blue whispering winds.

There is a train wailing into the night. The trains go across the mountains. It would be easy to catch a freight. They will say he has gone back to the blanket; I don't care. The dance at Christmas. . . .

A bunch of bums warming at a tiny fire talk politics and women and joke about the Relief and the WPA and smoke cigarettes. These men in caps and overcoats and dirty overalls living on the outskirts of civilization are free, but they pay the price of being free in civilization. They are outcasts. I remember a sociology professor lecturing on adjustment to society; hobos and prostitutes and criminals are individuals who never adjusted, he said. He could learn a lot if he came and listened to a bunch of bums talk. He would learn that work and a woman and a place to hang his hat are all the ordinary man wants. These are all he wants, but other men are not content to let him want only these. He must be taught to want radios and automobiles and a new suit every spring. Progress would stop if he did not want these things. I listen to hear if there is any talk of communism or socialism in the hobo jungles. There is none. At best there is a sort of disgusted philosophy about life. They seem to think there should be a better distribution of wealth, or more work, or something. But they are not rabid about it. The radicals live in the cities.

I find a fellow headed for Albuquerque, and talk road-talk with him. "It is hard to ride fruit cars. Bums break in. Better to wait for a cattle car going back to the Middle West, and ride that." We catch the next east-bound and walk the tops until we find a cattle car. Inside, we crouch near the forward wall, huddle, and try to sleep. I feel peaceful and content at last. I am going home. The cattle car rocks. I sleep.

Morning and the desert. Noon and the Salton Sea, lying more lifeless than a mirage under a somber sun in a pale sky. Skeleton mountains rearing on the skyline, thrusting out of the desert floor, all rock and shadow and edges. Desert. Good country for an Indian reservation. . . .

Yuma and the muddy Colorado. Night again, and I wait shivering for the dawn.

Phoenix. Pima country. Mountains that look like cardboard sets on a forgotten stage. Tucson. Papago country. Giant cacti that look like petrified hitchhikers along the highways. Apache country. At El Paso my road-buddy decides to go on to Houston. I leave him, and head north to the mesa country. Las Cruces and the terrible Organ Mountains, jagged peaks that instill fear and wondering. Albuquerque. Pueblos along the Rio Grande. On the boardwalk there are some Indian women in colored sashes selling bits of pottery. The stone age offering its art to the twentieth century. They hold up a piece and fix the tourists with black eyes until, embarrassed, he buys or turns away. I feel suddenly angry that my people should have to do such things for a living. . . .

Santa Fe trains are fast, and they keep them pretty clean of bums. I decide to hurry and ride passenger coaltenders. Hide in the dark, judge the speed of the train as it leaves, and then dash out, and catch it. I hug the cold steel wall of the tender and think of the roaring fire in the engine ahead, and of the passengers back in the dining car reading their papers over hot coffee. Beneath me there is blur of rails. Death would come quick if my hands should freeze and I fall. Up over the Sangre De Cristo range, around cliffs and through canyons to Denver. Bitter cold here, and I must watch out for Denver Bob. He is a railroad bull who has thrown bums from fast freights. I miss him. It is too cold, I suppose. On north to the Sioux country.

Small towns lit for the coming Christmas. On the streets of one I see a beam-shouldered young farmer gazing into a window filled with shining silver toasters. He is tall and wears a blue shirt buttoned, with no tie. His young wife by his side looks at him hopefully. He wants decorations for his place to hang his hat to please his woman....

Northward again. Minnesota, and great white fields of snow; frozen lakes, and dawn running in dusk without noon. Long forests wearing white. Bitter cold, and one night the northern lights. I am nearing home.

I reach Woodruff at midnight. Suddenly I am afraid, now that I am but twenty miles from home. Afraid of what my father will say, afraid of being looked on as a stranger by my own people. I sit by a fire and think about myself and all the other young Indians. We just don't seem to fit in anywhere—certainly not among the whites, and not among the older people. I think again about the learned sociology professor and his professing. So many things seem to be clear now that I am away from school and do not have to worry about some man's opinion of my ideas. It is easy to think while looking at dancing flames.

Morning. I spend the day cleaning up, and buying some presents for my family with what is left of my money. Nothing much, but a gift is a gift, if a man buys it with his last quarter. I wait until evening, then start up the track toward home.

Christmas Eve comes in on a north wind. Snow clouds hang over the pines, and the night comes early. Walking along the railroad bed, I feel the calm peace of snowbound forests on either side of me. I take my time; I am back in a world where time does not mean so much now. I am alone; alone but not nearly so lonely as I was back on the campus at school. Those are never lonely who love the snow and the pines; never lonely when the pines are wearing white shawls and snow crunches coldly underfoot. In the woods I know there are the tracks of deer and rabbit; I know that if I leave the rails and go into the woods I shall find them. I walk along feeling glad because my legs are light and my feet seem to know that they are home. A deer comes out of the woods just ahead of me, and stands silhouetted on the rails. The North, I feel, has welcomed me home. I watch him and am glad that I do not wish for a gun. He goes into the woods quietly, leaving only the design of his tracks in the snow. I walk on. Now and then I pass a field, white under the night sky, with houses at the far end. Snow comes from the chimneys of the houses, and I try to tell what sort of wood each is burning by the smoke; some burn pine, others aspen, others tamarack. There is one from which comes black coal smoke that rises lazily and drifts out over the tops of the trees. I like to watch houses and try to imagine what might be happening in them.

Just as a light snow begins to fall, I cross the reservation boundary; somehow it seems as though I have stepped into another world. Deep woods in a white-and-black winter night. A faint trail leading to the village.

The railroad on which I stand comes from a city sprawled by a lake—a city with a million people who walk around without seeing one another; a city sucking the life from all the country around; a city with stores and police and intellectuals and criminals and movies and apartment houses; a city with its politics and libraries and zoos.

Laughing, I go into the woods. As I cross a frozen lake I begin to hear the drums. Soft in the night the drums beat. It is like the pulse beat of the world. The white line of the lake ends at a black forest, and above the trees the blue winds are dancing.

I come to the outlying houses of the village. Simple box houses, etched black in the night. From one or two windows soft lamp light falls on the snow. Christmas here, too, but it does not mean much; not much in the way of parties and presents. Joe Sky will get drunk. Alex Bodidash will buy his children red mittens and a new sled. Alex is a Carlisle man, and tries to keep his home up to white standards. White standards. Funny that my people should be ever falling farther behind. The more they try to imitate whites the more tragic the result. Yet they want us to be imitation white men. About all we imitate well are their vices.

The village is not a sight to instill pride, yet I am not ashamed; one can never be ashamed of his own people when he knows they have dreams as beautiful as white snow on a tall pine.

Father and my brother and sister are seated around the table as I walk in. Father stares at me for a moment, then I am in his arms, crying on his shoulder. I give them the presents I have brought, and my throat tightens as I watch my sister save carefully bits of red string from the packages. I hide my feelings by wrestling with my brother when he strikes my shoulder in token of affection. Father looks at me, and I know he has many questions, but he seems to know why I have come. He tells me to go on alone to the lodge, and he will follow.

I walk along the trail to the lodge, watching the northern lights forming in the heavens. White waving ribbons that seem to pulsate with the rhythm of the drums. Clean snow creaks beneath my feet, and a soft wind sighs through the trees, singing to me. Everything seems to say "Be happy! You are home now—you are free. You are among friends—we are your friends; we, the trees, and the snow, and the lights." I follow the trail to the lodge.

My feet are light, my heart seems to sing to the music, and I hold my head high. Across white snow fields blue winds are dancing.

Before the lodge door I stop, afraid. I wonder if my people will remember me. I wonder—"Am I Indian, or am I white?" I stand before the door a long time. I hear the ice groan on the lake, and remember the story of the old woman who is under the ice, trying to get out, so she can punish some runaway lovers. I think to myself, "If I am white I will not believe that story; if I am Indian, I will know that there is an old woman under the ice." I listen for a while, and I know that there is an old woman under the ice. I look again at the lights, and go in.

Inside the lodge there are many Indians. Some sit on benches around the walls, others dance in the center of the floor around a drum. Nobody seems to notice me. It seems as though I were among a people I have never seen before. Heavy women with long black hair. Women with children on their knees—small children that watch with intent black eyes the movements of the dancers, whose small faces are solemn and serene. The faces of the old people are serene, too, and their eyes are merry and bright. I look at the old men. Straight, dressed in dark trousers and beaded velvet vests, wearing soft moccasins. Dark, lined faces intent on the music. I wonder if I am at all like them. They dance on, lifting their feet to the rhythm of the drums, swaying lightly, looking upward. I look at their eyes, and am startled at the rapt attention to the rhythm of the music.

The dance stops. The men walk back to the walls, and talk in low tones or with their hands. There is little conversation, yet everyone seems to be sharing some secret. A woman looks at a small boy wandering away, and he comes back to her.

Strange, I think, and then remember. These people are not sharing words—they are sharing a mood. Everyone is happy. I am so used to white people that it seems strange so many people could be together without someone talking. These Indians are happy because they are together, and because the night is beautiful outside, and the music is beautiful. I try hard to forget school and white people, and be one of these—my people. I try to forget everything but the night, and it is a part of me; that I am one with my people and we are all a part of something universal. I watch eyes, and see now that the old people are speaking to me. They nod slightly, imperceptibly, and their eyes laugh into mine. I look around the room. All the eyes are friendly; they all laugh. No one questions my being here. The drums begin to beat again, and I catch the invitation in the eyes of the old men. My feet begin to lift to the rhythm, and I look out beyond the walls into the night and see the lights. I am happy. It is beautiful. I am home.

1938

D'ARCY MCNICKLE
1904–1977

D'Arcy McNickle was born on January 18, 1904, in St. Ignatius, Montana, to William McNickle and Philomene Parenteau. As he was to write later in life, his mother and her family came to Montana to escape the aftermath of the failed Métis Revolution in present-day Saskatchewan. (Descendants of Cree and French trappers, the Métis tried to maintain control over their lands when the Canadian government wanted them settled by European immigrants; the hostilities are often referred to as The Riel, or The Northwest, Rebellion.) Whether or not Philomene's father, Isidore Plante Parenteau, was an active participant in the revolt, and indeed the amount of "Indian blood" he possessed, are points of debate among some present-day scholars; however, the debate is noteworthy for one simple reason: it so clearly represents the resonating effects of McNickle's life and works. He raised controversy about contemporary Native American identity and issues at every turn. It is sufficient to note here that in April 1905 Philomene renounced all claim to lands or rights as a member of the Cree, and that she and her three children were adopted into the Salish (Flathead) tribe. There is no doubt that McNickle identified as a Native American, as he often articulated, and that he was dedicated to the causes of indigenous peoples.

His mother and father divorced, and in 1914 he was sent, as so many other Native American children in similar situations were sent, to a federal boarding school, Chemawa in Salem, Oregon. He was to write of this experience in several works, including two of his novels, for it epitomizes the central conflict and dilemma faced by generations of tribal peoples on this continent after the incursion of the European: the ever-present attempts to undermine native cultures, in this case through "re-education" camps, but also the immense attraction—the power, glitter and wealth—of the "modern" lifestyle offered as an alternative.

Although McNickle portrays federal boarding schools in very bleak terms, he continued with his education at the University of Montana, majoring in English, and in 1925 he sold his eighty-acre allotment on the reservation to fund his study at Oxford University. Although he did not finish his degree, McNickle became a respected scholar, academic, and activist: he wrote well-received books on Native American history, as well as three novels, and numerous short stories; he was the first director of the Newberry Library's Center for the History of the American Indian, which now is named after him; he helped found the Department of Anthropology at the University of Saskatchewan, Regina; and he was a founding member of the Congress of American Indians. These are but a few of the accomplishments that seem to indicate his total assimilation into mainstream society, as some scholars have argued.

McNickle was, however, a self-proclaimed, vocal proponent of the Native American right of self-determination, one who succeeded in urban America, true, but who remained self-identified with the lifeways he left on the reservation and who drew a voice from native verbal arts and tribal perspectives. As his novels repeatedly proclaim, American Indians want only to be left alone to pursue their futures in their own ways. As history demonstrates and McNickle dramatizes, when this basic human right is abrogated, bad things happen.

Yet, his fiction is not always bleak and humorless, nor tragic in the usual, historical sense, for it is always underscored by a consistent reaffirmation in modern times of native values and beliefs; he provides insights into cultures that exist today after tens of thousands of years, despite very obvious recent changes in the landscape of this continent. Moreover, as the story "Hard Riding" shows us, attempts to impose nontraditional, nonindigenous patterns of behavior on native populations can have its humorous side. Employing his favorite character, the well-intentioned Euro-American, McNickle is able to show the inherent folly of an ethnocentric approach to intercultural interaction: the power figure is rendered powerless by those who give him what he wants and is given an abject lesson in the subtle strength of self-determination at the same time.

John Lloyd Purdy
Western Washington University

PRIMARY WORKS

Fiction: *The Surrounded*, 1936; *Runner in the Sun: A Story of Indian Maize*, 1954; *Wind From an Enemy Sky*, 1978; *The Hawk Is Hungry and Other Stories*, 1993; *D'Arcy McNickle's The Hungry Generations: The Evolution of a Novel*, ed. Birgit Hans, 2007. Other Prose: *They Came Here First*, 1949; *Indian Man: A Life of Oliver La Farge*, 1972; *Native American Tribalism: Indian Survival and Renewals*, 1973.

Hard Riding

Riding his gray mare a hard gallop in the summer dust, Brinder Mather labored with thought which couldn't quite come into focus.

The horse labored too, its gait growing heavy as loose sand fouled its footing; but at each attempt to break stride into a trot, there was the prick of spur point, a jerk at the reins. It was a habit with the rider.

"Keep going! Earn your feed, you hammerhead!"

Brinder was always saying that his horses didn't earn their feed. Yet he was the hardest rider in the country.

Feeling as he did about horses, he quite naturally had doubts about Indians. And he had to work with Indians. He was their superintendent ... a nurse to their helplessness, was the way he sometimes thought of it.

It was getting toward sundown. The eastward mirror of the sky reflected orange and crimson flame thwarting the prismatic heavens. It was after supper, after a hard day at the Agency office, and Brinder was anxious to get his task done and be home to rest. The heat of the day had fagged him. His focusing thought came out in words, audibly.

"They've been fooling with the idea for a month, more than a month, and I still can't tell what they'll do. Somehow I've got to put it over. Either put it over or drop it. I'll tell them that. Take it or leave it...."

Ahead, another mile, he saw the white school house, the windows ablaze with the evening sun. He wondered if those he had called together would be there, if they would all be there. A full turn-out, he reasoned, would indicate that they were interested. He could be encouraged if he saw them all on hand.

As he drew nearer, he observed that a group stood waiting. He tried to estimate the number ... twelve or fifteen. Others were still coming. There were riders in the distance coming by other roads. The frown relaxed on his heavy, sun-reddened face. For the moment he was satisfied. He had called the entire Tribal Council of twenty, and evidently they would all be on hand. Good!

He let his horse slow to less than a canter for the first time in the three-mile ride from the Agency.

"Hello, boys. Everybody coming tonight? Let's go inside."

He strode, tall and dignified, through the group.

They smiled to his words, saying nothing. One by one they followed him into the school room. He was always for starting things with a rush; they always hung back. It was a familiar pattern. He walked to the teacher's desk and spread out before him a sheaf of paper which he had brought in a heavy envelope.

In five years one got to know something about Indians. Even in one's first job as superintendent of a Reservation, five years was a good schooling.

The important thing, the first thing to learn, was not to let them stall you. They would do it every time if you let them. They would say to a new idea, "Let us talk about that" or "Give us time. We'll think about it." One had to know when to cut short. Put it over or drop it. Take it or leave it.

Not realizing that at the start, he had let these crazy Mountain Indians stall on him a long time before he had begun to get results. He had come to them with a simple idea and only now, after five years, was it beginning to work.

Cattle ... that was the idea. Beef cattle. Blooded stock. Good bulls. Fall round-ups. The shipment East. Cash profits. In language as simple as that he had finally got them to see his point. He had a special liking for cattle. It began long before he had ever seen an Indian, back home in New York State. Boyhood reading about hard riding and fast shooting on the cattle trails ... that was what started it. Then, in his first job in the Indian Service, he had worked under a hard-minded Scotchman whose record as a stockman was unbeatable. He had learned the gospel from him. He learned to talk the lingo.

"Indians don't know, more than that don't give a damn, about dragging their feet behind a plow. Don't say as I blame 'em. But Indians'll always ride horses. They're born to that. And if they're going to ride horses they might as well be riding herd on a bunch of steers. It pays money."

He put it that way, following his Scotch preceptor. He put it to the Indians, to Washington officials, and to anybody he could buttonhole for a few minutes. It was a complete gospel. It was appropriations of money from Congress for cattle purchases. It won flattering remarks from certain visitors who were always around inquiring about Indian welfare. In time, it won over the Indians. It should have won them sooner.

The point was just that, not to let them stall on you. After five years he had learned his lesson. Put it over, or drop it.

He had taken off his broad-brimmed cattleman's hat and laid it on the desk beside his papers. The hat was part of the creed. He surveyed the score of wordless, pensive, buckskin-smelling Indians, some slouched forward, holding their big hats between their knees; others, hats on, silently smoking.

He had to put it across, this thing he wanted them to do. He had to do it now, tonight, or else drop it. That was what he had concluded.

"I think you fellows have learned a lot since I been with you. I appreciate the way you co-operate with me. Sometimes it's kinda hard to make things clear, but once you see what it means to you, you're all for it. I like that." He paused and mopped his brow. The schoolroom was an oven. The meeting should have been held outside—but never mind.

"In our stock association, we run our cattle together on a common range. We share the costs of riding range, rounding up, branding, and buying breeding bulls. Every time you sell a steer you pay a five-dollar fee into the pot, and that's what pays the bills. That's one of the things I had to tell you about. You didn't understand at first, but once you did, you went ahead. Today, it's paying dividends.

"You never had as much cash profit in your life before. Your steers are better beef animals, because the breeding is better. We got the class in bulls. And you get better prices because you can dicker with the buyers. But you know all that. I'm just reminding you."

Someone coughed in the back of the room and Brinder, always on guard, like the cowboys contending with rustlers and sheepmen he used to read about, straightened his back and looked sharply. But it was only a cough, repeated several times—an irritating, ineffective kind of cigarette cough. No one else in the audience made a sound. All were held in the spell of Brinder's words, or at any rate were waiting for him to finish what he had to say.

"We have one bad defect yet. You know what I mean, but I'll mention it just the same. In other words, fellows, we all of us know that every year a certain number of cattle disappear. The wolves don't get them and they don't die of natural causes. They are always strong, fat, two- or three-year-old steers that disappear, the kind that wolves don't monkey with and that don't die naturally. I ain't pointing my finger at anybody, but you know as well's I do that there's a certain element on the Reservation that don't deserve fresh meat, but always has it. They're too lazy or too ornery or they just don't know what it's all about. But they get fresh meat just the same.

"I want you fellows to get this. Let it sink in deep. Every time a fat steer goes to feed some Slick Steve too lazy to earn his keep, some of you are out around seventy-five, eighty dollars. You lose that much. Ponder that, you fellows."

He rustled the papers on the desk, looking for a row of figures: number of beef animals lost in five years (estimated), their money value, in round numbers. He hurled his figures at them, cudgeling.

"Some of you don't mind the loss. Because it's poor people getting the meat. It keeps someone from starving. That's what you say. What I say is — that ain't a proper way to look at it. First of all, because it's stealing and we can't go to countenancing stealing, putting up with it, I mean. Nobody has to starve, remember that. If you want to do something on your own book for the old people who can't work, you can. You can do what you like with your money. But lazy people, these Slick Steves who wouldn't work on a bet, nobody should give it easy to them, that's what I'm saying."

He waited a moment, letting the words find their way home. "There's a solution, as I told you last month. We want to set up a court, a court of Indian judges, and you will deal with these fellows in your own way. Give a few of them six months in jail to think it over, and times will begin to change around here. . . ."

That was the very point he had reached the last time he talked to the Council, a month before. He had gone no further, then, because they had begun asking questions, and from their questions he had discovered that they hadn't the least idea what he was driving at. Or so they made it appear. "If we have a tribal court," somebody would ask, "do we have to put somebody in jail?" That, obviously, was intentionally naive. It was intended to stall him off. Or some old man would say: "If somebody has to go to jail, let the Superintendent do it. Why should we have to start putting our own people in jail?" Such nonsense as that had been talked.

Finally, the perennial question of money came up. Would the Government pay for the court? A treacherous question, and he had answered without flinching.

"That's another thing," he had said brightly. "We're going to get away from the idea of the Government paying for everything. Having your own business this way, making a profit from it, you can pay for this yourselves. That will make you independent. It will be your own court, not the Government's court, not the Superintendent's court. No. The court will be supported by the fee money you pay when you sell a steer."

That speech broke up the meeting. It was greeted by a confusion of talk in the native tongue which gradually subsided in form of one speaker, one of the ancients, who obviously was a respected leader. Afterwards, a young, English-speaking tribesman translated.

"The old man here, Looking Glass, says the Gover'ment don't give us nothing for nothing. The money it spends on us, that's our own money, he says. It belongs to us and they keep it there at Washington, and nobody can say how much it is or how much has been lost. He says, where is all that money that they can't afford to pay for this court? That's what he says."

There was the snare which tripped up most Agency plans, scratch an old Indian, and the reaction was always the same. "Where's the money the Government owes us? Where's our land? Where's our treaty?" They were like a whistle with only one stop, those old fellows. Their tune was invariable, relentless, and shrill. That was why one dreaded holding a meeting when the old men were present. Now the young fellows, who understood Agency plans....

Anyhow, here he was trying it again, going over the plan with great care and patience. Much of the misunderstanding had been ironed out in the meantime. So he had been led to believe.

"This court will put an end to all this trouble," he was going on, trying to gauge the effect of his words, watching for a reaction. At last it came. One of the old men was getting to his feet.

He was a small man, emaciated by age and thin living, yet neat looking. His old wife, obviously, took good care of his clothes, sewed buckskin patches on his overalls and kept him in new moccasins. He talked firmly, yet softly, and not for very long. He sat down as soon as he had finished and let the interpreter translate for him.

"The old man here, Big Face, says the court, maybe, is all right. They have talked it over among themselves, and maybe it's all right. Our agent, he says, is a good man. He rides too fast. He talks too fast. But he has a good heart, so maybe the court is all right. That's what Big Face says."

The words were good, and Brinder caught himself smiling, which was bad practice when dealing with the old fellows. They were masters at laying traps for the unwary—that, too, he had learned in five years. Their own expressions never changed, once they got going, and you could never tell what might be in their minds.

Just the same, he felt easier. Big Face, the most argumentative of the lot, had come around to accept this new idea, and that was something gained. The month had not been lost.

He had something more to say. He was getting to his feet again, giving a tug to his belt and looking around, as if to make sure of his following. He had been appointed spokesman. That much was clear.

He made a somewhat longer speech, in which he seemed to express agitation, perhaps uncertainty. One could never be sure of tone values. Sometimes the most excitable sounding passages of this strange tongue were very tame in English. Brinder had stopped smiling and waited for the translation.

"Big Face here says there's only one thing they can't decide about. That's about judges. Nobody wants to be a judge. That's what they don't like. Maybe the court is all right, but nobody wants to be judge."

Brinder was rather stumped by that. He rose to his feet, quickly, giving everyone a sharp glance. Was this the trap?

"Tell the old man I don't understand that. It is an honor, being a judge. People pay money to be a judge in some places. Tell Big Face I don't understand his objection."

The old man was on his feet as soon as the words had been translated for him.

"It's like this. To be a judge, you got to be about perfect. You got to know everything, and you got to live up to it. Otherwise, you got nothing to say to anybody who does wrong. Anybody who puts himself up to be that good, he's just a liar. And people will laugh at him. We are friends among ourselves and nobody interferes in another person's business. That's how it is, and nobody wants to set himself up and be a judge. That's what Big Face says."

There it was—as neatly contrived a little pitfall as he had ever seen. He had to admire it—all the time letting himself get furious. Not that he let them see it. No, in five years, he had learned that much. Keep your head, and when in doubt, talk your head off. He drew a deep breath and plunged into an explanation of all the things he had already explained, reminding them of the money they lost each year, of the worthless fellows who were making an easy living from their efforts, of the proper way to deal with the problem. He repeated all the arguments and threw in as many more as he could think of.

"You have decided all this. You agree the court is a good thing. But how can you have a court without judges? It's the judges that make a court."

He couldn't tell whether he was getting anywhere or not—in all likelihood, not. They were talking all together once more and it didn't look as if they were paying much attention to him. He waited.

"What's it all about?" he finally asked the interpreter, a young mixed-blood, who was usually pretty good about telling Brinder which way the wind of thought blew among the old people.

"I can't make out," the interpreter murmured, drawing closer to Brinder. "They are saying lots of things. But I think they're going to decide on the judges—they've got some kind of plan—watch out for it—now, one of the old men will speak."

It was Big Face raising to his feet once more. Looking smaller, more wizened than ever. The blurring twilight of the room absorbed some of his substance and made Brinder feel that he was losing his grip on the situation. A shadow is a difficult adversary and Big Face was rapidly turning into one.

"The agent wants this court. He thinks it's a good thing. So we have talked some more—and we agree. We will have this court." He paused briefly, allowing Brinder only a moment's bewilderment.

"Only we couldn't decide who would be judge. Some said this one, some said that one. It was hard...."

Brinder coughed. "Have you decided on any one, Big Face?" He no longer knew which way things were drifting but only hoped for the best.

The old fellow's eyes, misted by age, actually twinkled. In the body of councillors somebody laughed and coughed in the same breath. Feet stirred and bodies shifted. Something was in the air. Haltingly, Big Face named the men—the most amazing trio the Reservation had to offer.

"Walks-in-the-Ground—Jacob Gopher—Twisted Horn ..."

In the silence that followed, Brinder tried hard to believe he had heard the wrong names. A mistake had been made. It was impossible to take it seriously. These three men—no, it was impossible! The first, an aged imbecile dripping saliva—ready to die! The second, stone deaf and blind! The third, an utter fool, a half-witted clown, to whom no one listened.

"You mean this?" Brinder still could not see the full situation, but was afraid that the strategy was deliberate and final.

"Those will be the judges of this court," Big Face replied, smiling his usual friendly way.

"But these men can't be judges! They are too old, or else too foolish. No one will listen to them...," Brinder broke off short. He saw that he had stated the strategy of the old men especially as they had intended it. His friendliness withered away.

Big Face did not hesitate, did not break off smiling. "It is better, we think, that fools should be judges. If people won't listen to them, no one will mind."

Brinder had nothing to say, not just then. He let the front legs of his chair drop to the floor, picked up his hat. His face had paled. After five years—still to let this happen.... Using great effort, he turned it off as a joke. "Boys, you should of elected me judge to your kangaroo court. I would have made a crackerjack."

The Indians laughed and didn't know what he meant, not exactly. But maybe he was right.

1989

Navajo Painting and the "Studio Style" of Native American Art in the 1930s

IN SEPTEMBER 1932, NEWLY MINTED CHICAGO ART INSTITUTE GRADUATE DOROTHY Dunn (1903-1992) arrived in Santa Fe, New Mexico, to join the staff of the Santa Fe Indian School, a federal boarding school administered by the Bureau of Indian Affairs. Ostensibly hired to teach fifth grade, Dunn was actually intent on beginning an arts program that would encourage Native Americans of the Southwest to reclaim indigenous art forms and techniques. The goal was to free self-expression from the stereotypical images and symbols that she felt reduced Native American identities to romanticized "curios." Instead, Dunn wanted to encourage her students to create authentic (though not realistic) depictions of their tribal rituals, values, and emblems. Her mission in Santa Fe coincided with a reform initiative throughout Native American education that did away with the Bureau's coercive assimilation agenda—the original charter of the Santa Fe Indian School—to emphasize instead cultural self-awareness and heritage preservation.

Formally christened the Studio School at the beginning of Dunn's second year, her classroom and the style it promoted garnered immediate international attention and helped create a serious market for painting by Native American artists. Although Dunn left the Studio after only five years, her instructional principles dominated Native American fine arts pedagogy for decades to come. (The Studio School itself continued under the direction of Dunn's associate, Geronima Cruz Montoya, until the early 1960s, when it was succeeded by the Institute of American Indian Arts, or the IAIA). Equally important, the aesthetic vision Dunn promulgated proved the single-most defining measure of Native American subjectivity in painting until the 1960s, a fact that remains controversial given that Dunn herself was of Anglo-European ancestry. Because her idea of what constituted "true" indigenous expression was grounded in the same reverence for primitivism that inspired Picasso to steep his work in African tribal iconography, Dunn has been accused of shaping an oversimplified, excessively decorative, and historically/politically disengaged body of work in which the "traditions" being reconstituted are inflected with decidedly "modern" notions of their simplicity and elemental purity. While the argument demands discussion, it is also undeniable that as an institution, the Studio provided a space through which an incredible number of significant Native American talents discovered their *métier*—and while at an average age of fifteen, it should be remembered. Many of Dunn's students graduated from her tutelage to enjoy successful careers, including several of the Navajo painters represented here:

Harrison Begay (Haskay Yah Ne Yah) (b. 1914), Andrew Tsihnahjinnie (1916–2000), and Gerald Nailor (Toh Yah) (1917–1952). Those who did not pursue livelihoods in the arts, such as Mary Ellen—about whom not much is known—have nevertheless been rediscovered in recent years thanks to the assiduous collecting and advocacy Dunn maintained even after her 1937 departure from the Studio.

As is quickly apparent from the paintings reproduced in the following pages, the essential characteristic of the Studio style is the flat, two-dimensional perspective that eschews shade, perspective, portraiture, and other techniques of representational realism. Instead, the emphasis is on abstraction, linearity, formal balance, and negative space. These traits are the style's most obvious affinities with modernist painting in general, with the overall insistence on figuration suggesting a sort of sleek, archetypal essence of existence uncluttered by complexity and unhampered by modern indirection and purposeless. Dunn was not promoting the Studio School as a specifically modernist movement, however. She cited anthropological evidence to insist that the "naturalistic"[1] style, as she called it, was *the* authentic method of Native American expression: because it could be found on wall and rock painting dating back centuries, it represented a linkage to the past through which contemporary Native peoples could reach back beyond their history of white exploitation and domination to reconnect with "something elemental and real to be felt very deeply, if not quite understood," as she insisted in 1935. In this regard she was not unlike contemporaries who promoted African or Asian folk materials as models through which one could transcend the sullying forces of history.

Where Dunn did differ from many in the modern arts movement was in her aversion to incorporating past-day elements into the work, not for her found objects and contemporary effluvia in collage form—no newspapers, magazine bills, dime-store novels, as is often found in modernist painting. "Any production which revealed copy of unworthy exotic influences was discouraged," Dunn would recall in her lone major study, *American Indian Painting of the Southwest and Plains Areas* (1968), "not by forbiddance, but by suggestion of a variety of choices of tribal elements which might make a particular painting more authentic and interesting." In other words, as scholar W. Jackson Rushing puts it, Dunn "was subtly prescriptive, if well-intentioned."

Dunn's insistence on avoiding "exotic" elements accounts for the basic congruence of content, style, and medium among Studio students. The subject matter tends to be rituals and ceremonies. Even when the scope approaches a panorama—as in Sybil Yazzie's "Going to the Yeibichai" (1937)—there is rarely any semblance of landscape or vista. (Two exceptions might be Stanley Mitchell's "Along the Lake" [1936] and Quincy Tahoma's "Riders Resting" [1937].) Dunn was also adamant that students not employ models to render the human body in proportion or detail, which accounts for the emblematic quality of the

---

[1]What Dunn means by "naturalistic" is by no means comparable to literary naturalism, which emphasizes the Darwinian brutality of nature as opposed to its supposed balance and rationality. Nor was the Studio the only expression of the "flat art" style; preceding Dunn's students were turn-of-the century artists in San Ildefonso Pueblo and a group of youth from the St. Patrick's Mission School in Anadarko, Oklahoma, known variously as the Kiowa Five or Kiowa Six.

imagery in, for example, Nailor's untitled 1938 selection and Narciso Abeyta (Na So De)'s contemporaneous "Antelope Hunt" (in which the central antelope appears to be abstracted into the shape of a palette even). The Studio also advocated watercolor and tempera because texturally they reflected the harmonious relationship between land, sky, and self. Although she did not disallow students from employing oils, she did encourage them to dilute the paint with turpentine to flatten their color into "earth and vegetable" hues.

By the end of her short tenure at the Studio School, Dunn had brought together students from nearly a dozen different tribes. Navajo youth were a significant portion of the population, and as *American Indian Painting of the Southwest and Plains Areas* makes clear, Dunn prided herself on knowledge of their folk traditions, sandpainting in particular. The artwork here captures one of the more obvious instances of how mentorship and patronage can affect minority expression. As a teacher, Dorothy Dunn was in an even greater position of influence over the development of the style that the Studio School advanced than, say, patrons Carl Van Vechten and Charlotte Osgood Mason were with the aesthetics of the Harlem Renaissance movement. After the reputation of Dunn's program was severely reassessed in the 1960s, most former students would make a point to remember Dunn as a kindly maternal figure who gave them the tools and time to hone their talents. In the end, lingering questions over the construction of Studio Style authenticity do not mitigate the fact that the program produced works of great beauty. The accomplishments of her students demonstrate an enduring conundrum of art in general: while no work can be understood outside of the context of its production—something many modernist artists tried to deny—neither is its significance entirely contained by it.

Kirk Curnutt
Troy University-Montgomery, Alabama

GERARD NAILOR (TOH YAH)
1917–1952

untitled (1938)

Museum of Indian Arts and Culture

MARY ELLEN
1884–1980

Navajo Women with Corn (1941)

ANDREW TSIHNAHJINNIE
1916–2000

Fire Dance (1934)

Museum of Indian Arts and Culture

HARRISON BEGAY (HASKAY YAH NE YAH)
B. 1917

Navajos at a Dance (1939) or "Yeibicai" (1939)

Museum of Indian Arts and Culture

ROSALIE JAMES
UNKNOWN DATES

Night Singers and Drummer (1936)

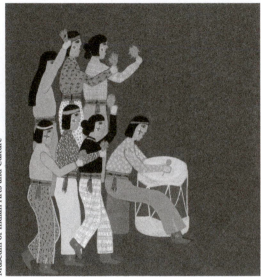

Museum of Indian Arts and Culture

SYBIL YAZZIE
UNKNOWN DATES

Going to the Yeibichai (1937)

QUINCY TAHOMA
1917–1956

Riders Resting (1937)

Museum of Indian Arts and Culture

■ STANLEY C. MITCHELL (CHE-CHILLY-TSOSIE) ■
B. 1920

Along the Lake (1936)

Museum of Indian Arts and Culture

NARCISO ABEYTA (NA SO DE)
1918–1998

Antelope Hunt (1938)

Museum of Indian Arts and Culture

ROBERT PENN WARREN
1905–1989

Robert Penn Warren was born and raised in Guthrie, Kentucky, a small town in the "Black Patch" tobacco country near the Tennessee border. Early on he developed deep loves for the countryside and for reading, particularly fiction and history. After failing his physical examination for the U.S. Naval Academy because of an eye injury, in 1921 he entered Vanderbilt University instead.

Warren's talent for writing was quickly noticed by his teachers, including John Crowe Ransom and Donald Davidson. Before long, he was an active member of the "Fugitives," a literary group centered at the university that met regularly to discuss philosophy and poetry. Warren at this time began writing his own verse and became close friends with Allen Tate, another "Fugitive" whose literary career, like Warren's, was then just beginning.

By the time he graduated from Vanderbilt in 1925 and was off to graduate study at the University of California, Berkeley (and later at Yale and then Oxford with a Rhodes scholarship), Warren had committed himself to a career of writing. His years at Vanderbilt with the Fugitives had been crucial in his early development. Perhaps most important, he established during this time a profound conviction for the worth of artistic pursuit, seeing, in his own words, "that poetry was a vital activity, that it related to ideas and life." Moreover, particularly through his friendship with Allen Tate, he immersed himself in the tremendous vitality and experimentation of literary modernism and began experimenting to discover his own poetic voice. Probably best known for his novel *All the King's Men*, Warren also published ten other novels, fifteen volumes of poetry, two plays, a biography of John Brown, and numerous books and essays on cultural and literary criticism, including the influential anthologies he edited with Cleanth Brooks, *Understanding Poetry*, *Understanding Fiction*, and *Modern Rhetoric*.

Warren's early poems show the strong influences of Tate and T. S. Eliot, and also, by way of Eliot and John Crowe Ransom, of the seventeenth-century metaphysical poets. His first volume of verse, *Thirty-Six Poems*, appeared in 1935, followed by *Eleven Poems on the Same Theme* (1942) and *Selected Poems: 1923–1943* (1944). Most of the poems from these volumes, as James Justus has pointed out, show Warren as a master craftsman experimenting with models and conventions of others and along the way "slowly learning how to reinvigorate models out of his own needs and with his own voice."

Not all of Warren's energies during this time were going exclusively into poetry. In 1930 he began his distinguished academic career by accepting an appointment at Southwestern College in Memphis, followed by appointments at Vanderbilt University (1931) and Louisiana State University (1934), where with Cleanth Brooks he edited the *Southern Review* until 1942. In 1942, he became a professor of English at the University of Minnesota, where he stayed until 1950 when he accepted a position at Yale University. Warren retired from Yale in 1973.

During the 1930s and 1940s, Warren was doing a great deal of writing other than poetry. He collaborated on several important anthologies of literature and rhetoric, and, even more importantly, began his career as writer of fiction. *Night Rider*, his first novel, appeared in 1939, followed by *At Heaven's Gate* (1943), his masterpiece, *All the King's Men* (1946), and *The Circus in the Attic and Other Stories* (1948). Seven other novels subsequently appeared along with a number of volumes of literary and cultural criticism.

Meanwhile, Warren's poetic output ceased from 1944 until 1953, when he brought out *Brother to Dragons: A Tale in Verse and Voices*. This striking work, an imaginative reconstruction of a historical event involving Thomas Jefferson's nephew written in voices, dialogue, and colloquy, marks the beginning of Warren's major phase as poet. *Brother to Dragons* opened up "a whole new sense of poetry," he later admitted. No less than twelve volumes of Warren's verse followed its publication. Warren's quest in his poetry was driven by a passion both to know himself and his world and to discover meaning and continuities despite the resistance of a naturalistic universe. This effort to achieve understanding, to transfigure the factual into the interpretative, lies at the heart of Warren's imaginative vision. "In this century, and moment, of mania," he writes in *Audubon*, "tell me a story."

Robert H. Brinkmeyer, Jr.
University of Arkansas

PRIMARY WORKS

Fiction: *Night Rider*, 1939; *At Heaven's Gate*, 1943; *All the King's Men*, 1946; *The Circus in the Attic and Other Stories*, 1948; *World Enough and Time*, 1950; *Band of Angels*, 1955; *The Cave*, 1959; *Wilderness*, 1961; *Flood: A Romance of Our Time*, 1961; *Meet Me in the Green Glen*, 1971; *A Place to Come To*, 1977. Poetry: *Thirty-Six Poems*, 1935; *Brother to Dragons: A Tale in Verse and Voices*, 1953; *Audubon: A Vision*, 1969; *Chief Joseph of the Nez Perce*, 1983; *New and Selected Poems*, 1923–1985, 1985. Nonfiction: *John Brown: The Making of a Martyr*, 1929; *Segregation: The Inner Conflict in the South*, 1957; *Selected Essays*, 1958; *The Legacy of the Civil War*, 1961; *Who Speaks for the Negro?*, 1965; *Homage to Theodore Dreiser*, 1971; *Democracy and Poetry*, 1975; *Jefferson Davis Gets His Citizenship Back*, 1975; *Portrait of a Father*, 1988; *New and Selected Essays*, 1989. Anthologies (with Cleanth Brooks): *Understanding Poetry*, 1938; *Understanding Fiction*, 1943; *Modern Rhetoric*, 1949.

Founding Fathers, Early-Nineteenth-Century Style, Southeast U.S.A.

They were human, they suffered, wore long black coat and gold
    watch chains.
They stare from daguerreotype with severe reprehension,
Or from genuine oil, and you'd never guess any pain
In those merciless eyes that now remark our own time's sad
    declension.   5

Some composed declarations, remembering Jefferson's language.
Knew pose of the patriot, left hand in crook of the spine or

With finger to table, while right invokes the Lord's just rage.
There was always a grandpa, or cousin at least, who had been a
    real Signer.   10

Some were given to study, read Greek in the forest, and these
Longed for an epic to do their own deeds right honor;
Were Nestor[1] by pigpen, in some tavern brawl played Achilles.[2]
In the ring of Sam Houston[3] they found, when he died, one word
    engraved: *Honor.*   15

Their children were broadcast, like millet seed flung in a wind
    flare.
Wives died, were dropped like old shirts in some corner of
    country.   20
Said, "Mister," in bed, the child-bride; hadn't known what to find
    there;
Wept all the next morning for shame; took pleasure in silk; wore
    the keys to the pantry.

"Will die in these ditches if need be," wrote Bowie, at the Alamo.   25
And did, he whose left foot, soft-catting, came forward, and breath
    hissed:
Head back, gray eyes narrow, thumb flat along knife-blade,
    blade low.
"Great gentleman," said Henry Clay,[4] "and a patriot." Portrait by
    Benjamin West.[5]   30
Or take those, the nameless, of whom no portraits remain,
No locket or seal ring, though somewhere, broken and rusted,
In attic or earth, the long Decherd,[6] stock rotten, has lain;
Or the mold-yellow Bible, God's Word, in which, in their strength,
    they also trusted.   35

Some wrestled the angel, and took a fall by the corncrib.
Fought the brute, stomp-and-gouge, but knew they were doomed
    in that glory.
All night, in sweat, groaned; fell at last with spit red and a
    cracked rib.   40
How sweet then the tears! Thus gentled, they roved the dark land
    with the old story.

---

[1] A king of Pylos in Greek legend; hero of the Trojan War.

[2] A warrior in Greek legend; hero of Homer's *Iliad.*

[3] Soldier and statesman of Tennessee and Texas, 1793–1863; commander-in-chief of Texan forces in war with Mexico, 1836.

[4] American statesman, 1777–1852; pivotal figure in political controversies concerning slavery and sectionalism in decades before Civil War.

[5] American painter, 1738–1820; best known for his historical paintings.

[6] Flintlock Kentucky rifle.

Some prospered, had black men and acres, and silver on table,
But remembered the owl call, the smell of burnt bear fat on
    dusk-air. 45
Loved family and friends, and stood it as long as able—
"But money and women, too much is ruination, am Arkansas-
    bound." So went there.

One of mine was a land shark, or so the book with scant praise 50
Denominates him. "A man large and shapeless,
Like a sack of potatoes set on a saddle," it says,
"Little learning but shrewd, not well trusted." Rides thus out of
    history, neck fat and napeless.

One fought Shiloh[7] and such, got cranky, would fiddle all night. 55
The boys nagged for Texas. "God damn it, there's nothing, God
    damn it,
In Texas"—but took wagons, went, and to prove he was right,
Stayed a year and a day—"hell, nothing in Texas"—had proved it,
    came back to black vomit, 60

And died, and they died, and are dead, and now their voices
Come thin, like the last cricket in frost-dark, in grass lost,
With nothing to tell us for our complexity of choices,
But beg us only one word to justify their own old life-cost.

So let us bend ear to them in this hour of lateness, 65
And what they are trying to say, try to understand,
And try to forgive them their defects, even their greatness,
For we are their children in the light of humanness, and under the
    shadow of God's closing hand.

                                 1956

Infant Boy at Midcentury

I. When the Century Dragged

When the century dragged, like a great wheel stuck at dead center;
When the wind that had hurled us our half-century sagged now,
And only velleity of air somewhat snidely nagged now,
With no certain commitment to compass, or quarter: then you
    chose to enter. 5

[7]Civil War battle, April 6 and 7, 1862, in
southern Tennessee.

You enter an age when the neurotic clock-tick
Of midnight competes with the heart's pulsed assurance of power.
You have entered our world at scarcely its finest hour.
And smile now life's gold Apollonian[1] smile at a sick dialectic.

You enter at the hour when the dog returns to his vomit,   10
And fear's moonflower spreads, white as girl-thigh, in our dusk of
    compromise;
When posing for pictures, arms linked, the same smile in their
    eyes,
Good and Evil, to iron out all differences, stage their meeting at
    summit.   15

You come in the year when promises are broken,
And petal fears the late, as fruit the early frost-fall;
When the young expect little, and the old endure total recall,
But discover no logic to justify what they had taken, or forsaken.   20

But to take and forsake now you're here, and the heart will
    compress
Like stone when we see that rosy heel learn,
With its first step, the apocalyptic power to spurn
Us, and our works and days, and onward, prevailing, pass   25

To pause, in high pride of unillusioned manhood,
At the gap that gives on the new century, and land,
And with calm heart and level eye command
That dawning perspective and possibility of human good.

2. Brightness of Distance

You will read the official histories—some true, no doubt.   30
Barring total disaster, the record will speak from the shelf.
And if there's disaster, disaster will speak for itself.
So all of our lies will be truth, and the truth vindictively out.

Remember our defects, we give them to you gratis.
But remember that ours is not the worst of times.   35
Our country's convicted of follies rather than crimes—
We throw out baby with bath, drop the meat in the fire where the
    fat is.

[1]Harmonious, ordered, balanced.

And in even such stew and stink as Tacitus[2]
Once wrote of, his generals, gourmets, pimps, poltroons,   40
He found persons of private virtue, the old-fashioned stout ones
Who would bow the head to no blast; and we know that such are
    yet with us.

He was puzzled how virtue found perch past confusion and wrath;
How even Praetorian[3] brutes, blank of love, as of hate,   45
Proud in their craftsman's pride only, held a last gate,
And died, each back unmarred as though at the barracks bath.

And remember that many among us wish you well;
And once, on a strange shore, an old man, toothless and through,
Groped a hand from the lattice of personal disaster to touch you.   50
He sat on the sand for an hour; said *ciao, bello,*[4] as evening fell.

And think, as you move past our age that grudges and grieves,
How eyes, purged of envy, will follow your sunlit chance.
Eyes will brighten to follow your brightness and dwindle of
    distance.   55
From privacy of fate, eyes will follow, as though from the shadow
    of leaves.

                                          1956

The Leaf

A

Here the fig lets down the leaf, the leaf
Of the fig five fingers has, the fingers
Are broad, spatulate, stupid,
Ill-formed, and innocent—but of a hand, and the hand,

To hide me from the blaze of the wide world, drops,   5
Shamefast, down. I am
What is to be concealed. I lurk
In the shadow of the fig. Stop.
Go no further. This is the place.

To this spot I bring my grief.   10
Human grief is the obscenity to be hidden by the leaf.

---

[2]Historian of imperial Rome, c. 55 B.C.–c. A.D. 118.   [4]Italian: Goodbye, beautiful one.
[3]Referring to the bodyguard of the Roman emperor.

B

We have undergone ourselves, therefore
What more is to be done for Truth's sake? I

Have watched the deployment of ants, I
Have conferred with the flaming mullet in a deep place.   15

Near the nesting place of the hawk, among
Snag-rock, high on the cliff, I have seen
The clutter of annual bones, of hare, vole, bird, white
As chalk from sun and season, frail
As the dry grass stem. On that   20

High place of stone I have lain down, the sun
Beat, the small exacerbation
Of dry bones was what my back, shirtless and bare, knew. I saw

The hawk shudder in the high sky, he shudders
To hold position in the blazing wind, in relation to   25
The firmament, he shudders and the world is a metaphor, his eye
Sees, white, the flicker of hare-scut, the movement of vole.

Distance is nothing, there is no solution, I
Have opened my mouth to the wind of the world like wine,
    I wanted   30
To taste what the world is, wind dried up

The live saliva of my tongue, my tongue
Was like a dry leaf in my mouth.

Destiny is what you experience, that
Is its name and definition, and is your name, for   35
The wide world lets down the hand in shame:
Here is the human shadow, there, of the wide world, the flame.

C

The world is fruitful, In this heat
The plum, black yet bough-bound, bursts, and the gold ooze is,
Of bees, joy, the gold ooze has striven   40
Outward, it wants again to be of
The goldness of air and—blessedly—innocent. The grape
Weakens at the juncture of the stem. The world

Is fruitful, and I, too,
In that I am the father   45
Of my father's father's father. I,
Of my father, have set the teeth on edge. But
By what grape? I have cried out in the night.

From a further garden, from the shade of another tree,
My father's voice, in the moment when the cicada ceases, has
  called to me.   50

D

The voice blesses me for the only
Gift I have given: *teeth set on edge.*

In the momentary silence of the cicada,
I can hear the appalling speed,   55
In space beyond stars, of
Light. It is

A sound like wind.

                1968

Evening Hawk

From plane of light to plane, wings dipping through
Geometries and orchids that the sunset builds,
Out of the peak's black angularity of shadow, riding
The last tumultuous avalanche of
Light above pines and the guttural gorge,   5
The hawk comes.
      His wing
Scythes down another day, his motion
Is that of the honed steel-edge, we hear
The crashless fall of stalks of Time.   10

The head of each stalk is heavy with the gold of our error.

Look! Look! he is climbing the last light
Who knows neither Time nor error, and under
Whose eye, unforgiving, the world, unforgiven, swings
Into shadow.   15

      Long now,
The last thrush is still, the last bat
Now cruises in his sharp hieroglyphics. His wisdom
Is ancient, too, and immense. The star
Is steady, like Plato, over the mountain.   20

If there were no wind we might, we think, hear
The earth grind on its axis, or history
Drip in darkness like a leaking pipe in the cellar.

         1975

Heart of Autumn

Wind finds the northwest gap, fall comes.
Today, under gray cloud-scud and over gray
Wind-flicker of forest, in perfect formation, wild geese
Head for a land of warm water, the *boom*, the lead pellet.

Some crumple in air, fall. Some stagger, recover control,   5
Then take the last glide for a far glint of water. None
Knows what has happened. Now, today, watching
How tirelessly V upon V arrows the season's logic,

Do I know my own story? At least, they know
When the hour comes for the great wing-beat. Sky-strider,   10
Star-strider—they rise, and the imperial utterance,
Which cries out for distance, quivers in the wheeling sky.

That much they know, and in their nature know
The path of pathlessness, with all the joy
Of destiny fulfilling its own name.   15
I have known time and distance, but not why I am here.

Path of logic, path of folly, all
The same—and I stand, my face lifted now skyward,
Hearing the high beat, my arms outstretched in the tingling
Process of transformation, and soon tough legs,   20

With folded feet, trail in the sounding vacuum of passage,
And my heart is impacted with a fierce impulse
To unwordable utterance—
Toward sunset, at a great height.

         1978

Amazing Grace in the Back Country

In the season of late August star-fall,
When the first crickets crinkled the dark,
There by woods, where oaks of the old forest-time
Yet swaggered and hulked over upstarts, the tent
Had been pitched, no bigger than one of   5
Some half-bankrupt carnival come
To town with fat lady, human skeleton, geek,
Man-woman and moth-eaten lion, and one
Boa constrictor for two bits seen
Fed a young calf or what; plus a brace   10
Of whores to whom menopause now
Was barely a memory, one with gold teeth and one
With game gam, but both
With aperture ready to serve
Any late-lingerers, and leave   15
A new and guaranteed brand of syphilis handy—yes,

The tent old and yellowed and patched,
Lit inside by three wire-hung gasoline lamps
That outside, through threadbare canvas, were muted to gold.
Here no carnival now—the tabernacle   20
To the glory of God the Most High, for now corn
Was laid by, business slack, such business as was, and
The late-season pain gnawing deep at the human bone
As the season burned on to its end.

God's Word and His glory—and I, aged twelve,   25
Sat there while an ex-railroad engineer
Turned revivalist shouted the Threat and the Promise, with sweat
On his brow, shirt plastered to belly, and
Eyes a-glaze with the mania of joy.
And now by my knees crouched some old-fool dame   30
In worn-out black silk, there crouching with tears
In here eyes as she tugged me to kneel
And save my pore twelve-year-old soul
Before too late. She wept.
She wept and she prayed, and I knew I was damned,   35
Who was guilty of all short of murder,
At least in my heart and no alibi there, and once
I had walked down a dark street, lights out in houses,
Uttering, "Lust—lust—lust,"
Like an invocation, out loud—and the word   40
So lovely, fresh-minted.

I saw others fall as though stricken. I heard
The shout of salvation. I stared
In the red-rimmed, wet eyes of the crazy old dame,
Whose name I never remembered, but knew   45
That she loved me—the Pore Little Lamb—and I thought
How old bones now creaked in God's name.

But the Pore Little Lamb, he hardened his heart,
Like a flint nigger-head[1] rounded slick in a creek-bed
By generations of flood, and suddenly   50
I found myself standing, then
Ran down an aisle, and outside,
Where cool air and dark filled my lungs, and fifty
Yards off, with my brow pressed hard
On the scaly bark of a hickory tree,   55
Vomited. Fumbling
In darkness, I found the spring
And washed my mouth. Humped there,

And knowing damnation, I stared
Through interstices of black brush to the muted gold glow   60
Of God's canvas, till in
The last hymn of triumph rose voices, and hearts
Burst with joy at amazing grace so freely given,
And moving on into darkness,

Voices sang of amazing grace, singing as they   65
Straggled back to the village, where voice after voice died away,
As singer by singer, in some dark house,
Found bed and lay down,
And tomorrow would rise and do all the old things to do,
Until that morning they would not rise, not ever.   70
And now, when all voices were stilled and the lamps
Long out in the tent, and stars
Had changed place in the sky, I yet lay
By the spring with one hand in cold black water
That showed one star in reflection, alone—and lay   75
Wondering and wondering how many
A morning would I rise up to greet,
And what grace find.

But that was long years ago. I was twelve years old then.

                                                                  1978

[1]Dark-colored rock.

Fear and Trembling

The sun now angles downward, and southward.
The summer, that is, approaches its final fulfillment.
The forest is silent, no wind-stir, bird-note, or word.
It is time to meditate on what the season has meant.

But what is the meaningful language for such meditation?   5
What is a word but wind through the tube of the throat?
Who defines the relation between the word *sun* and the sun?
What word has glittered on whitecap? Or lured blossom out?

Walk deeper, foot soundless, into the forest.
Stop, breath bated. Look southward, and up, where high leaves   10
Against sun, in vernal translucence, yet glow with the freshest
Young tint of the lost spring. Here now nothing grieves.

Can one, in fact, meditate in the heart, rapt and wordless?
Or find his own voice in the towering gust now from northward?
When boughs toss—is it in joy or pain and madness?   15
The gold leaf—is it whirled in anguish or ecstasy skyward?

Can the heart's meditation wake us from life's long sleep,
And instruct us how foolish and fond was our labor spent—
Us who now know that only at death of ambition does the deep
Energy crack crust, spurt forth, and leap   20

From grottoes, dark—and from the caverned enchainment?

                                                                 1980

■   ALLEN TATE   ■
                           1899–1979

John Orley Allen Tate was born in Kentucky in 1899 and attended Vanderbilt University in 1918. There he was instructed by John Crowe Ransom and Donald Davidson, was a friend of Robert Penn Warren, and helped to create *The Fugitive* (1922–1925), the most influential poetry magazine of literary modernism in the South. In 1924 he went to New York to become a freelance writer; he wrote many book reviews and two biographies, *Stonewall Jackson* (1928) and *Jefferson Davis* (1929). After the publication of *Mr. Pope and Other Poems* (1928), Tate received a Guggenheim Fellowship, which he spent in Europe among the

American expatriate literary community. He returned to live in the South, where he contributed to *I'll Take My Stand: The South and the Agrarian Tradition* (1930), the expression of the conservative movement known as Southern Agrarianism. This period in his life culminated in the publication of a historical novel of Civil War Virginia, *The Fathers* (1938). During the mid-1930s he abandoned the life of a freelance writer and became a college professor, most lastingly at the University of Minnesota (1951–1968), with periods as the Chair of Poetry at the Library of Congress (1943–1944) and as editor of the *Sewanee Review* (1944–1946). During these later years, his production of poetry declined markedly and he became most active as a literary critic associated with the New Criticism—a movement more famously urged by his friends Cleanth Brooks, Warren, and Ransom—and as a friend and patron of younger poets such as Robert Lowell. In his retirement, he returned to Tennessee, where he died in 1979.

Tate began his career as an admirer of H. L. Mencken, who excoriated the South as a cultural desert, moved to an interest in the French Symbolist poets (especially Baudelaire), then became devoted to T. S. Eliot, whose merits Tate was among the first to urge. Among the "Fugitive" poets, Tate pled the causes of cosmopolitanism, freedom from inhibition, the impossibility of general truth, and indifference to place. After having experienced New York and France, he began to reconsider these standpoints, though he never completely abandoned them. In "Ode to the Confederate Dead," Tate began to explore his mature theme: the delicate and fructifying tension between community and commitment on the one hand, and alienation and self-awareness on the other. Beginning with his essay "The Profession of Letters in the South" (1935) and continuing until "A Southern Mode of the Imagination" (1959), Tate applied this theme to southern literature, especially that of the Southern Renaissance.

Tate felt that if modernity was to salvage sanity, the intellectual must by act of will assert a meaningful social and religious order, almost irrespective of whether he accepted the general truth of that order. In the late 1920s and 1930s, Tate gave more attention to the social problem, though even in *I'll Take My Stand* he was drawn to make "Remarks on the Southern Religion." He argued that agrarianism—as opposed to urban industrial capitalism—would better lead to morality, prosperity, and community.

More rapidly than most of his confederates, however, he began to minimize the southern dimension of the cause by reaching out to other cultures. *The Fathers* was his last sustained venture in considering southern culture; its theme was the triumph of rapacious modernity over older traditions of noblesse oblige and civility. After 1938 Tate abandoned the attempt to make the South a repository of meaning and turned more strictly to religion; he converted to Roman Catholicism in 1952. In a world that Tate believed to be spinning into disorder, the forms of art seemed to him the nearest available, though very inadequate, consolation and bulwark.

Michael O'Brien
Jesus College, Cambridge

PRIMARY WORKS

The Fathers, 1938; *Essays of Four Decades*, 1968; *Memoirs and Opinions, 1926–1974*, 1975; *Collected Poems, 1919–1976*, 1977.

Ode to the Confederate Dead

Row after row with strict impunity
The headstones yield their names to the element,
The wind whirrs without recollection;
In the riven troughs the splayed leaves
Pile up, of nature the casual sacrament   5
To the seasonal eternity of death;
Then driven by the fierce scrutiny
Of heaven to their election in the vast breath,
They sought the rumour of mortality.

Autumn is desolation in the plot   10
Of a thousand acres where these memories grow
From the inexhaustible bodies that are not
Dead, but feed the grass row after rich row.
Think of the autumns that have come and gone!—
Ambitious November with the humors of the year,   15
With a particular zeal for every slab,
Staining the uncomfortable angels that rot
On the slabs, a wing chipped here, an arm there:
The brute curiosity of an angel's stare
Turns you, like them, to stone,   20
Transforms the heaving air
Till plunged to a heavier world below
You shift your sea-space blindly
Heaving, turning like the blind crab.

      Dazed by the wind, only the wind   25
      The leaves flying, plunge

You know who have waited by the wall
The twilight certainty of an animal,
Those midnight restitutions of the blood
You know—the immitigable pines, the smoky frieze   30
Of the sky, the sudden call: you know the rage,
The cold pool left by the mounting flood,
Of muted Zeno and Parmenides.
You who have waited for the angry resolution
Of those desires that should be yours tomorrow,   35
You know the unimportant shrift of death
And praise the vision
And praise the arrogant circumstance
Of those who fall

Rank upon rank, hurried beyond decision—   40
Here by the sagging gate, stopped by the wall.

      Seeing, seeing only the leaves
      Flying, plunge and expire

Turn your eyes to the immoderate past,
Turn to the inscrutable infantry rising   45
Demons out of the earth—they will not last.
Stonewall, Stonewall, and the sunken fields of hemp,
Shiloh, Antietam, Malvern Hill, Bull Run
Lost in that orient of the thick-and-fast
You will curse the setting sun.   50

      Cursing only the leaves crying
      Like an old man in a storm

You hear the shout, the crazy hemlocks point
With troubled fingers to the silence which
Smothers you, a mummy, in time.   55

          The hound bitch
Toothless and dying, in a musty cellar
Hears the wind only.

         Now that the salt of their blood
Stiffens the saltier oblivion of the sea,   60
Seals the malignant purity of the flood,
What shall we who count our days and bow
Our heads with a commemorial woe
In the ribboned coats of grim felicity,
What shall we say of the bones, unclean,   65
Whose verdurous anonymity will grow?
The ragged arms, the ragged heads and eyes
Lost in these acres of the insane green?
The gray lean spiders come, they come and go;
In a tangle of willows without light   70
The singular screech-owl's tight
Invisible lyric seeds the mind
With the furious murmur of their chivalry.

      We shall say only the leaves
      Flying, plunge and expire   75

We shall say only the leaves whispering
In the improbable mist of nightfall

That flies on multiple wing;
Night is the beginning and the end
And in between the ends of distraction   80
Waits mute speculation, the patient curse
That stones the eyes, or like the jaguar leaps
For his own image in a jungle pool, his victim.
What shall we say who have knowledge
Carried to the heart? Shall we take the act   85
To the grave? Shall we, more hopeful, set up the grave
In the house? The ravenous grave?

                    Leave now
The shut gate and the decomposing wall:
The gentle serpent, green in the mulberry bush,   90
Riots with his tongue through the hush—
Sentinel of the grave who counts us all!

                                 1928, 1937

EUDORA WELTY
1909–2002

Like that of Jane Austen, the canvas of Eudora Welty is small. She had, as she wrote in *One Writer's Beginnings* (1983), a "sheltered life," but one full of emotional daring. For nearly a century, Welty lived in the small town of Jackson, Mississippi, where she was born in 1909. Her artistic sensibility is the product of a childhood framed by family and rooted in story. And this sensibility accounts for one of her great strengths as a writer: her ability to infuse the tradition of southern manners with the complex emotional truths of the twentieth century South out of which she wrote.

Welty's formal education included attendance at Mississippi State College for Women, the University of Wisconsin, and the Columbia University School of Business; her first job, publicity assistant for the Works Progress Administration (WPA), helped to sharpen her eye and ear for the tasks of a fiction writer. Welty's first short story appeared in 1936 and, with the help of Robert Penn Warren and Cleanth Brooks, she published six other stories over the next three years. *A Curtain of Green*, Welty's first collection of stories, was published in 1941 with an excellent preface by Katherine Anne Porter. The forties also saw publication of Welty's first short novel (*The Robber Bridegroom*, 1942), a second collection of stories (*The Wide Net*, 1943), a second novel (*Delta Wedding*, 1946), and a collection of interrelated stories (*The Golden Apples*, 1949). *The Ponder Heart*, a short novel, appeared in 1954, and a collection entitled *The Bride of the*

Innesfallen was published the following year. In 1970 Welty's longest novel, *Losing Battles*, was published, and her WPA-inspired photographs, *One Time, One Place*, appeared in 1971. *The Optimist's Daughter*, a novel awarded the Pulitzer Prize in 1972, was followed by a collection of essays, *The Eye of the Story* (1978), *The Collected Stories of Eudora Welty* (1980), *One Writer's Beginnings* (1983), and the coedited *The Norton Book of Friendship* (1991). A collection of her book reviews (*A Writer's Eye*) appeared in 1994. Four years later, Library of America published two collections of Welty's work (*Eudora Welty: Complete Novels* and *Eudora Welty: Stories, Essays and Memoir*), edited by Richard Ford and Michael Kreyling. She was awarded the Medal of Arts in 1987, fourteen years before her death.

Although critics disagree about how Welty's fiction should be read, they have consistently recognized its importance. New Critics Robert Penn Warren and Cleanth Brooks included a sampling of Welty's short stories in their classic text *Understanding Fiction* (1943). Since then, Welty has been claimed not only by critics of southern gothic literature, folklore, and mythology, but also by modern and feminist critics. Her stories are a staple of American literature anthologies, and she continues to find an audience in colleges and universities across the country.

Welty said that she wrote out of an impulse "to praise," and her fiction is often a celebration of life in all its mystery and complexity. Her characters are imbued with a sense of place (an emotional and associational texture described by Welty in her essay "Place in Fiction") and are easily recognizable by their distinctive narrative voices. An admirer of William Faulkner's work, Welty had a similar interest in "the problems of the human heart in conflict with itself." In her work these problems are most often centered on a conflict between the desire to belong (whether to family or lover) and to preserve a separate identity. The root of this conflict is love, and Welty's stories, however grotesque or comic, transcend regionalism in their universal themes.

In as much as she grew up listening to and reading fairy tale, legend, and myth, Welty's narrative technique owes as much to an oral as to a written tradition. Welty's ability to hear the rhythms and patterns of speech is apparent in her narrative voices, which range from the hill country to the Mississippi Delta and the city. Her images are often grounded in the natural world, and her style is lyric and evocative.

Jennifer L. Randisi
Independent Scholar

PRIMARY WORKS

A Curtain of Green, 1941; *The Robber Bridegroom*, 1942; *The Wide Net*, 1943; *Delta Wedding*, 1946; *The Golden Apples*, 1949; *The Ponder Heart*, 1954; *The Bride of Innesfallen*, 1955; *Losing Battles*, 1970; *One Time, One Place*, 1971; *The Optimist's Daughter*, 1972; *The Eye of the Story*, 1978; *The Collected Stories of Eudora Welty*, 1980; *One Writer's Beginnings*, 1983; *A Writer's Eye: Collected Book Reviews*, 1994; *The Collected Stories*, 1998; *Country Churchyards*, 2000.

The Wide Net

This story is for John Fraiser Robinson

William Wallace Jamieson's wife Hazel was going to have a baby. But this was October, and it was six months away, and she acted exactly as though it would be tomorrow. When he came in the room she would not speak to him, but would look as straight at nothing as she could, with her eyes glowing. If he only touched her she stuck out her tongue or ran around the table. So one night he went out with two of the boys down the road and stayed out all night. But that was the worst thing yet, because when he came home in the early morning Hazel had vanished. He went through the house not believing his eyes, balancing with both hands out, his yellow cowlick rising on end, and then he turned the kitchen inside out looking for her, but it did no good. Then when he got back to the front room he saw she had left him a little letter, in an envelope. That was doing something behind someone's back. He took out the letter, pushed it open, held it out at a distance from his eyes.... After one look he was scared to read the exact words, and he crushed the whole thing in his hand instantly, but what it had said was that she would not put up with him after that and was going to the river to drown herself.

"Drown herself ... But she's in mortal fear of the water!"

He ran out front, his face red like the red plums hanging on the bushes there, and down in the road he gave a loud shout for Virgil Thomas, who was just going in his own house, to come out again. He could just see the edge of Virgil, he had almost got in, he had one foot inside the door.

They met half-way between the farms, under the shade tree.

"Haven't you had enough of the night?" asked Virgil. There they were, their pants all covered with dust and dew, and they had had to carry the third man home flat between them.

"I've lost Hazel, she's vanished, she went to drown herself."

"Why, that ain't like Hazel," said Virgil.

William Wallace reached out and shook him. "You heard me. Don't you know we have to drag the river?"

"Right this minute?"

"You ain't got nothing to do till spring."

"Let me go set foot inside the house and speak to my mother and tell her a story, and I'll come back."

"This will take the wide net," said William Wallace. His eyebrows gathered, and he was talking to himself.

"How come Hazel to go and do that way?" asked Virgil as they started out. William Wallace said, "I reckon she got lonesome."

"That don't argue—drown herself for getting lonesome. My mother gets lonesome."

"Well," said William Wallace. "It argues for Hazel."

"How long is it now since you and her was married?"

"Why, it's been a year."

"It don't seem that long to me. A year!"

"It was this time last year. It seems longer," said William Wallace, break-ing a stick off a tree in surprise. They walked along, kicking at the flowers on the road's edge. "I remember the day I seen her first, and that seems a long time ago. She was coming along the road holding a little frying-size chicken from her grandma, under her arm, and she had it real quiet. I spoke to her with nice manners. We knowed each other's names, being bound to, just didn't know each other to speak to. I says, 'Where are you taking the fryer?' and she says, 'Mind your manners,' and I kept on till after while she says, 'If you want to walk me home, take littler steps.' So I didn't lose time. It was just four miles across the field and full of blackberries, and from the top of the hill there was Dover below, looking sizeable-like and clean, spread out between the two churches like that. When we got down, I says to her, 'What kind of water's in this well?' and she says, 'The best water in the world.' So I drew a bucket and took out a dipper and she drank and I drank. I didn't think it was that remarkable, but I didn't tell her."

"What happened that night?" asked Virgil.

"We ate the chicken," said William Wallace, "and it was tender. Of course that wasn't all they had. The night I was trying their table out, it sure had good things to eat from one end to the other. Her mama and papa sat at the head and foot and we was face to face with each other across it, with I remember a pat of butter between. They had real sweet butter, with a tree drawed down it, elegant-like. Her mama eats like a man. I had brought her a whole hatful of berries and she didn't even pass them to her husband. Hazel, she would leap up and take a pitcher of new milk and fill up the glasses. I had heard how they couldn't have a singing at the church without a fight over her."

"Oh, she's a pretty girl, all right," said Virgil. "It's a pity for the ones like her to grow old, and get like their mothers."

"Another thing will be that her mother will get wind of this and come after me," said William Wallace.

"Her mother will eat you alive," said Virgil.

"She's just been watching her chance," said William Wallace. "Why did I think I could stay out all night."

"Just something come over you."

"First it was just a carnival at Carthage, and I had to let them guess my weight . . . and after that . . ."

"It was nice to be sitting on your neck in a ditch singing," prompted Vir-gil, "in the moonlight. And playing on the harmonica like you can play."

"Even if Hazel did sit home knowing I was drunk, that wouldn't kill her," said William Wallace. "What she knows ain't ever killed her yet. . . . She's smart, too, for a girl," he said.

"She's a lot smarter than her cousins in Beulah," said Virgil, "and espe-cially Edna Earle, that never did get to be what you'd call a heavy thinker. Edna Earle could sit and ponder all day on how the little tail of the 'C' got through the 'L' in a Coca-Cola sign."

"Hazel *is* smart," said William Wallace. They walked on. "You ought to see her pantry shelf, it looks like a hundred jars when you open the door. I don't see how she could turn around and jump in the river."

"It's a woman's trick."

"I always behaved before. Till the one night—last night."

"Yes, but the one night," said Virgil. "And she was waiting to take advantage."

"She jumped in the river because she was scared to death of the water and that was to make it worse," he said. "She remembered how I used to have to pick her up and carry her over the oak-log bridge, how she'd shut her eyes and make a deadweight and hold me round the neck, just for a little creek. I don't see how she brought herself to jump."

"Jumped backwards," said Virgil. "Didn't look."

When they turned off, it was still early in the pink and green fields. The fumes of morning, sweet and bitter, sprang up where they walked. The insects ticked softly, their strength in reserve; butterflies chopped the air, going to the east, and the birds flew carelessly and sang by fits and starts, not the way they did in the evening in sustained and drowsy songs.

"It's a pretty *day* for sure," said William Wallace. "It's a pretty *day* for it."

"I don't see a sign of her ever going along here," said Virgil.

"Well," said William Wallace. "She wouldn't have dropped anything. I never saw a girl to leave less signs of where she's been."

"Not even a plum seed," said Virgil, kicking the grass.

In the grove it was so quiet that once William Wallace gave a jump, as if he could almost hear a sound of himself wondering where she had gone. A descent of energy came down on him in the thick of the woods and he ran at a rabbit and caught it in his hands.

"Rabbit ... Rabbit ..." He acted as if he wanted to take it off to himself and hold it up and talk to it. He laid a palm against its pushing heart. "Now ... There now ..."

"Let her go, William Wallace, let her go." Virgil, chewing on an elderberry whistle he had just made, stood at his shoulder: "What do you want with a live rabbit?"

William Wallace squatted down and set the rabbit on the ground but held it under his hand. It was a little old, brown rabbit. It did not try to move. "See there?"

"Let her go."

"She can go if she wants to, but she don't want to."

Gently he lifted his hand. The round eye was shining at him sideways in the green gloom.

"Anybody can freeze a *rabbit*, that wants to," said Virgil, Suddenly he gave a far-reaching blast on the whistle, and the rabbit went in a streak. "Was you out catching cotton-tails, or was you out catching your wife?" he said, taking the turn to the open fields. "I come along to keep you on the track."

*   *   *

"Who'll we get now?" They stood on top of a hill and William Wallace looked critically over the countryside. "Any of the Malones?"

"I was always scared of the Malones," said Virgil. "Too many *of* them."

"This is my day with the net, and they would have to watch out," said William Wallace. "I reckon some Malones, and the Doyles, will be enough. The six Doyles and their dogs, and you and me, and two little nigger boys is enough, with just a few Malones."

"That ought to be enough," said Virgil, "no matter what."

"I'll bring the Malones, and you bring the Doyles," said William Wallace, and they separated at the spring.

When William Wallace came back, with a string of Malones just showing behind him on the hilltop, he found Virgil with the two little Rippen boys waiting behind him, solemn little towheads. As soon as he walked up, Grady, the one in front, lifted his hand to signal silence and caution to his brother Brucie, who began panting merrily and untrustworthily behind him.

Brucie bent readily under William Wallace's hand-pat, and gave him a dreamy look out of the tops of his round eyes, which were pure green-and-white like clover tops. William Wallace gave him a nickel. Grady hung his head; his white hair lay in a little tail in the nape of his neck.

"Let's let them come," said Virgil.

"Well, they can come then, but if we keep letting everybody come it is going to be too many," said William Wallace.

"They'll appreciate it, those little old boys," said Virgil. Brucie held up at arm's length a long red thread with a bent pin tied on the end; and a look of helpless and intense interest gathered Grady's face like a drawstring—his eyes, one bright with a sty, shone pleadingly under his white bangs, and he snapped his jaw and tried to speak. . . . "Their papa was drowned in the Pearl River," said Virgil.

There was a shout from the gully.

"Here come all the Malones," cried William Wallace. "I asked four of them would they come, but the rest of the family invited themselves."

"Did you ever see a time when they didn't," said Virgil. "And yonder from the other direction comes the Doyles, still with biscuit crumbs on their cheeks, I bet, now it's nothing to do but eat as their mother said."

"If two little niggers would come along now, or one big nigger," said William Wallace. And the words were hardly out of his mouth when two little Negro boys came along, going somewhere, one behind the other, stepping high and gay in their overalls, as though they waded in honeydew to the waist.

"Come here, boys. What's your names?"

"Sam and Robbie Bell."

"Come along with us, we're going to drag the river."

"You hear that, Robbie Bell?" said Sam.

They smiled.

The Doyles came noiselessly, their dogs made all the fuss. The Malones, eight giants with great long black eyelashes, were already stamping the ground and pawing each other, ready to go. Everybody went up together to see Doc.

Old Doc owned the wide net. He had a house on top of the hill and he sat and looked out from a rocker on the front porch.

"Climb the hill and come in!" he began to intone across the valley. "Harvest's over ... slipped up on everybody ... corn's all in, hogs gettin' ripe ... hay cut ... molasses made around here.... Big explosion's over, supervisors elected, some pleased, some not.... We're hearing talk of war!"

When they got closer, he was saying, "Many's been saved at revival, twenty-two last Sunday including a Doyle, ought to counted two. Hope they'll be a blessing to Dover community besides a shining star in Heaven. Now what?" he asked, for they had arrived and stood gathered in front of the steps.

"If nobody is using your wide net, could we use it?" asked William Wallace.

"You just used it a month ago," said Doc. "It ain't your turn."

Virgil jogged William Wallace's arm and cleared his throat. "This time is kind of special," he said. "We got reason to think William Wallace's wife Hazel is in the river, drowned."

"What reason have you got to think she's in the river drowned?" asked Doc. He took out his old pipe. "I'm asking the husband."

"Because she's not in the house," said William Wallace.

"Vanished?" and he knocked out the pipe.

"Plum vanished."

"Of course a thousand things could have happened to her," said Doc, and he lighted the pipe.

"Hand him up the letter, William Wallace," said Virgil. "We can't wait around till Doomsday for the net while Doc sits back thinkin'."

"I tore it up, right at the first," said William Wallace. "But I know it by heart. It said she was going to jump straight in the Pearl River and that I'd be sorry."

"Where do you come in, Virgil?" asked Doc.

"I was in the same place William Wallace sat on his neck in, all night, and done as much as he done, and come home the same time."

"You-all were out cuttin' up, so Lady Hazel has to jump in the river, is that it? Cause and effect? Anybody want to argue with me? Where do these others come in, Doyles, Malones, and what not?"

"Doc is the smartest man around," said William Wallace, turning to the solidly waiting Doyles, "but it sure takes time."

"These are the ones that's collected to drag the river for her," said Virgil.

"Of course I am not going on record to say so soon that *I* think she's drowned," Doc said, blowing out blue smoke.

"Do you think ..." William Wallace mounted a step, and his hands both went into fists. "Do you think she was *carried off?*"

"Now that's the way to argue, see it from all sides," said Doc promptly. "But who by?"

Some Malone whistled, but not so you could tell which one.

"There's no booger around the Dover section that goes around carrying off young girls that's married," stated Doc.

"She was always scared of the Gypsies." William Wallace turned scarlet. "She'd sure turn her ring around on her finger if she passed one, and look in the other direction so they couldn't see she was pretty and carry her off. They come in the end of summer."

"Yes, there are the Gypsies, kidnappers since the world began. But was it to be you that would pay the grand ransom?" asked Doc. He pointed his finger. They all laughed then at how clever old Doc was and clapped William Wallace on the back. But that turned into a scuffle and they fell to the ground.

"Stop it, or you can't have the net," said Doc. "You're scaring my wife's chickens."

"It's time we was gone," said William Wallace.

The big barking dogs jumped to lean their front paws on the men's chests.

"My advice remains, Let well enough alone," said Doc. "Whatever this mysterious event will turn out to be, it has kept one woman from talking a while. However, Lady Hazel is the prettiest girl in Mississippi, you've never seen a prettier one and you never will. A golden-haired girl." He got to his feet with the nimbleness that was always his surprise, and said, "I'll come along with you."

The path they always followed was the Old Natchez Trace. It took them through the deep woods and led them out down below on the Pearl River, where they could begin dragging it upstream to a point near Dover. They walked in silence around William Wallace, not letting him carry anything, but the net dragged heavily and the buckets were full of clatter in a place so dim and still.

Once they went through a forest of cucumber trees and came up on a high ridge. Grady and Brucie, who were running ahead all the way, stopped in their tracks; a whistle had blown and far down and far away a long freight train was passing. It seemed like a little festival procession, moving with the slowness of ignorance or a dream, from distance to distance, the tiny pink and gray cars like secret boxes. Grady was counting the cars to himself, as if he could certainly see each one clearly, and Brucie watched his lips, hushed and cautious, the way he would watch a bird drinking. Tears suddenly came to Grady's eyes, but it could only be because a tiny man walked along the top of the train, walking and moving on top of the moving train.

They went down again and soon the smell of the river spread over the woods, cool and secret. Every step they took among the great walls of vines and among the passion-flowers started up a little life, a little flight.

"We're walking along in the changing-time," said Doc. "Any day now the change will come. It's going to turn from hot to cold, and we can kill the hog that's ripe and have fresh meat to eat. Come one of these nights and we can wander down here and tree a nice possum. Old Jack Frost will be pinching things up. Old Mr. Winter will be standing in the door. Hickory tree there will be yellow. Sweet-gum red, hickory yellow, dogwood red, sycamore yellow." He went along rapping the tree trunks with his knuckle. "Magnolia and live-oak never die. Remember that. Persimmons will all get fit to eat, and the nuts will be dropping like rain all through the woods here. And run, little quail, run, for we'll be after you too."

They went on and suddenly the woods opened upon light, and they had reached the river. Everyone stopped, but Doc talked on ahead as though nothing had happened. "Only today," he said, "today, in October sun, it's all gold—sky and tree and water. Everything just before it changes looks to be made of gold."

William Wallace looked down, as though he thought of Hazel with the shining eyes, sitting at home and looking straight before her, like a piece of pure gold, too precious to touch.

Below them the river was glimmering, narrow, soft, and skin-colored, and slowed nearly to stillness. The shining willow trees hung round them. The net that was being drawn out, so old and so long-used, it too looked golden, strung and tied with golden threads.

Standing still on the bank, all of a sudden William Wallace, on whose word they were waiting, spoke up in a voice of surprise. "What is the name of this river?"

They looked at him as if he were crazy not to know the name of the river he had fished in all his life. But a deep frown was on his forehead, as if he were compelled to wonder what people had come to call this river, or to think there was a mystery in the name of the river they all knew so well, the same as if it were some great far torrent of waves that dashed through the mountains somewhere, and almost as if it were a river in some dream, for they could not give him the name of that.

"Everybody knows Pearl River is named the Pearl River," said Doc.

A bird note suddenly bold was like a stone thrown into the water to sound it.

"It's deep here," said Virgil, and jogged William Wallace. "Remember?"

William Wallace stood looking down at the river as if it were still a mystery to him. There under his feet, which hung over the bank, it was transparent and yellow like an old bottle lying in the sun, filling with light.

Doc clattered all his paraphernalia.

Then all of a sudden all the Malones scattered jumping and tumbling down the bank. They gave their loud shout. Little Brucie started after them, and looked back.

"Do you think she jumped?" Virgil asked William Wallace.

II

Since the net was so wide, when it was all stretched it reached from bank to bank of the Pearl River, and the weights would hold it all the way to the bottom. Jug-like sounds filled the air, splashes lifted in the sun, and the party began to move upstream. The Malones with great groans swam and pulled near the shore, the Doyles swam and pushed from behind with Virgil to tell them how to do it best; Grady and Brucie with his thread and pin trotted along the sandbars hauling buckets and lines. Sam and Robbie Bell, naked and bright, guided the old oarless rowboat that always drifted at the shore, and in it, sitting up tall with his hat on, was Doc—he went along without ever touching water and without ever taking his eyes off the net. William Wallace himself did everything but most of the time he was out of sight, swimming about under water or diving, and he had nothing to say any more.

The dogs chased up and down, in and out of the water, and in and out of the woods.

"Don't let her get too heavy, boys," Doc intoned regularly, every few minutes, "and she won't let nothing through."

"She won't let nothing through, she won't let nothing through," chanted Sam and Robbie Bell, one at his front and one at his back.

The sandbars were pink or violet drifts ahead. Where the light fell on the river, in a wandering from shore to shore, it was leaf-shaped spangles that trembled softly, while the dark of the river was calm. The willow trees leaned overhead under muscadine vines, and their trailing leaves hung like waterfalls in the morning air. The thing that seemed like silence must have been the endless cry of all the crickets and locusts in the world, rising and falling.

Every time William Wallace took hold of a big eel that slipped the net, the Malones all yelled, "Rassle with him, son!"

"Don't let her get too heavy, boys," said Doc.

"This is hard on catfish," William Wallace said once.

There were big and little fishes, dark and bright, that they caught, good ones and bad ones, the same old fish.

"This is more shoes than I ever saw got together in any store," said Virgil when they emptied the net to the bottom. "Get going!" he shouted in the next breath.

The little Rippens who had stayed ahead in the woods stayed ahead on the river. Brucie, leading them all, made small jumps and hops as he went, sometimes on one foot, sometimes on the other.

The winding river looked old sometimes, when it ran wrinkled and deep under high banks where the roots of trees hung down, and sometimes it seemed to be only a young creek, shining with the colors of wildflowers. Sometimes sandbars in the shapes of fishes lay nose to nose across, without the track of even a bird.

"Here comes some alligators," said Virgil. "Let's let them by."

They drew out on the shady side of the water, and three big alligators and four middle-sized ones went by, taking their own time.

"Look at their great big old teeth!" called a shrill voice. It was Grady making his only outcry, and the alligators were not showing their teeth at all.

"The better to eat folks with," said Doc from his boat, looking at him severely.

"Doc, you are bound to declare all you know," said Virgil. "Get going!"

When they started off again the first thing they caught in the net was the baby alligator.

"That's just what we wanted!" cried the Malones.

They set the little alligator down on a sandbar and he squatted perfectly still; they could hardly tell when it was he started to move. They watched with set faces his incredible mechanics, while the dogs after one bark stood off in inquisitive humility, until he winked.

"He's ours!" shouted all the Malones. "We're taking him home with us!"

"He ain't nothing but a little-old baby," said William Wallace.

The Malones only scoffed, as if he might be only a baby but he looked like the oldest and worst lizard.

"What are you going to do with him?" asked Virgil.

"Keep him."

"I'd be more careful what I took out of this net," said Doc.

"Tie him up and throw him in the bucket," the Malones were saying to each other, while Doc was saying, "Don't come running to me and ask me what to do when he gets big."

They kept catching more and more fish, as if there was no end in sight.

"Look, a string of lady's beads," said Virgil. "Here, Sam and Robbie Bell."

Sam wore them around his head, with a knot over his forehead and loops around his ears, and Robbie Bell walked behind and stared at them.

In a shadowy place something white flew up. It was a heron, and it went away over the dark treetops. William Wallace followed it with his eyes and Brucie clapped his hands, but Virgil gave a sigh, as if he knew that when you go looking for what is lost, everything is a sign.

An eel slid out of the net.

"Rassle with him, son!" yelled the Malones. They swam like fiends.

"The Malones are in it for the fish," said Virgil.

It was about noon that there was a little rustle on the bank.

"Who is that yonder?" asked Virgil, and he pointed to a little undersized man with short legs and a little straw hat with a band around it, who was following along on the other side of the river.

"Never saw him and don't know his brother," said Doc.

Nobody had ever seen him before.

"Who invited you?" cried Virgil hotly. "Hi ... !" and he made signs for the little undersized man to look at him, but he would not.

"Looks like a crazy man, from here," said the Malones.

"Just don't pay any attention to him and maybe he'll go away," advised Doc.

But Virgil had already swum across and was up on the other bank. He and the stranger could be seen exchanging a word apiece and then Virgil put out his hand the way he would pat a child and patted the stranger to the ground. The little man got up again just as quickly, lifted his shoulders, turned around, and walked away with his hat tilted over his eyes.

When Virgil came back he said, "Little-old man claimed he was harmless as a baby. I told him to just try horning in on this river and anything in it."

"What did he look like up close?" asked Doc.

"I wasn't studying how he looked," said Virgil. "But I don't like anybody to come looking at me that I am not familiar with." And he shouted, "Get going!"

"Things are moving in too great a rush," said Doc.

Brucie darted ahead and ran looking into all the bushes, lifting up their branches and looking underneath.

"Not one of the Doyles has spoke a word," said Virgil.

"That's because they're not talkers," said Doc.

All day William Wallace kept diving to the bottom. Once he dived down and down into the dark water, where it was so still that nothing stirred, not even a fish, and so dark that it was no longer the muddy world of the upper river but the dark clear world of deepness, and he must have believed this was the deepest place in the whole Pearl River, and if she was not here she would not be anywhere. He was gone such a long time that the others stared hard at the surface of the water, through which the bubbles came from below. So far down and all alone, had he found Hazel? Had he suspected down there, like some secret, the real, the true trouble that Hazel had fallen into, about which words in a letter could not speak . . . how (who knew?) she had been filled to the brim with that elation that they all remembered, like their own secret, the elation that comes of great hopes and changes, sometimes simply of the harvest time, that comes with a little course of its own like a tune to run in the head, and there was nothing she could do about it—they knew—and so it had turned into this. It could be nothing but the old trouble that William Wallace was finding out, reaching and turning in the gloom of such depths.

"Look down yonder," said Grady softly to Brucie.

He pointed to the surface, where their reflections lay colorless and still side by side. He touched his brother gently as though to impress him.

"That's you and me," he said.

Brucie swayed precariously over the edge, and Grady caught him by the seat of his overalls. Brucie looked, but showed no recognition. Instead, he backed away, and seemed all at once unconcerned and spiritless, and pressed the nickel William Wallace had given him into his palm, rubbing it into his skin. Grady's inflamed eyes rested on the brown water. Without warning he saw something . . . perhaps the image in the river seemed to be his father, the drowned man—with arms open, eyes open, mouth open. . . . Grady stared and blinked, again something wrinkled up his face.

And when William Wallace came up it was in an agony from submersion, which seemed an agony of the blood and of the very heart, so woeful he looked. He was staring and glaring around in astonishment, as if a long time had gone by, away from the pale world where the brown light of the sun and the river and the little party watching him trembled before his eyes.

"What did you bring up?" somebody called—was it Virgil?

One of his hands was holding fast to a little green ribbon of plant, root and all. He was surprised, and let it go.

It was afternoon. The trees spread softly, the clouds hung wet and tinted. A buzzard turned a few slow wheels in the sky, and drifted upwards. The dogs promenaded the banks.

"It's time we ate fish," said Virgil.

On a wide sandbar on which seashells lay they dragged up the haul and built a fire.

Then for a long time among clouds of odors and smoke, all half-naked except Doc, they cooked and ate catfish. They ate until the Malones groaned and all the Doyles stretched out on their faces, though for long after, Sam and Robbie Bell sat up to their own little table on a cypress stump and ate on and on. Then they all were silent and still, and one by one fell asleep.

"There ain't a thing better than fish," muttered William Wallace. He lay stretched on his back in the glimmer and shade of trampled sand. His sun-burned forehead and cheeks seemed to glow with fire. His eyelids fell. The shadow of a willow branch dipped and moved over him. "There is nothing in the world as good as ... fish. The fish of Pearl River." Then slowly he smiled. He was asleep.

But it seemed almost at once that he was leaping up, and one by one up sat the others in their ring and looked at him, for it was impossible to stop and sleep by the river.

"You're feeling as good as you felt last night," said Virgil, setting his head on one side.

"The excursion is the same when you go looking for your sorrow as when you go looking for your joy," said Doc.

But William Wallace answered none of them anything, for he was leaping all over the place and all, over them and the feast and the bones of the feast, trampling the sand, up and down, and doing a dance so crazy that he would die next. He took a big catfish and hooked it to his belt buckle and went up and down so that they all hollered, and the tears of laughter streaming down his cheeks made him put his hand up, and the two days' growth of beard began to jump out, bright red.

But all of a sudden there was an even louder cry, something almost like a cheer, from everybody at once, and all pointed fingers moved from William Wallace to the river. In the center of three light-gold rings across the water was lifted first an old hoary head ("It has whiskers!" a voice cried) and then in an undulation loop after loop and hump after hump of a long dark body, until there were a dozen rings of ripples, one behind the other, stretching all across the river, like a necklace.

"The King of the Snakes!" cried all the Malones at once, in high tenor voices and leaning together.

"The King of the Snakes," intoned old Doc in his profound bass.

"He looked you in the eye."

William Wallace stared back at the King of the Snakes with all his might.

It was Brucie that darted forward, dangling his little thread with the pin tied to it, going toward the water.

"That's the King of the Snakes!" cried Grady, who always looked after him.

Then the snake went down.

The little boy stopped with one leg in the air, spun around on the other, and sank to the ground.

"Git up," Grady whispered. "It was just the King of the Snakes. He went off whistling. Git up. It wasn't a thing but the King of the Snakes."

Brucie's green eyes opened, his tongue darted out, and he sprang up; his feet were heavy, his head light, and he rose like a bubble coming to the surface.

Then thunder like a stone loosened and rolled down the bank.

They all stood unwilling on the sandbar, holding to the net. In the eastern sky were the familiar castles and the round towers to which they were used, gray, pink, and blue, growing darker and filling with thunder. Lightning flickered in the sun along their thick walls. But in the west the sun shone with such a violence that in an illumination like a long-prolonged glare of lightning the heavens looked black and white; all color left the world, the goldenness of everything was like a memory, and only heat, a kind of glamor and oppression, lay on their heads. The thick heavy trees on the other side of the river were brushed with mile-long streaks of silver, and a wind touched each man on the forehead. At the same time there was a long roll of thunder that began behind them, came up and down mountains and valleys of air, passed over their heads, and left them listening still. With a small, near noise a mockingbird followed it, the little white bars of its body flashing over the willow trees.

"We are here for a storm now," Virgil said. "We will have to stay till it's over."

They retreated a little, and hard drops fell in the leathery leaves at their shoulders and about their heads.

"Magnolia's the loudest tree there is in a storm," said Doc.

Then the light changed the water, until all about them the woods in the rising wind seemed to grow taller and blow inward together and suddenly turn dark. The rain struck heavily. A huge tail seemed to lash through the air and the river broke in a wound of silver. In silence the party crouched and stooped beside the trunk of the great tree, which in the push of the storm rose full of a fragrance and unyielding weight. Where they all stared, past their tree, was another tree, and beyond that another and another, all the way down the bank of the river, all towering and darkened in the storm.

"The outside world is full of endurance," said Doc. "Full of endurance."

Robbie Bell and Sam squatted down low and embraced each other from the start.

"Runs in our family to get struck by lightnin'," said Robbie Bell. "Lightnin' drawed a pitchfork right on our grandpappy's cheek, stayed till he died.

Pappy got struck by some bolts of lightnin' and was dead three days, dead as that-there axe."

There was a succession of glares and crashes.

"This'n's goin' to be either me or you," said Sam. "Here come a little bug. If he go to the left, be me, and to the right, be you."

But at the next flare a big tree on the hill seemed to turn into fire before their eyes, every branch, twig, and leaf, and a purple cloud hung over it.

"Did you hear that crack?" asked Robbie Bell. "That were its bones."

"Why do you little niggers talk so much!" said Doc. "Nobody's profiting by this information."

"We always talks this much," said Sam, "but now everybody so quiet, they hears us."

The great tree, split and on fire, fell roaring to earth. Just at its moment of falling, a tree like it on the opposite bank split wide open and fell in two parts.

"Hope they ain't goin' to be no balls of fire come rollin' over the water and fry all the fishes with they scales on," said Robbie Bell.

The water in the river had turned purple and was filled with sudden currents and whirlpools. The little willow trees bent almost to its surface, bowing one after another down the bank and almost breaking under the storm. A great curtain of wet leaves was borne along before a blast of wind, and every human being was covered.

"Now us got scales," wailed Sam. "Us is the fishes."

"Hush up, little-old colored children," said Virgil. "This isn't the way to act when somebody takes you out to drag a river."

"Poor lady's-ghost, I bet it is scareder than us," said Sam.

"All I hoping is, us don't find her!" screamed Robbie Bell.

William Wallace bent down and knocked their heads together. After that they clung silently in each other's arms, the two black heads resting, with wind-filled cheeks and tight-closed eyes, one upon the other until the storm was over.

"Right over yonder is Dover," said Virgil. "We've come all the way. William Wallace, you have walked on a sharp rock and cut your foot open."

III

In Dover it had rained, and the town looked somehow like new. The wavy heat of late afternoon came down from the watertank and fell over everything like shiny mosquito-netting. At the wide place where the road was paved and patched with tar, it seemed newly embedded with Coca-Cola tops. The old circus posters on the store were nearly gone, only bits, the snowflakes of white horses, clinging to its side. Morning-glory vines started almost visibly to grow over the roofs and cling round the ties of the railroad track, where bluejays lighted on the rails, and umbrella chinaberry trees hung heavily over the whole town, dripping intermittently upon the tin roofs.

Each with his counted fish on a string, the members of the river-dragging party walked through the town. They went toward the town well, and there was Hazel's mother's house, but no sign of her yet coming out. They all drank a dipper of the water, and still there was not a soul on the street. Even the bench in front of the store was empty, except for a little corn-shuck doll.

But something told them somebody had come, for after one moment people began to look out of the store and out of the post office. All the bird dogs woke up to see the Doyle dogs and such a large number of men and boys materialize suddenly with such a big catch of fish, and they ran out barking. The Doyle dogs joyously barked back. The bluejays flashed up and screeched above the town, whipping through their tunnels in the chinaberry trees. In the café a nickel clattered inside a music box and a love song began to play. The whole town of Dover began to throb in its wood and tin, like an old tired heart, when the men walked through once more, coming around again and going down the street carrying the fish, so drenched, exhausted, and muddy that no one could help but admire them.

William Wallace walked through the town as though he did not see anybody or hear anything. Yet he carried his great string of fish held high where it could be seen by all. Virgil came next, imitating William Wallace exactly, then the modest Doyles crowded by the Malones, who were holding up their alligator, tossing it in the air, even, like a father tossing his child. Following behind and pointing authoritatively at the ones in front strolled Doc, with Sam and Robbie Bell still chanting in his wake. In and out of the whole little line Grady and Brucie jerked about. Grady, with his head ducked, and stiff as a rod, walked with a springy limp; it made him look forever angry and unapproachable. Under his breath he was whispering, "Sty, sty, git out of my eye, and git on somebody passin' by." He traveled on with narrowed shoulders, and kept his eye unerringly upon his little brother, wary and at the same time proud, as though he held a flying June-bug on a string. Brucie, making a twanging noise with his lips, had shot forth again, and he was darting rapidly everywhere at once, delighted and tantalized, running in circles around William Wallace, pointing to his fish. A frown of pleasure like the print of a bird's foot was stamped between his faint brows, and he trotted in some unknown realm of delight.

"Did you ever see so many fish?" said the people in Dover.

"How much are your fish, mister?"

"Would you sell your fish?"

"Is that all the fish in Pearl River?"

"How much you sell them all for? Everybody's?"

"Take 'em free," said William Wallace suddenly and loud. The Malones were upon him and shouting, but it was too late. "I don't want no more of 'em. I want my wife!" he yelled, just at the moment when Hazel's mother walked out of her front door.

"You can't head her mother off," said Virgil. "Here she comes in full bloom."

"What have you done with my child?" Hazel's mother shouted.

But William Wallace turned his back on her, that was all, and on everybody, for that matter, and that was the breaking-up of the party.

Just as the sun went down, Doc climbed his back steps, sat in his chair on the back porch where he sat in the evenings, and lighted his pipe. William Wallace hung out the net and came back and Virgil was waiting for him, so they could say good evening to Doc.

"All in all," said Doc, when they came up, "I've never been on a better river-dragging, or seen better behavior. If it took catching catfish to move the Rock of Gibraltar, I believe this outfit could move it."

"Well, we didn't catch Hazel," said Virgil.

"What did you say?" asked Doc.

"He don't really pay attention," said Virgil. "I said, 'We didn't catch Hazel.'"

"Who says Hazel was to be caught?" asked Doc. "She wasn't in there. Girls don't like the water—remember that. Girls don't just haul off and go jumping in the river to get back at their husbands. They got other ways."

"Didn't you ever think she was in there?" asked William Wallace. "The whole time?"

"Nary once," said Doc.

"He's just smart," said Virgil, putting his hand on William Wallace's arm. "It's only because we didn't find her that he wasn't looking for her."

"I'm beholden to you for the net, anyway," said William Wallace.

"You're welcome to borry it again," said Doc.

On the way home Virgil kept saying, "Calm down, calm down, William Wallace."

"If he wasn't such an old skinny man I'd have wrung his neck for him," said William Wallace. "He had no business coming."

"He's too big for his britches," said Virgil. "Don't nobody know everything. And just because it's his net. Why does it have to be his net?"

"If it wasn't for being polite to old men, I'd have skinned him alive," said William Wallace.

"I guess he don't really know nothing about wives at all, his wife's so deaf," said Virgil.

"He don't know Hazel," said William Wallace. "I'm the only man alive knows Hazel: would she jump in the river or not, and I say she would. She jumped in because I was sitting on the back of my neck in a ditch singing, and that's just what she ought to done. Doc ain't got no right to say one word about it."

"Calm down, calm down, William Wallace," said Virgil.

"If it had been you that talked like that, I'd have broke every bone in your body," said William Wallace. "Just let you talk like that. You're my age and size."

"But I ain't going to talk like that," said Virgil. "What have I done the whole time but keep this river-dragging going straight and running even, without no hitches? You couldn't have drug the river a foot without me."

"What are you talking about! Without who!" cried William Wallace. "This wasn't your river-dragging! It wasn't your wife!" He jumped on Virgil and they began to fight.

"Let me up." Virgil was breathing heavily.

"Say it was my wife. Say it was my river-dragging."

"Yours!" Virgil was on the ground with William Wallace's hand putting dirt in his mouth.

"Say it was my net."

"Your net!"

"Get up then."

They walked along getting their breath, and smelling the honeysuckle in the evening. On a hill William Wallace looked down, and at the same time there went drifting by the sweet sounds of music outdoors. They were having the Sacred Harp Sing on the grounds of an old white church glimmering there at the crossroads, far below. He stared away as if he saw it minutely, as if he could see a lady in white take a flowered cover off the organ, which was set on a little slant in the shade, dust the keys, and start to pump and play.... He smiled faintly, as he would at his mother, and at Hazel, and at the singing women in his life, now all one young girl standing up to sing under the trees the oldest and longest ballads there were.

Virgil told him good night and went into his own house and the door shut on him.

When he got to his own house, William Wallace saw to his surprise that it had not rained at all. But there, curved over the roof, was something he had never seen before as long as he could remember, a rainbow at night. In the light of the moon, which had risen again, it looked small and of gauzy material, like a lady's summer dress, a faint veil through which the stars showed.

He went up on the porch and in at the door, and all exhausted he had walked through the front room and through the kitchen when he heard his name called. After a moment, he smiled, as if no matter what he might have hoped for in his wildest heart, it was better than that to hear his name called out in the house. The voice came out of the bedroom.

"What do you want?" he yelled, standing stock-still.

Then she opened the bedroom door with the old complaining creak, and there she stood. She was not changed a bit.

"How do you feel?" he said.

"I feel pretty good. Not too good," Hazel said, looking mysterious.

"I cut my foot," said William Wallace, taking his shoe off so she could see the blood.

"How in the world did you do that?" she cried, with a step back.

"Dragging the river. But it don't hurt any longer."

"You ought to have been more careful," she said. "Supper's ready and I wondered if you would ever come home, or if it would be last night all over again. Go and make yourself fit to be seen," she said, and ran away from him.

After supper they sat on the front steps a while.

"Where were you this morning when I came in?" asked William Wallace when they were ready to go in the house.

"I was hiding," she said. "I was still writing on the letter. And then you tore it up."

"Did you watch me when I was reading it?"

"Yes, and you could have put out your hand and touched me. I was so close."

But he bit his lip, and gave her a little tap and slap, and then turned her up and spanked her.

"Do you think you will do it again?" he asked.

"I'll tell my mother on you for this!"

"Will you do it again?"

"No!" she cried.

"Then pick yourself up off my knee."

It was just as if he had chased her and captured her again. She lay smiling in the crook of his arm. It was the same as any other chase in the end.

"I will do it again if I get ready," she said. "Next time will be different, too."

Then she was ready to go in, and rose up and looked out from the top step, out across their yard where the China tree was and beyond, into the dark fields where the lightning-bugs flickered away. He climbed to his feet too and stood beside her, with the frown on his face, trying to look where she looked. And after a few minutes she took him by the hand and led him into the house, smiling as if she were smiling down on him.

1943

CHARLES REZNIKOFF
1894–1976

The chronology of the Objectivist movement is brief. In late 1930, Louis Zukofsky, the poet who coined the term "Objectivist," wrote Ezra Pound that he was preparing a critical article on the poetry of Charles Reznikoff but, in order to analyze the poetry, had become involved in trying to define two terms: *sincerity* and *objectification*. Pound, familiar with Zukofsky's work, had already convinced editor Harriet Monroe to allow Zukofsky to edit an issue of *Poetry*. Zukofsky then appended his article, entitled "Sincerity and Objectification: With Special Reference to the Work of Charles Reznikoff," to the February 1931 issue—the "Objectivists" issue—with an eye to providing what he later called a "standard" for his contributors. His primary example of the language of Objectivism was Reznikoff's one-line poem "Aphrodite Vrania"—"The ceaseless weaving of the uneven water." The poem strongly suggests in its sound the movement to which it refers.

Reznikoff was a product of the Jewish community in New York. Born in Brooklyn in 1894, he earned a law degree but practiced only briefly. For a few years in the 1930s, however, he worked at a legal publishing firm, where he helped condense and summarize court records for inclusion in legal reference works. Although he had begun to publish in the teens (he self-published some of his own work with hand-set plates beginning in the 1920s), his reading and writing in legal publishing had a profound effect on much of his later poetry. He began to see that court testimony uniquely documented a comprehensive cultural history, and from court records he extracted and further condensed stories and vignettes (published as his prose book *Testimony*, 1934) and transformed them and additional records into poems that filled two volumes when published some thirty years later. He came to appreciate the straightforward, unornamented prose of court testimony, which used metaphor sparsely if at all. The tools he developed in such writing served him well when he wrote *Holocaust*, based closely on courtroom accounts of the Nazi death camps.

Reznikoff had an apparently intuitive eye for the "historical particulars" that Zukofsky valued. He incorporated into even his earliest poetry details of daily life in New York—from street lamps to domestic tragedies—that he saw during his long walks through the city. He wrote drama and fiction, including fictionalized history, but seldom criticism. In the 1930s, he worked for a time in Hollywood but returned to New York and made a living as a freelance writer, translator, and researcher until his death in 1976. Reznikoff's work speaks of a significant project—one in which history shapes language, language in turn shapes history's readers, and poetry marks out the most artfully shaped language of the lived historical moment.

Randolph Chilton
College of St. Francis

PRIMARY WORKS

Rhythms, 1918; *Rhythms II*, 1919; *Poems*, 1920; *Uriel Accosta: A Play & A Fourth Group of Verse*, 1921; *Chatterton, the Black Death, and Meriwether Lewis*, 1922 (plays); *Coral and Captive Israel*, 1923 (plays); *Nine Plays*, 1927; *Five Groups of Verse*, 1927; *By the Waters of Manhattan: An Annual*, 1929 (anthology); *By the Waters of Manhattan*, 1930 (novel); *Jerusalem the Golden*, 1934; *Testimony*, 1934 (prose); *In Memoriam: 1933*, 1934; *Early History of a Sewing Machine Operator* (with Nathan Reznikoff), 1936 (prose); *Separate Way*, 1936; *Going To and Fro and Walking Up and Down*, 1941; *The Lionhearted*, 1944 (novel); *Inscriptions: 1944–1956*, 1959; *By the Waters of Manhattan: Selected Verse*, 1962; *Family Chronicle* (with Nathan and Sarah Reznikoff), 1963 (prose); *Testimony: The United States 1885–1890: Recitative*, 1965; *Testimony: The United States (1891–1900): Recitative*, 1968; *By the Well of Living and Seeing and The Fifth Book of the Maccabees*, 1969; *By the Well of Living & Seeing: New & Selected Poems 1918–1973*, 1974; *Holocaust*, 1975; *The Poems of Charles Reznikoff, 1918–1975*, 2005.

[How shall we mourn you who are killed and wasted]

How shall we mourn you who are killed and wasted,
sure that you would not die with your work unended,
as if the iron scythe in the grass stops for a flower?

1918

Aphrodite Vrania[1]

The ceaseless weaving of the uneven water.

1921

[The shoemaker sat in the cellar's dusk beside his bench]

The shoemaker sat in the cellar's dusk beside his bench and
    sewing-machine, his large, blackened hands, finger tips
    flattened and broad, busy.
Through the grating in the sidewalk over his window, paper
    and dust were falling year by year.   5

At evening Passover would begin. The sunny street was
    crowded. The shoemaker could see the feet of those who
    walked over the grating.
He had one pair of shoes to finish and he would be through.
His friend came in, a man with a long, black beard, in shabby,   10
    dirty clothes, but with shoes newly cobbled and blacked.
"Beautiful outside, really the world is beautiful."

A pot of fish was boiling on the stove. Sometimes the water
    bubbled over and hissed. The smell of the fish filled the
    cellar.   15
"It must be beautiful in the park now. After our fish we'll take
    a walk in the park." The shoemaker nodded.
The shoemaker hurried his work on the last shoe. The pot on
    the stove bubbled and hissed. His friend walked up and
    down the cellar in shoes newly cobbled and blacked.   20

1921

[1]The Greek goddess of love and beauty,
Aphrodite, combined with the Greek muse of
astronomy, Urania.

Hellenist[1]

As I, barbarian, at last, although slowly, could read Greek,
at "blue-eyed Athena"
I greeted her picture that had long been on the wall:
the head slightly bent forward under the heavy helmet,
as if to listen; the beautiful lips slightly scornful.   5

1934

[In steel clouds]

In steel clouds
to the sound of thunder
like the ancient gods:
our sky, cement;
the earth, cement;   5
our trees, steel;
instead of sunshine,
a light that has no twilight,
neither morning nor evening,
only noon   10

Coming up the subway stairs, I thought the moon
only another street-light—
a little crooked.

1934

[About an excavation]

About an excavation
a flock of bright red lanterns
has settled.

1934

The English in Virginia, April 1607[1']

They landed and could
see nothing but
meadows and tall
trees—

[1]Student of classical Greece.

[1']Based upon the *Works of Captain John Smith*,
edited by Edward Arber. [Reznikoff's note]

cypress, nearly three   5
   fathoms about at the
   roots,
rising straight for
   sixty or eighty feet
   without a branch.   10
In the woods were
   cedars, oaks, and
   walnut trees;
some beech, some elm,
   black walnut, ash,   15
   and sassafras; mul-
   berry trees in
   groves;
honey-suckle and
   other vines hanging   20
   in clusters on
   many trees.
They stepped on
   violets and other
   sweet flowers,   25
many kinds in many
   colors; straw-
   berries and rasp-
   berries were on
   the ground.   30
Blackbirds with red
   shoulders were
   flying about
and many small birds,
   some red, some blue;   35
the woods were full of deer;
and running
   everywhere
   fresh water—
   brooks, rundles,   40
   springs and creeks.
In the twilight,
   through the thickets
   and tall grass,
creeping upon all   45
   fours—the
   savages, their
   bows in their
   mouths.

                                                   1934

from **Testimony**[1]

I

The company had advertised for men to unload a steamer
    across the river. It was six o'clock in the morning, snowing,
    and still dark.
There was a crowd looking for work on the dock;
and all the while men hurried to the dock.   5
The man at the wheel
kept the bow of the launch
against the dock—
the engine running slowly;
and the men kept jumping   10
from dock to deck,
jostling each other,
and crowding into the cabin.

Eighty or ninety men were in the cabin as the launch pulled away.
There were no lights in the cabin, and no room to turn—whoever   15
    was sitting down could not get up, and whoever had his
    hand up could not get it down,
as the launch ran in the darkness
through the ice,
ice cracking   20
against the launch
bumping and scraping
against the launch,
banging up against it,
until it struck   25
a solid cake of ice,
rolled to one side, and slowly
came back to an even keel.

The men began to feel water running against their feet as if from
    a hose. "Cap," shouted one, "the boat is taking water! Put   30
    your rubbers on, boys!"
The man at the wheel turned.
"Shut up!" he said.
The men began to shout,
ankle-deep in water.   35
The man at the wheel turned
with his flashlight:

[1]Based on cases in the law reports. [Reznikoff's
note]

everybody was turning and pushing against each other;
those near the windows
were trying to break them,   40
in spite of the wire mesh
in the glass; those who had been near the door
were now in the river,
reaching for the cakes of ice,
their hands slipping off and   45
reaching for the cakes of ice.

II

Amelia was just fourteen and out of the orphan asylum; at her
  first job—in the bindery, and yes sir, yes ma'am, oh, so
  anxious to please.
She stood at the table, her blonde hair hanging about her   50
  shoulders, "knocking up" for Mary and Sadie, the stitchers
("knocking up" is counting books and stacking them in piles to
  be taken away).
There were twenty wire-stitching machines on the floor, worked
  by a shaft that ran under the table;   55
as each stitcher put her work through the machine,
she threw it on the table. The books were piling up fast
and some slid to the floor
(the forelady had said, Keep the work off the floor!);
and Amelia stooped to pick up the books—   60
three or four had fallen under the table
between the boards nailed against the legs.
She felt her hair caught gently;
put her hand up and felt the shaft going round and round
and her hair caught on it, wound and winding around it,   65
until the scalp was jerked from her head,
and the blood was coming down all over her face and waist.

1941

from **Holocaust**

Children

1

Once, among the transports, was one with children—two freight
  cars full.
The young men sorting out the belongings of those taken to the
  gas chambers
had to undress the children—they were orphans—   5

and then take them to the "lazarette."
There the S.S. men shot them.

2

A large eight-wheeled car arrived at the hospital
where there were children;
in the two trailers—open trucks—were sick women and men   10
lying on the floor.
The Germans threw the children into the trucks
from the second floor and the balconies—
children from one-year-old to ten;
threw them upon the sick in the trucks.   15
Some of the children tried to hold on to the walls,
scratched at the walls with their nails;
but the shouting Germans
beat and pushed the children towards the windows.

3

The children arrived at the camp in buses,   20
guarded by gendarmes of the French Vichy government.
The buses stopped in the middle of the courtyard
and the children were quickly taken off
to make room for the buses following.
Frightened but quiet,   25
the children came down in groups of fifty or sixty to eighty;
the younger children holding on to older ones.
They were taken upstairs to empty halls—
without any furniture
and only dirty straw bags on the floor, full of bugs: 30
children as young as two, three, or four years of age,
all in torn clothes and dirty,
for they had already spent two or three weeks in other camps,
uncared for;
and were now on their way to a death camp in Poland.   35
Some had only one shoe.
Many had diarrhea
but they were not allowed in the courtyard
where the water-closets were;
and, although there were chamber pots in the corridor
        of each story, these were too large for the small children.   40

The women in the camp who were also deportees
and about to be taken to other camps
were in tears:

they would get up before sunrise   45
and go into the halls where the children were—
in each a hundred to a hundred and twenty—
to mend the children's clothing;

but the women had no soap to clean the children,
no clean underwear to give them,   50
and only cold water with which to wash them.
When soup came for the children,
there were no spoons;
and it would be served in tins
but the tins were sometimes too hot for the children to hold.   55

After nine at night no one—except for three or four who had a
        permit—
was allowed to stay with the children.
Each room was then in darkness,
except for one bulb painted blue by blackout instructions.   60
The children would wake at night
calling for their mothers
and would then wake each other,
and sometimes all in the room would start crying out
and even wake the children in other rooms.   65

A visitor once stopped one of the children:
a boy of seven or eight, handsome, alert and gay.
He had only one shoe and the other foot was bare,
and his coat of good quality had no buttons.
The visitor asked him for his name   70
and then what his parents were doing;
and he said, "Father is working in the office
and Mother is playing the piano."
Then he asked the visitor if he would be joining his parents soon—
they always told the children they would be leaving soon to rejoin
        their parents—   75
and the visitor answered, "Certainly. In a day or two."
At that the child took out of his pocket
half an army biscuit he had been given in camp
and said, "I am keeping this half for Mother;"   80
and then the child who had been so gay
burst into tears.

4

Other children, also separated from their parents,
arrived in buses,

and were put down in the courtyard of the camp—   85
a courtyard surrounded by barbed wire
and guarded by gendarmes.
On the day of leaving for the death camp
they were awakened at five in the morning.
Irritable, half asleep, most of them refused to get up and go
     down to the courtyard.   90
Women—French volunteers, for they were still in France—
urged the children gently
to obey—they must!—and vacate the halls.
But many still would not leave the straw bags on which they slept   95
and then the gendarmes entered,
and took up the children in their arms;
the children screamed with fear,
struggled and tried to grasp each other.

5

Women guards at the women's section of the concentration camp   100
were putting little children into trucks
to be taken away to the gas chambers
and the children were screaming and crying, "Mamma, Mamma,"
even though the guards were trying to give them pieces of candy
     to quiet them.   105

1975

JOHN STEINBECK
1902–1968

John Steinbeck grew up in an Edenic slice of central California, the Salinas Valley. As a boy he rode his red pony, Jill, across tawny hills or along the lazy Salinas River that disappeared underground in summer. Twenty-five miles west on
the Pacific coast, the Steinbeck family owned a summer cottage near Monterey
Bay. On weekend jaunts to Pacific Grove, John and his three sisters splashed in
waves and peered into tide pools. He grew up loving the sea, open spaces, and
his family in equal measure. His mother Olive instilled in him a deep love for
language and legends, reading him the King James Bible, Greek myths, and
Arthurian tales. His father, John Adolph, taught him "loyalty to my friends,
respect for the law, love of country and instant and open revolt against tyranny,
whether it come from the bully in the schoolyard, the foreign dictator, or the
local demagogue," he wrote years later while defending playwright Arthur Miller,

who was called before the House Un-American Activities Committee (HUAC). John Steinbeck felt deep-seated and lifelong empathy for those who suffer needlessly at the hands of others.

His adolescence revolt was focused on his hometown of Salinas, a prosperous agricultural community of wealthy growers and shippers who, in John's eyes, slighted his middle-class family, particularly his father, an unsuccessful businessman. That homegrown elitism seared him, turning him into a writer at age fourteen. He spent the next fifteen years honing his craft—as an undergraduate at Stanford University (never completing a degree), as a young man in New York City in 1925 (the brief stint as laborer and reporter "beat the pants off me," he later admitted), and as a struggling writer, first in a remote Lake Tahoe cabin and then in the Pacific Grove cottage where he moved in 1930, composing stories that no one would publish.

Influenced profoundly by his plucky first wife, Carol Henning Steinbeck, and his ever-curious best friend, marine biologist Edward F. Ricketts, Steinbeck developed a more muscular prose than is evident in his first novel, *Cup of Gold* (1929), about pirate Henry Morgan. With Carol's nudging, he started writing about his own land, today known as "Steinbeck Country": early successes include *To a God Unknown* (1933), *The Pastures of Heaven* (1932), and stories later collected as *The Long Valley* (1938), including the four delicately wrought Red Pony stories. These tales about Jody Tifflin's stunned recognition of mortality were written as his mother, Olive, lay dying in 1933–1934. During those same sad months, to "cut against the gloom," he also wrote *Tortilla Flat*, a novel about Monterey *paisanos* who huddle together for camaraderie and joy. Steinbeck would revisit the themes of male friendship, reconfigured families, and homebuilding in several books, most notably *Cannery Row* (1945). In 1940, he and Ricketts collected marine invertebrates in Mexico's Sea of Cortez, a trip that resulted not only in *The Pearl* (1947), but also in a superb work of nonfiction, *Sea of Cortez* (1941), which lays out his and Ricketts's shared ecological perspective, considering humans as part of, not dominating, the natural world.

But Steinbeck is best known for novels about hardscrabble workers in 1930s California: *In Dubious Battle* (1936), *Of Mice and Men* (1937), and *The Grapes of Wrath* (1939). Each pits the powerless against the powerful, a theme that, in fact, weaves through most of his work. He was drawn to stories of ordinary folk, whether the Joads in *The Grapes of Wrath*, Soviet peasants in *A Russian Journal* (1948), Mexican revolutionaries in the film script for *Viva Zapata!* (1952), or Vietnam soldiers in "Letters to Alicia," 1966–1967, his last journalistic assignment. Throughout a career spanning four decades, Steinbeck remained an engaged artist, a man on the scene. In the last decade of his life he assessed American democracy and character in another triptych: *The Winter of Our Discontent* (1961), *Travels with Charley* (1962), and *America and Americans* (1966).

Steinbeck repeatedly insisted, however, that he was not a realist but wrote "layered" fiction that blends myth, ecology, history, and human behavior. In *The Grapes of Wrath*, layers might include the Biblical Exodus, migrant histories, and the ecological devastation of the Dust Bowl. In "The Promise," Jody's psychological growth is poised between the real and the imagined, between the dark cypress and the green tub where he "eliminated time and distance." And the "promise" of the title becomes increasingly nuanced and complex. In the 1950s and 1960s, Steinbeck's work focused more intensely on humanity's moral quandaries, most notably in *East of Eden* (1952), perhaps his most ambitious novel. It weaves together stories of his mother's family, the Hamiltons, and those of "symbol people," characters cast as Cain and Abel, wrestling with human frailty and guilt.

In 1962 he was awarded the Nobel Prize. In 1968 he died in New York City.

Susan Shillinglaw
San Jose State University

PRIMARY WORKS

The Pastures of Heaven, 1932; *To a God Unknown*, 1933; *Tortilla Flat*, 1935; *In Dubious Battle*, 1936; *Of Mice and Men*, 1937; *The Long Valley*, 1938; *The Grapes of Wrath*, 1939; *Sea of Cortez*, 1941; *The Moon is Down*, 1942; *Cannery Row*, 1945; *The Pearl*, 1945; *East of Eden*, 1952; *The Winter of Our Discontent*, 1961; *Travels With Charley*, 1962; *Journal of a Novel: The* East of Eden *Letters*, 1969; *Steinbeck: A Life in Letters*, eds. Elaine Steinbeck and Robert Wallsten, 1976; *Working Days: The Journals of The Grapes of Wrath*, ed. Robert DeMott, 1989; America and Americans *and Selected Nonfiction*, eds. Susan Shillinglaw and Jackson J. Benson, 2002.

from **The Red Pony**

III. The Promise

In a mid-afternoon of spring, the little boy Jody walked martially along the brush-lined road toward his home ranch. Banging his knee against the golden lard bucket he used for school lunch, he contrived a good bass drum, while his tongue fluttered sharply against his teeth to fill in snare drums and occasional trumpets. Some time back the other members of the squad that walked so smartly from the school had turned into the various little canyons and taken the wagon roads to their own home ranches. Now Jody marched seemingly alone, with highlifted knees and pounding feet; but behind him there was a phantom army with great flags and swords, silent but deadly.

The afternoon was green and gold with spring. Underneath the spread branches of the oaks the plants grew pale and tall, and on the hills the feed was smooth and thick. The sagebrushes shone with new silver leaves and the oaks wore hoods of golden green. Over the hills there hung such a green odor that the horses on the flats galloped madly, and then stopped, wondering; lambs, and even old sheep jumped in the air unexpectedly and landed on stiff legs, and went on eating; young clumsy calves butted their heads together and drew back and butted again.

As the grey and silent army marched past, led by Jody, the animals stopped their feeding and their play and watched it go by.

Suddenly Jody stopped. The grey army halted, bewildered and nervous. Jody went down on his knees. The army stood in long uneasy ranks for a moment, and then, with a soft sigh of sorrow, rose up in a faint grey mist and disappeared. Jody had seen the thorny crown of a horny-toad moving under the dust of the road. His grimy hand went out and grasped the spiked halo and held firmly while the little beast struggled. Then Jody turned the horny-toad over, exposing its pale gold stomach. With a gentle forefinger he stroked the throat and chest until the horny-toad relaxed, until its eyes closed and it lay languorous and asleep.

Jody opened his lunch pail and deposited the first game inside. He moved on now, his knees bent slightly, his shoulders crouched; his bare feet were wise and silent. In his right hand there was a long grey rifle. The brush along the road stirred restively under a new and unexpected population of grey tigers and grey bears. The hunting was very good, for by the time Jody reached the fork of the road where the mail box stood on a post, he had captured two more horny-toads, four little grass lizards, a blue snake, sixteen yellow-winged grasshoppers and a brown damp newt from under a rock. This assortment scrabbled unhappily against the tin of the lunch bucket.

At the road fork the rifle evaporated and the tigers and bears melted from the hillsides. Even the moist and uncomfortable creatures in the lunch pail ceased to exist, for the little red metal flag was up on the mail box, signifying that some postal matter was inside. Jody set his pail on the ground and opened the letter box. There was a Montgomery Ward catalog and a copy of the *Salinas Weekly Journal*. He slammed the box, picked up his lunch pail and trotted over the ridge and down into the cup of the ranch. Past the barn he ran, and past the used-up haystack and the bunkhouse and the cypress tree. He banged through the front screen door of the ranch house calling, "Ma'am, ma'am, there's a catalog."

Mrs. Tiflin was in the kitchen spooning clabbered milk into a cotton bag. She put down her work and rinsed her hands under the tap. "Here in the kitchen, Jody. Here I am."

He ran in and clattered his lunch pail on the sink. "Here it is. Can I open the catalog, ma'am?"

Mrs. Tiflin took up the spoon again and went back to her cottage cheese. "Don't lose it, Jody. Your father will want to see it." She scraped the last of the milk into the bag. "Oh, Jody, your father wants to see you before you go to your chores." She waved a cruising fly from the cheese bag.

Jody closed the new catalog in alarm. "Ma'am?"

"Why don't you ever listen? I say your father wants to see you."

The boy laid the catalog gently on the sink board. "Do you—is it something I did?"

Mrs. Tiflin laughed. "Always a bad conscience. What did you do?"

"Nothing, ma'am," he said lamely. But he couldn't remember, and besides it was impossible to know what action might later be construed as a crime.

His mother hung the full bag on a nail where it could drip into the sink. "He just said he wanted to see you when you got home. He's somewhere down by the barn."

Jody turned and went out the back door. Hearing his mother open the lunch pail and then gasp with rage, a memory stabbed him and he trotted away toward the barn, conscientiously not hearing the angry voice that called him from the house.

Carl Tiflin and Billy Buck, the ranch hand, stood against the lower pasture fence. Each man rested one foot on the lowest bar and both elbows on the top bar. They were talking slowly and aimlessly. In the pasture half a dozen horses nibbled contentedly at the sweet grass. The mare, Nellie, stood backed up against the gate, rubbing her buttocks on the heavy post.

Jody sidled uneasily near. He dragged one foot to give an impression of great innocence and nonchalance. When he arrived beside the men he put one foot on the lowest fence rail, rested his elbows on the second bar and looked into the pasture too. The two men glanced sideways at him.

"I wanted to see you," Carl said in the stern tone he reserved for children and animals.

"Yes, sir," said Jody guiltily.

"Billy, here, says you took good care of the pony before it died."

No punishment was in the air. Jody grew bolder. "Yes, sir, I did."

"Billy says you have a good patient hand with horses."

Jody felt a sudden warm friendliness for the ranch hand.

Billy put in. "He trained that pony as good as anybody I ever seen."

Then Carl Tiflin came gradually to the point. "If you could have another horse, would you work for it?"

Jody shivered. "Yes, sir."

"Well, look here, then. Billy says the best way for you to be a good hand with horses is to raise a colt."

"It's the *only* good way," Billy interrupted.

"Now, look here, Jody," continued Carl. "Jess Taylor, up to the ridge ranch, has a fair stallion, but it'll cost five dollars. I'll put up the money, you'll have to work it out all summer. Will you do that?"

Jody felt that his insides were shriveling. "Yes, sir," he said softly.

"And no complaining? And no forgetting when you're told to do something?"

"Yes, sir."

"Well, all right, then. Tomorrow morning you take Nellie up to the ridge ranch and get her bred. You'll have to take care of her, too, till she throws the colt."

"Yes, sir."

"You better get to the chickens and the wood now."

Jody slid away. In passing behind Billy Buck he very nearly put out his hand to touch the blue-jeaned legs. His shoulders swayed a little with maturity and importance.

He went to his work with unprecedented seriousness. This night he did not dump the can of grain to the chickens so that they had to leap over each other and struggle to get it. No, he spread the wheat so far and so carefully that the hens couldn't find some of it at all. And in the house, after listening to his mother's despair over boys who filled their lunch pails with slimy, suffocated reptiles, and bugs, he promised never to do it again. Indeed, Jody felt that all such foolishness was lost in the past. He was far too grown up ever to put horny-toads in his lunch pail any more. He carried in so much wood and built such a high structure with it that his mother walked in fear of an avalanche of oak. When he was done, when he had gathered eggs that had remained hidden for weeks, Jody walked down again past the cypress tree, and past the bunkhouse toward the pasture. A fat warty toad that looked out at him from under the watering trough had no emotional effect on him at all.

Carl Tiflin and Billy Buck were not in sight, but from a metallic ringing on the other side of the barn Jody knew that Billy Buck was just starting to milk a cow.

The other horses were eating toward the upper end of the pasture, but Nellie continued to rub herself nervously against the post. Jody walked slowly near, saying, "So, girl, so-o, Nellie." The mare's ears went back naughtily and her lips drew away from her yellow teeth. She turned her head around; her eyes were glazed and mad. Jody climbed to the top of the fence and hung his feet over and looked paternally down on the mare.

The evening hovered while he sat there. Bats and nighthawks flicked about. Billy Buck, walking toward the house carrying a full milk bucket, saw Jody and stopped. "It's a long time to wait," he said gently. "You'll get awful tired waiting."

"No I won't, Billy. How long will it be?"

"Nearly a year."

"Well, I won't get tired."

The triangle at the house rang stridently. Jody climbed down from the fence and walked to supper beside Billy Buck. He even put out his hand and took hold of the milk bucket to help carry it.

The next morning after breakfast Carl Tiflin folded a five-dollar bill in a piece of newspaper and pinned the package in the bib pocket of Jody's overalls. Billy Buck haltered the mare Nellie and led her out of the pasture.

"Be careful now," he warned. "Hold her up short here so she can't bite you. She's crazy as a coot."

Jody took hold of the halter itself and started up the hill toward the ridge ranch with Nellie skittering and jerking behind him. In the pasturage along the road the wild oat heads were just clearing their scabbards. The warm morning sun shone on Jody's back so sweetly that he was forced to take a serious stiff-legged hop now and then in spite of his maturity. On the fences the shiny blackbirds with red epaulets clicked their dry call. The meadowlarks sang like water, and the wild doves, concealed among the bursting leaves of the oaks, made a sound of restrained grieving. In the fields the rabbits sat sunning themselves, with only their forked ears showing above the grass heads.

After an hour of steady uphill walking, Jody turned into a narrow road that led up a steeper hill to the ridge ranch. He could see the red roof of the barn sticking up above the oak trees, and he could hear a dog barking unemotionally near the house.

Suddenly Nellie jerked back and nearly freed herself. From the direction of the barn Jody heard a shrill whistling scream and a splintering of wood, and then a man's voice shouting. Nellie reared and whinnied. When Jody held to the halter rope she ran at him with bared teeth. He dropped his hold and scuttled out of the way, into the brush. The high scream came from the oaks again, and Nellie answered it. With hoofs battering the ground the stallion appeared and charged down the hill trailing a broken halter rope. His eyes glittered feverishly. His stiff, erected nostrils were as red as flame. His black, sleek hide shone in the sunlight. The stallion came on so fast that he couldn't stop when he reached the mare. Nellie's ears went back; she whirled and kicked at him as he went by. The stallion spun around and reared. He struck the mare with his front hoof, and while she staggered under the blow, his teeth raked her neck and drew an ooze of blood.

Instantly Nellie's mood changed. She became coquettishly feminine. She nibbled his arched neck with her lips. She edged around and rubbed her shoulder against his shoulder. Jody stood half-hidden in the brush and watched. He heard the step of a horse behind him, but before he could turn, a hand caught him by the overall straps and lifted him off the ground. Jess Taylor sat the boy behind him on the horse.

"You might have killed," he said. "Sundog's a mean devil sometimes. He busted his rope and went right through a gate."

Jody sat quietly, but in a moment he cried, "He'll hurt her, he'll kill her. Get him away!"

Jess chuckled. "She'll be all right. Maybe you'd better climb off and go up to the house for a little. You could get maybe a piece of the pie up there."

But Jody shook his head. "She's mine, and the colt's going to be mine. I'm going to raise it up."

Jess nodded. "Yes, that's a good thing. Carl has good sense sometimes."

In a little while the danger was over. Jess lifted Jody down and then caught the stallion by its broken halter rope. And he rode ahead, while Jody followed, leading Nellie.

It was only after he had unpinned and handed over the five dollars, and after he had eaten two pieces of pie, that Jody started for home again. And Nellie followed docilely after him. She was so quiet that Jody climbed on a stump and rode her most of the way home.

The five dollars his father had advanced reduced Jody to peonage for the whole late spring and summer. When the hay was cut he drove a rake. He led the horse that pulled on the Jackson-fork tackle, and when the baler came he drove the circling horse that put pressure on the bales. In addition, Carl Tiflin taught him to milk and put a cow under his care, so that a new chore was added night and morning.

The bay mare Nellie quickly grew complacent. As she walked about the yellowing hillsides or worked at easy tasks, her lips were curled in a perpetual fatuous smile. She moved slowly, with the calm importance of an empress. When she was put to a team, she pulled steadily and unemotionally.

Jody went to see her every day. He studied her with critical eyes and saw no change whatever.

One afternoon Billy Buck leaned the many-tined manure fork against the barn wall. He loosened his belt and tucked in his shirttail and tightened the belt again. He picked one of the little straws from his hatband and put it in the corner of his mouth. Jody, who was helping Doubletree Mutt, the big serious dog, to dig out a gopher, straightened up as the ranch hand sauntered out of the barn.

"Let's go up and have a look at Nellie," Billy suggested.

Instantly Jody fell into step with him. Doubletree Mutt watched them over his shoulder; then he dug furiously, growled, sounded little sharp yelps to indicate that the gopher was practically caught. When he looked over his shoulder again, and saw that neither Jody nor Billy was interested, he climbed reluctantly out of the hole and followed them up the hill.

The wild oats were ripening. Every head bent sharply under its load of grain, and the grass was dry enough so that it made a swishing sound as Jody and Billy stepped through it. Halfway up the hill they could see Nellie and the iron-grey gelding, Pete, nibbling the heads from the wild oats. When they approached, Nellie looked at them and backed her ears and bobbed her head up and down rebelliously. Billy walked to her and put his hand under her mane and patted her neck, until her ears came forward again and she nibbled delicately at his shirt.

Jody asked, "Do you think she's really going to have a colt?"

Billy rolled the lids back from the mare's eyes with his thumb and forefinger. He felt the lower lip and fingered the black, leathery teats. "I wouldn't be surprised," he said.

"Well, she isn't changed at all. It's three months gone."

Billy rubbed the mare's flat forehead with his knuckle while she grunted with pleasure. "I told you you'd get tired waiting. It'll be five months more before you can see a sign, and it'll be at least eight months more before she throws the colt, about next January."

Jody sighed deeply. "It's a long time, isn't it?"

"And then it'll be about two years more before you can ride."

Jody cried out in despair, "I'll be grown up."

"Yep, you'll be an old man," said Billy.

"What color do you think the colt'll be?"

"Why, you can't ever tell. The stud is black and the dam is bay. Colt might be black or bay or gray or dappled. You can't tell. Sometimes a black dam might have a white colt."

"Well, I hope it's black, and a stallion."

"If it's a stallion, we'll have to geld it. Your father wouldn't let you have a stallion."

"Maybe he would," Jody said. "I could train him not to be mean."

Billy pursed his lips, and the little straw that had been in the corner of his mouth rolled down to the center. "You can't ever trust a stallion," he said critically. "They're mostly fighting and making trouble. Sometimes when they're feeling funny they won't work. They make the mares uneasy and kick hell out of the geldings. Your father wouldn't let you keep a stallion."

Nellie sauntered away, nibbling the drying grass. Jody skinned the grain from a grass stem and threw the handful into the air, so that each pointed, feathered seed sailed out like a dart. "Tell me how it'll be, Billy. Is it like when the cows have calves?"

"Just about. Mares are a little more sensitive. Sometimes you have to be there to help the mare. And sometimes if it's wrong, you have to—" he paused.

"Have to what, Billy?"

"Have to tear the colt to pieces to get it out, or the mare'll die."

"But it won't be that way this time, will it, Billy?"

"Oh, no. Nellie's thrown good colts."

"Can I be there, Billy? Will you be certain to call me? It's my colt."

"Sure, I'll call you. Of course I will."

"Tell me how it'll be."

"Why, you've seen the cows calving. It's almost the same. The mare starts groaning and stretching, and then, if it's a good right birth, the head and forefeet come out, and the front hoofs kick a hole just the way the calves do. And the colt starts to breathe. It's good to be there, 'cause if its feet aren't right maybe he can't break the sac, and then he might smother."

Jody whipped his leg with a bunch of grass. "We'll have to be there, then, won't we?"

"Oh, we'll be there, all right."

They turned and walked slowly down the hill toward the barn. Jody was tortured with a thing he had to say, although he didn't want to. "Billy," he began miserably, "Billy, you won't let anything happen to the colt, will you?"

And Billy knew he was thinking of the red pony, Gabilan, and of how it died of strangles. Billy knew he had been infallible before that, and now he was capable of failure. This knowledge made Billy much less sure of himself than he had been. "I can't tell," he said roughly. "All sorts of things might happen, and they wouldn't be my fault. I can't do everything." He felt badly about his lost prestige, and so he said, meanly, "I'll do everything I know, but I won't promise anything. Nellie's a good mare. She's thrown good colts before. She ought to this time." And he walked away from Jody and went into the saddle-room beside the barn, for his feelings were hurt.

Jody traveled often to the brushline behind the house. A rusty iron pipe ran a thin stream of spring water into an old green tub. Where the water spilled over and sank into the ground there was a patch of perpetually green grass. Even when the hills were brown and baked in the summer that little patch was green. The water whined softly into the trough all the year round. This place had grown to be a center-point for Jody. When he had been punished the cool green grass and the singing water soothed him. When he had been mean the biting acid of meanness left him at the brushline. When he sat in the grass and listened to the purling stream, the barriers set up in his mind by the stern day went down to ruin.

On the other hand, the black cypress tree by the bunkhouse was as repulsive as the water-tub was dear, for to this tree all the pigs came, sooner or later, to be slaughtered. Pig killing was fascinating, with the screaming and the blood, but it made Jody's heart beat so fast that it hurt him. After the pigs were scalded in the big iron tripod kettle and their skins were scraped and white, Jody had to go to the water-tub to sit in the grass until his heart grew quiet. The water-tub and the black cypress were opposites and enemies.

When Billy left him and walked angrily away, Jody turned up toward the house. He thought of Nellie as he walked, and of the little colt. Then suddenly he saw that he was under the black cypress, under the very singletree where the pigs were hung. He brushed his dry-grass hair off his forehead and hurried on. It seemed to him an unlucky thing to be thinking of his colt in the very slaughter place, especially after what Billy had said. To counteract any evil result of that bad conjunction he walked quickly past the ranch house, through the chicken yard, through the vegetable patch, until he came at last to the brushline.

He sat down in the green grass. The trilling water sounded in his ears. He looked over the farm buildings and across at the round hills, rich and yellow with grain. He could see Nellie feeding on the slope. As usual the water place eliminated time and distance. Jody saw a black, long-legged colt, butting against Nellie's flanks, demanding milk. And then he saw himself breaking a large colt to halter. All in a few moments the colt grew to be a magnificent animal, deep of chest, with a neck as high and arched as a seahorse's neck, with a tail that tongued and rippled like black flame. This horse was terrible to everyone but Jody. In the schoolyard the boys begged rides, and Jody smilingly agreed. But no sooner were they mounted than the black demon pitched them off. Why, that was his name, Black Demon! For a moment the trilling water and the grass and the sunshine came back, and then . . .

Sometimes in the night the ranch people, safe in their beds, heard a roar of hoofs go by. They said, "It's Jody, on Demon. He's helping out the sheriff again." And then . . .

The golden dust filled the air in the arena at the Salinas Rodeo. The announcer called the roping contests. When Jody rode the black horse to the starting chute the other contestants shrugged and gave up first place, for it was well known that Jody and Demon could rope and throw and tie a steer a great deal quicker than any roping team of two men could. Jody was not a boy any more, and Demon was not a horse. The two together were one glorious individual. And then . . .

The President wrote a letter and asked them to help catch a bandit in Washington. Jody settled himself comfortably in the grass. The little stream of water whined into the mossy tub.

The year passed slowly on. Time after time Jody gave up his colt for lost. No change had taken place in Nellie. Carl Tiflin still drove her to a light cart, and she pulled on a hay rake and worked the Jackson-fork tackle when the hay was being put into the barn.

The summer passed, and the warm bright autumn. And then the frantic morning winds began to twist along the ground, and a chill came into the air, and the poison oak turned red. One morning in September, when he had finished his breakfast, Jody's mother called him into the kitchen. She was pouring boiling water into a bucket full of dry midlings and stirring the materials to a steaming paste.

"Yes, ma'am?" Jody asked.

"Watch how I do it. You'll have to do it after this every other morning."

"Well, what is it?"

"Why, it's warm mash for Nellie. It'll keep her in good shape."

Jody rubbed his forehead with a knuckle. "Is she all right?" he asked timidly.

Mrs. Tiflin put down the kettle and stirred the mash with a wooden paddle. "Of course she's all right, only you've got to take better care of her from now on. Here, take this breakfast out to her!"

Jody seized the bucket and ran, down past the bunkhouse, past the barn, with the heavy bucket banging against his knees. He found Nellie playing with the water in the trough, pushing waves and tossing her head so that the water slopped out on the ground.

Jody climbed the fence and set the bucket of steaming mash beside her. Then he stepped back to look at her. And she was changed. Her stomach was swollen. When she moved, her feet touched the ground gently. She buried her nose in the bucket and gobbled the hot breakfast. And when she had finished and had pushed the bucket around the ground with her nose a little, she stepped quietly over to Jody and rubbed her cheek against him.

Billy Buck came out of the saddle-room and walked over. "Starts fast when it starts, doesn't it?"

"Did it come all at once?"

"Oh, no, you just stopped looking for a while." He pulled her head around toward Jody. "She's goin' to be nice, too. See how nice her eyes are! Some mares get mean, but when they turn nice, they just love everything." Nellie slipped her head under Billy's arm and rubbed her neck up and down between his arm and his side. "You better treat her awful nice now," Billy said.

"How long will it be?" Jody demanded breathlessly.

The man counted in whispers on his fingers. "About three months," he said aloud. "You can't tell exactly. Sometimes it's eleven months to the day, but it might be two weeks early, or a month late, without hurting anything."

Jody looked hard at the ground. "Billy," he began nervously, "Billy, you'll call me when it's getting born, won't you? You'll let me be there, won't you?"

Billy bit the tip of Nellie's ear with his front teeth. "Carl says he wants you to start right at the start. That's the only way to learn. Nobody can tell you anything. Like my old man did with me about the saddle blanket. He was a government packer when I was your size, and I helped him some. One day I left a wrinkle in my saddle blanket and made a saddle-sore. My old man didn't give me hell at all. But the next morning he saddled me up with a forty-pound stock saddle. I had to lead my horse and carry that saddle over a whole damn mountain in the sun. It darn near killed me, but I never left no wrinkles in a blanket again. I couldn't. I never in my life since then put on a blanket but I felt that saddle on my back."

Jody reached up a hand and took hold of Nellie's mane. "You'll tell me what to do about everything, won't you? I guess you know everything about horses, don't you?"

Billy laughed. "Why I'm half horse myself, you see," he said. "My ma died when I was born, and being my old man was a government packer in the mountains, and no cows around most of the time, why he just gave me mostly mare's milk." He continued seriously, "And horses know that. Don't you know it, Nellie?"

The mare turned her head and looked full into his eyes for a moment, and this is a thing horses practically never do. Billy was proud and sure of himself now. He boasted a little. "I'll see you get a good colt. I'll start you right. And if you do like I say, you'll have the best horse in the county."

That made Jody feel warm and proud, too; so proud that when he went back to the house he bowed his legs and swayed his shoulders as horsemen do. And he whispered, "Whoa, you Black Demon, you! Steady down there and keep your feet on the ground."

The winter fell sharply. A few preliminary gusty showers, and then a strong steady rain. The hills lost their straw color and blackened under the water, and the winter streams scrambled noisily down the canyons. The mushrooms and puffballs popped up and the new grass started before Christmas.

But this year Christmas was not the central day to Jody. Some undetermined time in January had become the axis day around which the months swung. When the rains fell, he put Nellie in a box stall and fed her warm food every morning and curried her and brushed her.

The mare was swelling so greatly that Jody became alarmed. "She'll pop wide open," he said to Billy.

Billy laid his strong square hand against Nellie's swollen abdomen. "Feel here," he said quietly. "You can feel it move. I guess it would surprise you if there were twin colts."

"You don't think so?" Jody cried. "You don't think it will be twins, do you, Billy?"

"No, I don't, but it does happen, sometimes."

During the first two weeks of January it rained steadily, Jody spent most of his time, when he wasn't in school, in the box stall with Nellie. Twenty times a day he put his hand on her stomach to feel the colt move. Nellie became more and more gentle and friendly to him. She rubbed her nose on him. She whinnied softly when he walked into the barn.

Carl Tiflin came to the barn with Jody one day. He looked admiringly at the groomed bay coat, and he felt the firm flesh over ribs and shoulders. "You've done a good job," he said to Jody. And this was the greatest praise he knew how to give. Jody was tight with pride for hours afterward.

The fifteenth of January came, and the colt was not born. And the twentieth came; a lump of fear began to form in Jody's stomach. "Is it all right?" he demanded of Billy.

"Oh, sure."

And again, "Are you sure it's going to be all right?"

Billy stroked the mare's neck. She swayed her head uneasily. "I told you it wasn't always the same time, Jody. You just have to wait."

When the end of the month arrived with no birth, Jody grew frantic. Nellie was so big that her breath came heavily, and her ears were close together and straight up, as though her head ached. Jody's sleep grew restless, and his dreams confused.

On the night of the second of February he awakened crying. His mother called to him, "Jody, you're dreaming. Wake up and start over again."

But Jody was filled with terror and desolation. He lay quietly a few moments, waiting for his mother to go back to sleep, and then he slipped his clothes on, and crept out in his bare feet.

The night was black and thick. A little misting rain fell. The cypress tree and the bunkhouse loomed and then dropped back into the mist. The barn door screeched as he opened it, a thing it never did in the daytime. Jody went to the rack and found a lantern and a tin box of matches. He lighted the wick and walked down the long straw-covered aisle to Nellie's stall. She was standing up. Her whole body weaved from side to side. Jody called to her, "So, Nellie, so-o, Nellie," but she did not stop her swaying nor look around. When he stepped into the stall and touched her on the shoulder she shivered under his hand. Then Billy Buck's voice came from the hayloft right above the stall.

"Jody, what are you doing?"

Jody started back and turned miserable eyes up toward the nest where Billy was lying in the hay. "Is she all right, do you think?"

"Why sure, I think so."

"You won't let anything happen, Billy, you're sure you won't?"

Billy growled down at him. "I told you I'd call you, and I will. Now you get back to bed and stop worrying that mare. She's got enough to do without you worrying her."

Jody cringed, for he had never heard Billy speak in such a tone. "I only thought I'd come and see," he said. "I woke up."

Billy softened a little then. "Well, you get to bed. I don't want you bothering her. I told you I'd get you a good colt. Get along now."

Jody walked slowly out of the barn. He blew out the lantern and set it in the rack. The blackness of the night and the chilled mist struck him and enfolded him. He wished he believed everything Billy said as he had before the pony died. It was a moment before his eyes, blinded by the feeble lantern-flame, could make any form of the darkness. The damp ground chilled his bare feet. At the cypress tree the roosting turkeys chattered a little in alarm, and the two good dogs responded to their duty and came charging out, barking to frighten away the coyotes they thought were prowling under the tree.

As he crept through the kitchen, Jody stumbled over a chair. Carl called from his bedroom. "Who's there? What's the matter there?"

And Mrs. Tiflin said sleepily. "What's the matter, Carl?"

The next second Carl came out of the bedroom carrying a candle, and found Jody before he could get into bed. "What are you doing out?"

Jody turned shyly away. "I was down to see the mare."

For a moment anger at being awakened fought with approval in Jody's father. "Listen," he said, finally, "there's not a man in this country that knows more about colts than Billy. You leave it to him."

Words burst out of Jody's mouth. "But the pony died——"

"Don't you go blaming that on him," Carl said sternly. "If Billy can't save a horse, it can't be saved."

Mrs. Tiflin called, "Make him clean his feet and go to bed, Carl. He'll be sleepy all day tomorrow."

It seemed to Jody that he had just closed his eyes to try to go to sleep when he was shaken violently by the shoulder. Billy Buck stood beside him, holding a lantern in his hand. "Get up," he said. "Hurry up." He turned and walked quickly out of the room.

Mrs. Tiflin called, "What's the matter? Is that you, Billy?"

"Yes, ma'am."

"Is Nellie ready?"

"Yes, ma'am."

"All right, I'll get up and heat some water in case you need it."

Jody jumped into his clothes so quickly that he was out the back door before Billy's swinging lantern was halfway to the barn. There was a rim of dawn on the mountain-tops, but no light had penetrated into the cup of the ranch yet. Jody ran frantically after the lantern and caught up to Billy just as he reached the barn. Billy hung the lantern to a nail on the stall-side and took off his blue denim coat. Jody saw that he wore only a sleeveless shirt under it.

Nellie was standing rigid and stiff. While they watched, she crouched. Her whole body was wrung with a spasm. The spasm passed. But in a few moments it started over again, and passed.

Billy muttered nervously, "There's something wrong." His bare hand disappeared. "Oh, Jesus," he said. "It's wrong."

The spasm came again, and this time Billy strained, and the muscles stood out on his arm and shoulder. He heaved strongly, his forehead beaded with perspiration. Nellie cried with pain. Billy was muttering, "It's wrong. I can't turn it. It's way wrong. It's turned all around wrong."

He glared wildly toward Jody. And then his fingers made a careful, careful diagnosis. His cheeks were growing tight and grey. He looked for a long questioning minute at Jody standing back of the stall. Then Billy stepped to the rack under the manure window and picked up a horseshoe hammer with his wet right hand.

"Go outside, Jody," he said.

The boy stood still and stared dully at him.

"Go outside, I tell you. It'll be too late."

Jody didn't move.

Then Billy walked quickly to Nellie's head. He cried. "Turn your face away, damn you, turn your face."

This time Jody obeyed. His head turned sideways. He heard Billy whispering hoarsely in the stall. And then he heard a hollow crunch of bone. Nellie chuckled shrilly. Jody looked back in time to see the hammer rise and fall again on the flat forehead. Then Nellie fell heavily to her side and quivered for a moment.

Billy jumped to the swollen stomach; his big pocketknife was in his hand. He lifted the skin and drove the knife in. He sawed and ripped at the tough belly. The air filled with the sick odor of warm living entrails. The other horses reared back against their halter chains and squealed and kicked.

Billy dropped the knife. Both of his arms plunged into the terrible ragged hole and dragged out a big, white, dripping bundle. His teeth tore a hole in the covering. A little black head appeared through the tear, and little slick, wet ears. A gurgling breath was drawn, and then another. Billy shucked off the sac and found his knife and cut the string. For a moment he held the little black colt in his arms and looked at it. And then he walked slowly over and laid it in the straw at Jody's feet.

Billy's face and arms and chest were dripping red. His body shivered and his teeth chattered. His voice was gone; he spoke in a throaty whisper. "There's your colt. I promised. And there it is. I had to do it—had to." He stopped and looked over his shoulder into the box stall. "Go get hot water and a sponge," he whispered. "Wash him and dry him the way his mother would. You'll have to feed him by hand. But there's your colt, the way I promised."

Jody stared stupidly at the wet, panting foal. It stretched on its chin and tried to raise its head. Its blank eyes were navy blue.

"God damn you," Billy shouted, "will you go now for the water? *Will you go?*"

Then Jody turned and trotted out of the barn into the dawn. He ached from his throat to his stomach. His legs were stiff and heavy. He tried to be glad because of the colt, but the bloody face, and the haunted, tired eyes of Billy Buck hung in the air ahead of him.

RICHARD WRIGHT
1908–1960

In 1941, Robert Park, one of the founders of the Chicago School of sociology, met thirty-three-year-old African American author Richard Wright and demanded to know, "How in hell did you happen?" The causes of Park's amazement are clear.

Born the son of Mississippi sharecroppers, Wright had managed to complete only an eighth-grade education. His early life had been marked by tremendous hardship. He had known intense physical hunger due to crippling poverty. He also suffered from what he later described as a kind of spiritual hunger because of what he regarded as the anti-intellectualism of members of his stern religious family, whose prohibitions compounded the general strictures imposed on a curious, young African American boy by life in the racist, segregated South. Yet by the time he met Park, Wright had overcome these limitations. He had transformed himself into the successful author of the bestselling *Native Son* (1940), an intense psychological novel set in Chicago about a young black man who is driven to commit murder by the forces of fear created by white oppression.

Wright's accomplishments were a testament to the failure of racism to effectively cripple his abilities and his aspirations. He chronicled the first part of his story in his autobiography of childhood, *Black Boy*, which was published to much acclaim in 1945. Like *Native Son* before it, *Black Boy* was chosen as a main selection by the influential Book of the Month Club. This publication not only increased Wright's renown in literary circles, but it gave him the remarkable ability to support himself financially with this writing.

As a young man, Wright had left the stifling atmosphere of the Arkansas and Mississippi of his childhood for Memphis and later for Chicago, following a path frequented by many others on what has become known as the "Great Migration" of African Americans out of the rural South. While in Chicago, Wright found intellectual kinship among members of and sympathizers with the Communist Party who encouraged him to publish his poetry in a number of left-wing journals. He then found his way to New York and from there to Paris, a move so transformational for Wright, who felt freer from racism there, that he was to spend the rest of his life living in France. His relocation and continued travels in Europe, Asia, and Africa provided fodder for thirteen more books, which included poetry, fiction, and nonfiction. Some of his prolific output was published posthumously, including a collection of haiku written near the end of his life, and most recently, the unfinished crime novel *A Father's Law*, published in 2008 with an introduction by his daughter Julia Wright.

Although Wright experimented throughout his career with genre, subject matter, and style, one constant remained—he strove to write works of social significance. As a young man living in Memphis, while reading the fiery writings of journalist H. L. Mencken, he came to the realization that words could be used as weapons, and he vowed to use language "to tell, to march, to fight." From the social realism and naturalism employed in his early indictments of American racism, to his exploration of existentialist philosophy in the novel *The Outsider* (1953), to his experimentation with creative nonfiction in *Black Power* (1954) and *Pagan Spain* (1957), Wright remained convinced that his role as a writer went beyond creating art for its own sake. He felt continually obligated to call out for social change, which he increasingly conceptualized of on an international scale. Throughout his career as a writer, Wright interjected his autobiographical voice into his creative work, casting himself as not only an artist and chronicler, but also as a participant and witness.

His first book, the collection of novellas *Uncle Tom's Children*, depicted black characters striking out against racism in more assertive ways than that of their literary predecessor, Harriet Beecher Stowe's longsuffering 1852 creation of the slave "Uncle Tom." Appearing originally in 1938, the collection was reprinted in a longer form, which included an autobiographical piece entitled "The Ethics of Jim Crow" in 1940. By augmenting the collection this way, Wright inserted himself alongside his fictional creations as a member of a generation who had to find new ways to come to terms with American racism. By intermingling literal and fictional truth, Wright does not give his readers the option of labeling the lynching in "Big Boy Leaves Home" as "just a story," but as a brutal reality with which both the writer and reader of conscience were obligated to grapple.

Jennifer Jensen Wallach
University of North Texas

PRIMARY WORKS

Uncle Tom's Children: Four Novellas, 1938, 1940; *Native Son*, 1940; *Native Son: The Biography of a Young American: A Play in Ten Scenes*, with Paul Green, 1941; *Twelve Million Black Voices*, 1941; *Black Boy: A Record of Childhood and Youth*, 1945; *The Outsider*, 1953; *Savage Holiday*, 1954; *Black Power: A Record of Reactions in a Land of Pathos*, 1954; *The Color Curtain: A Report on the Bandung Conference*, 1956; *Pagan Spain*, 1957; *White Man, Listen*, 1957; *The Long Dream*, 1958; *Eight Men*, 1961; *Lawd Today*, 1963; *American Hunger*, 1977; *Rite of Passage*, 1994; *Haiku: This Other World*, 1988; *A Father's Law*, 2008.

The Ethics of Living Jim Crow: An Autobiographical Sketch

I

My first lesson in how to live as a Negro came when I was quite small. We were living in Arkansas. Our house stood behind the railroad tracks. Its skimpy yard was paved with black cinders. Nothing green ever grew in that yard. The only touch of green we could see was far away, beyond the tracks, over where the white folks lived. But cinders were good enough for me and I never missed the green growing things. And anyhow, cinders were fine weapons. You could always have a nice hot war with huge black cinders. All you had to do was crouch behind the brick pillars of a house with your hands full of gritty ammunition. And the first woolly black head you saw pop out from behind another row of pillars was your target. You tried your very best to knock it off. It was great fun.

I never fully realized the appalling disadvantages of a cinder environment till one day the gang to which I belonged found itself engaged in a war with the white boys who lived beyond the tracks. As usual we laid down our cinder barrage, thinking that this would wipe the white boys out. But they replied with a steady bombardment of broken bottles. We doubled our cinder barrage, but they hid behind trees, hedges, and the sloping embankments of their lawns. Having no such fortifications, we retreated to the brick pillars of our homes. During the retreat a broken milk bottle caught me behind the ear, opening a deep gash which bled profusely. The sight of blood pouring over my face completely demoralized our ranks. My fellow-combatants left me standing paralyzed in the center of the yard, and scurried for their homes. A kind neighbor saw me and rushed me to a doctor, who took three stitches in my neck.

I sat brooding on my front steps, nursing my wound and waiting for my mother to come from work. I felt that a grave injustice had been done me. It was all right to throw cinders. The greatest harm a cinder could do was leave a bruise. But broken bottles were dangerous; they left you cut, bleeding, and helpless.

When night fell, my mother came from the white folks' kitchen. I raced down the street to meet her. I could just feel in my bones that she would understand. I knew she would tell me exactly what to do next time. I grabbed her hand and babbled out the whole story. She examined my wound, then slapped me.

"How come yuh didn't hide?" she asked me. "How come yuh awways fightin'?"

I was outraged, and bawled. Between sobs I told her that I didn't have any trees or hedges to hide behind. There wasn't a thing I could have used as a trench. And you couldn't throw very far when you were hiding behind the brick pillars of a house. She grabbed a barrel stave, dragged me home, stripped me naked, and beat me till I had a fever of one hundred and two. She would smack my rump with the stave, and, while the skin was still smarting, impart to me gems of Jim Crow wisdom. I was never to throw cinders any more. I was never to fight any more wars. I was never, never, under any conditions, to fight *white* folks again. And they were absolutely right in clouting me with the broken milk bottle. Didn't I know she was working hard every day in the hot kitchens of the white folks to make money to take care of me? When was I ever going to learn to be a good boy? She couldn't be bothered with my fights. She finished by telling me that I ought to be thankful to God as long as I lived that they didn't kill me.

All that night I was delirious and could not sleep. Each time I closed my eyes I saw monstrous white faces suspended from the ceiling, leering at me.

From that time on, the charm of my cinder yard was gone. The green trees, the trimmed hedges, the cropped lawns grew very meaningful, became a symbol. Even today when I think of white folks, the hard, sharp outlines of white houses surrounded by trees, lawns, and hedges are present somewhere in the background of my mind. Through the years they grew into an overreaching symbol of fear.

It was a long time before I came in close contact with white folks again. We moved from Arkansas to Mississippi. Here we had the good fortune not to live behind the railroad tracks, or close to white neighborhoods. We lived in the very heart of the local Black Belt. There were black churches and black preachers; there were black schools and black teachers; black groceries and black clerks. In fact, everything was so solidly black that for a long time I did not even think of white folks, save in remote and vague terms. But this could not last forever. As one grows older one eats more. One's clothing costs more. When I finished grammar school I had to go to work. My mother could no longer feed and clothe me on her cooking job.

There is but one place where a black boy who knows no trade can get a job, and that's where the houses and faces are white, where the trees, lawns, and hedges are green. My first job was with an optical company in Jackson, Mississippi. The morning I applied I stood straight and neat before the boss, answering all his questions with sharp yessirs and nosirs. I was very careful to pronounce my *sirs* distinctly, in order that he might know that I was polite, that I knew where I was, and that I knew he was a *white* man. I wanted that job badly.

He looked me over as though he were examining a prize poodle. He questioned me closely about my schooling, being particularly insistent about how much mathematics I had had. He seemed very pleased when I told him I had had two years of algebra.

"Boy, how would you like to try to learn something around here?" he asked me.

"I'd like it fine, sir," I said, happy. I had visions of "working my way up." Even Negroes have those visions.

"All right," he said. "Come on."

I followed him to the small factory.

"Pease," he said to a white man of about thirty-five, "this is Richard. He's going to work for us."

Pease looked at me and nodded.

I was then taken to a white boy of about seventeen.

"Morrie, this is Richard, who's going to work for us."

"Whut yuh sayin' there, boy!" Morrie boomed at me.

"Fine!" I answered.

The boss instructed these two to help me, teach me, give me jobs to do, and let me learn what I could in my spare time.

My wages were five dollars a week.

I worked hard, trying to please. For the first month I got along O.K. Both Pease and Morrie seemed to like me. I was not learning anything and nobody was volunteering to help me. Thinking they had forgotten that I was to learn something about the mechanics of grinding lenses, I asked Morrie one day to tell me about the work. He grew red.

"Whut yuh tryin' t' do, nigger, git smart?" he asked.

"Naw; I ain' tryin' t' git smart," I said.

"Well, don't, if yuh know whut's good for yuh!"

I was puzzled. Maybe he just doesn't want to help me, I thought. I went to Pease.

"Say, are you crazy, you black bastard?" Pease asked me, his gray eyes growing hard.

I spoke out, reminding him that the boss had said I was to be given a chance to learn something.

"Nigger, you think you're *white*, don't you?"

"Naw, sir!"

"Well, you're acting mighty like it!"

"But, Mr. Pease, the boss said . . ."

Pease shook his fist in my face.

"This is a *white* man's work around here, and you better watch yourself!"

From then on they changed toward me. They said good-morning no more. When I was just a bit slow in performing some duty, I was called a lazy black son-of-a-bitch.

Once I thought of reporting all this to the boss. But the mere idea of what would happen to me if Pease and Morrie should learn that I had "snitched" stopped me. And after all, the boss was a white man, too. What was the use?

The climax came at noon one summer day. Pease called me to his work-bench. To get to him I had to go between two narrow benches and stand with my back against a wall.

"Yes, sir," I said.

"Richard, I want to ask you something," Pease began pleasantly, not looking up from his work.

"Yes, sir," I said again.

Morrie came over, blocking the narrow passage between the benches. He folded his arms, staring at me solemnly.

I looked from one to the other, sensing that something was coming.

"Yes, sir," I said for the third time.

Pease looked up and spoke very slowly.

"Richard, *Mr.* Morrie here tells me you called me *Pease*."

I stiffened. A void seemed to open up in me. I knew this was the show-down.

He meant that I had failed to call him *Mr.* Pease. I looked at Morrie. He was gripping a steel bar in his hands. I opened my mouth to speak, to protest, to assure Pease that I had never called him simply *Pease*, and that I had never had any intentions of doing so, when Morrie grabbed me by the collar, ramming my head against the wall.

"Now, be careful, nigger!" snarled Morrie, baring his teeth. "*I* heard yuh call 'im *Pease!* 'N' if yuh say yuh didn't, yuh're callin' me a *lie*, see?" He waved the steel bar threateningly.

If I had said: No, sir, Mr. Pease, I never called you *Pease*, I would have been automatically calling Morrie a liar. And if I had said: Yes, sir, Mr. Pease, I called you *Pease*, I would have been pleading guilty to having uttered the worst insult that a Negro can utter to a southern white man. I stood hesitating, trying to frame a neutral reply.

"Richard, I asked you a question!" said Pease. Anger was creeping into his voice.

"I don't remember calling you *Pease*, Mr. Pease," I said cautiously. "And if I did, I sure didn't mean . . ."

"You black son-of-a-bitch! You called me *Pease*, then!" he spat, slapping me till I bent sideways over a bench. Morrie was on top of me, demanding:

"Didn't yuh call 'im *Pease*? If yuh say yuh didn't, I'll rip yo' gut string loose with this bar, yuh black granny dodger! Yuh can't call a white man a lie 'n' git erway with it, you black son-of-a-bitch!"

I wilted. I begged them not to bother me. I knew what they wanted. They wanted me to leave.

"I'll leave," I promised. "I'll leave right *now*."

They gave me a minute to get out of the factory. I was warned not to show up again, or tell the boss.

I went.

When I told the folks at home what had happened they called me a fool. They told me that I must never again attempt to exceed my boundaries. When you are working for white folks, they said, you got to "stay in your place" if you want to keep working.

II

My Jim Crow education continued on my next job, which was portering in a clothing store. One morning, while polishing brass out front, the boss and his twenty-year-old son got out of their car and half dragged and half kicked a Negro woman into the store. A policeman standing at the corner looked on, twirling his nightstick. I watched out of the corner of my eye, never slackening the strokes of my chamois upon the brass. After a few minutes, I heard shrill screams coming from the rear of the store. Later the woman stumbled out, bleeding, crying, and holding her stomach. When she reached the end of the block, the policeman grabbed her and accused her of being drunk. Silently, I watched him throw her into a patrol wagon.

When I went to the rear of the store, the boss and his son were washing their hands at the sink. They were chuckling. The floor was bloody and strewn with wisps of hair and clothing. No doubt I must have appeared pretty shocked, for the boss slapped me reassuringly on the back.

"Boy, that's what we do to niggers when they don't want to pay their bills," he said, laughing.

His son looked at me and grinned.

"Here, hava cigarette," he said.

Not knowing what to do, I took it. He lit his and held the match for me. This was a gesture of kindness, indicating that even if they had beaten the poor old woman, they would not beat me if I knew enough to keep my mouth shut.

"Yes, sir," I said, and asked no questions.

After they had gone, I sat on the edge of a packing box and stared at the bloody floor till the cigarette went out.

That day at noon, while eating in a hamburger joint, I told my fellow Negro porters what had happened. No one seemed surprised. One fellow, after swallowing a huge bite, turned to me and asked:

"Huh! Is tha' all they did t' her?"

"Yeah. Wasn't tha' enough?" I asked.

"Shucks! Man, she's a lucky bitch!" he said, burying his lips deep into a juicy hamburger. "Hell, it's a wonder they didn't lay her when they got through."

III

I was learning fast, but not quite fast enough. One day, while I was delivering packages in the suburbs, my bicycle tire was punctured. I walked along the hot, dusty road, sweating and leading my bicycle by the handle-bars.

A car slowed at my side.

"What's the matter, boy?" a white man called.

I told him my bicycle was broken and I was walking back to town.

"That's too bad," he said. "Hop on the running board."

He stopped the car. I clutched hard at my bicycle with one hand and clung to the side of the car with the other.

"All set?"

"Yes, sir," I answered. The car started.

It was full of young white men. They were drinking. I watched the flask pass from mouth to mouth.

"Wanna drink, boy?" one asked.

I laughed as the wind whipped my face. Instinctively obeying the freshly planted precepts of my mother, I said:

"Oh, no!"

The words were hardly out of my mouth before I felt something hard and cold smash me between the eyes. It was an empty whiskey bottle. I saw stars, and fell backwards from the speeding car into the dust of the road, my feet becoming entangled in the steel spokes of my bicycle. The white men piled out and stood over me.

"Nigger, ain' yuh learned no better sense'n tha' yet?" asked the man who hit me. "Ain' yuh learned t' say *sir* t' a white man yet?"

Dazed, I pulled to my feet. My elbows and legs were bleeding. Fists doubled, the white man advanced, kicking my bicycle out of the way.

"Aw, leave the bastard alone. He's got enough," said one.

They stood looking at me. I rubbed my shins, trying to stop the flow of blood. No doubt they felt a sot of contemptuous pity, for one asked:

"Yuh wanna ride t' town now, nigger? Yuh reckon yuh know enough t' ride now?"

"I wanna walk," I said, simply.

Maybe it sounded funny. They laughed.

"Well, walk, yuh black son-of-a-bitch!"

When they left they comforted me with:

"Nigger, yuh sho better be damn glad it wuz us yuh talked t' tha' way. Yuh're a lucky bastard, 'cause if yuh'd said tha' t' somebody else, yuh might've been a dead nigger now."

IV

Negroes who have lived South know the dread of being caught alone upon the streets in white neighborhoods after the sun has set. In such a simple situation as this the plight of the Negro in America is graphically symbolized. While white strangers may be in these neighborhoods trying to get home, they can pass unmolested. But the color of a Negro's skin makes him easily recognizable, makes him suspect, converts him into a defenseless target.

Late one Saturday night I made some deliveries in a white neighborhood. I was pedaling my bicycle back to the store as fast as I could, when a police car, swerving toward me, jammed me into the curbing.

"Get down and put up your hands!" the policemen ordered.

I did. They climbed out of the car, guns drawn, faces set, and advanced slowly.

"Keep still!" they ordered.

I reached my hands higher. They searched my pockets and packages. They seemed dissatisfied when they could find nothing incriminating. Finally, one of them said:

"Boy, tell your boss not to send you out in white neighborhoods after sundown."

As usual, I said:

"Yes, sir."

V

My next job was as hall-boy in a hotel. Here my Jim Crow education broadened and deepened. When the bell-boys were busy, I was often called to assist them. As many of the rooms in the hotel were occupied by prostitutes, I was constantly called to carry them liquor and cigarettes. These women were nude most of the time. They did not bother about clothing, even for bell-boys. When you went into their rooms, you were supposed to take their nakedness for granted, as though it startled you no more than a blue vase or a red rug. Your presence awoke in them no sense of shame, for you were not regarded as human. If they were alone, you could steal sidelong glimpses at them. But if they were receiving men, not a flicker of our eyelids could show. I remember one incident vividly. A new woman, a huge, snowy-skinned blonde, took a room on my floor. I was sent to wait upon her. She was in bed with a thick-set man; both were nude and uncovered. She said she wanted some liquor and slid out of bed and waddled across the floor to get her money from a dresser drawer. I watched her.

"Nigger, what in hell you looking at?" the white man asked me, raising himself upon his elbows.

"Nothing," I answered, looking miles deep into the blank wall of the room.

"Keep your eyes where they belong, if you want to be healthy!" he said.

"Yes, sir."

VI

One of the bell-boys I knew in this hotel was keeping steady company with one of the Negro maids. Out of a clear sky the police descended upon his home and arrested him, accusing him of bastardy. The poor boy swore he had had no intimate relations with the girl. Nevertheless, they forced him to marry her. When the child arrived, it was found to be much lighter in complexion than either of the two supposedly legal parents. The white men around the hotel made a great joke of it. They spread the rumor that some white cow must have scared the poor girl while she was carrying the baby. If you were in their presence when this explanation was offered, you were supposed to laugh.

VII

One of the bell-boys was caught in bed with a white prostitute. He was castrated and run out of town. Immediately after this all the bell-boys and hall-boys were called together and warned. We were given to understand that the boy who had been castrated was a "mighty, mighty lucky bastard." We were impressed with the fact that next time the management of the hotel would not be responsible for the lives of "trouble-makin' niggers." We were silent.

VIII

One night, just as I was about to go home, I met one of the Negro maids. She lived in my direction, and we fell in to walk part of the way home together. As we passed the white night-watchman, he slapped the maid on her buttock. I turned around, amazed. The watchman looked at me with a long, hard, fixed-under stare. Suddenly he pulled his gun and asked:

"Nigger, don't yuh like it?"

I hesitated.

"I asked yuh don't yuh like it?" he asked again, stepping forward.

"Yes, sir," I mumbled.

"Talk like it, then!"

"Oh, yes, sir!" I said with as much heartiness as I could muster.

Outside, I walked ahead of the girl, ashamed to face her. She caught up with me and said:

"Don't be a fool! Yuh couldn't help it!"

This watchman boasted of having killed two Negroes in self-defense.

Yet, in spite of all this, the life of the hotel ran with an amazing smoothness. It would have been impossible for a stranger to detect anything. The maids, the hall-boys, and the bell-boys were all smiles. They had to be.

IX

I had learned my Jim Crow lessons so thoroughly that I kept the hotel job till I left Jackson for Memphis. It so happened that while in Memphis

I applied for a job at a branch of the optical company. I was hired. And for some reason, as long as I worked there, they never brought my past against me.

Here my Jim Crow education assumed quite a different form. It was no longer brutally cruel, but subtly cruel. Here I learned to lie, to steal, to dissemble. I learned to play that dual role which every Negro must play if he wants to eat and live.

For example, it was almost impossible to get a book to read. It was assumed that after a Negro had imbibed what scanty schooling the state furnished he had no further need for books. I was always borrowing books from men on the job. One day I mustered enough courage to ask one of the men to let me get books from the library in his name. Surprisingly, he consented. I cannot help but think that he consented because he was a Roman Catholic and felt a vague sympathy for Negroes, being himself an object of hated. Armed with a library card, I obtained books in the following manner: I would write a note to the librarian, saying: "Please let this nigger boy have the following books." I would then sign it with the white man's name.

When I went to the library, I would stand at the desk, hat in hand, looking as unbookish as possible. When I received the books desired I would take them home. If the books listed in the note happened to be out, I would sneak into the lobby and forge a new one. I never took any chances guessing with the white librarian about what the fictitious white man would want to read. No doubt if any of the white patrons had suspected that some of the volumes they enjoyed had been in the home of a Negro, they would not have tolerated it for an instant.

The factory force of the optical company in Memphis was much larger than that in Jackson, and more urbanized. At least they liked to talk, and would engage the Negro help in conversation whenever possible. By this means I found that many subjects were taboo from the white man's point of view. Among the topics they did not like to discuss with Negroes were the following: American white women; the Ku Klux Klan; France, and how Negro soldiers fared while there; French women; Jack Johnson; the entire northern part of the United States; the Civil War; Abraham Lincoln; U. S. Grant; General Sherman; Catholics; the Pope; the Jews; the Republican Party; slavery; social equality; Communism; Socialism; the 13th and 14th Amendments to the Constitution; or any topic calling for positive knowledge or manly self-assertion on the part of the Negro. The most accepted topics were sex and religion.

There were many times when I had to exercise a great deal of ingenuity to keep out of trouble. It is a southern custom that all men must take off their hats when they enter an elevator. And especially did this apply to us blacks with rigid force. One day I stepped into an elevator with my arms full of packages. I was forced to ride with my hat on. Two white men stared at me coldly. Then one of them very kindly lifted my hat and placed it upon my armful of packages. Now the most accepted response for a Negro to make under such circumstances is to look at the white man out of the corner of his eye and grin. To have said: "Thank you!" would have made the white man *think* that you *thought* you were receiving from him a personal service. For such an act I have seen Negroes take a blow in the mouth. Finding the first alternative distasteful, and the second dangerous, I hit upon an acceptable course of action which fell safely between these two poles. I immediately—no sooner than my hat was lifted—pretended that my packages were about to spill, and appeared deeply distressed with keeping them in my arms. In this fashion I evaded having to acknowledge his service, and, in spite of adverse circumstances, salvaged a slender shred of personal pride.

How do Negroes feel about the way they have to live? I think this question can be answered in a single sentence. A friend of mine who ran an elevator once told me:

"Lawd, man! Ef it wuzn't fer them polices 'n' them ol' lynch-mobs, there wouldn't be nothin' but uproar down here!"

1937

Big Boy Leaves Home

I

Yo Mama don wear no drawers . . .

Clearly, the voice rose out of the woods, and died away. Like an echo another voice caught it up:

Ah seena when she pulled em off . . .

Another, shrill, cracking, adolescent:

N she washed 'em in alcohol . . .

Then a quartet of voices, blending in harmony, floated high above the tree tops:

N she hung 'em in the hall . . .

Laughing easily, four black boys came out of the woods into cleared pasture. They walked lollingly in bare feet, beating tangled vines and bushes with long sticks.

"Ah wished Ah knowed some mo lines t tha song."

"Me too."

"Yeah, when yuh gits t where she hangs em out in the hall yuh has t stop."

"Shucks, whut goes wid *hall?*"

"*Call.*"

"*Fall.*"

"*Wall.*"

"*Quall.*"

They threw themselves on the grass, laughing.

"Big Boy?"

"Huh?"

"Yuh know one thing?"

"Whut?"

"Yuh sho is crazy!"

"Crazy?"

"Yeah, yuh crazys a bed-bug!"

"Crazy bout whut?"

"Man, whoever hearda *quall*?"

"Yuh said yuh wanted something t go wid *hall*, didnt yuh?"

"Yeah, but whuts a *quall*?"

"Nigger, a *qualls* a *quall*."

They laughed easily, catching and pulling long green blades of grass with their toes.

"Waal, ef a *qualls* a *quall*, whut IS a *quall*?"

"Oh, Ah know."

"Whut?"

"Tha ol song goes something like this:

> Yo mama don wear no drawers,
> 　Ah seena when she pulled em off,
> N she washed em in alcohol,
> 　N she hung em out in the hall,
> 　N then she put em back on her QUALL!"

They laughed again. Their shoulders were flat to the earth, their knees propped up, and their faces square to the sun.

"Big Boy, yuhs CRAZY!"

"Don ax me nothin else."

"Nigger, yuhs CRAZY!"

They fell silent, smiling, drooping the lids of their eyes softly against the sunlight.

"Man, don the groun feel warm?"

"Jus lika bed."

"Jeesus, Ah could stay here ferever."

"Me too."

"Ah kin feel tha ol sun goin all thu me."

"Feels like mah bones is warm."

In the distance a train whistled mournfully.

"There goes number fo!"

"Hittin on all six!"

"Highballin it down the line!"

"Boun fer up Noth, Lawd, boun fer up North!"

They began to chant, pounding bare heels in the grass.

> Dis train boun fo Glory
> Dis train, Oh Hallelujah
> Dis train boun fo Glory
> Dis train, Oh Hallelujah
> Dis train boun fo Glory
> Ef yuh ride no need fer fret er worry

Dis train, Oh Hallelujah
Dis train . . .

Dis train don carry no gambler
Dis train, Oh Hallelujah
Dis train don carry no gambler
Dis train, Oh Hallelujah
Dis train don carry no gambler
No fo day creeper er midnight rambler
Dis train, Oh Hallelujah
Dis train . . .

When the song ended they burst out laughing, thinking of a train bound
for Glory.

"Gee, thas a good ol song!"

"Huuuuummmmmmmmmman . . ."

"Whut?"

"Geeee whiiiiiz . . ."

"Whut?"

"Somebody don let win! Das whut!"

Buck, Bobo, and Lester jumped up. Big Boy stayed on the ground, feigning sleep.

"Jeesus, tha sho stinks!"

"Big Boy!"

Big Boy feigned to snore.

"Big Boy!"

"Big Boy stirred as though in sleep.

"Big Boy!"

"Hunh?"

"Yuh rotten inside!"

"Rotten?"

"Lawd, cant yuh smell it?"

"Smell whut?"

"Nigger, yuh mus gotta bad col!"

"Smell whut?"

"NIGGER, YUH BROKE WIN!"

Big Boy laughed and fell back on the grass, closing his eyes.

"The hen whut cackles is the hen whut laid the egg."

"We ain no hens."

"Yuh cackled, didnt yuh?"

The three moved off with noses turned up.

"C mon!"

"Where yuh-all goin?"

"T the creek fer a swim."

"Yeah, les swim."

"Naw buddy naw!" said Big Boy, slapping the air with a scornful palm.

"Aw, c mon! Don be a heel!"

"N git *lynched*? Hell naw!"

"He ain gonna see us."

"How yuh know?"

"Cause he ain."

"Yuh-all go on. Ahma stay right here," said Big Boy.

"Hell, let im stay! C mon, les go," said Buck.

The three walked off, swishing at grass and bushes with sticks. Big Boy looked lazily at their backs.

"Hey!"

Walking on, they glanced over their shoulders.

"Hey, niggers!"

"C mon!"

Big Boy grunted, picked up his stick, pulled to his feet, and stumbled off.

"Wait!"

"C mon!"

He ran, caught up with them, leaped upon their backs, bearing them to the ground.

"Quit, Big Boy!"

"Gawddam, nigger!"

"Git t hell offa me!"

Big Boy sprawled in the grass beside them, laughing and pounding his heels in the ground.

"Nigger, whut yuh think we is, hosses?"

"How come yuh awways hoppin on us?"

"Lissen, wes gonna double-team on yuh one of these days n beat yo ol ass good."

Big Boy smiled.

"Sho nough?"

"Yeah, don yuh like it?"

"We gonna beat yuh sos yuh cant walk!"

"N dare yuh t do nothin erbout it!"

Big Boy bared his teeth.

"C mon! Try it now!"

The three circled around him.

"Say, Buck, yuh grab his feets!"

"N yuh git his head, Lester!"

"N Bobo, yuh git berhin n grab his arms!"

Keeping more than arm's length, they circled round and round Big Boy.

"C mon!" said Big Boy, feinting at one and then the other.

Round and round they circled, but could not seem to get any closer. Big Boy stopped and braced his hands on his hips.

"Is all three of yuh-all scareda me?"

"Les git im some other time," said Bobo, grinning.

"Yeah, we kin ketch yuh when yuh ain thinkin," said Lester.

"We kin trick yuh," said Buck.

They laughed and walked together.

Big Boy belched.

"Ahm hongry," he said.

"Me too."

"Ah wished Ah hada big hot pota belly-busters!"

"Cooked wid some good ol salty ribs . . ."

"N some good ol egg cornbread . . ."

"N some buttermilk . . ."

"N some hot peach cobbler swimmin in juice . . ."

"Nigger, hush!"

They began to chant, emphasizing the rhythm by cutting at grass with sticks.

> Bye n bye
> Ah wanna piece of pie
> Pies too sweet
> Ah wanna piece of meat
> Meats too red
> Ah wanna piece of bread
> Breads too brown
> Ah wanna go t town
> Towns too far
> Ah wanna ketch a car
> Cars too fas
> Ah fall n break mah ass
> Ahll understan it better bye n bye . . .

They climbed over a barbed-wire fence and entered a stretch of thick woods. Big Boy was whistling softly, his eyes half-closed.

"LES GIT IM!"

Buck, Lester, and Bobo whirled, grabbed Big Boy about the neck, arms, and legs, bearing him to the ground. He grunted and kicked wildly as he went back into weeds.

"Hol im tight!"

"Git his arms! Git his arms!"

"Set on his legs so he cant kick!"

Big Boy puffed heavily, trying to get loose.

"WE GOT YUH NOW, GAWDDAMMIT, WE GOT YUH NOW!"

"Thas a Gawddam lie!" said Big Boy. He kicked, twisted, and clutched for a hold on one and then the other.

"Say, yuh-all hep me hol his arms!" said Bobo.

"Aw, we got this bastard now!" said Lester.

"Thas a Gawddam lie!" said Big Boy again.

"Say, yuh-all hep me hol his arms!' called Bobo.

Big Boy managed to encircle the neck of Bobo with his left arm. He tightened his elbow scissors-like and hissed through his teeth:

"Yuh got me, ain yuh?"

"Hol im!"

"Les beat this bastard's ass!"

"Say, hep me hol his *arms*! Hes got aholda mah *neck*!" cried Bobo.

Big Boy squeezed Bobo's neck and twisted his head to the ground.

"Yuh got me, ain yuh?"

"Quit, Big Boy, yuh chokin me; yuh hurtin mah neck!" cried Bobo.

"Turn me loose!" said Big Boy.

"Ah ain got yuh! Its the others whut got yuh!" pleaded Bobo.

"Tell them others t git t hell offa me or Ahma break yo neck," said Big Boy.

"Ssssay, yyyuh-all gggit ooooffa Bbig Boy. Hhhes got me," gurgled Bobo.

"Cant yuh hol im?"

"Nnaw, hhes ggot mmah nneck . . ."

Big Boy squeezed tighter.

"N Ahma break it too less yuh tell em t git t hell offa me!"

"Ttturn mmmeee lllloose," panted Bobo, tears gushing.

"Cant yuh hol im, Bobo?" asked Buck.

"Nnaw, yuh-all tturn im lloose; hhhes got mah nnneck . . ."

"Grab his neck, Bobo . . ."

"Ah cant; yugurgur . . ."

To save Bobo, Lester and Buck got up and ran to a safe distance. Big Boy released Bobo, who staggered to his feet, slobbering and trying to stretch a crick out of his neck.

"Shucks, nigger, yuh almos broke mah neck," whimpered Bobo.

"Ahm gonna break yo ass nex time," said Big Boy.

"Ef Bobo coulda hel yuh we woulda had yuh," yelled Lester.

"Ah wuznt gonna let im do that," said Big Boy.

They walked together again, swishing sticks.

"Yuh see," began Big Boy, "when a ganga guys jump on yuh, all yuh gotta do is jus put the heat on one of them n make im tell the others t let up, see?"

"Gee, thas a good idee!"

"Yeah, thas a good idee!"

"But yuh almos broke mah neck, man," said Bobo.

"Ahma smart nigger," said Big Boy, thrusting out his chest.

II

They came to the swimming hole.

"Ah ain goin in," said Bobo.

"Done got scared?" asked Big Boy.

"Naw, Ah ain scared . . ."

"How come yuh ain goin in?"

"Yuh know ol man Harvey don errlow no niggers t swim in this hole."

"N jus las year he took a shot at Bob fer swimmin in here," said Lester.

"Shucks, ol man Harvey ain studyin bout us niggers," said Big Boy.

"Hes at home thinkin about his jelly-roll," said Buck.

They laughed.

"Buck, yo mins lowern a snakes belly," said Lester.

"Ol man Harveys too doggone ol t think erbout jelly-roll," said Big Boy.

"Hes dried up; all the saps done lef im," said Bobo.

"C mon, les go!" said Big Boy.

Bobo pointed.

"See tha sign over yonder?"

"Yeah."

"Whut it say?"

"NO TRESPASSIN," read Lester.

"Know whut tha mean?"

"Mean ain no dogs n niggers erllowed," said Buck.

"Waal, wes here now," said Big Boy. "Ef he ketched us even like this thered be trouble, so we just as waal go on in . . ."

"Ahm wid the nex one!"

"Ahll go ef anybody else goes!"

Big Boy looked carefully in all directions. Seeing nobody, he began jerking off his overalls.

"LAS ONE INS A OL DEAD DOG!"

"THAS YO MA!"

"THAS YO PA!"

"THAS BOTH YO MA N YO PA!"

They jerked off their clothes and threw them in a pile under a tree. Thirty seconds later they stood, black and naked, on the edge of the hole under a sloping embankment. Gingerly Big Boy touched the water with his foot.

"Man, this waters col," he said.

"Ahm gonna put mah cloes back on," said Bobo, withdrawing his foot.

Big Boy grabbed him about the waist.

"Like hell yuh is!"

"Git outta the way, nigger!" Bobo yelled.

"Throw im in!" said Lester.

"Duck im!"

Bobo crouched, spread his legs, and braced himself against Big Boy's body. Locked in each other's arms, they tussled on the edge of the hole, neither able to throw the other.

"C mon, les me n yuh push em in."

"O.K."

Laughing, Lester and Buck gave the two locked bodies a running push. Big Boy and Bobo splashed, sending up silver spray in the sunlight. When Big Boy's head came up he yelled:

"Yuh bastard!"

"Tha wuz yo ma yuh pushed!" said Bobo, shaking his head to clear the water from his eyes.

They did a surface dive, came up and struck out across the creek. The muddy water foamed. They swam back, waded into shallow water, breathing heavily and blinking eyes.

"C mon in!"

"Man, the waters fine!"

Lester and Buck hesitated.

"Les wet em," Big Boy whispered to Bobo.

Before Lester and Buck could back away, they were dripping wet from handsful of scooped water.

"Hey, quit!"

"Gawddam, nigger! Tha waters col!"

"C mon in!" called Big Boy.

"We jus as waal go on in now," said Buck.

"Look n see ef anybodys comin."

Kneeling, they squinted among the trees.

"Ain nobody."

"C mon, les go."

They waded in slowly, pausing each few steps to catch their breath. A desperate water battle began. Closing eyes and backing away, they shunted water into one another's faces with the flat palms of hands.

"Hey, cut it out!"

"Yeah, Ahm bout drownin!"

They came together in water up to their navels, blowing and blinking. Big Boy ducked, upsetting Bobo.

"Look out, nigger!"

"Don holler so loud!"

"Yeah, they kin hear yo ol big mouth a mile erway."

"This waters too col fer me."

"Thas cause it rained yistiddy."

They swam across and back again.

"Ah wish we hada bigger place t swim in."

"The white folks got plenty swimmin pools n we ain got none."

"Ah useta swim in the ol Mississippi when we lived in Vicksburg."

Big Boy put his head under the water and blew his breath. A sound came like that of a hippopotamus.

"C mon, les be hippos."

Each went to a corner of the creek and put his mouth just below the surface and blew like a hippopotamus. Tiring, they came and sat under the embankment.

"Look like Ah gotta chill."

"Me too."

"Les stay here n dry off."

"Jeeesus, Ahm col!"

They kept still in the sun, suppressing shivers. After some of the water had dried off their bodies they began to talk through clattering teeth.

"Whut would yuh do ef ol man Harveyd come erlong right now?"

"Run like hell!"

"Man, Ahd run so fas hed thinka black streaka lightnin shot pass im."

"But spose he hada gun?"

"Aw, nigger, shut up!"

They were silent. They ran their hands over wet, trembling legs, brushing water away. Then their eyes watched the sun sparkling on the restless creek.

Far away a train whistled.

"There goes number seven!"

"Headin fer up Noth!"

"Blazin it down the line!"

"Lawd, Ahm goin Noth some day."

"Me too, man."

"They say colored folks up Noth is got ekual rights."

They grew pensive. A black winged butterfly hovered at the water's edge. A bee droned. From somewhere came the sweet scent of honeysuckles. Dimly they could hear sparrows twittering in the woods. They rolled from side to side, letting sunshine dry their skins and warm their blood. They plucked blades of grass and chewed them.

"Oh!"

They looked up, their lips parting.

"Oh!"

A white woman, poised on the edge of the opposite embankment, stood directly in front of them, her hat in her hand and her hair lit by the sun.

"Its a woman!" whispered Big Boy in an underbreath. "A *white* woman!"

They stared, their hands instinctively covering their groins. Then they scrambled to their feet. The white woman backed slowly out of sight. They stood for a moment, looking at one another.

"Les git outta here!" Big Boy whispered.

"Wait till she goes erway."

"Les run, theyll ketch us here naked like this!"

"Mabbe theres a man wid her."

"C mon, les git our cloes," said Big Boy.

They waited a moment longer, listening.

"Whut t hell! Ahma git mah cloes," said Big Boy.

Grabbing at short tufts of grass, he climbed the embankment.

"Don run out here now!"

"C mon back, fool!"

Bobo hesitated. He looked at Big Boy, and then at Buck and Lester.

"Ahm goin wid Big Boy n git mah cloes," he said.

"Don run out there naked like tha, fool!" said Buck. "Yuh don know whos out there!"

Big Boy was climbing over the edge of the embankment.

"C mon," he whispered.

Bobo climbed after. Twenty-five feet away the woman stood. She had one hand over her mouth. Hanging by fingers, Buck and Lester peeped over the edge.

"C mon back; that womans sacred," said Lester.

Big Boy stopped, puzzled. He looked at the woman. He looked at the bundle of clothes. Then he looked at Buck and Lester.

"C mon, les git our cloes!"

He made a step.

"Jim!" the woman screamed.

Big Boy stopped and looked around. His hands hung loosely at his sides. The woman, her eyes wide, her hand over her mouth, backed away to the tree where their clothes lay in a heap.

"Big Boy, come back n wait till shes gone!"

Bobo ran to Big Boy's side.

"Les go home! Theyll ketch us here," he urged.

Big Boy's throat felt tight.

"Lady, we wanna git our cloes," he said.

Buck and Lester climbed the embankment and stood indecisively. Big Boy ran toward the tree.

"Jim!" the woman screamed. "Jim! Jim!"

Black and naked, Big Boy stopped three feet from her.

"We wanna git our cloes," he said again, his words coming mechanically.

He made a motion.

"You go away! You go away! I tell you, you go away!"

Big Boy stopped again, afraid. Bobo ran and snatched the clothes. Buck and Lester tried to grab theirs out of his hands.

"You go away! You go away! You go away!" the woman screamed.

"Les go!" said Bobo, running toward the woods.

CRACK!

Lester grunted, stiffened and pitched forward. His forehead struck a toe of the woman's shoes.

Bobo stopped, clutching the clothes. Buck whirled. Big Boy stared at Lester, his lips moving.

"Hes gotta gun; hes gotta gun!" yelled Buck, running wildly.

CRACK!

Buck stopped at the edge of the embankment, his head jerked backward, his body arched stiffly to one side; he toppled headlong, sending up a shower of bright spray to the sunlight. The creek bubbled.

Big Boy and Bobo backed away, their eyes fastened fearfully on a white man who was running toward them. He had a rifle and wore an army officer's uniform. He ran to the woman's side and grabbed her hand.

"You hurt, Bertha, you hurt?"

She stared at him and did not answer.

The man turned quickly. His face was red. He raised the rifle and pointed it at Bobo. Bobo ran back, holding the clothes in front of his chest.

"Don shoot me, Mistah, don shoot me . . ."

Big Boy lunged for the rifle, grabbing the barrel.

"You black sonofabitch!"

Big Boy clung desperately.

"Let go, you black bastard!"

The barrel pointed skyward.

CRACK!

The white man, taller and heavier, flung Big Boy to the ground. Bobo dropped the clothes, ran up, and jumped onto the white man's back.

"You black sonsofbitches!"

The white man released the rifle, jerked Bobo to the ground and began to batter the naked boy with his fists. Then Big Boy swung, striking the man in the mouth with the barrel. His teeth caved in, and he fell, dazed. Bobo was on his feet.

"C mon, Big Boy, les go!"

Breathing hard, the white man got up and faced Big Boy. His lips were trembling, his neck and chin wet with blood. He spoke quietly.

"Give me that gun, boy!"

Big Boy leveled the rifle and backed away.

The white man advanced.

"Boy, I say give me that gun!"

Bobo had the clothes in his arms.

"Run, Big Boy, run!"

The man came at Big Boy.

"Ahll kill yuh; Ahll kill yuh!" said Big Boy.

His fingers fumbled for the trigger.

The man stopped, blinked, spat blood. His eyes were bewildered. His face whitened. Suddenly, he lunged for the rifle, his hands outstretched.

CRACK!

He fell forward on his face.

"Jim!"

Big Boy and Bobo turned in surprise to look at the woman.

"Jim!" she screamed again, and fell weakly at the foot of the tree.

Big Boy dropped the rifle, his eyes wide. He looked around. Bobo was crying and clutching the clothes.

"Big Boy, Big Boy . . ."

Big Boy looked at the rifle, started to pick it up, but didn't. He seemed at a loss. He looked at Lester, then the white man; his eyes followed a thin stream of blood that seeped to the ground.

"Yuh done killed im," mumbled Bobo.

"Les go home!"

Naked, they turned and ran toward the woods. When they reached the barbed-wire fence they stopped.

"Les git our cloes on," said Big Boy.

They slipped quickly into overalls. Bobo held Lester's and Buck's clothes.

"Whut we gonna do wid these?"

Big Boy stared. His hands twitched.

"Leave em."

They climbed the fence and ran through the woods. Vines and leaves switched their faces. Once Bobo tripped and fell.

"C mon!" said Big Boy.

Bobo started crying, blood streaming from his scratches.

"Ahm scared!"

"C mon! Don cry! We wanna git home fo they ketches us!"

"Ahm scared!" said Bobo again, his eyes full of tears.

Big Boy grabbed his hand and dragged him along.

"C mon!"

III

They stopped when they got to the end of the woods. They could see the open road leading home, home to ma and pa. But they hung back, afraid. The thick shadows cast from the trees were friendly and sheltering. But the wide glare of sun stretching out over the fields was pitiless. They crouched behind an old log.

"We gotta git home," said Big Boy.

"Theys gonna lynch us," said Bobo, half-questioningly.

Big Boy did not answer.

"Theys gonna lynch us," said Bobo again.

Big Boy shuddered.

"Hush!" he said. He did not want to think of it. He could not think of it; there was but one thought, and he clung to that one blindly. He had to get home, home to ma and pa.

Their heads jerked up. Their ears had caught the rhythmic jingle of a wagon. They fell to the ground and clung flat to the side of a log. Over the crest of the hill came the top of a hat. A white face. Then shoulders in a blue shirt. A wagon drawn by two horses pulled into full view.

Big Boy and Bobo held their breath, waiting. Their eyes followed the wagon till it was lost in dust around a bend of the road.

"We gotta git home," said Big Boy.

"Ahm scared," said Bobo.

"C mon! Les keep t the fields."

They ran till they came to the cornfields. Then they went slower, for last year's corn stubbles bruised their feet.

They came in sight of a brickyard.

"Wait a minute," gasped Big Boy.

They stopped.

"Ahm goin on t mah home n yuh better go on t yos."

Bobo's eyes grew round.

"Ahm scared!"

"Yuh better go on!"

"Lemme go wid yuh; they'll ketch me . . ."

"Ef yuh kin git home mabbe yo folks kin hep yuh t git erway."

Big Boy started off. Bobo grabbed him.

"Lemme go wid yuh!"

Big Boy shook free.

"Ef yuh stay here theys gonna lynch yuh!" he yelled, running.

After he had gone about twenty-five yards he turned and looked; Bobo was flying through the woods like the wind.

Big Boy slowed when he came to the railroad. He wondered if he ought to go through the streets or down the track. He decided on the tracks. He could dodge a train better than a mob.

He trotted along the ties, looking ahead and back. His cheek itched, and he felt it. His hand came away smeared with blood. He wiped it nervously on his overalls.

When he came to his back fence he heaved himself over. He landed among a flock of startled chickens. A bantam rooster tried to spur him. He slipped and fell in front of the kitchen steps, grunting heavily. The ground was slick with greasy dishwater.

Panting, he stumbled through the doorway.

"Lawd, Big Boy, whuts wrong wid yuh?"

His mother stood gaping in the middle of the floor. Big Boy flopped wordlessly onto a stool, almost toppling over. Pots simmered on the stove. The kitchen smelled of food cooking.

"Whuts the matter, Big Boy?"

Mutely, he looked at her. Then he burst into tears. She came and felt the scratches on his face.

"Whut happened t yuh, Big Boy? Somebody been botherin yuh?"

"They after me, Ma! They after me ..."

"Who!"

"Ah ... Ah ... We ..."

"Big Boy, whuts wrong wid yuh?"

"He killed Lester n Buck," he muttered simply.

"Killed!"

"Yessum."

"Lester n Buck!"

"Yessum, Ma!"

"How killed?"

"He shot em, Ma!"

"Lawd Gawd in Heaven, have mercy on us all! This is mo trouble, mo trouble," she moaned, wringing her hands.

"N Ah killed im, Ma ..."

She stared, trying to understand.

"Whut happened, Big Boy?"

"We tried t git our cloes from the tree ..."

"Whut tree?"

"We wuz swimmin, Ma. N the white woman ..."

"*White* woman? ..."

"Yessum. She wuz at the swimmin hole ..."

"Lawd have mercy! Ah knowed yuh boys wuz gonna keep on till yuh got into somethin like this!"

She ran into the hall.

"Lucy!"

"Mam?"

"C mere!"

"Mam?"

"C mere, Ah say!"

"Whutcha wan, Ma? Ahm sewin."

"Chile, will yuh c mere like Ah ast yuh?"

Lucy came to the door holding an unfinished apron in her hands. When she saw Big Boy's face she looked wildly at her mother.

"Whuts the matter?"

"Wheres Pa?"

"Hes out front, Ah reckon."

"Git im, quick!"

"Whuts the matter, Ma?"

"Go git yo Pa, Ah say!"

Lucy ran out. The mother sank into a chair, holding a dish rag. Suddenly, she sat up.

"Big Boy, Ah thought yuh wuz at school?"

Big Boy looked at the floor.

"How come yuh didnt go t school?"

"We went t the woods."

She sighed.

"Ah done done all Ah kin fer yuh, Big Boy. Only Gawd kin hep yuh now."

"Ma, don let em git me; don let em git me . . ."

His father came into the doorway. He stared at Big Boy, then at his wife.

"Whuts Big Boy inter now?" he asked sternly.

"Saul, Big Boys done gone n got inter trouble wid the white folks."

The old man's mouth dropped, and he looked from one to the other.

"Saul, we gotta git im erway from here."

"Open yo mouth n talk! What yuh been doin?" The old man gripped Big Boy's shoulders and peered at the scratches on his face.

"Me n Lester n Buck n Bobo wuz out on ol man Harveys place swimmin . . ."

"Saul, its a *white* woman!"

Big Boy winced. The old man compressed his lips and stared at his wife. Lucy gaped at her brother as though she had never seen him before.

"Whut happened? Cant yuh-all talk?" the old man thundered, with a certain helplessness in his voice.

"We wuz swimmin," Big Boy began, "n then a white woman comes up t the hole. We got up right erway t git our cloes sos we could git erway, n she started screamin. Our cloes wuz right by the tree where she wuz standin, n when we started t git em she just screamed. We tol her we wanted our cloes . . . Yuh see, Pa, she wuz standin right *by* our cloes; n when we went t git em she jus screamed . . . Bobo got the cloes, n then he shot Lester . . ."

"*Who* shot Lester?"

"The white man."

"Whut white man?"

"Ah dunno, Pa. He wuz a soljer, n he had a rifle."

"A soljer?"

"Yessuh."

"A *soljer*?"

"Yessuh, Pa. A soljer."

The old man frowned.

"N then whut yuh-all do?"

"Waal, Buck said, 'Hes gotta gun!' N we started runnin. N then he shot Buck, n he fell in the swimmin hole. We didn't see im no mo ... He wuz close on us then. He looked at the white woman n then he started to shoot Bobo. Ah grabbed the gun, n we started fightin. Bobo jumped on his back. He started beatin Bobo. Then Ah hit im wid the gun. Then he started at me an Ah shot im. Then we run ..."

"Who seen?"

"Nobody."

"Wheres Bobo?"

"He went home."

"Anybody run after yuh-all?"

"Nawsuh."

"Yuh see anybody?"

"Nawsuh. Nobody but a white man. But he didnt see us."

"How long fo yuh-all lef the swimmin hole?"

"Little while ergo."

The old man nervously brushed his hand across his eyes and walked to the door. His lips moved, but no words came.

"Saul, whut we gonna do?"

"Lucy," began the old man, "go t Brother Sanders n tell im Ah said c mere; n go t Brother Jenkins n tell im Ah said c mere; n go t Elder Peters n tell im Ah said c mere. N don say nothin t nobody but whut Ah tol yuh. N when yuh it thu come straight back. Now go!"

Lucy dropped her apron across the back of a chair and ran down the steps. The mother bent over, crying and praying. The old man walked slowly over to Big Boy.

"Big Boy?"

Big Boy swallowed.

"Ahm talkin t yuh!"

"Yessuh."

"How come yuh didnt go t school this mawnin?"

"We went t the woods."

"Didnt yo ma send yuh t school?"

"Yessuh."

"How come yuh didnt go?"

"We went t the woods."

"Don yuh know thas wrong?"

"Yessuh."

"How come yuh go?"

Big Boy looked at his fingers, knotted them, and squirmed in his seat.

"AHM TALKIN T YUH!"

His wife straightened up and said reprovingly:

"Saul!"

The old man desisted, yanking nervously at the shoulder straps of his overalls.

"How long wuz the woman there?"

"Not long."

"Wuz she young?"

"Yessuh. Lika gal."

"Did yuh-all say anythin t her?"

"Nawsuh. We just said we wanted our cloes."

"N whut she say?"

"Nothin, Pa. She jus backed erway t the tree n screamed."

The old man stared, his lips trying to form a question.

"Big Boy, did yuh-all bother her?"

"Nawsuh, Pa. We didn't *touch* her."

"How long fo the white man come up?"

"Right erway."

"Whut he say?"

"Nothin. He jus cussed us."

Abruptly the old man left the kitchen.

"Ma, cant Ah go fo they ketches me?"

"Sauls doin whut he kin."

"Ma, Ma, Ah don wan em t ketch me . . ."

"Sauls doin whut he kin. Nobody but the good Lawd kin hep us now."

The old man came back with a shotgun and leaned it in a corner. Fascinatedly, Big Boy looked at it.

There was a knock at the front door.

"Liza, see whos there."

She went. They were silent, listening. They could hear her talking.

"Whos there?"

"Me."

"Who?"

"Me, Brother Sanders."

"C mon in. Sauls waitin fer yuh."

Sanders paused in the doorway, smiling.

"Yuh sent fer me, Brother Morrison?"

"Brother Sanders, wes in deep trouble here."

Sanders came all the way into the kitchen.

"Yeah?"

"Big Boy done gone n killed a white man."

Sanders stopped short, then came forward, his face thrust out, his mouth open. His lips moved several times before he could speak.

"A *white* man?"

"They gonna kill me; they gonna kill me!" Big Boy cried, running to the old man.

"Saul, cant we git im erway somewhere?"

"Here now, take it easy; take it easy," said Sanders, holding Big Boy's wrists.

"They gonna kill me; they gonna lynch me!"

Big Boy slipped to the floor. They lifted him to a stool. His mother held him closely, pressing his head to her bosom.

"Whut we gonna do?" asked Sanders.

"Ah done sent fer Brother Jenkins n Elder Peters."

Sanders leaned his shoulders against the wall. Then, as the full meaning of it all came to him, he exclaimed:

"Theys gonna git a mob! ..." His voice broke off and his eyes fell on the shotgun.

Feet came pounding on the steps. They turned toward the door. Lucy ran in crying. Jenkins followed. The old man met him in the middle of the room, taking his hand.

"Wes in bad trouble here, Brother Jenkins. Big Boy's done gone n killed a white man. Yuh-alls gotta hep me ..."

Jenkins looked hard at Big Boy.

"Elder Peters says hes comin," said Lucy.

"When all this happen?" asked Jenkins.

"Near bout a hour ergo, now," said the old man.

"Whut we gonna do?" asked Jenkins.

"Ah wanna wait till Elder Peters come," said the old man helplessly.

"But we gotta work fas ef we gonna do anythin," said Sanders. "Well git in trouble jus standin here like this."

Big Boy pulled away from his mother.

"Pa, lemme go now! Lemme go now!"

"Be still, Big Boy!"

"Where kin yuh go?"

"Ah could ketch a freight!"

"Thas *sho* death!" said Jenkins. "They'll be watchin em all!"

"Kin yuh-all hep me wid some money?" the old man asked.

They shook their heads.

"Saul, whut kin we do? Big Boy cant stay here."

There was another knock at the door.

The old man backed stealthily to the shotgun.

"Lucy go!"

Lucy looked at him, hesitating.

"Ah better go," said Jenkins.

It was Elder Peters. He came in hurriedly.

"Good evenin, everybody!"

"How yuh, Elder?"

"Good evenin."

"How yuh today?"

Peters looked around the crowded kitchen.

"Whuts the matter?"

"Elder, wes in deep trouble," began the old man. "Big Boy n some mo boys ..."

"... Lester n Buck n Bobo ..."

"... wuz over on ol man Harveys place swimmin ..."

"N he don like us niggers *none*," said Peters emphatically. He widened his legs and put his thumbs in the armholes of his vest.

"... n some white woman ..."

"Yeah?" said Peters, coming closer.

"... comes erlong n the boys tries t git their cloes where they done lef em under a tree. Waal, she started screamin n all, see? Reckon she thought the boys wuz after her. Then a white man in a soljers suit shoots two of em ..."

"... Lester n Buck ..."

"Huummm," said Peters. "Tha wuz ol man Harveys son."

"Harveys son?"

"Yuh mean the one tha wuz in the Army?"

"Yuh mean Jim?"

"Yeah," said Peters. "The papers said he wuz here for a vacation from his regiment. N tha woman the boys saw wuz jus erbout his wife ..."

They stared at Peters. Now that they knew what white person had been killed, their fears became definite.

"N whut else happened?"

"Big Boy shot the man ..."

"Harveys *son*?"

"He had t, Elder. He wuz gonna shoot im ef he didnt ..."

"Lawd!" said Peters. He looked around and put his hat back on.

"How long ergo wuz this?"

"Mighty near an hour, now, Ah reckon."

"Do the white folks know yit?"

"Don know, Elder."

"Yuh-all better git this boy outta here right now," said Peters. "Cause ef yuh don theres gonna be a lynchin ..."

"Where kin Ah go, Elder?" Big Boy ran up to him.

They crowded around Peters. He stood with his legs wide apart, looking up at the ceiling.

"Mabbe we kin hide im in the church till he kin git erway," said Jenkins. Peters' lips flexed.

"Naw, Brother, thall never do! Theyll git im there sho. N anyhow, ef they ketch im there itll ruin us all. We gotta git the boy outta town ..."

Sanders went up to the old man.

"Lissen," he said in a whisper. "Mah son, Will, the one whut drives fer the Magnolia Express Comny, is taking a truck o goods t Chicawgo in the mawnin. If we kin hide Big Boy somewhere till then, we kin put im on the truck ..."

"Pa, please, lemme go wid Will when he goes in the mawnin," Big Boy begged.

The old man stared at Sanders.

"Yuh reckon thas safe?"

"Its the only thing yuh *kin* do," said Peters.

"But where we gonna hide im till then?"

"Whut time yo boy leavin out in the mawnin?"

"At six."

They were quiet, thinking. The water kettle on the stove sang.

"Pa, Ah knows where Will passes erlong wid the truck out on Bullards Road. Ah kin hide in one of them ol kilns . . ."

"Where?"

"In one of them kilns we built . . ."

"But theyll git yuh there," wailed the mother.

"But there ain no place else fer im t go."

"Theres some holes big enough fer me t git in n stay till Will comes erlong," said Big Boy. "Please, Pa, lemme go fo they ketches me . . ."

"Let im go!"

"Please, Pa . . ."

The old man breathed heavily.

"Lucy, git his things!"

"Saul, theyll git im out there!" wailed the mother, grabbing Big Boy.

Peters pulled her away.

"Sister Morrison, ef yuh don let im go n git erway from here hes gonna be caught shos theres a Gawd in Heaven!"

Lucy came running with Big Boy's shoes and pulled them on his feet. The old man thrust a battered hat on his head. The mother went to the stove and dumped the skillet of corn pone into her apron. She wrapped it, and unbuttoning Big Boy's overalls, pushed it into his bosom.

"Heres somethin fer yuh t eat, n pray, Big Boy, cause thas all anybody kin do now . . ."

Big Boy pulled to the door, his mother clinging to him.

"Let im go, Sister Morrison!"

"Run fas, Big Boy!"

Big Boy raced across the yard, scattering the chickens. He paused at the fence and hollered back:

"Tell Bobo where Ahm hidin n tell im t c mon!"

IV

He made for the railroad, running straight toward the sunset. He held his left hand tightly over his heart, holding the hot pone of corn bread there. At times he stumbled over the ties, for his shoes were tight and hurt his feet. His throat burned from thirst; he had had no water since noon.

He veered off the track and trotted over the crest of a hill, following Bullard's Road. His feet slipped and slid in the dust. He kept his eyes straight ahead, fearing every clump of shrubbery, every tree. He wished it were night. If he could only get to the kilns without meeting anyone. Suddenly a thought came to him like a blow. He recalled hearing the old folks tell tales of bloodhounds, and fear made him run slower. None of them had thought of that. Spose blood-houns wuz put on his trail? Lawd! Spose a whole pack of em, foamin n howlin, tore im t pieces? He went limp and his feet dragged. Yeah, thas whut they wuz gonna send after im, blood-houns! N then thered be no way fer im t dodge! Why hadnt Pa let im take tha shotgun? He stopped. He oughta go back n git tha shotgun. And then when the mob came he would take some with him.

In the distance he heard the approach of a train. It jarred him back to a sharp sense of danger. He ran again, his big shoes sopping up and down in the dust. He was tired and his lungs were bursting from running. He wet his lips, wanting water. As he turned from the road across a plowed field he heard the train roaring at his heels. He ran faster, gripped in terror.

He was nearly there now. He could see the black clay on the sloping hillside. Once inside a kiln he would be safe. For a little while, at least. He thought of the shotgun again. If he only had something! Someone to talk to ... Thas right! Bobo! Bobod be wid im. Hed almost fergot Bobo. Bobod bringa gun; he knowed he would. N tergether they could kill the whole mob. Then in the mawning theyd git inter Will's truck n go far erway, t Chicawgo ...

He slowed to a walk, looking back and ahead. A light wind skipped over the grass. A beetle lit on his cheek and he brushed it off. Behind the dark pines hung a red sun. Two bats flapped against that sun. He shivered, for he was growing cold; the sweat on his body was drying.

He stopped at the foot of the hill, trying to choose between two patches of black kilns high above him. He went to the left, for there lay the one he, Bobo, Lester, and Buck had dug only last week. He looked around again; the landscape was bare. He climbed the embankment and stood before a row of black pits sinking four and five feet deep into the earth. He went to the largest and peered in. He stiffened when his ears caught the sound of a whir. He ran back a few steps and poised on his toes. Six foot of snake slid out of the pit and went into coil. Big Boy looked around wildly for a stick. He ran down the slope, peering into the grass. He stumbled over a tree limb. He picked it up and tested it by striking it against the ground.

Warily, he crept back up the slope, his stick poised. When about seven feet from the snake he stopped and waved the stick. The coil grew tighter, the whir sounded louder, and a flat head reared to strike. He went to the right, and the flat head followed him, the blue-black tongue darting forth; he went to the left, and the flat head followed him there too.

He stopped, teeth clenched. He had to kill this snake. Jus had t kill im! This wuz the safest pit on the hillside. He waved the stick again, looking at the snake before, thinking of a mob behind. The flat head reared higher. With stick over shoulder, he jumped in, swinging. The stick sang through the air, catching the snake on the side of the head, sweeping him out of coil. There was a brown writhing mass. Then Big Boy was upon him, pounding blows home, one on top of the other. He fought viciously, his eyes red, his teeth bared in a snarl. He beat till the snake lay still; then he stomped it with his heel, grinding its head into the dirt.

He stopped, limp, wet. The corners of his lips were white with spittle. He spat and shuddered.

Cautiously, he went to the hole and peered. He longed for a match. He imagined whole nests of them in there waiting. He put the stick into the hole and waved it around. Stooping, he peered again. It mus be awright. He looked over the hillside, his eyes coming back to the dead snake. Then he got to his knees and backed slowly into the hole.

When inside he felt there must be snakes all about him, ready to strike. It seemed he could see and feel them there, waiting tensely in coil. In the dark he imagined long white fangs ready to sink into his neck, his side, his legs. He wanted to come out, but kept still. Shucks, he told himself, ef there wuz any snakes in here they sho woulda done bit me by now. Some of his fear left, and he relaxed.

With elbows on ground and chin on palms, he settled. The clay was cold to his knees and thighs, but his bosom was kept warm by the hot pone of corn bread. His thirst returned and he longed for a drink. He was hungry, too. But he did not want to eat the corn pone. Naw, not now. Mabbe after erwhile, after Bobod came. Then theyd both eat the corn pone.

The view from his hole was fringed by the long tufts of grass. He could see all the way to Bullard's Road, and even beyond. The wind was blowing, and in the east the first touch of dusk was rising. Every now and then a bird floated past, a spot of wheeling black printed against the sky. Big Boy sighed, shifted his weight, and chewed at a blade of grass. A wasp droned. He heard number nine, far away and mournful.

The train made him remember how they had dug these kilns on long hot summer days, how they had made boilers out of big tin cans, filled them with water, fixed stoppers for steam, cemented them in holes with wet clay, and built fires under them. He recalled how they had danced and yelled when a stopper blew out of a boiler, letting out a big spout of steam and a shrill whistle. There were times when they had the whole hillside blazing and smoking. Yeah, yuh see, Big Boy wuz Casey Jones n wuz speedin it down the gleamin rails of the Southern Pacific. Bobo had number two on the Santa Fe. Buck wuz on the Illinoy Central. Lester the Nickel Plate. Lawd, how they shelved the wood in! The boiling water would almost jar the cans loose from the clay. More and more pine-knots and dry leaves would be piled under the cans. Flames would grow so tall they would have to shield their eyes. Sweat would pour off their faces. Then, suddenly, a peg would shoot high into the air, and

Pssseeeezzzzzzzzzzzzzzzzzzzzzz . . .

Big Boy sighed and stretched out his arm, quenching the flames and scattering the smoke. Why didnt Bobo c mon? He looked over the fields; there was nothing but dying sunlight. His mind drifted back to the kilns. He remembered the day when Buck, jealous of his winning, had tried to smash his kiln. Yeah, that ol sonofabitch! Naw, Lawd! He didnt go t say tha! Whut wuz he thinkin erbout? Cussin the dead! Yeah, po ol Buck wuz dead now. N Lester too. Yeah, it wuz awright fer Buck t smash his kiln. Sho. N he wished he hadnt socked ol Buck so hard tha day. He wuz sorry fer Buck now. N he sho wished he hadnt cussed po ol Bucks ma, neither. Tha wuz sinful! Mabbe Gawd would git im fer tha? But he didnt go t do it! Po Buck! Po Lester! Hed never treat anybody like tha ergin, never . . .

Dusk was slowly deepening. Somewhere, he could not tell exactly where, a cricket took up a fitful song. The air was growing soft and heavy. He looked over the fields, longing for Bobo . . .

He shifted his body to ease the cold damp of the ground, and thought back over the day. Yeah, hed been dam right erbout not wantin t go swimmin. N ef hed followed his right min hed neverve gone n got inter all this trouble. At first hed said naw. But shucks, somehow hed just went on wid the res. Yeah, he shoulda went on t school tha mawnin, like Ma told im t do. But, hell, who wouldnt git tireda awways drivin a guy t school! Tha wuz the big trouble, awways drivin a guy t school. He wouldnt be in all this trouble now ef it wuznt fer that Gawddam school! Impatiently, he took the grass out of his mouth and threw it away, demolishing the little red school house . . .

Yeah, ef they had all kept still n quiet when tha ol white woman showed-up, mabbe shedve went on off. But yuh never kin tell erbout these white folks. Mabbe she wouldntve went. Mabbe tha white man woulda killed all of em! All *fo* of em! Yeah, yuh never kin tell erbout white folks. Then, ergin, mabbe tha white woman woulda went on off n laffed. Yeah, mabbe tha white man woulda said: *Yuh nigger bastards git t hell outta here! Yuh know Gawddam well yuh don belong here*! N then they woulda grabbed their cloes n run like all hell . . . He blinked the white man away. Where wuz Bobo? Why didn't he hurry up n c mon?

He jerked another blade and chewed. Yeah, ef pa had only let im have the shotgun! He could stan off a whole mob wid a shotgun. He looked at the ground as he turned a shotgun over in his hands. Then he leveled it at an advancing white man. *Boooom*! The man curled up. Another came. He reloaded quickly, and let him have what the other had got. He too curled up. Then another came. He got the same medicine. Then the whole mob swirled around him, and he blazed away, getting as many as he could. They closed in; but, by Gawd, he had done his part, hadnt he? N the newspapersd say: NIGGER KILLS DOZEN OF MOB BEFO LYNCHED! Er mabbe theyd say: TRAPPED NIGGER SLAYS TWENTY BEFO KILLED! He smiled a little. Tha wouldnt be so bad, would it? Blinking the newspaper away, he looked over the fields. Where wuz Bobo? Why didnt he hurry up n c mon?

He shifted, trying to get a crick out of his legs. Shucks, he wuz gittin tireda this. N it wuz almos dark now. Yeah, there wuz a little bittie star way over yonder in the eas. Mabbe tha white man wuznt dead? Mabbe they wuznt even lookin fer im? Mabbe he could go back home now? Naw, better wait erwhile. Thad be bes. But, Lawd, ef he only had some water! He could hardly swallow, his throat was so dry. Gawddam them white folks! Thas all they wuz good fer, t run a nigger down lika rabbit! Yeah, they git yuh in a corner n then they let yuh have it. A thousan of em! He shivered, for the cold of the clay was chilling his bones. Lawd, spose they foun im here in this hole? N wid nobody t hep im? . . . But ain no use in thinkin erbout tha; wait till trouble come fo yuh start fightin it. But ef tha mob came one by one hed wipe em all out. Clean up the whole bunch. He caught one by the neck and choked him long and hard, choked him till his tongue and eyes popped out. Then he jumped upon his chest and stomped him like he had stomped that snake. When he had finished with one, another came. He choked him too. Choked till he sank slowly to the ground, gasping . . .

"Hoalo!"

Big Boy snatched his fingers from the white man's neck and looked over the fields. He saw nobody. Had someone spied him? He was sure that somebody had hollered. His heart pounded. But, shucks, nobody couldnt see im here in this hole . . . But mabbe theyd seen im when he wuz creepin up on im! Praps they wuz signalin fer the others? Yeah, they wuz creepin up on im! Mabbe he oughta git up n run . . . Oh! Mabbe tha wuz Bobo! Yeah, Bobo! He oughta clim out n see ef Bobo wuz lookin fer im . . . He stiffened.

"Hoalo!"

"Hoalo!"

"Wheres yuh?"

"Over here on Bullards Road!"

"C mon over!"

"Awright!"

He heard footsteps. Then voices came again, low and far away this time.

"Seen anybody?"

"Naw. Yuh?"

"Naw."

"Yuh reckon they got erway?"

"Ah dunno. Its hard t tell."

"Gawddam them sonofabitchin niggers!"

"We oughta kill ever black bastard in this country!"

"Waal, Jim got two of em, anyhow."

"But Bertha said there wuz *fo*!"

"Where in hell they hidin?"

"She said one of em wuz named Big Boy, or somethin like that."

"We went t his shack lookin fer im."

"Yeah?"

"But we didnt fin im."

"These niggers stick tergether; they don never tell on each other."

"We looked all thu the shack n couldnt fin hide ner hair of im. Then we drove the ol woman n man out n set the shack on fire . . ."

"Jeesus! Ah wished Ah coulda been there!"

"Yuh shoulda heard the ol nigger woman howl . . ."

"Hoalo!"

"C mon over!"

Big Boy eased to the edge and peeped. He saw a white man with a gun slung over his shoulder running down the slope. Wuz they gonna search the hill? Lawd, there wuz no way fer im t git erway now; he wuz caught! He shoulda knowed theyd git im here. N he didnt hava thing, notta thing t fight wid. Yeah, soon as the blood-houns came theyd fin im. Lawd, have mercy! Theyd lynch im right on the hill ... Theyd git im n tie im t a stake n burn im erlive! Lawd! Nobody but the good Lawd could hep im now, nobody ...

He heard more feet running. He nestled deeper. His chest ached. Nobody but the good Lawd could hep now. They wuz crowdin all round im n when they hada big crowd theyd close in on im. Then itd be over ... The good Lawd would have t hep im, cause nobody could hep im now, nobody ...

And then he went numb when he remembered Bobo. Spose Bobod come now? Hed be caught sho! Both of em would be caught! They'd make Bobo tell where he wuz! Bobo oughta not try to come now. Somebody oughta tell im ... But there wuz nobody; there wuz no way ...

He eased slowly back to the opening. There was a large group of men. More were coming. Many had guns. Some had coils of rope slung over shoulders.

"Ah tell yuh they still here, somewhere ..."

"But we looked all over!"

"What t hell! Wouldnt do t let em git erway!"

"Naw. Ef they git erway notta woman in this town would be safe."

"Say, whuts tha yuh got?"

"Er pillar."

"Fer whut?"

"Feathers, fool!"

"Chris! Thisll be hot ef we kin ketch them niggers!"

"Ol Anderson said he wuz gonna bringa barrela tar!"

"Ah got some gasoline in mah car ef yuh need it."

Big Boy had no feelings now. He was waiting. He did not wonder if they were coming after him. He just waited. He did not wonder about Bobo. He rested his cheek against the cold clay, waiting.

A dog barked. He stiffened. It barked again. He balled himself into a knot at the bottom of the hole, waiting. Then he heard the patter of dog feet.

"Look!"

"Whuts he got?"

"Its a snake!"

"Yeah, the dogs foun a snake!"

"Gee, its a big one!"

"Shucks, Ah wish he could fin one of them sonofabitchin niggers!"

The voices sank to low murmurs. Then he heard number twelve, its bell tolling and whistle crying as it slid along the rails. He flattened himself against the clay. Someone was singing:

> "We'll hang ever nigger t a sour apple tree ..."

When the song ended there was hard laughter. From the other side of the hill he heard the dog barking furiously. He listened. There was more than one dog now. There were many and they were barking their throats out.

"Hush, Ah hear them dogs!"

"When theys barkin like tha theys foun somethin!"

"Here they come over the hill!"

"WE GOT IM! WE GOT IM!"

There came a roar. Tha mus be Bobo; tha mus be Bobo ... In spite of his fear, Big Boy looked. The road, and half of the hillside across the road, were covered with men. A few were at the top of the hill, stenciled against the sky. He could see dark forms moving up the slopes. They were yelling.

"By Gawd, we got im!"

"C mon!"

"Where is he?"

"Theyre bringing im over the hill!"

"Ah got a rope fer im!"

"Say, somebody go n git the others!"

"Where is he? Cant we see im, Mister?"

"They say Berthas comin, too."

"Jack! Jack! Don leave me! Ah wanna see im!"

"Theyre bringin im over the hill, sweetheart!"

"AH WANNA BE THE FIRST T PUT A ROPE ON THA BLACK BASTARDS NECK!"

"Les start the fire!"

"Heat the tar!"

"Ah got some chains t chain im."

"Bring im over this way!"

"Chris, Ah wished Ah hada drink ..."

Big Boy saw men moving over the hill. Among them was a long dark spot. Tha mus be Bobo; tha mus be Bobo theys carryin ... They'll git im here. He oughta git up n run. He clamped his teeth and ran his hand across his forehead, bringing it away wet. He tried to swallow, but could not; his throat was dry.

They had started the song again:

"We'll hang ever nigger t a sour apple tree ..."

There were women singing now. Their voices made the song round and full. Song waves rolled over the top of pine trees. The sky sagged low, heavy with clouds. Wind was rising. Sometimes cricket cries cut surprisingly across the mob song. A dog had gone to the utmost top of the hill. At each lull of the song his howl floated full into the night.

Big Boy shrank when he saw the first tall flame light the hillside. Would they see im here? Then he remembered you could not see into the dark if you were standing in the light. As flames leaped higher he saw two men rolling a barrel up the slope.

"Say, gimme a han here, will yuh?"

"Awright, heave!"

"C mon! Straight up! Git t the other end!"

"Ah got the feathers here in this pillar!"

"BRING SOME MO WOOD!"

Big Boy could see the barrel surrounded by flames. The mob fell back, forming a dark circle. Theyd fin im here! He had a wild impulse to climb out and fly across the hills. But his legs would not move. He stared hard, trying to find Bobo. His eyes played over a long dark spot near the fire. Fanned by wind, flames leaped higher. He jumped. That dark spot had moved. Lawd, thas Bobo; thas Bobo . . .

He smelt the scent of tar, faint at first, then stronger. The wind brought it full into his face, then blew it away. His eyes burned and he rubbed them with his knuckles. He sneezed.

"LES GIT SOURVINEERS!"

He saw the mob close in around the fire. Their faces were hard and sharp in the light of the flames. More men and women were coming over the hill. The long dark spot was smudged out.

"Everbody git back!"

"Look! Hes gotta finger!"

"C MON! GIT THE GALS BACK FROM THE FIRE!"

"He's got one of his ears, see?"

"Whuts the matter!"

"A woman fell out! Fainted, Ah reckon . . ."

The stench of tar permeated the hillside. The sky was black and the wind was blowing hard.

"HURRY UP N BURN THE NIGGER FO IT RAINS!"

Big Boy saw the mob fall back, leaving a small knot of men about the fire. Then, for the first time, he had a full glimpse of Bobo. A black body flashed in the light. Bobo was struggling, twisting; they were binding his arms and legs.

When he saw them tilt the barrel he stiffened. A scream quivered. He knew the tar was on Bobo. The mob fell back. He saw a tar-drenched body glistening and turning.

"THE BASTARDS GOT IT!"

There was a sudden quiet. Then he shrank violently as the wind carried, like a flurry of snow, a widening spiral of white feathers into the night. The flames leaped tall as the trees. The scream came again. Big Boy trembled and looked. The mob was running down the slopes, leaving the fire clear. Then he saw a writhing white mass cradled in yellow flame, and heard screams, one on top of the other, each shriller and shorter than the last. The mob was quiet now, standing still, looking up the slopes at the writhing white mass gradually growing black, growing black in a cradle of yellow flame.

"PO ON MO GAS!"

"Gimme a lif, will yuh!"

Two men were struggling, carrying between them a heavy can. They set it down, tilted it, leaving it so that the gas would trickle down to the hollowed earth around the fire.

Big Boy slid back into the hole, his face buried in clay. He had no feelings now, no fears. He was numb, empty, as though all blood had been drawn from him. Then his muscles flexed taut when he heard a faint patter. A tiny stream of cold water seeped to his knees, making him push back to a drier spot. He looked up; rain was beating in the grass.

"Its rainin!"

"C mon, les git t town!"

"... don worry, when the fire git thu wid im hell be gone ..."

"Wait, Charles! Don leave me; its slippery here ..."

"Ahll take some of yuh ladies back in mah car ..."

Big Boy heard the dogs barking again, this time closer. Running feet pounded past. Cold water chilled his ankles. He could hear raindrops steadily hissing.

Now a dog was barking at the mouth of the hole, barking furiously, sensing a presence there. He balled himself into a knot and clung to the bottom, his knees and shins buried in water. The bark came louder. He heard paws scraping and felt the hot scent of dog breath on his face. Green eyes glowed and drew nearer as the barking, muffled by the closeness of the hole, beat upon his eardrums. Backing till his shoulders pressed against the clay, he held his breath. He pushed out his hands, his fingers stiff. The dog yawped louder, advancing, his bark rising sharp and thin. Big Boy rose to his knees, his hands before him. Then he flattened out still more against the bottom, breathing lungsful of hot dog scent, breathing it slowly, hard, but evenly. The dog came closer, bringing hotter dog scent. Big Boy could go back no more. His knees were slipping and slopping in the water. He braced himself, ready. Then, he never exactly knew how—he never knew whether he had lunged or the dog had lunged—they were together, rolling in the water. The green eyes were beneath him, between his legs. Dognails bit into his arms. His knees slipped backward and he landed full on the dog; the dog's breath left in a heavy gasp. Instinctively, he fumbled for the throat as he felt the dog twisting between his knees. The dog snarled, long and low, as though gathering strength. Big Boy's hands traveled swiftly over the dog's back, groping for the throat. He felt dognails again and saw green eyes, but his fingers had found the throat. He choked, feeling his fingers sink; he choked, throwing back his head and stiffening his arms. He felt the dog's body heave, felt dognails digging into his loins. With strength flowing from fear, he closed his fingers, pushing his full weight on the dog's throat. The dog heaved again, and lay still ... Big Boy heard the sound of his own breathing filling the hole, and heard shouts and footsteps above him going past.

For a long, long time he held the dog, held it long after the last footstep had died out, long after the rain had stopped.

V

Morning found him still on his knees in a puddle of rainwater, staring at the stiff body of a dog. As the air brightened he came to himself slowly. He held still for a long time, as though waking from a dream, as though trying to remember.

The chug of a truck came over the hill. He tried to crawl to the opening. His knees were stiff and a thousand needle-like pains shot from the bottom of his feet to the calves of his legs. Giddiness made his eyes blur. He pulled up and looked. Through brackish light he saw Will's truck standing some twenty-five yards away, the engine running. Will stood on the run-ningboard, looking over the slopes of the hill.

Big Boy scuffled out, falling weakly in the wet grass. He tried to call to Will, but his dry throat would make no sound. He tried again.

"Will!"

Will heard, answering:

"Big Boy, c mon!"

He tried to run and fell. Will came, meeting him in the tall grass.

"C mon," Will said, catching his arm.

They struggled to the truck.

"Hurry up!" said Will, pushing him onto the runningboard.

Will pushed back a square trapdoor which swung above the back of the driver's seat. Big Boy pulled through, landing with a thud on the bottom. On hands and knees he looked around in the semi-darkness.

"Wheres Bobo?"

Big Boy stared.

"Wheres Bobo?"

"They got im."

"When?"

"Las night."

"The mob?"

Big Boy pointed in the direction of a charred sapling on the slope of the opposite hill. Will looked. The trapdoor fell. The engine purred, the gears whined, and the truck lurched forward over the muddy road, sending Big Boy on his side.

For a while he lay as he had fallen, on his side, too weak to move. As he felt the truck swing around a curve he straightened up and rested his back against a stack of wooden boxes. Slowly, he began to make out objects in the darkness. Through two long cracks fell thin blades of daylight. The floor was of smooth steel, and cold to his thighs. Splinters and bits of sawdust danced with the rumble of the truck. Each time they swung around a curve he was pulled over the floor; he grabbed at corners of boxes to steady himself. Once he heard the crow of a rooster. It made him think of home, of ma and pa. He thought he remembered hearing somewhere that the house had burned, but could not remember where . . . It all seemed unreal now.

He was tired. He dozed, swaying with the lurch. Then he jumped awake. The truck was running smoothly, on gravel. Far away he heard two short blasts from the Buckeye Lumber Mill. Unconsciously, the thought sang through his mind: Its six erclock . . .

The trapdoor swung in. Will spoke through a corner of his mouth.

"How yuh comin?"

"Awright."

"How they git Bobo?"

"He wuz comin over the hill."

"Whut they do?"

"They burnt im ... Will, Ah wan some water; mah throats like fire ..."

"Well git some when we pass a fillin station."

Big Boy leaned back and dozed. He jerked awake when the truck stopped. He heard Will get out. He wanted to peep through the trapdoor, but was afraid. For a moment, the wild fear he had known in the hole came back. Spose theyd search n fin im? He quieted when he heard Will's footstep on the runningboard. The trapdoor pushed in. Will's hat came through, dripping.

"Take it, quick!"

Big Boy grabbed, spilling water into his face. The truck lurched. He drank. Hard cold lumps of brick rolled into his hot stomach. A dull pain made him bend over. His intestines seemed to be drawing into a tight knot. After a bit it eased, and he sat up, breathing softly.

The truck swerved. He blinked his eyes. The blades of daylight had turned brightly golden. The sun had risen.

The truck sped over the asphalt miles, sped northward, jolting him, shaking out of his bosom the crumbs of corn bread, making them dance with the splinters and sawdust in the golden blades of sunshine.

He turned on his side and slept.

1938

MARGARET WALKER
1915–1998

Margaret Abigail Walker was born July 7, 1915, in Birmingham, Alabama. She received her early education in New Orleans and completed her undergraduate education at Northwestern University in Evanston, Illinois, by the time she was nineteen years old. Although Walker had been writing and publishing before moving to Chicago as a student, it was there that her talent matured. A member of the Works Progress Administration (WPA), Walker shared intellectual, cultural, and professional interests with an important group of artists and writers who formed the Southside Writers Group, led by Richard Wright. Wright and Walker enjoyed a close friendship until he moved to New York in the late 1930s. When Walker left Chicago for graduate school at the University of Iowa in 1939, she was well on her way to becoming a major American poet.

In 1942, Walker completed the full manuscript of a volume she called *For My People*, the title poem of which had been written and published in Chicago five years earlier. *For My People* won the Yale Series of Younger Poets Award following its 1942 publication and brought her immediate recognition as the first African American woman to achieve national literary prominence.

Walker also began work on a historical novel based on her great grandmother, Elvira Ware Dozier, a project she would not finish until she returned to Iowa in the 1960s to complete her doctoral studies. *Jubilee* is the story of Vyry, whose commitment to her own set of values sustains her during difficult times both as a slave and later as a free woman. Walker's revisionist account of the Civil War and Reconstruction established a new tradition in southern American literature.

For most of her career, Walker lived in Jackson, Mississippi, where she taught English for thirty years. Married to Firnist James Alexander, Walker found time between writing and teaching to mother four children as well as a host of grandchildren.

Walker described herself as a "poet and dreamer who has tried to make her life a poem," a statement suggestive of the many influences and traditions found in her writing, the most notable of which is oratory. She works with sounds, rhythms, and meanings that are drawn from an African American cultural framework and that embrace classical mythology, Judeo-Christian humanism, and African spirituality. With precision of language and sharpness of imagery, Walker captures a wide range of feelings within Anglo-American and traditional African American literary forms. The "I" that frequently appears in her poetry reveals a collective voice reminiscent of Walt Whitman, yet it remains distinctive in its lyrical cadences.

As a writer-activist for the civil rights movement—which her writing helped to fuel and which she acknowledged as a major source of her work—Walker was the model for an entire generation of African American women writers, many of whose careers she midwived into existence through her efforts as a public spokesperson, literary sponsor, workshop leader, and conference organizer. Walker died in 1998 after a long illness.

Maryemma Graham
University of Kansas

PRIMARY WORKS

For My People, 1942; *Jubilee*, 1966; *Profits for a New Day*, 1970; *Richard Wright, Daemonic Genius: A Portrait of the Man, A Critical Look at His Work*, 1986; *This Is My Century: New and Collected Poems*, 1988; *How I Wrote Jubilee and Other Essays on Life and Literature*, 1990; *On Being Female, Black, and Free: Essays by Margaret Walker, 1932–1992*, ed. Maryemma Graham, 1997.

from **Jubilee**

No more auction block for me!

7. Cook in the Big House

Early in the spring of 1851 a fairly well-developed plot for an uprising among the slaves of Lee County, with the assistance of free Negroes and white abolitionists, became known to the High Sheriff of the county. How the news began to leak out and through what sources could not be determined by most Negroes. In the first place, the slaves on Marse John's plantation were not fully informed as to what nature the plot took nor how an uprising could take place. Brother Zeke was so troubled that he confided to his flock at their regular meeting place at the Rising Glory Church that it must be a false rumor since no definite plans had ever come to his knowledge. It was first suspected, however, by the guards or patter-rollers[1] and the drivers, who claimed that the Negroes were unusually hard to manage. And the neighboring whites claimed there were unusual movements in town among strange whites and in the county among free Negroes. At first the planters were not suspicious and hardly dared believe the piece-meal information they received. Why would their slaves want to do such a thing?

As Big Missy said to Marse John, "They are all well treated, and we love them and take good care of them just like a part of our family. When they are sick we nurse them back to health. We feed and clothe them and teach them the Christian religion. Our nigras are good and wouldn't try such a thing unless some criminal minds aided and abetted them, like abolitionists and free niggers from outside the state." Such monstrous activities were beyond the wildest imaginations of their good and happy childlike slaves!

Nevertheless, if there was such ingratitude lurking among them, after all the money that had been spent on food and clothes and doctor bills, the owners must be realistic and resort to drastic methods to counteract such activity. They must not wait too long to listen to reason. Hastily and secretly, Marse John and his planter friends gathered with this purpose. There they decided, as their drivers had suggested, that the first thing was to seek out the culprits and see that they were punished to the full extent of the law, chiefly by hanging. Thus they would make an example of them and put the fear of God in the rest of the slaves. Second, they must clamp down harder on the movements of all blacks, enforce the curfew laws and all of the Black Code, thereby rigorously maintaining control over their property, both land and chattel slaves. Finally, but not least, they must seek out all abolitionists guilty of giving aid and comfort to the black enemies of the Georgia people, and either force them out of the state or deal with them so harshly that they would willingly leave. As for the free Negroes, all of them should be called in for questioning and under threat of revoking their papers, forcing them back into slavery, they should be made to leave the state. Meanwhile, the planters should continue to question trusted slaves for any information and should keep watch for any signs of the development of the plot or for any unusual movements of the slaves. The guards and patter-rollers were ordered to search the slave cabins to make sure no weapons or firearms of any kind came into the possession of any black person, slave or free.

May Liza and Caline told Vyry and Lucy and Aunt Sally, "Marster and Big Missy done taking to whisper and shush all the time."

---

[1]Colloquial term for "patrollers," roving groups of whites responsible for keeping watch and maintaining control over the movement of blacks in the slave South.

"We act like we don't see nothing and don't hear nothing neither."

If any Negroes were caught in the woods or in the swamps they always said, "We's looking for greens and herbs for medicine and teas."

Many slaves, like Aunt Sally, had gardens around their cabins with collards growing almost into the door. These they cultivated when they did not go to the fields. But the tension was growing so they were forbidden any free activity. Marse John like his other planter friends redoubled his guards and patter-rollers and changed the curfew from nine o'clock to first dark or about one hour after sundown.

The growing tension exploded when the two Negro women accused of having killed their master and his mother by poisoning his food were convicted of murder and sentenced to be hanged. Like Aunt Sally and Vyry and Lucy, they worked in the kitchen of their Marster's Big House. When they were brought to the county jail for trial one afternoon it was quickly decided that they were guilty and had confessed the crime so that nothing was left but to hang them as soon as a judge could set the time and a hangman nearby could be summoned to do the deed.

This episode created a great disturbance among both planters and slaves. Among the planters' families there was unmistakable panic, and among the slaves there was great fear. Mutual distrust hung in the air between blacks and whites. In addition to the recent increase of guards on his place, Marse John, at the request of Grimes, purchased three additional bloodhounds for his plantation.

One of the murders had been committed several months before the second crime and the women were not at first suspected, but when the master died, a doctor confirmed suspicions expressed earlier when the man's mother died. The news traveled fast, and long before the date of the hanging had been set, the crime was common knowledge in every household.

The darkest day in Vyry's young life came without warning. Big Missy and Marse John had arranged to sell Aunt Sally. She would go first to Savannah and then by boat to New Orleans, where she would go on the auction block and be sold to the highest bidder. The morning she was ordered to go, she and Vyry went as usual to the kitchen. Big Missy came out in the kitchen after breakfast and told Aunt Sally to get her things together; there was a wagon in the backyard waiting to take her to Savannah. Now Aunt Sally was ready. She had her head-rag on and she had tied in a bundle the few things she had in the world including the few rags of clothes she wore. She had spread out one of her big aprons and tied them in it. Now she carried it in her arms. Tears were running down her fat black cheeks and she could not control her trembling lips. Vyry stood dazed and numb. Even when Aunt Sally hugged and kissed her, Vyry did not cry. She could not believe this was real, that she would be forced apart from Aunt Sally, that Aunt Sally was leaving and going somewhere. She heard Aunt Sally saying, "Goodbye, honey, don't yall forget to pray. Pray to God to send His chilluns a Moses, pray to Jesus to have mercy on us poor suffering chilluns.

Goodbye, honey, don't you forget Aunt Sally and don't forget to pray. Aunt Sally know she ain't never gwine see yall no more in this here sinful world, but I'm gwine be waiting for you on the other side where there ain't gwine be no more auction block. Goodbye, honey-child, goodbye."

Even then Vyry's eyes were dry. But then she saw poor old Aunt Sally clinging to Sam and Big Boy. She heard her sobbing pitifully, "Oh, Lord, when is you gwine send us that Moses? When you gwine set us peoples free? Jesus, how long? Marster, how long? They is taking all I got in the world from me, they is sending me way down yonder to that cruel auction block! Oh, Lord, how long is we gotta pray?" They were pulling her away but stumbling along crying and muttering she kept saying, "Oh, Lord, have mercy!"

Then Vyry found herself shaking like a leaf in a whirlwind. Salt tears were running in her mouth, and her short, sharp finger nails were digging in the palms of her hands. Suddenly she decided she would go with Aunt Sally, and just then Big Missy slapped her so hard she saw stars and when she saw straight again Aunt Sally was gone.

The first woman who came in from the fields to cook in the Big House did not suit anybody. Her food did not please Marse John and he said so, complaining and cursing at the same time. He grew more and more petulant at each meal, and Big Missy railed at him, "You are so cross and peevish you act like a child!" And he would swear, "Damn you, I was a fool! Had a good cook, been cooking ever since I was a boy, and I let you persuade me to sell her, damn you, don't you talk to me." To make it worse the house servants swore all-out war with the woman and would not help her do anything. She had never worked in the kitchen and knew nothing about where to find anything. She was confused by all the house servants whispering and muttering around her, even within earshot of the white folks. Caline said, "House servants and field hands just don't mix. I ain't no yard nigger myself and I don't have nothing to do with yard niggers. First place, they stinks!"

Vyry was still grieving over the loss of Aunt Sally, but she also resented the woman, and did no more than absolutely necessary to help her. Finally, Big Missy Salina admitted that the woman would have to go.

Then there was a brief interim when Big Missy tried several other women. After the field woman, an older woman from a nearby plantation was sold to Marse John and recommended as an excellent cook, but she ran away within twenty-four hours. They caught her, but Big Missy and Marster decided not to keep her but sent her back, instead, to her former master. The third woman was sickly and she coughed over the pots. In less than a month she grew so much worse that before they realized her trouble she was dead, dying one night on her own pallet after having cooked supper and worked all day. Vyry took her place in the emergency. Thus began her life as cook in the Big House. She always dated the time back to Aunt Sally's going away. Vyry knew the work thoroughly, having been accustomed to the kitchen from childhood. She had worked seven years under Aunt Sally and she not only had learned all she knew from her, but she cooked exactly like

Aunt Sally. Although Marse John was immediately pleased with the food, he thought she was too young to be entrusted with the responsibility of chief cook, and that the work would be too hard for her. When he said this to Missy Salina she decided at once that Vyry should be the cook. Vyry did not care. She had really had to do all the heavy work with the other women anyway, and she was glad to get the kitchen once more to herself. For a short time she was troubled with Big Missy coming into the kitchen, opening the pots to see what was in them, and giving shrill nervous orders which Vyry generally disregarded. After a terrible steaming burn Big Missy ceased to trouble Vyry, much to the girl's relief. The house servants were again satisfied, and the usual atmosphere of an uneasy peace seemed to descend once more over the household.

One morning Vyry was busy with the breakfast dishes when Big Missy came into the kitchen and said, "Vyry, there's a free nigger down at the stables shoeing Marster's horses. I guess you'd best take him a mouthful of something to eat. But mind, you'd better not give him anything fresh. See if you can't find some leftovers. Claims he's hungry and can't work. I don't see howcome he needs anything before dinnertime. He's only been working since six o'clock." Vyry said, "Yes'm. I'll see after him." Big Missy went off grumbling about free niggers being nothing but trouble, "and you mark my words, John'll be sorry for bringing him on this place."

Vyry finished her dishes and when she was ready to start dinner she fixed a plate of food and took it to the hired blacksmith. Rarely, indeed, did a free Negro come on the place to work. The overseers were afraid of the trouble free Negroes might make among the slaves, but there had not been a blacksmith on the place for a long time, so this man had been brought in from the nearby village where he owned his own smithy.

He was so busy working he did not hear Vyry's light step behind him, and when he turned and looked up, her milk-white face startled him. She was five and a half feet tall with her sandy hair roped high on her head. Her cold, bluish-gray eyes looked out without emotion. Her mouth was tight in a straight, hard line. He quickly recovered when he saw she wore the cheap calico and sack clothes of a slave.

"First off, I thought you was the young Missus. You look just like her."

"I'm a slave all right," snapped Vyry. "Here's your food. I ain't got no time for swapping gossip."

Then he stood up straight. He made no move to take the food, but giving her a long look said, "Ain't no hurry, is there? Or do they *pay* you to work so fast? I just wanted to know what might be your name?"

"Ain't got no name," said Vyry, and putting the food down on the ground she turned to walk away from him. But he was too quick for her. He jumped before her and caught her by the arm, "Easy, gal, I mean no harm. Bide a bit, and tell me who's your man?"

"You know who ain't, I reckon, and I'll thank you to turn me loose."

"Too good for a black man, hanh? I reckon the white folks got they eyes on you themselves."

"Don't know about that. I ain't had no trouble so far, and I ain't looking for none from black nor white."

He snickered. "Ain't feeding you saltpeter, hanh, to keep a good cook cooking?"

Vyry spoke out angrily, "Nigger, make haste and turn me loose!"

At that he narrowed his eyes and moved his hand.

"I may be a nigger, but I'm still a free man, and that's more'n you can say, Miss Stuck-up, with your ass on your shoulder. If you would marriage with me, I'd buy your freedom!" With that he turned to one side, looked her full in the eye, tossed back his massive black head, sparked his eyes, flashed his pearl-white teeth, and jingled the coins in his pocket. The word "freedom" caught her up short, and giving him a quick questioning glance she sized him up from head to toe. He had the strong, hard, muscular body that went with his trade and his shoulders were as big as a barrel. Black as a spade and stockily built, he looked like a powerful giant. There was just enough animal magnetism in him to trouble Vyry, and he was never more magnetic than now while she paused to weigh his words.

"You ain't got enough gold to buy me with what you jingling in your jeans." She said this half-scornfully, but she did not move now that she was perfectly free to go.

"I got a thousand gold pieces and a thousand silver pieces and I don't carry them in my jeans. I reckon they'll buy your freedom, or do you think you're worth more than that?"

"Show me your money first, and talk to me later."

"Why I got to show you? Can you buy, or can you sell?" Scornfully he chided her,

> White man got the eye for gold,
> And nigger man do what he told.

She continued just as pertly. "Then I gotta be getting back to my cooking. When you speaks to Marster bout buying my freedom so's I can marriage with you, I'll gossip with you then, till times gets better."

> Lil piece of wheat bread,
> Lil piece of pie,
> Gwine have that yaller gal,
> Or else I'll die.

1966

Southern Song

I want my body bathed again by southern suns, my soul
    reclaimed again from southern land. I want to rest
    again in southern fields, in grass and hay and clover

bloom; to lay my hand again upon the clay baked by a
    southern sun, to touch the rain-soaked earth and smell   5
    the smell of soil.

I want my rest unbroken in the fields of southern earth;
    freedom to watch the corn wave silver in the sun and
    mark the splashing of a brook, a pond with ducks and
    frogs and count the clouds.   10

I want no mobs to wrench me from my southern rest; no
    forms to take me in the night and burn my shack and
    make for me a nightmare full of oil and flame.

I want my careless song to strike no minor key; no fiend to
    stand between my body's southern song—the fusion of   15
    the South, my body's song and me.

        1942

For My People

For my people everywhere singing their slave songs repeatedly: their
    dirges and their ditties and their blues and jubilees, praying their
    prayers nightly to an unknown god, bending their knees humbly to
    an unseen power;

For my people lending their strength to the years, to the gone years 5
    and the now years and the maybe years, washing ironing cooking
    scrubbing sewing mending hoeing plowing digging planting
    pruning patching dragging along never gaining never reaping never
    knowing and never understanding;

For my playmates in the clay and dust and sand of Alabama back- 10
    yards playing baptizing and preaching and doctor and jail and
    soldier and school and mama and cooking and playhouse and
    concert and store and hair and Miss Choomby and company;

For the cramped bewildered years we went to school to learn to know
    the reasons why and the answers to and the people who and the 15
    places where and the days when, in memory of the bitter hours
    when we discovered we were black and poor and small and
    different and nobody cared and nobody wondered and nobody
    understood;

For the boys and girls who grew in spite of these things to be man and 20
    woman, to laugh and dance and sing and play and drink their wine

2588 ■ Modern Period: 1910–1945

and religion and success, to marry their playmates and bear
children and then die of consumption and anemia and lynching;

For my people thronging 47th Street in Chicago and Lenox Avenue in
New York and Rampart Street in New Orleans, lost disinherited   25
dispossessed and happy people filling the cabarets and taverns and
other people's pockets needing bread and shoes and milk and land
and money and something—something all our own;

For my people walking blindly spreading joy, losing time being lazy,
sleeping when hungry, shouting when burdened, drinking when   30
hopeless, tied and shackled and tangled among ourselves by the
unseen creatures who tower over us omnisciently and laugh;

For my people blundering and groping and floundering in the dark of
churches and schools and clubs and societies, associations and
councils and committees and conventions, distressed and   35
disturbed and deceived and devoured by money-hungry glory-
craving leeches, preyed on by facile force of state and fad and
novelty, by false prophet and holy believer;

For my people standing staring trying to fashion a better way from
confusion, from hypocrisy and misunderstanding, tryingto fashion   40
a world that will hold all the people, all the faces, all the adams and
eyes and their countless generations;

Let a new earth rise. Let another world be born. Let a bloody peace be
written in the sky. Let a second generation full of courage issue
forth; let a people loving freedom come to growth. Let a beauty   45
full of healing and a strength of final clenching be the pulsing in
our spirits and our blood. Let the martial songs be written, let the
dirges disappear. Let a race of men now rise and take control.

                                                                    1942

Ballad of the Hoppy-Toad

Ain't been on Market Street for nothing
With my regular washing load
When the Saturday crowd went stomping
Down the Johnny-jumping road,

Seen Sally Jones come running   5
With a razor at her throat,
Seen Deacon's daughter lurching
Like a drunken alley goat.

But the biggest for my money,
And the saddest for my throw   10
Was the night I seen the goopher man
Throw dust around my door.

Come sneaking round my doorway
In a stovepipe hat and coat;
Come sneaking round my doorway   15
To drop the evil note.

I run down to sis Avery's
And told her what I seen
"Root-worker's out to git me
What you reckon that there mean?"   20

Sis Avery she done told me,
"Now honey go on back
I knows just what will hex him
And that old goopher sack."

Now I done burned the candles   25
Till I seen the face of Jim
And I done been to church and prayed
But can't git rid of him.

Don't want to burn his picture
Don't want to dig his grave   30
Just want to have my peace of mind
And make that dog behave.

Was running through the fields one day
Sis Avery's chopping corn
Big horse come stomping after me   35
I knowed then I was gone.

Sis Avery grabbed that horse's mane
And not one minute late
Cause trembling down behind her
I seen my ugly fate.   40

She hollered to that horse to "Whoa!
I gotcha hoppy-toad."
And yonder come the goopher man
A-running down the road.

She hollered to that horse to "Whoa"   45
And what you wanta think?

Great-God-a-mighty, that there horse
Begun to sweat and shrink.

He shrunk up to a teeny horse
He shrunk up to a toad   50
And yonder come the goopher man
Still running down the road.

She hollered to that horse to "Whoa"
She said, "I'm killing him.
Now you just watch this hoppy-toad   55
And you'll be rid of Jim."

The goopher man was hollering
"Don't kill that hoppy-toad."
Sis Avery she said "Honey,
You bout to lose your load."   60

That hoppy-toad was dying
Right there in the road
And goopher man was screaming
"Don't kill that hoppy-toad."

The hoppy-toad shook one more time   65
And then he up and died
Old goopher man fell dying, too.
"O hoppy-toad," he cried.

                                                             1970

Solace

Now must I grieve and fret my little way
into death's darkness, ending all my day
in bitterness and pain, in striving and in stress;
go on unendingly again
to mock the sun with death   5
and mask all light with fear?
Oh no, I will not cease to lift my eyes
beyond those resurrecting hills;
a Fighter still, I will not cease to strive
and see beyond this thorny path a light.   10
I will not darken all my days
with bitterness and fear,
but lift my heart with faith and hope
and dream, as always, of a brighter place.

                                                             1988

The Crystal Palace

The Crystal Palace used to be
a place of elegance
Where "bourgie" black folks came to shoot
a game of pool
And dine in the small cafe   5
across the way.
The dance hall music rocked the night
and sang sweet melodies:
"Big fat mama with the meat shaking on her bones"
"Boogie woogie mama   10
Please come back home"
"I miss you loving papa
but I can't live on love alone"
The Crystal Palace
Used to be   15
most elegant.

1988

SAUNDERS REDDING
1906–1988

Of middle-class parentage, Jay Saunders Redding was born in Wilmington, Delaware, just three years after W.E.B. Du Bois posed his own probing questions in *The Souls of Black Folk*. His father, Lewis Alfred Redding, and his mother, Mary Ann Holmes Redding, had been educated to become teachers. His father's roots led back to slavery; his paternal grandmother was an escaped slave. His mother was mulatto; his maternal grandmother, a mixture of Irish, Indian, and black, was of a "free" background. For the young Saunders, an understanding of the importance of education for blacks and a consciousness of racial identity and awareness developed early.

After his early schooling in Wilmington (1912–1923), Redding attended Lincoln University in Pennsylvania for one year (1923–1924), then transferred to Brown University, from which he received his A.B. degree in 1928. After teaching at Morehouse College in Atlanta, he returned to Brown and was awarded an M.A. in 1932.

For more than half a century, Redding taught at a number of colleges and universities and built an outstanding career as writer and literary and cultural critic. He became one of the major "senior" scholars in African American literature and a much-sought-after mentor to new scholars in the field. Over the years, he taught at Louisville Municipal College, Southern University in Baton Rouge, State Teachers College at Elizabeth City, North Carolina, and Hampton Institute, among others. In his final professorial years he was Ernest I. White Professor of American Studies and Humane Letters at Cornell. He served also as director of the division of research and publication of the National Endowment for the Humanities, and he accepted a State Department assignment in India. In recognition of his scholarship, he was awarded several honorary doctorates, including one from his alma mater, Brown, and one from his home state university, the University of Delaware.

In literary history and criticism, Redding's *To Make a Poet Black* (1939) is a standard among early sources on African American literature. Including key writers from 1760 to 1939, the text had as its goal "to bring together factual material and critical opinion on American Negro literature in a sort of history of Negro thought in America." In 1940 Redding received a Rockefeller Grant to "Go out into Negro life in the South." The result was *No Day of Triumph* (1942), which won him the Mayflower Award from the North Carolina Historical Society for the best work that year by a North Carolinian. This book is an example of Redding's writing forte: the bringing together of the personal and the historic, with analysis and commentary.

Supported by a Guggenheim Award, Redding wrote his only novel, *Stranger and Alone* (1950), in which he scathingly attacks the black educator. This book received mixed critical attention in essays by Alain Locke, Ralph Ellison, Ann Petry, and others. As an illumination of the novel and an extension of the autobiography and social history of *No Day of Triumph,* one should read *On Being Negro in America* (1951), Redding's attempt to look back at self and race in his continued search for truth. His social histories—*They Came in Chains* (1950), *The Lonesome Road* (1958), and *The Negro* (1967)—treat some of the same issues as his other texts. Finally, in 1971, he and Arthur P. Davis published an anthology, *Cavalcade: Negro American Writing from 1760 to the Present,* revised with Joyce Ann Joyce and reissued after Redding's death. Letters written between 1938 and 1945 by Redding to James Weldon Johnson, Carl Van Vechten, and Richard Wright are housed at the Yale University Beinecke Rare Book and Manuscript Library.

Eleanor Q. Tignor
LaGuardia Community College

PRIMARY WORKS

To Make a Poet Black, 1939; *No Day of Triumph,* 1942; *Stranger and Alone,* 1950; *They Came in Chains,* 1950; *On Being Negro in America,* 1951; *The Lonesome Road,* 1958; *The Negro,* 1967; *J. Saunders Redding: Selected Writings,* ed. Faith Berry, 1988; *Cavalcade: Negro American Writing from 1760 to the Present,* 2 vols., ed. with Arthur P. Davis and Joyce Ann Joyce, 1991, 1992; *A Scholar's Conscience: Selected Writings of J. Saunders Redding, 1942–1977,* ed. Faith Berry, 1992.

from **No Day of Triumph**

Chapter One.
Troubled in Mind

1

Consciousness of my environment began with the sound of talk. It was not hysterical talk, not bravado, though it might well have been, for my father had bought in a neighborhood formerly forbidden, and we lived, I realize now, under an armistice. But in the early years, when we were a young family, there was always talk at our house; a great deal of it mere talk, a kind of boundless and robustious overflow of family feeling. Our shouts roared through the house with the exuberant gush of flood waters through an open sluice, for talk, generated by any trifle, was the power that turned the wheels of our inner family life. It was the strength and that very quality of our living that made impregnable, it seemed, even to time itself, the walls of our home. But it was in the beginning of the second decade of the century, when the family was an institution still as inviolate as the swing of the earth.

There was talk of school, of food, of religion, of people. There were the shouted recitations of poems and Biblical passages and orations from *Bryan, Phillips*, and *John Brown*.[1] My mother liked rolling *apostrophes*.[2] We children were all trained at home in the declining art of oratory and were regular contestants for prizes at school. My father could quote with appropriate gestures bits from *Beveridge*, whom he had never heard, and from *Teddy Roosevelt* and *Fred Douglass*,[3] whom he had. There was talk of the "race problem," reasonable and unembittered unless Grandma Redding was there, and then it became a kind of spiritual poison, its virulence destructive of its own immediate effects, almost its own catharsis. Some of the poison was absorbed.

I remember Grandma Redding coming on one of her visits and finding us playing in the back yard. My brother and sister were there and we were playing with Myrtle Lott and Elwood Carter, white children who were neighbors. Grandma came in the back way through the alley, as she always did, and when we heard the gate scrape against the bricks we stopped. She stepped into the yard and looked fixedly at us. Holding her ancient, sagging canvas bag under one arm, she slowly untied the ribbons of her black

---

[1]William Jennings Bryan (1860–1925), American orator, politician, and statesman; Democratic Party candidate who lost the presidential race, twice to William McKinley (1860, 1900) and once to William Howard Taft (1908); Wendell Phillips (1811–1884), American orator and reformer, active with William Lloyd Garrison's abolitionist group and later with the American Anti-Slavery Society; John Brown (1800–1859), American abolitionist, charged with treason for his attempted raid of a United States arsenal at Harpers Ferry, Virginia (now West Virginia).

[2]A figure of speech in which a person or thing not listening is addressed directly.
[3]William Henry Beveridge (1879–1963), British economist and author, took the position that the number of jobs should always exceed the number of workers; Theodore Roosevelt, 26th President of the United States (1901–1909); Frederick Douglass (1817?–1895), American slave who escaped to freedom, became an abolitionist, orator, and statesman.

bonnet. The gate fell shut behind her. Her eyes were like lashes on our faces. Reaching out her long arm, she held open the gate. Then she said, "Git. You white trash, git!" Our companions, pale with fright, ducked and scampered past her. When they had gone, Grandma nodded curtly to us. "Chillen," she said, and went into our house.

Grandma Redding's visits were always unannounced. She came the fifty-odd miles up from Still Pond, Maryland, as casually as if she had come from around the nearest corner. A sudden cold silence would fall, and there would be Grandma. I do not know how she managed to give the impression of shining with a kind of deadly hard glare, for she was always clothed entirely in black and her black, even features were as hard and lightless as stone. I never saw a change of expression on her features. She never smiled. In anger her face turned slowly, dully gray, but her thin nostrils never flared, her long mouth never tightened. She was tall and fibrous and one of her ankles had been broken when she was a girl and never properly set, so that she walked with a defiant limp.

She hated white people. In 1858, as a girl of ten, she had escaped from slavery on the eastern shore of Maryland with a young woman of eighteen. They made their way to Camden, New Jersey, but there was no work and little refuge there. Across the river, bustling Philadelphia swarmed with slave hunters. By subterfuge or by violence even free people were sometimes kidnaped and sent south. Near Bridgeton, New Jersey, the runaways heard, there was a free Negro settlement, but one night they were stopped on the docks by a constable who asked them for papers. They had none. Within two weeks after their escape they were slaves again. When my grandmother tried to run away from the flogging that was her punishment, Caleb Wrightson, her master, flung a chunk of wood at her and broke her ankle.

It was not until we were quite large children that Grandma Redding told us this story. She did not tell it for our pleasure, as one tells harrowing tales to children. It was without the dramatic effects that Grandma Conway delighted in. What *she* would have done with such a tale! No. Grandma Redding's telling was as bare and imageless as a lesson recited from the head and as coldly furious as the whine of a shot.

"An' ol' man Calub flane a hick'ry chunk an' brist my anklebone."

I can see her now as she sits stooped in the wooden rocker by the kitchen stove, her sharp elbows on her sharp knees and her long black fingers with their immense purple nails clawing upward at the air. Her undimmed eyes whipped at ours, and especially at mine, it seemed to me; her thin lips scarcely parted. She had just come in or was going out, for she wore her bonnet and it sat on the very top of her harsh, dull hair. Hatred shook her as a strong wind shakes a boughless tree.

"An' ol' man Calub stank lik'a pes'-house from the rottin' of his stomick 'fore he died an' went t' hell, an' his boys died in the wo' an' went to hell."

But her implacable hatred needed no historical recall, and so far as I remember, she never told the tale to us again.

But generally Grandma Redding's taciturnity was a hidden rock in the sea of our talk. The more swift the tide, the more the rock showed, bleak and unavoidable. At other times the talk flowed smoothly around her: the bursts of oratory and poetry, the chatter of people and events, the talk of schooling and sometimes of money and often of God. Even the talk of God did not arouse her. I think she was not especially religious; and in this, too, she was unlike Grandma Conway.

My grandmothers met at our house but once. They did not like each other.

2

Grandma Conway said "Good morning" as if she were pronouncing the will of God. A woman as squat and solid as a tree stump, she had a queer knurl of religious thought and character that no ax of eclecticism could cleave. She had great bouts of religious argument with whoever would argue with her. Even though her adversary sat but two feet away, she would shout out her disputes in a cracking voice and half-rise threateningly, her gray serge breast lifting and falling as if she had been running uphill. She often frightened our young friends in this manner, awed them into speechlessness; and when she had done this, her green-yellow eyes would blink very fast and her fat, yellow little fists would fly to her chest and beat gently there in laughter.

Grandma Conway was honest about God and often very moving. When she visited us, the family prayers on Sunday belonged to her. Her prayers seemed to bring Him into our dining room, transforming the flesh and blood reality of Grandma Conway into a greater reality of mystical communion. It was as if a sleep and a dream of God descended upon us all, replacing our earthly consciousness with another too penetrating to be born in wakefulness and too sublime to bear the weight of our gross senses. I would keep my gaze fastened upon Grandma for visual evidence against that awful Presence; or I looked around, feeling my elbows pressed deep into the fabroid of the chair seat, at my brother, my sisters, the quiet stillness of my mother's bent back, the upright, almost transfixed solidity of my father's shoulders. I would hear and smell the sausage frying, and the baked beans, and the hot rolls, and the coffee. But insensibly my eyes would close against the physical reality, which somehow even sight and sound and smell could not confirm, and I would be washed up onto a plane of awareness that terrified me.

"Come on feet of thunder, Holy One, but tread amongst us softly, and let us hear the rustling of your garments. It's like the sound the wind makes at night in the sycamore trees in front of my house on Columbus Street. I feel Your spirit hands uplifting me and Your Holy Presence cloaking me, Oh, Giver of all things good and perfect."

But often she talked to Him of the intimate trifles that enlivened her day, of her children and her children's children.

"Dear Father, the boy, Saunders, had a croup last night and his hacking and coughing kept me from my sleep."

So intimately and yet so reverently.

It was on one of these Sundays that my grandmothers met. Grandma Conway had been with us a month. Grandma Redding came as unceremoniously as she usually came, looking as if she had walked every step of the fifty miles from her home. When my mother went to the kitchen that morning, Grandma Redding was sitting on the back steps. Though it was August and hot, she wore the heavy black dress and the black woolen jacket which seemed to be her only garments. When she discovered that Grandma Conway was visiting us, she did not remove her bonnet, and, as I remember, there was some difficulty in inducing her to stay for prayers and breakfast.

The presence of the two old women filled us children with strange, jerky excitement. Even our mother was infected by it. I think we recognized more than the surface differences between our grandmothers. Separating their thoughts and characters was a deep gulf that could not be accounted for alone by the wide divergence of their experiences. It was something even more fundamental. It was what they were and would have been, even, I believe, had they lived through similar experiences. No bridge of time or thought or feeling could join them. They were of different earth. On the surface it looked as simple as this: one was yellow, the other black.

There was a pause of embarrassment just before we knelt for prayers. Grandma Conway, with the gracious magnanimity with which one sometimes yields to a rival, said to my father, "Maybe your ma would like to lead us in prayer this morning." My father looked embarrassed, drawing his hand over his bald head from crown to forehead and shooting an oblique glance at my mother. Mother said nothing. Then Grandma Redding said;

"No. Thank'ee. Lewis *wist*[4] I ain't no comp'ny-prayin' one. Let her pray."

We knelt at chairs around the square table. The odor of the breakfast was heavy in the room—coffee, fresh bread, and the Sunday smell of sliced bananas all mingled. The sun made a heavy shaft of light through each of the two windows and flecks of it escaping through the multitudinous small holes in the green shades danced upon the wall. More than the Sunday excitement of dressing for church filled us. Beyond the hard, straight shoulders of Grandma Redding I could see my older sister silently dancing on her knees. Behind me I could hear my mother's stepped-up breathing and the sound her dress made when she moved against the chair. The others knelt on the other side of the table. Lowering my face in my spread fingers, I waited for prayers to begin. Grandma Conway sighed heavily. I set myself against the coming of that awful Presence.

"God, our Holy Father, Chastiser of sin and evil, great Maker of all things pure and good and of the creatures that here on earth do dwell, be with us in our prayers this morning. There are many who cannot rise from their beds of pain this morning—dear Lord, be with them. There are many who went last night in health to bed and this morning lie cold in death. Be with them. And be with us. Thou can be everywhere. Thou art in the sun that..."

It was obvious to us who knew her prayers that the spirit had not descended upon her. Her prayer was not coming with that mellifluous and

[4]Knows.

intimate spontaneity with which she generally spoke to God. She was remembering perhaps too much of the Book of Common Prayer which she had studied as a child. My tension eased a little.

" ... Holy Father, these my children now, and my children's children. Mary here, and the man who made her a woman. You know all this, Father, but I'm getting old and my mind wanders. Make these children as Your Son. Keep not the cross from them, nor the crown of thorns, nor the cup of sorrow. Deny them not the chastening rod of truth if their young lives would be as lamps on the footpaths of eternity. And Redding's ma, Lord. She's with us this morning. She has her affliction, Holy One, and we can hardly notice it, but it's an affliction on her. Bless her. Teach her that affliction chasteneth a righteous heart and only the wicked are bowed down. Bless her, dear God, and bless us all. We ask it in the name ... "

Before my father could say "Amen," as was his custom, and we could rise from our knees, Grandma Redding's hard, grainy voice whanged out beside me. I felt the room's shocked stillness. Surprised and irritated a little at this fresh delay to breakfast, I peeped at her through my fingers. She was kneeling with her long back in a hard curve and her forearms spread along the chair seat. Her black hands grasped the uprights of the chair, so that her large knuckles stood out purple. Her eyes were not closed and her face was as hard as rock.

"Lis'en, Jesus. You *wist* I ain't got the words fer comp'ny prayers. This is all I want t'say. I been climbin' hills an' goin' down valleys be't sixty some years, an' the hills ain't no littler an' the valleys ain't no lesser. I ain't downright complainin', Jesus. I'm jes' tellin' You the way things is, be't You ain't been here in my lifetime. You ain't been here in be't than a thousan' years. Sence You been here, Gawd's done made a new lan' an' put a whole lot o' dif-f'unt things an' people on it all together, an' we'se all steered up ever' which way. We had slav'ry sence You been here. That's mean business. Now we got something else, an' that's mean business too. Devilment an' hate an' wo' an' some being one thing an' some another, that's all bad, mean business. We'se all skiverin' an' steered up. It ain't t'beginnin' an' it ain't the close. You understan' what's on my mind, Jesus.

"Now, bless these young'uns. Bless 'em on earth. It don't matter 'bout us ol' ones. We'se skitterin' down the rocky hill anyhow. Bless us in the everlastin'. But these young'uns, they's climbin' up. All I ast be You keep 'em from the knowin' an' the manbirthed sins o' blackness. We'se bent on knees to Your will, Lord Jesus. Amen."

This prayer probably had no lasting effect upon the others who heard it, but, young as I was, its impression upon me was profound. In time to come it was to be as a light thrown upon Grandma Redding's character, and, by reflection, upon Grandma Conway's. It was only later, of course, that I had any intellectual comprehension of the basis of the contrast between them. For many years I continued to think of Grandma Redding as a strange, bitterly choleric old woman and that her irascibility was somehow a part of her blackness. I could not help this absurdity then, for ours was an upper-class Negro family, the unwitting victim of our own culture complexes; deeply sensitive to the tradition of ridicule and inferiority attaching to color; hating the tradition and yet inevitably absorbing it.

Grandma Redding knew and admitted the debilitating force of that tradition, and out of her knowledge had come her prayer. There were dark ones among us, but none so black as Grandma Redding. I was dark. But here again we were victims of evasive and defensive thinking. To members of our immediate family the stigma of blackness did not apply. But Grandma Redding, whom, somehow, we never seemed to know very well, and her children—my father's brothers—were not of the family circle. And it applied to them. It was a crazy, irrational, paradoxical pattern, not made less so by those occasional upheaving disturbances in the general social order that rolled in on us in great breakers from the fathomless sea of the white world. We were a garrisoned island in that sea.

On the other hand, I thought of Grandma Conway and her kin—they were all mulattoes—as escaping the tradition. But, indeed, Grandma Conway was nearer the absurdity than I. I have always remembered with what garrulous delight she used to repeat:

"So this white gentleman, who lived in the next block, met us on the street one day. I had a big hat on Cora, you see, and you couldn't see her face without raising her head or taking off her hat. So he met us and says, bowing just as nice, 'Miss Cora'—that was to me. Your poor, dead Aunt Cora was named for me. 'Miss Cora,' he says, 'let me see this prize package under the big hat,' and he lifted her hat up. Cora was just as pretty! She was too pretty to live, dear Lord. He lifted her hat up, and when he saw her, he says, as if he'd been kicked in the stomach, 'Why, she's nearly white!' 'Yes, indeedy,' I said, 'and I intend to keep her that way.'"

And then her eyes behind her tiny oval glasses would screw up and her fat yellow hands would fly to her breast and beat there gently in laughter. Her laughter was not an exact comment, but it was only later that I realized this, for when we were young it seemed merely an amusing story.

My grandmothers did not meet again after that Sunday breakfast. It was as strained a meal as any I have ever sat through. Grandma Redding kept her bonnet on all through it. She drank only sweetened hot water and ate only the sliced bananas. As always, Grandma Conway, though silent, ate and drank heavily of black coffee sweetened almost to syrup, of the kidney stew and baked beans, and the crunchy rolls as large as buns. Even under ordinary circumstances, her appetite was amazing. My father quarreled with us a good deal that morning. My mother was silent. Eventually we all fell silent, hearing only the sucking sound that Grandma Redding's lips made on the edge of her cup and the explosive grunts of pleasure with which Grandma Conway munched her roll.

They never saw each other again, though each lived several years longer. In 1923 Grandma Redding, her face stone-set in pain, limped defiantly to her death, and three years later death caught up with Grandma Conway while she slept.

1942

PIETRO DI DONATO
1911–1992

An anomaly in American literature and eccentric in the true sense of being off-center, the primitivism of Pietro Di Donato burst like a meteor on the literary scene of the late Thirties. This mainly self-taught son of Italian immigrants was to immortalize his tragically killed worker father as the veritable Christ-figure of his classic novel *Christ in Concrete*, published in 1939 to extraordinary critical acclaim.

It was, perhaps, the precisely right moment for this novel to be acclaimed: the portrayal of exploited workers fit the social protest sympathies of the period, and the unique language that expressed in English the Italian rhythms and thought patterns of Di Donato's immigrant characters appealed to critics newly receptive to the linguistic innovations of modernism. The searching energy and the raw idealism behind Di Donato's literary debut was not again achieved; *Christ in Concrete* remains the classic expression of the Italian American experience in the thematic material of the young boy's seeking identity in a new and alien world that is as rejecting as the old one of tradition (which had been his father's) is closed to him. *Christ in Concrete* is the most searing and thorough representation of the condition of an immigrant suspended between two worlds and held in thrall to work and the job.

Christ in Concrete, which began as a short story in *Esquire*, is an autobiographical rendering of the most haunting, ineluctable event of Di Donato's life—the tragic accident that killed his father on a construction job just days before his own twelfth birthday, casting the young boy into his father's role as brick-layer and supporter of the destitute family. When, during the Great Depression of the Thirties, Di Donato was laid off the job, the circumstance brought about his Golden Age: "With unemployment and Home Relief I was permitted the leisure to think ... That sent me to the Northport Library and the discovery of the immortal minds of all countries. They gave me freedom...."

When it appeared in 1939, *Christ in Concrete* was hailed as "the epithet of the twentieth century." It was chosen over John Steinbeck's *The Grapes of Wrath* for the Book-of-the-Month Club, and Di Donato, the working man, was transformed into a literary lion only to have the too-instant celebrity status and financial affluence render him silent for the next two decades.

From 1942 Pietro Di Donato spent time in a Cooperstown, New York, camp as a conscientous objector during World War II; while there, he met the widowed Helen Dean, a former showgirl. They were married in 1943, became the parents of two sons, and subsequently moved to Long Island, where Di Donato continued to write. Much of Di Donato's internal conflict—the contradictory pull between sensual hedonism and idealism, between the attraction to the woman he married and the insane jealousy harbored toward the dead husband who preceded him, between his feeling of having betrayed his Italian American identity and his unsure place in American society—found expression in his next autobiographical novel, *This Woman*.

Critics were not impressed with this work, which was dramatized, or with his next novel, *Three Circles of Light*, which was called "a loose collection of episodes rather than a sustained narrative ... The novel's descent into sentimentality, bathos, and just plain scurrility is rapid." Subsequently Di Donato seems to have secured his identity within the framework of the reclaimed religious faith of his people, and he went on to write two religious biographies: *Immigrant Saint: The Life of Mother Cabrini* and *The Penitent*, which is the life of Maria Goretti.

Di Donato's short pieces, articles, and stories were collected in *Naked Author*. In 1978 his reportage on the kidnapping and murder of Aldo Moro, "Christ in Plastic," which appeared in *Penthouse* magazine, won the Overseas Press Club Award. At his best, as in *Christ in Concrete*, Di Donato's narrative patterns form, in their diversity, one of the richest linguistic textures to be found in the twentieth-century novel and make the bridge, for him and for his characters, between a lost and mythical Italy and a real but never realized America.

Helen Barolini

PRIMARY WORKS

Christ in Concrete, 1939, 1975; *This Woman*, 1958; *Immigrant Saint: The Life of Mother Cabrini*, 1960; *Three Circles of Light*, 1960; *The Penitent*, 1962; *Naked Author*, 1970.

Christ in Concrete

March whistled stinging snow against the brick walls and up the gaunt girders. Geremio, the foreman, swung his arms about, and gaffed the men on.

Old Nick, the "Lean," stood up from over a dust-flying brick pile, and tapped the side of his nose.

"Master Geremio, the devil himself could not break his tail any harder than we here."

Burly Vincenzo of the walrus mustache, and known as the "Snoutnose," let fall the chute door of the concrete hopper and sang over in the Lean's direction: "Mari-Annina's belly and the burning night will make of me once more a milk-mouthed stripling lad...."

The Lean loaded his wheelbarrow and spat furiously. "Sons of two-legged dogs ... despised of even the devil himself! Work! Sure! For America beautiful will eat you and spit your bones into the earth's hole! Work!" And with that his wiry frame pitched the barrow violently over the rough floor.

Snoutnose waved his head to and fro and with mock pathos wailed, "Sing on, oh guitar of mine...."

Short, cheery-faced Joe Chiappa, the scaffoldman, paused with hatchet in hand and tenpenny spike sticking out from small dicelike teeth to tell the Lean as he went by, in a voice that all could hear, "Ah, father of countless chicks, the old age is a carrion!"

Geremio chuckled and called to him: "Hey, little Joe, who are you to talk? You and big-titted Cola can't even hatch an egg, whereas the Lean has just to turn the doorknob of his bedroom and old Philomena becomes a balloon!"

Coarse throats tickled and mouths opened wide in laughter.

Mike, the "Barrel-mouth," pretended he was talking to himself and yelled out in his best English ... he was always speaking English while the rest carried on in their native Italian: "I don't know myself, but somebody whose gotta bigga buncha keeds and he alla times talka from somebody elsa!"

Geremio knew it was meant for him and he laughed. "On the tomb of Saint Pimplelegs, this little boy my wife is giving me next week shall be the last! Eight hungry little Christians to feed is enough for any man."

Joe Chiappa nodded to the rest. "Sure, Master Geremio had a telephone call from the next bambino. Yes, it told him it had a little bell there instead of a rose bush.... It even told him its name!"

"Laugh, laugh all of you," returned Geremio, "but I tell you that all my kids must be boys so that they some day will be big American builders. And then I'll help him to put the gold away in the basements for safekeeping!"

A great din of riveting shattered the talk among the fast-moving men. Geremio added a handful of "honest" tobacco to his corncob, puffed strongly, and cupped his hands around the bowl for a bit of warmth. The chill day caused him to shiver, and he thought to himself, Yes, the day is cold, cold ... but who am I to complain when the good Christ himself was crucified?

Pushing the job is all right (when has it been otherwise in my life?) but this job frightens me. I feel the building wants to tell me something; just as one Christian to another. I don't like this. Mr. Murdin tells me, "Push it up!" That's all he knows. I keep telling him that the underpinning should be doubled and the old material removed from the floors, but he keeps the inspector drunk and ... "Hey, Ashes-ass! Get away from under that pilaster! Don't pull the old work. Push it away from you or you'll have a nice present for Easter if the wall falls on you!" ... Well, with the help of God I'll see this job through. It's not my first, nor the.... "Hey, Patsy number two! Put more cement in that concrete we're putting up a building, not an Easter cake!"

Patsy hurled his shovel to the floor and gesticulated madly. "The padrone Jurdin-sa tells me, 'Too much, too much! Lil' bit is plenty!' And you tell me I'm stingy! The rotten building can fall after I leave!"

Six floors below, the contractor called: "Hey, Geremio! Is your gang of dagos dead?"

Geremio cautioned to the men: "On your toes, boys. If he writes out slips, someone won't have big eels on the Easter table."

The Lean cursed that "the padrone could take the job and shove it ... !"

Curly-headed Sandino, the roguish, pigeon-toed scaffoldman, spat a clod of tobacco juice and hummed to his own music.

... "Yes, certainly yes to your face, master padrone ... and behind, this to you and all your kind!"

The day, like all days, came to an end. Calloused and bruised bodies sighed, and numb legs shuffled towards shabby railroad flats....

"Ah, *bella casa mia*. Where my little freshets of blood, and my good woman await me. Home where my broken back will not ache so. Home where midst the monkey chatter of my *piccolinos* I will float off to blessed slumber with my feet on the chair and the head on the wife's soft full breast."

These great childhearted ones leave each other without words or ceremony, and as they ride and walk home, a great pride swells the breast....

"Blessings to Thee, oh Jesus. I have fought winds and cold. Hand to hand I have locked dumb stones in place and the great building rises. I have earned a bit of bread for me and mine."

The mad day's brutal conflict is forgiven, and strained limbs prostrate themselves so that swollen veins can send the yearning blood coursing and pulsating deliciously as though the body mountained leaping streams.

The job alone remained behind ... and yet, they too, having left the bigger part of their lives with it. The cold ghastly beast, the Job, stood stark, the eerie March wind wrapping it in sharp shadows of falling dusk.

That night was a crowning point in the life of Geremio. He bought a house! Twenty years he had helped to mold the New World. And now he was to have a house of his own! What mattered that it was no more than a wooden shack? It was his own!

He had proudly signed his name and helped Annunziata to make her x on the wonderful contract that proved them owners. And she was happy to think that her next child, soon to come, would be born under their own rooftree. She heard the church chimes, and cried to the children: "Children, to bed! It is near midnight. And remember, shut-mouth to the *paesanos*! Or they will send the evil eye to our new home even before we put foot."

The children scampered off to the icy yellow bedroom where three slept in one bed and three in the other. Coltishly and friskily they kicked about under the covers; their black iron-cotton stockings not removed ... what! and freeze the peanut-little toes?

Said Annunziata, "The children are so happy, Geremio; let them be, for even I would a Tarantella dance." And with that she turned blushing. He wanted to take her on her word. She patted his hands, kissed them, and whispered, "Our children will dance for us ... in the American style some day."

Geremio cleared his throat and wanted to sing. "Yes, with joy I could sing in a richer feeling than the great Caruso." He babbled little old-country couplets and circled the room until the tenant below tapped the ceiling.

Annunziata whispered: "Geremio, to bed and rest. Tomorrow is a day for great things ... and the day on which our Lord died for us."

The children were now hard asleep. Heads under the cover, over ... moist noses whistling, and little damp legs entwined.

In bed Geremio and Annunziata clung closely to each other. They mumbled figures and dates until fatigue stilled their thoughts. And with chubby Johnnie clutching fast his bottle and warmed between them ... life breathed heavily, and dreams entertained in far, far worlds, the nation-builder's brood.

But Geremio and Annunziata remained for a while staring into darkness, silently.

"Geremio?"

"Yes?"

"This job you are now working . . ."

"So?"

"You always used to tell me about what happened on the jobs . . . who was jealous, and who praised. . . ."

"You should know by now that all work is the same. . . ."

"Geremio. The month you have been on this job, you have not spoken a word about the work. . . . And I have felt that I am walking into a dream. Is the work dangerous? Why don't you answer . . . ?"

Job loomed up damp, shivery gray. Its giant members waiting.

Builders quietly donned their coarse robes, and waited.

Geremio's whistle rolled back into his pocket and the symphony of struggle began.

Trowel rang through brick and slashed mortar rivets were machine-gunned fast with angry grind Patsy number one check Patsy number two check the Lean three check Vincenzo four steel bellowed back at hammer donkey engines coughed purple Ashes-ass Pietro fifteen chisel point intoned stone thin steel whirred and wailed through wood liquid stone flowed with dull rasp through iron veins and hoist screamed through space Carmine the Fat twenty-four and Giacomo Sangini check. . . . The multitudinous voices of a civilization rose from the surroundings and melded with the efforts of the Job.

To the intent ear, Nation was voicing her growing pains, but, hands that create are attached to warm hearts and not to calculating minds. The Lean as he fought his burden on looked forward to only one goal, the end. The barrow he pushed, he did not love. The stones that brutalized his palms, he did not love. The great Good Job, he did not love. He felt a searing bitterness and a fathomless consternation at the queer consciousness that inflicted the ever mounting weight of structure that he HAD TO! HAD TO! raise above his shoulders! When, when and where would the last stone be? Never . . . did he bear his toil with the rhythm of song! Never . . . did his gasping heart knead the heavy mortar with lilting melody! A voice within him spoke in wordless language.

The language of worn oppression and the despair of realizing that his life had been left on brick piles. And always, there had been hunger and her bastard, the fear of hunger.

Murdin bore down upon Geremio from behind and shouted: "Goddamnit Geremio, if you're givin' the men two hours off today with pay, why the hell are they draggin' their tails? And why don't you turn that skinny old Nick loose, and put a young wop in his place?"

"Now, listen-a to me, Mister Murdin—"

"Don't give me that! And bear in mind that there are plenty of good barefoot men in the streets who'll jump for a day's pay!"

"Padrone—padrone, the underpinning gotta be make safe and—"

"Lissenyawopbastard! If you don't like it, you know what you can do!"

And with that he swung swaggering away.

The men had heard, and those who hadn't knew instinctively.

The new home, the coming baby, and his whole background, kept the fire from Geremio's mouth and bowed his head. "Annunziata speaks of scouring the ashcans for the children's bread in case I didn't want to work on a job where ... But am I not a man, to feed my own with these hands? Ah, but day will end and no boss in the world can then rob me of the joy of my home!"

Murdin paused for a moment before descending the ladder.

Geremio caught his meaning and jumped to, nervously directing the rush of work.... No longer Geremio, but a machinelike entity.

The men were transformed into single, silent, beasts. Snoutnose steamed through ragged mustache whip lashing sand into mixer Ashes-ass dragged under four-by-twelve beam Lean clawed wall knots jumping in jaws masonry crumbled dust billowed thundered choked....

At noon, Geremio drank his wine from an old-fashioned magnesia bottle and munched a great pepper sandwich ... no meat on Good Friday. Said one, "Are some of us to be laid off? Easter is upon us and communion dresses are needed and ..."

That, while Geremio was dreaming of the new house and the joys he could almost taste. Said he: "Worry not. You should know Geremio." It then all came out. He regaled them with his wonderful joy of the new house. He praised his wife and children one by one. They listened respectfully and returned him well wishes and blessings. He went on and on.... "Paul made a radio—all by himself mind you! One can hear Barney Google and many American songs! How proud he."

The ascent to labor was made, and as they trod the ladder, heads turned and eyes communed with the mute flames of the brazier whose warmth they were leaving, not with willing heart, and in that fleeting moment the breast wanted so, so much to speak, of hungers that never reached the tongue.

About an hour later, Geremio, called over to Pietro: "Pietro, see if Mister Murdin is in the shanty and tell him I must see him! I will convince him that the work must not go on like this ... just for the sake of a little more profit!"

Pietro came up soon. "The padrone is not coming up. He was drinking from a large bottle of whiskey and cursed in American words that if you did not carry out his orders—"

Geremio turned away disconcerted, stared dumbly at the structure and mechanically listed in his mind's eye the various violations of construction safety. An uneasy sensation hollowed him. The Lean brought down an old piece of wall and the structure palsied. Geremio's heart broke loose and out thumped the floor's vibrations, a rapid wave of heat swept him and left a chill touch in its wake. He looked about to the men, a bit frightened. They seemed usual, lifesize, and moved about with the methodical deftness that made the moment then appear no different than the task of toil had ever been.

Snoutnose's voice boomed into him. "Master Geremio, the concrete is rea—dy!"

"Oh, yes, yes, Vincenz." And he walked gingerly toward the chute, but, not without leaving behind some part of his strength, sending out his soul to wrestle with the limbs of Job, who threatened in stiff silence. He talked and joked with Snoutnose. Nothing said anything, nor seemed wrong. Yet a vague uneasiness was to him as certain as the foggy murk that floated about Job's stone and steel.

"Shall I let the concrete down now, Master Geremio?"

"Well, let me see—no, hold it a minute. Hey, Sandino! Tighten the chute cables!"

Snoutnose straightened, looked about, and instinctively rubbed the sore small of his spine. "Ah," sighed he, "all the men feel as I—yes, I can tell. They are tired but happy that today is Good Friday and we quit at three o'clock ... " And he swelled in human ecstasy at the anticipation of food, drink, and the hairy flesh-tingling warmth of wife, and then, extravagant rest. In truth, they all felt as Snoutnose, although perhaps with variations on the theme.

It was the Lean only who had lived, and felt otherwise. His soul, accompanied with time, had shredded itself in the physical war to keep the physical alive. Perhaps he no longer had a soul, and the corpse continued from momentum. May he not be the Slave, working on from the birth of Man— He of whom it was said, "It was not for Him to reason"? And probably He who, never asking, taking, nor wanting, created God and the creatables? Nevertheless, there existed in the Lean a sense of oppression suffered, so vast that the seas of time could never wash it away.

Geremio gazed about and was conscious of seeming to understand many things. He marveled at the strange feeling which permitted him to sense the familiarity of life. And yet—all appeared unreal, a dream pungent and nostalgic. Life, dream, reality, unreality, spiraling ever about each other. "Ha," he chuckled, "how and from where do these thoughts come?"

Snoutnose had his hand on the hopper latch and was awaiting the word from Geremio. "Did you say something, Master Geremio?"

"Why, yes, Vincenz, I was thinking—funny! A—yes, what is the time— yes, that is what I was thinking."

"My American can of tomatoes says ten minutes from two o'clock. It won't be long now, Master Geremio."

Geremio smiled. "No, about an hour ... and then, home."

"Oh, but first we stop at Mulberry Street, to buy their biggest eels, and the other finger-licking stuffs."

Geremio was looking far off, and for a moment happiness came to his heart without words, a warm hand stealing over. Snoutnose's words sang to him pleasantly, and he nodded.

"And Master Geremio, we ought really to buy the seafruits with the shells—you know, for the much needed steam they put into the—"

He flushed despite himself and continued. "It is true, I know it—especially the juicy clams ... uhmn, my mouth waters like a pump."

Geremio drew on his unlit pipe and smiled acquiescence. The men around him were moving to their tasks silently; feeling of their fatigue, but absorbed in contemplations the very same as Snoutnose's. The noise of labor seemed not to be noise, and as Geremio looked about, life settled over him a gray concert—gray forms, atmosphere, and gray notes.... Yes, his off-tone world felt so near, and familiar.

"Five minutes from two," swished through Snoutnose's mustache.

Geremio automatically took out his watch, rewound, and set it. Sandino had done with the cables. The tone and movement of the scene seemed to Geremio strange, differently strange, and yet, a dream familiar from a timeless date. His hand went up in motion to Vincenzo. The molten stone gurgled low, and then with heightening rasp. His eyes followed the stone-cementy pudding, and to his ears there was no other sound than its flow. From over the roofs somewhere, the tinny voice of Barney Google whined its way, hooked into his consciousness and kept itself a revolving record beneath his skull-plate.

"Ah, yes, Barney Google, my son's wonderful radio machine ... wonderful Paul." His train of thought quickly took in his family, home and hopes. And with hope came fear. Something within asked, Is it not possible to breathe God's air without fear dominating with the pall of unemployment? And the terror of production for Boss, Boss and Job? To rebel is to love all of the very little. To be obedient is to choke. Oh, dear Lord, guide my path.

Just then, the floor lurched and swayed under his feet. The slipping of the underpinning below rumbled up through the undetermined floors.

Was he faint or dizzy? Was it part of the dreamy afternoon? He put his hands in front of him and stepped back, and looked up wildly. "No! No!"

The men poised stricken. Their throats wanted to cry out and scream but didn't dare. For a moment they were a petrified and straining pageant. Then the bottom of their world gave way. The building shuddered violently, her supports burst with the crackling slap of wooden gunfire. The floor vomited upward. Geremio clutched at the air and shrieked agonizingly. "Brother, what have we done. Ahhh-h, children of ours!" With the speed of light, balance went sickenly awry and frozen men went flying explosively. Job tore down upon them madly. Walls, floors, beams became whirling, solid, splintering waves crashing with detonations that ground man and material in bonds of death.

The strongly shaped body that slept with Annunziata nights and was perfect in all the limitless physical quantities, thudded as a worthless sack amongst the giant debris that crushed fragile flesh and bone with centrifugal intensity.

Darkness blotted out his terror and the resistless form twisted, catapulted insanely in its directionless flight, and shot down neatly and deliberately between the empty wooden forms of a foundation wall pilaster in upright position, his blue swollen face pressed against the form and his arms outstretched, caught securely through the meat by the thin round bars of reinforcing steel.

The huge concrete hopper that was sustained by an independent structure of thick timber, wavered a breath or so, its heavy concrete rolling uneasily until a great sixteen-inch wall caught it squarely with all the terrific verdict of its dead weight and impelled it downward through joists, beams and masonry until it stopped short, arrested by two girders, an arm's length above Geremio's head; the gray concrete gushing from the hopper mouth, and sealing up the mute figure.

Giacomo had been thrown clear of the building and dropped six floors to the street gutter, where he lay writhing.

The Lean had evinced no emotion. When the walls descended, he did not move. He lowered his head. One minute later he was hanging in mid-air, his chin on his chest, his eyes tearing loose from their sockets, a green foam bubbling from his mouth and his body spasming, suspended by the shreds left of his mashed arms pinned between a wall and a girder.

A two-by-four hooked little Joe Chiappa up under the back of his jumper and swung him around in a circle to meet a careening I-beam. In the flash that he lifted his frozen cherubic face, its shearing edge sliced through the top of his skull.

When Snoutnose cried beseechingly, "Saint Michael!" blackness enveloped him. He came to in a world of horror. A steady stream, warm, thick, and sickening as hot wine bathed his face and clogged his nose, mouth and eyes. The nauseous syrup that pumped over his face clotted his mustache red and drained into his mouth. He gulped for air, and swallowed the rich liquid scarlet. As he breathed, the pain shocked him to oppressive semiconsciousness. The air was wormingly alive with cries, screams, moans and dust, and his crushed chest seared him with a thousand fires. He couldn't see, nor breathe enough to cry. His right hand moved to his face and wiped at the gelatinizing substance, but it kept coming on, and a heartbreaking moan wavered about him, not far. He wiped his eyes in subconscious despair. Where was he? What kind of a dream was he having? Perhaps he wouldn't wake up in time for work, and then what? But how queer; his stomach beating him, his chest on fire, he sees nothing but dull red, only one hand moving about, and a moaning in his face!

The sound and clamor of the rescue squads called to him from far off.

Ah, yes, he's dreaming in bed, and far out in the streets, engines are going to a fire. Oh poor devils! Suppose his house were on fire? With the children scattered about in the rooms he could not remember! He must do his utmost to break out of this dream! He's swimming under water, not able to raise his head and get to the air. He must get back to consciousness to save his children!

He swam frantically with his one right hand, and then felt a face beneath its touch. A face! It's Angelina alongside of him! Thank God, he's awake! He tapped her face. It moved. It felt cold, bristly and wet. "It moves so. What is this?" His fingers slithered about grisly sharp bones and in a gluey, stringy, hollow mass, yielding as wet macaroni. Gray light brought sight, and hysteria punctured his heart. A girder lay across his chest, his right hand clutched a grotesque human mask, and suspended almost on top of him was the twitching, faceless body of Joe Chiappa. Vincenzo fainted with an inarticulate sigh. His fingers loosed and the bodyless-headless face dropped and fitted to the side of his face while the drippings above came slower and slower.

The rescue men cleaved grimly with pick and axe.

Geremio came to with a start ... far from their efforts. His brain told him instantly what had happened and where he was. He shouted wildly. "Save me! Save me! I'm being buried alive!"

He paused exhausted. His genitals convulsed. The cold steel rod upon which they were impaled froze his spine. He shouted louder and louder. "Save me! I am hurt badly! I can be saved, I can—save me before it's too late!" But the cries went no farther than his own ears. The icy wet concrete reached his chin. His heart was appalled. "In a few seconds I shall be entombed. If I can only breathe, they will reach me. Surely they will!" His face was quickly covered, its flesh yielding to the solid, sharp-cut stones. "Air! Air!" screamed his lungs as he was completely sealed. Savagely, he bit into the wooden form pressed upon his mouth. An eighth of an inch of its surface splintered off. Oh, if he could only hold out long enough to bite even the smallest hole through to air! He must! There can be no other way! He is responsible for his family! He cannot leave them like this! He didn't want to die! This could not be the answer to life! He had bitten halfway through when his teeth snapped off to the gums in the uneven conflict. The pressure of the concrete was such, and its effectiveness so thorough, that the wooden splinters, stumps of teeth, and blood never left the choking mouth.

Why couldn't he go any farther?

Air! Quick! He dug his lower jaw into the little hollowed space and gnashed in choking agonized fury. "Why doesn't it go through? Mother of Christ, why doesn't it give? Can there be a notch, or two-by-four stud behind it? Sweet Jesu! No! No! Make it give.... Air! Air!"

He pushed the bone-bare jaw maniacally; it splintered, cracked, and a jagged fleshless edge cut through the form, opening a small hole to air. With a desperate burst the long-prisoned air blew an opening through the shredded mouth and whistled back greedily a gasp of fresh air. He tried to breathe, but it was impossible. The heavy concrete was settling immutably, and its rich cement-laten grout ran into his pierced face. His lungs would not expand, and were crushing in tighter and tighter under the settling concrete.

"Mother mine—mother of Jesu-Annunziata—children of mine—dear, dear, for mercy, Jesu-Guiseppe e 'Maria," his blue-foamed tongue called. It then distorted in a shuddering coil and mad blood vomited forth. Chills and fire played through him and his tortured tongue stuttered, "Mercy, blessed Father—salvation, most kind Father—Savior—Savior of His children help me—adored Savior—I kiss Your feet eternally—you are my God of infinite mercy—Hail Mary divine Virgin—Our Father who art in heaven hallowed be thy—name—our Father—my Father," and the agony excrucied with never-ending mount, "our Father—Jesu, Jesu, soon Jesu, hurry dear Jesu

Jesu! Je-sssu ... !" His mangled voice trebled hideously, and hung in jerky whimperings.

The unfeeling concrete was drying fast, and shrinking into monolithic density. The pressure temporarily desensitized sensation; leaving him petrified, numb and substanceless. Only the brain remained miraculously alive.

"Can this be death? It is all too strangely clear. I see nothing nor feel nothing, my body and senses are no more, my mind speaks as it never did before. Am I or am I not Geremio? But I am Geremio! Can I be in the other world? I never was in any other world except the one I knew of; that of toil, hardship, prayer ... of my wife who awaits with child for me, of my children and the first home I was to own. Where did I begin in this world? Where do I leave off? Why? I recall only a baffled life of cruelty from every direction. And hope was always as painful as fear, the fear of displeasing, displeasing the people and ideas whom I could never understand; laws, policemen, priests, bosses, and a rag with colors waving on a stick. I never did anything to these things. But what have I done with my life? Yes, my life! No one else's! Mine—mine—MINE—Geremio! It is clear. I was born hungry, and have always been hungry for freedom—life! I married and ran away to America so as not to kill and be killed in Tripoli for things they call 'God and Country.' I've never known the freedom I wanted in my heart. There was always an arm upraised to hit at me. What have I done to them? I did not want to make them toil for me. I did not raise my arm to them. In my life I could never breathe, and now without air, my mind breathes clearly for me. Wait! There has been a terrible mistake! A cruel crime! The world is not right! Murderers! Thieves! You have hurt me and my kind, and have taken my life from me! I have long felt it—yes, yes, yes, they have cheated me with flags, signs, and fear.... I say you can't take my life! Vincenz! Chiappa! Nick! Men! Do you hear me? We must follow the desires within us for the world has been taken from us; we, who made the world! Life!"

Feeling returned to the destroyed form.

"Ahhh-h, I am not dead yet. I knew it—you have not done with me. Torture away! I cannot believe you, God and Country, no longer!" His body was fast breaking under the concrete's closing wrack. Blood vessels burst like mashed flower stems. He screamed. "Show yourself now, Jesu! Now is the time! Save me! Why don't you come! Are you there! I cannot stand it— ohhh, why do you let it happen—it is bestial—where are you! Hurry, hurry, hurry! You do not come! You make me suffer, and what have I done? Come, come—come now—now save me, save me now! Now, now, now! If you are God, save me!"

The stricken blood surged through a weltering maze of useless pipes and exploded forth from his squelched eyes and formless nose, ears and mouth, seeking life in the indifferent stone.

"Aie—aie, aie—devils and saints—beasts! Where are you—quick, quick, it is death and I am cheated—cheat—ed! Do you hear, you whoring bastards who own the world? Ohhh-ohhh aie aie—hahahaha!" His bones cracked mutely and his sanity went sailing distorted in the limbo of the subconscious.

With the throbbing tones of an organ in the hollow background, the fighting brain disintegrated and the memories of a baffled lifetime sought outlet.

He moaned the simple songs cf barefoot childhood, scenes flashed desperately on and off in disassociated reflex, and words and parts of words came pitifully high and low from his inaudible lips, the hysterical mind sang cringingly and breathlessly, "Jesu my Lord my God my all Jesu my Lord my God my all Jesu my Lord my God my all Jesu my Lord my God my all," and on as the whirling tempo screamed now far, now near, and came in soul-sickening waves as the concrete slowly contracted and squeezed his skull out of shape.

1937

YOUNGHILL KANG
1903–1972

Younghill Kang was born in Hamkyong Province in northern Korea. Educated at first in the Confucian tradition, he later attended Christian schools, which were established all over Korea by American missionaries. Kang immigrated to the United States with only $4 in his pocket in 1921, just three years prior to the enactment of laws that excluded immigrants from Korea for more than three decades. Originally, Kang was interested in science, but he found himself uncomfortable in the laboratory and said that he was forced to write because he couldn't find what he wanted said expressed anywhere else. Describing himself as "self-educated," Kang read English and American classics voraciously, attending classes at Harvard and Boston Universities while working at various jobs to support himself. Between 1924 and 1927, Kang wrote in Korean and Japanese, and in 1928 he began writing in English with the help of his Wellesley-educated American wife, Frances Keeley. He found work as an editor at *Encyclopaedia Britannica* and obtained a position as a lecturer in the English Department at New York University, where he befriended Thomas Wolfe. At the time, Kang was working on *The Grass Roof*, a novel about a young man's life in Korea to the point of his departure for America. Wolfe read four chapters of the book and then took it to his own editor at Charles Scribner's Sons, where it was published in 1931. Between 1933 and 1935, Kang went to Germany and Italy with a Guggenheim Award in Creative Literature. In 1937, Scribner's published *East Goes West*, the story of a Korean in America.

An intensely lonely man, Younghill Kang was never afforded a permanent niche in American life. Always a visiting lecturer, he was never offered a stable teaching position. Instead, he traveled from speaking engagement to speaking engagement in an old Buick, spellbinding Rotary Club audiences with his recitations of Hamlet's soliloquy and his lectures on Korea. Widely read and possessing a remarkable memory, he lived with his wife, two sons, and a daughter, in genteel poverty in a ramshackle Long Island farmhouse overflowing with books. He is said to have commented that it was his great misfortune that Pearl Buck's Pulitzer Prize–winning novel about China, *The Good Earth*, was published in the same year as *The Grass Roof*, eclipsing his own tale of Asia.

Although he is best known for *The Grass Roof* and *East Goes West*, Kang also published translations of Korean literature, such as *Meditations of the Lover* and *Murder in the Royal Palace*, a children's book based on the first part of *The Grass Roof* (*The Happy Grove*, 1933), as well as a number of book reviews in the *New York Times* on Asian culture. Hospitalized in New York for postoperative hemorrhaging after a massive stroke, Kang died in 1972.

Kang considered *East Goes West* "more mature in style and technique" and more highly developed in content than *The Grass Roof*, which American critics generally preferred. Perhaps because they did not think that America and Americans should be part of a Korean immigrant's discourse territory, they applauded Kang's portrayal of Korea as a "planet of death," but they found fault with his criticism of American racism and prejudice.

Younghill Kang's work represents a new beginning in Asian American literature, a transition from the viewpoint of a guest or visitor acting as a "cultural bridge" to the perspective of the immigrant attempting to claim a permanent place in American life.

Elaine H. Kim
University of California, Berkeley

PRIMARY WORKS

The Grass Roof, 1931; *The Happy Grove*, 1933; *East Goes West: The Making of an Oriental Yankee*, 1937.

from **East Goes West**

Part One, Book Three

1

George and I were to leave New York about the same time. Pyun had found places for both, as he said he would. Since I could not cook, though George was charitable enough to recommend me, they said I must go as a houseboy, in company with another Korean, Mr. Pak.

"I know Mr. Pak," said George. "And you will have no trouble there."

I became optimistic then:

"My first American step, George, in economic life. I will make money now like Hung-Kwan Pang. On that I will become educated like J.P. Ok, A.B., B.D., M.S.T., M.A., Ph.D."

"I'm sure of Pak," George added, "but I am not sure of Pyun. Pyun has himself learned the American efficiency, though he would be ashamed to say that he is a good business man ... this shows he still has some

Orientality about him. But all the same he may be sending us both out just to get a commission."

"But he is a good friend of yours!"

"I do not like him much. In some ways he is an interesting type of Oriental successful in America.... Pyun's Utopia is not unlike that good old Epicurus[1] ... he believes in eating good meals. He also believes in hard work. So he spends his days in hard work and his nights in good times—a typical New Yorker. He really knows gin. Those who come for the party enjoy themselves and have no headache the next morning. He has an apartment uptown where I often go to play poker (mostly losing). He keeps the entire floor for himself, so he can bring his friends privately. (His friends are mostly girls.) But he will never get anywhere. He has no poetry, no romance! Just skating!"

"Remember," said George to me, "it is not always the money man who is the best dancer, the best drinker, or the best-dressed human being at all. He often leads the dullest existence. That is because he does not know how to create an enjoyable life. It may be that money does not come to the man who knows how to spend it for a good time. But then you can't afford to have a dull life. At any rate—make money: but don't sacrifice mystery to make money. When you say, 'Never mind—that will come when I accumulate wealth,' then it may be too late. To scorn delights and live laborious days, that will not do."

I was packed long before George, and presently Pak came in a taxicab with his two suitcases. They were old and worn, not so good-looking as George's. The handle of one was wrapped with strings. Pak was very big and tall, with a phlegmatic face. He had a stubborn hesitating accent; three times his tongue would flutter, sometimes even more, before he could utter a sentence.

He was a most typical Korean, an exile only in body, not in soul. Western civilization had rolled over him as water over a rock. He was a very strong nationalist; so he always sat in at the Korean Christian services, because they had sometimes to do with nationalism. With his hard-earned money, he supported all societies for Korean revolution against Japan. Most of his relations had moved out of Korea since the Japanese occupation— into Manchuria and Russia—but Pak still lived believing that the time must come to go back, and even now, with a little money sent in care of a brother-in-law, he had bought a minute piece of land to the north of Seoul. For fifteen years his single ambition had been to get back there and settle down. On Korean land, he wanted to raise 100 per cent Korean children, who would be just as patriotic as himself, and maybe better educated in the classics. But still he did not have enough money to travel back, get married, settle comfortably down. This made him rather suffering and gloomy, always looking on the dark side of things.

---

[1]Greek philosopher who held that sensuous pleasure was the highest good.

George went out and got some beer to cheer him up. Real beer it was, in a paper carton. Pak drank beer and light wines—never gin—and smoked Luckies, but very temperately.

Pak too was worried, not about George's job, but about his and mine.

"Eighty dollars a month for two. That is not much!" he sighed. And George agreed.

"What is the matter with Pyun? Is he trying all the worst places first?"

"That trick was played on me many times before," said Pak.

"I guess your place is all right. The woman has two kids. She must be normal."

Pak shook his head gloomily.

"Normal you say—or as I say, not—American woman is hard to understand," insisted Pak, shaking his head. "I have had only one good job in America. For seven years I had a good job. A very nice man. Very nice wife. Nobody ever was mad at me. But he was mad at her, she was mad at him. Finally both become so mad with each other, they divorce. Nobody can see a reason why. The man goes to live in New York hotel. The lady goes to live with a friend in California. I was so happy with both!" Pak was almost crying. "Neither could take me. The lady cried, saying good-by. Then the man came, separately crying. But—all up! Our home was broken. One month's pay, $100 from the man. From the lady, a wonderful letter recommending me. I use this letter ever since. But never find another job like that. No more jobs like that in America!"

"Well," said George philosophically, "Their jobs are like their marriages. In the American civilization, especially in New York civilization, a married woman is no more than a kept woman, and no kept woman could be kept long. Thus divorce comes. It costs money. But they have it. So social life is a burden to them...."

"Western marriage is no good in New York!" agreed Pak mournfully.

"But being a bachelor in New York is not bad!"

Pak didn't see it that way.

"Not good for a man to be unmarried. Indecent Western way."

"Look here, Pak, you are not Westernized," exclaimed George, rising up to preach. "You are not civilized. What is the matter with you? You can't enjoy the bachelor life when you have it. It is something we don't have in the Orient. This is one of the advantages of Western civilization. Listen, I read you advice."

George took down a big fat notebook. He put on his glasses.

"These are the wisest of Western men—the greatest of thinkers," he opened to his self-made index, hunting advice whether or not to get married. "(Not because they are wise and great, but because I agree in what they say.) First. Take Socrates. When asked whether to get married or stay single, Socrates said, 'Whichever, you will repent.' (You see, Socrates encouraged marriage 50 per cent. He lived in western classical times.) Another writer says, 'One was never married and this is his hell; another is, and that is his plague.' Hell may be bad, still it would not be as bad as plague. The wisest advice I know is that given by the great philosopher and thinker, Bacon, 'Young man—not yet! Elder man—never!'" And George shut the book with a whack, pleased with himself.

Pak still stood by his own conviction. He seemed not to have heard Jum's words at all.

"Forty-five years old I am. Not yet married. Already I lose at least five children by not marrying. And no children—no more me! This is fault! This is sin! This is crime ... of the race suicide!"

2

In the station Pak bought a newspaper, which he could not read. He only bought it to look at the advertisements. He had not had much education at home and none at all in America. I offered to read some to him. But he was only interested to know what had happened in the Korean revolution, which had already quieted down. At least in American papers.

We were met at our destination by a lady in a big shiny car, all enclosed, and she was driving it herself. I examined her somewhat curiously, remembering the stories of George and Pak. She looked very *artificial* to me and *not very friendly*.

"He talk not much English," said Pak, and, uneasy how I would behave, he nudged me. As we assembled our suitcases, he said in Korean:

"Leave everything to me. You just keep in the background. Be shy like a Korean bride."

I tried to be shy. But the lady would not allow me to do this. As we rolled through suburban green lawns and semi-countrified streets, she directed all her words at me.

"You are the houseboy, aren't you? What? No experience! I hope we won't have too hard a time to train you" ... and on and on.... My rôle seemed more a star than Pak's.

"And you must say 'Yes, *Madame.*'"

The car stopped. All around was free land, laid out for houses regularly with streets, but on it now were only small trees. There was one house. I did not care for the house. It ought out here to be a farmhouse but nobody attempted to make it a farm. It was a three-story concrete, very abrupt to look at in that flat space. There was a tiny hedge a little dog could jump and an artificial lawn with gravel paths. On the wind also you could smell the sea, but there was no sea smell about the house. It negated Nature, but the city was not transported yet. In a few years there would be many houses. I saw on the horizon another going up. I would not be able to recognize this place in 1975. Now, with neither society nor privacy, it was desolate.

"Get out," said the lady, who seemed a society-pioneer here. "And open the door for me. No, I mean you." And she pointed at me.

I had difficulty though to open the door for myself. Pak tried to open too, but it stuck. There was a trick in the button. The lady opened the door, turning around from her seat in front. Then my suitcase, which was on top of Pak's two suitcases, fell out, and opened and all my books fell out, and I fell out of the taxi after them. There I stood and didn't know whether to pick up my books or open the door for the lady. For she would have to step out on the books.

"Go round to the other door," said Pak to me in Korean. And he jumped out after me.

"Yes, Madame."

I tried to get there so fast that I stubbed my toe on Shakespeare and fell down. I jumped up and got the door open at last, and the lady had to step out in a kind of flower bed, while Pak crammed all my books back into the suitcase, and shut it, but only by one lock on one side: the other wouldn't close.

"That was very badly done," said the lady. "Leave the suitcases there—no, on the gravel, not on the lawn. Get into the car and try that over again."

This time I did very well. Pak breathed a sigh of relief.

"Now whenever I come in, you stand out here and open the car door...."

She was moving toward the house in illustration. I grabbed up my suitcase again and followed after. Pak too.

She opened the side door with her key.

"Here, you must help to take my coat and overshoes."

"Yes, Madame."

I dropped my suitcase again. Again it broke.

"Never mind now," she said in vexation, "just remember another time."

I picked up my books.

"I hope they have no germs," she said, shuddering as she saw the dingy Oriental covers of some second-hand books I bought in Yokohoma.

We went inside. Pak took off his coat the first thing. But I kept mine—a missionary had told me that a gentleman never takes off his short coat in the house; forever he must wear it just like shoes. The lady handed us two white aprons, badges of servitude, ordering us to try these on. Pak tied his around his armpits. But mine was too long. I tied it around my neck and stood attentively.

"No, no, not that way."

"Yes, Madame."

Dejectedly I tied it around my waist under the jacket. The upper part looked man now, the lower, woman. Certainly it was a very long skirt. It almost trailed on the floor. The lady was looking at me analytically.

"H'm! What is wrong with you? Well, these are the best I can do until I take your sizes. My former cook was a very tall Negro. He was able to do the work of two. *But I hired you to be presentable.* Tomorrow I will go into the city to get some white coats—if everything else is satisfactory," she added with emphasis.

A cultured Korean lady takes small and calm steps full of leisure. This American lady moved out vice versa.

We were late. We must rush to get the first dinner. I only peeled carrots and beans. Then I cut my finger. But I had to wait on table. Pak couldn't do it for me. O Lord! George had forgotten to tell me how. I had a short lesson from Pak.

"Fork on left, spoon on right ... pour water over right shoulder ... offer meat on left ... don't take away plate under soup bowl till end of soup...."

How was I to remember all this? It was like learning the Chinese book of rites in five minutes.

Then I forgot all when I brought in the soup. A girl of eighteen stood there in trousers and shirt like an American man, with long leather boots reaching to the knees. She sat down.

"Oh, I'm so hungry," said the girl. "I rode clear round the riding school.... My horse was in fine spirits and ... "

She caught sight of me and giggled. Her brother, a boy of twelve, laughed too.

I returned to the kitchen and described the girl to Pak.

"It's the way women dress on Long Island," I said.

Pak, however, took it as sinister.

"This job won't last," he gloomily shook his head. "Girl dressed like man, hair cut short, Westerners all like ten hells."

"But she has to, to ride on a horse."

"Yes! Rides on horse! Son-of-ingenuine-woman!"

The lady's bell rang peremptorily.

"Quick! Tell me what next."

But Pak couldn't. His tongue wouldn't move that fast.

"Get back," was all he said.

I went back in and the lady said, "Take the soup off."

"Through?" I said as softly as I could.

"You must say 'Yes, Madame.'"

What had Pak said? Don't take the plates under soup-bowls? I left the plates. It was wrong.

"Take these plates off!" said the lady angrily.

"Yes, Madame."

"Hey, give me some more water, Charley, before you go," said the boy.

"Yes, Madame."

The girl and the boy seemed to be giggling and laughing the whole time. They never took their eyes from me. I went into the kitchen again, where Pak was still mumbling to himself about the unnatural evils of Western civilization.

"What would my grandmother say? Running round over country on horseback dressed like men."

"How can I be there like Korean bride?" I asked indignantly. "The girl and boy are laughing at me all the time."

"Get back!" was all Pak said. "Before she rings. Here. Put napkin over arm."

I went in as noiselessly as I could. That was very noiseless. I was facing the boy and girl but the lady's back was to me. She didn't know I came in. I stood by the sideboard like a statue, napkin over the arm. The boy and girl were delighted.

"Ain't we got style?" said the boy. "We got a butler."

The lady laughed, "Peu! peu!" But she didn't see me.

Pretty soon I had to sneeze. I struggled for control. I must be Korean bride. No help. It was an awful sneeze. The lady jumped and said 'Oh!' She turned in a hurry—the boy and girl buried their faces in napkins and weakly howled. I too must laugh to look at them. "Hee!" I too put the napkin to my face. But the lady didn't laugh. "You may go!"

"Yes, Madame."

<h2 style="text-align:center">3</h2>

Pak worked slowly, but he did well, and he was a good cook. To me he was always kind. I complained to Pak about the lady, who interviewed me much more than Pak.

"It is not good that all the time she should get angry—not good for her, not good for me."

"No man can understand American ladies," he said patiently.

I had to work from morning to night. I had never worked so hard in all my life with no time to myself. First, beds to make. Pak helped me in this, for it was hard. Pak preached like George, be tight, but for a different reason.

"All Westerners roast the feet to freeze the nose. Western feet are cold, while Western nose is tough, tough as the elephant's trunk."

But next day the whole thing was to do over again. I was discouraged.

"All Westerners kick, these more than most," said Pak. "It is bad conscience maybe. I will buy big safety pins to pin the end sheets and blankets so they won't come off, after once being done, when the lady kicks at night."

Then there was so much dusting to do, all seeming an unnecessary labor to me. Surely such quantities of furniture were only in the way! In Korea, the beauty of a room is in its freespace. "The utility of a vase is in its emptiness." I did not believe Americans got much out of Shakespeare—American domesticity gave no time. And yet there were all sorts of labor-saving devices in the kitchen, even an electric egg-beater. I could not understand why I did not get through safely and quickly like George, with plenty of leisure time.

Whenever the lady saw me, she got nervous and irritated. Before she spoke, she would give one big artificial smile, and the bigger the smile was, the angrier she was going to be. She would preach:

"Always rearrange pillows after I—or any others—sit on the sofa...."

"Always put on a clean apron before coming out of the kitchen ... not one spotted with jam...."

"Never leave off your apron as if you were a guest in the house...."

"Dust under each chair with an oil rag, not with a feather...."

"Dry the saucepan before putting it away...."

"Dishwipers must be washed at once after being used; then hang them up carefully...."

"Never use the front door except to open it for others...."

"Don't stay here ... go ... after being called and serving ... "

This last was vice versa to the orders of Pak. Always when I came out of the dining room while the family sat at the table, he ordered, "Back!" He didn't want me in his way either.

It was interesting in a sense, being treated just like a dog or cat. One could see everything, and go unnoticed, except while being scolded. But how tired my feet got! How discouraged I was! How hungry to get away somewhere, even if I starved! *"To keep on is harder than being a prisoner,"* I thought. And I remembered George's advice not to scorn delight and live laborious days.

Still another day of chore work in domesticity began. It was a beautiful morning. I looked out through the window at the green fields of the first April, juicy and wet. Outside the spring odor was penetrating and lyrical. The perfume of the bursting sods and quickened rootlets all swaying in the west wind, intermingled with the salty tang of the sea. But inside it was tough and bitter, for I had slept too late, having gone to bed too late the night before. Shakespeare was to blame for it. He was too beautiful to be left unread, too poignant to be left uncried. I wished to write letters to my ideal as George did.

"From you I have been absent in the Spring...."

The clock indicated that I was an hour and a half late when I got up that morning. Pak did not wake me, because he thought I needed a little more sleep after the night before. He was too kind to me always. Alas, kindness was to spoil the whole business!

I went into the great white mechanized kitchen. Pak said:

"Fired!"

"Something is burning?" I cried, running to the electric stove.

"No. Fired! Job doesn't last!"

But hoping still to make good, I dragged the vacuum cleaner in to do the living room, my usual morning task. The girl, who was always the latest breakfast-getter, was already up, and so was her mother. They were standing, looking at the living room which was just as it had been left the night before, when the girl, who was already a candidate for somebody, entertained company.

The girl as usual giggled when she saw me. But the lady did not. She looked at me with a hard and spiteful smile:

"I have telephoned for a house servant, not a comedian."

1937

JOSE GARCIA VILLA
1908–1997

Jose Garcia Villa was born in Manila, Philippines, on August 5, 1908, and grew up in a society in flux. The American colonial government had succeeded in pacifying and in co-opting the elite that had fought for Philippine independence from Spain. The military dealt forcibly with any overt resistance to American rule. By the 1920s, when Villa was in his teens, the American colonial government had brought in a new language, new values, and new modes of perceiving and conduct, often at odds with the Old World values and the spirit of nationalism that had shaped the generation before him.

Villa lived that confrontation of cultures. His father, Simeon Villa, had fought in the Philippine revolution against Spain and had served as the personal physician of Emilio Aguinaldo, the leader of the revolution and eventually the first President of the Philippines before the United States seized control. Villa, however, was the product of an American-style education, immersed in the poetry and prose of the American and English Romantics and the fantasies being peddled by Hollywood and the American popular press.

His father wanted him to be a doctor and sent him to the College of Medicine of the University of the Philippines. Villa, however, felt that his talent lay elsewhere, first in painting and later in literature. Like many of his generation and class status, he chose to write in English, not Spanish nor Tagalog, thus alienating himself further from his elders and from the tradition of nationalistic writing that had emerged in the late nineteenth century against Spain and that persisted in the first decade of the twentieth century against American rule.

Villa became one of the pioneers of Philippine literature in English, writing stories for nationally circulated magazines and the campus papers in the late 1920s. As the decade drew to a close, Villa had established a name for himself as a short-story writer.

The Philippine short story in English was then not even a decade old—Paz Marquez Benitez's "Dead Stars," published in 1925, is usually credited as the first modern story in English by a Filipino. Many writers were still mastering the language and the short story form, trying out different styles in the process. Classic writers of the short story like Edgar Allan Poe and Guy de Maupassant and more contemporary practitioners like Sherwood Anderson and later, Ernest Hemingway, William Saroyan, and Dorothy Parker, among others, influenced its development. Villa more than once credited Anderson as his model, although he also imitated other writers. Thus, in "Footnote to Youth," the protagonist, like the 'grotesques' of Anderson's *Winesburg, Ohio*, gropes for answers to life's questions and struggles unsuccessfully to connect with others.

In 1930 Villa arrived in the United States to finish college. He had been suspended from the University of the Philippines for writing what the conservative social and university establishment thought were "obscene" poems, which he called "Man-Songs." One of these compared a woman's nipples to coconuts. He would be readmitted on the condition that he promise not to write similar things in the future. This incident and other clashes with his father led him to stay in the United States except for occasional visits to the Philippines.

At the University of New Mexico, he pursued short-story writing and even mimeographed a "little magazine" called *Clay*, where he published William Saroyan, Witter Bynner, and William Carlos Williams, among other writers. In 1933, his first and only book of short stories was published, *Footnote to Youth: Tales of the Philippines and Others*, by Charles Scribner's Sons. Edward J. O'Brien, then the editor of the annual *Best Short Stories*, declared that Villa was one of the most promising short-story writers of the time.

Villa abandoned fiction, however, to pursue poetry, adopting the pseudonym Doveglion (combining *dove*, *eagle*, and *lion*). Although he had dabbled in poetry earlier, even publishing two collections of poems in the Philippines (*Many Voices* [1939] and *Poems* [1941]), it was only after reading E. E. Cummings' *Collected Poems* (1938) that he realized the direction that his poetry was to take. Cummings' lyricism and experimental way with language were what would characterize Villa's poetry. Villa added a mystical or visionary dimension, drawing inspiration, it seems, from William Blake and John Donne, and in some poems a gnomic, paradoxical style of utterance reminiscent of Emily Dickinson. Thus one finds as subject in many of Villa's poems romantic or erotic love, the art of poetry itself, and the poet as a Genius and rebel who dares to wrestle with God.

In 1942, the Viking Press published *Have Come, Am Here*. The title of the book was properly annunciative, for with the book Villa received instant and almost universal recognition. The book was lauded by critics and poets like Mark Van Doren, Marianne Moore, Babette Deutsch, and Louis Untermeyer. Villa introduced a rhyme scheme, though used in only a few poems, that he calls "reversed consonance," where "the last sounded consonants of the last syllable, or the last principal consonants of a word, are reversed for the corresponding rhyme." Thus, *run* rhymes with *rain*, and *green* with *reign*. (See poem no. 1.)

Villa's second book of poems to be published in the United States did not come out until 1949. *Volume Two* was published by New Directions, which, in accordance with the reputation of New Directions, furthered Villa's bid to be taken as avant garde. His new experiment was the "comma poem", in which every word is separated by a comma unless another punctuation mark is used: thus, "The,soul,swarms,with,angels, / If,Soul,but,knew,it." (See his note on the commas on p. 1318.) He also introduced the Aphorisms, miniature poems that are often philosophical in tone. His preoccupation with God, love, and poetry also persisted, the speaking voice often Sphinx-like in utterance.

Readers were unimpressed, however, by the comma experiment, and as the American literary scene changed, Villa's reputation also began to wane. He essentially remained the kind of poet that he had been in 1942 when he surprised the American literary scene with his ecstatic and mysterious utterances, an inward-looking poet. Amid increasing pressure for one to produce committed art in the 1960s and later the vogue for hyphenated subjectivities, Villa remained committed to his own vision of art. His poems are brilliant explosions in a dark void—impressive and startling in their own right.

In 1953 he wrote his last and longest poem, "The Anchored Angel," which was published as the lead poem in the *Times Literary Supplement*. It was, in essence, the supreme reiteration of his vision of poetry and the poet.

His third American book of poems was *Selected Poems and New* (McDowell, Obolensky, 1958), where he introduced the Adaptations, conversions of prose into poems "through technical manipulation." Another volume of collected poems, mostly early poems that had not been published in the United States, appeared in 1979, entitled *Appassionata: Poems in Praise of Love* (King and Cowen). But Villa remained increasingly reclusive in his Greenwich Village apartment, where he conducted workshops with a small group of students until his death on February 7, 1997.

His death was virtually unheralded in the American press. In the Philippines, however, he had been declared National Artist for Literature in 1973 by the Philippine government and was fittingly given a state tribute.

Jonathan Chua
Ateneo de Manila University

PRIMARY WORKS

Footnote to Youth, 1933; *Have Come, Am Here*, 1942; *Volume Two*, 1949; *Selected Poems and New*, 1958; *Appassionata: Poems in Praise of Love*, 1979; *Doveglion: Collected Poems*, 2008; *The Anchored Angel: Selected Writings by Jose Garcia Villa*, 1999; *The Critical Villa: Essays in Literary Criticism by Jose Garcia Villa*, 2002.

Footnote to Youth

The sun was salmon and hazy in the west. Dodong thought to himself he would tell his father about Teang when he got home, after he had unhitched the carabao from the plow, and let it to its shed and fed it. He was hesitant about saying it, but he wanted his father to know. What he had to say was of serious import as it would mark a climacteric in his life. Dodong finally decided to tell it, at a thought came to him his father might refuse to consider it. His father was silent hard-working farmer who chewed areca nut, which he had learned to do from his mother, Dodong's grandmother.

I will tell it to him. I will tell it to him.

The ground was broken up into many fresh wounds and fragrant with a sweetish earthy smell. Many slender soft worms emerged from the furrows and then burrowed again deeper into the soil. A short colorless worm marched blindly to Dodong's foot and crawled calmly over it. Dodong go tickled and jerked his foot, flinging the worm into the air. Dodong did not bother to look where it fell, but thought of his age, seventeen, and he said to himself he was not young any more.

Dodong unhitched the carabao leisurely and gave it a healthy tap on the hip. The beast turned its head to look at him with dumb faithful eyes. Dodong gave it a slight push and the animal walked alongside him to its shed. He placed bundles of grass before it land the carabao began to eat. Dodong looked at it without interests.

Dodong started homeward, thinking how he would break his news to his father. He wanted to marry, Dodong did. He was seventeen, he had pimples on his face, the down on his upper lip already was dark–these meant he was no longer a boy. He was growing into a man–he was a man. Dodong felt insolent and big at the thought of it although he was by nature low in statue. Thinking himself a man grown, Dodong felt he could do anything.

He walked faster, prodded by the thought of his virility. A small angled stone bled his foot, but he dismissed it cursorily. He lifted his leg and looked at the hurt toe and then went on walking. In the cool sundown he thought wild you dreams of himself and Teang. Teang, his girl. She had a small brown face and small black eyes and straight glossy hair. How desirable she was to him. She made him dream even during the day.

Dodong tensed with desire and looked at the muscles of his arms. Dirty. This field work was healthy, invigorating but it begrimed you, smudged you terribly. He turned back the way he had come, then he marched obliquely to a creek.

Dodong stripped himself and laid his clothes, a gray undershirt and red kundiman shorts, on the grass. The he went into the water, wet his body over, and rubbed at it vigorously. He was not long in bathing, then he marched homeward again. The bath made him feel cool.

It was dusk when he reached home. The petroleum lamp on the ceiling already was lighted and the low unvarnished square table was set for supper. His parents and he sat down on the floor around the table to eat. They had fried fresh-water fish, rice, bananas, and caked sugar.

Dodong ate fish and rice, but did not partake of the fruit. The bananas were overripe and when one held them they felt more fluid than solid. Dodong broke off a piece of the cakes sugar, dipped it in his glass of water and ate it. He got another piece and wanted some more, but he thought of leaving the remainder for his parents.

Dodong's mother removed the dishes when they were through and went out to the batalan to wash them. She walked with slow careful steps and Dodong wanted to help her carry the dishes out, but he was tired and now felt lazy. He wished as he looked at her that he had a sister who could help his mother in the housework. He pitied her, doing all the housework alone.

His father remained in the room, sucking a diseased tooth. It was pain-ing him again, Dodong knew. Dodong had told him often and again to let the town dentist pull it out, but he was afraid, his father was. He did not tell that to Dodong, but Dodong guessed it. Afterward Dodong himself thought that if he had a decayed tooth he would be afraid to go to the dentist; he would not be any bolder than his father.

Dodong said while his mother was out that he was going to marry Teang. There it was out, what he had to say, and over which he had done so much thinking. He had said it without any effort at all and without self-consciousness. Dodong felt relieved and looked at his father expectantly. A decrescent moon outside shed its feeble light into the window, graying the still black temples of his father. His father looked old now.

"I am going to marry Teang," Dodong said.

His father looked at him silently and stopped sucking the broken tooth. The silence became intense and cruel, and Dodong wished his father would suck that troublous tooth again. Dodong was uncomfortable and then became angry because his father kept looking at him without uttering anything.

"I will marry Teang," Dodong repeated. "I will marry Teang."

His father kept gazing at him in inflexible silence and Dodong fidgeted on his seat.

"I asked her last night to marry me and she said. . .yes. I want your per-mission. I. . . want. . . it. . . ." There was impatient clamor in his voice, an exacting protest at this coldness, this indifference. Dodong looked at his father sourly. He cracked his knuckles one by one, and the little sounds it made broke dully the night stillness.

"Must you marry, Dodong?"

Dodong resented his father's questions; his father himself had married. Dodong made a quick impassioned easy in his mind about selfishness, but later he got confused.

"You are very young, Dodong."

"I'm. . . seventeen."

"That's very young to get married at."

"I. . . I want to marry. . .Teang's a good girl."

"Tell your mother," his father said.

"You tell her, tatay."

"Dodong, you tell your inay."

"You tell her."

"All right, Dodong."

"You will let me marry Teang?"

"Son, if that is your wish. . .of course. . ." There was a strange helpless light in his father's eyes. Dodong did not read it, so absorbed was he in himself

Dodong was immensely glad he had asserted himself. He lost his resentment for his father. For a while he even felt sorry for him about the diseased tooth. Then he confined his mind to dreaming of Teang and himself. Sweet young dreams!

Dodong stood in the sweltering noon heat, sweating profusely, so that his camiseta was damp. He was still as a tree and his thoughts were confused. His mother had told him not to leave the house, but he had left. He had wanted to get out of it without clear reason at all. He was afraid, he felt. Afraid of the house. It had seemed to cage him, to compares his thoughts with severe tyranny. Afraid also of Teang. Teang was giving birth in the house; she gave screams that chilled his blood. He did not want her to scream like that, he seemed to be rebuking him. He began to wonder madly if the process of childbirth was really painful. Some women, when they gave birth, did not cry.

In a few moments he would be a father. "Father, father," he whispered the word with awe, with strangeness. He was young, he realized now, contradicting himself of nine months comfortable. . . "Your son," people would soon be telling him. "Your son, Dodong."

Dodong felt tired standing. He sat down on a saw-horse with his feet close together. He looked at his callused toes. Suppose he had ten children. . . What made him think that? What was the matter with him? God!

He heard his mother's voice from the house:

"Come up, Dodong. It is over."

Suddenly he felt terribly embarrassed as he looked at her. Somehow he was ashamed to his mother of his youthful paternity. It made him feel guilty, as if he had taken something no properly his. He dropped his eyes and pretended to dust dirt off his kundiman shorts.

"Dodong," his mother called again. "Dodong."

He turned to look again and this time saw his father beside his mother.

"It is a boy," his father said. He beckoned Dodong to come up.

Dodong felt more embarrassed and did not move. What a moment for him. His parents' eyes seemed to pierce him through and he felt limp.

He wanted to hide from them, to run away.

"Dodong, you come up. You come up," he mother said.

Dodong did not want to come up and stayed in the sun.

"Dodong. Dodong."

"I'll. . . come up."

Dodong traced tremulous steps on the dry parched yard. He ascended the bamboo steps slowly. His heart pounded mercilessly in him. Within, he avoided his parents eyes. He walked ahead of them so that they should not see his face. He felt guilty and untrue. He felt like crying. His eyes smarted and his chest wanted to burst. He wanted to turn back, to go back to the yard. He wanted somebody to punish him.

His father thrust his hand in his and gripped it gently.

"Son," his father said.

And his mother: "Dodong. . ."

How kind were their voices. They flowed into him, making him strong.

"Teang?" Dodong said.

"She's sleeping. But you go on. . ."

His father led him into the small sawali room. Dodong saw Teang, his girl-wife, asleep on the papag with her black hair soft around her face. He did not want her to look that pale.

Dodong wanted to touch her, to push away that stray wisp of hair that touched her lips, but again that feeling of embarrassment came over him and before his parents he did not want to be demonstrative.

The hilot was wrapping the child, Dodong heard it cry. The thin voice pierced him queerly. He could not control the swelling of happiness in him.

"You give him to me. You give him to me," Dodong said.

Blas was not Dodong's only child. Many more children came. For six successive years a new child came along. Dodong did not want any more children, but they came. It seemed the coming of children could not be helped. Dodong got angry with himself sometimes.

Teang did not complain, but the bearing of children told on her. She was shapeless and thin now, even if she was young. There was interminable work to be done. Cooking. Laundering. The house. The children. She cried sometimes, wishing she had not married. She did not tell Dodong this, not wishing him to dislike her. Yet she wished she had not married. Not even Dodong, whom she loved. There has been another suitor, Lucio, older than Dodong by nine years, and that was why she had chosen Dodong. Young Dodong. Seventeen. Lucio had married another after her marriage to Dodong, but he was childless until now. She wondered if she had married Lucio, would she have borne him children. Maybe not, either. That was a better lot. But she loved Dodong. . .

Dodong whom life had made ugly.

One night, as he lay beside his wife, he rose and went out of the house. He stood in the moonlight, tired and querulous. He wanted to ask questions and somebody to answer him. He w anted to be wise about many things.

One of them was why life did not fulfill all of Youth's dreams. Why it must be so. Why one was forsaken... after Love.

Dodong would not find the answer. Maybe the question was not to be answered. It must be so to make youth Youth. Youth must be dreamfully sweet. Dreamfully sweet. Dodong returned to the house humiliated by himself. He had wanted to know a little wisdom but was denied it.

When Blas was eighteen he came home one night very flustered and happy. It was late at night and Teang and the other children were asleep. Dodong heard Blas's steps, for he could not sleep well of nights. He watched Blas undress in the dark and lie down softly. Blas was restless on his mat and could not sleep. Dodong called him name and asked why he did not sleep. Blas said he could not sleep.

"You better go to sleep. It is late," Dodong said.

Blas raised himself on his elbow and muttered something in a low fluttering voice.

Dodong did not answer and tried to sleep.

"Itay ...," Blas called softly.

Dodong stirred and asked him what it was.

"I am going to marry Tona. She accepted me tonight."

Dodong lay on the red pillow without moving.

"Itay, you think it over."

Dodong lay silent.

"I love Tona and... I want her."

Dodong rose from his mat and told Blas to follow him. They descended to the yard, where everything was still and quiet. The moonlight was cold and white.

"You want to marry Tona," Dodong said. He did not want Blas to marry yet. Blas was very young. The life that would follow marriage would be hard...

"Yes."

"Must you marry?"

Blas's voice stilled with resentment. "I will marry Tona."

Dodong kept silent, hurt.

"You have objections, Itay?" Blas asked acridly.

"Son... n-none..." (But truly, God, I don't want Blas to marry yet... not yet. I don't want Blas to marry yet....)

But he was helpless. He could not do anything. Youth must triumph... now. Love must triumph... now. Afterwards... it will be life.

As long ago Youth and Love did triumph for Dodong... and then Life.

Dodong looked wistfully at his young son in the moonlight. He felt extremely sad and sorry for him.

1933

Selected Poetry

1.

It's a hurricane of spirit—
That's genius! Not God can tear
It from itself, though He is the rose
In this skull that's seer.
Skull revolving rose: that's I!
I am in my skull and spy
Eternity and Now and Why.

It's a mastery of death—
And that's Love. It's the bequeathèd
Mind of Christ. It's I, it's Love,
What the great deaths reveal.
I revolve a skull, I rose!
I revolve a skull that knows
I make it speak God's voice!

2.

First, a poem must be magical,
Then musical as a sea-gull.
It must be a brightness moving
And hold secret a bird's flowering.
It must be slender as a bell,
And it must hold fire as well.
It must have the wisdom of the bows
And it must kneel like a rose.
It must be able to hear
The luminance of dove and deer.
It must be able to hide
What it seeks, like a bride.
And over all I would like to hover
God smiling from the poem's cover.

3.

Inviting a tiger for a weekend.
The gesture is not heroics but discipline.
The memoirs will be splendid.

Proceed to dazzlement, Augustine.
Banish little birds, graduate to tiger.
Proceed to dazzlement, Augustine.

Any tiger of whatever colour
The same as jewels any stone
Flames always essential morn.

The guest is luminous, peer of Blake.
The host is gallant, eye of Death.
If you will do this you will break

The little religions for my sake.
Invite a tiger for a weekend,
Proceed to dazzlement, Augustine.

4.

I have observed pink monks eating blue raisins.
And I have observed blue monks eating pink raisins.
Studiously have I observed.

Now, this is the way a pink monk eats a blue raisin:
Pink is he and it is blue and the pink
Swallows the blue. I swear this is true.

And the way a blue monk eats a pink raisin is this:
Blue is he and it is pink and the blue
Swallows the pink. And this also is truth.

Indeed I have observed and myself have partaken
Of blue and pink raisins. But my joy was different:
My joy was to see the blue and the pink counterpointing.

5.

God said, "I made a man
Out of clay—
　　But so bright he, he spun
Himself to brightest Day

Till he was all shining gold,
And oh,
　　He was lovely to behold!
But in his hands held he a bow

Aimed at me who created
Him. And I said,
　　'Wouldst murder m
Who am thy Fountainhead!'

Then spoke he the man of gold:
'I will not
    Murder thee! I do but
Measure thee. Hold

Thy peace.' And this I did.
But I was curious
    Of this so regal head.
'Give thy name!'—'Sir! Genius.'"

1942

from **Seven Poems**

A Note on the Commas

The reader of the following poems may be perplexed and puzzled at my use of the comma: it is a new, special and *poetic* use to which I have put it. The commas appear in the poems *functionally*, and thus not for eccentricity; and they are there also poetically, that is to say, not in their prose function. These poems were conceived *with* commas, as 'comma poems', in which the commas are an integral and essential part of the medium: regulating the poem's verbal density and time movement: enabling each word to attain a fuller tonal and sonal value, and the line movement to become more measured. The method may be compared to Seurat's architectonic and measured pointillism—where the points of color *are* themselves the medium as well as the technique of expression, and therefore functional and valid, as medium of art and as medium of personality. Only the uninitiate would complain that Seurat should have painted in strokes.

Regarding the time movement effected by the commas—a pause ensues after each comma, but a pause not as long as that commanded by its prose use: for this reason the usual space after the comma is omitted. The result is a lineal pace of dignity and movement.

I realize of course that this new poetic employment of the comma is an innovation which may disconcert some readers: for them I can only say that they can *still* read the poems by ignoring the commas if they find these in the way; personally I find that they even add visual distinction. With the more poetically and texturally sensitive reader, I believe that he will see with me the essentiality of the commas: the best test, which I have myself employed, is to copy out a poem *omitting* the commas and then to read this text comparatively with the comma'ed version: the loss is distinctly and immediately cognizable. Therein lies the justification for this—true enough—strange innovation.

7.

The,bright,Centipede,
Begins,his,stampede!
O,celestial,Engine,from,
What,celestial,province!
His,spiritual,might,
Golding,the,night—
His,spiritual,eyes,
Foretelling,my,Size;
His,spiritual,feet,
Stamping,in,heat,
The,radium,brain,
To,Spiritual,Imagination.

8.

My,whoseness,is,to,me,what,I,
  Am,to,the,Holy,
      Unghost—
It,moveth,me,
      As,it,

Progresses,me,to,unnight,noon,
  Day. Project,
      Me,Unghost!
Project,me,
      Elect,

Me,to,thy,kingdom,to,that,
  Stern,height.
      Knight,and,
Unnight,
      Me. In,

Strictest,supervision,knitme:
  To,the,Gibralt,
      Rock: to,the,
Radium,rock,
      Of,I.

To,the,Gibralt,rock: to,the,
  Radium,rock,of,
      I. O,halt,
And,halter,
      Me. Lead,

And,perish,me! Erect,me,to,where,
  All,eyesights,
    Break—
Let,all,eye-
    Sights,break!

1949

Aphorisms (a selection)

2

An,Epigram,
Is,an,epic,Weight,

Concealed,
In,a,gram's,Space.

6

A,genius,is,he,
That,can,make,
Portable,pyriamids.

25

Mathematician,excel,us,
Take,a,census,
Of,the,canaries,in,the,sun.

33

Only,the,hero,may,take,
A,snapshot,of,God:

And,then,it,would,be,
A,Self-Portrait.

41

Suspense—
The,fire,that,creates,Alaska.

69

A,Bee,flying,to,the,end,of,the,world,
To,find,one,Flower,wherein,to,lie,curled,

Is,a,fiction,is,a,lie,
That,will,keep,God,in,the,sky.

113

Fade,out,fade,out,
Pale,spermless,God:
Arise: Fire-testicled,God.

138

When,Nothing,is,so,well,said,
Or,so,well,done,

It,betrays,itself,and,becomes,
Something:

Like,apples,by,Cézanne,or,just,
Lines,by,Mondrian.

1949

JOVITA GONZÁLEZ
(1904-1983)

Jovita González was a folklorist, educator, and writer who dedicated her extra-ordinary career to the recovery and analysis of Texas-Mexican (or *Tejano*) culture. She was active in Texas folklore studies throughout the 1930s, producing a major master's thesis and numerous scholarly articles, giving frequent lectures as an expert in *Tejano* folklore, and even serving as president of the esteemed Texas Folklore Society, a position she held from 1930–1932. These were heady achievements for a Mexican American woman working in a field dominated by white male Texans and in a climate of heightened racial tensions between Mexicans and Anglos. While some have characterized her writings dismissively as "assimilationist" because of their emphasis on reform over revolution, critics such as José Limón and María Cotera have argued convincingly that her writings should be understood as political texts that use folklore and history to influence discourses on race relations between Anglos and Mexicans.

González was born on her grandparent's ranch near the old border town of Roma, Texas, in 1904. Throughout her early childhood, she mingled with those who lived and worked there and consequently developed a deep knowledge of and appreciation for *Tejano* culture, including its balladry, legends, folk remedies, food traditions, and the general practices of everyday life. While she expressed nostalgia for this period in her childhood, González came of age in a context of severe ethnic strife, which led to the dissolution of the Texas-Mexican ranching culture she loved. In response to the violence and civil disenfranchisement faced by Mexicans in the region, González's father moved the family to San Antonio, hoping that his daughters would attain the education they would need to negotiate the dramatic cultural and economic transformations taking place in their midst.

González excelled in her studies, earning a bachelor's degree in Spanish in 1927. From there she pursued a master's in the history department at the University of Texas at Austin. Supported by a Lapham scholarship, she spent the summer of 1929 traveling through remote regions of the Texas-Mexican borderlands, collecting materials for her thesis. The resulting work, "Social Life in Cameron, Starr, and Zapata Counties," was a remarkable contestation of Anglo-Texan historiography, one that celebrated Mexican contributions to Texas history and culture and worked to debunk negative stereotypes of *Tejanos*. While the manuscript was not published in her lifetime and was tepidly received by her Anglo-Texan thesis advisor—presumably because of its polemical nature—it has been used for decades as invaluable source material by researchers of South Texas culture.

González's thesis established the double focus that would be the hallmark of much of her later work. In Cotera's words, González strove to "help Anglo/Mexican race relations by clarifying dominant misconceptions about 'Latin Americans' among the Anglo community," and sought to "build pride within the Mexican American community regarding its long history and important cultural heritage in Texas." Such themes emerge in the historical novel González began work on in 1936, which traced the lives of a group of *Tejano* ranching families in the aftermath of the U.S.-Mexican War (1846–1848). Written with an Anglo-American woman named Margaret Eimer (who wrote under the pseudonym Eve Raleigh), the narrative, entitled *Caballero*, contrasts Anglo and Mexican characters that remain rigidly opposed to interethnic solidarity with those that cross ethnic lines in order to "collaborate" in a range of projects, including romantic relationships, artistic endeavors, and more pragmatic social and political ventures. As Cotera explains, the novel manifests González's belief that human understanding between different ethnic and racial groups was the key to harmony on the borderlands and contests the male-centered resistance strategies that marked emerging Mexican American institutions during González's own period. Though *Caballero* did not see publication until 1996, well after the deaths of its authors, it has become a highly prized text among scholars of Chicana/o studies, women's studies, and ethnic studies.

By the late 1930s, González's involvement with the Texas Folklore Society ended, most likely because of her disillusion with folklore studies as a means of transforming racist sensibilities, especially when such studies advocated a dehistoricized and depoliticized focus on "cultural appreciation." In the following piece, "Shades of the Tenth Muse," which she wrote in 1935 and which, like *Caballero*, remained unpublished during her lifetime, we see González's sense that a cultural pluralism that could constitute a viable model for race relations would have to go beyond mere "appreciation" by emphasizing mutual respect and understanding, a relationship modeled by the story's two characters.

While González published less frequently and made fewer public appearances after 1940, she remained active as an educator, teaching Spanish for twenty-one years before her retirement in 1967. Her literary, scholarly, and political legacy continues to be burnished as scholars recover and analyze the remarkable body of work she left behind.

Yolanda Padilla
University of Minnesota

PRIMARY WORKS

Folk-Lore of the Texas-Mexican Vaquero, 1927; *Tales and Songs of the Texas-Mexicans*, 1930; *Among My People*, 1932; *Caballero*, 1996; *Dew on the Thorn*, 1997; *The Woman who Lost Her Soul, and Other Stories*, 2000; *The Short Stories of Jovita Gonzalez*, 2000; *Life Along the Border: A Landmark Tejana Thesis*, 2006.

Shades of the Tenth Muses[1]

The air in the room is close and smoky; I can still smell the rosemary and lavender leaves I have just burnt in an incense burned to drive out the mosquitoes that have driven me insane with their monotonous, droning music. For, in spite of the family's efforts to have me work in the house I prefer my garage room with its screenless windows and door, its dizzy floor, the plants of which act like the keys of an old piano, and walls, hung with relics which I like to gather as I go from ranch to ranch in my quest for stories of the ranch folk. A faded Saint Teresa, in a more faded niche smiles her welcome every morning and a Virgin of Guadalupe reminds me daily that I am a descendant of a proud stoic race. Back of the desk, a collection of ranch spits is witness of my ranch heritage, an old, crude treasure chest holds my only possession, a manuscript which will sometime be sold, if I am among the fortunate. Hanging from a nail above is a home-spun, hand-woven coin bag, the very same which my grandfather was given by his mother on his wedding day with the admonition, "my son, may you and all who ever own it keep it filled with gold coins." It hangs there empty, for the descendant of that Don has never seen a gold coin, much less owned one.

In the place of honor, above my desk in a gold and black frame is a prayer, a letter written to the Almighty by my good friend Frost Woodhul, in which he asks for rain, not for himself, but for his friends in the ranches

---

[1]Presumably this is the only nonfolkloric story that Jovita González wrote in her writing career. Its original manuscript is in the E. E. Mireles & Jovita González de Mireles Papers, Special Collections & Archives, Texas A&M University-Corpus Christi Bell Library.

of northern Mexico—"Dear God in Heaven," it begins "Give us rain" . . . and ending "Yours truly."

It is late, too dark to write, the smell of rosemary and lavender is soothing and I fall—can I say asleep? Or am I transported three centuries back?

A figure glides in. It is a woman. She does not see me, or if she does she does not acknowledge my presence. She sits in the vacant chair by my desk. A radiance surrounds her, and I can see her face. She is beautiful, her features patrician and classical in their perfection resemble an ivory cameo, and her eyes are like black diamonds shining in the dark. I am not a bit surprised at the unexpected entrance of my uninvited guest, I even know who she is. She takes paper and pen and begins to write. I don't have to read over her shoulder. I know. She is Sor Juana Inés de la Cruz the spirit of her epoch and her race. I don't know how it happened; I do not even remember having left my place at the desk, yet I find myself resting in the couch. I can not be dreaming; the song of the mocking bird on the telephone past by my window tells me I am awake. And yet another figure equally strange has entered my room. She is a stately matron; her somber dress and serious expression mark her out as one who is always mournful and sad. She sits in the empty chair with a sign and looks around the room. Her eyes become fixed on the prayer. I can see terror and consternation on her face as she reads—"Oh God, our cows are dying; we're not crying. Our tears are dry much like our land. It's rained on every other hand." She clutches at her heart. She gasps at the sacrilegious words. She can not even utter a word.

A clear, silvery laugh bursts from the lips of the nun. "The prayer has shocked you has it not?" she asks.

"You call that prayer? It's blasphemy! Who dares to address God in such familiar terms?"

'I wouldn't say that," answered the nun in a careless drawling tone, "the man no doubt asks for what he wants in his own way. Let me see, who is the author? Frost Woodhul, Judge of Bexar County—not one of us; but I would like to know him. He's witty, I can see and wit, my dear, is a gift from the Angels."

"How can you!" gasps the somber figure. "What did you say his name was?"

"Woodhul, English, perhaps one of your colonials. Do you know him?"

"The Lord deliver me from that! He must be one of the pagan dwellers of Merrill Mount, one of Morton's infidels."

"It's a clever piece of nonsense though," the nun continued but seeing the look of anguish on her companion's face she said laughing,

"Perhaps he was merely joking."

"Joking about God? That's a sin that would bring fire and brimstone from heaven. Don't you have any religion?"

"Do I have any religion?" laughed the nun, "don't you see these garbs of a servant of the Lord?"

"A nun! And yet you'd like to meet that awful man?"

"My dear, religion and virtue should wear a happy face."

"I don't understand at all. You say you serve the Lord, don't you fear His wrath?"

"I have confidence in His love."

"Who are you? Your words and attitude dismay and yet surprise me."

"Who am I? I am Sister Joan of the Cross. I serve the Lord, and I also write when my duties permit me. People call me the Tenth Muse of New Spain."

"They call you that? What a coincidence! I am also called the Tenth Muse, but of New England."

"Then we should be friends, and know more of each other. Where are you from? Where do you live?"

"I live in Massachusetts, the governor of the colony is my husband, but I was born in England, dear England," Anne Bradstreet, for she is no other, replied sighing again, a tear rolling down her cheeks.

"Why do you weep?"

"For England, for my lovely home, for the friends I left there."

"Don't you like this new place where you live?"

"How can I like it? How can I like the savages, the discomforts of a new country? The ways are so strange! But I am convinced now it is the way of God and to it I must submit. Do you like your country?"

"Do I like it?" answered the nun with shining eyes. "You've never seen anything like the greenness of its valleys, and the blueness of the sky. The air is warm and soft, and the first things my eyes see at dawn are two volcanoes in the distance, covered with perpetual snow! I was born there just twelve leagues from the city of palaces, that's what we call Mexico, and there I would be now had it not been that my thirst for knowledge brought me to the city."

"Oh you like learning too?"

"Yes, I was but three when I learned to read and write, and when I was thirteen my parents presented me to the viceroy who had heard of my learning."

"And when I was seven," answered Anne, "I had as many as eight tutors in languages, dancing and music."

"Strange isn't it that we should like the same things! I love music too; often have I composed selections for the viceroy and his wife, and the Mother Superior."

"Somehow, I can not see you as a nun. You are so gay, so happy, so care free. Why did you enter the convent?"

"In the first place to serve God, and then too I needed a retreat, a quiet place to study, where I might work without interruption, and in the convent I found the things I longed for."

"Aren't you ever lonesome? Don't you crave for the companionship of others?"

"My dear Anne, you don't know much about us, do you?"

"No, I must admit I don't. I have always looked upon nuns and Popish things with distrust, even with fear. Won't you tell me about your life?"

"Delighted. We live in a big, beautiful convent surrounded by luxurious gardens. We never leave it, but we have a life of contentment and leisure. You see all of us there belong to the nobility. We have over two hundred servants who do the work and we lead a life of prayer and innocent pleasures. We are quite experts at making pastries, cakes and sweets, which we send to our friends, in particular to my friend the viceroy. During our leisure hours we embroider altar clothes, converse or play the harp. In the afternoon after vespers we hold open house. The viceroy, the notables and their ladies come. We discuss the events of the day, the gossip of the town, comment on the sermons preached, the last religious festival. There are times though, when the conversation is not so pleasant, and that is when we hear that an English pirate ship has captured a Spanish galleon loaded with gold and silver bars."

"English pirates! We never have been that! Our seamen might capture a Spanish treasure ship but always in a good fight!"

"I do not like to contradict. Pirate or patriot, it is the same. It merely is a matter of point of view. What was I saying? I've lost the trend."

"You discussed the events of the day."

"Oh yes. Our guests sing to us the latest songs, ballads, romances, provincial tunes and they also delight us with the latest dances."

"Dances? Dances? Dear me, dear me, and you a nun! Dancing is an instrument of Satan himself. And I always thought living in the convent was dull."

"Not when you realize our Spanish convents have not been invaded yet by northern prudery and Puritanism. But tell me, how do you employ your time?"

"I am the mother of eight children. I had eight birds hatch in one nest. Four bucks there were, and hens the rest. I nursed them up with pain and care, nor cost, nor labour did I spare. Till at the last they all had wing. And then I have my husband, if ever two were one, then surely we. If ever man were loved by wife then he; if ever wife was happy in a man, compare with me ye women if you can.

"Did you ever want to get married?"

"No I can not say I ever did. Many suitors wooed and made love to me, but no one would I have. I always thought myself superior to any man."

"You astound me, Juana."

"Why should they be our superiors? Have we not a mind like they? Do we not have a soul? Can we not think? Can we not love the same as they? Are they made of finer clay?"

"Let Greeks be Greeks, and women what they are. Men have precedence and still excel. It is but vain unjustly to wage war: Men can do best, and women know it well."

"I don't know such things! They are weak, silly creatures who can not take the blame for the sins they commit. Foolish, foolish men who blame women for the evil things they do, when they themselves are to blame for the sin women commit! Tell me who is more to blame, although both I think are sinners, the one who hungry sins for pay, or the one who pays to sin?"

Stop stop!" Anne called out covering her ears with both hands. "Your evil words pollute me, contaminate me! Have you no decency? No shame?"

"My dear Anne, there is nothing more decent than truth, and there is nothing shameful in seeing life as it is! However, if such things hurt your tender, sensible heart, we shall no more discuss them.

When you came in you told me you were the Tenth Muse; I am curious to know what you've done to merit such title. Have you published any of your poems?"

"I don't like to talk about it. It's too much like vanity, and vanity, as you no doubt know, is a thing of Satan. But if you'll tell me what you've written, perhaps I shall consider . . ."

"I don't mind telling you, I have written three plays and my poems have been published under the title of '*Works of the Only Poetess, Tenth Muse, Sister Juana Inés de la Cruz, Professed Religious in the Monastery of San Gerónimo of the Imperial City of Mexico, which in Various Metres, Languages and Styles, Discusses Many Matters with Elegant, Subtle, Clear, Ingenious, and Useful Verses; for Teaching, Recreation, and Admiration.*' It was published in 1689."

"Your title is as verbose as mine, '*The Tenth Muse Lately Sprung in America. Several Poems, Compiled with Great Variety of Wit and Learning, Full of Delight, Wherein Specially is Contained a Complete Discourse and Description of the Four Elements, Constitutions, Ages of Man, Lessons of the Year. Together with an Exact Epitome of the Four Monarchies, Viz. the Assyrian, Persian, Grecian, Roman, Also a Dialogue Between Old England and New, Concerning the Late Troubles. With Diverse Other Pleasant and Serious Poems.*'"

"As high sounding as mine. What style do you follow?"

"At first I imitated the 'fantastic school' of England, but in spite of that I am told that I made use of ingenious arguments. I would have liked to express my poetic nature, to set forth all that my heart felt, to express my loneliness for England, but I dared not."

"But why, why? Don't you know poets should express their feelings?"

"I dared not, I was touched with maladies of conscience. My Puritan instinct repressed me."

"Pooh, pooh! My dear Anne, you talk like an old woman! I've never been ashamed or afraid to express anything I wish. I discuss earthly love with the same freedom as I do love divine. Love is the spark that keeps us happy."

"Please, Juana, if you talk that way, I shall be forced to leave you. What time is it now?"

The nun looked out the window and without hesitation answered,

"It's eight o'clock by the evening star."

"Dear me, dear me, Simon must be wondering what has become of me. He loves his pipe early, and I must tuck him in bed by mine."

"Simon must be tucked in," giggled the nun to herself, and aloud to Anne she said,

"It has been a great honor and a pleasure to know another Tenth Muse. I thought I had the monopoly to the title. Come up and see me again."

"'Come up and see me.' Where have I heard that before?"

"Never mind, you wouldn't even recognize her name if I told it to you; but do come again."

"That I will my dear Juana," answered the New England Tenth Muse, kissing the nun on the forehead, "but please put that sinful prayer away, I shudder at the levity of it!"

"The one written by your countryman? I really must meet that man; he may not be a poet, but I bet he has a sense of humor and is clever."

Anne faded away. So Juana stood up, yawned, looked at me with what I thought was a wink, and following her companion she also disappeared in the dimness of space.

■ AMÉRICO PAREDES ■
1915–1999

Renowned as an ethnographer, literary critic, and social historian for nearly fifty years, Américo Paredes was one of the most respected of Mexican American intellectuals of the twentieth century and one of the founders of American ethnic studies. Paredes's historical importance rests on his foundational work in the 1950s and 1960s on the ballads, legends, and everyday folklife of Mexican Americans residing in the southwestern borderlands and on his later elaboration of that work during the 1970s and 1980s.

His initial scholarly contribution, *"With His Pistol in His Hand": A Border Ballad and Its Hero* (1958), is a masterful study of the ballads and social patterns of life along the Texas-Mexican border during the late nineteenth and early twentieth centuries. *"With His Pistol in His Hand"* rewrote the history of the U.S.-Mexican border region by going against the grain of the accepted analytical methods, disciplinary conventions, and historical thinking of the day. It combined literary, sociological, ethnographic, and historical analysis of traditional border ballads (*corridos*) to offer a different way of conceiving the history of the region by overturning the common wisdom and official histories of the relations between Anglos and Mexicans.

Before Paredes, the cultural politics of the borderlands was virtually the singular product of a white Euro-American imagination that responded exclusively to the hegemony of Euro-American material interests. After Paredes's work in the early 1950s and 1960s, the cultural politics of the region began to be recast in the mold of transculturalism, reflecting the multicultural and multiethnic histories of the American social world.

In the years immediately before his death, Paredes returned to another aspect of his life as a chronicler and critic of the southwestern borderlands. A novel, *George Washington Gómez* (1990); a collection of his poetry, *Between Two Worlds* (1991); and a collection of short stories, *The Hammon and the Beans and Other Stories* (1994), added an imaginative dimension to his work in the historical, ethnographic, and theoretical realms. Composed for the most part during the depression and World War II years in the U.S.-Mexican borderlands and also later in Japan, China, and Korea, the selections from his poetry and short fiction included here anticipate the insights of his later transdisciplinary work of social criticism and cultural intervention.

The literary works from this period can now be seen as part of a larger imaginative project to invent a figural discourse of transnational epic proportions that is appropriate to the construction of a new narrative of a modern American social and cultural history. For Paredes, this new pan-American history is not defined by geopolitical borderlines or by customs and immigration offices or Homeland Security checkpoints. Rather, it extends beyond these borders to include cultures and peoples that traverse national boundaries and inhabit the transnational borderlands of culture. Its geopolitical site is the region that Paredes would later come to call "Greater Mexico."

Here, Paredes is examining the emergence of a new transnational American consciousness that resides in the cognitive, social, and political-economic space "between two worlds" and that speaks a bicultural and bilingual tongue. The lyrical and narrative voices of *Between Two Worlds* and *The Hammon and the Beans* contest official discourses for the authority to assign different meanings and different directions to everyday borderland reality.

And yet not all the poems in *Between Two Worlds* or stories in *The Hammon and the Beans* are set in the borderlands. Some take us from the familiar space of the American southwest into the Asia Pacific theater of World War II, the postwar occupation of Japan, and the opening days of the Korean War, reflecting Paredes's experiences as a member of the U.S. Army and later as a humanitarian aid worker for the International Red Cross. In these works, the issues remain focused on the intersections of race, power, and conquest.

Now, however, having witnessed firsthand Japanese, Chinese, Korean, British, French, and American nationalisms at their worst in Asia as a member of the U.S. Army of Occupation of Japan, Paredes was shaken from the comfortable sense that being rooted in a homogeneous racial or ethnic community was a wholly positive thing. Because of his experiences in Asia, Paredes came to realize that ideas based on separatism, race hatred, racial supremacy, nationalisms, and prejudice of all kinds, in both their more and less virulent forms, sprouted from the same kinds of roots that had nourished his own sense of ethnic identity and racial pride.

To experience ethnic or racial identity under these conditions was thus in part to understand the contradictions of ethnic and racial identity. How might one conceive of national identity under these highly charged and difficult conditions? How might one do so in a world of evolving traditional ethnicities and emerging new ones? Within the limits of reason, what might serve as the desirable path to an acceptable future with a sense of accomplished community? How might changing ethnicities add to or detract from the sense of a larger national unity and national coherence? Such questions are the substance of the racial and nationalist matters that Paredes was observing in Japan and in his travels in Asia during the immediate postwar years. With minor variations, they remain the vital questions of our times.

In the struggles that he encountered both in the U.S.-Mexican borderlands and in postwar Asia, the defining line between justice and evil became as blurred and ambiguous as the line between luck and fate, between national and cultural commitment. At the same time, Paredes expresses something else in his writings from the pre- and postwar period—the nature of the aesthetics and politics of bilingualism, multiculturalism, and the transnational reality of life in the borderlands. Throughout the 1930s and 1940s, Paredes gained insights into the nature of American cultural diversity and its role in the achievement of social justice and the creation of a truly democratic society.

In the selections from this period of his life, we see Paredes's emerging recognition that the U.S.-Mexican borderlands comprised something very much like a multination state of polyethnic makeup, creating dynamic and perplexing pluralities of cultural and political identity rather than two independent national identities interacting in strictly binary terms. In this complex state of affairs between two worlds, American justice would rise or fall.

Honored in 1989 by the National Endowment for the Humanities as one of the initial recipients of the Charles Frankel Prize for lifelong contributions to the humanities and in 1990 by the Republic of Mexico as one of the first Mexican American inductees to the Order of the Aztec Eagle, Mexico's highest award to noncitizens for the advancement of Mexican culture, Paredes's historical position is assured.

Ramón Saldívar
Stanford University

PRIMARY WORKS

"With His Pistol in His Hand": A Border Ballad and Its Hero, 1958; *Between Two Worlds*, 1991; *The Hammon and the Beans and Other Stories*, 1994.

The Rio Grande

Muddy river, muddy river,
Moving slowly down your track
With your swirls and counter-currents,
As though wanting to turn back,

As though wanting to turn back   5
Towards the place where you were born,
While your currents swirl and eddy,
While you whisper, whimper, mourn;

So you wander down your channel
Always on, since it must be,   10
Till you die so very gently
By the margin of the sea.

All my pain and all my trouble
In your bosom let me hide,
Drain my soul of all its sorrow   15
As you drain the countryside,

For I was born beside your waters,
And since very young I knew
That my soul had hidden currents,
That my soul resembled you,   20

Troubled, dark, its bottom hidden
While its surface mocks the sun,
With its sighs and its rebellions,
Yet compelled to travel on.

When the soul must leave the body,   25
When the wasted flesh must die,
I shall trickle forth to join you,
In your bosom I shall lie;

We shall wander through the country
Where your banks in green are clad,   30
Past the shanties of rancheros,
By the ruins of old Bagdad,

Till at last your dying waters,
Will release their hold on me,
And my soul will sleep forever   35
By the margin of the sea.

1934

Night on the Flats

Hushed is the owl in the chaparral
As the moon rises from the sea,
Making the dwarfed mesquitès tall ...
        The White Woman walks in the moonlight.

Not a coyotè howls tonight,   5
It is a night of mystery,
Even the wind has died
        Of fright.

Even the stars so far above
Blink their little eyes in terror too,   10
While the lonely sage beneath the moon
Weeps glimmering tears of dew.
        The White Woman walks in the moonlight.

1934

The Four Freedoms

Lengua, Cultura, Sangre:—
es vuestro mi cantar,
sois piedra de los mares
y muro del hogar;
este país de "Cuatro Libertades"   5
nada nos puede dar.
Justicia ... ¿acaso existe?
La fuerza es la justicia,
palabras humorísticas: Justicia y Libertad.
Nos queda sólo la Raza,   10
nos queda sólo la Lengua;
hay que guardarlas siempre
y mantenerlas vivas
por una eternidad.

                                                              1941

Hastío

Nunca temí el dolor, sólo temía
que el corazón, cansado de sufrir,
insensible por fin en algún día
dejara de sentir.

Por eso fui soberbio y fui ladino   5
y débil, pues caí cobardemente
en la zanja a lo largo del camino
y me manché de fango pestilente.

En la negra tormenta que me abruma
soy el ala extraviada, que abatida,   10
no puede mucho más llevar a cuestas
la bajeza y el tedio de la vida.

                                                              1941

Moonlight on the Rio Grande

The moon is so bright it dazzles me
To look her in the eye,
She lies like a round, bright pebble
On the dark-blue velvet sky,
She hangs like a giant pebble   5

In the star-incrusted sky.
The Rio Grande is bent and brown
And slow, like an aged peon,
But silver the lazy wavelets
Which the bright moon shines upon,   10
As bright as the little silver bells
On the round hat of a peon.

1935

Guitarreros

Bajaron el toro prieto,
que nunca lo habían bajado . . .

Black against twisted black
The old mesquite
Rears up against the stars   5
Branch bridle hanging,
While the bull comes down from the mountain
Driven along by your fingers,
Twenty nimble stallions prancing up and down
        the *redil* of the guitars.   10

One leaning on the trunk, one facing—
Now the song:
Not cleanly flanked, not pacing,
But in a stubborn yielding that unshapes
And shapes itself again,   15
Hard-mouthed, zigzagged, thrusting,
Thrown not sung
One to the other.

The old man listens in his cloud
Of white tobacco smoke.   20
"It was so," he says,
"In the old days it was so."

1935

When It Snowed in Kitabamba

Captain Meniscus was a man who dearly loved order. One had to see him at his desk, his neat little profile bent over his tidily stacked papers, his rimless glasses shining in the light that came in through the spotless windows. He kept the town of Kitabamba as neat as a brand-new pin.

The captain loved to issue his little orders. The town, from such and such a street to street such and such, was hereby declared Area Number That. The inhabitants of Area Number That would comport themselves in this and this manner from hours A to B. Occupation personnel would comport themselves in the following manner in relation to indigenous personnel. This man could go so far down this street and no more. This one must not enter this building, but that one might. After a certain hour, certain people might not do certain things.

It would have pleased the captain if he could have believed that the world stopped in its tracks when he was not looking. But he was a practical man; he knew that these creatures he moved hither and yon, put in this square and that, had the annoying habit of creeping and crawling out of place the moment his attention was engaged elsewhere. But he did his best. No one could say that Captain Meniscus did not always do his best. And he worked hard.

Such was the case one cold day shortly before noon, the last day of the year to be exact, of a year that would live in history forever. Much had been accomplished, much had been done toward the making of a better world. Captain Meniscus had begun the year fighting the people he now governed. He was ending it in his office, working hard for them, for their reform. He had decided that he and all his staff would work late that New Year's Eve. It would set a good example, it would show the natives what was being done for them. His light would shine brightly until after midnight, while they played at their New Year's festivities.

And in working late on important days, Captain Meniscus was but following in the footsteps of the Old Man. The Old Man. Reverently he raised his eyes toward him, when Corporal Hogg interrupted by coming in. The captain, who never smoked, was conscious of Corporal Hogg's presence before he saw the man, just by the stale pipe odor.

Corporal Hogg was the company clerk, or sergeant major as the captain preferred to call him. He typed outgoing reports, filed incoming ones, and managed relations with interpreters and the other native help that was necessary for the captain to govern Kitabamba. Hogg spoke with a Texas drawl, a lazy way of speech in the captain's opinion. His uniform was buttoned and clean, yet it was not sharp as a soldier's should be. He was sloppy, Meniscus thought as Hogg's long bony figure approached his desk. But sloppy in a subtle sort of way that Meniscus found hard to reprimand because he could not quite define it.

The corporal came up, drawled a good morning and laid some papers on Meniscus' desk. He stood waiting, not quite lounging and not quite at attention, but somewhere in between. It irritated Meniscus, so that he looked out the window to control himself. He knew that he could easily come to hate Corporal Hogg. But Captain Meniscus had long ago decided he must never allow himself such a disorderly emotion as hate. It was not for an officer. Hate was out of place in an ordered mind which knew where it was going. So he gazed out the window until he was sure he could look at Hogg without a feeling of irritation.

He turned from the window to meet Hogg's lively, jeering eyes. Meniscus looked away again.

"You have the draft of the proclamation," Meniscus said. He preferred to make his questions sound like statements.

"Yes, sir," Hogg answered. He spoke in a very respectful tone, but he pushed the paper rudely at the captain. It was Meniscus' New Year's proclamation to the citizens of Kitabamba, to be published the next day. Tame enough in style, dignified but tame, the captain thought. He would have liked it in a more lofty tone, something on the order of Themistocles to the Athenians, "To you then, o citizens, I wish to advise what is best to do." But the thought that Corporal Hogg must type the draft had stopped him. It would be just like Hogg to remind him, rather innocently, that Themistocles had been a Navy man. So he had begun it in a more routine fashion, "In the name of the Supreme Commander, I wish to extend, to the people of Kitabamba ..." He read the draft carefully, making a few penciled corrections in a neat, almost feminine hand. Then he looked up at Hogg.

"You have the report from the village association."

"No sir," Hogg replied. "It hasn't come in yet."

"It has not come in," the captain said sharply, annoyed now at something with a definite cause. "There is no excuse for that."

"It got held up along the way ... sir. One must realize that it takes time, that it has to go round to many people ... sir."

Meniscus carefully noted Hogg's delayed "sirs," and the part they played in keeping Hogg from definite respect.

"Hogg," he said. "I hate this circumlocution, this circumnavigation of things." He pointed, looking Hogg straight in the face. Hogg turned to the wall with what was almost but not quite a faint smile. Hanging before the captain's desk was a large picture of the Old Man in a massive, hand-carved frame. It was a popular picture of him, one he liked himself, in which he was shown looking far into the distance, his chiseled profile raised as though he were sniffing the wind, a white silk scarf around his throat to hide the wrinkles on his aged neck. No one knew how old the Old Man was, and since it was rumored that he dyed his hair, it was hard to guess. But he looked very impressive, with his handsome, dignified face and his haughty expression, the cluster of stars on his shoulder and the shining, gold-braided cap hanging like an aureole over his high olympian forehead. Or like bay leaves. Captain Meniscus always thought of bay leaves when he looked at the braid on the Old Man's cap.

Under the Old Man's portrait was a long bamboo frame which contained a single sentence in large gothic print. The Old Man had once said those words in Captain Meniscus' presence, not to him but in his presence. Very close to him too.

Corporal Hogg kept his eyes dutifully fixed on the space between portrait and inscription while Meniscus said in his precise tones, "Look at those words, corporal; the words of him we all serve. Look at them, never forget them."

The inscription read, "The shortest distance between two points is a straight line." Hogg stared at the wall with a very sober face.

"Doing things after his manner is not at all impossible, corporal, if we keep those words in mind," Meniscus continued. "The *shortest* distance between *two* points is a *straight* line. Not a curve, corporal, not a series of angles, not one long meander. The straight line! That is the secret!"

"Yes sir," Hogg said. Meniscus was gratified by the meekness in the corporal's voice. Then Hogg turned from the picture and looked at him, the same bright levity in his eyes. Meniscus was annoyed once more. He looked away and said, "That is all you have."

"All the papers, yes sir," Hogg said.

"Nothing else to be noted, nothing circulating (he mouthed the word contemptuously), nothing circulating among the town gossips."

"Nothing, sir, except that it may snow."

The captain shook his head. "Too far south."

"That's what they say," the corporal said.

"There has never been any snow in Kitabamba. The records show that."

"That's not what the people say, sir. They say it has snowed. Twice in the memory of old men."

"Folktales," Meniscus said. "Our intelligence would mention it; there is nothing on record."

"It looks like snow," the corporal said, adding after a short silence, "sir."

The captain looked at him coldly. "Corporal," he said, "don't talk arrant nonsense."

The corporal looked at Meniscus with strangely mirthful eyes, his large, rather loose mouth set in an indefinite expression.

"That is all, corporal," the captain said.

Hogg straightened his shoulders a bit. "I'm going to lunch now," he said and walked out.

The captain waited for the room to lose Corporal Hogg's pipe smell. Probably smoked it to save his cigarettes for other purposes, Meniscus thought. Of course he could not censure the man for smoking a pipe. Especially since the Old Man smoked one too. But he had never noticed that the Old Man's pipe stank that way. He wondered whether Hogg might affect a pipe—he rejected the thought even as it formed in his mind. Not Hogg. He was too crude a man, despite his bookish learning.

If anything, Hogg might be suspected of disrespect. But Meniscus was not sure. It was no small thing to accuse a man of. Meniscus could not imagine a life in which there was not at least some reverence for the Old Man, in whose services he had been since he was young. He had come in as a private and had risen by perseverance, by courage and stick-to-itiveness, by a certain clear conception of his goals and a decisiveness in his movement toward them that he had never, could never have put into words until the Old Man himself (who was as well-known an orator as a strategist) had let fall those precious words which were now framed on the captain's wall.

Men like Hogg were too cynical. The corporal would come to no good end. Yet, he did his work well. Meniscus had no complaint on that score. And yet again, there were a lot of things about Hogg that were difficult to forgive. That song, for one. But how to prove that it was Hogg's? Meniscus knew better than to take a false step; he must be sure. But meanwhile the song was gaining in popularity, and the Army was disgraced each time it was sung. Even the urchins were singing it in the streets.

> Chewing gummo, chocoretto,
> Yamamoto was her name;
> All she had was gonorrhea,
> But I loved her just the same.

Captain Meniscus felt like spitting in disgust. It was not true! They were not lecherous carpetbaggers. They were not blackmarketeers. They were men with a mission to perform! And the natives? He had thought of banning the song, but he knew that would only attract more attention to it. Why didn't Hogg use his talents in a different direction? Why didn't he write a song about their mission instead of back-alley rot?

He knew there was no truth in the song. His men were good, clean American boys. Even Hogg, he thought, was guilty in imagination rather than in practice. Meniscus watched them all too closely; his MPs were too efficient to allow things like that. But the agents of a certain power would be glad to have it thought that his men were degenerates, as the song made them out. "*Arigato, sayonara*, Yankee soldier come again." Anger knotted the captain's throat. If he were only sure!

There was a timid knock at the open door and Amakata crept in. Amakata was a little man with crooked teeth and a mournful, embarrassed air. He wrinkled his brown face when he saw the captain, smiling an expectant smile. In he came, ducking his round, short-cropped head, his face expressionless despite the frozen, formal smile. He was dressed in old cavalry breeches; strips of cloth were wrapped around his legs. His feet, in straw sandals, were blue with cold.

"Well," the captain said, "don't stand there."

Amakata understood a bare dozen words of English. He smiled and bowed and began to dust with a dirty rag. Captain Meniscus watched him with growing impatience. Finally he said, "Amakata!"

At the sound of his name Amakata came and stood before the captain's desk. He bowed deeply, his hands touching his knees, then stood quietly before the captain.

"How old are you?" the captain demanded.

Amakata smiled and shrugged, bowed and smiled and looked repentant, as if to say, "I know I am a very stupid person. Pardon me for being so stupid." He did not have to understand what the captain was saying. To appear stupid and humble was his main job, and he knew it to perfection. He smiled and bowed low again.

Meniscus watched him, a chord of cruelty growing within him. Suddenly he shouted, "Don't loll before me like that, you bastard! Straighten up!"

Amakata stiffened into soldierly attention. He understood only the word bastard, but he recognized the tone of voice. Meniscus watched Amakata's painfully rigid form for a long while. Then he began to talk—coldly, evenly.

"You are a fool," the captain said. "Just look at you. Little better than an animal."

Amakata remained in agonized stiffness.

"You'll never get anywhere in life," Meniscus continued, his tone less cold now. "Do you know that? Why, you're almost middle-aged, man, almost middle-aged. And what have you done? You've wasted your life away."

He leaned back in his chair and put his locked hands over his stomach. "For generations," he went on, "where have you gone? I'll tell you. Nowhere. I've watched you, all of you. You never get to the point. Even when you take a wife, you have to send her a go-between to talk about the weather. You spend all your life, at least ninety-five percent of it, in lost motion."

The captain leaned forward and put an elbow on his desk. "But that is all past," he said softly, almost dreamily. "All that is past. Now you have begun a new life, all of you." Amakata perceived his change in tone, and he relaxed a bit, though he still remained at attention.

Meniscus lowered his voice almost to a whisper. "And then what?" he asked Amakata. "Then what? What when we go away? Won't you go right back to it? To your night soil and your open sewers and your conferences in the right-of-way? You will, won't you? Eh? Won't you?"

Amakata realized that a question was being asked of him and eagerly dipped into his stock of English words. Smiling broadly he nodded and said, "Yes s', yes s'."

"You will, will you!" Meniscus cried. "You will, you dirty bastard!"

Amakata saw that he should have used the other word. He stiffened into exquisite rigidity once more and shook his head. "No s'," he said, "no s'."

Meniscus let him stand in that muscle-straining stiffness for a few moments. Then he tore a sheet of paper from a pad, picked up a pencil and motioned Amakata nearer. The captain always acted on the assumption that the natives understood more English than they would admit. But this was important; it might very well be epoch-making. He pointed at the Old Man's picture.

Amakata was never surer of what was expected of him. He turned full toward the picture and bowed profoundly, much more profoundly than before the captain. Three times he bowed, while Meniscus watched him with a satisfied smile. Then Amakata turned toward the captain, who beckoned to him to lean over the desk.

"See?" the captain said, making a dot on one end of the page. "This is you. Now . . ." he made another dot at the other end of the page, ". . . this is where you are going. See? How do you get there? How is the best way to get there? Do you go to this corner first? To this other corner? Do you go back and forth like this? Do you go around under the paper like this? Of course not." He picked up a ruler and laid it between the two dots. "Like this! This is the way!" He pointed at the inscription on the wall and repeated it, slowly and distinctly.

Amakata was bewildered. There was nothing in his experience to help him guess the captain's meaning. He could not tell how this confusion of curves and angles that the captain had drawn on the paper was related to the portrait of the Supreme Person on the wall. He looked at Meniscus, his mouth open.

"Do you understand?" the captain said. Then, in an unprecedented impulse he repeated the question, brokenly, in Amakata's own tongue.

Amakata pounced greedily on the mispronounced words. "Yes," he said, also in his own tongue. "Yes, yes, yes!"

Captain Meniscus smiled, then scowled. He ordered Amakata back to his work, and for the next fifteen minutes he badgered him with orders which Amakata had to guess by a gesture or an intonation. The captain made him straighten the same thing again and again, made him wipe the dust off places he had wiped three or four times before. Amakata strained at the captain's every gesture, a horribly anxious expression on his face, hanging on every word of the incomprehensible flow that came from the captain's mouth. He began to sweat. Finally, when Captain Meniscus saw that Amakata's hands were beginning to shake, he was satisfied and let him go.

A short while later Amakata came into the office again, wearing a white jacket and with the captain's lunch upon a tray. Amakata put the tray on the captain's desk and left in a flurry of frantic bows, shutting the door behind him. Meniscus selected the least important of the documents in his "In" baskets and put them beside his tray. As he ate he glanced at them and initialed them.

After a while he became aware of a soft, feathery sound outside his window. It had begun to snow. He stopped, his fork halfway to his mouth, at the sight of the fat flakes falling, falling in a thick cottony shower upon the square outside. The captain let the fork clatter down upon his plate. There was no reason, no precedent for this. It seemed that the weather had willfully set out to contradict him. For a moment the captain pursed his little mouth and glared at the falling snow. Then his features assumed their habitual calm, and he turned back to his work and his lunch. But he found it hard to concentrate on either. A vague uneasiness seized him. He sat at his desk staring out the window at the snow. Not until Amakata came in with his tea did he resume his meal.

In the outer office there was a sound of running, then a stamping of feet. Corporal Hogg returning from his lunch. Captain Meniscus stopped work long enough to look at his watch and note that Hogg had taken more than an hour, as usual. Then he continued eating and reading, and thinking about the snow outside.

Other feet stamped in the outer office. Captain Meniscus heard the voice of Master Sergeant Fatt saying, "Hi, Lover Boy." Hogg answered in a lower tone, and he and Sergeant Fatt began a conversation that Meniscus could not hear. Fatt was the head of the MP unit, a man whom Meniscus liked and trusted. The captain had often hoped the sergeant would be a good influence on Hogg.

In the outer office Hogg and Fatt were talking in low tones. Hogg was sitting at his desk, fidding with his typewriter keys, while Fatt, big and beefy, sat sideways on the desk, his large, freckled hand supporting his holster. Fatt thought it his duty to be a friend to Hogg, since both were from Texas. Besides, he felt that he could use the corporal.

"The trouble with you," Fatt was saying, "is that you're interested in nothing but pom-pom."

Hogg looked at him with a playful sort of contempt. "What else is there?" he said.

"For God's sakes, man," Fatt said. "Do you think you'll be here forever?"

"I'll worry about that later. Right now I'll take the girls and the liquor. I get all I want on a carton a week. Why stick my neck out?"

"Some extra yen won't hurt you," Fatt said. "And there's no risk to it at all."

Hogg looked at him narrowly. "I'll think it over," he said.

Cigarettes brought thirty yen a pack. Thirty yen was two dollars in cash and about fifteen dollars in goods and services. Each man was issued a carton a week, enough to live a high life behind the captain's back. But Sergeant Fatt wanted more than fun. He wanted to make a killing in pearls. One carton of cigarettes could bring thousands and thousands of yen if one man kept selling it and his buddy, an MP, kept confiscating it from the buyers.

"I'll think it over," Hogg said, raising his voice as a sign that he wanted to end the conversation.

"Give it some thought," Fatt answered, also in a louder voice. "I'm doing it because I like you."

The captain had finished his meal. He put the papers he had initialed into an "Out" box. Then, with an angry look at the snow outside, he rose and went to the file cabinet by the wall. As he opened it, he heard the voices in the outer office. But he never took advantage of his discovery. His sense of honor, coupled with a serene confidence in himself, kept him from eavesdropping, though occasionally he could not help hearing snatches of conversation going on outside. He heard Hogg say, loudly and distinctly, that he would think it over and heard Fatt's reply.

"He's working on Hogg," Meniscus said to himself. "I hope he does the man some good."

Then Hogg said in lower tones, "By the way, aren't you going in to see old Straighten-Up-And-Fly-Right?"

Meniscus moved back to his desk, quickly and noiselessly. Hogg's last words did not anger him. He had known for a long time that Hogg had given him that nickname and that it had stuck, that even his MPs called him that behind his back. He was not pleased at Hogg's imprudence, but he did like the name. It had some of the flavor of "Old Rough and Ready." A fit epithet for a leader of men.

There were other names, vague echoes of which had reached his ears, such as "The Anointed" and "God's Little Acher." These Meniscus did not like, and the suspicion that Hogg circulated them behind his back was another cause of his feeling against the corporal. It was through no effort of his, Meniscus thought, that the natives looked upon the Old Man with awe and reverence. And if he, Captain Meniscus, was tinctured in the eyes of the native population by the overflow of this awe, why it made his mission easier.

He called Fatt. Fatt came in as though he were on parade, sharp in his flawless uniform. He marched up to the captain's desk, saluted and came to attention with a click of heels and a light stamp. He gave his name and the reason for his presence. Smiling, Meniscus put him at ease. The sight of Sergeant Fatt, his military bearing, his faultlessness and assurance, made the captain's heart glad. He listened good-humoredly while Fatt reported briefly on the arrests he had made, the patrols he had run in town.

"Very good, sergeant," he said. "Dictate a full report to the corporal."

Fatt saluted and came to attention again, waiting to be dismissed.

Meniscus smiled. "Sergeant," he said, "I've said it before, I will say it again. You will go far in the Army."

"Thank you sir," Fatt said.

"I admire your devotion to the unswerving path of duty," Meniscus said. "Stay on it. Remember, sergeant." Fatt looked up expectantly as Meniscus raised his hand. "Those words, sergeant."

"Yes sir," Fatt said.

Meniscus smiled paternally. "You may go," he said.

Fatt saluted, about-faced and marched out. After he left, the captain sighed. He took off his wristwatch and placed it on the desk, noting the time there was left before 3:19, when the train would arrive. He took out papers from an "In" box, put them neatly in order, taking only those which he knew he could finish by 3:19. He quickly divided the number of pages by the number of minutes until train time and began to work on them, checking the time now and then to make sure he was moving at the right speed.

Every day, with the arrival of the train, a little ritual was enacted at Kitabamba in which Meniscus was the chief actor and the crowd of townspeople both audience and supporting cast. Across the square was the railroad station, and from the doorstep of Meniscus' headquarters (straight as a piece of string stretched between the two points had been able to make it) a low narrow boardwalk ran unerringly to a post on the station platform. The post was marked with a sign which said, "Kitabamba, 27th Military Government Headquarters, Captain Meniscus commanding."

Here, day after day without fail, stopped the coach bearing the courier with the mail from General Headquarters. And at precisely the right moment, Captain Meniscus would start from the door of his own headquarters, just as the train—an express—drew into the station. As he stepped out, the local police force, drawn up for the occasion, saluted and presented their truncheons. The MPs guarding his route at scattered points parallel to the boardwalk stiffened into attention as he passed. Under the station portico, the local band was arrayed, and beyond the police and MP cordon every soul in town stood watching.

With perfect timing, Meniscus would march down the boardwalk, reaching the signpost just as the courier, a white-helmeted lieutenant, sprang from the coach. Like actors in a play, they would meet, precisely at the right moment, meet and salute each other smartly. Two soldiers of Meniscus' command, standing on either side, presented arms. Captain Meniscus and the courier exchanged pouches and saluted again, more smartly if possible. Then the captain about-faced and marched back along the boardwalk, his eyes on the door out of which he had come.

As Meniscus about-faced, the courier would jump back into the train, which pulled out immediately, signaling its departure with one shrill whistle. The whistle was the signal for the band under the station portico to strike up a shaky version of "America" or "Anchors Aweigh" or some other American piece in their repertoire. The military guard stationed around the square presented arms. The uniformed station personnel, native, saluted. To all this, Captain Meniscus seemed oblivious. He looked at none of it, nor at the crowd of gaping natives, sprinkled with a few soldiers off duty. Eyes straight on the door of his own headquarters, he returned on the same straight line, holding in the crook of his arm close to his heart the communications from the Old Man to him and the town of Kitabamba.

Of course, none of those communications ever were from the Old Man himself. But they were in his name, and the natives were convinced that every day at this hour the captain received a personal letter, in which each day his right and authority to rule, regulate and improve the town of Kitabamba were reaffirmed. This alone made the daily ceremony worth the effort. Every day the natives would gather in a great crowd around the edges of the square and in the station to see the captain parade from his office to the station and back again. The village stopped its activities at this hour. Those who had cameras and were bold enough to use them took pictures for their children and their children's children. Farmers from the surrounding countryside, who had come to the village to bring their produce or to buy salt, fish or seaweed paste, stayed beyond their expected visit to see the edifying sight. And Meniscus acted as if the crowd did not exist, even though it was for them that the whole thing was staged. While they watched, he came and went as though he and the courier were the only two persons in the world.

Captain Meniscus finished his allotted work at 3:18, one minute before the deadline he had set for himself. The minute passed but there was no sign of the train. The captain leaned back in his chair and looked out at the station directly across the square. It had stopped snowing. On this last day of such an important year, the crowd was larger than usual in spite of the snow. It was already gathered around the edges of the square, waiting for the train. The band was forming at the station. The captain looked at his watch—3:20. He wondered if his watch could be fast, but he immediately dismissed the thought. Rising, he went toward the window, going near the file cabinet in the corner to look beyond the station for a glimpse of smoke. As he did so, he caught a sound of humming in the outer room. It was Hogg's voice.

He's not singing that thing again! thought Meniscus. He went closer to the wall and made out the tune that Hogg was humming. His face softened. No, it was not the chewing gummo song; it was a march. "Ta-da-Da, ta-DA, ta-DA, DA. Tee-DUM, tee-DUM, tee-DUM, tee-DUMitty, DUM," Hogg sang. It was "The Captain's March." Meniscus smiled.

"The Captain's March." It was going to be the high point of the day's ceremony. For almost a month the band had been practicing the piece, which the rat-faced little bandmaster had composed in Meniscus' honor. Today it would be played in public for the first time as Meniscus marched back to his office with the message from the Old Man. To have a march composed in one's honor was no mean achievement, though he had successfully concealed his pride behind the detached, almost cold attitude with which he had treated the bandmaster. Then there was also Hogg. In spite of himself, the captain felt self-conscious when the natives paid him homage in front of Hogg. Hogg had agreed with the captain that it was quite an honor to have a march named after one. But his eyes seemed to be laughing when he said it. And not long afterwards he managed to let fall a remark about the way native musicians murdered Western music. On another occasion Meniscus had overheard Hogg telling Fatt, "It sounds just like an old radio commercial I once heard in West Texas. Advertising a cough medicine. Just exactly like it!" But Meniscus was not sure what Hogg had been referring to. In any case, it was heartening to hear Hogg now, humming "The Captain's March" to himself with such obvious enjoyment.

Then the captain heard Fatt's voice. "Come on. Sing it, man; sing it."

Hogg snickered. Then he sang, "When it snoooowed in Kitabamba, the MONkeys wrapped their TAILS around the TREES." He stopped. "Let's see. What rhymes with trees? Freeze?"

Fatt said, "How about 'The monkey's tails did freeze?'"

"Good, very good," Hogg answered with quiet mockery. "But we already have monkeys in the other line."

"Put Meniscus up there."

"Meniscus wrapped his tail around the trees?"

The captain waited to hear no more. He walked quickly to the door and threw it open. Fatt leaped to his feet, his red face turning sickly pale; Hogg looked down at his typewriter. Meniscus stood in the doorway, looking about the room furiously as though he expected to see iniquity in every corner of it. He opened his mouth to speak.

In the distance the train hooted its approach into the cold, snow-washed air. Meniscus snapped his mouth shut with an audible click. Fatt sprang out of attention and rushed outside, blowing his whistle and shouting orders to the guard. The captain followed him to the main door, but not before shooting one last vindictive glance at Hogg.

Outside the square looked unfamiliar in the snow. The boardwalk was half-hidden, a long white lump in the blankness of the square. The smoke of the engine now appeared at a curve on the far end of the yards. Meniscus waited one full minute. Then he straightened his uniform, put his cap at the right angle and walked out. He stopped outside the door, measuring the distance, casting his eye along the boardwalk faintly marked by ridges in the snow. Then, at precisely the right moment, he started walking across the square, directly toward the spot where he would meet the courier, straight as a bullet flying, walking as he had walked this route, this pilgrimage, so many times since he had been made military governor of Kitabamba.

As the captain stepped off, the band at the station gave a preliminary wheeze and then struck up "The Captain's March." Meniscus faltered at this unexpected change in the order of today's events. Then he caught the swing of the march and strode toward the station, his carriage stiff and military, his eyes forward. It was a good march, he thought proudly as he strode along. When it snoooowed—Damn that Hogg! Had him singing it too. This was the end! He must do something about that man. He shook his head to dispel Hogg from his thoughts, and it was at that moment that he slipped.

He had walked straight enough. Perhaps he had merely started too close to one edge of the boardwalk. As he took a longer step than usual in response to the rhythm of the band, his foot came down on the very edge of the walk. On dry boards it would not have mattered, but the wet snow beneath him gave way, and he slipped.

He slipped and went off the edge while the band played, and he fell face down in the snow.

He was up in an instant, disdaining to brush the snow from his face and his clothes, still erect and military, as if nothing had happened, as if this was part of the normal course of things. So he rose to his feet and stepped off again and again he fell. Again he rose and again he slipped and he fell again, again, and again and still again, to the rhythm of the lively march which rang crazily in his ears, "When it snoooowed in Kitabamba, the MONkeys wrapped their TAILS . . ."

The sharp, piercing shriek of Sergeant Fatt's whistle cut through the insane braying of the band. Fatt bounded across the snow, one hand on his whistle chain, the other cradling his flapping holster. He leaped on the station platform and gave the bandmaster a loud slap on the ear with his whistle hand. The music stopped abruptly and with it also ended Meniscus' efforts to get up and march. He lay across the boardwalk in the middle of the square, his face in the snow, his feet upraised behind him.

So he remained, immersed in a white silence, until he heard the squish of feet as Sergeant Fatt came cutting heavy-treaded through the blankness of the snow. Then Meniscus rose to his hands and knees, shaking the snow off his face, and slowly got to his feet. In the station the train left, with its customary whistle. At this familiar signal the band gave one convulsive wheeze and then squashed itself into silence again. Meniscus shook off Fatt's hand fumbling at his arm and turned to face the crowd, his eyes cold and commanding. He would stare them down. He would dare anyone to laugh.

The crowd was one huge, faceless blur. Captain Meniscus put his hand up to his bruised, near-sighted eyes and allowed Sergeant Fatt to lead him away.

Once in his office and wearing another pair of glasses, the captain felt more like himself. Like a part of himself, rather, because he felt as if a great segment of him had been torn out and that he was now but a portion of a man. Not daring to raise his eyes to the wall in front of his desk, he turned to look out the window instead. The crowd was still there, staring at him as he stood at the window looking out at them. It was the same crowd that had watched him every day. He looked out at them angrily, in the way he had wanted to look at them in the square minutes before, staring them down, daring anyone to laugh. But they did not laugh, they did not smile. They just looked at him with sadness in their eyes.

At first, when Meniscus had risen and fallen to the rhythm of the band, the crowd had been amused. They had watched delightedly, with open curious faces, this strange New Year's ceremony of the conqueror. Then they were puzzled, and when Fatt came running to stop the whole thing they understood. They understood and their faces were clouded over with an old and patient sadness that went far beyond Meniscus himself. So now, when the captain showed himself at the window, they looked at him with that same ancient sadness in their eyes. And the captain, seeing their faces and the pity and the fellowship in them, became enraged at the sight. He shouted to the guards outside to drive them away, to beat them, to hit them with their rifle butts.

The guards drove them away, but they did not beat them. They pushed at the crowd with rifles and clubs, calling at them in the flat, impersonal tone policemen sometimes use with crowds, "All right, break it up. *Hayaku. Hayaku.*"

The crowd broke up, leaving the square deserted. Master Sergeant Fatt came out and quietly dismissed the guard. In his office Captain Meniscus still stood at the window, looking at the soiled snow of the square. He muttered a curse, a foul unaccustomed oath that failed to drain any of the moil inside him. His eyes blurred. No, he told himself, fighting back his tears. No. And then he thought how much easier it would have been if they had laughed. But they had not laughed. He kept staring out the window at the dirty snow and at the wallow in the middle of the square, where he had danced his strange dance to the tune of the native band.

He turned as the door opened and Amakata came in, the courier's pouch in one hand and the captain's broken, twisted glasses in the other. Amakata ducked his head quickly, almost perfunctorily, in a bow that almost was a nod. Meniscus pointed to the desk and looked away. Amakata put down the pouch and the glasses and went out again.

The captain touched the broken glasses with the tips of his fingers. Then, out of habit, he opened the mail pouch and let its contents fall out on the desk. Something caught his eye—a letter from the chief of staff. His small-featured face lighted up. Quickly he tore open the envelope and read the letter, not once but twice. It was a commendation for his work in Kitabamba. He could have sworn that the Old Man's signature, over that of the chief of staff's, was in ink and not mimeographed. But that could not be. The Old Man never ... He moved toward the windows to see the signature in the light. It was mimeographed. But it didn't matter anyway. Not now.

He heard voices in the outer office and crept to the corner near the file cabinet. Hogg was saying, "Anyway, I think you're a son-of-a-bitch."

Then came Fatt's rumbling chuckle. "What did you want me to do? Hold him up by his little ankles?"

"You could have blown that damned whistle sooner. It's a hell of a deal, I tell you. The poor bastard!"

"But he looked so goddam funny for a minute there ..." Fatt choked back a laugh.

After a pause Hogg said, "Anyway, it serves him right, putting on those silly airs. I guess he doesn't know I'm on to him."

"You sure?"

"Sure I'm sure. He must have changed his name when he left town. I was just a kid, but I remember him. His brothers and sisters too, must have been ten of them. Or fifteen, I never counted them all."

"He'll never make colonel now."

"He'll never make major, for that matter. When this shit hits GHQ he won't be going anywhere. Might be busted, for all we know."

Fatt laughed. "He'd make a good company clerk," he said. Meniscus moved away from the window, trembling.

Hogg and Fatt heard the muffled shot, and when they came into Meniscus' office the little pistol was still in the captain's mouth. His head was among his papers. Hogg grew pale. "Jesus!" said Fatt. "Just look at that!"

They sent Amakata to get more witnesses before they moved the body, and as soon as Amakata was out of the door Fatt opened the desk drawers and began rummaging around.

"Hey!" said Hogg. "What are you doing there?"

"The stores key," Fatt replied. "Ah, here it is!" He displayed it triumphantly. "You can forget about that deal we talked about."

"What am I getting out of this?" Hogg demanded.

"Don't worry," Fatt said. "I'll fix you up."

Captain Meniscus had been the only commissioned officer in Kitabamba, so the detachment remained temporarily in charge of Master Sergeant Fatt until a new commanding officer arrived from headquarters. Meanwhile orders were received by wire to prepare the body for shipment to the Capital on the next day's train. The job fell to Amakata. He had no one to direct him because Sergeant Fatt was busy that night, carrying away several jeeploads of cigarettes, chewing gum, chocolate bars and other supplies from unit stores to the house of a friend. The new officer might arrive the next day, and one of the first things he would do was to carry out an inventory. Corporal Hogg was busy too, celebrating New Year's Eve. From his quarters in the rear of the building came sounds of music, laughter and women's voices.

So Amakata did the job assisted by his wife, a leathery faced old woman in a drab-looking kimono and hair done up in a bun. They laid by a clean uniform, and he undressed and washed the body. Without the uniform and no longer speaking those terrible foreign words, the captain was much the same as other corpses Amakata had seen in the past. As he was about to draw the pink dress trousers over the captain's legs, he stopped and looked toward his wife.

"Come," he said softly. "Look."

She came, holding the shirt she had been unbuttoning, and looked at the captain's hairless shins, barked raw like those of an errant schoolboy. "Poor thing!" she said. "It must have hurt him, with the cold."

Amakata drew the trousers over the captain's legs. "Yes," he said. "Poor thing."

In Corporal Hogg's quarters the geishas were singing "You Are My Sunshine."

1994

Ichiro Kikuchi

My name is Ichiro Kikuchi, and I am alive. Which might not be such a good thing. Being alive, I mean. Being Ichiro Kikuchi is all right. That's my legal name, my Japanese name. The legitimate son of Keigo Kikuchi and María de los Angeles Bermúdez de Kikuchi. My given name means "first born." The funny thing is that I am the only one.

My mother calls me Lupe because she had me baptized with a Mexican name soon after I was born. Juan Guadalupe. Juan for San Juan, the town where she was born, and Guadalupe for Our Lady, the Mother of all Mexicans. My mother had me baptized without letting my father know and my father was angry when he found out. But his anger did not last long, my mother says. He was never angry about anything for very long.

But I am glad my mother named me Guadalupe. It is because of her, the dark Virgin, that I am alive today. You smile, though you yourself are a Mexican, even if you are an American soldier. But it is true. Whether you see it as a miracle of the Virgin's, or whether you think it was just an accident. A lucky break, as you would say. My mother is convinced it was a miracle. My father says nothing because he does not know. And he says very little about anything these days, coughing his lungs out as he is. And it is best that he should die without knowing. Only I, my mother, and now you, know. And one other person, a sergeant in the American Army like you, a sergeant named Melguizo. But he does not want to know.

I'm telling you this because you are my friend. And because I trust you. Because you are a Mexican too, even though you are not a believer. And because you do not know much Japanese. I am sure that even if you would want to, you could not tell others here what I have told you. No, I do not mean to offend you. I know you will keep this to yourself at least until my mother and I can leave this country. When, I do not know.

Then we will be able to go back to our place outside of Cuernavaca, on the road to Acapulco. I often think of it. It is very beautiful, with acres of flowers and fruit trees. It is the way my father used to tell me Japan was, a beautiful country. But that was not the way Japan was when we got here five years ago. And it got much worse soon afterward, as you well know.

Outside Cuernavaca we had a large farm. We still have it. My uncle, my mother's brother, owns a half-interest in it, and he is keeping our interest for us. He has written my mother that we are welcome whenever we choose to go back. But we cannot go just yet.

My uncle and my father owned the farm. My uncle, being native-born, was legal owner of the land. My father put up half the money to buy the land, and he also contributed his knowledge of Japanese farming methods. We raised some fruit, but the richest and most beautiful harvest was the flowers. I thought there was nothing so beautiful as our farm.

But my father would tell me, "Wait till you go to Japan. It is so beautiful that you'll think this farm is a poor place compared to the country of your fathers." After I finished the primary grades, my father got a Japanese lady to teach me the Japanese language, but I learned to say only simple things in it. It was easy to speak, but I just could not learn how to read it. When I entered preparatory school, I studied English instead. My father was disappointed. He said, "Wait till you go to Japan. Then you will find it easy to learn Japanese. But I don't think you will ever know enough *kanji* to read a newspaper even." Those are the Chinese signs, you know. When my father talked like that my mother was very quiet.

A lot of things happened when I reached the age of eighteen. My birthday was celebrated with a big fiesta. Japanese friends and Mexican relatives came all the way from Fuanajuato and Jalisco. I had finished public school, and my mother wanted me to become a *licenciado* in something, she did not care in what. So I was thinking about what I would study at the university. And then one day my father comes home from Acapulco with his big surprise. He just came in and told us, "Get ready. We'll be leaving for Japan in three weeks." He had already booked passage for the three of us on a steamer coming from Chile on its way to Yokohama.

"But Kei!" my mother said. "People are fighting over there!"

"The war is far to the south," my father said. "We won't be in any danger."

What if the Americans attacked Japan, my mother wanted to know. We all knew how angry the Americans were because of all the Japanese victories. But my father was sure that Japan and the United States would never fight each other. It was all propaganda. But what about the university, my mother insisted. We would be gone only for a few months, and when we came back I could go to the university. Unless I fell in love with Japan, as my father hoped I would, and then I would want to stay. My mother looked gloomy.

I didn't fall in love with Japan, but I did stay here as you can see. Japan was a flower garden, my father had told me. When we landed in Yokohama what I saw was an armed camp. From Yokohama we came here to Tokyo, where my father's family is. Barely had we got here when war began with the United States. The neighbors did not like my mother and me very much, and it was even worse when Mexico declared war against Japan a few months later.

I had a difficult time, being only half Japanese and not knowing the language very well. They put me to work on the government radio broadcasting to Spanish America. I was not very good at it; still, it gave me a job to do. Everybody had to have a job. Three years later I was drafted. We had been hearing about the great battles our army and navy were winning, but everybody suspected we were losing. Now they were taking everybody in trousers—old men, schoolboys and people like me. My mother took it very hard, and I was sorry for her. But I felt worse about my father. He said he was very proud of me. He was supposed to feel that way, and I'm sure he was. But he was very sad, and a bit angry. Not at anybody but himself, I think.

Not long after, I was landing in the Philippines, exactly where I never knew. Our ship was one of the lucky ones; many others were sunk by your airplanes and submarines. My memories about combat, you say? Terror, bombs and artillery shells. Terror, smoke, confusion and retreat. We were not trained. We were given rifles, put on a ship and sent over. Perhaps I am trying to excuse the fact that we surrendered. We had been ordered to fight to the death, but a lot of others were surrendering too.

There were about fifteen of us. Among us was a boy named Yokoyama, Nobuo Yokoyama. He was small and near-sighted and was afraid all the time. We had known each other in Tokyo, and during the fighting he had stayed very close to me. I did my best to take care of him. He called me Elder Brother. And now I tried to set his mind at ease. "You don't have to be afraid anymore, Younger Brother," I told him. "The war is over for us."

We were taken as prisoners of a unit that had seen much fighting, from the looks of them. The man who was in command was talking to another, a sergeant. The sergeant was arguing, it appeared, but finally he saluted and came to where we were. He looked familiar somehow. He picked out a dozen of his own men, and they took us back some fifty meters toward their rear. All the others went ahead. When we stopped, the Americans guarding us took their spades from their packs and dropped them on the ground in front of us. Then they moved back and made signs to us that we should pick them up.

"They are going to put us to work," one of us said. But we soon understood what they wanted. We were ordered to dig a long, narrow trench. There was nothing we could do but obey, but we dug very slowly. Then Nobou began to cry. He was digging right next to me, and I could see the tears running down his face. A great rage seized me. "Hurry up!" I shouted. "If we must die, let it be over quickly! And let us die with dignity!" I began to dig as fast as I could, without looking at Nobuo, for if I looked at him I was sure I would start crying too.

The two top buttons of my shirt had been torn off, and as I dug the chain I wear around my neck spilled out, with the pendant at the end. The sergeant came up to me and shouted, "Hey, you! What is that you're wearing?"

I looked up at him, and now that he was close to me I saw why he had looked familiar. He was Mexican. Like you. An American Mexican. So I answered in Spanish, "A medallion. La Virgen de Guadalupe."

"Put down that spade," he said, also in Spanish. "Get out of that hole and come with me."

I was trembling as I climbed out of the hole, trembling and praying, giving thanks to La Guadalupana and to my mother, who had put the medallion around my neck when I was home for the last time. I did not look at Nobou. All I saw, all I knew was myself. I was alive, and that was all that mattered. The sergeant led me away, to the rear where I was put in a pen with some other prisoners. Not many of them. We were halfway there when I heard the volleys. I did not look back. I shuddered but I felt happy I was not there, back at the hole. I am a coward, I know. But it was not until later that I felt any regret, any shame.

I heard somebody call the sergeant Melguizo, that's how I know his name. I didn't see him again in the Philippines. It was only recenly that I met him at a street corner here in Tokyo.

"¡Melguizo!" I said. "¡Qué gusto de verte!"

He stared at me. "I don't know who you are," he said in English and walked away.

It was the same man, I am not mistaken. I wonder why he pretended not to know me. Why he wouldn't let me thank him. Is he ashamed of what he did for me?

My father does not know. He is the one who should never know about this at all. It was my mother who decided we should not tell him, because he would not understand. "Let him die happy," she said, "happy that he saw you come home. There are so many others who will not be so fortunate." She made me go see Nobuo Yokoyama's parents. "It is painful for parents to know that their son is dead," my mother told me. "But it is worse not to know at all."

So I went to see them and told them Nobou had died in combat, and that he had been buried in a grave dug by his comrades. And then I broke down and wept. They were moved. They thought I was weeping for Nobuo.

In a way it is easier to deceive my father, and again it is not. He can barely talk, so he does not ask many questions. But I wish he would not look so proud and happy every time he sees me. He still is walking around, though he gets weaker every day. But there still is a lot of life in him, I am sure. He was an air-raid warden during the fire-bombings. The section of town just downhill from where we live was set afire before dawn one day. There was a woman with three children, whose husband was in the army. When her house started burning, she shouted to the eldest to follow her, and she took the two younger ones out of the house. But the eldest girl did not come out, and she tried to go after her, but the neighbors held her back. Then my father went into the burning house and took the girl out. She was dead. The first bomb to land on the house did not explode. It went through the roof and hit the girl while she was in bed. They found that out later. My father got the girl's body out, but he damaged his lungs. Some people say he breathed fire and that his lungs were cooked. Perhaps it was the heat, perhaps the smoke. We don't know. Whatever it was, he's dying. Very slowly, but he's dying.

Just a few months ago, a consul from Mexico came to look after Mexican citizens caught here by the war. He has been very helpful. My mother and I have passports of our own now. Not my father, since he never was a Mexican citizen and is too sick to travel anyway. My uncle in Mexico, my mother's brother, has been very good to us too. As the consul told us, he could have kept all of our farm for himself, and it would have been legal. But he has written us, and the consul too, that he is waiting to welcome us home, and that half of the property still is my mother's and mine.

I suppose I will give up the idea of going to the university. I'll become a farmer just as my father was. But my mother says that she will see to it that I become a *licenciado*. Only God knows what will happen. And the Virgin. I have promised my mother I will go with her to the Virgin's shrine in Tepeyac and give thanks for the miracle that saved my life. But I don't think we should crawl on our knees there. Anyway, we are not there yet. We have not left Japan.

The consul has arranged everything for us, and my uncle has sent us money. But we will not leave until after my father dies. The consul is getting impatient. He would like to get our business out of the way, he says, before he returns to Mexico.

It is a terrible thing for us to be here, waiting for my father to die. Sometimes I wake up in the morning, and the first thing that comes to my mind is, "Perhaps he died during the night."

I get up and go look at him, and I am glad he's still with us. I really am. He was very brave, going into that burning house. My mother says the neighbors called him a hero. But that was before the war ended. There are no heroes now.

1994

Carved on the Walls—Poetry by Early Chinese Immigrants

ANGEL ISLAND IN SAN FRANCISCO BAY, NOW AN IDYLLIC STATE PARK, WAS THE point of entry for the majority of the approximately 175,000 Chinese immigrants who came to America between 1910 and 1940. Modeled after New York's Ellis Island, the site was the immigration detention headquarters for Chinese awaiting the outcomes of medical examinations and immigration papers. It was also the holding ground for deportees awaiting transportation back to the motherland.

The ordeal of immigration and detention left an indelible mark in the minds of many Chinese, a number of whom wrote poetry on the barrack walls, recording impressions of their voyage to America, their longing for families back home, and their outrage and humiliation at the treatment America accorded them. When the center's doors shut in 1940, one of the bitterest chapters in the history of Chinese immigration to America came to a close. The poems expressing the thoughts of the Chinese immigrants were locked behind those doors and forgotten until 1970, when they were discovered by park ranger Alexander Weiss and preserved in *Island: Poetry and History of Chinese Immigrants on Angel Island, 1910–1940* (1980).

The Chinese began emigrating to America in large numbers during the California Gold Rush. Political chaos and economic hardships at home forced them to venture overseas to seek a better livelihood. Despite their contributions to America—building the transcontinental railroad, developing the shrimp and abalone fisheries, the vineyards, new strains of fruit, reclaiming swamplands, and providing needed labor for California's growing agriculture and light industries—they were viewed as labor competition and undesirable aliens and were mistreated and discriminated against.

The Chinese Exclusion Act of 1882 was the inevitable culmination of a series of oppressive anti-Chinese laws and violent physical assaults upon the Chinese. For the first time in American history, members of a specific ethnic group—the Chinese—were refused entry. Only exempt classes, which included merchants, government officials, students, teachers, visitors, as well as those claiming U.S. citizenship, were admitted. The Angel Island Immigration Station was established in 1910 to process Chinese immigrants claiming citizenship and exempt statuses.

According to stories told by Chinese detainees, most immigrants went into debt to pay for passage to America. Upon arrival, they were given medical examinations and then locked up in dormitories segregated by sex to await hearings on their applications. To prevent collusion, no visitors were allowed prior to interrogation except missionaries. Women were sometimes taken outside for walks and men were allowed to exercise in a small, fenced-in yard. Otherwise, confined inside, they spent their waking hours worrying about their future, gambling, reading, sewing, or knitting. Three times a day, they were taken to the dining hall for meals, which, although cooked by Chinese staff, were barely edible.

Because the interrogation involved many detailed questions about one's family and village background, lengthy coaching books were memorized by prospective immigrants before coming to America. Inquiries usually lasted two to three days, during which time one's testimony had to be corroborated by witnesses. For those whose applications for entry were rejected, the wait could stretch to as long as two years while they awaited appeals. Most of the debarred swallowed their disappointment and stolidly awaited their fate. However, some committed suicide in the barracks or aboard returning ships. Still others vented their frustrations and anguish by writing or carving Chinese poems on the barrack walls as they waited for the results of appeals or orders for their deportation.

These poets of the exclusion era were largely Cantonese villagers from the Pearl River Delta region in Guangdong Province in South China. They were immigrants who sought to impart their experiences to men and women following in their footsteps. Their feelings of anger, frustration, uncertainty, hope and despair, self-pity, homesickness, and loneliness filled the walls of the detention barrack. Many of their poems were written in pencil or ink and eventually covered by coats of paint. Some, however, were first written in brush and then carved into the wood. The majority of the poems are undated and unsigned, probably for fear of retribution from the authorities.

All of the poems are written in the classical style, with frequent references or allusions to famous literary or heroic figures in Chinese legend and history, especially those who faced adversity. Because the early twentieth century saw an increasing national consciousness among the Chinese, many of the poems also voice resentment at being confined and bitterness that their weak motherland cannot intervene on their behalf. Most of the poems, however, bemoan the writer's own situation. A few are farewell verses written by deportees or messages of tribulations by transients to or from Mexico and Cuba.

The literary quality of the poems varies greatly. The style and language of some works indicate that the poets were well versed in the linguistic intricacies of poetic expression, while others, at best, can only be characterized as sophomoric attempts. Since most immigrants at that time did not have formal schooling beyond the primary grades and for obvious reasons were usually not equipped with rhyme books and dictionaries, many poems violate rules of rhyme and tone required in Chinese poetry.

The poems occupy a unique place in the literary culture of Asian America. These immigrant poets unconsciously introduced a new sensibility, a Chinese American sensibility using China as the source and America as a bridge to spawn a new cultural perspective. Their poetry is a legacy to Chinese Americans who would not be here today were it not for these predecessors' pioneering spirit. Their poetry is also a testimony to the indignity they suffered coming here.

The irony of exclusion was that it did not improve the white workingman's lot. Unemployment remained high and the wage level did not rise after the "cheap" competition had been virtually eliminated. As for the Chinese, their experiences on Angel Island and under the American exclusion laws, which were not repealed until 1943, laid the groundwork for the behavior and attitudes of an entire generation of Chinese Americans. The psychological scars—fear of officials, suspicion of outsiders, political apathy—still linger as a legacy in the Chinese American community today.

Him Mark Lai
Genny Lim
Judy Yung

PRIMARY WORK

Island: Poetry and History of Chinese Immigrants on Angel Island, 1910–1940, eds. Him Mark Lai, Genny Lim, and Judy Yung, 1991.

from **The Voyage**

5 *[Four days before the Qiqiao Festival]*

Four days before the Qiqiao Festival,[1]
I boarded the steamship for America.
Time flew like a shooting arrow.
Already, a cool autumn has passed.
Counting on my fingers, several months have elapsed.   5
Still I am at the beginning of the road.
I have yet to be interrogated.
My heart is nervous with anticipation.

8 *[Instead of remaining a citizen of China, I willingly became an ox]*

Instead of remaining a citizen of China, I willingly became an ox.
I intended to come to America to earn a living.
The Western styled buildings are lofty; but I have not the luck to
    live in them.
How was anyone to know that my dwelling place would be a
    prison?   5

---

[1]Better known as the "Festival of the Seventh Day of the Seventh Moon," the Qiqiao Festival is widely celebrated among the Cantonese. As the legend of the Cowherd (Niulang) and the Weaver Maiden (Zhinu) is told, the Weaver Maiden in heaven one day fell in love with a mortal Cowherd. After their marriage, her loom, which once wove garments for the gods, fell silent. Angered by her dereliction of duty, the gods ordered her back to work. She was separated from the Cowherd by the Silver Stream or Milky Way, with the Cowherd, in the Constellation Aquila and she, across the Heavenly River in the Constellation Lyra. The couple was allowed to meet only once a year on the seventh day of the seventh moon, when the Silver Stream is spanned by a bridge of magpies. On this day, maidens display toys, figurines, artificial fruits and flowers, embroidery, and other examples of their handiwork, so that men can judge their skills. It is also customary for girls to worship and make offerings of fruits to the gods.

from **The Detainment**

20 [Imprisonment at Youli, when will it end?]

Imprisonment at Youli,[1] when will it end?
Fur and linen garments have been exchanged; it is already another
    autumn.
My belly brims with discontent, too numerous to inscribe on
    bamboo slips.[2]   5
Snow falls, flowers wilt, expressing sorrow through the ages.

30 [After leaping into prison, I cannot come out]

After leaping into prison, I cannot come out.
From endless sorrows, tears and blood streak.
The *jingwei*[1'] bird carries gravel to fill its old grudge.
The migrating wild goose complains to the moon, mourning his
    harried life.   5
When Ziqing[2'] was in distant lands, who pitied and inquired after
    him?
When Ruan Ji[3] reached the end of the road, he shed futile tears.
The scented grass and hidden orchids complain of withering and
    falling.   10
When can I be allowed to rise above as I please?

           By Li Jingbo of Taishan District[4]

31 [There are tens of thousands of poems composed on these walls]

There are tens of thousands of poems composed on these walls.
They are all cries of complaint and sadness.

[1]King Wen (c. 12th century B.C.), founder of the Zhou state, was held captive at Youli because the last Shang king, Zhou (1154–1122 B.C., different Chinese character from the preceding), regarded him as a potential threat to Shang rule. His son King Wu (1134–1115 B.C.) later did defeat the Shang and establish the Zhou dynasty (1122–249 B.C.).

[2]This idea is taken from a proverb that alludes to crimes so numerous they will not even fit on slips made from all the bamboo in the Zhongnan mountains. The ancient Chinese often wrote on bamboo slips.

[1']According to a folk tale, the daughter of the legendary Yandi, while playing in the Eastern Sea, was drowned. Her soul changed to a bird called the "jingwei," who, resenting the fact that the ocean took her life, carried pebbles in her beak from the Western Mountains and dropped them into the ocean, hoping to fill it.

[2']Another name for Su Wu (140–60 B.C.), who during the Western Han dynasty (206 B.C.–24 A.D.) was sent by the Chinese government as envoy to Xiongnu, a nomadic people north of the Chinese empire. Su Wu was detained there for 19 years, but refused to renounce his loyalty to the Han emperor.

[3]Ruan Ji (A.D. 210–263), a scholar during the period of the Three Kingdoms (A.D. 220–280), was a person who enjoyed drinking and visiting mountains and streams. Often when he reached the end of the road, he would cry bitterly before turning back.

[4]A district southwest of the Pearl River Delta. The largest percentage of Chinese in the continental United States and Canada came from this district.

The day I am rid of this prison and attain success,
I must remember that this chapter once existed.
In my daily needs, I must be frugal.   5
Needless extravagance leads youth to ruin.
All my compatriots should be mindful.
Once you have some small gains, return home early.

By One From Xiangshan[1]

from **The Weak Shall Conquer**

35 [Leaving behind my writing brush and removing my sword, I came]

Leaving behind my writing brush and removing my sword, I came
    to America.
Who was to know two streams of tears would flow upon arriving
    here?
If there comes a day when I will have attained my ambition and
    become successful,   5
I will certainly behead the barbarians and spare not a single blade
    of grass.

38 [Being idle in the wooden building, I opened a window]

Being idle in the wooden building, I opened a window.
The morning breeze and bright moon lingered together.
I reminisce the native village far away, cut off by clouds and
    mountains?
On the little island the wailing of cold, wild geese can be faintly
    heard.   5
The hero who has lost his way can talk meaninglessly of the sword.
The poet at the end of the road can only ascend a tower.
One should know that when the country is weak, the people's
    spirit dies.   10
Why else do we come to this place to be imprisoned?

42 [The dragon out of water is humiliated by ants]

The dragon out of water is humiliated by ants;
The fierce tiger who is caged is baited by a child.

---

[1]A district in the Pearl River Delta, Xiangshan is the birth place of Sun Yat-sen (Sun Zhongshan, 1866–1925). After his death in 1925, the district name was changed to Zhongshan in Sun's memory.

As long as I am imprisoned, how can I dare strive for supremacy?
An advantageous position for revenge will surely come one day.

from **About Westerners**

51 [I hastened here for the sake of my stomach and landed promptly]

I hastened here for the sake of my stomach and landed promptly
    in jail.
Imprisoned, I am melancholy; even when I eat, my heart is
    troubled.
They treat us Chinese badly and feed us yellowed greens.[1]   5
My weak physique cannot take it; I am truly miserable.

55 [Shocking news, truly sad, reached my ears]

Shocking news, truly sad, reached my ears.
We mourn you. When will they wrap your corpse for return?
You cannot close your eyes.
Whom are you depending on to voice your complaints?
If you had foresight, you should have regretted coming here.   5
Now you will be forever sad and forever resentful.
Thinking of the village, one can only futilely face the Terrace for
    Gazing Homeward.[1']
Before you could fulfill your ambition, you were buried beneath
    clay and earth.   10
I know that even death could not destroy your ambition.

from **Deportees, Transients**

57 [On a long voyage I travelled across the sea]

On a long voyage I travelled across the sea.
Feeding on wind and sleeping on dew, I tasted hardships.
Even though Su Wu was detained among the barbarians, he would
    one day return home.[1"]

[1] Salted cabbage.

[1'] During the political turmoil in China at the end of the Western Jin dynasty (A.D. 265–316), two princesses fled to a distant region for safety and ended up marrying commoners in a village. They were often unhappy and longed for their old homes. Their fellow villagers then built a terrace that they could ascend to gaze in the direction of their home.

[1"] Another name for Su Wu (140–60 B.C.), who during the Western Han dynasty (206 B.C.–24 A.D.) was sent by the Chinese government as envoy to Xiongnu, a nomadic people north of the Chinese empire. Su Wu was detained there for 19 years, but refused to renounce his loyalty to the Han emperor.

When he encountered a snow storm, Wengong sighed, thinking of
    bygone years[2]   5
In days of old, heroes underwent many ordeals.
I am, in the end, a man whose goal is unfulfilled.
Let this be an expression of the torment which fills my belly.
Leave this as a memento to encourage fellow souls.   10
           13th Day of the 3rd Month in the 6th Year of the Republic[3]

64

Crude Poem Inspired by the Landscape

The ocean encircles a lone peak.
Rough terrain surrounds this prison.
There are few birds flying over the cold hills.
The wild goose messenger[1] cannot find its way.
I have been detained and obstacles have been put my way for half
    a year.   5
Melancholy and hate gather on my face.
Now that I must return to my country,
I have toiled like the *jingwei* bird in vain.[2′]

69 [Detained in this wooden house for several tens of days]

Detained in this wooden house for several tens of days,
It is all because of the Mexican exclusion law[1′] which
    implicates me.
It's a pity heroes have no way of exercising their prowess.
I can only await the word so that I can snap Zu's whip.[2″]   5

[2]The posthumous title of Han Yu (A.D. 768–824) scholar and official during the Tang dynasty (A.D. 618–907). In 819 he came under disfavor when he memorialized the throne against the elaborate ceremonies planned to welcome an alleged bone of Buddha. For this, he was exiled to Chaozhou in Guangdong province, then still an undeveloped region of jungles and swamps. On his way south, he bade farewell to his grandnephew at a snowy mountain pass, Lan Guan, in Shenxi, and composed a poem to express his feeling.

[3]March 13, 1917.

[1]*I.e.*, mail service.

[2′]According to a folk tale, the daughter of the legendary Yandi, while playing in the Eastern Sea, was drowned. Her soul changed to a bird called the "jingwei," who, resenting the fact that the ocean took her life, carried pebbles in her beak from the Western Mountains and dropped them into the ocean, hoping to fill it.

[1′]Angel Island was also used as a detention facility for transients to and from Cuba, Mexico, and other Latin American countries. In 1921 the Mexican government banned the immigration of Chinese labor into Mexico.

[2″]A contraction of "the whip of Zu Di." Zu Di (A.D. 266–321) was a general during the Western Jin dynasty (A.D. 265–316).When non–Chinese people seized control of the Yellow River Valley in the 4th century and the Chinese court had to retreat to the south, Zu Di swore to recover this lost territory. One of his friends, also a general, once said, "I sleep with my weapon awaiting the dawn. My ambition is to kill the barbarian enemy, but I am always afraid that Zu will crack the whip before me." Thus, the reference means to try hard and compete to be first.

From now on, I am departing far from this building.
All of my fellow villagers are rejoicing with me.
Don't say that everything within is Western styled.
Even if it is built of jade, it has turned into a cage.

1910–1940

CARLOS BULOSAN
1913–1956

The first Filipino writer to bring Filipino concerns to national attention, Carlos Bulosan came to Seattle in 1930, steerage class, inculcated with the ideals of brotherhood and equality he had learned in American schools in the Philippines. Arriving at the start of the Great Depression, he quickly learned the bitter truth that when jobs are scarce, minorities and immigrants become scapegoats, and the egalitarian rhetoric was far from reality for such as he. From the 1870s, the Chinese had been targets of such racial hatred; in the 1930s, the Filipinos were perceived as the latest influx of the "yellow horde" who worked for little pay, taking jobs away from whites. In his brief experience as a migrant laborer, Bulosan endured living conditions worse than those he had left behind. Bulosan found "that in many ways it was a crime to be a Filipino in California. I came to know that the public streets were not free to my people: we were stopped each time these vigilant patrolmen saw us driving a car. We were suspect each time we were seen with a white woman."

In Los Angeles, Bulosan met labor organizer Chris Mensalves. Together they organized a union of fish cannery workers, and Bulosan, working as a dishwasher, wrote for the union paper. Writing became a means of defining his life, and his concern for just treatment for Filipino workers became one of his major themes. In 1936 the effects of poverty and constant moving led to tuberculosis. Bulosan entered the hospital, and in 1938 he was discharged, after three operations for lung lesions and an extended convalescence. His enforced confinement became his education. Bulosan read at least a book a day, from Whitman and Poe through Hemingway, Dreiser, and Steinbeck.

With some of the most important Pacific action of World War II occurring in the Philippine Islands, names such as Bataan and Corregidor became household words, and the climate was right for Bulosan to rise to national prominence. The *Saturday Evening Post* paid nearly a thousand dollars for Bulosan's essay "Freedom from Want" (an essay that was illustrated by Norman Rockwell and displayed in the Federal Building in San Francisco); his work appeared in *The New Yorker*, *Harper's Bazaar*, *Town and Country*, *Poetry* and other prestigious magazines, and he was featured on the cover of news magazines. His book of reminiscences, *Laughter of My Father*, was broadcast to American soldiers around the world, and *Look* declared his autobiographic novel, *America Is in the Heart*, one of the fifty most important American books ever published.

However, Bulosan died in 1956, in poverty and obscurity. The political climate had changed, and narratives of the underdog, the remorselessly common person, were no longer appealing. In Asian American literature, though, Carlos Bulosan's impassioned work has an enduring place. In addition to "Freedom from Want," included here is "The End of the War," a bittersweet selection, perhaps: after the story's appearance in *The New Yorker* in 1944, Bulosan was sued for plagiarism by Italian American author Guido D'Agostino, whose "The Dream of Angelo Zara" (1942) provided its structural model. Although the suit was settled out of court, the charge hurt Bulosan's reputation. Nevertheless, "The End of the War" remains a powerful interrogation of the very notion of the American Dream, exploring the dichotomies of individuality and community and heritage and nationhood.

Amy Ling
late of University of Wisconsin–Madison

King-Kok Cheung
University of California, Los Angeles

PRIMARY WORKS

The Voice of Bataan, 1943; *The Dark People*, 1944; *Laughter of My Father*, 1944; *America Is in the Heart*, 1946; *The Power of the People*, 1977; *On Becoming Filipino: Selected Writings of Carlos Bulosan*, ed. E. San Juan, 1995.

The End of the War

It was a fine Sunday morning and the First Filipino Infantry was very quiet. Private Pascual Fidel, who was small even for a Filipino, opened his eyes and kicked the thick Army blankets off his body. His right hand reached for the shiny harmonica which was on the floor beside a pair of clean boots. He rubbed his eyes slowly and then began humming, "Amor, amor, amor," which he had heard on the radio some nights before. He tapped the harmonica on his knee, out of habit, put it in his mouth, and fumbled for the first note. Suddenly his hands stopped and he jumped up and ran around the room from cot to cot, looking. But his comrades had already left. With nothing on but his undershorts, he rushed through the door of the barracks and out into the bright sunlight, screaming for his cousin, "Pitong! Sergeant Pitong Tongkol!"

Sergeant Tongkol, who was in the same company of the First Filipino Infantry, stood watching three men planting poppies in a vacant space nearby. He looked up and saw Private Fidel running toward him. Anxious to know what it was all about, Sergeant Tongkol started to meet his cousin. They met in front of the mess hall, where most of the soldiers were now assembled.

"What is it, Cousin?" Sergeant Tongkol asked.

"I had a dream," Private Fidel said, when he had caught his breath.

"A dream?" Sergeant Tongkol said.

"It is a big dream," Private Fidel said. "It is bigger than this whole camp." He stopped and looked beyond Sergeant Tongkol at the distant low brown hills of northern California. Then, turning around slowly, he scanned the vastness of the valley that surrounded Camp Beale.

"What happened, Cousin?" Sergeant Tongkol asked.

"We were approaching Mindanao when it happened," Private Fidel said. "I remember it very well because I was playing monte with my brother Malong and your brother Ponso when it happened. I had a poor hand, so I wanted to cheat, because it was my last dollar." He spread an imaginary hand of cards in front of his cousin, and while Sergeant Tongkol became more and more impatient, Private Fidel deliberated as if he were actually playing cards. Finally he said, "Your brother Ponso put two dollars in the pot, but my brother Malong raised the bet. I had a pair of threes, but there was another three under my left foot. I remember it well because my eyes were not on my cards; they were glued to the approaching shore of southern Mindanao. I saw Ponso's helmet move in the morning light when I reached for the hidden card. Then it happened, suddenly and without ceremony."

"What happened?" Sergeant Tongkol asked.

"I ran to the railing of the ship and looked," Private Fidel continued. "I stood there for quite some time, not believing in what I saw. But it was true. They came to the shore and surrendered."

"What is true?" Sergeant Tongkol shouted. "Who surrendered? As your superior, Private Fidel, I order you to answer me!" He stepped back and stood at attention, waiting for his cousin to obey him.

"The Japs met us on the beach and surrendered," Private Fidel said. "A few minutes afterward, it was broadcast that Germany had also surrendered and the war came to a sudden end."

Sergeant Tongkol was stunned for a moment. Then, realizing the importance of the event, he grabbed his cousin and a rush of anxious words poured out of his mouth. "Are you sure, Cousin?" he asked. "Are you sure they were Japs? Did you see the large teeth of the yellow sons of the Rising Sun? Did you hear the broadcast that the war came to an end?"

"I'm sure, Sergeant Tongkol!" Private Fidel shouted.

Sergeant Tongkol relaxed his hold. His face was filled with sudden kindness. "Not so loud, Cousin," he said. "Here is my jacket. You might catch cold."

Private Fidel put the jacket on. It was so big that it hung like an overcoat. Filled now with the big dream, Sergeant Tongkol expanded his chest. Wild anticipation illumined his eyes and his dark face. He put his arm around Private Fidel, as though his cousin were a precious toy. "Let's tell the good news to my brother," Sergeant Tongkol said.

The two Filipino soldiers walked eagerly toward the mess hall, each with his arm around the other. It was always like that with Private Fidel and Sergeant Tongkol. They were the same age and in their native village, on the island of Luzon, they used to go together into the banana grove across the river and steal the choicest fruit. They sailed together to the United States when they were seventeen years old. They had worked together on a farm most of the time since, and they were never separated from each other except when one of them was in jail for gambling or selling something that did not belong to him. When the war came, they had volunteered together. But it had been hard on Private Fidel when, some months after their enlistment, his cousin Pitong was promoted. Pitong had always been his inferior in civilian life, especially when they were working on the farm. Sergeant Tongkol had been just a field hand, cutting lettuce or picking tomatoes or doing some unimportant job like that. But he, Private Fidel, was a bookkeeper or timekeeper or had some other important job. He resented his cousin's promotion and he had tried many times to work against him, but every time was discredited. He had resigned himself to his fate and did not even try for promotions except in his dreams, where one promotion after another came to him.

Mess Sergeant Ponso Tongkol was chopping string beans into a barrel with a long butcher knife. When the two soldiers approached him, he started chopping faster. His feet danced rhythmically as he jabbed the knife up and down. It was a stunt they always enjoyed. The two soldiers stood watching him. Suddenly Sergeant Pitong grabbed his brother. "The war has ended, Ponso!" he said.

One of the dancing feet stopped in mid-air. The butcher knife stopped moving up and down. Slowly, Ponso looked up from the barrel of chopped string beans and his eyes fastened on his brother's face. "You are kidding, Brother," he said. "But it is true, Ponso," Sergeant Pitong said.

Mess Sergeant Ponso sat down on the edge of the barrel and put the knife in his lap. "If it is true that the war has ended," he said, "why am I still preparing string beans for dinner?"

"It is in the dream that the war had ended," Private Fidel interrupted.

Sergeant Pitong pushed him away and planted himself in front of his brother. "We were approaching Mindanao when it happened," he began, glancing sideways at Private Fidel with his superior air. "I remember it vividly, because I was walking on the deck with his brother Malong."

"No, no!" Private Fidel protested. "I was there!"

"Let me tell it," Sergeant Pitong said. "This dream is not for a small potato like you, Private Fidel." Then he turned his back on him and faced the mess sergeant. "I was walking on the deck with Private Fidel's brother Malong when it happened. I was about to tell him about a champion gamecock I had when I was in Salinas, California. That rooster had the most beautiful pair of legs. I made lots of money betting on him, but it was not the money that I enjoyed as much as his dancing feet when he was in the ring with an adversary. Well, then, it was at this moment when it happened. The Japs came to the shore and surrendered. Then it was broadcast that the war had ended."

"Was the Son of Heaven with the soldiers?" Mess Sergeant Ponso asked.

"He was the first one to come to the shore," Sergeant Pitong said.

Private Fidel interrupted again. "He was *not* there. The Emperor was not there. I would have seen him and his white horse if they'd been there."

"He *was* there!" Sergeant Pitong said. "The Son of Heaven came to meet us with several generals. They were all smiling and willing to surrender."

"The salomabit!"[1] Mess Sergeant Ponso exclaimed. He gripped the handle of the butcher knife with both hands. "Then what did you do?"

"We started shouting and throwing away our guns," his brother said.

"Goddamit!" Mess Sergeant Ponso shouted, getting up from the barrel. Slowly he sat down again. "If I was only there," he said. The strong hands tightened around the knife. He was a much larger man than his brother. He got up once more and walked around a table, stabbing the air furiously with the knife.

"It was only a dream," Private Fidel said.

But Mess Sergeant Ponso did not hear him. He said, "Ten years I worked peacefully in America, minding my own business, when the salomabit come

---

[1]"Son of a bitch" in the Filipino idiom.

stabbing me at the back. Maybe it is not much I make, but I got the beautiful Ford from Detroit. When I come home at night from work, I ride it to town, pressing the horn and whistling. I ride and ride and I am happy. In the bank I got money—maybe not much, but it is my money. When I see the flag, I take the hat off and I say, "Thank you very much!" I like the color of the flag and I work hard. Why the *salomabit* come?" He drove the knife into the edge of the table with a terrific blow. Then he looked at his brother and cousin. "If only I was there!"

Private Fidel stepped back. He was not afraid of his cousin, but he kept his eyes on the knife nevertheless. Mess Sergeant Ponso pulled the knife out and wiped it with his apron. Then he produced a bottle of wine from the rice bin and filled three glasses. As though he had noticed Private Fidel for the first time, Mess Sergeant Ponso pulled a pair of pants from a hook on the wall and gave it to him. "Here," he said, "put these on. And then let's tell the good news to your brother."

The three soldiers hurried from the mess hall and went to the latrine, where Private Malong Fidel was on duty. When he saw them rushing toward him, he dropped the handle of his mop.

"The war has come to an end, Malong," Mess Sergeant Ponso said.

Private Malong stepped back against the wall of the latrine. . . . "Don't torture me," he said. "I'm too tired."

"But it's true!" Mess Sergeant Ponso shouted. "I saw the Son of Heaven himself, and his wife—"

Sergeant Pitong tried to interrupt, but his brother prevented him by putting a huge hand over his mouth.

"No, no!" Private Fidel cried. "I was there!" The loud voice of his cousin Ponso drowned him out.

Private Fidel had dreamed the big dream, but it was too big for him to hold. It was a dream that belonged to no one now, yet it was a dream for every soldier. Hearing it told by another person, Private Fidel knew that it was not his dream anymore. First it had become Sergeant Pitong's dream, then Mess Sergeant Ponso had taken it over. In a few minutes, it would be Malong's dream.

In utter defeat, Private Fidel backed out into the sunlight and returned to his barracks where he sat on his cot. He was surprised to notice that the harmonica was still in his hand. He tapped it on his knee, out of habit, and started to play, "Amor, Amor, Amor." After a while, he began playing with great joy and inspiration.

1944

Freedom from Want

If you want to know what we are, look upon the farms or upon the hard pavements of the city. You usually see us working or waiting for work, and you think you know us, but our outward guise is more deceptive than our history.

Our history has many strands of fear and hope, that snarl and converge at several points in time and space. We clear the forest and the mountains of the land. We cross the river and the wind. We harness wild beast and living steel. We celebrate labor, wisdom, peace of the soul.

When our crops are burned or plowed under, we are angry and confused. Sometimes we ask if this is the real America. Sometimes we watch our long shadows and doubt the future. But we have learned to emulate our ideals from these trials. We know there were men who came and stayed to build America. We know they came because there is something in America that they needed, and which needed them.

We march on, though sometimes strange moods fill our children. Our march toward security and peace is the march of freedom—the freedom that we should like to become a living part of. It is the dignity of the individual to live in a society of free man, where the spirit of understanding and belief exist; of understanding that all men are equal; that all men, whatever their color, race, religion, or estate, should be given equal opportunity to serve themselves and each other according to their needs and abilities.

But we are not really free unless we use what we produce. So long as the fruit of our labor is denied us, so long will want manifest itself in a world of slaves. It is only when we have plenty to eat—plenty of everything—that we begin to understand what freedom means. To us, freedom is not an intangible thing. When we have enough to eat, then we are healthy enough to enjoy what we eat. Then we have the time and ability to read and think and discuss things. Then we are not merely living but also becoming a creative part of life. It is only then that we become a growing part of democracy.

We do not take democracy for granted. We feel it grow in our working together—many millions of us working toward a common purpose. If it took us several decades of sacrifices to arrive at this faith, it is because it took us that long to know what part of America is ours.

Our faith has been shaken many times, and now it is put to question. Our faith is a living thing, and it can be crippled or chained. It can be killed by denying us enough food or clothing, by blasting away our personalities and keeping us in constant fear. Unless we are properly prepared, the powers of darkness will have good reason to catch us unaware and trample our life.

The totalitarian nations hate democracy. They hate us, because we ask for a definite guaranty of freedom of religion, freedom of expression, and freedom from fear and want. Our challenge to tyranny is the depth of our faith in a democracy worth defending. Although they spread lies about us, the way of life we cherish is not dead. The American dream is only hidden away, and it will push its way up and grow again.

We have moved down the years steadily toward the practice of democracy. We become animate in the growth of Kansas wheat or in the ring of Mississippi rain. We tremble in the strong winds of the Great Lakes. We cut timbers in Oregon just as the gold flowers blossom in Maine. We are multitudes in Pennsylvania mines, in Alaskan canneries. We are millions from

Puget Sound to Florida. In violent factories, crowded tenements, teeming cities. Our numbers increase hunger, disease, death, and fear.

But sometimes we wonder if we are really a part of America. We recognize the mainsprings of American democracy in our right to form unions and bargain through them collectively, our opportunity to sell our products at reasonable prices, and the privilege of our children to attend schools where they learn the truth about the world in which they live. We also recognize the forces which have been trying to falsify American history—the forces which drive many Americans to a corner of compromise with those who would distort the ideals of men that died for freedom.

Sometimes we walk across the land looking for something to hold on to. We cannot believe that the resources of this country are exhausted. Even when we see our children suffer humiliations, we can not believe that America has no more place for us. We realize that what is wrong is not in our system of government, but in the ideals which were blasted away by a materialistic age. We know that we can truly find and identify ourselves with a living tradition if we walk proudly in familiar streets. It is a great honor to walk on the American earth.

If you want to know what we are, look at the men reading books, searching in the dark pages of history for the lost word, the key to the mystery of living peace. We are factory hands, mill hands, searching, building, and molding structures. We are doctors, scientists, chemists, discovering and eliminating disease, hunger, and antagonism. We are soldiers, Navy men, citizens, guarding the imperishable dream of our fathers to live in freedom. We are the living dream of dead men. We are the living spirit of free men.

Everywhere we are on the march, passing through darkness into a sphere of economic peace. When we have the freedom to think and discuss things without fear, when peace and security are assured, when the futures of our children are ensured—then we have resurrected and cultivated the early beginnings of democracy. And America lives and becomes a growing part of our aspirations again.

We have been marching for the last one hundred and fifty years. We sacrifice our individual liberties, and sometimes we fail and suffer. Sometimes we divide into separate groups and our methods conflict, though we all aim at one common goal. The significant thing is that we march on without turning back. What we want is peace, not violence. We know that we thrive and prosper only in peace.

We are bleeding where clubs are smashing heads, where bayonets are gleaming. We are fighting where the bullet is crashing upon armorless citizens, where the tear gas is choking unprotected children. Under the lynch trees, amidst hysterical mobs. Where the prisoner is beaten to confess a crime he did not commit. Where the honest man is hanged because he told the truth.

We are the sufferers who suffer for natural love of man for another man, who commemorate the humanities of every man. We are the creators of abundance.

We are the desires of anonymous men. We are the subways of suffering, the well of dignities. We are the living testament of a flowering race.

But our march to freedom is not complete unless want is annihilated. The America we hope to see is not merely a physical but also a spiritual and an intellectual world. We are the mirror of what America is. If America wants us to be living and free, then we must be living and free. If we fail, then America fails.

What do we want? We want complete security and peace. We want to share the promises and fruits of American life. We want to be free from fear and hunger.

If you want to know what we are—We are Marching.

1943

ACKNOWLEDGMENTS

Sherwood Anderson. "The Book of the Grotesque" and "Hands," from *Winesburg, Ohio* (The Modern Library, 1919). "Death in the Woods," from *Death in the Woods and Other Stories* by Sherwood Anderson, pp. 3–23. Reprinted by permission of Harold Ober Associates Incorporated. Originally appeared in American Mercury (September 1926). Copyright © 1926 by Sherwood Anderson. Copyright renewed © 1953 by Eleanor Copenhaver Anderson.

Bruce Barton. "The Man Nobody Knows: A Discovery of the Real Jesus," from *The Man Nobody Knows* by Bruce Barton. Copyright © 1925 by Bruce Barton. Copyright renewed © 1953 by Bruce Barton. All rights reserved. Reprinted with the permission of Scribner, a Division of Simon & Schuster, Inc.

Gwendolyn Bennett. "Heritage," from *Opportunity* (National Urban League, 1923). "To Usward," published in *The Crisis*, May 1924, p. 19 and *Opportunity*, May 1924, pp. 143–144. Courtesy of Schomburg Center for Research in Black Culture. "Advice" and "Lines Written at the Grave of Alexandre Dumas," from *Caroling Dusk: An Anthology of Verse by Negro Poets*, edited by Countee Cullen, pp. 156–157, 159 (1927). Courtesy of Schomburg Center for Research in Black Culture.

Edward Bernays. From *Propaganda* by Edward Bernays. Copyright © 1928, 1955 by Edward Bernays. Used by permission of Ig Publishing, Inc. and the Estate of Edward Bernays.

Blind Blake. "Blues Lyrics - Early one morning when I was on my way home," from *Third Degree Blues* by Blind Blake. Used by permission of Document Records Ltd.

Louise Bogan. "Women," "The Sleeping Fury," "Roman Fountain," "After the Persian," "Dragonfly," and "Night," from *The Blue Estuaries* by Louise Bogan. Copyright © 1968 by Louise Bogan. Copyright renewed © 1996 by Ruth Limmer. Reprinted by permission of Farrar, Straus and Giroux, LLC.

Lucille Bogan. "Blues Lyrics - Comin a Time B.D. Womens Ain't Gonna Need No Men," from *B.D. Woman's Blues* by Lucille Bogan. Used by permission of Document Records Ltd.

Randolph Bourne. "Trans-National America." *The Atlantic Monthly* (July 1916).

Ishmon Bracey. "Blues Lyrics - Now She's the Meanest Woman That I've Ever Seen," from *Saturday Blues* by Ishmon Bracey. Used by permission of Peer International Corporation.

Sterling A. Brown. "When de Saints Go Ma'ching Home," "Strong Men," "Ma Rainey," "Remembering Nat Turner," and "Song of Triumph," from *The Collected Poems of Sterling A. Brown*, edited by Michael S. Harper. Copyright © 1980 by Sterling A. Brown. Reprinted by permission of HarperCollins Publishers. "Slim in Hell," from *Folk-Say IV: The Land Is Ours, Benjamin A Botkin* (University of Oklahoma Press, 1932); republished with permission of The University of Oklahoma Press. Permission conveyed through Copyright Clearance Center, Inc.

Carlos Bulosan. "The End of the War" and "The Freedom from Want," by Carlos Bulosan; Epifanio San Juan, *On Becoming Filipino: Selected Writings of Carlos Bulosan* (Temple University Press, 1995). Used by permission of University of Washington Libraries, Special Collections, Carlos Bulosan Papers, Acc0581.

Earnest Calkins. Republished with permission of *The Atlantic Monthly*, from Earnest Elmo Calkins, "Beauty: The New Business Tool," *Atlantic Monthly* (August 1927), pp. 153–55. Permission conveyed through Copyright Clearance Center, Inc.

Margaret Carter. "Blues Lyrics - I Need Plenty Grease in My Frying Pan 'Cause I Don't Want My Meat to Burn," from *I Want (Need)*

Plenty Grease in My Frying Pan by Margaret Carter. Used by permission of Document Records Ltd.

Willa Cather. "Coming, Aphrodite!," from *Youth and the Bright Medusa* (Knopf, 1920).

Robert H. Clancy. "Speech by Robert H. Clancy," April 8, 1924, *Congressional Record*, 68th Congress, 1st Session (Washington DC: Government Printing Office, 1924), Volume 65, pp. 5929–5932.

Ida Cox. "Blues Lyrics — I've Got a Disposition and a Way of My Own," from *Wild Women Don't Have the Blues*, written by Ida Cox. Copyright © 1961 Orpheum Music. All Rights Reserved. Used by permission.

Hart Crane. "Black Tambourine," "Chaplinesque," "At Melville's Tomb," "To Brooklyn Bridge," "The Broken Tower," and "The River," from *Complete Poems of Hart Crane*, edited by Marc Simon. Copyright © 1933, 1958, 1966 by Liveright Publishing Corporation. Copyright © 1986 by Marc Simon. Used by permission of Liveright Publishing Corporation.

Harry Crosby. "Harry Crosby's Reasons for Expatriating," from *Transition* (1928). Reprinted in *Altogether Elsewhere: Writers on Exile*, Marc Robinson, ed., (Boston: Faber & Faber, 1994), p. 208.

Countee Cullen. "Incident," "The Dark Tower," "Simon the Cyrenian Speaks," "Yet Do I Marvel," "Pagan Prayer," "Heritage," and "Scottsboro, Too, Is Worth Its Song," by Countee Cullen. Used by permission of the Estate of Ida M. Cullen.

E. E. Cummings. "Buffalo Bill's," "into the strenuous briefness," "the Cambridge ladies who live in furnished souls," "I like my body when it is with your," "my sweet old etcetera," "since feeling is first," "i sing of Olaf glad and big," "Picasso," "anyone lived in a pretty how town," "plato told," "what if a much of a which of a wind," and "pity this monster, manunkind," from *Complete Poems: 1904-1962* by E. E. Cummings, edited by George J. Firmage. Copyright © 1923, 1925, 1926, 1931, 1935, 1938, 1939, 1940, 1944, 1945, 1946, 1947, 1948, 1949, 1950, 1951, 1952, 1953, 1954, 1955, 1956, 1957, 1958, 1959, 1960, 1961, 1962, 1963, 1966, 1967, 1968, 1972, 1973, 1974, 1975, 1976, 1977, 1978, 1979, 1980, 1981, 1982, 1983, 1984, 1985, 1986, 1987, 1988, 1989, 1990, 1991 by the Trustees for the E.E. Cummings Trust. Copyright © 1973, 1976, 1978, 1979, 1981, 1983, 1985, 1991 by George James Firmage. Used by permission of Liveright Publishing Corporation.

Walter Davis. "Blues Lyrics - Poor People is Like Prisoners, But They Just Ain't Got on a Ball and Chain," from *Howling Wind Blues* by Walter Davis. Used by permission of Peer International Corporation.

Eugene V. Debs. "Sound Socialist Tactics," (1912), from *Eugene V. Debs Speaks*, Jean Y. Tussey, ed., (New York: Pathfinder Press, 1970).

Tom Dickson. "Blues Lyrics - I Don't Mind Workin, Captain, From Sun to Sun," from *Labor Blues* by Tom Dickson. Used by permission of Document Records Ltd.

Pietro Di Donato. "Tenement," from *Christ in Concrete* by Pietro di Donato. Copyright © 1937, 1965 by Pietro di Donato. Used by permission of Signet, a division of Penguin Group (USA) Inc.

Hilda Doolittle. "Sea Rose," "The Helmsman," "Oread," "Helen," "[43]," from *The Walls Do Not Fall* by H.D. (Hilda Doolittle), from *Collected Poems, 1912–1944*. Copyright © 1982 by The Estate of Hilda Doolittle. Reprinted by permission of New Directions Publishing Corp. "Tribute to the Angels [8]," "Tribute to the Angels [12]," "Tribute to the Angels [19]," "Tribute to the Angels [20]," "Tribute to the Angels [23]," "Tribute to the Angels [43]," from *Trilogy* by H.D. (Hilda Doolittle). Copyright © 1945 by Oxford University Press. Copyright renewed © 1973 by Norman Holmes Pearson. Reprinted by permission of New Directions Publishing Corp.

John Dos Passos. "The Body of an American" and "The Bitter Drink," from *U.S.A.*, pp. 540–545. Used by permission.

Mourning Dove (Okanogan). "Preface" and "The Spirit Chief Names the Animal People," from *Coyote Stories* by Mourning Dove, pp. 7–12, 17–26; Guie, Heister Dean. Copyright © 1990. Reproduced with permission of University of Nebraska Press in the format Textbook via Copyright Clearance Center.

Ernest Hemingway. "Hills Like White Elephants" is reprinted with the permission of Scribner, a Division of Simon & Schuster, Inc., from *Men without Women* by Ernest Hemingway. Copyright © 1927 by Charles Scribner's Sons. Copyright renewed © 1955 by Ernest Hemingway. All rights reserved.

Rosa Henderson. "Blues Lyrics - Got the Backwoods Blues But I Don't Want to Go Back Home," from *Back Woods Blues* by Rosa Henderson. Used by permission of Document Records Ltd.

Joe Hill. "The Preacher and the Slave," from *John Hill, Pie in the Sky* (Little Red Songbook, 4th edition, 1911).

Langston Hughes. "Goodbye Christ," "Advertisement for the Waldorf-Astoria," "Air Raid Over Harlem," "The Negro Speaks of Rivers," "Drum," "Negro," "Bad Luck Card," "I, Too," "Dream Variation," "Harlem," "Freedom Train," and "The Weary Blues," from *The Collected Poems of Langston Hughes* by Langston Hughes, edited by Arnold Rampersad with David Roessel, Associate Editor. Copyright © 1994 by The Estate of Langston Hughes. Used by permission of Alfred A. Knopf, a division of Random House, Inc. "The Same," is reprinted with permission from the January 1, 1926 issue of *The Nation*. For subscription information, call 1-800-333-8536. Portion of each week's *Nation* magazine can be accessed at http://www.thenation.com. "The Negro Artist and the Racial Mountain," reprinted from the June 23, 1926, issue of *The Nation*. For subscription information, call 1-800-333-8536. Portion of each week's *Nation* magazine can be accessed at http://www.thenation.com. "Big Meeting" and "Thank You M'am," from *Short Stories by Langston Hughes.* Copyright © 1996 by Ramona Bass and Arnold Rampersad. Reprinted by permission of Hill and Wang, a division of Farrar, Straus and Giroux, LLC. "When the Negro Was in Vogue" and "When the Negro Was in Vogue - Illustration/Text 1– Illustration/Text 7," from *The Big Sea* by Langston Hughes. Copyright © 1940 by Langston Hughes. Copyright renewed © 1968 by Arna Bontemps and George Houston Bass. Reprinted by permission of Hill and Wang, a division of Farrar, Straus and Giroux, LLC. "Radioactive Redcaps," from *The Best of Simple* by Langston Hughes. Copyright © 1961 by Langston Hughes. Copyright renewed © 1989 by George Houston Bass. Reprinted by permission of Hill and Wang, a division of Farrar, Straus and Giroux, LLC.

Zora Neale Hurston. "Sweat" and "The Gilded Six-Bits," from *The Complete Stories* by Zora Neale Hurston. Introduction copyright © 1995 by Henry Louis Gates, Jr., and Sieglinde Lemle. Compilation copyright © 1995 by Vivian Bowden, Lois J. Hurston Gaston, Clifford Hurston, Lucy Ann Hurston, and Winifred Hurston.

Blind Jefferson. "Blues Lyrics - Well, the Blues Come to Texas Loping Like a Mule…," from *Long Lonesome Blues* by Blind Jefferson. Used by permission of Document Records Ltd.

James Weldon Johnson. "Lift Every Voice and Sing" and "O Black and Unknown Bards," from *Saint Peter Relates an Incident* by James Weldon Johnson. Copyright © 1917, 1921, 1935 by James Weldon Johnson. Copyright renewed © 1963 by Grace Nail Johnson. Used by permission of Viking Penguin, a division of Penguin Group. Excerpts from *The Autobiography of an Ex-Colored Man* (Sherman, French & Co., 1912). "The Creation," from *God's Trombones* by James Weldon Johnson. Copyright © 1927 The Viking Press, Inc., renewed copyright © 1955 by Grace Nail Johnson. Used by permission of Viking Penguin, a division of Penguin Group (USA) Inc.

Robert Leroy Johnson. "Blues Lyrics — I've Got to Keep Moving, I've Got to Keep Moving," from *Hell Hound on My Trail*. 100% Written by Robert Leroy Johnson. Published by Music Publishing Company of America, Inc. Administered by Kobalt Music Publishing America, Inc.

Tommy Johnson. "Blues Lyrics — Crying, Sun Gonna Shine in My Back Door Some Day," from *Big Road Blues* by Tommy Johnson. Used by permission of Peer International Corporation.

Joseph Kalar. "Papermill," from *Papermill: Poems, 1927–1935.* Copyright © 2006 by the Board of Trustees of the University of Illinois. Used with permission of the poet and the University of Illinois Press.

Younghill Kang. "Part One, Book Three," from *East Goes West: The Making of an Oriental Yankee*. Copyright © 1937 and renewed © 1965 by Younghill Kang. Reprinted with the permission of The Permissions Company, Inc., on behalf of Kaya Press, www.kaya.com.

Him Lai. "The Voyage: Four days before the Qiqiao Festival...," "The Voyage: Instead of remaining a citizen of China, I willingly became an ox...," "The Detainment: Imprisonment at Youli...," "The Detainment: After leaping into prison, I cannot come out....," "The Detainment: There are tens of thousands of poems composed on these walls," "The Weak Shall Conquer: Leaving behind my writing brush and removing my sword, I came...," "The Weak Shall Conquer: Being idle in the wooden building, I opened a window," "The Weak Shall Conquer: The dragon out of water is humiliated by ants," "About Westerners: I hastened here for the sake of my stomach and landed promptly in jail," "About Westerners: Shocking news, truly sad, reached my ears," "Deportees, Transients: On a long voyage I travelled across the sea," "Deportees, Transients: Crude poem inspired by the landscape," "Deportees, Transients: Detained in this wooden house for several tens of days ...," from *Island: Poetry and History of Chinese Immigrants on Angel Island, 1910–1940*, edited by Him Mark Lai, Genny Lim, and Judy Yung. Copyright © 1991. Reprinted by permission of the University of Washington Press.

Nella Larsen. "Explanatory Notes," by Thadious M. Davis, from *Passing* by Nella Larsen. Copyright © 1997 by Thadious M. Davis. Used by permission of Penguin, a division of Penguin Group (USA) Inc.

Meridel LeSueur. "Annunciation," originally published by Platen Press, 1935. Reviewed in *The New Masses* by Nelson Algren, August 20, 1935, p. 25. Reprinted in *Ripening, Selected Work by Meridel Leseuer and Elaine Hedges*. Published 1990 by The Feminist Press, New York, NY 10011-2302. "Annunciation," reprinted with permission of International Publishers. Copyright © 1948, 1956, 1966 by International Publishers. Excerpt from *The Girl*, pp. 137–148. Copyright © 2006 by the Estate of Meridel LeSueur. Reprinted with the permission of The Permissions Company, Inc., on behalf of West End Press, Albuquerque, New Mexico, www.westendpress.org.

Furry Lewis. "Blues Lyrics — Mama Get Your Hatchet, Kill the Fly on Your Baby's Head," from *Creepers Blues* by Lewis Furry. Copyright © 1929 Universal Music Corp. Copyright renewed. All rights reserved. Used by permission.

Walter Lippmann. Walter Lippmann, *Drift and Mastery: An Attempt to Diagnose the Current Unrest* (New York: M. Kennerley, 1914)

Alain Locke. "The New Negro," by Alain Locke. Copyright © 1925 by Albert & Charles Boni, Inc. Introduction copyright © 1992 by Macmillan Publishing Company. All Rights Reserved. Reprinted with the permission of Scribner, a Division of Simon & Schuster, Inc.

Amy Lowell. "But near, Fright fully near, and rather terrifying, I understand you all, for in myself—Is that presumption? Yet indeed it's true—We are one family," from *Sisters* (North American Review, 1922). "A Lady," from *Sword Blades and Poppy Seed* by Amy Lowell (The Macmillan Company, 1914). "Patterns" from *Men, Women and Ghosts* by Amy Lowell (The Macmillan Company, 1916). "The Letter," "Summer Rain," "Venus Transiens," "Madonna of the Evening Flowers," "Opal," "Wakefulness," and "Grotesque," from *Pictures of the Floating World* by Amy Lowell (The Macmillan Company, 1919). "The Sisters," from *The Complete Poetical Works of Amy Lowell*. Copyright © 1955 by Houghton Mifflin Harcourt Publishing Company. Copyright renewed © 1983 by Houghton Mifflin Harcourt Publishing Company, Brinton P. Roberts, and G. D'Andelot Belin, Esquire. Reprinted by permission of Houghton Mifflin Harcourt Publishing Company. All rights reserved.

Bernarr Macfadden. Bernarr Macfadden, *Vitality Supreme* (New York: Physical Culture Publishing, 1922), xi–xii, pp. 1–3.

Ricardo Flores Magón. "Ricardo Flores Magon, *Land and Liberty* (Regeneracion, November 19, 1910)

Albert Maltz. "The Happiest Man on Earth," from *Afternoon in the Jungle: The Selected*

Reznikoff, edited by Seamus Cooney. Reprinted by permission of Black Sparrow Books, an imprint of David R.Godine, Publisher, Inc. Copyright © 2005 by the Estate of Charles Reznikoff.

Lola Ridge. "Stone Face." Used by permission.

Elizabeth Roberts. "Death at Bearwallow," from *The Haunted Mirror* by Elizabeth Madox Roberts. Copyright © 1932 by Elizabeth Madox Roberts; renewed © 1960 by Ivor S. Roberts. Used by permission of Viking Penguin, a division of Penguin Group (USA) Inc.

Edwin Robinson. "The Clerks," from *The Children of the Night* (Charles Scribner's Sons, 1897). "Aunt Imogen," from *Captain Craig* (The Riverside Publishing Company, 1902). "Momus," from *The Town Down the River* (Charles Scribner's Sons, 1910). "Eros Turannos," from *The Man Against the Sky: A Book of Poems* (The Macmillan Company, 1916). "The Tree in Pamela's Garden," from *Collected Poems* (The Macmillan Company, 1921). "Mr. Flood's Party," (The Nation, 1920).

Edwin Rolfe. "Asbestos," "Season of Death," "First Love," and "Elegia," from *Collected Poems* by Edward Rolfe. Copyright © 1993 by the Board of Trustees of the University of Illinois. Used with the permission of Mary Rolfe and the University of Illinois Press.

Franklin Delano Roosevelt. "This is preeminently the time to speak the truth, the whole truth, frankly and boldly," "I see millions of families trying to live on incomes so meager that the pall of family disaster hangs over them day by day....," from *the First Inaugural Address.* "The Four Freedoms." The Public Papers and Addresses of Franklin D. Roosevelt, 1940: War and Aid to Democracies, Franklin Delano Roosevelt Presidential Library and Museum, http://www.fdrlibrary.marist.edu/4free.html. "Executive Order 9006 and Western Defense Command Order for Relocation of Those of Japanese Ancestry ," from www.archives.gov.

Muriel Rukeyser. "Letter to the Front — To be a Jew in the Twentieth Century," "Absalom," and "The Minotaur," from *The Collected Poems of Muriel Rukeyser*, edited by Janet E. Kaufman & Anne F. Herzog, published by the University of Pittsburgh Press, Pittsburgh, PA 15260. Reprinted by permission of International Creative Management, Inc. Copyright © 2005 by Muriel Rukeyser.

George Schuyler. "Our Greatest Gift to America," originally published in *Ebony and Topaz* in 1927, reprinted in V. F. Calverton's Anthology of *American Negro Literature* (1929). From the periodical *Ebony and Topaz*. Copyright © 1927 by George Schuyler. Used by permission of the Esate. "The Negro-Art Hokum," reprinted with permission from the June 16, 1926, issue of *The Nation*. For subscription information, call 1-800-333-8536. A portion of each week's *Nation* magazine can be accessed at http://www.thenation.com

Gilbert Seldes. Excerpts from "The Great God Bogu," in *The Seven Lively Arts* (New York: Harper and Brothers, 1924). Reprinted by the permission of Russell & Volkening as agents for the author's estate. Copyright © 1924 by Gilbert Seldes. Renewed © 1952 by Gilbert Seldes.

Ellison Smith. Speech by Ellison DuRant Smith, April 9, 1924, Congressional Record, 68th Congress, 1st Session (Washington DC: Government Printing Office, 1924), vol. 65, 5961–5962.

Anne Spencer. "Lines to a Nasturtium," "Substitution," "For Jim, Easter Eve," from *Time's Unfading Garden*, J. Lee Greene, ed. (1977). Courtesy of the Anne Spencer House and Garden Museum Archives.

Harold Stearns. "The Intellectual Life," *Civilization and American Culture* (New York: Harcourt, Brace, 1920), 135–37, 141–43.

Gertrude Stein. "The Gentle Lena," from *Three Lives: Stories of The Good Anna, Melanctha and The Gentle Lena* (The Grafton Press, 1909). Excerpt from *The Making of Americans; Being a History of a Family's Progress* (New York: A & C, Boni, 1926). Reprinted by permission of The Estate of Gertrude Stein, through its literary executor, Mr. Stanford Gann, Jr. of Levin & Gann, P.A. "Susie Asado," "Ladies' Voices," and "Miss Furr and Miss Skeene," from *Geography and Plays* (The Four Seas Press, 1922). "Preciosilla," and

"Composition as Explanation," from *Composition as Explanation* (Hogarth Press, The Hogarth Essays, Second Series, No. 1, 1926). Reprinted by permission of The Estate of Gertrude Stein, through its Literary Executor, Mr. Stanford Gann, Jr. of Levin & Gann, P.A.

John Steinbeck. "Chapter 23," from *The Grapes of Wrath* by John Steinbeck. Copyright © 1939, renewed © 1967 by John Steinbeck. Used by permission of Viking Penguin, a division of Penguin Group (USA) Inc. "The Promise," from *The Red Pony* by John Steinbeck, copyright © 1933, 1937, 1938, copyright renewed © 1961, 1965, 1966 by John Steinbeck. Used by permission of Viking Penguin, a division of Penguin Group (USA) Inc.

Wallace Stevens. "Sunday Morning," "The Snowman," "Peter Quince at the Clavier," "Anecdote of the Jar," "A High-Toned Old Christian Woman," "Of Modern Poetry," and "Of Mere Being," from *The Collected Poems Of Wallace Stevens* by Wallace Stevens. Copyright © 1954 by Wallace Stevens and renewed © 1982 by Holly Stevens. Used by permission of Alfred A. Knopf, a division of Random House, Inc. "The Course of a Particular," from *The Palm at the End of the Mind* by Wallace Stevens, edited by Holly Stevens. Copyright © 1967, 1969, 1971 by Holly Stevens. Used by permission of Alfred A. Knopf, a division of Random House, Inc.

Lothrop Stoddard. Lothrop Stoddard, *The Rising Tide of Colored against White World-Supremacy* (New York: Scribners, 1920): p. 3.

Genevieve Taggard. "Up State—Depression Summer," "To the Negro People," "Ode in Time of Crisis," and "To the Veterans of the Abraham Lincoln Brigade," poems from *Calling Western Union.* Copyright © Harper & Bros., 1936, and Long View, Harper & Bros., 1942. Copyrights renewed and reprinted with the permission of Judith Benét Richardson.

Allen Tate. "Ode to the Confederate Dead," from *Collected Poems: 1919-1976* by Allen Tate. Copyright © 1977 by Allen Tate. Reprinted by permission of Farrar, Straus and Giroux, LLC. "I'll take my stand," from *I'll take My Stand: The South and The Agrarian Tradition* (Harper & Brothers, 1930), pp. xxxviii, xxxix,

xiii, xlvi. Used by permission of the Louisiana State University Press.

Frederick W. Taylor. "Introduction to The Principles of Scientific Management," (New York: Harper & Row, 1911), www.fordham.edu/halsall/mod/1911taylor.html.

Wallace Thurman. Excerpts from *Infants of the Spring* by Wallace Thurman. University Press of New England, 1992. "Nephews of Uncle Remus" and "Grist of the Mill," from *The Collected Writings of Wallace Thurman: A Harlem Renaissance Reader*, edited by Amiritjit Singh and Daniel M. Scott III (New Brunswick: Rutgers University Press, 2003).

Bessie Tucker. "Blues Lyrics — I Got All Cut to Pieces, Aah Aah, about a Man I Love," from *Got Cut All to Pieces* by Bessie Tucker. Used by permission of Document Records Ltd.

U.S. Congress. "Sedition Act (1918–1921)," from http://frwebgate.access.gpo.gov/cgi-bin/multidb.cgi.

Thorstein Veblen. Thorstein Veblen, *The Theory of the Leisure Class: A Study of Economic Institutions* (New York: Huebsch, 1912), pp. 73–76

Jose Garcia Villa. "Footnote to Youth," from *Footnote to Youth: Tales of the Philippines and Others* (Charles Scribner's Sons, 1933). Copyright and used by permission of John Edwin Cowen, Literary Trustee for the Jose Garcia Villa Estate. "Selected Poetry," from *Many Voices: Selected Poems* (Book Guild, 1939). Copyright and used by permission of John Edwin Cowen, Literary Trustee for the José Garcia Villa Estate.

Leonor Villegas de Magnon. "Laredo and the Constitutionalists," from *Laredo y los constitucionalistas* (La Cronica, 2 March 1911).

Margaret Walker. "Cook in the Big House," from *Jubilee* by Margaret Walker. Copyright © 1966 by Margaret Walker, renewed © 1994 by Margaret Walker Alexander. Reprinted by permission of Houghton Mifflin Harcourt Publishing Company. All rights reserved. "Southern Song," "For my People," "Solace," and "The Crystal Palace," from *This is My Century: New and Collected Poems.* Published by the

University of Georgia Press, Athens, Georgia 30602, www.ugapress.org. All rights reserved. Reprinted by permission of The University of Georgia Press. "Ballad of the Hoppy-Toad," from *Profits for a New Day* (1970), reprinted by permission of Broadside Press.

Robert Penn Warren. "Founding Fathers, Early Nineteenth-Century Style, Southeast USA," "Infant Boy at Midcentury," "The Leaf," and "Evening Hawk," from *New and Selected Poems, 1923–1985* (Random House, 1985). Copyright © 1976 by Robert Penn Warren. Reprinted by permission of William Morris Endeavor Entertainment, LLC on behalf of the author. "Heart of Autumn" and "Amazing Grace in the Back Country," from *Now and Then*. Copyright © 1978 by Robert Penn Warren. Reprinted by permission of William Morris Endeavor Entertainment, LLC, on behalf of the author. "Fear and Trembling," from *Rumor Verified*. Copyright © 1981 by Robert Penn Warren. Reprinted by permission of William Morris Endeavor Entertainment, LLC, on behalf of the author.

Booker Washington. "A Slave Among Slaves," "The Struggle for an Education," "Black Race and Red Race," "Two Thousand Miles for a Five-Minute Speech," and "The Atlanta Exposition Address," from *Up from Slavery*, by Booker T. Washington, (Doubleday, Page & Co., 1901).

Eudora Welty. "The Wide Net," from *The Wide Net and Other Stories*. Copyright © 1942 and renewed 1970 by Eudora Welty. Reprinted by permission of Houghton Mifflin Harcourt Publishing Company.

Edith Wharton. Edith Wharton, "The Valley of Childish Things," from *The Valley of Childish Things and Other Emblems* (*Century Magazine*, 1896). "Souls Belated," from *The Greater Inclination* (Charles Scribner's Sons, 1899). *The Other Two* (*Collier's Weekly*, Crowell-Collier Publishing Co., Feb. 13, 1904). "The Life Apart," is reprinted by permission of the Estate of Edith Wharton and the Watkins/Loomis Agency. "The Eyes," from *Tales of Men and Ghosts* (Charles Scribner's Sons, 1910). "Roman Fever," from *Roman Fever and Other Stories* by Edith Wharton, is reprinted with the permission of Scribner, an imprint of Simon & Schuster,

Inc. Copyright © 1934 by *Liberty Magazine*. Copyright renewed © 1962 by William R. Tyler. All rights reserved.

Peetie Wheatstraw. "Blues Lyrics - I Did More for You than You Understand," from *Ice and Snow* by Peetie Wheatstraw. Used by permission of Document Records Ltd. "When I Picked You Up, Baby, You Was Beat Just Like a Slave," from *No Count Woman* by Peetie Wheatstraw. Used by permission of Document Records Ltd.

Thomas S. Whitecloud. "Blue Winds Dancing," by Tom Whitecloud, from *Scribner's Magazine* 103 February 1938, reprinted with the permission of Scribner, an imprint of Simon & Schuster, Inc. Copyright © 1938 by Charles Scribner's Sons; copyright renewed © 1966. All rights reserved.

William Carlos Williams. "Danse Russe," "The Young Housewife," "Portrait of a Lady," "Spring and All," "The Red Wheelbarrow," "The Pot of Flowers," "The Rose," "To Elsie," "Young Sycamore," "The Flower," and "The Poor," by William Carlos Williams, from *Collected Poems, Vol. 1, 1909–1939*. Copyright © 1938 by New Directions Publishing Corp. Reprinted by permission of New Directions Publishing Corp. "Burning the Christmas Greens," "The Descent," and "The Pink Locust," by William Carlos Williams, from *Collected Poems, Vol. 2, 1939–1962*. Copyright © 1944 by William Carlos Williams. Reprinted by permission of New Directions Publishing Corp.

Richard Wright. "The Ethics of Living Jim Crow," from *Uncle Tom's Children* by Richard Wright, pp. 3–15. Copyright © 1937 by Richard Wright. Copyright renewed © 1965 by Ellen Wright. Reprinted by permission of HarperCollins Publishers. "Big Boy Leaves Home," from *Uncle Tom's Children* by Richard Wright, pp. 17–61. Copyright © 1936 by Richard Wright, renewed © 1964 by Ellen Wright. Reprinted by permission of HarperCollins Publishers.

Anzia Yezierska. "America and I," from *The Open Cage* by Anzia Yezierska. Copyright © 1979 by Louise Levitas Henriksen. Reprinted by permission of Persea Books, Inc., New York. All rights reserved.

INDEX OF AUTHORS, TITLES, AND FIRST LINES OF POEMS

LIST OF AUTHORS